Lecture Notes in Computer Science   14085

Founding Editors

Gerhard Goos
Juris Hartmanis

The series Lecture Notes in Computer Science (LNCS), including its subseries Lecture Notes in Artificial Intelligence (LNAI) and Lecture Notes in Bioinformatics (LNBI), has established itself as a medium for the publication of new developments in computer science and information technology research, teaching, and education.

LNCS enjoys close cooperation with the computer science R & D community, the series counts many renowned academics among its volume editors and paper authors, and collaborates with prestigious societies. Its mission is to serve this international community by providing an invaluable service, mainly focused on the publication of conference and workshop proceedings and postproceedings. LNCS commenced publication in 1973.

Helena Handschuh · Anna Lysyanskaya
Editors

Advances in Cryptology – CRYPTO 2023

43rd Annual International Cryptology Conference, CRYPTO 2023
Santa Barbara, CA, USA, August 20–24, 2023
Proceedings, Part V

 Springer

Editors
Helena Handschuh
Rambus Inc.
San Jose, CA, USA

Anna Lysyanskaya
Brown University
Providence, RI, USA

ISSN 0302-9743   ISSN 1611-3349 (electronic)
Lecture Notes in Computer Science
ISBN 978-3-031-38553-7   ISBN 978-3-031-38554-4 (eBook)
https://doi.org/10.1007/978-3-031-38554-4

This Springer imprint is published by the registered company Springer Nature Switzerland AG
The registered company address is: Gewerbestrasse 11, 6330 Cham, Switzerland

Preface

The 43rd International Cryptology Conference (CRYPTO 2023) was held at the University of California, Santa Barbara, California, USA, from August 20th to August 24th, 2023. It is an annual conference organized by the International Association for Cryptologic Research (IACR).

A record 479 papers were submitted for presentation at the conference, and 124 were selected, including two pairs of soft merges, for a total of 122 speaking slots. As a result of this record high, CRYPTO 2023 had three tracks for the first time in its history.

For the first time in its history as well, CRYPTO benefited from the great advice and tremendous help from six area chairs, covering the main areas of focus for the conference. These were Lejla Batina for Efficient and Secure Implementations, Dan Boneh for Public Key Primitives with Advanced Functionalities, Orr Dunkelman for Symmetric Cryptology, Leo Reyzin for Information-Theoretic and Complexity-Theoretic Cryptography, Douglas Stebila for Public-Key Cryptography and Muthuramakrishnan Venkitasubramaniam for Multi-Party Computation. Each of them helped lead discussions and decide which ones of the approximately 80 submissions in their area should be accepted. Their help was invaluable and we could not have succeeded without them.

To evaluate the submissions, we selected a program committee that consisted of 102 top cryptography researchers from all over the world. This was the largest program committee that CRYPTO has ever had, as well. Each paper was assigned to three program committee members who reviewed it either by themselves or with the help of a trusted sub-referee. As a result, we benefited from the expertise of almost 500 sub-referees. Together, they generated a staggering 1500 reviews. We thank our program committee members and the external sub-referees for the hard work of peer review which is the bedrock of scientific progress.

The review process was double-blind and confidential. In accordance with the IACR conflict-of-interest policy, the reviewing software we used (HotCRP) kept track of which reviewers had a conflict of interest with which authors (for example, by virtue of being a close collaborator or an advisor) and ensured that no paper was assigned a conflicted reviewer.

In order to be considered, submissions had to be anonymous and their length was limited to 30 pages excluding the bibliography and supplementary materials. After the first six or so weeks of evaluation, the committee chose to continue considering 330 papers; the remaining 149 papers were rejected, including five desk rejects. The majority of these received three reviews, none of which favored acceptance, although in limited cases the decision was made based on only two reviews that were in agreement. The papers that remained under consideration were invited to submit a response (rebuttal) to clarifications requested from their reviewers. Two papers were withdrawn during this second phase. Each of the 328 remaining papers received at least three reviews. After around five weeks of additional discussions, the committee made the final selection of the 124 papers that appear in these proceedings.

We would like to thank all the authors who submitted their papers to CRYPTO 2023. The vast majority of the submissions, including those that were ultimately not selected, were of very high quality, and we are very honored that CRYPTO was the venue that the authors chose for their work. We are additionally grateful to the authors of the accepted papers for the extra work of incorporating the reviewers' feedback and presenting their papers at the conference.

This year the Best Paper Award was awarded to Keegan Ryan and Nadia Heninger for their paper "Fast Practical Lattice Reduction Through Iterated Compression." The Best Early Career Paper Award went to Elizabeth Crites, Chelsea Komlo and Mary Maller for their paper "Fully Adaptive Schnorr Threshold Signatures." The runner up Best Early Career Paper was by Ward Beullens on "Graph-Theoretic Algorithms for the Alternating Trilinear Form Equivalence Problem." These three papers were subsequently invited to be submitted to the IACR Journal of Cryptology.

In addition to the presentations of contributed papers included in these proceedings, the conference also featured two plenary talks: Hugo Krawczyk delivered the IACR Distinguished Lecture, and Scott Aaronson gave an invited talk titled "Neurocryptography." The traditional rump session, chaired by Allison Bishop, took place on Tuesday, August 22nd, and featured numerous short talks.

Co-located cryptography workshops were held in the preceding weekend; they included the following seven events, "Crypto meets Artificial Intelligence—The Glowing Hot Topics in Cryptography," "MathCrypt—The Workshop on Mathematical Cryptology," "CFAIL—The Conference for Failed Approaches and Insightful Losses in Cryptography," "PPML—The Privacy-Preserving Machine Learning Workshop," "WAC6—The Workshop on Attacks in Cryptography 6," "ACAI—Applied Cryptology and Artificial Intelligence," and "RISE—Research Insights and Stories for Enlightenment." We gladly thank Alessandra Scafuro for serving as the Affiliated Events Chair and putting together such an enticing program.

All of this was possible thanks to Kevin McCurley and Kay McKelly without whom all of our review software would be crashing non-stop, and all of the Crypto presentations would be nothing but static. They are the true pillars of all of our IACR Crypto events and conferences. Last but not least we thank Britta Hale for serving as our General Chair and making sure the conference went smoothly and attendees had a great experience. Thank you to our industry sponsors, including early sponsors a16z, AWS, Casper, Google, JPMorgan, Meta, PQShield, and TII for their generous contributions, as well as to the NSF Award 2330160 for supporting Ph.D. student participants.

August 2023

Helena Handschuh
Anna Lysyanskaya

Organization

General Chair

Britta Hale   Naval Postgraduate School, USA

Program Co-chairs

Helena Handschuh   Rambus Inc., USA
Anna Lysyanskaya   Brown University, USA

Area Chairs

Lejla Batina *(for Efficient and*   Radboud University, the Netherlands
  Secure Implementations)
Dan Boneh *(for Public Key*   Stanford University, USA
  Primitives with Advanced
  Functionalities)
Orr Dunkelman *(for Symmetric*   University of Haifa, Israel
  Cryptology)
Leo Reyzin *(for*   Boston University, USA
  Information-Theoretic and
  Complexity-Theoretic
  Cryptography)
Douglas Stebila *(for Public-Key*   University of Waterloo, Canada
  Cryptography)
Muthu Venkitasubramaniam *(for*   Georgetown University, USA
  Multi-Party Computation)

Program Committee

Shweta Agrawal   IIT Madras, India
Ghada Almashaqbeh   University of Connecticut, USA
Benny Applebaum   Tel-Aviv University, Israel
Marshall Ball   New York University, USA
Fabrice Benhamouda   Algorand Foundation, USA

Nina Bindel   SandboxAQ, USA
Allison Bishop   Proof Trading and City University of New York,
                                        USA
Joppe W. Bos   NXP Semiconductors, Belgium
Raphael Bost   Direction Générale de l'Armement, France
Chris Brzuska   Aalto University, Finland
Benedikt Bünz   Stanford and Espresso Systems, USA
David Cash   University of Chicago, USA
Gaëtan Cassiers   TU Graz and Lamarr Security Research, Austria
Yilei Chen   Tsinghua University, China
Chitchanok Chuengsatiansup   The University of Melbourne, Australia
Kai-Min Chung   Academia Sinica, Taiwan
Carlos Cid   Simula UiB, Norway, and Okinawa Institute of
                                        Science and Technology, Japan
Sandro Coretti   IOHK, Switzerland
Geoffroy Couteau   CNRS, IRIF, Université Paris-Cité, France
Luca De Feo   IBM Research Europe, Switzerland
Gabrielle De Micheli   University of California, San Diego, USA
Jean Paul Degabriele   Technology Innovation Institute, UAE
Siemen Dhooghe   imec-COSIC, KU Leuven, Belgium
Itai Dinur   Ben-Gurion University, Israel
Christoph Dobraunig   Intel Labs, Intel Corporation, USA
Thomas Eisenbarth   University of Lübeck, Germany
Sebastian Faust   TU Darmstadt, Germany
Ben Fisch   Yale University, USA
Pierre-Alain Fouque   IRISA and University of Rennes, France
Georg Fuchsbauer   TU Wien, Austria
Chaya Ganesh   Indian Institute of Science, India
Rosario Gennaro   City University of New York, USA
Henri Gilbert   ANSSI, France
Niv Gilboa   Ben-Gurion University, Israel
Mike Hamburg   Rambus Inc., the Netherlands
David Heath   University of Illinois Urbana-Champaign, USA
Naofumi Homma   Tohoku University, Japan
Abhishek Jain   Johns Hopkins University, USA
Bhavana Kanukurthi   Indian Institute of Science, India
Shuichi Katsumata   PQShield, UK, and AIST, Japan
Jonathan Katz   University of Maryland and Dfns, USA
Nathan Keller   Bar-Ilan University, Israel
Lisa Kohl   CWI, the Netherlands
Ilan Komargodski   Hebrew University, Israel and NTT Research,
                                        USA

Anja Lehmann	Hasso-Plattner-Institute, University of Potsdam, Germany
Tancrède Lepoint	Amazon, USA
Benjamin Lipp	Max Planck Institute for Security and Privacy, Germany
Feng-Hao Liu	Florida Atlantic University, USA
Tianren Liu	Peking University, China
Patrick Longa	Microsoft Research, USA
Julian Loss	CISPA Helmholtz Center for Information Security, Germany
Fermi Ma	Simons Institute and UC Berkeley, USA
Mary Maller	Ethereum Foundation and PQShield, UK
Chloe Martindale	University of Bristol, UK
Alexander May	Ruhr-University Bochum, Germany
Florian Mendel	Infineon Technologies, Germany
Bart Mennink	Radboud University, the Netherlands
Brice Minaud	Inria and ENS, France
Kazuhiko Minematsu	NEC and Yokohama National University, Japan
Pratyush Mishra	Aleo Systems, USA
Tarik Moataz	MongoDB, USA
Jesper Buus Nielsen	Aarhus University, Denmark
Kaisa Nyberg	Aalto University, Finland
Miyako Ohkubo	NICT, Japan
Eran Omri	Ariel University, Israel
David Oswald	University of Birmingham, UK
Omkant Pandey	Stony Brook University, USA
Omer Paneth	Tel-Aviv University, Israel
Alain Passelègue	Inria and ENS Lyon, France
Arpita Patra	IISc Bangalore and Google Research, India
Léo Perrin	Inria, France
Thomas Peters	UCLouvain and FNRS, Belgium
Thomas Peyrin	Nanyang Technological University, Singapore
Stjepan Picek	Radboud University, the Netherlands
David Pointcheval	École Normale Supérieure, France
Antigoni Polychroniadou	J.P. Morgan AI Research, USA
Bart Preneel	University of Leuven, Belgium
Mariana Raykova	Google, USA
Christian Rechberger	TU Graz, Austria
Oscar Reparaz	Block, Inc., USA
Matthieu Rivain	CryptoExperts, France
Mélissa Rossi	ANSSI, France
Guy Rothblum	Apple, USA

Alexander Russell   University of Connecticut, USA
Paul Rösler   FAU Erlangen-Nürnberg, Germany
Kazue Sako   Waseda University, Japan
Alessandra Scafuro   North Carolina State University, USA
Patrick Schaumont   Worcester Polytechnic Institute, USA
Thomas Schneider   TU Darmstadt, Germany
André Schrottenloher   Inria, Univ. Rennes, CNRS, IRISA, France
Dominique Schröder   FAU Erlangen-Nürnberg, Germany
Benjamin Smith   Inria and École Polytechnique, France
Ling Song   Jinan University, China
Mehdi Tibouchi   NTT Social Informatics Laboratories, Japan
Yosuke Todo   NTT Social Informatics Laboratories, Japan
Alin Tomescu   Aptos Labs, USA
Dominique Unruh   University of Tartu, Estonia
Gilles Van Assche   STMicroelectronics, Belgium
Damien Vergnaud   Sorbonne Université, France
Jiayu Xu   Oregon State University, USA
Arkady Yerukhimovich   George Washington University, USA
Yu Yu   Shanghai Jiao Tong University, China

Additional Reviewers

Kasra Abbaszadeh   Christian Badertscher
Behzad Abdolmaleki   Shi Bai
Masayuki Abe   David Balbás
Ittai Abraham   Paulo Barreto
Hamza Abusalah   James Bartusek
Amit Agarwal   Andrea Basso
Akshima   Jules Baudrin
Gorjan Alagic   Balthazar Bauer
Martin Albrecht   Carsten Baum
Bar Alon   Josh Beal
Miguel Ambrona   Hugo Beguinet
Prabhanjan Ananth   Amos Beimel
Megumi Ando   Sana Belguith
Yoshinori Aono   Thiago Bergamaschi
Paula Arnold   Olivier Bernard
Gal Arnon   Sebastian Berndt
Arasu Arun   Ward Beullens
Gilad Asharov   Tim Beyne
Renas Bacho   Rishiraj Bhattacharyya
Matilda Backendal   Ritam Bhaumik

Mengda Bi

Alexander Bienstock

Bruno Blanchet

Olivier Blazy

Maxime Bombar

Xavier Bonnetain

Jonathan Bootle

Samuel Bouaziz-Ermann

Katharina Boudgoust

Alexandre Bouez

Charles Bouillaguet

Christina Boura

Clémence Bouvier

Ross Bowden

Pedro Branco

Anne Broadbent

Olivier Bronchain

Andreas Brüggemann

Anirudh Chandramouli

Eleonora Cagli

Matteo Campanelli

Pedro Capitão

Eliana Carozza

Kévin Carrier

Wouter Castryck

Pyrros Chaidos

Andre Chailloux

Suvradip Chakraborty

Gowri Chandran

Rohit Chatterjee

Albert Cheu

Céline Chevalier

Nai-Hui Chia

Arka Rai Choudhuri

Hien Chu

Hao Chung

Michele Ciampi

Valerio Cini

James Clements

Christine Cloostermans

Benoît Cogliati

Andrea Coladangelo

Jean-Sébastien Coron

Henry Corrigan-Gibbs

Craig Costello

Elizabeth Crites

Eric Crockett

Jan-Pieter D'Anvers

Antoine Dallon

Poulami Das

Gareth Davies

Hannah Davis

Dennis Dayanikli

Leo de Castro

Paola De Perthuis

Rafael del Pino

Cyprien Delpech de Saint Guilhem

Jeroen Delvaux

Patrick Derbez

Zach DeStefano

Lalita Devadas

Julien Devevey

Henri Devillez

Jean-François Dhem

Adam Ding

Yevgeniy Dodis

Xiaoyang Dong

Nico Döttling

Benjamin Dowling

Leo Ducas

Clément Ducros

Céline Duguey

Jesko Dujmovic

Christoph Egger

Maria Eichlseder

Reo Eriguchi

Andreas Erwig

Daniel Escudero

Thomas Espitau

Andre Esser

Simona Etinski

Thibauld Feneuil

Pouria Fallahpour

Maya Farber Brodsky

Pooya Farshim

Joël Felderhoff

Rex Fernando

Matthias Fitzi

Antonio Flórez-Gutiérrez

Cody Freitag

Sapir Freizeit
Benjamin Fuller
Phillip Gajland
Tarek Galal
Nicolas Gama
John Gaspoz
Pierrick Gaudry
Romain Gay
Peter Gaži
Yuval Gelles
Marilyn George
François Gérard
Paul Gerhart
Alexandru Gheorghiu
Ashrujit Ghoshal
Shane Gibbons
Benedikt Gierlichs
Barbara Gigerl
Noemi Glaeser
Aarushi Goel
Eli Goldin
Junqing Gong
Dov Gordon
Lénaïck Gouriou
Marc Gourjon
Jerome Govinden
Juan Grados
Lorenzo Grassi
Sandra Guasch
Aurore Guillevic
Sam Gunn
Aldo Gunsing
Daniel Günther
Chun Guo
Siyao Guo
Yue Guo
Shreyas Gupta
Hosein Hadipour
Mohammad Hajiabadi
Shai Halevi
Lucjan Hanzlik
Aditya Hegde
Rachelle Heim
Lena Heimberger
Paul Hermouet

Julia Hesse
Minki Hhan
Taiga Hiroka
Justin Holmgren
Alex Hoover
Akinori Hosoyamada
Kristina Hostakova
Kai Hu
Yu-Hsuan Huang
Mi-Ying Miryam Huang
Pavel Hubáček
Andreas Hülsing
Akiko Inoue
Takanori Isobe
Akira Ito
Ryoma Ito
Tetsu Iwata
Jennifer Jackson
Joseph Jaeger
Zahra Jafargholi
Jonas Janneck
Stanislaw Jarecki
Zhengzhong Jin
David Joseph
Daniel Jost
Nathan Ju
Seny Kamara
Chetan Kamath
Simon Holmgaard Kamp
Gabriel Kaptchuk
Vukašin Karadžić
Ioanna Karantaidou
Harish Karthikeyan
Mustafa Khairallah
Mojtaba Khalili
Nora Khayata
Hamidreza Khoshakhlagh
Eda Kirimli
Elena Kirshanova
Ágnes Kiss
Fuyuki Kitagawa
Susumu Kiyoshima
Alexander Koch
Dmitry Kogan
Konrad Kohbrok

Sreehari Kollath
Yashvanth Kondi
Venkata Koppula
Marina Krcek
Maximilian Kroschewski
Daniël Kuijsters
Péter Kutas
Qiqi Lai
Yi-Fu Lai
Philip Lazos
Jason LeGrow
Gregor Leander
Ulysse Léchine
Yi Lee
Charlotte Lefevre
Jonas Lehmann
Antonin Leroux
Baiyu Li
Chaoyun Li
Hanjun Li
Wenjie Li
Xin Li
Xingjian Li
Zhe Li
Mingyu Liang
Xiao Liang
Damien Ligier
Wei-Kai Lin
Helger Lipmaa
Guozhen Liu
Jiahui Liu
Linsheng Liu
Meicheng Liu
Qipeng Liu
Zeyu Liu
Chen-Da Liu-Zhang
Alex Lombardi
Johanna Loyer
Ji Luo
Vadim Lyubashevsky
Yiping Ma
Varun Madathil
Bernardo Magri
Luciano Maino
Monosij Maitra

Christian Majenz
Jasleen Malvai
Marian Margraf
Mario Marhuenda Beltrán
Erik Mårtensson
Ange Martinelli
Daniel Masny
Loïc Masure
Takahiro Matsuda
Kotaro Matsuoka
Christian Matt
Krystian Matusiewicz
Noam Mazor
Matthias Meijers
Fredrik Meisingseth
Pierre Meyer
Daniele Micciancio
Elena Micheli
Marine Minier
Helen Möllering
Charles Momin
Atsuki Momose
Hart Montgomery
Tal Moran
Tomoyuki Morimae
Kirill Morozov
Fabrice Mouhartem
Koksal Mus
Saachi Mutreja
Michael Naehrig
Marcel Nageler
Rishub Nagpal
Yusuke Naito
Anand Kumar Narayanan
Shoei Nashimoto
Ky Nguyen
Georgio Nicolas
Raine Nieminen
Valeria Nikolaenko
Oded Nir
Ryo Nishimaki
Olga Nissenbaum
Anca Nitulescu
Julian Nowakowski
Adam O'Neill

Sai Lakshmi Bhavana Obbattu
Maciej Obremski
Arne Tobias Ødegaard
Morten Øygarden
Cavit Özbay
Erdinc Ozturk
Jiaxin Pan
Dimitrios Papachristoudis
Aditi Partap
Anat Paskin-Cherniavsky
Rafael Pass
Sikhar Patranabis
Stanislav Peceny
Chris Peikert
Angelos Pelecanos
Alice Pellet-Mary
Octavio Perez-Kempner
Guilherme Perin
Trevor Perrin
Giuseppe Persiano
Pessl Peter
Spencer Peters
Duong Hieu Phan
Benny Pinkas
Bertram Poettering
Guru Vamsi Policharla
Jason Pollack
Giacomo Pope
Alexander Poremba
Eamonn Postlethwaite
Thomas Prest
Robert Primas
Luowen Qian
Willy Quach
Håvard Raddum
Shahram Rasoolzadeh
Divya Ravi
Michael Reichle
Jean-René Reinhard
Omar Renawi
Joost Renes
Nicolas Resch
Mahshid Riahinia
Silas Richelson
Jan Richter-Brockmann

Doreen Riepel
Peter Rindal
Bhaskar Roberts
Wrenna Robson
Sondre Rønjom
Mike Rosulek
Yann Rotella
Lior Rotem
Ron Rothblum
Adeline Roux-Langlois
Joe Rowell
Lawrence Roy
Keegan Ryan
Mark Ryan
Sherman S. M. Chow
Eric Sageloli
Antonio Sanso
Practik Sarkar
Yu Sasaki
Robert Schaedlich
Jan Schlegel
Martin Schläffer
Markus Schofnegger
Peter Scholl
Jan Schoone
Phillipp Schoppmann
Jacob Schuldt
Mark Schultz-Wu
Marek Sefranek
Nicolas Sendrier
Jae Hong Seo
Karn Seth
Srinath Setty
Yannick Seurin
Dana Shamir
Devika Sharma
Yaobin Shen
Yixin Shen
Danping Shi
Sina Shiehian
Omri Shmueli
Ferdinand Sibleyras
Janno Siim
Mark Simkin
Jaspal Singh

Amit Singh Bhati
Sujoy Sinha Roy
Naomi Sirkin
Daniel Slamanig
Christopher Smith
Tomer Solomon
Fang Song
Yifan Song
Pratik Soni
Jesse Spielman
Srivatsan Sridhar
Damien Stehlé
Marc Stevens
Christoph Striecks
Patrick Struck
Adam Suhl
Chao Sun
Siwei Sun
Berk Sunar
Ajith Suresh
Moeto Suzuki
Erkan Tairi
Akira Takahashi
Katsuyuki Takashima
Abdul Rahman Taleb
Quan Quan Tan
Er-Cheng Tang
Qiang Tang
Stefano Tessaro
Justin Thaler
Yan Bo Ti
Tyge Tiessen
Junichi Tomida
Dilara Toprakhisar
Andreas Trügler
Daniel Tschudi
Yiannis Tselekounis
Ida Tucker
Balazs Udvarhelyi
Rei Ueno
Florian Unterstein
Annapurna Valiveti
Gijs Van Laer
Wessel van Woerden
Akhil Vanukuri
Karolin Varner

Javier Verbel
Tanner Verber
Frederik Vercauteren
Corentin Verhamme
Psi Vesely
Fernando Virdia
Quoc-Huy Vu
Benedikt Wagner
Roman Walch
Hendrik Waldner
Han Wang
Libo Wang
William Wang
Yunhao Wang
Zhedong Wang
Hoeteck Wee
Mor Weiss
Weiqiang Wen
Chenkai Weng
Luca Wilke
Mathias Wolf
David Wu
Lichao Wu
Zejun Xiang
Tiancheng Xie
Alex Xiong
Anshu Yadav
Sophia Yakoubov
Hossein Yalame
Shota Yamada
Avishay Yanai
Kang Yang
Qianqian Yang
Tianqi Yang
Yibin Yang
Kan Yasuda
Eylon Yogev
Yang Yu
Arantxa Zapico
Hadas Zeilberger
Bin Zhang
Jiang Zhang
Ruizhe Zhang
Zhenda Zhang
Chenzhi Zhu
Jens Zumbraegel

Contents – Part V

Quantum Cryptography

Tracing Quantum State Distinguishers via Backtracking

Mark Zhandry[(✉)]

NTT Research, Sunnyvale, USA
mark.zhandry@ntt-research.com

Abstract. We show the following results:

- The post-quantum equivalence of indistinguishability obfuscation and differing inputs obfuscation in the restricted setting where the outputs differ on at most a polynomial number of points. Our result handles the case where the auxiliary input may contain a *quantum state*; previous results could only handle classical auxiliary input.
- Bounded collusion traitor tracing from general public key encryption, where the decoder is allowed to contain a *quantum state*. The parameters of the scheme grow polynomially in the collusion bound.
- Collusion-resistant traitor tracing with constant-size ciphertexts from general public key encryption, again for *quantum state decoders*. The public key and secret keys grow polynomially in the number of users.
- Traitor tracing with embedded identities in the keys, again for *quantum state decoders*, under a variety of different assumptions with different parameter size trade-offs.

Traitor tracing and differing inputs obfuscation with quantum decoders/auxiliary input arises naturally when considering the post-quantum security of these primitives. We obtain our results by abstracting out a core algorithmic model, which we call the Back One Step (BOS) model. We prove a general theorem, reducing many quantum results including ours to designing *classical* algorithms in the BOS model. We then provide simple algorithms for the particular instances studied in this work.

1 Introduction

The threat of quantum computers requires re-evaluation of some of the core aspects of modern cryptography. Due to Shor's algorithm [Sho94], cryptosystems based on factoring or discrete logs will be insecure. Even for cryptosystems based on so-called "post-quantum" building blocks, quantum computing may also yield new threat models, such as superposition attacks [KM10, Zha12, DFNS].

A perhaps more subtle issue is the following: even if the building blocks are quantum-immune and the threat model remains the same, the classical proof may not hold quantumly. Indeed, a classical proof converts a *classical* adversary into a *classical* algorithm for some underlying hard problem, while a post-quantum proof must convert a *quantum* adversary into a *quantum* algorithm. What works for classical adversaries may not work for quantum adversaries. The canonical

H. Handschuh and A. Lysyanskaya (Eds.): CRYPTO 2023, LNCS 14085, pp. 3–36, 2023.
https://doi.org/10.1007/978-3-031-38554-4_1

example of a proof technique that does not translate is rewinding, which is known to be problematic quantumly due to the no-cloning theorem [VDG98, ARU14][1]. Rewinding is most often discussed in the context of interactive proofs, where it is used to extract information from the adversary that would remain hidden against straight-line procedures. In this context, a number of positive results have been achieved quantumly [Wat06, Unr12, CMSZ21, LMS21].

In this work, we consider certain cases where rewinding arises, perhaps implicitly, in settings other than interactive proofs:

- It is known, classically, that indistinguishability obfuscation (iO) implies differing inputs obfuscation (diO) in the setting where the pairs of circuits being considered only differ on polynomially many points [BCP14]. The proof extracts a differing input from a distinguisher by testing the distinguisher on a variety of distributions over programs, using a type of binary search.
- In traitor tracing [CFN94], a coalition of malicious users group their secret keys into a pirate decoder program, and a tracing algorithm must identify at least one malicious user. Once identified, the malicious user(s) can be prosecuted. Essentially all traitor tracing schemes test the decoder on various distributions over ciphertexts, and use the corresponding decryption probabilities to accuse a user.

The unifying feature of both classes of results is that the extracted information is computed based on the success probabilities of a single adversary on various distributions of inputs. This is very different from the way information is typically extracted for interactive proofs, where the information is usually extracted from the adversary's outputs themselves.

When moving to the quantum setting for traitor tracing, Zhandry [Zha20] shows that if the pirate decoder contains a quantum state, then the classical tracing algorithms are no longer guaranteed to work. The malicious users of course want to design their decoder in such a way as to avoid tracing, and would therefore be incentivized to design a quantum state decoder to evade tracing. Being able to trace such quantum state decoders is therefore the natural model to consider in the post-quantum setting. Zhandry provides an initial positive result, showing how to trace even quantum decoders for schemes in the Private Linear Broadcast Encryption (PLBE) framework [BSW06], when the identity space is polynomial size[2]. However, the techniques are incapable of handling other important traitor tracing approaches, in particular:

- Traitor tracing with embedded identities, where the identity of a user is an arbitrary string, as opposed to an index in a polynomial-sized set. The first such tracing scheme is due to [NWZ16], who use the PLBE framework but

---

[1] A different example is the quantum random oracle model [BDF+11], though this model is conceptually closer to the superposition attacks mentioned above.

[2] Another limitation of Zhandry's work is that the PLBE must support public encryption for all distributions used during tracing, which is not true of the known succinct LWE-based scheme [GKW18].

with *exponentially many* identities. [NWZ16] and later [GKW19] also explore other structures for achieving embedded identities.

- Combinatorial traitor tracing, such as [CFN94, BN08, BP08], which achieve traitor tracing with short ciphertexts from general public key encryption, as opposed to algebraic tools.

When considering the restricted iO-diO equivalence in the quantum setting, it is most natural to consider a quantum auxiliary input, since the auxiliary input will be the adversary's state at some step in the protocol. However, the equivalence has a flavor similar to PLBE with super-polynomial identity spaces (as observed by [NWZ16]), and therefore is also not handled by the previous quantum techniques.

Thus, these important cases of traitor tracing and the iO-diO equivalence were previously open questions in the quantum decoder/auxiliary input setting.

This Work. In our work, we resolve these open questions. We start by defining an algorithmic model we call the Back One Step (BOS) model, which we show can be realized by any quantum program containing a quantum state. This is the core conceptual contribution of this work, and builds on ideas from Zhandry [Zha20] and Chiesa et al. [CMSZ21], which in turn build on Marriott and Watrous [MW04].

We then design new algorithms for the BOS model, for the instances arising from the aforementioned open problems. This step is entirely classical, and while the algorithms may not be trivial, they are fairly simple. Combining our results together, we achieve the following results:

- (Section 6) We prove the restricted iO-diO equivalence holds post-quantumly, even if the auxiliary input is a quantum state. Along the way, we give a definition of diO that address several subtleties in defining quantum security that we overcome.
- We construct tracing algorithms for several existing traitor tracing schemes, achieving a couple of "firsts" for tracing schemes for quantum decoders:
  - (Section 8) Bounded collision traitor tracing from general public key encryption, where the parameters grow polynomially with the collusion bound but are independent of the number of users.
  - (Section 8) Collusion-resistant traitor tracing from general public key encryption, where ciphertext size is independent of the number of users.
  - (Sections 7 and 9) Collusion-resistant *embedded identity* traitor tracing, under various assumptions with different parameter size trade-offs. In particular, assuming public key encryption, we get a scheme where the parameters grow polynomially in the number of users. Assuming Learning With Errors (LWE), we get such a scheme with succinct ciphertexts whose length is independent of the length of the embedded identities. Finally, assuming iO, we get a scheme with both succinct ciphertexts and where parameter sizes are independent of the number of users.

These schemes are identical to their classical counterparts, *except* for the tracing algorithm. They also match most of the best-known results for classical

traitor tracing under post-quantum assumptions, with the main exception being the LWE-based traitor tracing scheme with constant-sized parameters [GKW18], which still remains open in the quantum setting.
- In the full version, we show limitations of the BOS model, showing an artificial setting that can be solved classically, but for which there is no BOS model algorithm.

2 Technical Overview

2.1 A General View of Classical Tracing Algorithms

Essentially all modern classical traitor tracing algorithms can be framed as follows. There is a collection $\mathcal{D} = \{D_q\}_{q \in \mathcal{Q}}$ of distributions of ciphertexts for some index set $\mathcal{Q}$, and the adversary produces a decoder subject to the following guarantees:

- **Large success probability on source.** The distribution of "honest" ciphertexts is an element of $\mathcal{D}$, which we will denote as D_α for some distinguished $\alpha \in \mathcal{Q}$ that we call the source. Any useful decoder, by definition, has a "large" success probability on D_α.
- **Small success probability on sinks.** There is a collection of distributions $\{D_q\}_{q \in \Omega}$ for $q \in \Omega \subset \mathcal{Q}$, which we may call sinks, for which any coalition of users has "small" success probability.
- **Constant on adversary partition.** Any coalition of malicious users corresponds to a partition Π on $\mathcal{Q}$, such that the coalition, and therefore their decoder, cannot efficiently distinguish between distributions belonging to the same part of the partition. In other words, the decoder's decryption probability is roughly constant on each part of the partition.

The tracing algorithm therefore tests the decoder on various D_q, learning (estimates of) the decoder's success probabilities on D_q. The rough idea is that α and $q \in \Omega$ must have different success probabilities, so the tracer is guaranteed to see some jumps as it makes its queries. These jumps must be across different parts of the partition, revealing some information about the structure of the partition. The hope is that this information can identify at least one malicious user.

Abstracting out the details of generating the various distributions and estimating their success probability, we arrive at a model we might call the Globally Consistent Hidden Partition model, where the tracer simply queries (potentially adaptively) on various $q_i \in \mathcal{Q}$ and receives in response real numbers $o_i \in [0,1]$. We are guaranteed that any o_i, o_j which correspond to queries q_i, q_j lying in the same part of the partition Π will be close, that $q_i = \alpha$ will give "large" o_i, and that $q_i \in \Omega$ will give "small" o_i. The tracer then takes these o_i and uses them to learn information about the partition.

Example: PLBE. To make things concrete, we now illustrate how this view captures private linear broadcast encryption (PLBE). Here, there are N users, with identities $1, \ldots, N$. For any $q \in [0, N]$, one can encrypt to the set $[q] = \{1, \ldots, q\}$. Users in $[q]$ will be able to decrypt, while users outside of $[q]$ will not. An "honest" ciphertext is an encryption to all users, $q = N$. Moreover, any coalition of users will be unable to distinguish encryptions to $[a]$ and $[b]$, unless the coalition contains a user in the half-open interval $(a, b]$. In the view above, we would therefore have $\mathcal{Q} = [0, N]$, $\alpha = N$, and $\Omega = \{0\}$. For a coalition of users $a_1 < a_2 < \cdots < a_t \in [N]$, the partition Π therefore consists of the intervals $[0, a_1), [a_1, a_2), [a_2, a_3), \cdots, [a_t, N]$.

To trace, we split into two cases. In the case where N is polynomial, one simply estimates the success probabilities $o_0, o_1, \ldots, o_N$ on queries $0, 1, \cdots, N$. The usefulness of the decoder implies that $o_N \gg 0$, while PLBE security implies that $o_0 \approx 0$. Therefore, there must exist a q such that $|o_{q-1} - o_q| \gg 0$. But since o_i must be constant on the intervals in Π, we know that $q = a_i$ for some i. Thus we have identified a member of the coalition.

If N is exponential, then we cannot simply do a linear scan. However, a variant of a binary search will work, as shown in [BCP14, NWZ16]. In the binary search, we recurse left if there is a large gap between the pivot and the left value, while we recurse right if there is a large gap between the pivot and the right value. Importantly, we must make sure to pivot *both* left and right if there is a large gap in both directions. Otherwise, there is a possibility that every time we recurse, the gap gets divided by 2, and after a polynomial number of steps the gap is negligible but we have yet to accuse a user. Fortunately, it is proved by those works that there will never be more branches in the binary search than there are users in the coalition, so the overall search still takes polynomial time.

2.2 Moving to Quantum: Prior Results

When we move to allowing a quantum decoder, we must be much more careful. There are several issues, first pointed out by Zhandry [Zha20]. First is definitional: the success probability of the decoder is not necessarily known (nor even *knowable*) until it is *measured*, and any measurement necessarily alters the quantum state. Care must be taken to appropriately define traitor tracing to handle cases where the decoder may be in superposition of both high success probability and low success probability. Zhandry shows how to handle these definitional issues.

The second issue has to do with rewinding, which happens at two levels. First, estimating success probability on a distribution classically involves running the decoder on various samples from the distribution. But this implicitly requires being able to return the decoder to its original state every time, to ensure independent trials from the same distribution. As mentioned above, quantumly rewinding is problematic. In particular, each trial may alter the state of the decoder. Zhandry demonstrates that the classical approach of repeated sampling cannot, in general, yield an estimate of the decoder's success probability. Fortunately, Zhandry shows how to develop a quantum-compatible success probability estimation routine based on a technique of Marriott and Watrous [MW04].

Remark 2.1. Note that Zhandry's procedure requires security to hold when the adversary gets an arbitrary polynomial number of tracing ciphertexts; for traitor tracing from LWE [GKW18], this is not guaranteed. We inherit this limitation, and this is why we still cannot handle succinct traitor tracing from LWE.

A second level is that multiple success probabilities will have to be estimated, for various distributions of inputs. In the classical setting, it is assumed that each estimate of success probability is applied to the same initial decoder; in other words, the decoder is rewound to its initial state[3]. Otherwise, how can we make sense of gaps between estimated success probabilities, if the success probabilities has since changed and the previous estimates are no longer valid?

Zhandry gives a first step toward overcoming this problem, by showing that a *local* consistency property holds: if two *consecutive* estimates of success probabilities are on computationally indistinguishable distributions, then the estimated success probabilities will be close. However, estimated probabilities that are not consecutive may not obey this property. This gives rise to a variant of the tracing model above, which we will call the *Locally Consistent Hidden Partition Model*, that is identical to the Globally Consistent model above, except that (1) o_i, o_j corresponding to q_i, q_j in the same part are guaranteed close *only if* $|i - j| \leq 1$, and (2) $q_i = \alpha$ is guaranteed to yield a large r_i *only on the first query* $i = 1$. The good news is that the linear scan algorithm for PLBE with polynomial identity space fits within this model (provided the scan starts at N and goes to 0), allowing Zhandry to trace this particular case. On the other hand, the model seems inherently limited to PLBE: during any sequence of probability estimates, the estimate outcomes may be the sequence $1, 1, 1, \cdots, 1, 0, 0, 0, \cdots$. Such a sequence would satisfy the local consistency requirements, as long as the jump from 1 to 0 happens the first time a distribution D_q for $q \in \Omega$ is tested. But for a polynomial-length sequence, only a logarithmic number of bits of information can be extracted, namely the location of the jump between 1 and 0. Thus this model is incapable of handling a variety of traitor tracing scenarios, such as

– Embedded identities, where the whole point is to embed more than a logarithmic amount of information.
– Combinatorial traitor tracing, which usually follows a non-linear path. For example, traitor tracing based on fingerprinting codes [BN08, BP08] first extracts a very long "codeword" from the decoder, which is then further processed; in the locally consistent model it would be impossible to construct this codeword.

The Work of [KN22]. [KN22] shows how to watermark PRFs in a quantum decoder model. Most relevant to us, their algorithm surprisingly extracts more

---

[3] The usual terminology is that the decoder is "stateless".

than a logarithmic amount of information. See the full version for a brief interpretation of their technique and why it is likely limited to the case of no collusions, which is insufficient for our purposes.

2.3   Our Solution: The Back One Step (BOS) Model

A starting point for our results is the recent work of Chiesa et al. [CMSZ21]. They provide a powerful new rewinding technique, where they show that in some sense it is possible to "repair" a quantum state after a measurement. They apply their technique to the setting of interactive proofs, where they repair the quantum state of the adversary in order to rewind it many times. In this work, we show how to adapt the rewinding technique to our setting.

Before getting into the details of our approach, we highlight some conceptual differences between our settings:

- Chiesa et al. extract information from an adversary using the adversary's actual messages; the rewinds are used to obtain many such messages. The inputs for the different rewinds are typically all uniformly random and independent. In contrast, for traitor tracing, information is generally extracted by looking at success probabilities. The distributions tested will generally be far from uniform, in order to get differences in success probabilities.
- The decision tree in traitor tracing is rather deep. Consider for example the binary search algorithm for PLBE with large identities. In order to find a gap, we must explore a deep branch. We may not find anything, in which case we must return to the root and explore a different branch. In contrast, the rewinding in Chiesa et al. always returns the adversary to a state approximating the initial state of the adversary. In this sense, the decision tree is shallow, having only one level.
- The repair procedure can only repair a single feature of the adversary. This is inherent, since different quantities may correspond to "incompatible" observables, and in general quantum systems one cannot simultaneously "know" the values of incompatible observables. Chiesa et al. always repair just the original success probability of the adversary. This is enough for them, due to their shallow decision tree. Looking at our setting, however, always repairing to the initial setting will not work. For example, in the binary search case, if we just repair to the initial success probability, this allows us to return to the root of the binary search tree. But now the values at all points may have shifted around. So if we explore a branch and fail to find a gap, when we return to the root, the gap we are looking for may have moved into the branch we just abandoned. Even if we explore all branches, we may never end up actually finding the ever-moving gap.

In order to simplify the task of designing new tracing protocols to overcome these challenges, we propose an intermediate model which we call the Back One Step (BOS) model. The BOS model allows us to abstract away the complicated techniques of state repair in order to give a clean model of what the technique should be capable of. This model will then allow us to design novel tracing algorithms. Importantly, the task of designing algorithms in the model will be entirely classical, with all the quantum aspects hidden beneath the abstraction.

The Model. We now describe the BOS model: there is a collection $\mathcal{Q}$ of queries available. There is moreover a potentially *stateful* oracle which contains a secret partition Π of $\mathcal{Q}$. The oracle accepts a sequence of queries $q_1, \ldots, q_t \in \mathcal{Q}$, and answers queries with a bit $o_i \in \{0, 1\}$. Note that we discretized the o_i, to make the model simpler. We impose the following constraints:

- **Large value on source if first query.** A distinguished query $\alpha \in \mathcal{Q}$. If $q_1 = \alpha$, then $o_1 = 1$. There are no guarantees on subsequent queries to α, or if α is not the very first query.
- **Small values on sinks.** There is a collection $\Omega \subset \mathcal{Q}$, such that if $q_i \in \Omega$, then $o_i = 0$. This holds for *all* $i \in [t]$.
- **Local consistency.** For any two *consecutive* queries q_i, q_{i+1}, if q_i, q_{i+1} lie in the same part of the partition Π (and in particular, if $q_i = q_{i+1}$), then $o_i = o_{i+1}$. There is no such requirement for q_i, q_j with $|i - j| > 1$.
- **Single step rewinding.** Finally, if $q_{i+2} = q_i$, then $o_{i+2} = o_i$. Any other identical queries that may exist in the query sequence have no such restriction.

If we ignore the last requirement, note that we recover the model of Zhandry. The last requirement essentially says that we can make a query q_i, make an arbitrary different query q_{i+1}, and then rewind to the previous query q_i for query $i + 2$ and be guaranteed to recover the same output o_i a second time.

Realizing the BOS Model. By adapting the rewinding technique of Chiesa et al., we show how to instantiate a BOS oracle from any pirate decoder or diO adversary. The rough idea is to run the BOS algorithm, using Zhandry's [Zha20] success probability estimation routine to answer every query. This already ensures large values on the source (if the first query), small values on the sinks, and local consistency, following the same analysis as Zhandry. In order to ensure single step rewinding, we then add one more feature: if any query q_{i+2} is equal to q_i, instead of naively computing the success probability o_{q+2} using Zhandry, we instead use the quantum rewinding technique of Chiesa et al. to rewind to a state where query $q_{i+2} = q_i$ yields success probability essentially equal to o_q. Thus, we can answer the query with $o_{q+2} = o_q$, thereby guaranteeing single step rewinding.

Designing Algorithms for the BOS Model. The BOS oracle guarantees are much weaker than the Globally Consistent Hidden Partition Model, and as discussed above, many classical tracing algorithm crucially rely on these stronger consistency guarantees. Perhaps surprisingly, while local consistency alone does not appear enough for many tracing settings, the ability to rewind even a single step opens many doors. We design new algorithms for the BOS model for the various settings, crucially leveraging the ability to rewind a single step. Importantly, this design process is entirely classical, greatly simplifying the design task. We note that the algorithm for each result is different (aside from the iO/diO equivalence and basic embedded identity tracing scheme being the same).

We next briefly describe how the process works for tracing PLBE; for the other results see the main body of the paper.

The Case of PLBE. As explained above, in the case of PLBE, we have $Q = [0, N], \alpha = N, \Omega = \{0\}$, and $\Pi = \{[0, a_1), [a_1, a_2), [a_2, a_3), \cdots, [a_t, N]\}$. Our goal is to recover one of the a_i.

We know if the first query is on $\alpha = N$, then the response is $o_N = 1$. Likewise, we know if we ever query on 0, the response is $o_0 = 0$. In the classical case, we would identify an a_i via a binary search. We first assign a pivot to be $N/2$, and query on $N/2$. If the query response is $o_{N/2} = 1$, we know that at least one a_i lies in the interval $[1, N/2]$, so we can recurse on the interval $[0, N/2]$. If the query response is $o_{N/2} = 0$, then we know at least one a_i lies in the interval $[N/2 + 1, N]$, and so we can recurse on the interval $[N/2, N]$.

In the BOS model, we can try the same: after querying on N and receiving response 1, we query on $N/2$ and receive response $o_{N/2}$. If $o_{N/2} = 1$, we know by the rules of the BOS model that there is an a_i in the interval $[1, N/2]$, and if $o_{N/2} = 0$, we know by the rules of the BOS model that there is an a_i in the interval $[N/2 + 1, N]$. Moreover, in the case $o_{N/2} = 1$, we actually have the correct setup to recurse on $Q' = [0, N/2]$ by setting $\alpha' = N/2$, $\Omega' = \{0\}$, and Π' to be the partition of Q' induced by Q. Indeed, by local consistency, since the last query was on $N/2 = \alpha'$ and the response was 1, if the next query is on α' the response will be 1, guaranteeing a large response for the recursion. Small value on the sink, local consistency, and single step rewinding carry over as well.

On the other hand, let us see what happens if we try to recurse on $[N/2, N]$ in the case $o_{N/2} = 0$. We would naturally set $Q' = [N/2, N], \alpha' = N, \Omega = \{N/2\}$. We note that local consistency and single step rewinding still carry over to this case. Moreover, since the penultimate query was on $N = \alpha'$, single step rewinding guarantees that we get a large value on α' if it is the next query.

This leaves small values on sink. Initially, it is true that querying on the sink $N/2$ gives 0, as desired. But importantly this only holds initially, where the BOS model requires the sink to give 0 *always*. We can see where this leads to trouble by taking the recursion a couple steps forward. The next step is to query on $3N/4$, receiving $o_{3N/4}$. Suppose $o_{3N/4} = 1$. Then we recurse left on the interval $Q'' = [N/2, 3N/4]$ and query on $5N/8$. Suppose again that $o_{5N/8} = 1$, so we recurse on the interval $[N/2, 5N/8]$. At this point, we would want that $\Omega''' = \{N/2\}$. However, our last query on $N/2$ was three queries ago (with $3N/4$ and $5N/2$ between). Therefore, $o_{N/2}$ may have changed, and there is no longer any guarantee of having small values on the sinks. Without a small value on the sinks, the recursion will fail.

One attempt to fix this problem is, after querying on $3N/4$ and receiving $o_{3N/4} = 1$, we insert a query on $N/2$. By single step rewinding, we have, as desired, that the result is $o_{N/2} = 0$. However, this strategy fails when we move to the query on $5N/8$. Suppose now that $o_{5N/8} = 0$, meaning we recurse right on the interval $Q''' = [5N/8, 3N/4]$. Unfortunately, by inserting the new query on

$N/2$, the most recent query on $3N/4$ was now three queries ago (being followed by $N/2$ and $5N/8$). Therefore, we no longer have the guarantee that querying on the new source $\alpha''' = 3N/4$ gives a 1, and in fact it could be that all future queries give a 0, which clearly does not allow for extracting any information.

We now explain our solution. If $o_{N/2} = 1$, we recurse on $[0, N/2]$ as we would classically. In the case $o_{N/2} = 0$, we still query on $3N/4$ to get $o_{3N/4}$. Here, if $o_{3N/4} = 1$, we cannot recurse on the interval $[N/2, 3N/4]$. However, we *can* recurse on the interval $Q' = [0, 3N/4]$, since now $\Omega' = \{0\} = \Omega$ and so we guarantee small values on sinks throughout, not just on the next query.

What if $o_{3N/4} = 0$? In this case, we update the pivot to $7N/8$ as if we were recursing to the right. Importantly, however, we always keep the bottom of the domain as 0 to ensure small values on the sink. So if $o_{7N/8}$ gives 1, we recurse on the interval $[0, 7N/8]$. If $o_{7N/8} = 0$, we update the pivot to $15N/16$, and so on.

With this new algorithm, we can prove that we do indeed preserve all the properties of the BOS model in each step of the recursion, and will eventually reach the case where the interval is $[0, a]$ and the pivot is $a - 1$, and the last two queries were on $a, a-1$ giving $o_a = 1, o_{a-1} = 0$. We output a, as local consistency implies that a is one of the endpoints of the intervals in Π. Moreover, we can prove termination in a polynomial number of steps, namely $O(t \log^2 N)$ where t is the number of a_i.

3   Quantum Background

We assume basic familiarity with quantum computation. We distinguish between classical probabilistic polynomial time (PPT) algorithms and quantum polynomial time (QPT) algorithms. Sometimes we will consider programs that consist of a quantum state. Formally, these will consist of a quantum circuit C, and a quantum auxiliary input aux. To evaluate the program on input x, one evaluates C on $|x\rangle \otimes$ aux. We will denote such programs by $|P\rangle$ and the evaluation of such programs as $|P\rangle(x)$.

Almost Projective Measurements. We state a property of general measurements due to [Zha20] that captures when a measurement is "close" to being projective, in the sense that sequential applications of the measurement yield similar outcomes.

Definition 3.1. *A real-valued measurement* $\mathbf{M} = (M_p)_p$ *is* (ϵ, δ)-*almost projective if applying* $\mathbf{M}$ *twice in a row to a register* $\mathcal{H}$ *(initially containing any state* ρ*) produces measurement outcomes* p, p' *where* $\Pr[|p - p'| \leq \epsilon] \geq 1 - \delta$.

Quantum State Repair. We now recall quantum state repair from [CMSZ21].

Lemma 3.2 ([CMSZ21], **Lemma 4.10**). *Given a projective measurement* $\mathbf{P}$ *on register* $\mathcal{H}$ *that has outcomes in set* S *of size* N, *an* (ϵ, δ)-*almost projective measurement* $\mathbf{M}$ *on* $\mathcal{H}$, *and* $T \in \mathbb{N}, s \in S, p \in [0, 1]$, *there exists a procedure* $\mathrm{Repair}_{T,p,s}^{\mathbf{M},\mathbf{P}}$ *on* $\mathcal{H}$ *such that:*

- *(State is repaired with respect to* **M***) Consider applying the following operations to register* $\mathcal{H}$ *initially containing state* ρ*:*
  1. *First apply* **M** *to obtain* $p \in [0, 1]$,
  2. *Then apply* **P** *to obtain outcome* $s \in S$,
  3. *Then apply* Repair$_{T,p,s}^{\mathbf{M},\mathbf{P}}$,
  4. *And finally, apply* **M** *once more to obtain* $p' \in [0, 1]$.
  Then $\Pr[|p - p'| > 2\epsilon] \leq N\delta + N/T + 4\sqrt{\delta}$.
- *(Efficiency) The expected total number of calls that* Repair *makes to* **M** *and* **P** *is at most* $N + 4T\sqrt{\delta}$.

In other words, since **M** is almost projective, applying **M** twice in a row will give outcomes p, p' that are close. However, if **P** is applied in between these two measurements, there are no more guarantees on the closeness of p, p'. However, by applying Repair before the second application of **M**, we can once again ensure closeness of p, p'.

Mixtures of Projective Measurements. The following is taken from [Zha20]. We consider the following abstract setup. We have a collection $\mathcal{P} = \{\mathcal{P}_i\}_{i \in \mathcal{I}}$ of binary outcome projective measurements $\mathcal{P}_i = (P_i, Q_i)$ over the same Hilbert space $\mathcal{H}$. Here, P_i corresponds to output 0, and Q_i corresponds to output 1. We will assume we can efficiently measure the $\mathcal{P}_i$ for superpositions of i, meaning we can efficiently perform the following projective measurement over $\mathcal{I} \otimes \mathcal{H}$:

$$\left(\sum_i |i\rangle\langle i| \otimes P_i \, , \, \sum_i |i\rangle\langle i| \otimes Q_i \right) \tag{1}$$

Here, we call $\mathcal{P}$ a *collection of projective measurements*, and call $\mathcal{I}$ the *control*. For a distribution D over $\mathcal{I}$, let $\mathcal{P}_D$ be the POVM which samples a random $i \leftarrow D$, applies the measurement $\mathcal{P}_i$, and outputs the resulting bit. We call $\mathcal{P}_D$ a *mixture of projective measurements*. The POVM is given by the matrices (P_D, Q_D) where

$$P = \sum_{i \in \mathcal{I}} \Pr[i \leftarrow D] P_i \quad \text{and} \quad Q = \sum_{i \in \mathcal{I}} \Pr[i \leftarrow D] Q_i$$

Next, for $a \in \mathbb{R}$ and interval $[b, c] \subseteq \mathbb{R}$, denote the distance between a and $[b, c]$ as $|a - [b, c]| := \min_{x \in [b,c]} |a - x|$. For $a \in [b, c]$, the distance is 0 and for $a \notin [b, c]$, the distance is $\max(a - c, b - a)$. Let D_0, D_1 be two distributions over $\mathbb{R}$, with cumulative density functions f_0, f_1, respectively. Let $\epsilon \in \mathbb{R}$. The Shift distance with parameter ϵ is defined as:

$$\Delta_\epsilon(D_0, D_1) := \sup_{x \in \mathbb{R}} \left| f_0(x) - [f_1(x - \epsilon), f_1(x + \epsilon)] \right|$$

Let $\mathbf{M} = (M_i)_{i \in \mathcal{I}}$ and $\mathbf{N} = (N_j)_{j \in \mathcal{J}}$ be real-valued quantum measurements over the same quantum system $\mathcal{H}$. The shift distance between $\mathbf{M}, \mathbf{N}$, denoted $\Delta_\epsilon(\mathbf{M}, \mathbf{N})$ is defined as

$$\Delta_\epsilon(\mathbf{M}, \mathbf{N}) := \sup_{|\psi\rangle} \Delta_\epsilon(\mathbf{M}(|\psi\rangle), \mathbf{N}(|\psi\rangle))$$

Now, if $\mathcal{P}_D = (P_D, Q_D)$ is a mixture of projective measurements, we note that $Q_D = \mathbf{I} - P_D$, and therefore P_D, Q_D commute. In this case, $\mathcal{P}_D$ has a *projective implementation*, denoted $\mathsf{ProjImp}(\mathcal{P}_D)$, which is defined as follows. Let S be the set of eigenvalues of P_D, and R_i for i the projectors onto the associated eigenspaces. Then $\mathsf{ProjImp}(\mathcal{P}_D)$ is the projective measurement $(P_i)_{i \in S}$. Note that $S \subseteq [0, 1]$. Also note that applying $\mathcal{P}_D$ is equivalent to the following: first apply $\mathsf{ProjImp}(\mathcal{P}_D)$ to obtain outcome p, then interpret p as a probability and output 1 with probability p.

Lemma 3.3 ([Zha20], **Theorem 6.2**). *For any $\epsilon, \delta, \mathcal{P}, D$, there exists an algorithm $\mathsf{API}_{\epsilon,\delta}^{\mathcal{P},D}$ operating on $\mathcal{H}$ and making quantum queries to $\mathcal{P}, D$ which additionally outputs a number in some set $S \subseteq [0, 1]$ such that:*

- *There is a function $R = \mathsf{poly}(1/\epsilon, \log(1/\delta))$ such that the expected number of calls $\mathsf{API}_{\epsilon,\delta}^{\mathcal{P},D}$ makes to $\mathcal{P}$ and D, the running time of $\mathsf{API}_{\epsilon,\delta}^{\mathcal{P},D}$, and $|S|$ are all bounded by R.*
- *$\mathsf{API}_{\epsilon,\delta}^{\mathcal{P},D}$ is (ϵ, δ)-almost projective.*
- *$\Delta_\epsilon(\mathsf{API}_{\epsilon,\delta}^{\mathcal{P},D}, \mathsf{ProjImp}(\mathcal{P}_D)) \leq \delta$.*

Lemma 3.4 ([Zha20], **Theorem 6.5**). *Let ρ be an efficiently constructible mixed state over $\mathcal{H}$, and D_0, D_1 efficiently sampleable, computationally indistinguishable distributions. For any inverse polynomial ϵ, there exists a negligible δ such that $\Delta_\epsilon(\mathsf{ProjImp}(\mathcal{P}_{D_0})(\rho), \mathsf{ProjImp}(\mathcal{P}_{D_0})(\rho)) \leq \delta$.*

4   Cryptographic Notions

Note that we use superscripts like ^{IPP} and ^{TT} to disambiguate between algorithms belonging to different cryptosystems.

We assume the reader is familiar with the basic definitions of indistinguishability obfuscation (iO) and functional encryption. Post-quantum candidates for iO include [BGMZ18, CHVW19, Agr19, AP20, BDGM20, WW21, DQV+21]. Functional encryption can be built from iO [GGH+13]. It can even be made to have functions of unbounded complexity [AS16]. Functional encryption with bounded collusions can be built from public-key encryption [GVW12]; the parameters of the scheme grow polynomially in the collusion bound, and as well as the size of functions handled. Succinct ciphertexts independent of the function complexity can be obtained via subexponential LWE [GKP+13].

4.1   IPP Codes

A fingerprinting code [BS95] is used to fingerprint data. Fingerprinting codes have long been used to build traitor tracing schemes (e.g. [BN08, Sir06, BP08]). Note, however, that the fingerprinting codes explicitly cited in the literature are usually *binary* codes. Yet, the schemes provided can be generalized to non-binary codes, but require a different kind of code called an identifiable parent property (IPP) code [HvLT98]. We will use this generalization in order to abstract more schemes from the literature, so we here define IPP codes rather than fingerprinting codes. Note that the two notions coincide for binary codes.

An IPP code is a pair $(\mathsf{Gen}^{\mathsf{IPP}}, \mathsf{Trace}^{\mathsf{IPP}})$ of PPT algorithms such that:

- $\mathsf{Gen}^{\mathsf{IPP}}(1^\lambda, 1^N, 1^c)$ takes as input a security parameter, a number of users N, and a collusion bound c, all in unary. It outputs a tracing key tk, as well as N strings $w_1, \ldots, w_N \in \Sigma^\ell$. The w_i are called codewords
- $\mathsf{Trace}^{\mathsf{IPP}}(\mathsf{tk}, w^*)$ takes as input the tracing key and a codeword $w^* \in \Sigma^\ell$. It outputs a set $A \subseteq [N]$.

For a set of codewords $C \subseteq \Sigma^\ell$, let $F(C)$ be the "feasible set" of C, which is defined as follows. A word $w^* \in \Sigma \cup \{?\}$ is in $F(C)$ if, for each position $j \in [\ell]$, either $w_j^* = ?$ or there exists a codeword $w \in C$ such that $w_j^* = w_j$. In other words, $F(C)$ consists of all codewords in C, plus all codewords that can be obtained from C by potentially using a different codeword character in each position. Additionally, any entry can be set to ?. The condition of being in the feasible set of C is also called the "marking condition".

Remark 4.1. Where IPP codes differ from fingerprinting codes is in this marking condition. For a fingerprinting code, in any position j where $\{w_j\}_{w \in C}$ is not a single character, w_j^* is allowed to be *anything*. This condition better reflects the use in fingerprinting. However, the marking condition for IPP codes better reflects the use in traitor tracing.

Definition 4.2. *An IPP code* $(\mathsf{Gen}^{\mathsf{IPP}}, \mathsf{Trace}^{\mathsf{IPP}})$ *is δ-robust if, for all (potentially unbounded) algorithms $\mathcal{A}^{\mathsf{IPP}}$, for all polynomially bounded N, c, and for all $S \subseteq [N]$, $\mathcal{A}^{\mathsf{IPP}}$ wins the following experiment with probability at most $2^{-\lambda}$:*

- *Run* $(\mathsf{tk}, \{w_i\}_{i \in [N]}) \leftarrow \mathsf{Gen}^{\mathsf{IPP}}(1^\lambda, 1^N, 1^c)$.
- *Run* $w^* \leftarrow \mathcal{A}^{\mathsf{IPP}}(\{w_i\}_{i \in S})$
- *If the number of ? in w^* is more than $\delta\ell$, output "lose" and stop.*
- *Otherwise, run* $A \leftarrow \mathsf{Trace}^{\mathsf{IPP}}(\mathsf{tk}, w^*)$
- *Output "win" if (1) $w^* \in F(\{w_i\}_{i \in S})$ (w^* is feasible for the set of codewords given to $\mathcal{A}^{\mathsf{IPP}}$), and (2) either $A = \emptyset$ or $A \not\subseteq S$.*

Instantiations. In the case of binary alphabets, δ-robust IPP codes are also fingerprinting codes. Optimal fingerprinting codes with constant δ have $\ell = \Theta(c^2\lambda^2)$ [Tar03]. In the case of non-binary alphabets, less is known about IPP codes. However, the main traitor tracing scheme of [CFN94] can be seen as employing IPP codes with $\delta = 0$ and various parameters choices for ℓ, Σ, including $\ell = \Theta(c\lambda), |\Sigma| = \Theta(c^2\lambda)$.

4.2   Traitor Tracing with Quantum Decoders

We follow the definitions of traitor tracing given by Zhandry [Zha20]. The text is mostly taken from Zhandry, except we adjust the syntax to accommodate both ordinary and embedded-identity traitor tracing. A traitor tracing system for identity space $\mathcal{I}$ is a tuple $\Pi^{\mathsf{TT}} = (\mathsf{Gen}^{\mathsf{TT}}, \mathsf{Derive}^{\mathsf{TT}}, \mathsf{Enc}^{\mathsf{TT}}, \mathsf{Dec}^{\mathsf{TT}}, \mathsf{Trace}^{\mathsf{TT}})$ defined as follows:

- $\mathsf{Gen}^{\mathsf{TT}}(1^\lambda)$ is a classical probabilistic polynomial time (PPT) algorithm that takes as input the security parameter (in unary), and samples a public key pk and master secret key msk.
- $\mathsf{Derive}^{\mathsf{TT}}(\mathsf{msk}, \mathsf{id})$ is a classical PPT algorithm that takes as input the master secret key msk and an identity $\mathsf{id} \in \mathcal{I}$, and outputs a user secret key $\mathsf{sk}_{\mathsf{id}}$.
- $\mathsf{Enc}^{\mathsf{TT}}(\mathsf{pk}, m)$ is a classical PPT algorithm that takes as input the public key pk and a message m, and outputs a ciphertext c.
- $\mathsf{Dec}^{\mathsf{TT}}(\mathsf{sk}_{\mathsf{id}}, c)$ is a classical deterministic algorithm that takes as input a secret key $\mathsf{sk}_{\mathsf{id}}$ for user id and a ciphertext, and outputs a message m'.
- $\mathsf{Trace}^{\mathsf{TT}}(\mathsf{pk}, m_0, m_1, 1^{1/\epsilon}, |D\rangle)$ is a QPT algorithm that takes as input the public key pk, two messages m_0, m_1, and a parameter ϵ (whose reciprocal is an integer represented in unary), and a quantum state $|D\rangle$ representing a pirate decoder. It ultimately outputs a subset of $\mathcal{I}$, which are the accused users. Here, m_0, m_1 are two messages whose ciphertexts $|D\rangle$ supposedly distinguishes, and ϵ is a supposed lower bound on the distinguishing advantage.

We next define correctness and security.

Definition 4.3. *A traitor tracing system* Π^{TT} *is correct if, for all messages m and identities* $\mathsf{id} \in \mathcal{I}$,

$$\Pr\left[\mathsf{Dec}^{\mathsf{TT}}(\mathsf{sk}_{\mathsf{id}}, \mathsf{Enc}^{\mathsf{TT}}(\mathsf{pk}, m)) = m : \begin{matrix} (\mathsf{pk},\mathsf{msk}) \leftarrow \mathsf{Gen}^{\mathsf{TT}}(1^\lambda) \\ \mathsf{sk}_{\mathsf{id}} \leftarrow \mathsf{Derive}^{\mathsf{TT}}(\mathsf{msk},\mathsf{id}) \end{matrix}\right] \geq 1 - \mathsf{negl}(\lambda)$$

We now discuss security, adapting the software decoder model version of the definition of Zhandry [Zha20]. For a decoder $|D\rangle$, two messages m_0, m_1, and public key pk, consider the operation on $|D\rangle$:

- Choose a random bit $b \leftarrow \{0, 1\}$.
- Run $c \leftarrow \mathsf{Enc}^{\mathsf{TT}}(\mathsf{pk}, m_b)$ to get a random encryption of m_b.
- Run $b' \leftarrow |D\rangle(c)$.
- Output 1 if and only if $b = b'$; otherwise output 0.

Let $\mathcal{M}^{\mathsf{TT}} = (M_0, M_1)$ be the POVM given by this operation, which we call the *associated POVM* to the decoder. $\mathcal{M}^{\mathsf{TT}}$ has a projective implementation $\mathsf{ProjImp}(\mathcal{M}^{\mathsf{TT}}) = \{M'_p\}_p$, where each M'_p corresponds to the probability distribution on $\{0, 1\}$ that is 1 with probability p.

Tracing Experiment. For an adversary $\mathcal{A}^{TT}$, function $\epsilon(\cdot)$, and security parameter λ, we consider the following experiment on $\mathcal{A}^{TT}$:

- Run $(\mathsf{pk}, \mathsf{msk}) \leftarrow \mathsf{Gen}^{TT}(1^\lambda)$, and send pk to $\mathcal{A}^{TT}$.
- $\mathcal{A}^{TT}$ then makes an arbitrary number of classical queries on identities $\mathsf{id} \in \mathcal{I}$; in response it receives $\mathsf{sk_{id}}$. Let S be the set of id queried by $\mathcal{A}^{TT}$.
- Next, $\mathcal{A}^{TT}$ outputs $(|D\rangle, m_0, m_1)$ for decoder $|D\rangle$ and messages m_0, m_1.
- Apply the measurement $\mathsf{ProjImp}(\mathcal{M}^{TT})$ to $|D\rangle$, obtaining a probability p. Let $\mathsf{Live}_\epsilon^{TT}$ be the event that $p \geq 1/2 + \epsilon$.
- Finally run $A \leftarrow \mathsf{Trace}^{TT}(\mathsf{pk}, m_0, m_1, 1^{1/\epsilon}, |D\rangle)$ to get a set of accused users. Let $\mathsf{Fail}_\epsilon^{TT}$ as the event that $A \not\subseteq S$ (an accused user was not one of the queried users). We define the event $\mathsf{Success}_\epsilon^{TT}$ as the event that $A \neq \emptyset$ (some user is accused).

Definition 4.4. *A tracing system is* quantum traceable *if for all quantum polynomial time adversaries $\mathcal{A}^{TT}$ and for every inverse polynomial ϵ, there is a negligible* negl *such that* $\Pr[\mathsf{Fail}_\epsilon^{TT}] < \mathsf{negl}(\lambda)$ *and* $\Pr[\mathsf{Live}_\epsilon^{TT} \wedge \neg\mathsf{Success}_\epsilon^{TT}] < \mathsf{negl}(\lambda)$.

Variations. The usual setting of traitor tracing has $\mathbf{I} = [N]$ for a polynomial N. In this case, we often set N to be an explicit input to Gen^{TT}, and the parameters of the scheme may depend on N. A bounded collusion traitor tracing scheme additionally has another parameter c given to Gen^{TT}, and security only is required to hold if $|S| \leq c$. Traitor tracing with *embedded identities* has for $\mathcal{I} = \{0,1\}^n$ for integer n. Therefore, identities are now polynomial-length strings. Here, n may be an input to Gen^{TT} and the parameters of the scheme may depend on n. Note that some versions of embedded identity traitor tracing will have $\mathcal{I} = \{0,1\}^*$, meaning there is no a priori bound on the length of identity strings. Finally, we consider schemes with private tracing, where Gen^{TT} outputs a special tracing key tk, which is inputted into Trace^{TT}, and security only holds if tk is kept secret.

4.3 Defining Differing Inputs Obfuscation

We now define differing-inputs obfuscation (diO) in the quantum setting. To the best of our knowledge, diO has not been defined in the quantum setting, and it turns out that the task is somewhat subtle. In the full version, we briefly explain the challenges of providing such a definition. Below, we adapt the definition of traitor tracing for quantum decoders to give a strong definition of quantum-secure diO.

Let $m(\lambda), n(\lambda), s(\lambda)$ be polynomials, and consider a quantum polynomial time algorithm $\mathsf{Samp}(1^\lambda)$ which samples (1) a pair of classical circuits C_0, C_1 of size $s(\lambda)$, input length $n(\lambda)$ and output length $m(\lambda)$, and (2) a *quantum* side information aux. Consider a distinguishing adversary $\mathcal{A}$. Consider the following operation on aux:

- Choose a random bit $b \leftarrow \{0,1\}$.
- Run $\hat{C} \leftarrow \mathsf{diO}(1^\lambda, C_b)$ to get an obfuscation of a random choice of C_0, C_1.
- Run $b' \leftarrow \mathcal{A}(\hat{C}, C_0, C_1, \mathsf{aux})$.

– Output 1 if and only if $b' = b$; otherwise output 0.

Let $\mathcal{M}^{\mathsf{diO}} = (M_0, M_1)$ be the POVM given by this operation, which we call the *associated POVM* to the sampler. $\mathcal{M}^{\mathsf{diO}}$ has a projective implementation $\mathsf{ProjImp}(\mathcal{M}^{\mathsf{diO}}) = \{M'_p\}_p$, where each M'_p corresponds to the probability distribution on $\{0, 1\}$ that is 1 with probability p.

Now consider an extractor $\mathcal{E}$ which takes as input C_0, C_1, aux as well as a parameter ϵ whose reciprocal is given in unary (so $1^{1/\epsilon}$), so that if $\mathcal{E}$ runs in polynomial time, then it runs in time polynomial in λ whenever ϵ is an inverse polynomial in λ. We define the following experiment, parameterized by $\mathcal{S}, \mathcal{A}, \mathcal{E}$ as well as a function ϵ:

– Run $(C_0, C_1, \mathsf{aux}) \leftarrow \mathcal{S}(1^\lambda)$. Let $\mathcal{H}$ be the register containing aux.
– Apply $\mathsf{ProjImp}(\mathcal{M}^{\mathsf{diO}})$ to $\mathcal{H}$, resulting in probability p.
– If $p > \frac{1}{2} + \epsilon(\lambda)$, we say that event $\mathsf{Live}^{\mathsf{diO}}_\epsilon$ happens.
– Next, run $\mathcal{E}$ on $\mathcal{H}$, obtaining an input x or symbol $\perp$
– If $x \neq \perp$ but $C_0(x) = C_1(x)$, we say event $\mathsf{Fail}^{\mathsf{diO}}_\epsilon$ happens.
– If $x \neq \perp$ and $C_0(x) \neq C_1(x)$, we say event $\mathsf{Success}^{\mathsf{diO}}_\epsilon$ happens.

Definition 4.5 (Post-Quantum Differing-inputs Obfuscation). *A post-quantum differing-inputs obfuscator (diO) is a PPT algorithm* diO *such that:*

– diO$(1^\lambda, C)$ *is equivalent to* C *with overwhelming probability over the randomness of* diO.
– *For every QPT adversary* $\mathcal{A}$ *and sampler* $\mathcal{S}$, *there exists a QPT* $\mathcal{E}$ *such that for every inverse polynomial function* $\epsilon = \epsilon(\lambda)$, *there exists a negligible* $\mathsf{negl} = \mathsf{negl}(\lambda)$ *such that* $\Pr[\mathsf{Fail}^{\mathsf{diO}}_\epsilon] < \mathsf{negl}$ *and* $\Pr[\mathsf{Live}^{\mathsf{diO}}_\epsilon \wedge \neg\mathsf{Success}^{\mathsf{diO}}_\epsilon] < \mathsf{negl}$.

5   Hidden Partitions and the BOS Model

A partition Π of a set T is a collection of subsets $\Pi = \{S_1, \ldots, S_n\}$ such that $T = \cup_i S_i$ and the S_i are disjoint. The sets S_i are called parts of Π. Given partition $\Pi = \{S_1, \ldots, S_n\}$ of T and $\Pi' = \{S'_1, \ldots, S'_{n'}\}$ of T', we can define the product partition $\Pi \times \Pi'$ of $T \times T'$ as $\Pi \times \Pi' = \{S_i \times S'_j\}_{(i,j) \in [n] \times [n']}$. We can similarly define the product of several partitions.

The Basic Setup. Fix a set $\mathcal{Q}$, $\alpha \in \mathcal{Q}$ a distinguished element, and $\Omega \subseteq \mathcal{Q}$ a distinguished subset. Also fix a relation $R(\Pi, w)$ that takes as input partitions Π of $\mathcal{Q}$ and strings $w \in \{0, 1\}^*$ and outputs a bit.

5.1   The Quantum Hidden Partition Problem

Given $\mathcal{Q}, \alpha, \Omega, R$ as above, consider a QPT $\mathcal{S}(1^\lambda)$, called a quantum hidden partition sampler (QHPS) that samples $(|P\rangle, \Pi, \mathcal{D}, \mathsf{aux}) \leftarrow \mathcal{S}(1^\lambda)$ such that:

- $|P\rangle$ is a quantum state program taking inputs in some domain $\mathcal{X}$ and outputting a bit.
- Π is a partition of $\mathcal{Q}$, and
- $\mathcal{D}: \mathcal{Q} \to \mathcal{X} \times \{0,1\}$ is a PPT algorithm mapping $\mathcal{Q}$ to $\mathcal{X} \times \{0,1\}$.

Now consider two experiments involving a QHPS $\mathcal{S}$ and a quantum adversary $\mathcal{A}$. The first, called the *sink indistinguishability* experiment, works as follows:

- First run $(|P\rangle, \Pi, \mathcal{D}) \leftarrow \mathcal{S}(1^\lambda)$, and give $|P\rangle$ to $\mathcal{A}$.
- Throughout, $\mathcal{A}$ may make *classical* queries to $\mathcal{D}$, sending $q \in \mathcal{Q}$, and receiving independent samples $(x,b) \leftarrow \mathcal{D}(q)$. Repeated queries on the same q will give independent samples.
- Eventually $\mathcal{A}$ outputs a sink $q^* \in \Omega$. In response, run $(x^*, b^*) \leftarrow \mathcal{D}(q^*)$ and send x^* to $\mathcal{A}$.
- $\mathcal{A}$ outputs a guess b' for b^*. The experiment outputs $o = b' \oplus b^*$;

We say $\mathcal{A}$ wins the sink indistinguishability experiment if $o = 0$ (equivalently, $b' = b^*$).

The second experiment, called the *partition indisitnguishability* experiment, works as follows:

- First run $(|P\rangle, \Pi, \mathcal{D}) \leftarrow \mathcal{S}(1^\lambda)$, and give $|P\rangle$ to $\mathcal{A}$.
- Throughout, $\mathcal{A}$ may make *classical* queries to $\mathcal{D}$, sending $q \in \mathcal{Q}$, and receiving independent samples $(x,b) \leftarrow \mathcal{D}(q)$.
- Eventually $\mathcal{A}$ outputs two queries q_0^*, q_1^*. If q_0^*, q_1^* are in the same part of Π, output a random bit o and abort. Otherwise, choose a random bit c and run $(x,b) \leftarrow \mathcal{D}(q_c^*)$ and send (x^*, b^*) to $\mathcal{A}$.
- $\mathcal{A}$ outputs a guess c' for c. The experiment outputs $o = c' \oplus c$; $\mathcal{A}$ wins if $o = 0$.

We say $\mathcal{A}$ wins the partition indistinguishability experiment if $o = 0$.

Definition 5.1. *$\mathcal{S}$ is a valid QHPS if for any QPT adversaries $\mathcal{A}_0, \mathcal{A}_1$, there exists negligible functions $\mathsf{negl}_0, \mathsf{negl}_1$ such that the probability $\mathcal{A}_0$ wins the sink indistinguishability experiment is at most $\mathsf{negl}_0(\lambda)$, and the probability $\mathcal{A}_1$ wins the partition indistinguishability experiment is at most $\mathsf{negl}_1(\lambda)$.*

Consider the POVM which runs $(x,b) \leftarrow \mathcal{D}(\alpha)$, and run $|P\rangle(x)$ to obtain a bit b'. The POVM outputs 1 if $b' = b$. This POVM has a projective implementation, which we denote $\mathsf{ProjImp}(\mathcal{D}(\alpha))$. Now, consider the following experiment with algorithm $\mathcal{T}$:

- First run $(|P\rangle, \Pi, \mathcal{D}) \leftarrow \mathcal{S}(1^\lambda)$.
- Next apply $\mathsf{ProjImp}(\mathcal{D}(\alpha))$ to the register $\mathcal{H}$ containing $|P\rangle$, obtaining probability p.
- Run $\mathcal{T}$ on $1^{1/\epsilon}$ and $\mathcal{H}$. $\mathcal{T}$ can make queries to $\mathcal{D}$. Importantly, on query q, $\mathcal{T}$ can obtain a superposition of samples from $\mathcal{D}(q)$. The output is a string w or an abort symbol $\perp$.

Let $\mathsf{Live}_\epsilon^{\mathsf{BOS}}$ be the event that $p \geq \frac{1}{2} + \epsilon$. The event $\mathsf{Live}_\epsilon^{\mathsf{BOS}}$ corresponds to $|P\rangle$ being able to predict the bit b with advantage at least ϵ. Let $\mathsf{Success}_\epsilon^{\mathsf{BOS}}$ be the event that $\mathcal{T}$ outputs a $w \neq \perp$ such that $R(\Pi, w) = 1$, and let $\mathsf{Fail}_\epsilon^{\mathsf{BOS}}$ be the event that $\mathcal{T}$ outputs a $w \neq \perp$ such that $R(\Pi, w) = 0$.

Definition 5.2. $\mathcal{Q}, \alpha, \Omega, R$ *is solvable if there exists a* $\mathcal{T}^{\mathcal{D}}(|P\rangle, \epsilon)$ *that runs in time polynomial in* λ *and* $1/\epsilon$ *and makes quantum queries to* $\mathcal{D}$*, such that for any valid QHPS* $\mathcal{S}$ *and inverse-polynomial* ϵ *there is a negligible* negl *such that* $\Pr[\mathsf{Live}_\epsilon^{\mathsf{BOS}} \wedge \neg\mathsf{Success}_\epsilon^{\mathsf{BOS}}] \leq \mathsf{negl}(\lambda)$ *and* $\Pr[\mathsf{Fail}_\epsilon^{\mathsf{BOS}}] \leq \mathsf{negl}(\lambda)$.

In other words, $\mathcal{T}$ should almost always succeed if $|P\rangle$ starts out live, and $\mathcal{T}$ should almost never output a w that is not accepted by R (outputting $\perp$ instead if it cannot succeed).

5.2   The BOS Model

Now consider a stateful interactive potentially randomized algorithm O which takes as a secret input a partition Π, and then receives a sequence of queries $q_1, q_2, \cdots \in \mathcal{Q}$ and produces a corresponding sequence of outputs $o_1, o_2, \cdots \in \{0, 1\}$. We will denote an interactive algorithm $\mathcal{A}$ interacting with O and outputting w as $w \leftarrow \mathcal{A} \Leftrightarrow O(\Pi)$.

Definition 5.3. O *is a* BOS oracle *if, for any partition* Π *and any poly-length sequence of queries* $q_1, q_2, \ldots$, $O(\Pi)$ *satisfies each of the following guarantees:*

- **Accepts first distinguished query.** *If* $q_1 = \alpha$, *then* $o_1 = 1$.
- **Rejects sinks.** *For any* i, *if* $q_i \in \Omega$, *then* $o_i = 0$.
- **Local consistency.** *For any two consecutive queries* q_i, q_{i+1}, *if* $q_i, q_{i+1} \in P \in \Pi$ *(that is, if* q_i, q_{i+1} *are in the same part of the partition* Π*), then* $o_i = o_{i+1}$.
- **Single step rewinding.** *For any* i, *if* $q_{i+2} = q_i$, *then* $o_{i+2} = o_i$.

Definition 5.4. *A PPT algorithm* $\mathcal{A}$ *solves* R *(with the associated* $\mathcal{Q}, \alpha, \Omega$*) in the* BOS model *if, for any BOS oracle* O *and any partition* Π *of* Q*, then* $\Pr[R(\Pi, w) = 1 : w \leftarrow \mathcal{A} \Leftrightarrow O(\Pi)] = 1$.

5.3   From BOS to Solving Quantum Hidden Partitions

Here, we present the main technical tool of this paper:

Theorem 5.5. *For any* $R, \mathcal{Q}, \alpha, \Omega$, *if there exists an algorithm* $\mathcal{A}$ *which solves* R *in the* BOS model *in polynomial time, then* $R, \mathcal{Q}, \alpha, \Omega$ *is solvable.*

We now prove Theorem 5.5. We first assume without loss of generality that $\mathcal{A}$ has the following properties:

- $q_1 = \alpha$. To see why this is without loss of generality, let $\mathcal{A}$ solve R in the BOS model, and let $\mathcal{A}'$ be $\mathcal{A}$, except that if the first query is *not* α, $\mathcal{A}'$ inserts a dummy query to α as the first query, and then ignores the response. It is easy to see that the oracle seen by $\mathcal{A}$ as a subroutine of $\mathcal{A}'$ is still a BOS algorithm, and so $\mathcal{A}'$ still solves R.
- If $o_i = 0$, then $q_{i+1} = q_{i-1}$. A simple inductive argument then shows that any $o_i = 0$ is always preceded by an $o_{i-1} = 1$. To see why this is without loss of generality, let $\mathcal{A}$ solve R in the BOS model, and let $\mathcal{A}'$ be $\mathcal{A}$ except that if $o_i = 0$ and $q_{i+1} \neq q_{i-1}$, then $\mathcal{A}'$ makes a final query on q_{i-1}, immediately stops making queries (including not querying on q_{i+1}), and answers every subsequent query by $\mathcal{A}$ with 0. The oracle seen by $\mathcal{A}$ as a subroutine of $\mathcal{A}'$ is still a BOS algorithm, so $\mathcal{A}'$ still solves R. But the new $\mathcal{A}'$ will always query on $q_{i+1} = q_{i-1}$ if $o_i = 0$.

We call an $\mathcal{A}$ with the above properties *normal form*. We describe the algorithm $\mathcal{T}$ given a normal form $\mathcal{A}$:

Algorithm 5.6. *Let $\mathcal{A}$ be any normal form algorithm in the BOS model. Consider a quantum program $|P\rangle$ stored in register $\mathcal{H}$. First, define the following:*

- *Let r be an upper bound on the number of queries made by $\mathcal{A}$.*
- *Let $\epsilon' = \epsilon/2r, \delta = 2^{-\lambda}, T = 1/\sqrt{\delta}$.*
- *Let $\mathsf{Pred} = \{\mathsf{Pred}_x\}_x$ be the collection of projective measurements applied to $\mathcal{H}$ corresponding to running $|P\rangle$ on input x.*
- *Let $\mathsf{EST}(q)$ be the algorithm $\mathsf{API}^{\mathsf{Pred},\mathcal{D}(q)}_{\epsilon'/4,\delta}$, where API is the algorithm in Lemma 3.3. We will dilate $\mathsf{EST}(q)$ so that it is a projective measurement. This means that $\mathsf{EST}(q)$ acts on register $\mathcal{H} \times \mathcal{I}_q$, where $\mathcal{I}_q$ are the anilla registers used to purify, with a different register used for every query.*

We now give the algorithm $\mathcal{T}^{\mathcal{D}}(|P\rangle, 1^{1/\epsilon})$. Run $\mathcal{A}$, which makes queries $q_1, \dots, q_r$. To answer each query q_i, do the following:

1. *Define $p_{q_0} = 1/2 + \epsilon$.*
2. *If $q_i \neq q_{i-2}$:*
   (a) *Create the register $\mathcal{I}_{q_i}$, replacing any existing register with that name.*
   (b) *Then run $\mathsf{EST}(q_i)$, obtaining measurement outcome p_{q_i}, replacing any existing value for p_{q_i}.*
   (c) *If $p_{q_i} \leq p_{q_{i-1}} - \epsilon'$, answer the query with $o_{q_i} = 0$.*
   (d) *If $p_{q_i} > p_{q_{i-1}} - \epsilon'$, answer the query with $o_{q_i} = 1$.*
   (e) *If $i = 1$ and $o_{q_1} = 0$ (that is, this is the first query and the query response is 0) then immediately abort and output $\bot$.*
3. *Otherwise, if $q_i = q_{i-2}$:*
   (a) *Run the algorithm $\mathsf{Repair}^{\mathsf{EST}(q_{i-1}),\mathsf{EST}(q_{i-2})}_{T,p_{q_{i-1}},p_{q_{i-2}}}$.*
   (b) *Update p_{q_i} to $p_{q_{i-2}} - \epsilon'$, and answer the query with $o_{q_i} = o_{q_{i-2}}$.*

When $\mathcal{A}$ terminates and outputs w, $\mathcal{T}$ outputs w.

We now prove that $\mathcal{T}$ solves $\mathcal{Q}, \alpha, \Omega, R$. We first need the following lemma:

Lemma 5.7. *Suppose $\mathcal{T}$ does not abort in Step 2e. Then except with negligible probability, every query q_i that $\mathcal{T}$ responds with 1 will have $p_{q_i} \geq 1/2 + \epsilon - i \times \epsilon'$.*

Proof. We prove by induction on i. Since $p_{q_0} = 1/2 + \epsilon$, $\mathcal{T}$ does not abort in Step 2e only if $p_{q_1} > p_{q_0} - \epsilon' = 1/2 + \epsilon - 1 \times \epsilon'$. Now we inductively assume the lemma holds for all queries before query i, and prove it holds for query i. We break into three cases:

- $q_i = q_{i-2}$. In this case, $o_{q_i} = o_{q_{i-2}}$, so if $\mathcal{T}$ responds with 1, then $\mathcal{T}$ must have responded two queries ago with 1 as well. By the inductive hypothesis, this means $p_{q_{i-2}} \geq 1/2 + \epsilon - (i-2) \times \epsilon'$. But now we update p_{q_i} to $p_{q_{i-2}} - \epsilon' \geq 1/2 + \epsilon - (i-1) \times \epsilon' \geq 1/2 + \epsilon - i \times \epsilon'$.
- $q_i \neq q_{i-1}$, and $o_{q_{i-1}} = 1$. In this case, by induction, we have $p_{q_{i-1}} \geq 1/2 + \epsilon - (i-1) \times \epsilon'$. If $o_{q_i} = 1$, then it must be that $q_i \geq q_{i-1} - \epsilon' \geq 1/2 + \epsilon - i \times \epsilon'$.
- $q_i \neq q_{i-2}$ and $o_{q_{i-1}} = 0$. By the assumption that $\mathcal{A}$ is valid, this is impossible.

This completes the proof of Lemma 5.7. □

We now prove the following lemma:

Lemma 5.8. *If $\mathcal{T}$ does not abort in Step 2e, then except with negligible probability the oracle $\mathcal{T}$ presents to $\mathcal{A}$ is a BOS oracle.*

Proof. We prove the properties of a BOS oracle.

- **First distinguished query**: Recall we assumed $q_1 = \alpha$. If $\mathcal{T}$ does not abort in Step 2e, then $\mathcal{T}$ responds to the query with 1.
- **Sinks**: Consider a query $q_i \in \Omega$. We claim that $\mathsf{EST}(q_i)$ gives measurement outcome p_{q_i} that is at most $\frac{1}{2} + \epsilon'$, except with negligible probability. First consider replacing $\mathsf{EST}(q_i) = \mathsf{API}_{\epsilon'/4,\delta}^{\mathsf{Pred},\mathcal{D}(q_i)}$ (which produces p_{q_i}) with $\mathsf{ProjImp}(\mathcal{D}(q_i))$, giving outcome p'. By Lemma 3.3, since $\Delta_{\epsilon'/4}(\mathsf{EST}(q_i), \mathsf{ProjImp}(\mathcal{D}(q_i)) \leq \delta$, we have $|p' - p_{q_i}| < \epsilon'/4$ except with negligible probability.
  Then we note that p' must be at most $1/2 + \mathsf{negl} \leq 1/2 + \epsilon'/4$, except with negligible probability. Indeed, if this were not the case, then the bit b produced by $\mathcal{D}(q)$ could be predicted with non-negligible probability. Thus we have that $|p_{q_i} - \frac{1}{2}| \leq \epsilon'/2 \leq \epsilon'$. Now that $p_{q_i} \leq \frac{1}{2} + \epsilon'$, we use Lemma 5.7. If $o_{q_i} = 1$, then $p_{q_i} \geq 1/2 + \epsilon - i\epsilon' \geq 1/2 + \epsilon - r\epsilon' > 1/2 + \epsilon'$ since $(r+1)\epsilon' < \epsilon$, we therefore have that o_{q_i} must be 0.
- **Local consistency**: Suppose q_i, q_{i+1} lie in the same part of Π. We claim that the measurement outcomes p_{q_i} and $p_{q_{i+1}}$ satisfy $p_{q_{i+1}} \geq p_{q_i} - \epsilon'$. Indeed, consider replacing $\mathsf{EST}(q_{i+1}) = \mathsf{API}_{\epsilon'/4,\delta}^{\mathsf{Pred},\mathcal{D}(q_{i+1})}$ (which produces $p_{q_{i+1}}$) with each of the following:
  - $\mathsf{EST}(q_i) = \mathsf{API}_{\epsilon'/4,\delta}^{\mathsf{Pred},\mathcal{D}(q_i)}$, giving outcome p'. Since the last measurement on $\mathcal{H}$ was also $\mathsf{EST}(q_i)$, by being almost projective via Lemma 3.3, we have $|p' - p_{q_i}| < \epsilon'/4$ except with negligible probability.

- ProjImp$(\mathcal{D}(q_i))$, giving outcome p''. Again by Lemma 3.3, since $\Delta_{\epsilon'/4}(\text{EST}(q_i), \text{ProjImp}(\mathcal{D}(q_i)) \leq \delta$, we have $|p'' - p'| < \epsilon'/4$ except with negligible probability.
- ProjImp$(\mathcal{D}(q_{i+1}))$, giving p'''. Since q_i, q_{i+1} are in the same part of Π, the distributions $\mathcal{D}(q_i)$ and $\mathcal{D}(q_{i+1})$ are computationally indistinguishable. Therefore, by Lemma 3.4, $|p''' - p'| \leq \epsilon'/4$ except with negligible probability.
- EST(q_{i+1}), giving $p_{q_{i+1}}$. As above, by Lemma 3.3, we have $|p_{q_{i+1}} - p'''| \leq \epsilon'/4$ except with negligible probability. Putting the above inequalities together shows that $|p_{q_{i+1}} - p_{q_i}| \leq \epsilon'$ except with negligible probability.
  - **Single-step Rewinding**: If $q_i = q_{i-2}$, then Lemma 3.2 and the fact that EST(q_i) is almost projective immediately gives us that $|p_{q_i} - p_{q_{i-2}}| \leq \epsilon'/2 \leq \epsilon'$ except with probability $N\delta + N/T + 4\sqrt{\delta} = N\delta + (N+4)\sqrt{\delta}$, which is negligible.

One issue with the above proof is that in order to actually turn a bit predictor in the sink proof or a distinguisher in the local consistency proof into algorithms for the sink and partition indistinguishability games, the adversary needs to be able to run API, which in turn needs to get superpositions of samples from $\mathcal{D}(q)$. While $\mathcal{T}$ is allowed such queries, we do not allow adversaries for the sink and partition indistinguishability games such quantum access. However, following Zhandry [Zha12], we can simulate such superpositions of samples with a polynomial number of samples, thus getting an algorithm for these games which only makes classical queries. This completes the proof of Lemma 5.8.   □

Now suppose $\text{Live}_\epsilon^{\text{BOS}}$ happens. In this case, by Lemma 3.3, $\Delta_{\epsilon'/4}(\text{EST}(\alpha), \text{ProjImp}(\mathcal{D}(\alpha))) \leq \delta$. This means, except with negligible probability δ, $p_\alpha = p_{q_1}$ will be at least $\epsilon - \epsilon'/4 \geq p_{q_0} - \epsilon'$. Thus, $\mathcal{T}$ will not abort in Step 2e. Therefore, by Lemma 5.8, $\mathcal{T}$ presents a BOS oracle to $\mathcal{A}$, meaning $\mathcal{A}$ outputs a w such that $R(\Pi, w) = 1$. Thus $\text{Live}_\epsilon^{\text{BOS}} \wedge \neg\text{Success}_\epsilon^{\text{BOS}}$ happens except with negligible probability.

We now turn to proving that $\text{Fail}_\epsilon^{\text{BOS}}$ happens with negligible probability. For $\text{Fail}_\epsilon^{\text{BOS}}$ to happen, we must have (1) that $\mathcal{T}$ does *not* abort in Step 2e, and (2) that $\mathcal{T}$ fails to output a w such that $R(\Pi, w) = 1$. But by Lemma 5.8, if $\mathcal{T}$ does not abort, then it presents a BOS oracle to $\mathcal{A}$ except with negligible probability, meaning $R(\Pi, w) = 1$. Thus $\text{Fail}_\epsilon^{\text{BOS}}$ happens with negligible probability. This completes the proof of Theorem 5.5.   □

6   The Quantum iO to diO Transformation

In this section, we prove that iO implies diO for circuits with a polynomial number of differing inputs. This was shown classically by [BCP14], and we show that the same result holds quantumly as well using our BOS model.

6.1   The Hidden Partition

Here we give the *boundary* hidden partition, denoted with the superscript ^{Bnd}. Let $N = 2^n$ and we interpret the domain $\{0,1\}^n$ as the interval $[N]$. We set $\mathcal{Q}^{\mathsf{Bnd}} = [0, N]$, $\alpha^{\mathsf{Bnd}} = N$, $\Omega^{\mathsf{Bnd}} = \{0\}$. We say a partition Π of $\mathcal{Q}^{\mathsf{Bnd}}$ is *contiguous* if each part of Π is an interval $[a, b]$, so that $\Pi = \{[0, a_1 - 1], [a_1, a_2 - 1], \ldots, [a_{k-1}, a_k - 1], [a_k, N]\}$. For a contiguous partition, we say that $a_1, \ldots, a_k$ are the boundaries. Let $R^{\mathsf{Bnd}}(\Pi, w)$ be the following relation:

- Output 1 if Π is *not* contiguous.
- Output 1 if Π is contiguous and w is a boundary of Π.
- Output 0 if Π is contiguous but w is not a boundary of Π.

The first condition means that we trivially win for all non-contiguous Π, and can focus on the case of contiguous Π, where the goal is to find a boundary of Π.

We now explain how diO leads to an instance of the quantum hidden partition problem relative to $\mathcal{Q}^{\mathsf{Bnd}}, \alpha^{\mathsf{Bnd}}, \Omega^{\mathsf{Bnd}}, R^{\mathsf{Bnd}}$. We interpret a circuit sampler $\mathcal{S}$ and adversary $\mathcal{A}$ as a quantum hidden partition sampler $\mathcal{S}^{\mathsf{diO}}$, where $|P\rangle(\hat{C})$ is the algorithm that runs $\mathcal{A}$ on aux and $\hat{C}$. The algorithm $\mathcal{D}$, on input $q \in \mathcal{Q}^{\mathsf{Bnd}}$, chooses a random bit b, and then outputs $(\hat{C}_b, b)$, where $\hat{C}_0$ is an obfuscation of C_0, and $\hat{C}_1$ is an obfuscation of the program

$$C^{(0)} = C_0$$
$$C^{(q)}(x) = \begin{cases} C_1(x) & \text{if } x \le q \\ C_0(x) & \text{if } x > q \end{cases} \quad \text{for } 0 < q < N$$
$$C^{(N)} = C_1$$

Finally, the partition Π is the contiguous partition whose boundaries are exactly the differing inputs of C_0, C_1.

Lemma 6.1. *Assuming* diO *is a secure iO, the QHPS* $\mathcal{S}^{\mathsf{diO}}$ *is valid with respect to* $\mathcal{Q}^{\mathsf{Bnd}}, \alpha^{\mathsf{Bnd}}, \Omega^{\mathsf{Bnd}}, R^{\mathsf{Bnd}}$.

Proof. The unique sink is 0, and note that $C^{(0)} = C_0$, and so the response $\hat{C}$ to a query on $q = 0$ is independent of the bit b. Thus the probability any adversary can predict b (and therefore win the sink indistinguishability experiment) is exactly $1/2$.

Next, observe that $C^{(q)}$ is equivalent to $C^{(q')}$ for $q' > q$ as long as C_0, C_1 have no differing inputs in the interval $[q, q' - 1]$. Thus, if there are no differing inputs in $[q, q' - 1]$, by iO we have that no efficient adversary can distinguish query responses from the same part of Π. Therefore, the probability of winning the partition indistinguishability experiment is $1/2 + \mathsf{negl}$. □

6.2   The BOS Algorithm

Algorithm 6.2 (BOS Algorithm $\mathcal{A}^{\mathsf{Bnd}}$). *Initialize integers $a, b \in [0, N]$. Set $a = N, b = 0$, and query on a, which by definition gives response $o = 1$. Then do the following for at most $O(k \log^2 N)$ steps, where k is an upper bound on the number of parts in Π:*

1. *Query on b, obtaining response o.*
2. *If $o = 1$: set $(a, b) = (b, 0)$ and go to Step 1.*
3. *Else ($o = 0$):*
   (a) *If $b \neq a - 1$: Query on a, set $b = \lfloor (a + b)/2 \rfloor$ (a remains unchanged), and go to Step 1.*
   (b) *Else ($b = a - 1$): output a.*

If the algorithm has not terminated in $O(k \log^2 N)$ steps, output $\perp$.

Theorem 6.3. $\mathcal{A}^{\mathsf{Bnd}}$ *solves* $(Q^{\mathsf{Bnd}}, \alpha^{\mathsf{Bnd}}, \Omega^{\mathsf{Bnd}}, R^{\mathsf{Bnd}})$ *in the BOS model.*

Proof. We first observe the following invariants:

- Any time the algorithm goes to Step 1, the most recent previous query was on a. This is because either we return to Step 1 following Step 3a which queries a, or because we return to Step 1 in Step 2, which sets a to b, after having just queried b.
- At *any* point, one of the most recent two queries was on a.
- The only time a is updated is in Step 2, immediately after which the most recent query on a yielded 1.
- By local consistency and single step rewinding, at all times the most recent query on a yielded 1.
- Whenever the algorithm terminates in Step 3b, the most recent queries were on a and $b = a - 1$, and the responses were 1 and 0 respectively. By local consistency, this means a is a boundary.

To prove correctness, it therefore suffices to guarantee that A_{Boundary} eventually terminates in Step 3b, which is equivalent to showing that it reaches Step 3b in at most $O(k \log^2 N)$ steps given a contiguous partition.

Toward that end, we observe that every time Step 3 is invoked, either we terminate in Step 3b or the difference $a - b$ is approximately halved. Thus Step 3 can only be called in at most $O(\log N)$ consecutive iterations without terminating in Step 3b. Moreover, by local consistency, if we invoke Step 3, it must be that there is a boundary in the interval $[b, a]$, and so after completing Step 3a (which updates b), there must be a boundary in $[b - (a - b), a]$.

On the other hand, after every call to Step 2 must follow a call to Step 3, since b was set to 0, which is guaranteed to have query response 0. Moreover, every time we call Step 2, we there must have been a boundary in the interval $[b - (a - b), a]$ (before updating a, b), because the previous iteration would have called Step 3. Thus, if we let c be the closest boundary less than a, every call to Step 2 must either (1) at least halve the distance between a and c (2) set a to be less than c. (1) can only happen $O(\log N)$ times consecutively, and (2) can only happen k times in total since there are only k boundaries. Thus the total number of times Step 2 is called is at most $O(k \log N)$.

Putting everything together gives an upper bound of $O(k \log^2 N)$ total steps before terminating in Step 3b, thus proving the correctness of Algorithm A^{Bnd}. $\square$

Corollary 6.4. *Any iO is also diO for S where the number of differing inputs is bounded by a polynomial.*

Proof. We note that $\mathsf{Live}^{\mathsf{diO}}, \mathsf{Success}^{\mathsf{diO}}, \mathsf{Fail}^{\mathsf{diO}}$ are identical to the events $\mathsf{Live}^{\mathsf{BOS}}$, $\mathsf{Success}^{\mathsf{BOS}}$ and $\mathsf{Fail}^{\mathsf{BOS}}$. Then combining Algorithm A^{Bnd} with Theorem 5.5 gives extractor $\mathcal{E} = \mathcal{T}$, proving diO. $\square$

7 Post-quantum Tracing with Embedded Identities

Here, we show how to build embedded identity traitor tracing from functional encryption, specifically a special case called private linear broadcast encryption (PLBE). PLBE with polynomial index space was first formalized by [BSW06] to build ordinary traitor tracing in the classical setting, and the result was upgraded to the quantum setting by [Zha20], though only in the setting of polynomial identity spaces. Using PLBE with exponential index space to build embedded identity traitor tracing was proposed by [NWZ16] for the classical setting. Here, we upgrade their result to the quantum setting.

Construction 7.1. *Let Π^{FE} be a functional encryption scheme. We construct the traitor tracing scheme $\Pi^{\mathsf{TT}} = (\mathsf{Gen}^{\mathsf{TT}}, \mathsf{Derive}^{\mathsf{TT}}, \mathsf{Enc}^{\mathsf{TT}}, \mathsf{Dec}^{\mathsf{TT}}, \mathsf{Trace}^{\mathsf{TT}})$, where we define $\mathsf{Gen}^{\mathsf{TT}}, \mathsf{Derive}^{\mathsf{TT}}, \mathsf{Enc}^{\mathsf{TT}}, \mathsf{Dec}^{\mathsf{TT}}$ below:*

- $\mathsf{Gen}^{\mathsf{TT}}(1^\lambda, N) = \mathsf{Gen}^{\mathsf{FE}}(1^\lambda)$
- $\mathsf{Derive}^{\mathsf{TT}}(\mathsf{msk}, \mathsf{id}) = \mathsf{Derive}^{\mathsf{FE}}(\mathsf{msk}, f_{\mathsf{id}})$ *where* $f_{\mathsf{id}}(x, m) = \begin{cases} m & \text{if } x \geq \mathsf{id} \\ \bot & \text{otherwise} \end{cases}$
- $\mathsf{Enc}^{\mathsf{TT}}(\mathsf{pk}, m) = \mathsf{Enc}^{\mathsf{FE}}(\mathsf{pk}, (N, m))$
- $\mathsf{Dec}^{\mathsf{TT}}(\mathsf{sk}_{\mathsf{id}}, c) = \mathsf{Dec}^{\mathsf{FE}}(\mathsf{sk}_{\mathsf{id}}, c)$

7.1 The Hidden Partition

We use the same hidden partition $\mathcal{Q}^{\mathsf{Bnd}}, \alpha^{\mathsf{Bnd}}, \Omega^{\mathsf{Bnd}}, R^{\mathsf{Bnd}}$ as in Sect. 6. We now explain how Construction 7.1 leads to an instance of the quantum hidden partition problem relative to this partition. We interpret an adversary A^{TT} interacting in the tracing experiment as a quantum hidden partition sampler $\mathcal{S}^{\mathsf{TT}}$, where $|P\rangle$ is the decoder $|D\rangle$ outputted by A^{TT}, Π is the contiguous partition whose boundaries are the identities queried by A^{TT}. Finally $\mathcal{D}$, on input q, encrypts (q, m_b) for a random choice of b to get ciphertext c, and outputs (c, b).

Lemma 7.2. *Assuming Π^{FE} is an adaptively secure FE scheme, the QHPS $\mathcal{S}^{\mathsf{TT}}$ is valid for $\mathcal{Q}^{\mathsf{Bnd}}, \alpha^{\mathsf{Bnd}}, \Omega^{\mathsf{Bnd}}, R^{\mathsf{Bnd}}$.*

Proof. The unique sink is 0, and note that encryptions of $(0, m)$ computationally hide m, since the only secret keys are f_{id} for $id > 0$. Thus the probability the adversary can predict b (and therefore win the sink indistinguishability experiment) is at most $1/2 + \mathsf{negl}$.

Next, observe that encryptions of (q, m) and (q', m) for $q' > q$ decrypt identically under any secret key except those for id in the interval $[q, q' - 1]$. Thus, by FE security, the encryptions are indistinguishable unless the adversary has an $id \in [q, q' - 1]$, meaning no efficient adversary can distinguish query responses from the same part of Π. Therefore, the probability of winning the partition indistinguishability experiment is $1/2 + \mathsf{negl}$. $\qquad\square$

Corollary 7.3. *Assuming* Π^{FE} *is an adaptively secure FE scheme, Construction 7.1 is quantum traceable.*

Proof. Let $\mathcal{T}(|P\rangle, 1^{1/\epsilon})$ be the algorithm guaranteed by Theorem 5.5 and the existence of $\mathcal{A}^{\mathsf{Bnd}}$. Then set $\mathsf{Trace}^{\mathsf{TT}}(\mathsf{pk}, m_0, m_1, 1^{1/\epsilon}, |\mathsf{D}\rangle)$ to be $\mathcal{T}^{\mathcal{D}}(|\mathsf{D}\rangle, 1^{1/\epsilon})$ where $\mathcal{D}$ is the sampler above obtained from pk, m_0, m_1. Now consider the events $\mathsf{Live}_\epsilon^{\mathsf{BOS}}, \mathsf{Success}_\epsilon^{\mathsf{BOS}}, \mathsf{Fail}_\epsilon^{\mathsf{BOS}}$ for the QHPS described above, and the events $\mathsf{Live}_\epsilon^{\mathsf{TT}}, \mathsf{Success}_\epsilon^{\mathsf{TT}}, \mathsf{Fail}_\epsilon^{\mathsf{TT}}$ for the tracing experiment with Π^{TT} from Construction 7.1. We see that the events exactly coincide; in particular $D(\alpha)$ is identical to running $\mathsf{Enc}^{\mathsf{TT}}(\mathsf{pk}, m_b)$ for a random choice of b. Thus, by the guarantees of Theorem 5.5, Π^{TT} in Construction 7.1 is secure. $\qquad\square$

8   Traitor Tracing from Collusion-Resistant IPP Codes

In [BN08, Sir06, BP08], it was shown how to construct collusion-secure traitor tracing with constant-sized ciphertexts from binary fingerprinting codes [BS95]. The scheme, described momentarily, naturally generalizes to larger alphabets (at the cost of larger ciphertexts). However, the code needed for the generalization is not a fingerprinting code, but a collusion resistant identifiable parent property (IPP) code [HvLT98], which has a different marking condition. It turns out that IPP codes and fingerprinting codes coincide for binary codes. But by generalizing to larger alphabets (and using IPP codes) we can abstract other existing combinatorial schemes in the literature such as [CFN94].

We now recall the scheme, which is parameterized by a parameter t.

Construction 8.1. *Let* $(\mathsf{Gen}^{\mathsf{PK}}, \mathsf{Enc}^{\mathsf{PK}}, \mathsf{Dec}^{\mathsf{PK}})$ *be a public key encryption scheme and* $(\mathsf{Gen}^{\mathsf{IPP}}, \mathsf{Trace}^{\mathsf{IPP}})$ *a* δ-*robust fingerprinting code. Define the following algorithms, which depend on a parameter* σ *that may be a function of* δ, λ, ℓ:

- $\mathsf{Gen}^{\mathsf{TT}}(1^\lambda, 1^N, 1^c)$[4]: *Run* $(\mathsf{tk}', w_1, \dots, w_N) \leftarrow \mathsf{Gen}^{\mathsf{IPP}}(1^\lambda, 1^N, 1^c)$. *For* $j \in [\ell]$ *and* $\sigma \in \Sigma$, *run* $(\mathsf{ek}_{j,\sigma}, \mathsf{dk}_{j,\sigma}) \leftarrow \mathsf{Gen}^{\mathsf{PK}}(\lambda)$. *Output*

$$\mathsf{pk} = \{\mathsf{ek}_{j,\sigma}\}_{j\in[\ell],\sigma\in\Sigma} \text{ (the public key)}$$
$$\mathsf{tk} = (\{\mathsf{dk}_{j,\sigma}\}_{j\in[\ell],\sigma\in\Sigma}, \mathsf{tk}') \text{ (the tracing key)}$$
$$\mathsf{sk}_i = (\{\mathsf{dk}_{j,w_{i,j}}\}_{j\in[\ell]}, w_i) \text{ for } i \in [N] \text{ (the secret key for user } i)$$

---

[4] Recall that N is the total identity space, and c is the collusion bound.

- $\mathsf{Enc}^{\mathsf{TT}}(\mathsf{pk}, m)$: *Choose a random subset* $T \subseteq [\ell]$ *of size* t. *Let* $m_j, j \in T$ *be a* t-*out-of-*t *secret sharing of* m: m_j *are uniform conditioned on* $\oplus_{j \in T} m_j = m$. *For each* $j \in T, \sigma \in \Sigma$, *compute* $c_{j,\sigma} = \mathsf{Enc}^{\mathsf{PK}}(\mathsf{ek}_{j,\sigma}, m_j)$. *Output* $c = (T, \{c_{j,\sigma}\}_{j \in T, \sigma \in \Sigma})$.
- $\mathsf{Dec}^{\mathsf{TT}}(\mathsf{sk}_i, c)$: *For each* $j \in T$, *run* $m'_j \leftarrow \mathsf{Dec}^{\mathsf{PK}}(\mathsf{dk}_{j,w_{i,j}}, c_{j,w_{i,j}})$. *Then output* $m' = \oplus_{j \in T} m'_j$.

Quantum Tracing Challenges. In the classical setting, tracing works by first extracting a codeword w^* from the decoder D, and then traces w^* using the fingerprinting code. The first step is accomplished roughly by replacing $c_{i,\sigma}$ with junk and seeing if D still decrypts. Based on this information, the tracer can determine if w_i^* should be one of the symbols in Σ or ?. By doing this for each $i \in [\ell]$, the tracer extracts an entire codeword w^*.

We can easily mimic the above strategy in the quantum setting to derive a measurement for each i which computes w_i^*. The problem is that the measurements for each i might be incompatible, which means that the tracing algorithm cannot apply these measurements simultaneously. If applied sequentially, it could be that after computing the first several positions, the decoder becomes dead. There is no guarantee that an entire codeword w^* can be computed.

More abstractly, any tracing algorithm that works within the globally consistent hidden partition model is likely only able to extract logarithmically many bits, which is insufficient for obtaining a full codeword for the fingerprinting code.

8.1　The Hidden Partition

We will assume the alphabet Σ is equal to $[1, s]$. Let $\mathcal{Q}^{\mathsf{Prod}} = [0, s]^\ell$ and $\alpha^{\mathsf{Prod}} = s^\ell$. Let $\Omega_\delta^{\mathsf{Prod}}$ be the set of vectors w where the number of 0's is more than $\delta\ell$. We call a partition Π of $\mathcal{Q}$ valid if it is equal to a product partition $\Pi_1 \times \cdots \times \Pi_\ell$ where each Π_i is a contiguous partition of $[0, s]$ (recall contiguous partitions defined in Sect. 6).

Given a valid partition, let $(a_{i,j})_j$ for $i \in [\ell]$ be the boundaries of Π_i. Let $R_\delta^{\mathsf{Prod}}(\Pi, w)$ be the following relation:

- Output 1 if Π is *not* valid.
- Output 1 if (1) Π is valid with boundaries $(a_{i,j})_{i,j}$, (2) for all $i \in [\ell]$, $w_i = ?$ or $w_i \in (a_{i,j})_j$, and (3) the number of ? in w is at most $\delta\ell$.
- Output 0 in all other cases.

The first condition means that we trivially win for all non-valid Π, and can focus on the case of valid Π, where the goal is to find a string w that does not have too many ? and matches the boundaries of the product partition.

We now explain how the tracing experiment for Construction 8.1 leads to a QHPS relative to $(\mathcal{Q}^{\mathsf{Prod}}, \alpha^{\mathsf{Prod}}, \Omega_\delta^{\mathsf{Prod}}, R_\delta^{\mathsf{Prod}})$. Given an adversary $\mathcal{A}^{\mathsf{TT}}$, we define the QHPS $\mathcal{S}^{\mathsf{Prod}}$ as follows: first run the tracing experiment with $\mathcal{A}^{\mathsf{TT}}$, until $\mathcal{A}^{\mathsf{TT}}$ outputs $(|\mathsf{D}\rangle, m_0^*, m_1^*)$. Then set $|P\rangle = |\mathsf{D}\rangle$. Let S be the set of id queried by

$\mathcal{A}^{\mathsf{TT}}$, and let S' be the corresponding set of codewords in the IPP code given to the users in S. Let Π be the valid partition generated by S'.

Finally, let $\mathcal{D}(q)$ be the algorithm which does the following: choose a random subset $T \subseteq [\ell]$ of size t. Choose a random bit b, and let $m = m_b^*$. Then let $m_j, j \in T$ be a t-out-of-t secret sharing of m: m_j are uniform conditioned on $\oplus_{j \in T} m_j = m$. For each $j \in T, \sigma \in \Sigma$, compute

$$c_{j,\sigma} = \begin{cases} \mathsf{Enc}^{\mathsf{PK}}(\mathsf{ek}_{j,\sigma}, m_j) & \text{if } \sigma \leq q_j \\ \mathsf{Enc}^{\mathsf{PK}}(\mathsf{ek}_{j,\sigma}, 0) & \text{otherwise} \end{cases}$$

Output $c = (T, \{c_{j,\sigma}\}_{j \in T, \sigma \in \Sigma})$ and b. In other words, $\mathcal{D}(q)$ outputs an encryption of a random choice of m_b^*, except that it replaces the ciphertext components $c_{j,\sigma}$ with junk (importantly, independent of b) if $q_j < \sigma$.

The QHPS then outputs $(|P\rangle, \Pi, \mathcal{D})$.

Lemma 8.2. *Assuming Π^{PK} is semantically secure and either (1) $t \geq (1 - \delta)\ell$ or (2) $\binom{(1-\delta)\ell}{t}/\binom{\ell}{t}$ is negligible, then $\mathcal{S}^{\mathsf{Prod}}$ is valid for $\mathcal{Q}^{\mathsf{Prod}}, \alpha^{\mathsf{Prod}}, \Omega^{\mathsf{Prod}}, R^{\mathsf{Prod}}$.*

Proof. Let $q \in \Omega^{\mathsf{Prod}}$. Then q has strictly more than $\delta\ell$ zeros; call this set $\mathcal{Z}$. If $T \cap \mathcal{Z} \neq \emptyset$, then the share m_j inside $T \cap \mathcal{Z}$ is information-theoretically hidden given c. Since the m_j form a t-out-of-t secret sharing, this means if $T \cap \mathcal{Z} \neq \emptyset$, then b is statistically hidden. Thus, to prove the sink indistinguishability problem is hard, we just need to show that $T \cap \mathcal{Z} \neq \emptyset$ with overwhelming probability. A simple combinatorial argument shows that

$$\Pr[T \cap \mathcal{Z} \neq \emptyset] = 1 - \Pr[T \cap \mathcal{Z} = \emptyset] = 1 - \frac{\binom{\ell - |\mathcal{Z}|}{t}}{\binom{\ell}{t}} \geq 1 - \frac{\binom{(1-\delta)\ell - 1}{t}}{\binom{\ell}{t}}$$

$$= 1 - \left(\frac{(1-\delta)\ell - t}{(1-\delta)\ell}\right)\left(\frac{\binom{(1-\delta)\ell}{t}}{\binom{\ell}{t}}\right)$$

If $t > (1 - \delta)\ell$, then $\binom{(1-\delta)\ell}{t} = 0$. If $t = (1 - \delta)\ell$, then $(1 - \delta)\ell - t = 0$. In either case, $\Pr[T \cap \mathcal{Z} \neq \emptyset] = 1$. Alternatively, if $\binom{(1-\delta)\ell}{t}/\binom{\ell}{t}$ is negligible, then $\Pr[T \cap \mathcal{Z} \neq \emptyset] \geq 1 - \mathsf{negl}$. Thus, under the conditions of Lemma 8.2, the sink indisitnguishability problem is hard.

We now turn to the partition indisitnguishability experiment. Suppose q_1, q_2 are in the same part of Π, and consider the distributions $\mathcal{D}(q_1)$ and $\mathcal{D}(q_2)$. We will argue they are indistinguishable. Toward that end, consider some $j \in [\ell]$. Since q_1, q_2 are in the same part of Π, then $q_{1,j}$ and $q_{2,j}$ are in the same part of Π_j. If we assume wlog that $q_{1,j} \leq q_{2,j}$, then Π_i has no boundary in $(q_{1,j}, q_{2,j}]$. Now consider a ciphertext component $c_{j,\sigma}$. If $\sigma \leq q_{1,j}$, then the distributions of $c_{j,\sigma}$ under $\mathcal{D}(q_1)$ and $\mathcal{D}(q_2)$ are identical. Likewise if $\sigma > q_{2,j}$. On the other hand, for $\sigma \in (q_{1,j}, q_{2,j}]$, $\mathcal{A}^{\mathsf{TT}}$ does not have the secret key $\mathsf{dk}_{j,\sigma}$. By the semantic security of Π^{PK}, the adversary cannot distinguish $c_{j,\sigma}$ under $\mathcal{D}(q_1)$ and $\mathcal{D}(q_2)$.

By a hybrid over all j, no efficient adversary can distinguish $\mathcal{D}(q_1)$ from $\mathcal{D}(q_2)$, proving the hardness of the partition indistinguishability experiment. $\square$

8.2   The BOS Algorithm

Algorithm 8.3 (BOS Algorithm $\mathcal{A}^{\mathsf{Prod}}$). *Initialize $x \in [0, s]^\ell$, and set $x = s^\ell$. Now query on x, which by definition gives 1. Then do the following for $i = 1, \ldots, \ell + 1$:*

1. *For $a = s, \ldots, 1$:*
   (a) *Set $x' = x$, except that x'_i is set to $a - 1$.*
   (b) *Query on x', receiving response o'.*
   (c) *If $o' = 0$, query on x, break the loop in Step 1, and proceed to the next iteration of the main loop over i.*
   (d) *Otherwise, set $x = x'$, and proceed to the next iteration of the loop over a in Step 1.*
2. *If the loop in Step 1 terminated with all responses o' being 1, then set $x_i = 0$. Then proceed to the next iteration of the main loop over i.*

In the end, output w, which is x but with every 0 replaced by ?.

Theorem 8.4. $\mathcal{A}^{\mathsf{Prod}}$ *solves* $(\mathcal{Q}^{\mathsf{Prod}}, \alpha^{\mathsf{Prod}}, \Omega_\delta^{\mathsf{Prod}}, R_\delta^{\mathsf{Prod}})$ *in the BOS model.*

Proof. We maintain the invariant that each time we exit an iteration of the main loop over i, the last query was on x and the response was 1. There are two cases:

- We exited the iteration from Step 1c. But in this step we query on x, so x is the most recent query at exit. Moreover, x was queried in the last iteration of the loop over a in Step 1, and the result must have been 1 in order to proceed to this iteration. Therefore, x was queried two queries ago and resulted in response 1. By single step rewinding, the latest query on x must also give 1.
- We exited the iteration from Step 2. But here the most recent query was on x', it resulted in query response 1, and in Step 1d we set $x = x'$.

We also see that if we exit the loop of Step 1 via Step 1c, then the adjacent queries x and x' resulted in different outcomes, meaning a is a boundary of Π_i.

The result is that the final x is a string where all the non-zero terms are boundaries of the respective component partition, and $x \notin \Omega^{\mathsf{Prod}}$ (since the query output was no 0), meaning the number of 0's in x is at most $\delta\ell$. Thus when we replace 0's with ?'s to get w, we have that $R^{\mathsf{Prod}}(\Pi, w) = 1$. We finally note that the number of queries $\mathcal{A}^{\mathsf{Prod}}$ makes is at most $O(s\ell)$, which is polynomial. $\square$

Corollary 8.5. *Assuming Π^{PK} is a secure PKE scheme, Construction 8.1 is quantum traceable.*

9   Tracing Embedded Identities with Short Ciphertexts

In Construction 7.1 from Sect. 7, the string x is n bits long, where n is the bit length of identities. It is also part of the message inputted to $\mathsf{Enc}^{\mathsf{FE}}$ of the underlying functional encryption scheme. Therefore, the ciphertext size must grow with the bit length of identities. As observed by [NWZ16], this is *not* inherent to traitor tracing. They instead propose a different structure where ciphertexts may be independent of the identity length. We now recall their construction:

Construction 9.1. *Let* Π^{FE} *be a functional encryption scheme. We construct the traitor tracing scheme* $\Pi^{\mathsf{TT}} = (\mathsf{Gen}^{\mathsf{TT}}, \mathsf{Derive}^{\mathsf{TT}}, \mathsf{Enc}^{\mathsf{TT}}, \mathsf{Dec}^{\mathsf{TT}}, \mathsf{Trace}^{\mathsf{TT}})$, *where we define* $\mathsf{Gen}^{\mathsf{TT}}, \mathsf{Derive}^{\mathsf{TT}}, \mathsf{Enc}^{\mathsf{TT}}, \mathsf{Dec}^{\mathsf{TT}}$ *below:*

- $\mathsf{Gen}^{\mathsf{TT}}(1^\lambda) = \mathsf{Gen}^{\mathsf{FE}}(1^\lambda)$
- $\mathsf{Derive}^{\mathsf{TT}}(\mathsf{msk}, \mathsf{id})$: *choose a random* $\tau \in [N]$ *where* $N = 2^\lambda$. *Then return*

$$\mathsf{sk}_{\tau,\mathsf{id}} \leftarrow \mathsf{Derive}^{\mathsf{FE}}(\mathsf{msk}, f_{\tau,\mathsf{id}}) \text{ where } f_{\tau,\mathsf{id}}(i, x, m) = \begin{cases} m & \text{if } x \geq 2 * \tau - \mathsf{id}_i \\ \bot & \text{otherwise} \end{cases}.$$

  Note here that $x \in [0, 2N] = [0, 2^{\lambda+1}]$ *and* $i \in [n]$, *so the inputs to* $\mathsf{Enc}^{\mathsf{TT}}$ *are bounded by* $O(\lambda)$ *bits long, independent of* n. *Thus if* Π^{FE} *has succinct ciphertexts, so will* Π^{TT}.
- $\mathsf{Enc}^{\mathsf{TT}}(\mathsf{pk}, m) = \mathsf{Enc}^{\mathsf{FE}}(\mathsf{pk}, (1, N, m))$
- $\mathsf{Dec}^{\mathsf{TT}}(\mathsf{sk}_{\tau,\mathsf{id}}, c) = \mathsf{Dec}^{\mathsf{FE}}(\mathsf{sk}_{\tau,\mathsf{id}}, c)$

Tracing. The classical ideal behind the structure above is the following: first apply the tracing algorithm for Construction 7.1 setting $i = 1$. The result is that the tracing algorithm outputs $2\tau - \mathsf{id}_1$ from some secret key. Since id_1 is a single bit, this reveals uniquely both τ and the first bit of the associated identity. Then, by varying i and testing on ciphertexts encrypting $(i, 2\tau - 1, m)$, one can learn the rest of the bits of id. Essentially, we know if the first phase accused $2\tau - \mathsf{id}_1$, there must be a gap in the success probabilities of the decoder on encryptions of $(1, 2\tau - \mathsf{id}_1, m)$ and $(1, 2\tau - \mathsf{id}_1 - 1, m)$. Call these two probabilities p_0 and p_1, respectively, which are far apart. Since the τ of various secret keys are unique whp, by the security of functional encryption, we know that the decryption probability for $(i, 2\tau - \mathsf{id}_i, m)$ must be close to p_0, and the decryption probability for $(i, 2\tau - \mathsf{id}_i - 1, m)$ must be close to p_1. Put another way, the decryption probability for $(i, 2\tau - 1, m)$ will be close to $p_{1-\mathsf{id}_i}$, thus revealing id_i.

Quantumly, we can employ the same strategy to recover τ, id_1. However, recovering the rest of the bits of id will not work as in the classical case. This is because the probabilities p_0, p_1 may change as we further interrogate the decoder, so we cannot simply compare with the previous value. We therefore need to develop a new quantum algorithm for the problem.

9.1 The Hidden Partition

Let $Q^{\mathsf{Short}} = [n] \times [0, 2N]$ where $N = 2^\lambda$. Let $\alpha^{\mathsf{Short}} = (1, 2N)$. Let $\Omega^{\mathsf{Short}} = \{(i, 0)\}$. Consider a sequence $(\tau^{(1)}, \mathsf{id}^{(1)}), \ldots, (\tau^{(t)}, \mathsf{id}^{(t)})$ where $\mathsf{id}^{(j)} \in \{0,1\}^*$ and $\tau^{(j)} \in [N]$ with $\tau^{(1)} < \tau^{(2)} < \cdots < \tau^{(t)}$. This gives rise to a partition $\Pi = \{S_0, \ldots, S_t\}$ of Q^{Short} consisting of sets $S_j = \{(i, x) : 2\tau^{(j)} - \mathsf{id}_i^{(j)} \leq x < 2\tau^{(j+1)} - \mathsf{id}_i^{(j+1)}\}$ for $j = 1, \ldots, t-1$, $S_0 = \{(i, x) : x < 2\tau^{(1)} - \mathsf{id}_i^{(1)}\}$, and $S_t = \{(i, x) : 2\tau^{(t)} - \mathsf{id}_i^{(t)} \leq x\}$. We call Π of this form *contiguous*, and we call $(\tau^{(j)}, \mathsf{id}^{(j)})$ the boundaries of Π. Let $R^{\mathsf{Short}}(\Pi, w)$ be the following relation:

- Output 1 if Π is *not* valid
- Output 1 if Π is valid, and w is a boundary of Π.

– Output 0 if Π is valid but w is not a boundary of Π.

We now explain how Construction 9.1 leads to the quantum hidden partition problem relative to this partition. We interpret an adversary $\mathcal{A}^{\mathsf{TT}}$ interacting in the tracing experiment as a quantum hidden partition sampler $\mathcal{S}^{\mathsf{TT}}$, where $|P\rangle$ is the decoder $|D\rangle$ outputted by $\mathcal{A}^{\mathsf{TT}}$, Π is the contiguous partition whose boundaries are the identities queried by $\mathcal{A}^{\mathsf{TT}}$. Finally $\mathcal{D}$, on input (i, q), encrypts $((i, q), m_b)$ for a random choice of b to get ciphertext c, and outputs (c, b).

Lemma 9.2. *Assuming* Π^{FE} *is a secure FE scheme, the QHPS is valid for* $Q^{\mathsf{Short}}, \alpha^{\mathsf{Short}}, \Omega^{\mathsf{Short}}, R^{\mathsf{Short}}$

Proof. The sinks have the form $(i, 0)$, and note that encryptions of $((i, 0), m)$ computationally hide m, since the only secret keys are f_{id} for $\mathsf{id} > 0$. Thus the probability the adversary can predict b (and therefore win the sink indistinguishability experiment) is at most $1/2 + \mathsf{negl}$.

Next, observe that encryptions of $((i, q), m)$ and $((i', q'), m)$ decrypt identically if (i, q) and (i', q') are in the same part of Π. Thus, by FE security, the encryptions are indistinguishable if they lie in the same part. Therefore, the probability of winning the partition indistinguishability experiment is $1/2 + \mathsf{negl}$. $\qquad\square$

9.2   The BOS Algorithm

Algorithm 9.3 (BOS Algorithm $\mathcal{A}^{\mathsf{Short}}$**).** *Initialize integers* $a, b \in [0, 2N]$ *and* $i \in [n]$. *Set* $a = 2N, b = 0$, *and query on* $(1, a)$, *which by definition gives response* $o = 1$. *Then do the following for at most* $O(kn \log^2 N)$ *steps, where* k *in an upper bound on the number of parts in* Π:

1. *Query on* $(1, b)$, *obtaining response* o.
2. *If* $o = 1$, *set* $(a, b) = (b, 0)$ *and go to Step 1.*
3. *Else* $(o = 0)$:
   (a) *If* $b \neq (a-1)$: *Query on* $(1, a)$, *set* $b = \lfloor (a+b)/2 \rfloor$ *(a remains unchanged), and go to Step 1.*
   (b) *Else* $(b = a - 1)$: *Query on* $(1, a)$, *parse* a *as* $2\tau - \mathsf{id}_1$, *and do the following for* $i = 2, \dots, n$:
      i. *Query on* $(i, 2\tau - 1)$, *receiving response* o.
      ii. *If* $o = 0$, *query on* $(1, a)$, *set* $\mathsf{id}_i = 0$, *and proceed to the next* i.
      iii. *Else* $(o = 1)$:
         A. *Query on* $(i, 2\tau - 2)$, *receiving response* o'.
         B. *If* $o' = 0$, *set* $\mathsf{id}_i = 1$, *query on* $(i, 2\tau - 1)$ *and then* $(1, a)$ *and proceed to the next* i.
         C. *Else* $(o' = 1)$, *set* $(a, b) = (a - 1, 0)$, *clear* τ, id, *exit the loop over* i *in Step 3b, and go to Step 1.*
      If the loop over i *in Step 3b completes (that is, if we never have* $o' = 1$), *output* (τ, id).

Theorem 9.4. $\mathcal{A}^{\mathsf{Short}}$ *solves* $(\mathcal{Q}^{\mathsf{Short}}, \alpha^{\mathsf{Short}}, \Omega^{\mathsf{Short}}, R^{\mathsf{Short}})$ *in the BOS model.*

Proof. The proof is an adaptation of the proof of Theorem 6.3 for $\mathcal{A}^{\mathsf{Bnd}}$. As in Theorem 6.3, we will eventually find $a, b = a - 1$ where the previous query was on $(1, a - 1)$ and gave 0, and the query before was on $(1, a)$ and gave 1. This is Step 3b. By local consistency, $a = 2\tau - \mathsf{id}_1$ for some (τ, id) that defined the partition. We then query on $(1, a)$ again, which by single step rewinding gives 1.

It remains to show that id is obtained in its entirety. This is done by trying to ascertain if $(i, 2\tau - 1)$ lies in the same part as $(1, a)$ or $(1, a - 1)$. This is done by querying on $(i, 2\tau - 1)$. If the result is 0 (Step 3(b)ii), we know by local consistency (and the fact that the last query was on $(1, a)$ and gave 1) that $(i, 2\tau - 1)$ cannot be in the same part as $(1, a)$. So we set $\mathsf{id}_i = 0$ and move on to the next bit of id. In order to guarantee that the last query response was 1, we query again on $(1, a)$, which, by single-step rewinding will give 1.

If $o = 1$, we do not immediately learn which part $(i, 2\tau - 1)$ is in. So we also query on $(i, 2\tau - 2)$ to get response o' (Step 3(b)iiiA). If the response is now 0, we know that $(i, 2\tau - 1)$ and $(i, 2\tau - 2)$ are in different parts, meaning $(i, 2\tau - 1)$ is in the same part as $(1, a)$. Thus we set $\mathsf{id}_i = 1$ and move on to the next bit of id (Step 3(b)iiiB). But first we query again on $(i, 2\tau - 1)$, which by single-step rewinding gives 1. Then we query on $(1, a)$, which gives 1 by local consistency.

If on the other hand the response o' is once again 1, then we learn nothing about id_i. However, in this case, we have exactly the setup of a new hidden partition with $N = \tau - 1$. In particular, we know there must be a (τ', id') with $\tau' < \tau$. We therefore proceed back to Step 1 but with the new $N = \tau - 1$. A simple inductive argument shows that we will eventually find such a (τ', id'). This completes the proof.   □

Corollary 9.5. *Assuming FE, Construction 9.1 is quantum traceable.*

Proof. Let $\mathcal{T}(|P\rangle, 1^{1/\epsilon})$ be the algorithm guaranteed by Theorem 5.5 and the existence of $\mathcal{A}^{\mathsf{Short}}$. Then set $\mathsf{Trace}^{\mathsf{TT}}(\mathsf{pk}, m_0, m_1, 1^{1/\epsilon}, |D\rangle)$ to be $\mathcal{T}^{\mathcal{D}}(|D\rangle, 1^{1/\epsilon})$ where $\mathcal{D}$ is the sampler obtained from pk, m_0, m_1 described in Sect. 9.1. Now consider the events $\mathsf{Live}_\epsilon^{\mathsf{BOS}}, \mathsf{Success}_\epsilon^{\mathsf{BOS}}, \mathsf{Fail}_\epsilon^{\mathsf{BOS}}$ for the QHPS described in Sect. 9.1, and the events $\mathsf{Live}_\epsilon^{\mathsf{TT}}, \mathsf{Success}_\epsilon^{\mathsf{TT}}, \mathsf{Fail}_\epsilon^{\mathsf{TT}}$ for the tracing experiment with Π^{TT} from Construction 9.1; in particular $D(\alpha)$ is identical to running $\mathsf{Enc}^{\mathsf{TT}}(\mathsf{pk}, m_b)$ for a random choice of b. We see that the events exactly coincide. Thus, by the guarantees of Theorem 5.5, Π^{TT} in Construction 9.1 is secure.   □

Acknowledgements. We thank Fermi Ma for helpful discussions.

References

[Agr19] Agrawal, S.: Indistinguishability obfuscation without multilinear maps: new methods for bootstrapping and instantiation. In: Ishai, Y., Rijmen, V. (eds.) EUROCRYPT 2019. Part I, volume 11476 of LNCS, pp. 191–225. Springer, Heidelberg (2019). https://doi.org/10.1007/978-3-030-17653-2_7

[AP20] Agrawal, S., Pellet-Mary, A.: Indistinguishability obfuscation without maps: attacks and fixes for noisy linear FE. In: Canteaut, A., Ishai, Y. (eds.) EUROCRYPT 2020. Part I, volume 12105 of LNCS, pp. 110–140. Springer, Heidelberg (2020). https://doi.org/10.1007/978-3-030-45721-1_5

[ARU14] Ambainis, A., Rosmanis, A., Unruh, D.: Quantum attacks on classical proof systems: the hardness of quantum rewinding. In: 55th FOCS, pp. 474–483. IEEE Computer Society Press, October 2014

[AS16] Ananth, P.V., Sahai, A.: Functional encryption for turing machines. In: Kushilevitz, E., Malkin, T. (eds.) TCC 2016-A. Part I, vol. 9562 of LNCS, pp. 125–153. Springer, Heidelberg (2016). https://doi.org/10.1007/978-3-662-49096-9_6

[BCP14] Boyle, E., Chung, K.-M., Pass, R.: On extractability obfuscation. In: Lindell, Y. (ed.) TCC 2014. LNCS, vol. 8349, pp. 52–73. Springer, Heidelberg (2014). https://doi.org/10.1007/978-3-642-54242-8_3

[BDF+11] Boneh, D., Dagdelen, Ö., Fischlin, M., Lehmann, A., Schaffner, C., Zhandry, M.: Random Oracles in a quantum world. In: Lee, D.H., Wang, X. (eds.) ASIACRYPT 2011. LNCS, vol. 7073, pp. 41–69. Springer, Heidelberg (2011). https://doi.org/10.1007/978-3-642-25385-0_3

[BDGM20] Brakerski, Z., Döttling, N., Garg, S., Malavolta, G.: Candidate iO from homomorphic encryption schemes. In: Canteaut, A., Ishai, Y. (eds.) EUROCRYPT 2020. Part I, volume 12105 of LNCS, pp. 79–109. Springer, Heidelberg (2020). https://doi.org/10.1007/978-3-030-45721-1_4

[BGMZ18] Bartusek, J., Guan, J., Ma, F., Zhandry, M.: Return of GGH15: provable security against zeroizing attacks. In: Beimel, A., Dziembowski, S. (eds.) TCC 2018. Part II, volume 11240 of LNCS, pp. 544–574. Springer, Heidelberg (2018). https://doi.org/10.1007/978-3-030-03810-6_20

[BN08] Boneh, D., Naor, M.: Traitor tracing with constant size ciphertext. In: Ning, P., Syverson, P.F., Jha, S. (eds.) ACM CCS 2008, pp. 501–510. ACM Press, October 2008

[BP08] Billet, Q., Phan, D.H.: Efficient traitor tracing from collusion secure codes. In: Safavi-Naini, R. (ed.) ICITS 2008. LNCS, vol. 5155, pp. 171–182. Springer, Heidelberg (2008). https://doi.org/10.1007/978-3-540-85093-9_17

[BS95] Boneh, D., Shaw, J.: Collusion-secure fingerprinting for digital data (extended abstract). In: Coppersmith, D. (ed.) CRYPTO 1995. LNCS, vol. 963, pp. 452–465. Springer, Heidelberg (1995). https://doi.org/10.1007/3-540-44750-4_36

[BSW06] Boneh, D., Sahai, A., Waters, B.: Fully collusion resistant traitor tracing with short ciphertexts and private keys. In: Vaudenay, S. (ed.) EUROCRYPT 2006. LNCS, vol. 4004, pp. 573–592. Springer, Heidelberg (2006). https://doi.org/10.1007/11761679_34

[CFN94] Chor, B., Fiat, A., Naor, M.: Tracing traitors. In: Desmedt, Y. (ed.) CRYPTO 1994. LNCS, vol. 839, pp. 257–270. Springer, Heidelberg (1994). https://doi.org/10.1007/3-540-48658-5_25

[CHVW19] Chen, Y., Hhan, M., Vaikuntanathan, V., Wee, H.: Matrix PRFs: constructions, attacks, and applications to obfuscation. In: Hofheinz, D., Rosen, A. (eds.) TCC 2019. Part I, volume 11891 of LNCS, pp. 55–80. Springer, Heidelberg (2019). https://doi.org/10.1007/978-3-030-36030-6_3

[CMSZ21] Chiesa, A., Ma, F., Spooner, N., Zhandry, M.: Post-quantum succinct arguments. In: Proceedings of FOCS 2021 (2021)

[DFNS]   Damgård, I., Funder, J., Nielsen, J.B., Salvail, L.: Superposition attacks on cryptographic protocols. In: Padró, C. (ed.) ICITS 2013. LNCS, vol. 8317, pp. 142–161. Springer, Cham (2014). https://doi.org/10.1007/978-3-319-04268-8_9

[DQV+21] Devadas, L., Quach, W., Vaikuntanathan, V., Wee, H., Wichs, D.: Succinct LWE sampling, random polynomials, and obfuscation. In: Nissim, K., Waters, B. (eds.) TCC 2021. Part II, volume 13043 of LNCS, pp. 256–287. Springer, Heidelberg (2021). https://doi.org/10.1007/978-3-030-90453-1_9

[GGH+13] Garg, S., Gentry, C., Halevi, S., Raykova, M., Sahai, A., Waters, B.: Candidate indistinguishability obfuscation and functional encryption for all circuits. In: 54th FOCS, pp. 40–49. IEEE Computer Society Press, October 2013

[GKP+13] Goldwasser, S., Kalai, Y.T., Popa, R.A., Vaikuntanathan, V., Zeldovich, N.: Reusable garbled circuits and succinct functional encryption. In: Boneh, D., Roughgarden, T., Feigenbaum, J. (eds.) 45th ACM STOC, pp. 555–564. ACM Press, June 2013

[GKW18]   Goyal, R., Koppula, V., Waters, B.: Collusion resistant traitor tracing from learning with errors. In: Diakonikolas, I., Kempe, D., Henzinger, M. (eds.) 50th ACM STOC, pp. 660–670. ACM Press, June 2018

[GKW19]   Goyal, R., Koppula, V., Waters, B.: New approaches to traitor tracing with embedded identities. In: Hofheinz, D., Rosen, A. (eds.) TCC 2019. Part II, volume 11892 of LNCS, pp. 149–179. Springer, Heidelberg (2019). https://doi.org/10.1007/978-3-030-36033-7_6

[GVW12]   Gorbunov, S., Vaikuntanathan, V., Wee, H.: Functional encryption with bounded collusions via multi-party computation. In: Safavi-Naini, R., Canetti, R. (eds.) CRYPTO 2012. LNCS, vol. 7417, pp. 162–179. Springer, Heidelberg (2012). https://doi.org/10.1007/978-3-642-32009-5_11

[HvLT98] Hollmann, H.D.L., van Lint, J.H., Linnartz, J.-P., Tolhuizen, L.M.G.M.: On codes with the identifiable parent property. J. Comb. Theory Ser. A **82**(2), 121–133 (1998)

[KM10]   Kuwakado, H., Morii, M.: Quantum distinguisher between the 3-round Feistel cipher and the random permutation. In: 2010 IEEE International Symposium on Information Theory, pp. 2682–2685 (2010)

[KN22]   Kitagawa, F., Nishimaki, R.: Watermarking PRFs against quantum adversaries. In: Dunkelman, O., Dziembowski, S. (eds.) EUROCRYPT 2022, Part III, vol. 13277. LNCS, pp. 488–518. Springer, Heidelberg (2022). https://doi.org/10.1007/978-3-031-07082-2_18

[LMS21]   Lombardi, A., Ma, F., Spooner, N.: Post-quantum zero knowledge, revisited (or: how to do quantum rewinding undetectably). Cryptology ePrint Archive, Report 2021/1543 (2021). https://eprint.iacr.org/2021/1543

[MW04]   Marriott, C., Watrous, J.: Quantum Arthur-Merlin games. In: Proceedings of 19th IEEE Annual Conference on Computational Complexity, pp. 275–285 (2004)

[NWZ16]   Nishimaki, R., Wichs, D., Zhandry, M.: Anonymous traitor tracing: how to embed arbitrary information in a key. In: Fischlin, M., Coron, J.-S. (eds.) EUROCRYPT 2016. Part II, vol. 9666 of LNCS, pp. 388–419. Springer, Heidelberg (2016). https://doi.org/10.1007/978-3-662-49896-5_14

[Sho94]   Shor, P.W.: Algorithms for quantum computation: discrete logarithms and factoring. In: 35th FOCS, pp. 124–134. IEEE Computer Society Press, November 1994

[Sir06] Sirvent, T.: Traitor tracing scheme with constant ciphertext rate against powerful pirates. Cryptology ePrint Archive, Report 2006/383 (2006). https://eprint.iacr.org/2006/383

[Tar03] Tardos, G.: Optimal probabilistic fingerprint codes. In: 35th ACM STOC, pp. 116–125. ACM Press, June 2003

[Unr12] Unruh, D.: Quantum proofs of knowledge. In: Pointcheval, D., Johansson, T. (eds.) EUROCRYPT 2012. LNCS, vol. 7237, pp. 135–152. Springer, Heidelberg (2012). https://doi.org/10.1007/978-3-642-29011-4_10

[VDG98] Van De Graaf, J.: Towards a formal definition of security for quantum protocols. Ph.D. thesis, Universite de Montreal (1998)

[Wat06] Watrous, J.: Zero-knowledge against quantum attacks. In: Kleinberg, J.M. (ed.) 38th ACM STOC, pp. 296–305. ACM Press, May 2006

[WW21] Wee, H., Wichs, D.: Candidate obfuscation via oblivious LWE sampling. In: Canteaut, A., Standaert, F.-X. (eds.) EUROCRYPT 2021. Part III, vol. 12698 of LNCS, pp. 127–156. Springer, Heidelberg (2021). https://doi.org/10.1007/978-3-030-77883-5_5

[Zha12] Zhandry, M.: How to construct quantum random functions. In: 53rd FOCS, pp. 679–687. IEEE Computer Society Press, October 2012

[Zha20] Zhandry, M.: Schrödinger's pirate: how to trace a quantum decoder. In: Pass, R., Pietrzak, K. (eds.) TCC 2020. Part III, vol. 12552 of LNCS, pp. 61–91. Springer, Heidelberg (2020). https://doi.org/10.1007/978-3-030-64381-2_3

Black-Hole Radiation Decoding Is Quantum Cryptography

Zvika Brakerski[✉]

Weizmann Institute of Science, Rehovot, Israel
zvika.brakerski@weizmann.ac.il

Abstract. We propose to study equivalence relations between phenomena in high-energy physics and the existence of standard cryptographic primitives, and show the first example where such an equivalence holds. A small number of prior works showed that high-energy phenomena *can be explained* by cryptographic hardness. Examples include using the existence of one-way functions to explain the hardness of decoding black-hole Hawking radiation (Harlow and Hayden 2013, Aaronson 2016), and using pseudorandom quantum states to explain the hardness of computing AdS/CFT dictionary (Bouland, Fefferman and Vazirani, 2020).

In this work we show, for the former example of black-hole radiation decoding, that it also *implies* the existence of secure quantum cryptography. In fact, we show an existential equivalence between the hardness of black-hole radiation decoding and a variety of cryptographic primitives, including bit-commitment schemes and oblivious transfer protocols (using quantum communication). This can be viewed (with proper disclaimers, as we discuss) as providing a physical justification for the existence of secure cryptography. We conjecture that such connections may be found in other high-energy physics phenomena.

1 Introduction

The idea that computational considerations play a significant role in the most foundational laws of nature is gradually becoming well-accepted in physical research. Such ideas are recently coming up increasingly frequently in the context of understanding the plausible properties of the (still out-of-reach) theory of quantum gravity.

One of the notable examples of this principle, which is the focus of this work, is due to Harlow and Hayden [HH13] (henceforth HH). They were considering the extent to which "effective field theory" (EFT, the combination of quantum field theory and the general theory of relativity which is applicable in "mild" gravitational conditions) provides accurate predictions about the physical universe. It is known that EFT is not applicable if gravity is very strong, but until

For the most up-to-date version of this work, please refer to https://arxiv.org/abs/2211.05491.

Z. Brakerski—Supported by the Israel Science Foundation (Grant No. 3426/21), and by the European Union Horizon 2020 Research and Innovation Program via ERC Project REACT (Grant 756482).

H. Handschuh and A. Lysyanskaya (Eds.): CRYPTO 2023, LNCS 14085, pp. 37–65, 2023.
https://doi.org/10.1007/978-3-031-38554-4_2

recently it was widely conjectured to otherwise be universally applicable. Recent thought experiments involving black-holes are now challenging this conjecture and putting forth the question of the limits of applicability of EFT.

Whereas the singularity region of the black-hole (its "center") has extreme gravity and is not expected to be described by EFT, the event horizon of the black-hole (its "boundary") does not have particularly strong gravity. EFT therefore predicts that the near horizon area emits radiation known as Hawking radiation, which in turn is strongly believed to carry out information that fell into the black-hole throughout its history, in some scrambled form.[1] This means that, at some point, the entropy outside the black-hole must decrease. In other words, at some point, the outgoing Hawking radiation must be correlated with the previously-emitted ("historic") radiation. State-of-the-art models for black-holes predict that this should happen almost immediately after the halfway point of the evaporation (this is known as "Page time"), and that shortly after the Page time, outgoing radiation is almost fully quantumly entangled with the history. On the other hand, the general theory of relativity predicts that the near horizon area is not highly impacted by gravity (it is not very "curved") and therefore the near-horizon area contains "ordinary" vacuum that can be described by "standard" quantum field theory. The Hawking radiation therefore originates from the vacuum ground state in the horizon-area. According to quantum field theory, this ground state is strongly spatially entangled. Therefore, the outgoing Hawking radiation must be almost fully entangled with so-called "modes" in the near-horizon area. If a quantum system (the outgoing radiation) is (almost) fully entangled with another system (the near-horizon modes) then it cannot exhibit (almost) any correlation with another quantum system (the historic radiation). To resolve this difficulty, the "complementarity principle" was invoked. That is, it was suggested that if the outgoing radiation is maximally entangled with two different systems, then the two *must actually be the same system*. Indeed, one of these systems (the historic radiation) lives "outside" the black-hole, and the other (the near-horizon modes) lives "inside" the black-hole. Therefore, perhaps the Hilbert space of the universe simply presents itself so that a part of it is accessible in two different ways, from inside and outside the black-hole.

This is a very appealing solution, but it has been challenged by the so-called "firewall paradox" of Almheiri, Marolf, Polchinski and Sully [AMPS13], who proposed the following thought experiment. An observer (Alice) can collect the historic radiation, and leisurely decode it. Alice can then verify that the decoded value is indeed correlated with the outgoing radiation. Finally, Alice can "jump in" together with the radiation bit, and check that it is also correlated with the inside modes. Thus Alice witnesses a violation of the monogamy of entanglement, which is a fundamental feature of quantum theory. The conclusion of [AMPS13] is that the near-horizon area is not in a vacuum ground state, but rather in a very high-energy state that allows for the outgoing radiation to not be entangled

---

[1] The reason that Hawking radiation is believed to carry information, is that otherwise the evolution of the wave-function of the universe would not be unitary, which seems implausible in the context of well accepted physical theory.

with the near-horizon modes. If this is indeed the case, then EFT is inapplicable in the near-horizon area, despite it not having extreme gravitational conditions.

HH proposed to rescue complementarity using a computational argument. They argue that while Alice can in principle decode the historic radiation and distill a correlation with the outgoing radiation, the *computational complexity* of this process may be prohibitive. In particular, the near-horizon modes will not survive long enough until the end of this calculation, so Alice can never witness a monogamy violation. It is therefore suggested that the ability to perform high-complexity tasks falls outside of the descriptive power of EFT, similarly to the setting of a strong gravitational field. See [Aar16, Sect. 6] for additional discussion of the firewall paradox from a computational perspective.

The HH decoding problem considers a quantum state defined over 3-subsystems HBR, where H represents the interior of the black-hole, B is the outgoing radiation which for simplicity is assumed to contain a single bit, and R is the historic radiation. The state is set up so that BR are information-theoretically maximally correlated, that is there exists a *possibly inefficient* quantum process that takes R as input and "distills" it into a single qubit register D that is maximally entangled with B (the state of BD is close to $|\text{epr}\rangle = \frac{|00\rangle + |11\rangle}{\sqrt{2}}$). The HH decoding problem is to efficiently implement such a procedure that takes R and produce D that is highly entangled with B.[2] They show that this problem is potentially intractable *in the worst case* (i.e. there is no efficient process that solves *every possible* HBR), unless an implausible complexity-theoretic result follows. Specifically, that all languages that have a statistical zero-knowledge protocol also have a quantum polynomial-time algorithm (**SZK** $\subseteq$ **BQP**).

Aaronson [Aar16] showed a similar result, but under a different computational assumption. He relied on the existence of injective one-way functions (injOWF) that are secure against quantum inverters. In a nutshell, injOWF is an injective function f such that $f(x)$ can be computed in time poly($|x|$), but f cannot be inverted in polynomial time. Aaronson suggests that this subsumes the result of HH, since **SZK**-hardness implies the existence of OWF [Ost91]. We believe that this claim is true in spirit but formally it is not completely accurate.[3]

---

[2] The description of the quantum operations in [HH13] and in followups [Sus13, Aar16] is in terms of unitaries that are efficient/inefficient to implement. We find this unnecessarily cumbersome and consider general quantum procedures, which correspond to completely positive trace preserving (CPTP) channels. Such channels can always be "purified" into unitary form, so this does not limit the generality of the discussion.

[3] This is not the focus of this work, so we choose not to elaborate too much on this point. In a nutshell, there are two gaps in the claim of [Aar16]. One is that [Ost91] refers to *average-case hardness* in **SZK**, whereas the HH argument only assumes *worst-case hardness*. To an extent, HH rely on a weaker assumption but also prove a weaker claim: they only show that there does not exist an efficient decoder that decodes *all* possible black-holes, whereas Aaronson shows that there is a (single) potential black-hole that resists all efficient decoders. The second point is that [Ost91] shows that average-case **SZK** hardness implies one-wayness, but not necessarily injectivity.

Aaronson further suggests that the existence of injOWF implies a stronger sense of decoding-intractability, as follows. HH and Aaronson's first result presented a system in which BD cannot be brought to the EPR state, but it was still trivial to infer classical correlations between B and R. Namely to produce a D that is classically correlated with B. In Aaronson's second construction, classical correlations are shown to be intractable to detect. This is done using Goldreich and Levin's hard-core-predicate construction [GL89]. We point out that, whereas finding classical correlation becomes intractable in this latter construction, it becomes trivial to find *phase correlations*, namely, correlations between BD when both registers are presented in the Hadamard basis. In this sense, Aaronson's second construction does not actually give a qualitative improvement over the first one. Indeed, it appears that prior works were not very concerned with the possibility that some correlation between B and R may be efficiency detectable, so long as recovering perfect quantum correlation was intractable.

1.1   This Work: Gravitational Cryptology

The arguments of [HH13, Aar16] show that under computational/cryptographic assumptions, it is possible to resolve an quantum-gravity "paradox". That is, in our terminology, a cryptology-induced gravitational phenomenon. In this work, we improve this connection, by showing that *even milder* cryptographic constructs, namely ones that are not known to imply OWF at all (whether injective or not) already give rise to potential "black-hole radiation" whose decoding is intractable. We show that these extremely mild assumptions also allow us to construct "radiation" which is not only intractable to decode, but one that is *computationally indistinguishable from being completely uncorrelated* with the historic radiation R. Therefore, it is impossible for any efficient process to extract *any* correlation between B and R.

We then turn our attention to show the complementary result. Namely, to show that if there exists a black-hole with hard-to-decode radiation, then such a physical phenomena would imply the existence of cryptographic objects! We believe that such a result has not been previously shown in the quantum context. To some extent, one can view this as providing some physical justification to the existence of cryptography.[4]

Putting the two results together, we get an *existential equivalence* between the hardness of decoding Hawking radiation, using a proper asymptotic formalism that we propose (see Technical Overview below for additional details), and the ability to securely realize a variety of cryptographic objects. This variety

---

[4] At the same time, we caution from over-interpreting our result. The hardness of radiation decoding has been suggested as a possible solution to an apparent paradox, under a specific set of assumptions about the behavior of quantum gravity and black-holes. Therefore our result is only meaningful in the context of these physical assumptions. Nevertheless, the argument that firewalls should be avoided rests on physical understanding of the universe, and being able to derive computational conclusions from it appears worthwhile. See additional discussion in Sect. 1.3 below.

includes: bit-commitment schemes (which allow a party to fix a binary value without revealing it to another party, but such that the other party can later verify what that fixed value was), oblivious transfer protocols (a protocol where in the beginning one party holds two bits a_0, a_1, and the other holds a bit b, and in the end the latter party holds a_b, without learning $a_{\bar{b}}$ and without the first party learning b itself), secure multiparty computation protocols (where parties can jointly and securely compute arbitrary functions on their inputs), and (non-trivial) quantum zero-knowledge proof protocols for languages in the complexity class **QIP**. In fact, we rely on a sequence of works, summarized in [BCQ22], that shows that all of the above cryptographic primitives are existentially equivalent to a very basic object that is called EFI in [BCQ22]. EFI is simply a pair of distributions (over quantum states) that are statistically distinguishable but computationally indistinguishable.[5] We show that this cryptographic object corresponds to hard-to-decode Hawking radiation.

Having shown an equivalence between finding a non-trivial correlation between B and R is equivalent to the existence of a cryptographic primitive, we go back to consider the implications on the [AMPS13] experiment. We notice that in the experiment, Alice processes R, compares it with B and then jumps into the black-hole. Whereas any non-trivial correlation between BR would suggest that something strange is going on, Alice's level of confidence may be quite low, and in particular may not be worth jumping into the black-hole to find out the answer. It would be quite unsatisfactory if cryptology is only implied by extremely-hard-to-decode "black-holes".[6] We therefore show that even "mildly hard to decode" black-holes imply EFI. Therefore, by our prior result, that mildly-hard-to-decode black-holes imply potential extremely-hard-to-decode black-holes. Our notion of mild-hardness is one where Alice attempts to decode R, and declares whether she succeeded or not. A *high-confidence decoder* is one that declares success reasonably often (i.e. with non-negligible probability), and, conditioned on declaring success, it produces a distilled qubit D such that BD are extremely correlated (the fidelity with an EPR pair is very close to 1).

1.2 Technical Overview

In order to show anything about the Black-Hole Radiation Decoding problem (which we denote by BHRD), we must provide a formal definition. We provide a somewhat more quantitative description compared to the one appearing in prior works [HH13, Sus13, Aar16, Aar22a]. Similarly to those prior works, we consider an efficiently generatable quantum state that represents the state of the black-hole interior H, the historic radiation R and the next outgoing bit of radiation B.

---

[5] EFI stands for Efficient (to sample), Far (statistically), and Indistinguishable (computationally). For a formal definition, see Definition 2.6.

[6] Alice can boost her confidence by performing the experiment many times and relying on concentration bounds. This would require her to chase after multiple radiation particles once inside the black-hole. This is not unreasonable but we view it as less elegant compared to our solution.

We are guaranteed that BR are very strongly correlated, in the sense that there exists an *inefficient* quantum procedure that takes R as input and produces single qubit D such that BD form an EPR pair.[7] In our formulation we allow a little slackness so that BD are allowed to only be very close to an EPR pair (in the sense that their fidelity with the EPR state is negligibly close to 1). The decoding problem is to efficiently "distill" this entanglement.

But how much entanglement should be hard to distill? In prior works [HH13, Aar16], the intractability was shown for getting fidelity 1 (or close to 1), and the counterexamples provided in fact exhibited weak non-trivial correlation. We notice that if we wish to completely avoid the firewall paradox, we need to rule out BD having any sort of non-trivial correlation. Therefore, we consider a *radiation decoder* $\mathcal{A}$ to be successful if it manages to take R as input, and produce D such that the projection of BD on the EPR state (or rather, the square of its absolute value) is non-negligibly greater than $1/4$. Note that $1/4$ correlation can easily be achieved by outputting D in a maximally mixed state (that is, completely uncorrelated with B). However, as we mentioned above, we show an amplification theorem that shows that if there exists a state for which "high confidence" decoding is hard then there is also one for which any non-trivial decoding is hard.[8]

Cryptology-Induced Gravitational Phenomena. We show that EFI imply a hard-to-decode state as follows. Our hard-to-decode state will start from an EPR pair in registers BT. It will then apply $X^x Z^z$ on the T part of the EPR, and use *a commitment scheme* to produce commitments to both x and z. The register R will constitute of T and the commitments to x, z. We use a cryptographic primitive known as a *non-interactive statistically-binding bit-commitment* which is essentially equivalent to EFI (see e.g. [Yan20]). Intuitively, for the purpose of this work, a commitment string is similar to an encryption, in the sense that it computationally hides a well-defined committed value. We can thus think of the radiation decoding task as the task of unmasking T. This is information-theoretically possible, since a commitment to a value x allows us to recover x using an inefficient procedure. However, to a computationally bounded adversary, a commitment to x is indistinguishable from a commitment to a fixed value (say 0). Therefore, a computationally bounded decoder cannot deduce any information about x, z from the commitments, and its view is therefore equivalent to seeing T masked with an unknown random Pauli. This is equivalent to T being maximally mixed, and in particular independent of (i.e. in tensor product with) B. Therefore a computationally bounded decoder cannot detect *any* correlation between B and R without violating the properties of the commitment and thus of the EFI.

---

[7] As noted above, our formulation is in terms of quantum channels and not in terms of unitaries.

[8] We recall that high-confidence decoding means that with some non-negligible probability, the decoder declares success and produces D such that the fidelity of BD with EPR is $1 - o(1)$.

We note that, as explained above, in our construction, B and R are computationally indistinguishable from being in a tensor product, and therefore it is impossible to find any correlation between them. Therefore, our result is stronger than prior ones by [HH13, Aar16]. Indeed, in hindsight, one can view the previous results of [HH13, Aar16] as having a similar structure, but only masking either in the X or Z "basis" but not in both, thus not achieving the strong computational tensor-product property that we achieve, and using stronger computational assumptions.

Superdense Decoding, Gravitationally-Induced Cryptology. To show the converse result, that BHRD-hardness implies EFI, we show an equivalence between the BHRD problem and another problem that we call "superdense decoding". Essentially we observe that distilling D that is jointly EPR with B is *quantitatively* the same task as being able to decode two classical bits that are superdense-encoded in B. A more detailed description follows.

We recall that when two parties share an EPR pair on registers BD, it is possible to transfer two classical bits x, z from one to the other using a single qubit of communication. This is done by applying a Pauli operation $X^x Z^z$ on B and then sending B to the holder of D. One can verify that the x, z values generate a set of orthogonal states (the Bell/EPR basis) on BD, and thus x, z can be recovered. We present a formal argument that the task of decoding D from some register R is equivalent to the task of decoding a superdense encoding of x, z over B. That is, a superdense decoder S takes two registers BR, where B encodes random values x, z using the superdense encoding procedure, and its goal is to produce the classical values x, z. The *advantage* of the superdense decoder is the probability that it recovered both x, z correctly.

Showing that a radiation decoder implies a superdense decoder (on the same initial state HBR) is fairly straightforward. If D that is in EPR with the original B can be decoded from R, then we can apply the regular superdense decoding to recover x, z. For the converse, we rely on quantum teleportation. Assume we have a "good" superdense decoder S, and we wish to derive from it a good radiation decoder $\mathcal{A}$. The superdense decoder produces a classical output x, z out of a pair of registers BR, whereas the radiation decoder is required to produce a quantum register D out of the radiation R. To do this, we give S as input the R for which we want to decode the radiation, but we give it a "fake" B which is a half-EPR of a freshly generated EPR pair. We show that a successful superdense decoding corresponds to *teleporting* an implicit qubit D onto the other end of the EPR pair of "fake B". Therefore, even though the superdense decoder only returns a classical value, we can use this value to obtain the decoded radiation qubit D.

The correspondence between the two problems is *exact*. Namely, the probability of recovering x, z by a superdense decoder is identical to the fidelity of the radiation decoder output with an EPR pair, and this is achieved with roughly the same complexity (in both directions). Thus, the superdense decoding problem provides a convenient proxy for the radiation decoding problem, only now we have a problem with a classical interface (random classical bits x, z go in, get encoded quantumly, sent to a quantum decoder, but the output of this decoder is again a classical value that is compared against x, z).

To generate EFI from a superdense-hard state, we consider an instance of the superdense decoding problem in registers BR, together with the "correct answer" x, z. We define two distributions over quantum states. One that outputs $BRxz$ and one that outputs BRu_1u_2, where u_1, u_2 are random bits that are drawn independently of x, z. The two distributions are clearly distinguishable by an inefficient procedure that superdense-decodes BR and compares the outcome with the two classical bits provided. We show that distinguishing the two with any non-negligible probability allows us to "learn" about the values of the actual x, z and thus to obtain non-negligible advantage against the superdense decoding problem.

Amplification. We are given a state which is only hard to superdense-decode with high confidence. Namely, it is hard to come up with a decoder that declares "success" with non-negligible probability, and upon declaring success, correctly decodes the state with probability $1 - o(1)$. We would like to show that even such a hard-to-decode state implies EFI. The argument above is clearly insufficient, since it is possible that the two distributions obtained are always distinguishable to within a non-negligible advantage.

Our amplification result is achieved using repetition. We first show that if we get a sequence of decoding instances, and are tasked with correctly decoding *all of them*, then we cannot succeed with any non-negligible probability. We then use a hard-core bit construction to show a pair of EFI distributions.

For the first part, we consider a challenge that consists of an n-tuple of independent decoding instances that we call "slots". We consider the task of correctly decoding all slots with non-negligible probability. We show that given such a decoder, that succeeds with non-negligible probability ϵ, it is possible to identify a slot i and an event E_i, such that E_i occurs with probability at least ϵ, and when E_i occurs, the probability that the decoding of the i-th slot succeeds is roughly $1 - 1/n$. The proof of this "Estimation Lemma" uses elementary probability theoretic techniques. Specifically, E_i is simply the event that all slots $< i$ were decoded correctly. We show that at least for some of the i's, if all previous slots were correct, then the i-th slot will also decode correctly.

This establishes the hardness of decoding all n slots with non-negligible probability. The EFI construction follows by considering an instance that contains n slots as before, but also the inner product of the concatenation of all correct answers with a random vector a, in addition to a itself. This is exactly the Goldreich-Levin hard core bit [GL89]. We set one of the EFI distributions to have the correct inner product value, and the other to have its negation. This means that a distinguisher between the two amounts to calculating the value of the inner product. We then use a result by Adcock and Cleve [AC02] that shows a quantum algorithm that converts such an inner-product predictor into one that produces the entire pre-image of the inner product. This completes the amplification algorithm.

1.3   Discussion and Other Related Work

Our work suggests that, to some extent, the existence of cryptographic hardness could rely on a natural phenomena. The desire to find physical substantiation for cryptography is not new. Indeed, one can make a (classical) thermodynamical argument that the increase of entropy in complex systems implies that some processes (like scrambling an egg or breaking a glass) are "efficiently occurring but intractable to invert". The argument that is implied by this work follows a similar high level logic, but the quantitative nature of the black-hole radiation decoding problem allows us to draw quantitative conclusions and explicitly point out to the connection between the (proposed) properties of physical theory, and computational hardness.

It is nevertheless important to state as clearly as possible what we need to assume in order to derive the conclusion that cryptographic hardness is "implied" by nature.

1. We assume that the description of black-hole dynamics is indeed as accepted physical theory suggests. This includes the unitarity of the evolution of black-holes and the applicability of "known physics" (effective field theory) in the near-horizon area.
2. We assume that there is some cosmological censorship of the firewall paradox that prevents the [AMPS13] experiment from being successfully carried out "under normal circumstances". Namely, given that we live in "moderate gravity space" and haven't encountered random firewalls popping into existence, we should not expect any experiment we conduct to bring them up in the specific moderate gravity space in the near-horizon area.
3. We accept the translation of the decoding problem from a physical system into an information theoretic task of decoding a qubit of information. Or at least that a more accurate description does not significantly change the nature of the problem.
4. We state the decoding problem as an average case problem, namely we require a black-hole which is hard to decode against all efficient decoders. We furthermore assume that this hardness needs to be super-polynomial. It may be the case that some concrete hardness would be required, rather than just assuming hardness against all polynomial time decoders. For example, [HH13, Footnote 4] suggests that exponential hardness of the decoding problem should be sought out. We note that our reductions are quite generic and tight, and asymptotically preserve the hardness of the decoding problem versus that of the obtained cryptographic primitive. They can therefore be applied to any "degree of hardness" of the decoding problem.

Whereas each of these axioms can be challenged, we believe that they are at least consistent with the way science currently views the physical world. Therefore, while we cannot formally deduce cryptographic hardness from nature, we can at least view the above as some justification that cryptography is a natural part of our current view of the universe.

Quantum Cryptography vs. Classical Cryptography. In this work we show that the black-hole radiation decoding problem is equivalent to the existence of quantum-cryptographic objects, namely EFI. However, it remains unsettled whether it has implications on the landscape of *classical* cryptography. Aaronson [Aar16] raised the question whether radiation decoding remains intractable even in the extreme case where $\mathbf{P=PSPACE}$ (where in particular classical cryptography does not exist). Our work frames this question in the context of the relation between quantum cryptography and classical complexity. It was recently shown by Kretschmer [Kre21] that (in a quantum-relativized world) quantum cryptography, and in particular EFI, could exist even if $\mathbf{BQP=QMA}$ (which is a setting where in particular classical cryptography can always be efficiently quantumly broken). The same work also showed that some forms of quantum cryptography cannot exist if $\mathbf{P=PSPACE}$, but this refers to so-called pseudorandom quantum states which are plausibly stronger primitives than EFI. It remains an intriguing open problem whether EFI could exist even if $\mathbf{P=PSPACE}$, and this work shows the implications to the radiation-decoding problem.

Gravitational Non-malleability, Black-Hole Dynamics. Kim, Tang and Preskill [KTP20] were considering the question of whether complementarity between the emitted radiation and the black-hole interior implies that the outside system could effect the black-hole interior by applying operations on the system R. They used cryptography, and in particular pseudorandom quantum states [JLS18] in order to show that under the assumption that the emitted radiation is pseudorandom (and thus "sufficiently scrambled"), it is not possible to act on it *efficiently* in a way that would effect the black-hole interior in a non-negligible manner. This is an additional evidence that the connection between cryptography and gravitational phenomena may not be incidental. Nevertheless, it is not known whether black-hole dynamics would actually emit the radiation in a pseudorandom manner. Indeed, coming up with a satisfactory description of information processing in black-hole dynamics is a grand goal, and our work is another evidence that cryptographic research may play a significant role in pursuing it.

Gravitational Cryptology in AdS/CFT? Cryptographic tools have recently been used by Bouland, Fefferman and Vazirani [BFV20] in order to characterize computational properties of the so-called AdS/CFT correspondence [Mal98]. At a high level, AdS/CFT is a class of quantum gravity theories that are based on a duality between "quantum gravity in the universe" (AdS, this is often called "the bulk") and "quantum fields on the boundary of the universe" (CFT).[9] It is shown in [BFV20] that quantum gravity theories such as AdS/CFT are either hard to use in the sense that the AdS to CFT translation is computationally intractable, or that they can solve computational problems that are intractable to "standard" quantum computers. Their work relied on the conjectured security

---

[9] To be precise, our universe is not AdS, so AdS/CFT theories do not directly apply to universes like our own. Nevertheless, it is believed that AdS/CFT hints to a duality relation that could exist in our universe as well.

of an explicit construction of a cryptographic object (a pseudorandom quantum state [JLS18]). Gheorghiu and Hoban [GH20] later proposed a path towards establishing a similar argument based on a well studied cryptographic problem (Learning with Errors [Reg05]).

The idea that the AdS/CFT mapping is potentially cryptographically hard, at least in some instances, could lead to a speculation that gravitational cryptology could be emergent in that context as well. Is it possible that the properties of quantum gravity *necessitate* cryptographic hardness in the AdS/CFT map? Can we think of the CFT description as an encryption of the AdS space? Interestingly, Aaronson (attributing to a discussion with Gottesman and Harlow about a proposal by Susskind) [Aar22b] proposed that such cryptographic hardness would posses *homomorphic* properties. This is since the evolution of the system in the bulk, according to the laws of physics, is represented by the evolution in the CFT, but the "plaintext" is intractable to recover. Many parts of this analogy remain unclear and await further investigation.

2   Preliminaries

The Security Parameter. The notion of a security parameter is one of the most fundamental in cryptography and is used to provide an asymptotic notion of efficiency and security, especially in cases where the input lengths do not immediately translate to a complexity measure (e.g. algorithms that do not take an input).

All algorithms we consider take an additional implicit input called the *security parameter* and usually denoted by λ. The complexity of the algorithm is defined as a function of λ. Therefore, in fact, every algorithm we consider constitutes of an ensemble of algorithms, one for each value of λ. Efficient algorithms are ones that run in time $\text{poly}(\lambda)$ for some polynomial, and a negligible function is one that vanishes faster than any inverse polynomial function in λ.

Quantum States and Registers. We use standard notation for quantum states and quantum registers. Quantum states are vectors in complex Hilbert space. For the purpose of this work, we consider Hilbert spaces composed of qubits, namely of the form $\bigotimes_{i=1}^{n} \mathbb{C}^2 \cong \mathbb{C}^{2^n}$, where n is the number of qubits. We associate Hilbert spaces with "registers" that manifest the local property of individual qubits. Registers are denoted by capital letters such as $A, B, \ldots$, and the concatenation of registers corresponds to the tensor product of their respective Hilbert spaces. Every n-qubit Hilbert space can naturally be written as a sequence of n single qubit registers $A_1 \cdots A_n$. We can thus refer to the register $A_1 A_3$, which corresponds to the first and third qubits in the sequence. We may sometimes use more than one partitioning for the same Hilbert space, for example if $n = 5$ we may consider a 2-qubit register B and an 3-qubit register C, and define $B = A_1 A_3$, $C = A_2 A_4 A_5$. In this case BC represents a Hilbert space that is isomorphic to $A_1 \cdots A_5$. Likewise CB is isomorphic to BC.

We use standard Dirac notation for quantum states. We recall that quantum states are fully characterized by their density matrix and that "pure quantum states" are ones represented by a rank-1 density matrix. The density matrix of a quantum state that is supported over a number of registers, say A,B is denoted ρ_{AB}, and the reduced density matrix over register A is denoted ρ_A. A register is said to contain a classical value if its reduced density matrix is diagonal in the computational basis (see below). We often refer to classical values by denoting them in lowercase letters.

A pure state $|\psi\rangle$ over m qubits is a *purification* of a (possibly mixed) state ρ over $n \leq m$ qubits, if letting A, B be registers of length $n, (m - n)$ respectively, and setting $\rho_{AB} = |\psi\rangle\langle\psi|$, it holds that $\rho_A = \rho$. Every state has a purification of length $m = 2n$.

Every qubit Hilbert space is associated with a basis that we refer to as the "computational basis" and denoted $\{|0\rangle, |1\rangle\}$. We also refer to the "Hadamard basis" $\{|+\rangle, |-\rangle\}$ which is defined respective to the computational basis by applying the Hadamard unitary operator.

We use standard notation for quantum gates (unitary operators) such as Pauli operators X, Z, Hadamard H and controlled X/Z operations: CNOT : $|xy\rangle \rightarrow |x, x \oplus y\rangle$, CZ : $|xy\rangle \rightarrow (-1)^{xy}|x, y\rangle$. When we wish to apply a gate or unitary on a specific register, we denote it in subscript. For example, in a system containing registers $ABCD$, if B is a single qubit register then H_B denotes the operation of applying the Hadamard gate on the register B (and acting as identity on ACD).

We let $|\text{epr}\rangle$ denote the standard two-qubit EPR state $|\text{epr}\rangle = \frac{|00\rangle + |11\rangle}{\sqrt{2}}$, and also consider the "EPR/Bell basis" $\{|\text{epr}_{xz}\rangle = (I \otimes X^x Z^z)|\text{epr}\rangle\}_{x,z \in \{0,1\}}$. Naturally, $|\text{epr}\rangle = |\text{epr}_{00}\rangle$. We note that $(H \otimes I)\text{CNOT}|\text{epr}_{xz}\rangle = |xz\rangle$.

Quantum Channels. A quantum channel is a CPTP (completely positive trace preserving) map between density operators, where the input and output can be defined over different Hilbert spaces. We refer to the Hilbert space of the input as the "source" and that of the output as the "target". Given two registers S, T whose associated Hilbert spaces correspond to those of the source and target spaces of a channel $\mathcal{C}$, we let $\mathcal{C}[S \rightarrow T]$ denote the application of the channel on the quantum state stored in register S, and storing the output in the register T. We think of the application of a channel as destroying the source register S and generating the target register T.

The computational complexity of a quantum channel refers to the minimal quantum circuit size that implements it. The atomic operations in quantum circuits are the application of a unitary on a constant number of qubits (say at most 3 qubits), introducing additional single-qubit registers that are initialized to the zero state, and discarding single-qubit registers (thus tracing them out of the total state of the system). It follows from the above that generating a random classical bit, and applying constant-arity classical gates can also be performed by a quantum circuit at a constant cost.

An ensemble (indexed by the security parameter) of quantum channels is efficiently implementable if its complexity is bounded by $p(\lambda)$ for some polynomial p. An ensemble of quantum states is efficiently generatable if there exists an efficient channel that generates them (starting from an empty, or 0-dimensional, register).

For any quantum channel $\mathcal{C}$, there exists a unitary $U_{\mathcal{C}}$ such that $\mathcal{C}[S \to T]$ is equivalent to the following. Consider registers A, A' such that the dimensions of SA and TA' match, apply the unitary $U_{\mathcal{C}}$ on $SA = A'T$ and trace out A'. Note that this unitary is not unique (although it is possible to define such a unitary canonically). The channel $\mathcal{C}$ is efficiently implementable if there exists such a $U_{\mathcal{C}}$ which is efficiently implementable. The unitary $U_{\mathcal{C}}$ is a *purification* of $\mathcal{C}$. If a channel (efficiently) generates some quantum state, a purification of the channel (efficiently) generates a purification of the state.

In terms of notation, we may refer to "a channel from register A to register B" when we mean that the channel is defined over the Hilbert spaces induced by these registers. Such a channel can be applied on other registers that are associated with Hilbert spaces of the same dimension as A, B.

Measurements and Distinguishers. For the purpose of this work, we use the following definition of a measurement. A quantum measurement $\mathcal{T}$ of a state in a register S is a quantum channel from S to a classical register t. A computational basis measurement of an n-qubit register corresponds to applying the operator $\sum_{x \in \{0,1\}^n} |x\rangle\langle x|\rho_S|x\rangle\langle x|$. More generally measurement in a basis represented by a unitary U corresponds to the operator $\sum_{x \in \{0,1\}^n} U|x\rangle\langle x|U^\dagger \rho_S U|x\rangle\langle x|U^\dagger$. Any projector Π on the Hilbert space associated with a register S induces a binary (two-outcome) measurement on S by $|1\rangle\langle 1| \operatorname{Tr}[\Pi \rho_S] + |0\rangle\langle 0| \operatorname{Tr}[(I - \Pi)\rho_S]$. That is, $\Pr[t = 1] = \operatorname{Tr}[\Pi \rho_S]$. We refer to such a measurement as "applying the projector Π", and refer to the outcome 1 as an "accepting" event for the measurement. We denote $\Pi_{\mathrm{EQ}} = |00\rangle\langle 00| + |11\rangle\langle 11|$.

A distinguisher between two distributions is a quantum channel whose target is a single classical bit. Such a channel $\mathcal{D}[S \to t]$ can always be represented by an operator $0 \leq \mathcal{D} \leq I$ over S (note the slight overloading of notation for both the channel and the operator), s.t. $\operatorname{Tr}[\mathcal{D}\rho_S]$ is the probability that the channel outputs the value 1 (when ρ_S is the state of S). The *advantage* of a distinguisher in distinguishing two distributions ρ_0, ρ_1 is $\operatorname{Tr}[\mathcal{D}(\rho_1 - \rho_0)] \in [-1, 1]$.[10] The maximal distinguishing advantage between two distributions is called their *statistical distance* (or total variation distance) and is equal to $\|\rho_1 - \rho_0\|_1$.

Consider an ensemble of pairs of distributions (indexed by the security parameter λ). We say that two distributions are *statistically indistinguishable* if their statistical distance as a function of λ is a negligible function. We say that two distributions are *computationally indistinguishable* if every *efficient* distinguisher (a sequence of distinguishers with complexity polynomial in λ), has negligible advantage.

The following propositions are straightforward.

Proposition 2.1. *Consider two distributions ρ_0, ρ_1, and define $\rho'_0 = \frac{1}{2}I \otimes \rho_0$ and $\rho'_1 = \frac{1}{2}\sum_b |b\rangle\langle b| \otimes \rho_b$. Then if there exists $\mathcal{D}'$ with advantage ϵ against ρ'_0, ρ'_1,*

---

[10] We use a *signed* definition of advantage, where positive advantage reflects positive correlation between the output of the distinguisher and the "label" of the input state, and negative advantage represents negative correlation.

then there exists $\mathcal{D}$ with advantage $\epsilon/2$ against ρ_0, ρ_1 with essentially the same complexity.

Proof. Given $\mathcal{D}'$ as in the statement, define $\mathcal{D}$ as follows. Given an input in a register S, initialize a register B to the state $|1\rangle\langle 1|$ and run $\mathcal{D}'$ on BS. The result follows by calculation.

Proposition 2.2. *Consider two distributions ρ_0, ρ_1 and let $\mathcal{D}$ be a distinguisher with advantage ϵ. Then the following experiment succeeds with probability $1/2 + \epsilon/2$.*

1. *Initialize registers BS in state $\frac{1}{2}\sum_b |b\rangle\langle b| \otimes \rho_b$.*
2. *Apply $\mathcal{D}[S \rightarrow D]$.*
3. *Apply Π_{EQ} on BD (i.e. output the negation of their XOR in the computational basis).*

Proof. Let O be the operator associated with $\mathcal{D}$. Define $\delta_b = \mathrm{Tr}[O\rho_b]$. Then the state of BD after the application of $\mathcal{D}$ is

$$\tfrac{1}{2}\left((1-\delta_0)|00\rangle\langle 00| + \delta_0|01\rangle\langle 01| + \delta_1|11\rangle\langle 11| + (1-\delta_1)|10\rangle\langle 10|\right). \qquad (1)$$

The success probability is thus $\frac{1}{2}(1 - \delta_0 + \delta_1) = 1/2 + \epsilon/2$.

Quantum Teleportation and Superdense Coding. One of the most basic features of quantum information is the ability to teleport a quantum state using classical communication. Let $TDBB'$ be a quadruple of quantum registers, where T, D, B are all single-qubit registers, and B' is of an arbitrary dimension. Consider an initial state where $\rho_{BB'} = \rho_0$ is arbitrary and $\rho_{TD} = |\mathrm{epr}\rangle\langle \mathrm{epr}|$. Then if we measure DB in the Bell basis, namely apply $(H_B \otimes I_D)\mathrm{CNOT}_{BD}$ and measure in the computational basis, and obtain an outcome x, z, then it holds that post-measurement: $\rho_{TB'} = ((X^x Z^z)_B \otimes I_{B'})(\rho_0)_{BB'}$. Namely, given the values of x, z it is possible to recover T to have the exact same state as the original B.

A related phenomenon is that of superdense coding, which allows us to send two bits of classical information using just one qubit, assuming that the parties pre-share an EPR pair. Let BD be a register that is initialized to $|\mathrm{epr}\rangle$. Now to encode two classical bits x, z, apply $X^x Z^z$ on the register D, and send it to the holder of B. Now once BD are measured in the Bell basis, x, z are recovered.

The Quantum Goldreich-Levin Theorem. The following is a quantum version of the famous Goldreich-Levin theorem [GL89]. This version was proven by Adcock and Cleve in [AC02], although it is not stated as a standalone theorem but rather as Eq. (16) which describes an algorithm presented in Fig. 1 and is proven as the first part of the proof of [AC02, Theorem 2].

Theorem 2.3 ([AC02, Eq. (16)]). *Let $n \in \mathbb{N}$, $x \in \{0,1\}^n$ and let $\{U_r\}_{\{0,1\}^n}$ be a set of m-qubit unitaries. Define the unitary U that applies U_r controlled by a value r received in an additional register, formally: $U = \sum_r |r\rangle\langle r| \otimes U_r$. Then the quantum circuit $\mathcal{R}^{U,U^\dagger}$ described in Fig. 1 has the following property.*

If, on average over r, the first qubit of $U_r|0^m\rangle$ is ϵ-correlated with $r \cdot x = \sum_{i=1}^{n} r_i x_i \pmod 2$, namely

$$\mathbb{E}_r\left[\|(I \otimes \langle r \cdot x|)U_r|0^m\rangle\|^2\right] \geq 1/2 + \epsilon, \tag{2}$$

then it holds that

$$\left|\langle x, 0^m, 1|\mathcal{R}^{U,U^\dagger}|0^{n+m+1}\rangle\right| \geq 2\epsilon. \tag{3}$$

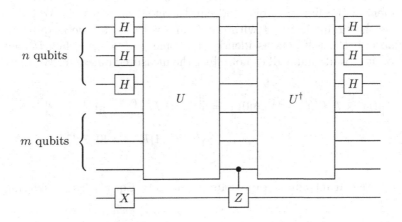

Fig. 1. Quantum circuit $\mathcal{R}^{U,U^\dagger}$.

The following immediate corollary follows from examining the algorithm in Fig. 1.

Corollary 2.4. *In the setting of Theorem 2.3, if there exists a pure state $|\varphi\rangle$ such that*

$$\left|\mathbb{E}_r\left[\|(I \otimes \langle r \cdot x|)U_r|\varphi\rangle\|^2\right] - 1/2\right| \geq \epsilon, \tag{4}$$

then it holds that

$$\left\|(\langle x| \otimes I)\mathcal{R}^{U,U^\dagger}|0^n\rangle|\varphi\rangle|0\rangle\right\|^2 \geq (2\epsilon)^2, \tag{5}$$

and therefore it is possible to recover the value of x with probability at least $(2\epsilon)^2$ by measuring the first n qubits in the computational basis.

Furthermore, if U_r acts as identity on a part of $|\varphi\rangle$, then $\mathcal{R}$ does not require access to this part of its input. In other words, the above holds even in the presence of quantum auxiliary input.

Proof. Let us start by considering the case where

$$\mathbb{E}_r \left[\left\| (I \otimes \langle r \cdot x|) U_r |\varphi\rangle \right\|^2 \right] \geq 1/2 + \epsilon. \tag{6}$$

Notice that in the corollary we only argue about the outcome of the measurement of the first n qubits of the state in the computational basis, and not about the entire output state. For this purpose, replacing the m-qubit state $|0^m\rangle$ with $|\varphi\rangle$ does not matter since we can imagine a (possibly inefficient) unitary W that generates $|\varphi\rangle$ from $|0\rangle$, then we can apply Theorem 2.3 with a unitary U' which first applies W to create $|\varphi\rangle$ and then applies U. This would be identical to applying U with the state $|\varphi\rangle$ as input. For applying $U'^\dagger$, we would need to apply $U^\dagger$ followed by $W^\dagger$, but the latter does not affect the outcome of the measurement of the first n qubits and can therefore be omitted. We have that we can use the circuit in Fig. 1 with our U and with $|\varphi\rangle$ as the m-qubit input. Furthermore, if U itself acts as identity on some part of $|\varphi\rangle$, then $U^\dagger$ acts as identity on it as well, and it does not effect the measured outcome. We therefore get

$$\left\| (\langle x| \otimes I) \mathcal{R}^{U,U^\dagger} |0^n\rangle |\varphi\rangle |0\rangle \right\|^2 = \left\| (\langle x| \otimes I) \mathcal{R}^{U',U'^\dagger} |0^{n+m+1}\rangle \right\|^2$$

$$\geq \left| \langle x, 0^m, 1| \mathcal{R}^{U',U'^\dagger} |0^{n+m+1}\rangle \right|^2$$

$$\geq (2\epsilon)^2.$$

Finally, we can introduce an absolute value into Eq. (4) by considering the case where

$$\mathbb{E}_r \left[\left\| (I \otimes \langle r \cdot x|) U_r |\varphi\rangle \right\|^2 \right] \leq 1/2 - \epsilon. \tag{7}$$

Here, can just consider U'_r that always flips the last bit of the output. For U' we have the "correct" expected value of at least $1/2 - \epsilon$, so we can apply Theorem 2.3. However, flipping the last bit in U' is equivalent to conjugating the controlled-Z gate in Fig. 1 by X on the control qubit. This is equivalent to applying an additional Z gate on the last qubit right after the controlled Z operation, which again does not change the measured value of the first n qubits. Therefore, applying the algorithm on U would yield the same outcome as applying it on U' and the corollary follows.

An Estimation Lemma. We use the following lemma. The proof is straightforward and is deferred to Appendix A.

Lemma 2.5. *Let $n \in \mathbb{N}$ and let $(\Gamma_1, \ldots, \Gamma_n)$ be an arbitrary set of events over some probability space. Define $\Upsilon_i = \bigwedge_{j=1}^i \Gamma_j$ and let Υ_0 be the universal event. Denote $\epsilon = \Pr[\Upsilon_n]$. Finally denote $\alpha_i = \Pr[\Gamma_i | \Upsilon_{i-1}]$. Then for all $\delta \in (0,1)$*

$$\Pr_{i \in [n]} \left[\alpha_i > 1 - \frac{\ln(1/\epsilon)}{\delta n} \right] \geq 1 - \delta . \tag{8}$$

If particular for any value of t, setting $\delta = 1/2$, $n > 2t \ln(1/\epsilon)$, we get that there exists a value of i (in fact, for half the values of i), $\alpha_i > 1 - 1/t$.

2.1   EFI Quantum States

The notion of efficiently generatable, statistically far but computationally indistinguishable pair of quantum states (EFI) was recently explicitly introduced in [BCQ22], extending ideas from [Yan20], as a generalization of a similar notion that existed in classical cryptography [Gol90].

Definition 2.6 (EFI). *An Efficiently Sampleable, Statistically Far and Computationally Indistinguishable pair of distributions (EFI) is an ensemble of equal-dimension pairs of quantum states such that the following all hold:*

(E) Each element in the pair, as an individual ensemble, is efficiently generatable.
(F) The two ensembles are not statistically indistinguishable.
(I) The two ensembles are computationally indistinguishable.

We also consider the notion of "strong EFI" for which condition (F) is strengthened as

(F!) The two ensembles have statistical distance $1 - \eta$, where η is a negligible function.

We may strengthen this notion even further and define "perfect EFI" via

(F!!) The two ensembles have statistical distance 1.

We note that by using repetition, strong EFI exists if and only if "standard" EFI exists (however, this equivalence is not known for perfect EFI).

Proposition 2.7. *Strong EFI exists if and only if EFI exists.*

We may now make the cryptographic assumption that EFI exist.

Assumption 1. EFI exist.

It has been shown in [BCQ22], also relying on prior work, that the existence of EFI is equivalent to that of a few cryptographic objects.

Theorem 2.8. *EFI exists if and only if any of the following cryptographic primitives exist:*[11]

1. *Quantum bit commitments.*
2. *Quantum oblivious transfer protocols.*
3. *Quantum secure multiparty computation protocols for non-trivial functionalities.*
4. *Non-trivial quantum computational zero-knowledge proofs for the complexity class* QIP = PSPACE.

---

[11] This refers to the standard adversarial cryptographic model, without making physical assumptions about limits on storage or use of special hardware.

3   Black-Hole Radiation Decoding

We provide our formal definition for the problem of decoding black-hole radiation. We define, from the beginning, the general version in which the decoder is allowed to declare failure. Essentially, we require that with non-negligible probability failure is not declared, and when this happens, the radiation decoder distills a qubit from the radiation that is highly entangled with a qubit inside the horizon. This is defined in terms of fidelity with the EPR state. A successful decoding will lead to non-trivial fidelity of more than $1/4$ (which is the fidelity of the EPR state with completely unentangled qubits). The formal definition follows.

Definition 3.1 (Black-Hole Radiation Decoder). *Let $|\psi\rangle_{HBR}$ be a pure state supported over 3 registers HBR, where B is a single-qubit register. A radiation decoder (or just "decoder" when the context is clear) is a quantum channel $\mathcal{D}[R \to DF]$, where D, F are each a single-qubit register. We refer to F as the "failure qubit" and to D as the "decoded value".*

For $\gamma, \epsilon \in [0, 1]$ We say that $\mathcal{D}$ is (γ, ϵ)-decoder (against $|\psi\rangle$) if the following holds. Consider the experiment where HBR are initialized to $|\psi\rangle_{HBR}$, and then $\mathcal{D}[R \to DF]$ is applied. Then the reduced density matrix of FBD is

$$\rho_{FBD} = \gamma'|0\rangle\langle 0|_F \otimes (\rho_0)_{BD} + (1 - \gamma')|1\rangle\langle 1|_F \otimes (\rho_1)_{BD}, \tag{9}$$

for some $\gamma' \geq \gamma$, and unit trace ρ_0, ρ_1, and in addition $\langle \mathrm{epr}|\rho_0|\mathrm{epr}\rangle \geq (1/4) + (3/4)\epsilon$.

We use the following terminology for asymptotic families of decoders:

- *A $(1, 1 - \eta)$-decoder with negligible η is a strong decoder.*
- *A (γ, ϵ)-decoder which is computationally efficient and for which $\gamma \cdot \epsilon$ is non-negligible, is an effective decoder. If in addition $\epsilon = 1 - o(1)$, we call it a high confidence decoder.*

The scaling for ϵ is chosen so that the effective range of ϵ is $[0, 1]$ (this unfortunately leads to an asymmetry between $\epsilon > 0$ and $\epsilon < 0$ but it will not be problematic for us).

Assumption 2 (Black-Hole Radiation Decoding (BHRD)). There exists an ensemble of efficiently generated pure states as per Definition 3.1, for which there exists a strong (inefficient) decoder, but there does not exist an effective decoder.

The following is a simple observation.

Proposition 3.2. *If there exists a (γ, ϵ)-decoder against a state $|\psi\rangle$ then there also exists a $(1, \gamma \cdot \epsilon)$-decoder against $|\psi\rangle$.*

Proof. Given a (γ, ϵ)-decoder $\mathcal{A}'$, consider a decoder $\mathcal{A}[R \to DF]$ as follows that first runs the original $\mathcal{A}'[R \to D'F']$ and measures the register F'. If $f' = 0$ then set $D = D'$, otherwise set D to contain a maximally mixed state. Set F to $|0\rangle\langle 0|$. The result follows by calculation.

3.1   The Superdense Decoding Problem

We introduce a computational problem that is related to the well known notion of quantum superdense coding. We relate it to the problem of radiation decoding and show that the two are essentially equivalent. We believe that the superdense formulation of the problem may be a useful one, and indeed this formulation plays an important role in our constructions of EFI in Sect. 5.

The formal definition follows. We wish to emphasize that both the radiation decoder and the superdense decoder are defined with respect to the a state (or an ensemble of states) over HBR, but whereas a radiation decoder only takes R as input, a superdense decoder takes BR as input (where a classical challenge is encoded into the register B).

Definition 3.3. *Let $|\psi\rangle_{HBR}$ be a pure state supported over 3 registers HBR, where B is a single-qubit register. A Decoder is a quantum channel $S[BR \rightarrow PF]$, where P is a two-qubit register and F is a single-qubit register. We consider the following experiment:*

1. *Initialize the registers HBR to $|\psi\rangle_{HBR}$.*
2. *Sample two random bits x, z.*
3. *Apply the Pauli mask $X^x Z^z$ to the register B (this is also known as a quantum one-time-pad encryption).*
4. *Apply $S[BR \rightarrow PF]$.*
5. *Measure P, F in the computational basis to obtain values $(x', z'), f$.*

For $\gamma, \epsilon \in [0, 1]$, we say that S is (γ, ϵ)-superdense-decoder (against $|\psi\rangle$) if $\Pr[f = 0] \geq \gamma$ and $\Pr[(x', z') = (x, z)|f = 0] \geq 1/4 + (3/4)\epsilon$.

The following lemma establishes the connection between superdense decoding and radiation decoding (in any parameter regime).

Lemma 3.4. *Let $|\psi\rangle_{HBR}$ be a pure state supported over 3 registers HBR, where B is a single-qubit register. Then there exists a (γ, ϵ)-radiation decoder against $|\psi\rangle$ if and only if there exists a (γ, ϵ)-superdense decoder against $|\psi\rangle$ with comparable computational complexity.*

Proof. Let $|\psi\rangle_{HBR}$ be as in the lemma statement. We consider both directions of the lemma.

Radiation-Decoder Implies Superdense-Decoder. This direction is almost immediate. Given a radiation decoder $\mathcal{A}$, we can use it to decode the radiation R. If the experiment is successful, then whenever in the original experiment BD constitute an EPR pair, we can use standard superdense decoding procedure to recover x, z.

More formally, let $\mathcal{A}$ be a (γ, ϵ)-radiation decoder. We define a superdense decoder $S[BR \rightarrow PF]$ as follows.

1. Apply $\mathcal{A}[R \rightarrow DF]$.
2. Measure BD in the Bell basis and store the outcome in P.

The parameters (γ, ϵ) remain the same by the properties of superdense coding.

Superdense-Decoder Implies Radiation-Decoder. Let $\mathcal{S}$ be a (γ, ϵ)-superdense decoder. We start by noticing that applying a quantum one-time pad to a register is equivalent to performing quantum teleportation onto a different variable. Thus, the experiment from Definition 3.3 is equivalent to the following.

1. Initialize the registers HBR to $|\psi\rangle_{HBR}$.
2. Initialize two single-qubit registers DT to $|\text{epr}\rangle_{DT}$.
3. Measure BD in the Bell basis to obtain values x, z. (This is the process of teleporting the register B into the register T via the register D.)
4. Apply $\mathcal{S}[TR \rightarrow PF]$.
5. Measure P in the computational basis to obtain values (x', z').

We therefore conclude that in the above experiment, $\mathcal{S}$ outputs F which takes the value 0 with probability at least γ, and letting f being the measured value of F, we have $\Pr[(x', z') = (x, z) | f = 0] \geq 1/4 + (3/4)\epsilon$.

We note that step 3 in the above experiment (the BD measurement) commutes with all following steps of the experiment until the final one. Let us therefore defer it until the end of the experiment.

We now define a radiation decoder $\mathcal{A}[R \rightarrow DF]$ as follows.

1. Initialize two single-qubit registers DT to $|\text{epr}\rangle_{DT}$.
2. Apply $\mathcal{S}[TR \rightarrow PF]$.
3. Measure P in the computational basis to obtain values x', z'.
4. Apply $Z^{z'} X^{x'}$ to D.
5. Output DF.

Measuring the value of F in the computational basis to obtain a value f, we have that $\Pr[f = 0] \geq \gamma$ by the properties of $\mathcal{S}$. Now let us consider the reduced density matrix of PBD conditioned on $f = 0$ (this is a trace-1 density matrix). This matrix can be written as

$$\rho_{PBD} = \sum_{x', z'} c_{x', z'} |x', z'\rangle\langle x', z'|_P \otimes (\rho_{x', z'})_{BD}, \tag{10}$$

where $c_{x', z'}$ are real values summing to 1, and $\rho_{x', z'}$ are proper trace-1 density matrices. We know that the probability of measuring BD in the Bell basis and obtaining values that are equal to (x', z') is $1/4 + (3/4)\epsilon$. We notice that the success probability would have been the same if we performed $X^{x'} Z^{z'}$ on D and applied the $|\text{epr}\rangle\langle\text{epr}|$ projector, which is exactly the success probability of $\mathcal{A}$, conditioned on $f = 0$. This concludes this case.

4 Cryptology-Induced Gravitational Phenomena

We show that Assumption 1 implies Assumption 2. An efficiently generatable state $|\psi\rangle_{HBR}$ for which it is hard to decode entanglement. We in fact show that the existence of EFI also implies such states where it is impossible to detect *any* correlation between the B and R registers. In other words, BR are computationally indistinguishable from being in tensor product. This is therefore a stronger result than that of [HH13, Aar16], where some classical or Hadamard correlations can be efficiently recovered.

Theorem 4.1. *If there exists an EFI pair as per Assumption 1 then there exists an ensemble of hard-to-decode radiation states as per Assumption 2.*

Proof. Consider a strong EFI pair of states (recalling Proposition 2.7, EFI implies strong EFI). By considering the purification of the generating channel of the pair of states, there exist efficiently generatable ensembles of *pure* states $\{|\varphi_b\rangle\}_{b\in\{0,1\}}$ over registers HR' such that $\text{Tr}_H\left[|\varphi_b\rangle\langle\varphi_b|_{HR'}\right]$ are strong EFI.

Consider the ensemble of states defined over registers $H'BTH_1R_1'H_2R_2'$ as

$$|\psi\rangle = \frac{1}{2\sqrt{2}} \sum_{b,x,z\in\{0,1\}} |xz\rangle_{H'}|b\rangle_B(X^xZ^z|b\rangle_T)|\varphi_x\rangle_{H_1R_1'}|\varphi_z\rangle_{H_2R_2'} . \tag{11}$$

We denote $H = H'H_1H_2$, $R = TR'$ so that $|\psi\rangle$ is defined over HBR.

Efficient Generation. The above state is generated in the following steps:

1. Generate an EPR pair in BT.
2. Generate $|++\rangle$ in H'.
3. Apply a "quantum one-time pad" X^xZ^z, controlled by H' on the qubit in T. (This is equivalent to converting BT to $|\text{epr}_{xz}\rangle$, controlled by the values xz in H').
4. Encode x, z using the EFI. Formally, controlled by the individual bits of H', generate either $|\varphi_0\rangle$ or $|\varphi_1\rangle$ in $H_1'R_1'$ controlled by the first qubit of H', and likewise in $H_2'R_2'$ controlled by the second qubit of H'.

Inefficient Decoder. By the strong EFI property, there exists a possibly inefficient channel $\mathcal{D}$ so that $\mathcal{D}[R' \to D]$ distinguishes $|\varphi_1\rangle\langle\varphi_1|$ from $|\varphi_0\rangle\langle\varphi_0|$ with $(1 - \eta)$ advantage, for a negligible η.

We now show an inefficient $(1, 1 - (4/3)\eta)$-radiation decoder $\mathcal{A}[R \to TF]$ (note that the register T will be our output register).

1. Apply $\mathcal{D}[R_1' \to D_1]$.
2. Apply $\mathcal{D}[R_2' \to D_2]$.
3. Apply CZ_{D_2T}.
4. Apply CNOT_{D_1T}.
5. Initialize F to $\rho_F = |0\rangle\langle0|$.

To analyze, let us consider the state of $H'BTD_1D_2$ after the two applications of $\mathcal{D}$. Consider an experiment where the CZ and CNOT gates are controlled by H_2', H_1' instead of D_2, D_1. In that case, essentially by definition, BT is exactly in $|\text{epr}\rangle$. Therefore, the probability that BT is not measured in $|\text{epr}\rangle$ in the experiment is at most the probability that H' is not equal to D_1D_2, which is at most η by Proposition 2.2 and the union bound: $2 \cdot (1 - (1/2 + (1 - \eta)/2)) = \eta$.

No Effective Decoder. Assume there exists an efficient (γ, ϵ)-radiation-decoder $\mathcal{A}$ for the state $|\psi\rangle$. We show how it can be used to construct an efficient distinguisher $\mathcal{D}$ for the EFI with advantage $\gamma \cdot \epsilon$. This would show that an effective decoder contradicts the computational indistinguishability property of the EFI.

We will use a hybrid argument. We describe a sequence of experiments (hybrids) that will allow us to draw the required conclusion.

- Hybrid 0. This is the standard radiation decoding game as per Definition 3.1, where $\mathcal{A}$ attempts to decode the radiation in encoded in $|\psi\rangle$.
- Hybrid 1. In this experiment, we change the way $|\psi\rangle$ is generated. In particular we generate $H_2 R_2'$ to always contain $|\varphi_0\rangle$, regardless of the value of x.
- Hybrid 2. In this experiment, we again change the way $|\psi\rangle$ is generated. We keep $H_2 R_2'$ as in the previous hybrid, but now we also generate $H_1 R_1'$ to always contain $|\varphi_0\rangle$, regardless of the value of z.

We let γ_i denote the probability of measuring 0 in F in Hybrid i, and by ϵ_i the probability of measuring EPR in BD conditioned on measuring 0 in F. We argue that it must be the case that $|\gamma_i \epsilon_i - \gamma_{i+1}\epsilon_{i+1}|$, are negligible. Otherwise, by Proposition 2.1, it would allow us to distinguish the EFI states.

Finally, it must be the case that in Hybrid 2, even when F measures to 0, the probability to measure $|\text{epr}\rangle$ in BD, no matter how D is generated, is exactly $1/4$. In fact, in Hybrid 2, it is indeed the case that R and B are in tensor product, since R_1', R_2' are independent of x, z, and therefore T is in maximally mixed state. Indeed, in this hybrid there simply does not exist *any* correlation between B and R. Since the reduced density matrix of B is maximally mixed, we have that the probability of measuring EPR is exactly $1/4$. The theorem thus follows.

5 Gravitationally-Induced Cryptology

We start by showing the "vanilla" version of our claim. We consider the following two distributions.

Definition 5.1. *Let $|\psi\rangle$ be an efficiently generatable ensemble of states over registers HBR. We consider the following EFI candidate distribution. Specifically, the distribution ρ_b for $b \in \{0, 1\}$ is defined as follows.*

1. *Initialize HBR to $|\psi\rangle_{HBR}$.*
2. *Sample uniformly $x, z \in \{0, 1\}$.*
3. *Apply $(X^x Z^z)_B$.*
4. *If $b = 0$ set $x' = x$, $z' = z$, otherwise (if $b = 1$) sample $x', z' \in \{0, 1\}$ uniformly at random.*
5. *Output BR and $x'z'$.*

Theorem 5.2. *Let $|\psi\rangle$ be efficiently generatable, strongly decodable but not effectively decodable, as per Assumption 2. Then the pair of distributions in Definition 5.1 is EFI as per Assumption 1.*

Proof. Since $|\psi\rangle$ is strongly radiation-decodable, it is also strongly superdense decodable. We show an inefficient distinguisher for the EFI candidate as follows. Given as input $BRx'z'$, apply the inefficient $(1, 1 - \eta)$-superdense decoder to BR to obtain values $x''z''$. If these values are equal to $x'z'$ output 0, otherwise output 1. The probability that this distinguisher outputs 1 on ρ_0 is at most $(4/3)\eta$. The probability that it outputs 1 on ρ_1 is at least $(3/4)(1 - (4/3)\eta)$. The distinguishing gap thus follows.

On the other hand, let $\mathcal{D}$ be a distinguisher between ρ_0, ρ_1 as per Definition 5.1, with advantage δ. We show that there exists a $(1, \delta/12)$-superdense decoder $\mathcal{S}$ against $|\psi\rangle$ with roughly the same complexity. Thus, by Lemma 3.4, there is also a radiation decoder against $|\psi\rangle$ and the theorem would follow.

Our superdense decoder, upon receiving an input in registers BR, does the following.

1. Sample $x', z' \in \{0, 1\}$ uniformly at random.
2. Apply $\mathcal{D}[BRx'z' \to T]$ and measures the outcome in the computational basis to obtain a value t.
3. If $t = 0$, set P to the classical value $xz = x'z'$, otherwise set P to a maximally mixed state. Set F to $|0\rangle\langle 0|$.

Note that by definition, this $\mathcal{S}$ has $\gamma = 1$. We show that its ϵ is related to the distinguishing advantage δ. To this end, we let δ_b denote the probability that $\mathcal{D}$ outputs 0 on ρ_b. We denote by $\delta_\perp$ the probability that $\mathcal{D}$ outputs 0 when its input consists of properly generated BR, along with $x'z'$ that are sampled to be *not equal* to the actual xz. A simple calculation implies that $\delta_1 = \frac{1}{4}\delta_0 + \frac{3}{4}\delta_\perp$. By the definition of $\mathcal{D}$ we have that $\delta_0 - \delta_1 = \delta$.

The probability that $\mathcal{S}$ outputs the correct values x, z in the superdense decoding experiment is therefore:

$$\frac{1}{4}\delta_1 \cdot 1 + \frac{1}{4}(1 - \delta_1) \cdot \frac{1}{4} + \frac{3}{4}(1 - \delta_\perp) \cdot \frac{1}{4} . \tag{12}$$

The three terms in this expression are as follows:

1. If $x'z'$ were sampled identically to the real xz, which happens with probability $1/4$ then:
   (a) With probability δ_1, $\mathcal{D}$ outputs 0 and we output the correct value. This event therefore has a total probability of $\frac{1}{4}\delta_1 \cdot 1$.
   (b) With probability $(1 - \delta_1)$, $\mathcal{D}$ outputs 1 and we output a random value, which hits the correct value with probability $1/4$. This event therefore has a total probability of $\frac{1}{4}(1 - \delta_1) \cdot \frac{1}{4}$.
2. If $x'z'$ were sampled to not be equal to xz, which happens with probability $3/4$, then we can only win if $\mathcal{D}$ outputs 1, which happens with probability $(1 - \delta_\perp)$, and in addition the randomly sampled output hits the correct values xz, which happens with probability $1/4$. This event therefore has a total probability of $\frac{3}{4}(1 - \delta_\perp) \cdot \frac{1}{4}$.

The 3 terms above sum to $\frac{1}{4} + \frac{\delta}{16}$. It follows that indeed $\epsilon = (4/3) \cdot (\delta/16)$ and the result follows.

5.1 Amplifying the Result

We now show a candidate for EFI which is proven to remain EFI even if the underlying state is only mildly hard to decode.

Definition 5.3. *Let $|\psi\rangle$ be an ensemble of states, and let $n = n(\lambda)$ be a parameter. We consider the following EFI candidate distribution. Specifically, the distributions ρ_0, ρ_1 that are defined as follows.*

1. *Consider registers $H_i B_i R_i$, for $i \in [n]$, initialize each triple $H_i B_i R_i$ to $|\psi\rangle_{H_i B_i R_i}$.*
2. *Sample uniformly random strings $\vec{x}, \vec{z} \in \{0,1\}^n$.*
3. *For all i, apply $(X^{x_i} Z^{z_i})_{B_i}$.*
4. *Sample uniformly random strings $\vec{a}, \vec{a}' \in \{0,1\}^n$.*
5. *Calculate $c = (\vec{a} \cdot \vec{x}) \oplus (\vec{a}' \cdot \vec{z})$, where the inner product is over the binary field.*
6. *The output of ρ_b contains the following:*

$$\left(\{B_i R_i\}_{i \in [n]}, (\vec{a}, \vec{a}'), c' = c \oplus b \right). \tag{13}$$

We now prove that it suffices that $|\psi\rangle$ is mildly hard to decode in order to imply that the above construction is EFI. For the sake of convenience, we split our argument into two lemmas. One that considers the efficiency of generation, and the existence of an inefficient distinguisher, and the other that converts an efficient distinguisher into an efficient high-confidence decoder.

Lemma 5.4. *Let $|\psi\rangle$ be efficiently generatable and strongly (possibly inefficiently) decodable as per Assumption 2. Then the pair of distributions in Definition 5.3 is efficiently generatable and statistically distinguishable for any polynomial $n(\lambda)$.*

Proof. Since $|\psi\rangle$ is efficiently generatable, then our ρ_b are also efficiently generatable for every polynomial n, since the generation of ρ_b contains a generation of polynomially many copies of $|\psi\rangle$ as well as a polynomial number of elementary computational steps.

Next we show that ρ_0, ρ_1 are inefficiently distinguishable, given that there exists a strong radiation decoder $\mathcal{A}$ against $|\psi\rangle$. We use Lemma 3.4 to argue that there also exists a strong $(1, 1 - \eta)$-superdense decoder $\mathcal{S}$ against $|\psi\rangle$ and use $\mathcal{S}$ to derive a distinguisher between ρ_0, ρ_1 with advantage at least $1 - 2n\eta$. Since η is negligible and n is polynomial, then $2n\eta$ is also negligible. To see the above, we consider a distinguisher $\mathcal{D}$ that takes as input a register S containing $\left(\{B_i R_i\}_{i \in [n]}, (\vec{a}, \vec{a}'), c' \right)$ and $\mathcal{D}[S \to T]$ acts as follows:

1. Apply $\mathcal{S}[B_i R_i \to P_i F_i]$, for all i.
2. Measure P_i in the computational basis to obtain two classical bits (x_i', z_i').
3. Setting $\vec{x}' = (x_1, \ldots, x_k)$, $\vec{z}' = (z_1, \ldots, z_k)$, compute $b' = c' \oplus (\vec{a} \cdot \vec{x}') \oplus (\vec{a}' \cdot \vec{z}')$.
4. Initialize a register T to the classical value b' and produce this register as the output.

We note that since $\mathcal{B}$ has $\gamma = 1$, we need not measure the register F_i since it is guaranteed to always be identical to 0.

To see the distinguishing gap of $\mathcal{D}$ defined above, we notice that since $\mathcal{S}$ is a strong decoder and therefore with all but η probability, $(x_i', z_i') = (x_i, z_i)$. Applying the union bound, we get that this holds for all i with all but $n\eta$ probability. If this indeed holds then, by definition, $b' = b$. The distinguishing advantage thus follows.

The next lemma establishes that an efficient distinguisher against our EFI candidate would result in a high-confidence decoder, so long as n is chosen to be sufficiently large, specifically $n(\lambda) = \omega(\log \lambda)$.

Lemma 5.5. *Let $|\psi\rangle$ be efficiently generatable, and consider the pair of distributions in Definition 5.3. If the aforementioned distributions are efficiently distinguishable with non-negligible advantage, then there is a (γ, ϵ)-decoder with polynomially-related computational complexity against $|\psi\rangle$, where γ is non-negligible, and $\epsilon = 1 - O(\log(\lambda)/n)$.*

Proof. For the remainder of the proof, let $|\psi\rangle$ be an ensemble of states and let $\mathcal{D}$ be an efficient distinguisher between the pair of distributions of Definition 5.3, with non-negligible advantage δ. We show that there exists an effective radiation decoder $\mathcal{A}$ against $|\psi\rangle$. We will do this by first presenting a superdense decoder $\mathcal{S}$ against $|\psi\rangle$ and then applying Lemma 3.4 to derive the final conclusion.

From Distinguishing to Batch-Decoding. We start by showing that the existence of $\mathcal{D}$ also implies the existence of an efficient *batch-decoder* $\mathcal{B}$ that succeeds with probability at least $\delta' = \text{poly}(\delta)$ in the following experiment.

1. Consider registers $H_i B_i R_i$, for $i \in [n]$, initialize each triple $H_i B_i R_i$ to $|\psi\rangle_{H_i B_i R_i}$.
2. Sample uniformly random strings $\vec{x}, \vec{z} \in \{0, 1\}^n$.
3. For all i, apply $(X^{x_i} Z^{z_i})_{B_i}$.
4. Apply $\mathcal{B}[\{B_i R_i\}_{i \in [n]} \to Q]$, where Q is a $2n$-qubit register.
5. Measure Q in the computational basis to obtain values $\vec{x}', \vec{z}' \in \{0, 1\}^n$.
6. The experiment succeeds if $(\vec{x}', \vec{z}') = (\vec{x}, \vec{z})$.

In other words, with probability δ', $\mathcal{B}$ is able to recover all x_i, z_i values for all i, given only access to the registers $B_i R_i$.

The existence of $\mathcal{B}$ is implied from that of $\mathcal{D}$ by Corollary 2.4 (the quantum Goldreich-Levin theorem). To apply the corollary, we need to construct the required unitary U from the distinguisher $\mathcal{D}$, using a standard argument.

Let $\delta_{\vec{x}, \vec{z}}$ denote the advantage of $\mathcal{D}$ over fixed values of $\vec{x}, \vec{z}$. With probability at least $\delta/2$ over $\vec{x}, \vec{z}$, it holds that $|\delta_{\vec{x}, \vec{z}}| \geq \delta/2$. Consider the channel $\mathcal{D}'$ that, given as input $(\{B_i R_i\}_{i \in [n]}, (\vec{a}, \vec{a}'))$ (note that c' is not given) samples a random value $t' \in \{0, 1\}$, applies $\mathcal{D}$ on $(\{B_i R_i\}_{i \in [n]}, (\vec{a}, \vec{a}'), t')$ to obtain a value t, and outputs $t' \oplus t$. It is not hard to verify that the probability that $t' \oplus t = c = (\vec{a} \cdot \vec{x}) \oplus (\vec{a}' \cdot \vec{z})$ is exactly equal to $1/2 + \delta_{\vec{x}, \vec{z}}/2$. The unitary U is derived from the purification of the channel $\mathcal{D}'$, in addition to acting as identity on the registers

H_i which are not provided to $\mathcal{D}$. The state $|\varphi\rangle$ in the corollary is the pure state in $\{H_iB_iR_i\}_{i\in[n]}$ conditioned on the values of $\vec{x},\vec{z}$, which are constants for the purpose of the corollary.

It follows that with probability at least $\delta/2$ over $\vec{x},\vec{z}$, the correct values are recovered with probability at least $(\delta/2)^2$, which implies that $\mathcal{B}$ succeeds in decoding $\vec{x},\vec{z}$ with probability at least $\delta' = (\delta/2)^3$.

Corollary 2.4 can therefore be applied and the performance of $\mathcal{B}$ follows.

From Batch-Decoding to Single-Instance Decoding. We now use the batch decoder $\mathcal{B}$ to obtain a (regular) effective superdense decoder $\mathcal{S}$ as follows.

We consider the following random variables, with reference to the experiment of $\mathcal{B}$ above. We denote by Γ_i the event where $(x_i', z_i') = (x_i, z_i)$, and note that all Γ_i are defined over the same probability space. We can now invoke the estimation lemma (Lemma 2.5) to deduce that for at least half of the values $i \in [n]$ it holds that

$$\alpha_i = \Pr\left[\Gamma_i \middle| \bigwedge_{j=1}^{i-1} \Gamma_i\right] > 1 - \frac{2\ln(1/\delta')}{n}. \tag{14}$$

Since we know that $\delta' = \mathrm{poly}(\lambda)$, it holds that $\frac{2\ln(1/\delta')}{n} = O(\log(\lambda)/n)$.

We also recall that for all i it holds that

$$\Pr\left[\bigwedge_{j=1}^{i-1} \Gamma_i\right] \geq \Pr\left[\bigwedge_{j=1}^{n} \Gamma_i\right] \geq \delta'. \tag{15}$$

It therefore follows that in $\mathrm{poly}(1/\delta, n, \lambda) = \mathrm{poly}(\lambda)$ time, it is possible to estimate all values α_i to within additive error $O(\log\lambda/n)$, with global estimation error $O(\log\lambda/n)$, using the Chernoff bound. This is because the batch-decoding experiment can be ran efficiently (in polynomial time).

We therefore devise our superdense decoder $\mathcal{S}[BR \to PF]$ as follows.

1. Using $\mathcal{B}$, estimate the values of all α_i to within $O(\log\lambda/n)$ with $O(\log\lambda/n)$ total estimation error, as described above.
2. Let i^* be such that the estimated α_{i^*} is the highest.
3. For all $i \neq i^*$ generate B_iR_i along with x_i, z_i as in the batch-decoding experiment.
4. Set $B_{i^*}R_{i^*} = BR$.
5. Run $\mathcal{B}[\{B_iR_i\}_{i\in[n]} \to Q]$. Measure Q in the computational basis to obtain $\vec{x}', \vec{z}' \in \{0,1\}^n$.
6. If for all $i < i^*$ it holds that $(x_i', z_i') = (x_i, z_i)$, set F to the classical value 0 and set P to the classical values x_i', z_i'.
7. Otherwise set F to the classical value 1 and set P to an arbitrary value.

It follows from the above argument that $\mathcal{S}$ is a (γ, ϵ) superdense decoder against $|\psi\rangle$ with $\gamma \geq \delta'$ and $\epsilon \geq (1 - O(\log\lambda/n))$.

Finally, applying Lemma 3.4, we deduce that we can also obtain a (γ, ϵ)-radiation decoder with the same parameters, which completes the proof of our lemma.

Acknowledgements. We thank Scott Aaronson, Ran Canetti, Isaac Kim and Luowen Qian for valuable feedback. We also thank anonymous reviewers for their comments.

A   Proof of Estimation Lemma

Lemma A.1 (Lemma 2.5, Restated). *Let $n \in \mathbb{N}$ and let $(\Gamma_1, \ldots, \Gamma_n)$ be an arbitrary set of events over some probability space. Define $\Upsilon_i = \bigwedge_{j=1}^{i} \Gamma_j$ and let Υ_0 be the universal event. Denote $\epsilon = \Pr[\Upsilon_n]$. Finally denote $\alpha_i = \Pr[\Gamma_i | \Upsilon_{i-1}]$. Then for all $\delta \in (0,1)$*

$$\Pr_{i \in [n]} \left[\alpha_i > 1 - \frac{\ln(1/\epsilon)}{\delta n} \right] \geq 1 - \delta. \tag{16}$$

Proof. By definition it holds that

$$\alpha_i = \frac{\Pr[\Gamma_i \wedge \Upsilon_{i-1}]}{\Pr[\Upsilon_{i-1}]} = \frac{\Pr[\Upsilon_i]}{\Pr[\Upsilon_{i-1}]}. \tag{17}$$

Then by a telescopic product it holds that

$$\prod_{i=1}^{n} \alpha_i = \Pr[\Upsilon_n] = \epsilon, \tag{18}$$

or alternatively

$$\frac{\ln(1/\epsilon)}{n} = \mathop{\mathbb{E}}_{i \in [n]} \left[\ln(1/\alpha_i) \right]. \tag{19}$$

We can apply Markov's inequality (since $\ln(1/\alpha_i)$ is positive) to conclude that for all $\delta \in (0,1)$:

$$\Pr_{i} \left[\ln(1/\alpha_i) \geq \frac{\ln(1/\epsilon)}{\delta n} \right] \leq \delta. \tag{20}$$

Therefore with probability at least $1 - \delta$ over i, we have that $\ln(1/\alpha_i) < \frac{\ln(1/\epsilon)}{\delta n}$, which implies that $1/\alpha_i < e^{\frac{\ln(1/\epsilon)}{\delta n}}$. That is

$$\alpha_i > e^{-\frac{\ln(1/\epsilon)}{\delta n}} \geq 1 - \frac{\ln(1/\epsilon)}{\delta n}. \tag{21}$$

This concludes the proof of the lemma.

References

[Aar16] Aaronson, S.: The complexity of quantum states and transformations: from quantum money to black holes. CoRR, abs/1607.05256 (2016)

[Aar22a] Aaronson, S.: Introduction to quantum information science II lecture notes (2022). https://www.scottaaronson.com/qisii.pdf

[Aar22b] Aaronson, S.: On black holes, holography, the quantum extended church-turing thesis, fully homomorphic encryption, and brain uploading (2022). Blog Post on Shtetl-Optimized, The Blog of Scott Aaronson https://scottaaronson.blog/?p=6599. Attributed to discussions with Daniel Gottesman, Daniel Harlow and Leonard Susskind

[AC02] Adcock, M., Cleve, R.: A quantum Goldreich-Levin theorem with cryptographic applications. In: Alt, H., Ferreira, A. (eds.) STACS 2002. LNCS, vol. 2285, pp. 323–334. Springer, Heidelberg (2002). https://doi.org/10.1007/3-540-45841-7_26

[AMPS13] Almheiri, A., Marolf, D., Polchinski, J., Sully, J.: Black holes: complementarity or firewalls? J. High Energy Phys. **2013**(2), 1–20 (2013). https://doi.org/10.1007/JHEP02(2013)062

[BCQ22] Brakerski, Z., Canetti, R., Qian, L.: On the computational hardness needed for quantum cryptography. Cryptology ePrint Archive, Paper 2022/1181 (2022). https://eprint.iacr.org/2022/1181

[BFV20] Bouland, A., Fefferman, B., Vazirani, U.V.: Computational pseudorandomness, the wormhole growth paradox, and constraints on the ADS/CFT duality (abstract). In: Vidick, T. (ed.) 11th Innovations in Theoretical Computer Science Conference, ITCS 2020, 12–14 January 2020, Seattle, Washington, USA, LIPIcs, vol. 151, pp. 63:1–63:2. Schloss Dagstuhl - Leibniz-Zentrum für Informatik (2020)

[GH20] Gheorghiu, A., Hoban, M.J.: Estimating the entropy of shallow circuit outputs is hard (2020)

[GL89] Goldreich, O., Levin, L.A.: A hard-core predicate for all one-way functions. In: Johnson, D.S. (ed.) Proceedings of the 21st Annual ACM Symposium on Theory of Computing, 14–17 May 1989, Seattle, Washington, USA, pp. 25–32. ACM (1989)

[Gol90] Goldreich, O.: A note on computational indistinguishability. Inf. Process. Lett. **34**(6), 277–281 (1990)

[HH13] Harlow, D., Hayden, P.: Quantum computation vs. firewalls. J. High Energy Phys. **2013**, (85) (2013)

[JLS18] Ji, Z., Liu, Y.-K., Song, F.: Pseudorandom quantum states. In: Shacham, H., Boldyreva, A. (eds.) CRYPTO 2018. LNCS, vol. 10993, pp. 126–152. Springer, Cham (2018). https://doi.org/10.1007/978-3-319-96878-0_5

[Kre21] Kretschmer, W.: Quantum pseudorandomness and classical complexity. In: Hsieh, M.-H. (ed.) 16th Conference on the Theory of Quantum Computation, Communication and Cryptography, TQC 2021, 5–8 July 2021, Virtual Conference, LIPIcs, vol. 197, pp. 2:1–2:20. Schloss Dagstuhl - Leibniz-Zentrum für Informatik (2021)

[KTP20] Kim, I., Tang, E., Preskill, J.: The ghost in the radiation: robust encodings of the black hole interior. J. High Energy Phys. **2020**(6), 1–65 (2020). https://doi.org/10.1007/JHEP06(2020)031

[Mal98] Maldacena, J.M.: The large n limit of superconformal field theories and supergravity. Adv. Theor. Math. Phys. **2**, 231 (1998)

[Ost91] Ostrovsky, R.: One-way functions, hard on average problems, and statisti-
         cal zero-knowledge proofs. In: Proceedings of the Sixth Annual Structure
         in Complexity Theory Conference, Chicago, Illinois, USA, 30 June–3 July
         1991, pp. 133–138. IEEE Computer Society (1991)
[Reg05] Regev, O.: On lattices, learning with errors, random linear codes, and cryp-
         tography. In: Gabow, H.N., Fagin, R. (eds.) Proceedings of the 37th Annual
         ACM Symposium on Theory of Computing, Baltimore, MD, USA, 22–24
         May 2005, pp. 84–93. ACM (2005)
[Sus13] Susskind, L.: Black hole complementarity and the Harlow-Hayden conjec-
         ture (2013)
[Yan20] Yan, J.: General properties of quantum bit commitments. Cryptology ePrint
         Archive, Paper 2020/1488 (2020). https://eprint.iacr.org/2020/1488

Cloning Games: A General Framework for Unclonable Primitives

Prabhanjan Ananth[1]($\boxtimes$), Fatih Kaleoglu[1], and Qipeng Liu[2]

[1] University of California, Santa Barbara, CA, USA
prabhanjan@cs.ucsb.edu, kaleoglu@ucsb.edu
[2] Simons Institute for the Theory of Computing, Berkeley, CA, USA

Abstract. The powerful no-cloning principle of quantum mechanics can be leveraged to achieve interesting primitives, referred to as unclonable primitives, that are impossible to achieve classically. In the past few years, we have witnessed a surge of new unclonable primitives. While prior works have mainly focused on establishing feasibility results, another equally important direction, that of understanding the relationship between different unclonable primitives is still in its nascent stages. Moving forward, we need a more systematic study of unclonable primitives.

To this end, we introduce a new framework called *cloning games*. This framework captures many fundamental unclonable primitives such as quantum money, copy-protection, unclonable encryption, single-decryptor encryption, and many more. By reasoning about different types of cloning games, we obtain many interesting implications to unclonable cryptography, including the following:

1. We obtain the first construction of information-theoretically secure single-decryptor encryption in the one-time setting.
2. We construct unclonable encryption in the quantum random oracle model based on BB84 states, improving upon the previous work, which used coset states. Our work also provides a simpler security proof for the previous work.
3. We construct copy-protection for single-bit point functions in the quantum random oracle model based on BB84 states, improving upon the previous work, which used coset states, and additionally, providing a simpler proof.
4. We establish a relationship between different challenge distributions of copy-protection schemes and single-decryptor encryption schemes.
5. Finally, we present a new construction of one-time encryption with certified deletion.

1 Introduction

Unclonable cryptography is a prominent research area that lies at the intersection of quantum computing and cryptography. This research area consists of many

© International Association for Cryptologic Research 2023
H. Handschuh and A. Lysyanskaya (Eds.): CRYPTO 2023, LNCS 14085, pp. 66–98, 2023.
https://doi.org/10.1007/978-3-031-38554-4_3

fascinating primitives that solve cryptographic problems using quantum information that are impossible to solve using only classical technology. At the heart of this area is the no-cloning principle of quantum mechanics [WZ82, Die82], which states that no universal cloner can clone arbitrary quantum states. Since Wiesner put forward quantum money in 1983 [Wie83], a novel unclonable primitive that protects digital money against counterfeiting attacks, there have been a myriad of interesting unclonable primitives proposed over the years. They include variants of quantum money [AC12, Zha19, Shm22], quantum one-time programs [BGS13], copy-protection [Aar09, AL21, ALL+21, CLLZ21], tokenized signatures [BS16, CLLZ21, Shm22], unclonable encryption [Got02, BL20], secure software leasing [AL21, KNY21, BJL+21], encryption with certified deletion [BI20] and certified zero-knowledge [HMNY22].

We discuss three unclonable primitives that are the main focus of this work[1].

Unclonable Encryption. Roughly speaking, an unclonable encryption scheme, introduced by [BL20], is a type of symmetric key encryption scheme that protects ciphertexts, encoded in quantum states, from being illegally distributed. To formalize this, we first consider the following security experiment. The adversary participating in the security experiment is referred to as a cloning adversary, consisting of three algorithms, namely $\mathcal{A}$, $\mathcal{B}$ and $\mathcal{C}$. $\mathcal{A}$ receives a quantum state in the *setup phase*. The quantum state is a ciphertext, which is an encryption of a message m computed using a private key k. Then, $\mathcal{A}$ sends a bipartite state to the spatially separated parties $(\mathcal{B}, \mathcal{C})$ during the *splitting phase*. Finally, $\mathcal{B}$ and $\mathcal{C}$ are asked to simultaneously pass verification in the *challenge phase*. In more detail, in the challenge phase, $\mathcal{B}$ and $\mathcal{C}$ both receive the classical decryption key k and $\mathcal{B}$ outputs $b_{\mathcal{B}}$ while $\mathcal{C}$ outputs $b_{\mathcal{C}}$. We say that $(\mathcal{A}, \mathcal{B}, \mathcal{C})$ wins if $b_{\mathcal{B}} = b_{\mathcal{C}} = m$.

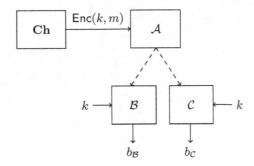

[1] An (impatient) reader familiar with the above primitives could skip directly to Sect. 1.1. We still recommend going through the discussion before reading Sect. 1.1.

With the above security experiment in mind, there are two ways to define security.

- *Unclonability.* In this case, m is sampled uniformly at random from the message space. We say that the scheme is ε-secure if the probability that the adversary $(\mathcal{A}, \mathcal{B}, \mathcal{C})$ wins is ε. Ideally, we would require that ε is negligible in $|m|$.
- *Unclonable-Indistinguishability.* In this case, m is sampled uniformly at random[2] from some adversarially chosen set $\{m_0, m_1\}$. Similar to the above property, we can define ε-security. Ideally, we would require ε to be negligibly close to 0.5.

Public-key unclonable encryption schemes have also been considered by [AK21, AKL+22].

Copy-Protection. Quantum copy-protection, introduced in [Aar09], is a functionality-preserving compiler that transforms programs into quantum states. Moreover, we require that the resulting copy-protected state should not allow the adversary to copy the functionality of the state.

The security experiment against cloning adversaries of the form $(\mathcal{A}, \mathcal{B}, \mathcal{C})$ is formalized as follows[3]. $\mathcal{A}$ receives an unclonable copy-protected program $\rho_f :=$ $\mathsf{CP}(f)$, which can be used to evaluate a classical function f[4]. In the challenge phase, $\mathcal{B}$ and $\mathcal{C}$ receive inputs $x_\mathcal{B}, x_\mathcal{C}$, sampled from a *challenge distribution* and are asked to output $b_\mathcal{B}, b_\mathcal{C}$. $(\mathcal{A}, \mathcal{B}, \mathcal{C})$ wins if $b_\mathcal{B} = f(x_\mathcal{B})$ and $b_\mathcal{C} = f(x_\mathcal{C})$, respectively.

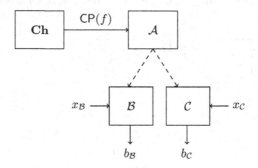

---

[2] We note that the security in the literature is stated slightly differently. $\mathcal{A}$ is given encryption of a message m_b, where b is picked uniformly at random and $\mathcal{B}, \mathcal{C}$ are expected to simultaneously guess b. We note that this formulation is identical to the above formulation.

[3] The original formulation by [Aar09] is weaker than what is stated here. We follow the game-based definition by [CMP20].

[4] We only consider classes of unlearnable functions which are functions that cannot be efficiently learned from its input and output behavior. Copy-protection for learnable functions is impossible.

Ideally, we would like to say that a copy-protection scheme is secure if the probability that $(\mathcal{A}, \mathcal{B}, \mathcal{C})$ wins is negligible in the output lengths. However, such a statement would be false if we are not careful in choosing the distributions from which f is sampled and $x_\mathcal{B}, x_\mathcal{C}$ are sampled. For example, if f is sampled from a distribution with support size one, then the adversary $(\mathcal{A}, \mathcal{B}, \mathcal{C})$ clearly knows the function being copy-protected and can thus easily violate the security. Even if f is sampled from a high-entropy distribution, we should also require $x_\mathcal{B}$ and $x_\mathcal{C}$ to come from high-entropy distributions for the definition to be meaningful. For example, if we set $x_\mathcal{C}$ to be a fixed element, then $(\mathcal{A}, \mathcal{B}, \mathcal{C})$ can always win by $\mathcal{A}$ first computing the value of the function $f(x_\mathcal{C})$ and then handing over the copy-protected state to $\mathcal{B}$ and then handing over $f(x_\mathcal{C})$ to $\mathcal{C}$. Moreover, our definition should be robust in even handling functions with single-bit outputs. This suggests that we must carefully examine the challenge distribution when evaluating results on constructions of copy-protection schemes.

Single-Decryptor Encryption. A single-decryptor encryption, introduced in [GZ20, CLLZ21], enables a user to delegate their decryption key, represented as a quantum state, such that the delegated key cannot be used to illegally distribute two or more decryption keys that can decrypt ciphertexts.

Formally, $\mathcal{A}$ receives an unclonable decryption key ρ_{sk} for an encryption scheme where the encryption procedure and the message space are both classical. In the challenge phase, $\mathcal{B}$ and $\mathcal{C}$ respectively receive ciphertexts $\mathsf{ct}_\mathcal{B}, \mathsf{ct}_\mathcal{C}$ encrypting messages $m_\mathcal{B}, m_\mathcal{C}$. They are then expected to output $b_\mathcal{B}, b_\mathcal{C}$ respectively. $(\mathcal{A}, \mathcal{B}, \mathcal{C})$ wins if $b_\mathcal{B} = m_\mathcal{B}$ and $b_\mathcal{C} = m_\mathcal{C}$.

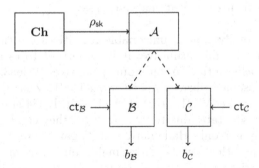

Depending on the specification of the distributions from which the ciphertexts are sampled and how $b_\mathcal{B}, b_\mathcal{C}$ are defined, there are many ways to define security for single-decryptor encryption.

- We could require $\mathsf{ct}_\mathcal{B} = \mathsf{ct}_\mathcal{C}$ (referred to as *identical* ciphertext distribution), in which case $m_\mathcal{B} = m_\mathcal{C}$, or we could require that $\mathsf{ct}_\mathcal{B}$ and $\mathsf{ct}_\mathcal{C}$ be sampled independently (referred to as *independent* ciphertext distribution).
- Analogous to the unclonable encryption setting, we could require that the messages $m_\mathcal{B}, m_\mathcal{C}$ are picked from the uniform distribution, or they are sampled from a set of two messages chosen by $(\mathcal{A}, \mathcal{B}, \mathcal{C})$.

1.1   Complexity of Unclonable Primitives

Most prior works on unclonable encryption, copy-protection, single-decryptor encryption, and other unclonable primitives mainly focus on feasibility. A few exceptions include the works of [CMP20, AK21, SW22], who make partial progress in understanding the relationship between unclonable encryption, copy-protection, and single-decryptor encryption.

In order to achieve a deeper understanding of the area, we need to move beyond the feasibility results and investigate how different primitives are related to each other. There are many reasons why we should care about understanding the relationship between unclonable primitives, and we discuss some of them below.

Computational Assumptions. Firstly, it leads to a better understanding of the computational assumptions necessary in the conception of unclonable primitives. While some primitives require powerful cryptographic tools such as post-quantum indistinguishability obfuscation, some other primitives can even be conceived information-theoretically. It would be interesting to classify the unclonable primitives based on the computational assumptions necessary to construct them. In classical cryptography, via Impagliazzo's five worlds [Imp95] and numerous black-box separations [IR90], we have a solid understanding of the minimal computational assumptions necessary for the existence of primitives. We have just begun to understand the assumptions necessary for achieving cryptographic primitives in the quantum world [AQY22, MY22, BCQ22]. Investigating the implications between the unclonable primitives will help us classify these primitives based on their computational hardness.

Types of States. Secondly, not all unclonable primitives use the same types of states. Given any unclonable primitive, it is important to establish the types of states needed to achieve this notion. Some primitives [Wie83, BI20, BL20] use BB84 states [BB84], some utilize subspace states [AC12, Zha19] and others take advantages of coset states [VZ21, CLLZ21, AKL+22]. BB84 states are preferred over subspace and coset states due to two facts: (a) they can be prepared easily (the preparation requires only Hadamard and X gates), and (b) each qubit is unentangled with the other qubits. Since maintaining entanglement has been challenging in the existing quantum systems, understanding the feasibility of cryptographic systems using unentangled states is important. We currently have a limited understanding of whether BB84 states are sufficient for constructing many primitives. For instance, copy-protection for point functions with single-bit output seems to require coset states [AKL+22] whereas copy-protection for point functions with multi-bit output requires only BB84 states [CMP20].

Challenge Distributions. Unclonable primitives are often associated with challenge distributions. Thus, different feasibility results on the same unclonable primitive assuming different challenge distributions can be qualitatively incomparable. As was seen in the examples of unclonable encryption, copy-protection and single-decryptor encryption, the security of an unclonable primitive can be defined as a game between a challenger and an adversary composed of three parts $(\mathcal{A}, \mathcal{B}, \mathcal{C})$. First, $\mathcal{A}$ receives an unclonable state (a.k.a. a quantum token) from the challenger, and it outputs a bipartite state shared by $\mathcal{B}$ and $\mathcal{C}$. Then, $\mathcal{B}$ and $\mathcal{C}$ receive samples from a distribution, called a *challenge distribution*, and they output answers.

It is often the case that security proven with respect to one challenge distribution does not necessarily imply security proven for a different challenge distribution. For instance, as was discussed earlier in the context of copy-protection, the choice of challenge distribution can qualitatively affect the type of result we get. Discerning the relationship between security notions of different challenge distributions will enable us to compare different results based on the challenge distributions they consider. Indeed, even in the literature, constructions of copy-protection for point functions have considered different challenge distributions [CMP20, BJL+21, AKL+22], which makes their results difficult to compare. Besides point functions, copy-protection was only known under certain distributions (product distributions).

Porting Classical Techniques. It turns out to be challenging to adopt many standard techniques employed to prove the security of cryptographic systems in the classical cryptography literature to the unclonable setting. Let us take an example. Traditionally, encrypting multiple bits can be generically reduced to encrypting single-bit messages in parallel using a simple hybrid argument. The same transformation fails when applied to the setting of unclonable encryption. Even standard search-to-decision reductions, such as Goldreich-Levin [GL89], commonly used in the classical cryptography literature, cannot be directly ported to the unclonable setting. In the context of unclonable encryption, [AKL+22] discuss the challenges associated with using Goldreich-Levin and more in Sect. 1.1 of their work.

1.2 Our Contributions

In order to better understand the relationship between the unclonable primitives, we propose a new framework called *Cloning Games*. Firstly, we observe that many[5] fundamental unclonable primitives can be cast as cloning games. We establish the relationship between large classes of cloning games. There are two directions we undertake to establish the relationship between cloning games.

1. In the first approach, we show that, under some conditions, the relationship between different cloning games can be reduced to the existence of classical reductions between two non-interactive assumptions. This approach gives a new toolkit to help us use classical techniques and computational assumptions to build unclonable primitives. We give an overview of this approach in Sect. 2.2.

---

[5] As far as we know, all unclonable primitives can be cast as cloning games by making reasonable minor modifications to the framework.

2. In the second approach, using new techniques, we refurbish existing constructions of primitives into generic transformations between cloning games. This approach leads to new constructions of primitives with improved features over prior works. An overview of this approach is given in Sect. 2.3.

As a consequence of the above two approaches, we obtain new results in unclonable cryptography.

Single-Decryptor Encryption. Existing constructions of single-decryptor encryption in the public-key setting, are based on post-quantum indistinguishability obfuscation [GZ20, CLLZ21]. It is worth investigating whether we can achieve single-decryptor encryption in the private-key setting based on well-studied assumptions. Indeed, even in the one-time setting, it was not known how to achieve single-decryptor encryption without relying on strong assumptions. By one-time setting, we mean that the adversary only gets one ciphertext computed using the private key. We show the following.

Theorem 1 (Informal). *There exists an information-theoretically secure one-time single-decryptor encryption scheme for single-bit messages.*

The ciphertext distribution we consider in the above result is the following: The challenger chooses the messages $m_B \xleftarrow{\$} \{0,1\}$ and $m_C \xleftarrow{\$} \{0,1\}$. It then encrypts m_B (resp., m_C) and gives the ciphertext to B (resp., C). Then, B and C are supposed to simultaneously guess which bit was encrypted. The security of our construction states that the success probability of any adversary is negligibly close to 0.5.

Although our construction is only for 1-bit messages, we hope the toolkit we develop can be applied to obtain single-decryptor encryption for multi-bit messages in future work.

Unclonable Encryption and Copy-Protection. We revisit recent works that leveraged coset states to achieve unclonable primitives. Specifically, we focus on two constructions of unclonable-indistinguishable encryption and copy-protection for point functions by [AKL+22]. We show that these two constructions can be obtained from *any* encryption scheme satisfying the unclonability property in the quantum random oracle model. Ours is the first work to formally establish the relationship between unclonability and unclonable-indistinguishability properties.

Theorem 2. *Assuming the existence of one-time encryption satisfying unclonability, there exists an encryption scheme satisfying unclonable-indistinguishability in the quantum random oracle model.*

Assuming the existence of one-time encryption satisfying unclonability, there exists a copy-protection scheme for 1-bit output point functions in the quantum random oracle model.

Unclonable encryption can be constructed from BB84 states [BL20], and hence, as a consequence, we can obtain unclonable-indistinguishable encryption and copy-protection for point functions leveraging just BB84 states.

Corollary 1 (Informal). *There exists a (one-time) encryption scheme satisfying unclonable indistinguishability property, based on BB84 states, in the quantum random oracle model.*

There exists copy-protection for 1-bit output point functions, based on BB84 states, in the quantum random oracle model.

In fact, [AK21] showed that encryption satisfying unclonability can be obtained from a variety of monogamy of entanglement games [TFKW13]. Consequently, we obtain both unclonable-indistinguishable encryption and copy-protection schemes based on a variety of quantum states, not just BB84 states.

Moreover, by plugging in the generic transformation from [AK21], we achieve public-key unclonable encryption based on BB84 states.

Relationship between Challenge Distributions. In both copy-protection and single-decryptor encryption, the choice of challenge distribution plays a role in determining the usefulness of constructions. This makes comparing results difficult. For instance, a priori, it is unclear how to compare two different works constructing copy-protection for the same class of functions but with different challenge distributions. Similarly, even for single-decryptor encryption, schemes with different ciphertext distributions might be incomparable.

We make progress in understanding the relationship between different challenge distributions. Although our result is more general, for the current discussion, let us focus on two types of distributions:

- *Identical*: Both $\mathcal{B}$ and $\mathcal{C}$ get the same challenge (challenge refers to input in the case of copy-protection and ciphertext in the case of single-decryptor encryption), drawn from some distribution.
- *Independent*: $\mathcal{B}$ and $\mathcal{C}$ each get two challenges chosen independently from some distribution.

Although being quite similar, the relationship between security under identical-challenge cloning experiments and independent-challenge cloning experiments was not known, as all the security proofs of general copy-protection schemes [ALL+21, CLLZ21] were established with respect to independent-challenge distributions[6], and their security with respect to identical-challenge distributions was not analyzed. Indeed, it turns out that the proof techniques in [ALL+21, CLLZ21] were tailored to the independent challenge setting and they did not generalize to the identical challenge setting.

We address this issue by showing the following.

Theorem 3 (Informal). *A copy-protection scheme secure for a class of multi-bit output functions in the independent challenge distribution setting is also secure in the identical challenge distribution setting.*

---

[6] With the exception of copy-protection of point functions [CMP20, AKL+22].

A single-decryptor encryption scheme in the independent challenge distribution setting is also secure in the identical challenge distribution setting.

For the result on copy-protection, we remark that besides the fact that the output length of the functions is large (more precisely, depends on the security parameter), our result is general and applies to any class of functions. For the result of single-decryptor encryption, we consider the definition where the adversary is given the encryption of a message chosen from the uniform distribution and is supposed to predict the entire message.

In fact, in the technical sections, we prove a stronger theorem that generalizes for arbitrary correlated distributions instead of just identical distributions! More precisely, suppose $\mathcal{D}_\mathcal{B}$ (resp., $\mathcal{D}_\mathcal{C}$) is the challenge distribution for $\mathcal{B}$ (resp., $\mathcal{C}$). Let $\mathcal{D}$ be the challenge distribution on $\mathcal{B}$'s and $\mathcal{C}$'s challenge spaces, as long as the marginal distribution on $\mathcal{B}$ (or $\mathcal{C}$ respectively) of $\mathcal{D}$ corresponds to $\mathcal{D}_\mathcal{B}$ (or $\mathcal{D}_\mathcal{C}$, respectively). We show that a secure copy-protection scheme when the challenge distribution is $\mathcal{D}_\mathcal{B} \times \mathcal{D}_\mathcal{C}$, is also secure when the challenge distribution is $\mathcal{D}$. Similar conclusions also hold for single-decryptor encryption schemes.

Encryption with Certified Deletion. Another well-studied unclonable primitive is encryption with certified deletion [BI20]. Certified deletion can be thought of as a weaker form of unclonability, where the adversary is asked to provide a classical certificate of deletion before learning the secret key.[7] While it is unknown whether unclonable encryption is information theoretically possible, encryption with certified deletion is known to be information theoretically possible [BI20, BK22]. We give an alternate construction and proof of security of this construction that is based on the techniques used for bounding monogamy-of-entanglement games [TFKW13]. Our techniques are conceptually different from the existing works [BI20, BK22] who used entropic arguments to argue the same. En route, we formally define the notion of *deletion games*, a subclass[8] of cloning games.

2 Technical Overview

We first discuss our definition of cloning games, why it captures many existing unclonable primitives, and then present techniques to relate different cloning games.

2.1 Definitional Contribution: Cloning Games

A cloning game consists of the following four procedures (Setup, GenT, GenC, Ver):

---

[7] In contrast, unclonability allows $\mathcal{B}$ and $\mathcal{C}$ to both learn the secret key before passing verification. Note that we use the word "weaker" qualitatively in this sentence, and do *not* claim that unclonability implies the existence of certified deletion in general.

[8] Although this is not true for the initial definition we use to introduce cloning games, deletion games are captured after considering a natural extension of cloning games, where $\mathcal{B}$ and $\mathcal{C}$ are not treated symmetrically.

- A setup procedure Setup, on input a security parameter, outputs a secret key sk.
- A token generation procedure GenT that takes as input the secret key sk, a message and outputs a quantum state ρ. As we will see later, ρ is expected to have some unclonability properties.
- A challenge generation procedure GenC, which takes sk, m together with random coins r, and outputs a challenge ch.
- Finally, a verification procedure Ver, that takes sk, m, ch together with an alleged answer (which can be either a classical string or a quantum state) and outputs either 0 (reject) or 1 (accept).

  We also consider another (stateful) variant where Ver gets as input r, which are the random coins used in GenC.

We require that a cloning game satisfies two properties: correctness and security. First, we discuss correctness.

Correctness. The correctness property says that there always exists an (efficient) quantum algorithm $\mathcal{A}_{\mathcal{G}}$ if all the procedures are executed honestly and in the order of (Setup, GenT, GenC, $\mathcal{A}_{\mathcal{G}}$), the verification procedure should almost always output 1 (accept). That is, $\mathcal{A}_{\mathcal{G}}$ takes as input the state produced by GenT and the challenge produced by GenC and outputs an answer ans that is accepted by Ver with probability negligibly close to 1.

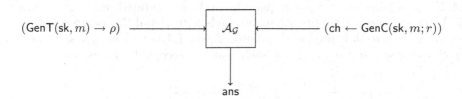

Instantiations. Before we discuss security, we demonstrate the power of cloning games by showing a couple of examples. Below, we show that both unclonable encryption and copy-protection can be cast as cloning games.

Unclonable Encryption. We cast unclonable encryption as a cloning game (Setup, GenT, GenC, Ver) below.

- Setup in the cloning game corresponds to the key generation of the unclonable encryption scheme. That is, Setup produces the secret key, denoted by sk, of the encryption scheme,
- GenT corresponds to the encryption algorithm,
- GenC produces the challenge ch = sk,

- Ver takes as input (sk, m, ch, ans) and outputs 1 if and only if ans $= m$.
- $\mathcal{A_G}$ corresponds to the decryption algorithm. On input the ciphertext state produced by GenT and the secret key, i.e., ch, it outputs the message m.

Copy-Protection. We can similarly cast copy-protection using cloning games, as shown below. We do not need to define Setup for copy-protection of classical programs and thus sk $= \perp$.

- GenT takes $sk = \perp$, message $m = f$, where f is the program to be copy-protection and outputs a quantum state ρ. That is, GenT corresponds to the copy-protection algorithm,
- GenC takes as input $sk = \perp$, $m = f$ and samples a challenge ch $:= x$ according to the distribution.
- Ver corresponds to the evaluation algorithm of the copy-protection scheme. That is, it takes input ch $:= x$ and f, and tests whether $f(x) = $ ans.
- $\mathcal{A_G}$ corresponds to the evaluation algorithm. On input the copy-protected state of f and the challenge input x, it outputs $f(x)$.

Similarly, single decryptor encryption, tokenized signatures, primitives with certified deletion, and many others can be cast as cloning games. We refer the reader to the main body for more details.

Security. In the security experiment, we consider cloning adversaries of the form $(\mathcal{A}, \mathcal{B}, \mathcal{C})$. $\mathcal{A}$ receives as input a quantum state ρ generated using GenT(sk, m). $\mathcal{A}$ then computes a bipartite state and sends it to $\mathcal{B}$ and $\mathcal{C}$. Both $\mathcal{B}$ and $\mathcal{C}$ then receive ch, where ch is produced by GenC(sk, m). $(\mathcal{A}, \mathcal{B}, \mathcal{C})$ wins if ans$_\mathcal{B}$ produced by $\mathcal{B}$ and ans$_\mathcal{C}$ produced by $\mathcal{C}$ are such that Ver accepts both ans$_\mathcal{B}$ and ans$_\mathcal{C}$.

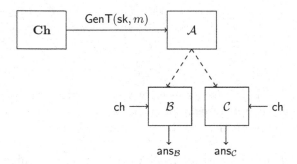

To define the security, we first define the *trivial success probability* of the adversaries in the cloning game. We say that the cloning game is secure as long as any cloning adversary cannot succeed with probability significantly larger than the trivial success probability. The trivial success probability is calculated as follows: $\mathcal{A}$ gives the quantum token to $\mathcal{B}$, and then $\mathcal{B}$ computes the correct answer ans_B. On the other hand, C outputs its best guess ans_C. The probability that (A, B, C) wins is precisely the trivial success probability.

The trivial success probability in an encryption scheme satisfying unclonability[9] is $\frac{1}{|M|}$, where M is the message space, and the trivial success probability in a scheme satisfying unclonable-indistinguishability is $\frac{1}{2}$.

Computational Complexity of the Attackers. We did not remark on the computational complexity of (A, B, C). In this work, we mainly work with attackers where A, B, and C are all computationally unbounded adversaries. Nevertheless, we can consider more general settings, where all of them run in quantum polynomial time.

Message Distributions. In the security experiment, m is sampled from some distribution D. There are two main types of distributions we consider in this work: (1) D is uniform and, (2) D_{m_0,m_1} is a distribution parameterized by two messages m_0, m_1 and it outputs m_0 or m_1 with equal probability $1/2$. When considering D_{m_0,m_1}, we allow the adversary to choose the messages m_0, m_1.

Search and Decision Games. We consider a specific type of cloning games, called *search* games, where the verification algorithm Ver is defined as follows: on input $(\mathsf{sk}, m, \mathsf{ch}, \mathsf{ans})$, it outputs 1 (or Valid) if and only if $\mathsf{ans} = m$. We can consider two different security notions of search games.

- *Unclonable-Search* security: the message distribution D is uniform and,
- *Unclonable-Indistinguishability* security: the message distribution is D_{m_0,m_1}, where (m_0, m_1) is the pair of messages chosen by the cloning adversary.

In the context of unclonable encryption, the above two notions correspond to unclonability and unclonable-indistinguishability properties.

We also define *decision* games, where $\mathsf{ans}_B, \mathsf{ans}_C \in \{0, 1\}$.

Extensions and Stateful games. For some applications, we need to generalize the algorithms of the cloning games further. Firstly, we can generalize the challenge generation phase to the asymmetric setting, where both B and C do not necessarily receive the same challenge. This is formalized by defining an extended algorithm $\widetilde{\mathsf{GenC}}$ which samples two random strings r_B and r_C such that B (resp., C) receives a challenge generated using r_B (resp., r_C). Furthermore, we generalize the verification algorithm Ver to also take as input the randomness used in the challenge generation algorithm. This way, the pair of algorithms (GenC, Ver) acts as a *stateful* verifier, hence the term stateful games.

---

[9] Please refer to the definition of unclonability of an unclonable encryption scheme in the introduction.

Challenge Distributions. Finally, we need to remark on how the randomness for the challenge generation is generated. There are two popular options:

- *Identical challenge distribution*: in this case, $\widetilde{\mathsf{GenC}}$ generates $r_B = r_C$.
- *Independent challenge distribution*: in this case, $\widetilde{\mathsf{GenC}}$ generates r_B, r_C such that r_B and r_C are chosen independently.

We also consider more general challenge distributions where r_B and r_C are arbitrarily correlated.

2.2   Part I: Implications via Classical Reductions

In the classical cryptography literature, there is an abundance of techniques developed to show the relationship between different primitives. Ideally, we would like to draw inspiration from these techniques and/or rehash them to develop new relationships between unclonable primitives.

We develop a new framework to relate cloning games using classical reductions. This new framework presents a new approach of using classical techniques to build unclonable primitives.

Specifically, we show that the implication of a cloning game $\mathcal{G} = (\mathsf{Setup}, \mathsf{GenT}, \mathsf{GenC}, \mathsf{Ver})$ to another cloning game $\mathcal{G}' = (\mathsf{Setup}', \mathsf{GenT}', \mathsf{GenC}', \mathsf{Ver}')$ can be based on a classical reduction that transforms a probabilistic polynomial-time solver for one assumption into a solver for a different assumption, where the assumptions are closely related to the games $\mathcal{G}, \mathcal{G}'$.

For the implication to hold, we require some extra (and mild) conditions. In the simplest case, $\mathsf{Setup} = \mathsf{Setup}'$ and $\mathsf{GenT}' = \mathsf{GenT}$. More generally, we require that the distribution of the states generated by GenT is close (in trace distance) to the distribution of the states generated by GenT'. Additionally, we require that in both games, the trivial success probability is negligible[10].

Implications. As a result of the above implication, we obtain two interesting sets of results.

Firstly, we can show that many unclonable primitives (for instance, copy-protection and single-decryptor encryption schemes) secure with respect to independent challenge distribution are also secure with respect to an arbitrary challenge distribution, as long as the marginals of the latter distribution correspond to the independent challenge distribution. This follows from the fact that changing the challenge distribution corresponds to only modifying the algorithms GenC and Ver.

Secondly, we show that any unclonable encryption scheme generically implies the existence of single-decryptor encryption. The transformation leverages the classic Goldreich-Levin technique [GL89]. The setup and token generation of single-decryptor encryption are the same as the setup and token generation of unclonable encryption. In particular, to generate the unclonable decryption key

---

[10] Our theorem is more general than what is stated here; refer to the full version for more details.

in a single-decryptor scheme, we sample a long random message x and encrypt x to get $|ct_x\rangle$, using the unclonable encryption scheme. To encrypt a message m in the single-decryptor scheme, we first sample random coins r (of the same length as m) and let the ciphertext be $(r, \langle r, x \rangle \oplus m)$ together with the key to recover x from the encryption $|ct_x\rangle$. Since the setup and the token generation algorithms remain the same, and only GenC and Ver need to be modified, we obtain this implication.

From Classical Reductions to Reductions Between Cloning Games. We establish the relationship between cloning games using classical reductions in the following steps:

- In the first step, we define a new notion of classical reductions called classical *non-local* reductions. We then show that many natural classical (local) reductions can be upgraded to classical non-local reductions.
- In the second step, we show how to generically lift classical non-local reductions into reductions between cloning games. Specifically, we obtain a reduction between two games $\mathcal{G}$ and $\mathcal{G}'$ such that a cloning adversary for $\mathcal{G}$ can be converted into a cloning adversary for $\mathcal{G}'$. The transformation only works in the setting when the challenge distribution associated with $\mathcal{G}$ corresponds to an independent challenge distribution.
- In the third and final step, we show that, for any cloning game $\mathcal{G}$, a cloning adversary succeeding in violating the security of $\mathcal{G}$ with respect to an arbitrary challenge distribution $\mathcal{D}$ can also succeed in violating the security of $\mathcal{G}$ with respect to independent challenge distribution, corresponding to the marginals of $\mathcal{D}$.

Using the third step, we can now get an improved result in Step 2. Specifically, the reduction between $\mathcal{G}$ and $\mathcal{G}'$ holds even if the challenge distribution associated with $\mathcal{G}$ corresponds to an arbitrary challenge distribution, as long as the marginal distributions for $\mathcal{B}$ and $\mathcal{C}$ remain the same.

We remark that in the third step, we only consider cloning games with trivial success probability to be negligible. Thus, the resulting reductions between cloning games only hold for this setting. Alternately, if we start with a cloning game $\mathcal{G}$ with respect to the independent challenge distribution then we can still apply the first and second step to obtain a reduction between $\mathcal{G}$ and $\mathcal{G}'$ even if the trivial success probability is not negligible.

Step I: From Classical (Local) Reductions to Classical Non-Local Reductions. A reduction transforms a solver for a non-interactive assumption P into a solver for another non-interactive assumption Q. Henceforth, we refer to reductions commonly studied in the literature, as *local* reductions.

In this work, we consider a notion of reductions called *non-local reductions*. First, we need to define non-local solvers. Suppose $\mathfrak{A}$ is a non-interactive assumption (for example, learning with errors). Then, a non-local solver for $\mathfrak{A}$ consists of two algorithms $(\mathcal{B}, \mathcal{C})$ such that each of $\mathcal{B}$ and $\mathcal{C}$ receives samples/challenges

$ch_{\mathcal{B}}, ch_{\mathcal{C}}$ from $\mathfrak{A}$ and is supposed to solve the samples they receive. Throughout the process, $\mathcal{B}$ and $\mathcal{C}$ cannot speak to each other, although they could have exchanged some common information, denoted by ρ, before receiving $ch_{\mathcal{B}}, ch_{\mathcal{C}}$. The samples $ch_{\mathcal{B}}, ch_{\mathcal{C}}$ can be arbitrarily correlated. We denote the distribution that samples $(ch_{\mathcal{B}}, ch_{\mathcal{C}})$ to be $\mathcal{D}_{\mathfrak{A}}$.

A *non-local* reduction is a transformation that converts a *non-local* $\mathcal{D}_P$-solver $(\mathcal{B}_P, \mathcal{C}_P)$ for assumption P into a *non-local* $\mathcal{D}_Q$-solver $(\mathcal{B}_Q, \mathcal{C}_Q)$ for assumption Q, for some challenge distributions $\mathcal{D}_P$ and $\mathcal{D}_Q$. It turns out that we can lift local reductions into non-local reductions in the classical setting (i.e., when the solvers are classical algorithms) as long as the distribution $\mathcal{D}_Q$ is an independent challenge distribution and the trivial success probability of Q is small (for example, negligible)[11].

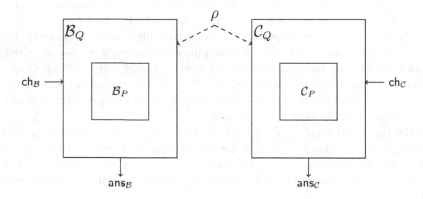

Step II: Lifting Classical Non-Local Reductions to Reductions Between Cloning Games. To lift classical non-local reductions to reductions between cloning games, we take inspiration from a recent work by [BBK22] (henceforth, referred to as BBK), who showed a lifting theorem that lifts classical reductions into post-quantum reductions. Suppose we would like to convert a solver for assumption P into a solver for assumption Q. The difficulty in porting classical reductions into post-quantum reductions stems from the fact that the Q-solver could run the P-solver multiple times. Since the state of the P-solver could drastically change from one execution to the other (due to the difficulty of rewinding), potentially, there could no longer be any guarantees from the P-solver after the first execution.

To solve this issue, BBK prove a novel lifting theorem in three steps.

– Persistence theorem: in the first step, they show how to transform a P-solver into another one, where the success probability of the P-solver does not decrease a lot even after executing it multiple times. In other words, the

---

[11] One example of trivial success probability being large is non-local decision games, where $\mathcal{B}$ and $\mathcal{C}$ try to produce binary answers simultaneously.

P-solver does not lose the ability to solve instances of P even after multiple executions. In more detail, suppose the P-solver, on input ρ, solved an instance of P with probability p. Then we can convert the P-solver into another one, whose success probability is at least $p - \epsilon$, for some small $\epsilon > 0$, even after multiple executions.

Ideally, we would like the P-solver to be stateless, i.e., it does not know whether it has ever been executed in the past, in order for us to successfully reduce to the problem of solving Q.

- From persistence to memoryless: In the next step, they convert a persistent solver into another one that is indistinguishable from a P-solver that is memoryless. A solver is memoryless if the only thing it can remember is the number of times it has been executed so far.
- From memoryless to stateless: In the final step, they convert the solver from the second step into another solver that is indistinguishable from a stateless solver. Roughly speaking, a stateless solver is one that does not remember any information from one execution to the next.

Our strategy to lift non-local reductions into reductions between cloning games is to use the BBK approach. Similar to their work, we can define the notion of persistent, memoryless, and stateless non-local solvers. Due to some nice structural properties of their transformation, it turns out that the persistent to stateless transformation (the second and third steps above) extends directly to the non-local setting.

Showing the non-local version of their persistence theorem (first bullet above) requires more work. To see why, let us first recall the BBK approach to prove the persistence theorem. They use two procedures, namely value estimation (ValEst) and repair (Repair) procedures, first defined by [CMSZ02].

- ValEst has the guarantee that given an input state ρ and a verification algorithm Ver, it outputs a number (probability) p such that $\mathbb{E}[p] = p_{\mathsf{acc}}$ and p_{acc} is the probability that Ver accepts ρ. If the output of ValEst is p, let the leftover state be ρ_p.
- Suppose we have computed the P-solver on ρ_p. The residual state ρ'_p could be far from ρ_p and more importantly, might not provide any guarantees. We would like to restore the success probability on the residual state ρ'_p obtained after running the P-solver. The procedure Repair does just that. It takes as input potentially disturbed state ρ'_p and outputs another state ρ^* such that the success probability on ρ^* is close to the success probability on the original state ρ.

The persistence theorem is proven as follows: each time before computing the P-solver, first run ValEst procedure, and then after the execution of the P-solver run the Repair procedure. Roughly speaking, by the guarantees of ValEst and Repair, we have that the underlying P-solver does not lose its ability to solve the assumption P even after executing it multiple times.

Non-local Persistence Theorem. Before we describe the non-local persistence theorem, we first set up some terminology. We start with a non-local *classical* non-local reduction which reduces a P-non-local solver to a Q-non-local solver. A P-solver consists of $(\mathcal{B}_P, \mathcal{C}_P)$ and is associated with the challenge distribution $\mathcal{D}_P$. On the other hand, a Q-solver consists of $(\mathcal{B}_Q, \mathcal{C}_Q)$ and is associated with challenge distribution $\mathcal{D}_Q$. We want to upgrade this *classical* non-local reduction to the setting when both the P-solver and Q-solver can be quantum. For simplicity, we consider the case when both $\mathcal{D}_P$ and $\mathcal{D}_Q$ are both product distributions.

We now consider a non-local version of the persistence theorem. Informally speaking, we require that the P-non-local solver continues to be a good solver for P even after multiple executions. A natural approach to prove this theorem would be to extend the BBK approach to the non-local setting:

- Before computing the P-non-local solver on its state, first run ValEst procedure.
- After computing on the state, run the Repair procedure.

Unfortunately, we do not know how to execute the above steps. The reason is that the Q-solver itself is non-local and hence, cannot perform any global operations on the state. However, what it can do is to alternately apply value estimation and repair procedures locally. That is, $\mathcal{B}_Q$ (resp., $\mathcal{C}_Q$) applies the value estimation and repair procedures on $\mathcal{B}_P$ (resp., $\mathcal{C}_P$). While this sounds promising, this leads to a new issue: we need the guarantee that the P-solver $(\mathcal{B}_P, \mathcal{C}_P)$ is *simultaneously* persistent. Even if we locally apply the procedures above on $(\mathcal{B}_P, \mathcal{C}_P)$ such that both $\mathcal{B}_P$ and $\mathcal{C}_P$ are persistent, this does not mean that they are simultaneously persistent! It could very well be the case when $\mathcal{B}_P$ succeeds, then $\mathcal{C}_P$ does not (or vice versa), but still both of them are persistent.

To address this issue, let us first consider a simple case when the state shared by $\mathcal{B}_P$ and $\mathcal{C}_P$ are unentangled. In this special case, there is a clear relationship between the local and global value estimation and repair procedures. In particular, the following holds:

- Suppose applying (ValEst $\otimes$ ValEst) on the shared state of $(\mathcal{B}_P, \mathcal{C}_P)$ yields $(p_{\mathcal{B}}, p_{\mathcal{C}})$ then it holds that $\mathbb{E}[p_{\mathcal{B}} \cdot p_{\mathcal{C}}]$ equals the output of the (global) ValEst on the initial state of $(\mathcal{B}_P, \mathcal{C}_P)$.

Using this, we can relate global persistence to local persistence.

To generalize this to the case when the initial states of $(\mathcal{B}_P, \mathcal{C}_P)$ could be entangled, we look at the specific implementation details of the estimation procedure ValEst by [CMSZ02]. The value estimation procedure ValEst is a sequence of alternating projections, denoted by Π_1, Π_2, followed by a computational basis measurement determining the success probability p.

Suppose the initial state of $(\mathcal{B}_P, \mathcal{C}_P)$ is in the Hilbert space $\mathcal{H} = \mathcal{H}_{\mathcal{B}} \otimes \mathcal{H}_{\mathcal{C}}$. We decompose both $\mathcal{H}_{\mathcal{B}}$ and $\mathcal{H}_{\mathcal{C}}$ into subspaces that are invariant under the projections Π_1, Π_2 using Jordan's lemma [Jor75]. Therefore, we can rewrite the initial state of $(\mathcal{B}_P, \mathcal{C}_P)$ to be in the span of $\{|\psi_i^{\mathcal{B}}\rangle|\psi_j^{\mathcal{C}}\rangle\}$, where $\{|\psi_i^{\mathcal{B}}\rangle\}$ (resp., $\{|\psi_j^{\mathcal{C}}\rangle\}$) is in the corresponding Jordan subspaces of $\mathcal{H}_{\mathcal{B}}$ (resp., $\mathcal{H}_{\mathcal{C}}$).

Using an observation made by [CMSZ02], we can think of ValEst as first performing a Jordan subspace measurement (that projects the state onto one of the Jordan subspaces) followed by performing a sequence of alternating measurements Π_1, Π_2. In other words, we can think of applying value estimation locally, i.e., (ValEst $\otimes$ ValEst), as first performing the Jordan subspace measurement to obtain a joint state $|\psi_i^{\mathcal{B}}\rangle|\psi_j^{\mathcal{C}}\rangle$, for some i, j, followed by alternating measurements. Notice that once we apply the Jordan subspace measurement, the states become unentangled! Thus, we reduce to the above simple case, and the rest of the analysis follows.

Step III: Relating Challenge Distributions: From Independent to Identical. In Step II, in order to be able to run the value estimation and the repair procedures locally, it was crucial that the underlying P-solver was defined for an *independent* challenge distribution. It would be interesting to generalize to the case when the underlying challenge distribution is arbitrary. For this overview, we focus on the case when the challenge distribution is identical, although the proof generalizes to arbitrary challenge distributions as well. Specifically, we demonstrate a reduction from a cloning game $\mathcal{G}$ satisfying unclonable security with respect to independent challenges to $\mathcal{G}$ satisfying unclonable security with respect to identical challenges. For the reduction to work, we crucially use the fact that the trivial success probability in both the games is negligible. An interesting point to note here is that the reduction does not change the description of the game.

We give an overview of our reduction. Let $|\sigma\rangle_{\mathbf{BC}}$ be the (entangled) quantum state shared by Bob and Charlie (the two non-local quantum adversaries) after Alice's (the splitting adversary) stage. We additionally define projections Π_r^B and Π_r^C for every possible random coins r:

Π_r^B: Run Bob on its own register $\sigma[\mathbf{B}]$ with the challenge corresponding to random coins r, project onto Bob's output being accepted and uncompute;

Π_r^C: Run Charlie on its own register $\sigma[\mathbf{C}]$ with the challenge corresponding to random coins r, project onto Charlie's output being accepted and uncompute;

By definition, the success probability in the independent challenge case is:

$$\delta = \mathsf{Tr}\left[\left(\frac{1}{|R|} \sum_r \Pi_r^B \right) \otimes \left(\frac{1}{|R|} \sum_r \Pi_r^C \right) |\sigma\rangle\langle\sigma| \right], \tag{1}$$

where R is the random coin space.

Since $\Pi^B := \frac{1}{|R|} \sum_r \Pi_r^B$ is a POVM, let $\{|\phi_p\rangle\}_{p \in \mathbb{R}}$ be the set of eigenvectors with eigenvalues $p \in [0,1]$[12]. Similarly, let $\{|\psi_q\rangle\}_{q \in \mathbb{R}}$ be the set of eigenvectors with eigenvalues $q \in [0,1]$ for $\Pi^C := \frac{1}{|R|} \sum_r \Pi_r^C$. Therefore, we can always write

---

[12] There can be multiple eigenvectors with the same eigenvalues. In the overview, we assume that eigenvalues are unique.

$|\sigma\rangle_{BC}$ under the bases $\{|\phi_p\rangle\}$ and $\{|\psi_q\rangle\}$[13]:

$$|\sigma\rangle = \sum_{p,q} \alpha_{p,q} |\phi_p\rangle |\psi_q\rangle.$$

From the above decomposition of $|\sigma\rangle$ and Eq. 1, we have $\delta = \sum_{p,q} |\alpha_{p,q}|^2 pq$.

Let $\eta \in [0,1]$ be a threshold we will pick later. The quantum state can be written as the summation of three terms:

$$|\sigma\rangle = \sum_{q<\eta} \alpha_{p,q} |\phi_p\rangle |\psi_q\rangle + \sum_{p<\eta,q>\eta} \alpha_{p,q} |\phi_p\rangle |\psi_q\rangle + \sum_{p>\eta,q>\eta} \alpha_{p,q} |\phi_p\rangle |\psi_q\rangle.$$

We denote the first term by $|\sigma_C\rangle$, indicating that Charlie's success probability is bounded by η; the second term by $|\sigma_B\rangle$, indicating that Bob's success probability is bounded by η; and the last term by $|\rho\rangle$, none of the probabilities is below η. Thus, $|\sigma\rangle = |\sigma_C\rangle + |\sigma_B\rangle + |\rho\rangle$.

First, we note that the success probability when executed on the state $|\sigma_C\rangle + |\sigma_B\rangle$ is at most η under both independent challenges and identical challenges. However, $\frac{|\rho\rangle}{\||\rho\rangle\|^2}$ could be such that the success probability when executed on this state maybe large (even as large as 1). In the next step, we show that although ρ may have a large probability under identical challenges, $\||\rho\rangle\|^2$ is relatively small. Because $\delta := \sum_{p,q} |\alpha_{p,q}|^2 pq$, we have:

$$\||\rho\rangle\|^2 = \sum_{p>\eta,q>\eta} |\alpha_{p,q}|^2 \implies \||\rho\rangle\|^2 \leq \delta/\eta^2.$$

Therefore, the success probability of $|\sigma\rangle$ under identical challenges is:

$$\delta = \frac{1}{|R|} \sum_r \left\| \Pi_r^B \otimes \Pi_r^C |\sigma\rangle \right\|^2$$

$$\leq \frac{3}{|R|} \sum_r \left(\left\| \Pi_r^B \otimes \Pi_r^C |\sigma_C\rangle \right\|^2 + \left\| \Pi_r^B \otimes \Pi_r^C |\sigma_B\rangle \right\|^2 + \|\rho\|^2 \right)$$

$$\leq 3 \left(\eta + \delta/\eta^2 \right).$$

By picking $\eta = \delta^{1/3}$, the resulting probability is $6 \cdot \delta^{1/3}$. Specifically, if δ is negligible then so is the resulting quantity.

2.3   Part II: Generalizing Existing Results

Unclonable Search to Unclonable Indistinguishability. Our first focus is a cloning game with unclonable search security (a concrete example is unclonable encryption with standard unclonable security) whose distribution $\mathcal{D}$ is uniform over all possible messages. We show a generic reduction that turns such

---

[13] There is a one-to-one mapping between $\{|\phi_p\rangle\}, \{|\psi_q\rangle\}$ and the vectors $\{|\psi_i^B\rangle\}, \{|\psi_j^C\rangle\}$ defined in the Jordan's lemma.

a game into another cloning game with unclonable indistinguishability security whose underlying distribution is $\mathcal{D}_{m_0,m_1}$ for any m_0, m_1 in the message space, in the quantum random oracle model (QROM, introduced by [BDF+11]). Since unclonable encryption with standard unclonable security exists [BL20], this gives a direct corollary for unclonable encryption with unclonable indistinguishability security in the QROM, from BB84/Wiesner states, improving the previous result by [AKL+22].

Unclonable Security for High-Entropy Message Distributions. As a first step in the reduction, we make the following observation. Suppose we start with a cloning game satisfying unclonable security. If the message is sampled from a high min-entropy distribution instead of being sampled uniformly at random, unclonable security still holds. In particular, we prove that when m is sampled from a source with min-entropy h instead of from a uniform source, its unclonable search security will be $2^h \cdot \delta$; where δ is the unclonable search security under the uniform message distribution. For instance, if m is sampled uniformly at random from a set S then by appropriately choosing $|S|$ (for example, it is exponential sized), we can prove that $2^h \delta$ is still negligible and thus establish its augmented unclonable security.

As a concrete example, we obtain the following corollary: the unclonable encryption with standard unclonable security in [BL20] also satisfies this augmented unclonable security. In other words, even if P_m is provided as oracle, it will not help Bob and Charlie to simultaneously recover m.

Augmented Security. Next, we first define stronger unclonable search security, which we call *augmented unclonable security*. The cloning game is defined in the same way, except now all attackers have oracle access to a point function $P_m(\cdot)$, which outputs 1 if and only if the input equals to m, where m is the message used to generate the token given to the adversary. We claim that the definition of unclonable search security can be generically upgraded to obtain augmented security.

Our first observation is that, we can enlarge the set of all accepting inputs of $P_m(\cdot)$ (originally only m) to a large random set S consisting of m, with its security staying roughly the same. More concretely, S will be defined as an exponentially large (but negligibly small compared to the number of all possible messages) set consisting of a single m, and the rest are random messages. As P_m and P_S only differ on exponentially many but sparse random inputs, query-bounded adversaries can not distinguish which oracle is given.

Next, the augmented unclonable security is then argued under a random message m and oracle access to P_S. In this case, we can instead think of an alternate but equivalent process of sampling m: first sample an exponentially large random set S then sample a message m is uniformly at random from S. After changing the sampling order, we can argue that even if the adversary is given the description of the set S, unclonable security still holds. This holds from our earlier observation that unclonable security holds even if the message is sampled from a high min-entropy distribution.

From Augmented Security to Unclonable-Indistinguishability Security. Finally, we show that starting from a cloning game satisfying augmented unclonability property $\mathcal{G}$, we can obtain a game $\mathcal{G}'$ satisfying unclonable indistinguishability property. The token generation of $\mathcal{G}'$ on input a message m, first samples a long random message x, runs the token generation of $\mathcal{G}$ on x and then outputs this token along with $H(x) \oplus m$, where H is a hash function. In the proof of security, H is treated as a random hash function that the adversary has oracle access to.

To prove unclonable indistinguishability, we look at the state $|\psi\rangle_{BC}$ output by Alice, where Alice has oracle access to H punctured at the input x. For the sake of the proof, we treat the hash function both Bob and Charlie have access to, separately. We use H_B to denote the hash function Bob has access to and H_C to denote the hash function Charlie has access to. Correspondingly, we can define the POVM Π^B that runs $\mathcal{B}$ with oracle access to H_B that is programmed on x to output 0 or 1 with equal probability, projects onto the output being correct and then uncomputes. Similarly, we define Π^C as well. In order to make sure we can implement Π^B and Π^C efficiently, we give the adversary oracle access to $P_x(\cdot)$.

Let $\{|\phi_p\rangle\}_{p \in \mathbb{R}}$ be the set of eigenvectors with respect to Π^B with eigenvalues $p \in [0, 1]$. Similarly, let $\{|\psi_q\rangle\}_{q \in \mathbb{R}}$ be the set of eigenvectors with eigenvalues $q \in [0, 1]$ with respect to Π^C. We can then rewrite $|\psi\rangle_{BC}$ in terms of the eigenbases of Π^B and Π^C.

$$|\psi\rangle = \sum_{q \approx 0.5} \alpha_{p,q} |\phi_p\rangle|\psi_q\rangle + \sum_{\substack{p \approx 0.5 \\ |q-0.5| \gg 0}} \alpha_{p,q} |\phi_p\rangle|\psi_q\rangle + \sum_{\substack{|p-0.5| \gg 0 \\ |q-0.5| \gg 0}} \alpha_{p,q} |\phi_p\rangle|\psi_q\rangle.$$

Once we do this, we show the following:

- $\sum_{p,q} |\alpha_{p,q}|^2$ is negligible. We show this by reducing to the unclonability property.
- Once we show bullet 1, we can then show that Bob and Charlie cannot simultaneously succeed with probability significantly better than 0.5 in the case when it receives as input $|\psi\rangle$. The analysis of this was shown in [AKL+22].

2.4   Generalized Cloning Games

Another way we can extend the notion of cloning games is by allowing asymmetric verification for $\mathcal{B}$ and $\mathcal{C}$ by allowing different algorithms ($\mathsf{GenC}_\mathcal{B}$, $\mathsf{GenC}_\mathcal{C}$, $\mathsf{Ver}_\mathcal{B}$, $\mathsf{Ver}_\mathcal{C}$) in the verification phase. We call this more general class of games *asymmetric cloning games*.

Deletion Games. As a special case, we define *deletion games*, in which $\mathsf{GenC}_\mathcal{B}$ outputs no challenge, so that $\mathcal{B}$ is effectively supposed to produce a classical certificate of deletion. In this context, we can define search games based on the algorithms ($\mathsf{GenC}_\mathcal{C}$, $\mathsf{Ver}_\mathcal{C}$), with $\mathcal{C}$ understood to be the party tasked to perform the intended functionality of the token. With these modifications, unclonable search security and unclonable indistinguishable security are defined the same as before. We show how to how to go from the former to the latter using the Quantum Goldreich-Levin Lemma[14] [AC02]. In order to achieve unclonable search security, we show that the construction[15] of [BI20] satisfies unclonable search security using monogamy-of-entanglement games [TFKW13], which have been commonly used in unclonable cryptography [BL20, CLLZ21, CV21]. Specifically, we show that the success probability of any adversary $(\mathcal{A}, \mathcal{B}, \mathcal{C})$ in the following game is exponentially small in λ:

- $(\mathcal{A}, \mathcal{B}, \mathcal{C})$ prepares a bipartite state ρ shared between $\mathcal{A}$ and the referee Ref. $\mathcal{A}$ splits the state between $\mathcal{B}$ and $\mathcal{C}$.
- Ref makes a measurement in basis H^θ for a random $\theta \in \{0, 1\}^\lambda$
- $\mathcal{B}$ outputs x_B. $\mathcal{C}$ receives θ and outputs x_C.
- $(\mathcal{A}, \mathcal{B}, \mathcal{C})$ wins if $x_C = x$ and $x_{B,i} = x_i$ whenever $\theta_i = 1$.

This suffices due to a well-known reduction from cloning games to monogamy-of-entanglement games using EPR pairs. Thus, we provide a different method to achieve information theoretic encryption with certified deletion. Although our method is incomparable to previous methods for achieving the same result [BI20, BK22], we believe our approach may be more intuitive for some readers.

Relating Search and Decision Games. We give one more transformation, which starts with a cloning search game and ends up with a cloning decision game. The first one uses augmented security above and applies it to the construction of [AKL+22] for copy-protection in the QROM. We generalize the proof for a class of cloning games, and as a special case, we achieve copy-protection for point functions using BB84 states in the QROM. Since the ideas employed in this part are similar to Sect. 2.3, we omit the details.

2.5 Future Directions

Relationship Between Challenge Distributions for Decision Games. In this work, we show that when a cloning game has negligible soundness (similar to a search game) with an independent distribution, the cloning game with the corresponding identical distribution is also secure. We leverage this theorem to many applications, including copy-protection and single-decryptor encryption schemes. However, this theorem does not apply when the soundness is a constant. An interesting open problem is to generalize the result to the case with constant security error (for example, unclonable-indistinguishability). Generalizing this result would present a pathway towards achieving unclonable encryption scheme with unclonable-indistinguishability in the plain model, that is currently open.

---

[14] Unlike our result on single-decryptor encryption, which asks for the usual, stronger property of unclonability, here we do not need the simultaneous version of the Goldreich-Levin Lemma because we are in the weaker, certified deletion setting.

[15] A simplified version of it without additional properties. The authors show in [BI20] that the construction already satisfies the stronger notion of unclonable indistinguishable security, yet the proof is more involved.

Removing Random Oracles from BB84-based Constructions. Another approach to obtain unclonable encryption with unclonable-indistinguishability in the plain model is to remove the need for random oracle in the Corollary 1. Currently, the random oracle is essential, and we do not know how to get rid of it. Still, we believe that removing QROM in the theorem statement is a promising direction and will help us understand the relationship between various unclonable primitives and the computational assumptions they need.

Domain Extension. Suppose we have a cloning game for messages of n bits. Is it possible to generically transform this into another cloning game for $2n$ bits? Naive repetition does not work well with cloning games and hence, it would be interesting to come up with interesting techniques for domain extension. One application of this is domain extension for unclonable encryption. Suppose we have an encryption scheme that can encrypt n bits and we would like to transform this into a different scheme encrypting $2n$ bits. It would also be interesting to study domain extension for the challenge space as well. This would have implications to domain extension for single-decryptor encryption.

Generalizing the Non-Local Lifting Theorem Our non-local lifting theorem in the full version is restricted in that the classical reductions need to be black-box and non-adaptive. These restrictions propagate from the work of [BBK22], and removing them will allow for more classical reductions to be lifted to the quantum setting.

3   Cloning Games - Definitions

We would like to capture all cryptographic games where the adversary needs to clone a particular functionality of a given quantum token. The quantum token could be a copy-protected program, signature token, unclonable ciphertext, unclonable decryption key, or any quantum state that serves some functionality which could only be used by one party at a given time. We start off with basic definitions and give generalizations in the full version.

Definition 1 (Cloning Game). *A cloning game consists of a tuple of efficient algorithms* $\mathcal{G} = (\mathsf{Setup}, \mathsf{GenT}, \mathsf{GenC}, \mathsf{Ver})$:

- **Key Generation:** $\mathsf{Setup}(1^\lambda)$ *is a PPT algorithm which takes as input a security parameter* 1^λ *in unary. It outputs a secret key* $\mathsf{sk} \in \{0,1\}^*$. *We will assume without loss of generality*[16] *that* sk *always contains the security parameter* 1^λ.
- **Token Generation:** $\mathsf{GenT}(\mathsf{sk}, m)$ *is a QPT algorithm that takes as input a secret key* sk *and a message* $m \in \{0,1\}^*$. *It outputs a quantum token* ρ.
- **Challenge Generation:** $\mathsf{GenC}(\mathsf{sk}, m)$ *takes as input a secret key* sk *and a message* m. *It outputs a classical challenge* $\mathsf{ch} \in \{0,1\}^*$.

---

[16] This is in order to simplify the notation for the rest of the algorithms. We will sometimes make this inclusion explicit, and other times it is understood implicitly.

– **Verification:** $\mathsf{Ver}(\mathsf{sk}, m, \mathsf{ch}, \mathsf{ans})$ *takes as input a secret key* sk, *a message* m, *a challenge* ch, *and an answer* ans. *It outputs either* 0 *(reject) or* 1 *(accept).*

3.1 Correctness

Before we talk about cloning experiments, we should specify what property of a quantum token ρ we would like to be unclonable. Intuitively, the property will be captured by the ability to honestly pass verification using the token ρ. This brings us to the definition of correctness for a cloning game:

Definition 2 (Correctness). *Let* $\delta : \mathbb{Z}^+ \rightarrow [0,1]$. *We say that* $\mathcal{G}$ *has* δ-*correctness if there exists an efficient quantum algorithm* $\mathcal{A}_{\mathcal{G}}$ *such that for all messages* $m \in \mathcal{M}$:

$$\Pr\left[\mathsf{Ver}(\mathsf{sk},m,\mathsf{ch},\mathsf{ans})=1 \ : \ \begin{array}{l}\mathsf{sk}\leftarrow\mathsf{Setup}(1^\lambda)\\ \rho\leftarrow\mathsf{GenT}(\mathsf{sk},m)\\ \mathsf{ch}\leftarrow\mathsf{GenC}(\mathsf{sk},m)\\ \mathsf{ans}\leftarrow\mathcal{A}_{\mathcal{G}}(\rho,\mathsf{ch})\end{array}\right] \geq \delta(\lambda)$$

If $\delta = 1$ *(or* $\delta(\lambda) = 1 - \mathsf{negl}(\lambda)$*), we say* $\mathcal{G}$ *has* perfect *(or* statistical*) correctness. In this work, we will mainly focus on statistically correct cloning games.*

Note: In the correctness definition above, $\mathcal{A}_{\mathcal{G}}$ should be considered an honest user of the primitive.

3.2 Special Types of Cloning Games

Next, we define some special cases, with terminology borrowed from classical security notions.

Definition 3 (Cloning Search Game). *Let* $\mathcal{G} = (\mathsf{Setup}, \mathsf{GenT}, \mathsf{GenC}, \mathsf{Ver})$ *be a cloning game such that* $\mathsf{Ver}(\mathsf{sk}, m, \mathsf{ch}, \mathsf{ans})$ *accepts if and only if* $\mathsf{ans} = m$. *Then,* $\mathcal{G}$ *is called a* cloning search game.

Definition 4 (Cloning Decision Game). *Let* $\mathcal{G} = (\mathsf{Setup}, \mathsf{GenT}, \mathsf{GenC}, \mathsf{Ver})$ *be a cloning game such that the answer* ans *taken as input by* Ver *is one bit, i.e.* $\mathsf{ans} \in \{0, 1\}$. *Then,* $\mathcal{G}$ *is called a* cloning decision game.

We additionally define the notion of a *cloning encryption game* when we discuss unclonable encryption in Sect. 3.4.

3.3 Security

Cloning Experiment. We will define notions of security for a cloning game in terms of a security experiment. Given a token ρ, an adversary should not be able to generate two (possibly entangled) quantum tokens which can simultaneously pass verification. We will formalize this intuition below.

Definition 5 (Cloning Experiment). *A cloning experiment, denoted by* $\mathfrak{CE}_{\mathcal{G},\mathcal{D}}$, *is a security game played between a referee* Ref *and a cloning adversary* $(\mathcal{A}, \mathcal{B}, \mathcal{C})$. *It is parameterized by a cloning game* $\mathcal{G} = (\mathsf{Setup}, \mathsf{GenT}, \mathsf{GenC}, \mathsf{Ver})$ *and a distribution* $\mathcal{D}$ *over the message space* $\mathcal{M}$. *The experiment is described as follows:*

- *Setup Phase:*
  - *All parties get a security parameter* 1^λ *as input.*
  - Ref *samples a message* $m \leftarrow \mathcal{D}$.
  - Ref *computes* $\mathsf{sk} \leftarrow \mathsf{Setup}(1^\lambda)$ *and* $\rho \leftarrow \mathsf{GenT}(\mathsf{sk}, m)$.
  - Ref *sends* ρ *to* $\mathcal{A}$.
- *Splitting Phase:*
  - $\mathcal{A}$ *computes a bipartite state* ρ' *over registers* B, C.
  - $\mathcal{A}$ *sends* $\rho'[B]$ *to* $\mathcal{B}$ *and* $\rho'[C]$ *to* $\mathcal{C}$.
- *Challenge Phase:*
  - Ref *independently samples* $\mathsf{ch}_\mathcal{B}, \mathsf{ch}_\mathcal{C} \leftarrow \mathsf{GenC}(\mathsf{sk}, m)$.
  - Ref *sends* $\mathsf{ch}_\mathcal{B}$ *to* $\mathcal{B}$ *and* $\mathsf{ch}_\mathcal{C}$ *to* $\mathcal{C}$.
  - $\mathcal{B}$ *and* $\mathcal{C}$ *send back answers* $\mathsf{ans}_\mathcal{B}$ *and* $\mathsf{ans}_\mathcal{C}$, *respectively.*
  - Ref *computes bits* $b_\mathcal{B} \leftarrow \mathsf{Ver}(\mathsf{sk}, m, \mathsf{ch}_\mathcal{B}, \mathsf{ans}_\mathcal{B})$ *and* $b_\mathcal{C} \leftarrow \mathsf{Ver}(\mathsf{sk}, m, \mathsf{ch}_\mathcal{C}, \mathsf{ans}_\mathcal{C})$.
  - *The outcome of the game is denoted by* $\mathfrak{CE}_{\mathcal{G},\mathcal{D}}(1^\lambda, (\mathcal{A}, \mathcal{B}, \mathcal{C}))$, *which equals 1 if* $b_\mathcal{B} = b_\mathcal{C} = 1$, *indicating that the adversary has won, and 0 otherwise, indicating that the adversary has lost.*

Trivial Success. As a baseline for unclonable security, we will consider *trivial* attacks that do not require any cloning operation. The best we can hope is that such attacks are optimal, hence the definitions below.

Definition 6 (Trivial Cloning Attack).

We say that $(\mathcal{A}, \mathcal{B}, \mathcal{C})$ *is a* trivial cloning attack *against a cloning experiment* $\mathfrak{CE}_{\mathcal{G},\mathcal{D}}$ *if* $\mathcal{A}$ *upon receiving a token* ρ, *sends the product state* $|\bot\rangle\langle\bot| \otimes \rho$ *to* $\mathcal{B}$ *and* $\mathcal{C}$. *In other words, only* $\mathcal{C}$ *gets the token* ρ. *We denote by* $\mathsf{TRIV}(\mathfrak{CE}_{\mathcal{G},\mathcal{D}})$ *the set of trivial attacks against* $\mathfrak{CE}_{\mathcal{G},\mathcal{D}}$.

Remark 1. Note that due to the symmetry between $\mathcal{B}$ and $\mathcal{C}$, the definition of trivial cloning attack could be equivalently defined so that only $\mathcal{B}$ gets the token ρ.

Definition 7 (Trivial Success Probability for Cloning Games). *We define the trivial success probability of a cloning experiment* $\mathfrak{CE}_{\mathcal{G},\mathcal{D}}$ *as*

$$p^{\mathsf{triv}}(\mathcal{G}, \mathcal{D}) := \sup_{(\mathcal{A},\mathcal{B},\mathcal{C}) \in \mathsf{TRIV}(\mathfrak{CE}_{\mathcal{G},\mathcal{D}})} \Pr\left[1 \leftarrow \mathfrak{CE}_{\mathcal{G},\mathcal{D}}(1^\lambda, (\mathcal{A}, \mathcal{B}, \mathcal{C}))\right].$$

Unclonable Security. We present the security definition of cloning games below.

Definition 8 (Unclonable Security). *Let* $\mathcal{G}$ *be a cloning game,* $\mathcal{D}$ *be a distribution over the message space* $\mathcal{M}$, *and* $\varepsilon : \mathbb{Z}^+ \to [0, 1]$. *We say that* $\mathcal{G}$ *has* $(\mathcal{D}, \varepsilon)$ unclonable security *if for all QPT cloning adversaries* $(\mathcal{A}, \mathcal{B}, \mathcal{C})$ *we have:*

$$\Pr\left[1 \leftarrow \mathfrak{CE}_{\mathcal{G},\mathcal{D}}(1^\lambda, (\mathcal{A}, \mathcal{B}, \mathcal{C}))\right] \leq p^{\mathsf{triv}}(\mathcal{G}, \mathcal{D}) + \varepsilon(\lambda).$$

If $|\mathcal{M}| = 1$, *we will simply write* ε *unclonable security.*

Security for Search Games. For the special case of search games, we consider two definitions below.

Definition 9 (Unclonable Search Security). *If $\mathcal{G}$ is a cloning search game with $(\mathcal{D}, \varepsilon)$ unclonable security, we additionally say that $\mathcal{G}$ has $(\mathcal{D}, \varepsilon)$ unclonable search security.*

Remark 2. Note that even though the definitions above are valid for any distribution $\mathcal{D}$, to get meaningful security one needs to choose $\mathcal{D}$ appropriately for the context. For instance, if the cloning game $\mathcal{G}$ represents copy-protection for point functions, it is appropriate to pick $\mathcal{D}$ in a balanced way so that the trivial success probability $p^{\text{triv}}(\mathcal{G}, \mathcal{D})$ is bounded away from 1. As long as this is the case, $(\mathcal{D}, \varepsilon)$ unclonable security (for small ε) is non-trivial[17] in the sense that it is classically impossible and it uses the power of no-cloning. On the other hand, when $p^{\text{triv}}(\mathcal{G}, \mathcal{D}) \approx 1$ unclonable security becomes trivial and achieved by uninteresting constructions including classical games.

Definition 10 (Unclonable Indistinguishable Security). *Let $\mathcal{D}_{m_0, m_1}$ denote the distribution that outputs messages m_0 and m_1 with probability $1/2$ each. We say that a search game $\mathcal{G}$ has ε unclonable indistinguishable security if it has $(\mathcal{D}_{m_0, m_1}, \varepsilon)$ unclonable search security for any pair of messages $m_0, m_1 \in \mathcal{M}$.*

In Definitions 8 to 10, if $(\mathcal{A}, \mathcal{B}, \mathcal{C})$ is not required to be efficient, then we say that $\mathcal{G}$ has *information theoretic* unclonable (search/indistinguishable) security.

3.4 Examples

In this section, we demonstrate the comprehensiveness of cloning games by casting popular unclonable primitives as cloning games. We restrict our attention to primitives with symmetric verification, and those with asymmetric verification, such as secure software leasing or certified deletion, require a slightly more general syntax, which will be defined in the full version.

Copy-Protection. Let $\mathcal{F}$ be the class of functions of the form $f : \mathcal{X} \to \mathcal{Y}$, parameterized implicitly by a security parameter λ, and let $\mathcal{D}$ be a distribution over $\mathcal{F}$. A copy-protection scheme for $\mathcal{D}$ is a pair of efficient algorithms (CP, Eval):

- CP$(1^\lambda, d_f)$ takes as input description d_f of a function $f : \mathcal{X} \to \mathcal{Y}$ and outputs a copy-protected quantum program ρ_f.
- Eval$(1^\lambda, \rho_f, x)$ takes as input a quantum program ρ_f and an input $x \in \mathcal{X}$. It outputs a value $y \in \mathcal{Y}$.

(CP, Eval) defines a cloning game $\mathcal{G}_{\text{CP}}^{\mathcal{D}'} = (\text{Setup}, \text{GenT}, \text{GenC}, \text{Ver})$ for any family of distributions $\mathcal{D}' = \left(\mathcal{D}'_f\right)_{f \in \mathcal{F}}$ over $\mathcal{F}$ as follows. Note that, $\mathcal{D}'$ defines a distribution on challenge inputs, therefore, it specifies GenC.

---

[17] We assume statistical correctness here.

- The message space $\mathcal{M}$ is the set of function descriptions d_f for all $f \in \mathcal{F}$.
- Setup(1^λ) outputs sk $= 1^\lambda$, i.e. there is no secret key.
- GenT(sk, m) parses the input as $m = d_f$, then it computes $\rho_f \leftarrow \mathsf{CP}(1^\lambda, d_f)$ and outputs ρ_f.
- GenC(sk, m) parses $m = d_f$ and samples input $x \leftarrow \mathcal{D}'_f$.[18]
- Ver(sk, m, ch, ans) parses $m = d_f$, ch $= x$. It accepts if and only if ans $= f(x)$.

Correctness: We require that $\mathcal{G}_{\mathsf{CP}}$ has statistical correctness, to ensure that the copy-protected program is reusable. More specifically, $\mathcal{A}_{\mathcal{G}_{\mathsf{CP}}}(\rho, \mathsf{ch})$ runs Eval(ρ, ch).[19]

Security: We consider a game-based definition of copy-protection, first defined by [CMP20, BJL+21]. We say that (CP, Eval) is secure for a class of distributions $\mathcal{D}'$ if $\mathcal{G}_{\mathsf{CP}}^{\mathcal{D}'}$ has $(\mathcal{D}, \varepsilon)$ unclonable security. For optimal security, we require ε to be negligible.

Unclonable Encryption. Below, we define unclonable encryption [BL20] as a cloning game. We focus our attention to one-time secret-key setting, in which case unclonable encryption is synonymous with cloning encryption games defined in Definition 11. It is known in the literature that construction in this simple setting can be generically lifted to achieve unclonable encryption with additional properties, such as public-key encryption [AK21]. We note, however, that unclonable encryption with such properties can still be expressed as a cloning game by modifying the syntax of a cloning encryption game. We state the correspondence below, which is easy to verify.

Definition 11 (Cloning Encryption Game). *A cloning search game* $\mathcal{G} =$ (Setup, GenT, GenC, Ver) *is called a* cloning encryption game *if* GenC(sk, m) *outputs* sk *with probability 1 for all* (sk, m).

Fact 4 (Informal). *An unclonable encryption scheme for a message space* $\mathcal{M}$ *exists with unclonable (unclonable indistinguishable) security if and only if a cloning encryption game* $\mathcal{G}$ *for* $\mathcal{M}$ *with unclonable (unclonable indistinguishable) security exists.*

There are two types of security we will consider for unclonable encryption: (1) $(\mathcal{U}_{\mathcal{M}}, \varepsilon)$ unclonable security and (2) ε unclonable indistinguishable security. These security definitions together with δ-correctness are on par with the original definitions of [BL20].[20] Note that since GenC is deterministic, it has a unique extension.

---

[18] Here we make the natural assumption that correctness and security are defined with respect to the same distribution $\mathcal{D}'_f$. Intuitively, the scheme should protect against cloning the functionality of the honest evaluator.

[19] Note that this captures the average-input correctness as opposed to per-input correctness.

[20] Although (2) was defined in a slightly different way in [BL20], the difference is inconsequential, and our version has been used in follow-up works such as [AKL+22]. We also mention that [BL20] considered perfect correctness.

Single Decryptor Encryption. We define single-decryptor encryption as a tuple of efficient algorithms (Gen, GenT', Enc, Dec), adapted from the definition of (secret-key) single-decryptor encryption (with honestly generated keys) in [GZ20]:

1. Gen(1^λ) takes as input a security parameter and outputs a classical secret key sk.
2. GenT'(sk) takes as input a classical secret key and it outputs a quantum decryption key ρ_{dk}.
3. Enc(sk, x) takes as input a secret key and a classical message. It outputs a classical ciphertext ct.
4. Dec(ρ, ct) takes as input a quantum decryption key and a classical ciphertext. It outputs a classical message x'.

(Gen, GenT', Enc, Dec) defines a stateful cloning game $\mathcal{G}^{\mathcal{D}_\mathcal{X}}_{\mathsf{SDE}}$ = (Setup, GenT, GenC, Ver), parameterized by a distribution $\mathcal{D}_\mathcal{X}$, where $\mathcal{X}$ is the set of classical messages encrypted by this scheme, as follows:

- Setup(1^λ) runs $sk \leftarrow$ Gen(1^λ) and outputs sk = sk.
- There is no message, i.e. $m = \perp$.
- GenT(sk, m) computes $\rho_{dk} \leftarrow$ GenT'(sk) and outputs ρ_{dk}.
- GenC(sk, m; r_{GenC}) samples $x \xleftarrow{\$} \mathcal{X}$ using random coins r_{GenC}. It outputs $c \leftarrow$ Enc(sk, x).
- Ver(sk, m, ch, ans, r_{GenC}) computes x as above using r_{GenC}. Then it accepts if and only if ans = x.

Correctness. We say that (Gen, GenT', Enc, Dec) has correctness if $\mathcal{G}^{\mathcal{D}_\mathcal{X}}_{\mathsf{SDE}}$ has perfect correctness for any distribution $\mathcal{D}_\mathcal{X}$. More specifically, $\mathcal{A}_{\mathcal{G}_{\mathsf{SDE}}}(\rho_{dk}, \mathsf{ch})$ runs Dec(ρ_{dk}, ch).

Security. We say that (Gen, GenT', Enc, Dec) has ε unclonable security if $\mathcal{G}^{\mathcal{U}_\mathcal{X}}_{\mathsf{SDE}}$ has ε unclonable security[21].

In other words, the ability to decrypt a random classical message is the unclonable property of the quantum decryption key. For optimal security, we require that ε is negligible.

Quantum Money. Next, we give examples of cloning games with quantum verification. We focus on quantum money, first introduced by Wiesner [Wie83]. We consider a public-key variant of quantum money considered by [AC12, Zha19]. We note that the description below can be suitably adapted to case private-key quantum money as a cloning game. A public-key quantum money scheme is a tuple of efficient algorithms (Gen, Mint, VerToken):

- Gen(1^λ) takes as input a security parameter and outputs a public-secret key pair (pk, sk).

---

[21] We omit the message distribution due to the lack of message.

- Mint(sk) takes as input a secret key and outputs a classical serial number s and a quantum banknote ρ_s.
- VerToken(pk, s, ρ) takes as input a public key, a serial number, and a quantum state. It outputs 0 (reject) or 1 (accept).

(Gen, Mint, VerToken) defines a cloning game $\mathcal{G}_{\mathsf{QM}} = (\mathsf{Setup}, \mathsf{GenT}, \mathsf{GenC}, \mathsf{Ver})$ as follows:

- We set $m = \bot$, i.e. there is no message.
- Setup(1^λ) runs $(pk, sk) \leftarrow \mathsf{Gen}(1^\lambda)$ and outputs $\mathsf{sk} = (pk, sk)$
- GenT(sk, m) parses the input as $\mathsf{sk} = (pk, sk)$, runs $(s, \rho_s) \leftarrow \mathsf{Mint}(sk)$, and outputs $\rho \otimes |s\rangle\langle s| \otimes |pk\rangle\langle pk|$.
- GenC(sk, m) outputs $\mathsf{ch} = \bot$, i.e. no challenge.
- Ver$(\mathsf{sk}, m, \mathsf{ch}, \sigma_{\mathsf{ans}})$ parses $\mathsf{sk} = (pk, sk)$ and outputs $b \leftarrow \mathsf{VerToken}(pk, \sigma_{\mathsf{ans}})$

Correctness. We say that the quantum money scheme has correctness if $\mathcal{G}_{\mathsf{QM}}$ has statistical correctness. Note that $\mathcal{A}_{\mathcal{G}_{\mathsf{QM}}}$ can simply output the quantum banknote it receives to satisfy Definition 2 (correctness). Furthermore, it can be assumed without loss of generality that the optimal $\mathcal{A}_{\mathcal{G}_{\mathsf{QM}}}$ acts as identity (i.e. outputs ρ as is) since there is no challenge. Therefore, this fully captures the usual definition of correctness for quantum money schemes.

Security. We say that the quantum money scheme is secure if $\mathcal{G}_{\mathsf{QM}}$ has ε unclonable security. For optimal security, we require that ε is negligible. Note that unclonable security as we defined only gives 1-to-2 unclonability, but it can be generalized to k-to-$k+1$ unclonability. Alternatively, one can define a quantum-money mini scheme in our framework, which is necessary and sufficient for constructing public-key quantum money [AC12].

4   Results

We state our main results, with proofs deferred to the appendix due to space restrictions. Theorems 5 and 6 show the existence of unclonable encryption and copy-protection for point-functions, respectively, in the QROM. The proofs can be found in the full version.

Theorem 5 (Search to Indistinguishability). *Let* $\mathcal{G} = (\mathsf{Setup}, \mathsf{GenT}, \mathsf{GenC}, \mathsf{Ver})$ *be a statistically correct cloning search game with message space* $\mathcal{M} = \{0,1\}^\ell$, *where* $\ell = \mathsf{poly}(\lambda)$, *such that* $p^{\mathsf{triv}}(\mathcal{G}, \mathcal{U}_{\mathcal{M}})$ *is negligible and* $\mathsf{GenC}(\mathsf{sk}, m)$ *does not depend[22] on* m. *Suppose that* $\mathcal{G}$ *has* $(\mathcal{U}_{\mathcal{M}}, |\mathcal{M}|^{-\delta})$ *unclonable search security for some* $\delta > 0$. *Let* $n = \mathsf{poly}(\lambda)$, *and define a cloning search game* $\mathcal{G}' = (\mathsf{Setup}', \mathsf{GenT}', \mathsf{GenC}', \mathsf{Ver}')$ *in QROM as follows:*

---

[22] This requirement can be lifted by extending the definition of stateful cloning games and having GenC know the random coins of GenT' (in this case m). We keep the syntax simple for there is no known application to the more general case.

- $\mathcal{G}'$ has message space $\mathcal{M}' = \{0,1\}^n$.
- Let $H : \mathcal{M} \to \mathcal{M}'$ be a random oracle.
- $\mathsf{Setup}'(1^\lambda)$ runs $\mathsf{sk} \leftarrow \mathsf{Setup}(1^\lambda)$. It outputs $\mathsf{sk}' = \mathsf{sk}$.
- $\mathsf{GenT}'(\mathsf{sk}', m')$ parses the input as $\mathsf{sk}' = (\mathsf{sk}, m)$. It samples $m \leftarrow \mathcal{U}_\mathcal{M}$ and computes $\rho \leftarrow \mathsf{GenT}(sk, m)$, then it outputs the token $\rho' = \rho \otimes |m' \oplus H(m)\rangle\langle m' \oplus H(m)|$ and random coins $r_{\mathsf{GenT}'} = m$
- $\mathsf{GenC}'(\mathsf{sk}', m')$ parses the input as $\mathsf{sk}' = \mathsf{sk}$. It computes $\mathsf{ch} \leftarrow \mathsf{GenC}(sk, m)$ (recall that by assumption this does not require knowledge of m) and outputs ch.
- $\mathcal{G}'$ is a search game, which defines Ver'.

Then, $\mathcal{G}'$ has statistical correctness and negl unclonable indistinguishable security.

Theorem 6 (Search to Decision).

Let $\mathcal{G} = (\mathsf{Setup}, \mathsf{GenT}, \mathsf{GenC}, \mathsf{Ver})$ be a statistically correct cloning encryption game with message space $\mathcal{M} = \{0,1\}^\ell$, where $\ell = \mathsf{poly}(\lambda)$, such that

- $\mathsf{Setup}(1^\lambda)$ outputs a uniformly random key $\mathsf{sk} \xleftarrow{\$} \mathcal{K}$, where $|\mathcal{K}|^{-1}$ is negligible in λ.
- $\mathcal{G}$ is $\mathcal{U}_\mathcal{M}$-evasive.
- $\mathcal{G}$ has $(\mathcal{U}_\mathcal{M}, |\mathcal{M}|^{-\delta})$ unclonable search security for some $\delta > 0$

Define a cloning decision game $\mathcal{G}' = (\mathsf{Setup}', \mathsf{GenT}', \mathsf{GenC}', \mathsf{Ver}')$ in QROM as follows:

- Let $\mathcal{M}'$ be an arbitrary message space.
- Let $H : \mathcal{M} \to \{0,1\}^n$ and $G : \mathcal{M}' \to \mathcal{K}$ be random oracles, where $n = \Omega(\lambda)$.
- $\mathsf{Setup}'(1^\lambda)$ outputs $\mathsf{sk}' = \bot$
- $\mathsf{GenT}'(\mathsf{sk}', m')$ samples $m \leftarrow \mathcal{U}_\mathcal{M}$. It computes $\rho \leftarrow \mathsf{GenT}(G(m'), m)$. It outputs $\rho' = \rho \otimes |H(m)\rangle\langle H(m)|$.
- $\mathsf{GenC}'(\mathsf{sk}', m')$ is an algorithm which does not depend on sk', and outputs a value $\mathsf{ch}' \in \mathcal{M}'$.
- $\mathsf{Ver}'(\mathsf{sk}', m', \mathsf{ch}', \mathsf{ans}')$ accepts if $\mathsf{ans}' = [\mathsf{ch}' == m']$.

Then, $\mathcal{G}'$ has statistical correctness and $(\mathcal{D}', \mathsf{negl})$ independent-challenge unclonable security for any unlearnable distribution $\mathcal{D}'$ over $\mathcal{M}$.

Theorem 7. There exists a single-decryptor encryption scheme in the plain model with information-theoretic independent-challenge security.

Theorem 7 above follows as a corollary of a general main theorem we prove in the full version, which shows that classical non-adaptive black-box reductions can be generically lifted to relate the unclonable security of cloning games.

In the full version, we also show how to extend the definition of cloning games to capture more unclonable primitives including primitives with certified deletion, and give an alternate construction/proof to show the feasibility of encryption with certified deletion in the plain model.

Acknowledgements. PA and FK are supported by a gift from Cisco.

References

[Aar09] Aaronson, S.: Quantum copy-protection and quantum money. In: 2009 24th Annual IEEE Conference on Computational Complexity, pp. 229–242. IEEE (2009) (cit. on pp. 2, 3)

[AC02] Adcock, M., Cleve, R.: A quantum Goldreich-Levin theorem with cryptographic applications. In: Alt, H., Ferreira, A. (eds.) STACS 2002. LNCS, vol. 2285, pp. 323–334. Springer, Heidelberg (2002). https://doi.org/10.1007/3-540-45841-7_26 (cit. on p. 22)

[AC12] Aaronson, S., Christiano, P.: Quantum money from hidden subspaces. In: Proceedings of the Forty-Fourth Annual ACM Symposium on Theory of Computing (STOC 2012). Association for Computing Machinery, New York (2012), pp. 41–60. https://doi.org/10.1145/2213977.2213983. ISBN:9781450312455 (cit. on pp. 2, 5, 28, 29)

[AK21] Ananth, P. Kaleoglu, F. Unclonable ecryption, revisited. In: Nissim, K., Waters, B. (eds.) TCC 2021. LNCS, vol. 13042, pp. 299–329. Springer, Cham (2021). https://doi.org/10.1007/978-3-030-90459-3_11 (cit. on pp. 3, 5, 8, 27)

[AKL+22] Ananth, P., Kaleoglu, F., Li, X., Liu, Q., Zhandry, M.: On the feasibility of unclonable encryption, and more. In: Dodis, Y., Shrimpton, T. (eds.). Advances in Cryptology – CRYPTO 2022, pp. 212–241. Springer, Cham (2022). https://doi.org/10.1007/978-3-031-15979-4_8. ISBN:978-3-031-15979-4 (cit. on pp. 3, 5-8, 20-22, 27)

[AL21] Ananth, P., La Placa, R.L..: Secure software leasing. In: Canteaut, A., Standaert, F.-X. (eds.) EUROCRYPT 2021. LNCS, vol. 12697, pp. 501–530. Springer, Cham (2021). https://doi.org/10.1007/978-3-030-77886-6_17 (cit. on p. 2)

[ALL+21] Aaronson, S., Liu, J., Liu, Q., Zhandry, M., Zhang, R.: New approaches for quantum copy-protection. In: Malkin, T., Peikert, C. (eds.) Advances in Cryptology - CRYPTO 2021, pp. 526–555. Springer, Cham (2021). https://doi.org/10.1007/978-3-030-84242-0_19. ISBN:978-3-030-84242-0 (cit. on pp. 2, 8)

[AQY22] Ananth, P., Qian, L., Yuen, H.: Cryptography from pseudorandom quantum states. In: Annual International Cryptology Conference, pp. 208–236. Springer, Cham (2022). https://doi.org/10.1007/978-3-031-15802-5_8 (cit. on p. 5)

[BB84] Bennett, C., Brassard, G.: Quantum cryptography: public key distribution and coin tossing, vol. 560, pp. 175–179 (1984). https://doi.org/10.1016/j.tcs.2011.08.039 (cit. on p. 5)

[BBK22] Bitansky, N., Brakerski, Z., Kalai, Y.T.: Constructive post-quantum reductions. In: Dodis, Y., Shrimpton, T. (eds.) Advances in Cryptology – CRYPTO 2022. Springer, Cham (2022), pp. 654–683. https://doi.org/10.1007/978-3-031-15982-4_22. ISBN:978-3-031-15982-4 (cit. on pp. 15, 23)

[BCQ22] Brakerski, Z., Canetti, R., Qian, L.: On the computational hardness needed for quantum cryptography. arXiv preprint arXiv:2209.04101 (2022) (cit. on p. 5)

[BDF+11] Boneh, D., Dagdelen, Ö., Fischlin, M., Lehmann, A., Schaffner, C., Zhandry, M.: Random oracles in a quantum world. In: Lee, D.H., Wang, X. (eds.) ASIACRYPT 2011. LNCS, vol. 7073, pp. 41–69. Springer, Heidelberg (2011). https://doi.org/10.1007/978-3-642-25385-0_3 (cit. on p. 20)

[BGS13] Broadbent, A., Gutoski, G., Stebila, D.: Quantum one-time programs. In: Canetti, R., Garay, J.A. (eds.) CRYPTO 2013. LNCS, vol. 8043, pp. 344–360. Springer, Heidelberg (2013). https://doi.org/10.1007/978-3-642-40084-1_20 (cit. on p. 2)

[BI20] Broadbent, A., Islam, R.: Quantum encryption with certified deletion. In: Pass, R., Pietrzak, K. (eds.) TCC 2020. LNCS, vol. 12552, pp. 92–122. Springer, Cham (2020). https://doi.org/10.1007/978-3-030-64381-2_4 (cit. on pp. 2, 5, 9, 22)

[BJL+21] Broadbent, A., Jeffery, S., Lord, S., Podder, S., Sundaram, A.: Secure software leasing without assumptions. In: Nissim, K., Waters, B. (eds.) TCC 2021. LNCS, vol. 13042, pp. 90–120. Springer, Cham (2021). https://doi.org/10.1007/978-3-030-90459-3_4 (cit. on pp. 2, 6, 27)

[BK22] Bartusek, J., Khurana, D.: Cryptography with Certified Deletion (2022). https://doi.org/10.48550/ARXIV.2207.01754 (cit. on pp. 9, 22)

[BL20] Broadbent, A., Lord, S.: Uncloneable quantum encryption via oracles. In: Schloss Dagstuhl - Leibniz-Zentrum für Informatik (2020). https://doi.org/10.4230/LIPICS.TQC.2020.4 (cit. on pp. 2, 5, 8, 20, 22, 27)

[BS16] Ben-David, S., Sattath, O.: Quantum Tokens for Digital Signatures (2016). https://doi.org/10.48550/ARXIV.1609.09047 (cit. on p. 2)

[CLLZ21] Coladangelo, A., Liu, J., Liu, Q., Zhandry, M.: Hidden cosets and applications to unclonable cryptography. In: Malkin, T., Peikert, C. (eds.) CRYPTO 2021. LNCS, vol. 12825, pp. 556–584. Springer, Cham (2021). https://doi.org/10.1007/978-3-030-84242-0_20 (cit. on pp. 2, 4, 5, 7, 8, 22)

[CMP20] Coladangelo, A., Majenz, C., Poremba, A.: Quantum copy-protection of compute-and-compare programs in the quantum random oracle model (2020). 13865. https://doi.org/10.48550/ARXIV.2009 (cit. on pp. 3, 5, 6, 8, 27)

[CMSZ02] Chiesa, A., Ma, F., Spooner, N., Zhandry, M.: Post-quantum succinct arguments: breaking the quantum rewinding barrier. In: 62nd FOCS, pp. 49–58. IEEE Computer Society (2022). (cit. on pp. 16–18)

[CV21] Culf, E., Vidick, T.: A monogamy-of-entanglement game for subspace coset states. arXiv preprint arXiv:2107.13324 [cs.CR] (2021) (cit. on p. 22)

[Die82] DGBJ Dieks. Communication by EPR devices. Phys. Lett. A **92**(6), 271–272 (1982) (cit. on p. 2)

[GL89] Goldreich, O., Levin, L.A.: A hard-core predicate for all one-way functions. In: Proceedings of the Twenty-First Annual ACM Symposium on Theory of Computing, Seattle (STOC 1989), pp. 25–32. Association for Computing Machinery (1989). https://doi.org/10.1145/73007.73010. ISBN:0897913078 (cit. on pp. 6, 13)

[Got02] Gottesman, D.: Uncloneable Encryption (2002). https://doi.org/10.48550/ARXIV.QUANT-PH/0210062 (cit. on p. 2)

[GZ20] Georgiou, M., Zhandry, M.: Unclonable decryption keys. In: IACR Cryptol. ePrint Arch (2020), p. 877 (cit. on pp. 4, 7, 28)

[HMNY22] Hiroka, T., Morimae, T., Nishimaki, R., Yamakawa, T.: Certified everlasting zero-knowledge proof for QMA. In: Annual International Cryptology Conference, pp. 239–268. Springer, Cham (2022). https://doi.org/10.1007/978-3-031-15802-5_9(cit. on p. 2)

[Imp95] Impagliazzo, R.: A personal view of average-case complexity. In: Proceedings of Structure in Complexity Theory. Tenth Annual IEEE Conference, pp. 134–147. IEEE (1995) (cit. on p. 5)

[IR90] Impagliazzo, R., Rudich, S.: Limits on the provable consequences of one-way permutations. In: Goldwasser, S. (ed.) CRYPTO 1988. LNCS, vol. 403, pp. 8–26. Springer, New York (1990). https://doi.org/10.1007/0-387-34799-2_2 (cit. on p. 5)

[Jor75] Jordan, C.: Essai sur la géométrie à n dimensions fre. In: Bulletin de la Société Mathématique de France 3, pp. 103–174 (1875) (cit. on p. 17)

[KNY21] Kitagawa, F. Nishimaki, R. Yamakawa, T. Secure software leasing from standard assumptions. In: Nissim, K., Waters, B. (eds.) TCC 2021. LNCS, vol. 13042, pp. 31–61. Springer, Cham (2021). https://doi.org/10.1007/978-3-030-90459-3_2 (cit. on p. 2)

[MY22] Morimae, T., Yamakawa, T.: Quantum commitments and signatures without one-way functions. In: Annual International Cryptology Conference, pp. 269–295. Springer, Cham (2022). https://doi.org/10.1007/978-3-031-15802-5_10 (cit. on p. 5)

[Shm22] Shmueli, O.: Public-key Quantum money with a classical bank. In: Proceedings of the 54th Annual ACM SIGACT Symposium on Theory of Computing, pp. 790–803 (2022) (cit. on p. 2)

[SW22] Sattath, O., Wyborski, S.: Uncloneable decryption from quantum copy protection. arXiv preprint arXiv:2203.05866 (2022) (cit. on p. 5)

[TFKW13] Tomamichel, M., Fehr, S., Kaniewski, J.d., Wehner, S.: A monogamy-of-entanglement game with applications to device-independent quantum cryptography. New J. Phys. **15**(10), 103002 (2013). https://doi.org/10.1088/1367-2630/15/10/103002 (cit. on pp. 8, 9, 22)

[VZ21] Vidick, T., Zhang, T.: Classical proofs of quantum knowledge. In: Canteaut, A., Standaert, F.-X. (eds.) EUROCRYPT 2021. LNCS, vol. 12697, pp. 630–660. Springer, Cham (2021). https://doi.org/10.1007/978-3-030-77886-6_22 (cit. on p. 5)

[Wie83] Wiesner, S.: Conjugate coding. ACM Sigact News **15**(1), 78 88 (1983) (cit. on pp. 2, 5, 28)

[WZ82] Wootters, W.K., Zurek, W.H.: A single quantum cannot be cloned. Nature **299**(5886), pp. 802–803 (1982) (cit. on p. 2)

[Zha19] Zhandry, M.: Quantum lightning never strikes the same state twice. In: Ishai, Y., Rijmen, V. (eds.) EUROCRYPT 2019. LNCS, vol. 11478, pp. 408–438. Springer, Cham (2019). https://doi.org/10.1007/978-3-030-17659-4_14 (cit. on pp. 2, 5, 28)

Publicly-Verifiable Deletion
via Target-Collapsing Functions

James Bartusek[1($\boxtimes$)], Dakshita Khurana[2], and Alexander Poremba[3]

[1] University of California, Berkeley, USA
bartusek.james@gmail.com
[2] University of Illinois Urbana-Champaign, Champaign, USA
dakshita@illinois.edu
[3] California Institute of Technology, Pasadena, USA
aporemba@caltech.edu

Abstract. We build quantum cryptosystems that support publicly-verifiable deletion from standard cryptographic assumptions. We introduce target-collapsing as a weakening of collapsing for hash functions, analogous to how second preimage resistance weakens collision resistance; that is, target-collapsing requires indistinguishability between superpositions and mixtures of preimages of an honestly sampled image.

We show that target-collapsing hashes enable publicly-verifiable deletion (PVD), proving conjectures from [Poremba, ITCS'23] and demonstrating that the Dual-Regev encryption (and corresponding fully homomorphic encryption) schemes support PVD under the LWE assumption. We further build on this framework to obtain a variety of primitives supporting publicly-verifiable deletion from weak cryptographic assumptions, including:

- Commitments with PVD assuming the existence of injective one-way functions, or more generally, *almost-regular* one-way functions. Along the way, we demonstrate that (variants of) target-collapsing hashes can be built from almost-regular one-way functions.
- Public-key encryption with PVD assuming trapdoored variants of injective (or almost-regular) one-way functions. We also demonstrate that the encryption scheme of [Hhan, Morimae, and Yamakawa, Eurocrypt'23] based on pseudorandom group actions has PVD.
- X with PVD for $X \in \{$attribute-based encryption, quantum fully-homomorphic encryption, witness encryption, time-revocable encryption$\}$, assuming X and trapdoored variants of injective (or almost-regular) one-way functions.

1 Introduction

Recent research has explored the exciting possibility of combining quantum information with computational hardness to enable classically infeasible cryptographic tasks. Beginning with proposals such as unforgeable money [28], this list has recently grown to include the possibility of provably deleting cryptographic information encoded into quantum states [2,5–7,9,15–17,21,27].

© International Association for Cryptologic Research 2023
H. Handschuh and A. Lysyanskaya (Eds.): CRYPTO 2023, LNCS 14085, pp. 99–128, 2023.
https://doi.org/10.1007/978-3-031-38554-4_4

In this work, we further investigate the task of provable deletion of information via destructive measurements. We focus on building primitives that satisfy *publicly-verifiable deletion* (PVD). This deletion property allows any participant in possession of a quantum encoding to publish a publicly-verifiable classical certificate proving that they deleted[1] the underlying plaintext. This is in contrast to the weaker *privately-verifiable deletion* property, where deletion can be verified only by parties that hold a secret verification key, and this key must remain hidden from the party holding the ciphertext. Public verification is more desirable due to its stronger security guarantee: secret verification keys do not need to be stored in hidden locations, and security continues to hold even when the verification key is leaked. Furthermore, clients can outsource verification of deletion by publishing the verification key itself.

Our approach to building publicly verifiable deletion departs from templates used in prior works on deletion. While most prior works, building on [9,27], rely on the combination of a quantum information-theoretic tool such as Wiesner encodings/BB84 states [8,28] and a cryptographic object such as an encryption scheme, our work enables publicly-verifiable deletion by directly using simple cryptographic properties of many-to-one hash functions.

The Template, in a Nutshell. When illustrating our approach to publicly-verifiable deletion, it will help to first consider enabling this for a simple cryptographic primitive: a commitment scheme. That is, we consider building a statistically binding non-interactive quantum bit commitment scheme where each commitment is accompanied by a classical, *public* verification key vk. A receiver holding the commitment may generate a classical proof that they deleted the committed bit b, and this proof can be publicly verified against vk. We would like to guarantee that as long as verification accepts, the receiver has information-theoretically removed b from their view and will be unable to recover it given unbounded resources, despite previously having the bit b determined by their view.

To allow verification to be a public operation, it is natural to imagine the certificate or proof of deletion to be a hard-to-find solution to a public puzzle. For instance, the public verification key could be an image y of a (one-way) function, and the certificate of deletion a valid pre-image $f^{-1}(y)$ of this key. Now, the commitment itself must encode the committed bit b in such a way that the ability to generate $f^{-1}(y)$ given the commitment implies information-theoretic deletion of b. This can be enabled by encoding b in the *phase* of a state supported on multiple pre-images of y.

---

[1] In this work, we focus on *information-theoretic* deletion of computationally hidden secrets, where the guarantee is that after deletion, even an unbounded adversary cannot recover the plaintext that was previously determined by their view [6].

Namely, given an appropriate *two-to-one* function f, a commitment[2] to a bit b can be

$$\mathsf{Com}(b) = \left(y, |0, x_0\rangle_\mathsf{A} + (-1)^b |1, x_1\rangle_\mathsf{A}\right)$$

where $(0, x_0), (1, x_1)$ are the two pre-images of (a randomly sampled) image y.

Given an image y and a state on register A, a valid certificate of deletion of the underlying bit could be any pre-image of y, which for a well-formed commitment will be obtained by measuring the A register in the computational basis. It is easy to see that an immediate *honest* measurement of the A register implies information-theoretic erasure of the phase b. But a malicious adversary holding the commitment may decide to perform arbitrary operations on this state in an attempt to find a pre-image y without erasing b.

In this work, we analyze (minimal) requirements on the cryptographic hardness of f in the template above, so that the ability to computationally find any preimage of y given the commitment necessarily implies *information-theoretic* erasure of b. A useful starting point, inspired by recent conjectures in [21], is the *collapsing* property of hash functions. This property was first introduced in [26] as a quantum strengthening of collision-resistance.

Collapsing Functions. The notion of *collapsing* considers an experiment where a computationally bounded adversary prepares an arbitrary superposition of preimages of f on a register A, after which the challenger tosses a random coin c. If $c = 0$, the challenger measures register A, otherwise it measures a register containing the hash y of the value on register A, thus leaving A holding a superposition of preimages of y. The register A is returned to the adversary, and we say that f is collapsing if the adversary cannot guess c with better than negligible advantage. Constructions of collapsing hash functions are known based on LWE [25], low-noise LPN [30], and more generally on special types of collision-resistant hashes. They have played a key role in the design of post-quantum protocols, especially in settings where proofs of security of these protocols rely on *rewinding* an adversary.

It is easy to see that

$$\mathsf{Com}(b) = \left(y, |0, x_0\rangle + (-1)^b |1, x_1\rangle\right)$$

computationally hides the bit b as long as the function f used to build the commitment above is *collapsing*. Indeed, collapsing implies that the superposition $|0, x_0\rangle + (-1)^b |1, x_1\rangle$ is computationally indistinguishable from the result of measurement in the computational basis, and the latter perfectly erases the phase b. However, PVD requires something stronger: we must show that any adversary that generates a valid pre-image of y given the superposition $|0, x_0\rangle + (-1)^b |1, x_1\rangle$,

---

[2] Technically, it is only an appropriate purification of the scheme described here that will satisfy binding; we ignore this detail for the purposes of this overview.

must have *information-theoretically* deleted b from its view, despite b being information-theoretically present in the adversary's view before generating the certificate. We show via a careful proof that this is indeed the case for collapsing f. Proving this turns out to be non-trivial. Indeed, a similar construction in [21] based on the Ajtai hash function [3] relied on an unproven conjecture, which we prove in this work by developing new techniques.

In addition, we show how f in the template above can be replaced with functions that satisfy weaker properties than collapsing, yielding PVD from regular variants of one-way functions. We discuss these results below.

1.1   Our Results

We introduce new properties of (hash) functions, namely target-collapsing, generalized target-collision-resistance. We will show that hash functions satisfying these properties (1) can be based on (regular) variants of one-way functions and (2) imply publicly-verifiable deletion in many settings. Our results also use an intermediate notion, a variant of target-collapsing that satisfies certified everlasting security. Before discussing our results, we motivate and discuss these new definitions informally below.

Definitions

Target-Collapsing and Generalized Target-Collision-Resistant Functions. Towards better understanding the computational assumptions required for PVD, we observe that in the deletion experiment for the commitment above, the superposition $|x_0\rangle + (-1)^b |x_1\rangle$ is prepared by an *honest committer*. This indicates that the collapsing requirement, where security is required to hold even for an adversarial choice of superposition over preimages, may be overkill.

Inspired by this, we consider a natural weakening called *target-collapsing*, where *the challenger (as opposed to the adversary)* prepares a superposition of preimages of a random image y of f on register A. After this, the challenger tosses a random coin c. If $c = 0$, it does nothing to A, otherwise it measures A in the computational basis. The register A is returned to the adversary, and we say that a hash function is target-collapsing if a computationally bounded adversary cannot guess c with better than negligible advantage.

As highlighted above, this definition weakens collapsing to allow the challenger (instead of the adversary) to prepare the preimage register. The weakening turns out to be significant because we show that target-collapsing functions are realizable from relatively weak cryptographic assumptions – namely variants of one-way functions – which are unlikely to imply (standard) collapsing or collision-resistant hash functions due to known black-box separations [22].

To enable these instantiations from weaker assumptions, we first further generalize target-collapsing so that when $c = 1$, the challenger applies a *binary-outcome measurement* M to A (as opposed to performing a computational basis measurement resulting in a singleton preimage). Thus, a template commitment with PVD from generalized target-collapsing hashes has the form:

$$\mathsf{Com}(b) = \left(y, \sum_{x:f(x)=y,M(x)=0} |x\rangle + (-1)^b \sum_{x:f(x)=y,M(x)=1} |x\rangle \right).$$

We show that this commitment satisfies PVD as long as f is target-collapsing w.r.t. the measurement M, and satisfies an additional property of "generalized" target-collision-resistance (TCR), that we discuss next.

Generalized target-collision-resistance is a quantum generalization of the (standard) cryptographic property of second pre-image resistance/target-collision-resistance. Very roughly, this considers an experiment where the challenger first prepares a superposition of preimages of a random image y of f on register A. After this, the challenger applies a measurement (e.g., a binary-outcome measurement) M on A to obtain outcome μ and sends A to the adversary. We require that no polynomially-bounded adversary given register A can output *any* preimage x' of y such that $M(x') \neq M(\mu)$ (except with negligible probability)[3].

Certified Everlasting Target-Collapsing. In order to show PVD, instead of directly relying on target-collapsing (which only considers computationally bounded adversaries), we introduce a stronger notion that we call *certified everlasting* target-collapsing. This considers the following experiment: as before, the challenger prepares a superposition of preimages of a random image y of f on register A. After this, the challenger tosses a random coin c. If $c = 0$, it does nothing to A, otherwise it applies measurement M to A. The register A is returned to the adversary, after which the adversary is required to return a pre-image of y as its "deletion certificate". While such a certificate can be obtained via an honest measurement of the register A, the *certified everlasting target-collapsing* property requires that the following *everlasting* security guarantee hold. As long as the adversary is computationally bounded at the time of generating a valid deletion certificate, verification of this certificate implies that the bit c is *information-theoretically* erased from the adversary's view, and cannot be recovered even given unbounded resources. That is, if the adversary indeed returns a valid pre-image, they will never be able to guess whether or not the challenger applied measurement M.

New Constructions and Theorems

Main Theorem. Now, we are ready to state the main theorem of our paper. In a nutshell, this says that any (hash) function f that satisfies both target-collapsing and (generalized) target-collision resistance also satisfies *certified everlasting* target-collapsing.

---

[3] We remark that this notion can also be seen as a generalization of "conversion hardness" defined in [14].

Theorem 1. *(Informal). If f satisfies target-collapsing and generalized target-collision-resistance with respect to measurement M, then f satisfies* certified everlasting target-collapsing *with respect to the measurement M.*

We also extend recent results from the collapsing literature [11,12,30] to show that for the case of binary-outcome (in fact, polynomial-outcome) measurements M, generalized TCR with respect to M actually implies target-collapsing with respect to M. Thus, we obtain the following corollary.

Corollary 1. *(Informal). If f satisfies generalized target-collision-resistance with respect to a* binary-outcome *measurement M, then f satisfies* certified everlasting target-collapsing *with respect to the measurement M.*

Resolving the Strong Gaussian Collapsing Conjecture [21]. We now apply the main theorem and its corollary to build various cryptographic primitives with PVD. First, we immediately **prove** the following "strong Gaussian-collapsing"[4] conjecture from [21], which essentially conjectures that the Ajtai hash function (based on the hardness of SIS) satisfies a certain form of key-leakage security after deletion. This follows from our main theorem because the Ajtai hash function is known to be collapsing [19,21] and collision-resistant (which implies that it is target-collapsing and target-collision-resistant when preimages are sampled from the Gaussian distribution).

Conjecture 1 (Strong Gaussian-Collapsing Conjecture, [21]).
There exist parameters $n, m, q \in \mathbb{N}$ with $m \geq 2$ and $\sigma > 0$ such that, for every efficient quantum algorithm $\mathcal{A}$, it holds that

$$\Big| \Pr[\mathsf{StrongGaussCollapseExp}_{\mathcal{A},n,m,q,\sigma}(0) = 1] -$$
$$\Pr[\mathsf{StrongGaussCollapseExp}_{\mathcal{A},n,m,q,\sigma}(1) = 1] \Big| \leq \mathrm{negl}(\lambda)$$

with respect to the experiment defined in Fig. 1.

This conjecture, from [21] considers a slightly weaker notion of certified collapsing which resembles the notion of certified deletion first proposed by Broadbent and Islam [9]. Here, the adversary is not computationally unbounded once a valid deletion certificate is produced; instead, the challenger simply reveals some additional secret information (in the case of the strong Gaussian-collapsing experiment, the challenger reveals a short trapdoor vector for the Ajtai hash function[5]).

---

[4] Here, "Gaussian" refers to a quantum superposition of Gaussian-weighted vectors, where the distribution assigns probability proportional to $\rho_\sigma(\mathbf{x}) = \exp(-\pi \|\mathbf{x}\|^2 / \sigma^2)$ for vectors $\mathbf{x} \in \mathbb{Z}^m$ and parameter $\sigma > 0$.

[5] In the strong Gaussian-collapsing experiment it is crucial that the trapdoor is only revealed after a valid certificate is presented; otherwise, the adversary can easily distinguish the collapsed from the non-collapsed world by applying the Fourier transform and using the trapdoor to distinguish LWE samples from uniformly random vectors [21].

StrongGaussCollapseExp$_{\mathcal{A},n,m,q,\sigma}(b)$:

1. The challenger samples $\bar{\mathbf{A}} \xleftarrow{\$} \mathbb{Z}_q^{n \times (m-1)}$ and prepares the Gaussian state

$$|\psi\rangle_{XY} = \sum_{\mathbf{x} \in \mathbb{Z}_q^m} \rho_\sigma(\mathbf{x}) |\mathbf{x}\rangle_X \otimes |\mathbf{A} \cdot \mathbf{x} \ (\mathrm{mod} \ q)\rangle_Y,$$

   where $\mathbf{A} = [\bar{\mathbf{A}} \ \| \ \bar{\mathbf{A}} \cdot \bar{\mathbf{x}} \ (\mathrm{mod} \ q)] \in \mathbb{Z}_q^{n \times m}$ is a matrix with $\bar{\mathbf{x}} \xleftarrow{\$} \{0,1\}^{m-1}$.
2. The challenger measures Y in the computational basis, resulting in

$$|\psi_{\mathbf{y}}\rangle_{XY} = \sum_{\substack{\mathbf{x} \in \mathbb{Z}_q^m: \\ \mathbf{A}\mathbf{x}=\mathbf{y} \ (\mathrm{mod} \ q)}} \rho_\sigma(\mathbf{x}) |\mathbf{x}\rangle_X \otimes |\mathbf{y}\rangle_Y.$$

3. If $b = 0$, the challenger does nothing. Else, if $b = 1$, the challenger measures system X in the computational basis. The challenger then sends system X to $\mathcal{A}$, together with the matrix $\mathbf{A} \in \mathbb{Z}_q^{n \times m}$ and the string $\mathbf{y} \in \mathbb{Z}_q^n$.
4. $\mathcal{A}$ sends a classical witness $\mathbf{w} \in \mathbb{Z}_q^m$ to the challenger.
5. The challenger checks if $\mathbf{w}$ satisfies $\mathbf{A} \cdot \mathbf{w} = \mathbf{y} \ (\mathrm{mod} \ q)$ and $\|\mathbf{w}\| \leq \sigma\sqrt{m/2}$. If true, the challenger sends the trapdoor vector $\mathbf{t} = (\bar{\mathbf{x}}, -1) \in \mathbb{Z}^m$ to $\mathcal{A}$, where $\mathbf{A} \cdot \mathbf{t} = \mathbf{0} \ (\mathrm{mod} \ q)$. Else, the challenger outputs a random bit $b' \leftarrow \{0,1\}$ and the game ends.
6. $\mathcal{A}$ returns a bit b', which is retured as the output of the experiment.

Fig. 1. The strong Gaussian-collapsing experiment [21].

Following results from [21], we obtain the following cryptosystems with PVD, for the first time from standard cryptographic assumptions.

Theorem 2. *(Informal) Assuming the hardness of* LWE *and* SIS *with appropriate parameters, there exists public-key encryption and (leveled) fully-homomorphic encryption with* PVD.

Next, we ask whether one necessarily needs to rely on concrete, highly structured assumptions such as LWE in order to achieve publicly-verifiable deletion, or whether weaker generic assumptions suffice. We present a more general approach to building primitives with PVD from weaker, generic assumptions.

Commitments with PVD *from Regular One-Way Functions.* We first formulate the notion of a *balanced binary-measurement* TCR hash, which is any function that is TCR with respect to some appropriately balanced binary-outcome measurement. By balanced, we mean that the set of preimages of a random image will have significant weight on preimages that correspond to both measurement outcomes (this will roughly be required to guarantee the binding property of our commitment/correctness properties of our encryption schemes). By roughly following the template described above, we show that such hashes generically imply commitments with PVD. Next, we show that such "balanced" functions can be based on (almost-)regular one-way functions[6] By carefully instantiating this outline, we obtain the following results.

Theorem 3. *(Informal). Assuming the existence of almost-regular one-way functions, there exists a balanced binary-outcome TCR hash, and consequently there exist commitments with PVD.*

Public-Key Encryption with PVD from Regular Trapdoor Functions. Next, we take this framework to the public-key setting, showing that any balanced binary-outcome TCR hash with an additional "trapdoor" property generically implies a public-key encryption scheme with PVD. The additional property roughly requires the existence of a trapdoor for f that enables recovering the phase term from the quantum commitments discussed above: we call this *trapdoor phase-recoverability.* We show that balanced binary-outcome TCR, with trapdoor phase-recoverability, can be based on injective trapdoor one-way functions or pseudorandom group actions (the latter builds on [14]).

Theorem 4. *(Informal). Assuming the existence of injective trapdoor one-way functions or pseudorandom group actions, there exists a balanced binary-outcome TCR hash with trapdoor phase-recoverability, and consequently there exists public-key encryption with PVD.*

We also show that injectivity requirement on the trapdoor function can be further relaxed to a notion of "superposition-invertible" trapdoor regular one-way function for the results above. Informally, this is a regular one-way function, where a trapdoor allows one to obtain a uniform superposition over all preimages of a given image. This is an example of a *generic assumption* that is not known to, and perhaps is unlikely to, imply classical public-key encryption – but does imply PKE with quantum ciphertexts, and in fact even one that supports PVD. The only other assumption in this category is the concrete assumption that pseudorandom group actions exist [14].

Theorem 5. *(Informal). Assuming the existence of superposition-invertiable regular trapdoor functions, there exists a balanced binary-outcome TCR hash with trapdoor phase-recoverability and consequently, there exists public-key encryption with PVD.*

Advanced Encryption with PVD from Weak Assumptions Finally, we show that hybrid encryption gives rise to a generic compiler for encryption with PVD, obtaining the following results.

---

[6] This is a generalization of regular one-way functions where preimage sets for different images should be polynomially related in size.

Theorem 6. *(Informal). Assuming the existence of injective trapdoor one-way functions or pseudorandom group actions, and $X \in \{attribute\text{-}based\ encryption,\ quantum\ fully\text{-}homomorphic\ encryption,\ witness\ encryption,\ timed\text{-}release encryption\}$, there exists X with* PVD.

Prior to this work, while there existed encryption schemes with PVD from non-standard assumptions such as one-shot signatures [17], conjectured strong collapsing [21] or post-quantum indistinguishability obfuscation [7], no basic or advanced cryptosystems supporting PVD were known from standard assumptions. We provide a more detailed overview of prior work below.

1.2   Prior Work

The first notion resembling *certified deletion* was introduced by Unruh [27] who proposed a (private-key) quantum timed-release encryption scheme that is *revocable*, i.e. it allows a user to *return* the ciphertext of a quantum timed-release encryption scheme, thereby losing all access to the data. Unruh's scheme uses conjugate coding [8,28] and relies on the *monogamy of entanglement* in order to guarantee that revocation necessarily erases information about the plaintext. Broadbent and Islam [9] introduced the notion of *certified deletion* and constructed a private-key quantum encryption scheme with the aforementioned feature which is inspired by the quantum key distribution protocol [8,24]. In contrast with Unruh's [27] notion of revocable quantum ciphertexts which are eventually returned and verified, Broadbent and Islam [9] consider certificates which are entirely classical. Moreover, the security definition requires that, once the certificate is successfully verified, the plaintext remains hidden even if the secret key is later revealed. Inspired by the notion of quantum copy-protection [1], Ananth and La Placa [4] defined a form of quantum software protection called *secure software leasing* whose anti-piracy notion requires that the encoded program is returned and verified.

Using a hybrid encryption scheme, Hiroka, Morimae, Nishimaki and Yamakawa [17] extended the scheme in [9] to both public-key and attribute-based encryption with privately-verifiable certified deletion via *receiver non-committing encryption* [10,18]. Hiroka, Morimae, Nishimaki and Yamakawa [16] considered *certified everlasting zero-knowledge proofs* for QMA via the notion of *everlasting security* which was first formalized by Müller-Quade and Unruh [20]. Bartusek and Khurana [6] revisited the notion of certified deletion and presented a unified approach for how to generically convert any public-key, attribute-based, fully-homomorphic, timed-release or witness encryption scheme into an equivalent quantum encryption scheme with certified deletion. In particular, they considered a stronger notion called *certified everlasting security* which allows the adversary to be computationally unbounded once a valid deletion certificate is submitted. This is also the definition we consider in this work. In the same spirit, Hiroka, Morimae, Nishimaki and Yamakawa [15] gave a *certified everlasting* functional encryption scheme which allows the receiver of the ciphertext to obtain the outcome specific function applied the plaintext, but nothing else. In other very recent work, Ananth, Poremba and Vaikuntanathan [5] used Gaussian superpositions to construct (key)-revocable cryptosystems, such as public-key encryption, fully homomorphic encryption and pseudorandom functions assuming the hardness of LWE, and Agarwal et al. [2] introduced a generic compiler for adding key-revocability to a variety of cryptosystems. In these systems, the cryptographic key consists of a quantum state which can later be *certifiably revoked* via a quantum channel – in contrast with the classical deletion certificates for ciphertexts considered in this work.

Cryptosystems with Publicly Verifiable Deletion. First, in addition to their results in the setting of private verification, [17] also gave a public-key encryption scheme with certified deletion which is *publicly verifiable* assuming the existence of one-shot signatures (which rely on strong black-box notions of obfucation) and extractable witness encryption. Using *Gaussian superpositions*, Poremba [21] proposed *Dual-Regev*-based public-key and fully homomorphic encryption schemes with certified deletion which are publicly verifiable and proven secure assuming the (then unproven) *strong Gaussian-collapsing conjecture* — a strengthening of the collapsing property of the Ajtai hash. Finally, a recent work [7] relies on post-quantum indistinguishability obfuscation (iO) to obtain both publicly verifiable deletion and publicly verifiable key revocation. This is a strong assumption for which we have candidates, but no constructions based on standard (post-quantum) assumptions at this time.

2   Technical Overview

In this overview, we begin by discussing the key ideas involved in proving our main theorem. We show how to prove publicly verifiable deletion for a toy protocol that relies on stronger assumptions than the ones that we actually rely on in our actual technical sections.

Next, we progressively relax these assumptions to instantiate broader frameworks, including the one from [21], obtaining public-key encryption and fully-homomorphic encryption with PVD from LWE/SIS.

Finally, we further generalize this to enable constructions from weak cryptographic assumptions – including commitments with PVD from variants of one-way functions and PKE with PVD from trapdoored variants of the same assumption. We also discuss a hybrid approach that enables a variety of advanced encryption schemes supporting PVD.

2.1   Proving Our Main Theorem

Consider the toy commitment

$$\mathsf{Com}(b) = \big(y, |0, x_0\rangle + (-1)^b |1, x_1\rangle\big)$$

where $(0, x_0), (1, x_1)$ are preimages of y under a structured two-to-one function f, where every image has a preimage that begins with a 0 and another that begins with a 1. We note that this commitment can be efficiently prepared by first preparing a superposition over all preimages

$$\sum_{b\in\{0,1\},x\in\{0,1\}^\lambda} |b,x\rangle$$

on a register X, then writing the output of f applied on X to register Y, and finally measuring the contents of register Y to obtain image y. The register X contains $|0,x_0\rangle + |1,x_1\rangle$, which can be converted to $|0,x_0\rangle + (-1)^b|1,x_1\rangle$ via (standard) phase kickback.

To show that the commitment satisfies publicly-verifiable deletion, we consider an adversary $\mathcal{A} = (\mathcal{A}_1, \mathcal{A}_2)$ where $\mathcal{A}_1$ is (quantum) polynomial time and $\mathcal{A}_2$ is unbounded, participating in the following experiment.

- The challenger samples $b \leftarrow \{0,1\}$ and runs $\mathsf{Expmt}_0(b)$, described below.
  $\underline{\mathsf{Exmpt}_0(b)}$:
    1. Prepare $\left(|0,x_0\rangle + (-1)^b|1,x_1\rangle, y\right)$ on registers A, B and send them to $\mathcal{A}_1$.
    2. $\mathcal{A}_1$ outputs a (classical) deletion certificate γ,[7] and left-over state ρ.
    3. If $f(\gamma) \neq y$, output a uniformly random bit $b' \leftarrow \{0,1\}$, otherwise output $b' = \mathcal{A}_2(\rho)$.
- The advantage of $\mathcal{A}$ is defined to be $\mathsf{Adv}_{\mathcal{A}}^{\mathsf{Expmt}_0} = \left| \Pr[b' = b] - \frac{1}{2} \right|$.

We discuss how to prove the following.

Claim. (Informal). For every $\mathcal{A} = (\mathcal{A}_1, \mathcal{A}_2)$ where $\mathcal{A}_1$ is (quantum) computationally bounded,

$$\mathsf{Adv}_{\mathcal{A}}^{\mathsf{Expmt}_0} = \mathrm{negl}(\lambda),$$

as long as f is target collapsing and target collision-resistant w.r.t. a computational basis measurement of the pre-image register.

Overview of the Proof of Claim 2.1. To prove this claim, we must show that b is information-theoretically *removed* from the leftover state of any $\mathcal{A}_1$ that generates a valid pre-image of y, despite the fact that the adversary's view contains b at the beginning of the experiment.

Proof techniques for this type of experiment were recently introduced in [6] in the context of *privately verifiable deletion* via BB84 states. Inspired by their method, our first step is to defer the dependence of the experiment on the bit b. In more detail, we will instead imagine sampling the distribution by guessing a uniformly random $c \leftarrow \{0,1\}$, and initializing the adversary with $(|x_0\rangle + (-1)^c|x_1\rangle, y)$. The challenger later obtains input b and aborts the experiment (outputs $\perp$) if $c \neq b$. Since c was a uniformly random guess, the trace distance between the $b = 0$ and $b = 1$ outputs of this modified experiment is at least half the trace distance between the outputs of the original experiment.

---

[7] If the $\mathcal{A}_1$ outputs a quantum state as their certificate, the state is measured in the computational basis to obtain a classical certificate γ.

Moreover, we can further delay the process of obtaining input b, and then abort or not until *after* the adversary outputs a certificate of deletion. That is, we can consider a *purification* where a register C contains a superposition $|0\rangle + |1\rangle$ of two choices for c, and is later measured to determine bit c. This experiment is discussed in detail below.

$\underline{\mathsf{Expmt}_1(b)}$: The experiment proceeds as follows.

1. Prepare the $|+\rangle$ state on an ancilla register C, and a superposition of preimages $|x_0\rangle + |x_1\rangle$ of a random y on register A.
2. Then, controlled on the contents of register C, do the following: if the control bit is 0, do nothing, and otherwise flip the phase on x_1 (via phase kickback), changing the contents of A to $|x_0\rangle - |x_1\rangle$. This means that the overall state is

$$\frac{1}{\sqrt{2}} \sum_{c \in \{0,1\}} |c\rangle_C \otimes |0, x_0\rangle_A + (-1)^c |1, x_1\rangle_A$$

Send A to $\mathcal{A}_1$.
3. Obtain from $\mathcal{A}_1$ a purported certificate of deletion γ.
4. If $f(\gamma) \neq y$, abort, and otherwise measure register C to obtain output c, and abort if $c \neq b$. In the case of abort, output a uniformly random bit $b' \leftarrow \{0, 1\}$.
5. If no aborts occurred, output $b' = \mathcal{A}_2(\rho)$.

We note that the event $c = b$ occurs with probability exactly $\frac{1}{2}$, and since measurements on separate subsystems commute, we have that

$$\mathsf{Adv}_{\mathcal{A}}^{\mathsf{Expmt}_1} \geq \frac{1}{2} \mathsf{Adv}_{\mathcal{A}}^{\mathsf{Expmt}_0}. \tag{1}$$

where $\mathsf{Adv}_{\mathcal{A}}^{\mathsf{Expmt}_1} = \left| \Pr[\mathsf{Expmt}_1(b) = b] - \frac{1}{2} \right|$ for $b \leftarrow \{0, 1\}$.

Once the dependence of the experiment on b has been deferred, as above, we can consider another experiment (described below) where the challenger measures the contents of register A *before* sending it to $\mathcal{A}_1$. Intuitively, performing this measurement *removes* information about b from $\mathcal{A}_1$'s view in a manner that is computationally undetectable by $\mathcal{A}_1$ (due to the target-collapsing property of f).

$\underline{\mathsf{Expmt}_2(b)}$: The experiment proceeds as follows.

– Prepare the $|+\rangle$ state on an ancilla register C, and a superposition of preimages $|x_0\rangle + |x_1\rangle$ of a random y on register A. *Next, measure register A in the computational basis.*

  Then, controlled on the contents of register C, do the following: if the control bit is 0, do nothing, and otherwise flip the phase on x_1. This means that the overall state is a uniform mixture of the states

$$\frac{1}{\sqrt{2}} \sum_{c \in \{0,1\}} |c\rangle_C \otimes |0, x_0\rangle_A \text{ and } \frac{1}{\sqrt{2}} \sum_{c \in \{0,1\}} (-1)^c |c\rangle_C \otimes |1, x_1\rangle_A$$

Finally, send A to $\mathcal{A}_1$.
- Obtain from $\mathcal{A}_1$ a purported certificate of deletion γ.
- If $f(\gamma) \neq y$, abort, otherwise measure register C to obtain output c, and abort if $c \neq b$. In the case of abort, output a uniformly random bit $b' \leftarrow \{0,1\}$.
- If no aborts occurred, output $b' = \mathcal{A}_2(\rho)$.

As described above, the target-collapsing property of f implies that $\mathcal{A}_1$ cannot (computationally) distinguish the register A obtained in $\mathsf{Expmt}_2(b)$ from the one obtained in $\mathsf{Expmt}_1(b)$. However, this is not immediately helpful: information about which experiment $\mathcal{A}_1$ participated in could potentially be encoded into $\mathcal{A}_1$'s left-over state ρ, so that it remains computationally hidden from $\mathcal{A}_1$ but can be extracted by (unbounded) $\mathcal{A}_2$. And it is after all the output of $\mathcal{A}_2$ that determines the advantage of $\mathcal{A}$. Because of $\mathcal{A}_2$ being unbounded and the experiments only being *computationally* indistinguishable, even if we could show that $\mathsf{Adv}_{\mathcal{A}}^{\mathsf{Expmt}_2} = \mathrm{negl}(\lambda)$, it is unclear how to use this to show our desired claim, i.e., $\mathsf{Adv}_{\mathcal{A}}^{\mathsf{Expmt}_0} = \mathrm{negl}(\lambda)$. It may appear that the proof is stuck.

To overcome this issue, we will aim to identify an *efficiently computable predicate* of the challenger's system, which will *imply* the following (inefficient) property: when $\mathcal{A}_1$ outputs a valid deletion certificate, even an unbounded $\mathcal{A}_2$ cannot determine whether it participated in $\mathsf{Expmt}_1(b)$ or $\mathsf{Expmt}_2(b)$, i.e., $\mathcal{A}_1$'s left-over state is information-theoretically independent of b.

Identifying an Efficiently Computable Predicate. Observe that in $\mathsf{Expmt}_2(b)$, the ancilla register C is *unentangled* with the rest of the experiment. In fact, the ancilla register is exactly $|+\rangle$ when we give the adversary $|0, x_0\rangle$ on register A, and $|-\rangle$ when we give the adversary $|1, x_1\rangle$ on register A. Moreover, in $\mathsf{Expmt}_2(b)$, the target-collision-resistance of f implies that the computationally-bounded $\mathcal{A}_1$ given x_0 cannot output x_1 as their deletion certificate (and vice-versa).

This, along with the fact that the certificate *must* be a pre-image of y means that the following guarantee holds (except with negligible probability) in $\mathsf{Expmt}_2(b)$:

> When the adversary outputs a valid certificate γ, a projection of the pre-image register onto $|+\rangle$ succeeds if $\gamma = (0, x_0)$ and a projection of the pre-image register onto $|-\rangle$ succeeds if $\gamma = (1, x_1)$.

At this point, we can rely on the target-collapsing property of f to prove the following claim: the *efficient projection* described above also succeeds except with negligible probability in $\mathsf{Expmt}_1(b)$, when the adversary generates a valid deletion certificate. If this claim is not true, then since the experiments (including $\mathcal{A}_1$) run in quantum polynomial time until the point that the deletion certificate is generated, and the projection is efficient, one can build a reduction that contradicts target-collapsing of f. This reduction obtains a challenge (which is either a superposition when the challenger did not measure, or a mixture if the challenger did measure) on register A, prepares ancilla C as in $\mathsf{Expmt}_1(b)$, then follows steps 2, 3 identically to $\mathsf{Expmt}_1(b)$. Next, given a deletion certificate (β, x_β), the reduction projects C onto $|0\rangle + (-1)^\beta |1\rangle$, outputting 1 if the projection succeeds and 0 otherwise.

Introducing an Alternative Experiment. Having established that the projection above must succeed in $\mathsf{Expmt}_1(b)$ except with negligible probability, we can now consider an alternative experiment $\mathsf{Expmt}_{\mathsf{alt}}(b)$. This is identical to $\mathsf{Expmt}_1(b)$, except that the challenger *additionally* projects register C onto $|0\rangle + (-1)^{\beta}|1\rangle$ when the adversary generates a valid certificate (β, x_{β}). We established above that the projection is successful in $\mathsf{Expmt}_1(b)$ except with negligible probability, and this implies that

$$\mathsf{Adv}_{\mathcal{A}}^{\mathsf{Expmt}_{\mathsf{alt}}} \geq \mathsf{Adv}_{\mathcal{A}}^{\mathsf{Expmt}_1} - \mathsf{negl}(\lambda) \tag{2}$$

where as before, $\mathsf{Adv}_{\mathcal{A}}^{\mathsf{Expmt}_{\mathsf{alt}}} = \left| \Pr[\mathsf{Expmt}_{\mathsf{alt}}(b) = b] - \frac{1}{2} \right|$ for $b \leftarrow \{0, 1\}$.

Crucially, in $\mathsf{Expmt}_{\mathsf{alt}}(b)$, the bit c is determined by a measurement on register C which is *unentangled* with the system and in either the $|+\rangle$ or $|-\rangle$ state (due to the projective measurement that we just applied). Thus, measuring C in the computational basis results in a uniformly random and independent c. By definition of the experiment (abort when $b \neq c$, continue otherwise) – this implies that the bit b is set in a way that is uniformly random and independent of the adversary's view, and thus

$$\mathsf{Adv}_{\mathcal{A}}^{\mathsf{Expmt}_{\mathsf{alt}}} = 0 \tag{3}$$

Now, Eq. (1, 2, 3) together yield the desired claim, that is, $\mathsf{Adv}_{\mathcal{A}}^{\mathsf{Expmt}_0} = \mathsf{negl}(\lambda)$.

This completes a simplified overview of our key ideas, assuming the existence of a perfectly 2-to-1 function f where every image y has preimages $((0, x_0), (1, x_1))$, and where f satisfies both target-collapsing and target-collision-resistance. Unfortunately, we do not know how to build functions satisfying these clean properties from simple generic assumptions. Instead, we will generalize the template above, where the first generalization will no longer require f be 2-to-1.

Generalizing the Template. First, note that we can replace $|0, x_0\rangle$ and $|1, x_1\rangle$ with superpositions over two disjoint sets of preimages of y separated via an efficient binary-outcome measurement, namely

$$\mathsf{Com}(b) = \sum_{x:f(x)=y,M(x)=0} |x\rangle + (-1)^b \sum_{x:f(x)=y,M(x)=1} |x\rangle$$

We can even consider measurements M that have arbitrarily many outcomes. Proof ideas described above also generalize almost immediately to show that for any M, Com satisfies PVD as long as f is target-collapsing and target-collision resistant w.r.t. M. In fact, we can generalize this even further (see our main results in the full version) to consider arbitrary (as opposed to uniform) distributions over pre-images, as well as to account for any auxiliary information that may be sampled together with the description of the hash function.

Certified Everlasting Target-Collapsing. As discussed in the results section, our actual technical proofs proceed in two parts. (1) Show that for any M, a function f that is target-collapsing and target-collision resistant w.r.t. M is also *certified everlasting* target-collapsing w.r.t. M, and (2) show that f being *certified everlasting* target-collapsing implies that Com satisfies publicly verifiable deletion.

Recall that *certified* everlasting target collapsing requires that an adversary that outputs a valid deletion certificate information-theoretically loses the bit b determining whether they received a superposition or a mixture of preimages. Our proof of certified everlasting target-collapsing follows analogously to the proof sketched above. In short, we defer measurement of a bit b which decides whether the adversary is given a superposition or a mixture, and then rely on target-collapsing and target-collision-resistance to argue that an efficient projection on the challenger's state (almost) always succeeds when the adversary outputs a valid certificate. We finally show that success of this projection implies that the adversary's state is information-theoretically independent of b.

The certified everlasting target-collapsing property almost immediately implies certified deletion security of Com via a hybrid argument:

- In Hyb_0, the adversary obtains register A containing

$$\mathsf{Com}(0) = \sum_{x:f(x)=y,M(x)=0} |x\rangle + \sum_{x:f(x)=y,M(x)=1} |x\rangle$$

- In Hyb_1, the measurement M is applied to A before sending it to the adversary.
- In Hyb_2, the adversary obtains register A containing

$$\mathsf{Com}(1) = \sum_{x:f(x)=y,M(x)=0} |x\rangle - \sum_{x:f(x)=y,M(x)=1} |x\rangle$$

The certified everlasting hiding property of f guarantees that all hybrids are statistically close when the adversary outputs a valid deletion certificate. Moreover, these experiments abort and output a random bit when the adversary does not output a valid certificate, and it is easy to show (by computational indistinguishability) that the probability of generating a valid certificate remains negligibly close between experiments.

TCR Implies Target-Collapsing for Polynomial-Outcome Measurements. We also show that when M has polynomially many possible outcomes, then TCR implies target-collapsing with respect to M. This follows from techniques that were recently developed in the literature on collapsing versus collision resistant hash functions [11,12,30]. In a nutshell, these works showed that any distinguisher that distinguishes mixtures from superpositions over preimages for an *adversarially chosen* image y, can be used to swap between pre-images, and therefore find a collision for y. We observe that their technique is agnostic to whether the image y is chosen randomly (in the targeted setting) or adversarially. Furthermore, it also extends to swapping superpositions over sets of pre-images to superpositions over other sets. These allow us to prove that TCR with respect to any polynomial-outcome measurement M implies target-collapsing with respect to M.

2.2 Publicly-Verifiable Deletion via Gaussian Superpositions

We revisit the *Dual-Regev* public-key and (leveled) fully homomorphic encryption schemes with publicly-verifiable deletion proposed by Poremba [21] and conjectured to be secure under the *strong Gaussian-collapsing property*. By applying our main theorem to the Ajtai hash function, we obtain a proof of the conjecture, which allows us to show the certified everlasting security of the aforementioned schemes assuming the hardness of the LWE assumption.

The constructions introduced in [21] exploit the the duality between LWE and SIS [23], and rely on the fact that one encode Dual-Regev ciphertexts via Gaussian superpositions. Below, we give a high-level sketch of the basic public-key construction.

- To generate a pair of keys (sk, pk), sample a random $\mathbf{A} \in \mathbb{Z}_q^{n \times (m+1)}$ together with a particular short trapdoor vector $\mathbf{t} \in \mathbb{Z}^{m+1}$ such that $\mathbf{A} \cdot \mathbf{t} = \mathbf{0} \pmod{q}$. Let pk $= \mathbf{A}$ and sk $= \mathbf{t}$.
- To encrypt a single bit $b \in \{0, 1\}$ using pk $= \mathbf{A}$, generate the following pair for a random $\mathbf{y} \in \mathbb{Z}_q^n$:

$$\mathsf{vk} \leftarrow (\mathbf{A}, \mathbf{y})$$
$$|\mathsf{CT}\rangle \leftarrow \sum_{\mathbf{s} \in \mathbb{Z}_q^n} \sum_{\mathbf{e} \in \mathbb{Z}_q^{m+1}} \rho_{q/\sigma}(\mathbf{e}) \, \omega_q^{-\langle \mathbf{s}, \mathbf{y} \rangle} |\mathbf{s}^\mathsf{T} \mathbf{A} + \mathbf{e}^\mathsf{T} + b \cdot (0, \dots, 0, \lfloor \tfrac{q}{2} \rfloor)\rangle,$$

where vk is a public verification key and $|\mathsf{CT}\rangle$ is the ciphertext for $\sigma > 0$.
- To decrypt $|\mathsf{CT}\rangle$ using sk, measure in the computational basis to obtain $\mathbf{c} \in \mathbb{Z}_q^{m+1}$, and output 0, if $\mathbf{c}^\mathsf{T} \cdot \mathsf{sk} \in \mathbb{Z}_q$ is closer to 0 than to $\lfloor \tfrac{q}{2} \rfloor$, and output 1, otherwise. Here sk $= \mathbf{t}$ is chosen such that $\mathbf{c}^\mathsf{T} \cdot \mathsf{sk}$ yields an approximation of $b \cdot \lfloor \tfrac{q}{2} \rfloor$ from which we can recover b.

To delete the ciphertext $|\mathsf{CT}\rangle$, perform a measurement in the Fourier basis. Poremba [21] showed that the Fourier transform of $|\mathsf{CT}\rangle$ results in the *dual* quantum state given by

$$|\widehat{\mathsf{CT}}\rangle = \sum_{\substack{\mathbf{x} \in \mathbb{Z}_q^{m+1}: \\ \mathbf{A}\mathbf{x} = \mathbf{y} \pmod{q}}} \rho_\sigma(\mathbf{x}) \, \omega_q^{\langle \mathbf{x}, b \cdot (0, \dots, 0, \lfloor \tfrac{q}{2} \rfloor) \rangle} |\mathbf{x}\rangle.$$

In other words, a Fourier basis measurement of $|\mathsf{CT}\rangle$ will necessarily erase all information about the plaintext $b \in \{0, 1\}$ and results in a *short* vector $\pi \in \mathbb{Z}_q^{m+1}$ such that $\mathbf{A} \cdot \pi = \mathbf{y} \pmod{q}$. To publicly verify a deletion certificate, simply check whether a certificate π is a solution to the (inhomogenous) SIS problem specified by vk $= (\mathbf{A}, \mathbf{y})$. Due to the hardness of the SIS problem, it is computationally difficult to produce a valid deletion certificate from $(\mathbf{A}, \mathbf{y})$ alone.

Our approach to proving certified everlasting security of the Dual-Regev public-key and fully-homomorphic encryption schemes with publicly-verifiable deletion in [21] is as follows. First, we observe that the Ajtai hash function is both target-collapsing and target-collision-resistant with respect to the discrete Gaussian distribution. Here, the former follows from LWE as a simple consequence of the *Gaussian-collapsing property* previously shown by Poremba [19,21], whereas the latter follows immediately from the quantum hardness of SIS. Thus, our main theorem implies that the Ajtai hash function is certified-everlasting target-collapsing. Finally, as a simple corollary of our theorem, we obtain a proof of the *strong Gaussian-collapsing conjecture* in [21], which we stated in Conjecture 1. We also note that the aforementioned conjecture considers a weaker notion of certified collapsing which resembles the notion of certified deletion first proposed by Broadbent and Islam [9]. Here, the adversary is not computationally unbounded once a valid deletion certificate is produced; instead, the challenger simply reveals additional secret information (in the case of the strong Gaussian-collapsing experiment, this is a short trapdoor vector for the Ajtai hash function). Our notion of certified everlasting target-collapsing is significantly stronger; in particular, it implies the weaker collapsing scenario considered by Poremba [21]. This follows from the fact that the security reduction can simply brute-force search for a short trapdoor solution for the Ajtai hash once it enters the phase in which it is allowed to be computationally unbounded. We exploit this fact in the proof of Conjecture 1.

2.3   Weakening Assumptions for Publicly-Verifiable Deletion

Next, we look for instantiations of the above template from *generic* cryptographic assumptions, as opposed to structured specific assumptions such as LWE. Here, all of our instantiations only require us to consider functions that are target-collision-resistant and target-collapsing w.r.t. binary-outcome measurements (and as discussed above, TCR implies certified-everlasting target-collapsing in this setting). In addition, for the case of commitments, in order for the commitment to satisfy binding[8], we require that there is a measurement that can distinguish

$$\sum_{x:f(x)=y,M(x)=0} |x\rangle + \sum_{x:f(x)=y,M(x)=1} |x\rangle$$

from

$$\sum_{x:f(x)=y,M(x)=0} |x\rangle - \sum_{x:f(x)=y,M(x)=1} |x\rangle$$

with probability δ for any constant $0 < \delta \leq 1$. For the case of public-key encryption, we similarly require that a trapdoor be able to recover the phase with

---

[8] We actually prove that a purification of the template commitment described above satisfies honest-binding [29]. Namely, the committer generates the state above but leaves registers containing the image y (and the key, if f is a keyed function) unmeasured, and holds on to these registers for the opening phase. It can later either open the commitment by sending these registers to a receiver, or request deletion, by measuring them and publishing y (and any keys for the function).

constant probability. We then resort to standard amplification techniques to boost correctness error from constant to (negligibly close to) 0. We note that this amplification would also work if the phase was recoverable with inverse-polynomial δ (as opposed to constant); however, we focus on constant δ because of simplicity, and because it suffices for our instantiations.

In the template above, we observe that a measurement can find the phase with inverse polynomial probability whenever the sets

$$\sum_{x:f(x)=y,M(x)=0} |x\rangle \quad \text{and} \quad \sum_{x:f(x)=y,M(x)=1} |x\rangle$$

are somewhat "balanced", i.e. for a random image y, for sets $S_0 = \{x : f(x) = y, M(x) = 0\}$ and $S_1 = \{x : f(x) = y, M(x) = 1\}$, we have that $\frac{|S_0|}{|S_1|}$ is a fixed constant. We show in ?? and ?? that commitments and PKE with PVD can be obtained from appropriate variants of TCR functions following this template.

Now, our goal is to build such TCR functions from generic assumptions. A natural idea would be to start with any one-way function f and compose it with a random two-to-one hash h defined on its range[9]. Then, any output y of the composed function $(h \circ f)$ is associated with two elements $\{z_0, z_1\} = h^{-1}(y)$ in the range of f, and the binary-outcome measurement would measure one of z_0 or z_1. Recalling that we eventually want to prove target-collision-resistance, the hope would be that just given a superposition over the preimages of, say, z_0, the one-wayness of f would imply the difficulty of finding a preimage of z_1[10]. This could give the type of TCR property we need.

Technical Bottlenecks, and a Resolution. Unfortunately, there are two issues with the approach proposed above. First, f may be extremely unbalanced, so that the relative sizes of the sets of preimages of two random points y_1, y_2, i.e. $|\{x : f(x) = y_1\}|$ and $|\{x : f(x) = y_2\}|$ in its image may have very different sizes, that are not polynomially related with each other. There may even be many points in the co-domain/range that have *zero* preimages (for a general OWF, we cannot guarantee that its image is equal to its range). A second related issue is that the above sketched reduction to one-wayness may not work. Let's say we choose h to be a two-to-one function defined by a random shift Δ, i.e. $h(x) = h(x \oplus \Delta)$. Then we are essentially asking that it be hard to invert a random *range* element of f, as opposed to $f(x)$ for a random *domain* element x, which is the standard one-wayness assumption.

We don't know how to make this approach work from arbitrary one-way functions, which we leave as an open question. Instead, we appeal to a result

---

[9] The *co-domain* of a function $f : \{0,1\}^n \to \{0,1\}^m$ is $\{0,1\}^m$, and we will also refer to this as the *range* of the function in this paper. The *image* is the set of all actual output values of f, i.e. the set $\{y : \exists x \text{ such that } f(x) = y\}$. The co-domain/range may in general be a superset of the image of a function.

[10] More concretely, a purported reduction to one-wayness when given challenge image z_1, can sample a random image z_0 with its preimages, then find h s.t. $h(z_0) = h(z_1)$, thereby using a TCR adversary to find a preimage of the given challenge z_1.

of [13], who in the classical context of building statistically hiding commitments, show the following result. By appropriately combining an (almost)-*regular*[11] one-way function with universal hash functions, it *is* possible to obtain a function f with exactly the required properties: sufficiently balanced, and one-way over its *range*. The former property means that an overwhelming fraction of range elements have similar-sized preimage sets, while the latter property says that an element y sampled randomly from the range of the function cannot be inverted except with negligible probability. This resolves both the difficulties above.

Given such a balanced function f, we apply a random two-to-one hash h defined by a shift Δ to the range of this f. We prove that this implies the flavor of target-collision-restistant hash that we need to construct commitments with PVD.

Public-Key Encryption with PVD. Next, we note that the construction above *also* yields a public-key encryption scheme, as long as there is a trapdoor that allows recovery of the phase b given the state

$$y, \quad \sum_{x:f(x)=y,M(x)=0} |x\rangle + (-1)^b \sum_{x:f(x)=y,M(x)=1} |x\rangle$$

We call this property "trapdoor phase-recoverability". We show that this property is achievable from generic assumptions, even those that are not known to imply classical PKE.

– Specifically, trapdoor phase-recoverability is implied by a trapdoored variant of (almost) regular one-way functions, for which a trapdoor to the function allows recovery of a uniform superposition over all preimages of any given image y. This then allows efficient projection onto $\sum_{x:f(x)=y,M(x)=0}|x\rangle +$ $(-1)^b \sum_{x:f(x)=y,M(x)=1}|x\rangle$ for any efficient M. We also note that this property is satisfied by any (standard) trapdoored injective function. But it is also satisfied by functions such as the Ajtai function that are not necessarily injective. Indeed, it is unclear how to build classical public-key encryption, or even PKE with classical ciphertexts, given a general trapdoor phase-recoverable function. Nevertheless, we formalize the above ideas in the full version of this article in order to build PKE schemes with quantum ciphertexts, that also support PVD.
– Additionally, we show that a recent public-key encryption scheme of [14] from pseudorandom group actions also satisfies trapdoor phase-recoverability: in fact, the decryption algorithm in [14] relies on recovering the phase from a similar superposition, given a trapdoor.

---

[11] An almost regular one-way function generalizes regular one-way functions to require only that for any two images y_1, y_2 of the function, the sizes of preimage sets of y_1, y_2 are polynomially related. In particular, injective functions, and (standard) regular functions also satisfy almost-regularity.

Hybrid Encryption with PVD. Finally, we observe that we can use any encryption scheme Enc to encrypt the trapdoor td associated with the above construction, and security will still hold. That is, if Enc is semantically-secure, then our techniques extend to show that a ciphertext of the form

$$y, \sum_{x:f(x)=y,M(x)=0} |x\rangle + (-1)^b \sum_{x:f(x)=y,M(x)=1} |x\rangle, \mathsf{Enc}(\mathsf{td})$$

where td is the trapdoor for f, still supports publicly-verifiable deletion of the bit b. Thus, our approach can be seen as a way to *upgrade* cryptographic schemes Enc with special properties to satisfy PVD. In particular, we prove that instantiating Enc appropriately with attribute-based encryption, fully-homomorphic encryption, witness encryption, or timed-release encryption gives us the same scheme supporting PVD.

2.4   Discussion and Directions for Future Work

Our work demonstrates a strong relationship between weak security properties of (trapdoored) one-way functions and publicly-verifiable deletion. In particular, previous work [21] conjectured that collapsing functions, which are a quantum strengthening of collision-resistant hashes, lead to cryptosystems with publicly-verifiable deletion. Besides proving this conjecture, we also show that collapsing/collision-resistance, which are considered stronger assumptions than one-wayness, are actually not necessary for PVD.

Indeed, weakenings called target-collapsing and generalized-target-collision-resistance, that can be obtained from (regular) variants of one-way functions, suffice for publicly-verifiable deletion. Analogously to their classical counterparts, we believe that these primitives will be of independent interest. Indeed, a natural question that this work leaves open is whether variants of these primitives that suffice for publicly-verifiable deletion can be based on *one-way functions* without the regularity constraint. It is also interesting to further understand relationships and implications between target-collision-resistance and target-collapsing, including when these properties may or may not imply each other. It may also be useful to understand if these weaker properties can suffice in place of stronger properties such as collapsing and collision-resistance in other contexts, including the design of post-quantum protocols.

Finally, note that we rely on trapdoored variants of these primitives to build public-key encryption schemes. Here too, in addition to obtaining PKE with PVD from any injective trapdoor one-way function (TDF), it becomes possible to relax assumptions to only require (almost)-regularity and trapdoor phase-recoverability – properties that can plausibly be achieved from weaker concrete assumptions than injective TDFs. These are new examples of complexity assumptions that yield public-key encryption with quantum ciphertexts, but may be too weak to obtain PKE with classical ciphertexts. It is an interesting question to further investigate the weakest complexity assumptions that may imply public-key encryption, with or without PVD.

3   Main Theorem: Certified Everlasting Target-Collapsing

In this section, we prove our main theorem.

3.1   Definitions

First, we present our definitions of target-collapsing and (generalized) target-collision-resistance. We parameterize our definitions by a distribution $\mathcal{D}$ over preimages and a measurement function $\mathcal{M}$. Note that when $\mathcal{M}$ is the identity function, the notion of $(\mathcal{D}, \mathcal{M})$-target-collapsing corresponds to a notion where the entire preimage register is measured in the computational basis. In this case we drop parameterization by $\mathcal{M}$ and just say $\mathcal{D}$-target-collapsing. Also, when $\mathcal{D}$ is the uniform distribution, we drop parameterization by $\mathcal{D}$ and just say $\mathcal{M}$-target-collapsing.

Definition 1 ($(\mathcal{D}, \mathcal{M})$-Target-Collapsing Hash Function). *Let $\lambda \in \mathbb{N}$ be the security parameter. A hash function family given by $\mathcal{H} = \{H_\lambda : \{0,1\}^{m(\lambda)} \to \{0,1\}^{n(\lambda)}\}_{\lambda \in \mathbb{N}}$ is $(\mathcal{D}, \mathcal{M})$-target-collapsing for some distribution $\mathcal{D} = \{D_\lambda\}_{\lambda \in \mathbb{N}}$ over $\{\{0,1\}^{m(\lambda)}\}_{\lambda \in \mathbb{N}}$ and family of functions $\mathcal{M} = \{\{M[h] : \{0,1\}^{m(\lambda)} \to \{0,1\}^{k(\lambda)}\}_{h \in H_\lambda}\}_{\lambda \in \mathbb{N}}$ if, for every QPT adversary $\mathcal{A} = \{\mathcal{A}_\lambda\}_{\lambda \in \mathbb{N}}$,*

$$| \Pr[\mathsf{TargetCollapseExp}_{\mathcal{H}, \mathcal{A}, \mathcal{D}, \mathcal{M}, \lambda}(0) = 1] -$$
$$\Pr[\mathsf{TargetCollapseExp}_{\mathcal{H}, \mathcal{A}, \mathcal{D}, \mathcal{M}, \lambda}(1) = 1]| \leq \mathrm{negl}(\lambda).$$

Here, the experiment $\mathsf{TargetCollapseExp}_{\mathcal{H}, \mathcal{A}, \mathcal{D}, \mathcal{M}, \lambda}(b)$ is defined as follows:

1. *The challenger prepares the state*

$$\sum_{x \in \{0,1\}^{m(\lambda)}} \sqrt{D_\lambda(x)} |x\rangle$$

   on register X, and samples a random hash function $h \xleftarrow{\$} H_\lambda$. Then, it coherently computes h on X (into a fresh $n(\lambda)$-qubit register Y) and measures system Y in the computational basis, which results in an outcome $y \in \{0,1\}^{n(\lambda)}$.
2. *If $b = 0$, the challenger does nothing. Else, if $b = 1$, the challenger coherently computes $M[h]$ on X (into a fresh $k(\lambda)$-qubit register V) and measures system V in the computational basis. Finally, the challenger sends the outcome state in system X to $\mathcal{A}_\lambda$, together with the string $y \in \{0,1\}^{n(\lambda)}$ and a description of the hash function h.*
3. *$\mathcal{A}_\lambda$ returns a bit b', which we define as the output of the experiment.*

We also define an analogous notion of $(\mathcal{D}, \mathcal{M})$-target-collision-resistance, as follows. Similarly to above, we drop the parameterization by $\mathcal{M}$ in the case that it is the identity function, and we drop the parameterization by $\mathcal{D}$ in the case that it is the uniform distribution. Notice that target-collision-resistance (without parameterization) then coincides with the classical notion where a uniformly random input is sampled, and the adversary must find a collision with respect to this input (this is also sometimes called second-preimage resistance, or weak collision-resistance).

Definition 2 ($(\mathcal{D}, \mathcal{M})$-Target-Collision-Resistant Hash Function). *A hash function family $\mathcal{H} = \{H_\lambda : \{0,1\}^{m(\lambda)} \to \{0,1\}^{n(\lambda)}\}_{\lambda \in \mathbb{N}}$ is $(\mathcal{D}, \mathcal{M})$-target-collision-resistant for some distribution $\mathcal{D} = \{D_\lambda\}_{\lambda \in \mathbb{N}}$ over $\{\{0,1\}^{m(\lambda)}\}_{\lambda \in \mathbb{N}}$ and family of functions $\mathcal{M} = \{\{M[h] : \{0,1\}^{m(\lambda)} \to \{0,1\}^{k(\lambda)}\}_{h \in H_\lambda}\}_{\lambda \in \mathbb{N}}$ if, for every QPT adversary $\mathcal{A} = \{\mathcal{A}_\lambda\}_{\lambda \in \mathbb{N}}$,*

$$|\Pr[\mathsf{TargetCollRes}_{\mathcal{H}, \mathcal{A}, \mathcal{D}, \mathcal{M}, \lambda} = 1]| \leq \mathrm{negl}(\lambda).$$

Here, the experiment $\mathsf{TargetCollRes}_{\mathcal{H}, \mathcal{A}, \mathcal{D}, \mathcal{M}, \lambda}$ is defined as follows:

1. *The challenger prepares the state*

$$\sum_{x \in \{0,1\}^{m(\lambda)}} \sqrt{D_\lambda(x)} |x\rangle$$

   on register X, and samples a random hash function $h \xleftarrow{\$} H_\lambda$. Next, it coherently computes h on X (into a fresh $n(\lambda)$-qubit system Y) and measures system Y in the computational basis, which results in an outcome $y \in \{0,1\}^{n(\lambda)}$. Next, it coherently computes $M[h]$ on X (into a fresh $k(\lambda)$-qubit register V) and measures system V in the computational basis, which results in an outcome v. Finally, its sends the outcome state in system X to $\mathcal{A}_\lambda$, together with the string $y \in \{0,1\}^{n(\lambda)}$ and a description of the hash function h.
2. *$\mathcal{A}_\lambda$ responds with a string $x \in \{0,1\}^{m(\lambda)}$.*
3. *The experiment outputs 1 if $h(x) = y$ and $M[h](x) \neq v$.*

Finally, we define the notion of a *certified everlasting* target-collapsing hash.

Definition 3. *A hash function family $\mathcal{H} = \{H_\lambda : \{0,1\}^{m(\lambda)} \to \{0,1\}^{n(\lambda)}\}_{\lambda \in \mathbb{N}}$ is certified everlasting $(\mathcal{D}, \mathcal{M})$-target-collapsing for some distribution $\mathcal{D} = \{D_\lambda\}_{\lambda \in \mathbb{N}}$ over $\{\{0,1\}^{m(\lambda)}\}_{\lambda \in \mathbb{N}}$ and family of functions $\mathcal{M} = \{\{M[h] : \{0,1\}^{m(\lambda)} \to \{0,1\}^{k(\lambda)}\}_{h \in H_\lambda}\}_{\lambda \in \mathbb{N}}$ if for every two-part adversary $\mathcal{A} = \{\mathcal{A}_{0,\lambda}, \mathcal{A}_{1,\lambda}\}_{\lambda \in \mathbb{N}}$, where $\{\mathcal{A}_{0,\lambda}\}_{\lambda \in \mathbb{N}}$ is QPT and $\{\mathcal{A}_{1,\lambda}\}_{\lambda \in \mathbb{N}}$ is unbounded, it holds that*

$$\left|\Pr\left[\mathsf{EvTargetCollapseExp}_{\mathcal{H}, \mathcal{A}, \mathcal{D}, \mathcal{M}, \lambda}(0) = 1\right] - \Pr\left[\mathsf{EvTargetCollapseExp}_{\mathcal{H}, \mathcal{A}, \mathcal{D}, \mathcal{M}, \lambda}(1) = 1\right]\right| \leq \mathrm{negl}(\lambda).$$

Here, the experiment $\mathsf{EvTargetCollapseExp}_{\mathcal{H}, \mathcal{A}, \mathcal{D}, \mathcal{M}, \lambda}(b)$ is defined as follows:

1. *The challenger prepares the state*

$$\sum_{x \in \{0,1\}^{m(\lambda)}} \sqrt{D_\lambda(x)} |x\rangle$$

   on register X, and samples a random hash function $h \xleftarrow{\$} H_\lambda$. Then, it coherently computes h on X (into a fresh $n(\lambda)$-qubit system Y) and measures system Y in the computational basis, which results in an outcome $y \in \{0,1\}^{n(\lambda)}$.

2. *If $b = 0$, the challenger does nothing. Else, if $b = 1$, the challenger coherently computes $M[h]$ on X (into an auxiliary $k(\lambda)$-qubit system V) and measures system V in the computational basis. Finally, the challenger sends the outcome state in system X to $\mathcal{A}_{0,\lambda}$, together with the string $y \in \{0,1\}^{n(\lambda)}$ and a description of the hash function h.*
3. *$\mathcal{A}_{0,\lambda}$ sends a classical certificate $\pi \in \{0,1\}^{m(\lambda)}$ to the challenger and initializes $\mathcal{A}_{1,\lambda}$ with its residual state.*
4. *The challenger checks if $h(\pi) = y$. If true, $\mathcal{A}_{1,\lambda}$ is run until it outputs a bit b'. Otherwise, $b' \leftarrow \{0,1\}$ is sampled uniformly at random. The output of the experiment is b'.*

3.2   Main Theorem

Our main theorem is the following.

Theorem 7. *Let $\mathcal{H} = \{H_\lambda\}_{\lambda \in \mathbb{N}}$ be a hash function family that is both $(\mathcal{D}, \mathcal{M})$-target-collapsing and $(\mathcal{D}, \mathcal{M})$-target-collision-resistant, for some distribution $\mathcal{D}$ and efficiently computable family of functions $\mathcal{M}$. Then, $\mathcal{H}$ is certified everlasting $(\mathcal{D}, \mathcal{M})$-target-collapsing.*

Proof. Throughout the proof, we will leave the security parameter implicit, defining $H := H_\lambda, D := D_\lambda, m := m(\lambda), n := n(\lambda), k := k(\lambda), \mathcal{A}_0 := \mathcal{A}_{0,\lambda}$, and $\mathcal{A}_1 := \mathcal{A}_{1,\lambda}$. Next, we define

$$|\psi\rangle_X := \sum_{x \in \{0,1\}^m} \sqrt{D(x)}|x\rangle.$$

For $h \in H, y \in \{0,1\}^m$, we define a unit vector

$$|\psi_{h,y}\rangle_X \propto \sum_{x \in \{0,1\}^m : h(x) = y} \sqrt{D(x)}|x\rangle.$$

Finally, for $h \in H, y \in \{0,1\}^m, v \in \{0,1\}^k$ we define a unit vector

$$|\psi_{h,y,v}\rangle_X \propto \sum_{x \in \{0,1\}^m : h(x) = y, M[h](x) = v} \sqrt{D(x)}|x\rangle.$$

We consider the following hybrids.

- $\mathsf{Exp}_0(b)$:
  1. The challenger prepares $|\psi\rangle_X$, samples a random hash function $h \xleftarrow{\$} H_\lambda$, coherently computes h on X into a fresh n-qubit register Y, and measures Y in the computational basis to obtain $y \in \{0,1\}^n$ and a left-over state $|\psi_{h,y}\rangle_X$.
  2. If $b = 0$, the challenger does nothing. Else, if $b = 1$, the challenger computes $M[h]$ on X into a fresh k-qubit register V, and measures V in the computational basis. Finally, the challenger sends the left-over state in system X to $\mathcal{A}_0$, together with the string $y \in \{0,1\}^n$ and a classical description of h.

3. $\mathcal{A}_0$ sends a classical certificate $\pi \in \{0,1\}^m$ to the challenger and initializes $\mathcal{A}_1$ with its residual state.
4. The challenger checks if $h(\pi) = y$. If true, $\mathcal{A}_1$ is run until it outputs a bit b'. Otherwise, $b' \leftarrow \{0,1\}$ is sampled uniformly at random. The output of the experiment is b'.

– $\mathsf{Exp}_1(b)$:

1. The challenger prepares $|\psi\rangle_X$, samples a random hash function $h \xleftarrow{\$} H_\lambda$, coherently computes h on X into a fresh n-qubit register Y, and measures Y in the computational basis to obtain $y \in \{0,1\}^n$ and a left-over state $|\psi_{h,y}\rangle_X$.
2. The challenger computes $M[h]$ on X into a fresh k-qubit register V to obtain a state

$$\propto \sum_{x \in \{0,1\}^m : h(x)=y} \sqrt{D(x)}|x\rangle_X |M[h](x)\rangle_V.$$

Then, the challenger samples a random string $z \xleftarrow{\$} \{0,1\}^k$, prepares a $|+\rangle$ state in system C, and applies a controlled-Z^z operation from C to V, which results in a state

$$\propto \sum_{c \in \{0,1\}} |c\rangle_C \otimes \sum_{x \in \{0,1\}^m : h(x)=y} \sqrt{D(x)}|x\rangle_X \mathsf{Z}^{c \cdot z}|M[h](x)\rangle_V$$

$$= \sum_{c \in \{0,1\}} |c\rangle_C \otimes \sum_{x \in \{0,1\}^m : h(x)=y} \sqrt{D(x)}(-1)^{c \cdot \langle M[h](x),z \rangle}|x\rangle_X |M[h](x)\rangle_V.$$

Finally, the challenger uncomputes the V register by again computing $M[h]$ from X to V, and sends system X to $\mathcal{A}_0$, together with $y \in \{0,1\}^n$ and a classical description of h.

3. $\mathcal{A}_0$ sends a classical certificate $\pi \in \{0,1\}^m$ to the challenger and initializes $\mathcal{A}_1$ with its residual state.
4. The challenger checks if $h(\pi) = y$. Then, the challenger measures system C to obtain $c' \in \{0,1\}$ and checks that $c' = b$. If both checks are true, $\mathcal{A}_1$ is run until it outputs a bit b'. Otherwise, $b' \leftarrow \{0,1\}$ is sampled uniformly at random. The output of the experiment is b'.

– $\mathsf{Exp}_2(b)$:

1. The challenger prepares $|\psi\rangle_X$, samples a random hash function $h \xleftarrow{\$} H_\lambda$, coherently computes h on X into a fresh n-qubit register Y, and measures Y in the computational basis to obtain $y \in \{0,1\}^n$ and a left-over state $|\psi_{h,y}\rangle_X$.
2. The challenger computes $M[h]$ on X into a fresh k-qubit register V. Then, the challenger samples a random string $z \xleftarrow{\$} \{0,1\}^k$, prepares a $|+\rangle$ state in system C, applies a controlled-Z^z operation from C to V, and finally uncomputes the V register by again computing $M[h]$ from X to V. Note that this results in a state

$$\propto \sum_{c\in\{0,1\}} |c\rangle_C \otimes \sum_{x\in\{0,1\}^m:h(x)=y} (-1)^{c\cdot\langle M[h](x),z\rangle} |x\rangle_X.$$

Finally, it sends system X to $\mathcal{A}_0$, together with $y \in \{0,1\}^n$ and a classical description of h.

3. $\mathcal{A}_0$ sends a classical certificate $\pi \in \{0,1\}^m$ and initializes $\mathcal{A}_1$ with its residual state.

4. The challenger checks if $h(\pi) = y$. Then, the challenger applies the following projective measurement to system C:

$$\left\{|\phi_\pi^z\rangle\langle\phi_\pi^z|, I - |\phi_\pi^z\rangle\langle\phi_\pi^z|\right\} \quad \text{where} \quad |\phi_\pi^z\rangle := \frac{1}{\sqrt{2}}\left(|0\rangle + (-1)^{\langle M[h](\pi),z\rangle}|1\rangle\right),$$

and checks that the first outcome is observed. Finally, the challenger measures system C to obtain $c' \in \{0,1\}$ and checks that $c' = b$. If all three checks are true, $\mathcal{A}_1$ is run until it outputs a bit b'. Otherwise, $b' \leftarrow \{0,1\}$ is sampled uniformly at random. The output of the experiment is b'.

Finally, we also use the following hybrid which is convenient for the sake of the proof.

– $\mathsf{Exp}_3(b)$:

1. The challenger prepares $|\psi\rangle_X$, samples a random hash function $h \xleftarrow{\$} H_\lambda$, coherently computes h on X into a fresh n-qubit register Y, and measures Y in the computational basis to obtain $y \in \{0,1\}^n$ and a left-over state $|\psi_{h,y}\rangle_X$.

2. The challenger computes $M[h]$ on X into a fresh k-qubit register V. Then, the challenger measures V in the computational basis to obtain $v \in \{0,1\}^k$. Next, the challenger samples a random string $z \xleftarrow{\$} \{0,1\}^k$, prepares a $|+\rangle$ state in system C, applies a controlled-Z^z operation from C to V, and finally uncomputes the V register by again computing $M[h]$ from X to V. Note that this results in the state

$$\frac{1}{\sqrt{2}}\left(|0\rangle_C + (-1)^{\langle v,z\rangle}|1\rangle_C\right) \otimes |\psi_{h,y,v}\rangle_X.$$

Finally, the challenger sends system X to $\mathcal{A}_0$, together with $y \in \{0,1\}^n$ and a classical description of h.

3. $\mathcal{A}_0$ sends a classical certificate $\pi \in \{0,1\}^m$ to the challenger and initializes $\mathcal{A}_1$ with its residual state.

4. The challenger checks if $h(\pi) = y$. Then, the challenger applies the following projective measurement to system C:

$$\left\{|\phi_\pi^z\rangle\langle\phi_\pi^z|, I - |\phi_\pi^z\rangle\langle\phi_\pi^z|\right\} \quad \text{where} \quad |\phi_\pi^z\rangle := \frac{1}{\sqrt{2}}\left(|0\rangle + (-1)^{\langle M[h](\pi),z\rangle}|1\rangle\right),$$

and checks that the first outcome is observed. Finally, the challenger measures system C to obtain $c' \in \{0,1\}$ and checks that $c' = b$. If all three checks are true, $\mathcal{A}_1$ is run until it outputs a bit b'. Otherwise, $b' \leftarrow \{0,1\}$ is sampled uniformly at random. The output of the experiment is b'.

Before we analyze the probability of distinguishing between the consecutive hybrids, we first show that the following statements hold for the final experiment $\mathsf{Exp}_3(b)$.

Claim. The probability that the challenger accepts the deletion certificate π in Step 4 of $\mathsf{Exp}_3(b)$ and $M[h](\pi) \neq v$ is negligible. That is,

$$\Pr_{h,y,v} [h(\pi) = y \ \wedge \ M[h](\pi) \neq v \ : \ \pi \leftarrow \mathcal{A}_0(h, y, |\psi_{h,y,v}\rangle)] \leq \mathsf{negl}(\lambda),$$

where the probability is over the challenger preparing $|\psi\rangle$, sampling h, and measuring y and v as described in $\mathsf{Exp}_3(b)$ to produce the left-over state $|\psi_{h,y,v}\rangle$.

Proof. This follows directly from the assumed $(\mathcal{D}, \mathcal{M})$-target-collision resistance of $\mathcal{H}$, since the above probability is exactly $\Pr[\mathsf{TargetCollRes}_{\mathcal{H},\mathcal{A},\mathcal{D},\mathcal{M},\lambda} = 1]$.

Claim. The probability that the challenger accepts the deletion certificate π in Step 4 of $\mathsf{Exp}_3(b)$ and the subsequent projective measurement on system C fails (returns the second outcome) is negligible.

Proof. This follows directly from Sect. 3.2, which implies that except with negligible probability, the register C is in the state

$$\frac{1}{\sqrt{2}} \left(|0\rangle + (-1)^{\langle v,z \rangle} |1\rangle \right)$$

at the time the challenger applies the projective measurement.

For any experiment $\mathsf{Exp}_i(b)$, we define the advantage

$$\mathsf{Adv}(\mathsf{Exp}_i) := | \Pr[\mathsf{Exp}_i(0) = 1] - \Pr[\mathsf{Exp}_i(1) = 1] |.$$

Claim.
$$\mathsf{Adv}(\mathsf{Exp}_2) = 0.$$

Proof. First note that in the case that the challenger rejects because either the deletion certificate is invalid or their projection fails, the experiment does not involve b, and thus the advantage of the adversary is 0. Second, in the case that the challenger's projection succeeds, the register C is either in the state

$$\frac{1}{\sqrt{2}}(|0\rangle + (-1)^{\langle \pi,z \rangle} |1\rangle) \quad \text{or} \quad \frac{1}{\sqrt{2}}(|0\rangle - (-1)^{\langle \pi,z \rangle} |1\rangle)$$

for some $z \in \{0,1\}^k$, and thereby completely unentangled from the rest of the system. Notice that the challenger's measurement of system C with outcome c' results in a uniformly random bit, which completely masks b. Therefore, the experiment is also independent of b in this case, and thus the adversary's overall advantage in Exp_2 is 0.

Next, we argue the following.

Claim.

$$|\mathsf{Adv}(\mathsf{Exp}_2) - \mathsf{Adv}(\mathsf{Exp}_1)| \leq \mathsf{negl}(\lambda).$$

Proof. Recall that Sect. 3.2 shows that the projective measurement performed by the challenger in Step 4 of Exp_3 succeeds with overwhelming probability. We now argue that the same is also true in Exp_2. Suppose for the sake of contradiction that there is a non-negligible difference between the success probabilities of the measurement. We now show that this implies the existence of an efficient distinguisher $\mathcal{A}'$ that breaks the $(\mathcal{D}, \mathcal{M})$-target-collapsing property of the hash family $\mathcal{H} = \{H_\lambda\}_{\lambda \in \mathbb{N}}$.

$\mathcal{A}'$ receives (y, h) and a state on register X from its challenger. Next, it computes $M[h]$ on X into a fresh k-qubit register V, samples a random string $z \xleftarrow{\$} \{0,1\}^k$, prepares a $|+\rangle$ state in system C, applies a controlled-Z^z operation from C to V, and then uncomputes register V by again applying $M[h]$ from X to V. Then, it runs $\mathcal{A}$ on (y, h, X), which outputs a certificate π.

Finally, $\mathcal{A}'$ applies the following projective measurement to system C:

$$\left\{ |\phi_\pi^z\rangle\langle\phi_\pi^z|, I - |\phi_\pi^z\rangle\langle\phi_\pi^z| \right\} \quad \text{where} \quad |\phi_\pi^z\rangle := \frac{1}{\sqrt{2}}\left(|0\rangle + (-1)^{\langle\pi, z\rangle}|1\rangle \right),$$

and outputs 1 if the measurement succeeds and 0 otherwise. If there is a non-negligible difference in success probabilities of this measurement between $\mathsf{Exp}_3(b)$ and $\mathsf{Exp}_2(b)$ (for any $b \in \{0,1\}$), then $\mathcal{A}'$ breaks $(\mathcal{D}, \mathcal{M})$-target-collapsing of $\mathcal{H}$.

Now, recall that $\mathsf{Exp}_2(b)$ is identical to $\mathsf{Exp}_1(b)$, except that the challenger applies an additional a measurement in Step 4. Because the measurement succeeds with overwhelming probability, it follows from Gentle Measurement that the advantage of the adversary must remain the same up to a negligible amount. This proves the claim.

Claim.

$$\mathsf{Adv}(\mathsf{Exp}_1) = \mathsf{Adv}(\mathsf{Exp}_0)/2.$$

Proof. First note that in $\mathsf{Exp}_1(b)$, we can imagine measuring register C to obtain c' and aborting if $c' \neq b$ before the challenger sends any information to the adversary. This follows because register C is disjoint from the adversary's registers. Next, by the random Pauli-Z twirl property, we have the following guarantees about the state on system X given to the adversary in $\mathsf{Exp}_1(b)$.

- In the case $c' = b = 0$, the reduced state on register X is $|\psi_{h,y}\rangle$.
- In the case that $c' = b = 1$, the reduced state on register X is a mixture over $|\psi_{h,y,v}\rangle$ where v is the result of measuring register V in the computational basis.

Thus, this experiment is identical to $\mathsf{Exp}_0(b)$, except that we decide to abort and output a uniformly random bit b' with probability $1/2$ at the beginning of the experiment.

Putting everything together, we have that $\mathsf{Adv}(\mathsf{Exp}_0) \leq \mathsf{negl}(\lambda)$, which completes the proof.

Acknowledgements. D.K. was supported in part by NSF CAREER CNS-2238718, NSF CNS-2247727 and DARPA SIEVE. This material is based upon work supported by the Defense Advanced Research Projects Agency through Award HR00112020024.

A.P. is partially supported by AFOSR YIP (award number FA9550-16-1-0495), the Institute for Quantum Information and Matter (an NSF Physics Frontiers Center; NSF Grant PHY-1733907) and by a grant from the Simons Foundation (828076, TV).

References

1. Aaronson, S.: Quantum copy-protection and quantum money. In: 2009 24th Annual IEEE Conference on Computational Complexity, pp. 229–242. IEEE (2009)
2. Agarwal, S., et al.: public key encryption with secure key leasing. In: Eurocrypt 2023 (to appear) (2023). https://doi.org/10.1007/978-3-031-30545-0_20
3. Ajtai, M.: Generating hard instances of lattice problems (extended abstract). In: Miller, G,L., (ed.) Proceedings of the Twenty-Eighth Annual ACM Symposium on the Theory of Computing, Philadelphia, Pennsylvania, USA, 22–24 May 1996, pp. 99–108. ACM (1996). https://doi.org/10.1145/237814.237838
4. Ananth, P., La Placa, R.L.: Secure software leasing. In: Canteaut, A., Standaert, F.-X. (eds.) EUROCRYPT 2021. LNCS, vol. 12697, pp. 501–530. Springer, Cham (2021). https://doi.org/10.1007/978-3-030-77886-6_17
5. Ananth, P., Poremba, A., Vaikuntanathan, V.: Revocable Cryptography from Learning with Errors. Cryptology ePrint Archive, Paper 2023/325 (2023). https://eprint.iacr.org/2023/325
6. Bartusek, J., Khurana, D.: Cryptography with Certified Deletion. Cryptology ePrint Archive, Paper 2022/1178 (2022). https://eprint.iacr.org/2022/1178
7. Bartusek, J., et al.: Obfuscation and Outsourced Computation with Certified Deletion. Cryptology ePrint Archive, Paper 2023/265. (2023). https://eprint.iacr.org/2023/265
8. Bennett, C.H., Brassard, G.: Quantum cryptography: Public key distribution and coin tossing. In: Proceedings of IEEE International Conference on Computers, Systems, and Signal Processing. Bangalore, p. 175 (1984)
9. Broadbent, A., Islam, R.: Quantum encryption with certified deletion. In: Pass, R., Pietrzak, K. (eds.) TCC 2020. LNCS, vol. 12552, pp. 92–122. Springer, Cham (2020). https://doi.org/10.1007/978-3-030-64381-2_4
10. Canetti, R., et al.: Adaptively secure multi-party computation. In: Proceedings of the Twenty-Eighth Annual ACM Symposium on Theory of Computing. STOC 1996, Philadelphia, Pennsylvania, USA, pp. 639–648. Association for Computing Machinery (1996). https://doi.org/10.1145/237814.238015, isbn: 0897917855
11. Cao, S., Xue, R.: The Gap Is Sensitive to Size of Preimages: Collapsing Property Doesn't Go Beyond Quantum Collision-Resistance for Preimages Bounded Hash Functions. Springer-Verlag (2022)
12. Dall'Agnol, M., Spooner, N.: On the necessity of collapsing. Cryptology ePrint Archive, Paper 2022/786 (2022). https://eprint.iacr.org/2022/786
13. Haitner, I., Horvitz, O., Katz, J., Koo, C.-Y., Morselli, R., Shaltiel, R.: Reducing complexity assumptions for statistically-hiding commitment. J. Cryptol. **22**(3), 283–310 (2007). https://doi.org/10.1007/s00145-007-9012-8

14. Hhan, M., Morimae, T., Yamakawa, T.: From the hardness of detecting super-positions to cryptography: quantum public key encryption and commitments. In: Eurocrypt 2023 (2023) (to appear). https://doi.org/10.1007/978-3-031-30545-0_22
15. Hiroka, et al.: Certified Everlasting Functional Encryption. Cryptology ePrint Archive, Paper 2022/969 (2022). https://eprint.iacr.org/2022/969
16. Hiroka. T., et al.: Certified everlasting zero-knowledge proof for QMA. In: Dodis, Y., Shrimpton, T., (eds.) Advances in Cryptology - CRYPTO 2022–42nd Annual International Cryptology Conference, CRYPTO 2022, Santa Barbara, CA, USA, 15–18 August 2022, Proceedings, Part I., vol. 13507. LNCS, pp. 239–268. Springer (2022). https://doi.org/10.1007/978-3-031-15802-5_9
17. Hiroka, T., Morimae, T., Nishimaki, R., Yamakawa, T.: Quantum encryption with certified deletion, revisited: public key, attribute-based, and classical communication. In: Tibouchi, M., Wang, H. (eds.) ASIACRYPT 2021. LNCS, vol. 13090, pp. 606–636. Springer, Cham (2021). https://doi.org/10.1007/978-3-030-92062-3_21
18. Jarecki, S., Lysyanskaya, A.: Adaptively secure threshold cryptography: introducing concurrency, removing erasures. In: Preneel, B. (ed.) EUROCRYPT 2000. LNCS, vol. 1807, pp. 221–242. Springer, Heidelberg (2000). https://doi.org/10.1007/3-540-45539-6_16
19. Liu, Q., Zhandry, M.: Revisiting Post-quantum Fiat-Shamir. In: Boldyreva, A., Micciancio, D. (eds.) CRYPTO 2019. LNCS, vol. 11693, pp. 326–355. Springer, Cham (2019). https://doi.org/10.1007/978-3-030-26951-7_12
20. Müller-Quade, J., Unruh, D.: Long-term security and universal composability. In: Vadhan, S.P. (ed.) TCC 2007. LNCS, vol. 4392, pp. 41–60. Springer, Heidelberg (2007). https://doi.org/10.1007/978-3-540-70936-7_3
21. Poremba, A.: Quantum proofs of deletion for learning with errors. In: Kalai, Y.T., (ed.)14th Innovations in Theoretical Computer Science Conference, ITCS 2023, 10–13 January, vol. 251. LIPIcs. Schloss Dagstuhl - Leibniz-Zentrum füur Informatik, pp. 90:1–90:14. MIT, Cambridge, Massachusetts, USA (2023). https://doi.org/10.4230/LIPIcs.ITCS.2023.90
22. Simon, D.R.: Finding collisions on a one-way street: Can secure hash functions be based on general assumptions? In: Nyberg, K. (ed.) EUROCRYPT 1998. LNCS, vol. 1403, pp. 334–345. Springer, Heidelberg (1998). https://doi.org/10.1007/BFb0054137
23. Stehlé, D., Steinfeld, R., Tanaka, K., Xagawa, K.: Efficient public key encryption based on ideal lattices. In: Matsui, M. (ed.) ASIACRYPT 2009. LNCS, vol. 5912, pp. 617–635. Springer, Heidelberg (2009). https://doi.org/10.1007/978-3-642-10366-7_36
24. Tomamichel, M., Leverrier, A.: A largely self-contained and complete security proof for quantum key distribution. In: Quantum 1, p. 14 (July 2017), ISSN: 2521–327X. https://doi.org/10.22331/q-2017-07-14-14
25. Unruh, D.: Collapse-binding quantum commitments without random oracles. In: Cheon, J.H., Takagi, T. (eds.) ASIACRYPT 2016. LNCS, vol. 10032, pp. 166–195. Springer, Heidelberg (2016). https://doi.org/10.1007/978-3-662-53890-6_6
26. Unruh, D.: Computationally binding quantum commitments. In: Fischlin, M., Coron, J.-S. (eds.) EUROCRYPT 2016. LNCS, vol. 9666, pp. 497–527. Springer, Heidelberg (2016). https://doi.org/10.1007/978-3-662-49896-5_18
27. Unruh, D.: Revocable quantum timed-release encryption. J. ACM **62**(6) (2015). https://doi.org/10.1145/2817206, ISSN: 0004–5411
28. Wiesner, S.: Conjugate coding. In: SIGACT News, vol. 15(1), pp. 78–88 (Jan 1983) . https://doi.org/10.1145/1008908.1008920, ISSN: 0163–5700

29. Yan, J.: General properties of quantum bit commitments (extended abstract). In: Agrawal, S., Lin, D. (eds.) ASIACRYPT 2022. LNCS, vol. 13794. Springer, Cham (2022). https://doi.org/10.1007/978-3-031-22972-5_22
30. Zhandry, M.: New constructions of collapsing hashes. In: Dodis, Y., Shrimpton, T. (eds.) Advances in Cryptology - CRYPTO 2022–42nd Annual International Cryptology Conference, CRYPTO 2022, Santa Barbara, CA, USA, 15–18 August 2022, Proceedings, Part III. LNCS, vol. 13509, pp. 596–624. Springer (2022). https://doi.org/10.1007/978-3-031-15982-4_20

On Concurrent Multi-party Quantum Computation

Vipul Goyal[1,2($\boxtimes$)], Xiao Liang[1], and Giulio Malavolta[3]

[1] NTT Research, Sunnyvale, USA
[2] CMU, Pittsburgh, USA
vipul@cmu.edu
[3] Max Planck Institute for Security and Privacy, Bochum, Germany

Abstract. Recently, significant progress has been made toward quantumly secure multi-party computation (MPC) in the *stand-alone* setting. In sharp contrast, the picture of *concurrently* secure MPC (or even 2PC), for both classical and quantum functionalities, still remains unclear. Quantum information behaves in a fundamentally different way, making the job of adversaries harder and easier at the same time. Thus, it is unclear if the positive or negative results from the classical setting still apply. This work initiates a systematic study of *concurrent* secure computation in the quantum setting. We obtain a mix of positive and negative results.

We first show that assuming the existence of post-quantum one-way functions (PQ-OWFs), concurrently secure 2PC (and thus MPC) for quantum functionalities is impossible. Next, we focus on the *bounded-concurrent* setting, where we obtain *simulation-sound* zero-knowledge arguments for both **NP** and **QMA**, assuming PQ-OWFs. This is obtained by a new design of simulation-sound gadget, relying on the recent post-quantum non-malleable commitments by Liang, Pandey, and Yamakawa [arXiv:2207.05861], and the quantum rewinding strategy recently developed by Ananth, Chung, and La Placa [CRYPTO'21] for bounded-concurrent post-quantum ZK.

Moreover, we show that our technique is general enough—It also leads to quantum-secure bounded-concurrent coin-flipping protocols, and eventually *general-purpose* 2PC and MPC, for both classical and quantum functionalities. All these constructions can be based on the quantum hardness of Learning with Errors.

Keywords: Concurrent · Secure Computation · Quantum

1 Introduction

Secure multi-party computation (MPC) [23,43] enables two or more mutually distrustful parties to compute any functionality without compromising the privacy of their inputs. Since its introduction, MPC has soon become a cornerstone

© International Association for Cryptologic Research 2023
H. Handschuh and A. Lysyanskaya (Eds.): CRYPTO 2023, LNCS 14085, pp. 129–161, 2023.
https://doi.org/10.1007/978-3-031-38554-4_5

of cryptography. Most papers study MPC only in the so-called *stand-alone* setting, which guarantees the privacy of honest parties for a *single* execution of the underlying protocol.

More realistic setting is the *concurrent setting* where parties might participate in multiple session at a time. A broad study of MPC in the concurrent setting was undertaken starting with the work of Feige and Shamir [19,20] on *witness-indistinguishable proofs* in the concurrent setting, and Dwork, Naor and Sahai [18] on *concurrent zero-knowledge proofs*. Unfortunately broad impossibility results for concurrent *self composition* [4,31,32] as well as general composition like *universal composability* [10–12] were soon obtained thereafter.

To overcome this limitation, a number of settings were studied to bypass these results, including

- Standard ideal-world security notion but in weaker real-world model: For example, bounded concurrency [31], CRS model [13], hardware token model [29], etc.
- Weaker notions of security: For example, super-polynomial-time simulation [35,39], input indistinguishable computation [34], simulation with the ability to receive multiple outputs [24,25], etc.

Concurrent MPC in the Quantum Era. All the above impossibility results are in the classical setting. However, it is known that quantum information behaves in a fundamentally different way. For example, the no-cloning theorem [42] might allow us to restrict the ability of the adversary to copy messages. *This raises the tantalizing possibility that assuming laws of quantum physics, concurrently secure computation maybe possible after all!* However, one should also note that, e.g., no cloning also makes the design of the simulator harder since the simulator is no longer free to rewind the (quantum) adversary as in the classical setting. *This on the other hand raises the tantalizing possibility that assuming laws of quantum physics, even results in the weaker setting such as bounded-concurrent secure computation maybe impossible to obtain!*

> Our goal in this paper is to initiate a systematic study of concurrently secure computation in the quantum setting.

1.1 Our Results

Notation. We call a protocol *post-quantum* if the honest parties and their communication channels are entirely *classical* but the adversary is allowed to be a quantum machine. We use PQ-MPCC (resp. PQ-2PCC) to denote post-quantum multi-party (resp. two-party) secure computation for *classical* functionalities. Similarly, we use MPQC (resp. 2PQC) to denote secure multi-party (resp. two-party) computation for *quantum* functionalities (over quantum channels), where both the honest parties and the adversaries could be quantum machines.

First, we obtain the following no-go theorem ruling out concurrently secure 2PQC protocols. It can be viewed as a generalization of the [4] impossibility to quantum functionalities.

Theorem 1 (Impossibility). *Assuming the existence of PQ-OWFs, it is impossible to build concurrently secure 2PQC (and thus MPQC) protocols (even assuming quantum computation and communication).*

We remark that assuming the existence of post-quantum one-way functions (PQ-OWFs), concurrently secure PQ-2PCC (and thus PQ-MPCC) is impossible. This follows from an observation that the impossibility results in [4] for concurrently secure 2PCC *in the classical world* extend to the post-quantum setting directly. We do not claim this as our contribution. In contrast, the proof of Theorem 1 is not immediate because of quantum computational and communication.

Next, we investigate possibilities in the *bounded-concurrent* model, where a bound m is a priori fixed (so the protocol design can depend on m) and the adversary is allowed to participate in at most m simultaneous executions of the *same* protocol[1]. This model is interesting because it does not rely on any setup assumptions or relaxations of the security (e.g., super-polynomial-time simulation). It has been demonstrated in the classical setting (e.g., [31,36,37]) that a crucial step to build composable computation protocols is to obtain *simulation-sound* ZK systems secure in the (bounded) concurrent setting. Simulation soundness [40] is a form of non-malleability; It requires that the soundness of each of the protocols in the (bounded) concurrent setting is preserved *even when the other protocols are simulated at the same time with the roles of the prover and verifier reversed* (see Def. 4). Intuitively, this notion is crucial for composable 2PC/MPC because it provides a tool for the simulator to "cheat" while ensuring that the adversary cannot, in the concurrent setting.

However, bounded-concurrent simulation-sound ZK arguments are not known in the quantum setting. Therefore, we first propose a new approach to build post-quantum bounded-concurrent simulation-sound ZK arguments. At a high-level, we take the bounded-concurrent ZK argument from [3] and build simulation soundness into it. Moreover, we will show that our technique is general enough—It also leads to bounded-concurrent coin-flipping protocols, and eventually general-purpose 2PC and MPC, for both classical and quantum functionalities. (See for Sect. 2 details.) We summarize the positive results in the following theorem.

Theorem 2 (Positive Results). *There exist constructions, secure against quantum-polynomial-time (QPT) adversaries, for the following tasks in the bounded-concurrent setting:*

1. *Simulation-sound ZK arguments for **NP**, based on the minimal assumption of PQ-OWFs. Honest parties of this protocol do not need to perform any quantum computation/communication;*
2. *Simulation-sound ZK arguments for **QMA**, assuming the existence of PQ-OWFs;*

---

[1] We follow the convention that the term "bounded-concurrent" actually means bounded *self* composition.

3. *Two-party coin-flipping, multi-party coin-flipping, PQ-2PCC and PQ-MPCC, assuming the quantum hardness of Learning with Errors; Honest parties of these protocols do not need to perform any quantum computation/communication;*
4. *2PQC and MPQC, assuming the quantum hardness of Learning with Errors.*

1.2 Organization

Due to space constraints, this proceeding version contains only the construction of bounded-concurrent simulation-sound zero-knowledge arguments for **NP** and **QMA** (in Sect. 4), and the impossibility of (unbounded) concurrent quantum multi-party computation (in Sect. 5). We refer to the full version [26] for the remaining results claimed in Theorem 2.

1.3 Related Work

In the classical setting, Lindell [31] presented the first m-concurrent two-party protocol for any *a priori* fixed m. Pass and Rosen [37] then improved Lindell's results from $O(m)$ rounds to constant rounds. Subsequently, Pass [36] presented a constant-round *multi-party* protocol (and under improved assumptions). The state of the art is from [21], which can be understood as a black-box version[2] of [36].

In the quantum setting, a recent line of research gave a beautiful characterization of *stand-alone* MPC. For classical functionalities, after Watrous' breakthrough work on post-quantum zero-knowledge [41], the works of [15,28,33] considered variants of quantum-secure computation protocols in the two-party setting. Recently, constant-round PQ-MPC was also achieved [1,30]. For quantum functionalities, [17] obtained the first 2PQC protocol. Later, MPQC with dishonest majority was obtained [2,5,6,16,27,30].

In contrast, the situation of *concurrently secure* MPC in the quantum setting is less satisfactory. The closest work in this regard is the recent results by Ananth, Chung, and La Placa [3], who built a bounded-concurrently secure protocol for the special case of zero-knowledge arguments.[3] In the plain model, important questions regarding the (im)possibility of composable secure two-party/multi-party computation in the quantum world remained open before the current work.

2 Technical Overview

2.1 Overview of [3]

We first recall the bounded-concurrent post-quantum zero-knowledge (PQ-ZK) arguments from [3]. Let $Q(\lambda)$ be a polynomial of the security parameter λ that

---

[2] [21] obtained the same results as [36] while making only block-box use of the underlying primitives.

[3] [3] also obtained a zero-knowledge *proof of knowledge* protocol. This protocol is bounded-concurrent ZK, but [3] only established its proof of knowledge property in the *stand-alone* setting.

denotes the number of concurrent sessions. The [3] protocol proceeds in two stages:

- **Preamble Stage:** the prover P and verifier V repeat sequentially for $\ell_{\text{slot}} := 120Q^7\lambda$ times the following basic slot: P sends a statistically binding commitment SBCom to a random bit a, V replies by sending another random bit b (in plain). Such a slot is said to *match* if the bit a committed in P's SBCom equals to V's bit b.

- **Proof Stage:** P and V run a witness-indistinguishable (WI) argument where P proves to V that *either* the concerned statement x is true (dubbed the true statement) *or* there are more than Th $:= 60Q^7\lambda + Q^4\lambda$ slots match from the above stage (dubbed the trapdoor statement).

The idea behind the Q-concurrent ZK property of this protocol is as follows:[4] A simulator can always rewind a particular slot until it matches. Therefore, if one can find a proper way to rewind the slots so that the trapdoor statement becomes true for all the sessions, then the simulator can just use the trapdoor to finish the **Proof Stage**.

However, since the adversary is a quantum machine, finding a proper rewinding strategy in this Q-concurrent setting is not easy. [3] makes use of Watrous' quantum rewinding lemma [41]. Roughly, this lemma allows one to rewind a quantum adversary under the condition that *the decision of rewinding should be (almost) independent of the adversary's internal (quantum) state.* [3] designs a special *block rewinding* strategy as follows: Let T denote the total number of messages across all sessions in the Q-concurrent execution of their protocol. They partition these T messages into $L := 24Q^6\lambda$ equal-size blocks $\{B_1, \ldots, B_L\}$. That is, block B_1 contains the first $\frac{T}{L} = 10Q^2$ messages[5], block B_2 contains the next $10Q^2$ messages, and so on (messages are ordered according to their order of appearing in the execution). Note that the adversary can stagger the messages of a particular session across the different blocks such that the first message of a slot is in one block but the second message of this slot could be in a different block.

As the execution goes on, the simulator monitors each block B_j to see if there is a slot fully nested[6] in B_j. If not, it tosses a random coin to decide whether to rewind the execution of the whole block B_j; Otherwise (i.e., there are at least one fully nested slot), it chooses at random a fully nested slot in B_j, and rewind the execution of the whole block B_j iff the chosen slot matches.

Observe that if there is no fully nested slots in a block, it would be rewound with probability exactly $\frac{1}{2}$; Otherwise, it would be rewound with probability $\frac{1}{2} \pm \mathsf{negl}(\lambda)$ (due to the computationally hiding property of SBCom). Thus, any block would be rewound with probability $\frac{1}{2} \pm \mathsf{negl}(\lambda)$, *independent of the adversary's behavior*, thus satisfying the condition of Watrous rewinding lemma, which implies that this block rewinding strategy will not change the adversary's view.

---

[4] The soundness of this protocol is less relevant to this overview.

[5] Assuming the SBCom is non-interactive, each slot consists of two messages. The total number T is then $\ell_{\text{slot}} \cdot 2 \cdot Q = 240Q^8\lambda$, which implies that $\frac{T}{L} = 10Q^2$.

[6] That is, both messages of this slot are contained in block B_j.

On the other hand, [3] also shows that by their choice of parameters, the above rewinding strategy will make the trapdoor statement available in each session. Roughly, that is because in each session, there are approximately $\frac{\ell_{slot}}{2} = 60Q^7\lambda$ matching slots *even if there are no rewindings* (as each slot will *naturally* match with probability $\frac{1}{2} \pm \mathsf{negl}(\lambda)$); Then, by a combinatorial argument, the authors manage to show that the above rewinding strategy will contribute at least $Q^4\lambda$ extra matching slots in each session. Thus, the total number of matching slots in each session will exceed the threshold $\mathsf{Th} = 60Q^7\lambda + Q^4\lambda$. This eventually completes the proof of the Q-concurrent ZK property.

2.2   Getting Simulation Soundness

Our first goal is to build simulation-sound ZK arguments in the bounded-concurrent setting. In this setting, a polynomial $Q(\lambda)$ (of the security parameter λ) is a priori fixed so the protocol design can depend on Q. It considers an adversary $\mathcal{A}$ (dubbed the MIM adversary) participates in $2Q$ instances of the same protocol *simultaneously*; In Q instances (dubbed the *left* sessions), $\mathcal{A}$ controls the verifiers talking to honest provers; In the other Q instances (dubbed the *right* sessions), $\mathcal{A}$ controls the provers talking to honest verifiers. Each of the sessions is associated with an ID (or tag), and no right-session ID is equal to any left-session IDs.[7] Henceforth, we will refer to this setting as the *Q-Q MIM execution* if the Q is known. Simulation soundness requires the existence of a simulator who could simulate the view of $\mathcal{A}$ in this Q-Q MIM execution *without the witness for any of the left sessions*, while ensuring that $\mathcal{A}$ cannot generate a convincing proof for a false statement in any of the right sessions *even in this simulated execution*.

The [3] protocol does not satisfy this requirement, because in the man-in-the-middle setting, when the simulator performs their rewinding strategy to generate matching slots in left sessions, the MIM adversary may also be able to make extra slots match in some right sessions so that she can use the trapdoor witness to cheat in these right sessions.

Our idea is to equip the slots in [3] with a certain simulation-sound property, while retaining the overall structure of their protocol so that we can re-use their block rewinding strategy. This will eventually yield a protocol so that in the Q-Q MIM setting, a simulator can use the trapdoor on the left (due to the [3] block rewinding strategy), but the MIM adversary cannot in any of the right sessions (due to the simulation soundness that we will add to the [3] slots.)

Organization. In the sequel, we first give a warm-up discussion in Sect. 2.3 about how to build a certain flavor of simulation soundness into a single [3] slot (i.e., in the 1-1 MIM setting). Next, we show how to generalize this result to the Q-Q MIM setting in Sect. 2.4. Then, we show that this bounded-concurrent simulation-sound component can be used to build more applications including

---

[7] Without IDs, a man-in-the-middle attack can not be prevented. See [36] for related discussions.

bounded-concurrent simulation-sound ZK arguments for both **NP** and **QMA** (Sect. 2.5), secure 2PC for both classical and quantum functionalities (in Sect. 2.6), and secure MPC for both classical and quantum functionalities (in Sect. 2.7). Finally, we discuss the impossibility of (unbounded) concurrent 2PC for quantum functionalities in Sect. 2.8.

2.3 Simulation-Sound Gadgets: 1-1 MIM Setting

Intuition. In this subsection, we consider the man-in-the-middle execution of the [3] slot. That is, a MIM adversary $\mathcal{A}$ participates in two instances of the [3] slot simultaneously; $\mathcal{A}$ corrupts the sender (the role of the played by the prover in the [3] slot) in one instance (dubbed the *right* slot) and corrupts the receiver (the role of the played by the verifier in the [3] slot) in the other (dubbed the *left* slot). We will modify the [3] slot so that in this MIM execution, the right slot matches with probability almost $\frac{1}{2}$, *even if conditioned on the left* slot *matching*.

To do that, we ask the receiver to commit to the bit b in advance using a post-quantum statistically-binding commitment SBCom, and ask the sender to commit to the bit a using a constant-round post-quantum non-malleable commitment, followed by the receiver's decommitment to b. In the MIM execution, the receiver's SBCom will allow us to learn the bit b *non-uniformly* in the left slot. Then, a non-uniform reduction to the sender's non-malleable commitment will show that the match probability of the right slot cannot deviate from $\frac{1}{2}$ even if conditioned on the left slot matching. This construction is shown in Prot. 1, where ENMC is a post-quantum constant-round statistically-binding commitment that is both *non-malleable* and *extractable*. For a reason that will become clear later, we additionally require ENMC to be *first-message binding*, which roughly means that the first message of ENMC already statistically determines the committed value. The ENMC from [30] satisfies this property.

Protocol 1: A 1-1 Simulation-Sound Gadget

This protocol is between a sender (dubbed S) and a receiver (dubbed R); Both of them take a string id $\in \{0,1\}^{\lambda}$ as the common input, denoting the ID associated with this execution.

1. R samples $b \xleftarrow{\$} \{0,1\}$ and commits to it using SBCom.
2. S samples $a \xleftarrow{\$} \{0,1\}$ and commits to it using ENMC, where S and R use id as the ID (or tag) for this ENMC.
3. R sends b together with the decommitment information w.r.t. the SBCom in Step 1.

(Through out this overview, we assume for simplicity that both SBCom and ENMC are *perfectly* binding and that the MIM adversary $\mathcal{A}$ does not abort the execution before it completes. In the main body, we will show that these assumptions can be removed easily.)

Let T denote the transcript (i.e., all the messages exchanged on both the left and right sides) resulted from the above MIM execution. We claim that

$$\Pr_{T \leftarrow \text{MIM}}[a = b] = \frac{1}{2}, \tag{1}$$

where b is the value committed in the left SBCom by $\mathcal{A}$, and a is the value committed in the left ENMC by S. Equation (1) follows simply from the fact that the left (honest) S samples a uniformly at random, after $\mathcal{A}$'s b committed in SBCom was fixed.

We also claim that

$$\Pr_{T \leftarrow \text{MIM}}[\widetilde{a} = \widetilde{b}] = \frac{1}{2} \pm \text{negl}(\lambda), \tag{2}$$

where $\widetilde{b}$ is the value committed in the right SBCom by R, and $\widetilde{a}$ is the value committed in the right ENMC by $\mathcal{A}$. Equation (2) follows from the computationally hiding property of SBCom and the extractability of ENMC. In more details, if Eq. (2) is false, then we can extract the $\widetilde{a}$ (due to the extractability of the right-side ENMC) and break the computationally hiding property of the right-side SBCom using $\widetilde{a}$ as a reasonable guess for the value $\widetilde{b}$ committed in SBCom.

Next, we prove a lemma establishing a certain flavor of simulation soundness of Protocol 1 in the MIM execution. Intuitively, this lemma says that *even if we conditioned on the left side $a = b$, $\mathcal{A}$ cannot force $\widetilde{a} = \widetilde{b}$ on the right side with probability significantly different from half. This is essentially due to the non-malleability of ENMC.

Lemma 1. *Assuming* $\text{id} \neq \widetilde{\text{id}}$, *it holds that* $\Pr_{T \leftarrow \text{MIM}}[\widetilde{a} = \widetilde{b} \mid a = b] = \frac{1}{2} \pm \text{negl}(\lambda)$.

Proof. Recall that $\mathcal{A}$ is in charge of the schedule of messages. We use the *first message of the left* ENMC as a pivot to divide all possible schedules into two mutually exclusive and collectively exhaustive types and show Lemma 1 for them using different strategies.

- **Type-1:** They are the schedules where the right ENMC *starts* after (or in parallel with) *the first messages of the left* ENMC. (An example is depicted in Fig. 1a.)
- **Type-2:** They are the schedules where the right ENMC *starts* before *the first message of the left* ENMC. (An example is depicted in Fig. 1b.)

Proof for **Type-1** Schedules. We assume for contradiction that Lemma 1 is false and build an adversary $\mathcal{A}_{\text{NM}}$ who can break the (non-uniform) non-malleability of ENMC. W.l.o.g., we assume

$$\Pr_{T \leftarrow \text{MIM}}[\widetilde{a} = \widetilde{b} \mid a = b] \geq \frac{1}{2} + \frac{1}{\text{poly}(\lambda)}. \tag{3}$$

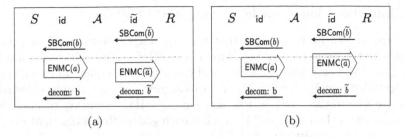

(a)   (b)

Fig. 1. Different Schedules for the MIM Execution of Protocol 1

A standard calculation with Eq. (1) , Eq. (2) and Inequality (3) implies that

$$\Pr_{\mathcal{T}\leftarrow\text{MIM}}[\widetilde{a} = \widetilde{b} \mid a \neq b] \leq \frac{1}{2} - \frac{1}{\text{poly}(\lambda)} + \text{negl}(\lambda). \tag{4}$$

We now build the adversary $\mathcal{A}_{\text{NM}}$ against the non-malleability of ENMC.

- $\mathcal{A}_{\text{NM}}$ internally emulates the MIM game until the moment when $\mathcal{A}$ sends the left-side SBCom to b. $\mathcal{A}_{\text{NM}}$ then pauses the execution and performs brute-force search to learn the value b. We remark that this step is not efficient. But it happens before the beginning of the ENMCs on both sides (due to **Type-1** schedules). Thus, the information in this step can be thought as a *non-uniform* advice to $\mathcal{A}_{\text{NM}}$.
- $\mathcal{A}_{\text{NM}}$ starts to participate in the non-malleability game: She sets $m_0 := b$ and $m_1 := 1 - b$, and sends (m_0, m_1) to the external non-malleability challenger Ch. By the definition of non-malleability, Ch will flip a random coin b and performs a MIM execution of ENMC with $\mathcal{A}_{\text{NM}}$. $\mathcal{A}_{\text{NM}}$ simply relays messages so that these external ENMCs are used as the left and right ENMCs for the internal emulation of the MIM game with $\mathcal{A}$.

Notice that if Ch chooses to commit to m_0 (resp. m_1) on the left, the view of the internal $\mathcal{A}$ is identical to that from the MIM execution conditioned on $a = b$ (resp. $a \neq b$) on the left. Thus, $\mathcal{A}_{\text{NM}}$'s advantage in winning the non-malleability game is exactly the difference between the LHS of Inequality (3) and the LHS of Inequality (4), which is *lower-bounded* by $\frac{2}{\text{poly}(\lambda)} - \text{negl}(\lambda)$. This breaks the non-malleability of ENMC.

Proof for **Type-2** Schedules. Security in this case simply follows from the first-message binding property of the right ENMC. That is, the message $\widetilde{a}$ committed in the ENMC is determined by its first message; For **Type-2** schedules, this message is fixed before the beginning of the left ENMC. Therefore, conditioning on $a = b$ on the left does not change the probability of $\widetilde{a} = \widetilde{b}$ for **Type-2** schedules. Lemma 1 then follows directly from Eq. (2) in this case.

This completes the proof of Lemma 1. □

2.4   Simulation-Sound Gadgets: Q-Q MIM Setting

Intuition. In this part, we show that the "simulation soundness" of Protocol 1 extends to the more demanding many-many MIM setting. That is, consider a many-many MIM execution of a protocol consisting of sequential repetitions of the gadget shown in Protocol 1. We want to argue that: even if one performs the [3] block rewinding strategy in this many-many MIM execution to make some gadgets match on the left, it still holds that each gadget (in all the *right* sessions) matches with probability almost $\frac{1}{2}$.

Here, the challenge is that the [3] block rewinding needs to be performed over a coherent execution of the concerned protocol. However, the simulation soundness shown in Lemma 1 is regarding the *de-coherent* execution of a gadget, and in a *straight-line* execution (i.e., where there is no rewindings). Generalizing Lemma 1 to this setting requires new ideas. Roughly, we will introduce extra intermediate hybrids (in addition to those in [3]) to make the execution de-coherent for the blocks that the Watrous rewinding has not reached. Then, by a careful design of induction-type arguments, we manage to reduce the simulation soundness in the Q-Q MIM setting to that in the straight-line 1-1 MIM setting shown in Lemma 1. We provide more details below.

Simulation-Sound Gadgets in the Q-Q MIM Setting. To ensure simulation soundness in the Q-Q MIM setting, we simply repeat the basic gadget in Protocol 1 for sufficiently many times:

Protocol 2: Simulation-Sound Gadgets Secure in the Q-Q MIM Setting

Let $Q(\lambda)$ be a polynomial of λ, denoting the maximum number of concurrent sessions. Both S and R take a string id $\in \{0,1\}^\lambda$ as the common input. Repeat the following steps for $k = 1$ to $\ell_{\mathsf{gad}} := 120Q^7\lambda$:

1. R samples $b_k \xleftarrow{\$} \{0,1\}$ and commits to it using SBCom.
2. S samples $a_k \xleftarrow{\$} \{0,1\}$ and commits to it using ENMC, where S and R use id:k as the ID for this ENMC execution so that each ENMC uses a different ID.
3. R sends b_k together with the decommitment information w.r.t. the SBCom in Step 1.

Terminology. We call each repetition of Step 1 to Step 3 a gadget. We say that the k-th gadget *matches* if the a_k committed by S in Step 2 is equal to the b_k *validly* decommitted by R in Step 3. We emphasize that this condition of match is always well-defined regardless of the honesty of S (or R), because both SBCom and ENMC are perfectly binding.

Similar as [3], we partition all the messages into $L := 24Q^6\lambda$ equal-size blocks $\{B_1, \ldots, B_L\}$, in the same manner as we explained when recalling the [3] protocol.[8] In the following, we define a sequence of games (or hybrids) G_0 and $\{G_j\}_{j \in [L]}$, the "simulation soundness" of Protocol 2 will appear in the form of two lemmas (Lemma 2 and 3) related to these games.

Game G_0: This is the Q-Q MIM execution of Protocol 2 described above, but executed *coherently*. At the end of this game, we measure (in computational basis) and output the transcript (i.e., all the messages exchanged on both the left and right sides).

Also, we additionally setup L single-qubit registers $\otimes_{j=1}^{L} W_j$, which will be used for Watrous rewinding only in later games. To explain the meaning of these registers, let us briefly recall the Watrous rewinding lemma. It considers a quantum circuit U operating on the tensor of a single-qubit Watrous control register W and another multi-qubit register; As long as the output of U induces a distribution on W that is (almost) independent on the other input register, U can be converted into a new circuit W that on the same input is guaranteed to yield the (almost) same output of U *conditioned on the* Watrous control register *being 0*. Here, each W_j will be used as the Watrous control register for the rewinding of block B_j. We use a similar strategy as in [3] to ensure that they are (almost) independent of the adversary's behavior: If block B_j does not contain any fully nested gadget from any left sessions (dubbed left gadget), W_j is set to 0 with probability $1/2$; Otherwise (i.e., there exists at least one fully nested left gadget), W_j is set to 0 iff a randomly-chosen fully nest left gadget in B_j matches.

Game G_j ($\forall j \in [L]$): This game is identical to G_{j-1} except that it uses Watrous rewinding for block B_j, using the W_j (defined in G_0) as the Watrous control register.

Two Critical Properties of Protocol 2. We prove two lemmas (Lemma 2 and 3) that play a central role in all the positive results in this work.

The following Lemma 2 says that in a hybrid G_j, if a left session is finished before the last messages of block B_j, then the total number of matching gadgets in that session is *large enough*, which means that it exceeds a certain threshold Th that we choose properly.

Lemma 2 (Enough Matching Gadgets). *Let* $\mathsf{Th} := 60Q^7\lambda + Q^4\lambda$. *For all* $j \in [L]$, *let* Σ_j *denote the indices of left sessions that completes before the last message of block B_j. Then, it holds that for all hybrid G_j ($\forall j \in [L]$) and all* $i \in \Sigma_j$ *that in hybrid G_j, the number of matching gadgets in the left session i is greater than* Th, *except for with negligible probability.*

(Proof Sketch for Lemma 2). The proof of this lemma is almost identical to [3], where the authors also need to prove that there are enough matching "slots" (i.e., our gadgets in their term). Intuitively, it is because the natural execution will contribute $\frac{\ell_{gad}}{2} = 60Q^7\lambda$ matching gadgets, and the block rewinding will in additional contribute $Q^4\lambda$ matching ones in each left session. We refer to [26] for a formal treatment.   □

---

[8] But notice that we are in the Q-Q MIM setting. Both the left and right sessions contribute messages to blocks.

Definition 1. *For a Q-Q MIM execution of Protocol 2 we say that the* invariant condition *holds iff*

$$\forall i \in [Q], k \in [\ell_{\text{gadget}}], \quad \Pr\left[\widetilde{a}_k^{(i)} = \widetilde{b}_k^{(i)}\right] = \frac{1}{2} \pm \mathsf{negl}(\lambda),$$

where $\widetilde{a}_k^{(i)}$ is the value committed in the k-th ENMC *(i.e., the* ENMC *of the k-th gadget) in the i-th right session, $\widetilde{b}_k^{(i)}$ is the value committed in the k-th* SBCom *(i.e., the* SBCom *in the k-th gadget) of the i-th right session, and the probability is taken over the Q-Q MIM execution.*

Lemma 3 (Indistinguishability and Invariant Condition). *The view of the adversary in all the games $\{G_0, G_1, \ldots, G_L\}$ are computationally indistinguishable. Moreover, the* invariant condition *(as per Def. 1) holds in all the games, assuming no left-session ID is equal to any right-session ID.*

(Proof Sketch for Lemma 3). We first prove that $\mathcal{A}$'s view is indistinguishable in games $\{G_0, G_1, \ldots, G_L\}$. This follows from a rather straight-forward manner from Watrous' rewinding lemma. To see that, recall that for any $j \in [L]$, the only difference between G_{j-1} and G_j is: G_j will finish block B_j using Watrous rewinding with W_j playing the role of the Watrous control register. Therefore, the indistinguishability of the views will follow once we show that W_i is set to 0 (almost) independent of $\mathcal{A}$'s behavior. This simply follows from the way we definition of W_j (defined in G_0):

1. If there is no fully nested left gadgets in block B_j, W_j is set to 0 with probability exactly $1/2$;
2. Otherwise, the game will pick a fully nested left gadget at random and set W_j to 0 iff that gadget matches. Note that a left gadget matches with probability exactly $1/2$ as well, because the left honest sender $S^{(i)}$ (of the i-th left session) samples the bit $a_k^{(i)}$ uniformly at random (in all left session $i \in [Q]$ and all its gadget $k \in [\ell_{\text{gad}}]$).

Therefore, the Watrous control register is set to 0 with probability exactly $1/2$, independent of $\mathcal{A}$'s behavior. This establishes the view indistinguishability of $\mathcal{A}$ in all the games. We note that this proof (for view indistinguishability) is not new to this work. A similar argument already appears in [3].

Invariant Condition. In the following, we prove the invariant condition. *This proof relies on new techniques developed in this work.*

This proof is of the form of mathematical induction. We first establish the invariant condition in game G_0. Next, we show that for all $j \in [L]$, if the invariant condition holds in game G_{j-1}, then it must hold in game G_j as well.

Invariant condition in G_0. In game G_0, there is no Watrous rewinding; All the blocks are executed in straight-line. This makes the proof of invariant condition straightforward—If $\mathcal{A}$ manages to break the invariant condition for the k-th gadget in the i-th right session, then we can extract the $\widetilde{a}_k^{(i)}$ (due to the extractability of ENMC) and break the computationally hiding property of SBCom using $\widetilde{a}_k^{(i)}$ as a reasonable guess for the value $\widetilde{b}_k^{(i)}$ committed in the corresponding SBCom.

One caveat is that we define G_0 to be a *coherent* execution. But the above argument is in the de-coherent setting, where all the messages are classical. This is not a problem because of the following observation: due to the deferred measurement principle, the classical transcript[9] resulted from G_0 is identically distributed as that from the real (de-coherent) Q-Q MIM execution. Since the invariant condition is information-theoretically determined by the transcript, proving it in the de-coherent Q-Q MIM execution is equivalent to proving it in (the coherent) game G_0.

Invariant condition in G_j. Assume that the invariant condition holds in G_{j-1}. We now show that it must hold in G_j as well. Similar as in the above proof for G_0, game G_j is a *coherent* execution. We will instead consider a new game G_j' that *de-coherentizes* the blocks in G_j that are not reached by Watrous rewinding.

- **Game G_j' ($j \in [L]$):** This game is identical to G_j, except that at the end of block B_j, it measures (in computational basis) the transcript so far, and then finish the remaining execution de-coherently.

As we argued before, the invariant condition in G_j' is equivalent to that in G_j, due to the deferred measurement principle. In the following, we focus on an arbitrary gadget $k \in [\ell_{\mathsf{gad}}]$ and right session $i \in [Q]$ in G_j'; we denote this gadget by $\widetilde{\mathsf{gadget}}_k^{(i)}$.

Note that the only difference between G_{j-1}' and G_j' is the Watrous rewinding performed by G_j' for block B_j. By definition, this rewinding could happen for two reasons: (i) there is no left gadget fully nested in block B_j, but we decide to perform a "dummy" rewinding (w.p. $1/2$); (ii) there exists at least one left gadget fully nested in block B_j, and the randomly selected gadget does not match. First, note that Case (i) is degenerated, because it corresponds to a "dummy" rewinding that essentially does not change the transcript. For this case, the invariant condition in G_j' is inherited from that in G_{j-1}'. Therefore, in this proof sketch, we only focus on Case (ii).[10]

Recall that the schedule of messages is controlled by $\mathcal{A}$. Similar as in the proof of Lemma 1, we divide the possible schedules into different types and prove the invariant condition for them one by one. This time, we use the last message of block B_{j-1} as the pivot:

Type-1 Schedules: The first message of ENMC to $\widetilde{a}_k^{(i)}$ happens before (or in parallel with) the final message of B_{j-1}. This is an easy case. Note that G_{j-1}' and G_j' are identical until the end of block B_{j-1}, by when the the first message of the $\widetilde{\mathsf{gadet}}_k^{(i)}$ ENMC is already fixed. By the first-message binding property

---

[9] Recall that the transcript output by G_0 is classical, because G_0 measured it at the end of the execution.

[10] We refer to [26] for a formal treatment of Case (i) and how we combine Cases (i) and (ii).

of ENMC, this already fixed the committed value $\widetilde{a}_k^{(i)}$ and thus the invariant condition. Therefore, the invariant condition in G'_j is inherited from that in G'_{j-1}.

Type-2 Schedules: The first message of ENMC to $\widetilde{a}_k^{(i)}$ happens after the final message of B_{j-1}. Recall that we are in Case (ii), i.e., G'_j rewinds block B_j because the randomly sampled left gadget (fully nested in B_j) does not match. Let us denote this selected left gadget by $\mathsf{gadget}_v^{(u)}$ (i.e., it happens to be the v-th gadget of some u-th left session).

Here, the key observation is: the transcript resulted from G'_j is actually identical to that from G'_{j-1} *but conditioned on* $\mathsf{gadget}_v^{(u)}$ *matches* (i.e., $a_v^{(u)} = b_v^{(u)}$). This is because that the effect of Watrous rewinding is to "kill" the branch in the superposition that corresponds to the Watrous control register being 1, and only retain the branch that corresponds to the Watrous control register being 0. It then follows from this observation that proving the invariant condition in G'_j is equivalent to proving that in G'_{j-1} *but conditioned on* $\mathsf{gadget}_v^{(u)}$ *matches*.[11] As a vigilant reader may already notice, this is exactly what we have proven in Lemma 1 for the 1–1 "simulation soundness" of Protocol 1.[12] Thus, the same argument applies here to finish the proof of the invariant condition. In more details, we will view all the execution except for $\mathsf{gadget}_v^{(u)}$ and $\widetilde{\mathsf{gadget}}_k^{(i)}$ as a new MIM adversary, and view $\mathsf{gadget}_v^{(u)}$ and $\widetilde{\mathsf{gadget}}_k^{(i)}$ as the left and right gadgets in the 1–1 MIM setting. This configuration matches exactly the proof of Protocol 1. This finishes the proof of Lemma 3.   □

2.5   Bounded-Concurrent Simulation-Sound ZK Arguments for NP and QMA

We show how to use Protocol 2 to build a bounded-concurrent simulation-sound ZK argument protocol Π_{SSZK} for **NP**. The idea is to first execute a **Preamble** stage where the prover and the verifier run Protocol 2. Then, they will execute a WI argument to prove *either* the concerned statement x is true, *or* there are more than $\mathsf{Th} = 60Q^7\lambda + Q^4\lambda$ matching gadgets from the execution of Protocol 2 in the **Preamble** stage; An honest prover will use the real witness w (for $x \in \mathcal{L}$) for this stage. This protocol Π_{SSZK} is presented in Protocol 3 below.

Protocol 3: Π_{SSZK}: Q-Q Simulation-Sound ZK Arguments for NP (Informal)

A prover (dubbed P_{id}) and a verifier (dubbed V_{id}) agree on an ID $\mathsf{id} \in \{0,1\}^\lambda$ and an statement x from some **NP** language $\mathcal{L}$; P_{id} additionally holds a witness w for $x \in \mathcal{L}$.

---

[11] Here, we mean (invariant condition in G'_j) $\equiv$ (invariant condition in G'_{j-1} conditioned on $\mathsf{gadget}_v^{(u)}$ matches).

[12] Note that neither $\mathsf{gadget}_v^{(u)}$ nor $\widetilde{\mathsf{gadget}}_k^{(i)}$ is interleaved with Watrous rewinding in G_{j-1} (due to **Type-2** schedules).

1. **Preamble:** These two parties run Protocol 2 (using id as the ID), where P_{id} acts as the sender S and V_{id} acts as the receiver R.
2. **WI:** Then, they run a WI argument where P_{id} proves that *either* x is in $\mathcal{L}$ *or* there are more than $\mathsf{Th} = 60Q^7\lambda + Q^4\lambda$ matching gadgets from the execution of Protocol 2 in Stage 1. An honest P_{id} will always use the real witness w (for $x \in \mathcal{L}$) to perform this WI.

To prove simulation soundness of Π_{SSZK} in the Q-Q MIM setting,[13] we need to construct a simulator $\mathcal{S}$ in the Q-Q MIM execution of Π_{SSZK}, who can simulate the view of the MIM adversary $\mathcal{A}$ *without* using the real witness w in any of the Q left sessions; Meanwhile, we need to make sure that even in this simulated execution, $\mathcal{A}$ cannot convince the honest verifier on a false statement in any of the Q right sessions.

Intuitively, the properties (i.e., Lemma 2 and 3) of Protocol 2 performed in the **Preamble** will allow us to construct the desired simulator $\mathcal{S}$ so that $\mathcal{S}$ is able to use the trapdoor (i.e., more than $\mathsf{Th} = 60Q^7\lambda + Q^4\lambda$ gadgets match) to cheat in the **WI** stage against the adversary in each left sessions (due to Lemma 2), and meanwhile ensure that the adversary cannot use the trapdoor and must behave honestly in all right sessions (due to the invariant condition[14] claimed in Lemma 3). However, we cannot use Lemma 2 and 3 *in a modular way*, because we only proved them for the Q-Q MIM execution of Protocol 2 *itself*, where there are no other protocols. It is unclear if they still hold when Protocol 2 is composed with other messages (i.e., the **WI** stage messages). Nevertheless, we will show in the following that the proofs of Lemma 2 and 3 are robust enough to "tolerate" the **WI** stage.

We again partition all the messages in the Q-Q MIM execution of Π_{SSZK} into $L = 24Q^6\lambda$ equal-size blocks, and define the same hybrids G_0 and $\{G_j\}_{j\in[L]}$ as in Sect. 2.4. This time, these blocks and hybrids are defined w.r.t. Π_{SSZK}. That is, in each session, there exist **WI** messages (after the execution of the Protocol 2 instance) that contribute to the total number T of messages in the Q-Q MIM execution. But each block still contain T/L blocks, and the rule to rewind a block does not change (i.e., it is still based on if there are fully nested left gadgets as before).

Additionally, we insert the following hybrid H_{j-1} between G_{j-1} and G_j:[15]

Hybrid H_{j-1} ($\forall j \in [L]$): This hybrid is identical to G_{j-1} (defined on Page 11) except that it additionally monitors the execution of block B_j, and for all left sessions of Π_{SSZK} whose **WI** stage *starts* in block B_j, it switches to using the trapdoor (i.e., more than Th gadgets match) to finish that **WI** stage.

---

[13] Completeness and soundness of Π_{SSZK} follow from standard techniques. We refer to the main body for details.

[14] Note that the invariant condition only help us to upper bound the *expected* number of matching right gadgets. But using a proper concentration bound, we can also show that $\mathcal{A}$ cannot make more than Th gadgets match.

[15] That is, the current order of hybrids is: $G_0 \rightarrow H_0 \rightarrow G_1 \rightarrow H_1 \rightarrow G_2 \rightarrow \cdots \rightarrow G_{L-1} \rightarrow H_{L-1} \rightarrow G_L$.

Notice that if we manage to show Lemma 2 and 3 for this new sequence of hybrids (with the intermediate H_j's), the Q-Q simulation soundness of Π_{SSZK} is established. Because in G_L, we are able to use the trapdoor to cheat in the **WI** stage against the adversary in all left sessions (due to Lemma 2); Meanwhile, the adversary cannot use the trapdoor and thus cannot prove false statements in all right sessions (due to the invariant condition[16] claimed in Lemma 3). It turns out the only step that requires new ideas is the switch from G_{j-1} to the new hybrid H_{j-1}. In the following, we focus on the challenges and how we resolve them.

Indistinguishability. We first claim that the view of $\mathcal{A}$ is computationally indistinguishable between G_{j-1} and H_{j-1} ($\forall j \in [L]$). Recall that G_{j-1} performs Watrous rewinding only for the first $j - 1$ blocks $\{B_1, \ldots, B_{j-1}\}$. In particular, it means that the WI that *starts* in block B_j will be executed in straight-line. Since the only difference between G_{j-1} and H_{j-1} is the witness used in this WI, the view indistinguishability follows directly from the WI property.

There are two issues to address in the above argument. First, recall that both G_{j-1} and H_{j-1} are coherent executions, so we cannot use the WI property, which is about the de-coherent execution of the **WI** stage. This can be resolved using the same technique as for Lemma 3—We consider an intermediate hybrid G'_{j-1} (resp. H'_{j-1}) that is identical to G_{j-1} (resp. H_{j-1}) but execute the blocks $\{B_j, \ldots, B_L\}$ (i.e., the blocks Watrous rewinding has not reached) de-coherently. In this way, we can perform the reduction to the WI property as explained above.

Second, we need to show that the trapdoor will indeed become available when H_{j-1} needs it. We want to prove this using (a similar argument as for) Lemma 2—When the **WI** stage of some left session *starts* in block B_j, it means the **Preamgle** stage of this left session must complete before block B_j. It then follows from Lemma 2 that the trapdoor witness of this left session must be available. However, the result in Lemma 2 is about G_j that performs Watrous rewinding up to block B_j, but the current hybrid G'_{j-1} only performs rewinding up to B_{j-1}. It is possible that one less gadget is made match in G'_{j-1} (i.e., the one fully nested in block B_j and picked by Watrous' rewinding). Fortunately, this does not affect the availability of trapdoor in G'_{j-1} because the bound in Lemma 2 is derived asymptotically on the security parameter λ, and it still holds even if one less gadget matches. Another related issue is: Compared with the G_j considered in Lemma 2, there are more messages in each session (i.e., the **WI** stage) in G'_{j-1}. But this does not affect the asymptotic bound in Lemma 2 either, because the **WI** stage contribute to each session only a constant number (particularly, independent of λ) of extra messages.

Invariant Condition. We also need to prove the invariant condition (as per Def. 1) in H_{j-1}. A simple solution is to require the **WI** stage to be *statistically* WI. In this way, the switch of witness in H_{j-1} does not affect the invariant condition as the WI execution contains no information of the used witness at all. However,

---

[16] Note that the invariant condition only help us to upper bound the *expected* number of matching right gadgets. But using a proper concentration bound, we can also show that $\mathcal{A}$ cannot make more than Th gadgets match.

constant-round[17] statistical WI arguments are not unknown from the *minimal* assumption of PQ-OWFs. We thus take a different proof approach (that allows us to keep using the computational WI arguments).

We will keep using the H'_{j-1} defined above, because of its advantage that the blocks after B_{j-1} are de-coherent (again, due to the deferred measurement principle, invariant condition in H'_{j-1} implies that in H_{j-1}). We divide all possible schedules into two types in the same manner as in the proof of Lemma 3 (shown on Page 13). **Type-1** schedules can be handled in exactly the same manner as on Page 13. However, we cannot re-use the same proof for **Type-2** schedules, because the change in the current H'_{j-1} is to switch the WI witness; And the ENMC is non-malleable only w.r.t. another ENMC (but not w.r.t. the concerned WI argument).

Instead, we re-use the proof for G_0 (shown on Page 12) for **Type-2** schedules—If $\mathcal{A}$ manages to break the invariant condition, then we can extract the $\widetilde{a}_k^{(i)}$ (due to the extractability of ENMC) and break the computationally hiding property of SBCom using $\widetilde{a}_k^{(i)}$ as a reasonable guess for the value $\widetilde{b}_k^{(i)}$ committed in the corresponding SBCom. However, there is one difficulty in the current setting. **Type-2** schedules in H'_{j-1} only guarantees the ENMC to $\widetilde{a}_k^{(i)}$ starts after the final message of B_{j-1} (and thus is executed de-coherently and in straight-line). However, it is possible that the SBCom to $\widetilde{b}_k^{(i)}$ happens within some block B_z with $z \leq j-1$; Since this B_z is performed using Watrous rewinding, we *cannot* view the concerned $\widetilde{\text{gadget}}_k^{(i)}$ as a straight-line, de-coherent execution and perform the above reduction to the hiding property of SBCom.

To solve this issue, we define another hybrid H''_{j-1}, which is identical to H'_{j-1} except that it guess at random the block index z and stop performing the Watrous rewinding for block B_z, while executing other blocks in the same manner as H'_{j-1}. In this way, if the SBCom to $\widetilde{b}_k^{(i)}$ appears within B_z, it will be a de-coherent execution. Moreover, H''_{j-1} is equivalent to H'_{j-1} with probability $1/2$. I.e., they are equivalent as long as the Watrous control register W_z (for the picked z) is set to 0 in hybrid H''_{j-1}, and as we proved earlier, each Watrous control register will be set to 0 with probability exactly $1/2$. Then, we can perform the above reduction to the hiding of SBCom in the new hybrid H''_{j-1}. This approach only incurs an $\frac{1}{2} \cdot \frac{1}{\ell_{\text{gad}}}$ multiplicative loss on the adversary's advantage in winning the hiding game, where the term $\frac{1}{2}$ is due to the fact that $H''_{j-1} \equiv H'_{j-1}$ with probability $\frac{1}{2}$, and the term $\frac{1}{\ell_{\text{gad}}}$ is due to the fact that H''_{j-1} needs to guess *correctly* in which block B_z the SBCom to $\widetilde{b}_{i,k}$ will appear. Since ℓ_{gad} is a polynomial of λ, the reduction still works.

Extension to QMA. Notice that the above security proof for Π_{SSZK} makes use of its **WI** stage in a "black-box" manner. That is, all the claims above hold as long as the **WI** stage is constant-round, computationally WI, and computationally

---

[17] If the WI argument is not constant-round, the above proof of indistinguishability may not goes through anymore. Because it is unclear if the asymptotic bound in Lemma 2 still holds.

sound. In particular, this is true even if this **WI** stage involves quantum communication. Therefore, a bounded-concurrent simulation-sound ZK argument for **QMA** can be constructed by replacing the **WI** stage for **NP** in Π_{SSZK} with a WI argument for **QMA**, where again the prover proves *either* the **QMA** statement is true *or* the trapdoor statement is true. We remark that such a constant-round WI argument for **QMA** is know from PQ-OWFs in [14].[18]

2.6 More Applications: Coin-Flipping Protocols, PQ-2PCC, and 2PQC

To build these applications, we want to follow the same template as in Sect. 2.5. That is, we ask the parties to run a **Preamble** stage involving executions of Protocol 2. Then, the parties execute some extra components implementing the desired functionality (e.g., the **WI** stage in our Π_{SSZK} protocol). As long as the "extra components" are constant-round and have a straight-line security proof, the proof techniques in Sect. 2.5 will generalize to this new construction.

But coin-flipping protocols, or general-purpose 2PC in general, have crucial differences with zero-knowledge arguments:

1. For the Q-Q MIM execution of zero-knowledge arguments, we only need to deal with "fixed-role" corruptions. That is, we know for sure that the MIM adversary corrupts the verifiers of all the left sessions and corrupts the provers of all the right sessions. In contrast, for the Q-concurrent execution of 2PC protocols, it is possible that $\mathcal{A}$ corrupts P_1 of some sessions and P_2 of other sessions (this is typically referred to as *interchangeable-role* corruptions).

2. ZK arguments require *simulation-based* security against corrupted verifiers (i.e., the ZK property), and in this case, the corrupted party (i.e., the verifier) does not have private input. On the other hand, the security requirement against corrupted provers (i.e., the soundness property) is *game-based*. Namely, to prove soundness, the reduction does not need to extract private input (i.e., a potential witness) from a malicious prover. In contrast, for 2PC protocols, we always require a simulation-based security no matter which party is corrupted, and the simulator needs to extract the private input of the corrupted party explicitly. Indeed, this is one of the reasons why ZK arguments are typically easier to build than general-purpose 2PC protocols.

To address Issue 1, we require that P_1 and P_2 in each session execute two sequential instances of Protocol 2 *in opposite directions* in the **Preamble** stage. That is, they first run an instance of Protocol 2 where P_1 acts as the sender S, and then another instance where P_2 acts as the sender S. In the security proof,[19] the schedule of the Q-concurrent execution of the protocol (to be constructed) can be "recast" to a similar pattern as the Q-Q MIM execution of the ZK protocol discussion in Sect. 2.5 with the adversary sitting in the middle. To do that,

---

[18] In more detail, [14] constructed a constant-round ε-ZK argument for **QMA** using only PQ-OWFs. It is well-known that ε-ZK implies WI.

[19] W.l.o.g., we assume that exactly one party is corrupted in each session, in this Q-concurrent execution of 2PCC.

we simply put Q instances of Protocol 2 *where the receiver is corrupted* on the left, and put the other Q instances of Protocol 2 *where the sender is corrupted* on the right. This matches exactly the Q-Q MIM setting where we proved security of Protocol 2 (and the Q-Q simulation-sound ZK in Sect. 2.5). Intuitively, this allows us to construct a simulator who is able to use the trapdoor in each session when simulating the behavior of honest parties for the MIM adversary $\mathcal{A}$; Meanwhile, $\mathcal{A}$ cannot use any trapdoor. However, to make the the proof work, we have to make sure that the other components (except for the **Preamble** stage) in each session have only constant rounds and their security proof does not involve rewinding. (E.g., for the Π_{SSZK} in Sect. 2.5, the **WI** stage plays the role of "other components".) We need to instantiate these components carefully to satisfy this requirement (see the following application-specific discussions).

To address Issue 2, our idea is application-specific. In the sequel, we discuss the case of coin-flipping protocols, 2PC for classical functionalities and quantum functionalities one by one.

Two-Party Coin-Flipping Protocols. We start with a canonical construction: Each party P_b ($b \in \{0, 1\}$) sequentially commits to a random share r_b using an *extractable* commitment scheme. Then, they sequentially reveal the committed r_b, *without giving the associated decommitment information*. Finally, they sequentially give a ZK argument to prove that the revealed r_b is indeed the value committed earlier. The coin-flipping result is defined by $r := r_0 \oplus r_1$. To prove the security, a simulator can extract the committed share r_b from the extractable commitment given by the corrupted party, then enforce the coin-flipping result to the r from the ideal functionality by setting $r_{1-b} := r \oplus r_b$ as the (simulated) revealed share and cheating in the ZK argument (using the ZK simulator).

As discussed earlier, if we find a constant-round, straight-line version of the above canonical two-party coin-flipping protocol, and add it after the aforementioned **Preamble** stage, then we will obtain a secure construction re-using the same proof techniques shown in Sect. 2.5:

- For the commitment to share r_b, we ask each party P_b to use a post-quantum statistically binding commitment, and then perform a constant-round *post-quantum secure function evaluation* (SFE) [7], so that if the other party P_{1-b} knows the trapdoor,[20] the SFE will reveal the committed value; Otherwise, the SFE reveals nothing.
- Note that after revealing the r_b's, each party also needs to prove their honesty for the execution so far. Instead of using a ZK argument, we ask each party to give a WI argument, where the prover proves that *either* the revealed r_b, the commitment, and the SFE are generated honestly and consistently, *or* the trapdoor statement is true.

---

[20] Specifically, trapdoor in this setting is the witness for the following trapdoor statement: More than $\mathsf{Th} = 60Q^7\lambda + Q^4\lambda$ gadgets match in the Protocol 2 instance (from the **Preamble** stage) where P_{1-b} acts as the sender S.

Extension to General-Purpose PQ-2PCC. Bounded concurrent PQ-2PCC can be constructed by taking a (stand-alone-secure) PQ-2PCC protocol Π_{2PCC} *in the CRS model* and using the above bounded-concurrent two-party coin-flipping protocol to generate its CRS. Similar as in the previous constructions, as long as Π_{2PCC} is constant-round and has a straight-line simulator (in the CRS model), the same proof techniques can be re-used to show its security in the bounded-concurrent setting. We remark that such a Π_{2PCC} is known from the quantum hardness of learning with Errors (LWE) (by combining [22,38]).

Extension to General-Purpose 2PQC. This part is similar to our generalization of Π_{sszk} from **NP** to **QMA** (shown on Page 17)—The above construction of the PQ-2PCC protocol makes use of the Π_{2PCC} in a rather "black-box" manner. That is, all the claims above hold as long as the Π_{2PCC} is constant-round and straight-line simulatable in the CRS model. In particular, it does *not* rely on the fact that the Π_{2PCC} messages are classical. Therefore, a bounded-concurrent 2PQC can be constructed by replacing the Π_{2PCC} in the above protocol with a constant-round, straight-line simulatable (in the CRS model) 2PC for *quantum functionalities*.

2.7 Generalization to the Multi-party Setting

The above results for two-party coin-flipping and secure computation for both classical and quantum functionalities generalizes to the multi-party setting, if we setup the parameters of the Protocol 2 instances in the **Preamble** stage carefully.

Let us consider the direct generalization of the two-part protocol in Sect. 2.6 to the n-party case. Compared with the two-party protocol, the main difference is the **Preamble** stage (other stages are less relevant in this overview and thus suppressed). In the two-party setting, the **Preamble** stage consists of two executions of Protocol 2, where in one execution, P_1 plays the roles of the sender S and in the other, P_2 plays the roles of the sender S. In the n-party setting, there will be two executions of Protocol 2 between *every pair of parties* P_i and P_j in the **Preamble** stage.

Here, the key observation is: *The **Preamble** stage in the n-party setting can be understood as $\binom{n}{2}$ concurrent executions of two-party **Preamble Stages**.* The analysis of the two-party setting (i.e., Sect. 2.6) shows that if we set the parameter $\ell_{gad} = 120Q^7\lambda$ in Protocol 2, then the **Preamble** stage will provide "simulation soundness" in the Q-concurrent execution. Therefore, using the above observation, if we set $\ell_{gad} = 120\widehat{Q}^7\lambda$ with a new $\widehat{Q} := \binom{n}{2} \cdot Q$, then the **Preamble** stage will provide "simulation soundness" in the Q-concurrent execution *of the n-party protocol*. Remaining steps of the security proof are almost identical to that for the two-party setting. We refer to [26] for details.

2.8 Impossibility of (Unbounded) Concurrent 2PQC

We provide a sketch of the impossibility for concurrent 2PC in the quantum settings, where the adversary is allowed to be quantum, and the protocol is computing a quantum functionality. Our approach is based on the classical result of Barak et al. [4], but with important differences that we explain in the following.

To better understand the challenges involved, let us first recall the high-level intuition for the impossibility of concurrent zero-knowledge with respect to an oracle $\mathcal{O}$, described in [4]. Let Π be an ℓ-round zero-knowledge protocol to prove the knowledge of a pre-image of a one-way function, the oracle $\mathcal{O}$ plays the role of the verifier, except that in the last round it outputs some secret information, if the (interactive) proof verifies. The idea of the separation consists of the following two steps:

1. An adversary interacting in with an honest prover (the real, concurrent protocol) can trivially recover the secret by simply forwarding the messages of the honest prover to $\mathcal{O}$. Since the honest prover is assumed to succeed, then the adversary can recover the secret with certainty.
2. An adversary interacting with an ideal functionality (the ideal settings) cannot recover the secret, since that would require to complete a proof for a witness that the adversary does not posses.

Although this captures the main idea, the proof is actually more subtle, especially for Step 2. The issue is that the oracle $\mathcal{O}$ is not allowed to keep a state across different queries and therefore the adversary may try to break the zero-knowledge proof by "rewinding" the verifier (represented by the oracle $\mathcal{O}$) or scheduling messages in the wrong order. The way this is solved classically is to let the verifier *sign* the transcript of the protocol in such a way that in the later query it can enforce a straight-line execution of the protocol.

Unfortunately, quantumly this idea does not work, since there is no well-defined notion of "transcript" of quantum protocols, as quantum states cannot in general be copied. The way we solve this issue (which significantly complicates the analysis) is to let the oracle compute the internal state (which could be a quantum state), authenticate it with a quantum authentication code[21], and return it as an output. Then the adversary will be forced to feed the same state in the next query (thus forcing a straight-line execution); Otherwise, the authentication process will fail and the oracle will just return $\perp$. Interestingly, in our proof we need a strong notion of security for quantum authentication codes, namely simulation security. Fortunately for us, the work of Broadbent and Wainewright [9] shows that the Clifford code and the trap code satisfy our desired notion of security.

Finally, to lift the theorem from an oracle separation to an actual impossibility, we need to get rid of the oracle $\mathcal{O}$ and substitute it with a two-party functionality, which is not allowed to depend on the protocol Π. In [4], this is done by substituting the ℓ invocations of the oracle with garbled circuits (which will be given as part of the parties' inputs) and letting the functionality compute the encoding for

---

[21] Note that a good quantum authentication code also serves as an encryption scheme. Therefore, given this authenticated internal state to the adversary does not reveal information about the verifier's secrets.

the inputs. This way, the adversary can *simulate* the calls to $\mathcal{O}$ by simply evaluating the garbled circuits. It turns out that the same idea works in our settings, using recent results on quantum garbled circuits [8]. The only subtlety is that we need the garbling scheme to satisfy *adaptive security*, i.e., the distinguisher should be allowed to choose the input adaptively, after it obtains the garbled circuit. To complete the proof, we show that this can be achieved with a simple generic transformation. For more details, we refer the reader to Sect. 5.

3   Preliminaries

Additional preliminaries are provided in the full version of this work [26, Section 3], which includes the definitions of post-quantum extractable commitments, post-quantum non-malleable commitments, quantumly secure bounded-concurrent secure computation, the Watrous' quantum rewinding lemma, and Azuma-Hoeffding Inequality.

Basic Notations. Let $\lambda \in \mathbb{N}$ denote security parameter. For a positive integer n, let $[n]$ denote the set $\{1, 2, ..., n\}$. For a finite set $\mathcal{X}$, $x \xleftarrow{\$} \mathcal{X}$ means that x is uniformly chosen from $\mathcal{X}$. We denote by $\mathsf{poly}(\cdot)$ an unspecified polynomial and by $\mathsf{negl}(\cdot)$ an unspecified negligible function. For two probabilities $p_1(\lambda)$ and $p_2(\lambda)$, we will often use $p_1 = p_2 \pm \mathsf{negl}(\lambda)$ as a shorthand for $|p_1 - p_2| \leq \mathsf{negl}(\lambda)$.

For indistinguishability, we may consider random variables over bit strings or over quantum states. This will be clear from the context. For ensembles of random variables $\mathcal{X} = \{X_i\}_{\lambda \in \mathbb{N}, i \in I_\lambda}$ and $\mathcal{Y} = \{Y_i\}_{\lambda \in \mathbb{N}, i \in I_\lambda}$ over the same set of indices $I = \bigcup_{\lambda \in \mathbb{N}} I_\lambda$ and a function $\varepsilon(\cdot)$, we use $\mathcal{X} \overset{c}{\approx}_\varepsilon \mathcal{Y}$ to mean that for any non-uniform QPT[22] algorithm $\mathcal{A}$, there exists a negligible function $\mathsf{negl}(\cdot)$ such that for all $\lambda \in \mathbb{N}$, $i \in I_\lambda$, we have

$$| \Pr[\mathcal{A}(X_i)] - \Pr[\mathcal{A}(Y_i)]| \leq \varepsilon(\lambda) + \mathsf{negl}(\lambda).$$

We say that $\mathcal{X}$ and $\mathcal{Y}$ are ε-computationally indistinguishable if the above holds. In particular, when the above holds for $\varepsilon = 0$, we say that $\mathcal{X}$ and $\mathcal{Y}$ are computationally indistinguishable, and simply write $\mathcal{X} \overset{c}{\approx} \mathcal{Y}$. Statistical indistinguishability (denoted by "$\overset{s}{\approx}_\varepsilon$" and "$\overset{s}{\approx}$") can be defined similarly but for computationally unbounded adversaries. Moreover, we write $\mathcal{X} \overset{\text{i.d.}}{=\!=\!=} \mathcal{Y}$ to mean that X_i and Y_i are distributed identically for all $i \in I$.

OR-Composition of NP Languages. For an **NP** language $\mathcal{L}$ and a true statement in this language $x \in \mathcal{L}$, we use $\mathcal{R}_\mathcal{L}(x)$ ($\mathcal{R}$ stands for "relation") to denote the set of all witnesses for x. We will refer to the OR-composition of **NP** languages, which is defined in Def. 2.

Definition 2 (OR-Composition of NP Languages). *Let $\mathcal{L}_1$ and $\mathcal{L}_2$ be two* **NP** *languages. The OR-composition of them (dubbed $\mathcal{L}_1 \vee \mathcal{L}_2$) is the new* **NP** *language defined as follows:*

---

[22] Unless stated differently, throughout this paper, computational indistinguishability is always w.r.t. non-uniform QPT adversaries.

$$\mathcal{L}_1 \vee \mathcal{L}_2 := \{(x_1, x_2) \mid x_1 \in \mathcal{L}_1 \vee x_2 \in \mathcal{L}_2\}.$$

3.1   Post-Quantum Bounded-Concurrent Simulation-Sound ZK Arguments

For any interactive protocol $\langle P, V \rangle$, we use $\langle \{P_i\}_{i \in [m]}, \{V_i\}_{i \in [m]} \rangle$ to denote the concurrent execution of m instances of $\langle P, V \rangle$, where the i-th instance is the execution of $\langle P, V \rangle$ with P_i acting as the prover and V_i acting as the verifier. When defining soundness, we consider the setting where the provers are corrupted; In this case, we write the execution as $\langle P^*, \{V_i\}_{i \in [m]} \rangle$, meaning that a malicious P^* controls all the provers in the m sessions. Similarly, for properties like zero-knowledge, we can define $\langle \{P_i\}_{i \in [m]}, V^* \rangle$, where the verifiers are corrupted.

Definition 3 (Post-Quantum Bounded-Concurrent Interactive Arguments). *Let* $\langle P, V \rangle$ *be an interactive protocol between a classical PPT prover* P *and a classical PPT verifier* V. *Let* $m(\lambda)$ *be a polynomial of* λ. *For any priori fixed* m, $\langle P, V \rangle$ *is a post-quantum* m-*bounded concurrent interactive argument for an* **NP** *language* $\mathcal{L}$ *if it satisfies the following requirements:*

1. **(Completeness.)** *For any* $(x_1, \ldots, x_m) \in \mathcal{L}^m$ *and any* $(w_1, \ldots, w_m)$ *such that* $w_i \in \mathcal{R}_\mathcal{L}(x_i)$ *for all* $i \in [m]$, *it holds that:*

$$Pr[All\, V_i\text{'s accept in } \langle \{P_i(x_i, w_i)\}_{i \in [m]}, \{V_i(x_i)\}_{i \in [m]} \rangle] = 1.$$

2. **(Computational Soundness.)** *For any (non-uniform) QPT prover* $P^* = \{P^*_\lambda, \rho_\lambda\}_{\lambda \in \mathbb{N}}$ *and any* $(x_1, \ldots, x_m) \in (\{0,1\}^\lambda)^m$, *it holds that*

$$Pr[\exists i \text{ s.t. } (x_i \notin \mathcal{L}) \wedge (d_i = 1) : (d_1, \ldots, d_m) \leftarrow \mathsf{OUT}_V(\langle P^*_\lambda(x_1, \ldots, x_m; \rho_\lambda), \{V_i(x_i)\}_{i \in [m]} \rangle)] = \mathsf{negl}(\lambda),$$

   where d_i *denotes the output of* V_i *in the execution* $\langle P^*_\lambda(x_1, \ldots, x_m; \rho_\lambda), \{V_i(x_i)\}_{i \in [m]} \rangle$, *indicating if* V_i *accepts (when* $d_i = 1$*) or rejects (when* $d_i = 0$*) in the* i-*th session.*

Man-in-the-Middle Execution. Let $m(\lambda)$ be a polynomial of λ. Let $\langle P, V \rangle$ be an interactive argument system for a language $\mathcal{L} \in \mathbf{NP}$ with witness relation $\mathcal{R}_\mathcal{L}$. For any (non-uniform) QPT adversary $\mathcal{A} = \{\mathcal{A}_\lambda, \rho_\lambda\}_{\lambda \in \mathbb{N}}$, consider the following m-m man-in-the-middle (MIM) setting:

- *m* Left Sessions: $\mathcal{A}_\lambda$, on input $(\{x_1, \ldots, x_m\}; \rho_\lambda)$, executes m instances of $\langle P, V \rangle$ with m honest provers $\{P_i(x_i, w_i)\}_{i \in [m]}$. $\mathcal{A}_\lambda$ plays the role of the verifier in all of these m sessions. Similar as for non-malleable commitments, each session is associated with an identity (or tag). We use id_i to denote the identity of the i-th left session.

- m Right Sessions: The same $\mathcal{A}_\lambda$ with the same input executes anther m instances of $\langle P, V \rangle$ with m honest verifiers $\{V_i\}_{i \in [m]}$. $\mathcal{A}_\lambda$ plays the role of the (potentially malicious) provers in all of these m sessions, trying to prove a statement $\widetilde{x}_i$ in the i-th right session. We use $\widetilde{\mathsf{id}}_i$ to denote the identity of the i-th right session.

We emphasize that $\mathcal{A}_\lambda$ participates in the above executions *simultaneously*, taking full control over the schedule of messages on both sides; The statements $\{x_1, \ldots, x_m\}$ proven in the left sessions are given to the corresponding P_i's and $\mathcal{A}_\lambda$ prior to the experiment; In contrast, the statements $\{\widetilde{x}_1, \ldots, \widetilde{x}_m\}$ proven in the right interaction the identities used on both sides are chosen by $\mathcal{A}_\lambda$ during the experiment. Let $\mathsf{View}_{\mathcal{A}_\lambda}(\rho_\lambda, x_1, \ldots, x_m)$ denote the view of $\mathcal{A}_\lambda$ in the above experiment.

Definition 4 (Post-Quantum   Bounded-Concurrently   Simulation -Sound ZK). *Let $m(\lambda)$ be a polynomial of λ. For any priori fixed m, an m-concurrent post-quantum interactive argument system $\langle P, V \rangle$ for an* **NP** *language $\mathcal{L}$ (as per Def. 3) is post-quantum m-concurrent simulation-sound if there exists a QPT machine $\mathcal{S}$ (simulator) such that for any (potentially non-uniform) QPT adversary $\mathcal{A} = \{\mathcal{A}_\lambda, \rho_\lambda\}_{\lambda \in \mathbb{N}}$, the following hold:*

1. **(Indistinguishable Simulation.)** *It holds that*

$$\{\mathsf{View}_{\mathcal{A}_\lambda}(\rho_\lambda, x_1, \ldots, x_m)\}_{\lambda \in \mathbb{N}, \; x_1, \ldots, x_m \in \mathcal{L} \cap \{0,1\}^\lambda} \overset{c}{\approx} \{\mathcal{S}(1^\lambda, \rho_\lambda, x_1, \ldots, x_m)\}_{\lambda \in \mathbb{N}, \; x_1, \ldots, x_m \in \mathcal{L} \cap \{0,1\}^\lambda}.$$

2. **(Simulation Soundness.)** *For any $x_1, \ldots, x_m \in \mathcal{L} \cap \{0,1\}^\lambda$ and any left-session IDs $\{\mathsf{id}_j\}_{j \in [m]}$, it holds that*

$$\Pr\left[\begin{array}{l} \exists i \in [m] \; s.t. \; (\widetilde{x}_i \notin \mathcal{L}) \;\wedge\; (\widetilde{d}_i = 1) \\ \wedge \; (\forall j \in [m], \; \mathsf{id}_j \neq \widetilde{\mathsf{id}}_i) \end{array} : \mathsf{View} \leftarrow \mathcal{S}(1^\lambda, \rho_\lambda, x_1, \ldots, x_m) \right] \leq \mathsf{negl}(\lambda),$$

where $\{\widetilde{\mathsf{id}}_i\}_{i \in [m]}$ are the IDs of the right sessions as specified in View, $\widetilde{x}_i$ is the statement in the i-th right session as specified in View, and $\widetilde{d}_i$ is the verifier's decision bit in the i-the right session as specified in View, indicating if it accepts $(\widetilde{d}_i = 1)$ or rejects $(\widetilde{d}_i = 0)$ this execution.

Remark 1 (On m-Concurrent ZK). We remark that m-concurrent simulation soundness (as per Def. 4) implies m-concurrent ZK. Thus, we do not need to define bounded-concurrent zero-knowledge separately. The interested reader can find the definition of post-quantum bounded-concurrent ZK in, e.g., [3, Section 3.1].

4   Bounded-Concurrent Simulation-Sound ZK Arguments for NP and QMA

4.1   Construction for NP

Our construction for **NP** makes use of the following building blocks:

- A constant-round statistically binding and computationally hiding commitment SBCom. Let $\Gamma_{\text{SBC.C}}$ denote the round complexity of its Commit Phase, and $\Gamma_{\text{SBC.D}}$ the round complexity of its Decommit Phase. Let $\Gamma_{\text{SBC}} := \Gamma_{\text{SBC.C}} + \Gamma_{\text{SBC.D}}$. We use Naor's commitment as SBCom.
- A constant-round post-quantum non-malleable commitment ENMC that is also ε-simulation extractable and first-message binding. Let Γ_{ENMC} denote its round complexity. We use the construction from [30] as our ENMC.
- A constant-round post-quantum witness indistinguishable argument WI. Let Γ_{WI} denote its round complexity. It is known that such a WI can be obtained assuming only post-quantum OWFs.

Protocol 4: Post-Quantum Bounded-Concurrent Simulation-Sound Zero-Knowledge Argument

---

Let $Q(\lambda)$ be a polynomial of λ, denoting the maximum number of concurrent sessions. Prover P takes as input λ, $x \in L$, and $w \in \mathcal{R}_{\mathcal{L}}(x)$; Verifier V takes as input λ and $x \in \mathcal{L}$. P and V agree on an id $\in \{0,1\}^\lambda$ as the ID for this execution of the protocol.

1. In this stage, P (resp. V) samples a random string $\beta_P \xleftarrow{\$} \{0,1\}^\lambda$ (resp. $\beta_V \xleftarrow{\$} \{0,1\}^\lambda$) sends it to V (resp. P). The purpose of β_P and β_V is as follows: In later steps, both P and V need to perform Naor's commitments for several times (recall that Naor's commitment remains secure even if polynomially-many instances use the same first-round message). We stipulate that whenever P (resp. V) needs to make a Naor's commitment to some value, it uses β_V (resp. β_P) as the first message of the two-round Naor's commitment. In this way, we can assume w.l.o.g. that all the Naor's commitments in our construction are non-interactive (i.e., single-round).

2. **(Com-and-Guess Stage.)** For $k = 1$ to $\ell_{\text{gad}} := 120Q^7\lambda$:

   (a) V samples $b_k \xleftarrow{\$} \{0,1\}$ and commits to it using SBCom. Note that this is a non-interactive execution of Naor's commitment, as we explained in Stage 1.

   (b) P samples $a_k \xleftarrow{\$} \{0,1\}$ and commits to it using ENMC. Note that the ENMC requires an ID. P and V will use id:k (according to some standard encoding) as the ID for this ENMC so that each ENMC is executed using a different ID. (Recall that id is the ID for this SSZK.) Also recall that the first two messages of ENMC constitute a Naor's commitment. As discussed in Stage 1, one can think treat this Naor's commitment as being non-interactive; We denote this message as $\text{com}_k = \text{Com}_{\beta_V}(a_k; r_k)$.

   (c) V sends b_k together with the decommitment information w.r.t. the SBCom in Step 2a. P continues only if this decommitment is valid.

Terminology: We call each repetition of Step 2a to Step 2c a gadget. Naturally, we call the ℓ_{gad} defined above the total number of gadgets. The k-th gadget *matches* if the a_k committed by P in Step 2b is equal to the b_k *validly* decommitted by V in Step 2c. We emphasize that this matching condition is always well-defined regardless of the honesty of P (or V), because both SBCom and ENMC are *statistically* binding.

3. **(WI Stage.)** P and V execute an instance of WI where P proves that *either* x is in the language *or* no less than $\mathsf{Th} := 60Q^7\lambda + Q^4\lambda$ gadgets are matching. Formally, P proves that $\left(x, \{(\beta_V, \mathsf{com}_k, b_k)\}_{k=1}^{\ell_{\mathsf{gad}}}\right) \in \mathcal{L} \vee \mathcal{L}_{\mathsf{match}}^{\ell_{\mathsf{gad}}, \mathsf{Th}}$ (see Def. 2), where $\mathcal{L}_{\mathsf{match}}^{\ell_{\mathsf{gad}}, \mathsf{Th}}$ denotes the following language

$$\left\{ \{(\beta_V, \mathsf{com}_k, b_k)\}_{j=1}^{\ell_{\mathsf{gad}}} : \begin{array}{l} \exists G \subseteq [\ell_{\mathsf{gad}}], \ \exists \{(a_k, r_k)\}_{k \in G} \text{ s.t. } |G| \geq \mathsf{Th} \wedge \\ \forall k \in G, \ a_k = b_k \ \wedge \ \mathsf{com}_k = \mathsf{Com}_{\beta_V}(a_k; r_k) \end{array} \right\}, \quad (5)$$

where by our parameter setting $\ell_{\mathsf{gad}} = 120Q^7\lambda$ and $\mathsf{Th} = 60Q^7\lambda + Q^4\lambda$.
Terminology: Later in the security proof, we will refer to $w \in \mathcal{R}_\mathcal{L}(x)$ as the real witness, and refer to the witness for $\{(\beta_V, \mathsf{com}_k, b_k)\}_{k=1}^{\ell_{\mathsf{gad}}} \in \mathcal{L}_{\mathsf{match}}^{\ell_{\mathsf{gad}}, \mathsf{Th}}$ as the trapdoor witness. Of course, the trapdoor witness should not exist even for a cheating prover, which we will show when proving soundness. But our ZK simulator will set up the trapdoor witness and make use of it. Also, we emphasize that the honest P always finishes this stage using the real witness.

Security Proof. The security of Protocol 4 is established by the following Theorem 3. To prove Theorem 3, first note that completeness follows straightforwardly from the description in Protocol 4. Thus, we only need to establish the Q-concurrent soundness (to show that it is a Q-concurrent interactive argument system) and Q-concurrent simulation soundness, which are provided in the full versions [26].

Theorem 3. *For any $Q(\lambda)$ that is a polynomial of the security parameter λ, Protocol 4 is a Q-concurrent simulation-sound ZK argument (as per Def. 4).*

4.2   Extension to QMA

As discussed in the technical overview, we remark that the proof of Theorem 3 makes use of the Stage 3 WI of Protocol 4 in a "black-box" manner. That is, all the claims/lemmas above hold as long as the Stage 3 WI is constant-round, computationally WI, and computationally sound. In particular, this is true even if this Stage 3 WI involves quantum communication.

Therefore, a bounded-concurrent simulation-sound ZK argument for **QMA** can be constructed by replacing the Stage 3 WI for **NP** in Protocol 4 with a WI argument for **QMA**, where again the prover proves *either* the **QMA** statement is true *or* the trapdoor statement is true. (We refer to [14, Section 6.4] for definitions of **QMA**, WI arguments for **QMA**, etc.) We remark that such a constant-round WI argument for **QMA** is known from the existence of PQ-OWFs in [14]. In more detail, [14] constructed a constant-round ε-ZK argument for **QMA** using only PQ-OWFs. It is well-known that ε-ZK implies WI. This leads to the following theorem:

Theorem 4. *Assuming the existence of PQ-OWFs, bounded-concurrent simulation-sound ZK arguments for* **QMA** *exist.*

5 Impossibility of (Unbounded) Concurrent 2PQC

In this section, we show that there exists a functionality for which realizing an unbounded concurrent 2PQC is impossible, even with quantum communication. We need the following building blocks: (1) Quantum MAC that achieves a simulation-based security; (2) A quantum circuits garbling scheme that is *adaptively* secure (i.e., the distinguisher can choose the input state adaptively, possibly depending on the garbled circuit) and has *decomposable* input encoding (i.e., each of the input qubits is encoded individually). Due to space constraints, we refer to the full versions [26] for related definitions and constructions.

5.1 Oracle Separation

Our impossibility result will follow closely the outline of [4], although with some non-trivial modification to handle the quantum nature of the protocol. We will start with the following warm-up result in an oracular model, which will be a useful intermediate step for our final result.

Lemma 4. *Let f be a one-way function, and let R_f be the following NP-relation*

$$R_f = \{(x, w) : f(w) = x\}.$$

Let Π^{ZK} be a stand-alone zero-knowledge proof of knowledge for R_f with $\ell = \ell(\lambda)$ prover messages. There exists a functionality $\mathcal{G}$, a distribution $\mathcal{D}$, a function secret, *and a polynomial-time adversary $\mathcal{A}$ such that:*

- *In a concurrent execution scheduled by $\mathcal{A}$ of one copy of Π^{ZK} (with $\mathcal{A}$ playing the role of the verifier) and ℓ ideals calls to $\mathcal{G}$ with $\mathcal{A}$ providing the second input and receiving the output, if the inputs to the honest parties are chosen from $d \leftarrow \mathcal{D}$, then $\mathcal{A}$ learns* secret(d) *with probability one.*
- *In any execution of ℓ copies of the ideal calls to $\mathcal{G}$ and a copy of the ideal functionality $\mathcal{F}^{\mathsf{ZK}}$, with honest inputs chosen from $d \leftarrow \mathcal{D}$, any polynomial time adversary $\widetilde{\mathcal{A}}$ will only output* secret(d) *with negligible probability.*

(Proof Sketch). Due to space constraints, we only provide the intuition behind this lemma and refer to the full version [26] for the formal proof.

The functionality $\mathcal{G}$ is very similar to that used in [4]. It is essentially the next-message function of the verifier of the zero-knowledge proof of knowledge protocol Π^{ZK}. It also supports a special call that return the secret to the adversary $\mathcal{A}$ if $\mathcal{A}$ *manages to make a query that results in an acceptance decision of the Π^{ZK} verifier (underlying the $\mathcal{G}$).* Then,

1. When $\mathcal{A}$ interacts with an honest prover, she can trivially recover the secret by simply forwarding the messages of the honest prover to $\mathcal{G}$. Since the honest prover is assumed to succeed, then the adversary can recover the secret with certainty.

2. When $\mathcal{A}$ interacts with an ideal functionality (the ideal settings), she cannot recover the secret, since that would require to complete a proof for a witness that the adversary does not posses, which otherwise breaks the hiding of the secret (which is implemented as a post-quantum OWF pre-image).

This proof differs from [4] in that the protocol Π^{ZK} is quantum, which means both the communication (translating to the queries made to G) and the verifier (translating to G's internal behavior) are quantum. We take care of this using a quantum MAC *with simulation-based security* to protect the verifier's internal state (simulated by G) and to make sure that $\mathcal{A}$ makes the queries in correct order. We refer to [26] for details.   □

5.2   Impossibility of Concurrent 2PQC

Here we state and prove the main theorem of this section.

Theorem 5. *Assume the existence of post-quantum OWFs. Then there exists a functionality $\mathcal{F}$ such that, for any two-party protocol Π to compute $\mathcal{F}$ there exists a polynomial $t = t(\lambda)$, a distribution $\mathcal{D}$, a function* secret, *and a polynomial-time adversary $\mathcal{A}$ such that:*

- *In a concurrent execution scheduled by $\mathcal{A}$ of l copies of Π with parties receiving inputs from the chosen from $d \leftarrow \mathcal{D}$, then $\mathcal{A}$ learns* secret(d) *with probability negligibly close to one.*
- *In an ideal execution where the parties get access to t copies of the ideal functionality $\mathcal{F}$ and receive inputs chosen from $d \leftarrow \mathcal{D}$, then any polynomial time adversary $\widetilde{\mathcal{A}}$ will only output* secret(d) *with negligible probability.*

Proof. Let f be a post-quantum OWF. We provide the description of the ideal functionality $\mathcal{F}$ below.

- Sender Input: A flag $j \in \{0, 1, 2, 3\}$, a statement x (which is supposed to be an image of f), a witness w (which is supposed to be the pre-image satisfying $f(w) = x$), a string r, an index i, a state $\mathbf{e}$, two bit-strings $\widetilde{a}$ and $\widetilde{b}$, and two bits c and d.
- Receiver Input: A flag $j' \in \{0, 1, 2, 3\}$, a statement x, and a qubit $\mathbf{x}$.
- Upon receiving the input from both parties, the functionality computes its output to the Receiver (while the sender does not receive anything) as follows:
    - If $j = j' = 0$: Check if $f(w) = x$ and return 1 if this is the case; Return 0 otherwise.
    - If $j = j' = 1$: Compute $X^{\widetilde{a}} Z^{\widetilde{b}} \mathsf{QGEncode}(i, r, \mathbf{e}, \mathbf{x})$.
    - If $j = j' = 2$: Return $(\widetilde{a}, \widetilde{b})$.
    - If $j = j' = 3$: Return (c, d).

- If $j \neq j'$: Return $\perp$.

Let Π be a protocol to implement $\mathcal{F}$, we can derive protocols Π^{ZK} and Π^{Encode} for the zero knowledge and the input encoding functions, respectively. Let $\ell = \ell(\lambda)$ be the number of rounds needed for Π^{ZK} and let $\mathcal{G}$ be the (quantum) functionality as defined in the proof of Lemma 4. We assume that the adversary is given as input ℓ copies of the garbled circuits for the function computed by $\mathcal{G}$ (where the sender's inputs to the $\mathcal{G}$ functionality, which are all classical, are hardwired to the function description) and we set $t = (m + 2n) \cdot \ell + 1$, where m is the the size (i.e., the number of qubits) of each garbled circuit.

Recall that each garbled circuit corresponds to a state $\widetilde{R}$. On the other hand, the sender of $\mathcal{F}$ is given as input the registers $\mathbf{e}_{1,i}$ and the strings r_i, for all $i \in [n]$, and the strings $\widetilde{x}$ and $\widetilde{z}$ corresponding to the encoding information for each garbled circuit. For each of the ℓ iterations, we assume that the sender behaves as follows. We only describe the inputs of the sender that influence the output, whereas for the other inputs we assume that the sender sends something arbitrary. The following actions are performed in sequence:

- First, it sends all of the $(i, r_i, \mathbf{e}_{1,i})$ to the functionality in sequence along with two random bit-strings (a_i, b_i), setting $j = 1$.
- Then, it sends all of the (a_i, b_i), setting $j = 2$.
- Finally, it sends all bits $(\widetilde{x}_i, \widetilde{z}_i)$ from the encoding in sequence, setting $j = 3$.

Given this protocol, we make the following claims.

- **Claim:** In the real world, there is an adversary that learns the secret with probability negligibly close to one.

The attack is identical to the one describe in Lemma 4, where the attacker just forwards the prover messages to the ideal functionality, except that it forwards them qubit-by-qubit to $\mathcal{F}$, setting $j = 1$. Afterwards it queries the functionality on input $j = 2$ and $j = 3$ for m queries, receiving the keys for the quantum one-time pad. This allows it to retrieve the encoded input and evaluate each quantum garbled circuit. By the correctness of the quantum garbling scheme, the output of this procedure is statistically close to the message of $\mathcal{G}$, and thus the attack succeeds with roughly the same probability.

- **Claim:** In the ideal world, no adversary can learn the secret with non-negligible probability.

We show this with a reduction to the same claim, except where the function implemented by $\mathcal{G}$ is queried as an oracle, which was already proven in Lemma 4. First observe that the parties need to agree on the flag $j = j'$ to obtain a non-$\perp$ output, and therefore we can assume without loss of generality that the attacker queries the functionality in the correct order.

The reduction proceeds as follows: For every message of the adversary with flags $j = j' = 1$, the reduction returns the first register of a series of freshly sampled maximally entangled states (one for each qubit of the encoding). The reduction stores the input qubit ψ_i sent be the adversary and, after n queries, it sends the adjoint state ψ to the ideal functionality $\mathcal{G}$. It receives the state ϕ as output and runs

$$(\widetilde{E}_1, \ldots, \widetilde{E}_n, \widetilde{Q}) \leftarrow \mathsf{QGSim}(1^\lambda, \mathsf{par}, \phi).$$

For each encoding $\widetilde{E}_i$, the reduction teleports it into the previously sampled maximally entangled state and sends the teleportation measurements with flag $j = j' = 2$. Then teleports also $\widetilde{Q}$ into the view of the adversary (same as done by the adaptive simulator) and sends the teleportation measurements with flag $j = j' = 3$. Note that, except for the fact that the garbled circuit is computed with a simulator, the reduction perfectly simulates the view of the adversary. By the security of the garbling scheme, the distribution induced by the reduction is computationally indistinguishable from the original one, and therefore any advantage of the adversary carries over to the settings where $\mathcal{G}$ is queried as an oracle, except for a negligible factor. By the proof of Lemma 4, we can therefore bound this to a negligible function.   □

Acknowledgment. We thank Kai-Min Chung for helpful discussions regarding [3]. We also thank the CRYPTO'23 reviewers for their constructive feedback.

G.M. is partially funded by the German Federal Ministry of Education and Research (BMBF) in the course of the 6GEM research hub under grant number 16KISK038, and by the Deutsche Forschungsgemeinschaft (DFG, German Research Foundation) under Germany's Excellence Strategy - EXC 2092 CASA - 390781972.

Work partially done when X.L. was at Rice University, supported by Nai-Hui Chia's NSF award FET-2243659.

References

1. Agarwal, A., Bartusek, J., Goyal, V., Khurana, D., Malavolta, G.: Post-quantum multi-party computation. In: Canteaut, A., Standaert, F.-X. (eds.) EUROCRYPT 2021. LNCS, vol. 12696, pp. 435–464. Springer, Cham (2021). https://doi.org/10.1007/978-3-030-77870-5_16

2. Alon, B., Chung, H., Chung, K.-M., Huang, M.-Y., Lee, Y., Shen, Y.-C.: Round efficient secure multiparty quantum computation with identifiable abort. In: Malkin, T., Peikert, C. (eds.) CRYPTO 2021. LNCS, vol. 12825, pp. 436–466. Springer, Cham (2021). https://doi.org/10.1007/978-3-030-84242-0_16

3. Ananth, P., Chung, K.-M., Placa, R.L.L.: On the concurrent composition of quantum zero-knowledge. In: Malkin, T., Peikert, C. (eds.) CRYPTO 2021. LNCS, vol. 12825, pp. 346–374. Springer, Cham (2021). https://doi.org/10.1007/978-3-030-84242-0_13

4. Barak, B., Prabhakaran, M., Sahai, A.: Concurrent non-malleable zero knowledge. In: 47th Annual Symposium on Foundations of Computer Science, pp. 345–354. IEEE Computer Society Press, Berkeley, CA, USA (Oct 21–24) (2006). https://doi.org/10.1109/FOCS.2006.21

5. Bartusek, J., Coladangelo, A., Khurana, D., Ma, F.: On the round complexity of secure quantum computation. In: Malkin, T., Peikert, C. (eds.) CRYPTO 2021. LNCS, vol. 12825, pp. 406–435. Springer, Cham (2021). https://doi.org/10.1007/978-3-030-84242-0_15

6. Bartusek, J., Coladangelo, A., Khurana, D., Ma, F.: One-way functions imply secure computation in a quantum world. In: Malkin, T., Peikert, C. (eds.) CRYPTO 2021. LNCS, vol. 12825, pp. 467–496. Springer, Cham (2021). https://doi.org/10.1007/978-3-030-84242-0_17

7. Brakerski, Z., Döttling, N.: Two-message statistically sender-private OT from LWE. In: Beimel, A., Dziembowski, S. (eds.) TCC 2018. LNCS, vol. 11240, pp. 370–390. Springer, Cham (2018). https://doi.org/10.1007/978-3-030-03810-6_14

8. Brakerski, Z., Yuen, H.: Quantum garbled circuits. In: Proceedings of the 54th Annual ACM SIGACT Symposium on Theory of Computing, pp. 804–817 (2022)

9. Broadbent, A., Wainewright, E.: Efficient simulation for quantum message authentication. In: Nascimento, A.C.A., Barreto, P. (eds.) ICITS 2016. LNCS, vol. 10015, pp. 72–91. Springer, Cham (2016). https://doi.org/10.1007/978-3-319-49175-2_4

10. Canetti, R.: Universally composable security: A new paradigm for cryptographic protocols. In: 42nd Annual Symposium on Foundations of Computer Science, pp. 136–145. IEEE Computer Society Press, Las Vegas, NV, USA (Oct 14–17) (2001). https://doi.org/10.1109/SFCS.2001.959888

11. Canetti, R., Fischlin, M.: Universally composable commitments. In: Kilian, J. (ed.) CRYPTO 2001. LNCS, vol. 2139, pp. 19–40. Springer, Heidelberg (2001). https://doi.org/10.1007/3-540-44647-8_2

12. Canetti, R., Kushilevitz, E., Lindell, Y.: On the Limitations of Universally Composable Two-Party Computation without Set-up Assumptions. In: Biham, E. (ed.) EUROCRYPT 2003. LNCS, vol. 2656, pp. 68–86. Springer, Heidelberg (2003). https://doi.org/10.1007/3-540-39200-9_5

13. Canetti, R., Lindell, Y., Ostrovsky, R., Sahai, A.: Universally composable two-party and multi-party secure computation. In: 34th Annual ACM Symposium on Theory of Computing, pp. 494–503. ACM Press, Montréal, Québec, Canada (May 19–21) (2002). https://doi.org/10.1145/509907.509980

14. Chia, N.H., Chung, K.M., Liang, X., Yamakawa, T.: Post-quantum simulatable extraction with minimal assumptions: Black-box and constant-round. In: Dodis, Y., Shrimpton, T. (eds.) Advances in Cryptology - CRYPTO 2022, Part III. Lecture Notes in Computer Science, vol. 13509, pp. 533–563. Springer, Heidelberg, Germany, Santa Barbara, CA, USA (Aug 15–18, 2022). https://doi.org/10.1007/978-3-031-15982-4_18

15. Damgård, I., Lunemann, C.: Quantum-secure coin-flipping and applications. In: Matsui, M. (ed.) Advances in Cryptology - ASIACRYPT 2009. Lecture Notes in Computer Science, vol. 5912, pp. 52–69. Springer, Heidelberg, Germany, Tokyo, Japan (Dec 6–10) (2009). https://doi.org/10.1007/978-3-642-10366-7_4

16. Dulek, Y., Grilo, A.B., Jeffery, S., Majenz, C., Schaffner, C.: Secure multi-party quantum computation with a dishonest majority. In: Canteaut, A., Ishai, Y. (eds.) EUROCRYPT 2020. LNCS, vol. 12107, pp. 729–758. Springer, Cham (2020). https://doi.org/10.1007/978-3-030-45727-3_25

17. Dupuis, F., Nielsen, J.B., Salvail, L.: Actively secure two-party evaluation of any quantum operation. In: Safavi-Naini, R., Canetti, R. (eds.) CRYPTO 2012. LNCS, vol. 7417, pp. 794–811. Springer, Heidelberg (2012). https://doi.org/10.1007/978-3-642-32009-5_46

18. Dwork, C., Naor, M., Sahai, A.: Concurrent zero-knowledge. In: 30th Annual ACM Symposium on Theory of Computing, pp. 409–418. ACM Press, Dallas, TX, USA (May 23–26) (1998). https://doi.org/10.1145/276698.276853

19. Feige, U.: Alternative models for zero knowledge interactive proofs. Ph.D. thesis, Ph. D. thesis, Weizmann Institute of Science, Rehovot, Israel (1990)

20. Feige, U., Shamir, A.: Witness indistinguishable and witness hiding protocols. In: 22nd Annual ACM Symposium on Theory of Computing. pp. 416–426. ACM Press, Baltimore, MD, USA (May 14–16) (1990). https://doi.org/10.1145/100216.100272

21. Garg, S., Liang, X., Pandey, O., Visconti, I.: Black-box constructions of bounded-concurrent secure computation. In: Galdi, C., Kolesnikov, V. (eds.) SCN 2020. LNCS, vol. 12238, pp. 87–107. Springer, Cham (2020). https://doi.org/10.1007/978-3-030-57990-6_5

22. Garg, S., Srinivasan, A.: Two-round multiparty secure computation from minimal assumptions. In: Nielsen, J.B., Rijmen, V. (eds.) EUROCRYPT 2018. LNCS, vol. 10821, pp. 468–499. Springer, Cham (2018). https://doi.org/10.1007/978-3-319-78375-8_16

23. Goldreich, O., Micali, S., Wigderson, A.: How to play any mental game or A completeness theorem for protocols with honest majority. In: Aho, A. (ed.) 19th Annual ACM Symposium on Theory of Computing, pp. 218–229. ACM Press, New York City, NY, USA (May 25–27) (1987). https://doi.org/10.1145/28395.28420

24. Goyal, V., Jain, A.: On concurrently secure computation in the multiple ideal query model. In: Johansson, T., Nguyen, P.Q. (eds.) EUROCRYPT 2013. LNCS, vol. 7881, pp. 684–701. Springer, Heidelberg (2013). https://doi.org/10.1007/978-3-642-38348-9_40

25. Goyal, V., Jain, A., Ostrovsky, R.: Password-authenticated session-key generation on the internet in the plain model. In: Rabin, T. (ed.) CRYPTO 2010. LNCS, vol. 6223, pp. 277–294. Springer, Heidelberg (2010). https://doi.org/10.1007/978-3-642-14623-7_15

26. Goyal, V., Liang, X., Malavolta, G.: On concurrent multi-party quantum computation (2023). https://eprint.iacr.org/2023/827

27. Grilo, A.B., Lin, H., Song, F., Vaikuntanathan, V.: Oblivious transfer is in MiniQCrypt. In: Canteaut, A., Standaert, F.-X. (eds.) EUROCRYPT 2021. LNCS, vol. 12697, pp. 531–561. Springer, Cham (2021). https://doi.org/10.1007/978-3-030-77886-6_18

28. Hallgren, S., Smith, A., Song, F.: Classical cryptographic protocols in a quantum world. In: Rogaway, P. (ed.) CRYPTO 2011. LNCS, vol. 6841, pp. 411–428. Springer, Heidelberg (2011). https://doi.org/10.1007/978-3-642-22792-9_23

29. Katz, J.: Universally composable multi-party computation using tamper-proof hardware. In: Naor, M. (ed.) EUROCRYPT 2007. LNCS, vol. 4515, pp. 115–128. Springer, Heidelberg (2007). https://doi.org/10.1007/978-3-540-72540-4_7

30. Liang, X., Pandey, O., Yamakawa, T.: A new approach to post-quantum non-malleability. Cryptology ePrint Archive, Report 2022/907 (2022). https://eprint.iacr.org/2022/907

31. Lindell, Y.: Bounded-concurrent secure two-party computation without setup assumptions. In: 35th Annual ACM Symposium on Theory of Computing, pp. 683–692. ACM Press, San Diego, CA, USA (Jun 9–11) (2003). https://doi.org/10.1145/780542.780641

32. Lindell, Y.: Lower bounds for concurrent self composition. In: Naor, M. (ed.) TCC 2004. LNCS, vol. 2951, pp. 203–222. Springer, Heidelberg (2004). https://doi.org/10.1007/978-3-540-24638-1_12

33. Lunemann, C., Nielsen, J.B.: Fully simulatable quantum-secure coin-flipping and applications. In: Nitaj, A., Pointcheval, D. (eds.) AFRICACRYPT 2011. LNCS, vol. 6737, pp. 21–40. Springer, Heidelberg (2011). https://doi.org/10.1007/978-3-642-21969-6_2

34. Micali, S., Pass, R., Rosen, A.: Input-indistinguishable computation. In: 47th Annual Symposium on Foundations of Computer Science, pp. 367–378. IEEE Computer Society Press, Berkeley, CA, USA (Oct 21–24) (2006). https://doi.org/10.1109/FOCS.2006.43

35. Pass, R.: Simulation in quasi-polynomial time, and its application to protocol composition. In: Biham, E. (ed.) EUROCRYPT 2003. LNCS, vol. 2656, pp. 160–176. Springer, Heidelberg (2003). https://doi.org/10.1007/3-540-39200-9_10

36. Pass, R.: Bounded-concurrent secure multi-party computation with a dishonest majority. In: Babai, L. (ed.) 36th Annual ACM Symposium on Theory of Computing, pp. 232–241. ACM Press, Chicago, IL, USA (Jun 13–16) (2004). https://doi.org/10.1145/1007352.1007393

37. Pass, R., Rosen, A.: Bounded-concurrent secure two-party computation in a constant number of rounds. In: 44th Annual Symposium on Foundations of Computer Science, pp. 404–415. IEEE Computer Society Press, Cambridge, MA, USA (Oct 11–14) (2003). https://doi.org/10.1109/SFCS.2003.1238214

38. Peikert, C., Vaikuntanathan, V., Waters, B.: A framework for efficient and composable oblivious transfer. In: Wagner, D. (ed.) CRYPTO 2008. LNCS, vol. 5157, pp. 554–571. Springer, Heidelberg (2008). https://doi.org/10.1007/978-3-540-85174-5_31

39. Prabhakaran, M., Sahai, A.: New notions of security: Achieving universal composability without trusted setup. In: Babai, L. (ed.) 36th Annual ACM Symposium on Theory of Computing, pp. 242–251. ACM Press, Chicago, IL, USA (Jun 13–16) (2004). https://doi.org/10.1145/1007352.1007394

40. Sahai, A.: Non-malleable non-interactive zero knowledge and adaptive chosen-ciphertext security. In: 40th Annual Symposium on Foundations of Computer Science, pp. 543–553. IEEE Computer Society Press, New York, NY, USA (Oct 17–19) (1999). https://doi.org/10.1109/SFFCS.1999.814628

41. Watrous, J.: Zero-knowledge against quantum attacks. In: Kleinberg, J.M. (ed.) 38th Annual ACM Symposium on Theory of Computing, pp. 296–305. ACM Press, Seattle, WA, USA (May 21–23) (2006).https://doi.org/10.1145/1132516.1132560

42. Wootters, W.K., Zurek, W.H.: A single quantum cannot be cloned. Nature 299(5886), 802–803 (1982)

43. Yao, A.C.C.: How to generate and exchange secrets (extended abstract). In: 27th Annual Symposium on Foundations of Computer Science, pp. 162–167. IEEE Computer Society Press, Toronto, Ontario, Canada (Oct 27–29) (1986). https://doi.org/10.1109/SFCS.1986.25

Simple Tests of Quantumness Also Certify Qubits

Zvika Brakerski[1(✉)], Alexandru Gheorghiu[2(✉)],
Gregory D. Kahanamoku-Meyer[3,4(✉)], Eitan Porat[1(✉)],
and Thomas Vidick[1,5(✉)]

[1] Weizmann Institute of Science, Rehovot, Israel
zvika.brakerski@weizmann.ac.il
[2] Chalmers University of Technology, Gothenburg, Sweden
[3] Lawrence Berkeley National Laboratory, Berkeley, CA, USA
[4] University of California, Berkeley, CA, USA
[5] California Institute of Technology, Pasadena, CA, USA

Abstract. A test of quantumness is a protocol that allows a classical verifier to certify (only) that a prover is not classical. We show that tests of quantumness that follow a certain template, which captures recent proposals such as [KCVY21, KLVY22], can in fact do much more. Namely, the same protocols can be used for *certifying a qubit*, a building-block that stands at the heart of applications such as certifiable randomness and classical delegation of quantum computation.

Certifying qubits was previously only known to be possible based on families of post-quantum trapdoor claw-free functions (TCF) with an advanced "adaptive hardcore bit" property, which have only been constructed based on the hardness of the Learning with Errors problem [BCM+21] and recently isogeny-based group actions [AMR23]. Our framework allows certification of qubits based only on the existence of post-quantum TCF, without the adaptive hardcore bit property, or on quantum fully homomorphic encryption. These can be instantiated, for example, from Ring Learning with Errors. This has the potential to improve the efficiency of qubit certification and derived functionalities.

On the technical side, we show that the *quantum soundness* of any such protocol can be reduced to proving a bound on a simple algorithmic task: informally, answering "two challenges simultaneously" in the protocol. Our reduction formalizes the intuition that these protocols demonstrate quantumness by leveraging the impossibility of rewinding a general quantum prover. This allows us to prove tight bounds on the quantum soundness of [KCVY21] and [KLVY22], showing that no quantum polynomial-time prover can succeed with probability larger than $\cos^2 \frac{\pi}{8} \approx 0.853$. Previously, only an upper bound on the success probability of classical provers, and a lower bound on the success probability of quantum provers, were known. We then extend this proof of quantum soundness to show that provers that approach the quantum soundness bound must perform almost anti-commuting measurements. This certifies that the prover holds a qubit.

The full version of this paper can be found at https://arxiv.org/abs/2303.01293.

© International Association for Cryptologic Research 2023
H. Handschuh and A. Lysyanskaya (Eds.): CRYPTO 2023, LNCS 14085, pp. 162–191, 2023.
https://doi.org/10.1007/978-3-031-38554-4_6

1   Introduction

A *cryptographic test of quantumness*[1] is an interactive protocol allowing a classical polynomial-time *verifier* to determine, with high confidence, that a (possibly quantum) polynomial-time *prover* with which the verifier is interacting is non-classical. More precisely, it should be the case that there exists a quantum polynomial-time prover that succeeds with high probability in the protocol (*quantum completeness*) whereas no classical polynomial-time prover can succeed with comparable probability (*classical soundness*). Ideally, the former statement should hold with a "simple" quantum prover (i.e. one performing small quantum circuits), and the latter statement should hold based on the weakest possible cryptographic assumption.

A simple example of a test of quantumness consists in asking the prover to factor a large integer chosen by the verifier. While this proposal satisfies both completeness and soundness at the coarsest level, it suffers from two important limitations. The first is that demonstrating success for the quantum prover requires executing Shor's quantum algorithm for factoring [Sho94], which although quantum polynomial-time requires a large circuit to be executed (roughly, $\tilde{O}(\lambda)$ qubits and $\tilde{O}(\lambda^2)$ circuit size, where λ is the bit-length of the integer).

The second, even more significant limitation, is that it is unclear how to build any other interesting cryptographic primitive on top of such a protocol. Indeed, beyond the near-term demonstration of a quantum advantage the impetus for studying tests of quantumness comes from their potential use as building blocks towards more complex protocols in quantum cryptography, such as protocols for certified randomness [BCM+21, MVV22], for testing that a quantum prover is able to coherently manipulate a certain number of qubits ("tests for quantum space") [FWZ22, GMP22], or for classical delegation of quantum computations [Mah18, GV19, Zha22]. Currently, the only known protocols for such tasks all have at their heart a simple test of quantumness. In fact, to the best of our knowledge for all known protocols the test of quantumness is the same—it is the test introduced in [BCM+21].[2] The soundness of this test was originally shown based on the post-quantum hardness of the Learning With Errors (LWE) problem [Reg09], and more recently the same test (in fact, the same underlying assumption of post-quantum TCF with adaptive hardcore bit) was also shown sound based on isogeny-based group actions [AMR23], an advanced post-quantum cryptographic assumption.

The pervasiveness of the test of quantumness from [BCM+21] for advanced cryptographic applications begs the question—can new tests of quantumness be

---

[1] Also sometimes referred to as *proof of quantumness* [BKVV20].

[2] The one exception is the recent test of quantumness by Yamakawa and Zhandry [YZ22], which also achieves certifiable randomness generation, albeit by relying on a conjecture of Aaronson and Ambainis [AA14]. We exclude "quantum supremacy" demonstrations such as [AA11, AAB+19] because (i) they are not efficiently verifiable, and (ii) except for a single exception [BBF+21], they are not known to lead to any interesting cryptographic task.

found, that preserve the versatility of the previous test and its potential for applications but simplify, or at least diversify, the range of assumptions on which the test is based? Besides its intrinsic interest, answering this question may lead to more versatile as well as more prover-efficient tests; the test [BCM+21] requires quite an aggressive setting of parameters for LWE which hampers its practical applicability (see however the proof of principle demonstration in [ZKML+21]).

Recently there has been progress on this question in two different directions. Firstly, in [BKVV20] the authors introduce a test that is sound in the (quantum) random oracle model, assuming only the existence of trapdoor claw-free functions (defined later). Going even further [YZ22] show a *non-interactive* test of quantumness in the random oracle model. Secondly, very recently there have been two new proposals in the standard model. The test from [KCVY21] is a 6-message protocol whose soundness can be based on any family of trapdoor claw-free functions. The test from [KLVY22] is a 4-message protocol, that can be instantiated based on any two-player nonlocal game with a quantum advantage, and whose soundness relies on the existence of a quantum homomorphic encryption scheme, with some specific properties (which are known to hold for e.g. the scheme in [Mah20]).

However, these latter tests of quantumness suffer from an important limitation: prior to our work, it was not known how they could be expanded into a test for certified randomness, a test for a qubit (defined informally below), let alone a delegation protocol. This is simply because it was unknown how to analyze the behavior of malicious quantum provers in the protocol! For these protocols, only quantum *completeness* was known, but it was not known if the proposed honest strategy for the quantum prover is optimal. For example, for the proposals in [KCVY21,KLVY22] it was not even known if the success probability demonstrated by the honest quantum prover (in both cases, $\cos^2 \frac{\pi}{8} \approx 0.853\ldots$) was the optimal success probability—it was left open if there could be a quantum prover that succeeds with probability 1.

The main technical difficulty is that for showing soundness against classical adversaries, one can use classical rewinding-type arguments. This is no longer possible against quantum provers: quantum rewinding is notoriously delicate, and while some general results have started to appear (e.g. [CMSZ21]) they do not apply to the above tests. In fact, in some sense they *should not* apply, because the goal of the test is to demonstrate a quantum advantage through the quantum demonstration of a *non-rewindable* task.

1.1 Our Results

We break the "quantum soundness barrier" by showing that $\cos^2 \frac{\pi}{8}$ is indeed the optimal success probability for the protocols introduced in [KCVY21,KLVY22]. In fact, we show a general bound that applies to a broad class of protocols encompassing the above two. Furthermore, we are able to show that the measurement operators used by any near-optimal prover must satisfy a form of approximate anti-commutation. Such anti-commutation is a key signature of quantumness, which is informally known as a "test for a qubit" in the literature (see e.g. [Vid20, Lecture 2] for more on this). A very similar statement forms the basis for the certified randomness protocol in [BCM+21]. Our results thus open the door for making use of the protocols from [KCVY21, KLVY22] for the same applications as the one from [BCM+21], from certified randomness to delegated computation [Mah18, GV19]. The main advantage of our protocol is that its analysis does not require the infamous "adaptive hardcore bit" property used in [BCM+21]. As a result, we can instantiate it with any family of trapdoor claw-free functions, such as can be constructed from e.g. the ring-LWE problem, leading to more efficient protocols and better parameters.[3]

Before describing our results, and their proof, in more detail, we give a high-level overview of our "template protocol" (see Fig. 1 for a summary), which specifies a general format for a test of quantumness to which our results apply. Our template is divided into two phases. The first phase, Phase A, is a setup phase in which the verifier and prover exchange classical information that, informally, enables the quantum prover to create the "right" initial state. For example, for the protocol from [KCVY21] the result of Phase A is that the honest prover has returned to the verifier a string y, which has two preimages x_0 and x_1 under a claw-free function f, as well as an n-bit string d, and furthermore the prover holds the quantum state

$$\frac{1}{\sqrt{2}}\left(|r \cdot x_0\rangle + (-1)^{d \cdot (x_0 \oplus x_1)}|r \cdot x_1\rangle\right),$$

for some uniformly random string r that is communicated to the prover at some point during the phase. (Note that the protocol of [BCM+21] can also be cast in this language, although the equivalent of Phase B has a different structure so that protocol does not fully fall under the template we describe here.) Note that a "phase" is allowed to take place over multiple rounds of interaction. Phase A may also incorporate a test executed by the verifier, in which case the verifier is allowed to end the protocol outright with a flag signifying acceptance or rejection of the prover. (The "preimage test" in [BCM+21, KCVY21] is an example of such a test that occurs in Phase A).

Assuming no such flag has been raised, the protocol proceeds to Phase B. This phase is very simple: the prover is sent a uniformly random challenge bit $m \in \{0, 1\}$ and required to respond with a bit $b \in \{0, 1\}$. The verifier classically computes a correct value $\hat{c}_m = \hat{c}_m(\text{rand}, \text{trans})$, where rand are the verifier's private random bits and trans the classical communication transcript from Phase A, and the verifier accepts if and only if $(-1)^b = \hat{c}_m$.

Our main result is a reduction from classical, respectively quantum, soundness of the protocol template to a specific guessing task. Informally, we show the following.

Theorem 1.1 (Main theorem, informal). *Suppose that no classical (resp. quantum) polynomial-time algorithm may produce a guess for the parity $\hat{c}_0 \cdot \hat{c}_1$*

---

[3] We recall that the use of adaptive hardcore bits in [BCM+21] led to a significant degradation in the parameters for LWE that could be used.

that is correct with a non-negligible advantage.[4] *Then no classical (resp. quantum) polynomial-time prover can succeed in the protocol template with probability larger than* $\frac{3}{4}$ *(resp.* $\cos^2 \frac{\pi}{8}$*) by more than a negligible amount.*

The strength of this result is that it reduces an a priori complex task—bounding the success probability of a classical or quantum prover in an interactive protocol—to showing limitations on adversaries in a much simpler, non-interactive task. In particular, as we will see from the examples (Sect. 5), in virtually all known cases the hardness of the parity-predicting task considered in the theorem is essentially immediate from the computational hardness assumption that underlies the protocol. For example, in the protocol from [KCVY21] the product $\hat{c}_0 \cdot \hat{c}_1$ turns out to equal $r \cdot (x_0 \oplus x_1)$. A prover who can predict this quantity with advantage ε for a uniformly random r can, via the Golreich-Levin theorem, recover $x_0 \oplus x_1$ with a related advantage. Since Phase A of this version of the protocol verifies that the prover also knows either x_0 or x_1, we conclude that the prover is able to recover a claw (x_0, x_1), violating the claw-free property of the underlying function family.

The conceptually most appealing feature of our theorem is that it "explains" the bounds $\frac{3}{4}$ and $\cos^2 \frac{\pi}{8}$ that had been observed without justification for previous tests of quantumness, e.g. [KCVY21,KLVY22]. In particular, as already mentioned $\cos^2 \frac{\pi}{8}$ was established as a lower bound, but not an upper bound, on the maximum success probability of a quantum prover in those works. As such our result can be interpreted as a form of computational "quantum non-rewinding" result, which precisely establishes the extent to which a classical or quantum procedure may produce guesses for two quantities whose parity is known to be hard to predict.

Going beyond quantum soundness, we also establish that any quantum prover which succeeds close to the optimum probability must do so by using two binary measurements in Phase B of the protocol that are close to maximally anti-commuting measurements. This is what is generally known as a "test for a qubit" in the quantum information literature. Informally,

Theorem 1.2 (Qubit test, informal). *Suppose that a quantum polynomial-time prover succeeds in the protocol template with probability at least* $\cos^2 \frac{\pi}{8} - \varepsilon$*. Let S_0 and S_1 be the two binary observables associated with the prover's measurements on a Phase B challenge of $m = 0$ and $m = 1$ respectively. Then S_0 and S_1 are within distance $O(\sqrt{\varepsilon})$ of a pair of perfectly anti-commuting measurements.*[5]

This result is formalized in Theorem 4.7. While more technical, the statement will be familiar to researchers in the area of self-testing, and it is well-known to have powerful consequences. In [BCM+21] a similar statement is used to obtain

---

[4] Here, $\hat{c}_0$ and $\hat{c}_1$ are defined conditional on a transcript for Phase A of the protocol template. We refer to Theorem 4.4 for a more precise formulation.

[5] Here, "distance" should be measured using the appropriate norm. We use the standard "state-dependent norm" from self-testing. See Theorem 4.7 for the precise formulation.

certified randomness, and this has been expanded in [GV19] to obtain verifiable classical delegation of quantum computation. In a work of Merkulov and Arnon-Friedman [MA23] the connection with certified randomness is made explicit. They show that the specific bound on the anti-commutator obtained in our qubit test implies precise quantitative bounds on the randomness generated in a single execution of our (and other) protocols, as well as on the accumulation of randomness across many sequential executions.

Related work. While writing our results, we learned that Natarajan and Zhang [NZ23] had independently obtained directly related, yet strictly incomparable, results. Natarajan and Zhang focus on the protocol from [KLVY22] (whereas our result applies more generically), when specialized to the CHSH nonlocal game, and establish its quantum soundness as well as the property of "test for a qubit." This part of the results is common to both our works. However, they go further by showing that the test for a qubit can be leveraged to implement a complete protocol for verifiable delegation of quantum computations, an application which we do not investigate (though we expect our qubit test to also yield a quantum verification protocol by making use of the history state construction as in [Mah18]).

1.2 Technical Overview

Beyond its conceptual clarity, another appealing feature of our main result is that its proof is simple! We sketch the argument here. Let's start by observing that the statement for classical soundness is almost immediate. This is because a prover who is able to predict $\hat{c}_0$ with probability p_0, and $\hat{c}_1$ with probability p_1, such that $\frac{1}{2}(p_0 + p_1) = \frac{3}{4} + \varepsilon$, must, by a union bound, be able to predict both $\hat{c}_0$ and $\hat{c}_1$, and hence their product, with probability at least $\frac{1}{2} + 2\varepsilon$. If the latter is hard, then the prover cannot exist.

Now, let us think about the quantum case. Here the argument is more delicate, because the "union bound" does not apply. If it was known that the quantum prover responds correctly on at least one of the challenges with probability close to 1, then we could use a tool such as the gentle measurement lemma (see e.g. [Wil11, Lemma 9.4.1]) to perform the rewinding. However, in general this will not be the case—and indeed, it *cannot* be the case, since we expect that there should be a quantum advantage!

The central question is thus the following: what is the smallest possible probability p such that a quantum prover who can predict either $\hat{c}_0$, or $\hat{c}_1$, with overall probability p (on average over the choice of a uniform $m \in \{0, 1\}$), can also predict $\hat{c}_0 \cdot \hat{c}_1$ with non-negligible advantage? We show that the answer is the famous probability $\cos^2 \frac{\pi}{8} \approx 0.853$. This probability already appears in the analysis of the nonlocal game CHSH,[6] and it is not a coincidence. We explain why. Recall that in the CHSH game, two isolated provers Alice and Bob are given uniformly

---

[6] CHSH is a well known two-prover protocol, which allows to certify quantum correlations between two non-communicating provers.

generated inputs $x, y \in \{0, 1\}$ respectively, and are tasked with generating bits $a, b \in \{0, 1\}$ respectively, where

$$a \oplus b = x \wedge y \tag{1}$$

Observe that this condition means that, on input $y = 0$ we must have $b_0 = a$, whereas on input $y = 1$ we must have $b_1 = a \oplus x$. Therefore, Bob's task is to find two measurement operators whose outcomes satisfy $b_0 \oplus b_1 = x$. But x is Alice's input, which Bob has no information at all about! The question of finding an optimal strategy in the CHSH game is then reduced to finding measurements for Bob that lead to the highest probability of success for (1), while knowing that the parity $b_0 \oplus b_1$ is a bit that is information-theoretically impossible for Bob to predict. It then immediately follows—using the same argument as above—that the maximum success probability for a classical Bob is $\frac{3}{4}$. And it is also known, albeit harder to prove, that the maximum quantum success probability is $\cos^2 \frac{\pi}{8}$, and that this can only be achieved using a pair of anti-commuting measurements for Bob.

Working out the actual result in our setting requires a bit more work. This is because the situation is not completely analogous to that of CHSH; in particular the state on which Bob (here, the quantum prover in Phase B of the protocol template) makes his measurement is the result of an interaction with the verifier, not of a measurement by Alice on some prior entangled state. While the technical setup differs, ultimately we are able to apply similar tools to those applied in quantum information theory for the analysis of non-local games. In particular, we make a careful use of Jordan's lemma to reduce the analysis to a 2-dimensional problem (for this it is crucial that the verifier's challenge in the last round consists of a single bit). Having reduced the problem to two dimensions we quantify the tension between the tasks of succeeding in the protocol, and the potential of the quantum prover for predicting the parity with $\hat{c}_0 \cdot \hat{c}_1$. Carefully working out this tension leads to the optimal quantitative tradeoffs that are expressed in our main theorem.

1.3   Open Questions

Our template protocol does not capture all known tests of quantumness. Two notable exceptions are the test of quantumness by Brakerski et al. [BCM+21] and the ones that operate in the random oracle model [BKVV20, YZ22]. It may seem surprising that the test from [BCM+21] does not fit our framework, as indeed it is quite similar, though more demanding cryptographically, to the test from [KCVY21]. It is possible that a small variation on the test could be made to fit our template, but we do not investigate this. Regarding the test from [YZ22], it operates in the random oracle model, which we did not attempt to incorporate in our framework. More importantly, it is non-interactive, which makes it unclear how our ideas could be used.

A test of quantumness that we believe should fall within a modified version of our framework is the application of the compiler from [KLVY22] to the Magic

Square game. The Magic Square game is a nonlocal game which has the advantage that the optimal quantum winning probability is exactly 1. This could lead to a test of quantumness with quantum completeness 1, which is convenient for applications. We leave this question open for future work.

By formalizing the common structure underlying many simple tests of quantumness, our results suggest a hierarchy of "capabilities", that builds from a test of quantumness based on the non-rewinding property of quantum systems, to a test for a qubit, followed potentially by tests for certified randomness and delegated computation. An interesting conceptual question is to determine what is the minimal basis for achieving these capabilities, and whether the advanced ones can always, or almost always, be reduced to the more elementary ones, as seems to be the case in our framework. A specific direction that would be worthwhile investigating is whether certified randomness can be "accumulated" in a generic fashion from the family of protocols that we consider here.

The first author is supported by the Israel Science Foundation (Grant No. 3426/21), and by the European Union Horizon 2020 Research and Innovation Program via ERC Project REACT (Grant 756482). The second author is supported by the Knut and Alice Wallenberg Foundation through the Wallenberg Centre for Quantum Technology (WACQT). The third author is supported by the U.S. Department of Energy, Office of Science, Office of Advanced Scientific Computing Research, under the Accelerated Research in Quantum Computing (ARQC) program. The fifth author is supported by a grant from the Simons Foundation (828076, TV), MURI Grant FA9550-18-1-0161, AFOSR Grant FA9550-21-S-0001, and a research grant from the Center for New Scientists at the Weizmann Institute of Science.

2 Preliminaries

2.1 Notation

We use $\mathrm{negl}(\lambda)$ to denote any negligible function of λ, i.e. a function $f : \mathbb{N} \to \mathbb{R}_+$ such that $f(\lambda)p(\lambda) \to_{\lambda \to \infty} 0$ for all polynomials p. Given two strings r_0, r_1 we write $r_0 \| r_1$ for their concatenation.

2.2 Quantum Goldreich-Levin

We state a quantum version of the Goldreich-Levin theorem, which is taken from [AC02].

Definition 2.1. *A* quantum inner product *query (with bias ε) is a unitary transformation U_{IP} together with an auxiliary m-qubit quantum state $|\psi\rangle$ on $n + m + t$ qubits, or its inverse $U_{\mathrm{IP}}^\dagger$, such that U_{IP} satisfies the following two properties:*

1. *There is a string $a \in \{0,1\}^n$ such that if $x \in \{0,1\}^n$ is chosen randomly according to the uniform distribution and the last qubit of $U_{\mathrm{IP}}|x\rangle|\psi\rangle|0^t\rangle$ is measured, the value $w \in \{0,1\}$ obtained is such that $\Pr(w = a \cdot x) \geq \frac{1}{2} + \varepsilon$.*

2. For any $x \in \{0,1\}^n$ and $y \in \{0,1\}^t$, the state of the first n qubits of $U_{\text{IP}} |x\rangle |\psi\rangle |y\rangle$ is x.

Theorem 2.2. *There exists a quantum algorithm that returns the string a with probability greater than or equal to $4\varepsilon^2$ using a U_{IP} query and a $U_{\text{IP}}^\dagger$ query. The number of auxilliary qubit operation used by this procedure is $O(1)$.*

2.3   Jordan's Lemma

Lemma 2.3. *Let Q_0 and Q_1 be two orthogonal projections on a (finite-dimensional) Hilbert space $\mathcal{H}$. Then there is a decomposition $\mathcal{H} = \oplus_i \mathcal{H}_i$ where for each i, $\mathcal{H}_i$ has dimension at most 2 and furthermore, the decomposition is stabilized by both Q_0 and Q_1. In particular, whenever $\dim(\mathcal{H}_i) = 2$ we can find a basis of $\mathcal{H}_i$ in which*

$$Q_0 = \begin{pmatrix} 1 & 0 \\ 0 & 0 \end{pmatrix} \quad and \quad Q_1 = \begin{pmatrix} c_i^2 & c_i s_i \\ c_i s_i & s_i^2 \end{pmatrix}, \tag{2}$$

where $c_i = \cos(\alpha_i)$ and $s_i = \sin(\alpha_i)$, $\alpha_i \in [-\pi, \pi)$.

3   Protocol Template

We introduce a general template that a test of quantumness may take. The template divides the test into two phases, *Phase A* and *Phase B*. Phase A is a "setup phase" in which the verifier and prover exchange classical information that, informally, guarantees that the prover has properly set up their workspace. The phase may include some tests, at the end of which the verifier may decide to abort the phase and either accept or reject the prover's actions outright. This possibility is captured by an outcome flag $\in \{\text{acc}, \text{rej}, \text{cont}\}$ that the verifier may return. Here, flag $=$ cont means that no decision has been taken and the protocol should proceed to Phase B. In Phase B, a single-bit challenge m is issued by the verifier to the prover, who responds with a single-bit outcome b. The value b returned by the prover is checked against a correct value $\hat{c}_m$ that is computed by the verifier as a function of its private randomness rand, the transcript trans of the interaction in the first phase, and the challenge bit m. This template is summarized in Fig. 1.

Our main results bound the maximum success probability of classical or quantum provers in any such protocol, assuming that a specific prediction task associated with the protocol is hard (informally, predicting the parity $\hat{c}_0 \cdot \hat{c}_1$). To formulate the results we need to model the behavior of an arbitrary prover in the protocol. Such a prover is specified by a Hilbert space $\mathcal{H}_\mathsf{P}$, an initial quantum state $|\psi\rangle \in \mathcal{H}_\mathsf{P} \otimes \mathcal{H}_\mathsf{E}$, where $\mathcal{H}_\mathsf{E}$ models an "environment" to which the prover does not have access (nor the verifier), and two families of measurements corresponding to the prover's actions in the two phases of the protocol (Fig. 1). We emphasize that while Phase B naturally consists of a single round of interaction, Phase A may consist of multiple rounds of interaction. In this case, the actions of

Fix a security parameter λ.

Phase A:

1. The verifier and prover interact classically. At the end of the interaction, the verifier returns a `flag` $\in \{$`acc`, `rej`, `cont`$\}$. Let `rand` denote the verifier's random bits used in that phase, `trans` the transcript of the interaction, and $|\psi_{\text{trans}}\rangle \in \mathcal{H}_{\text{PE}}$ the state of the prover and the environment at the end of the interaction.

Phase B (executed only in case `flag` = `cont`):

1. The verifier sends a uniformly random challenge $m \in \{0, 1\}$ to the prover.
2. The prover returns a bit $b \in \{0, 1\}$ to the verifier.
3. The verifier accepts if and only if $(-1)^b = \hat{c}_m$, where $\hat{c}_m = \hat{c}_m(\text{rand}, \text{trans}) \in \{-1, 1\}$ is a value computed by the verifier.

Fig. 1. Our template for a test of quantumness.

the prover in Phase A are described by multiple families of measurements, which incorporate any unitaries that the prover may apply to update its quantum state from one round to the next. Since our analysis will for the most part focus on the prover's behavior in the second phase, we abstract some of the details in the following definition.

Definition 3.1 (Quantum Device). *A quantum device $\mathfrak{D}$ is specified by:*

- *Hilbert spaces $\mathcal{H}_P$ and $\mathcal{H}_E$, and a family of states $\{|\psi_{trans}\rangle_{PE} : trans \in \mathcal{T}\}$ on $\mathcal{H}_P \otimes \mathcal{H}_E$ together with a distribution μ on $\mathcal{T}$. Here $\mathcal{T}$ is used to denote the space of possible transcripts.*
- *For each $m \in \{0, 1\}$, a projective measurement $\{\Pi_b^m\}$ on $\mathcal{H}_P$.[7]*

A quantum device can be used to specify a quantum prover in the template protocol as follows. The prover starts the protocol in a state $|\psi\rangle \in \mathcal{H}_P \otimes \mathcal{H}_E$. In Phase A, the verifier and the prover interact. This interaction results in a transcript `trans`, obtained with probability $\mu(\text{trans})$, and a post-interaction state $|\psi_{\text{trans}}\rangle_{\text{PE}}$. Note that the fact that $(\text{trans}, |\psi_{\text{trans}}\rangle)$ must be produced through a valid execution of Phase A of the protocol is implicit in the definition of a device. In the second phase, after having received m the prover measures $\mathcal{H}_P$ using $\{\Pi_b^m\}$ and returns the obtained outcome b. This is without loss of generality, as the measurement operators may incorporate any m-dependent unitary that the prover applies to their state after having received the verifier's challenge bit.

---

[7] By Naimark's theorem the requirement that the measurement is projective is without loss of generality, up to enlarging the prover's Hilbert space with a single auxiliary qubit.

4   Soundness Analysis

In this section we show that general statements on the soundness of the protocol template can be derived from a simple assumption about the hardness of predicting the parity $\hat{c}_0 \cdot \hat{c}_1$ of the correct answers on challenges $m = 0$ and $m = 1$. Specifically, we establish *classical soundness* (a bound on the maximum probability of success of any classical prover in the protocol), *quantum soundness* (the same, for quantum provers), and the property of being a *test for a qubit* (informally, that any quantum prover that succeeds with near-optimal probability must do so by performing measurements in Phase B such that the measurement applied for $m = 0$ and the one applied for $m = 1$ are close to maximally anti-commuting).

4.1   The Parity Adversary

We start by showing that any device that succeeds in the protocol template with some probability can be turned into an algorithm for predicting the parity of the verifier's two decision bits $\hat{c}_0$ and $\hat{c}_1$ in Phase B of the protocol. Although rather simple, observing such a transformation in the general setup of the protocol template is arguably our main conceptual contribution. Specifically, we construct the following.

Definition 4.1. *Let $\delta, \kappa : \mathbb{N} \to [0, 1]$. We say that a pair $\mathcal{A} = (\mathcal{A}_1, \mathcal{A}_2)$ of (classical or quantum) polynomial-time algorithms is a (classical or quantum) parity adversary with advantage (κ, δ) on (some instantiation of) the template protocol if the following hold. Firstly, $\mathcal{A}_1$ and $\mathcal{A}_2$ have the following structure:*

- *$\mathcal{A}_1$ is a family of algorithms for the prover in an interaction with the verifier for Phase A of the template protocol. In particular, $\mathcal{A}_1$ is initialized in a quantum state $|\psi\rangle \in \mathcal{H}_{PE}$ and completes the interaction by returning a transcript $\textbf{trans}$ and a post-interaction state $|\psi_{\textbf{trans}}\rangle \in \mathcal{H}_{PE}$.*
- *$\mathcal{A}_2$ takes as input the output $(\textbf{trans}, |\psi_{\textbf{trans}}\rangle)$ of $\mathcal{A}_1$. It returns a bit $b \in \{0, 1\}$. ($\mathcal{A}_2$ does not interact with the verifier.)*

Secondly, it holds that the interaction of $\mathcal{A}_1$ with the verifier results in $\textbf{flag} = \textbf{rej}$ with probability at most $\kappa(\lambda)$, and furthermore

$$\mathop{\mathrm{E}}_{\textbf{trans} \leftarrow \mathcal{A}_1(1^\lambda)} \left| \mathop{\mathrm{Pr}}_{b \leftarrow \mathcal{A}_2(1^\lambda, \textbf{trans}, |\psi_{\textbf{trans}}\rangle)} \left((-1)^b = \hat{c}_0 \cdot \hat{c}_1 \right) - \frac{1}{2} \right| \leq \delta(\lambda) \, ,$$

where the outer expectation is taken over $\textbf{trans}$ generated from $\mathcal{A}_1$ and is taken conditioned on $\textbf{flag} = \textbf{cont}$, the inner probability is taken over b generated from $\mathcal{A}_2$ on input $\textbf{trans}$ and $|\psi_{\textbf{trans}}\rangle$, and for $m \in \{0, 1\}$, $\hat{c}_m$ is computed from $\textbf{trans}$ and the verifier's private coins $\textbf{rand}$ used when interacting with $\mathcal{A}_1$ as in Phase B of the template protocol.

Let $\mathfrak{D}$ be a device for the protocol template (Definition 3.1). Let $\mathcal{A}_1$ execute Phase A of the protocol by interacting the device with the verifier, resulting in a transcript $\mathtt{trans}$ obtained with probability $\mu(\mathtt{trans})$ and a post-execution state $|\psi_{\mathtt{trans}}\rangle \in \mathcal{H}_{\mathsf{PE}}$. Let $\mathcal{A}_2$ perform the following actions. $\mathcal{A}_2$ first applies the projective measurement $\{\Pi_b^0\}$ on $\mathcal{H}_{\mathsf{P}}$ to obtain a $b_0 \in \{0, 1\}$. Then $\mathcal{A}_2$ applies the projective measurement $\{\Pi_b^1\}$ on $\mathcal{H}_{\mathsf{P}}$ to obtain a $b_1 \in \{0, 1\}$. Finally, $\mathcal{A}_2$ returns $b_0 \oplus b_1$. This construction is summarized in Fig. 2.

Fix a device $\mathfrak{D}$ for the protocol template.
- Algorithm $\mathcal{A}_1$: Execute Phase A of the protocol template to obtain $(\mathtt{trans}, |\psi_{\mathtt{trans}}\rangle)$ and a flag $\mathtt{flag}$ returned by the verifier.
- Algorithm $\mathcal{A}_2$: If $\mathtt{flag} = \mathtt{cont}$,
  1. Measure $\mathcal{H}_{\mathsf{P}}$ using the two-outcome measurement $\{\Pi_0^0, \Pi_1^0\}$. Let $b_0 \in \{0, 1\}$ be the outcome obtained.
  2. Measure using the two-outcome measurement $\{\Pi_0^1, \Pi_1^1\}$. Let $b_1 \in \{0, 1\}$ be the outcome obtained.
  3. Return $b_0 \oplus b_1$.

Fig. 2. A parity adversary.

Given a choice of random bits $\mathtt{rand}$ and a transcript $\mathtt{trans}$, define projections on $\mathcal{H}_{\mathsf{P}}$ by

$$Q_0 = \Pi_{\hat{c}_0}^0 \qquad \text{and} \qquad Q_1 = \Pi_{\hat{c}_1}^1 . \tag{3}$$

Lemma 4.2. *Conditioned on $\mathtt{flag} = \mathtt{cont}$ and $\mathtt{trans}$ having been obtained after the execution of $\mathcal{A}_1$, the parity adversary defined in Fig. 2 returns an outcome $b \in \{0, 1\}$ such that*

$$\begin{aligned} p_{\mathrm{xor}} &= p_{\mathrm{xor}}(\boldsymbol{rand}, \boldsymbol{trans}) \\ &:= \Pr\left((-1)^b = \hat{c}_0 \cdot \hat{c}_1\right) \\ &= \left\| (Q_1 Q_0 + (Id - Q_1)(Id - Q_0)) |\psi_{trans}\rangle \right\|^2 . \end{aligned}$$

Proof. It holds that $(-1)^{b_0 \oplus b_1} = \hat{c}_0 \cdot \hat{c}_1$ if and only if either $((-1)^{b_0} = \hat{c}_0$ and $(-1)^{b_1} = \hat{c}_1)$ or $((-1)^{b_0} \neq \hat{c}_0$ and $(-1)^{b_1} \neq \hat{c}_1)$. By definition, the probability of the first event is $\|Q_1 Q_0 |\psi_{\mathtt{trans}}\rangle\|^2$ and the probability of the second event is $\|(Id - Q_1)(Id - Q_0)|\psi_{\mathtt{trans}}\rangle\|^2$. Using that Q_1 and $(Id - Q_1)$ are orthogonal, the lemma follows.

4.2   Classical and Quantum Soundness

In this section we show that a precise bound on the classical and quantum soundness of the protocol template can be obtained from the following assumption.

Assumption 1. *There is a function* $s : \mathbb{N} \times [0,1] \to [0,1]$ *such that for any (classical or quantum) polynomial-time parity adversary* $\mathcal{A}$ *with advantage* (κ, δ), *it holds that* $\delta(\lambda) \leq s(\lambda, \kappa(\lambda))$.

Note that Assumption 1 will in general be conditional on the hardness of some computational problem, such as the Learning with Errors problem. In the examples from Sect. 5 we will give various instantiations of the assumption. As we will see, given a concrete protocol that fits the protocol template it is generally quite straightforward to show that the assumption holds (often, it will hold for a function $s(\lambda) = \text{negl}(\lambda)$, and the possibility for executing a test in Phase A will not even be used). However, the conclusion that we obtain on quantum soundness of the protocol template will comparatively be quite strong.

Let $\mathfrak{D}$ be a (classical or quantum) polynomial-time device for the protocol template. Recall the definition of the projections Q_0 and Q_1 in (3) (which implicitly depend on the verifier's private randomness `rand` and the transcript `trans` from Phase A). By definition the probability that $\mathfrak{D}$ succeeds in Phase B of the protocol, conditioned on `flag = cont` and $m \in \{0,1\}$, is

$$p_m = \|Q_m |\psi_{\text{trans}}\rangle\|^2 . \tag{4}$$

Thus the probability that the device succeeds in Phase B of the protocol is

$$\frac{1}{2}(p_0 + p_1) = \frac{1}{2}\|Q_0|\psi_{\text{trans}}\rangle\|^2 + \frac{1}{2}\|Q_1|\psi_{\text{trans}}\rangle\|^2 . \tag{5}$$

By Jordan's lemma (Lemma 2.3) there is a decomposition $\mathcal{H}_{\text{PE}} = \oplus_i \mathcal{H}_i$ such that for all i, $\dim(\mathcal{H}_i) \leq 2$ and moreover $\mathcal{H}_i$ is invariant under both Q_0 and Q_1. For $\gamma \in \{1,2\}$ let $\mathcal{S}_\gamma$ be the collection of indices i such that $\dim(\mathcal{H}_i) = \gamma$ and let $\mathcal{S} = \mathcal{S}_1 \cup \mathcal{S}_2$.

Fix an index $i \in \mathcal{S}$. Let $|u_i\rangle$ be the normalized projection of $|\psi_{\text{trans}}\rangle$ on $\mathcal{H}_i$, and let $t_i = |\langle u_i | \psi_{\text{trans}}\rangle|^2$. If $i \in \mathcal{S}_1$ then the restrictions of Q_0 and Q_1 to $\mathcal{H}_i$ take the form

$$Q_0 = \left(\cos^2 \alpha_i\right) \quad \text{and} \quad Q_1 = \left(\cos^2 \beta_i\right) ,$$

where $\alpha_i, \beta_i \in \{0, \frac{\pi}{2}\}$. If $i \in \mathcal{S}_2$ then there exists a state in $\mathcal{H}_i$ which is orthogonal to $|u_i\rangle$, denote it by $|u_i^\perp\rangle$. The pair $\{|u_i\rangle, |u_i^\perp\rangle\}$ is an orthonormal basis for $\mathcal{H}_i$ in which Q_0 and Q_1 take the form

$$Q_0 = \begin{pmatrix} \cos^2(\alpha_i) & \cos(\alpha_i)\sin(\alpha_i) \\ \cos(\alpha_i)\sin(\alpha_i) & \sin^2(\alpha_i) \end{pmatrix} \tag{6}$$

and

$$Q_1 = \begin{pmatrix} \cos^2(\beta_i) & \cos(\beta_i)\sin(\beta_i) \\ \cos(\beta_i)\sin(\beta_i) & \sin^2(\beta_i) \end{pmatrix} \tag{7}$$

respectively, for some $\alpha_i, \beta_i \in [-\pi/2, \pi/2)$.[8] With these notations, starting from (4) one easily verifies that

$$p_0 = \sum_i t_i \cos^2(\alpha_i) \, ,$$

$$p_1 = \sum_i t_i \cos^2(\beta_i) \, . \tag{8}$$

We summarize our findings so far in the following claim.

Claim 4.3. *The probability that the device $\mathfrak{D}$ succeeds in the protocol template, conditioned on $(\mathbf{rand}, \mathbf{trans})$ and $\mathbf{flag} = \mathbf{cont}$ having been obtained in Phase A, is*

$$\frac{1}{2}(p_0 + p_1) = \sum_i \frac{t_i}{2}(\cos^2(\alpha_i) + \cos^2(\beta_i)) \, . \tag{9}$$

Furthermore, the parity adversary derived from $\mathfrak{D}$ as in Fig. 2 has advantage (also conditioned on $\mathbf{rand}$ and $\mathbf{trans}$)

$$\delta = \left| p_{\mathrm{xor}} - \frac{1}{2} \right| \, . \tag{10}$$

where

$$p_{\mathrm{xor}} = \sum_i t_i \cos^2(\alpha_i - \beta_i) \tag{11}$$

Proof. The first part of the claim follows directly from (8). The second part follows by direct calculation using the expression from Lemma 4.2. Specifically, starting from the expressions in (6) and (7) we obtain

$$Q_1 Q_0 + (\mathrm{Id} - Q_1)(\mathrm{Id} - Q_0) = \begin{pmatrix} c^2\hat{c}^2 + s^2\hat{s}^2 + 2c\hat{c}s\hat{s} & \hat{c}^2 cs + s^2\hat{c}\hat{s} - \hat{s}^2 cs - c^2\hat{c}\hat{s} \\ c^2\hat{c}\hat{s} + \hat{s}^2 cs - s^2\hat{c}\hat{s} - \hat{c}^2 cs & s^2\hat{s}^2 + c^2\hat{c}^2 + cs\hat{c}\hat{s} \end{pmatrix}$$

$$= \begin{pmatrix} \cos^2(\alpha_i - \beta_i) & \cos(\alpha_i - \beta_i)\sin(\alpha_i - \beta_i) \\ -\cos(\alpha_i - \beta_i)\sin(\alpha_i - \beta_i) & \cos^2(\alpha_i - \beta_i) \end{pmatrix} \, ,$$

where for the middle expression we used the shorthand $c = \cos(\alpha_i)$, $s = \sin(\alpha_i)$, $\hat{c} = \cos(\beta_i)$ and $\hat{s} = \sin(\beta_i)$ and for the last line we used the trigonometric identities

$$\cos(\alpha_i - \beta_i) = \cos(\alpha_i)\cos(\beta_i) + \sin(\alpha_i)\sin(\beta_i) \, ,$$
$$\sin(\alpha_i - \beta_i) = \sin(\alpha_i)\cos(\beta_i) - \cos(\alpha_i)\sin(\beta_i) \, .$$

This allows us to verify that $\|(Q_1 Q_0 + (\mathrm{Id} - Q_1)(\mathrm{Id} - Q_0))|u_i\rangle\|^2 = \cos^2(\alpha_i - \beta_i)$, establishing the claim.

---

[8] Without loss of generality, both Q_0 and Q_1 have rank exactly 1 in $\mathcal{H}_i$. In all other cases, the 2-dimensional space $\mathcal{H}_i$ can be further decomposed as a sum of two invariant 1-dimensional spaces.

Theorem 4.4 (Classical and quantum soundness). *Suppose that Assumption 1 holds for some function $s(\lambda, \kappa)$. Then the maximum probability with which a classical (resp. quantum) polynomial-time prover which succeeds in Phase A of the protocol template with probability at least $1 - \kappa$ may succeed in Phase B is $\frac{3}{4} + \frac{1}{2} s(\lambda, \kappa)$ (resp. $\cos^2 \frac{\pi}{8} + s(\lambda, \kappa)$).*

Proof. For the proof, we fix a device $\mathfrak{D}$ and use the notation introduced towards the proof of Claim 4.3.

We first show classical soundness. In this case, $\mathcal{S}_2 = \emptyset$ and thus by (11),

$$p_{\text{xor}} = \sum_{i:\alpha_i=\beta_i} t_i \,.$$

It follows that, from (9),

$$p_0 + p_1 = \sum_i t_i (\cos^2(\alpha_i) + \cos^2(\beta_i))$$

$$\leq \sum_{i:\alpha_i=\beta_i} 2t_i + \sum_{i:\alpha_i\neq\beta_i} t_i = 2p_{\text{xor}} + (1 - p_{\text{xor}})$$

$$\leq \frac{3}{2} + \delta \,,$$

Here the second line uses $\sum_i t_i = 1$ and (11) and the third uses (10). We then have that the probability with which the classical prover succeeds in Phase B is $\frac{1}{2}(p_0 + p_1) \leq \frac{3}{4} + \frac{1}{2} s(\lambda, \kappa)$, since by Assumption 1, $\delta \leq s(\lambda, \kappa)$.

Next we show quantum soundness. We use the following inequality (derived in Appendix A), valid for any α, β:

$$\cos^2(\alpha) + \cos^2(\beta) \leq |2\cos^2(\alpha - \beta) - 1| + 2\cos^2(\pi/8) \qquad (12)$$

It follows that, starting from (9),

$$\frac{1}{2}(p_0 + p_1) = \frac{1}{2}\sum_i t_i(\cos^2(\alpha_i) + \cos^2(\beta_i))$$

$$\leq \sum_i t_i \left|\cos^2(\alpha_i - \beta_i) - \frac{1}{2}\right| + \cos^2\frac{\pi}{8}$$

$$\leq \delta + \cos^2\frac{\pi}{8} \,,$$

where the second line follows from (12) together with the fact that $\sum_i t_i = 1$ and the third follows from (11). We therefore have that $\frac{1}{2}(p_0 + p_1) \leq s(\lambda, \kappa) + \cos^2\frac{\pi}{8}$ as claimed.

4.3 Qubit Test

In this section we go beyond quantum soundness and show that the protocol template can be used to certify that any prover which succeeds with probability close to the quantum optimum of $\omega = \cos^2\frac{\pi}{8}$ "has a qubit." The key technical step is given by the following proposition.

Proposition 4.5. *Let $\mathfrak{D}$ be a polynomial-time quantum device that is such that* $\Pr(flag = rej) \leq \kappa$ *in Phase A of the protocol template, and that succeeds with probability $\omega - \varepsilon$ in Phase B (conditioned on $flag = cont$ having been returned in Phase A). Let (t_i), (α_i), (β_i) be defined as in the start of Sect. 4.2. Then there is an $\eta = O(\varepsilon + \sqrt{s})$ such that for all but a fraction at most η of transcripts* $trans$ *(such that $flag = cont$) and indices i, as measured by (t_i), it holds that*

$$\left| \alpha_i \pm \frac{\pi}{8} \right| \leq \eta \quad \text{and} \quad \left| \beta_i + \alpha_i \right| \leq \eta ,$$

for some choice of sign $\pm$ (depending on i).

Proof. Recall the set S, and let

$$S' = \{i : \alpha_i \notin [-3\pi/16, 3\pi/16]\} \cup \{i : \beta_i \notin [-3\pi/16, 3\pi/16]\} .$$

We start by bounding $\sum_{i \in S'} t_i$. For this, we first observe the following inequality. For $\alpha \in [-\pi/2, -3\pi/16] \cup [3\pi/16, \pi/2]$ it holds that

$$\cos^2(\alpha - \beta) - \frac{1}{2} \geq 100 \left(\frac{\cos^2 \alpha + \cos^2 \beta}{2} - 0.851 \right) . \tag{13}$$

This is because for the range of α indicated, the right-hand side is always less than -0.5 (while the left-hand side is always at least -0.5), as can be verified by direct calculation. Using both (12) and (13) it follows from (9) that

$$100(\omega - \varepsilon) \leq \sum_i t_i \left(\cos^2(\alpha_i - \beta_i) - \frac{1}{2} \right) + 85.1 \sum_{i \in S'} t_i + 100\omega \sum_{i \notin S'} t_i .$$

Using Assumption 1 and $\sum_i t_i = 1$ we get that

$$\sum_{i \in S'} t_i \leq \frac{1}{\omega - 0.851} \varepsilon + O(s(\lambda, \kappa)) = O(\varepsilon + s) . \tag{14}$$

Since the function $x \mapsto \cos^2(x)$ is strictly concave on $[-3\pi/16, 3\pi/16]$, for $\alpha, \beta \in [-3\pi/16, 3\pi/16]$ it holds that

$$\zeta \cos^2(\alpha) + (1 - \zeta) \cos^2(\beta) = \zeta \cos^2(\alpha) + (1 - \zeta) \cos^2(-\beta) \leq \cos^2(\zeta\alpha - (1 - \zeta)\beta) , \tag{15}$$

for all $\zeta \in [0, 1]$. Taking $\zeta = \frac{1}{2}$, we have

$$\frac{1}{2} \left(\cos^2 \alpha + \cos^2 \beta \right) \leq \cos^2 \left(\frac{\alpha - \beta}{2} \right) . \tag{16}$$

It follows that

$$\frac{1}{2} \sum_{i \notin S'} t_i (\cos^2(\alpha_i) + \cos^2(\beta_i)) \leq \sum_{i \notin S'} t_i \cos^2 \left(\frac{\alpha_i - \beta_i}{2} \right) . \tag{17}$$

Starting from expression (9) we then deduce that,

$$\omega - \varepsilon = \frac{1}{2} \sum_i t_i \left(\cos^2(\alpha_i) + \cos^2(\beta_i) \right)$$

$$\leq \sum_{i \notin S'} t_i \cos^2 \left(\frac{\alpha_i - \beta_i}{2} \right) + O(\varepsilon + s)$$

$$\leq \sum_i \frac{t_i}{2} \left(1 + |\cos(\alpha_i - \beta_i)| \right) + O(\varepsilon + s)$$

$$\leq \frac{1}{2} + \frac{1}{2} \sqrt{\sum_i t_i \cos^2(\alpha_i - \beta_i)} + O(\varepsilon + s) , \qquad (18)$$

where the second line uses (14) and (17), the third line adds non-negative terms for $i \in S'$ and uses the trigonometric identity $\cos^2(x/2) = \frac{1}{2}(1 + \cos(x))$, and the last is by concavity of the square root function. By Assumption 1 the right-hand side is at most

$$\frac{1}{2} + \frac{1}{2\sqrt{2}} + O(\varepsilon + s) + O(\sqrt{s}) = \omega + O(\varepsilon + \sqrt{s}) .$$

Hence all inequalities in the derivation of (18) must be tight up to $O(\varepsilon + \sqrt{s})$. We show that this implies the following bounds.

Claim 4.6. *The following inequalities hold:*

$$\sum_i t_i \left(|\alpha_i - \beta_i| - \frac{\pi}{4} \right)^2 = O(\varepsilon + \sqrt{s}) . \qquad (19)$$

$$\sum_i t_i (\alpha_i + \beta_i)^2 = O(\varepsilon + \sqrt{s}) . \qquad (20)$$

Proof. We first prove (19). For this we exploit near-tightness of the application of Jensen's inequality on the last line of (18). This immediately implies that

$$\sum_i t_i \left(|\cos(\alpha_i - \beta_i)| - \sqrt{\sum_{i'} t_{i'} \cos^2(\alpha_{i'} - \beta_{i'})} \right)^2 = O(\varepsilon + \sqrt{s}) .$$

By definition, $\left| \sum_{i'} t_{i'} \cos^2(\alpha_{i'} - \beta_{i'}) - \frac{1}{2} \right| \leq s$, hence

$$\sum_i t_i \left(|\cos(\alpha_i - \beta_i)| - \frac{1}{\sqrt{2}} \right)^2 = O(\varepsilon + \sqrt{s}) .$$

Using that for $x \in [0, \pi]$,

$$\left| \cos(x) - \frac{1}{\sqrt{2}} \right| \geq \frac{1}{2} \left| x - \frac{\pi}{4} \right| ,$$

Equation (19) follows. To show (20), we similarly use near-tightness in the second line of (18), using the strict concavity expressed in (16).

Applying Markov's inequality to the conclusions of Claim 4.6, the proposition follows.

To formulate the qubit test we introduce the observables

$$S_0 = 2Q_0 - \text{Id} \quad \text{and} \quad S_1 = 2Q_1 - \text{Id} . \tag{21}$$

The next theorem states that the observables S_0 and S_1 must be close to anti-commuting, as measured by the squared norm of the anti-commutator when evaluated on the state $|\psi_{\text{trans}}\rangle$.

Theorem 4.7. *Suppose that Assumption 1 holds for some function $s(\lambda, \kappa)$. Let $\mathfrak{D}$ be a polynomial-time quantum device that is such that $\Pr(\text{flag} = \text{rej}) \leq \kappa$ in Phase A of the protocol template, and that succeeds with probability $\omega - \varepsilon$ in Phase B (conditioned on $\text{flag} = \text{cont}$ having been returned in Phase A). Then, on average over $(\text{rand}, \text{trans})$ and $|\psi_{\text{trans}}\rangle$ generated in Phase A of the protocol and conditioned on $\text{flag} = \text{cont}$, it holds that*

$$\langle \psi_{\text{trans}} | \{S_0, S_1\}^2 | \psi_{\text{trans}} \rangle = O(\varepsilon + \sqrt{s}) , \tag{22}$$

where $\{S_0, S_1\} = S_0 S_1 + S_1 S_0$.

Before giving the proof of the theorem, which follows from Proposition 4.5 by direct calculation, we motivate it by discussing its implications. A first, rather immediate consequence of a bound such as (22) is that there exists an isometry $V : \mathcal{H}_{\text{PE}} \to \mathbb{C}^2 \otimes \mathcal{H}'_E$ such that, under the isometry, $S_0 \simeq_{O(\sqrt{\varepsilon})} \sigma_Z \otimes \text{Id}_{\mathcal{H}'_E}$ and $S_1 \simeq_{O(\sqrt{\varepsilon})} \sigma_X \otimes \text{Id}_{\mathcal{H}'_E}$. Here, $\simeq$ measures distance in the appropriate state-dependent norm, and σ_Z and σ_X are the canonical Pauli matrices. This statement is standard in the self-testing literature. (For a proof and more details, see for example [GV19, Lemma 2.9]. A more extensive discussion appears in [Vid20, Lecture 2].) This statement formalizes the intuition that any successful prover in the qubit test must "have a qubit:" the operations that it performs in Phase B of the protocol template are essentially equivalent, up to isometry, with measurements in the standard (σ_Z) or Hadamard (σ_X) basis on a qubit.

This statement, of being a "test of a qubit," is powerful. In [BCM+21] a similar statement is used to obtain certifiable randomness. In [MA23] it is shown that the specific bound shown in Theorem 4.7 suffices to obtain precise quantitative bounds on the amount of randomness generated in an execution of our template protocol, as well as on the accumulation of randomness through multiple sequential executions. As a consequence of our work, their results also imply that certified randomness accumulation can be achieved using any of the concrete instantiations given in Sect. 5. In [MV21] this is expanded in a test for an EPR pair, which can lead to protocols for device-independent quantum key distribution as in [MDCA21]. In [GV19] the qubit test forms the basis for a protocol for classical delegation of quantum computation. While we do not work out any of these applications, our results open the door to developing them based on any protocol that follows our template (such as the examples given in Sect. 5) by using known techniques.

Proof (Proof of Theorem 4.7). We use the notation introduced at the start of Sect. 4.2. Fix an index $i \in S_2$. Then

$$S_0 = \begin{pmatrix} \cos(2\alpha_i) & \sin(2\alpha_i) \\ \sin(2\alpha_i) & -\cos(2\alpha_i) \end{pmatrix} \quad \text{and} \quad S_1 = \begin{pmatrix} \cos(2\beta_i) & \sin(2\beta_i) \\ \sin(2\beta_i) & -\cos(2\beta_i) \end{pmatrix}. \tag{23}$$

This allows us to compute

$$S_0 S_1 + S_1 S_0 = 2\cos(2(\alpha_i - \beta_i)) \, \mathrm{Id} \, .$$

In particular,

$$\langle u_i | \{S_0, S_1\}^2 | u_i \rangle \leq 4\cos^2\left(2(\alpha_i - \beta_i)\right).$$

Using $\cos^2(x) \leq (x - \pi/2)^2$ for $x \in [\pi/4, 3\pi/4]$ it follows that whenever $2(\alpha_i - \beta_i) \in [-\pi/4, 3\pi/4]$,

$$\langle u_i | \{S_0, S_1\}^2 | u_i \rangle \leq 16\left(\left|\alpha_i - \beta_i\right| - \frac{\pi}{4}\right)^2.$$

Using Proposition 4.5 all but a fraction $O(\varepsilon + \sqrt{s})$ of indices i satisfy this condition, and furthermore for these i the right-hand side is $O(\varepsilon + \sqrt{s})$. The theorem follows.

5   Applications

We give three applications. First we consider the protocol from [KCVY21]. This protocol is based on trapdoor claw-free functions, for which we recall the definition in the next section. Next we introduce a slightly simplified version of that protocol, and show that its proof of security follows in a completely direct way from our methods. Third we consider the general compiler from [KLVY22] and apply it to the CHSH game.

5.1   Trapdoor Claw-Free Functions

The main cryptographic primitive upon which the concrete protocols we describe rely on is the *trapdoor claw-free function family* (TCF), which is defined as follows.

Definition 5.1. *Let λ be a security parameter, $\mathcal{K}$ a set of keys, and $\mathcal{X}_k$ and $\mathcal{Y}_k$ finite sets for each $k \in \mathcal{K}$. A family of functions*

$$\mathcal{F} = \{f_k : \mathcal{X}_k \to \mathcal{Y}_k\}_{k \in \mathcal{K}}$$

is called a trapdoor claw-free (TCF) function family if the following conditions hold:

1. ***Efficient Function Generation.** There exists an efficient probabilistic algorithm Gen which given a security parameter λ in unary generates a key $k \in \mathcal{K}$ and the associated trapdoor t_k:*

$$(k, t_k) \leftarrow \mathrm{Gen}(1^\lambda)$$

2. **Trapdoor Injective Pair.** For all keys $k \in \mathcal{K}$, the following conditions hold.
   (a) *Injective pair:* There exists a perfect matching R_k on $\mathcal{X}_k$ such that for all $(x_0, x_1) \in R_k$, $f_k(x_0) = f_k(x_1)$.
   (b) *Trapdoor:* There exists an efficient deterministic algorithm Inv_k such that for all $y \in \mathcal{Y}_k$ and (x_0, x_1) such that $f_k(x_0) = f_k(x_1) = y$, $\mathrm{Inv}(t_k, y) = (x_0, x_1)$.
3. **Claw-free.** For any non-uniform probabilistic polynomial time Turing machine $\mathcal{A}$,

$$\Pr\left(f_k(x_0) = f_k(x_1) \wedge x_0 \neq x_1 | (x_0, x_1) \leftarrow \mathcal{A}(k) \right) = negl(\lambda) \,,$$

where the probability is over both the choice of k and the random coins of $\mathcal{A}$.
4. **Efficient Superposition.** There exists a polynomial-time quantum algorithm that on input a key k prepares the state

$$\frac{1}{\sqrt{|\mathcal{X}_k|}} \sum_{x \in \mathcal{X}_k} |x\rangle |f_k(x)\rangle \,. \tag{24}$$

Note that the third condition, claw-freeness, may be required to hold with regard to quantum adversaries, or only with regard to classical adversaries, depending on the application.

Trapdoor claw-free functions can be constructed based on a diversity of concrete assumptions. In [KCVY21] two constructions are given, based on Rabin's function and based on the Decisional Diffie-Hellman problem. Neither assumption is secure against quantum adversaries (only classical ones). In [BCM+21] a variant called "noisy" trapdoor claw-free function is constructed based on the Learning with Errors (LWE) problem. Furthermore, in [BKVV20] this was extended to Ring-LWE, which is expected to be more efficient than standard LWE. It is straightforward to verify that the noisy type of TCF can also be used in our protocol; for the sake of clarity we describe the protocols using simpler "non-noisy" TCFs.

5.2   The 3-Round Protocol from [KCVY21]

In Fig. 3 we recall the 3-round (6-message) test of quantumness from [KCVY21], which we refer to as the *KCVY protocol*. The protocol depends on a TCF family, of which we recall the definition in Definition 5.1.

In [KCVY21] it is shown that there exists an honest quantum prover that succeeds with probability 1 in the preimage test, and with probability $\omega = \cos^2 \frac{\pi}{8}$ in the equation test. We complement their result by showing that any quantum polynomial-time prover that succeeds with probability at least $1 - \kappa$ in the preimage test can succeed in the equation test with probability at most $\omega + O(\sqrt{\kappa}) + negl(\lambda)$. We do this by applying our main result, Theorem 4.4, to the KCVY protocol. The main observation needed is that for a given y, d the product $\hat{c}_0 \cdot \hat{c}_1 = (-1)^{r \cdot (x_0 \oplus x_1)}$. By the claw-freeness property, this quantity should be hard to predict for a uniformly random r—as long as there is also a means of recovering x_0 or x_1, which is guaranteed by the preimage test. This allows us to establish Assumption 1 for this protocol and therefore use Theorem 4.4.

Fix a TCF family (Gen, Inv) and a security parameter λ.

1. The verifier samples $(k, t_k) \leftarrow \text{Gen}(1^\lambda)$ and sends k to the prover. The prover returns a string $y \in \mathcal{Y}_k$ to the verifier.

2. The verifier computes $(x_0, x_1) \leftarrow \text{Inv}(t_k, y)$. The verifier decides to perform either of the following with probability $\frac{1}{2}$ each:

   (a) (Preimage test:) The verifier requests a preimage. The prover responds with a string x. The verifier accepts if and only if $x \in \{x_0, x_1\}$.

   (b) (Equation test:)

      i. The verifier chooses $r \in \{0, 1\}^n$ uniformly at random and sends r to the prover. The prover responds with $d \in \{0, 1\}^n$.

      ii. The verifier sends a uniformly random $m \in \{0, 1\}$ to the prover. The prover responds with a bit $b \in \{0, 1\}$.

      iii. The verifier accepts if and only if $(-1)^b = \hat{c}_m$, where $\hat{c}_m$ is defined in Table 1.

Fig. 3. The KCVY protocol.

Table 1. Here, $|\phi_{r,d}\rangle$ denotes the prover's state after step (b)i. in the protocol. The $\hat{c}$ column describes the c that will likely be sent from an honest error-free prover in the equation test of the KCVY protocol, in case where $m = 0$ or $m = 1$.

$\|\phi_{r,d}\rangle$	$r \cdot (x_0 \oplus x_1)$	$d \cdot (x_0 \oplus x_1)$	$\hat{c}_0\ (m = 0)$	$\hat{c}_1\ (m = 1)$
$\|0\rangle$	0	0	+1	+1
$\|1\rangle$	0	0	−1	−1
$\|+\rangle$	1	0	+1	−1
$\|-\rangle$	1	1	−1	+1

Theorem 5.2 (Quantum soundness of the KCVY protocol). *Suppose that a quantum polynomial-time prover succeeds in the preimage test with probability $p = 1 - \kappa$, and in the equation test with probability q. Then*

$$q \leq \cos^2 \frac{\pi}{8} + \frac{\sqrt{\kappa}}{2} + negl(\lambda) .$$

We remark that in principle using the same proof strategy as for the theorem, we could show that the KCVY protocol leads to a qubit test. We omit the details here and show this property for the simplified variant of the protocol introduced in the next section.

Proof. We first observe that the KCVY protocol fits the protocol template from Fig. 1 with the following adaptations. We incorporate all steps of the protocol except (b)ii. (b)iii. in Phase A. In particular, the choice of executing a preimage test or an equation test is made in Phase A. If the preimage test is chosen, then Phase A terminates with the result of that test, flag = acc or flag = rej. If the equation test is chosen, then step (b)i. is executed in Phase A, `flag = cont`, and steps (b)ii. (b)iii. are executed in Phase B.

Now we need to show that Assumption 1 is satisfied. Suppose that $\mathcal{A}_1$ succeeds with probability $1 - \kappa$ in Phase A, and that $\mathcal{A}_2$ has advantage δ in the parity guessing task. We first use $(\mathcal{A}_1, \mathcal{A}_2)$ to construct a quantum algorithm $\mathcal{A}'$ with the following properties. When given as input $(y, |\psi_y\rangle)$ generated from the first round of the KCVY protocol (Fig. 3),

1. On input $m' = 0$, $\mathcal{A}'$ returns x_0 or x_1 with probability at least $1 - \kappa$.
2. On input $m' = 1$, $\mathcal{A}'$ returns $x_0 \oplus x_1$ with probability at least $4\delta^2$.

To get the input for $\mathcal{A}'$, we first execute $\mathcal{A}_1$ for the first round of the protocol only. This yields a string y and a post-measurement state $|\psi_y\rangle$. Now, if $m' = 0$ then $\mathcal{A}'$ executes the remaining actions of $\mathcal{A}_1$ corresponding to the preimage test. By supposition, the first item is satisfied. If $m' = 1$ then $\mathcal{A}'$ proceeds as follows. $\mathcal{A}'$ creates the state

$$|\tilde{\psi}_y\rangle = \frac{1}{\sqrt{2^n}} \sum_{r \in \{0,1\}^n} |r\rangle \otimes |\psi_y\rangle .$$

Let U be the following unitary. U first coherently executes the remainder of $\mathcal{A}_1$ on this state, treating the first register as the verifier's question r in step (b)i, and writes the outcome $d \in \{0,1\}^n$ in an ancilla register. Then, U coherently executes $\mathcal{A}_2$ on all registers, writing the outcome b in another ancilla register. Observe that this unitary satisfies the two conditions of Definition 2.1, for $\varepsilon = \delta$ and the string $a = x_0 \oplus x_1$. This is because $\hat{c}_0 \cdot \hat{c}_1 = r \cdot (x_0 \oplus x_1)$, as can be verified from Table 1. Finally, $\mathcal{A}'$ on input $m' = 1$ executes the algorithm of Theorem 2.2 (the quantum Goldreich-Levin theorem). By Theorem 2.2, the second item above is satisfied.

To conclude we show the following.

Claim 5.3. *For any quantum polynomial time $\mathcal{A}'$ satisfying the two items above, it holds that*

$$\delta \leq \frac{1}{2} \kappa^{1/2} + negl(\lambda)$$

Proof. We construct an algorithm $\mathcal{A}''$ that returns both x_0 and x_1, thus violating the claw-free property of the TCF. $\mathcal{A}''$ is very simple: as above, it first executes $\mathcal{A}_1$ for the first round of the protocol, yielding a string y and state $|\psi_y\rangle$. Then, it simply executes $\mathcal{A}'$ on this state with input $m' = 1$, and then immediately executes $\mathcal{A}'$ again on the resulting state with input $m' = 0$. By item 2, with probability $4\delta^2$ the first execution of $\mathcal{A}'$ obtains $x_0 \oplus x_1$. Let P is the projection on this outcome being obtained (i.e. we model $\mathcal{A}'$ as a projective measurement and P is the projection associated with the outcome $x_0 \oplus x_1$). We have that $\langle \psi_y | P | \psi_y \rangle \geq 4\delta^2$. This then implies that $|\langle \psi_y | P | \psi_y \rangle|^2 \geq 4\delta^2 \|P|\psi_y\rangle\|^2$, or in other words, the trace distance between the original state, and the post-measurement state conditioned on the outcome being $x_0 \oplus x_1$, is at most $\sqrt{1 - 4\delta^2}$. Therefore, when subsequently executing $\mathcal{A}'$ on input $m' = 0$ the outcome is x_0 or x_1 with probability at least $1 - \kappa - \sqrt{1 - 4\delta^2}$. As long as this quantity is non-negligible, the claw-free property is violated. The claim follows.

The theorem follows from Claim 5.3 by applying Theorem 4.4.

5.3   A Simplified Protocol

We introduce a simplified variant of the KCVY protocol described in the previous section. This variant is described in Fig. 4. Our variant introduces a small innovation that allows us to do away with the preimage test entirely. The idea is that, instead of sending a single string $r \in \{0, 1\}^n$ with which the prover computes the inner products $r \cdot x_0$ and $r \cdot x_1$, the verifier sends separate strings $r_0, r_1 \in \{0, 1\}^n$ and computes the inner products $r_0 \cdot x_0$ and $r_1 \cdot x_1$.[9] Then, predicting the parity $(r_0 \cdot x_0) \oplus (r_1 \cdot x_1)$ is equivalent to computing the value of $r' \cdot (x_0 \| x_1)$ for a random string $r' = r_0 \| r_1$, which by the quantum Goldreich-Levin theorem is as hard as predicting the string $x_0 \| x_1$ and thus also the claw (x_0, x_1).

Fix a TCF family (Gen, Inv) and a security parameter λ.
1. The verifier samples $(k, t_k) \leftarrow \text{Gen}(1^\lambda)$ and sends k to the prover. The prover returns a string $y \in \mathcal{Y}_k$ to the verifier.
2. The verifier chooses $r_0, r_1 \leftarrow \{0, 1\}^n$ uniformly at random and sends them to the prover. The prover returns a string $d \in \{0, 1\}^n$.
3. The verifier sends a challenge $m \in \{0, 1\}$ chosen uniformly at random to the prover. The prover responds with a bit $b \in \{0, 1\}$.
4. The verifier computes $(x_0, x_1) \leftarrow \text{Inv}(t_k, y)$. They accept if and only if $(-1)^b = \hat{c}_m$, where $\hat{c}_m$ is defined in (25).

Fig. 4. A simpler variant of the KCVY protocol.

Honest Prover. Because the protocol in Fig. 4 is new, we start by arguing quantum completeness: we describe the actions of an honest quantum prover in the protocol.

Proposition 5.4. *There exists a polynomial-time quantum prover who succeeds in the simplified KCVY protocol from Fig. 4 with probability* $\cos^2(\pi/8)$.

---

[9] This does require a minor extra property of the TCF, which states that "x_0" type preimages can be efficiently distinguished from "x_1" type preimages; this property can be shown to hold for all TCF constructions of which we are aware.

Proof. Fix a TCF family (Gen, Inv), a security parameter λ and a key $(k, t_k) \leftarrow$ Gen(1^λ) as generated by the verifier in the protocol. Furthermore, assume that $\mathcal{X}_k \subseteq \{0,1\}^n$ for some $n = n(\lambda)$.

The prover proceeds as in the original protocol for the first round, yielding a string $y \in \mathcal{Y}_k$ and the post-measurement state

$$\frac{1}{\sqrt{2}} \left(|x_0\rangle + |x_1\rangle \right) .$$

Upon receiving $r_0, r_1 \in \{0,1\}^n$, the prover computes an ancilla qubit which differentiates x_0 and x_1, yielding

$$\frac{1}{\sqrt{2}} \left(|0\rangle|x_0\rangle + |1\rangle|x_1\rangle \right) .$$

With the ancilla, the prover can use controlled operations to compute the state

$$\frac{1}{\sqrt{2}} \left(|0\rangle|x_0\rangle|r_0 \cdot x_0\rangle + |1\rangle|x_1\rangle|r_1 \cdot x_1\rangle \right) .$$

The prover then uncomputes the ancilla. After a Hadamard transformation on the register containing x_0 and x_1, the state becomes

$$\frac{1}{\sqrt{2^{2n+1}}} \sum_{d \in \{0,1\}^n} |d\rangle \left((-1)^{d \cdot x_0}|r_0 \cdot x_0\rangle + (-1)^{d \cdot x_1}|r_1 \cdot x_1\rangle \right) .$$

Measuring the first register to obtain a particular string d, the post-measurement state is

$$\frac{(-1)^{d \cdot x_0}}{\sqrt{2}} \left(|r_0 \cdot x_0\rangle + (-1)^{d \cdot (x_0 \oplus x_1)}|r_1 \cdot x_1\rangle \right) .$$

The prover now returns the string d to the verifier. They receive a challenge $m \in \{0,1\}$. Let

$$\alpha = r_0 \cdot x_0 \oplus r_1 \cdot x_1 = r' \cdot (x_0||x_1) , \qquad \beta = d \cdot (x_0 \oplus x_1) ,$$

and

$$\hat{c}_m = \hat{c}_m(r, x_0, x_1, d) = (1 - \alpha) \cdot (-1)^{r_0 \cdot x_0} + \alpha(-1)^\beta \cdot (-1)^m . \qquad (25)$$

Finally, the prover measures the remaining qubit in the basis $\{|\pi/8\rangle, |5\pi/8\rangle\}$ if $m = 0$, and in the basis $\{|-\pi/8\rangle, |3\pi/8\rangle\}$ in case $m = 1$, where $|\theta\rangle = \cos(\theta)|0\rangle + \sin(\theta)|1\rangle$. Let $b \in \{0,1\}$ be the outcome obtained. It is straightforward to see that in all cases they return the correct answer $(-1)^b = \hat{c}_m$ with probability $\cos^2(\pi/8)$.

Soundness. We now argue both classical and quantum soundness of the protocol, by applying Theorem 4.4. We obtain the following.

Theorem 5.5 (Classical and quantum soundness of the simplified protocol). *The maximum probability with which a classical (resp. quantum) polynomial-time prover may succeed in the 3-round protocol from Fig. 4 is $\frac{3}{4} + negl(\lambda)$ (resp. $\cos^2 \frac{\pi}{8} + negl(\lambda)$).*

Proof. We emphasize that the proof is particularly simple. To show the theorem, it suffices to (a) show that the protocol can be formatted as an instance of our protocol template, and (b) show that Assumption 1 holds for some function $s(\lambda, \kappa)$.

Step (a) is very direct: we simply combine the first two rounds of the protocol into Phase A, and the last round into Phase B. Step (b) is a bit more interesting, yet still straightforward. The main observation is that for a given y, d and r, the product $\hat{c}_0 \cdot \hat{c}_1 = (-1)^{r \cdot (x_0 \| x_1)}$. Therefore, an adversary able to predict the product can—via the quantum Goldreich Levin algorithm—recover a claw (x_0, x_1).

In more detail, let $\mathcal{A} = (\mathcal{A}_1, \mathcal{A}_2)$ be a parity adversary. Since there is no test in Phase A of the protocol, we can assume that $\kappa = 0$. Suppose that $\mathcal{A}_2$ has advantage δ in the parity guessing task. We use $(\mathcal{A}_1, \mathcal{A}_2)$ to construct a quantum algorithm $\mathcal{A}'$ that returns a claw (x_0, x_1) with probability at least $4\delta^2$. The construction of $\mathcal{A}'$ is similar to the case $m' = 1$ in the proof of Theorem 5.2. We first execute $\mathcal{A}_1$ for the first round of the protocol, yielding $(y, |\psi_y\rangle)$. We then create

$$|\tilde{\psi}_y\rangle = \frac{1}{\sqrt{2^{2n}}} \sum_{r \in \{0,1\}^{2n}} |r\rangle |\psi_y\rangle .$$

We define the following unitary U on this state. U coherently executes $\mathcal{A}_1$ for the second round of the protocol, treating the first register as the verifier's question, and writes the outcome $d \in \{0,1\}^n$ in an ancilla register. Then, U coherently executes $\mathcal{A}_2$ on all registers, writing the outcome b in another ancilla register. This unitary satisfies the two conditions of Definition 2.1, for $\varepsilon = \delta$ and the string $a = x_0 \| x_1$. This is because $\hat{c}_0 \cdot \hat{c}_1 = (-1)^{r \cdot (x_0 \| x_1)}$, as can be verified from (25). We now define $\mathcal{A}'$ to execute the algorithm of Theorem 2.2. By Theorem 2.2, $\mathcal{A}'$ returns a claw (x_0, x_1) with probability $4\delta^2$. By the claw-free property, it follows that $\delta = negl(\lambda)$. This proves the theorem.

Similarly, we apply Theorem 4.7 to obtain the following consequence.

Corollary 5.6 (Qubit test from the simplified KCVY protocol). *Suppose that a quantum prover succeeds with probability $\omega - \varepsilon$ in the protocol from Fig. 4. Let $\{\Pi_b^m\}$ be the projective measurement applied by the prover in the third round of the protocol and $S_m = \Pi_0^m - \Pi_1^m$. Then, on average over the transcript **trans** obtained in the first two rounds of the protocol it holds that*

$$\langle \psi_{trans} | \{S_0, S_1\}^2 | \psi_{trans} \rangle = O(\varepsilon) ,$$

where $\{S_0, S_1\} = S_0 S_1 + S_1 S_0$ and $|\psi_{trans}\rangle$ is the state of the prover at the end of the second round.

Proof. We apply Theorem 4.7. We already verified that Assumption 1 holds, for $s = \text{negl}(\lambda)$, in the proof of Theorem 5.5. Theorem 4.7 gives a bound on $\langle \psi_{\text{trans}} | \{S_0, S_1\}^2 | \psi_{\text{trans}} \rangle$. Here the observables S_m, $m \in \{0, 1\}$, are defined from $\{\Pi_b^m\}$ using the definition of $\hat{c}_m$, see (21). However, Since the squared anti-commutator $\{S_0, S_1\}^2$ is invariant under exchanges $S_0 \leftarrow -S_0$ or $S_1 \leftarrow -S_1$. Therefore, the bound from Theorem 4.7 also applies for the simpler definition of $S_m = \Pi_0^m - \Pi_1^m$.

5.4   The KLVY Protocol

In [KLVY22] the authors introduce a general "compiler" that takes any 2-prover nonlocal game and transforms it into a 2-round test of quantumness.[10] They prove that the resulting protocol has classical soundness equal to the classical value of the nonlocal game, up to an additive term that is negligible in the security parameter λ, assuming the security of a quantum fully homomorphic encryption scheme with specific properties—namely, that it allows classical encryption of classical messages and that it satisfies a natural "aux-input correctness" property which they define. (Both properties are satisfied by the scheme from [Mah20].)

Here we apply our general results to recover classical soundness of the KLVY protocol, when applied to the celebrated nonlocal game CHSH, which is based on the Bell inequality by Clauser et al. [CHSH69]. Furthermore, we show quantum soundness of the same protocol (the authors were only able to establish quantum completeness; our bound matches theirs) and that the protocol can be used as a test for a qubit.

The KLVY protocol for the CHSH game is described in Fig. 5. For the definition of a quantum fully homomorphic encryption scheme, and the specific properties required here, we refer to [KLVY22, Definition 2.3].

Fix a quantum homomorphic encryption scheme (Gen, Enc, Eval, Dec) and a security parameter λ.

1. The verifier samples $sk \leftarrow \text{Gen}(1^\lambda)$. They sample an $x \in \{0, 1\}$ uniformly at random and set $\hat{x} \leftarrow \text{Enc}(sk, x)$. They send $\hat{x}$ to the prover. The prover responds with a ciphertext $\hat{a}$.
2. The verifier sends $m \in \{0, 1\}$ chosen uniformly at random to the prover. The prover responds with a bit $b \in \{0, 1\}$.
3. The verifier computes $a \leftarrow \text{Dec}(sk, \hat{a})$. They accept if and only if $(-1)^b = \hat{c}_m$, where $\hat{c}_m = (-1)^a (-1)^{xm}$.

Fig. 5. The KLVY protocol, specialized to the CHSH game.

---

[10] Their results apply to k-prover nonlocal games; here we only consider the case where $k = 2$.

Theorem 5.7 (Classical and quantum soundness of the KLVY protocol for the CHSH game). *The maximum probability with which a classical (resp. quantum) polynomial-time prover may succeed in the 2-round protocol from Fig. 4 is $\frac{3}{4} + negl(\lambda)$ (resp. $\cos^2 \frac{\pi}{8} + negl(\lambda)$).*

Proof. Similarly to the proof of Theorem 5.5, it suffices to (a) show that the protocol can be reformatted as an instance of our protocol template, and (b) show that Assumption 1 holds for some function $s(\lambda, \kappa)$.

Step (a) is very direct: the first round of the protocol is Phase A, and the second round is Phase B. Step (b) is also straightforward. The main observation is that $\hat{c}_0 \cdot \hat{c}_1 = (-1)^x$. However, x was only given in encrypted form to the prover. So, by semantic security of the homomorphic encryption scheme it should not be able to predict it with any non-negligible advantage.

We proceed with the details. Let $\mathcal{A} = (\mathcal{A}_1, \mathcal{A}_2)$ be a parity adversary. Since there is no test in Phase A of the protocol, we can assume that $\kappa = 0$. Suppose that $\mathcal{A}_2$ has advantage δ in the parity guessing task. By definition $(\mathcal{A}_1, \mathcal{A}_2)$ can be combined into a quantum polynomial-time algorithm that returns a guess for x that is correct with probability $\frac{1}{2} + \delta$. It follows that $\delta = negl(\lambda)$, concluding the proof. $\square$

Similarly, we apply Theorem 4.7 to obtain the following consequence.

Corollary 5.8 (Qubit test from the KLVY protocol for the CHSH game). *Suppose that a quantum prover succeeds with probability $\omega - \varepsilon$ in the protocol from Fig. 5. Let $\{\Pi_b^m\}$ be the projective measurement applied by the prover in the second round of the protocol and $S_m = \Pi_0^m - \Pi_1^m$. Then, on average over the transcript **trans** obtained in the first round of the protocol it holds that*

$$\langle \psi_{trans} | \{S_0, S_1\}^2 | \psi_{trans} \rangle = O(\varepsilon) \,,$$

where $\{S_0, S_1\} = S_0 S_1 + S_1 S_0$ and $|\psi_{trans}\rangle$ is the state of the prover at the end of the first round.

Proof. We apply Theorem 4.7. We already verified that Assumption 1 holds, for $s = negl(\lambda)$, in the proof of Theorem 5.7. Since $\hat{c}_0 = (-1)^a$, the observable S_0 as defined in (21) is the same observable as S_0 defined in the corollary. The observable S_1 defined in (21) is $S_1 = 2\Pi_{a+x}^1 - \text{Id}$, where a, x are determined by the transcript of the first phase. Theorem 4.7 gives a bound on $\langle \psi_{\text{trans}} | \{S_0, S_1\}^2 | \psi_{\text{trans}} \rangle$. Since this quantity is invariant under exchange $S_1 \leftarrow -S_1$, the corollary follows for the simpler definition of $S_1 = \Pi_0^1 - \Pi_1^1$. $\square$

Acknowledgments. We thank Ilya Merkulov and Rotem Arnon-Friedman for discussions in the early stages of this work.

A   A Trigonometric Identity

Lemma A.1. *The following inequality holds for all $\alpha, \beta \in [0, 2\pi]$:*

$$\cos^2(\alpha) + \cos^2(\beta) \leq |2\cos^2(\alpha - \beta) - 1| + 2\cos^2(\pi/8)$$

Proof. Using $\cos^2(\phi) = \frac{1}{2}(1 + \cos(2\phi))$ and that $\cos^2(\pi/8) = \frac{1}{2}\left(1 + \frac{1}{\sqrt{2}}\right)$, we can rewrite the inequality as

$$\frac{1}{2}(2 + \cos(2\alpha) + \cos(2\beta)) \leq |2\cos^2(\alpha - \beta) - 1| + 1 + \frac{1}{\sqrt{2}},$$

which after simplification and using the cosine sum rule becomes

$$\cos(\alpha + \beta)\cos(\alpha - \beta) \leq |2\cos^2(\alpha - \beta) - 1| + \frac{1}{\sqrt{2}}.$$

Let $x = \alpha + \beta, y = \alpha - \beta$, so that it will suffice to show

$$\cos(x)\cos(y) \leq |2\cos^2(y) - 1| + \frac{1}{\sqrt{2}}.$$

Note that if $\cos(x)$ and $\cos(y)$ have opposite signs, the inequality is trivially satisfied, as the left-hand side will be non-positive while the right-hand side is always positive. Without loss of generality we restrict to the case where $\cos(x) \geq 0$ and $\cos(y) \geq 0$ (the case where they're both negative is analogous). As $\cos(x) \leq 1$, it's sufficient to show that

$$\cos(y) \leq |2\cos^2(y) - 1| + \frac{1}{\sqrt{2}}.$$

Taking $t = \cos(y)$, with $0 \leq t \leq 1$, it suffices to show

$$t \leq |2t^2 - 1| + \frac{1}{\sqrt{2}}.$$

Suppose first that $2t^2 - 1 \geq 0$ which means (since $t \geq 0$) that $t \geq \frac{1}{\sqrt{2}}$. In this case, we have to show that

$$0 \leq 2t^2 - t - 1 + \frac{1}{\sqrt{2}}.$$

This follows from noting that $2t^2 - t - 1 + \frac{1}{\sqrt{2}}$ has roots $t_1 = \frac{1}{2} - \frac{1}{\sqrt{2}}$ and $t_2 = \frac{1}{\sqrt{2}}$ and is positive for all $t \leq t_1$ and $t \geq t_2$. Since we assumed $t \geq \frac{1}{\sqrt{2}}$ the result follows.

Now suppose that $2t^2 - 1 \leq 0$ which means (since $t \geq 0$) that $0 \leq t \leq \frac{1}{\sqrt{2}}$. In this case, we have to show that

$$0 \leq -2t^2 - t + 1 + \frac{1}{\sqrt{2}}.$$

Here, the roots are $t_1 = -\frac{1}{2} - \frac{1}{\sqrt{2}}$ and $t_2 = \frac{1}{\sqrt{2}}$ and the expression is positive for all $t_1 \leq t \leq t_2$. Since $0 \leq t \leq \frac{1}{\sqrt{2}}$, the inequality is satisfied, concluding the proof.

References

AA11. Aaronson, S., Arkhipov, A.: The computational complexity of linear optics. In: Proceedings of the 43rd Annual ACM Symposium on Theory of Computing, pp. 333–342 (2011)

AA14. Aaronson, S., Ambainis, A.: The need for structure in quantum speedups. Theor. Comput. **10**(1), 133–166 (2014)

AAB+19. Arute, F., et al.: Quantum supremacy using a programmable superconducting processor. Nature **574**, 505–510 (2019)

AC02. Adcock, M., Cleve, R.: A quantum Goldreich-Levin theorem with cryptographic applications. In: Alt, H., Ferreira, A. (eds.) STACS 2002. LNCS, vol. 2285, pp. 323–334. Springer, Heidelberg (2002). https://doi.org/10.1007/3-540-45841-7_26

AMR23. Alamati, N., Malavolta, G., Rahimi, A.: Candidate trapdoor claw-free functions from group actions with applications to quantum protocols. In: Kiltz, E., Vaikuntanathan, V. (eds.) Theory of Cryptography. TCC 2022. Lecture Notes in Computer Science, vol. 13747, pp. 266–293. Springer, Cham (2022). https://doi.org/10.1007/978-3-031-22318-1_10

BBF+21. Bassirian, R., Bouland, A., Fefferman, B., Gunn, S., Tal, A.: On certified randomness from quantum advantage experiments. arXiv preprint arXiv:2111.14846 (2021)

BCM+21. Brakerski, Z., Christiano, P., Mahadev, U., Vazirani, U., Vidick, T.: A cryptographic test of quantumness and certifiable randomness from a single quantum device. J. ACM (JACM) **68**(5), 1–47 (2021)

BKVV20. Brakerski, Z., Koppula, V., Vazirani, U., Vidick, T.: Simpler proofs of quantumness. In: 15th Conference on the Theory of Quantum Computation, Communication and Cryptography, TQC 2020. Schloss Dagstuhl-Leibniz-Zentrum für Informatik (2020)

CHSH69. Clauser, J.F., Horne, M.A., Shimony, A., Holt, R.A.: Proposed experiment to test local hidden-variable theories. Phys. Rev. Lett. **23**(15), 880 (1969)

CMSZ21. Chiesa, A., Ma, F., Spooner, N., Zhandry, M.: Post-quantum succinct arguments. CoRR, abs/2103.08140 (2021). Appeared in FOCS 2021

FWZ22. Fu, H., Wang, D., Zhao, Q.: Computational self-testing of multi-qubit states and measurements. arXiv preprint arXiv:2201.13430 (2022)

GMP22. Gheorghiu, A., Metger, T., Poremba, A.: Quantum cryptography with classical communication: parallel remote state preparation for copy-protection, verification, and more. arXiv preprint arXiv:2201.13445 (2022)

GV19. Gheorghiu, A., Vidick, T.: Computationally-secure and composable remote state preparation. In: 2019 IEEE 60th Annual Symposium on Foundations of Computer Science (FOCS), pp. 1024–1033. IEEE (2019)

KCVY21. Kahanamoku-Meyer, G.D., Choi, S., Vazirani, U.V., Yao, N.Y.: Classically-verifiable quantum advantage from a computational Bell test. CoRR, abs/2104.00687 (2021)

KLVY22. Kalai, Y., Lombardi, A., Vaikuntanathan, V., Yang, L.: Quantum advantage from any non-local game. arXiv preprint arXiv:2203.15877 (2022)

MA23. Merkulov, I., Arnon-Friedman, R.: Entropy accumulation under post-quantum cryptographic assumptions (2023, to appear). To appear on arXiv, March 2023

Mah18. Mahadev, U.: Classical verification of quantum computations. In: 2018 IEEE 59th Annual Symposium on Foundations of Computer Science (FOCS), pp. 259–267. IEEE (2018)

Mah20. Mahadev, U.: Classical homomorphic encryption for quantum circuits. SIAM J. Comput., FOCS18-189 (2020)

MDCA21. Metger, T., Dulek, Y., Coladangelo, A., Arnon-Friedman, R.: Device-independent quantum key distribution from computational assumptions. New J. Phys. **23**(12), 123021 (2021)

MV21. Metger, T., Vidick, T.: Self-testing of a single quantum device under computational assumptions. Quantum **5**, 544 (2021)

MVV22. Mahadev, U., Vazirani, U., Vidick, T.: Efficient certifiable randomness from a single quantum device. arXiv preprint arXiv:2204.11353 (2022)

NZ23. Natarajan, A., Zhang, T.: Bounding the quantum value of compiled non-local games: from CHSH to BQP verification (2023). Manuscript

Reg09. Regev, O.: On lattices, learning with errors, random linear codes, and cryptography. J. ACM (JACM) **56**(6), 1–40 (2009)

Sho94. Shor, P.W.: Algorithms for quantum computation: discrete logarithms and factoring. In: Proceedings 35th Annual Symposium on Foundations of Computer Science, pp. 124–134. IEEE (1994)

Vid20. Vidick, T.: Cours FSMP, Fall'20: Interactions with quantum devices (2020). http://users.cms.caltech.edu/~vidick/teaching/fsmp/fsmp.pdf

Wil11. Wilde, M.M.: From classical to quantum Shannon theory. arXiv preprint arXiv:1106.1445 (2011)

YZ22. Yamakawa, T., Zhandry, M.: Verifiable quantum advantage without structure. In: 2022 IEEE 63rd Annual Symposium on Foundations of Computer Science (FOCS), pp. 69–74. IEEE (2022)

Zha22. Zhang, J.: Classical verification of quantum computations in linear time. In: 2022 IEEE 63rd Annual Symposium on Foundations of Computer Science (FOCS), pp. 46–57. IEEE (2022)

ZKML+21. Zhu, D., et al.: Interactive protocols for classically-verifiable quantum advantage. arXiv preprint arXiv:2112.05156 (2021)

Cryptography with Certified Deletion

James Bartusek[1] and Dakshita Khurana[2(✉)]

[1] UC Berkeley, Berkeley, USA
[2] UIUC, Champaign, USA
dakshita@illinois.edu

Abstract. We propose a unifying framework that yields an array of cryptographic primitives with certified deletion. These primitives enable a party in possession of a quantum ciphertext to generate a classical certificate that the encrypted plaintext has been information-theoretically deleted, and cannot be recovered even given unbounded computational resources.

- For $X \in \{\text{public-key}, \text{attribute-based}, \text{fully-homomorphic}, \text{witness}, \text{timed-release}\}$, our compiler converts any (post-quantum) X encryption to X encryption with certified deletion. In addition, we compile statistically-binding commitments to statistically-binding commitments with certified everlasting hiding. As a corollary, we also obtain statistically-sound zero-knowledge proofs for QMA with certified everlasting zero-knowledge assuming statistically-binding commitments.
- We also obtain a strong form of everlasting security for two-party and multi-party computation in the dishonest majority setting. While simultaneously achieving everlasting security against *all* parties in this setting is known to be impossible, we introduce *everlasting security transfer (EST)*. This enables *any one* party (or a subset of parties) to dynamically and certifiably information-theoretically delete other participants' data after protocol execution. We construct general-purpose secure computation with EST assuming statistically-binding commitments, which can be based on one-way functions or pseudorandom quantum states.

We obtain our results by developing a novel proof technique to argue that a bit b has been *information-theoretically deleted* from an adversary's view once they output a valid deletion certificate, despite having been previously *information-theoretically determined* by the ciphertext they held in their view. This technique may be of independent interest.

1 Introduction

Deletion in a Classical World. On classical devices, data is stored and exchanged as a string of bits. There is nothing that can prevent an untrusted device with access to such a string from making arbitrarily many copies of it. Thus, it seems hopeless to try to *force* an untrusted device to delete classical data. Even if the string is merely a ciphertext encoding an underlying plaintext, there is no way to prevent a server from keeping that ciphertext around in memory forever. If

H. Handschuh and A. Lysyanskaya (Eds.): CRYPTO 2023, LNCS 14085, pp. 192–223, 2023.
https://doi.org/10.1007/978-3-031-38554-4_7

at some point in the future, the security of the underlying encryption scheme is broken either via brute-force or major scientific advances, or if the key is compromised and makes its way to the server, the server will be able to recover the underlying plaintext. This may be unacceptable in situations where extremely sensitive data is being transmitted or computed upon.

In fact, there has recently been widespread interest in holding data collectors accountable in responding to "data deletion requests" from their clients, as evidenced by data deletion clauses in legal regulations adopted by the European Union [17] and California [1]. Unfortunately, the above discussion shows that these laws cannot be cryptographically enforced against malicious data collectors, though there has been recent work on cryptographically *formalizing* what it means for *honest* data collectors to follow such guidelines [19].

Deletion in a Quantum World. The *uncertainty principle* [24], which lies at the foundation of quantum mechanics, completely disrupts the above classical intuition. It asserts the existence of pairs of measurable quantities such that precisely determining one quantity (e.g. the position of an electron) implies the *inability* to determine the other (e.g. the momentum of the electron). While such effects only become noticeable at an extreme microscopic scale, the pioneering work of Wiesner [43] suggested that the peculiar implications of the uncertainty principle could be leveraged to perform seemingly impossible "human-scale" information processing tasks.

Given the inherent "destructive" properties of information guaranteed by the uncertainty principle, provable data deletion appears to be a natural information processing task that, while impossible classically, may become viable quantumly. Surprisingly, the explicit study of data deletion in a quantum world has only begun recently. However, over the last few years, this question has been explored in many different contexts. Initial work studied deletion in the context of non-local games [18] and information-theoretic proofs of deletion with partial security [12], while the related notion of *revocation* was introduced in [41].

The work of [11] first considered certified deletion in the context of encryption schemes, leveraging the uncertainty principle to obtain one-time pad encryption with certified deletion. This caused a great deal of excitement, leading to many recent followup works on deletion in a cryptographic context: device-independent security of one-time pad encryption with certified deletion [32], public-key and attribute-based encryption with certified deletion [25], commitments and zero-knowledge with certified everlasting hiding [27], and most recently fully-homomorphic encryption with certified deletion [39].

This Work. Our work makes new definitional, conceptual and technical contributions. Our key contribution is a new proof technique to show that many natural encryption schemes satisfy security with certified deletion. This improves prior work in many ways, as we summarize below.

1. **A unified framework.** We present a simple compiler that relies on conjugate coding/BB84 states [6,43] to bootstrap semantically-secure cryptosystems to semantically-secure cryptosystems with certified deletion. For any

$X \in \{$public-key encryption, attribute-based encryption, witness encryption, timed-release encryption, statistically-binding commitment$\}$, we immediately obtain "X with certified deletion" by plugging X into our compiler. This compiler builds on [11], who used BB84 states in the context of certified deletion for one-time pad encryption.

2. **Stronger definitions.** We consider a strong definition of security with certified deletion for public-key primitives, which stipulates that if an adversary in possession of a quantum ciphertext encrypting bit b issues a certificate of deletion which passes verification, then the bit b must now be *information-theoretically* hidden from the adversary.

   Previous definitions of public-key and fully-homomorphic encryption with certified deletion [25,39] considered a weaker experiment, inspired by [11], where after deletion, the adversary is explicitly given the secret key, but is still required to be computationally bounded. For the public-key setting, we consider this prior definition to capture a (strong) *security against key leakage* property, as opposed to a *certified deletion* property[1]. In the full version [5], we show that the everlasting flavor of our definition implies prior definitions. Intuitively, this is because for public-key schemes, an adversary can sample a secret key on its own given sufficient computational resources. Moreover, in the case of fully-homomorphic encryption (FHE), prior work [39] considered definitions (significantly) weaker than semantic security.[2] We obtain the first semantically-secure FHE with certified deletion from standard LWE.

3. **Simpler constructions and weaker assumptions.** Our compiler removes the need to rely on complex cryptographic primitives such as non-committing encryption and indistinguishability obfuscation as in [25], or idealized models such as random oracles as in [27,41], or complex quantum states (such as Gaussian coset states) as in [39], instead yielding simple schemes satisfying certified deletion for a range of primitives from BB84 states and minimal assumptions.

   In fact, reliance on non-committing encryption was a key reason that prior techniques did not yield homomorphic encryption schemes with certified deletion, since compact homomorphic encryption schemes cannot simultaneously be non-committing [29]. Our work builds simple homomorphic encryption schemes that support certified deletion by eliminating the need to rely on non-committing properties, and instead only relying on semantic security of an underlying encryption scheme.

4. **Overcoming barriers to provable security.** How can one prove that a bit b has been *information-theoretically deleted* from an adversary's view once

---

[1] In contrast, in the one-time pad encryption setting as considered by [11], the original encrypted message is already information-theoretically hidden from the adversary, so to obtain any interesting notion of certified deletion, one must explicitly consider leaking the secret key.

[2] Subsequent to the original posting of our paper on arXiv, an update to [39] was posted with somewhat different results. We provide a comparison between our work and the updated version of [39] in Sect. 1.3.

they produce a valid deletion certificate, while it was previously information-theoretically *determined* by the ciphertext they hold in their view?

Prior work [25,27,39,41] resorted to either idealized models or weaker definitions, and constructions with layers of indirection, in order to get around this barrier. We develop a novel proof technique that resolves this issue by (1) carefully deferring the dependence of the experiment on the plaintext bit, and (2) identifying an efficiently checkable predicate on the adversary's state after producing a valid deletion certificate. We rely on semantic security of encryption to show that this predicate must hold, and we argue that if the predicate holds, the adversary's left-over state is statistically independent of the plaintext bit. This allows us to prove certified deletion security for simple and natural schemes.

5. **New implications to secure computation: Everlasting Security Transfer (EST).** We introduce the concept of *everlasting security transfer*. Everlasting security guarantees (malicious) security against a participant in a secure two-(or multi-)party computation protocol even if the participant becomes computationally unbounded after protocol execution. We introduce and build secure computation protocols where participants are able to *transfer* everlasting security properties from one party to another, even after the protocol ends.

We elaborate on our results in more detail below, then we provide an overview of our techniques.

1.1   Our Results

Warmup: Secret Sharing With Certified Deletion. We begin by considering certified deletion in the context of one of the simplest cryptographic primitives: information-theoretic, two-out-of-two secret sharing. Here, a dealer Alice would like to share a classical secret bit b between two parties Bob and Charlie, such that

1. **(Secret sharing.)** The individual views of Bob and Charlie perfectly hide b, while the joint view of Bob and Charlie can be used to reconstruct b, and
2. **(Certified deletion.)** Bob may generate a deletion certificate for Alice, guaranteeing that b has been *information theoretically removed* from the *joint* view of Bob and Charlie.

That is, as long as Bob and Charlie do not collude at the time of generating the certificate of deletion, their joint view upon successful verification of this certificate is guaranteed to become independent of b. As long as the certificate verifies, b will be perfectly hidden from Bob and Charlie *even if* they decide to later collude.

To build such a secret sharing scheme, we start by revisiting the usage of conjugate coding/BB84 states to obtain encryption with certified deletion, which was first explored in [11]. While the construction in [11] relies on a seeded randomness extractor in combination with BB84 states, we suggest a simpler alternative that replaces the seeded extractor with the XOR function. Looking ahead, this simplification combined with other proof techniques will help generically lift our secret sharing scheme to obtain several encryption schemes with certified deletion.

Consider a random string $x \leftarrow \{0,1\}^\lambda$, and a random set of bases $\theta \leftarrow \{0,1\}^\lambda$ (where 0 corresponds to the standard basis and 1 corresponds to the Hadamard basis). To obtain a scheme with certifiable deletion, we will build on the intuition that it is impossible to recover x given only BB84 states $|x\rangle_\theta$ without knowledge of the basis θ. Furthermore, measuring $|x\rangle_\theta$ in an incorrect basis θ' will destroy (partial) information about x.

Thus to secret-share a bit b in a way that supports deletion, the dealer will sample $x \leftarrow \{0,1\}^\lambda$ and bases $\theta \leftarrow \{0,1\}^\lambda$. Bob's share is then

$$|x\rangle_\theta$$

and Charlie's share is

$$\theta, b' = b \oplus \bigoplus_{i:\theta_i=0} x_i$$

That is, in Charlie's share, b is masked by the bits of x that are encoded in the standard basis.

We note that Bob's share contains only BB84 states while Charlie's share is entirely classical. Bob can now produce a certificate of deletion by returning the results of measuring all his BB84 states in the Hadamard basis, and Alice will accept as a valid certificate any string x' such that $x_i = x_i'$ for all i where $\theta_i = 1$. We show that this scheme is indeed a two-out-of-two secret sharing scheme that satisfies certified deletion as defined above.

A Conceptually Simple and Generic Compiler. As our key technical contribution, we upgrade the secret sharing with certified deletion scheme to the public-key setting by encrypting Charlie's share. In more detail, to encrypt a bit b with respect to any encryption scheme, we first produce two secret shares of b as described above, and then release a ciphertext that contains (1) Bob's share in the clear and (2) an encryption of Charlie's share. To certifiably delete a ciphertext, one needs to simply measure the quantum part of the ciphertext (i.e., Bob's share) in the Hadamard basis. Intuitively, since information about the bases (Charlie's share) is hidden at the time of producing the certificate of deletion, generating a certificate that verifies must mean information theoretically losing the description of computational basis states.

This method of converting a two-party primitive (i.e. secret sharing with certified deletion) into one-party primitives (i.e. encryption schemes with certified deletion) is reminiscent of other similar compilers in the literature, for instance those converting probabilistically checkable proofs to succinct arguments [7,28]. In our case, just like those settings, while the intuition is relatively simple, the proof turns out to be fairly non-trivial.

Our Main Theorem. In (almost) full generality, our main theorem says the following.[3] Consider an arbitrary family of distributions $\{\mathcal{Z}_\lambda(\theta)\}_{\lambda \in \mathbb{N}, \theta \in \{0,1\}^\lambda}$ and an arbitrary class $\mathscr{A}$ of computationally bounded adversaries $\mathcal{A} = \{\mathcal{A}_\lambda\}_{\lambda \in \mathbb{N}}$, such that $\mathcal{Z}_\lambda(\theta)$ semantically hides θ against $\mathcal{A}_\lambda$. Then, consider the following distribution $\widetilde{Z}_\lambda^{\mathcal{A}_\lambda}(b)$ over quantum states, parameterized by a bit $b \in \{0,1\}$.

– Sample $x, \theta \leftarrow \{0,1\}^\lambda$ and initialize $\mathcal{A}_\lambda$ with

$$\mathcal{Z}_\lambda(\theta), b \oplus \bigoplus_{i:\theta_i=0} x_i, |x\rangle_\theta.$$

– $\mathcal{A}_\lambda$'s output is parsed as a bitstring $x' \in \{0,1\}^\lambda$ and a residual state on register A'.
– If $x_i = x_i'$ for all i such that $\theta_i = 1$ then output A', and otherwise output a special symbol $\perp$.

Then,

Theorem 1. *For every $\mathcal{A} \in \mathscr{A}$, the trace distance between $\widetilde{Z}_\lambda^{\mathcal{A}_\lambda}(0)$ and $\widetilde{Z}_\lambda^{\mathcal{A}_\lambda}(1)$ is* negl(λ).

Intuitively, this means that as long as the adversary $\mathcal{A}_\lambda$ is computationally bounded *at the time of producing any deletion certificate* x' that properly verifies (meaning that x_i' is the correct bit encoded at index i for any indices encoded in the Hadamard basis), their left-over state *statistically* contains only negligible information about the original encrypted bit b. That is, once the certificate verifies, information about b cannot be recovered information-theoretically even given unbounded time from the adversary's residual state.

This theorem is both quite simple and extremely general. The quantum part that enables certified deletion only involves simple BB84 states, and we require no additional properties of the underlying distribution $\mathcal{Z}_\lambda$ except for the fact that $\mathcal{Z}_\lambda(\theta)$ and $\mathcal{Z}_\lambda(0^\lambda)$ are indistinguishable to some class of adversaries.[4] We now discuss our (immediate) applications in more detail.

---

[3] In order to fully capture all of our applications, we actually allow $\mathcal{Z}_\lambda$ to operate on all inputs, including the BB84 states. See Sect. 3 for the precise details.

[4] It may seem counter-intuitive that the certified deletion guarantees provided by our theorem hold even when instantiating $\mathcal{Z}_\lambda$ with general semantically secure schemes, such as a fully-homomorphic encryption scheme. In particular, what if an adversary evaluated the FHE to recover a classical encryption of b, and then reversed their computation and finally produced a valid deletion certificate? This may seem to contradict everlasting security, since a classical ciphertext could be used to recover b given unbounded time. However, this attack is actually not feasible. After performing FHE evaluation coherently, the adversary would obtain a register holding a superposition over classical ciphertexts encrypting b, but with different random coins. Measuring this superposition to obtain a single classical ciphertext would collapse the state, and prevent the adversary from reversing their computation to eventually produce a valid deletion certificate. Indeed, our Theorem rules out this (and all other) efficient attacks.

Public-Key, Attribute-Based and Witness Encryption. Instantiating the distribution $\mathcal{Z}_\lambda$ with the encryption procedure for any public-key encryption scheme, we obtain a public-key encryption scheme with certified deletion.

We also observe that we can instantiate the distribution $\mathcal{Z}_\lambda$ with the encryption procedure for any *attribute-based* encryption scheme, and immediately obtain an attribute-based encryption scheme with certified deletion. Previously, this notion was only known under the assumption of indistinguishability obfuscation, and also only satisfied the weaker key leakage style definition discussed above [25]. Finally, instantiating $\mathcal{Z}_\lambda$ with any *witness encryption* scheme implies a witness encryption scheme with certified deletion.

Fully-Homomorphic Encryption. Next, we consider the question of computing on encrypted data. We observe that, if $\mathcal{Z}_\lambda$ is instantiated with the encryption procedure Enc for a *fully-homomorphic* encryption scheme [9,20,21], then given $|x\rangle_\theta$, $\mathsf{Enc}(\theta, b \oplus \bigoplus_{i:\theta_i=0} x_i)$, one could run a homomorphic evaluation procedure in superposition to recover (a superposition over) $\mathsf{Enc}(b)$. Additionally, given multiple ciphertexts, one can even compute arbitrary functionalities over the encrypted plaintexts. Moreover, if such evaluation is done *coherently* (without performing measurements), then it can be reversed and the deletion procedure can subsequently be run on the original ciphertexts.

This immediately implies what we call a "blind delegation with certified deletion" protocol, which allows a computationally weak client to utilize the resources of a computationally powerful server, while (i) keeping its data hidden from the server during the protocol, and (ii) ensuring that its data is *information-theoretically* deleted from the server afterwards, by requesting a certificate of deletion. We show that, as long as the server behaves honestly during the "function evaluation" phase of the protocol, then even if it is arbitrarily malicious after the function evaluation phase, it cannot both pass deletion verification and maintain any information about the client's original plaintexts.

Recently, Poremba [39] also constructed a fully-homomorphic encryption scheme satisfying a weaker notion of certified deletion.[5] In particular, the guarantee in [39] is that from the perspective of any server that passes deletion with *sufficiently high probability*, there is significant entropy in the client's original *ciphertext*. This does not necessarily imply anything about the underlying plaintext, since a ciphertext encrypting a fixed bit b may be (and usually will be) highly entropic. Moreover, their construction makes use of relatively complicated and highly entangled *Gaussian coset states* in order to obtain these deletion properties. In summary, our framework simultaneously strengthens the security (to standard semantic security of the plaintext) and simplifies the construction of fully-homomorphic encryption with certified deletion. We also remark that neither our work nor [39] considers security against servers that may be malicious during the function evaluation phase of the blind delegation with certified deletion protocol. We leave obtaining security against fully malicious servers as an interesting direction for future research.

---

[5] We discuss comparisons with a recently updated version of [39] in Sect. 1.3.

Commitments and Zero-Knowledge. Next, we consider *commitment schemes.* A fundamental result in quantum cryptography states that one cannot use quantum communication to build a commitment that is simultaneously statistically hiding and statistically binding [34,35]. Intriguingly, [27] demonstrated the feasibility of statistically-binding commitments with a *certified everlasting hiding* property, where hiding is computational during the protocol, but becomes information-theoretic after the receiver issues a valid deletion certificate. However, their construction relies on the idealized quantum random oracle model. Using our framework, we show that *any* (post-quantum) statistically-binding computationally-hiding commitment implies a statistically-binding commitment with certified everlasting hiding. Thus, we obtain statistically-binding commitments with certified everlasting hiding in the plain model from post-quantum one-way functions, and even from plausibly weaker assumptions like *pseudorandom quantum states* [3,37].

Following implications in [27] from commitments with certified deletion to zero-knowledge, we also obtain interactive proofs for NP (and more generally, QMA) with *certified everlasting zero-knowledge*. These are proofs that are statistically sound, and additionally the verifier may issue a classical certificate *after the protocol ends* showing that the verifier has information-theoretically deleted all secrets about the statement being proved. Once a computationally bounded verifier issues a valid certificate, the proof becomes *statistically* zero-knowledge (ZK). Similarly to the case of commitments, while proofs for QMA or NP are unlikely to simultaneously satisfy *statistical soundness* and *statistical ZK*, [27] previously introduced and built statistically sound, certified everlasting ZK proofs in the random oracle model. On the other hand, we obtain a construction in the plain model from any statistically-binding commitment.

Timed-Release Encryption. As another immediate application, we consider the notion of *revocable* timed-release encryption. Timed-release encryption schemes (also known as time-lock puzzles) have the property that, while ciphertexts can eventually be decrypted in some polynomial time, it takes *at least* some (parallel) $T(\lambda)$ time to do so. [41] considered adding a *revocable* property to such schemes, meaning that the recipient of a ciphertext can either eventually decrypt the ciphertext in $\geq T(\lambda)$ time, or issue a certificate of deletion proving that they will *never* be able to obtain the plaintext. [41] constructs semantically-secure revocable timed-release encryption assuming post-quantum timed-release encryption, but with the following drawbacks: the certificate of deletion is a *quantum state*, and the underlying scheme must either be *exponentially* hard or security must be proven in the idealized quantum random oracle model.

We can plug any post-quantum timed-release encryption scheme into our framework, and obtain revocable timed-released encryption from (polynomially-hard) post-quantum timed-released encryption, with a classical deletion certificate. Note that, when applying our main theorem, we simply instantiate the class of adversaries to be those that are $T(\lambda)$-parallel time bounded.

Secure Computation With Everlasting Security Transfer (EST). Secure computation allows mutually distrusting participants to compute on joint private inputs while revealing no information beyond the output of the computation. The first templates for secure computation that make use of quantum information were proposed in a combination of works by Crépeau and Kilian [13], and Kilian [31]. For a while [36,46] it was believed that *unconditionally secure computation* could be realized based on a specific cryptographic building block: an *unconditionally secure quantum bit commitment.* Unfortunately, beliefs that unconditionally secure quantum bit commitments exist [10] were subsequently proven false [34,35], and the possibility of unconditional secure computation was also ruled out [33].

As such, secure computation protocols must either assume an honest majority or necessarily rely on computational hardness to achieve security against adversaries that are computationally bounded. But this may be troublesome when participants wish to compute on extremely sensitive data, such as medical or government records. In particular, consider a server that computes on highly sensitive data and keeps information from the computation around in memory forever. Such a server may be able to eventually recover data if the underlying hardness assumption breaks down in the future. In this setting, it is natural to ask: Can we use computational assumptions to design "everlasting" secure protocols against an adversary that is computationally bounded during protocol execution but becomes *computationally unbounded* after protocol execution?

Unfortunately, everlasting secure computation against *every participant in a protocol* is *also* impossible [40] for most natural two-party functionalities (or multi-party functionalities against dishonest majority corruptions). For the specific case of two parties, this means that it is impossible to achieve everlasting security against *both* players, without relying on special tools like trusted/ideal hardware. Nevertheless, it is still possible to obtain everlasting (or even the stronger notion of statistical) security against one unbounded participant (see eg., [30] and references therein). But in *all existing protocols*, which party may be unbounded and which one must be assumed to be computationally bounded must necessarily be fixed *before protocol execution*. We ask if this is necessary. That is,

> *Can participants transfer everlasting security from one party*
> *to another even after a protocol has already been executed?*

We show that the answer is yes, under the weak cryptographic assumption that (post-quantum) statistically-binding computationally-hiding bit commitments exist. These commitments can in turn be based on one-way functions [38] or even pseudo-random quantum states [3,37].

We illustrate our novel security property by considering it in the context of Yao's classic millionaire problem [45]. Stated simply, this toy problem requires two millionaires to securely compute who is richer without revealing to each other or anyone else information about their wealth. That is, the goal is to only reveal the bit indicating whether $x_1 > x_2$ where x_1 is Alice's private input and x_2 is Bob's private input. In our extension, the millionaires would also like (certified) everlasting security against the wealthier party, while maintaining standard simulation-based security against the other party. Namely, if $x_1 > x_2$ then the protocol should satisfy certified everlasting security against Alice and standard simulation-based security against computationally bounded Bob; and if it turns out that $x_2 \geq x_1$, then the protocol should satisfy certified everlasting security against Bob and simulation-based security against bounded Alice.

More generally, our goal is to enable any one party (or a subset of parties) to dynamically and certifiably information-theoretically delete other participants' inputs, during or even after a secure computation protocol completes. At the same time, the process of deletion should not destroy standard simulation-based security.

We build a two-party protocol that is (a) designed to be secure against computationally *unbounded Alice* and computationally *bounded Bob*. In addition, even after the protocol ends, (b) Bob has the capability to generate a proof whose validity certifies that the protocol has now become secure against *unbounded Bob* while remaining secure against *bounded Alice*. In other words, verification of the proof implies that everlasting security roles have switched: this is why we call this property *everlasting security transfer*. This implies zero-knowledge proofs for NP/QMA with certified everlasting ZK as a special case. We also extend this result to obtain *multi-party computation* where even after completion of the protocol, any arbitrary subset of parties can certifiably, information-theoretically remove information about the other party inputs from their view.

At a high level, we build these protocols by carefully combining Theorem 1 with additional techniques to ensure that having one party generate a certificate of deletion does not ruin standard (simulation-based, computational) security against the other party.

In what follows, we provide a detailed overview of our techniques.

1.2 Techniques

We first provide an overview of our proof of Theorem 1.

Our construction and analysis include a couple of crucial differences from previous work on certified deletion. First, our analysis diverges from recent work [11,39] that relies on "generalized uncertainty relations" which provide lower bounds on the sum of entropies resulting from two incompatible measurements, and instead builds on the simple but powerful "quantum cut-and-choose" formalism of Bouman and Fehr [8]. Next, we make crucial use of an *unseeded* randomness extractor (the XOR function), as opposed to a seeded extractor, as used by [11].

Delaying the Dependence on b. A key tension that must be resolved when proving a claim like Theorem 1 is the following: how to *information-theoretically* remove the bit b from the adversary's view, when it is initially information-theoretically *determined* by the adversary's input. Our first step towards a proof is a simple change in perspective. We will instead imagine sampling the distribution by *guessing* a uniformly random $b' \leftarrow \{0,1\}$, and initializing the adversary with $|x\rangle_\theta, b', \mathcal{Z}_\lambda(\theta)$. Then, we abort the experiment (output $\perp$) if it happens that $b' \neq b \oplus \bigoplus_{i:\theta_i=0} x_i$. Since b' was a uniformly random guess, we always abort with probability exactly $1/2$, and thus the trace distance between the $b = 0$ and $b = 1$ outputs of this experiment is at least half the trace distance between the outputs of the original experiment.[6]

Now, the bit b is only used by the experiment to determine whether or not to output $\perp$. This is not immediately helpful, since the result of this "abort decision" is of course included in the output of the experiment. However, we can make progress by delaying this abort decision (and thus, the dependence on b) until *after* the adversary outputs x' and their residual state on register A'. To do so, we will make use of a common strategy in quantum cryptographic proofs: replace the BB84 states $|x\rangle_\theta$ with halves of EPR pairs $\frac{1}{\sqrt{2}}(|00\rangle + |11\rangle)$. Let C be the register holding the "challenger's" halves of EPR pairs, and A be the register holding the other halves, which is part of the adversary's input. This switch is perfectly indistinguishable from the adversary's perspective, and it allows us to *delay* the measurement of C in the θ-basis (and thus, delay the determination of the string x and subsequent abort decision), until after the adversary outputs (x', A').

We still have not shown that when the deletion certificate is accepted, information about b doesn't exist in the output of the experiment. However, note that at this point it suffices to argue that $\bigoplus_{i:\theta_i=0} x_i$ is distributed like a uniformly random bit, even conditioned on the adversary's "side information" on register A' (which may be entangled with C). This is because, if $\bigoplus_{i:\theta_i=0} x_i$ is uniformly random, then the outcome of the abort decision, whether $b' = b \oplus \bigoplus_{i:\theta_i=0} x_i$, is also a uniformly random bit, regardless of b.

Identifying an Efficiently-Checkable Predicate. To prove that $\bigoplus_{i:\theta_i=0} x_i$ is uniformly random, we will need to establish that the measured bits $\{x_i\}_{i:\theta_i=0}$ contain sufficient entropy. To do this, we will need to make some claim about the structure of the state on registers $\mathsf{C}_{i:\theta_i=0}$. These registers are measured in the computational basis to produce $\{x_i\}_{i:\theta_i=0}$, so if we could claim that these registers are in a Hadamard basis state, we would be done. We won't quite be able to claim something this strong, but we don't need to. Instead, we will rely on the following claim: consider any (potentially entangled) state on systems X and Y, such that the part of the state on system Y is in a superposition of Hadamard basis states $|u\rangle_1$ where each u is a vector of somewhat low Hamming weight.[7] Then, measuring Y in the computational basis and computing the XOR of the resulting bits produces a bit that is *uniformly random and independent* of system

---

[6] One might be concerned that extending this argument to multi-bit messages may eventually reduce the advantage by too much, since the entire message must be guessed. However, it actually suffices to prove Theorem 1 for single bit messages and then use a bit-by-bit hybrid argument to obtain security for any polynomial-length message.

[7] It suffices to require that the relative Hamming weight of each u is $< 1/2$.

X.[8] This claim can be viewed as saying that XOR is a good (seedless) randomness extractor for the quantum source of entropy that results from measuring certain structured states in the conjugate basis. Indeed, such a claim was developed to remove the need for *seeded* randomness extraction in applications like quantum oblivious transfer [2], and it serves a similar purpose here.[9]

Thus, it suffices to show that the state on registers $C_{i:\theta_i=0}$ is only supported on low Hamming weight vectors in the Hadamard basis. A priori, it is not clear why this would even be true, since C, A are initialized with EPR pairs, and the adversary, who has access to A, can simply measure its halves of these EPR pairs in the computational basis. However, recall that the experiment we are interested in only outputs the adversary's final state when its certificate of deletion is valid, and moreover, a valid deletion certificate is a string x' that matches x in all the *Hadamard* basis positions. Moreover, which positions will be checked is semantically hidden from the adversary. Thus, in order to be sure that it passes the verification, an adversary should intuitively be measuring most of its registers A in the Hadamard basis.

Reducing to Semantic Security. One remaining difficulty in formalizing this intuition is that if the adversary knew θ, it could decide which positions to measure in the Hadamard basis to pass the verification check, and then measure $A_{i:\theta_i=0}$ in the computational basis in order to thwart the above argument from going through. And in fact, the adversary *does* have information about θ, encoded in the distribution $\mathcal{Z}_\lambda(\theta)$.

This is where the assumption that $\mathcal{A}_\lambda$ cannot distinguish between $\mathcal{Z}_\lambda(\theta)$ and $\mathcal{Z}_\lambda(0^\lambda)$ comes into play. We interpret the condition that registers $C_{i:\theta_i=0}$ must be in a superposition of low Hamming weight vectors in the Hadamard basis (or verification doesn't pass) as an efficient predicate (technically a binary projective measurement) that can be checked by a reduction to the indistinguishability of distributions $\mathcal{Z}_\lambda(\theta)$ and $\mathcal{Z}_\lambda(0^\lambda)$. Thus, this predicate must have roughly the same probability of being true when the adversary receives $\mathcal{Z}_\lambda(0^\lambda)$. But now, since θ is independent of the adversary's view, we can show *information-theoretically* that this predicate must be true with overwhelming probability.

We note that the broad strategy of identifying an efficiently-checkable predicate which implies the *uncheckable property that some information is random and independent of the adversary's view* has been used in similar (quantum cryptographic) contexts by Gottesman [22] in their work on the related concept of

---

[8] This proof strategy is inspired by the techniques of [8], who show a similar claim using a *seeded* extractor.

[9] If we had tried to rely on generic properties of a seeded randomness extractor, as done in [11], we would still have had to deal with the fact the adversary's view includes an encryption of the seed, which is required to be *uniform and independent* of the source of entropy. Even if the challenger's state can be shown to produce a sufficient amount of min-entropy when measured in the standard basis, we cannot immediately claim that this source of entropy is perfectly independent of the seed of the extractor. Similar issues with using seeded randomness extraction in a related context are discussed by [41] in their work on revocable timed-release encryption.

uncloneable (or perhaps more accurately, *tamper-detectable*) encryption[10] and by Unruh [41] in their work on revocable timed-release encryption.

Application: A Variety of Encryption Schemes with Certified Deletion. For any $X \in$ {public-key encryption, attribute-based encryption, witness encryption, statistically-binding commitment, timed-release encryption}, we immediately obtain "X with certified deletion" by instantiating the distribution $\mathcal{Z}_\lambda$ with the encryption/encoding procedure for X, and additionally encrypting/encoding the bit $b \oplus \bigoplus_{i:\theta_i=0} x_i$ to ensure that semantic security holds regardless of whether the adversary deletes the ciphertext or not.

Similarly, if $\mathcal{Z}_\lambda$ is instantiated with the encryption procedure for a *fully-homomorphic* encryption scheme [9,20,21], then the scheme also allows for arbitrary homomorphic operations over the ciphertext. We also note that such a scheme can be used for blind delegation with certified deletion, allowing a weak client to outsource computations to a powerful server and subsequently verify deletion of the plaintext. In particular, a server may perform homomorphic evaluation coherently (i.e. by not performing any measurements), and return the register containing the output to the client. The client can coherently decrypt this register to obtain a classical outcome, then reverse the decryption operation and return the output register to the server. Finally, the server can use this register to reverse the evaluation operation and recover the original ciphertext. Then, the server can prove deletion of the original plaintext as above, i.e. measure the quantum state associated with this ciphertext in the Hadamard basis, and report the outcomes as their certificate.

Application: Secure Computation with Everlasting Security Transfer (EST). Recall that in building two-party computation with EST, the goal is to build protocols (a) secure against *unbounded Alice* and computationally *bounded Bob* such that, during or even after the protocol ends, (b) Bob can generate a proof whose validity certifies that the protocol has now become secure against *unbounded Bob* while remaining secure against *bounded Alice*.

Our goal is to realize two-party secure computation with EST from minimal cryptographic assumptions. We closely inspect a class of protocols for secure computation that do not a-priori have any EST guarantees, and develop techniques to equip them with EST.

In particular, we observe that a key primitive called quantum oblivious transfer (QOT) is known to unconditionally imply secure computation of *all classical (and quantum) circuits* [14,16,31]. Namely, given OT with information-theoretic security, it is possible to build secure computation with everlasting

---

[10] In this notion, the adversary is an eavesdropper who sits between a ciphertext generator Alice and a ciphertext receiver Bob (using a symmetric-key encryption scheme), who attempts to learn some information about the ciphertext. The guarantee is that, *either* the eavesdropper gains information-theoretically no information about the underlying plaintext, *or* Bob can detect that the ciphertext was tampered with. While this is peripherally related to our setting, [22] does not consider public-key encryption, and moreover Bob's detection procedure is quantum.

(and even unconditional) security against unbounded participants. We recall that information-theoretically secure OT cannot exist in the plain model, even given quantum resources [33]. However, for the case of EST, we establish a general sequential composition theorem (in the full version [5]) which shows that oblivious transfer with EST can be plugged into the above unconditional protocols to yield secure computation protocols with EST.

Furthermore, a recent line of work [4,8,13,15,23] establishes *ideal* commitments[11] as the basis for QOT. Intuitively, these are commitments that satisfy the (standard) notion of simulation-based security against computationally bounded quantum committers and receivers. Namely, for every adversarial committer (resp., receiver) that interacts with an honest receiver (resp., committer) in the real protocol, there is a simulator that interacts with the ideal commitment functionality and generates a simulated state that is indistinguishable from the committer's (resp., receiver's) state in the real protocol. Our composition theorem combined with [4] also immediately shows that ideal commitments *with EST* imply QOT with EST. Thus, the problem reduces to building ideal commitments with EST.

Constructing Ideal Commitments with EST. An ideal commitment with EST satisfies statistical simulation-based security against unbounded committers, and computational simulation-based security against bounded receivers. Furthermore, after an optional delete/transfer phase succeeds, everlasting security is *transfered*: that is, then the commitment satisfies statistical (simulation-based) security against unbounded receivers, and remains computationally (simulation-based) secure against bounded committers.

To build ideal commitments with EST, we start with any commitment that satisfies standard computational hiding, and a strong form of binding: namely, simulation-based security against an unbounded malicious committer. At a high level, this means that there is an efficient extractor that can extract the input committed by an unbounded committer, thereby statistically simulating the view of the adversarial committer in its interaction with the ideal commitment functionality. We call this a *computationally-hiding statistically-efficiently-extractable* (CHSEE) commitment, and observe that prior work ([4]) builds such commitments from black-box use of any statistically-binding, computationally-hiding commitment. Our construction of ideal commitments with EST starts with CHSEE commitments, and proceeds in two steps, where the first involves new technical insights and the second follows from ideas in prior work [4].

Step 1: One-Sided Ideal Commitments with EST. While CHSEE commitments satisfy simulation-based security against a malicious committer, they do not admit security transfer. Therefore, our first step is to add the EST property to CHSEE commitments, which informally additionally allows receivers to

---

[11] The term "ideal committment" can sometimes refer to the commitment *ideal funtionality*, but in this work we use the term ideal commitment to refer to a *real-world protocol* that can be shown to securely implement the commitment ideal functionality.

certifiably, information-theoretically, delete the committed input. We call the resulting primitive *one-sided ideal commitments with EST*. The word "one-sided" denotes that these commitments satisfy simulation-based security against any malicious committer, but are not necessarily simulation-secure against malicious receivers. Instead, these commitments semantically hide the committed bit from a malicious receiver and furthermore, support certified everlasting hiding against malicious receivers.

We observe that invoking Theorem 1 while instantiating $\mathcal{Z}_\lambda$ with a CHSEE commitments already helps us add the certified everlasting hiding property to any CHSEE commitment. While this ensures the desired certified everlasting security against malicious receivers, the scheme appears to become insecure against malicious committers after certified deletion!

To see why, recall that the resulting commitment is now $|x\rangle_\theta$, $\mathsf{Com}\,(\theta, b')$, where Com is a CHSEE commitment and $b' = b \oplus \bigoplus_{i:\theta_i=0} x_i$. In particular, to simulate (i.e., to extract the bit committed by) a malicious committer $\mathcal{C}^*$, a simulator must extract the bases θ and masked bit b' from the CHSEE commitment, measure the accompanying state $|\psi\rangle$ in basis θ to recover x, and then XOR the parity $\bigoplus_{i:\theta_i=0} x_i$ with b' to obtain the committed bit b. Thus, the simulator will have to first measure qubits of $|\psi\rangle$ that correspond to $\theta_i = 0$ in the computational basis to recover x_i values at these positions. If the committer makes a delete request after this point, the simulator must measure *all positions* in the Hadamard basis to generate the certificate of deletion. But consider a cheating committer that (maliciously) generates the qubit at a certain position (say $i = 1$) as a half of an EPR pair, keeping the other half to itself. Next, this committer commits to $\theta_i = 0$ (i.e., computational basis) corresponding to the index $i = 1$. The simulation strategy outlined above will first measure the first qubit of $|\psi\rangle$ in the computational basis, and then later in the Hadamard basis to generate a deletion certificate. On the other hand, an honest receiver will only ever measure this qubit in the Hadamard basis to generate a deletion certificate. This makes it easy for such a committer to distinguish simulation from an honest receiver strategy, simply by measuring its half of the EPR pair in the Hadamard basis, thereby breaking simulation security post-deletion.

To prevent this attack, we modify the scheme so that the committer $\mathcal{C}^*$ *only ever obtains* the receiver's outcomes of Hadamard basis measurements on indices where the committed $\theta_i = 1$. In particular, we make the delete phase interactive: the receiver will first commit to all measurement outcomes in Hadamard bases, $\mathcal{C}^*$ will then decommit to θ, and then finally the receiver will *only* open the committed measurement outcomes on indices i where $\theta_i = 1$. Against malicious receivers, we prove that this scheme is computationally hiding before deletion, and is certified everlasting hiding after deletion. Against a malicious committer, we prove statistical simulation-based security before deletion, and show that computational simulation-based security holds *even after deletion*.

Step 2: Ideal Commitments with EST. Next, we upgrade the one-sided ideal commitments with EST obtained above to build (full-fledged) ideal commitments with EST. Recall that the one-sided ideal commitments with EST do not satisfy simulation-based security against malicious receivers. Intuitively, simulation-based security against malicious receivers requires the existence of a simulator that interacts with a malicious receiver to produce a state in the commit phase, that can later be opened (or *equivocated*) to a bit that is only revealed to the simulator at the end of the commit phase. We show that this property can be generically obtained (with EST) by relying on a previous compiler, namely an *equivocality compiler* from [4]. We defer additional details of this step to the full version [5] since this essentially follows from ideas in prior work [4]. This also completes an overview of our techniques.

Roadmap. We refer the reader to Sect. 3 for the proof of our main theorem, Sect. 4 for secret sharing and public-key encryption with certified deletion, and the full version [5] for additional cryptosystems with certified deletion including details on building secure computation with everlasting security transfer.

1.3 Concurrent and Independent Work

Subsequent to the original posting of our paper on arXiv, an updated version of [39] was posted with some independent new results on fully-homomorphic encryption with certified deletion. The updated FHE scheme with certified deletion is shown to satisfy standard semantic security, but under a newly introduced conjecture that a particular hash function is "strong Gaussian-collapsing". Proving this conjecture based on a standard assumption such as LWE is left as an open problem in [39]. Thus, the FHE scheme presented in our paper is the first to satisfy certified deletion based on a standard assumption (and in addition satisfies *everlasting hiding*). On the other hand, the updated scheme of [39] also satisfies the property of publicly-verifiable deletion, which we do not consider in this work.

Also, a concurrent and independent work of Hiroka et al. [26] was posted shortly after the original posting of our paper. In [26], the authors construct public-key encryption schemes satisfying the definition of security that we use in this paper: certified everlasting security. However, their constructions are either in the *quantum random oracle model*, or require a *quantum* certificate of deletion. Thus, our construction of PKE with certified everlasting security, which is simple, in the plain model, and has a classical certificate of deletion, subsumes these results. On the other hand, [26] introduce and construct the primitive of (bounded-collusion) *functional encryption* with certified deletion, which we do not consider in this work.

2   Preliminaries

Let λ denote the security parameter. We write negl($\cdot$) to denote any *negligible* function, which is a function f such that for every constant $c \in \mathbb{N}$ there exists $N \in \mathbb{N}$ such that for all $n > N$, $f(n) < n^{-c}$.

Given an alphabet A and string $x \in A^n$, let $h(x)$ denote the Hamming weight (number of non-zero indices) of x, and $\omega(x) := h(x)/n$ denote the *relative Hamming weight* of x. Given two strings $x, y \in \{0,1\}^n$, let $\Delta(x,y) := \omega(x \oplus y)$ denote the *relative Hamming distance* between x and y.

2.1 Quantum Preliminaries

A register X is a named Hilbert space $\mathbb{C}^{2^n}$. A pure quantum state on register X is a unit vector $|\psi\rangle^{\mathsf{X}} \in \mathbb{C}^{2^n}$, and we say that $|\psi\rangle^{\mathsf{X}}$ consists of n qubits. A mixed state on register X is described by a density matrix $\rho^{\mathsf{X}} \in \mathbb{C}^{2^n \times 2^n}$, which is a positive semi-definite Hermitian operator with trace 1.

A *quantum operation* F is a completely-positive trace-preserving (CPTP) map from a register X to a register Y, which in general may have different dimensions. That is, on input a density matrix ρ^{X}, the operation F produces $F(\rho^{\mathsf{X}}) = \tau^{\mathsf{Y}}$ a mixed state on register Y. We will sometimes write a quantum operation F applied to a state on register X and resulting in a state on register Y as $\mathsf{Y} \leftarrow F(\mathsf{X})$. Note that we have left the actual mixed states on these registers implicit in this notation, and just work with the names of the registers themselves.

A *unitary* $U : \mathsf{X} \to \mathsf{X}$ is a special case of a quantum operation that satisfies $U^\dagger U = UU^\dagger = \mathbb{I}^{\mathsf{X}}$, where $\mathbb{I}^{\mathsf{X}}$ is the identity matrix on register X. A *projector* Π is a Hermitian operator such that $\Pi^2 = \Pi$, and a *projective measurement* is a collection of projectors $\{\Pi_i\}_i$ such that $\sum_i \Pi_i = \mathbb{I}$.

Let Tr denote the trace operator. For registers X, Y, the *partial trace* Tr^{Y} is the unique operation from X, Y to X such that for all $(\rho, \tau)^{\mathsf{X}, \mathsf{Y}}$, $\mathsf{Tr}^{\mathsf{Y}}(\rho, \tau) = \mathsf{Tr}(\tau)\rho$. The *trace distance* between states ρ, τ, denoted $\mathsf{TD}(\rho, \tau)$ is defined as

$$\mathsf{TD}(\rho, \tau) := \frac{1}{2}\|\rho - \tau\|_1 := \frac{1}{2}\mathsf{Tr}\left(\sqrt{(\rho - \tau)^\dagger(\rho - \tau)}\right).$$

We will often use the fact that the trace distance between two states ρ and τ is an upper bound on the probability that any (unbounded) algorithm can distinguish ρ and τ. When clear from context, we will write $\mathsf{TD}(\mathsf{X}, \mathsf{Y})$ to refer to the trace distance between a state on register X and a state on register Y.

Lemma 1 (Gentle measurement [44]**).** *Let ρ^{X} be a quantum state and let $(\Pi, \mathbb{I} - \Pi)$ be a projective measurement on X such that $\mathsf{Tr}(\Pi\rho) \geq 1 - \delta$. Let*

$$\rho' = \frac{\Pi\rho\Pi}{\mathsf{Tr}(\Pi\rho)}$$

be the state after applying $(\Pi, \mathbb{I} - \Pi)$ to ρ and post-selecting on obtaining the first outcome. Then, $\mathsf{TD}(\rho, \rho') \leq 2\sqrt{\delta}$.

We will make use of the convention that 0 denotes the computational basis $\{|0\rangle, |1\rangle\}$ and 1 denotes the Hadamard basis $\left\{ \frac{|0\rangle + |1\rangle}{\sqrt{2}}, \frac{|0\rangle - |1\rangle}{\sqrt{2}} \right\}$. For a bit $r \in \{0,1\}$, we write $|r\rangle_0$ to denote r encoded in the computational basis, and $|r\rangle_1$

to denote r encoded in the Hadamard basis. For strings $x, \theta \in \{0,1\}^\lambda$, we write $|x\rangle_\theta$ to mean $|x_1\rangle_{\theta_1}, \ldots, |x_\lambda\rangle_{\theta_\lambda}$.

A non-uniform quantum polynomial-time (QPT) machine $\{\mathcal{A}_\lambda, |\psi\rangle_\lambda\}_{\lambda \in \mathbb{N}}$ is a family of polynomial-size quantum machines $\mathcal{A}_\lambda$, where each is initialized with a polynomial-size advice state $|\psi_\lambda\rangle$. Each $\mathcal{A}_\lambda$ is in general described by a CPTP map. Similar to above, when we write $\mathsf{Y} \leftarrow \mathcal{A}(\mathsf{X})$, we mean that the machine $\mathcal{A}$ takes as input a state on register X and produces as output a state on register Y, and we leave the actual descriptions of these states implicit. Finally, a quantum *interactive* machine is simply a sequence of quantum operations, with designated input, output, and work registers.

2.2   The XOR Extractor

We make use of a result from [2] which shows that the XOR function is a good randomness extractor from certain *quantum* sources of entropy, even given quantum side information. We include a proof here for completeness.

Imported Theorem 2 ([2]). *Let X be an n-qubit register, and consider any quantum state $|\gamma\rangle^{\mathsf{A},\mathsf{X}}$ that can be written as*

$$|\gamma\rangle^{\mathsf{A},\mathsf{X}} = \sum_{u:h(u)<n/2} |\psi_u\rangle^{\mathsf{A}} \otimes |u\rangle^{\mathsf{X}},$$

where $h(\cdot)$ denotes the Hamming weight. Let $\rho^{\mathsf{A},\mathsf{P}}$ be the mixed state that results from measuring X in the Hadamard basis to produce a string $x \in \{0,1\}^n$, and writing $\bigoplus_{i \in [n]} x_i$ into a single qubit register P. Then it holds that

$$\rho^{\mathsf{A},\mathsf{P}} = \mathsf{Tr}^{\mathsf{X}}(|\gamma\rangle \langle \gamma|) \otimes \left(\frac{1}{2} |0\rangle \langle 0| + \frac{1}{2} |1\rangle \langle 1|\right).$$

Proof. First, write the state on registers $\mathsf{A}, \mathsf{X}, \mathsf{P}$ that results from applying Hadamard to X and writing the parity, denoted by $p(x) := \bigoplus_{i \in [n]} x_i$, to P:

$$\frac{1}{2^{n/2}} \sum_{x \in \{0,1\}^n} \left(\sum_{u:h(u)<n/2} (-1)^{u \cdot x} |\psi_u\rangle^{\mathsf{A}}\right) |x\rangle^{\mathsf{X}} |p(x)\rangle^{\mathsf{P}} := \frac{1}{2^{n/2}} \sum_{x \in \{0,1\}^n} |\phi_x\rangle^{\mathsf{A}} |x\rangle^{\mathsf{X}} |p(x)\rangle^{\mathsf{P}}.$$

Then, tracing out the register X, we have that

$$\rho^{\mathsf{A},\mathsf{P}} = \frac{1}{2^n} \sum_{x \in \{0,1\}^n} |\phi_x\rangle |p(x)\rangle \langle p(x)| \langle \phi_x|$$

$$= \frac{1}{2^n} \sum_{x:p(x)=0} |\phi_x\rangle \langle \phi_x| \otimes |0\rangle \langle 0| + \frac{1}{2^n} \sum_{x:p(x)=1} |\phi_x\rangle \langle \phi_x| \otimes |1\rangle \langle 1|$$

$$= \frac{1}{2^n} \sum_{x:p(x)=0} \left(\sum_{u_1,u_2:h(u_1),h(u_2)<n/2} (-1)^{(u_1 \oplus u_2) \cdot x} |\psi_{u_1}\rangle \langle \psi_{u_2}| \right) \otimes |0\rangle \langle 0|$$

$$+ \frac{1}{2^n} \sum_{x:p(x)=1} \left(\sum_{u_1,u_2:h(u_1),h(u_2)<n/2} (-1)^{(u_1 \oplus u_2) \cdot x} |\psi_{u_1}\rangle \langle \psi_{u_2}| \right) \otimes |1\rangle \langle 1|$$

$$= \sum_{u_1,u_2:h(u_1),h(u_2)<n/2} |\psi_{u_1}\rangle \langle \psi_{u_2}|$$

$$\otimes \left(\frac{1}{2^n} \sum_{x:p(x)=0} (-1)^{(u_1 \oplus u_2) \cdot x} |0\rangle \langle 0| + \frac{1}{2^n} \sum_{x:p(x)=1} (-1)^{(u_1 \oplus u_2) \cdot x} |1\rangle \langle 1| \right)$$

$$= \sum_{u:h(u)<n/2} |\psi_u\rangle \langle \psi_u| \otimes \left(\frac{1}{2} |0\rangle \langle 0| + \frac{1}{2} |1\rangle \langle 1| \right)$$

$$= \mathsf{Tr}^{\mathsf{X}}(|\gamma\rangle \langle \gamma|) \otimes \left(\frac{1}{2} |0\rangle \langle 0| + \frac{1}{2} |1\rangle \langle 1| \right),$$

where the 5th equality is due to the following claim, plus the observation that $u_1 \oplus u_2 \neq 1^n$ for any u_1, u_2 such that $h(u_1) < n/2$ and $h(u_2) < n/2$.

Claim. For any $u \in \{0,1\}^n$ such that $u \notin \{0^n, 1^n\}$, it holds that

$$\sum_{x:p(x)=0} (-1)^{u \cdot x} = \sum_{x:p(x)=1} (-1)^{u \cdot x} = 0.$$

Proof. For any such $u \notin \{0^n, 1^n\}$, define $S_0 = \{i : u_i = 0\}$ and $S_1 = \{i : u_i = 1\}$. Then, for any $y_0 \in \{0,1\}^{|S_0|}$ and $y_1 \in \{0,1\}^{|S_1|}$, define $x_{y_0,y_1} \in \{0,1\}^n$ to be the n-bit string that is equal to y_0 when restricted to indices in S_0 and equal to y_1 when restricted to indices in S_1. Then,

$$\sum_{x:p(x)=0} (-1)^{u \cdot x} = \sum_{y_1 \in \{0,1\}^{|S_1|}} \sum_{y_0 \in \{0,1\}^{|S_0|}:p(x_{y_0,y_1})=0} (-1)^{u \cdot x_{y_0,y_1}}$$

$$= \sum_{y_1 \in \{0,1\}^{|S_1|}} 2^{|S_0|-1}(-1)^{1^{|S_1|} \cdot y_1} = 2^{|S_0|-1} \sum_{y_1 \in \{0,1\}^{|S_1|}} (-1)^{p(y_1)} = 0,$$

where the second equality can be seen to hold by noting that for any fixed $y_1 \in \{0,1\}^{|S_1|}$, there are exactly $2^{|S_0|-1}$ strings $y_0 \in \{0,1\}^{|S_0|}$ such that the parity of x_{y_0,y_1} is 0. Finally, the same sequence of equalities can be seen to hold for $x : p(x) = 1$.

2.3   Quantum Rewinding

We will make use of the following lemma from [42].

Lemma 2. *Let $\mathcal{Q}$ be a quantum circuit that takes n qubits as input and outputs a classical bit b and m qubits. For an n-qubit state $|\psi\rangle$, let $p(|\psi\rangle)$ denote the probability that $b = 0$ when executing $\mathcal{Q}$ on input $|\psi\rangle$. Let $p_0, q \in (0,1)$ and $\epsilon \in (0, 1/2)$ be such that:*

- *For every n-qubit state $|\psi\rangle$, $p_0 \leq p(|\psi\rangle)$,*
- *For every n-qubit state $|\psi\rangle$, $|p(|\psi\rangle) - q| < \epsilon$,*
- *$p_0(1 - p_0) \leq q(1 - q)$,*

Then, there is a quantum circuit $\widehat{\mathcal{Q}}$ of size $O\left(\frac{\log(1/\epsilon)}{4 \cdot p_0(1-p_0)}|\mathcal{Q}|\right)$, taking as input n qubits, and returning as output m qubits, with the following guarantee. For an n qubit state $|\psi\rangle$, let $\mathcal{Q}_0(|\psi\rangle)$ denote the output of $\mathcal{Q}$ on input $|\psi\rangle$ conditioned on $b = 0$, and let $\widehat{\mathcal{Q}}(|\psi\rangle)$ denote the output of $\widehat{\mathcal{Q}}$ on input $|\psi\rangle$. Then, for any n-qubit state $|\psi\rangle$,

$$\mathsf{TD}\left(\mathcal{Q}_0(|\psi\rangle), \widehat{\mathcal{Q}}(|\psi\rangle)\right) \leq 4\sqrt{\epsilon}\frac{\log(1/\epsilon)}{p_0(1 - p_0)}.$$

3   Main Theorem

Theorem 3. *Let $\{\mathcal{Z}_\lambda(\cdot, \cdot, \cdot)\}_{\lambda \in \mathbb{N}}$ be a quantum operation with three arguments: a λ-bit string θ, a bit b', and a λ-bit quantum register A. Let $\mathscr{A}$ be a class of adversaries[12] such that for all $\{\mathcal{A}_\lambda\}_{\lambda \in \mathbb{N}} \in \mathscr{A}$, and for any string $\theta \in \{0,1\}^\lambda$, bit $b' \in \{0,1\}$, and state $|\psi\rangle^{\mathsf{A},\mathsf{C}}$ on λ-bit register A and arbitrary size register C,*

$$\left|\Pr[\mathcal{A}_\lambda(\mathcal{Z}_\lambda(\theta, b', \mathsf{A}), \mathsf{C}) = 1] - \Pr[\mathcal{A}_\lambda(\mathcal{Z}_\lambda(0^\lambda, b', \mathsf{A}), \mathsf{C}) = 1]\right| = \mathsf{negl}(\lambda).$$

That is, $\mathcal{Z}_\lambda$ is semantically-secure against $\mathcal{A}_\lambda$ with respect to its first input. For any $\{\mathcal{A}_\lambda\}_{\lambda \in \mathbb{N}} \in \mathscr{A}$, consider the following distribution $\left\{\widetilde{\mathcal{Z}}_\lambda^{\mathcal{A}_\lambda}(b)\right\}_{\lambda \in \mathbb{N}, b \in \{0,1\}}$ over quantum states, obtained by running $\mathcal{A}_\lambda$ as follows.

- *Sample $x, \theta \leftarrow \{0,1\}^\lambda$ and initialize $\mathcal{A}_\lambda$ with*

$$\mathcal{Z}_\lambda\left(\theta, b \oplus \bigoplus_{i:\theta_i=0} x_i, |x\rangle_\theta\right).$$

- *$\mathcal{A}_\lambda$'s output is parsed as a string $x' \in \{0,1\}^\lambda$ and a residual state on register A'.*

---

[12] Technically, we require that for any $\{\mathcal{A}_\lambda\}_{\lambda \in \mathbb{N}} \in \mathscr{A}$, every adversary $\mathcal{B}$ with time and space complexity that is linear in λ more than that of $\mathcal{A}_\lambda$, is also in $\mathscr{A}$.

– If $x_i = x'_i$ for all i such that $\theta_i = 1$ then output A', and otherwise output a special symbol $\bot$.

Then,

$$\mathsf{TD}\left(\widetilde{\mathcal{Z}}_\lambda^{\mathcal{A}_\lambda}(0), \widetilde{\mathcal{Z}}_\lambda^{\mathcal{A}_\lambda}(1)\right) = \mathrm{negl}(\lambda).$$

Remark 1. We note that, in fact, the above theorem is true as long as x, θ are $\omega(\log\lambda)$ bits long.

Proof. We define a sequence of hybrid distributions.

– $\mathsf{Hyb}_0(b)$: This is the distribution $\left\{\widetilde{\mathcal{Z}}_\lambda^{\mathcal{A}_\lambda}(b)\right\}_{\lambda\in\mathbb{N}}$ described above.
– $\mathsf{Hyb}_1(b)$: This distribution is sampled as follows.
  • Prepare λ EPR pairs $\frac{1}{\sqrt{2}}(|00\rangle + |11\rangle)$ on registers $(\mathsf{C}_1, \mathsf{A}_1), \ldots, (\mathsf{C}_\lambda, \mathsf{A}_\lambda)$. Define $\mathsf{C} := \mathsf{C}_1, \ldots, \mathsf{C}_\lambda$ and $\mathsf{A} := \mathsf{A}_1, \ldots, \mathsf{A}_\lambda$.
  • Sample $\theta \leftarrow \{0,1\}^\lambda, b' \leftarrow \{0,1\}$, measure register C in basis θ to obtain $x \in \{0,1\}^\lambda$, and initialize $\mathcal{A}_\lambda$ with $\mathcal{Z}_\lambda(\theta, b', \mathsf{A})$.
  • If $b' = b \oplus \bigoplus_{i:\theta_i=0} x_i$ then proceed as in Hyb_0 and otherwise output $\bot$.
– $\mathsf{Hyb}_2(b)$: This is the same as $\mathsf{Hyb}_1(b)$ except that measurement of register C to obtain x is performed after $\mathcal{A}_\lambda$ outputs x' and ρ.

We define $\mathsf{Advt}(\mathsf{Hyb}_i) := \mathsf{TD}\left(\mathsf{Hyb}_i(0), \mathsf{Hyb}_i(1)\right)$. Then, we have that

$$\mathsf{Advt}(\mathsf{Hyb}_1) \geq \mathsf{Advt}(\mathsf{Hyb}_0)/2,$$

which follows because $\mathsf{Hyb}_1(b)$ is identically distributed to the distribution that outputs $\bot$ with probability $1/2$ and otherwise outputs $\mathsf{Hyb}_0(b)$. Next, we have that

$$\mathsf{Advt}(\mathsf{Hyb}_2) = \mathsf{Advt}(\mathsf{Hyb}_1),$$

which follows because the register C is disjoint from the registers that $\mathcal{A}_\lambda$ operates on. Thus, it remains to show that

$$\mathsf{Advt}(\mathsf{Hyb}_2) = \mathrm{negl}(\lambda).$$

To show this, we first define the following hybrid.

– $\mathsf{Hyb}'_2(b)$: This is the same as Hyb_2 except that $\mathcal{A}_\lambda$ is initialized with $\mathcal{Z}_\lambda(0^\lambda, b', \mathsf{A})$.

Now, for any $b \in \{0,1\}$, consider the state on register C immediately after $\mathcal{A}_\lambda$ outputs (x', A') in $\mathsf{Hyb}'_2(b)$. For any $\theta \in \{0,1\}^\lambda$, define sets $\theta_0 := \{i : \theta_i = 0\}$ and $\theta_1 := \{i : \theta_i = 1\}$, and define the projector

$$\Pi_{x',\theta} := \left(H^{\otimes|\theta_1|}|x'_{\theta_1}\rangle\langle x'_{\theta_1}|H^{\otimes|\theta_1|}\right)^{\mathsf{C}_{\theta_1}} \otimes \sum_{\substack{y\in\{0,1\}^{|\theta_0|}\ \text{s.t.}\\ \Delta(y,x'_{\theta_0})\geq 1/2}} \left(H^{\otimes|\theta_0|}|y\rangle\langle y|H^{\otimes|\theta_0|}\right)^{\mathsf{C}_{\theta_0}},$$

where $\Delta(\cdot, \cdot)$ denotes relative Hamming distance. Then, let $\Pr[\Pi_{x',\theta}, \mathsf{Hyb}'_2(b)]$ be the probability that a measurement of $\{\Pi_{x',\theta}, \mathbb{I} - \Pi_{x',\theta}\}$ accepts (returns the outcome associated with $\Pi_{x',\theta}$) in $\mathsf{Hyb}'_2(b)$.

Claim. For any $b \in \{0,1\}$, $\Pr[\Pi_{x',\theta}, \mathsf{Hyb}_2'(b)] = \mathrm{negl}(\lambda)$.

Proof. Consider running $\mathsf{Hyb}_2'(b)$ until $\mathcal{A}_\lambda$ outputs x' and a state on register A' that may be entangled with the challenger's state on register C. Note that we can sample $\theta \leftarrow \{0,1\}^\lambda$ independently since it is no longer in $\mathcal{A}_\lambda$'s view. Then since $\Pi_{x',\theta}$ is diagonal in the Hadamard basis for any (x', θ), we have that

$$\Pr[\Pi_{x',\theta}, \mathsf{Hyb}_2'(b)] = \Pr_{x',\theta,y}\left[y_{\theta_1} = x'_{\theta_1} \wedge \Delta\left(y_{\theta_0}, x'_{\theta_0}\right) \geq 1/2\right],$$

where the second probability is over $\mathcal{A}_\lambda$ outputting x', the challenger sampling $\theta \leftarrow \{0,1\}^\lambda$, and the challenger measuring register C in the Hadamard basis to obtain y. For any fixed string x', this probability can be bound by standard Hoeffding inequalities. For example, in [8, Appendix B.3], it is shown to be bounded by $4e^{-\lambda(1/2)^2/32} = \mathrm{negl}(\lambda)$, which completes the proof.

Now we consider the corresponding event in $\mathsf{Hyb}_2(b)$, denoted $\Pr[\Pi_{x',\theta}, \mathsf{Hyb}_2(b)]$.

Claim. For any $b \in \{0,1\}$, $\Pr[\Pi_{x',\theta}, \mathsf{Hyb}_2(b)] = \mathrm{negl}(\lambda)$.

Proof. This follows by a direct reduction to semantic security of $\{\mathcal{Z}_\lambda(\cdot, \cdot, \cdot)\}_{\lambda \in \mathbb{N}}$ with respect to its first input. The reduction samples $\theta \leftarrow \{0,1\}^\lambda$, $b' \leftarrow \{0,1\}$, prepares λ EPR pairs on registers (A, C), and sends (θ, b', A) to its challenger. It receives either $\mathcal{Z}_\lambda(\theta, b', \mathsf{A})$ or $\mathcal{Z}_\lambda(0^\lambda, b', \mathsf{A})$, which its sends to $\mathcal{A}_\lambda$. After $\mathcal{A}_\lambda$ outputs (x', A'), the reduction measures $\{\Pi_{x',\theta}, \mathbb{I} - \Pi_{x',\theta}\}$ on register C. Note that the complexity of this reduction is equal to the complexity of $\mathcal{A}_\lambda$ plus an extra λ bits of space and an extra linear time operation, so it is still in $\mathscr{A}$. If $\Pr[\Pi_{x',\theta}, \mathsf{Hyb}_2(b)]$ is non-negligible this can be used to distinguish $\mathcal{Z}_\lambda(\theta, b', \mathsf{A})$ from $\mathcal{Z}_\lambda(0^\lambda, b', \mathsf{A})$, due to Sect. 3.

Finally, we can show the following claim, which completes the proof.

Claim. $\mathsf{Advt}(\mathsf{Hyb}_2) = \mathrm{negl}(\lambda)$.

Proof. First, we note that for any $b \in \{0,1\}$, the global state of $\mathsf{Hyb}_2(b)$ immediately after $\mathcal{A}_\lambda$ outputs x' is within negligible trace distance of a state $\tau_{\mathsf{Ideal}}^{\mathsf{C},\mathsf{A}'}$ in the image of $\mathbb{I} - \Pi_{x',\theta}$. This follows immediately from Sect. 3 and Gentle Measurement (Lemma 1). Now, consider measuring registers C_{θ_1} of $\tau_{\mathsf{Ideal}}^{\mathsf{C},\mathsf{A}'}$ to determine whether the experiment outputs $\perp$. That is, the procedure measures C_{θ_1} in the Hadamard basis and checks if the resulting string is equal to x'_{θ_1}. There are two options.

- If the measurement fails, then the experiment outputs $\perp$, independent of whether $b = 0$ or $b = 1$, so there is 0 advantage in this case.
- If the measurement succeeds, then we know that the state on register C_{θ_0} is only supported on vectors $H^{\otimes|\theta_0|}|y\rangle$ such that $\Delta(y, x'_{\theta_0}) < 1/2$, since $\tau_{\mathsf{Ideal}}^{\mathsf{C},\mathsf{A}'}$ was in the image of $\mathbb{I} - \Pi_{x',\theta}$. These registers are then measured in the computational basis to produce bits $\{x_i\}_{i:\theta_i=0}$, and the experiment outputs $\perp$ if

$\bigoplus_{i:\theta_i=0} x_i \neq b' \oplus b$ and otherwise outputs the state on register A'. Note that (i) this decision is the *only* part of the experiment that depends on b, and (ii) it follows from Theorem 2 that the bit $\bigoplus_{i:\theta_i=0} x_i$ is *uniformly random and independent* of the register A', which is disjoint (but possibly entangled with) C. Thus, there is also 0 advantage in this case.

Indeed, Theorem 2 says that making a Hadamard basis measurement of a register that is in a superposition of computational basis vectors with relative Hamming weight $< 1/2$ will produce a set of bits $\{x_i\}_{i:\theta_i=0}$ such that $\bigoplus_{i:\theta_i=0} x_i$ is a uniformly random bit, even given potentially entangled quantum side information. We can apply this lemma to our system on $\mathsf{C}_{\theta_0}, \mathsf{A}'$ by considering a change of basis that maps $H^{\otimes|\theta_0|} |x'_{\theta_0}\rangle \to |0^{|\theta_0|}\rangle$. That is, the change of basis first applies Hadamard gates, and then an XOR with the fixed string x'_{θ_0}. Applying such a change of basis maps C_{θ_0} to a state that is supported on vectors $|y\rangle$ such that $\omega(y) < 1/2$, and we want to claim that a *Hadamard* basis measurement of the resulting state produces $\{x_i\}_{i:\theta_i=0}$ such that $\bigoplus_{i:\theta_i=0} x_i$ is uniformly random and independent of A'. This is exactly the statement of Theorem 2.

This completes the proof, since we have shown that there exists a single distribution, defined by $\tau^{\mathsf{C},\mathsf{A}'}_{\mathsf{Ideal}}$, that is negligibly close to both $\mathsf{Hyb}_2(0)$ and $\mathsf{Hyb}_2(1)$.

4   Cryptography with Certified Everlasting Security

4.1   Secret Sharing

We give a simple construction of a 2-out-of-2 secret sharing scheme where there exists a designated party that the dealer can ask to produce a certificate of deletion of their share. If this certificate verifies, then the underlying plaintext is information theoretically deleted, even given the other share.

Definition. First, we augment the standard syntax of secret sharing to include a deletion algorithm Del and a verification algorithm Ver. Formally, consider a secret sharing scheme $\mathsf{CD\text{-}SS} = (\mathsf{Share}, \mathsf{Rec}, \mathsf{Del}, \mathsf{Ver})$ with the following syntax.

- $\mathsf{Share}(m) \to (s_1, s_2, \mathsf{vk})$ is a quantum algorithm that takes as input a classical message m, and outputs a quantum share s_1, a classical share s_2 and a (potentially quantum) verification key vk.
- $\mathsf{Rec}(s_1, s_2) \to \{m, \bot\}$ is a quantum algorithm that takes as input two shares and outputs either a message m or a $\bot$ symbol.
- $\mathsf{Del}(s_1) \to \mathsf{cert}$ is a quantum algorithm that takes as input a quantum share s_1 and outputs a (potentially quantum) deletion certificate cert.
- $\mathsf{Ver}(\mathsf{vk}, \mathsf{cert}) \to \{\top, \bot\}$ is a (potentially quantum) algorithm that takes as input a (potentially quantum) verification key vk and a (potentially quantum) deletion certificate cert and outputs either $\top$ or $\bot$.

We say that $\mathsf{CD\text{-}SS}$ satisfies correctness of deletion if the following holds.

Definition 1 (Correctness of deletion). CD-SS = (Share, Rec, Del, Ver) *satisfies* correctness of deletion *if for any* m, *it holds with* $1 - \mathrm{negl}(\lambda)$ *probability over* $(s_1, s_2, \mathsf{vk}) \leftarrow \mathsf{Share}(m)$, $\mathsf{cert} \leftarrow \mathsf{Del}(s_1)$, $\mu \leftarrow \mathsf{Ver}(\mathsf{vk}, \mathsf{cert})$ *that* $\mu = \top$.

Next, we define certified deletion security for a secret sharing scheme.

Definition 2 (Certified deletion security).

  Let $\mathcal{A} = \{\mathcal{A}_\lambda\}_{\lambda \in \mathbb{N}}$ *denote an unbounded adversary and* b *denote a classical bit. Consider experiment* $\mathsf{EV\text{-}EXP}_\lambda^{\mathcal{A}}(b)$ *which describes everlasting security given a deletion certificate, and is defined as follows.*

- *Sample* $(s_1, s_2, \mathsf{vk}) \leftarrow \mathsf{Share}(b)$.
- *Initialize* $\mathcal{A}_\lambda$ *with* s_1.
- *Parse* $\mathcal{A}_\lambda$'s *output as a deletion certificate* cert *and a residual state on register* A'.
- *If* $\mathsf{Ver}(\mathsf{vk}, \mathsf{cert}) = \top$ *then output* (A', s_2), *and otherwise output* $\bot$.

Then CD-SS = (Share, Rec, Del, Ver) *satisfies certified deletion security if for any unbounded adversary* $\mathcal{A}$, *it holds that*

$$\mathsf{TD}\left(\mathsf{EV\text{-}EXP}_\lambda^{\mathcal{A}}(0), \mathsf{EV\text{-}EXP}_\lambda^{\mathcal{A}}(1)\right) = \mathrm{negl}(\lambda),$$

Corollary 1. *The scheme* CD-SS = (Share, Rec, Del, Ver) *defined as follows is a secret sharing scheme with certified deletion.*

- $\mathsf{Share}(m)$: *sample* $x, \theta \leftarrow \{0,1\}^\lambda$ *and output*

$$s_1 := |x\rangle_\theta \, , s_2 := \left(\theta, b \oplus \bigoplus_{i:\theta_i = 0} x_i \right), \quad \mathsf{vk} := (x, \theta).$$

- $\mathsf{Rec}(s_1, s_2)$: *parse* $s_1 := |x\rangle_\theta \, , s_2 := (\theta, b')$, *measure* $|x\rangle_\theta$ *in the* θ-*basis to obtain* x, *and output* $b = b' \oplus \bigoplus_{i:\theta_i = 0} x_i$.
- $\mathsf{Del}(s_1)$: *parse* $s_1 := |x\rangle_\theta$ *and measure* $|x\rangle_\theta$ *in the Hadamard basis to obtain a string* x', *and output* $\mathsf{cert} := x'$.
- $\mathsf{Ver}(\mathsf{vk}, \mathsf{cert})$: *parse* vk *as* (x, θ) *and* cert *as* x' *and output* $\top$ *if and only if* $x_i = x_i'$ *for all* i *such that* $\theta_i = 1$.

Proof. Correctness of deletion follows immediately from the description of the scheme. Certified deletion security, i.e.

$$\mathsf{TD}\left(\mathsf{EV\text{-}EXP}_\lambda^{\mathcal{A}}(0), \mathsf{EV\text{-}EXP}_\lambda^{\mathcal{A}}(1)\right) = \mathrm{negl}(\lambda)$$

follows by following the proof strategy of Theorem 3. This setting is slightly different than the setting considered in the proof of Theorem 3 since here we consider unbounded $\mathcal{A}_\lambda$ that are not given access to θ while Theorem 3 considers bounded $\mathcal{A}_\lambda$ that are given access to an encryption of θ. However, the proof is almost identical, defining hybrids as follows.

$\mathsf{Hyb}_0(b)$: This is the distribution $\left\{\mathsf{EV\text{-}EXP}_\lambda^{\mathcal{A}_\lambda}(b)\right\}_{\lambda \in \mathbb{N}}$ described above.

$\mathsf{Hyb}_1(b)$: This distribution is sampled as follows.
- Prepare λ EPR pairs $\frac{1}{\sqrt{2}}(|00\rangle + |11\rangle)$ on registers $(\mathsf{C}_1, \mathsf{A}_1), \ldots, (\mathsf{C}_\lambda, \mathsf{A}_\lambda)$. Define $\mathsf{C} := \mathsf{C}_1, \ldots, \mathsf{C}_\lambda$ and $\mathsf{A} := \mathsf{A}_1, \ldots, \mathsf{A}_\lambda$.
- Sample $\theta \leftarrow \{0,1\}, b' \leftarrow \{0,1\}$, measure register C in basis θ to obtain $x \in \{0,1\}^\lambda$, and initialize $\mathcal{A}_\lambda$ with register A.
- If $b' = b \oplus \bigoplus_{i:\theta_i=0} x_i$ then proceed as in Hyb_0 and otherwise output $\bot$.

$\mathsf{Hyb}_2(b)$: This is the same as $\mathsf{Hyb}_1(b)$ except that measurement of register C to obtain x is performed after $\mathcal{A}_\lambda$ outputs x' and A'.

Indistinguishability between these hybrids closely follows the proof of Theorem 3. The key difference is that $\mathsf{Hyb}_2'(b)$ is identical to $\mathsf{Hyb}_2(b)$ except that s_2 is set to $(b', 0^\lambda)$. Then, $\Pr[\Pi_{x',\theta}, \mathsf{Hyb}_2'(b)] = \mathsf{negl}(\lambda)$ follows identically to the proof in Theorem 3, whereas $\Pr[\Pi_{x',\theta}, \mathsf{Hyb}_2(b)] = \mathsf{negl}(\lambda)$ follows because the view of $\mathcal{A}_\lambda$ is identical in both hybrids. The final claim, that $\mathsf{Advt}(\mathsf{Hyb}_2) = \mathsf{negl}(\lambda)$ follows identically to the proof in Theorem 3.

Remark 2 (One-time pad encryption). We observe that the above proof, which considers unbounded $\mathcal{A}_\lambda$ who don't have access to θ until after they produce a valid deletion certificate, can also be used to establish the security of a simple one-time pad encryption scheme with certified deletion. The encryption of a bit b would be the state $|x\rangle_\theta$ together with a one-time pad encryption $k \oplus b \oplus \bigoplus_{i:\theta_i=0} x_i$ with key $k \leftarrow \{0,1\}$. The secret key would be (k, θ). Semantic security follows from the one-time pad, while certified deletion security follows from the above secret-sharing proof. This somewhat simplifies the construction of one-time pad encryption with certified deletion of [11], who required a seeded extractor.

4.2   Public-Key Encryption

In this section, we define and construct post-quantum public-key encryption with certified deletion for classical messages, assuming the existence of post-quantum public-key encryption for classical messages.

Public-Key Encryption With Certified Deletion. First, we augment the standard syntax to include a deletion algorithm Del and a verification algorithm Ver. Formally, consider a public-key encryption scheme $\mathsf{CD\text{-}PKE} = (\mathsf{Gen}, \mathsf{Enc}, \mathsf{Dec}, \mathsf{Del}, \mathsf{Ver})$ with syntax

- $\mathsf{Gen}(1^\lambda) \to (\mathsf{pk}, \mathsf{sk})$ is a classical algorithm that takes as input the security parameter and outputs a public key pk and secret key sk.
- $\mathsf{Enc}(\mathsf{pk}, m) \to (\mathsf{ct}, \mathsf{vk})$ is a quantum algorithm that takes as input the public key pk and a message m, and outputs a (potentially quantum) verification key vk and a quantum ciphertext ct.
- $\mathsf{Dec}(\mathsf{sk}, \mathsf{ct}) \to \{m, \bot\}$ is a quantum algorithm that takes as input the secret key sk and a quantum ciphertext ct and outputs either a message m or a $\bot$ symbol.

- Del(ct) → cert is a quantum algorithm that takes as input a quantum ciphertext ct and outputs a (potentially quantum) deletion certificate cert.
- Ver(vk, cert) → {⊤, ⊥} is a (potentially quantum) algorithm that takes as input a (potentially quantum) verification key vk and a (potentially quantum) deletion certificate cert and outputs either ⊤ or ⊥.

We say that CD-PKE satisfies correctness of deletion if the following holds.

Definition 3 (Correctness of deletion). CD-PKE = (Gen, Enc, Dec, Del, Ver) *satisfies* correctness of deletion *if for any* m, *it holds with* $1 - \mathrm{negl}(\lambda)$ *probability over* $(\mathsf{pk}, \mathsf{sk}) \leftarrow \mathsf{Gen}(1^\lambda), (\mathsf{ct}, \mathsf{vk}) \leftarrow \mathsf{Enc}(\mathsf{pk}, m), \mathsf{cert} \leftarrow \mathsf{Del}(\mathsf{ct}), \mu \leftarrow \mathsf{Ver}(\mathsf{vk}, \mathsf{cert})$ *that* $\mu = \top$.

Next, we define certified deletion security. Our definition has multiple parts, which we motivate as follows. The first experiment is the everlasting security experiment, which requires that conditioned on the (computationally bounded) adversary producing a valid deletion certificate, their left-over state is information-theoretically independent of b. However, we still want to obtain meaningful guarantees against adversaries that do not produce a valid deletion certificate. That is, we hope for standard semantic security against arbitrarily malicious but computationally bounded adversaries. Since such an adversary can query the ciphertext generator with an arbitrarily computed deletion certificate, we should include this potential interaction in the definition, and require that the response from the ciphertext generator still does not leak any information about b.[13] Note that, in our constructions, the verification key vk is actually completely independent of the plaintext b, and thus for our schemes this property follows automatically from semantic security.

Definition 4 (Certified deletion security). CD-PKE = (Gen, Enc, Dec, Del, Ver) *satisfies* certified deletion security *if for any non-uniform QPT adversary* $\mathcal{A} = \{\mathcal{A}_\lambda, |\psi\rangle_\lambda\}_{\lambda \in \mathbb{N}}$, *it holds that*

$$\mathsf{TD}\left(\mathsf{EV\text{-}EXP}_\lambda^{\mathcal{A}}(0), \mathsf{EV\text{-}EXP}_\lambda^{\mathcal{A}}(1)\right) = \mathrm{negl}(\lambda),$$

and

$$\left| \Pr\left[\mathsf{C\text{-}EXP}_\lambda^{\mathcal{A}}(0) = 1\right] - \Pr\left[\mathsf{C\text{-}EXP}_\lambda^{\mathcal{A}}(1) = 1\right] \right| = \mathrm{negl}(\lambda),$$

where the experiment $\mathsf{EV\text{-}EXP}_\lambda^{\mathcal{A}}(b)$ *considers everlasting security given a deletion certificate, and is defined as follows.*

- *Sample* $(\mathsf{pk}, \mathsf{sk}) \leftarrow \mathsf{Gen}(1^\lambda)$ *and* $(\mathsf{ct}, \mathsf{vk}) \leftarrow \mathsf{Enc}(\mathsf{pk}, b)$.

---

[13] One might expect that the everlasting security definition described above already captures this property, since whether the certificate accepts or rejects is included in the output of the experiment. However, this experiment does not include the output of the adversary in the case that the certificate is rejected. So we still need to capture the fact that the *joint* distribution of the final adversarial state and the bit indicating whether the verification passes semantically hides b.

- *Initialize* $\mathcal{A}_\lambda(|\psi_\lambda\rangle)$ *with* pk *and* ct.
- *Parse* $\mathcal{A}_\lambda$'s *output as a deletion certificate* cert *and a residual state on register* A'.
- *If* Ver(vk, cert) = ⊤ *then output* A', *and otherwise output* ⊥.

and the experiment C-EXP$_\lambda^\mathcal{A}(b)$ *is a strengthening of semantic security, defined as follows.*

- *Sample* (pk, sk) ← Gen(1^λ) *and* (ct, vk) ← Enc(pk, b).
- *Initialize* $\mathcal{A}_\lambda(|\psi_\lambda\rangle)$ *with* pk *and* ct.
- *Parse* $\mathcal{A}_\lambda$'s *output as a deletion certificate* cert *and a residual state on register* A'.
- *Output* $\mathcal{A}_\lambda$ (A', Ver(vk, cert)).

Now we can formally define the notion of public-key encryption with certified deletion.

Definition 5 (Public-key encryption with certified deletion). CD-PKE = (Gen, Enc, Dec, Del, Ver) *is a secure public-key encryption scheme with certified deletion if it satisfies (i) correctness of deletion (Definition 3), and (ii) certified deletion security (Definition 4).*

Then, we have the following corollary of Theorem 3.

Corollary 2. *Given any post-quantum semantically-secure public-key encryption scheme* PKE = (Gen, Enc, Dec), *the scheme* CD-PKE = (Gen, Enc', Dec', Del, Ver) *defined as follows is a public-key encryption scheme with certified deletion.*

- Enc'(pk, m) : *sample* $x, \theta \leftarrow \{0, 1\}^\lambda$ *and output*

$$\mathsf{ct} := \left(|x\rangle_\theta, \mathsf{Enc}\left(\mathsf{pk}, \left(\theta, b \oplus \bigoplus_{i:\theta_i=0} x_i \right) \right) \right), \quad \mathsf{vk} := (x, \theta).$$

- Dec'(sk, ct) : *parse* ct := $(|x\rangle_\theta, \mathsf{ct}')$, *compute* $(\theta, b') \leftarrow$ Dec(sk, ct'), *measure* $|x\rangle_\theta$ *in the* θ-*basis to obtain* x, *and output* $b = b' \oplus \bigoplus_{i:\theta_i=0} x_i$.
- Del(ct) : *parse* ct := $(|x\rangle_\theta, \mathsf{ct}')$ *and measure* $|x\rangle_\theta$ *in the Hadamard basis to obtain a string* x', *and output* cert := x'.
- Ver(vk, cert) : *parse* vk *as* (x, θ) *and* cert *as* x' *and output* ⊤ *if and only if* $x_i = x_i'$ *for all* i *such that* $\theta_i = 1$.

Proof. Correctness of deletion follows immediately from the description of the scheme. For certified deletion security, we consider the following:

- First, we observe that

$$\mathsf{TD}\left(\mathsf{EV\text{-}EXP}_\lambda^\mathcal{A}(0), \mathsf{EV\text{-}EXP}_\lambda^\mathcal{A}(1) \right) = \mathsf{negl}(\lambda)$$

follows from Theorem 3 and the semantic security of PKE by setting the distribution $\mathcal{Z}_\lambda(\theta, b', \mathsf{A})$ to sample (pk, sk) ← Gen(1^λ), and output (A, Enc(pk, (θ, b')))), and setting the class of adversaries $\mathcal{A}$ to be all non-uniform families of QPT adversaries $\{\mathcal{A}_\lambda, |\psi_\lambda\rangle\}_{\lambda \in \mathbb{N}}$.

– Next, we observe that

$$\left| \Pr\left[\text{C-EXP}_\lambda^{\mathcal{A}}(0) = 1 \right] - \Pr\left[\text{C-EXP}_\lambda^{\mathcal{A}}(1) = 1 \right] \right| = \text{negl}(\lambda)$$

follows from the fact that the encryption scheme remains (computationally) semantically secure even when the adversary is given the verification key x corresponding to the challenge ciphertext, since the bit b remains encrypted with Enc.

This completes our proof.

The notion of certified deletion security can be naturally generalized to consider multi-bit messages, as follows.

Definition 6 (Certified deletion security for multi-bit messages). CD-PKE = (Gen, Enc, Dec, Del, Ver) *satisfies* certified deletion security *if for any non-uniform QPT adversary* $\mathcal{A} = \{\mathcal{A}_\lambda, |\psi\rangle_\lambda\}_{\lambda \in \mathbb{N}}$, *it holds that*

$$\text{TD}\left(\text{EV-EXP}_\lambda^{\mathcal{A}}(0), \text{EV-EXP}_\lambda^{\mathcal{A}}(1) \right) = \text{negl}(\lambda),$$

and

$$\left| \Pr\left[\text{C-EXP}_\lambda^{\mathcal{A}}(0) = 1 \right] - \Pr\left[\text{C-EXP}_\lambda^{\mathcal{A}}(1) = 1 \right] \right| = \text{negl}(\lambda),$$

where the experiment $\text{EV-EXP}_\lambda^{\mathcal{A}}(b)$ *considers everlasting security given a deletion certificate, and is defined as follows.*

- *Sample* (pk, sk) $\leftarrow$ Gen(1^λ). *Initialize* $\mathcal{A}_\lambda(|\psi_\lambda\rangle)$ *with* pk *and parse its output as* (m_0, m_1).
- *Sample* (ct, vk) $\leftarrow$ Enc(pk, m_b).
- *Run* $\mathcal{A}_\lambda$ *on input* ct *and parse* $\mathcal{A}_\lambda$'s *output as a deletion certificate* cert, *and a residual state on register* A'.
- *If* Ver(vk, cert) = $\top$ *then output* A', *and otherwise output* $\bot$.

and the experiment $\text{C-EXP}_\lambda^{\mathcal{A}}(b)$ *is a strengthening of semantic security, defined as follows.*

- *Sample* (pk, sk) $\leftarrow$ Gen(1^λ). *Initialize* $\mathcal{A}_\lambda(|\psi_\lambda\rangle)$ *with* pk *and parse its output as* (m_0, m_1).
- *Sample* (ct, vk) $\leftarrow$ Enc(pk, m_b).
- *Run* $\mathcal{A}_\lambda$ *on input* ct *and parse* $\mathcal{A}_\lambda$'s *output as a deletion certificate* cert, *and a residual state on register* A'.
- *Output* $\mathcal{A}_\lambda$ (A', Ver(vk, cert)).

A folklore method converts any public-key bit encryption scheme to a public-key string encryption scheme, by separately encrypting each bit in the underlying string one-by-one and appending all resulting ciphertexts. Semantic security of the resulting public-key encryption scheme follows by a hybrid argument, where one considers intermediate hybrid experiments that only modify one bit of the underlying plaintext at a time. We observe that the same transformation from bit encryption to string encryption also preserves certified deletion security, and this follows by a similar hybrid argument. That is, as long as the encryption scheme for bits satisfies certified deletion security for single-bit messages per Definition 4, the resulting scheme for multi-bit messages satisfies certified deletion security according to Definition 6.

In the full version [5], we show how to build on this framework to obtain several advanced primitives with certified everlasting security, including *attribute-based encryption* and *fully-homormphic encryption*.

Acknowledgments. We thank Bhaskar Roberts and Alex Poremba for comments on an earlier draft, and for noting that quantum fully-homomorphic encryption is not necessary for our FHE with certified deletion scheme, classical fully-homomorphic encryption suffices.

D.K. was supported in part by DARPA, NSF 2112890 and NSF 2247727. This material is based on work supported by DARPA under Contract No. HR001120C0024. Any opinions, findings and conclusions or recommendations expressed in this material are those of the author(s) and do not necessarily reflect the views of the United States Government or DARPA.

References

1. California Consumer Privacy Act (CCPA)
2. Agarwal, A., Bartusek, J., Khurana, D., Kumar, N.: A new framework for quantum oblivious transfer. CoRR abs/2209.04520 (2022). https://doi.org/10.48550/arXiv.2209.04520
3. Ananth, P., Qian, L., Yuen, H.: Cryptography from pseudorandom quantum states. To appear in CRYPTO (2022). https://ia.cr/2021/1663
4. Bartusek, J., Coladangelo, A., Khurana, D., Ma, F.: One-way functions imply secure computation in a quantum world. In: Malkin, T., Peikert, C. (eds.) CRYPTO 2021. LNCS, vol. 12825, pp. 467–496. Springer, Cham (2021). https://doi.org/10.1007/978-3-030-84242-0_17
5. Bartusek, J., Khurana, D.: Cryptography with certified deletion. Cryptology ePrint Archive, Paper 2022/1178 (2022). https://eprint.iacr.org/2022/1178
6. Bennett, C.H., Brassard, G.: Quantum cryptography: public key distribution and coin tossing. In: Proceedings of the IEEE International Conference on Computers, Systems, and Signal Processing, pp. 175–179 (1984)
7. Biehl, I., Meyer, B., Wetzel, S.: Ensuring the integrity of agent-based computations by short proofs. In: Rothermel, K., Hohl, F. (eds.) MA 1998. LNCS, vol. 1477, pp. 183–194. Springer, Heidelberg (1998). https://doi.org/10.1007/BFb0057658
8. Bouman, N.J., Fehr, S.: Sampling in a quantum population, and applications. In: Rabin, T. (ed.) CRYPTO 2010. LNCS, vol. 6223, pp. 724–741. Springer, Heidelberg (2010). https://doi.org/10.1007/978-3-642-14623-7_39
9. Brakerski, Z., Vaikuntanathan, V.: Efficient fully homomorphic encryption from (standard) lwe. In: 2011 IEEE 52nd Annual Symposium on Foundations of Computer Science, pp. 97–106 (2011). https://doi.org/10.1109/FOCS.2011.12

10. Brassard, G., Crépeau, C., Jozsa, R., Langlois, D.: A quantum bit commitment scheme provably unbreakable by both parties. In: 34th FOCS, pp. 362–371. IEEE Computer Society Press (1993). https://doi.org/10.1109/SFCS.1993.366851
11. Broadbent, A., Islam, R.: Quantum encryption with certified deletion. In: Pass, R., Pietrzak, K. (eds.) TCC 2020. LNCS, vol. 12552, pp. 92–122. Springer, Cham (2020). https://doi.org/10.1007/978-3-030-64381-2_4
12. Coiteux-Roy, X., Wolf, S.: Proving erasure. In: IEEE International Symposium on Information Theory, ISIT 2019, Paris, France, 7–12 July 2019, pp. 832–836 (2019). https://doi.org/10.1109/ISIT.2019.8849661
13. Crépeau, C., Kilian, J.: Achieving oblivious transfer using weakened security assumptions (extended abstract). In: 29th FOCS, pp. 42–52. IEEE Computer Society Press (1988). https://doi.org/10.1109/SFCS.1988.21920
14. Crépeau, C., van de Graaf, J., Tapp, A.: Committed oblivious transfer and private multi-party computation. In: Coppersmith, D. (ed.) CRYPTO 1995. LNCS, vol. 963, pp. 110–123. Springer, Heidelberg (1995). https://doi.org/10.1007/3-540-44750-4_9
15. Damgård, I., Fehr, S., Lunemann, C., Salvail, L., Schaffner, C.: Improving the security of quantum protocols via commit-and-open. In: Halevi, S. (ed.) CRYPTO 2009. LNCS, vol. 5677, pp. 408–427. Springer, Heidelberg (2009). https://doi.org/10.1007/978-3-642-03356-8_24
16. Dulek, Y., Grilo, A.B., Jeffery, S., Majenz, C., Schaffner, C.: Secure multi-party quantum computation with a dishonest majority. In: Canteaut, A., Ishai, Y. (eds.) EUROCRYPT 2020. LNCS, vol. 12107, pp. 729–758. Springer, Cham (2020). https://doi.org/10.1007/978-3-030-45727-3_25
17. European Commission: Regulation (EU) 2016/679 of the European Parliament and of the Council of 27 April 2016 on the protection of natural persons with regard to the processing of personal data and on the free movement of such data, and repealing Directive 95/46/EC (General Data Protection Regulation) (Text with EEA relevance) (2016). https://eur-lex.europa.eu/eli/reg/2016/679/oj
18. Fu, H., Miller, C.A.: Local randomness: examples and application. Phys. Rev. A **97**, 032324 (2018). https://doi.org/10.1103/PhysRevA.97.032324
19. Garg, S., Goldwasser, S., Vasudevan, P.N.: Formalizing data deletion in the context of the right to be forgotten. In: Canteaut, A., Ishai, Y. (eds.) EUROCRYPT 2020. LNCS, vol. 12106, pp. 373–402. Springer, Cham (2020). https://doi.org/10.1007/978-3-030-45724-2_13
20. Gentry, C.: Fully homomorphic encryption using ideal lattices. In: Proceedings of the Forty-First Annual ACM Symposium on Theory of Computing, STOC 2009, pp. 169–178. Association for Computing Machinery, New York (2009). https://doi.org/10.1145/1536414.1536440
21. Gentry, C., Sahai, A., Waters, B.: Homomorphic encryption from learning with errors: conceptually-simpler, asymptotically-faster, attribute-based. In: Canetti, R., Garay, J.A. (eds.) CRYPTO 2013. LNCS, vol. 8042, pp. 75–92. Springer, Heidelberg (2013). https://doi.org/10.1007/978-3-642-40041-4_5
22. Gottesman, D.: Uncloneable encryption. Quant. Inf. Comput. **3**, 581–602 (2003)
23. Grilo, A.B., Lin, H., Song, F., Vaikuntanathan, V.: Oblivious transfer is in MiniQCrypt. In: Canteaut, A., Standaert, F.-X. (eds.) EUROCRYPT 2021. LNCS, vol. 12697, pp. 531–561. Springer, Cham (2021). https://doi.org/10.1007/978-3-030-77886-6_18
24. Heisenberg, W.: Über den anschaulichen Inhalt der quantentheoretischen Kinematik und Mechanik. Zeitschrift fur Physik **43**(3–4), 172–198 (1927). https://doi.org/10.1007/BF01397280

25. Hiroka, T., Morimae, T., Nishimaki, R., Yamakawa, T.: Quantum encryption with certified deletion, revisited: public key, attribute-based, and classical communication. In: Tibouchi, M., Wang, H. (eds.) ASIACRYPT 2021. LNCS, vol. 13090, pp. 606–636. Springer, Cham (2021). https://doi.org/10.1007/978-3-030-92062-3_21
26. Hiroka, T., Morimae, T., Nishimaki, R., Yamakawa, T.: Certified everlasting functional encryption. Cryptology ePrint Archive, Paper 2022/969 (2022). https://eprint.iacr.org/2022/969, https://eprint.iacr.org/2022/969
27. Hiroka, T., Morimae, T., Nishimaki, R., Yamakawa, T.: Certified everlasting zero-knowledge proof for QMA. CRYPTO (2022). https://ia.cr/2021/1315
28. Kalai, Y.T., Raz, R.: Probabilistically checkable arguments. In: Halevi, S. (ed.) CRYPTO 2009. LNCS, vol. 5677, pp. 143–159. Springer, Heidelberg (2009). https://doi.org/10.1007/978-3-642-03356-8_9
29. Katz, J., Thiruvengadam, A., Zhou, H.-S.: Feasibility and infeasibility of adaptively secure fully homomorphic encryption. In: Kurosawa, K., Hanaoka, G. (eds.) PKC 2013. LNCS, vol. 7778, pp. 14–31. Springer, Heidelberg (2013). https://doi.org/10.1007/978-3-642-36362-7_2
30. Khurana, D., Mughees, M.H.: On statistical security in two-party computation. In: Pass, R., Pietrzak, K. (eds.) TCC 2020. LNCS, vol. 12551, pp. 532–561. Springer, Cham (2020). https://doi.org/10.1007/978-3-030-64378-2_19
31. Kilian, J.: Founding cryptography on oblivious transfer. In: 20th ACM STOC, pp. 20–31. ACM Press (1988). https://doi.org/10.1145/62212.62215
32. Kundu, S., Tan, E.Y.Z.: Composably secure device-independent encryption with certified deletion (2020). https://doi.org/10.48550/ARXIV.2011.12704, https://arxiv.org/abs/2011.12704
33. Lo, H.K.: Insecurity of quantum secure computations. Phys. Rev. A **56**, 1154–1162 (1997). https://doi.org/10.1103/PhysRevA.56.1154, https://link.aps.org/doi/10.1103/PhysRevA.56.1154
34. Lo, H.K., Chau, H.F.: Is quantum bit commitment really possible? Phys. Rev. Lett. **78**(17), 3410 (1997)
35. Mayers, D.: Unconditionally secure quantum bit commitment is impossible. Phys. Rev. Lett. **78**(17), 3414 (1997)
36. Mayers, D., Salvail, L.: Quantum oblivious transfer is secure against all individual measurements. In: Proceedings Workshop on Physics and Computation. PhysComp 1994, pp. 69–77. IEEE (1994)
37. Morimae, T., Yamakawa, T.: Quantum commitments and signatures without one-way functions. To appear in CRYPTO (2022). https://ia.cr/2021/1691
38. Naor, M.: Bit commitment using pseudo-randomness. In: Brassard, G. (ed.) CRYPTO 1989. LNCS, vol. 435, pp. 128–136. Springer, New York (1990). https://doi.org/10.1007/0-387-34805-0_13
39. Poremba, A.: Quantum proofs of deletion for learning with errors. Cryptology ePrint Archive, Report 2022/295 (2022). https://ia.cr/2022/295
40. Unruh, D.: Everlasting multi-party computation. In: Canetti, R., Garay, J.A. (eds.) CRYPTO 2013. LNCS, vol. 8043, pp. 380–397. Springer, Heidelberg (2013). https://doi.org/10.1007/978-3-642-40084-1_22
41. Unruh, D.: Revocable quantum timed-release encryption. In: Nguyen, P.Q., Oswald, E. (eds.) EUROCRYPT 2014. LNCS, vol. 8441, pp. 129–146. Springer, Heidelberg (2014). https://doi.org/10.1007/978-3-642-55220-5_8
42. Watrous, J.: Zero-knowledge against quantum attacks. In: Kleinberg, J.M. (ed.) 38th ACM STOC, pp. 296–305. ACM Press (2006). https://doi.org/10.1145/1132516.1132560

43. Wiesner, S.: Conjugate coding. SIGACT News **15**, 78–88 (1983)

44. Winter, A.J.: Coding theorem and strong converse for quantum channels. IEEE Trans. Inf. Theory **45**(7), 2481–2485 (1999). https://doi.org/10.1109/18.796385, https://doi.org/10.1109/18.796385

45. Yao, A.C.C.: Protocols for secure computations (extended abstract). In: 23rd FOCS, pp. 160–164. IEEE Computer Society Press (1982). https://doi.org/10.1109/SFCS.1982.38

46. Yao, A.C.C.: Security of quantum protocols against coherent measurements. In: 27th ACM STOC, pp. 67–75. ACM Press (1995). https://doi.org/10.1145/225058.225085

Secure Computation with Shared EPR Pairs (Or: How to Teleport in Zero-Knowledge)

James Bartusek[1], Dakshita Khurana[2(✉)], and Akshayaram Srinivasan[3]

[1] UC Berkeley, Berkeley, USA
[2] UIUC, Champaign, USA
dakshita@illinois.edu
[3] Tata Institute of Fundamental Research, Mumbai, India
akshayaram.srinivasan@tifr.res.in

Abstract. Can a sender non-interactively transmit one of two strings to a receiver without knowing which string was received? Does there exist minimally-interactive secure multiparty computation that only makes (black-box) use of symmetric-key primitives? We provide affirmative answers to these questions in a model where parties have access to shared EPR pairs, thus demonstrating the cryptographic power of this resource.

– First, we construct a one-shot (i.e., single message) string oblivious transfer (OT) protocol with random receiver bit in the shared EPR pairs model, assuming the (sub-exponential) hardness of LWE.
  Building on this, we show that *secure teleportation through quantum channels* is possible. Specifically, given the description of any quantum operation Q, a sender with (quantum) input ρ can send a single classical message that securely transmits $Q(\rho)$ to a receiver. That is, we realize an ideal quantum channel that takes input ρ from the sender and provably delivers $Q(\rho)$ to the receiver without revealing any other information.
  This immediately gives a number of applications in the shared EPR pairs model: (1) non-interactive secure computation of unidirectional *classical* randomized functionalities, (2) NIZK for QMA from standard (sub-exponential) hardness assumptions, and (3) a non-interactive *zero-knowledge* state synthesis protocol.
– Next, we construct a two-round (round-optimal) secure multiparty computation protocol for classical functionalities in the shared EPR pairs model that is *unconditionally-secure* in the (quantum-accessible) random oracle model.

Classically, both of these results cannot be obtained without some form of correlated randomness shared between the parties, and the only known approach is to have a trusted dealer set up random (string) OT correlations. In the quantum world, we show that shared EPR pairs (which are simple and can be deterministically generated) are sufficient. At the heart of our work are novel techniques for making use of entangling operations to generate string OT correlations, and for instantiating the Fiat-Shamir transform using correlation-intractability in the quantum setting.

© International Association for Cryptologic Research 2023
H. Handschuh and A. Lysyanskaya (Eds.): CRYPTO 2023, LNCS 14085, pp. 224–257, 2023.
https://doi.org/10.1007/978-3-031-38554-4_8

1   Introduction

Understanding the nature of shared entanglement is one of the most prominent goals of quantum information science, and its study has repeatedly unearthed surprisingly strong properties. A remarkable example of this is the quantum teleportation protocol of [15], which demonstrated that shared EPR pairs [32], the most basic entangled resource, are "complete" for quantum communication using classical channels. That is, if Alice and Bob share EPR pairs a priori, then Alice can communicate an arbitrary state ρ to Bob by sending just a single classical message. In particular, this result positions shared EPR pairs at the center of proposals for building a quantum internet.

1.1   Our Contributions

In this work, we investigate the *cryptographic* power of shared EPR pairs.

Secure Teleportation through a Quantum Channel. First, we revisit the setting of quantum teleportation, which shows that shared EPR pairs and one-way classical communication give rise to a quantum channel implementing the identity map $\rho \to \rho$. We ask: what if Alice would instead like to send her state ρ to Bob through some arbitrary quantum map $\rho \to Q(\rho)$?[1]

Note that this is trivial given quantum teleportation if we allow either Alice or Bob to compute the map $\rho \to Q(\rho)$ for themselves. However, we are interested in guaranteeing that the effect of the protocol would be (computationally) "no different" than the effect of Alice inputting ρ to an "ideal" channel Q, and Bob receiving $Q(\rho)$ on the other side, *even if* Alice or Bob attempt to save extra information from or deviate from the protocol. In particular, we require each of the following three properties to hold against arbitrarily malicious adversaries: (1) Alice would not learn any side information created during the computation of $Q(\rho)$, (2) Bob would learn nothing about ρ beyond $Q(\rho)$, and (3) Bob would be convinced that the state he received was actually computed as the output of the map Q (on some input ρ). We show that this is possible under the sub-exponential hardness of learning with errors (LWE), a standard post-quantum security assumption.

Informal Theorem 1. *For any efficient quantum map Q, there exists a protocol for "secure teleportation through Q" in the shared EPR pairs model assuming the sub-exponential hardness of LWE. That is, there exists a one-shot[2] protocol in the shared EPR pairs model that computes the ideal functionality $\rho \to Q(\rho)$.*

---

[1] We will also allow for preserving entanglement that ρ may have with its environment, so technically we consider Q to map a state on Alice's input register $\mathcal{A}$ to a state on Bob's output register $\mathcal{B}$.

[2] We use one-shot, one-message, and non-interactive interchangeably to refer to a protocol that consists of a single message from a sender to a receiver.

Building Block: One-shot String OT. The main building block for this protocol, and the key technical contribution of this paper, is a one-shot protocol for (random receiver bit) *string oblivious transfer* (OT) in the shared EPR pairs model, which realizes an ideal funtionality that takes two strings m_0, m_1 from a sender Alice, and delivers (b, m_b) to Bob for a uniformly random bit b.[3]

Informal Theorem 2. *Assuming the sub-exponential hardness of LWE, there exists a simulation-secure one-shot protocol for (random receiver bit) string OT in the shared EPR pairs model.*

Given such an OT protocol, we rely on two key previous results to obtain our final implication to secure teleportation through quantum channels: (1) [34] showed how to construct a one-message protocol for secure computation of any unidirectional *classical* randomized functionality f that maps $x \to f(x; r)$ given a one-message protocol for string OT, and (2) [8] (building on the work of [19]) showed (implicitly) how to construct a one-message protocol for secure computation of any unidirectional *quantum* functionality given a one-message protocol for unidirectional classical functionalities.

Correlation Interactability. There have been many recent works that show how to instantiate random oracles with a concrete hash function family and base the security of (classical) primitives such as NIZKs and SNARGs on standard cryptographic assumptions [18,21,23–25,40,41,45,46,48,49,54]. These works proceed by constructing a special hash function family that satisfies the cryptographic notion of *correlation-intractability* [22]. Ours is the first to apply correlation-intractability to a setting that involves *quantum communication*, addressing technical barriers along the way. In fact, we obtain our one-message string OT protocol (refer to Informal Theorem 2) by utilizing correlation-intractability, which we discuss further in Sect. 2.

The Multiparty Setting. Next, we consider the *multiparty* setting, where all pairs of parties have access to shared EPR pairs. If each party has their own private input x_i, and their goal is to compute $C(x_1, \ldots, x_n)$ for some (classical) circuit C, they will have to use at least two rounds of interaction as single round protocols are susceptible to resetting attacks [39].

Classically, two rounds are known to suffice for secure multiparty computation, under the (minimal) assumption that two-round (chosen-input) oblivious transfer [13,36] protocols exist.[4] In the classical setting, OT is a "public-key-style" primitive that provably cannot be built from "minicrypt-style" primitives, including hash functions modeled as a random oracle [42]. On the other hand, a line of work beginning with [28] and culminating with [9,38] established that

---

[3] Note that it is impossible to obtain a one-shot protocol for fixed receiver bit OT, since Bob does not send any message.

[4] In chosen-input OT, the receiver specifies their input bit b, and they receive the message m_b. We contrast this with the notion of OT discussed above, where the receiver's bit b is chosen uniformly at random.

with quantum communication, it is possible to obtain oblivious transfer, and thus multiparty computation, from one-way functions or potentially even weaker assumptions [7,47,53]. However, these protocols require many rounds, and the possibility of achieving *round-optimal* (two-round) secure computation without public-key primitives was left open.

In this work, we show that round-optimal secure computation that makes black-box use of symmetric-key primitives (specifically, a random oracle) can be obtained in the shared EPR pairs model.

Informal Theorem 3. *There exists a two-round secure multiparty computation protocol in the shared EPR pairs model with either of the following properties.*

- *Unconditional security in the quantum-accesible random oracle model (QROM).*
- *Computational security assuming (the black-box use of) non-interactive extractable commitments and hash functions that are correlation-intractable for efficient functions.*

Discussion: Towards Weaker Correlated Randomness. In the classical world, it can be shown that without any form of correlated randomness shared between the parties, it is impossible to obtain either one-shot OT or two-round MPC (even with public-key primitives). Furthermore, we show in the full version [11] that one-shot (random receiver bit) string OT is impossible in the classical common reference string model, even when parties can compute and communicate quantumly. On the other hand, we remark that both our results can be obtained (even in the classical world) with an "OT correlations" setup, which assumes that a trusted dealer has sampled random strings x_0, x_1 and bit b and delivered x_0, x_1 to the sender and b, x_b to the receiver. For the case of string OT, this consequence is immediate and for the case of two-round MPC, this result follows from the work of Garg et al. [35].

Our results state that in the quantum world, shared EPR pairs are sufficient to obtain (i) one-shot (random receiver bit) string OT and (ii) two-round MPC from symmetric-key primitives. As noted in [2], shared EPR pairs are a fundamentally different resource than OT correlations. Indeed, OT correlations are *specific* to OT, while, as indicated above, shared EPR pairs are known to be broadly useful and have been widely studied independent of OT. Moreover, an OT correlations setup requires private (hidden) randomness, while generating EPR pairs is a fully deterministic quantum process.[5] Our work can thus be viewed as a step towards realizing secure computation protocols using weaker

---

[5] In particular, any (even semi-honest) dealer that sets up OT correlations can learn the parties' private inputs by observing the resulting transcript of communication, while this is not necessarily true of an EPR pair setup, by monogamy of entanglement. We also remark that obtaining OT correlations from *any* deterministically generated shared quantum state is non-trivial. In particular, if the parties shared a (deterministically generated) superposition over classical OT correlations, the receiver could simply decide not to measure the register holding their choice bit, and obtain a superposition over the sender's strings, which violates the security of OT.

forms of correlated randomness. Finally, we remark that, unlike the case of one-shot OT, it may be possible to achieve two-round MPC from symmetric-key primitives in the classical common reference string model (i.e., without shared EPR pairs), and we leave this as an intriguing open question for future study.

1.2   Applications

We now discuss several applications of our one-shot string OT construction and secure teleportation through quantum channel protocol.

Non-interactive Computation of Unidirectional Functionalities. The study of non-interactive protocols for unidirectional classical functionalities was initiated by [34]. Such functionalities are defined by a classical circuit f, take an input x from the sender, (potentially) sample some random coins r, and deliver $f(x; r)$ to the receiver. They showed the possibility (or impossibility) of achieving them in a model where the sender and the receiver have access to an *one-way communication channel*. In particular, they showed that ideal string OT channel suffices to build non-interactive secure computation of unidirectional classical functionalities. On the other hand, the work of Agrawal et al. [4] showed that bit OT channels provably do *not* suffice for non-interactive secure computation.[6]

Using our one-shot string OT construction, we can instantiate the results of Garg et al. [34] and obtain non-interactive secure computation of unidirectional functionalities in the shared EPR pairs model, assuming sub-exponential LWE.

The works of [5,34] also discuss several applications of non-interactive secure computation of unidirectional classical functionalities, and we mention one intriguing application here. The modern internet relies on a public-key infrastructure, where certificate authorities validate public keys by signing them under their own signing key.[7] A single message protocol for unidirectional classical functionalities would enable key authorities to *non-interactively* generate and send freshly sampled and signed public key secret key pairs to clients, *without* learning the client's secret key. Moreover, the client would not learn the secret signing key of the authority who sent their fresh pair. Thus, we show that there is a truly non-interactive solution to this widespread key certification functionality in a world where nodes are connected by shared EPR pairs.[8]

NIZKs for QMA. Our secure teleportation through quantum channels immediately gives a non-interactive zero-knowledge (NIZK) for QMA in the shared EPR pairs model, by letting the channel Q compute a QMA verification circuit

---

[6] A followup work of [5] showed that, assuming *ideal obfuscation*, there exists a protocol over a bit OT channel with $1/\text{poly}(\lambda)$ security.

[7] Note that despite the existence of quantum key distribution [14], public-key infrastructure would still likely be required for the quantum internet, since QKD requires authenticated classical channels.

[8] We do stress that our model assumes the EPR pairs are generated honestly, for example by an honest network administrator. Otherwise, such secure one-message protocols would be impossible to achieve.

and output the resulting bit to the receiver. The only previous NIZK for QMA in the shared EPR pairs model is due to [52], who argued security in the quantum random oracle model.[9] Thus, we obtain the first such protocol from a standard (sub-exponential) hardness assumption.

Non-interactive Zero-Knowledge State Synthesis. Many recent works consider the problem of quantum *state synthesis* [1,43,55], which studies the efficiency of preparing a complex quantum state with the help of an oracle or untrusted powerful prover. That is, given the implicit description of a quantum circuit Q, can a verifier prepare $|\psi\rangle = Q |0^n\rangle$ with the help of a prover, and be convinced that they end up with the correct state?

In fact, [55] asked whether there is any meaningful notion of *zero-knowledge* state synthesis. In this work, we propose one way to define zero-knowledge state synthesis. Roughly, we consider any *family* of circuits $\{Q_w\}_w$ parameterized by a potentially secret witness w, and require that a prover help the verifier prepare $|\psi_w\rangle = Q_w |0^n\rangle$ without leaking the witness w. We formalize our definition in the full version [11] and show that our secure teleportation protocol immediately gives a *one-message* solution to this task in the shared EPR pairs model. We stress that there may be other meaningful ways to define zero-knowledge state synthesis, and we leave a more thorough exploration of definitions and applications of zero-knowledge state synthesis to future work.

Non-interactive Quantum Cryptography. Finally, we observe that the full power of non-interactive secure computation of unidirectional quantum functionalities gives rise to quantum analogues of the classical applications mentioned above. For example, a certificate authority could non-interactively prepare and send signed key pairs for encryption schemes with *unclonable* or *revocable* decryption keys [3,6,10,26,37], where decryption keys are quantum states that can either provably not be distributed or verifiably be destroyed. The novel guarantee is that even the certificate authority itself will not learn the (description of) the decryption key.[10] As another example, a bank could non-interactively distribute signed *quantum money* states (technically, the serial number would be signed), without ever learning the classical description of the state. In particular, while valid money states could be provably generated and distributed non-interactively, no one (not even the bank) would ever learn a classical description that would enable cloning.

1.3 Related Works

This work continues a long line of research that studies the power of shared entanglement as a resource. We show that shared EPR pairs, which already have

---

[9] We also remark that [12] achieve NIZK for QMA in the (incomparable) common reference string model, but they argue security using classical oracles, or alternatively assuming indistinguishability obfuscation and the non-black-box use of a hash function modeled as a random oracle.

[10] In this setting, *publicly-verifiable* revocation [10] seems crucial to ensure that no one need know the classical description of the secret key.

a long history of study in communication [15, 16], cryptography [2, 31, 33, 51], and error-correction [20], can be leveraged to obtain perhaps surprisingly powerful secure computation tasks.

We also compare our results with the prior work of [2], which also studies oblivious transfer in the shared EPR pairs model. They achieve a one-message protocol for *bit* OT, where the sender's inputs are one bit each, and explicitly leave open the problem of building *string* OT, which we address in this work. We note that bit OT is not known to be complete for one-message secure computation [4, 34]. Moreover, security of the protocols in [2] are all argued in the quantum random oracle model, while we argue security *without* random oracles, and based on concrete properties of hash functions instead.

Concurrent Work. Finally, we mention a concurrent and independent work [27] that was posted recently to the arXiv. Their results and techniques are orthogonal to ours: in particular, they obtain two-message OT in the CRS model assuming NIZK (and an assumption on hash functions), whereas we obtain one-message OT from sub-exponential LWE, as well as unconditional two-round MPC in the QROM, both in the shared EPR pairs model. We do not believe that (a simple modification of) either work's results or techniques immediately subsumes or improves results in the other. We also remark that both our work and [27] leave open the intriguing question of obtaining minimally-interactive (two-round) MPC in the CRS model without the use of public-key primitives.

2   Technical Overview

2.1   One-Shot String OT

In this subsection, we focus on our key technical contribution, which is a construction of one-shot string OT in the shared EPR pairs model. Throughout this section, we define *one-shot string OT* as a one-message protocol that takes two strings m_0, m_1 from the sender, and delivers m_b to the receiver for a random bit $b \leftarrow \{0, 1\}$. For more discussion on our applications, we refer the reader to the full version [11].

A string OT skeleton. As mentioned earlier, [2] constructed a one-shot *bit* OT protocol in the shared EPR pairs model (where the sender's inputs are one bit each). However, their techniques don't appear to extend easily to the setting of one-shot *string* OT, for arbitrary length strings. In fact, [4, 34] showed that in the non-interactive setting, it is impossible to obtain string OT from bit OT. We additionally observe that prior quantum OT templates [2, 28] only obtain "bitwise" correlations by sending unentangled BB84 states or by immediately measuring each EPR pair independently.

To get around this barrier, our idea is to directly obtain string correlations from shared entanglement. This can be done by first *entangling* the separate EPR pairs in a special way before performing measurements.

Setup: An EPR pair on registers $(\mathcal{S}^{\text{ctl}}, \mathcal{R}^{\text{ctl}})$ and λ EPR pairs on registers $(\mathcal{S}^{\text{msg}}, \mathcal{R}^{\text{msg}})$.

Sender's message:

- Sample $x \leftarrow \{0,1\}^\lambda$ and for each $i \in [\lambda]$ such that $x_i = 1$, apply a CNOT gate from $\mathcal{S}^{\text{ctl}}$ to $\mathcal{S}_i^{\text{msg}}$.
- Measure $\mathcal{S}^{\text{msg}}$ in the standard basis to obtain $v \in \{0,1\}^\lambda$, and measure $\mathcal{S}^{\text{ctl}}$ in the Hadamard basis to delete the control bit.
- Given input (m_0, m_1), send $\widetilde{m}_0 = m_0 \oplus v, \widetilde{m}_1 = m_1 \oplus v \oplus x$.

Receiver's computation:

- Measure $\mathcal{R}^{\text{ctl}}, \mathcal{R}^{\text{msg}}$ in the standard basis to obtain b, v', and output $(b, m_b = \widetilde{m}_b \oplus v')$.

Fig. 1. An (insecure) skeleton for one-shot string OT

Our approach is illustrated in Fig. 1. Note that after the sender applies the random CNOT gates and measures $\mathcal{S}^{\text{msg}}$ to obtain v, the remaining state of the system is

$$\frac{1}{\sqrt{2}} |0\rangle_{\mathcal{S}^{\text{ctl}}} |0\rangle_{\mathcal{R}^{\text{ctl}}} |v\rangle_{\mathcal{R}^{\text{msg}}} + \frac{1}{\sqrt{2}} |1\rangle_{\mathcal{S}^{\text{ctl}}} |1\rangle_{\mathcal{R}^{\text{ctl}}} |v \oplus x\rangle_{\mathcal{R}^{\text{msg}}}.$$

Thus, tracing out $\mathcal{S}^{\text{ctl}}$, we see that the receiver has a uniform mixture over $|0, v\rangle$ and $|1, v \oplus x\rangle$, where $v, v \oplus x$ are uniformly random strings from their perspective, exactly as desired. Unfortunately, since the sender's control register is entangled with the receiver's, the sender could know exactly which bit b the receiver obtains by measuring $\mathcal{S}^{\text{ctl}}$ in the standard basis. Thus, we instead ask that the sender "delete" their control bit by measuring it in the *Hadamard* basis. Of course, a malicious (or even specious) sender may not follow these instructions, rendering this protocol insecure. However, this protocol serves as the foundation for our eventual secure realization of one-shot string OT.

Measurement check. Next, we add a mechanism for "forcing" the sender to delete their control bit. We build on the commitment-based cut-and-choose approach [2, 17, 28] as follows. Suppose the sender really did behave honestly, and measured $\mathcal{S}^{\text{ctl}}$ in the Hadamard basis to obtain a bit h. Then, the state on the receiver's side will be

$$|\psi_{v,x,h}\rangle := \frac{1}{\sqrt{2}} \left(|0, v\rangle + (-1)^h |1, v \oplus x\rangle\right).$$

So if the receiver was given (v, x, h), they could measure $(\mathcal{R}^{\text{ctl}}, \mathcal{R}^{\text{msg}})$ in the

$$\{|\psi_{v,x,h}\rangle\langle\psi_{v,x,h}|, \mathbb{I} - |\psi_{v,x,h}\rangle\langle\psi_{v,x,h}|\}$$

basis and accept if the first outcome is observed. Of course, sending (v, x, h) to the receiver would render the protocol insecure because the receiver could now obtain both v and $v \oplus x$. Instead, we apply a variant of the Fiat-Shamir-based non-interactive measurement check subprotocol of [2], using a non-interactive commitment scheme Com and a hash function H:

- Repeat the skeleton protocol ℓ times in parallel, and have the sender commit to all descriptions $\mathsf{cm}_1 = \mathsf{Com}(v_1, x_1, h_1), \ldots, \mathsf{cm}_\ell = \mathsf{Com}(v_\ell, x_\ell, h_\ell)$.
- Hash $T = H(\mathsf{cm}_1, \ldots, \mathsf{cm}_\ell)$ to obtain a subset $T \subset [\ell]$ of commitments.
- The sender sends $(\mathsf{cm}_1, \ldots, \mathsf{cm}_\ell)$ along with openings to $\{\mathsf{cm}_i\}_{i \in T}$.
- For each $i \in T$, the receiver measures registers $\mathcal{R}_i^{\mathsf{ctl}}, \mathcal{R}_i^{\mathsf{msg}}$ in basis

$$\{|\psi_{v_i, x_i, h_i}\rangle\langle\psi_{v_i, x_i, h_i}|, \mathbb{I} - |\psi_{v_i, x_i, h_i}\rangle\langle\psi_{v_i, x_i, h_i}|\}$$

and aborts if any of these measurements reject. Otherwise, the parties continue the protocol using indices $i \in \overline{T}$.

Now, assuming H behaves as a random oracle, we should be able to claim that conditioned on the receiver not aborting, their states on registers $\{\mathcal{R}_i^{\mathsf{ctl}}, \mathcal{R}_i^{\mathsf{msg}}\}_{i \in \overline{T}}$ should be "close" to the honest states $\{|\psi_{v_i, x_i, h_i}\rangle\}_{i \in \overline{T}}$. We can make this precise by arguing that after an appropriate change of basis, the states $\{\mathcal{R}_i^{\mathsf{ctl}}\}_{i \in \overline{T}}$ are in a superposition of Hadamard basis states that are close in Hamming distance to the honest state $H^{\otimes |\overline{T}|} |h_{\overline{T}}\rangle$, where $h_{\overline{T}}$ are the bits $\{h_i\}_{i \in \overline{T}}$. If this is the case, then by the "XOR extractor" lemma of [2], measuring these bits in the standard basis and XORing the results together would produce a bit b that is truly uniformly random and independent of the sender's view. Thus, we should be able to extract a perfectly random receiver's bit by *combining* correlations obtained from multiple instances $i \in \overline{T}$ of the skeleton protocol.

Defining two sender strings. Unfortunately, if we XOR together the correlations from all $i \in \overline{T}$, it is no longer clear how to define the two sender strings. Indeed, the receiver will obtain one out of two of each pair $\{(v_i, v_i \oplus x_i)\}_{i \in \overline{T}}$, which means one out of $2^{|T|}$ possible sets of strings! However, note that if the sender had used the same offset x for each repetition, then if the receiver XORs together one out of two of each $\{(v_i, v_i \oplus x)\}_{i \in \overline{T}}$, they obtain either $\bigoplus_{i \in \overline{T}} v_i$ or $x \oplus \bigoplus_{i \in \overline{T}} v_i$ depending on the parity of their choice bits. Of course, since we are opening the commitments on indices $i \in T$, the receiver would learn x, rendering this approach insecure.

Our solution is to make use of this "common offset" approach in a less direct manner. In addition to the ℓ repetitions of the skeleton protocol described above, the sender will sample an independent collection of strings $t_1, \ldots, t_\ell, \Delta$ and include commitments

$$\widehat{\mathsf{cm}}_{1,0} = \mathsf{Com}(t_1), \widehat{\mathsf{cm}}_{1,1} = \mathsf{Com}(t_1 \oplus \Delta), \ldots, \widehat{\mathsf{cm}}_{\ell,0} = \mathsf{Com}(t_\ell), \widehat{\mathsf{cm}}_{\ell,1} = \mathsf{Com}(t_\ell \oplus \Delta)$$

in their message. Then, the sender will use the random strings $(v_1, v_1 \oplus x_1), \ldots, (v_\ell, v_\ell \oplus x_\ell)$ to mask the *openings* for the commitments $(\widehat{\mathsf{cm}}_{1,0}, \widehat{\mathsf{cm}}_{1,1}), \ldots, (\widehat{\mathsf{cm}}_{\ell,0}, \widehat{\mathsf{cm}}_{\ell,1})$. The effect of this is that the receiver will be able to open one out of two of each pair of commitments $\{\widehat{cm}_{i,0}, \widehat{cm}_{i,1}\}_{i \in \overline{T}}$, obtaining either $\bigoplus_{i \in \overline{T}} t_i$ or $\Delta \oplus \bigoplus_{i \in \overline{T}} t_i$.

Finally, to maintain security, we require that the sender computes a non-interactive zero-knowledge (NIZK) argument that they sampled $\{\widehat{cm}_{i,b}\}_{i \in [\ell], b \in \{0,1\}}$ as commitments to pairs of strings that all share the same offset Δ.

Using correlation-intractability. This nearly completes the description of our protocol. Turning to the security proof, our goal is to reduce to a standard cryptographic assumption. Fortunately, the flavors of commitments and zero-knowledge we require are known from LWE. However, we also need some security from the Fiat-Shamir hash function H. In [2] this hash was modeled as a random oracle, and it was left open whether one could obtain security in the plain model.

Classically, a recent exciting line of work has shown how to securely instantiate the Fiat-Shamir transform from standard cryptographic assumptions in many settings [18, 21, 23–25, 40, 41, 45, 46, 48, 49, 54]. These works rely on the notion of *correlation-intractability* (CI), which is a property of the hash function H requiring that for some relation R over inputs and outputs, the adversary can't find any input x such that $(x, H(x)) \in R$. In particular, it is known how to obtain CI for efficiently computable *functions* from LWE [21, 54]. Moreover, [40] showed to extend this result to CI for efficiently verifiable product relations R, where the range of H is the t-wise cartesian product of a set Y, and each input x is associated with sets $S_{x,1}, \ldots, S_{x,t} \subset Y$ such that $(x, (y_1, \ldots, y_t)) \in R$ iff each $y_i \in S_{x,i}$. The property of efficient verifiability states that there is an efficient (classical) algorithm that, given (x, i, y_i), determines whether $y_i \in S_{x,i}$.

Recall that in our protocol, we apply H to a set of ℓ commitments in order to obtain the description of a subset $T \subset [\ell]$ of commitments to open. Intuitively, we want it to be difficult for the sender to find a set of commitments $(cm_1, \ldots, cm_\ell)$ to strings $(v_1, x_1, h_1), \ldots, (v_\ell, x_\ell, h_\ell)$ such that $T = H(cm_1, \ldots, cm_\ell)$ is a "bad" set, meaning that the receiver's registers $\{(\mathcal{R}_i^{\mathsf{ctl}}, \mathcal{R}_i^{\mathsf{msg}})\}_{i \in T}$ are "close" to the states $\{|\psi_{v_i, x_i, h_i}\rangle\}_{i \in T}$ (so the receiver won't abort) but the registers $\{(\mathcal{R}_i^{\mathsf{ctl}}, \mathcal{R}_i^{\mathsf{msg}})\}_{i \in \overline{T}}$ are "far" from the states $\{|\psi_{v_i, x_i, h_i}\rangle\}_{i \in \overline{T}}$. Thus, given an input $(cm_1, \ldots, cm_\ell)$, it appears that determining whether or not a potential output T is "bad" requires (at least) applying some *quantum measurement* to the receiver's registers. Unfortunately, all prior work has used CI in a purely classical setting, and extending the notion of efficiently verifiable relation to handle *quantum* verification algorithms appears to be beyond the reach of current techniques (though this may be an interesting direction for future research).

Instead, we take a different approach. Suppose that the sender's choices of $x_1, \ldots, x_\ell$ were fixed before the protocol begins. Then, we could pre-measure the receiver's registers even before initializing the malicious sender to obtain $(v_1, h_1), \ldots, (v_\ell, h_\ell)$. That is, we could first apply CNOTs from $\mathcal{R}_i^{\mathsf{ctl}}$ to each of the qubits in $\mathcal{R}_i^{\mathsf{msg}}$ controlled on x_i, and then measure $\mathcal{R}_i^{\mathsf{ctl}}$ in the Hadamard basis to obtain h_i and measure $\mathcal{R}_i^{\mathsf{msg}}$ in the standard basis to obtain v_i. Then given just this classical data, we can distinguish between honest commitments cm_i to (v_i, x_i, h_i) and dishonest commitments cm_i to some other string (as long as the commitment is efficiently extractable). If we split ℓ into t disjoint groups and parse T as t different subsets of $[\ell/t]$, then we can formulate a classically efficiently verifiable product relation R where $((\mathsf{cm}_1, \ldots, \mathsf{cm}_\ell), T) \in R$ iff all $\{\mathsf{cm}_i\}_{i \in T}$ are honest and "many" $\{\mathsf{cm}_i\}_{i \in \overline{T}}$ are dishonest.

Now, while we cannot guarantee that a malicious sender will sample any fixed $(x_1, \ldots, x_\ell)$, we can *guess* beforehand which $x_1, \ldots, x_\ell$ they will use, and simply give up on reducing to CI if the guess is wrong. Using complexity leveraging (and setting the security parameter of the CI hash function large enough), we can hope that this is enough to still break *sub-exponentially-secure* CI. It turns out that this strategy can only be made to work if our guessing loss depends only on the security parameter λ, and *not* on the number of repetitions ℓ (which must depend on the level of security required from the CI hash). Thus, we make one final tweak to the protocol. The sender will be required to sample $x_1, \ldots, x_\ell$ as the output of a pseudorandom generator with seed s of length $\{0, 1\}^\lambda$, and prove using the NIZK that they have done so honestly. Then, in the reduction to CI, it suffices to guess a λ-bit string s rather than a $\lambda\ell$-bit string $(x_1, \ldots, x_\ell)$. This allows us to eventually reduce security to the sub-exponential hardness of LWE.

Unconditional Protocols in the QROM. We remark that it appears plausible to obtain more efficient and unconditionally secure variants of our non-interactive protocols in the (quantum) random oracle model. In particular, following [2], we expect that the measure-and-reprogram technique [30] in the quantum random oracle model can be used in place of correlation intractability, which would remove the need for sampling $x_1, \ldots, x_\ell$ as the output of a PRG, and remove complexity leveraging in the approach outlined above. It also may be possible to rely on *black-box* commit-and-prove sigma protocols (e.g., variants of the protocol in [50]) to prove that commitments to pairs of strings share a common offset, thereby making our protocol black-box and unconditionally secure in the QROM. We leave a formalization and detailed analysis of this approach, and more generally an exploration of one-message protocols in the QROM, to future work.

2.2   Two-Round MPC

In this section, we give a brief overview of our approach to building two-round MPC in the shared EPR model, which is presented in the full version [11]. Our starting point is a three-round chosen-input string OT protocol from [2], which can be viewed as a two-round protocol in the shared EPR model. In order to use this protocol to build two-round MPC, we take the following steps.

1. Show that the protocol is "black-box friendly". That is, we split the protocol into an *input-independent* phase that uses both quantum measurements and cryptographic operations, and an *input-dependent* phase that is fully classical and information-theoretic.
2. Appeal to existing compilers (e.g. [29, 44]) to obtain a "black-box friendly" MPC protocol in the shared EPR pair model. Again, we have (1) an input-independent phase at the beginning where every party performs a measurement on their halves of EPR pairs, broadcasts a message, and performs some crytographic checks, and (2) an input-dependent multi-round phase that is entirely classical and information-theoretic.
3. Use the [36] round-compressing compiler and two-round OT in the shared EPR pair model to compress this black-box-friendly protocol into a two-round MPC in the shared EPR pair model. Crucially, the compiler only has to operate on the second (multi-round input-dependent) phase, and thus we obtain a final protocol that makes black-box use of cryptography.

We stress that to make the above compiler work, we need to start with an OT protocol in which all *cryptographic operations* and *quantum computations* are performed *independently* of the parties' inputs and *before* the second message. That is, it does not follow from any two-round quantum OT protocol.

If we start with the protocol from [2] that was proven secure in the quantum random oracle model, then we obtain a final MPC protocol in the quantum random oracle model. In addition, we prove that a slight variant of the [2] protocol is secure *without* random oracles, assuming non-interactive extractable commitments and correlation-intractability for efficient functions. Interestingly, while we use a similar approach as described above, we do not have to resort to subexponential assumptions here. Roughly, this is because the [2] protocol is built from "bitwise" rather than "stringwise" correlations, and it suffices for the reduction to correctly guess a random subset of the adversary's bitwise measurements.

3   Preliminaries

Let λ denote the security parameter. We write $\mathsf{negl}(\cdot)$ to denote any *negligible* function, which is a function f such that for every constant $c \in \mathbb{N}$ there exists $N \in \mathbb{N}$ such that for all $n > N$, $f(n) < n^{-c}$. We write $\mathsf{non\text{-}negl}(\cdot)$ to denote any function f that is not negligible. That is, there exists a constant c such that for infinitely many n, $f(n) \geq n^{-c}$.

3.1   Quantum Information

A register $\mathcal{X}$ is a named Hilbert space $\mathbb{C}^{2^n}$. A pure quantum state on register $\mathcal{X}$ is a unit vector $|\psi\rangle^{\mathcal{X}} \in \mathbb{C}^{2^n}$, and we say that $|\psi\rangle^{\mathcal{X}}$ consists of n qubits. A mixed state on register $\mathcal{X}$ is described by a density matrix $\rho^{\mathcal{X}} \in \mathbb{C}^{2^n \times 2^n}$, which is a positive semi-definite Hermitian operator with trace 1.

A *quantum operation* (also referred to as quantum map or quantum channel) Q is a completely-positive trace-preserving (CPTP) map from a register $\mathcal{X}$ to a register $\mathcal{Y}$, which in general may have different dimensions. That is, on input a density matrix $\rho^{\mathcal{X}}$, the operation Q produces $\tau^{\mathcal{Y}} \leftarrow Q(\rho^{\mathcal{X}})$ a mixed state on register $\mathcal{Y}$. We will sometimes write a quantum operation Q applied to a state on register $\mathcal{X}$ and resulting in a state on register $\mathcal{Y}$ as $\mathcal{Y} \leftarrow Q(\mathcal{X})$. Note that we have left the actual mixed states on these registers implicit in this notation, and just work with the names of the registers themselves.

A *unitary* $U : \mathcal{X} \rightarrow \mathcal{X}$ is a special case of a quantum operation that satisfies $U^\dagger U = UU^\dagger = \mathbb{I}^{\mathcal{X}}$, where $\mathbb{I}^{\mathcal{X}}$ is the identity matrix on register $\mathcal{X}$. A *projector* Π is a Hermitian operator such that $\Pi^2 = \Pi$, and a *projective measurement* is a collection of projectors $\{\Pi_i\}_i$ such that $\sum_i \Pi_i = \mathbb{I}$.

Let Tr denote the trace operator. For registers $\mathcal{X}, \mathcal{Y}$, the *partial trace* $\mathrm{Tr}^{\mathcal{Y}}$ is the unique operation from $\mathcal{X}, \mathcal{Y}$ to $\mathcal{X}$ such that for all $(\rho, \tau)^{\mathcal{X}, \mathcal{Y}}$, $\mathrm{Tr}^{\mathcal{Y}}(\rho, \tau) = \mathrm{Tr}(\tau)\rho$. The *trace distance* between states ρ, τ, denoted $\mathsf{TD}(\rho, \tau)$ is defined as

$$\mathsf{TD}(\rho, \tau) := \frac{1}{2}\|\rho - \tau\|_1 := \frac{1}{2}\mathrm{Tr}\left(\sqrt{(\rho - \tau)^\dagger(\rho - \tau)}\right).$$

The trace distance between two states ρ and τ is an upper bound on the probability that any (unbounded) algorithm can distinguish ρ and τ. When clear from context, we will write $\mathsf{TD}(\mathcal{X}, \mathcal{Y})$ to refer to the trace distance between a state on register $\mathcal{X}$ and a state on register $\mathcal{Y}$.

Lemma 1 (Gentle measurement [56]). *Let $\rho^{\mathcal{X}}$ be a quantum state and let $(\Pi, \mathbb{I} - \Pi)$ be a projective measurement on $\mathcal{X}$ such that $\mathrm{Tr}(\Pi\rho) \geq 1 - \delta$. Let*

$$\rho' = \frac{\Pi\rho\Pi}{\mathrm{Tr}(\Pi\rho)}$$

be the state after applying $(\Pi, \mathbb{I} - \Pi)$ to ρ and post-selecting on obtaining the first outcome. Then, $\mathsf{TD}(\rho, \rho') \leq 2\sqrt{\delta}$.

A non-uniform quantum polynomial-time (QPT) machine $\{\mathsf{Adv}_\lambda, |\psi\rangle_\lambda\}_{\lambda \in \mathbb{N}}$ is a family of polynomial-size quantum machines Adv_λ, where each is initialized with a polynomial-size advice state $|\psi_\lambda\rangle$. Each Adv_λ is in general described by a CPTP map. Similar to above, when we write $\mathcal{Y} \leftarrow \mathsf{Adv}(\mathcal{X})$, we mean that the machine Adv takes as input a state on register $\mathcal{X}$ and produces as output a state on register $\mathcal{Y}$, and we leave the actual description of these states implicit. Finally, a quantum *interactive* machine is simply a sequence of quantum operations, with designated input, output, and work registers.

Finally we will often use $\approx_c$ as a shorthand to denote *computational* indistinguishability between two families of distributions (over quantum states), and $\approx_s$ as a shorthand to denote *statistical* indistinguishability (or negligible closeness in trace distance) between two families of distributions.

3.2   Correlation Intractability

Definition 1 (Correlation intractable hash function). *Let* $\{\mathcal{X}_\lambda, \mathcal{Y}_\lambda\}_{\lambda \in \mathbb{N}}$ *be families of finite sets. An efficiently computable keyed hash function family* $\{H_\lambda : \{0,1\}^{k(\lambda)} \times \mathcal{X}_\lambda \rightarrow \mathcal{Y}_\lambda\}_{\lambda \in \mathbb{N}}$ *with keys of length* $k(\lambda)$ *is* $\epsilon(\lambda)$-*correlation intractable for a relation ensemble* $\{R_\lambda \subseteq \mathcal{X}_\lambda \times \mathcal{Y}_\lambda\}_{\lambda \in \mathbb{N}}$ *if for any QPT adversary* $\{\mathsf{Adv}_\lambda\}_{\lambda \in \mathbb{N}}$,

$$\Pr\left[(x, H_\lambda(\mathsf{hk}, x)) \in R_\lambda : \begin{array}{l} \mathsf{hk} \leftarrow \{0,1\}^{k(\lambda)} \\ x \leftarrow \mathsf{Adv}_\lambda(\mathsf{hk}) \end{array}\right] \leq \epsilon(\lambda).$$

We say that $\{H_\lambda\}_{\lambda \in \mathbb{N}}$ *is* sub-exponentially *correlation intractable for* $\{R_\lambda\}_{\lambda \in \mathbb{N}}$ *if it is* $2^{-\lambda^\delta}$-*correlation intractable for some constant* $\delta > 0$.

Definition 2 (Sparse, efficiently verifiable, approximate product relations [40]). *A relation* $R \subseteq \mathcal{X} \times \mathcal{Y}^t$ *is an efficiently verifiable* α-*approximate product relation with sparsity* ρ *if the following hold.*

- **Approximate product.** *For every* x, *the set* $R_x := \{y : (x, y) \in R\}$ *consists of* $y = (y_1, \ldots, y_t) \in \mathcal{Y}^t$ *such that*

$$|\{i \in [t] : y_i \in S_i\}| \geq \alpha t$$

  for some sets $S_{1,x}, \ldots, S_{t,x} \subseteq \mathcal{Y}$ *that may depend on* x.
- **Efficiently verifiable.** *There is a polynomial-size circuit* C *such that for every* x, *the sets* $S_{1,x}, \ldots, S_{t,x}$ *are such that for any* $i, y_i \in S_{i,x}$ *if and only if* $C(x, y_i, i) = 1$.
- **Sparse.** *For every* x, *the sets* $S_{1,x}, \ldots, S_{t,x}$ *are such that for all* $i, |S_{i,x}| \leq \rho |\mathcal{Y}|$.

Imported Theorem 4 ([40]). *Assuming the existence of an efficiently computable keyed hash function family that is* $\epsilon(\lambda)$-*correlation intractable for any efficient function, there exists an efficiently computable keyed hash function family* $\{H_\lambda : \{0,1\}^{k(\lambda)} \times \mathcal{X}_\lambda \rightarrow \mathcal{Y}_\lambda^{t(\lambda)}\}_{\lambda \in \mathbb{N}}$ *that is* $\epsilon(\lambda)$-*correlation intractable for any efficiently verifiable* α-*approximate product relation ensemble* $\{R_\lambda \subseteq \mathcal{X}_\lambda \times \mathcal{Y}_\lambda^{t(\lambda)}\}_{\lambda \in \mathbb{N}}$ *with sparsity* ρ, *as long as* $\rho < \alpha$ *and* $t(\lambda) \geq \lambda/(\alpha - \rho)^3$.

Imported Theorem 5 ([21,54]). *Assuming the* $\epsilon(\lambda)$-*hardness of LWE, there exists an efficiently computable keyed hash function family that is* $\epsilon(\lambda)$-*correlation intractable for any efficient function.*

Definition 3 (Programmability). *A hash function family* $\{H_\lambda : \{0,1\}^{k(\lambda)} \times \mathcal{X}_\lambda \to \mathcal{Y}_\lambda\}_{\lambda \in \mathbb{N}}$ *is* programmable *if for any* $\lambda, x \in \mathcal{X}_\lambda$, *and* $y \in \mathcal{Y}_\lambda$,

$$\Pr_{\mathsf{hk} \leftarrow \{0,1\}^{k(\lambda)}} [H_\lambda(\mathsf{hk}, x) = y] = \frac{1}{2^{m(\lambda)}},$$

and there exists a PPT sampling algorithm $\mathsf{Samp}(1^\lambda, x, y)$ *that samples from the conditional distribution*

$$\mathsf{hk} : H_\lambda(\mathsf{hk}, x) = y.$$

Remark 1. [21] show a simple transformation that generically adds the above notion of programmability to natural correlation intractable hash functions.

In the full version [11], we present additional preliminaries covering commitments, zero-knowledge, and quantum leftover hashing.

3.3   Secure Computation

An ideal functionality $\mathcal{F}$ is an interactive (classical or quantum) machine specifying some distributed computation. In this work, we will specifically focus on *two-party* functionalities between party A and party B. In some cases, party B will have a random input, or no input. The ideal functionalities we will consider in this work are specified in Fig. 2.

Security with abort. In what follows, we will by default consider the notion of security with abort, where the ideal functionality $\mathcal{F}$ is always modified to (1) know the identity of the corrupt party (if one exists) and (2) be slightly reactive: after the parties have provided input, the functionality computes outputs and sends output to the corrupt party only (if it expects output). Then the functionality awaits either a "deliver" or "abort" command from the corrupted party. Upon receiving "deliver", the functionality delivers the honest party output. Upon receiving "abort", the functionality instead delivers an abort message $\perp$ to the honest party. In the case where the corrupt party does not expect output, the functionality $\mathcal{F}$ still awaits a "deliver" or "abort" from the corrupt party before delivering output (or $\perp$) to the honest party.

The real-ideal paradigm. A two-party protocol $\Pi_\mathcal{F}$ for computing the functionality $\mathcal{F}$ consists of two families of quantum interactive machines $\{\mathsf{A}_\lambda\}_{\lambda \in \mathbb{N}}, \{\mathsf{B}_\lambda\}_{\lambda \in \mathbb{N}}$. An adversary intending to attack the protocol by corrupting one of the parties can be described by a family of quantum interactive machines $\{\mathsf{Adv}_\lambda\}_{\lambda \in \mathbb{N}}$ and a family of initial quantum states $\{|\psi_\lambda\rangle^{\mathcal{X},\mathcal{A},\mathcal{D}}\}_{\lambda \in \mathbb{N}}$ on registers $(\mathcal{X}, \mathcal{A}, \mathcal{D})$, where $\mathcal{X}$ is the honest party's input register, $\mathcal{A}$ is the adversary's input register, and $\mathcal{D}$ is given directly to the distinguisher. That is, the honest party takes as input the state on register $\mathcal{X}$, Adv_λ takes as input the state on register $\mathcal{A}$, and they interact in the protocol $\Pi_\mathcal{F}$. Then, the honest party outputs a state on register $\mathcal{X}'$, Adv_λ outputs a state on register $\mathcal{A}'$, and we define the random variable $\Pi_\mathcal{F}[\mathsf{Adv}_\lambda, |\psi_\lambda\rangle]$ to consist of the resulting state on registers

---

Ideal functionalities

Setup: Parties A and B, security parameter λ.

$\mathcal{F}_{\mathsf{OT}}$

- $\mathcal{F}_{\mathsf{OT}}$ receives input $m_0, m_1 \in \{0,1\}^\lambda$ from A and $b \in \{0,1\}$ from B.
- $\mathcal{F}_{\mathsf{OT}}$ delivers m_b to B.

$\mathcal{F}_{\mathsf{ROT}}$

- $\mathcal{F}_{\mathsf{ROT}}$ receives input $m_0, m_1 \in \{0,1\}^\lambda$ from A.
- $\mathcal{F}_{\mathsf{ROT}}$ samples a bit $b \leftarrow \{0,1\}$ and delivers (b, m_b) to B.

$\mathcal{F}_{\mathsf{CL}}[C]$

- C is a classical circuit with two inputs, one of length $n_1 = n_1(\lambda)$ and one of length $n_2 = n_2(\lambda)$.
- $\mathcal{F}_{\mathsf{CL}}[C]$ receives input $x \in \{0,1\}^{n_1}$ from A.
- $\mathcal{F}_{\mathsf{CL}}[C]$ samples a string $r \leftarrow \{0,1\}^{n_2}$ and delivers $C(x, r)$ to B.

$\mathcal{F}_{\mathsf{QU}}[Q]$

- Q is a quantum operation that takes as input a state on register $\mathcal{X}$ of $n = n(\lambda)$ qubits and outputs a state on register $\mathcal{Y}$.
- $\mathcal{F}_{\mathsf{QU}}[Q]$ receives as input a state on register $\mathcal{X}$ from A.
- $\mathcal{F}_{\mathsf{QU}}[Q]$ computes $Q(\mathcal{X}) = \mathcal{Y}$ and delivers $\mathcal{Y}$ to B.

Fig. 2. Ideal functionalities considered in this work.

$(\mathcal{X}', \mathcal{A}', \mathcal{D})$, which will be given to a distinguisher. In the case where the honest party has no input, we don't include a register $\mathcal{X}$, and just consider families $\{|\psi_\lambda\rangle^{\mathcal{A}, \mathcal{D}}\}_{\lambda \in \mathbb{N}}$ on registers $\mathcal{A}$ and $\mathcal{D}$. In the case where the honest party has a classical input, we assume that $\mathcal{X}$ is in a standard basis state. In other words, we consider families $\{(x_\lambda, |\psi_\lambda\rangle^{\mathcal{A}, \mathcal{D}})\}_{\lambda \in \mathbb{N}}$, where each x_λ is a classical string.

An *ideal-world* protocol $\widetilde{\Pi}_{\mathcal{F}}$ for functionality $\mathcal{F}$ consists of "dummy" parties $\widetilde{A}$ and $\widetilde{B}$ that have access to an additional "trusted" party that implements $\mathcal{F}$. That is, $\widetilde{A}$ and $\widetilde{B}$ only interact directly with $\mathcal{F}$, providing inputs and receiving outputs, and do not interact with each other. We consider the execution of ideal-world protocols in the presence of a simulator, described by a family of quantum interactive machines $\{\mathsf{Sim}_\lambda\}_{\lambda \in \mathbb{N}}$ that controls either party $\widetilde{A}$ or $\widetilde{B}$. The execution of the protocol in the presence of the simulator also begins with a family of states $\{|\psi_\lambda\rangle^{\mathcal{X}, \mathcal{A}, \mathcal{D}}\}_{\lambda \in \mathbb{N}}$ on registers $(\mathcal{X}, \mathcal{A}, \mathcal{D})$ as described above, and we define the analogous random variable $\widetilde{\Pi}_{\mathcal{F}}[\mathsf{Sim}_\lambda, |\psi_\lambda\rangle]$.

Secure realization. We define what it means for a protocol to securely realize an ideal functionality.

Definition 4 (Secure realization). *A protocol $\Pi_{\mathcal{F}}$ securely realizes the functionality $\mathcal{F}$ if for any QPT adversary $\{\mathsf{Adv}_\lambda\}_{\lambda \in \mathbb{N}}$ corrupting party $M \in \{A, B\}$, there exists a QPT simulator $\{\mathsf{Sim}_\lambda\}_{\lambda \in \mathbb{N}}$ corrupting party M such that for any QPT distinguisher $\{\mathsf{D}_\lambda\}_{\lambda \in \mathbb{N}}$ and polynomial-size family of states $\{|\psi_\lambda\rangle^{\mathcal{X},\mathcal{A},\mathcal{D}}\}_{\lambda \in \mathbb{N}}$,*

$$\left| \Pr[1 \leftarrow \mathsf{D}_\lambda(\Pi_{\mathcal{F}}[\mathsf{Adv}_\lambda, |\psi_\lambda\rangle])] - \Pr[1 \leftarrow \mathsf{D}_\lambda(\widetilde{\Pi}_{\mathcal{F}}[\mathsf{Sim}_\lambda, |\psi_\lambda\rangle])] \right| = \mathrm{negl}(\lambda).$$

3.4 The XOR Extractor

Informal Theorem 6 ([2]). *Let $\mathcal{X}$ be an n-qubit register, and consider any quantum state $|\gamma\rangle^{\mathcal{A},\mathcal{X}}$ that can be written as*

$$|\gamma\rangle^{\mathcal{A},\mathcal{X}} = \sum_{u:\mathrm{hw}(u)<n/2} |\psi_u\rangle^{\mathcal{A}} |u\rangle^{\mathcal{X}},$$

where $\mathrm{hw}(\cdot)$ denotes the Hamming weight. Let $\rho^{\mathcal{A},\mathcal{P}}$ be the mixed state that results from measuring $\mathcal{X}$ in the Hadamard basis to produce a string $x \in \{0,1\}^n$, and writing $\bigoplus_{i \in [n]} x_i$ into a single qubit register $\mathcal{P}$. Then it holds that

$$\rho^{\mathcal{A},\mathcal{P}} = Tr^{\mathcal{X}}(|\gamma\rangle\langle\gamma|) \otimes \left(\frac{1}{2}|0\rangle\langle0| + \frac{1}{2}|1\rangle\langle1| \right)^{\mathcal{P}}.$$

4 One-Shot String Oblivious Transfer

4.1 Construction

In this section, we give our construction of one-shot (random receiver bit) string oblivious transfer in the shared EPR pairs model.

Ingredients

- Non-interactive extractable commitment $(\mathsf{Com}, \mathsf{ExtGen}, \mathsf{Ext})$ in the common random string model. This is known from LWE.
- A programmable hash function family $\{H_\lambda\}_{\lambda \in \mathbb{N}}$ that is sub-exponentially correlation intractable for efficiently verifiable approximate product relations with constant sparsity (Sect. 3.2). This is known from the sub-exponential hardness of LWE (Theorems 4 and 5).
- Non-interactive zero-knowledge argument $(\mathsf{NIZK.Prove}, \mathsf{NIZK.Ver}, \mathsf{NIZK.Sim})$ in the common random string model. This is known from LWE.
- Pseudorandom generator PRG.

Parameters

- Security parameter λ.
- Correlation intractable hash security parameter $\lambda_{\mathsf{CI}} := \lambda^{1/\delta}$, where $\delta > 0$ is the constant such that $\{H_{\lambda_{\mathsf{CI}}}\}_{\lambda_{\mathsf{CI}} \in \mathbb{N}}$ is $2^{-\lambda_{\mathsf{CI}}^{\delta}}$-correlation intractable.
- Size of commitment key $h = h(\lambda)$.
- Size of NIZK crs $n = n(\lambda)$.
- Size of hash key $k = k(\lambda_{\mathsf{CI}})$.
- Approximation parameter $\alpha = 1/120$.
- Number of repetitions in each group $c = 480$.
- Sparsity $\rho = \frac{\binom{(1-\alpha)c}{(1/2)c}}{2^c} < \alpha$.
- Product parameter $t = t(\lambda_{\mathsf{CI}}) = 180^3 \lambda_{\mathsf{CI}} \geq \lambda_{\mathsf{CI}}/(\alpha - \rho)^3$.
- Total number of repetitions $\ell = \ell(\lambda) = c \cdot t = \mathrm{poly}(\lambda)$.
- PRG range $\{0,1\}^{2\lambda\ell}$.
- CI hash range $\mathcal{Y}^t$, where $\mathcal{Y}$ is the set of subsets of $[c]$ of size $c/2$. We will also parse $T \in \mathcal{Y}^t$ as a subset of $[\ell]$ of size $\ell/2$.

We remark that we have not tried to fully optimize the constants in the parameters above.

Setup

- ℓ collections of EPR pairs indexed by $i \in [\ell]$. Each collection consists of one "control" pair $\{\mathcal{S}_i^{\mathsf{ctl}}, \mathcal{R}_i^{\mathsf{ctl}}\}$ and 2λ "message" pairs on registers $\{\mathcal{S}_{i,j}^{\mathsf{msg}}, \mathcal{R}_{i,j}^{\mathsf{msg}}\}_{j \in [2\lambda]}$. For each $i \in [\ell]$, we define $\mathcal{S}_i := (\mathcal{S}_i^{\mathsf{ctl}}, \mathcal{S}_{i,1}^{\mathsf{msg}}, \ldots, \mathcal{S}_{i,2\lambda}^{\mathsf{msg}})$ and $\mathcal{R}_i := (\mathcal{R}_i^{\mathsf{ctl}}, \mathcal{R}_{i,1}^{\mathsf{msg}}, \ldots, \mathcal{R}_{i,2\lambda}^{\mathsf{msg}})$.
- Commitment key $\mathsf{ck} \leftarrow \{0,1\}^h$.
- NIZK common random string $\mathsf{crs} \leftarrow \{0,1\}^n$.
- Correlation intractable hash key $\mathsf{hk} \leftarrow \{0,1\}^k$.

Note that a shared uniformly random string can be obtained by measuring shared EPR pairs in the same basis, and thus this entire Setup can be obtained with just shared EPR pairs.

Finally, given a commitment key ck for Com and a set $\overline{T} \subset [\ell]$, we define the NP language $\mathcal{L}_{\mathsf{ck},\overline{T}}$ of instance-witness pairs as follows.

$$\left(\left(\{\widehat{\mathsf{cm}}_{i,0}, \widehat{\mathsf{cm}}_{i,1}\}_{i \in \overline{T}}, \{\mathsf{cm}_i\}_{i \in [\ell]} \right), \left(\{t_i\}_{i \in \overline{T}}, \Delta, s \right) \right) \in \mathcal{L}_{\mathsf{ck},\overline{T}}$$

if and only if[11]

$$\forall i \in \overline{T}, \widehat{\mathsf{cm}}_{i,0} \in \mathsf{Com}(\mathsf{ck}, t_i) \wedge \widehat{\mathsf{cm}}_{i,1} \in \mathsf{Com}(\mathsf{ck}, t_i \oplus \Delta), \text{ and}$$
$$\forall i \in [\ell], \mathsf{cm}_i \in \mathsf{Com}(\mathsf{ck}, (\cdot, x_i, \cdot)), \text{where } (x_1, \ldots, x_\ell) := \mathsf{PRG}(s).$$

Now, our protocol is described in Fig. 3.

---

[11] Technically, the random coins used to compute the commitments must also be included in the witness.

One-shot protocol for $\mathcal{F}_{\mathsf{ROT}}$

<u>Sender message.</u>   Input strings $m_0, m_1 \in \{0,1\}^\lambda$.

1. Sample a PRG seed $s \leftarrow \{0,1\}^\lambda$ and set $(x_1, \ldots, x_\ell) := \mathsf{PRG}(s)$, where each $x_i \in \{0,1\}^{2\lambda}$.
2. For each $i \in [\ell]$:
   - For each $j \in [2\lambda]$ such that $x_{i,j} = 1$, apply a CNOT gate from register $\mathcal{S}_i^{\mathsf{ctl}}$ to register $\mathcal{S}_{i,j}^{\mathsf{msg}}$.
   - Measure $\{\mathcal{S}_{i,j}^{\mathsf{msg}}\}_{j \in [2\lambda]}$ in the standard basis to obtain $v_i \in \{0,1\}^{2\lambda}$ and measure $\mathcal{S}_i^{\mathsf{ctl}}$ in the Hadamard basis to obtain $h_i \in \{0,1\}$.
   - Compute $\mathsf{cm}_i := \mathsf{Com}(\mathsf{ck}, (v_i, x_i, h_i); r_i)$, where $r_i \leftarrow \{0,1\}^\lambda$ are the random coins used for commitment.
3. Compute $T = H_\lambda(\mathsf{hk}, (\mathsf{cm}_1, \ldots, \mathsf{cm}_\ell)) \subseteq [\ell]$ and let $\overline{T} := [\ell] \setminus T$.
4. Sample $\Delta \leftarrow \{0,1\}^\lambda$ and for each $i \in \overline{T}$:
   - Sample $t_i \leftarrow \{0,1\}^\lambda$ and compute $\widehat{\mathsf{cm}}_{i,0} := \mathsf{Com}(\mathsf{ck}, t_i; r_{i,0})$ and $\widehat{\mathsf{cm}}_{i,1} := \mathsf{Com}(\mathsf{ck}, t_i \oplus \Delta; r_{i,1})$ where $r_{i,0}, r_{i,1} \leftarrow \{0,1\}^\lambda$ are the random coins used for commitment.
   - Define $z_{i,0} = (t_i, r_{i,0}) \oplus v_i$, $\quad z_{i,1} = (t_i \oplus \Delta, r_{i,1}) \oplus v_i \oplus x_i$.
5. Define
$$\widetilde{m}_0 := m_0 \oplus \bigoplus_{i \in \overline{T}} t_i, \quad \widetilde{m}_1 := m_1 \oplus \Delta \oplus \bigoplus_{i \in \overline{T}} t_i.$$
6. Compute $\pi \leftarrow \mathsf{NIZK.Prove}\left(\mathsf{crs}, \left(\{\widehat{\mathsf{cm}}_{i,0}, \widehat{\mathsf{cm}}_{i,1}\}_{i \in \overline{T}}, \{\mathsf{cm}_i\}_{i \in [\ell]}\right), \left(\{t_i\}_{i \in \overline{T}}, \Delta, s\right)\right)$ for the language $\mathcal{L}_{\mathsf{ck}, \overline{T}}$.
7. Send $\left(\{\mathsf{cm}_i\}_{i \in [\ell]}, \{v_i, x_i, h_i, r_i\}_{i \in T}, \{\widehat{\mathsf{cm}}_{i,0}, \widehat{\mathsf{cm}}_{i,1}, z_{i,0}, z_{i,1}\}_{i \in \overline{T}}, \pi, \widetilde{m}_0, \widetilde{m}_1\right)$ to the receiver.

<u>Receiver computation.</u>   In what follows, abort and output $\perp$ if any check fails.

1. Compute $T = H_\lambda(\mathsf{hk}, (\mathsf{cm}_1, \ldots, \mathsf{cm}_\ell))$ and check that for all $i \in T$, $\mathsf{cm}_i = \mathsf{Com}(\mathsf{ck}, (v_i, x_i, h_i); r_i)$.
2. For each $i \in T$, define $|\psi_{v_i, x_i, h_i}\rangle := \frac{1}{\sqrt{2}}\left(|0, v_i\rangle + (-1)^{h_i} |1, v_i \oplus x_i\rangle\right)$, and measure register $\mathcal{R}_i$ in the basis $\{|\psi_{v_i, x_i, h_i}\rangle\langle\psi_{v_i, x_i, h_i}|, \mathbb{I} - |\psi_{v_i, x_i, h_i}\rangle\langle\psi_{v_i, x_i, h_i}|\}$. Check that for all $i \in T$, the first outcome is observed.
3. Check that $\mathsf{NIZK.Ver}\left(\mathsf{crs}, \left(\{\widehat{\mathsf{cm}}_{i,0}, \widehat{\mathsf{cm}}_{i,1}\}_{i \in \overline{T}}, \{\mathsf{cm}_i\}_{i \in [\ell]}\right), \pi\right) = \top$.
4. For each $i \in \overline{T}$, measure register $\mathcal{R}_i$ in the standard basis to obtain $b_i \in \{0,1\}$ and $v_i' \in \{0,1\}^{2\lambda}$, compute $(t_i', r_i') = z_{i,b_i} \oplus v_i'$, and check that for each $i \in \overline{T}$, $\widehat{\mathsf{cm}}_{i,b_i} = \mathsf{Com}(\mathsf{ck}, t_i'; r_i')$.
5. Output
$$b := \bigoplus_{i \in \overline{T}} b_i, \quad m_b := \widetilde{m}_b \oplus \bigoplus_{i \in \overline{T}} t_i'.$$

Fig. 3. A protocol for one-shot random string OT in the shared EPR pair model.

4.2   Security

Theorem 7. *The protocol in Fig. 3 securely realizes (Definition 4) the functionality $\mathcal{F}_{\mathsf{ROT}}$. Thus, assuming the sub-exponential hardness of LWE, there exists a one-message protocol for $\mathcal{F}_{\mathsf{ROT}}$ in the shared EPR pair model.*

The proof of this theorem follows from receiver security, which is shown in Lemma 2 and sender security, which is more straightforward and is deferred to the full version [11].

Lemma 2. *The protocol in Fig. 3 is secure against a malicious sender.*

Proof. Let $\{\mathsf{Adv}_\lambda\}_{\lambda \in \mathbb{N}}$ be a QPT adversary corrupting the sender, which takes as input register $\mathcal{A}$ of $\{|\psi_\lambda\rangle^{\mathcal{A},\mathcal{D}}\}_{\lambda \in \mathbb{N}}$. Note that we don't consider a register $\mathcal{X}$ holding the honest party's input, since an honest receiver has no input. We will define a sequence of hybrids, beginning with the real distribution $\Pi_{\mathcal{F}_{\mathsf{ROT}}}[\mathsf{Adv}_\lambda, |\psi_\lambda\rangle]$ and ending with the distribution $\widetilde{\Pi}_{\mathcal{F}_{\mathsf{ROT}}}[\mathsf{Sim}_\lambda, |\psi_\lambda\rangle]$ defined by a simulator $\{\mathsf{Sim}_\lambda\}_{\lambda \in \mathbb{N}}$. Each hybrid is a distribution described by applying an operation to the input register $\mathcal{A}$, and a QPT distinguisher will obtain the output of this distribution along with the register $\mathcal{D}$. We drop the dependence of the hybrids on λ for convenience.

$\underline{\mathcal{H}_0(\mathcal{A})}$

- Prepare ℓ collections of EPR pairs on registers $\{\mathcal{S}_i, \mathcal{R}_i\}_{i \in [\ell]}$, and sample $\mathsf{ck} \leftarrow \{0,1\}^h$, $\mathsf{crs} \leftarrow \{0,1\}^n$, and $\mathsf{hk} \leftarrow \{0,1\}^k$.
- Run Adv_λ on input $\mathcal{A}, \{\mathcal{S}_i\}_{i \in [\ell]}, \mathsf{ck}, \mathsf{crs}, \mathsf{hk}$ until it outputs a message

$$\left(\{\mathsf{cm}_i\}_{i \in [\ell]}, \{v_i, x_i, h_i, r_i\}_{i \in T}, \{\widehat{\mathsf{cm}}_{i,0}, \widehat{\mathsf{cm}}_{i,1}, z_{i,0}, z_{i,1}\}_{i \in \overline{T}}, \pi, \widetilde{m}_0, \widetilde{m}_1\right)$$

and a state on register $\mathcal{A}'$.
- Run the Receiver's honest computation on the sender's message to obtain an output (b, m_b) or $\perp$. Output either $(\mathcal{A}', (b, m_b))$ or $(\mathcal{A}', \perp)$.

$\underline{\mathcal{H}_1(\mathcal{A})}$

- Prepare ℓ collections of EPR pairs on registers $\{\mathcal{S}_i, \mathcal{R}_i\}_{i \in [\ell]}$, and sample $(\mathsf{ck}, \mathsf{ek}) \leftarrow \mathsf{ExtGen}(1^\lambda)$, $\mathsf{crs} \leftarrow \{0,1\}^n$, and $\mathsf{hk} \leftarrow \{0,1\}^k$.
- Run Adv_λ on input $\mathcal{A}, \{\mathcal{S}_i\}_{i \in [\ell]}, \mathsf{ck}, \mathsf{crs}, \mathsf{hk}$ until it outputs a message

$$\left(\{\mathsf{cm}_i\}_{i \in [\ell]}, \{v_i, x_i, h_i, r_i\}_{i \in T}, \{\widehat{\mathsf{cm}}_{i,0}, \widehat{\mathsf{cm}}_{i,1}, z_{i,0}, z_{i,1}\}_{i \in \overline{T}}, \pi, \widetilde{m}_0, \widetilde{m}_1\right)$$

and a state on register $\mathcal{A}'$.
- Run the Receiver's honest computation on the sender's message to obtain an output (b, m_b) or $\perp$. Output either $(\mathcal{A}', (b, m_b))$ or $(\mathcal{A}', \perp)$.

$\underline{\mathcal{H}_2(\mathcal{A})}$

- Prepare ℓ collections of EPR pairs on registers $\{\mathcal{S}_i, \mathcal{R}_i\}_{i \in [\ell]}$, and sample $(\mathsf{ck}, \mathsf{ek}) \leftarrow \mathsf{ExtGen}(1^\lambda)$, $\mathsf{crs} \leftarrow \{0,1\}^n$, and $\mathsf{hk} \leftarrow \{0,1\}^k$.

– Run Adv_λ on input $\mathcal{A}, \{\mathcal{S}_i\}_{i\in[\ell]}, \mathsf{ck}, \mathsf{crs}, \mathsf{hk}$ until it outputs a message

$$\left(\{\mathsf{cm}_i\}_{i\in[\ell]}, \{v_i, x_i, h_i, r_i\}_{i\in T}, \{\widehat{\mathsf{cm}}_{i,0}, \widehat{\mathsf{cm}}_{i,1}, z_{i,0}, z_{i,1}\}_{i\in\overline{T}}, \pi, \tilde{m}_0, \tilde{m}_1\right)$$

and a state on register $\mathcal{A}'$.
– Run Steps 1–3 of the Receiver's honest computation on the sender's message.
– We will now *coherently* apply the check described in Step 4 to the registers $\{\mathcal{R}_i\}_{i\in\overline{T}}$. First we introduce some notation. For commitment key ck, commitment $\widehat{\mathsf{cm}}$, and two strings $z_0, z_1 \in \{0,1\}^{2\lambda}$, let $\Pi[\mathsf{ck}, \widehat{\mathsf{cm}}, z_0, z_1]$ be a projection onto strings $(b, v') \in \{0,1\}^{1+2\lambda}$ such that $\widehat{\mathsf{cm}} = \mathsf{Com}(\mathsf{ck}, t; r)$, where $(t, r) := z_b \oplus v'$.
Attempt to project registers $\{\mathcal{R}_i\}_{i\in\overline{T}}$ onto

$$\bigotimes_{i\in\overline{T}} \Pi[\mathsf{ck}, \widehat{\mathsf{cm}}_{i,0}, z_{i,0}, z_{i,1}]^{\mathcal{R}_i},$$

and aborts if the projection fails.
– If there was an abort, output $(\mathcal{A}', \bot)$. Otherwise, for each $i \in \overline{T}$, measure register $\mathcal{R}_i$ in the standard basis to obtain $b_i \in \{0,1\}$ and $v'_i \in \{0,1\}^{2\lambda}$, and compute $(t'_i, r'_i) = z_{i,b_i} \oplus v'_i$. Then, define

$$b := \bigoplus_{i\in\overline{T}} b_i, \quad m_b := \tilde{m}_b \oplus \bigoplus_{i\in\overline{T}} t'_i,$$

and output $(\mathcal{A}', (b, m_b))$.

$\mathcal{H}_3(\mathcal{A})$

– Prepare ℓ collections of EPR pairs on registers $\{\mathcal{S}_i, \mathcal{R}_i\}_{i\in[\ell]}$, and sample $(\mathsf{ck}, \mathsf{ek}) \leftarrow \mathsf{ExtGen}(1^\lambda)$, $\mathsf{crs} \leftarrow \{0,1\}^n$, and $\mathsf{hk} \leftarrow \{0,1\}^k$.
– Run Adv_λ on input $\mathcal{A}, \{\mathcal{S}_i\}_{i\in[\ell]}, \mathsf{ck}, \mathsf{crs}, \mathsf{hk}$ until it outputs a message

$$\left(\{\mathsf{cm}_i\}_{i\in[\ell]}, \{v_i, x_i, h_i, r_i\}_{i\in T}, \{\widehat{\mathsf{cm}}_{i,0}, \widehat{\mathsf{cm}}_{i,1}, z_{i,0}, z_{i,1}\}_{i\in\overline{T}}, \pi, \tilde{m}_0, \tilde{m}_1\right)$$

and a state on register $\mathcal{A}'$.
– Run Steps 1–3 of the Receiver's honest computation on the sender's message.
– Attempt to project registers $\{\mathcal{R}_i\}_{i\in\overline{T}}$ onto

$$\bigotimes_{i\in\overline{T}} \Pi[\mathsf{ck}, \widehat{\mathsf{cm}}_{i,0}, z_{i,0}, z_{i,1}]^{\mathcal{R}_i},$$

and abort if the projection fails.
– For each $i \in \overline{T}, b \in \{0,1\}$, compute $t_{i,b} \leftarrow \mathsf{Ext}(\mathsf{ek}, \widehat{\mathsf{cm}}_{i,b})$. Abort if any $t_{i,b} = \bot$ or if there does not exist Δ such that $t_{i,1} = \Delta \oplus t_{i,0}$ for all $i \in \overline{T}$.
– If there was an abort, output $(\mathcal{A}', \bot)$. Otherwise, for each $i \in \overline{T}$, measure register $\mathcal{R}_i$ in the standard basis to obtain $b_i \in \{0,1\}$ and $v'_i \in \{0,1\}^{2\lambda}$, and compute $(t'_i, r'_i) = z_{i,b_i} \oplus v'_i$. Then, define

$$b := \bigoplus_{i\in\overline{T}} b_i, \quad m_b := \tilde{m}_b \oplus \bigoplus_{i\in\overline{T}} t'_i,$$

and output $(\mathcal{A}', (b, m_b))$.

$\underline{\mathcal{H}_4(\mathcal{A})}$

- Prepare ℓ collections of EPR pairs on registers $\{\mathcal{S}_i, \mathcal{R}_i\}_{i \in [\ell]}$, and sample $(\mathsf{ck}, \mathsf{ek}) \leftarrow \mathsf{ExtGen}(1^\lambda)$, $\mathsf{crs} \leftarrow \{0,1\}^n$, and $\mathsf{hk} \leftarrow \{0,1\}^k$.
- Run Adv_λ on input $\mathcal{A}, \{\mathcal{S}_i\}_{i \in [\ell]}, \mathsf{ck}, \mathsf{crs}, \mathsf{hk}$ until it outputs a message

$$\left(\{\mathsf{cm}_i\}_{i \in [\ell]}, \{v_i, x_i, h_i, r_i\}_{i \in T}, \{\widehat{\mathsf{cm}}_{i,0}, \widehat{\mathsf{cm}}_{i,1}, z_{i,0}, z_{i,1}\}_{i \in \overline{T}}, \pi, \widetilde{m}_0, \widetilde{m}_1\right)$$

and a state on register $\mathcal{A}'$.
- Run Steps 1–3 of the Receiver's honest computation on the sender's message.
- Attempt to project registers $\{\mathcal{R}_i\}_{i \in \overline{T}}$ onto

$$\bigotimes_{i \in \overline{T}} \Pi[\mathsf{ck}, \widehat{\mathsf{cm}}_{i,0}, z_{i,0}, z_{i,1}]^{\mathcal{R}_i},$$

and abort if the projection fails.
- For each $i \in \overline{T}, b \in \{0,1\}$, compute $t_{i,b} \leftarrow \mathsf{Ext}(\mathsf{ek}, \widehat{\mathsf{cm}}_{i,b})$. Abort if any $t_{i,b} = \bot$ or if there does not exist Δ such that $t_{i,1} = \Delta \oplus t_{i,0}$ for all $i \in \overline{T}$.
- If there was an abort, output $(\mathcal{A}', \bot)$. Otherwise, for each $i \in \overline{T}$, measure register $\mathcal{R}_i^{\mathsf{ctl}}$ in the standard basis to obtain $b_i \in \{0,1\}$. Then, define

$$b := \bigoplus_{i \in \overline{T}} b_i, \quad m_0 := \bigoplus_{i \in \overline{T}} t_{i,0}, \quad m_1 := \widetilde{m}_1 \oplus \Delta \oplus \bigoplus_{i \in \overline{T}} t_{i,0},$$

and output $(\mathcal{A}', (b, m_b))$.

$\underline{\mathcal{H}_5(\mathcal{A})}$

- Prepare ℓ collections of EPR pairs on registers $\{\mathcal{S}_i, \mathcal{R}_i\}_{i \in [\ell]}$, and sample $(\mathsf{ck}, \mathsf{ek}) \leftarrow \mathsf{ExtGen}(1^\lambda)$, $\mathsf{crs} \leftarrow \{0,1\}^n$, and $\mathsf{hk} \leftarrow \{0,1\}^k$.
- Run Adv_λ on input $\mathcal{A}, \{\mathcal{S}_i\}_{i \in [\ell]}, \mathsf{ck}, \mathsf{crs}, \mathsf{hk}$ until it outputs a message

$$\left(\{\mathsf{cm}_i\}_{i \in [\ell]}, \{v_i, x_i, h_i, r_i\}_{i \in T}, \{\widehat{\mathsf{cm}}_{i,0}, \widehat{\mathsf{cm}}_{i,1}, z_{i,0}, z_{i,1}\}_{i \in \overline{T}}, \pi, \widetilde{m}_0, \widetilde{m}_1\right)$$

and a state on register $\mathcal{A}'$.
- Run Steps 1–3 of the Receiver's honest computation on the sender's message.
- We will insert a measurement on the registers $\{\mathcal{R}_i\}_{i \in \overline{T}}$. Before specifying this measurement, we introduce some notation.
  - For $\{(v_i, x_i, h_i)\}_{i \in \overline{T}}$ and a string $e \in \{0,1\}^{|\overline{T}|}$, define

$$\Pi[e, \{(v_i, x_i, h_i)\}_{i \in \overline{T}}]^{\{\mathcal{R}_i\}_{i \in \overline{T}}}$$
$$:= \bigotimes_{i:e_i=0} |\psi_{v_i, x_i, h_i}\rangle\langle\psi_{v_i, x_i, h_i}|^{\mathcal{R}_i} \otimes \bigotimes_{i:e_i=1} \mathbb{I} - |\psi_{v_i, x_i, h_i}\rangle\langle\psi_{v_i, x_i, h_i}|^{\mathcal{R}_i}.$$

  - For $\{(v_i, x_i, h_i)\}_{i \in \overline{T}}$ and a constant $\gamma \in [0,1]$, define

$$\Pi[\gamma, \{(v_i, x_i, h_i)\}_{i \in \overline{T}}]^{\{\mathcal{R}_i\}_{i \in \overline{T}}}$$
$$:= \sum_{e \in \{0,1\}^{|S|}: \mathsf{hw}(e) < \gamma|\overline{T}|} \Pi[e, \{(v_i, x_i, h_i)\}_{i \in \overline{T}}]^{\{\mathcal{R}_i\}_{i \in \overline{T}}}.$$

Compute $(v_i, x_i, h_i) \leftarrow \mathsf{Ext}(\mathsf{ek}, \mathsf{cm}_i)$ for each $i \in \overline{T}$. Attempt to project registers $\{\mathcal{R}_i\}_{i \in \overline{T}}$ onto

$$\Pi\left[1/30, \{(v_i, x_i, h_i)\}_{i \in \overline{T}}\right],$$

and abort if this projection fails.

- Attempt to project registers $\{\mathcal{R}_i\}_{i \in \overline{T}}$ onto

$$\bigotimes_{i \in \overline{T}} \Pi[\mathsf{ck}, \widehat{\mathsf{cm}}_{i,0}, z_{i,0}, z_{i,1}]^{\mathcal{R}_i},$$

and abort if the projection fails.

- For each $i \in \overline{T}, b \in \{0,1\}$, compute $t_{i,b} \leftarrow \mathsf{Ext}(\mathsf{ek}, \widehat{\mathsf{cm}}_{i,b})$. Abort if any $t_{i,b} = \bot$ or if there does not exist Δ such that $t_{i,1} = \Delta \oplus t_{i,0}$ for all $i \in \overline{T}$.
- If there was an abort, output $(\mathcal{A}', \bot)$. Otherwise, for each $i \in \overline{T}$, measure register $\mathcal{R}_i^{\mathsf{ctl}}$ in the standard basis to obtain $b_i \in \{0,1\}$. Then, define

$$b := \bigoplus_{i \in \overline{T}} b_i, \quad m_0 := \bigoplus_{i \in \overline{T}} t_{i,0}, \quad m_1 := \tilde{m}_1 \oplus \Delta \oplus \bigoplus_{i \in \overline{T}} t_{i,0},$$

and output $(\mathcal{A}', (b, m_b))$.

$\mathcal{H}_6(\mathcal{A})$

- Prepare ℓ collections of EPR pairs on registers $\{\mathcal{S}_i, \mathcal{R}_i\}_{i \in [\ell]}$, and sample $(\mathsf{ck}, \mathsf{ek}) \leftarrow \mathsf{ExtGen}(1^\lambda)$, $\mathsf{crs} \leftarrow \{0,1\}^n$, and $\mathsf{hk} \leftarrow \{0,1\}^k$.
- Run Adv_λ on input $\mathcal{A}, \{\mathcal{S}_i\}_{i \in [\ell]}, \mathsf{ck}, \mathsf{crs}, \mathsf{hk}$ until it outputs a message

$$\left(\{\mathsf{cm}_i\}_{i \in [\ell]}, \{v_i, x_i, h_i, r_i\}_{i \in T}, \{\widehat{\mathsf{cm}}_{i,0}, \widehat{\mathsf{cm}}_{i,1}, z_{i,0}, z_{i,1}\}_{i \in \overline{T}}, \pi, \tilde{m}_0, \tilde{m}_1\right)$$

and a state on register $\mathcal{A}'$.

- Run Steps 1–3 of the Receiver's honest computation on the sender's message.
- Compute $(v_i, x_i, h_i) \leftarrow \mathsf{Ext}(\mathsf{ek}, \mathsf{cm}_i)$ for each $i \in \overline{T}$. Attempt to project registers $\{\mathcal{R}_i\}_{i \in \overline{T}}$ onto

$$\Pi\left[1/30, \{(v_i, x_i, h_i)\}_{i \in \overline{T}}\right],$$

and abort if this projection fails.

- Attempt to project registers $\{\mathcal{R}_i\}_{i \in \overline{T}}$ onto

$$\bigotimes_{i \in \overline{T}} \Pi[\mathsf{ck}, \widehat{\mathsf{cm}}_{i,0}, z_{i,0}, z_{i,1}]^{\mathcal{R}_i},$$

and abort if the projection fails.

- Attempt to project registers $\{\mathcal{R}_i\}_{i \in \overline{T}}$ onto

$$\Pi\left[1/2, \{(v_i, x_i, h_i)\}_{i \in \overline{T}}\right],$$

and abort if this projection fails.

- For each $i \in \overline{T}, b \in \{0,1\}$, compute $t_{i,b} \leftarrow \mathsf{Ext}(\mathsf{ek}, \widehat{\mathsf{cm}}_{i,b})$. Abort if any $t_{i,b} = \bot$ or if there does not exist Δ such that $t_{i,1} = \Delta \oplus t_{i,0}$ for all $i \in \overline{T}$.

- If there was an abort, output $(\mathcal{A}', \perp)$. Otherwise, for each $i \in \overline{T}$, measure register $\mathcal{R}_i^{\mathsf{ctl}}$ in the standard basis to obtain $b_i \in \{0, 1\}$. Then, define

$$b := \bigoplus_{i \in \overline{T}} b_i, \quad m_0 := \bigoplus_{i \in \overline{T}} t_{i,0}, \quad m_1 := \tilde{m}_1 \oplus \Delta \oplus \bigoplus_{i \in \overline{T}} t_{i,0},$$

and output $(\mathcal{A}', (b, m_b))$.

$\underline{\mathcal{H}_7(\mathcal{A})}$

- Prepare ℓ collections of EPR pairs on registers $\{\mathcal{S}_i, \mathcal{R}_i\}_{i \in [\ell]}$, and sample $(\mathsf{ck}, \mathsf{ek}) \leftarrow \mathsf{ExtGen}(1^\lambda)$, $\mathsf{crs} \leftarrow \{0,1\}^n$, and $\mathsf{hk} \leftarrow \{0,1\}^k$.
- Run Adv_λ on input $\mathcal{A}, \{\mathcal{S}_i\}_{i \in [\ell]}, \mathsf{ck}, \mathsf{crs}, \mathsf{hk}$ until it outputs a message

$$\left(\{\mathsf{cm}_i\}_{i \in [\ell]}, \{v_i, x_i, h_i, r_i\}_{i \in T}, \{\widehat{\mathsf{cm}}_{i,0}, \widehat{\mathsf{cm}}_{i,1}, z_{i,0}, z_{i,1}\}_{i \in \overline{T}}, \pi, \tilde{m}_0, \tilde{m}_1\right)$$

and a state on register $\mathcal{A}'$.
- Run Steps 1–3 of the Receiver's honest computation on the sender's message.
- Compute $(v_i, x_i, h_i) \leftarrow \mathsf{Ext}(\mathsf{ek}, \mathsf{cm}_i)$ for each $i \in \overline{T}$. Attempt to project registers $\{\mathcal{R}_i\}_{i \in \overline{T}}$ onto

$$\Pi\left[1/30, \{(v_i, x_i, h_i)\}_{i \in \overline{T}}\right],$$

and abort if this projection fails.
- Attempt to project registers $\{\mathcal{R}_i\}_{i \in \overline{T}}$ onto

$$\bigotimes_{i \in \overline{T}} \Pi[\mathsf{ck}, \widehat{\mathsf{cm}}_{i,0}, z_{i,0}, z_{i,1}]^{\mathcal{R}_i},$$

and abort if the projection fails.
- Attempt to project registers $\{\mathcal{R}_i\}_{i \in \overline{T}}$ onto

$$\Pi\left[1/2, \{(v_i, x_i, h_i)\}_{i \in \overline{T}}\right],$$

and abort if this projection fails.
  For each $i \subset \overline{T}, b \in \{0,1\}$, compute $t_{i,b} \leftarrow \mathsf{Fxt}(\mathsf{ek}, \widehat{\mathsf{cm}}_{i,b})$. Abort if any $t_{i,b} = \perp$ or if there does not exist Δ such that $t_{i,1} = \Delta \oplus t_{i,0}$ for all $i \in \overline{T}$.
- If there was an abort, output $(\mathcal{A}', \perp)$. Otherwise, sample $b \leftarrow \{0,1\}$. Then, define

$$m_0 := \bigoplus_{i \in \overline{T}} t_{i,0}, \quad m_1 := \tilde{m}_1 \oplus \Delta \oplus \bigoplus_{i \in \overline{T}} t_{i,0},$$

and output $(\mathcal{A}', (b, m_b))$.

$\underline{\mathcal{H}_8(\mathcal{A})}$

- Prepare ℓ collections of EPR pairs on registers $\{\mathcal{S}_i, \mathcal{R}_i\}_{i \in [\ell]}$, and sample $(\mathsf{ck}, \mathsf{ek}) \leftarrow \mathsf{ExtGen}(1^\lambda)$, $\mathsf{crs} \leftarrow \{0,1\}^n$, and $\mathsf{hk} \leftarrow \{0,1\}^k$.
- Run Adv_λ on input $\mathcal{A}, \{\mathcal{S}_i\}_{i \in [\ell]}, \mathsf{ck}, \mathsf{crs}, \mathsf{hk}$ until it outputs a message

$$\left(\{\mathsf{cm}_i\}_{i \in [\ell]}, \{v_i, x_i, h_i, r_i\}_{i \in T}, \{\widehat{\mathsf{cm}}_{i,0}, \widehat{\mathsf{cm}}_{i,1}, z_{i,0}, z_{i,1}\}_{i \in \overline{T}}, \pi, \tilde{m}_0, \tilde{m}_1\right)$$

and a state on register $\mathcal{A}'$.

- Run Steps 1–3 of the Receiver's honest computation on the sender's message.
- Attempt to project registers $\{\mathcal{R}_i\}_{i \in \overline{T}}$ onto

$$\bigotimes_{i \in \overline{T}} \Pi[\mathsf{ck}, \widehat{\mathsf{cm}}_{i,0}, z_{i,0}, z_{i,1}]^{\mathcal{R}_i},$$

and abort if the projection fails.
- For each $i \in \overline{T}, b \in \{0,1\}$, compute $t_{i,b} \leftarrow \mathsf{Ext}(\mathsf{ek}, \widehat{\mathsf{cm}}_{i,b})$. Abort if any $t_{i,b} = \perp$ or if there does not exist Δ such that $t_{i,1} = \Delta \oplus t_{i,0}$ for all $i \in \overline{T}$.
- If there was an abort, output $(\mathcal{A}', \perp)$. Otherwise, sample $b \leftarrow \{0,1\}$. Then, define

$$m_0 := \bigoplus_{i \in \overline{T}} t_{i,0}, \quad m_1 := \tilde{m}_1 \oplus \Delta \oplus \bigoplus_{i \in \overline{T}} t_{i,0},$$

and output $(\mathcal{A}', (b, m_b))$.

$\mathcal{H}_9(\mathcal{A})/\mathsf{Sim}(\mathcal{A})$

- Prepare ℓ collections of EPR pairs on registers $\{\mathcal{S}_i, \mathcal{R}_i\}_{i \in [\ell]}$, and sample $(\mathsf{ck}, \mathsf{ek}) \leftarrow \mathsf{ExtGen}(1^\lambda)$, $\mathsf{crs} \leftarrow \{0,1\}^n$, and $\mathsf{hk} \leftarrow \{0,1\}^k$.
- Run Adv_λ on input $\mathcal{A}, \{\mathcal{S}_i\}_{i \in [\ell]}, \mathsf{ck}, \mathsf{crs}, \mathsf{hk}$ until it outputs a message

$$(\{\mathsf{cm}_i\}_{i \in [\ell]}, \{v_i, x_i, h_i, r_i\}_{i \in T}, \{\widehat{\mathsf{cm}}_{i,0}, \widehat{\mathsf{cm}}_{i,1}, z_{i,0}, z_{i,1}\}_{i \in \overline{T}}, \pi, \tilde{m}_0, \tilde{m}_1)$$

and a state on register $\mathcal{A}'$.
- Run Steps 1–3 of the Receiver's honest computation on the sender's message.
- Attempt to project registers $\{\mathcal{R}_i\}_{i \in \overline{T}}$ onto

$$\bigotimes_{i \in \overline{T}} \Pi[\mathsf{ck}, \widehat{\mathsf{cm}}_{i,0}, z_{i,0}, z_{i,1}]^{\mathcal{R}_i},$$

and abort if the projection fails.
- For each $i \in \overline{T}, b \in \{0,1\}$, compute $t_{i,b} \leftarrow \mathsf{Ext}(\mathsf{ek}, \widehat{\mathsf{cm}}_{i,b})$. Abort if any $t_{i,b} = \perp$ or if there does not exist Δ such that $t_{i,1} = \Delta \oplus t_{i,0}$ for all $i \in \overline{T}$.
- If there was an abort, send $\perp$ to the ideal functionality, and output $\mathcal{A}'$. Otherwise, define

$$m_0 := \bigoplus_{i \in \overline{T}} t_{i,0}, \quad m_1 := \tilde{m}_1 \oplus \Delta \oplus \bigoplus_{i \in \overline{T}} t_{i,0},$$

send (m_0, m_1) to the ideal functionality, and output $\mathcal{A}'$.

Observe that $\mathcal{H}_9(\mathcal{A})$ describes the behavior of a simulator Sim that operates on input register $\mathcal{A}$, and interacts with the ideal functionality $\mathcal{F}_{\mathsf{ROT}}$. Thus, The following sequence of claims completes the proof.

Claim 8. $\mathcal{H}_0 \approx_c \mathcal{H}_1$.

Proof. This follows directly from the extractability of the commitment. □

Claim 9. $\mathcal{H}_1 \equiv \mathcal{H}_2$.

Proof. The only difference is that we have applied the Step 4 check coherently before measuring in the standard basis. Since these measurements commute, these hybrids describe the same distribution. □

Claim 10. $\mathcal{H}_2 \approx_s \mathcal{H}_3$.

Proof. The newly introduced abort condition will only be triggered with negligible probability due to the soundness of the NIZK and the extractability of the commitment. □

Claim 11. $\mathcal{H}_3 \approx_s \mathcal{H}_4$.

Proof. We are now defining m_0, m_1 based on the strings extracted by Ext rather than the strings measured by the Receiver. Since the strings measured by the Receiver must be valid commitment openings, this only introduces a negligible difference due to the extractability of the commitment. □

Claim 12. $\mathcal{H}_4 \approx_s \mathcal{H}_5$.

Proof. By Gentle Measurement (Lemma 1), it suffices to argue that the projection introduced in $\mathcal{H}_5$ will succeed with probability $1 - \mathsf{negl}(\lambda)$. So towards contradiction, assume that the projection fails with non-negligible probability. We will eventually use this assumption to break the correlation intractability of H. First, consider the following experiment.

$\underline{\mathsf{Exp}_1}$

- Prepare ℓ collections of EPR pairs on registers $\{\mathcal{S}_i, \mathcal{R}_i\}_{i \in [\ell]}$. Sample $(\mathsf{ck}, \mathsf{ek}) \leftarrow \mathsf{ExtGen}(1^\lambda)$, $\mathsf{crs} \leftarrow \{0,1\}^n$, and $\mathsf{hk} \leftarrow \{0,1\}^k$.
- Run Adv_λ on input $\mathcal{A}, \{\mathcal{S}_i\}_{i \in [\ell]}, \mathsf{ck}, \mathsf{crs}, \mathsf{hk}$, and receive a message that includes $\{\mathsf{cm}_i\}_{i \in [\ell]}, \{\widehat{\mathsf{cm}}_{i,0}, \widehat{\mathsf{cm}}_{i,1}\}_{i \in \overline{T}}, \pi$.
- Compute $T = H_\lambda(\mathsf{hk}, (\mathsf{cm}_1, \ldots, \mathsf{cm}_\ell))$, check that for all $i \in T$, $\mathsf{cm}_i = \mathsf{Com}(\mathsf{ck}, (v_i, x_i, h_i); r_i)$, and that $\mathsf{NIZK.Ver}\left(\mathsf{crs}, (\{\widehat{\mathsf{cm}}_{i,0}, \widehat{\mathsf{cm}}_{i,1}\}_{i \in \overline{T}}, \{\mathsf{cm}_i\}_{i \in [\ell]}), \pi\right) = \top$, and abort if not.
- For each $i \in [\ell]$, compute $(v_i, x_i, h_i) \leftarrow \mathsf{Ext}(\mathsf{ek}, \mathsf{cm}_i)$, and abort if any are $\bot$.
- For each $i \in [\ell]$, measure registers $\mathcal{R}_i$ in the basis $\{|\psi_{v_i, x_i, h_i}\rangle\langle\psi_{v_i, x_i, h_i}|, \mathbb{I} - |\psi_{v_i, x_i, h_i}\rangle\langle\psi_{v_i, x_i, h_i}|\}$ and define the bit $e_i = 0$ if the first outcome is observed and $e_i = 1$ if the second outcome is observed.
- Output 1 if (i) there exists an $s \in \{0,1\}^\lambda$ such that $(x_1, \ldots, x_\ell) = \mathsf{PRG}(s)$,[12] (ii) $e_i = 0$ for all $i \in T$, and (iii) $e_i = 1$ for at least $1/30$ fraction of $i : i \in \overline{T}$.

---

[12] Note that this step is not efficient to implement, but this will not be important for our arguments.

We claim that $\Pr[\mathsf{Exp}_1 \to 1] = \mathsf{non\text{-}negl}(\lambda)$. This nearly follows from the assumption that the measurement introduced in $\mathcal{H}_5$ rejects with non-negligible probability, except for the following two differences. One difference from $\mathcal{H}_3$ is that in Exp_1, we are using $\{(v_i, x_i, h_i)\}_{i \in T}$ extracted from $\{\mathsf{cm}_i\}_{i \in T}$ to measure registers $\{\mathcal{R}_i\}_{i \in T}$, rather than the strings sent by the adversary. However, this introduces a negligible difference due to the extractability of the commitment scheme. The other difference is that we require $(x_1, \ldots, x_\ell)$, which are extracted from $\{\mathsf{cm}_i\}_{i \in [\ell]}$, to be in the image of $\mathsf{PRG}(\cdot)$. However, by extractability of the commitment scheme and soundness of the NIZK, the probability that the procedure does not abort and this fails to occur is negligible. Next, consider the following experiment.

Exp_2

- Prepare ℓ collections of EPR pairs on registers $\{\mathcal{S}_i, \mathcal{R}_i\}_{i \in [\ell]}$. Sample $(\mathsf{ck}, \mathsf{ek}) \leftarrow \mathsf{ExtGen}(1^\lambda)$, $\mathsf{crs} \leftarrow \{0,1\}^n$, and $\mathsf{hk} \leftarrow \{0,1\}^k$.
- Sample $s^* \leftarrow \{0,1\}^\lambda$ and set $(x_1^*, \ldots, x_\ell^*) = \mathsf{PRG}(s^*)$. For each $i \in [\ell]$ and $j \in [2\lambda]$ such that $x_{i,j} = 1$, apply a CNOT gate from register $\mathcal{R}_i^{\mathsf{ctl}}$ to $\mathcal{R}_{i,j}^{\mathsf{msg}}$, then measure $\mathcal{R}_i^{\mathsf{ctl}}$ in the Hadamard basis to obtain h_i^* and measure $\mathcal{R}_{i,1}^{\mathsf{msg}}, \ldots, \mathcal{R}_{i,2\lambda}^{\mathsf{msg}}$ in the standard basis to obtain v_i^*.
- Run Adv_λ on input $\mathcal{A}, \{\mathcal{S}_i\}_{i \in [\ell]}, \mathsf{ck}, \mathsf{crs}, \mathsf{hk}$, and receive a message that includes $\{\mathsf{cm}_i\}_{i \in [\ell]}$.
- Compute $T = H_\lambda(\mathsf{hk}, (\mathsf{cm}_1, \ldots, \mathsf{cm}_\ell))$ and $(v_i, x_i, h_i) \leftarrow \mathsf{Ext}(\mathsf{ek}, \mathsf{cm}_i)$ for each $i \in [\ell]$.
- Output 1 if (i) $(x_1, \ldots, x_\ell) = (x_1^*, \ldots, x_\ell^*)$, (ii) $(v_i, h_i) = (v_i^*, h_i^*)$ for all $i \in T$, and (iii) $(v_i, h_i) \neq (v_i^*, h_i^*)$ for at least $1/30$ fraction of $i : i \in T$.

It follows that $\Pr[\mathsf{Exp}_2 \to 1] = \mathsf{non\text{-}negl}(\lambda)/2^\lambda > 1/2^{\lambda_{\mathsf{Cl}}^\delta}$, since the guess of s^* is uniformly random and independent of the adversary's view. Finally, we will show that Exp_2 can be used to break the correlation intractability of H, but first we introduce some notation.

- For each $(\mathsf{ek}, s^*, \{v_i^*, h_i^*\}_{i \in [\ell]})$, define the relation $R[\mathsf{ek}, s^*, \{v_i^*, h_i^*\}_{i \in [\ell]}]$ as follows. Recalling that $\ell = c \cdot t$, we will associate each $i \in [\ell]$ with a pair (ι, κ) for $\iota \in [t], \kappa \in [c]$. Also, for each set of strings $\{\mathsf{cm}_i\}_{i \in [\ell]}$, we fix $(v_i, x_i, h_i) := \mathsf{Ext}(\mathsf{ek}, \mathsf{cm}_i)$ for each $i \in [\ell]$. Then the domain will consist of strings $\{\mathsf{cm}_i\}_{i \in [\ell]}$ such that (i) $(x_1, \ldots, x_\ell) = \mathsf{PRG}(s^*)$, (ii) $|i : (v_i, h_i) = (v_i^*, h_i^*)| \leq (1 - 1/60)\ell$, and (iii) for each $\iota \in [t]$, $|\kappa : (v_{(\iota,\kappa)}, h_{(\iota,\kappa)}) = (v_{(\iota,\kappa)}^*, h_{(\iota,\kappa)}^*)| \geq (1/2)c$.
- For each $\{\mathsf{cm}_i\}_{i \in [\ell]}$ in the domain of $R[\mathsf{ek}, s^*, \{v_i^*, h_i^*\}_{i \in [\ell]}]$, define the sets $\{S_{\iota, \{\mathsf{cm}_i\}_{i \in [\ell]}}\}_{\iota \in [t]}$ as follows. If $(1/2)c \leq |\kappa : (v_{(\iota,\kappa)}, h_{(\iota,\kappa)}) = (v_{(\iota,\kappa)}^*, h_{(\iota,\kappa)}^*)| \leq (1 - 1/120)c$, let $S_{\iota, \{\mathsf{cm}_i\}_{i \in [\ell]}}$ consist of subsets $C \subset [c]$ of size $c/2$ such that for all $\kappa \in C$, $(v_{(\iota,\kappa)}, h_{(\iota,\kappa)}) = (v_{(\iota,\kappa)}^*, h_{(\iota,\kappa)}^*)$. Otherwise, let $S_{\iota, \{\mathsf{cm}_i\}_{i \in [\ell]}} = \emptyset$.
- Define the set $R[\mathsf{ek}, s^*, \{v_i^*, h_i^*\}_{i \in [\ell]}]_{\{\mathsf{cm}_i\}_{i \in [\ell]}}$ to consist of all $y = (C_1, \ldots, C_t)$ such that $C_\iota \in S_{\iota, \{\mathsf{cm}\}_{i \in [\ell]}}$ for all ι such that $S_{\iota, \{\mathsf{cm}_i\}_{i \in [\ell]}} \neq \emptyset$. We claim that there are always at least $1/120$ fraction of $\iota \in [t]$ such that $S_{\iota, \{\mathsf{cm}_i\}_{i \in [\ell]}} \neq \emptyset$. To see this, note that $S_{\iota, \{\mathsf{cm}_i\}_{i \in [\ell]}} \neq \emptyset$ iff $|\kappa : (v_{(\iota,\kappa)}, h_{(\iota,\kappa)}) \neq (v_{(\iota,\kappa)}^*, h_{(\iota,\kappa)}^*)| >$

$(1/120)c$. However, if less $1/120$ fraction of ι satisfies this condition, then the fraction of $i \in [\ell]$ such that $(v_i, h_i) \neq (v_i^*, h_i^*)$ is at most $(1/120) + (1/120)(1-1/120) < 1/60$, which would contradict the fact that $\{\mathsf{cm}_i\}_{i \in [\ell]}$ is in the domain of $R[\mathsf{ek}, s^*, \{v_i^*, h_i^*\}_{i \in [\ell]}]\{\mathsf{cm}_i\}_{i \in [\ell]}$.

Thus, $R[\mathsf{ek}, s^*, \{v_i^*, h_i^*\}_{i \in [\ell]}]$ is an α-approximate efficiently verifiable product relation for $\alpha = 1/120$ with sparsity $\rho = \binom{(1-\alpha)c}{(1/2)c}/2^c < \alpha$.

Now, whenever $\mathsf{Exp}_2 = 1$, it must be the case that $\{\mathsf{cm}_i\}_{i \in [\ell]}$ is in the domain of $R[\mathsf{ek}, s^*, \{v_i^*, h_i^*\}_{i \in [\ell]}]$, and $T \in R[\mathsf{ek}, s^*, \{v_i^*, h_i^*\}_{i \in [\ell]}]\{\mathsf{cm}_i\}_{i \in [\ell]}$. Thus, we can break correlation intractability as follows. Begin running Exp_2, but don't sample hk. Once ek, s^* are sampled and $\{v_i^*, h_i^*\}_{i \in [\ell]}$ are measured, declare the relation $R[\mathsf{ek}, s^*, \{v_i^*, h_i^*\}_{i \in [\ell]}]$. Then, receive hk from the correlation intractability challenger, continue running Exp_2 until $\{\mathsf{cm}_i\}_{i \in [\ell]}$ is obtained, and output this to the challenger. The above analysis shows that this breaks correlation intractability for the relation $R[\mathsf{ek}, s^*, \{v_i^*, h_i^*\}_{i \in [\ell]}]$.   □

Claim 13. $\mathcal{H}_5 \approx_s \mathcal{H}_6$.

Proof. By Gentle Measurement (Lemma 1), it suffices to show that the projection introduced in $\mathcal{H}_6$ will succeed with probability $1 - \mathsf{negl}(\lambda)$. To do so, we will rule out one bad case. For each $i \in \overline{T}$, define the bit $f_i = 0$ if and only if $\widehat{\mathsf{cm}}_{i,0} = \mathsf{Com}(\mathsf{ck}, t_{i,0}; r_{i,0})$ and $\widehat{\mathsf{cm}}_{i,1} = \mathsf{Com}(\mathsf{ck}, t_{i,1}; r_{i,1})$, where $(t_{i,0}, r_{i,0}) = z_{i,0} \oplus v_i$, $(t_{i,1}, r_{i,1}) = z_{i,1} \oplus v_i \oplus x_i$, and $(v_i, x_i, h_i) := \mathsf{Ext}(\mathsf{ek}, \mathsf{cm}_i)$. Now we claim that if the fraction of $i \in \overline{T}$ such that $f_i = 1$ is $\geq 1/2 - 1/30$, then the attempted projection onto

$$\bigotimes_{i \in \overline{T}} \Pi[\mathsf{ck}, \widehat{\mathsf{cm}}_{i,0}, z_{i,0}, z_{i,1}]^{\mathcal{R}_i}$$

performed during Step 4 of the receiver's computation would have failed with probability $1 - \mathsf{negl}(\lambda)$. To see this, consider any state $|\psi\rangle^{\{\mathcal{R}_i\}_{i \in [\ell]}, \mathcal{X}}$ in the image of $\Pi\left[1/30, \{(v_i, x_i, h_i)\}_{i \in \overline{T}}\right]$, where $\mathcal{X}$ is an arbitrary auxiliary register. Then, defining $\gamma = 1/30$, we write $|\psi\rangle$ as

$$|\psi\rangle := \sum_{e \in \{0,1\}^{|\overline{T}|} : \mathsf{hw}(e) < \gamma |\overline{T}|} \left(\bigotimes_{i : e_i = 0} |\psi_{v_i, x_i, h_i}\rangle^{\mathcal{R}_i} \right) \otimes |\psi_e\rangle^{\{\mathcal{R}_i\}_{i : e_i = 1}, \mathcal{X}},$$

where $|\psi_e\rangle$ is some unit vector that is orthogonal to $|\psi_{v_i,x_i,h_i}\rangle$ for all i such that $e_i = 1$. Then,

$$
\left\| \bigotimes_{i\in \overline{T}} \Pi[\mathsf{ck}, \widehat{\mathsf{cm}}_{i,0}, z_{i,0}, z_{i,1}] |\psi\rangle \right\|^2
$$

$$
\leq \left\| \sum_{e\in\{0,1\}^{|\overline{T}|}:\mathsf{hw}(e)<\gamma|\overline{T}|} \bigotimes_{i:e_i=0} \Pi[\mathsf{ck}, \widehat{\mathsf{cm}}_i, z_{i,0}, z_{i,1}] |\psi_{v_i,x_i,h_i}\rangle^{\mathcal{R}_i} \right\|^2
$$

$$
\leq \binom{|\overline{T}|}{\gamma|\overline{T}|} \sum_{e\in\{0,1\}^{|\overline{T}|}:\mathsf{hw}(e)<\gamma|\overline{T}|} \left\| \bigotimes_{i:e_i=0} \Pi[\mathsf{ck}, \widehat{\mathsf{cm}}_i, z_{i,0}, z_{i,1}] |\psi_{v_i,x_i,h_i}\rangle^{\mathcal{R}_i} \right\|^2
$$

$$
\leq \binom{|\overline{T}|}{\gamma|\overline{T}|}^2 \cdot 2^{-(1/2-2\gamma)|\overline{T}|} \leq (3/\gamma)^{2\gamma|\overline{T}|} \cdot 2^{-(1/2-2\gamma)|\overline{T}|}
$$

$$
= 2^{|\overline{T}|(2\gamma\log(3/\gamma)-(1/2-2\gamma))} = \mathsf{negl}(\lambda)
$$

where the second inequality is Cauchy-Schwartz, the third inequality follow from the fact that there are at least $1/2 - 2\gamma$ fraction of indices where $f_i = 1$ and $e_i = 0$, and the final equality follows because $\gamma = 1/30$ is such that $2\gamma\log(3/\gamma) - (1/2 - 2\gamma) = O(1)$ and $|\overline{T}| = \ell/2 = \Omega(\lambda)$, so the exponent is $\Omega(\lambda)$.

Thus it suffices to consider the case where the fraction of $i \in \overline{T}$ such that $f_i = 1$ is $< 1/2 - 1/30$. So consider any state $|\psi\rangle^{\{\mathcal{R}_i\}_{i\in[\ell]},\mathcal{X}}$ in the image of $\Pi\left[1/30, \{(v_i, x_i, h_i)\}_{i\in\overline{T}}\right]$, which we can write as

$$
|\psi\rangle := \sum_{e\in\{0,1\}^{|\overline{T}|}:\mathsf{hw}(e)<|\overline{T}|/30} \left(\bigotimes_{i:e_i=0} |\psi_{v_i,x_i,h_i}\rangle^{\mathcal{R}_i} \right) \otimes |\psi_e\rangle^{\{\mathcal{R}_i\}_{i:e_i=1},\mathcal{X}}.
$$

Then,

$$
\Pi[\mathsf{ck}, \widehat{\mathsf{cm}}_{i,0}, z_{i,0}, z_{i,1}] |\psi\rangle
$$

$$
= \sum_{e\in\{0,1\}^{|\overline{T}|}:\mathsf{hw}(e)<|\overline{T}|/30} \left(\bigotimes_{i:e_i=0\wedge f_i=0} \Pi[\mathsf{ck}, \widehat{\mathsf{cm}}_{i,0}, z_{i,0}, z_{i,1}] |\psi_{v_i,x_i,h_i}\rangle \right)
$$

$$
\otimes \left(\bigotimes_{i:e_i=1\vee f_i=1} \Pi[\mathsf{ck}, \widehat{\mathsf{cm}}_{i,0}, z_{i,0}, z_{i,1}] \right) |\psi_e\rangle
$$

$$
= \sum_{e\in\{0,1\}^{|\overline{T}|}:\mathsf{hw}(e)<|\overline{T}|/30} \left(\bigotimes_{i:e_i=0\wedge f_i=0} |\psi_{v_i,x_i,h_i}\rangle \right) \otimes \left(\bigotimes_{i:e_i=1\vee f_i=1} \Pi[\mathsf{ck}, \widehat{\mathsf{cm}}_{i,0}, z_{i,0}, z_{i,1}] \right) |\psi_e\rangle
$$

$$
= \sum_{e'\in\{0,1\}^{|\overline{T}|}:\mathsf{hw}(e')<|\overline{T}|/2} \left(\bigotimes_{i:e_i'=0} |\psi_{v_i,x_i,h_i}\rangle \right) \otimes |\psi_{e'}\rangle
$$

$$
\in \mathsf{Im}\left(\Pi\left[1/2, \{(v_i, x_i, h_i)\}_{i\in\overline{T}}\right] \right),
$$

where the $|\psi_{e'}\rangle$ are some set of unit vectors. $\square$

Claim 14. $\mathcal{H}_6 \equiv \mathcal{H}_7$.

Proof. It suffices to show that in $\mathcal{H}_6$, the bit $b = \bigoplus_{i \in \overline{T}} b_i$ sampled by measuring registers $\{\mathcal{R}_i^{\mathsf{ctl}}\}_{i \in \overline{T}}$ of $|\psi\rangle^{\{\mathcal{R}_i\}_{i \in [\ell]}, \mathcal{X}}$ in the standard basis is uniformly random, even conditioned on the auxiliary register $\mathcal{X}$ (which includes the view of the adversarial sender). This follows from Theorem 6 by applying a change of basis. In more detail, define the unitary U_{v_i, x_i, h_i} to be applied to $\mathcal{R}_i$ as follows: For each $j \in [2\lambda]$ such that $x_{i,j} = 1$ apply a CNOT gate from $\mathcal{R}_{i,j}^{\mathsf{ctl}}$ to $\mathcal{R}_{i,j}^{\mathsf{msg}}$, then apply a classically controlled phase flip Z^{h_i} to $\mathcal{R}_i^{\mathsf{ctl}}$, and finally apply a Hadamard gate to $\mathcal{R}_i^{\mathsf{ctl}}$. In particular,

$$U_{v_i, x_i, h_i} |\psi_{v_i, x_i, h_i}\rangle = |0\rangle |v_i\rangle .$$

Thus, for any $|\psi\rangle \in \mathsf{Im}(\Pi\,[1/2, \{(v_i, x_i, h_i)\}_{i \in \overline{T}}])$, it holds that registers $\{\mathcal{R}_i^{\mathsf{ctl}}\}_{i \in \overline{T}}$ of $(\bigotimes_{i \in \overline{T}} U_{v_i, x_i, h_i}) |\psi\rangle$ are in a superposition of standard basis states with Hamming weight $< |\overline{T}|/2$. Since applying $U_{v_i, x_i, h_i}^\dagger$ to a standard basis measurement of $\mathcal{R}_i^{\mathsf{ctl}}$ yields a Hadamard basis measurement of $\mathcal{R}_i^{\mathsf{ctl}}$, Theorem 6 directly implies that the bit $b = \bigoplus_{i \in \overline{T}} b_i$ is uniformly random, even conditioned on the auxiliary register $\mathcal{X}$. $\qquad\square$

Claim 15. $\mathcal{H}_7 \approx_s \mathcal{H}_8$.

Proof. We are removing the two measurements introduced in hybrids $\mathcal{H}_5$ and $\mathcal{H}_6$, and indistinguishability follows from the same arguments used in the corresponding claims 12 and 13. $\qquad\square$

Claim 16. $\mathcal{H}_8 \equiv \mathcal{H}_9$.

Proof. This is just a syntactic switch, routing information through the ideal functionality $\mathcal{F}_{\mathsf{ROT}}$. $\qquad\square$

Acknowledgments. D. Khurana was supported in part by NSF CAREER CNS-2238718 and NSF CNS-2247727, DARPA SIEVE. This material is based upon work supported by the Defense Advanced Research Projects Agency through Award HR00112020024. A. Srinivasan is supported in part by a SERB startup grant and Google India Research Award.

References

1. Aaronson, S.: The complexity of quantum states and transformations: from quantum money to black holes (2016)
2. Agarwal, A., Bartusek, J., Khurana, D., Kumar, N.: A new framework for quantum oblivious transfer. In: Hazay, C., Stam, M. (eds.) Advances in Cryptology – EUROCRYPT 2023. EUROCRYPT 2023. LNCS, vol. 14004, pp. 363–393. Springer, Cham (2023). https://doi.org/10.1007/978-3-031-30545-0_13

3. Agarwal, S., Kitagawa, F., Nishimaki, R., Yamada, S., Yamakawa, T.: Public key encryption with secure key leasing. In: Hazay, C., Stam, M. (eds.) Advances in Cryptology – EUROCRYPT 2023. EUROCRYPT 2023. LNCS, vol. 14004, pp. 581–610. Springer, Cham (2023). https://doi.org/10.1007/978-3-031-30545-0_20
4. Agrawal, S., et al.: Cryptography from one-way communication: on completeness of finite channels. In: Moriai, S., Wang, H. (eds.) ASIACRYPT 2020. LNCS, vol. 12493, pp. 653–685. Springer, Cham (2020). https://doi.org/10.1007/978-3-030-64840-4_22
5. Agrawal, S., et al.: Secure computation from one-way noisy communication, or: anti-correlation via anti-concentration. In: Malkin, T., Peikert, C. (eds.) CRYPTO 2021. LNCS, vol. 12826, pp. 124–154. Springer, Cham (2021). https://doi.org/10.1007/978-3-030-84245-1_5
6. Ananth, P., Poremba, A., Vaikuntanathan, V.: Revocable cryptography from learning with errors. Cryptology ePrint Archive, Paper 2023/325 (2023). https://eprint.iacr.org/2023/325
7. Ananth, P., Qian, L., Yuen, H.: Cryptography from pseudorandom quantum states. In: Dodis, Y., Shrimpton, T. (eds.) Advances in Cryptology - CRYPTO 2022–42nd Annual International Cryptology Conference, CRYPTO 2022, Santa Barbara, CA, USA, 15–18 August 2022, Proceedings, Part I. LNCS, vol. 13507, pp. 208–236. Springer, Cham (2022). https://doi.org/10.1007/978-3-031-15802-5_8
8. Bartusek, J., Coladangelo, A., Khurana, D., Ma, F.: On the round complexity of secure quantum computation. In: Malkin, T., Peikert, C. (eds.) CRYPTO 2021. LNCS, vol. 12825, pp. 406–435. Springer, Cham (2021). https://doi.org/10.1007/978-3-030-84242-0_15
9. Bartusek, J., Coladangelo, A., Khurana, D., Ma, F.: One-way functions imply secure computation in a quantum world. In: Malkin, T., Peikert, C. (eds.) CRYPTO 2021. LNCS, vol. 12825, pp. 467–496. Springer, Cham (2021). https://doi.org/10.1007/978-3-030-84242-0_17
10. Bartusek, J.: Obfuscation and outsourced computation with certified deletion. Cryptology ePrint Archive, Paper 2023/265 (2023). https://eprint.iacr.org/2023/265
11. Bartusek, J., Khurana, D., Srinivasan, A.: Secure computation with shared EPR pairs (or: How to teleport in zero-knowledge). Cryptology ePrint Archive, Paper 2023/564 (2023). https://eprint.iacr.org/2023/564
12. Bartusek, J., Malavolta, G.: Indistinguishability obfuscation of null quantum circuits and applications. In: Braverman, M. (ed.) 13th Innovations in Theoretical Computer Science Conference, ITCS 2022, 31 January–3 February 2022, Berkeley, CA, USA. LIPIcs, vol. 215, pp. 15:1–15:13. Schloss Dagstuhl - Leibniz-Zentrum für Informatik (2022)
13. Benhamouda, F., Lin, H.: k-round multiparty computation from k-round oblivious transfer via garbled interactive circuits. In: Nielsen, J.B., Rijmen, V. (eds.) EUROCRYPT 2018. LNCS, vol. 10821, pp. 500–532. Springer, Cham (2018). https://doi.org/10.1007/978-3-319-78375-8_17
14. Bennett, C.H., Brassard, G.: Quantum cryptography: public key distribution and coin tossing. In: Proceedings of the IEEE International Conference on Computers, Systems, and Signal Processing, pp. 175–179 (1984)
15. Bennett, C.H., Brassard, G., Crépeau, C., Jozsa, R., Peres, A., Wootters, W.K.: Teleporting an unknown quantum state via dual classical and Einstein-Podolsky-Rosen channels. Phys. Rev. Lett. **70**, 1895–1899 (1993)
16. Bennett, C.H., Wiesner, S.J.: Communication via one- and two-particle operators on Einstein-Podolsky-Rosen states. Phys. Rev. Lett. **69**, 2881–2884 (1992)

17. Bouman, N.J., Fehr, S.: Sampling in a quantum population, and applications. In: Rabin, T. (ed.) CRYPTO 2010. LNCS, vol. 6223, pp. 724–741. Springer, Heidelberg (2010). https://doi.org/10.1007/978-3-642-14623-7_39
18. Brakerski, Z., Koppula, V., Mour, T.: NIZK from LPN and Trapdoor Hash via correlation intractability for approximable relations. In: Micciancio, D., Ristenpart, T. (eds.) CRYPTO 2020. LNCS, vol. 12172, pp. 738–767. Springer, Cham (2020). https://doi.org/10.1007/978-3-030-56877-1_26
19. Brakerski, Z., Yuen, H.: Quantum garbled circuits. In: Proceedings of the 54th Annual ACM SIGACT Symposium on Theory of Computing, STOC 2022, pp. 804–817. Association for Computing Machinery, New York (2022)
20. Brun, T., Devetak, I., Hsieh, M.-H.: Correcting quantum errors with entanglement. Science (New York, N.Y.) **314**, 436–439 (2006)
21. Canetti, R.: Fiat-Shamir: from practice to theory. In: Proceedings of the 51st Annual ACM SIGACT Symposium on Theory of Computing, STOC 2019, pp. 1082–1090. Association for Computing Machinery, New York (2019)
22. Canetti, R., Goldreich, O., Halevi, S.: The random oracle methodology, revisited. J. ACM **51**(4), 557–594 (2004)
23. Choudhuri, A.R., Garg, S., Jain, A., Jin, Z., Zhang, J.: Correlation intractability and SNARGs from sub-exponential DDH (2022). https://eprint.iacr.org/2022/1486
24. Choudhuri, A.R., Jain, A., Jin, Z.: Non-interactive batch arguments for NP from standard assumptions. IACR Cryptol. ePrint Arch., 2021:807 (2021)
25. Choudhuri, A.R., Jain, A., Jin, Z.: SNARGs for P from LWE. IACR Cryptol. ePrint Arch., p. 808 (2021)
26. Coladangelo, A., Liu, J., Liu, Q., Zhandry, M.: Hidden Cosets and applications to unclonable cryptography. In: Malkin, T., Peikert, C. (eds.) CRYPTO 2021. LNCS, vol. 12825, pp. 556–584. Springer, Cham (2021). https://doi.org/10.1007/978-3-030-84242-0_20
27. Colisson, L., Muguruza, G., Speelman, F.: Oblivious transfer from zero-knowledge proofs, or how to achieve round-optimal quantum oblivious transfer and zero-knowledge proofs on quantum states (2023)
28. Crépeau, C., Kilian, J.: Achieving oblivious transfer using weakened security assumptions (extended abstract). In: 29th FOCS, pp. 42–52. IEEE Computer Society Press, October 1988
29. Crépeau, C., van de Graaf, J., Tapp, A.: Committed oblivious transfer and private multi-party computation. In: Coppersmith, D. (ed.) CRYPTO 1995. LNCS, vol. 963, pp. 110–123. Springer, Heidelberg (1995). https://doi.org/10.1007/3-540-44750-4_9
30. Don, J., Fehr, S., Majenz, C., Schaffner, C.: Security of the Fiat-Shamir transformation in the quantum random-oracle model. In: Boldyreva, A., Micciancio, D. (eds.) CRYPTO 2019. LNCS, vol. 11693, pp. 356–383. Springer, Cham (2019). https://doi.org/10.1007/978-3-030-26951-7_13
31. Dupuis, F., Lamontagne, P., Salvail, L.: Fiat-Shamir for proofs lacks a proof even in the presence of shared entanglement (2022)
32. Einstein, A., Podolsky, B., Rosen, N.: Can quantum-mechanical description of physical reality be considered complete? Phys. Rev. **47**, 777–780 (1935)
33. Ekert, A.K.: Quantum cryptography based on Bell's theorem. Phys. Rev. Lett. **67**, 661–663 (1991)

34. Garg, S., Ishai, Y., Kushilevitz, E., Ostrovsky, R., Sahai, A.: Cryptography with one-way communication. In: Gennaro, R., Robshaw, M. (eds.) CRYPTO 2015. LNCS, vol. 9216, pp. 191–208. Springer, Heidelberg (2015). https://doi.org/10.1007/978-3-662-48000-7_10
35. Garg, S., Ishai, Y., Srinivasan, A.: Two-round MPC: information-theoretic and black-box. In: Beimel, A., Dziembowski, S. (eds.) TCC 2018. LNCS, vol. 11239, pp. 123–151. Springer, Cham (2018). https://doi.org/10.1007/978-3-030-03807-6_5
36. Garg, S., Srinivasan, A.: Two-round multiparty secure computation from minimal assumptions. In: Nielsen, J.B., Rijmen, V. (eds.) EUROCRYPT 2018. LNCS, vol. 10821, pp. 468–499. Springer, Cham (2018). https://doi.org/10.1007/978-3-319-78375-8_16
37. Georgiou, M., Zhandry, M.: Unclonable decryption keys. Cryptology ePrint Archive, Paper 2020/877 (2020). https://eprint.iacr.org/2020/877
38. Grilo, A.B., Lin, H., Song, F., Vaikuntanathan, V.: Oblivious transfer is in MiniQCrypt. In: Canteaut, A., Standaert, F.-X. (eds.) EUROCRYPT 2021. LNCS, vol. 12697, pp. 531–561. Springer, Cham (2021). https://doi.org/10.1007/978-3-030-77886-6_18
39. Halevi, S., Lindell, Y., Pinkas, B.: Secure computation on the web: computing without simultaneous interaction. In: Rogaway, P. (ed.) CRYPTO 2011. LNCS, vol. 6841, pp. 132–150. Springer, Heidelberg (2011). https://doi.org/10.1007/978-3-642-22792-9_8
40. Holmgren, J., Lombardi, A., Rothblum, R.D.: Fiat-Shamir via list-recoverable codes (or: Parallel repetition of GMW is not zero-knowledge). In: Proceedings of the 53rd Annual ACM SIGACT Symposium on Theory of Computing, STOC 2021, pp. 750–760. Association for Computing Machinery, New York (2021)
41. Hulett, J., Jawale, R., Khurana, D., Srinivasan, A.: SNARGs for P from sub-exponential DDH and QR. In: Dunkelman, O., Dziembowski, S. (eds.) Advances in Cryptology - EUROCRYPT 2022–41st Annual International Conference on the Theory and Applications of Cryptographic Techniques, Trondheim, Norway, 30 May–3 June 2022, Proceedings, Part II, LNCS, vol. 13276, pp. 520–549. Springer, Cham (2022). https://doi.org/10.1007/978-3-031-07085-3_18
42. Impagliazzo, R., Rudich, S.: Limits on the provable consequences of one-way permutations. In: Goldwasser, S. (ed.) CRYPTO 1988. LNCS, vol. 403, pp. 8–26. Springer, New York (1990). https://doi.org/10.1007/0-387-34799-2_2
43. Irani, S., Natarajan, A., Nirkhe, C., Rao, S., Yuen, H.: Quantum search-to-decision reductions and the state synthesis problem. In: Proceedings of the 37th Computational Complexity Conference, CCC 2022, Dagstuhl, DEU 2022. Schloss Dagstuhl-Leibniz-Zentrum fuer Informatik (2022)
44. Ishai, Y., Prabhakaran, M., Sahai, A.: Founding cryptography on oblivious transfer – efficiently. In: Wagner, D. (ed.) CRYPTO 2008. LNCS, vol. 5157, pp. 572–591. Springer, Heidelberg (2008). https://doi.org/10.1007/978-3-540-85174-5_32
45. Jain, A., Jin, Z.: Non-interactive Zero Knowledge from Sub-exponential DDH. In: Canteaut, A., Standaert, F.-X. (eds.) EUROCRYPT 2021. LNCS, vol. 12696, pp. 3–32. Springer, Cham (2021). https://doi.org/10.1007/978-3-030-77870-5_1
46. Jawale, R., Kalai, Y.T., Khurana, D., Zhang, R.: SNARGs for bounded depth computations and PPAD hardness from sub-exponential LWE. In: Khuller, S., Williams, V.V. (eds.) STOC 2021: 53rd Annual ACM SIGACT Symposium on Theory of Computing, Virtual Event, Italy, 21–25 June 2021, pp. 708–721. ACM (2021)

47. Ji, Z., Liu, Y.-K., Song, F.: Pseudorandom quantum states. In: Shacham, H., Boldyreva, A. (eds.) CRYPTO 2018. LNCS, vol. 10993, pp. 126–152. Springer, Cham (2018). https://doi.org/10.1007/978-3-319-96878-0_5

48. Kalai, Y., Lombardi, A., Vaikuntanathan, V.: SNARGs and PPAD hardness from the decisional Diffie-Hellman assumption. In: Hazay, C., Stam, M. (eds) Advances in Cryptology – EUROCRYPT 2023. EUROCRYPT 2023. LNCS, vol. 14005. Springer, Cham (2023). https://doi.org/10.1007/978-3-031-30617-4_16

49. Kalai, Y.T., Vaikuntanathan, V., Zhang, R.Y.: Somewhere statistical soundness, post-quantum security, and SNARGs. Cryptology ePrint Archive, Report 2021/788 (2021). https://ia.cr/2021/788

50. Khurana, D., Ostrovsky, R., Srinivasan, A.: Round optimal black-box "Commit-and-Prove". In: Beimel, A., Dziembowski, S. (eds.) TCC 2018. LNCS, vol. 11239, pp. 286–313. Springer, Cham (2018). https://doi.org/10.1007/978-3-030-03807-6_11

51. Kobayashi, H.: Non-interactive quantum perfect and statistical zero-knowledge. In: Ibaraki, T., Katoh, N., Ono, H. (eds.) ISAAC 2003. LNCS, vol. 2906, pp. 178–188. Springer, Heidelberg (2003). https://doi.org/10.1007/978-3-540-24587-2_20

52. Morimae, T., Yamakawa, T.: Classically verifiable NIZK for QMA with preprocessing. In: Agrawal, S., Lin, D. (eds.) Advances in Cryptology - ASIACRYPT 2022, pp. 599–627. Springer, Cham (2022). https://doi.org/10.1007/978-3-031-22972-5_21

53. Morimae, T., Yamakawa, T.: One-Wayness in quantum cryptography. CoRR, abs/2210.03394 (2022)

54. Peikert, C., Shiehian, S.: Noninteractive zero knowledge for NP from (plain) learning with errors. In: Boldyreva, A., Micciancio, D. (eds.) CRYPTO 2019. LNCS, vol. 11692, pp. 89–114. Springer, Cham (2019). https://doi.org/10.1007/978-3-030-26948-7_4

55. Rosenthal, G., Yuen, H.S.: Interactive proofs for synthesizing quantum states and unitaries. In: ITCS (2022)

56. Winter, A.J.: Coding theorem and strong converse for quantum channels. IEEE Trans. Inf. Theory **45**(7), 2481–2485 (1999)

Quantum Linear Key-Recovery Attacks Using the QFT

André Schrottenloher[✉][iD]

Univ Rennes, Inria, CNRS, IRISA, Rennes, France
andre.schrottenloher@inria.fr

Abstract. The Quantum Fourier Transform is a fundamental tool in quantum cryptanalysis. In symmetric cryptanalysis, hidden shift algorithms such as Simon's, which rely on the QFT, have been used to obtain structural attacks on some very specific block ciphers. The Fourier Transform is also used in classical cryptanalysis, for example in FFT-based linear key-recovery attacks introduced by Collard et al. (ICISC 2007). Whether such techniques can be adapted to the quantum setting has remained so far an open question.

In this paper, we introduce a new framework for quantum linear key-recovery attacks using the QFT. These attacks loosely follow the classical method of Collard et al., in that they rely on the fast computation of a *correlation state* in which experimental correlations, rather than being directly accessible, are encoded in the amplitudes of a quantum state. The experimental correlation is a statistic that is expected to be higher for the good key, and on some conditions, the increased amplitude creates a speedup with respect to an exhaustive search of the key. The same method also yields a new family of structural attacks, and new examples of quantum speedups beyond quadratic using classical known-plaintext queries.

Keywords: Linear cryptanalysis · Quantum cryptanalysis · Fast Walsh-Hadamard Transform · Quantum Fourier Transform

1 Introduction

Quantum cryptanalysis can be said to have started with Shor's algorithm [49], which showed that cryptosystems based on the hardness of factoring and computing discrete logarithms, which are secure classically, could be broken using a quantum computer. While Shor's algorithm provides an exponential speedup, at the other end of the spectrum, Grover's quantum search algorithm [25] provides a quadratic acceleration for NP problems, which is optimal for black-box search [4]. Asymptotically, it halves the level of security for key-recovery provided by all ciphers.

Since then, many quantum algorithms have been designed and applied in cryptanalysis. In symmetric cryptanalysis, which is the main focus of this paper, they can be classified in two ways.

© International Association for Cryptologic Research 2023
H. Handschuh and A. Lysyanskaya (Eds.): CRYPTO 2023, LNCS 14085, pp. 258–291, 2023.
https://doi.org/10.1007/978-3-031-38554-4_9

Q1/Q2. Following a widely used terminology [29,30,34,35], Q1 adversaries are those which are capable of *offline* quantum computations, but only work from *classical* data. This is the most commonly used threat model in post-quantum cryptography, underlying the ongoing standardization process organized by NIST [45]. In contrast, Q2 adversaries are capable of *quantum access* to oracles holding secret data (e.g., encryption, decryption, signing). It is known since Kuwakado and Morii [39] that some symmetric cryptosystems are especially vulnerable to Q2 adversaries, while remaining secure against Q1 ones. For example, the Even-Mansour cipher is broken in Q2 [40] and secure in Q1 [2]. All Q2 breaks known to date rely on structure-finding algorithms: Simon's [50], Shor's, Kuperberg's [38], Bernstein-Vazirani [5], Deutsch-Josza [21].

Below Quadratic/Above Quadratic. Starting from Grover's algorithm, one can build a family of *nested search* algorithms which reach at most a quadratic speedup. Most dedicated quantum attacks on symmetric cryptosystems so far belong to this family, with the notable exception of quantum slide attacks [34]. Notably, this category includes some Q2 attacks [35], collision attacks on hash functions [31] and a wide range of key-recovery techniques [12,20,24].

Better speedups than quadratic do not necessarily require Q2 queries, but all such attacks to date use the Quantum Fourier Transform in one way or another, usually a subcomponent of a structure-finding algorithm (Simon, Shor, *etc.*). The offline-Simon algorithm of Bonnetain et al. [11] was shown to reach a Q1 speedup of 2.5 for key-recovery on some block cipher constructions [13], i.e., from $\mathcal{O}(2^{2.5n})$ to $\widetilde{\mathcal{O}}(2^n)$. Yamakawa and Zhandry achieved a more fundamental separation result [53]. They demonstrated that under a random oracle assumption, one can build a classically secure one-way function, which is quantumly invertible. That is, Q1 exponential speedups on various primitives (hash functions, block ciphers) are theoretically possible. However this separation has not been converted into an attack on practical constructions. Recently, Hosoyamada [29] achieved a (Q2) quantum speedup beyond quadratic on some types of integral distinguishers. His attack relies on a modified subroutine of Simon's algorithm and can be seen, like ours, as a *statistical* attack using the QFT.

Motivation and Contribution. The classical (fast) Fourier Transform is also a major tool of classical cryptanalysis. In particular, since the work of Collard et al. [16] it is used to speed up linear key-recovery attacks. It leads to the best attacks on well studied ciphers such as PRESENT [23], and several variants exist such as FFT-based zero correlation linear attacks [9].

In the quantum setting, it would seem natural to replace the FFT by the QFT, but this is not an easy task, and previous works on quantum linear attacks [29,35] left it as an open problem.

In this paper, we solve (partially) this question, and introduce a new way to use the QFT in quantum key-recovery attacks. Our framework applies to the setting introduced by Collard et al. However, it comes with various limitations, and does not necessarily reach the same number of rounds as classical attacks.

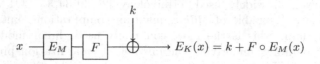

Fig. 1. Case considered by Collard et al. [16]. Under a guess of k, we have access to the middle rounds E_M (or a random permutation) and we compute the correlation of a linear approximation of E_M.

But it can also do more: we show a 2.5 speedup on a structural attack, in a case where the offline-Simon algorithm [11,13] seems inapplicable.

Main Feature: The Correlation State. In Fig. 1, we represent the situation considered by Collard et al. The cipher is divided into two parts: the middle rounds E_M and the last round F. A linear approximation (α, β) of E_M, with a large correlation, serves as a distinguisher which allows to find the subkey k.

More precisely, given a candidate z for this last subkey, we compose E_K with $F^{-1}(z + \cdot)$, and observe the correlation of the linear approximation (α, β), which we name the "experimental correlation" $\widehat{\text{cor}}(z)$. We defer the precise definition of $\widehat{\text{cor}}(z)$ to Sect. 2. All we need for the attack is to remark that, when $z = k$, the partial decryption of the last round gives us access to the middle rounds E_M. Due to the linear approximation of E_M, we will observe a larger correlation. When $z \neq k$, we only see a random permutation, and the experimental correlation is smaller.

One could evaluate each $\widehat{\text{cor}}(z)$ in time N for a total $\mathcal{O}(N \times 2^{|k|})$. However, Collard et al. showed how to evaluate all correlations in time $\widetilde{\mathcal{O}}(N + 2^{|k|})$ using a fast Walsh-Hadamard transform.

We aim to transfer this strategy to the quantum setting. Instead of computing experimental correlations individually, we will produce a *correlation state*:

$$|\text{Cor}\rangle := \frac{1}{\sqrt{\sum_z \widehat{\text{cor}}(z)^2}} \sum_z \widehat{\text{cor}}(z)|z\rangle \ .$$

Encoding correlations in the amplitude is also what Hosoyamada [29] did for quantum distinguishers. However, the quantum state that he constructed was a superposition of linear masks. We have a superposition of candidate keys instead, since we are targeting key-recovery attacks. In this context, the construction of $|\text{Cor}\rangle$ is more technical. It requires both the QFT and a *state preparation* technique, which is common in quantum algorithms. In fact, the principle is similar to [18], where the QFT is used to compute a *discrete convolution* of functions in the amplitudes of a quantum state.

From there, since the good subkey guess is expected to have a higher correlation, we use quantum amplitude amplification subroutines to complete the search for the key. This is the main limitation of our algorithm. Indeed, the speedup with respect to exhaustive search depends directly on the quality of the linear approximation (its *expected linear potential*, or ELP). This can be seen in the statement of our main theorem, given in Sect. 4:

Theorem 1. *In the situation of Fig. 1, let* $t = 1.005\sqrt{\mathrm{ELP}}2^{n/2}$, *where* ELP *is the ELP of the linear approximation* (α, β). *There exists a quantum algorithm that takes no input and returns (after measurement) the master key with probability* $\geq \frac{1}{2}$. *This algorithm has complexity:*

$$\frac{\pi^2}{8t}2^{|K|/2}r(E)\mathrm{Tof}\,(E) + \frac{\pi^2}{8t}2^{n/2}\mathrm{Tof}\,(\mathsf{CORCOMP}) \tag{1}$$

where $\mathrm{Tof}\,(E)$ *is the gate count of* E, $r(E)$ *the number of trial encryptions to test a key, and* $\mathrm{Tof}\,(\mathsf{CORCOMP})$ *is the gate count of computing the correlation state* $|\mathsf{Cor}\rangle$. *The attack succeeds with probability* 0.271.

Another limitation of this algorithm is that it queries the data in superposition. This means that our attacks will fall either in the Q2 setting, where we can directly query the block cipher, or in the model of *quantum-accessible classical memory*, where we make the queries classically and store them in a database with fast quantum access.

New Structural Attack. When the experimental correlation for the right key becomes really large, the cipher E_M basically degenerates into a linear function, and our algorithm becomes a structural attack. We observe that this attack is different from the offline-Simon algorithm [11]. While offline-Simon typically requires chosen-plaintext queries, classical known-plaintext queries are sufficient in our case. Indeed, we use the QFT to compute a *statistic* (the correlation) instead of recovering a hidden structure.

Outline. In Sect. 2 we give preliminaries of linear cryptanalysis, notably the statistical models of experimental correlations of right and wrong key guesses, which are essential for our framework. In Sect. 3 we give some preliminaries of quantum algorithms. Our new algorithm is introduced in Sect. 4 and extended to multiple linear cryptanalysis in Sect. 5. Our applications are given in Sect. 6. We conclude the paper with several open questions in Sect. 7.

2 Preliminaries on Linear Cryptanalysis

In this section we give preliminaries on classical linear cryptanalysis, linear distinguishers and key-recovery attacks. We also recall *quantum* linear attacks which were proposed in [35]. From now on, we use $\cdot$ to denote the scalar product of vectors in $\mathbb{F}_2^n$ and $+$ for addition modulo 2 of bit-strings (including single bits).

$$x \longrightarrow \boxed{E'_K} \boxed{F_k} \longrightarrow E_K(x) = F_k \circ E'_K(x)$$

Fig. 2. Case considered in Matsui's Algorithm 2.

2.1 Classical Linear Cryptanalysis

Linear cryptanalysis was introduced by Matsui [42] in order to attack the DES block cipher [43]. Let E_K be an n-bit block cipher instantiated with a given key K. A (keyless) *linear approximation* of E_K is a pair of n-bit *masks* $(\alpha, \beta) \in (\mathbb{F}_2^n)^2$. The *correlation* of this approximation is:

$$\mathrm{cor}_K(\alpha, \beta) := \frac{1}{2^n} \sum_{x \in \mathbb{F}_2^n} (-1)^{\alpha \cdot x + \beta \cdot E_K(x)} \ . \tag{2}$$

Linear cryptanalysis exploits approximations with a large correlation. Matsui proposed two algorithms, Algorithm 1 and Algorithm 2, to perform a key-recovery. We will focus here on Algorithm 2, which targets a block cipher of the form $E_K = F_k \circ E'_K$, where E'_K has a correlated linear approximation and F_k is a keyed permutation (e.g., the last round) in which only a subset of the master key K, denoted k, intervenes. This is represented in Fig. 2.

Algorithm 2 starts from a database D of N known plaintext-ciphertext pairs, and for each possible value z of k, it uses the database to compute the *experimental correlation*:

$$\widehat{\mathrm{cor}}(z) := \frac{1}{N} \sum_{(x,y) \in D} (-1)^{\alpha \cdot x + \beta \cdot F_z^{-1}(y)} \ . \tag{3}$$

Since it is a sum of N terms, this requires a total time $N \times 2^{|k|}$. The right key k is expected to be the one with the highest correlation (in absolute value). More generally, one keeps a certain proportion of subkeys having the largest correlations, and for each of these subkeys, one completes the key by exhaustive search.

ELP. As it can be seen in Eq. 2, the correlation is a key-dependent quantity. The quality of an approximation (α, β) is measured over all the keys, using the *expected linear potential* (ELP):

$$\mathrm{ELP}(\alpha, \beta) := \frac{1}{2^{|K|}} \sum_{K \in \mathbb{F}_2^{|K|}} \mathrm{cor}_K(\alpha, \beta)^2 \ . \tag{4}$$

Statistical models for the experimental correlation were first formalized for single linear approximations [10,17] and then extended [7,8] for multiple linear approximations. These models depend on a factor B: $B = 1$ if the plaintexts are chosen uniformly at random with repetition and $B = \frac{2^n - N}{2^n - 1}$ if they are distinct. In particular, if $N = 2^n$ (we know the whole codebook) we have $B = 0$. They also depend on whether the approximation has a *dominant trail*, or if it is a linear hull with many trails having a high correlation. In our applications, we focus on the second case. Here the experimental correlation for right and wrong keys follows normal distributions with different variances.

Assumption 1 (Right-key randomization hypothesis). The experimental correlation for the right subkey k ($\widehat{\mathrm{cor}}(k)$) is a random variable over k with normal distribution $\mathcal{N}(0, \sigma_R^2)$ where $\sigma_R^2 = \frac{B}{N} + \mathrm{ELP}$.

Assumption 2 (Wrong-key randomization hypothesis). Given a subkey k, the experimental correlation for wrong subkey guesses z ($\widehat{\mathrm{cor}}(z)$) is a random variable over z with normal distribution $\mathcal{N}(0, \sigma_W^2)$ where $\sigma_W^2 = \frac{B}{N} + 2^{-n}$.

If we want to keep only a proportion 2^{-a} of possible subkeys, we define a threshold $T = \sigma_W \Phi^{-1}(1 - 2^{-a-1})$, where Φ is the cumulative density function of $\mathcal{N}(0, 1)$. We will then keep all keys z with $|\widehat{\mathrm{cor}}(z)| \geq T$. This approach succeeds if the right key belongs indeed to this set, and the probability of this event is:

$$p := 2 - 2\Phi\left(\frac{\sigma_W}{\sigma_R}\Phi^{-1}(1 - 2^{-a-1})\right) .$$

Intuitively, for a constant a and p, we need σ_R to be bigger than σ_W by at least a constant factor, which gives that $N \times \mathrm{ELP}$ should be constant. So the data complexity of the attack is of order $N = \mathcal{O}(\mathrm{ELP}^{-1})$.

2.2 Multiple Linear Cryptanalysis

Linear cryptanalysis becomes more powerful when we can use *multiple* linear approximations α_i, β_i [33]. These approximations do not need to relate to the same key and state bits [6].

Consider M approximations. The correlation is replaced by the *capacity*:

$$C(K) = \sum_{i=1}^{M} \mathrm{cor}_K(\alpha_i, \beta_i)^2 . \tag{5}$$

The capacity is estimated by summing the correlations for representative families of trails for each approximation. If we can include all M approximations in this computation, we obtain an estimate C such that: $\mathrm{Exp}_K(C(K)) \simeq C + M2^{-n}$ and $\mathrm{Var}_K(C(K)) \simeq \frac{2}{M}C^2$ (Theorem 4.5 in [7]). The corresponding experimental statistic is:

$$\widehat{q}(z) = \sum_{i=1}^{M} \widehat{\mathrm{cor}}_i(z)^2 . \tag{6}$$

We use the results of [7] (Theorem 6) for the distributions of the statistics of the right and wrong key, which hold under an assumption of independence of the approximations.

Assumption 3 (Right-key randomization hypothesis, multiple). The statistic $\widehat{q}(k)$ for the right subkey k is a random variable over K following a normal distribution $\mathcal{N}(\mu_R, \sigma_R^2)$ where

$$\begin{cases} \mu_R = \frac{B}{N}M + \mathrm{Exp}_K(C(K)) \\ \sigma_R^2 = 2\frac{B^2}{N^2}M + 4\frac{B}{N}\mathrm{Exp}_K(C(K)) + \mathrm{Var}_K(C(K)) \ . \end{cases} \tag{7}$$

Assumption 4 (Wrong-key randomization hypothesis, multiple). Given a subkey k, the statistic $\widehat{q}(z)$ for wrong subkey guesses z follows a multiple of a χ^2 distribution with M degrees of freedom: $\frac{B+N2^{-n}}{N}\chi_M^2$, so with average and variance:

$$\begin{cases} \mu_W = M\left(\frac{B}{N} + 2^{-n}\right) \\ \sigma_W^2 = 2M\left(\frac{B}{N} + 2^{-n}\right)^2 \ . \end{cases} \tag{8}$$

With $B = 0$ and $N = 2^n$, these parameters are simplified into:

$$\begin{cases} \mu_R = \mathrm{Exp}_K(C(K)) \simeq C + M2^{-n}, \sigma_R^2 = \mathrm{Var}_K(C(K)) \simeq \frac{2}{M}C^2 \\ \mu_W = M2^{-n}, \sigma_W^2 = 2M2^{-2n} \ . \end{cases} \tag{9}$$

2.3   Advanced Key-Recovery Attacks and the FFT

Once the linear approximation has been chosen, we must find the best strategy to evaluate the experimental correlations $\widehat{\mathrm{cor}}(z)$ for all z and filter out the z exceeding a selected threshold. One can usually do better than the generic $N \times 2^{|k|}$ using an early-abort technique. We guess only the necessary key bits to compute a sequence of intermediate tables, which count the number of plaintext-ciphertext pairs leading to certain internal state values. An example of this technique can be found in [51]. However, on many ciphers like PRESENT [23] or SIMON [41], the best key-recovery attacks use the FFT approach introduced by Collard et al. [16].

We focus on the situation studied in [16], represented in Fig. 1, which is closer to our situation in the quantum setting. We note that it was extended afterwards in [23] with key additions in both the first and last rounds.

Hadamard Transform. The *Walsh-Hadamard Transform* (WHT) is a special case of the discrete Fourier transform. Given a function $f : \mathbb{F}_2^n \to \mathbb{C}$, its transform $\widehat{f}$ is defined as:

$$\widehat{f} : \begin{cases} \mathbb{F}_2^n \to & \mathbb{C} \\ x \mapsto & \sum_{y \in \mathbb{F}_2^n}(-1)^{x \cdot y}f(y) \end{cases} \tag{10}$$

Note that by convention, we do not normalize it (contrary to the quantum Hadamard transform). The Fast Walsh-Hadamard Transform (FWHT) algorithm is a special case of FFT which evaluates the WHT of f in time $\mathcal{O}(n2^n)$.

Considering the database D of N known-plaintext queries, we let "$(x, *) \in D$" be the predicate that determines if x is among the plaintexts, $(*, x) \in D$ to determine if x is among the ciphertexts, and for a given x, we let $D(x)$ and $D^{-1}(x)$ be the corresponding ciphertext (resp. plaintext).

Recall that for each $z \in \mathbb{F}_2^n$, we need to evaluate the experimental correlation:

$$\widehat{\mathrm{cor}}(z) = \frac{1}{N} \sum_{(x,*) \in D} (-1)^{\alpha \cdot x + \beta \cdot F^{-1}(z + D(x))}$$

$$= \frac{1}{N} \sum_{y \in \mathbb{F}_2^n} \mathbf{1}\left[(*, y) \in D\right] (-1)^{\alpha \cdot D^{-1}(y)} (-1)^{\beta \cdot F^{-1}(z+y)} .$$

Adapting [16], we introduce the pair of functions f, g:

$$\forall x \in \mathbb{F}_2^n \begin{cases} f(x) := \mathbf{1}\left[(*, x) \in D\right] (-1)^{\alpha \cdot D^{-1}(x)} \\ g(x) := (-1)^{\beta \cdot F^{-1}(x)} \end{cases} \tag{11}$$

The experimental correlation is actually the *discrete convolution* of f and g at z:

$$\widehat{\mathrm{cor}}(z) = \frac{1}{N} \sum_{y \in \mathbb{F}_2^n} f(y)g(y + z) := \frac{1}{N} (f \star g)(z) . \tag{12}$$

In order to evaluate $(f \star g)$, we use the *convolution theorem*: the convolution of two functions is equal, under a Fourier Transform, to the pointwise product of their Fourier Transforms. In our case:

$$(f \star g) = \frac{1}{2^n} \widehat{f} \cdot \widehat{g} . \tag{13}$$

The complexity to compute all correlations is thus reduced from $N2^{|k|}$ to $\mathcal{O}(n(N + 2^{|k|}))$, since we only need to do WHTs and pointwise products of vectors of length $2^{|k|}$.

2.4   Quantum Linear Cryptanalysis

In [35, Section 7], Kaplan et al. showed that quantum search (Grover search and Amplitude Amplification) could be used to speedup some classical linear key-recovery attacks. The proposed attack is a last-rounds attack similar to Matsui's algorithm 2, using either Q1 or Q2 queries.

With Q1 queries, it has a complexity $\mathcal{O}\left(N + 2^{|k|/2}\sqrt{N}\right)$ (and then the partial key must be completed). Note that this assumes that the good subkey k can be identified by its correlation, and that there are no false positives. While the first step (obtaining the data) is not accelerated, the second uses a Grover search on the possible values of k, and approximate counting to estimate the correlation for a given k (in time $\sqrt{N}$).

If quantum queries are given, then the data collection step is not required anymore, and the complexity becomes $\mathcal{O}\left(2^{|k|/2}\sqrt{N}\right)$. Also, this method uses a single linear approximation. In the case of *multiple* linear cryptanalysis, it may work only if we can guess globally the $|k|$ bits of key required for *all* linear approximations at the same time, which is rarely the case in advanced attacks.

Thus, an important characterization of these known attacks is that they cannot reach more rounds than the classical attacks that use a *single approximation and no FFT*.

New Approach for Distinguishers. Recently Hosoyamada [29] used a procedure inspired by Simon's algorithm to speedup some linear distinguishers. The main idea is that, using a single Q2 query to a function $f : \{0,1\}^n \to \{0,1\}^n$, one can produce a superposition:

$$\frac{1}{\sqrt{2^n}} \sum_{(\alpha,\beta)\in(\mathbb{F}_2^n)^2} \sum_x (-1)^{\alpha\cdot x+\beta\cdot f(x)}|\alpha\rangle|\beta\rangle .$$

It can be seen that the correlations appear directly in the amplitudes. Thus, to distinguish a function f having a correlated approximation (α, β), it suffices to estimate the corresponding amplitude, with typically a quadratic speedup with respect to classical estimates of the correlation.

The important difference with [35] is that this approach also speeds up multidimensional linear distinguishers. Besides, for some *multiple multi-dimensional integral distinguishers*, the amplitude on the component α, β can become so large that the speedup is better than quadratic. However, extending this to key-recovery attacks remains an open question.

The similarity of this approach with our work is evident, as in both cases, one obtains a quantum state with amplitudes encoding a *statistic* (the correlation). The difference is that we have a superposition of *keys*, instead of a superposition of masks. The subroutine that computes our own correlation state is also much different from the one in [29]. In Hosoyamada's attacks, the statistic appears with a singe Hadamard transform, while our procedure involves a discrete convolution, which will be detailed in Sect. 4.

3   Preliminaries of Quantum Computing

In this section, we collect some important preliminaries of quantum computing and detail the important building block of *state preparation*.

3.1   Quantum Computing Basics

We assume some basic knowledge of the quantum circuit model, e.g., quantum gates, operators, measurements [44]. In this paper, we will measure the time complexity of a quantum circuit as its *Toffoli* gate count, written Tof (). Indeed, all the circuits that we consider below are entirely made of Clifford and Toffoli gates; Clifford gates are often considered cheaper.

qRAM and Q2 queries. A quantum algorithm can make use of different types of memory: classical memory, but also *quantum-accessible* and *quantum* memory, which is often denoted as qRAM. In this paper we consider quantum-accessible classical memory (QRACM). This is a special hardware holding classical bits, but allowing *quantum access*, i.e., an efficient implementation of the following unitary:

$$|b\rangle|i\rangle \xrightarrow{\text{qRAM}(y_1,\ldots,y_M)} |b + y_i\rangle|i\rangle \qquad (14)$$

where M is the number of bits of the QRACM and $y_1, \ldots, y_M$ its contents. Notice that such a circuit could be implemented using about $\mathcal{O}(M)$ standard gates. In the *QRACM model*, we allow such access in time $\mathcal{O}(1)$.

When analyzing a block cipher E_K in the Q2 model, we assume that superposition queries are available via a unitary: $|x\rangle|0\rangle \mapsto |x\rangle|E_K(x)\rangle$. Such an operator can also be realized by storing classical queries in QRACM, which is why our attacks can use either QRACM, Q2 queries, or both. From this perspective, we consider a QRACM query to cost as much as a block cipher query.

Elementary Arithmetic Operations. We recall gate counts for some standard arithmetic operations, which can be found in the literature.

- Addition: adding two integers modulo 2^n can be done with $2n - 1$ Toffoli gates [52]. A *controlled* addition circuit can be done with $3n + 3$ Toffoli gates.
- Comparison: comparing two n-bit numbers can be done with the same cost as an addition or subtraction (e.g., we can subtract the numbers and observe the sign of the result), so we consider a cost of $2n - 1$ Toffoli gates as well.
- Multiplication: multiplying two integers modulo 2^n can be done with a sequence of n controlled additions and shifts (see e.g. Appendix A and B in [27]). We evaluate the corresponding number of Toffoli gates to $\sum_{i=1}^{n} 3(n - i) + 3n = \frac{3}{2}n^2 + \frac{3}{2}n$.

3.2 Quantum Search

Quantum Amplitude Amplification [14] (QAA) is a generalization of Grover's algorithm [25] which amplifies the probability of success of any quantum algorithm. Let $\mathcal{A}$ be a quantum algorithm that produces a superposition of a "good state" $|\psi_G\rangle$ and a "bad state" $|\psi_B\rangle$ of the form:

$$\mathcal{A}|0\rangle = \sqrt{p}|\psi_G\rangle|1\rangle + \sqrt{1 - p^2}|\psi_B\rangle|0\rangle \qquad (15)$$

where p is the probability of success of $\mathcal{A}$. Let O_{test} be an operator which flips the phase in the case 1 only. Let O_0 be an operator called *inversion around zero*, that flips the phase of the basis vector $|0\rangle$ (and only this one). The QAA starts from the output of $\mathcal{A}$: $|\psi_0\rangle := \mathcal{A}|0\rangle$ and constructs a sequence of states $|\psi_{i+1}\rangle := -\mathcal{A}O_0\mathcal{A}^{\dagger}O_{\text{test}}|\psi_i\rangle$. Its main property is:

Lemma 1 (From [14]). *Let θ be such that $\theta = \arcsin\sqrt{p}$. Then:* $|\psi_i\rangle = \sin((2i + 1)\theta)|\psi_G\rangle|1\rangle + \cos((2i + 1)\theta)|\psi_B\rangle|0\rangle$.

This is shown with a geometric argument: the QAA operator $-\mathcal{A}O_0\mathcal{A}^{\dagger}O_{\text{test}}$ realizes a rotation of angle 2θ in the plane spanned by $|\psi_G\rangle|1\rangle$ and $|\psi_B\rangle|0\rangle$.

Exhaustive Key Search. For a block cipher E_K, exhaustive key search using Grover's algorithm consists in finding among all possible keys the one that matches a few known plaintext-ciphertext pairs. This requires $\frac{\pi}{2}2^{|K|/2}r(E)\text{Tof}(E)$ Toffoli gates, where $r(E)$ is the number of trial encryptions required to discriminate the good key with certainty. In fact, the factor $r(E)$ can be amortized to 1 [19], both in exhaustive search and in our attacks. However, we will keep it to simplify the analysis.

Exact QAA and Unknown Success Probability. When the success probability is known exactly, it is possible to construct the state $|\psi_G\rangle$ exactly using a final *partial* rotation that reaches an angle $\frac{\pi}{2}$ [14]. The total number of iterates is thus $\left\lceil \frac{\pi}{4\arcsin\sqrt{p}} \right\rceil \leq \frac{\pi}{4\sqrt{p}} + 1$. The implementation of this final operator is handled via the Solovay-Kitaev theorem (see e.g. [48] for efficient implementations of arbitrary rotation operators). As it will not dominate the complexity anyway, we will not enter its details here.

When an interval on the success probability is known, performing an Exact QAA is still a good strategy: the relative error on p does not increase after amplification.

Lemma 2 (Lemma 5 in [12]). *Assume that $\mathcal{A}$ has a success probability $p' \in [p(1-\varepsilon); p(1+\varepsilon)]$ for $\varepsilon \leq \frac{1}{2}$. After running an exact QAA that assumes a success probability exactly equal to p, the success probability becomes greater than $1-\varepsilon^2$.*

3.3 State Preparation for Amplitude Products

One of the main ideas of our algorithm is to perform computations *in the amplitude*. In particular, we need to multiply the amplitudes of a quantum state by values given separately by an oracle.

Let X be a set (identified with a set of bit-strings). Let $\mathcal{A}$ and $\mathcal{B}$ be two unitary operators (quantum circuits without measurements) such that: $\mathcal{A}|0\rangle = \sum_{x \in X} \alpha_x |x\rangle$ and $\mathcal{B}|x\rangle = |x\rangle|f(x)\rangle$, where $f : X \to]-2^n; 2^n[$. In other words, we have a quantum circuit that produces a superposition and another that computes an integer function. Our goal is to multiply the amplitudes by $f(x)$ and re-normalize, that is, obtain the state:

$$\frac{1}{\sqrt{\sum_{x \in X} \alpha_x^2 f(x)^2}} \sum_{x \in X} \alpha_x f(x) |x\rangle .$$

This is a generalization of *state preparation*, where we would have $\alpha_x = 1/\sqrt{|X|}$, and a problem similar to *quantum rejection sampling* [46], where one wants to enforce the final amplitudes instead of multiplying. A generic method for black-box state preparation was given by Grover [26], but it relies on heavy quantum arithmetic circuits. In this paper, we use the more lightweight method of Sanders *et al.* [47]. The main subroutine is given in Algorithm 1. At step 3 in the algorithm, if the sign of $f(x)$ is encoded in a qubit, the phase flip by $\text{sgn}(f(x))$ can be implemented with a Z gate controlled by this qubit.

Algorithm 1. Main subroutine of quantum state preparation (from [47], adapted to handle negative values).

1: Call $\mathcal{A}$ $\triangleright \sum_x \alpha_x |x\rangle$
2: Apply $\mathcal{B}$ $\triangleright \sum_x \alpha_x |x\rangle |f(x)\rangle$
3: Flip the phase depending on the sign of $f(x)$ $\triangleright \sum_x \alpha_x \text{sgn}(f(x)) |x\rangle |f(x)\rangle$
4: Create a uniform superposition over $[0; 2^n - 1]$ in a new register, using Hadamard gates
$$\triangleright \sum_x \alpha_x \text{sgn}(f(x)) |x\rangle |f(x)\rangle \frac{1}{2^{n/2}} \sum_{0 \leq y \leq 2^n - 1} |y\rangle$$
5: Compare the value of y with $|f(x)|$ and write the result in a new output qubit
6: Apply $\mathcal{B}$ to uncompute $f(x)$
$$\triangleright \sum_x \alpha_x \text{sgn}(f(x)) |x\rangle \frac{1}{2^{n/2}} \left(\sum_{0 \leq y \leq |f(x)| - 1} |y\rangle |0\rangle + \sum_{|f(x)| \leq y \leq 2^n - 1} |y\rangle |1\rangle \right)$$
7: Apply Hadamard gates on the register holding y

Lemma 3. *There exists a unitary U such that:*

$$U|0\rangle = \sum_x \alpha_x \frac{f(x)}{2^n} |x\rangle |0\rangle + |\phi\rangle$$

where $|\phi\rangle$ is a non-normalized state where the last qubits are not zero. The Toffoli gate count of U is upper bounded by:

$$\text{Tof}(U) \leq 2\text{Tof}(\mathcal{B}) + \text{Tof}(\mathcal{A}) + 2n - 1 .$$

Proof. After running Algorithm 1, we obtain a state of the form:

$$\sum_x \alpha_x \text{sgn}(f(x)) \frac{|f(x)|}{2^n} |x\rangle |0\rangle |0\rangle + |\phi\rangle \tag{16}$$

where $|\phi\rangle$ is a non-normalized state with either the last flag equal to 1, or the y register different from zero. □

Afterwards, we must amplify the part of the state with flag zero, in order to obtain the exact superposition that we want.

4 Our New Algorithm

Recall the situation presented in Sect. 2.3: the experimental correlations for key guesses can be expressed as a convolution. In the quantum setting, with a similar sequence of operations, we will compute the convolution in the amplitudes:

$$\frac{1}{\sqrt{\sum_z (f \star g)(z)^2}} \sum_z (f \star g)(z) |z\rangle .$$

We know that the right key guess will have a higher amplitude in this superposition. However, as it remains rather small, trying to measure directly this state would be useless. Instead, we use this as the starting point of another QAA which tries to complete the whole key.

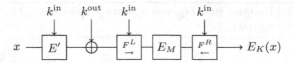

Fig. 3. Our generic attack. While E' is a permutation, both F_L (computed forwards) and F_R (computed backwards) are non-invertible functions which determine the value in the input and output masks.

4.1   Situation

We now consider the generic situation depicted in Fig. 3, which is a hybrid between [16] and [23]. The block cipher E_K is separated into multiple steps. The middle layer E_M, which has the linear approximation (α, β), will contain several rounds of E_K. We will then append several rounds before and after E_M. We define the forward and backward functions F^L and F^R, which compute partially through these rounds to obtain the input and output bits (respectively) of the linear approximation. They are not invertible. Finally, we append a few more rounds at the beginning of the cipher via a function E'.

We define 3 subsets of key bits: • k^{in} are the *inner* key bits, used in E', F^L, F^R (they need to be guessed first); • k^{out} are the *outer* key bits, XORed between E' and F^L, and handled by the WHT; • k^c are the key bits which allow to complete the master key. They are used in E_M only.

We assume that there are s bit relations between k^{in} and k^{out}, and that a choice of agreeing $k^{\text{in}}, k^{\text{out}}, k^c$ determines completely the master key. We also assume that $|k^{\text{out}}| = n$, i.e., like in Collard et al.'s initial attack, the FWHT is computed on the whole state size. With all these definitions, we have: $|K| = (|k^{\text{in}}| + |k^{\text{out}}| - s) + |k^c|$.

We assume that E_M admits a linear approximation (α, β) without a dominant trail, with a certain ELP. A database D of N known plaintext queries $(x, E_K(x))$ is given. We use the abbreviation "$x \in D$" to denote that the plaintext x belongs to the database and $D(x) := E_K(x)$ in that case. For each guess of inner key z^{in} and outer key z^{out}, the experimental correlation is:

$$\widehat{\text{cor}}(z^{\text{in}}, z^{\text{out}}) = \frac{1}{N} \sum_{x \in D} (-1)^{\beta \cdot F_{z^{\text{in}}}^R(D(x))} (-1)^{\alpha \cdot F_{z^{\text{in}}}^L(z^{\text{out}} + E'_{z^{\text{in}}}(x))}$$

$$= \frac{1}{N} \sum_{x \in \mathbb{F}_2^n} \mathbf{1}\left[x \in D\right] (-1)^{\beta \cdot F_{z^{\text{in}}}^R(D(x))} (-1)^{\alpha \cdot F_{z^{\text{in}}}^L(z^{\text{out}} + E'_{z^{\text{in}}}(x))}$$

$$= \frac{1}{N} \sum_{x \in \mathbb{F}_2^n} \mathbf{1}\left[E_{z^{\text{in}}}'^{-1}(x) \in D\right] (-1)^{\beta \cdot F_{z^{\text{in}}}^R \circ D \circ E_{z^{\text{in}}}'^{-1}(x)} (-1)^{\alpha \cdot F_{z^{\text{in}}}^L(z^{\text{out}} + x)} \ .$$

Thus, even in the case of reduced data, we can still define the experimental correlations as the convolution of two functions. For each z^{in}, we define:

$$\forall x \in \mathbb{F}_2^n, \begin{cases} f_{z^{\text{in}}}(x) = \mathbf{1}\left[E_{z^{\text{in}}}'^{-1}(x) \in D\right] (-1)^{\beta \cdot F_{z^{\text{in}}}^R \circ D \circ E_{z^{\text{in}}}'^{-1}(x)} \\ g_{z^{\text{in}}}(x) = (-1)^{\alpha \cdot F_{z^{\text{in}}}^L(z^{\text{out}} + x)} \end{cases} \tag{17}$$

$$\widehat{\mathrm{cor}}(z^{\mathrm{in}}, z) = \frac{1}{2^n} \left(f_{z^{\mathrm{in}}} \star g_{z^{\mathrm{in}}} \right)(z)$$

$$|\mathrm{Cor}_{z^{\mathrm{in}}}\rangle = \frac{1}{\sqrt{\sum_z \widehat{\mathrm{cor}}(z^{\mathrm{in}}, z)^2}} \sum_z \widehat{\mathrm{cor}}(z^{\mathrm{in}}, z)|z\rangle \ .$$

By assumption, in the state $|\mathrm{Cor}_{k^{\mathrm{in}}}\rangle$, there is a bigger amplitude on the basis state k^{out}. This is what we want to exploit; we start with the construction of $|\mathrm{Cor}_{z^{\mathrm{in}}}\rangle$, and around this, we build several layers of QAA to complete the search for the good key.

4.2   Construction and Analysis of $|\mathrm{Cor}\rangle$

First, we must make some assumptions. We assume that efficient unitaries are given for F_R, F_L and E', of gate counts Tof (F_R), Tof (F_L) and Tof (E'). In order to compute $f_{z^{\mathrm{in}}}$, we need either: • Q2 queries (in that case, $N = 2^n$); • a large QRACM storing the database D. In both cases, we have access to two unitaries:

$$\begin{cases} \mathsf{INIT} \ : |0\rangle \mapsto \frac{1}{\sqrt{N}} \sum_{x \in D} |x\rangle \\ \mathsf{QUERY} \ : |x\rangle|0\rangle \mapsto |x\rangle|D(x)\rangle \end{cases} \tag{18}$$

where INIT can be implemented with an appropriate data structure, and QUERY is either a Q2 query, or a QRACM query which is undefined if $x \notin D$.

Finally, we need a unitary that computes the Fourier coefficients of $g_{z^{\mathrm{in}}}$. In some cases this may be done with a precomputation, but otherwise, we will have to implement this unitary "by hand":

$$\mathsf{GFOURIER} : |z^{\mathrm{in}}\rangle|x\rangle|0\rangle \mapsto |z^{\mathrm{in}}\rangle|x\rangle|\widehat{g_{z^{\mathrm{in}}}}(x)\rangle \ . \tag{19}$$

For $z^{\mathrm{in}} = k^{\mathrm{in}}$, let G be an upper bound on the absolute value of Fourier coefficients of $g_{k^{\mathrm{in}}}$. For a random permutation, G is of order $\mathcal{O}(\sqrt{n}2^{n/2})$, as we show in Appendix A.

Lemma 4. *There exists an algorithm* $\mathsf{CORCOMP}$ *returning a state of the form:*

$$\mathsf{CORCOMP}|z^{\mathrm{in}}\rangle|0\rangle = |z^{\mathrm{in}}\rangle|\mathrm{Cor}_{z^{\mathrm{in}}}\rangle \ .$$

The Toffoli gate count of $\mathsf{CORCOMP}$ *is given by:*

$$\begin{aligned} \mathrm{Tof}\,(\mathsf{CORCOMP}) \leq \left(\frac{\pi}{2} \frac{G}{2^{n/2}} + 3 \right) \Bigg[&\mathrm{Tof}\,(\mathsf{INIT}) + 2\mathrm{Tof}\,(\mathsf{QUERY}) \\ &+ 2\mathrm{Tof}\,(\mathsf{GFOURIER}) + \mathrm{Tof}\,(E') + \mathrm{Tof}\,(E'^{-1}) \\ &+ 2\mathrm{Tof}\,(F^R) + (2\lceil \log_2 G \rceil - 1) + 2(n + \lceil \log_2 G \rceil) \Bigg] \ . \end{aligned} \tag{20}$$

Proof. We start from Algorithm 2. In the superposition at the end, the probability to measure the flag 1 is equal to:

$$p := \frac{1}{G^2 2^{2n}} \sum_z (\widehat{f_{z^{\mathrm{in}}}} \widehat{g_{z^{\mathrm{in}}}})^2 = \frac{1}{G^2 2^n} \sum_z \left(f_{z^{\mathrm{in}}} \star g_{z^{\mathrm{in}}} \right)(z)^2 = \frac{2^n}{G^2} \sum_z \widehat{\mathrm{cor}}(z^{\mathrm{in}}, z)^2 \ .$$

Algorithm 2. Subroutine of CORCOMP (Lemma 4). It runs in two phases: 1. Computation of f in the amplitude (Steps 1 to 8), 2. Fourier transform and multiplication by $\widehat{g}$ (Steps 9 to 10).

Input: state $|z^{\text{in}}\rangle|0_n\rangle$

1: Initialize ancilla registers $\hspace{3cm}\triangleright |z^{\text{in}}\rangle|0_n\rangle|0_n\rangle|0_n\rangle$

2: Apply INIT $\hspace{3cm}\triangleright |z^{\text{in}}\rangle\frac{1}{\sqrt{N}}\sum_{x\in D}|x\rangle|0_n\rangle|0_n\rangle$

3: Change of variable in the sum
$$\triangleright |z^{\text{in}}\rangle\frac{1}{\sqrt{N}}\sum_{x\in \mathbb{F}_2^n}\mathbf{1}\left[E_{z^{\text{in}}}'^{-1}(x)\in D\right]|E_{z^{\text{in}}}'^{-1}(x)\rangle|0_n\rangle|0_n\rangle$$

4: Apply QUERY
$$\triangleright |z^{\text{in}}\rangle\frac{1}{\sqrt{N}}\sum_{x}\mathbf{1}\left[E_{z^{\text{in}}}'^{-1}(x)\in D\right]|E_{z^{\text{in}}}'^{-1}(x)\rangle|E_K\circ E_{z^{\text{in}}}'^{-1}(x)\rangle|0_n\rangle$$

5: Apply F^R
$$\triangleright |z^{\text{in}}\rangle\frac{1}{\sqrt{N}}\sum_{x}\mathbf{1}\left[E_{z^{\text{in}}}'^{-1}(x)\in D\right]|E_{z^{\text{in}}}'^{-1}(x)\rangle|E_K\circ E_{z^{\text{in}}}'^{-1}(x)\rangle|F^R\circ E_K\circ E_{z^{\text{in}}}'^{-1}(x)\rangle$$

6: Compute the dot-product with α in the phase
$$\triangleright |z^{\text{in}}\rangle\frac{1}{\sqrt{N}}\sum_{x}f_{z^{\text{in}}}(x)|E_{z^{\text{in}}}'^{-1}(x)\rangle|E_K\circ E_{z^{\text{in}}}'^{-1}(x)\rangle|F^R\circ E_K\circ E_{z^{\text{in}}}'^{-1}(x)\rangle$$
This unitary is implemented with a series of controlled-Z gates: one for each nonzero bit of α, where the control qubit is the corresponding bit of $F^R\circ E_K\circ E_{z^{\text{in}}}'^{-1}(x)$

7: Re-apply F^R and QUERY $\hspace{1.5cm}\triangleright |z^{\text{in}}\rangle\frac{1}{\sqrt{N}}\sum_{x}f_{z^{\text{in}}}(x)|E_{z^{\text{in}}}'^{-1}(x)\rangle|0_n\rangle|0_n\rangle$

8: Apply E' in place (needs to compute E' and E'^{-1})
$$\triangleright |z^{\text{in}}\rangle\frac{1}{\sqrt{N}}\sum_{x}f_{z^{\text{in}}}(x)|x\rangle|0_n\rangle|0_n\rangle$$

9: Apply H $\hspace{3cm}\triangleright |z^{\text{in}}\rangle\frac{1}{\sqrt{N2^n}}\sum_{x}\widehat{f_{z^{\text{in}}}}(x)|x\rangle|0_n\rangle|0_n\rangle$
$\hspace{6cm}\triangleright$ Forget about the ancilla registers

10: Apply the state preparation technique of Lemma 3
$$\triangleright |z^{\text{in}}\rangle\left(|\phi\rangle+\frac{1}{G\sqrt{N2^n}}\sum_y(\widehat{f_{z^{\text{in}}}}\widehat{g_{z^{\text{in}}}})(y)|y\rangle|0\rangle\right)$$
$\triangleright$ Here $|\phi\rangle$ is a non-normalized vector whose details are insignificant for the rest of the algorithm

---

To estimate $\sum_z\widehat{\text{cor}}(z^{\text{in}},z)^2$, we neglect the case of the good key $z=k^{\text{out}}$, since its contribution to the sum will remain negligible. We use only the wrong-key randomization hypothesis, assuming that the $\widehat{\text{cor}}(z^{\text{in}},z)$ for wrong z^{in} and z follow a normal distribution $\mathcal{N}(0,2^{-n})$ (since we have the full codebook). So $2^{n/2}\widehat{\text{cor}}(z^{\text{in}},z)$ follows a normal distribution $\mathcal{N}(0,1)$ and $2^n\sum_z\widehat{\text{cor}}(z^{\text{in}},z)^2$ follows a $\chi^2_{2^n}$ distribution with mean 2^n and variance 2^{n+1}. Using Chebyshev's inequality:

$$\Pr\left(\left|2^n\sum_z\widehat{\text{cor}}(z^{\text{in}},z)^2-2^n\right|\geq 10\cdot 2^{(n+1)/2}\right)\leq\frac{1}{100}\ . \tag{21}$$

Thus, with 99% chance over the run of the attack, we have the bound on p:

$$\left|p-\frac{2^n}{G^2}\right|\leq\frac{10\cdot 2^{(n+1)/2}}{G^2}\ . \tag{22}$$

The Toffoli gate count is given by putting together the different operations.

In order to eliminate the component $|0\rangle$, we apply an Exact QAA over Algorithm 2, assuming that the success probability is exactly $\frac{2^n}{G^2}$. The term $2(n+$

$\lceil \log_2 G \rceil$) is due to the inversion around zero in the QAA. The minor relative error on the success probability does not disrupt QAA computations (see Lemma 2).

Finally, we apply a final Hadamard transform to obtain the correlations. □

From now on, unless stated otherwise, we will consider $N = 2^n$ (full codebook available), as it simplifies the computations and makes INIT trivial. Besides, we will always neglect the terms $T(E') + T(E'^{-1}) + 2T(F^R) + (2 \lceil \log_2 G \rceil - 1) + 2(n + \lceil \log_2 G \rceil)$, as we expect all of them to cost much less than complete block cipher evaluations. The cost of each iterate becomes dominated by 2Tof (QUERY) + 2Tof (GFOURIER).

Analysis of $|Cor_{k^{in}}\rangle$. Our attack works because the amplitude on the right key in $|Cor_{k^{in}}\rangle$ is bigger. To quantify how much, we need to bound $|\widehat{cor}(k^{in}, k^{out})|$. We write both an upper and a lower bound using some threshold t, as:

$$t2^{-n/2} \leq |\widehat{cor}(k^{in}, k^{out})| \leq 2t2^{-n/2} . \tag{23}$$

For fixed t, since $\frac{|\widehat{cor}(k^{in}, k^{out})|}{\sqrt{ELP}}$ follows a normal distribution $\mathcal{N}(0, 1)$, the probability that this event happens (over the run of the attack) is equal to:

$$2 \left(\Phi \left(\frac{2t2^{-n/2}}{\sqrt{ELP}} \right) - \Phi \left(\frac{t2^{-n/2}}{\sqrt{ELP}} \right) \right) .$$

Later on, we will see that the complexity of the attack is proportional to $\frac{1}{t}$. In order to minimize it for a given ELP, we must choose $c = \frac{t2^{-n/2}}{\sqrt{ELP}}$ such that $2c(\Phi(2c) - \Phi(c))$ is maximal. Via numerical optimization we find that $c = 1.005$ gives the maximal value 0.272. For this value of c we also have $2(\Phi(2c) - \Phi(c)) = 0.271$. Thus by selecting $t = 1.005\sqrt{ELP}2^{n/2}$ we are ensured that Eq. 23 holds with probability at least 0.271.

4.3   QAA Layers

Starting from the computation of $|Cor_{z^{in}}\rangle$, several layers of QAA are necessary to complete our algorithm, given in Algorithm 3. We analyze each level carefully in a bottom-up approach, starting from the innermost level and computing the probability of success of each QAA.

As we have seen, CORCOMP outputs a superposition of outer keys; however it does not take into account the relations with the inner key. Classically, these relations reduce the number of degrees of freedom and can be used in conjunction with a pruned Walsh transform [23]. However, in our case they are problematic. To eliminate them, we need to perform another layer of QAA.

Lemma 5. *There exists an algorithm* CORFILT *such that:*

$$CORFILT|z^{in}\rangle|0\rangle = |z^{in}\rangle 2^{s/2} \sum_{z^{in}, z^{out} \ agree} \widehat{cor}(z^{in}, z^{out})|z^{out}\rangle . \tag{24}$$

Algorithm 3. QAA architecture for the key-recovery, using CORCOMP as building block, in the situation represented on Figure 3.

Input: access to E_K (Q2 or QRACM)
Output: returns the master key K or fails

1: **Run QAA over the following:**
2:    Create a uniform superposition of z^{in}
3:    **Run QAA over the following:**
4:       Run CORCOMP
5:       Test if z^{in} agree with z^{out}
6:    **EndQAA**
7:    **Run QAA over the following:**
8:       Create a uniform superposition of z^c
9:       Write 1 if z^{in}, z^{out}, z^c leads to the correct K
10:   **EndQAA**
11:   Check if the flag is 1
12: **EndQAA**

CORFILT (Lemma 5)

SETUP (Lemma 6)

Its gate count is given by:

$$\text{Tof} (\text{CORFILT}) = \left(\frac{\pi}{2}2^{s/2} + 3\right) \text{Tof} (\text{CORCOMP}) \tag{25}$$

Proof. Note that we have simplified the writing by approximating $\sum_z \widehat{\text{cor}}(z)^2 \simeq 1$.

The structure of CORFILT is simply an Exact QAA performed over the output of CORCOMP, to force that z^{out} agrees with z^{in}. The number of iterates depends on the probability, on the output of CORCOMP, that z^{in} and z^{out} agree. For a given z^{in}, and setting aside the right key case, this is a sum of 2^{n-s} squared random correlations. So by similar arguments as above, this sum is highly concentrated around its mean 2^{-s}. This gives the number of iterates that we need to make.   □

At this point, we have a quantum algorithm that on input z^{in}, creates a "filtered correlation state". The right key in this state has an amplitude proportional to the experimental correlation. It remains to complete the key and check. Recall that to discriminate the right key with certainty, we will perform $r(E)$ trial encryptions.

Lemma 6. *There exists a quantum algorithm* SETUP *such that:*

$$\text{SETUP}|0\rangle = 2^{(s-|k^{in}|)/2} \sum_{z^{in}, z^{out} \; agreeing} \widehat{\text{cor}}(z^{in}, z^{out})|z^{in}\rangle|z^{out}\rangle|\text{good}\rangle \tag{26}$$

where $\text{good} = 1 \iff z^{in}, z^{out} = k^{in}, k^{out}$. *Its gate count is:*

$$\text{Tof} (\text{SETUP}) = \text{Tof} (\text{CORFILT}) + \frac{\pi}{2}2^{|k^c|/2}r(E)\text{Tof} (E) . \tag{27}$$

Proof. The algorithm runs as follows. We first create a uniform superposition over z^{in}, then we apply CORFILT, then we use an Exact QAA over the remaining key bits z^c to mark exactly the good subkeys by trial encryptions. We simply run this QAA and set the flag good to 1 if it outputs the good key. Indeed, if $z^{in}, z^{out} \neq k^{in}, k^{out}$, the completed key is never good and the QAA returns a uniform superposition of bad keys (so we always write 0). If $z^{in}, z^{out} = k^{in}, k^{out}$, we find the good key with certainty, so we always write 1.   □

Our algorithm is obtained by applying a QAA on SETUP.

Theorem 1. *Let $t = 1.005\sqrt{ELP}2^{n/2}$. There exists a quantum algorithm that takes no input and returns (after measurement) the master key with probability $\geq \frac{1}{2}$. This algorithm has complexity:*

$$\frac{\pi^2}{8t}2^{|K|/2}r(E)\text{Tof}(E) + \frac{\pi^2}{8t}2^{(n+|k^{in}|)/2}\text{Tof}(\text{CORCOMP}) \qquad (28)$$

and succeeds with probability 0.271 over the run of the attack.

Proof. We apply a QAA on SETUP, by amplifying the part which leads to a flag 1, i.e., the good subkey k^{in}, k^{out}. By Eq. 23 and the definition of t, with probability 0.271, the corresponding amplitude can be bounded by:

$$t2^{(s-|k^{in}|-n)/2} \leq 2^{(s-|k^{in}|)/2}|\widehat{\text{cor}}(k^{in}, k^{out})| \leq 2t2^{(s-|k^{in}|-n)/2} . \qquad (29)$$

This amplitude determines the number of iterates that we need to perform in the QAA. Given the upper bound, the maximal number that we can apply before over-amplifying is:

$$\left\lfloor \frac{\pi}{4}\left(\arcsin\frac{2t}{2^{(|k^{in}|-s+n)/2}}\right)^{-1} \right\rfloor \simeq \frac{\pi}{4}\frac{2^{(|k^{in}|-s+n)/2}}{2t} = \frac{\pi}{8t}2^{(|k^{in}|-s+n)/2}$$

The corresponding success probability, i.e., the probability to measure a flag 1 at the end, can be lower bounded as:

$$\sin^2\left(\left(2\frac{\pi}{8t}2^{(|k^{in}|-s+n)/2} + 1\right)\sqrt{2^{(s-|k^{in}|)/2}|\widehat{\text{cor}}(k^{in}, k^{out})|}\right) \geq \sin^2\frac{\pi}{4} = \frac{1}{2} .$$

We obtain the complexity as:

$$\frac{\pi}{4t}2^{(|k^{in}|-s+n)/2}\text{Tof}(\text{SETUP}) .$$

We replace Tof (SETUP) by its formula and develop to conclude.   □

If the first term is dominant, it differs from the complexity of Grover search ($\frac{\pi}{2}2^{\kappa/2}r\text{Tof}(E)$) by a factor $\frac{\pi}{4t}$. However Grover search succeeds with overwhelming probability, while this one succeeds only with probability $0.271\times0.5 \simeq 0.1355$. The difference in *average* complexity is of a factor: $\frac{\pi}{4t}/0.1355$.

We conclude that we can only use an ELP such that:

$$\frac{\pi}{4}/0.1355 < t = 1.005 \cdot 2^{n/2}\sqrt{ELP} \implies ELP \geq 2^{-n+5.06} .$$

5 Multiple Linear Cryptanalysis Using the QFT

With *multiple* linear approximations, the statistics have a much smaller variance, so it becomes easier to distinguish the right key from the other ones. In this section, we show that this also helps quantum attacks.

Multidimensional linear cryptanalysis [28] is a case in which one considers a set of linear approximations whose masks form a linear subspace. This makes the statistical analysis more robust to dependencies. We have not tried to use it, but it could plausibly replace multiple linear cryptanalysis in this section.

5.1 Intuition

We consider the structure of Fig. 3, but this time, we introduce M linear approximations: α_i, β_i (we use subscripts to denote the different cases). While the outer key bits k^{out} remain the same in all cases, the inner key bits k_i^{in} can be different, and the number of relations between k_i^{in} and k^{out} (denoted s_i) can vary.

We consider these approximations to be statistically independent. Let k^{in} be a superset of all subkey guesses k_i^{in}. The statistic of interest is denoted $\widehat{q}(k^{\text{in}}, k)$:

$$\widehat{q}(k^{\text{in}}, k) = \sum_{i=1}^{M} \widehat{\text{cor}}_i(k_i^{\text{in}}, k)^2 \ .$$

For the right subkey, we expect this statistic to be higher. Instead of trying to compute it by hand, we notice already that for individual approximations α_i, β_i, we can obtain the state:

$$|\text{Cor}_{z_i^{\text{in}}}\rangle \simeq \sum_{z} \widehat{\text{cor}}_i(z_i^{\text{in}}, z)|z\rangle \ ,$$

where the normalization follows from $\sum_z \widehat{\text{cor}}_i(z_i^{\text{in}}, z)^2 \simeq 1$. Thus, if we compute this for all M approximations in superposition over i, we obtain:

$$|\text{Cor}_{z^{\text{in}}}\rangle := \frac{1}{\sqrt{M}} \sum_i |\text{Cor}_{z_i^{\text{in}}}\rangle|i\rangle = \frac{1}{\sqrt{M}} \sum_{i,z} \widehat{\text{cor}}_i(z_i^{\text{in}}, z)|z\rangle|i\rangle \ . \tag{30}$$

Despite the presence of i, a subsequent QAA layer will only care on the total amplitude that is put on a given key guess. Here, if we have $z^{\text{in}} = k^{\text{in}}$, the total amplitude on k is $\sqrt{\frac{\widehat{q}(k^{\text{in}}, k)}{M}}$, which depends on the multiple linear cryptanalysis statistic. There is no computational overhead, because we *do not compute* the statistic; it simply appears in the amplitude.

5.2 Computation of the Correlation State

We start by computing the state $|\text{Cor}_{z^{\text{in}}}\rangle$ defined in Eq. 30 above. This means that:

- The partial computations of the cipher (E', F^R) must now take into account the dependency on i. They might cost more, but remain insignificant;
- The functions f, g in the convolution can depend on i, although we simply write them $f_{z_i^{in}}, g_{z_i^{in}}$ to simplify notation;
- We need a quantum circuit GFMULT to compute the Fourier coefficients of these different functions:

$$\text{GFMULT} : |z_i^{in}\rangle|x\rangle|i\rangle|0\rangle \mapsto |z_i^{in}\rangle|x\rangle|i\rangle|\widehat{g_{z_i^{in}}}(x)\rangle \ .$$

- We need an all-encompassing bound G on the Fourier coefficients of $g_{k_i^{in}}$, valid for all i simultaneously.

Fortunately in our applications, the different g are actually all similar functions, and there is no big difference in computing their Fourier coefficients.

Lemma 7. *There exists an algorithm* CORMULT *such that:*

$$\text{CORMULT}|z_i^{in}\rangle|i\rangle|0\rangle = |z_i^{in}\rangle|i\rangle \sum_z \widehat{\text{cor}}_i(z_i^{in}, z)|z\rangle$$

$$\text{Tof}\,(\text{CORMULT}) = \left(\frac{\pi}{2}\frac{G}{2^{n/2}} + 3\right)(2\text{Tof}\,(\text{GFMULT}) + 2\text{Tof}\,(\text{QUERY})) \ .$$

Proof. We run Algorithm 2 in superposition over $|i\rangle$. By an analysis similar to Lemma 4, the subroutine outputs:

$$|z_i^{in}\rangle|i\rangle \left(\frac{2^{n/2}}{G}\left(\sum_z \widehat{\text{cor}}_i(z_i^{in}, z)|z\rangle\right)|1\rangle + |*\rangle|0\rangle\right) \ . \tag{31}$$

Then, we use an Exact QAA to amplify the component 1. Note that we have simplified the writing by approximating the sum of correlations to 1.   □

Before we analyze the amplitude on the right key, we must (like before) use the relations between z_i^{in} and z. These relations differ depending on i, but *there should be the same amount* for all i. This is because the correlations are rescaled by a quantity $2^{s_i/2}$, where s_i is the amount of relations. We can only obtain the statistic $\widehat{q}(z)$ if all the s_i are equal.

Lemma 8. *There exists an algorithm* FILTEREDMULT *such that:*

$$\text{FILTEREDMULT}|z_i^{in}\rangle|i\rangle|0\rangle = |z_i^{in}\rangle|i\rangle 2^{s/2} \sum_{z_i^{out}\ agrees} \widehat{\text{cor}}_i(z_i^{in}, z_i^{out})|z_i^{out}\rangle$$

$$\text{Tof}\,(\text{FILTEREDMULT}) = \frac{\pi}{2}2^{s/2}\text{Tof}\,(\text{CORMULT}) \ .$$

Proof. On the output of CORMULT, we apply an Exact QAA.   □

5.3 QAA Layers

With the same structure as in Sect. 4.3, we add other QAA layers to complete our algorithm.

We start by completing the subkeys. Like before, we use an Exact QAA which marks the key guesses $(z_i^{\text{in}}, z_i^{\text{out}}) = (k_i^{\text{in}}, k_i^{\text{out}})$. The resulting algorithm is the "setup" on which we will apply QAA again. Notice that from now on, since all keys have the same amount of relations, we have $\forall i, j, |k_i^{\text{in}}| = |k_j^{\text{in}}|, |k_i^c| = |k_j^c|$.

Lemma 9. *There exists an algorithm* SETUPMULT *such that:*

$$\text{SETUPMULT}|0\rangle = \sum_{i, z_i^{\text{in}}, z_i^{\text{out}} \text{ agree}} \frac{2^{(s - |k^{\text{in}}|)/2}}{\sqrt{M}} \widehat{\text{cor}}_i(z_i^{\text{in}}, z_i^{\text{out}})|i\rangle|z_i^{\text{in}}, z_i^{\text{out}}\rangle|\text{good}\rangle$$

$$\text{Tof}\,(\text{SETUPMULT}) \leq \text{Tof}\,(\text{FILTEREDMULT}) + \frac{\pi}{2}2^{|k^c|/2}r(E)\text{Tof}\,(E)$$

Proof. The algorithm runs as follows. We first create a uniform superposition over i and z_i^{in}, then we apply FILTEREDMULT, then we mark the good subkeys with an Exact QAA. There are $\frac{\pi}{4}2^{|k^c|/2}$ iterates; each iterate calls E a total of $2r(E)$ times. □

Finally, we apply QAA on top of this algorithm, where we just want to find a subkey guess $z_i^{\text{in}}, z_i^{\text{out}}$ (whichever the i) which completes into the good key.

Theorem 2. *Assuming $M \gg 1$, there exists an algorithm which outputs a good guess $i, k_i^{\text{in}}, k_i^{\text{out}}$, with probability of success $\geq 1 - \frac{18}{M}$, in time:*

$$T := \frac{1}{\sqrt{2^n C/M + 1}} \left(\frac{\pi^2}{4}2^{|K|/2}r\text{Tof}\,(E) + \frac{\pi^2}{4}2^{(n + |k^{\text{in}}|)/2}\text{Tof}\,(\text{CORMULT}) \right).$$
$$(32)$$

Proof. On the output of SETUPMULT, the total probability of measuring the flag 1, which corresponds exactly to the good subkeys for different paths, is equal to:

$$p := \sum_i \frac{2^{s - |k^{\text{in}}|}}{M} \widehat{\text{cor}}_i(k_i^{\text{in}}, k_i^{\text{out}})^2 = \frac{2^{s - |k^{\text{in}}|}}{M} \widehat{q}(k^{\text{in}}, k^{\text{out}}).$$
$$(33)$$

By the right-key randomization hypothesis, $\widehat{q}(k^{\text{in}}, k^{\text{out}})$ follows a normal distribution with mean $C + M2^{-n}$ and variance $\frac{2}{M}C^2$ where C is the capacity of the multiple approximation. Thus, with overwhelming probability, we have:

$$C\left(1 - \frac{3\sqrt{2}}{\sqrt{M}}\right) + M2^{-n} \leq \widehat{q}(k^{\text{in}}, k^{\text{out}}) \leq C\left(1 + \frac{3\sqrt{2}}{\sqrt{M}}\right) + M2^{-n}$$
$$(34)$$

Thus, we can bound $p'(1 - \varepsilon) \leq p \leq p'(1 + \varepsilon)$ where $p' = 2^{s - |k^{\text{in}}|}\left(\frac{C}{M} + 2^{-n}\right)$ and $\varepsilon = \frac{3\sqrt{2}}{\sqrt{M}}$. We conclude with Lemma 2. □

If the first term in Eq. 32 is dominant, then we can have an advantage with respect to Grover search. The main interest in using the multiple cryptanalysis statistic is that we have reduced the variance on the right key case, allowing a good probability of success for this procedure (instead of the 0.1355 given by Theorem 1).

6   Applications

In this section, we give several examples of our technique. We start with the block ciphers FLY [36] and PIPO [37]. In both cases our QFT-based algorithm can reach more rounds than previous quantum linear attacks, like classical FFT-based cryptanalysis. We assume either Q2 queries (in which case they are not the dominant cost anyway), or QRACM queries, with a QRACM containing the whole codebook. Because we use large ELPs in both cases, it would be possible to reduce the data complexity (but this complicates the analysis).

6.1   Linear Characteristics on FLY and PIPO

Both ciphers have similar structures: a 64-bit state, S-Boxes of 8 bits, a linear layer which is a simple bit permutation (like PRESENT), and a trivial key schedule. FLY is defined only with 128-bit keys, with 20 rounds. The round function is represented on Fig. 4: it applies a round key addition, followed by 8 parallel S-Boxes of 8 bits (the S-Box LITTLUN-1 which is also defined in [36]) and a permutation of the bits.

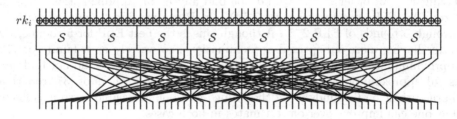

Fig. 4. FLY round function (Fig. 5.2 in [36].

We consider the simple key-schedule KS1 proposed for a case where related-key security is not required. The master key K of 128 bits is divided into two halves: $K = k_0 \| k_1$ and the round keys alternate between k_0 and $k_0 \oplus k_1$. In the following, we replace $(k_0, k_0 \oplus k_1)$ by (k_0, k_1), since this makes no difference. For other details of the specification which are irrelevant for our attack (such as round constants) we refer to [36].

The bit-permutation in PIPO is different, but it has the same property that the 8 bits of each S-Box are distributed to the 8 S-Boxes of the next round. There are two versions: PIPO-128 and PIPO-256 with respectively 13 and 17

Table 1. Results on linear characteristics.

Cipher	Rounds	M	ELP
FLY	8	64	2^{-58}
PIPO	5	112	$\geq 2^{-52}$
PIPO	5	24	2^{-50}

rounds (i.e., 14 and 18 subkey additions). In both cases, the master key K is cut into $|K|/64$ subkeys which are XORed alternatively to the state. The authors [37] claimed attacks for up to 9 / 13 and 11 / 17 rounds, but without details. In [32], quantum circuits for PIPO were given, using respectively $1248 = 2^{10.29}$ and $1632 = 2^{10.67}$ Toffoli gates for the two versions. For FLY, a quick look at its 8-bit S-Box shows that it contains 12 nonlinear operations (AND and OR) which can be implemented with 12 Toffoli gates. For 11 complete rounds this gives the count of $8 \times 11 \times 24 = 2112 = 2^{11.04}$ Toffoli gates.

Search for Linear Distinguishers. In both cases, we follow the approach of [1] to search for linear trails in a restricted family of masks. We use all masks which activate at most 2 S-Boxes, and at most 2 S-Boxes before the previous permutation layer. This forms a family of 6000 masks. We compute the 6000×6000 sparse correlation matrix through a single round, then obtain the ELPs for multiple rounds via matrix multiplication. In our attacks, we only use trails that activate *exactly* two S-Boxes at the rounds before and after.

Results (Table 1). On FLY, we find 64 approximations through 8 full rounds having ELP of order 2^{-58}. We did not find any useful approximation through 9 rounds (ELPs are too close to 2^{-64}). On PIPO, we find 24 approximations through 5 rounds of ELP 2^{-50}. Although this is the best ELP for 5 rounds, we prefer having more suboptimal approximations, so we rely on a family of 112 approximations of ELPs between $2^{-51.8}$ and 2^{-52}. Likewise, we did not find any useful approximations for 6 rounds. Nevertheless, the authors of [37] report a characteristic on 6 rounds using the branch-and-bound technique, so it is likely that one can improve over our estimates in both cases.

6.2   Attacks on FLY and PIPO-128

On FLY and PIPO-128, which have the same structure, we can propose a similar attack pattern. Following Fig. 3, we remove the block E' and append two rounds before (this corresponds to F_L) and one round after (F_R) the distinguisher.

In the case of FLY, the distinguisher contains 8 rounds, so the outer key k^{out} is k_0 and the inner key k^{in} contains $\leq 16 + 16$ bits of k_1 (because only two S-Boxes are active in these rounds). Whichever the linear approximation considered, due to the regularity of the bit permutation, there are exactly 4 bit relations between the 16 bits of k_1 that appear in the second and last rounds, so $|k^{\text{in}}| = 28$.

In the case of PIPO, we have the same scheduling but the distinguisher spans 5 rounds, so the outer key is k_0 and the inner key contains exactly 16 bits of k_0 and 16 bits of k_1. We have $|k^{in}| = 32$ and $s = 16$ bits of relation between k^{in} and k^{out}.

In both cases, we use multiple linear cryptanalysis and Theorem 2. Using M linear approximations with capacity C, our algorithm succeeds with probability $1 - \frac{18}{M}$ and runs in time:

$$T = \frac{1}{\sqrt{2^n C/M + 1}} \left[\frac{\pi^2}{4} 2^{|K|/2} r(E)T(E) + \frac{\pi^2}{4} 2^{\frac{n+|k^{in}|}{2}} \text{Tof (CORMULT)} \right] . \quad (35)$$

We take $r(E) = 3$, as 3 plaintext-ciphertext pairs are enough for checking the key.

Computing the Fourier Coefficients. We must implement the circuit GFMULT, which computes $\widehat{g_{z_i^{in}}}(x) = \sum_y (-1)^{x \cdot y} (-1)^{\beta \cdot F_{z^{in}}^L(y)}$ in superposition over z^{in} (current inner key guess), i and x. We show how to reduce this to a feasible computation, using the structure of F^L. We expect that this will also be possible in general for a small number of rounds in any SPN cipher.

All linear approximations considered activate two S-Boxes before the distinguisher. Thus, if we cut the input x into $x_0, \dots, x_7$ and the inner key z into bits $z_0, z_1, \dots, z_{15}$, we can simplify $F_z^L(x)$ into:

$$F_z^L(x) = S_0' [z_0 + S_0(x_0), z_1 + S_1(x_1), \dots, z_7 + S_7(x_7)],$$
$$S_1' [z_8 + S_8(x_0), z_9 + S_9(x_1), \dots, z_{15} + S_{15}(x_7)] \quad (36)$$

where all these functions are simply applying S-Boxes and selecting some input and output bits, up to permutations of these bits.

By merging S_0' and S_1' with the scalar product on β, we can rewrite this as:

$$g_z(x) = S_0' [z_0 + S_0(x_0), z_1 + S_1(x_1), \dots, z_7 + S_7(x_7)] \times$$
$$S_1' [z_8 + S_8(x_0), z_9 + S_9(x_1), \dots, z_{15} + S_{15}(x_7)] \quad (37)$$

where S_0' and S_1' are functions into $\{-1, 1\}$. The independence between these different parts is the key to a faster computation of $\widehat{g_z}$. Indeed:

$$\widehat{g_z}(y) = \sum_x (-1)^{x \cdot y} g_z(x)$$

$$= \sum_{\substack{u_0, \dots, u_{15}}} \sum_{\substack{x_0 | z_0 + S_0(x_0) = u_0 \\ z_8 + S_8(x_0) = u_8}} \cdots \sum_{\substack{x_7 | z_7 + S_7(x_7) = u_7 \\ z_{15} + S_{15}(x_7) = u_{15}}} (-1)^{x \cdot y} g_z(x)$$

$$= \sum_{\substack{u_0, \dots, u_{15}}} \prod_{i=0}^{7} \underbrace{\left(\sum_{\substack{x_i \\ S_i(x_i) = u_i \\ S_{i+8}(x_i) = u_{i+8}}} (-1)^{x_i \cdot y_i} \right)}_{:= h_i(y_i, u_i, u_{i+8})} \begin{array}{l} S_0'(u_0 + z_0, \dots, u_7 + z_7) \\ \times S_1'(u_8 + z_8, \dots, u_{15} + z_{15}) \end{array} .$$

At this point, we already arrive at a feasible cost using some precomputations (and QRACM tables). But we can reduce this cost further by noticing that it is easier to compute $\widehat{g_z}$ *directly into the amplitude.*

Amplitude Computation Pattern. We start from the state:

$$\sum_y \widehat{f_z}(y)|y\rangle$$

We first append a 16-bit value u, in uniform superposition:

$$\sum_y \sum_u \widehat{f_z}(y)|y\rangle|u\rangle .$$

We compute digitally the functions h_i, their product, and both S_0' and S_1':

$$\sum_y \sum_u \widehat{f_z}(y)|y\rangle|u\rangle|S_0'(u+z)S_1'(u+z)\prod_i h_i(y_i, u_i, u_{i+8})\rangle .$$

If we consider that the products of h_i are a sum of $(2^6)^8 = 2^{48}$ independent variables taking value ± 1, then by the argument of Lemma 10, the value to multiply in the amplitude is upper bounded by $2^{24}H$ where:

$$H := \sqrt{6(\ln 100 + 49\ln 2 + \ln M)} \simeq \sqrt{2^{7.85} + 6\ln M} .$$

After doing the product in the amplitude, we obtain a quantum state of the form:

$$\alpha \sum_y \sum_u \widehat{f_z}(y)\left(\prod_{i=0}^{7} h_i(y_i, u_i, u_{i+8})S_0'(u+z)S_1'(u+z)\right)|y\rangle|u\rangle|0\rangle + |\Phi\rangle$$

where $|\Phi\rangle$ is a non-normalized bad state and α is such that we project on 0 with probability about $\frac{1}{H^2}$.

Next, we apply a Hadamard transform on the u register. The "0" component of the state evolves as follows:

$$\frac{\alpha}{\sqrt{2^{16}}} \sum_y \sum_{u,v} \widehat{f_z}(y)\left(\prod_{i=0}^{7} h_i(y_i, u_i, u_{i+8})S_0'(u+z)S_1'(u+z)\right)(-1)^{u\cdot v}|y\rangle|v\rangle .$$

Thus, the component $v = 0$ has amplitude about $\frac{1}{H2^8}$, and it corresponds to the state $\sum_y \widehat{f_z}(y)\widehat{g_z}(y)|y\rangle$ that we want. In total, we can create the correlation state via a procedure which performs $\frac{\pi}{4}H2^8$ iterates of QAA. Each iterate queries f_z twice and does the following operations: compute the h_i (8×2^8 S-Box computations), their product (7 multiplications of 32-bit integers, i.e., 1584×7 Toffolis) and S_0, S_1' (2 S-Box computations) twice. Using a Toffoli count of 12 for the FLY S-Box (less for the PIPO S-Box), this gives an additional gate count of $35688 = 2^{15.12}$ Toffolis, and:

$$\text{Tof (CORMULT)} = \frac{\pi}{2}2^8\sqrt{2^{7.85} + 6\ln M}\left(\text{Tof (QUERY)} + 2^{15.12}\right) . \tag{38}$$

In both our attacks we have $M \leq 112$ so we can write: Tof $(\mathsf{CORMULT}) \leq 2^{27.78}$. We will also consider that Tof (QUERY) is dominated by the second term. Indeed, it performs either a query to the cipher (around 2^{11} Toffolis) or a QRACM query.

Results. For PIPO, we have $M = 112$ and $C = M \times 2^{-52}$, thus:

$$\text{Tof} = 2^{-6.00} \times \left(2^{2.89} \times 2^{64} \times 2^{10.29} + 2^{1.30} \times 2^{32+16} \times 2^{27.78}\right)$$
$$= 2^{-6.00} \left(2^{77.18} + 2^{77.08}\right) = 2^{72.13} \ .$$

The success probability is $1 - \frac{18}{M} = 0.84$. This compares favorably to an exhaustive search of the key in T-gate count $2^{74.94}$ (multiplying the count of [37] for PIPO-128 with a factor $\frac{\pi}{2}2^{64}$).

For FLY, we have a smaller capacity $C = M \times 2^{-58}$, but benefit from 4 bit-relations which reduce a little the complexity. Furthermore, there is one less level of QAA since there are no relations to enforce between k^{in} and k^{out}.

$$\text{Tof} = 2^{-3.01} \times \left(2^{2.89} \times 2^{64} \times 2^{10.67} + 2^{0.65} \times 2^{32+14} \times 2^{27.78}\right)$$
$$= 2^{-3.01} \left(2^{77.56} + 2^{74.43}\right) = 2^{74.71} \ .$$

These results are summarized in Table 2. In both cases, the quantum linear attacks from [35] are applicable, but reach one less round.

Table 2. Summary of attacks. "Data" in the Q2 setting is the total number of Q2 queries performed during the attack.

Attack	Rounds	Time (Toffoli gates)	Success prob.	Data	Memory
PIPO-128					
Classical search	13/13	2^{128}	1	3	negl.
Quantum search (Q1)	13/13	$2^{74.94}$	1	3	negl.
Linear QFT (Q1)	8/13	$2^{72.13}$	0.84	2^{64}	2^{71} QRACM
Linear QFT (Q2)	8/13	$2^{72.13}$	0.84	$2^{61.96}$	negl.
FLY					
Classical search	20/20	2^{128}	1	3	negl.
Quantum search (Q1)	20/20	$2^{75.69}$	1	3	negl.
Linear QFT (Q1)	11/20	$2^{74.11}$	0.72	2^{64}	2^{71} QRACM
Linear QFT (Q2)	11/20	$2^{74.11}$	0.72	$2^{59.31}$	negl.

6.3   Discussion on Other Applications

We have tried to apply our technique to other block ciphers, but the reduced-round attacks that we obtained required more time and memory only to reach the same number of rounds as the previous quantum linear cryptanalysis from [35].

Present. For PRESENT, linear attacks using the FWHT give the best results classically (up to 29 rounds out of 31 for the 128-bit key version [22]). However, we quickly run into the following problem: the simple quantum linear attack (without QFT) can work with relatively smaller ELPs, while our attack needs relatively bigger ones (e.g., $2^{-n+5.06}$ for Theorem 1).

More precisely, we tried the multiple linear cryptanalysis version with one-bit masks. We decided to append three rounds before the approximation and two rounds after, for an outer key of 64 bits and an inner key of $4 + 4 + 16 + 16 = 40$ bits. We used a family of 56 approximations on 22 rounds with ELPs between $2^{-60.8}$ and $2^{-61.5}$ (the constraint on this family is that there should be the same number of relations between the inner key and the outer key for all approximations). Unfortunately, the speedup becomes so small that the $\frac{\pi^2}{4}$ constant of Theorem 2 exceeds the gain.

Removing one round, we would have used 21-round approximations with ELP approximately 2^2 times larger. This would have given a speedup of a factor at most 2 with respect to exhaustive search. This is the best number of rounds $(21 + 2 + 3 = 26)$ that we can report. But using a single 22-round approximation from the family above, we can have a better time with [35].

NOEKEON. We studied the linear attack on NOEKEON given in [15]. Here the key and blocks have the same length of 128 bits. The classical data complexity being at least around 2^{120}, the only way to compete with Grover search is the Q2 model. Here the formula of Theorem 1 becomes:

$$\frac{\pi^2}{8t} 2^{128/2} r(E) \mathrm{Tof}\,(E) + \frac{\pi^2}{8t} 2^{128/2} \mathrm{Tof}\,(\mathsf{CORCOMP})\ . \tag{39}$$

However, the computation of the correlation state is always more costly than a single query to the cipher, and the factor t does not compensate this enough. Like in the case of PRESENT, the ELP would need to be larger than what the standard linear attack can use.

6.4   Structural Attacks and a Beyond-Quadratic Speedup

Replacing E_M by a key addition in Fig. 3, and removing the inner key k^{in} from F^L, we obtain the structure represented in Fig. 5. Here, our algorithm can achieve a better speedup than quadratic, up to 2.5 precisely, like the offline-Simon algorithm [13]. On a construction like this, offline-Simon needs at least $2^n(1 - \mathcal{O}(1/n))$ classical known-plaintext queries (Lemma 1 in [13]). However, our algorithm can use *any* number of known-plaintext queries. Its cost is dominated by QRACM queries.

Theorem 3. *Let t be the gate cost of a QRACM query and a cipher evaluation. Given N classical known-plaintext queries to the E_K of Fig. 5, there exists a quantum algorithm recovering K in $\mathcal{O}\left(2^{|k^{\mathrm{in}}|/2} \frac{2^{n/2}}{\sqrt{N}} \sqrt{n}(n + t) + n2^n\right)$ gates, using $\mathcal{O}(n2^n)$ bits of QRACM.*

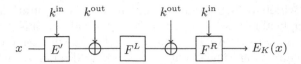

Fig. 5. Generic Structural Attack.

Proof. We follow the analysis in Sect. 4.2, using an arbitrary boolean mask $\alpha = \beta = (1, 0, \ldots, 0)$. Because there is no dependency on z^{in} in the middle permutation Π, we can precompute its Walsh-Hadamard transform in $\mathcal{O}(n2^n)$ and store it in $\mathcal{O}(n2^n)$ bits of QRACM. For the good key k^{in}, the wrong experimental correlations are of order $\mathcal{O}\left(\frac{\sqrt{N}}{2^n}\right)$, while the right key guess reaches exactly $\frac{N}{2^n}$: indeed, the correlation of a linear function is 1. Computing the correlation state takes $\mathcal{O}(\sqrt{n})$ iterates (because of the bound on Fourier coefficients for a random function of Lemma 10) of a procedure using $\mathcal{O}(n + t)$ gates (a comparator and a query to the QRACM).

After creating the correlation state for a given z^{in}, we complete the setup by performing a trial encryption. With a uniform superposition over z^{in}, the right key $k^{\text{in}}, k^{\text{out}}$, marked with 1, has an amplitude equal to: $\frac{1}{2^{|k^{\text{in}}|/2}} \times \frac{1}{\sqrt{N \times 2^n}} N = \mathcal{O}\left(\sqrt{N} 2^{-(|k^{\text{in}}|+n)/2}\right)$. Therefore, the key is found using $\mathcal{O}\left(2^{(|k^{\text{in}}|+n)/2}/\sqrt{N}\right)$ iterates of QAA. □

In particular, if QRACM queries are considered as costly as block cipher evaluations (typically $\mathcal{O}(n^2)$ gates), then the gate count at the minimal point $N = 2^n(1 - \mathcal{O}(1/n))$ is *smaller* than the one of offline-Simon, which requires n block cipher calls and $\mathcal{O}(n^3)$ gates per iterate.

7   Conclusion and Open Problems

In this paper, we have introduced a new technique in quantum key-recovery attacks on block ciphers. After Hosoyamada [29] showed that one could use the Quantum Fourier Transform in a statistical cryptanalysis, this technique shows that we can use it in key-recovery attacks. From the perspective of quantum algorithms, we have switched from Simon's algorithm, which is limited to strong algebraic structures, to computing a discrete convolution. However, this new perspective opens several important questions.

Technical Limitations. Our framework yields only two types of key-recovery attacks: Q2 attacks with an overall small memory footprint, or Q1 attacks that require a large amount of QRACM. (It is not necessary to have the full codebook, though we considered this to simplify our study.) Indeed, to construct efficiently the correlation states, we need to query the data in superposition, whether it is a classical database, or a quantum query.

QRACM is widely recognized as a strong model of computation, which limits the practical applicability of quantum cryptanalytic algorithms (even more than large classical memories). An important question is whether one can remove this memory requirement. The situation seems indeed reminiscent of the offline-Simon algorithm of [11]. In offline-Simon, quantum queries which were initially performed at each Grover iterate end up being done only once, and reused from one iterate to the next. The situation here is more challenging: we use a quantum amplitude amplification, and the queries are embedded in the amplified algorithm. This is why the technique of [11] does not work so far.

Computing Fourier Coefficients. While the construction of the *correlation state* is central to our work, it is also quite technical, due to the computation of Fourier coefficients into the amplitudes of a quantum state. In our applications, we have shown that this could be done efficiently by considering the structure of the functions involved. As a future work, we plan to give a generic algorithm and complexity analysis for the relevant cases in FFT-based linear cryptanalysis, e.g., a small number of rounds of any SPN structure. However, more generally, we do not know if there exists a competitive generic algorithm for this task.

Problem 1. Let $f, g : \mathbb{F}_2^n \to \{-1, 1\}$ be two functions. Given query access to g, given a black box that produces $\sum_x \widehat{f}(x)|x\rangle$, produce $\sum_x \widehat{g}(x)\widehat{f}(x)|x\rangle$.

Assuming that the Fourier coefficients of g and f are distributed somewhat uniformly, we can produce the state $\sum_x \widehat{g}(x)\widehat{f}(x)|x\rangle$ with $\mathcal{O}(2^{n/2})$ queries to both functions: we simply start with $\sum_x \widehat{g}(x)|x\rangle \sum_y \widehat{f}|y\rangle$ and amplify the part of the state where $x = y$. But if we use this in Theorem 1, we will need at least $|K| \geq 2n$ to obtain a speedup with respect to exhaustive search, leaving this generic method useless for most applications.

Finding the Largest Correlation. After building the correlation state, we need to find the key which has the largest experimental correlation. In general, the problem that we would like to solve is the following.

Problem 2. Given a black-box quantum that produces a state $\sum_x \alpha_x|x\rangle$, where the amplitude are distributed according to a centered Gaussian, and either: • all of them are below a threshold t; • exactly one of them is above the threshold t; determine the case and/or find the corresponding coordinate.

This problem is not specific to symmetric cryptanalysis, as it appears in quantum algorithms for dual lattice sieving attacks [3]. In the worst case, the experimental correlations have a standard deviation of $\mathcal{O}(2^{-n/2})$ and the largest one is only of order $\mathcal{O}(2^{n/2})$ as well. Here, we do not know of any algorithm faster than $\mathcal{O}(2^n)$. Unfortunately, this case seems typical in both applications (lattice sieving and linear cryptanalysis).

A related problem is *zero-correlation* attacks, where the experimental correlation of the right subkey, instead of being bigger, is exactly zero.

Problem 3. Given a black-box quantum that produces a state $\sum_x \alpha_x |x\rangle$, where the amplitude are distributed according to a centered Gaussian, and either:
• one of them is exactly zero; • or not; determine the case and/or find the corresponding coordinate.

Again, when the others have a standard deviation $\mathcal{O}(2^{-n/2})$, no algorithm better than $\mathcal{O}(2^n)$ is known. Consequently, we do not know how to exploit this property, which would be very useful for key-recovery attacks.

Acknowledgments. The author thanks Xavier Bonnetain, Antonio Flórez-Gutiérrez, María Naya-Plasencia and the anonymous reviewers from CRYPTO for helpful discussions and comments. This work has been partially supported by the French Agence Nationale de la Recherche through the DeCrypt project under Contract ANR-18-CE39-0007, and through the France 2030 program under grant agreement No. ANR-22-PETQ-0008 PQ-TLS.

A   Appendix: Bounding Fourier Coefficients

Lemma 10. *Let $f_i : \{0,1\}^n \to \{-1,1\}$, $1 \le i \le M$ be a family of independent random functions. With probability at least 0.99, it holds that:*

$$\forall z, \forall i, |\widehat{f_i}(z)| \le 2^{n/2}\sqrt{6(\ln 100 + (n+1)\ln 2 + \ln M)} \ . \tag{40}$$

Proof. Let $f : \{0,1\}^n \to \{-1,1\}$ be a random function. We want to bound the maximum of its Fourier coefficients: $\max_z |\widehat{f}(z)|$.

We consider each coefficient separately, although they are not independent. For each z, $\widehat{f}(z)$ is a random variable over f equal to: $2\mathrm{Bin}(2^n, 1/2) - 2^n = 2\left(\mathrm{Bin}(2^n, 1/2) - 2^{n-1}\right)$. We use a Chernoff bound:

$$\forall \delta, \forall z, \Pr_f(|\mathrm{Bin}(2^n, 1/2) - 2^{n-1}| \ge \delta 2^{n-1}) \le 2\exp\left(\frac{-\delta^2 2^n}{6}\right)$$

$$\Pr_f(|\widehat{f}(z)| \ge \delta 2^n) \le 2\exp\left(\frac{-\delta^2 2^n}{6}\right)$$

$$\implies \forall \delta, \forall z, \Pr_f(|\widehat{f}(z)| \ge \delta\sqrt{2^n}) \le 2\exp\left(\frac{-\delta^2}{6}\right)$$

$$\implies \forall \delta, \Pr_f(\exists z, |\widehat{f}(z)| \ge \delta\sqrt{2^n}) \le 2^{n+1}\exp\left(\frac{-\delta^2}{6}\right) \ .$$

We find a value of δ for which this probability is smaller than $1/100$:

$$\ln(2^{n+1}) - \frac{\delta^2}{6} \le -\ln 100 \implies \delta \ge \sqrt{6(\ln 100 + (n+1)\ln 2)} \ .$$

References

1. Abdelraheem, M.A.: Estimating the probabilities of low-weight differential and linear approximations on PRESENT-like ciphers. In: Kwon, T., Lee, M.-K., Kwon, D. (eds.) ICISC 2012. LNCS, vol. 7839, pp. 368–382. Springer, Heidelberg (2013). https://doi.org/10.1007/978-3-642-37682-5_26

2. Alagic, G., Bai, C., Katz, J., Majenz, C.: Post-quantum security of the even-mansour cipher. In: EUROCRYPT (3). Lecture Notes in Computer Science, vol. 13277, pp. 458–487. Springer, Heidelberg (2022). https://doi.org/10.1007/978-3-031-07082-2_17

3. Albrecht, M.R., Shen, Y.: Quantum augmented dual attack. IACR Cryptol. ePrint Arch, p. 656 (2022). https://eprint.iacr.org/2022/656

4. Bennett, C.H., Bernstein, E., Brassard, G., Vazirani, U.V.: Strengths and weaknesses of quantum computing. SIAM J. Comput. **26**(5), 1510–1523 (1997). https://doi.org/10.1137/S0097539796300933

5. Bernstein, E., Vazirani, U.V.: Quantum complexity theory. SIAM J. Comput. **26**(5), 1411–1473 (1997). https://doi.org/10.1137/S0097539796300921

6. Biryukov, A., De Cannière, C., Quisquater, M.: On multiple linear approximations. In: Franklin, M. (ed.) CRYPTO 2004. LNCS, vol. 3152, pp. 1–22. Springer, Heidelberg (2004). https://doi.org/10.1007/978-3-540-28628-8_1

7. Blondeau, C., Nyberg, K.: Improved parameter estimates for correlation and capacity deviates in linear cryptanalysis. IACR Trans. Symmetric Cryptol. **2016**(2), 162–191 (2016). https://doi.org/10.13154/tosc.v2016.i2.162-191

8. Blondeau, C., Nyberg, K.: Joint data and key distribution of simple, multiple, and multidimensional linear cryptanalysis test statistic and its impact to data complexity. Des. Codes Cryptogr., 319–349 (2016). https://doi.org/10.1007/s10623-016-0268-6

9. Bogdanov, A., Geng, H., Wang, M., Wen, L., Collard, B.: Zero-correlation linear cryptanalysis with FFT and improved attacks on ISO standards camellia and CLEFIA. In: Lange, T., Lauter, K., Lisoněk, P. (eds.) SAC 2013. LNCS, vol. 8282, pp. 306–323. Springer, Heidelberg (2014). https://doi.org/10.1007/978-3-662-43414-7_16

10. Bogdanov, A., Rijmen, V.: Linear hulls with correlation zero and linear cryptanalysis of block ciphers. Des. Codes Cryptogr. **70**(3), 369–383 (2012). https://doi.org/10.1007/s10623-012-9697-z

11. Bonnetain, X., Hosoyamada, A., Naya-Plasencia, M., Sasaki, Yu., Schrottenloher, A.: Quantum attacks without superposition queries: the offline simon's algorithm. In: Galbraith, S.D., Moriai, S. (eds.) ASIACRYPT 2019. LNCS, vol. 11921, pp. 552–583. Springer, Cham (2019). https://doi.org/10.1007/978-3-030-34578-5_20

12. Bonnetain, X., Naya-Plasencia, M., Schrottenloher, A.: Quantum security analysis of AES. IACR Trans. Symmetric Cryptol. **2019**(2), 55–93 (2019). https://doi.org/10.13154/tosc.v2019.i2.55-93

13. Bonnetain, X., Schrottenloher, A., Sibleyras, F.: Beyond quadratic speedups in quantum attacks on symmetric schemes. In: EUROCRYPT (3). Lecture Notes in Computer Science, vol. 13277, pp. 315–344. Springer, Heidelberg (2022). https://doi.org/10.1007/978-3-031-07082-2_12

14. Brassard, G., Hoyer, P., Mosca, M., Tapp, A.: Quantum amplitude amplification and estimation. Contemp. Math. **305**, 53–74 (2002)

15. Broll, M., Canale, F., Flórez-Gutiérrez, A., Leander, G., Naya-Plasencia, M.: Generic framework for key-guessing improvements. In: Tibouchi, M., Wang, H. (eds.) ASIACRYPT 2021. LNCS, vol. 13090, pp. 453–483. Springer, Cham (2021). https://doi.org/10.1007/978-3-030-92062-3_16

16. Collard, B., Standaert, F.-X., Quisquater, J.-J.: Improving the time complexity of matsui's linear cryptanalysis. In: Nam, K.-H., Rhee, G. (eds.) ICISC 2007. LNCS, vol. 4817, pp. 77–88. Springer, Heidelberg (2007). https://doi.org/10.1007/978-3-540-76788-6_7

17. Daemen, J., Rijmen, V.: Probability distributions of correlation and differentials in block ciphers. J. Math. Cryptol. **1**(3), 221–242 (2007)

18. van Dam, W., Hallgren, S., Ip, L.: Quantum algorithms for some hidden shift problems. SIAM J. Comput. **36**(3), 763–778 (2006). https://doi.org/10.1137/S009753970343141X

19. Davenport, J.H., Pring, B.: Improvements to quantum search techniques for block-ciphers, with applications to AES. In: Dunkelman, O., Jacobson, Jr., M.J., O'Flynn, C. (eds.) SAC 2020. LNCS, vol. 12804, pp. 360–384. Springer, Cham (2021). https://doi.org/10.1007/978-3-030-81652-0_14

20. David, N., Naya-Plasencia, M., Schrottenloher, A.: Quantum impossible differential attacks: applications to AES and SKINNY. IACR Cryptol. ePrint Arch., p. 754 (2022)

21. Deutsch, D., Jozsa, R.: Rapid solution of problems by quantum computation. Proc. Roy. Soc. Lond. Ser. A: Math. Phys. Sci. **439**(1907), 553–558 (1992)

22. Flórez-Gutiérrez, A.: Optimising linear key recovery attacks with affine walsh transform pruning. In: ASIACRYPT (4). Lecture Notes in Computer Science, vol. 13794, pp. 447–476. Springer, Heidelberg (2022). https://doi.org/10.1007/978-3-031-22972-5_16

23. Flórez-Gutiérrez, A., Naya-Plasencia, M.: Improving key-recovery in linear attacks: application to 28-round PRESENT. In: Canteaut, A., Ishai, Y. (eds.) EUROCRYPT 2020. LNCS, vol. 12105, pp. 221–249. Springer, Cham (2020). https://doi.org/10.1007/978-3-030-45721-1_9

24. Frixons, P., Naya-Plasencia, M., Schrottenloher, A.: Quantum boomerang attacks and some applications. In: AlTawy, R., Hülsing, A. (eds.) SAC 2021. LNCS, vol. 13203, pp. 332–352. Springer, Cham (2022). https://doi.org/10.1007/978-3-030-99277-4_16

25. Grover, L.K.: A fast quantum mechanical algorithm for database search. In: STOC, pp. 212–219. ACM (1996). https://doi.org/10.1145/237814.237866

26. Grover, L.K.: Synthesis of quantum superpositions by quantum computation. Phys. Rev. Lett. **85**(6), 1334 (2000)

27. Häner, T., Roetteler, M., Svore, K.M.: Optimizing quantum circuits for arithmetic. arXiv preprint arXiv:1805.12445 (2018)

28. Hermelin, M., Nyberg, K.: Multidimensional linear distinguishing attacks and boolean functions. Cryptogr. Commun. **4**(1), 47–64 (2012). https://doi.org/10.1007/s12095-011-0053-3

29. Hosoyamada, A.: Quantum speed-up for multidimensional (zero correlation) linear and integral distinguishers. Cryptology ePrint Archive, Paper 2022/1558 (2022). https://eprint.iacr.org/2022/1558

30. Hosoyamada, A., Sasaki, Yu.: Quantum Demiric-Selçuk meet-in-the-middle attacks: applications to 6-round generic feistel constructions. In: Catalano, D., De Prisco, R. (eds.) SCN 2018. LNCS, vol. 11035, pp. 386–403. Springer, Cham (2018). https://doi.org/10.1007/978-3-319-98113-0_21

31. Hosoyamada, A., Sasaki, Yu.: Finding hash collisions with quantum computers by using differential trails with smaller probability than birthday bound. In: Canteaut, A., Ishai, Y. (eds.) EUROCRYPT 2020. LNCS, vol. 12106, pp. 249–279. Springer, Cham (2020). https://doi.org/10.1007/978-3-030-45724-2_9
32. Jang, K., et al.: Grover on pipo. Electronics 10(10), 1194 (2021)
33. Kaliski, B.S., Robshaw, M.J.B.: Linear cryptanalysis using multiple approximations. In: Desmedt, Y.G. (ed.) CRYPTO 1994. LNCS, vol. 839, pp. 26–39. Springer, Heidelberg (1994). https://doi.org/10.1007/3-540-48658-5_4
34. Kaplan, M., Leurent, G., Leverrier, A., Naya-Plasencia, M.: Breaking symmetric cryptosystems using quantum period finding. In: Robshaw, M., Katz, J. (eds.) CRYPTO 2016. LNCS, vol. 9815, pp. 207–237. Springer, Heidelberg (2016). https://doi.org/10.1007/978-3-662-53008-5_8
35. Kaplan, M., Leurent, G., Leverrier, A., Naya-Plasencia, M.: Quantum differential and linear cryptanalysis. IACR Trans. Symmetric Cryptol. 2016(1), 71–94 (2016). https://doi.org/10.13154/tosc.v2016.i1.71-94
36. Karpman, P., Grégoire, B.: The littlun s-box and the fly block cipher. In: NIST Lightweight Cryptography Workshop (informal proceedings) (2016)
37. Kim, H., et al.: PIPO: a lightweight block cipher with efficient higher-order masking software implementations. In: Hong, D. (ed.) ICISC 2020. LNCS, vol. 12593, pp. 99–122. Springer, Cham (2021). https://doi.org/10.1007/978-3-030-68890-5_6
38. Kuperberg, G.: Another subexponential-time quantum algorithm for the dihedral hidden subgroup problem. In: TQC. LIPIcs, vol. 22, pp. 20–34. Schloss Dagstuhl - Leibniz-Zentrum für Informatik (2013)
39. Kuwakado, H., Morii, M.: Quantum distinguisher between the 3-round feistel cipher and the random permutation. In: ISIT, pp. 2682–2685. IEEE (2010)
40. Kuwakado, H., Morii, M.: Security on the quantum-type even-mansour cipher. In: ISITA, pp. 312–316. IEEE (2012). https://ieeexplore.ieee.org/document/6400943/
41. Leurent, G., Pernot, C., Schrottenloher, A.: Clustering effect in SIMON and SIMECK. In: Tibouchi, M., Wang, H. (eds.) ASIACRYPT 2021. LNCS, vol. 13090, pp. 272–302. Springer, Cham (2021). https://doi.org/10.1007/978-3-030-92062-3_10
42. Matsui, M.: Linear cryptanalysis method for DES cipher. In: Helleseth, T. (ed.) EUROCRYPT 1993. LNCS, vol. 765, pp. 386–397. Springer, Heidelberg (1994). https://doi.org/10.1007/3-540-48285-7_33
43. Matsui, M.: The first experimental cryptanalysis of the data encryption standard. In: Desmedt, Y.G. (ed.) CRYPTO 1994. LNCS, vol. 839, pp. 1–11. Springer, Heidelberg (1994). https://doi.org/10.1007/3-540-48658-5_1
44. Nielsen, M.A., Chuang, I.: Quantum computation and quantum information (2002)
45. NIST: Submission requirements and evaluation criteria for the post-quantum cryptography standardization process (2016). https://csrc.nist.gov/CSRC/media/Projects/Post-Quantum-Cryptography/documents/call-for-proposals-final-dec-2016.pdf
46. Ozols, M., Roetteler, M., Roland, J.: Quantum rejection sampling. ACM Trans. Comput. Theory 5(3), 11:1–11:33 (2013). https://doi.org/10.1145/2493252.2493256
47. Sanders, Y.R., Low, G.H., Scherer, A., Berry, D.W.: Black-box quantum state preparation without arithmetic. Phys. Rev. Lett. 122(2), 020502 (2019)
48. Selinger, P.: Efficient clifford+ t approximation of single-qubit operators. arXiv preprint arXiv:1212.6253 (2012)
49. Shor, P.W.: Algorithms for quantum computation: discrete logarithms and factoring. In: FOCS, pp. 124–134. IEEE Computer Society (1994). https://doi.org/10.1109/SFCS.1994.365700

50. Simon, D.R.: On the power of quantum computation. SIAM J. Comput. **26**(5), 1474–1483 (1997). https://doi.org/10.1137/S0097539796298637
51. Sun, L., Wang, W., Wang, M.: Improved attacks on `GIFT-64`. In: AlTawy, R., Hülsing, A. (eds.) SAC 2021. LNCS, vol. 13203, pp. 246–265. Springer, Cham (2022). https://doi.org/10.1007/978-3-030-99277-4_12
52. Takahashi, Y., Tani, S., Kunihiro, N.: Quantum addition circuits and unbounded fan-out. arXiv preprint arXiv:0910.2530 (2009)
53. Yamakawa, T., Zhandry, M.: Verifiable quantum advantage without structure. In: FOCS, pp. 69–74. IEEE (2022). https://doi.org/10.1109/FOCS54457.2022.00014

Tighter QCCA-Secure Key Encapsulation Mechanism with Explicit Rejection in the Quantum Random Oracle Model

Jiangxia Ge[1,2] , Tianshu Shan[1,2] , and Rui Xue[1,2(✉)]

[1] State Key Laboratory of Information Security, Institute of Information
Engineering, Chinese Academy of Sciences, Beijing 100093, China
{gejiangxia,shantianshu,xuerui}@iie.ac.cn
[2] School of Cyber Security, University of Chinese Academy of Sciences,
Beijing 100049, China

Abstract. Hofheinz et al. (TCC 2017) proposed several key encapsulation mechanism (KEM) variants of Fujisaki-Okamoto (FO) transformation, including $FO^{\not\perp}, FO_m^{\not\perp}, QFO_m^{\not\perp}, FO^{\perp}, FO_m^{\perp}$ and $QFO_m^{\perp}$, and they are widely used in the post-quantum cryptography standardization launched by NIST. These transformations are divided into two types, the implicit and explicit rejection type, including $\{FO^{\not\perp}, FO_m^{\not\perp}, QFO_m^{\not\perp}\}$ and $\{FO^{\perp}, FO_m^{\perp}, QFO_m^{\perp}\}$, respectively. The decapsulation algorithm of the implicit (resp. explicit) rejection type returns a pseudorandom value (resp. an abort symbol $\perp$) for an invalid ciphertext.

For the implicit rejection type, the IND-CCA security reduction of $FO^{\not\perp}$ in the quantum random oracle model (QROM) can avoid the quadratic security loss, as shown by Kuchta et al. (EUROCRYPT 2020). However, for the explicit rejection type, the best known IND-CCA security reduction in the QROM presented by Hövelmanns et al. (ASIACRYPT 2022) for $FO_m^{\perp}$ still suffers from a quadratic security loss. Moreover, it is not clear until now whether the implicit rejection type is more secure than the explicit rejection type.

In this paper, a QROM security reduction of $FO_m^{\perp}$ without incurring a quadratic security loss is provided. Furthermore, our reduction achieves IND-qCCA security, which is stronger than the IND-CCA security. To achieve our result, two steps are taken: The first step is to prove that the IND-qCCA security of $FO_m^{\perp}$ can be tightly reduced to the IND-CPA security of $FO_m^{\perp}$ by using the online extraction technique proposed by Don et al. (EUROCRYPT 2022). The second step is to prove that the IND-CPA security of $FO_m^{\perp}$ can be reduced to the IND-CPA security of the underlying public key encryption (PKE) scheme without incurring quadratic security loss by using the Measure-Rewind-Measure One-Way to Hiding Lemma (EUROCRYPT 2020).

In addition, we prove that (at least from a theoretic point of view), security is independent of whether the rejection type is explicit ($FO_m^{\perp}$) or implicit ($FO_m^{\not\perp}$) if the underlying PKE scheme is weakly γ-spread.

© International Association for Cryptologic Research 2023
H. Handschuh and A. Lysyanskaya (Eds.): CRYPTO 2023, LNCS 14085, pp. 292–324, 2023.
https://doi.org/10.1007/978-3-031-38554-4_10

Keywords: Fujisaki-Okamoto transformation · quantum random oracle · key encapsulation mechanism · quantum chosen-ciphertext attack

1 Introduction

The Fujisaki-Okamoto (FO) transformation [10] combines a public key encryption (PKE) scheme and a symmetric key encryption (SKE) scheme to obtain a hybrid scheme that is secure against the indistinguishability under chosen-ciphertext attacks (IND-CCA) in the random oracle model (ROM) [2]. It is known as the first generic transformation from an arbitrary OW-CPA-secure PKE to an IND-CCA-secure PKE in the ROM. Dent [8] introduced the first key encapsulation mechanism (KEM) variant of FO obtaining an IND-CCA-secure KEM in the ROM. Hofheinz et al. [14] provided a fine-grained and modular toolkit of transformations including $\mathsf{T}, \mathsf{U}^{\not\perp}, \mathsf{U}^{\perp}, \mathsf{U}_m^{\not\perp}$, $\mathsf{U}_m^{\perp}, \mathsf{QU}_m^{\not\perp}$ and $\mathsf{QU}_m^{\perp}$. They then presented the KEM variants of FO as $\mathsf{FO}^{\not\perp}, \mathsf{FO}^{\perp}, \mathsf{FO}_m^{\not\perp}, \mathsf{FO}_m^{\perp}, \mathsf{QFO}_m^{\not\perp}$ and $\mathsf{QFO}_m^{\perp}$ by combining T with $\mathsf{U}^{\not\perp}, \mathsf{U}^{\perp}, \mathsf{U}_m^{\not\perp}, \mathsf{U}_m^{\perp}, \mathsf{QU}_m^{\not\perp}$ and $\mathsf{QU}_m^{\perp}$, respectively. Here $\not\perp$ (resp. $\perp$) indicates that the transformation belongs to the implicit (resp. explicit) rejection type, which means that a pseudorandom value (resp. an abort symbol $\perp$) is returned if the ciphertext fails to decapsulate. In what follows, we refer to above KEM variants of FO as FO-like transformations.

As FO-like transformations are frequently used in the NIST post-quantum cryptography standardisation process [23], the post-quantum security of FO-like transformations have drawn much attention. In the post-quantum setting, the ROM should be lifted to the quantum random oracle model (QROM) [4], and thus the IND-CCA security reduction of FO-like transformations in the QROM is more concerned. To this problem, a sequence of works has been given [16–18]. The core tool used in their reductions is the One-Way to Hiding (O2H) Lemma [1,25], and their reductions all suffer from a quadratic security loss.

For the implicit rejection type of FO-like transformations, Kuchta et al. proposed a new O2H variant named Measure-Rewind-Measure One-Way to Hiding (MRM O2H) Lemma [20], with which an IND-CCA security reduction of $\mathsf{FO}^{\not\perp}$ in the QROM avoiding the quadratic security loss is provided. For the explicit rejection type of FO-like transformations, the best known reduction is provided by Hövelmanns et al. [15]. They proved the IND-CCA security of $\mathsf{FO}_m^{\perp}$ in the QROM and their reduction still suffers from a quadratic security loss. The core tool used in their reduction is a new O2H variant named semi-classical OWTH in the eQROM_f, which can be considered as the combination of the extractable RO-simulator [9] and the semi-classical O2H [1].

In addition to avoiding the quadratic security loss, Xagawa and Yamakawa [26] also considered the QROM security of FO-like transformations against quantum adversaries that can mount quantum superposition queries to the decapsulation oracle. They introduced a new security notion for KEM named indistinguishability under quantum chosen-ciphertext attacks (IND-qCCA) by following the notion of Boneh and Zhandry [5], and provided an IND-qCCA security reduction of SXY in the QROM. Here SXY designed in [26] is identical to $U_m^{\not\perp}$. Liu and Wang [21] modified the definition of disjoint simulatability secure proposed in [26] and applied the MRM O2H lemma to prove that the transformation KC defined in [24] can transform a OW-CPA-secure deterministic public key encryption (DPKE) scheme with correctness errors into a modified disjoint simulatability secure PKE scheme. Furthermore, they proved that transformation SXY ∘ KC and SXY ∘ KC ∘ T can also achieve the IND-qCCA security.

Compared with the implicit rejection type, the explicit rejection type of FO-like transformations is more natural and has a positive performance on the robustness [13]. Unfortunately, the best known QROM reduction of the explicit rejection type FO-like transformations provided by Hövelmanns et al. [15] still suffers from a quadratic security loss, and their IND-CCA security reduction seems to be insufficient to prove the IND-qCCA security[1]. Hence, a natural question arises:

> Is it possible to give an IND-qCCA security reduction of the explicit rejection type of FO-like transformations in the QROM avoiding quadratic security loss?

In addition, the impact of the different rejection type of the FO-like transformations on the security of the final scheme is also discussed in the literature. Bindel et al. [3] proved that the transformation $FO^{\not\perp}$ (resp. $FO^{\perp}$) is secure iff $FO_m^{\not\perp}$ (resp. $FO_m^{\perp}$) is secure. They also showed that the security of $FO_m^{\perp}$ implies security of $FO_m^{\not\perp}$, and that the security of $FO_m^{\not\perp}$ implies security of $QFO_m^{\perp}$. Further, Hövelmanns et al. [15] showed that the security of $FO_m^{\perp}$ implies security of all remaining FO-like transformations. However, it is not clear until now whether the security of $FO_m^{\not\perp}$ implies security of $FO_m^{\perp}$, and thus the results of [3,15] do not imply that the implicit rejection type of FO-like transformations is as secure as their explicit rejection counterparts. Therefore, there still exists an open problem on the implicit and explicit rejection types of FO-like transformations as follows:

> Is the explicit rejection type as secure as their implicit rejection counterparts? In other words, does the security of $FO_m^{\not\perp}$ imply the security of $FO_m^{\perp}$?

1.1 Our Contribution

Avoiding the quadratic security loss, an IND-qCCA security reduction of $FO_m^{\perp}$ in the QROM is provided (Corollary 1), and the corresponding security bound is

---

[1] Indeed, in the IND-CCA security reduction of [15], **Game G_1** records the decapsulation query c_i $(i = 1, \ldots, q_D)$ and computes $eCO.E(c_i)$ for each c_i via the extraction interface $eCO.E$ in its end. The record procedure is available in the IND-CCA security reduction. However, due to the quantum no-cloning principle, it is infeasible to perfectly record the quantum decapsulation queries in the IND-qCCA security reduction.

shown in Table 1. Compared with security bounds of $FO_m^\perp$ provided in [9, 15], our security bound of $FO_m^\perp$ is much tighter, and we achieve a stronger (IND-qCCA) security[2] with the same or even weaker requirements.

Table 1. Security bounds of different transformations in the QROM. Here q is the total number of query times to the random oracles, d and w is the query depth and query width of the random oracles, q_D is the adversary's query times to the decapsulation oracle. ϵ is the security bound of the underlying PKE scheme P.

Transformation	Underlying security	Achieved security	Requirement	Security bound($\approx$)
$FO_m^\perp$ [9]	OW-CPA	IND-CCA	P is weakly γ-spread	$q \cdot \sqrt{\epsilon}$
$FO_m^\perp$ [15]	OW-CPA	IND-CCA	P is γ-spread	$(d+q_D) \cdot \sqrt{w \cdot \epsilon}$
$FO_m^\perp$ Our work	IND-CPA	IND-qCCA	P is weakly γ-spread	$d(d + q_D) \cdot \epsilon$

Moreover, in the QROM, we prove that $FO_m^{\not\perp}$ is IND-qCCA-secure if $FO_m^\perp$ is IND-qCCA-secure (Theorem 5), and conversely that $FO_m^\perp$ is IND-qCCA-secure if $FO_m^{\not\perp}$ is IND-qCCA-secure (Theorem 6).

In more detail, in the proof of Theorem 5, we tightly reduce the IND-qCCA security of $FO_m^{\not\perp}$ to the IND-qCCA security of $FO_m^\perp$.

As for the Theorem 6, let $(\epsilon^\perp, T^\perp, S^\perp)$ denote the success probability, running time and memory space of an adversary against the IND-qCCA security of $FO_m^\perp$, respectively, and let $(\epsilon^{\not\perp}, T^{\not\perp}, S^{\not\perp})$ denote the success probability, running time and memory space of a reduction algorithm against the IND-qCCA security of $FO_m^{\not\perp}$, respectively. In the proof of Theorem 6, suppose that the underlying PKE scheme is weakly γ-spread, we prove that (Here q_D and q is the notion used in Table 1.)

$$\epsilon^\perp \leq \epsilon^{\not\perp} + O(q_D \cdot 2^{-\gamma/2}), \quad T^{\not\perp} \approx T^\perp + O(q^2), \quad S^{\not\perp} \approx S^\perp + O(q).$$

This indicates that the IND-qCCA security of $FO_m^\perp$ can be reduced to the IND-qCCA security of $FO_m^{\not\perp}$ with an additional error of $O(q_D \cdot 2^{-\gamma/2})$, a quadratic running time expansion, and a linear space expansion of the reduction algorithm.

Overall, assuming that the underlying PKE scheme is weakly γ-spread, it can be concluded that the explicit rejection type of FO-like transformations is as secure as their implicit rejection counterparts. This implies that the security of FO-like transformations is independent of the rejection type if the underlying PKE scheme is weakly γ-spread.

---

[2] If a PKE/KEM scheme is IND-qCCA-secure, it is also IND-CCA-secure, because classical decryption/decapsulation queries can be implemented by quantum decryption/decapsulation queries. That is why we say that IND-qCCA security is a stronger security.

1.2 Technical Overview

Our IND-qCCA security reduction of $FO_m^\perp$ in the QROM can be decomposed into two steps as shown in Fig. 1:

1. In the first step, we prove that, in the QROM, the IND-qCCA security of $FO_m^\perp$ can be tightly reduced to the IND-CPA security of $FO_m^\perp$ (Theorem 2).
2. In the second step, we prove that, in the QROM, $U_m^\perp$ can transform a OW-CPA-secure DPKE scheme dPKE into an IND-CPA-secure KEM scheme $U_m^\perp[dPKE]$ without the quadratic security loss (Theorem 3). Then combining with Lemma 8 and the property that $FO_m^\perp = U_m^\perp \circ T$, we prove that, in the QROM, the IND-CPA security of $FO_m^\perp$ can be reduced to the IND-CPA security of the underlying randomized PKE scheme P without the quadratic security loss.

$$\begin{array}{ccc} \text{IND-CPA} & \xrightarrow{\text{Theorem 2}} & \text{IND-qCCA} \\ FO_m^\perp & & FO_m^\perp \end{array}$$

$$\begin{array}{ccccc} \text{IND-CPA} & \xrightarrow{\text{T}} & \text{OW-CPA} & \xrightarrow{U_m^\perp} & \text{IND-CPA} \\ \text{δ-correct P} & \text{Lemma 8 [3]} & \text{dPKE} & \text{Theorem 3} & U_m^\perp[dPKE] \end{array}$$

Fig. 1. Two steps of the IND-qCCA security reduction of $FO_m^\perp$ in the QROM.

Here we first consider the second step. Using the MRM O2H lemma, it is straightforward to prove Theorem 3. We stress that this lemma requires the simulator simulates both H and G and we circumvent this problem by using the Lemma 4 in [21] (i.e. Lemma 9 in our paper.).

For the first step, we prove Theorem 2 via a series of hybrid games from G_0 to G_6, where game G_0 is the IND-qCCA game of $FO_m^\perp$ with adversary $\mathcal{A}$ in the QROM. Define $\mathrm{Adv}(G_i, G_{i+1}) := |\Pr[1 \leftarrow G_i] - \Pr[1 \leftarrow G_{i+1}]|$ for $i = 0, \ldots, 5$. In the proof of Theorem 2, our basic idea is to analyze the upper bound of $\mathrm{Adv}(G_i, G_{i+1})$ for $i = 0, \ldots, 5$, and finally construct an IND-CPA adversary $\tilde{\mathcal{A}}$ against $FO_m^\perp$ in the QROM by the adversary $\mathcal{A}$ in game G_6. The overview of games G_1 to G_6 are as follows.

- Game G_1 is identical with G_0, except the extractable RO-simulator $\mathcal{S}(f_1) := \{eCO.RO, eCO.E_{f_1}\}$ is introduced and the quantum queries to random oracle H is simulated by the RO-interface eCO.RO. In game G_1, $\mathcal{A}$'s quantum queries to H have been recorded in database imperfectly.
- From game G_2 to G_3, we gradually change the simulation of the quantum accessible decapsulation oracle, and finally simulate it without secret key sk in game G_3.
- From game G_4 to G_6, our aim is to make the database just before adversary $\mathcal{A}$ performs its operation be irrelevant to the challenge plaintext m^*.

In the following, we describe the difference between every two adjacent games of games $\mathbf{G_1}, \ldots, \mathbf{G_6}$ and analyze them at a high level.

Game $\mathbf{G_1}$-$\mathbf{G_2}$: In order to simulate the quantum accessible decapsulation oracle qDeca without sk, our idea is to use the extraction-interface of the extractable RO-simulator to read out the information recorded in the database and prepare replies to the qDeca. We emphasize that this simulating can only read the database and cannot update or change it. However, the simulation of qDeca in game $\mathbf{G_1}$ has no such limitation because it can query H (which is simulated by eCO.RO) and update the database at certain points. Therefore, we design the following game $\mathbf{G_2}$ in our proof to clarify the error produced when changing the simulation of qDeca from updating the database to reading it.

- Game $\mathbf{G_2}$: This game is the same as game $\mathbf{G_1}$, except that the operation $\mathsf{eCO.E}_{f_1} \circ O_G \circ \mathsf{eCO.E}_{f_1}$ as shown in Fig. 2 is used to simulate qDeca.

Here $\mathsf{eCO.E}_{f_1}$ maps $|c, D, m\rangle$ to $|c, D, m \oplus x\rangle$, $x = \mathsf{Dec}_{sk}(c)$ if $\mathsf{Dec}_{sk}(c) \neq \perp$ and $\mathsf{Enc}_{pk}(\mathsf{Dec}_{sk}(c), D(\mathsf{Dec}_{sk}(c))) = c$. Otherwise $x = \perp^3$. Operation O_G simulates the random oracle G and we set $G(\perp) = \perp$.

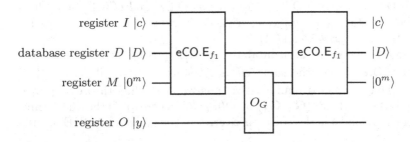

Fig. 2. Operation $\mathsf{eCO.E}_{f_1} \circ O_G \circ \mathsf{eCO.E}_{f_1}$. Here I/O is input/output register of qDeca, M is the internal register used by operation $\mathsf{eCO.E}_{f_1} \circ O_G \circ \mathsf{eCO.E}_{f_1}$.

For any computational basis state $|c, D, y\rangle$ on registers IDO that satisfies $\mathsf{Dec}_{sk}(c) \neq \perp$ and $D(\mathsf{Dec}_{sk}(c)) = \perp$, it is easily verified that the qDeca in game $\mathbf{G_2}$ returns state $|c, D, y \oplus \perp\rangle$ for input state $|c, D, y\rangle$ since $G(\perp) = \perp$. However, the qDeca in game $\mathbf{G_1}$ may not return $|c, D, y \oplus \perp\rangle$, because the simulation of qDeca in game $\mathbf{G_1}$ can update the database to a uniform superposition of database $D \cup (\mathsf{Dec}_{sk}(c), y)$ for $y \in \{0, 1\}^n$.

The difference between game $\mathbf{G_1}$ and $\mathbf{G_2}$ above actually corresponds to the classical event GUESS in the ROM reduction of $\mathsf{FO}_m^\perp$ provided in [15], i.e., the adversary queries a ciphertext c to the decapsulation oracle satisfying that $\mathsf{Dec}_{sk}(c)(\neq \perp)$ is never queried to H before but $\mathsf{Enc}_{pk}(\mathsf{Dec}_{sk}(c), H(\mathsf{Dec}_{sk}(c))) = c$. The probability that GUESS occurs can be upper bounded by $2^{-\gamma}$ if the

---

^{3} For simplify, we do not consider the case of $c = c^*$ here. c^* is the challenge ciphertext.

underlying PKE scheme is γ-spread, since $H(x)$ is uniformly random in $\{0,1\}^n$ if x is never queried to H, and the maximum number of elements y meeting $\mathsf{Enc}_{pk}(x,y) = c$ in $\{0,1\}^n$ is $2^{n-\gamma}$.

We analyze the difference between game $\mathbf{G_1}$ and $\mathbf{G_2}$ in a similar way, that is to say, even if the database is updated to a uniform superposition of database $D \cup (\mathsf{Dec}_{sk}(c), y)$ for $y \in \{0,1\}^n$ in game $\mathbf{G_1}$, there are not many $y \in \{0,1\}^n$ such that

$$\mathsf{eCO.E}_{f_1}|c, D \cup (\mathsf{Dec}_{sk}(c), y), m\rangle = |c, D \cup (\mathsf{Dec}_{sk}(c), y), m \oplus \mathsf{Dec}_{sk}(c)\rangle$$

if the underlying PKE scheme is weakly γ-spread. We stress that we finally (upper) bound $\mathrm{Adv}(\mathbf{G_1}, \mathbf{G_2})$ by $8q_D \cdot 2^{-\gamma/2}$ since decapsulation oracle qDeca is quantum accessible in our reduction.

Game $\mathbf{G_2}$-$\mathbf{G_3}$: Game $\mathbf{G_3}$ is the same as game $\mathbf{G_2}$ except that the extractable RO-simulator is changed to $\mathcal{S}(f_2) := \{\mathsf{eCO.RO}, \mathsf{eCO.E}_{f_2}\}$.

For computational basis state $|c, D, m\rangle$ on registers IDM, $\mathsf{eCO.E}_{f_2}$ extracts the minimum x satisfying $\mathsf{Enc}_{pk}(x, D(x)) = c$ and returns state $|c, D, m \oplus x\rangle$ if such x exists. Otherwise, returns state $|c, D, m \oplus \perp\rangle$. Note that the implementation of $\mathsf{eCO.E}_{f_2}$ does not need sk because it no longer cares about if above x also equals $\mathsf{Dec}_{sk}(c)$ like $\mathsf{eCO.E}_{f_1}$. However, $\mathsf{eCO.E}_{f_1}$ and $\mathsf{eCO.E}_{f_2}$ may have different effect on state $|c, D, m\rangle$ that triggers decryption errors (x exists s.t. $\mathsf{Enc}_{pk}(x, D(x)) = c$ but $x \neq \mathsf{Dec}_{sk}(c)$).

In the proof of Theorem 2, a database set $R_{pk,sk}^D$ is defined. We find that $\mathsf{eCO.E}_{f_1}$ and $\mathsf{eCO.E}_{f_2}$ have the same effect on state $|c, D, m\rangle$ if $D \notin R_{pk,sk}^D$. Then, we use the compressed semi-classical one-way to hiding theorem[4] proved in [11] to (upper) bound $\mathrm{Adv}(\mathbf{G_2}, \mathbf{G_3})$ by $O(q_H)\sqrt{\delta}$, where q_H is the query times to random oracle H and δ is the correctness error of the underlying PKE scheme.

Game $\mathbf{G_3}$-$\mathbf{G_4}$-$\mathbf{G_5}$: Note that game $\mathbf{G_3}$ uses operation $\mathsf{eCO.E}_{f_2} \circ O_G \circ \mathsf{eCO.E}_{f_2}$, which no longer needs sk, to simulate qDeca. However, the challenge ciphertext c^* $(= \mathsf{Enc}_{pk}(m^*, H(m^*)))$ still needs classically query H (which is simulated using $\mathsf{eCO.RO}$) by challenge plaintext m^* to generate. The database state just before adversary $\mathcal{A}$ performs its operations in game $\mathbf{G_3}$ can be written as

$$\mathsf{StdDecomp}_{m^*}|D^\perp \cup (m^*, H(m^*))\rangle,$$

where database $D^\perp$ only contains $(\perp, 0^n)$ pairs, $\mathsf{StdDecomp}_{m^*}$ is the local decompression procedure defined in [28], and we also denote it as S_{m^*} in what follows for convenience. Obviously, this state contains the information of m^*, hence a new adversary without m^* unable to simulate game $\mathbf{G_3}$ for $\mathcal{A}$.

---

[4] Actually, this theorem is a generalization of the compress oracle O2H theorem (Theorem 10) in [7], since the quantum oracle algorithm in this theorem can also make database read queries.

To circumvent this problem, our idea is as follows. Let O be a new random oracle that has the same input/output length as H, roughly speaking, if the extractable RO-simulator $\mathcal{S}(f_2)$ in game $\mathbf{G_3}$ perfectly simulates random oracle H at point m^*, we can equivalently compute c^* as $\mathsf{Enc}_{pk}(m^*, O(m^*))$ and the database state just before adversary $\mathcal{A}$ performs its operation at this time is irrelevant to m^*. What we need to do next is to ensure that $\mathcal{A}$ will get $O(m^*)$ accordingly when querying H (which is simulated using eCO.RO) by m^* and design a simulation method for qDeca following the modification of the computation of c^*.

Unfortunately, the extractable RO-simulator $\mathcal{S}(f_2)$ in game $\mathbf{G_3}$ cannot perfectly simulate the random oracle H at point m^*. Note that state $\mathsf{S}_{m^*}|D^\perp \cup (m^*, H(m^*))\rangle$ is a superposition of $|D^\perp \cup (m^*, y)\rangle$ for $y \in \{0,1\}^n$ and $|D^\perp\rangle$ [28], the extraction-interface eCO.E$_{f_2}$ used in game $\mathbf{G_3}$ may disturb this superposition state. Then, we design game $\mathbf{G_4}$ as follows in our reduction.

– Game $\mathbf{G_4}$: It is the same as game $\mathbf{G_3}$ except that S_{m^*} is performed before and after the applying of eCO.E$_{f_2}$. Thus, a new extractable RO-simulator

$$\mathcal{S}'(f_2) := \{\mathsf{eCO.RO}, \mathsf{S}_{m^*} \circ \mathsf{eCO.E}_{f_2} \circ \mathsf{S}_{m^*}\}$$

is applied in this game.

The $\mathrm{Adv}(\mathbf{G_3}, \mathbf{G_4})$ can be easily upper bounded by using the operator norm $\|[\mathsf{eCO.E}_{f_2}, \mathsf{S}_{m^*}]\|$ since S_{m^*} is an involution [28].

In contrast to game $\mathbf{G_3}$, the extractable RO-simulator $\mathcal{S}'(f_2)$ in game $\mathbf{G_4}$ perfectly simulates the random oracle H at point m^*. Intuitively, the operation $\mathsf{S}_{m^*} \circ \mathsf{eCO.E}_{f_2} \circ \mathsf{S}_{m^*}$ seems to implement one classical compressed standard oracle query at point m^*, except that the operation CNOT is changed to eCO.E$_{f_2}$. Indeed, it is precisely because of this query-like structure, $\mathsf{S}_{m^*} \circ \mathsf{eCO.E}_{f_2} \circ \mathsf{S}_{m^*}$ will not cause disturbance to $\mathsf{S}_{m^*}|D^\perp \cup (m^*, H(m^*))\rangle$ like eCO.E$_{f_2}$. We observe that the internal joint state of game $\mathbf{G_4}$ before and after the implementation of operation $\mathsf{S}_{m^*} \circ \mathsf{eCO.E}_{f_2} \circ \mathsf{S}_{m^*}$ can always be written as [5]

$$\sum_{Z,D} \mathsf{S}_{m^*} |Z, D \cup (m^*, H(m^*))\rangle.$$

Hence, the random oracle H in game $\mathbf{G_4}$, which is simulated using eCO.RO, will always return $H(m^*)$ for the input m^* and $H(m^*)$ is a uniformly random value in $\{0,1\}^n$. Thus, the extractable RO-simulator $\mathcal{S}'(f_2)$ in game $\mathbf{G_4}$ perfectly simulates the random oracle H at the point m^*.

As for the decapsulation oracle qDeca, it is simulated by operation

$$\underline{\mathsf{S}_{m^*} \circ \mathsf{eCO.E}_{f_2} \circ \mathsf{S}_{m^*}} \circ O_G \circ \underline{\mathsf{S}_{m^*} \circ \mathsf{eCO.E}_{f_2} \circ \mathsf{S}_{m^*}}$$

in game $\mathbf{G_4}$. In our reduction, we prove that the extraction result of the operation $\mathsf{S}_{m^*} \circ \mathsf{eCO.E}_{f_2} \circ \mathsf{S}_{m^*}$ acting on state $\mathsf{S}_{m^*}|c, D \cup (m^*, H(m^*)), m\rangle$ is the same as the

---

[5] (Here we abbreviate other registers that may entangled with the database register (e.g. registers of the adversary) as Z.)

extraction result of the operation $eCO.E_{f_2}$ acting on state $|c, D, m\rangle$. Therefore, if c^* is computed as $Enc_{pk}(m^*, O(m^*))$ in game $\mathbf{G_4}$, we can equivalently use the operation $eCO.E_{f_2} \circ O_G \circ eCO.E_{f_2}$ to simulate qDeca. That is to say, game $\mathbf{G_4}$ and following game $\mathbf{G_5}$ are identical.

- Game $\mathbf{G_5}$: This game is like game $\mathbf{G_4}$, except for the following modifications: A new random oracle O is introduced and the challenge ciphertext c^* is generated as $Enc_{pk}(m^*, O(m^*))$. The decapsulation oracle qDeca in this game is simulated by the operation $eCO.E_{f_2} \circ O_G \circ eCO.E_{f_2}$. When adversary $\mathcal{A}$ queries H by $|x, y\rangle$, a conditional operation U as follows is applied.

$$U|x, y, D\rangle = \begin{cases} eCO.RO|x, y, D\rangle & (x \neq m^*) \\ |x, y \oplus O(m^*), D\rangle & (x = m^*). \end{cases}$$

Game $\mathbf{G_5}$-$\mathbf{G_6}$: However, another problem arises in game $\mathbf{G_5}$, the conditional operation U still needs m^* to perform a test checking if $x = m^*$. In game $\mathbf{G_6}$, the conditional operation U is replaced by a new conditional operation U' as

$$U'|x, y, D\rangle = \begin{cases} eCO.RO|x, y, D\rangle & (Enc_{pk}(x, O(x)) \neq c^*) \\ |x, y \oplus O(m^*), D\rangle & (Enc_{pk}(x, O(x)) = c^*). \end{cases}$$

Obviously, if x' satisfying $Enc_{pk}(x', O(x')) = Enc_{pk}(m^*, O(m^*))$ does not exist, games $\mathbf{G_5}$ and $\mathbf{G_6}$ are identical. Indeed, if the underlying PKE scheme is δ-correct, the probability that such x' exists is at most 2δ by using the Lemma 4 in [21].

As for the relation between the security of $FO_m^\perp$ and $FO_m^{\not\perp}$, it is easy to prove that the IND-qCCA security of $FO_m^\perp$ implies the IND-qCCA security of $FO_m^{\not\perp}$[6]. The proof in the opposite direction heavily relies on Theorem 2 and contains the following two steps:

1. By using Theorem 2, we obtain that any IND-qCCA adversary against $FO_m^\perp$ can be transformed to an IND-CPA adversary against $FO_m^\perp$.
2. Then we prove that any IND-CPA adversary against $FO_m^\perp$ can be efficiently transformed to an IND-qCCA adversary against $FO_m^{\not\perp}$.

Related Work. The reduction from the IND-CCA security of $FO_m^\perp$ in the QROM to the IND-CPA security of $FO_m^\perp$ has been argued in [15]. Their IND-CPA security of $FO_m^\perp$ is in the $eQROM_{Enc}$, in which the random oracle H is simulated by an extractable RO-simulator $\mathcal{S}(Enc) := \{eCO.RO, eCO.E_{Enc}\}$ and the decapsulation oracle is simulated by using the extraction-interfaces $eCO.E_{Enc}$. They then reduced the IND-CPA security of $FO_m^\perp$ in the $eQROM_{Enc}$ to the OW-CPA security of the underlying PKE by using the semi-classical OWTH in the $eQROM_f$, which brings a quadratic security loss to their reduction.

---

[6] Note that any IND-qCCA adversary against $FO_m^{\not\perp}$ can be efficiently transformed to an IND-qCCA adversary against $FO_m^\perp$.

In contrast, we reduce the IND-qCCA security of $FO_m^\perp$ in the QROM to the IND-CPA security of $FO_m^\perp$ in the QROM (not $eQROM_{Enc}$), which enables us to use the MRM O2H lemma and avoid the quadratic security loss.

Recently, Ge et al. [11] proved a lifting theorem for a class of games called the oracle-hiding game, and then proved the IND-qCCA security of $FO_m^\perp$ in the QROM by directly applying that lifting theorem. However, their reduction still has a quadratic security loss. Additionally, by combining Theorem 2 of [21] and Theorem 5.1 of [26], the transformation HU ∘ KC can transform an OW-CPA-secure DPKE scheme into an IND-qCCA-secure KEM scheme in the QROM. The corresponding reduction also avoids the quadratic security loss, and HU ∘ KC is also an explicit rejection type KEM transformation. However, compared with the $FO_m^\perp$, the encapsulation and decapsulation algorithms of HU ∘ KC are more complicated, and the underlying PKE scheme of HU ∘ KC is restricted to DPKE scheme.

2   Preliminaries

2.1   Notation

By $[x = y]$ we denote a bit that is 1 if $x = y$ and 0 otherwise. $H : \mathcal{X} \to \mathcal{Y}$ represents a function with domain $\mathcal{X}$ and codomain $\mathcal{Y}$, and Ω_H is the set of all such functions. For a finite set S, we denote the sampling of a uniformly random element x by $x \xleftarrow{\$} S$. $x \leftarrow \mathcal{D}$ represents that the chosen x is subject to distribution $\mathcal{D}$. Let $y \leftarrow \mathcal{A}(x)$ denote that the algorithm $\mathcal{A}$ outputs y on input x, and let $y \leftarrow \mathbf{G}$ denote that the game $\mathbf{G}$ finally returns y. For a function or algorithm $\mathcal{A}$, $\mathsf{Time}(\mathcal{A})$ (resp. $\mathsf{Space}(\mathcal{A})$) denotes the time complexity (resp. memory space) of (an algorithm computing) $\mathcal{A}$.

2.2   Quantum Random Oracle Model

We refer to [22] for detailed basics of quantum computation and quantum information. In Appendix A of our full version [12], we provide an overview of important quantum notions that are used in this paper.

Here we first briefly introduce the quantum random oracle model (QROM). The random oracle model (ROM) is an ideal model in which a uniformly random function $H : \mathcal{X} \to \mathcal{Y}$ is selected and all parties have access to H. In the quantum setting, the QROM is considered and the adversary has quantum access to the random oracle in this model [4]. In the QROM, we take the random oracle H as a unitary operation O_H such that $O_H : |x, y\rangle \mapsto |x, y \oplus H(x)\rangle$.

Next, we introduce two lemmas that are used throughout this paper.

Lemma 1 (Simulate the QROM [27]). *Let O be a random oracle, and H be a function uniformly chosen from the set of $2q$-wise independent functions. For any adversary $\mathcal{A}$ with any input z and at most q quantum queries, we have*

$$\Pr[1 \leftarrow \mathcal{A}^H(z)] = \Pr[1 \leftarrow \mathcal{A}^O(z)].$$

Lemma 2 (Measure-Rewind-Measure One-Way to Hiding [20], Lemma 3.3). *Let $H, G : \mathcal{X} \to \mathcal{Y}$ be random functions, z be a random value, and $S \subseteq \mathcal{X}$ be a random set such that $H(x) = G(x)$ for every $x \notin S$. The tuple (H, G, S, z) may have arbitrary joint distribution $\mathcal{D}$. Furthermore, let $\mathcal{A}^O$ be a quantum oracle algorithm (not necessarily unitary) that makes at most q queries to oracle O. Let d be the query depth of $\mathcal{A}$'s oracle O queries. Then we can construct an algorithm $\mathcal{B}^{H,G}(z)$ such that $\mathsf{Time}(\mathcal{B}) \approx 2 \cdot \mathsf{Time}(\mathcal{A})$, $\mathsf{Space}(\mathcal{B}) \approx O(\mathsf{Space}(\mathcal{A}) + \mathsf{Time}(\mathcal{A}))$ and*

$$| \Pr[1 \leftarrow \mathcal{A}^H(z) : (H, G, S, z) \leftarrow \mathcal{D}] - \Pr[1 \leftarrow \mathcal{A}^G(z) : (H, G, S, z) \leftarrow \mathcal{D}]|$$
$$\leq 4d \cdot \Pr\left[T \cap S \neq \varnothing : T \leftarrow \mathcal{B}^{H,G}(z), (H, G, S, z) \leftarrow \mathcal{D}\right].$$

Here $\mathcal{B}^{H,G}(z)$ makes at most $3q$ queries in total to random functions H and G.

Remark 1. Here we omit the detailed construction of algorithm $\mathcal{B}^{H,G}(z)$ since it is slightly complicated. We emphasize that the property that $\mathsf{Time}(\mathcal{B}) \approx 2 \cdot \mathsf{Time}(\mathcal{A})$ and the fact that $\mathcal{B}^{H,G}(z)$ makes at most $3q$ queries in total are both easily obtained from the detailed construction of $\mathcal{B}^{H,G}(z)$ as presented in [20]. The property $\mathsf{Space}(\mathcal{B}) \approx O(\mathsf{Space}(\mathcal{A}) + \mathsf{Time}(\mathcal{A}))$ is proved by Jiang et al. in [19]. According to the analysis in [19], $\mathcal{B}^{H,G}(z)$ requires $\mathcal{A}$'s quantum gate operations to be explicitly described and accessed, resulting in the need for additional quantum memory space (or quantum register) to implement a unitary variant[7] of $\mathcal{A}$ if $\mathcal{A}$ is not unitary.

2.3 Compressed Oracle Technique

The compressed oracle technique was introduced by Zhandry in [28]. Roughly speaking, its core idea is to purify the quantum random oracle and use the purified version to record information about the quantum queries. In this section, we only introduce the database model and a specific version of the compressed oracle called the compressed standard oracle. Additionally, we set the query upper bound for the compressed standard oracle to a constant value of $q > 0$.

Definition of the Database: Let $\perp \notin \{0,1\}^m$ and $\perp \notin \{0,1\}^n$. A database D is a q-pair collection of pairs $(x, y) \in \{0,1\}^m \times \{0,1\}^n$ and $(\perp, 0^n)$ as:

$$D = ((x_1, y_1), (x_2, y_2), \ldots, (x_i, y_i), (\perp, 0^n), \ldots, (\perp, 0^n)),$$

where $(x_j, y_j) \in \{0,1\}^m \times \{0,1\}^n$ $(j = 1, \ldots, i)$, $x_1 < x_2 < \cdots < x_i$, and all $(\perp, 0^n)$ pairs are at the end of the collection. Let $\mathbf{D}_q$ be the set of all these databases. For a $x \in \{0,1\}^m$, we will write $D(x) = y$ if y exists such that $(x, y) \in D$, and $D(x) = \perp$ otherwise. Let $n(D)$ be the number of pairs $(x, y) \in D$ that $x \neq \perp$.

For a pair $(x, y) \in \{0,1\}^m \times \{0,1\}^n$ and a database $D \in \mathbf{D}_q$ with $n(D) < q$ and $D(x) = \perp$, write $D \cup (x, y)$ to be the new database obtained by first deleting a

---

[7] Unitary variants of quantum oracle algorithms is explained in Appendix A of [12].

$(\perp, 0^n)$ pair, then inserting (x, y) appropriately into D and maintain the ordering of the x values.

A quantum register D_q defined over set $\mathbf{D}_q$ is a complex Hilbert space with orthonormal basis $\{|D\rangle\}_{D \in \mathbf{D}_q}$, where the basis state $|D\rangle$ is labeled by the elements of $\mathbf{D}_q$. As mentioned in Appendix A of our full version [12], this basis is the computational basis. We also refer to D_q as the database register. For a database $D \in \mathbf{D}_q$ that $n(D) < q$ and $D(x) = \perp$, define a superposition state on the database register D_q as

$$|D \cup (x, \hat{r})\rangle := \frac{1}{\sqrt{2^n}} \sum_{y \in \{0,1\}^n} (-1)^{y \cdot r} |D \cup (x, y)\rangle,$$

where $x \in \{0,1\}^m$ and $r \in \{0,1\}^n$.

For a $x \in \{0,1\}^m$, the local decompression procedure $\mathsf{StdDecomp}_x$ acts on the database register D_q as follows:

- For $D \in \mathbf{D}_q$, if $D(x) = \perp$ and $n(D) < q$, $\mathsf{StdDecomp}_x |D\rangle = |D \cup (x, \hat{0^n})\rangle$.
- For $D \in \mathbf{D}_q$, if $D(x) = \perp$ and $n(D) < q$, $\mathsf{StdDecomp}_x |D \cup (x, \hat{0^n})\rangle = |D\rangle$ and

$$\mathsf{StdDecomp}_x |D' \cup (x, \hat{r})\rangle = |D' \cup (x, \hat{r})\rangle (r \neq 0^n).$$

- For $D \in \mathbf{D}_q$ that $D(x) = \perp$ and $n(D) = q$, $\mathsf{StdDecomp}_x |D\rangle = |D\rangle$.

For any $x \in \{0,1\}^m$, it is obvious that $\mathsf{StdDecomp}_x$ is a unitary operation and

$$\mathsf{StdDecomp}_x \circ \mathsf{StdDecomp}_x = \mathbf{I}.$$

Here $\mathbf{I}$ is the identity operator.

Definition 1 (Compressed Standard Oracle). *Let* X *(resp.* Y*) be the quantum register defined over* $\{0,1\}^m$ *(resp.* $\{0,1\}^n$*). Let* $|D^\perp\rangle$ *be the initial state on database register* D_q*, where* $D^\perp \in \mathbf{D}_q$ *is the database containing* q *pairs* $(\perp, 0^n)$*. A query to the compressed standard oracle with input/output register* X/Y *is implemented by performing the following unitary operation* CStO *on registers* XYD_q*.*

$$\mathsf{CStO} := \sum_{x \in \{0,1\}^m} |x\rangle\langle x|_{\mathsf{X}} \otimes \mathsf{StdDecomp}_x \circ \mathsf{CNOT}^x_{\mathsf{YD}_q} \circ \mathsf{StdDecomp}_x.$$

For state $|y, D\rangle$ *(* $y \in \{0,1\}^n$*,* $D \in \mathbf{D}_q$*),* $\mathsf{CNOT}^x_{\mathsf{YD}_q} |y, D\rangle = |y \oplus D(x), D\rangle$ *if* $D(x) \neq \perp$*,* $\mathsf{CNOT}^x_{\mathsf{YD}_q} |y, D\rangle = |y, D\rangle$ *if* $D(x) = \perp^8$*.*

Zhandry proved that the compressed standard oracle is perfectly indistinguishable from the quantum random oracle.

---

[8] The property that $\mathsf{CNOT}^x_{\mathsf{YD}_q}$ acts trivially on the state $|y, D\rangle$ satisfies $D(x) = \perp$, as defined in [9], is actually equivalent to the property that "$y \oplus \perp = y$" defined in [28].

Lemma 3 ([28]). *For any adversary making at most q queries, the compressed standard oracle defined in Definition 1 and quantum random oracle $H : \{0,1\}^m \to \{0,1\}^n$ are perfectly indistinguishable.*

Let X (resp. Y) be the quantum register defined over a finite set $\mathcal{X}$ (resp. $\mathcal{Y}$). For any function f with domain $\mathcal{X} \times \mathbf{D}_q$ and codomain $\mathcal{Y}$, define the unitary operation Read_f acting on registers $\mathsf{XD}_q\mathsf{Y}$ as

$$\mathsf{Read}_f|x, D, y\rangle = |x, D, y + f(x, D)\rangle, \tag{1}$$

where $+ : \mathcal{Y} \times \mathcal{Y} \to \mathcal{Y}$ is a group operation on $\mathcal{Y}$. Note that Read_f does not change the database in the computational basis state, it only computes $f(x, D)$ and returns the result in register Y. We call Read_f a database read operation.

We now recall the compressed semi-classical oracle and the compressed semi-classical one-way to hidding lemma from [11].

Compressed Semi-Classical Oracle: Let S be a subset of $\mathbf{D}_q$. Define a function f_S such that $f_S(D) = 1$ if $D \in S$, and $f_S(D) = 0$ otherwise. The compressed semi-classical oracle $\mathcal{O}_S^{CSC}$ performs the following operation on input state $\sum \alpha_{z,D}|z, D\rangle$:

1. Initialize a single qubit register L with $|0\rangle_\mathsf{L}$, transform state $\sum \alpha_{z,D}|z, D\rangle|0\rangle_\mathsf{L}$ into state $\sum \alpha_{z,D}|z, D\rangle|f_S(D)\rangle_\mathsf{L}$.
2. Measure L and output the measurement outcome.

Denote by Find the event that $\mathcal{O}_S^{CSC}$ ever returns 1.

Theorem 1 (Compressed Semi-Classical One-Way to Hidding [11], Theorem 3). *Let $H : \{0,1\}^m \to \{0,1\}^n$ be a quantum random oracle that is implemented by the compressed standard oracle with database register D_q. Let S be a subset of $\mathbf{D}_q$ that $D^\perp \notin S$ and z be a random string. The tuple (S, z) may have arbitrary joint distribution $\mathcal{D}$. Let $H\backslash S$ be an oracle that first queries H and then queries $\mathcal{O}_S^{CSC}$.*

Let $\mathcal{A}$ be a quantum oracle algorithm (not necessarily unitary) that makes at most $q_1 \leq q$[9] (resp. q_2) queries to oracle H (resp. oRead_f). Here f is a function with domain $\mathcal{X} \times \mathbf{D}_q$ and codomain $\mathcal{Y}$, and oracle oRead_f is implemented by the database read operation Read_f defined in (1). Define

$$P_{\text{left}} := \Pr\left[1 \leftarrow \mathcal{A}^{H,\mathsf{oRead}_f}(z) : (S, z) \leftarrow \mathcal{D}\right],$$

$$P_{\text{right}} := \Pr[1 \leftarrow \mathcal{A}^{H\backslash S,\mathsf{oRead}_f}(z) : (S, z) \leftarrow \mathcal{D}],$$

$$P_{\text{find}} := \Pr[\mathsf{Find} \text{ occurs in } \mathcal{A}^{H\backslash S,\mathsf{oRead}_f}(z) : (S, z) \leftarrow \mathcal{D}].$$

Then

$$|P_{\text{left}} - P_{\text{right}}| \leq \sqrt{(q_1 + 1) \cdot P_{\text{find}}}, \quad \left|\sqrt{P_{\text{left}}} - \sqrt{P_{\text{right}}}\right| \leq \sqrt{(q_1 + 1) \cdot P_{\text{find}}}.$$

---

[9] In fact, even if $q_1 > q$, Theorem 1 is still valid. We require $q_1 \leq q$ here because we have set the query upper bound for the compressed standard oracle to a constant value of q.

Define $\mathsf{J}_S := \sum_{D \in S} |D\rangle\langle D|$ *as a projector on the database register* D_q, *let* CStO *be as in Definition 1. Then we have*

$$P_{\mathrm{find}} \leq q_1 \cdot \underset{(S,z) \leftarrow \mathcal{D}}{\mathbb{E}} \| [\mathsf{J}_S, \mathsf{CStO}] \|^2.$$

2.4 The Extractable RO-Simulator

In [9], Don et al. generalized the compressed standard oracle and defined the extractable RO-simulator. Roughly speaking, this simulator simulates the quantum random oracle H by using the compressed standard oracle, and has an extraction-interface that can output a x satisfying $f(x, H(x)) = t$ for an input t. In the following, we present the details of the extractable RO-simulator and introduce a lemma that will be used in the next section. We stress that, similar to Sect. 2.3, the database register used here is also D_q. Therefore, unlike the inefficient version defined in [9], the extractable RO-simulator described here is efficient.

Let f be an arbitrary but fixed function with domain $\{0,1\}^m \times \{0,1\}^n$ and codomain $\mathcal{Y}$. For a fixed $t \in \mathcal{Y}$, we define relation $R_t^f \subset \{0,1\}^m \times \{0,1\}^n$ and corresponding parameter $\Gamma_{R_t^f}$ as

$$R_t^f := \{(x,y) \in \{0,1\}^m \times \{0,1\}^n | f(x,y) = t\},$$
$$\Gamma_{R_t^f} := \max_{x \in \{0,1\}^m} |\{y \in \{0,1\}^n | f(x,y) = t\}|.$$

For relation R_t^f, we define following projectors on the database register D_q:

$$\Sigma^x := \sum_{\substack{D \, s.t. \, (x,D(x)) \in R_t^f \\ x' < x, (x', D(x')) \notin R_t^f}} |D\rangle\langle D| \; (x \in \{0,1\}^m), \quad \Sigma^\perp := \mathbf{I} - \sum_{x \in \{0,1\}^m} \Sigma^x.$$

Then we define a measurement $\mathbb{M}^{R_t^f}$ on database register D_q to be the set of projectors $\{\Sigma^x\}_{x \in \{0,1\}^m \cup \perp}$.

Indeed, the measurement $\mathbb{M}^{R_t^f}$ returns the smallest x such that $(x, D(x)) \in R_t^f$. If such x does not exist, $\mathbb{M}^{R_t^f}$ will return $\perp$. Similar to [9], we also consider the purified measurement $\mathbb{M}^{R_t^f}_{\mathsf{D}_q\mathsf{P}}$ corresponding to $\mathbb{M}^{R_t^f}$, which is a unitary operation that acts on registers $\mathsf{D}_q\mathsf{P}$ as

$$\mathbb{M}^{R_t^f}_{\mathsf{D}_q\mathsf{P}} |D, p\rangle = \sum_{x \in \{0,1\}^m \cup \perp} \Sigma^x |D\rangle |p \oplus x\rangle.$$

Here P is a quantum register defined over $\{0,1\}^{m+1}$[10], $D \in \mathsf{D}_q$ and $p \in \{0,1\}^{m+1}$.

---

[10] Here we embed the set $\{0,1\}^m \cup \perp$ into the set $\{0,1\}^{m+1}$ as explained in Appendix A of [12].

Definition 2 (The Extractable RO-Simulator (efficient version)). *The extractable RO-simulator $\mathcal{S}(f)$ with an internal database register D_q is a black-box oracle with two interfaces: the RO-interface $\mathsf{eCO.RO}$ and the extraction-interface $\mathsf{eCO.E}_f$. $\mathcal{S}(f)$ prepares its database register D_q to be in state $|D^\perp\rangle$ at the beginning, where $D^\perp \in \mathbf{D}_q$ is the database containing q pairs $(\perp, 0^n)$. Then, the RO-interface $\mathsf{eCO.RO}$ and the extraction-interface $\mathsf{eCO.E}_f$ act as follows:*

- *Let X (resp. Y) be the quantum register defined over $\{0,1\}^m$ (resp. $\{0,1\}^n$), T be the quantum register defined over $\mathcal{Y}$.*
- *$\mathsf{eCO.RO}$: For any quantum RO-query on query registers XY, $\mathcal{S}(f)$ implements a compressed standard oracle query on registers XYD_q by the CStO defined in Definition 1.*
- *$\mathsf{eCO.E}_f$: For any quantum extraction-query on query registers TP, $\mathcal{S}(f)$ applies*

$$\mathsf{Ext}_f := \sum_{t \in \mathcal{Y}} |t\rangle\langle t|_\mathsf{T} \otimes \mathsf{M}_{\mathsf{D}_q\mathsf{P}}^{R_t^f} \tag{2}$$

to registers $\mathsf{TD}_q\mathsf{P}$.

Moreover, by the Theorem 4.3 of [9], the total runtime of $\mathcal{S}(f)$ is bounded[11] by

$$T_{\mathcal{S}} = O(q_{RO} \cdot q_E \cdot \mathrm{Time}[f] + q_{RO}^2),$$

where $q_{RO}(\leq q)$[12] and q_E are the number of queries to $\mathsf{eCO.RO}$ and $\mathsf{eCO.E}_f$, respectively.

The $\mathsf{eCO.RO}$ (resp. $\mathsf{eCO.E}_f$) can also be classically queried. In this case, the query registers XY (resp. TP) are measured after applying the unitary operation CStO (resp. Ext_f). The $\mathsf{eCO.RO}$ can also be queried in parallel, and k-parallel queries to $\mathsf{eCO.RO}$ are processed by sequentially implementing CStO k times [6].

In addition, for any computational basis state $|t, D, p\rangle$ on register $\mathsf{TD}_q\mathsf{P}$, it is straightforward to check that

$$\mathsf{Ext}_f|t, D, p\rangle = |t, D, p \oplus g(t, D)\rangle. \tag{3}$$

Here function $g : \mathcal{Y} \times \mathbf{D}_q \to \{0,1\}^{m+1}$ on input (t, D) outputs the smallest value x that satisfies $(x, D(x)) \in R_t^f$. If such x does not exist, function g outputs $\perp$. Therefore, by the definition of the database read operation given in Sect. 2.3, Ext_f can also be considered as a database read operation.

Lemma 4 ([11] Lemma 2). *For any $x \in \{0,1\}^m$, let $\mathsf{StdDecomp}_x$ and CStO be the unitary operation defined in Sect. 2.3, then*

$$\|[\mathsf{Ext}_f, \mathsf{StdDecomp}_x]\| \leq 16 \cdot \sqrt{\max_{t \in \mathcal{Y}} \Gamma_{R_t^f}/2^n}, \quad \|[\mathsf{CStO}, \Sigma^\perp]\| \leq 8 \cdot \sqrt{\Gamma_{R_t^f}/2^n}.$$

Here $[A, B] := AB - BA$ is the commutator of two operations A, B acting on a quantum register.

---

[11] Although [9] defined an inefficient version of the extractable RO-simulator, the total runtime of the efficient version is given instead in the Theorem 4.3 of [9].

[12] This is because we have set the query upper bound for the compressed standard oracle to a constant value of q.

3   From $\mathsf{IND\text{-}CPA}_{\mathsf{FO}_m^\perp[P]}$ to $\mathsf{IND\text{-}qCCA}_{\mathsf{FO}_m^\perp[P]}$

In this section, we prove that, in the QROM, the IND-qCCA security of KEM scheme $\mathsf{FO}_m^\perp[P, H, G]$ can be tightly reduced to its IND-CPA security. Particularly, our reduction does not require the perfect correctness property of the underlying randomized PKE scheme P. The formal definitions of cryptographic primitives, correctness and spreadness used in this section are shown in Appendix B of our full version [12].

Transformation. $\mathsf{FO}_m^\perp$: Let P = (Gen, Enc, Dec) be a randomized PKE with message space $\mathcal{M}(= \{0,1\}^m)$, randomness space $\{0,1\}^n$ and ciphertext space $\mathcal{C}$. Let $H : \mathcal{M} \to \{0,1\}^n$ and $G : \{0,1\}^* \to \{0,1\}^{n'}$ be hash functions. We associate

$$\mathsf{KEM}_m^\perp := \mathsf{FO}_m^\perp[P, H, G] = (\mathsf{Gen}, \mathsf{Enca}_m, \mathsf{Deca}_m^\perp).$$

The constituting algorithms of $\mathsf{KEM}_m^\perp$ are given in Fig. 3.

$\underline{\mathsf{Gen}}$	$\underline{\mathsf{Encap}_m(pk)}$	$\underline{\mathsf{Deca}_m^\perp(sk, c)}$
$(pk, sk) \leftarrow \mathsf{Gen}$	$m \xleftarrow{\$} \mathcal{M}$	$m' = \mathsf{Dec}_{sk}(c)$
return (pk, sk)	$c = \mathsf{Enc}_{pk}(m, H(m))$	**if** $m' = \perp$
	$K = G(m)$	**return** $\perp$
	return (K, c)	**else if** $c \neq \mathsf{Enc}_{pk}(m'; H(m'))$
		return $\perp$
		return $K = G(m')$

Fig. 3. Key Encapsulation Mechanism $\mathsf{KEM}_m^\perp = (\mathsf{Gen}, \mathsf{Enca}_m, \mathsf{Deca}_m^\perp)$.

Before we prove the main result of this section, we first describe how to simulate a quantum accessible decapsulation oracle qDeca for $\mathsf{KEM}_m^\perp$.

Denote by I/O the input/output register of qDeca, where I is defined over $\mathcal{C}$ and O is defined over $\{0,1\}^{n'+1}$ [13]. As shown in Fig. 3, decapsulation algorithm $\mathsf{Deca}_m^\perp$ needs to query H and G in its process. Specifically, it queries H to perform the re-encryption check (i.e., check if $c = \mathsf{Enc}_{pk}(m', H(m'))$), and then queries G by m' to produce the key K if m' passes the re-encryption check. Following this process, a unitary operation U_m acting on registers IM is presented as follows:

---

[13] Here we embed the set $\{0,1\}^{n'} \cup \perp$ (resp. $\{0,1\}^m \cup \perp$) into the set $\{0,1\}^{n'+1}$ (resp. $\{0,1\}^{m+1}$) as explained in Appendix A of [12]..

$$U_m|c\rangle_{\mathsf{I}}|0^m\rangle_{\mathsf{M}} = \begin{cases} |c\rangle_{\mathsf{I}}|m'\rangle_{\mathsf{M}} & \text{if } m' := \mathsf{Dec}_{sk}(c) \neq \bot \wedge \mathsf{Enc}_{pk}(m', H(m')) = c \\ |c\rangle_{\mathsf{I}}|\bot\rangle_{\mathsf{M}} & \text{otherwise.} \end{cases}$$

Here M is a quantum register defined over $\{0,1\}^{m+113}$. With this operation, the re-encryption check can be performed in superposition. The quantum circuit implementation of U_m is shown in Appendix C of our full version [12], which two queries to H is needed.

To simulate qDeca on input state $|c\rangle_{\mathsf{I}}|y\rangle_{\mathsf{O}}$, the following unitary operation is performed on state $|c\rangle_{\mathsf{I}}|y\rangle_{\mathsf{O}}|0^m\rangle_{\mathsf{M}}$:

$$U_{\mathsf{qD}} := (U_m)^\dagger \circ O_G \circ U_m, \tag{4}$$

where unitary operation O_G maps $|m'\rangle_{\mathsf{M}}|y\rangle_{\mathsf{O}}$ to $|m'\rangle_{\mathsf{M}}|y \oplus G(m')\rangle_{\mathsf{O}}$, and we set $G(\bot) = \bot$. The register M used by U_m can be viewed as the internal register of U_{qD}, it stores the plaintext m'. Note that this register is always in state $|0^m\rangle_{\mathsf{M}}$ before and after once simulation of qDeca.

Theorem 2 ($\mathsf{IND\text{-}CPA_{KEM_m^\perp}}$ $\overset{\mathsf{QROM}}{\Rightarrow}$ $\mathsf{IND\text{-}qCCA_{KEM_m^\perp}}$). *Let P be a randomized PKE scheme that is δ-correct and weakly γ-spread. Let $\mathcal{A}$ be an IND-qCCA adversary against $\mathsf{KEM}_{m\perp}$ in the QROM, making at most q_H, q_G and q_D queries to random oracle H, random oracle G and decapsulation oracle qDeca*[14], respectively. Let d_H (resp. d_G) be the query depth of $\mathcal{A}$'s random oracle H (resp. G) queries. Let w_H (resp. w_G) be the query width of $\mathcal{A}$'s random oracle H (resp. G) queries.*

Then there exists an IND-CPA adversary $\tilde{\mathcal{A}}$ against $\mathsf{KEM}_m^\perp$ in the QROM such that

$$\mathsf{Adv}_{\mathsf{KEM}_m^\perp,\mathcal{A}}^{\mathsf{IND\text{-}qCCA}} \leq \mathsf{Adv}_{\mathsf{KEM}_m^\perp,\tilde{\mathcal{A}}}^{\mathsf{IND\text{-}CPA}} + 8\sqrt{q_H(q_H+1)\cdot\delta} + (64q_H+2)\cdot\delta + 40q_D\cdot 2^{-\gamma/2}.$$

The adversary $\tilde{\mathcal{A}}$ makes at most $2q_H$ (resp. $q_G + q_D$) queries to random oracle H (resp. G). The query depth of $\tilde{\mathcal{A}}$ to random oracle H (resp. G) is $2d_H$ (resp. $d_G + q_D$). The running time and memory space of $\tilde{\mathcal{A}}$ is bounded as $\mathsf{Time}(\tilde{\mathcal{A}}) \approx \mathsf{Time}(\mathcal{A}) + O(q_H q_D + q_H^2)$ and $\mathsf{Space}(\tilde{\mathcal{A}}) \approx \mathsf{Space}(\mathcal{A}) + O(q_H)$, respectively.

Proof. To prove this theorem, a series of hybrid games are defined (see also Fig. 4).

---

[14] Here and in what follows, we following [16] to make the convention that q_H and q_G counts the total number of times H and G is queried in the security game, respectively.

GAMES G_0-G_6		$G(|x_G, y_G\rangle)$	$//G_0$-G_6
1, $(pk, sk) \leftarrow$ Gen	$//G_0$-G_6	12, **return** $O_G|x_G, y_G\rangle = |x_G, y_G \oplus G(x_G)\rangle$	
2, $H \xleftarrow{\$} \Omega_H, G \xleftarrow{\$} \Omega_G, O \xleftarrow{\$} \Omega_H$	$//G_0$-G_6	qDeca* $(|c, y\rangle)$	$//G_0$-G_1
3, $b \xleftarrow{\$} \{0, 1\}, m^* \xleftarrow{\$} \mathcal{M}$	$//G_0$-G_6	13, **if** $c = c^*$ **return** $|c, y \oplus \bot\rangle$	
4, $c^* = \mathsf{Enc}_{pk}(m^*, H(m^*))$	$//G_0$-G_6	**else return**	
5, $K_0^* = G(m^*), K_1^* \xleftarrow{\$} \mathcal{K}$	$//G_0$-G_6	$(\mathsf{U}_m)^\dagger \circ O_G \circ \mathsf{U}_m|c, y\rangle$	$//G_0$
6, $b' \leftarrow \mathcal{A}^{H, G, \mathsf{qDeca}^*}(pk, c^*, K_b^*)$	$//G_0$-G_1	$(\tilde{\mathsf{U}}_m)^\dagger \circ O_G \circ \tilde{\mathsf{U}}_m|c, y\rangle$	$//G_1$
$\quad b' \leftarrow \mathcal{A}^{H, G, \mathsf{qDeca}^\diamond}(pk, c^*, K_b^*)$	$//G_2$-G_6	qDeca$^\diamond$ $(|c, y\rangle)$	$//G_2$-G_6
7, **return** $[b = b']$	$//G_0$-G_6	14, **if** $c = c^*$ **return** $|c, y \oplus \bot\rangle$	
		else return	
$H(|x_H, y_H\rangle)$	$//G_0$-G_6	$\mathsf{eCO.E}_f \circ O_G \circ \mathsf{eCO.E}_f|c, y\rangle$	
8, **return** $|x_H, y_H \oplus H(x_H)\rangle$	$//G_0$	$\mathcal{S}(f) = \{\mathsf{eCO.RO}, \mathsf{eCO.E}_f\}$	$//G_1$-G_6
9, **query** eCO.RO **by** $|x_H, y_H\rangle$	$//G_1$-G_4	15, eCO.RO: **apply** CStO	$//G_1$-G_6
10, **if** $x_H = m^*$	$//G_5$	16, $\mathsf{eCO.E}_f$: $f = f_1$, **apply** Ext_{f_1}	$//G_1$-G_2
$\quad$ **return** $|x_H, y_H \oplus O(x_H)\rangle$		$\mathsf{eCO.E}_f$: $f = f_2$, **apply** Ext_{f_2}	$//G_3$
$\quad$ **else query** eCO.RO **by** $|x_H, y_H\rangle$		$\mathsf{eCO.E}_f$: $f = f_2$,	$//G_4$
11, **if** $\mathsf{Enc}_{pk}(x_H, O(x_H)) = c^*$	$//G_6$	$\quad\quad$ **apply** $\mathsf{S}_{m^*} \circ \mathsf{Ext}_{f_2} \circ \mathsf{S}_{m^*}$	
$\quad$ **return** $|x_H, y_H \oplus O(x_H)\rangle$		$\mathsf{eCO.E}_f$: $f = f_2$, **apply** Ext_{f_2}	$//G_5$-G_6
$\quad$ **else query** eCO.RO **by** $|x_H, y_H\rangle$			

Fig. 4. Games G_0 to G_6 in the proof of Theorem 2. In these games, the adversary $\mathcal{A}$ can make parallel quantum queries to H and G and quantum queries to qDeca*. In this figure, for brevity, we just write the input state of H, G and qDeca* as $|x_H, y_H\rangle$, $|x_G, y_G\rangle$ and $|c, y\rangle$, respectively. We also stress that the $H(m^*)$ used to compute c^* ($= \mathsf{Enc}_{pk}(m^*, H(m^*))$) in game G_1 to G_4 is generated by classically query eCO.RO with input m^*.

Game G_0: This is the IND-qCCA game of $\mathsf{KEM}_m^\bot$ with adversary $\mathcal{A}$ in the QROM. The decapsulation oracle qDeca* in this game is identical to qDeca that is simulated by U_{qD} as defined in (4), except that qDeca* returns $\bot$ if $c = c^*$.

$$\mathsf{Adv}_{\mathsf{KEM}_m^\bot, \mathcal{A}}^{\mathsf{IND\text{-}qCCA}} = \left| \Pr[1 \leftarrow G_0] - \frac{1}{2} \right|. \tag{5}$$

We recall that the input/output register of the decapsulation oracle is denoted as I/O, and U_{qD} also has an internal register M. Here we denote the private register of adversary $\mathcal{A}$ as A, which contains the query registers of the random oracle H and G.

Define $\mathsf{P}_{c^*} := |c^*\rangle\langle c^*|$ as a projector on the input register I, $\mathsf{U}_\bot$ as a unitary operation that acts on the output register O and maps $|y\rangle$ to $|y \oplus \bot\rangle$. Then the decapsulation oracle qDeca* in game G_0 is simulated by the unitary operation

$$\mathsf{U}_{\mathsf{qD}}^0 := \mathsf{U}_\bot \circ \mathsf{P}_{c^*} + (\mathsf{U}_m)^\dagger \circ O_G \circ \mathsf{U}_m \circ (\mathbf{I} - \mathsf{P}_{c^*}).$$

Let D_{q_H} be the database register defined over set $\mathbf{D}_{q_H}$ (Sect. 2.3). Let $S(f_1) := \{eCO.RO, eCO.E_{f_1}\}$ be the extractable RO-simulator with internal database register D_{q_H} (Definition 2), where function $f_1 : \mathcal{M} \times \{0,1\}^n \cup \bot \to \mathcal{C} \cup \bot$ is that

$$f_1(x,y) = \begin{cases} c \text{ if } y \neq \bot \wedge \mathsf{Enc}_{pk}(x,y) = c \wedge x = \mathsf{Dec}_{sk}(c) \\ \bot \text{ otherwise.} \end{cases}$$

Game $\mathbf{G_1}$: This game is identical to game $\mathbf{G_0}$, except that the extractable RO-simulator $S(f_1) := \{eCO.RO, eCO.E_{f_1}\}$ is introduced and the queries to random oracle H are answered by querying the RO-interface eCO.RO.

In game $\mathbf{G_1}$, the decapsulation oracle qDeca* is simulated by the unitary operation

$$\mathrm{U}_{\mathsf{qD}}^1 := \mathrm{U}_\bot \circ \mathrm{P}_{c^*} + (\tilde{\mathrm{U}}_m)^\dagger \circ O_G \circ \tilde{\mathrm{U}}_m \circ (\mathbf{I} - \mathrm{P}_{c^*}).$$

Here $\tilde{\mathrm{U}}_m$ acts the same as U_m, except that the internal two random oracle H queries are answered by querying eCO.RO.

In game $\mathbf{G_1}$, although the extractable RO-simulator $S(f_1)$ is used to answer the queries to random oracle H, the extraction-interface eCO.E$_{f_1}$ is never queried. By using Lemma 3, we have

$$\Pr[1 \leftarrow \mathbf{G_0}] = \Pr[1 \leftarrow \mathbf{G_1}]. \tag{6}$$

Game $\mathbf{G_2}$: This game is identical to game $\mathbf{G_1}$, except that the decapsulation oracle qDeca* is replaced with qDeca°.

Instead of using $\tilde{\mathrm{U}}_m$ to perform the re-encryption check in superposition, the decapsulation oracle qDeca° in game $\mathbf{G_2}$ queries eCO.E$_{f_1}$ to directly extract plaintext m' that passes the re-encryption check from the database register. Moreover, the decapsulation oracle qDeca° in game $\mathbf{G_2}$ is simulated by the unitary operation

$$\mathrm{U}_{\mathsf{qD}}^2 := \mathrm{U}_\bot \circ \mathrm{P}_{c^*} + \mathsf{Ext}_{f_1} \circ O_G \circ \mathsf{Ext}_{f_1} \circ (\mathbf{I} - \mathrm{P}_{c^*})$$

that acts on the registers $\mathsf{IOD}_{q_H}\mathsf{M}$, where $\mathsf{Ext}_{f_1} := \sum_{c \in \mathcal{C}} |c\rangle\langle c|_\mathsf{I} \otimes \mathrm{M}_{\mathsf{D}_{q_H}\mathsf{M}}^{R_c^{f_1}}$ acts on registers $\mathsf{ID}_{q_H}\mathsf{M}$[15]. Similar to (3) in Sect. 2.4, the unitary operation Ext_{f_1} can also be rewritten as

$$\mathsf{Ext}_{f_1}|c, D, m\rangle_{\mathsf{ID}_{q_H}\mathsf{M}} = |c, D, m \oplus x\rangle_{\mathsf{ID}_{q_H}\mathsf{M}}.$$

Here x is the smallest value that satisfies $f_1(x, D(x)) = c$. If such x does not exist, Ext_{f_1} returns $\bot$ in register M.

Indeed, we can prove the following lemma and the detailed proof is shown in Appendix D.1 of our full version [12].

Lemma 5. $|\Pr[1 \leftarrow \mathbf{G_1}] - \Pr[1 \leftarrow \mathbf{G_2}]| \leq 8q_D \cdot 2^{-\gamma/2}.$

---

[15] Note that the codomain of function f_1 is the union of $\mathcal{C}$ and $\bot$. However, we ignore the extraction with input $\bot$ in Ext_{f_1}, which is different from its definition as shown in Definition 2. That is to say, we restrict the adversary $\mathcal{A}$ from querying the decapsulation oracle by $\bot$ in our reduction. Indeed, this is reasonable since $\bot \notin \mathcal{C}$.

Game G_3: This game is the same as game G_2, except that the extractable RO-simulator is replaced to $\mathcal{S}(f_2) := \{\text{eCO.RO}, \text{eCO.E}_{f_2}\}$, where function $f_2 : \mathcal{M} \times \{0,1\}^n \to \mathcal{C} \cup \bot$ is that $f_2(x, y) = \text{Enc}_{pk}(x, y)$.

In game G_3, the decapsulation oracle $\text{qDeca}^\diamond$ is simulated by the unitary operation

$$U_{qD}^3 := U_\bot \circ P_{c^*} + \text{Ext}_{f_2} \circ O_G \circ \text{Ext}_{f_2} \circ (\mathbf{I} - P_{c^*}) \qquad (7)$$

that acts on registers IOD_{q_H}M, where $\text{Ext}_{f_2} := \sum_{c \in \mathcal{C}} |c\rangle\langle c|_{\mathsf{I}} \otimes M_{D_{q_H}\text{M}}^{R_c^{f_2}}$ acts on registers ID_{q_H}M. Similar with Ext_{f_1}, the unitary operation Ext_{f_2} can be rewritten as

$$\text{Ext}_{f_2}|c, D, m\rangle_{\text{ID}_{q_H}\text{M}} = |c, D, m \oplus x\rangle_{\text{ID}_{q_H}\text{M}}.$$

Here x is the smallest value satisfies $f_2(x, D(x)) = c$. If such x does not exist, Ext_{f_2} returns $\bot$ in register M. We note that the implementation of Ext_{f_2} does not require sk since the computation of function f_2 only uses pk. Therefore, the implementation of U_{qD}^3 also does not require sk.

Compared with f_1, function f_2 directly computes $\text{Enc}_{pk}(x, y)$ and ignores the check of whether x equals $\text{Dec}_{sk}(c)$, where $c = \text{Enc}_{pk}(x, y)$. Hence, for any computational basis state $|c, D, m\rangle_{\text{ID}_{q_H}\text{M}}$, if Ext_{f_1} does not map it to $|c, D, m \oplus \bot\rangle_{\text{ID}_{q_H}\text{M}}$, then Ext_{f_2} will also be unable to map it to $|c, D, m \oplus \bot\rangle_{\text{ID}_{q_H}\text{M}}$. Indeed, Ext_{f_2} may have a different return than Ext_{f_1} only on the following type of input state:

(a) $|c, D, m\rangle_{\text{ID}_{q_H}\text{M}}: c \neq c^*$, Ext_{f_1} maps it to $|c, D, m \oplus \bot\rangle_{\text{ID}_{q_H}\text{M}}$, but Ext_{f_2} does not.

(b) $|c, D, m\rangle_{\text{ID}_{q_H}\text{M}}: c \neq c^*$, neither Ext_{f_1} nor Ext_{f_2} maps it to $|c, D, m \oplus \bot\rangle_{\text{ID}_{q_H}\text{M}}$, but the return state of Ext_{f_1} and Ext_{f_2} is different.

For a fixed (pk, sk) pair, define a set of database as

$$R_{pk,sk}^D := \{D | D \in \mathbf{D}_{q_H}, \exists x \text{ s.t. } D(x) \neq \bot \wedge \text{Enc}_{pk}(x, D(x)) = c \wedge \text{Dec}_{sk}(c) \neq x\}. \qquad (8)$$

It is straightforward to check that the database D in state $|c, D, m\rangle_{\text{ID}_{q_H}\text{M}}$ of types (a) and (b) above must satisfy $D \in R_{pk,sk}^D$. Hence, we can conclude that the extraction-interfaces eCO.E_{f_1} and eCO.E_{f_2} proceed identically for any input state $|c, D, m\rangle_{\text{ID}_{q_H}\text{M}}$ if $D \notin R_{pk,sk}^D$.

By using Theorem 1, we can prove the following lemma. The detailed proof is shown in Appendix D.3 of our full version [12].

Lemma 6. $|\Pr[1 \leftarrow G_2] - \Pr[1 \leftarrow G_3]| \leq 8 \cdot \sqrt{q_H(q_H + 1) \cdot \delta} + 64 q_H \cdot \delta.$

Game G_4: This game is the same as game G_3, except that the extraction interface eCO.E_{f_2} is implemented by unitary operation $S_{m^*} \circ \text{Ext}_{f_2} \circ S_{m^*}$. Here, S_{m^*} is the abbreviation of StdDecomp_x defined in Sect. 2.3.

Obviously, the decapsulation oracle $\text{qDeca}^\diamond$ in game G_4 is simulated by unitary operation

$$U_{qD}^4 := U_\bot \circ P_{c^*} + \underline{S_{m^*} \circ \text{Ext}_{f_2} \circ S_{m^*}} \circ O_G \circ \underline{S_{m^*} \circ \text{Ext}_{f_2} \circ S_{m^*}} \circ (\mathbf{I} - P_{c^*}).$$

For a fixed (pk, sk) pair, one can check that the parameter $\Gamma_{R_c^{f_2}}$ related to function f_2 defined in Sect. 2.4 satisfies

$$\max_{c \in \mathcal{C}} \Gamma_{R_c^{f_2}} / 2^n \leq \gamma(pk, sk),$$

since the underlying PKE scheme P is weakly γ-spread. Then, by Lemma 4,

$$\|[\mathsf{Ext}_{f_2}, \mathsf{S}_{m^*}]\| \leq 16 \cdot \sqrt{\max_{c \in \mathcal{C}} \Gamma_{R_c^{f_2}} / 2^n} \leq 16 \cdot \sqrt{\gamma(pk, sk)}.$$

Notice that $\mathsf{S}_{m^*} \circ \mathsf{S}_{m^*} = \mathbf{I}$, thus we can conclude that $\mathsf{S}_{m^*} \circ \mathsf{Ext}_{f_2} \circ \mathsf{S}_{m^*}$ is indistinguishable from Ext_{f_2} except for an error of $16 \cdot \sqrt{\gamma(pk, sk)}$.

In game $\mathbf{G_4}$, the query times to decapsulation oracle $\mathsf{qDeca}^\diamond$ are at most q_D, thus the unitary operation $\mathrm{U}_{\mathsf{qD}}^4$ is implemented at most q_D times. Then, for a fixed (pk, sk) pair, it is easy to obtain

$$|\Pr[1 \leftarrow \mathbf{G_3} : (pk, sk)] - \Pr[1 \leftarrow \mathbf{G_4} : (pk, sk)]| \leq 32 q_D \cdot \sqrt{\gamma(pk, sk)}.$$

Here $\Pr[1 \leftarrow \mathbf{G} : (pk, sk)]$ is the probability that game $\mathbf{G}$ returns 1 for fixed (pk, sk). By averaging the (pk, sk), we obtain

$$|\Pr[1 \leftarrow \mathbf{G_3}] - \Pr[1 \leftarrow \mathbf{G_4}]| \leq 32 q_D \cdot \sqrt{\mathop{\mathbb{E}}_{(pk,sk) \leftarrow \mathsf{Gen}} \gamma(pk, sk)} \stackrel{(a)}{\leq} 32 q_D \cdot 2^{-\gamma/2}. \quad (9)$$

Here (a) uses the fact that the underlying PKE scheme P is weakly γ-spread.

In game $\mathbf{G_4}$, c^* is computed by $H(m^*)$, which is generated by classically querying the RO-interface eCO.RO with m^*. As defined in Definition 2, eCO.RO is implemented by the unitary operation CStO. Indeed, by the definition of the CStO (Definition 1), the joint state of game $\mathbf{G_4}$ just before $\mathcal{A}$ performs its first query to $\mathsf{qDeca}^\diamond$ can be written as

$$\sum_{z,c,y,D} \alpha_{z,c,y,D} \mathsf{S}_{m^*} |z, c, y, D \cup (m^*, H(m^*))\rangle_{\mathsf{AIOD}_{q_H}} |0^m\rangle_\mathsf{M}.$$

Then, for any basis state

$$|\psi\rangle := \mathsf{S}_{m^*} |z, c, y, D \cup (m^*, H(m^*)), 0^m\rangle,$$

suppose unitary operation Ext_{f_2} maps state $|z, c, y, D \cup (m^*, H(m^*)), 0^m\rangle$ to state $|z, c, y, D \cup (m^*, H(m^*)), m\rangle$, we have

$$\mathsf{S}_{m^*} \circ \mathsf{Ext}_{f_2} \circ \mathsf{S}_{m^*} |\psi\rangle = \mathsf{S}_{m^*} \circ \mathsf{Ext}_{f_2} |z, c, y, D \cup (m^*, H(m^*)), 0^m\rangle$$
$$= \mathsf{S}_{m^*} |z, c, y, D \cup (m^*, H(m^*)), m\rangle. \quad (10)$$

Therefore, if we abbreviate the other registers as R, the internal joint state of game $\mathbf{G_4}$ before and after the implementation of $\mathsf{S}_{m^*} \circ \mathsf{Ext}_{f_2} \circ \mathsf{S}_{m^*}$ always can be written as

$$\sum_{r,D} \beta_{r,D} |r, D \cup \mathsf{S}_{m^*}(m^*, H(m^*))\rangle_{\mathsf{RD}_{q_H}}.$$

Now, by the definition of the CStO (Definition 1), we can conclude that the random oracle H query (which is simulated by eCO.RO) with m^* makes by $\mathcal{A}$ in game $\mathbf{G_4}$ will return $H(m^*)$ again, thus the extractable RO-simulator $\mathcal{S}(f_2) = \{\text{eCO.RO}, \mathsf{S}_{m^*} \circ \text{eCO.E}_{f_2} \circ \mathsf{S}_{m^*}\}$ of game $\mathbf{G_4}$ perfectly simulates the random oracle H at point m^*.

In addition, we can prove the following lemma.

Lemma 7. *For any basis state* $|z, c, y, D\rangle$*, suppose* $c \neq c^*$*,*

$$\mathsf{Ext}_{f_2} |z, c, y, D \cup (m^*, H(m^*)), 0^m\rangle = |z, c, y, D \cup (m^*, H(m^*)), m\rangle$$

and $\mathsf{Ext}_{f_2} |z, c, y, D, 0^m\rangle = |z, c, y, D, m'\rangle$*, then we have* $m = m'$*.*

Proof. We recall that $c^* = \mathsf{Enc}_{pk}(m^*, H(m^*))$. Denote database $D \cup (m^*, H(m^*))$ as D', then we have $D'(m^*) = H(m^*)$. By the definition of function f_2, if the value $m \neq \bot$, it satisfies that $D'(m) \neq \bot$ and $\mathsf{Enc}_{pk}(m, D'(m)) = c$. Then we can conclude that m cannot be m^*, because $m = m^*$ implies $\mathsf{Enc}_{pk}(m^*, D'(m^*)) = c$, which is contradictory to $c \neq c^*$.

So even if database $D \cup (m^*, H(m^*))$ contains more information than D, the return of Ext_{f_2} on input state $|z, c, y, D \cup (m^*, H(m^*)), 0^m\rangle$ is irrelevant to that additional information. Thus, Ext_{f_2} returns the same value on state $|z, c, y, D \cup (m^*, H(m^*)), 0^m\rangle$ and $|z, c, y, D, 0^m\rangle$, i.e., $m = m'$. $\qquad\square$

By using above lemma and (10), we obtain that the return of operation $\mathsf{S}_{m^*} \circ \mathsf{Ext}_{f_2} \circ \mathsf{S}_{m^*}$ acting on state

$$\mathsf{S}_{m^*} |z, c, y, D \cup (m^*, H(m^*)), 0^m\rangle (c \neq c^*)$$

is identical to the return of operation Ext_{f_2} acting on state $|z, c, y, D, 0^m\rangle$. This implies that even if we do not query eCO.RO by m^* to generate c^* in game $\mathbf{G_4}$, and generate it as $\mathsf{Enc}_{pk}(m^*, O(m^*))$ instead ($O \xleftarrow{\$} \Omega_H$), the operation $\mathsf{S}_{m^*} \circ \mathsf{Ext}_{f_2} \circ \mathsf{S}_{m^*}$ in game $\mathbf{G_4}$ can then be reduced to operation Ext_{f_2} directly. In other words, we can transform game $\mathbf{G_4}$ to the following game $\mathbf{G_5}$ equivalently.

Game $\mathbf{G_5}$: Compared with game $\mathbf{G_4}$, this game has two modifications:

- The simulation of random oracle H is changed. Let $O \xleftarrow{\$} \Omega_H$ be a new random oracle, when H is queried with state $|x, y\rangle_{\mathsf{XY}}$, a conditional operation to registers XY is applied:
  - Query eCO.RO if $x \neq m^*$, query random oracle O with input/output register $\mathsf{X/Y}$ if $x_i = m^*$.
  The simulation of parallel queries can be done in a similar manner. We note that the c^* in this game is computed as $\mathsf{Enc}_{pk}(m^*, O(m^*))$.
- The extraction-interface eCO.E$_{f_2}$ is implemented by the unitary operation Ext_{f_2}. Therefore, the decapsulation oracle $\mathsf{qDeca}^\diamond$ in this game is simulated by the unitary operation $\mathsf{U}^3_{\mathsf{qD}}$ defined in (7).

$$\Pr[1 \leftarrow \mathbf{G_4}] = \Pr[1 \leftarrow \mathbf{G_5}]. \tag{11}$$

Notice that game $\mathbf{G_5}$ needs m^* to implement a conditional operation when simulating H. In the following game $\mathbf{G_6}$, a new conditional operation without using m^* is implemented instead.

Game G_6: This game is the same as G_5, except that a new conditional operation as follows is implemented to simulate random oracle H.

- Query eCO.RO if $\mathsf{Enc}_{pk}(x, O(x)) \neq c^*$, query random oracle O with input/output register X/Y if $\mathsf{Enc}_{pk}(x, O(x)) = c^*$.

Define a subset of message space $\mathcal{M}$ as

$$S_{pk,sk,O}^{collision} := \{m | \exists m' \neq m, \mathsf{Enc}_{pk}(m, O(m)) = \mathsf{Enc}_{pk}(m', O(m'))\}.$$

It is obvious that games G_5 and G_6 are identical if $m^* \notin S_{pk,sk,O}^{collision}$ for $(pk, sk) \leftarrow \mathsf{Gen}$ and $O \xleftarrow{\$} \Omega_H$. By using Lemma 9 and the δ-correct property of the underlying PKE scheme P, we obtain

$$|\Pr[1 \leftarrow G_5] - \Pr[1 \leftarrow G_6]| \leq 2\delta. \tag{12}$$

Now, we define an IND-CPA adversary $\tilde{\mathcal{A}}$ against $\mathsf{KEM}_m^\perp$ in the QROM as follows. To avoid confusion, we denote the two random oracles quantum accessible to $\tilde{\mathcal{A}}$ in the IND-CPA game of $\mathsf{KEM}_m^\perp$ as H' and G'.

1. The input of $\tilde{\mathcal{A}}$ is (pk, c^*, K_b^*), where $c^* = \mathsf{Enc}_{pk}(m^*, H'(m^*))$.
2. $\tilde{\mathcal{A}}$ initializes register M with state $|0^m\rangle$, prepares database register D_{q_H}, and implements the extractable RO-simulator $\mathcal{S}(f_2) = \{\mathsf{eCO.RO}, \mathsf{eCO.E}_{f_2}\}$. Then $\tilde{\mathcal{A}}$ runs adversary $\mathcal{A}$, simulates game G_6 for it, and output $\mathcal{A}$'s output.
   (a) When $\mathcal{A}$ queries random oracle H in parallel with state $|x_1, y_1\rangle_{X_1Y_1} \cdots |x_{w_H}, y_{w_H}\rangle_{X_{w_H}Y_{w_H}}$ on w_H pairs input/output registers, $\tilde{\mathcal{A}}$ answers it by applying a conditional operation to registers $X_iY_i (i = 1, \ldots, w_H)$ sequentially:
      i. For the registers $X_iY_i\mathsf{D}_{q_H}$, implement the RO-interface eCO.RO if $\mathsf{Enc}_{pk}(x_i, H'(x_i)) \neq c^*$, query random oracle H' with input/output register X_i/Y_i if $\mathsf{Enc}_{pk}(x_i, H'(x_i)) = c^*$.
   (b) When $\mathcal{A}$ queries random oracle G, $\tilde{\mathcal{A}}$ answers it by querying random oracle G' directly.
   (c) When $\mathcal{A}$ queries decapsulation oracle qDeca with input state $|c, y\rangle_{IO}$, $\tilde{\mathcal{A}}$ answers it by implementing unitary operation

$$\mathsf{U}_\perp \circ \mathsf{P}_{c^*} + \mathsf{Ext}_{f_2} \circ O_{G'} \circ \mathsf{Ext}_{f_2} \circ (\mathbf{I} - \mathsf{P}_{c^*})$$

   on registers $\mathsf{IOD}_{q_H}\mathsf{M}$. Here, $O_{G'}$ represents querying random oracle G' with input/output register M/O.

One can check that, adversary $\tilde{\mathcal{A}}$ makes at most $2q_H$ (resp. $q_G + q_D$) queries to H' (resp. G'), the query depth of $\tilde{\mathcal{A}}$ to H' (resp. G') is $2d_H$ (resp. $d_G + d_D$). As for the running time, since $\tilde{\mathcal{A}}$ implements eCO.RO and $\mathsf{eCO.E}_{f_2}$ at most q_H and $2q_D$ times, respectively, the running time of $\tilde{\mathcal{A}}$ can be bounded as $\mathsf{Time}(\tilde{\mathcal{A}}) \approx \mathsf{Time}(\mathcal{A}) + O(q_H q_D + q_H^2)$ by the Definition 2. As for the memory space, note that $\tilde{\mathcal{A}}$ needs to prepare database register D_{q_H} to implement the extractable RO-simulator $\mathcal{S}(f_2)$, hence, we have $\mathsf{Space}(\tilde{\mathcal{A}}) \approx \mathsf{Space}(\mathcal{A}) + O(q_H)$.

Obviously, we have

$$\mathrm{Adv}_{\mathsf{KEM}_m^\perp, \tilde{\mathcal{A}}}^{\mathsf{IND\text{-}CPA}} = \left| \Pr[1 \leftarrow \mathbf{G_6}] - \frac{1}{2} \right|. \tag{13}$$

Finally, combining Lemma 5 and Lemma 6 with (5), (6), (9), (11), (12) and (13), we obtain

$$\mathrm{Adv}_{\mathsf{KEM}_m^\perp, \mathcal{A}}^{\mathsf{IND\text{-}qCCA}} \leq \mathrm{Adv}_{\mathsf{KEM}_m^\perp, \tilde{\mathcal{A}}}^{\mathsf{IND\text{-}CPA}} + 8\sqrt{q_H(q_H+1) \cdot \delta} + (64q_H + 2) \cdot \delta + 40q_D \cdot 2^{-\gamma/2}.$$

$\square$

4 From IND-CPA$_\mathsf{P}$ to IND-CPA$_{\mathsf{FO}_m^\perp [\mathsf{P}]}$

In this section, we prove that, in the QROM, the IND-CPA security of KEM scheme $\mathsf{FO}_m^\perp[\mathsf{P}, H, G]$ can be reduced to the IND-CPA security of PKE scheme P without the quadratic security loss. Similar to Theorem 2, our reduction does not require the perfect correctness property of the PKE scheme P.

Before we prove the main result of this section, we first review the transformation T and $\mathsf{U}_m^\perp$ introduced in [14].

Transformation T: Let P = (Gen,Enc,Dec) be a randomized PKE scheme with message space $\mathcal{M}(= \{0,1\}^m)$ and randomness space $\{0,1\}^n$. Let $H : \mathcal{M} \rightarrow \{0,1\}^n$ be a hash function. We associate PKE scheme $\mathsf{T}[\mathsf{P}, H] := (\mathsf{Gen}, \mathsf{Enc_1}, \mathsf{Dec_1})$. The constituting algorithms of $\mathsf{T}[\mathsf{P}, H]$ are given in Fig. 5.

Gen	$\mathsf{Dec_1}(sk, c)$
$(pk, sk) \leftarrow \mathsf{Gen}$	$m' = \mathsf{Dec}_{sk}(c)$
return (pk, sk)	**if** $m' = \perp$
	return $\perp$
$\mathsf{Enc_1}(pk, m)$	**else if** $c \neq \mathsf{Enc}_{pk}(m'; H(m'))$
$c = \mathsf{Enc}_{pk}(m; H(m))$	**return** $\perp$
return c	**return** m'

Fig. 5. PKE scheme $\mathsf{T}[\mathsf{P}, H] = (\mathsf{Gen}, \mathsf{Enc_1}, \mathsf{Dec_1})$.

We introduce the following two lemmas about transformation T. Note that the final upper bound of the first lemma avoids the quadratic security loss.

Lemma 8 (Security of T in the QROM [3], Theorem 1). *For any adversary $\mathcal{A}$ against the OW-CPA security of PKE scheme $\mathsf{T}[\mathsf{P}, H]$ making q_H queries* to H with depth d_H, there exists an adversary $\mathcal{B}$ against the IND-CPA security of PKE scheme P such that

$$\mathrm{Adv}^{\mathsf{OW\text{-}CPA}}_{\mathsf{T}[\mathsf{P},H],\mathcal{A}} \le (d_H + 2) \cdot \left(\mathrm{Adv}^{\mathsf{IND\text{-}CPA}}_{\mathsf{P},\mathcal{B}} + \frac{8(q_H + 1)}{|\mathcal{M}|} \right),$$

$\mathsf{Time}(\mathcal{B}) \approx \mathsf{Time}(\mathcal{A})$ and $\mathsf{Space}(\mathcal{B}) \approx \mathsf{Space}(\mathcal{A})$.

Lemma 9 ([21], Lemma 4). *Let* $\mathsf{P}=(\mathsf{Gen},\mathsf{Enc},\mathsf{Dec})$ *with message space* $\mathcal{M}$ *and randomness space* $\{0,1\}^n$ *be* δ-*correct. Define a set with respect to fixed* $(pk, sk) \leftarrow \mathsf{Gen}$ *and* $H : \mathcal{M} \to \{0,1\}^n$:

$$S^{collision}_{pk,sk,H} := \{ m \in \mathcal{M} | \exists m' \ne m, \mathsf{Enc}_{pk}(m', H(m')) = \mathsf{Enc}_{pk}(m, H(m)) \}.$$

Then we have

$$\Pr[m \in S^{collision}_{pk,sk,H} | (pk, sk) \leftarrow \mathsf{Gen}, H \xleftarrow{\$} \Omega_H, m \xleftarrow{\$} \mathcal{M}] \le 2\delta.$$

Gen	Enca (pk)	Deca (sk, c)
$(pk, sk) \leftarrow \mathsf{Gen}$	$m \xleftarrow{\$} \mathcal{M}$	$m' = \mathsf{dDec}_{sk}(c)$
return (pk, sk)	$c = \mathsf{dEnc}_{pk}(m)$	**if** $m' = \bot$
	$K = G(m)$	**return** $\bot$
	return (K, c)	**else return** $K = G(m')$

Fig. 6. KEM scheme $\mathsf{U}^{\perp}_m[\mathsf{dPKE}, G] = (\mathsf{Gen}, \mathsf{Enca}, \mathsf{Deca})$.

Transformation $\mathsf{U}^{\perp}_m$: Let $\mathsf{dPKE} = (\mathsf{Gen},\mathsf{dEnc},\mathsf{dDec})$ be a DPKE scheme with message space $\mathcal{M}(= \{0,1\}^m)$. Let $G : \mathcal{M} \to \{0,1\}^n$ be a hash function. We associate KEM scheme $\mathsf{U}^{\perp}_m[\mathsf{dPKE}, G] := (\mathsf{Gen}, \mathsf{Enca}, \mathsf{Deca})$. The constituting algorithms of $\mathsf{U}^{\perp}_m[\mathsf{dPKE}, G]$ are given in Fig. 6.

Obviously, we have $\mathsf{FO}^{\perp}_m[\mathsf{P}, H, G] = \mathsf{U}^{\perp}_m[\mathsf{T}[\mathsf{P}, H], G]$. Next, we prove the following theorem, which indicates that the IND-CPA security of $\mathsf{U}^{\perp}_m[\mathsf{dPKE}, G]$ in the QROM can be reduced to the OW-CPA security of dPKE without the quadratic security loss.

Theorem 3 (OW-CPA$_{\mathsf{dPKE}}$ $\overset{\mathsf{QROM}}{\Rightarrow}$ IND-CPA$_{\mathsf{U}^{\perp}_m[\mathsf{dPKE},G]}$). *Let* $\mathcal{A}$ *be an IND-CPA adversary against* $\mathsf{U}^{\perp}_m[\mathsf{dPKE},G]$ *in the QROM making at most* q_G *queries to random oracle* G *with depth* d_G. *Then there exists an* OW-CPA *adversary* $\tilde{\mathcal{A}}$ *against* dPKE *such that*

$$\mathrm{Adv}^{\mathsf{IND\text{-}CPA}}_{\mathsf{U}^{\perp}_m[\mathsf{dPKE},G],\mathcal{A}} \le 2d_G \cdot \mathrm{Adv}^{\mathsf{OW\text{-}CPA}}_{\mathsf{dPKE},\tilde{\mathcal{A}}} + 2d_G \cdot \Pr[E_{\mathsf{dPKE}}].$$

Here E_{dPKE} *is the event that*

$$E_{\mathsf{dPKE}} : m \xleftarrow{\$} \mathcal{M}, \exists m' \ne m, \mathsf{dEnc}_{pk}(m) = \mathsf{dEnc}_{pk}(m').$$

The running time and memory space of $\tilde{\mathcal{A}}$ *is bounded as* $\mathsf{Time}(\tilde{\mathcal{A}}) \approx 2 \cdot \mathsf{Time}(\mathcal{A}) + O(q_G)$ *and* $\mathsf{Space}(\tilde{\mathcal{A}}) \approx O(\mathsf{Space}(\mathcal{A}) + \mathsf{Time}(\mathcal{A}))$, *respectively.*

Proof. Define two games $\mathbf{G}_{b=0}$ and $\mathbf{G}_{b=1}$ as shown in Fig. 7. Here $\mathcal{D}$ is a joint distribution of (G, H, m^*, pk), where $G \xleftarrow{\$} \Omega_G$, $m^* \xleftarrow{\$} \mathcal{M}$, H is identical to G, except that $H(m^*)$ is a fresh random value uniformly sampled from $\{0,1\}^n$, and pk is sampled by $(pk, sk) \leftarrow$ Gen. Then we have

$$\mathrm{Adv}^{\mathsf{IND\text{-}CPA}}_{U_m^\perp[\mathsf{dPKE},G],\mathcal{A}} = \frac{1}{2} | \Pr[1 \leftarrow \mathbf{G}_{b=0}] - \Pr[1 \leftarrow \mathbf{G}_{b=1}]|. \tag{14}$$

<u>$\mathbf{G}_{b=0}$</u>
1, $(G, H, m^*, pk) \leftarrow \mathcal{D}$
2, $b = 0$
   $c^* = \mathsf{dEnc}_{pk}(m^*)$
   $K_0^* = G(m^*)$, $K_1^* \xleftarrow{\$} \{0,1\}^n$
3, $b' \leftarrow \mathcal{A}^G(pk, c^*, K_b^*)$
4, **return** b'

<u>$\mathbf{G}_{b=1}$</u>
1, $(G, H, m^*, pk) \leftarrow \mathcal{D}$
2, $b = 1$
   $c^* = \mathsf{dEnc}_{pk}(m^*)$
   $K_0^* = G(m^*)$, $K_1^* \xleftarrow{\$} \{0,1\}^n$
3, $b' \leftarrow \mathcal{A}^G(pk, c^*, K_b^*)$
4, **return** b'

<u>$\mathbf{NG}_{b=0}$</u>
1, $(G, H, m^*, pk, c^*, K) \leftarrow \mathcal{D}_1$
2, $b' \leftarrow \mathcal{A}^G(pk, c^*, K)$
3, **return** b'

<u>$\mathbf{NG}_{b=1}$</u>
1, $(G, H, m^*, pk, c^*, K) \leftarrow \mathcal{D}_1$
2, $b' \leftarrow \mathcal{A}^H(pk, c^*, K)$
3, **return** b'

Fig. 7. Game $\mathbf{G}_{b=0}$, $\mathbf{G}_{b=1}$, $\mathbf{NG}_{b=0}$ and $\mathbf{NG}_{b=1}$.

Next, we rewrite game $\mathbf{G}_{b=0}$ and $\mathbf{G}_{b=1}$ to new games $\mathbf{NG}_{b=0}$ and $\mathbf{NG}_{b=1}$, respectively, as shown in Fig. 7. The $\mathcal{D}_1$ in games $\mathbf{NG}_{b=0}$ and $\mathbf{NG}_{b=1}$ are joint distributions identical to $\mathcal{D}$, except that two additional values c^* and K are sampled, where $c^* = \mathsf{dEnc}_{pk}(m^*)$ and $K = G(m^*)$. Then we have

$$\Pr[1 \leftarrow \mathbf{G}_{b=0}] = \Pr[1 \leftarrow \mathbf{NG}_{b=0}], \ \Pr[1 \leftarrow \mathbf{G}_{b=1}] = \Pr[1 \leftarrow \mathbf{NG}_{b=1}]. \tag{15}$$

Define $z := (pk, c^*, K)$ and $z' := (G, H, m^*, pk, c^*, K)$, we obtain

$$\begin{aligned} \Pr[1 \leftarrow \mathbf{NG}_{b=0}] &= \Pr[1 \leftarrow \mathcal{A}^G(z) : z' \leftarrow \mathcal{D}_1], \\ \Pr[1 \leftarrow \mathbf{NG}_{b=1}] &= \Pr[1 \leftarrow \mathcal{A}^H(z) : z' \leftarrow \mathcal{D}_1]. \end{aligned} \tag{16}$$

By applying Lemma 2 with $\mathcal{X} = \mathcal{M}$, $\mathcal{Y} = \{0,1\}^n$, $S = \{m^*\}$, and $z = (pk, c^*, K)$, there exists an adversary $\mathcal{B}$ that makes oracle queries to G and H and satisfies

$$| \Pr[1 \leftarrow \mathcal{A}^G(z) : z' \leftarrow \mathcal{D}_1] - \Pr[1 \leftarrow \mathcal{A}^H(z) : z' \leftarrow \mathcal{D}_1]|$$
$$\leq 4d_G \cdot \Pr[T \cap S \neq \varnothing : T \leftarrow \mathcal{B}^{G,H}(z), z' \leftarrow \mathcal{D}_1]. \tag{17}$$

The running time of $\mathcal{B}$ is $\mathsf{Time}(\mathcal{B}) \approx 2 \cdot \mathsf{Time}(\mathcal{A})$, the memory space of $\mathcal{B}$ is $\mathsf{Space}(\mathcal{B}) \approx O(\mathsf{Space}(\mathcal{A}) + \mathsf{Time}(\mathcal{A}))$, and $\mathcal{B}$ makes at most $3q_G$ queries in total to oracles H and G.

Now, we construct an adversary $\tilde{A}$ that against the OW-CPA security of dPKE as follows.

1. $\tilde{A}$ gets the challenge ciphertext $c^* = \mathsf{dPKE}_{pk}(m^*)$ and public key pk.
2. $\tilde{A}$ samples K uniformly from $\{0,1\}^n$ and chooses a $3q_G$-wise function f uniformly.
3. $\tilde{A}$ uses (pk, c^*, K) as input to run adversary $\mathcal{B}$:
   (a) When $\mathcal{B}$ queries H with state $|x, y\rangle_{\mathsf{IO}}$ on input/output register I/O, $\tilde{A}$ answers by applying unitary operation O_f to registers IO directly, where $O_f|x, y\rangle \to |x, y \oplus f(x)\rangle$.
   (b) When $\mathcal{B}$ queries G with state $|x, y\rangle_{\mathsf{I}_1 \mathsf{O}_1}$ on input/output register $\mathsf{I}_1/\mathsf{O}_1$, $\tilde{A}$ answers by applying a conditional operation to registers $\mathsf{I}_1 \mathsf{O}_1$:
   Apply O_f if $\mathsf{dPKE}_{pk}(x) \neq c^*$, apply U_K if $\mathsf{dPKE}_{pk}(x) = c^*$, where $U_K|x, y\rangle_{\mathsf{I}_1 \mathsf{O}_1} = |x, y \oplus K\rangle_{\mathsf{I}_1 \mathsf{O}_1}$.
4. After $\mathcal{B}$ returns its output T, $\tilde{A}$ searches x that satisfies $\mathsf{dPKE}_{pk}(x) = c^*$ from T and output the minimum one. If such x does not exist, $\tilde{A}$ output $\bot$.

One can check that the running time of $\tilde{A}$ is $\mathsf{Time}(\tilde{A}) \approx \mathsf{Time}(\mathcal{B}) + O(q_G)$, the memory space of $\tilde{A}$ is $\mathsf{Space}(\tilde{A}) \approx \mathsf{Space}(\mathcal{B})$.

The adversary $\tilde{A}$ cannot get m^* to simulate H and G directly. In the above construction, $\tilde{A}$ tests if x equals m^* by checking if $\mathsf{dPKE}_{pk}(x)$ equals c^*. Therefore, similar to the event $m^* \notin \mathsf{S}_{pk,sk,O}^{collision}$ used in the game $\mathbf{G_6}$ of the proof of Theorem 2, if the following event E_{dPKE} does not occur, the adversary $\tilde{A}$ simulates the oracle H and G for $\mathcal{B}$ perfectly.

$$E_{\mathsf{dPKE}} : m^* \xleftarrow{\$} \mathcal{M}, \exists m' \neq m^*, \mathsf{dEnc}_{pk}(m^*) = \mathsf{dEnc}_{pk}(m').$$

Then, we have

$$\Pr[T \cap S \neq \varnothing : T \leftarrow \mathcal{B}^{G,H}(z), z' \leftarrow \mathcal{D}_1] \leq \mathsf{Adv}_{\mathsf{dPKE}, \tilde{A}}^{\mathsf{OW\text{-}CPA}} + \Pr[E_{\mathsf{dPKE}}]. \quad (18)$$

Combining (14), (15), (16), (17) and (18), we finally obtain

$$\mathsf{Adv}_{U_m^\bot[\mathsf{dPKE}, G], \mathcal{A}}^{\mathsf{IND\text{-}CPA}} \leq 2d_G \cdot \mathsf{Adv}_{\mathsf{dPKE}, \tilde{A}}^{\mathsf{OW\text{-}CPA}} + 2d_G \cdot \Pr[E_{\mathsf{dPKE}}].$$

$\square$

Theorem 4 (IND-CPA$_\mathsf{P}$ $\overset{\mathrm{QROM}}{\Rightarrow}$ IND-CPA$_{\mathsf{FO}_m^\bot[\mathsf{P}, H, G]}$). *Let $\mathcal{A}$ be an* IND-CPA *adversary against* $\mathsf{FO}_m^\bot[\mathsf{P}, H, G]$ *in the QROM that making at most q_H and q_G queries to random oracle H and G, respectively. Let d_H (resp. d_G) be the query depth of $\mathcal{A}$'s random oracle H (resp. G) queries. Then there exists an* IND-CPA *adversary $\mathcal{B}$ against* P *such that*

$$\mathsf{Adv}_{\mathsf{FO}_m^\bot[\mathsf{P}, H, G], \mathcal{A}}^{\mathsf{IND\text{-}CPA}} \leq 2d_G(d_H + 2) \cdot \mathsf{Adv}_{\mathsf{P}, \mathcal{B}}^{\mathsf{IND\text{-}CPA}} + 16d_G(d_H + 2)\frac{(q_H + 1)}{|\mathcal{M}|} + 4d_G \cdot \delta.$$

The running time and memory space of $\mathcal{B}$ is bounded as $\mathsf{Time}(\mathcal{B}) \approx 2 \cdot \mathsf{Time}(\mathcal{A}) + O(q_G)$ *and* $\mathsf{Space}(\mathcal{B}) \approx O(\mathsf{Space}(\mathcal{A}) + \mathsf{Time}(\mathcal{A}))$, *respectively.*

Proof. Since $\mathsf{FO}_m^\perp[\mathsf{P}, H, G] = \mathsf{U}_m^\perp[\mathsf{T}[\mathsf{P}, H], G]$, we have

$$\mathrm{Adv}_{\mathsf{FO}_m^\perp[\mathsf{P},H,G],\mathcal{A}}^{\mathsf{IND\text{-}CPA}} = \mathrm{Adv}_{\mathsf{U}_m^\perp[\mathsf{T}[\mathsf{P},H],G],\mathcal{A}}^{\mathsf{IND\text{-}CPA}}$$

$$\overset{(a)}{\leq} 2d_G \cdot \mathrm{Adv}_{\mathsf{T}[\mathsf{P},H],\tilde{\mathcal{A}}}^{\mathsf{OW\text{-}CPA}} + 2d_G \cdot \Pr[E_{\mathsf{T}[\mathsf{P},H]}]$$

$$\overset{(b)}{\leq} 2d_G \cdot \mathrm{Adv}_{\mathsf{T}[\mathsf{P},H],\tilde{\mathcal{A}}}^{\mathsf{OW\text{-}CPA}} + 4d_G \cdot \delta$$

$$\overset{(c)}{\leq} 2d_G(d_H + 2) \cdot \mathrm{Adv}_{\mathsf{P},\mathcal{B}}^{\mathsf{IND\text{-}CPA}} + 16d_G(d_H + 2)\frac{(q_H + 1)}{|\mathcal{M}|} + 4d_G \cdot \delta.$$

Here (a) and (c) uses the Theorem 3 and Lemma 8, respectively. (b) uses the Lemma 9.

By the result of Theorem 3, the running time of $\tilde{\mathcal{A}}$ is $\mathsf{Time}(\tilde{\mathcal{A}}) \approx 2 \cdot \mathsf{Time}(\mathcal{A}) + O(q_G)$. By the result of Lemma 8, the running time of $\mathcal{B}$ is $\mathsf{Time}(\mathcal{B}) \approx \mathsf{Time}(\tilde{\mathcal{A}})$. Therefore the running time of $\mathcal{B}$ is $\mathsf{Time}(\mathcal{B}) \approx 2 \cdot \mathsf{Time}(\mathcal{A}) + O(q_G)$. The memory space of $\mathcal{B}$ can be obtained in a similar way. $\square$

Combining Theorem 2 and Theorem 4, we obtain following result.

Corollary 1 (IND-CPA$_\mathsf{P}$ $\overset{\mathsf{QROM}}{\Rightarrow}$ IND-qCCA$_{\mathsf{FO}_m^\perp[\mathsf{P},H,G]}$). *Let* P *be a randomized PKE scheme that is δ-correct and weakly γ-spread. Let $\mathcal{A}$ be an* IND-qCCA *adversary against* $\mathsf{KEM}_m^\perp := \mathsf{FO}_m^\perp[\mathsf{P}, H, G]$ *in the* QROM, *making at most q_H, q_G and q_D queries to random oracle H, random oracle G and decapsulation oracle* qDeca*, respectively. Let d_H (resp. d_G) be the query depth of $\mathcal{A}$'s random oracle H (resp. G) queries.*

Then there exists an IND-CPA *adversary $\mathcal{B}$ against* P *such that*

$$\mathrm{Adv}_{\mathsf{KEM}_m^\perp,\mathcal{A}}^{\mathsf{IND\text{-}qCCA}} \leq 2(d_G + q_D)(2d_H + 2) \cdot \mathrm{Adv}_{\mathsf{P},\mathcal{B}}^{\mathsf{IND\text{-}CPA}} + 40q_D \cdot 2^{-\gamma/2}$$

$$+ 8\sqrt{q_H(q_H + 1) \cdot \delta} + (64q_H + 4d_G + 4q_D + 2) \cdot \delta$$

$$+ 16(d_G + q_D)(2d_H + 2)\frac{(2q_H + 1)}{|\mathcal{M}|}.$$

The running time and memory space of $\mathcal{B}$ is bounded as $\mathsf{Time}(\mathcal{B}) \approx 2 \cdot \mathsf{Time}(\mathcal{A}) + O(q_H q_D + q_H^2 + q_G)$ *and* $\mathsf{Space}(\mathcal{B}) \approx O(\mathsf{Space}(\mathcal{A}) + \mathsf{Time}(\mathcal{A}) + q_H)$, *respectively.*

5 Explicit Rejection and Implicit Rejection

In this section, we prove that, in the QROM, $\mathsf{FO}_m^{\not\perp}$ is IND-qCCA-secure if $\mathsf{FO}_m^\perp$ is IND-qCCA-secure and vice versa.

Transformation. $\mathsf{FO}_m^{\not\perp}$: Let P = (Gen, Enc, Dec) be a randomized PKE scheme with message space $\mathcal{M}(= \{0,1\}^m)$ and randomness space $\{0,1\}^n$. Let $H : \mathcal{M} \to \{0,1\}^n$ and $G : \{0,1\}^* \to \{0,1\}^{n'}$ be hash functions. Let F be a pseudorandom function (PRF) with key space $\mathcal{K}^{prf}$. We associate

$$\mathsf{KEM}_m^{\not\perp} := \mathsf{FO}_m^{\not\perp}[\mathsf{P}, H, G] = (\mathsf{Gen}^{\not\perp}, \mathsf{Enca}_m, \mathsf{Deca}_m^{\not\perp}).$$

The constituting algorithms of $\mathsf{KEM}_m^{\not\perp}$ are given in Fig. 8.

$$\underline{\text{Gen}^{\perp}}$$

$(pk, sk) \leftarrow \text{Gen}$

$s \xleftarrow{\$} \mathcal{K}^{prf}$

$sk' := (sk, s)$

return (pk, sk')

$$\underline{\text{Encap}_m (pk)}$$

$m \xleftarrow{\$} \mathcal{M}$

$c = \text{Enc}_{pk} (m; H(m))$

$K = G(m)$

return (K, c)

$$\underline{\text{Deca}_m^{\perp} (sk' = (sk, s), c)}$$

$m' = \text{Dec}_{sk} (c)$

if $m' = \perp$

    return $\text{F}(s, c)$

else if $c \neq \text{Enc}_{pk} (m'; H(m'))$

    return $\text{F}(s, c)$

return $K = G(m')$

Fig. 8. KEM scheme $\text{KEM}_m^{\perp} = (\text{Gen}^{\perp}, \text{Enca}_m, \text{Deca}_m^{\perp})$.

Theorem 5 (Explicit → implicit). *Let* P *be a randomized PKE scheme. Let* $\mathcal{A}$ *be an* IND-qCCA *adversary against* $\text{KEM}_m^{\perp}$ *in the QROM. Then there exists an* IND-qCCA *adversary* $\mathcal{B}$ *against* $\text{KEM}_m^{\perp}$ *such that*

$$\text{Adv}_{\text{KEM}_m^{\perp}, \mathcal{A}}^{\text{IND-qCCA}} = \text{Adv}_{\text{KEM}_m^{\perp}, \mathcal{B}}^{\text{IND-qCCA}} .$$

The running time and memory space of $\mathcal{B}$ *is bounded as* $\text{Time}(\mathcal{A}) \approx \text{Time}(\mathcal{B})$ *and* $\text{Space}(\mathcal{A}) \approx \text{Space}(\mathcal{B})$, *respectively.*

Proof. The only difference between the adversary in the IND-qCCA game of $\text{KEM}_m^{\perp}$ and $\text{KEM}_m^{\perp}$ is that the former gets $\perp$ from the decapsulation oracle for an input c failed to decapsulate, the latter instead gets pseudorandom value $\text{F}(s, c)$. Indeed, the former adversary can also choose s itself and compute $\text{F}(s, c)$ after it gets $\perp$ from the decapsulation oracle for input c. Following this way, we construct an adversary $\mathcal{B}$ against the IND-qCCA security of $\text{KEM}_m^{\perp}$ as follows:

1. $\mathcal{B}$ chooses PRF key $s \xleftarrow{\$} \mathcal{K}^{prf}$ and runs adversary $\mathcal{A}$.
2. $\mathcal{B}$ answers the random oracle H/G queries of $\mathcal{A}$ by querying H/G directly.
3. $\mathcal{B}$ initializes a register K defined over $\{0, 1\}^{n'+116}$ with state $|0^{n'}\rangle_K$. When $\mathcal{A}$ queries the decapsulation oracle with input state $|c\rangle_I |y\rangle_O$, $\mathcal{B}$ answers by applying following operations sequentially:
   (a) Query the decapsulation oracle with input state $|c\rangle_I |0^{n'}\rangle_K$, suppose the output state is $|c\rangle_I |k\rangle_K$.
   (b) If $k = \perp$, perform unitary operation $U_s : |c\rangle_I |y\rangle_O \to |c\rangle_I |y \oplus \text{F}(s, c)\rangle_O$. Otherwise, perform unitary operation $U_{XOR} : |y\rangle_O |k\rangle_K \to |y \oplus k\rangle_O |k\rangle_K$.
   (c) Query the decapsulation oracle with input state $|c\rangle_I |k\rangle_K$, now the register K is guaranteed to contain $0^{n'}$.
4. $\mathcal{B}$ finally outputs $\mathcal{A}$'s output.

Obviously, adversary $\mathcal{B}$ perfectly simulates the IND-qCCA game of $\text{KEM}_m^{\perp}$ for adversary $\mathcal{A}$ and the running time (resp. memory space) of $\mathcal{B}$ is nearly the same

---

[16] Here we embed the set $\{0, 1\}^{n'} \cup \perp$ into the set $\{0, 1\}^{n'+1}$ as explained in Appendix A of [12].

as the running time (resp. memory space) of $\mathcal{A}$. Thus

$$\mathsf{Adv}^{\mathsf{IND\text{-}qCCA}}_{\mathsf{KEM}^{\not\perp}_m,\mathcal{A}} = \mathsf{Adv}^{\mathsf{IND\text{-}qCCA}}_{\mathsf{KEM}^{\perp}_m,\mathcal{B}}.$$

$\square$

Theorem 6 (Implicit → explicit). *Let* P *be a randomized PKE scheme that is* δ-*correct and weakly* γ-*spread. Let* $\mathcal{A}$ *be an* IND-qCCA *adversary against* $\mathsf{KEM}^{\perp}_m$ *that making at most* q_H, q_G *and* q_D *queries to random oracle* H, *random oracle* G *and decapsulation oracle* qDeca*, *respectively.*

Then there exists an IND-qCCA *adversary* $\mathcal{B}$ *against* $\mathsf{KEM}^{\not\perp}_m$ *such that*

$$\mathsf{Adv}^{\mathsf{IND\text{-}qCCA}}_{\mathsf{KEM}^{\perp}_m,\mathcal{A}} \leq \mathsf{Adv}^{\mathsf{IND\text{-}qCCA}}_{\mathsf{KEM}^{\not\perp}_m,\mathcal{B}} + 8\sqrt{q_H(q_H+1)\cdot\delta} + (64q_H+2)\cdot\delta + 40q_D\cdot 2^{-\gamma/2}.$$

The running time and memory space of $\mathcal{B}$ *is bounded as* $\mathsf{Time}(\mathcal{B}) \approx \mathsf{Time}(\mathcal{A}) +$ $O(q_H q_D + q_H^2)$ *and* $\mathsf{Space}(\mathcal{B}) \approx \mathsf{Space}(\mathcal{A}) + O(q_H)$, *respectively.*

Proof. By using Theorem 2, there exists an IND-CPA adversary $\tilde{\mathcal{A}}$ against $\mathsf{KEM}^{\perp}_m$ such that

$$\mathsf{Adv}^{\mathsf{IND\text{-}qCCA}}_{\mathsf{KEM}^{\perp}_m,\mathcal{A}} \leq \mathsf{Adv}^{\mathsf{IND\text{-}CPA}}_{\mathsf{KEM}^{\perp}_m,\tilde{\mathcal{A}}} + 8\sqrt{q_H(q_H+1)\cdot\delta} + (64q_H+2)\cdot\delta + 40q_D\cdot 2^{-\gamma/2}. \quad (19)$$

The running time and memory space of $\tilde{\mathcal{A}}$ is bounded as $\mathsf{Time}(\tilde{\mathcal{A}}) \approx \mathsf{Time}(\mathcal{A}) +$ $O(q_H q_D + q_H^2)$ and $\mathsf{Space}(\tilde{\mathcal{A}}) \approx \mathsf{Space}(\mathcal{A}) + O(q_H)$, respectively.

We note that, in the IND-qCCA game of $\mathsf{KEM}^{\not\perp}_m$, the PRF key s chosen as part of the secret key is useless if the adversary never queries the decapsulation oracle. This implies that, even though the IND-qCCA adversary against $\mathsf{KEM}^{\not\perp}_m$ does not know the PRF key s, it can still perfectly simulate the IND-CPA game of $\mathsf{KEM}^{\perp}_m$ for the adversary $\tilde{\mathcal{A}}$. Now, we construct an IND-qCCA adversary $\mathcal{B}$ against $\mathsf{KEM}^{\not\perp}_m$ as follows:

1. $\mathcal{B}$ runs adversary $\tilde{\mathcal{A}}$ and $\mathcal{B}$ never queries the decapsulation oracle.
2. $\mathcal{B}$ answers the random oracle H/G queries of $\tilde{\mathcal{A}}$ by querying H/G directly.
3. $\mathcal{B}$ finally outputs $\tilde{\mathcal{A}}$'s output.

It is straightforward to check that adversary $\mathcal{B}$ perfectly simulates the IND-CPA game of $\mathsf{KEM}^{\perp}_m$ for adversary $\tilde{\mathcal{A}}$, and the running time (resp. memory space) of $\mathcal{B}$ is nearly the same as the running time (resp. memory space) of $\tilde{\mathcal{A}}$. Thus

$$\mathsf{Adv}^{\mathsf{IND\text{-}CPA}}_{\mathsf{KEM}^{\perp}_m,\tilde{\mathcal{A}}} = \mathsf{Adv}^{\mathsf{IND\text{-}qCCA}}_{\mathsf{KEM}^{\not\perp}_m,\mathcal{B}}.$$

Combining above equation with (19), we obtain our result. $\square$

Remark 2. In Theorem 6, different from Corollary 1, we note that our reduction only introduces a linear memory space expansion $O(q_H)$. The reason is that the adversary $\tilde{\mathcal{A}}$ in Theorem 2 only invokes adversary $\mathcal{A}$ once in a black-box manner, and it just uses an additional database register D_{q_H} to process the oracle queries of $\mathcal{A}$.

Acknowledgments. We thank the anonymous reviewers of CRYPTO 2023, and Shujiao Cao for their insightful comments and suggestions. This work is supported by National Natural Science Foundation of China (Grants No. 62172405).

References

1. Ambainis, A., Hamburg, M., Unruh, D.: Quantum security proofs using semiclassical oracles. In: Boldyreva, A., Micciancio, D. (eds.) CRYPTO 2019. LNCS, vol. 11693, pp. 269–295. Springer, Cham (2019). https://doi.org/10.1007/978-3-030-26951-7_10
2. Bellare, M., Rogaway, P.: Random oracles are practical: A paradigm for designing efficient protocols. In: CCS '93, Proceedings of the 1st ACM Conference on Computer and Communications Security, Fairfax, Virginia, USA, November 3–5, 1993, pp. 62–73. ACM (1993). https://doi.org/10.1145/168588.168596
3. Bindel, N., Hamburg, M., Hövelmanns, K., Hülsing, A., Persichetti, E.: Tighter proofs of CCA security in the quantum random oracle model. In: Hofheinz, D., Rosen, A. (eds.) TCC 2019. LNCS, vol. 11892, pp. 61–90. Springer, Cham (2019). https://doi.org/10.1007/978-3-030-36033-7_3
4. Boneh, D., Dagdelen, Ö., Fischlin, M., Lehmann, A., Schaffner, C., Zhandry, M.: Random oracles in a quantum world. In: Lee, D.H., Wang, X. (eds.) ASIACRYPT 2011. LNCS, vol. 7073, pp. 41–69. Springer, Heidelberg (2011). https://doi.org/10.1007/978-3-642-25385-0_3
5. Boneh, D., Zhandry, M.: Secure signatures and chosen ciphertext security in a quantum computing world. In: Canetti, R., Garay, J.A. (eds.) CRYPTO 2013. LNCS, vol. 8043, pp. 361–379. Springer, Heidelberg (2013). https://doi.org/10.1007/978-3-642-40084-1_21
6. Chung, K.-M., Fehr, S., Huang, Y.-H., Liao, T.-N.: On the compressed-oracle technique, and post-quantum security of proofs of sequential work. In: Canteaut, A., Standaert, F.-X. (eds.) EUROCRYPT 2021. LNCS, vol. 12697, pp. 598–629. Springer, Cham (2021). https://doi.org/10.1007/978-3-030-77886-6_21
7. Czajkowski, J., Majenz, C., Schaffner, C., Zur, S.: Quantum lazy sampling and game-playing proofs for quantum indifferentiability. Cryptology ePrint Archive, Paper 2019/428 (2019). https://eprint.iacr.org/2019/428
8. Dent, A.W.: A designer's guide to KEMs. In: Paterson, K.G. (ed.) Cryptography and Coding 2003. LNCS, vol. 2898, pp. 133–151. Springer, Heidelberg (2003). https://doi.org/10.1007/978-3-540-40974-8_12
9. Don, J., Fehr, S., Majenz, C., Schaffner, C.: Online-extractability in the quantum random-oracle model. In: Advances in Cryptology - EUROCRYPT 2022–41st Annual International Conference on the Theory and Applications of Cryptographic Techniques, Trondheim, Norway, May 30 - June 3, 2022, Proceedings, Part III, pp. 677–706. Springer (2022). https://doi.org/10.1007/978-3-031-07082-2_24
10. Fujisaki, E., Okamoto, T.: Secure integration of asymmetric and symmetric encryption schemes. J. Cryptol. **26**(1), 80–101 (2011). https://doi.org/10.1007/s00145-011-9114-1
11. Ge, J., Shan, T., Xue, R.: On the fujisaki-okamoto transform: from classical cca security to quantum cca security. Cryptology ePrint Archive, Paper 2023/792 (2023). https://eprint.iacr.org/2023/792
12. Ge, J., Shan, T., Xue, R.: Tighter qcca-secure key encapsulation mechanism with explicit rejection in the quantum random oracle model. Cryptology ePrint Archive, Paper 2023/862 (2023). https://eprint.iacr.org/2023/862

13. Grubbs, P., Maram, V., Paterson, K.G.: Anonymous, robust post-quantum public key encryption. In: Advances in Cryptology - EUROCRYPT 2022–41st Annual International Conference on the Theory and Applications of Cryptographic Techniques, Trondheim, Norway, May 30 - June 3, 2022, Proceedings, Part III, pp. 402–432. Springer (2022). https://doi.org/10.1007/978-3-031-07082-2_15

14. Hofheinz, D., Hövelmanns, K., Kiltz, E.: A modular analysis of the fujisaki-okamoto transformation. In: Theory of Cryptography Conference, pp. 341–371. Springer (2017). https://doi.org/10.1007/978-3-319-70500-2_12

15. Hövelmanns, K., Hülsing, A., Majenz, C.: Failing gracefully: Decryption failures and the fujisaki-okamoto transform. In: Advances in Cryptology - ASIACRYPT 2022–28th International Conference on the Theory and Application of Cryptology and Information Security, Taipei, Taiwan, December 5–9, 2022, Proceedings, Part IV, pp. 414–443. Springer (2022)

16. Jiang, H., Zhang, Z., Chen, L., Wang, H., Ma, Z.: IND-CCA-secure key encapsulation mechanism in the quantum random oracle model, revisited. In: Shacham, H., Boldyreva, A. (eds.) CRYPTO 2018. LNCS, vol. 10993, pp. 96–125. Springer, Cham (2018). https://doi.org/10.1007/978-3-319-96878-0_4

17. Jiang, H., Zhang, Z., Ma, Z.: Key encapsulation mechanism with explicit rejection in the quantum random oracle model. In: Lin, D., Sako, K. (eds.) PKC 2019. LNCS, vol. 11443, pp. 618–645. Springer, Cham (2019). https://doi.org/10.1007/978-3-030-17259-6_21

18. Jiang, H., Zhang, Z., Ma, Z.: Tighter security proofs for generic key encapsulation mechanism in the quantum random oracle model. In: Ding, J., Steinwandt, R. (eds.) PQCrypto 2019. LNCS, vol. 11505, pp. 227–248. Springer, Cham (2019). https://doi.org/10.1007/978-3-030-25510-7_13

19. Jiang, H., Zhang, Z., Ma, Z.: On the non-tightness of measurement-based reductions for key encapsulation mechanism in the quantum random oracle model. In: Tibouchi, M., Wang, H. (eds.) ASIACRYPT 2021. LNCS, vol. 13090, pp. 487–517. Springer, Cham (2021). https://doi.org/10.1007/978-3-030-92062-3_17

20. Kuchta, V., Sakzad, A., Stehlé, D., Steinfeld, R., Sun, S.-F.: Measure-rewind-measure: tighter quantum random oracle model proofs for one-way to hiding and CCA Security. In: Canteaut, A., Ishai, Y. (eds.) EUROCRYPT 2020. LNCS, vol. 12107, pp. 703–728. Springer, Cham (2020). https://doi.org/10.1007/978-3-030-45727-3_24

21. Liu, X., Wang, M.: QCCA-secure generic key encapsulation mechanism with tighter security in the quantum random oracle model. In: Garay, J.A. (ed.) PKC 2021. LNCS, vol. 12710, pp. 3–26. Springer, Cham (2021). https://doi.org/10.1007/978-3-030-75245-3_1

22. Nielsen, M.A., Chuang, I.L.: Quantum Computation and Quantum Information (10th Anniversary edition). Cambridge University Press (2016)

23. NIST: National institute for standards and technology. post quantum crypto project. https://csrc.nist.gov/projects/post-quantum-cryptography (2017)

24. Saito, T., Xagawa, K., Yamakawa, T.: Tightly-secure key-encapsulation mechanism in the quantum random oracle model. In: Nielsen, J.B., Rijmen, V. (eds.) EUROCRYPT 2018. LNCS, vol. 10822, pp. 520–551. Springer, Cham (2018). https://doi.org/10.1007/978-3-319-78372-7_17

25. Unruh, D.: Revocable quantum timed-release encryption. J. ACM **62**(6), 49:1–49:76 (2015). https://doi.org/10.1145/2817206

26. Xagawa, K., Yamakawa, T.: (Tightly) QCCA-Secure key-encapsulation mechanism in the quantum random oracle model. In: Ding, J., Steinwandt, R. (eds.) PQCrypto 2019. LNCS, vol. 11505, pp. 249–268. Springer, Cham (2019). https://doi.org/10.1007/978-3-030-25510-7_14

27. Zhandry, M.: Secure identity-based encryption in the quantum random oracle model. In: Safavi-Naini, R., Canetti, R. (eds.) CRYPTO 2012. LNCS, vol. 7417, pp. 758–775. Springer, Heidelberg (2012). https://doi.org/10.1007/978-3-642-32009-5_44

28. Zhandry, M.: How to record quantum queries, and applications to quantum indifferentiability. In: Boldyreva, A., Micciancio, D. (eds.) CRYPTO 2019. LNCS, vol. 11693, pp. 239–268. Springer, Cham (2019). https://doi.org/10.1007/978-3-030-26951-7_9

Post-quantum Cryptography

A Detailed Analysis of Fiat-Shamir with Aborts

Julien Devevey[1]([✉]), Pouria Fallahpour[1], Alain Passelègue[1,2],
and Damien Stehlé[1,3]

[1] ENS de Lyon, Lyon, France
{julien.devevey,pouria.fallahpour}@ens-lyon.fr
[2] Inria Lyon, Lyon, France
alain.passelegue@inria.fr
[3] CryptoLab Inc., Lyon, France
damien.stehle@cryptolab.co.kr

Abstract. Lyubashevky's signatures are based on the Fiat-Shamir with Aborts paradigm. It transforms an interactive identification protocol that has a non-negligible probability of aborting into a signature by repeating executions until a loop iteration does not trigger an abort. Interaction is removed by replacing the challenge of the verifier by the evaluation of a hash function, modeled as a random oracle in the analysis. The access to the random oracle is classical (ROM), resp. quantum (QROM), if one is interested in security against classical, resp. quantum, adversaries. Most analyses in the literature consider a setting with a bounded number of aborts (i.e., signing fails if no signature is output within a prescribed number of loop iterations), while practical instantiations (e.g., Dilithium) run until a signature is output (i.e., loop iterations are unbounded).

In this work, we emphasize that combining random oracles with loop iterations induces numerous technicalities for analyzing correctness, run-time, and security of the resulting schemes, both in the bounded and unbounded case. As a first contribution, we put light on errors in all existing analyses. We then provide two detailed analyses in the QROM for the bounded case, adapted from Kiltz *et al* [EUROCRYPT'18] and Grilo *et al* [ASIACRYPT'21]. In the process, we prove the underlying Σ-protocol to achieve a stronger zero-knowledge property than usually considered for Σ-protocols with aborts, which enables a corrected analysis. A further contribution is a detailed analysis in the case of unbounded aborts, the latter inducing several additional subtleties.

Keywords: Fiat-Shamir with aborts · Lyubashevsky's signature · QROM

1 Introduction

The Fiat-Shamir heuristic [FS86] transforms a public-coin interactive proof system into a digital signature, by replacing the public coins of the verifier with

© International Association for Cryptologic Research 2023
H. Handschuh and A. Lysyanskaya (Eds.): CRYPTO 2023, LNCS 14085, pp. 327–357, 2023.
https://doi.org/10.1007/978-3-031-38554-4_11

hash function evaluations. In the random oracle model (ROM), the publicly available hash function is modeled as a uniform function, which the adversary is given (classical) access to. One of the most famous instances of the Fiat-Shamir heuristic is Schnorr's signature [Sch89], whose security relies on the discrete logarithm problem (heuristically, in the ROM). If considering quantum adversaries, two adaptations are required: first, the discrete logarithm hardness assumption must be replaced by another one that is conjectured to be quantum-resistant; second, the adversary should be granted quantum access to the random oracle (QROM) as it can query the hash function in quantum superposition.

In [Lyu09, Lyu12], Lyubashevsky proposed a lattice-based signature scheme that is reminiscent of Schnorr's. A key difference is that the underlying interactive proof system has a non-negligible probability of aborting. Aborting allows to make the signature distribution independent of the signing key and is necessary to avoid attacks against the signature schemes (see [ASY22, Sect. 4.1]). To handle the aborts, the protocol execution is repeated within a loop, until no abort occurs in the current loop iteration. Similarly to the Fiat-Shamir heuristic, one may replace the non-final verifier steps by hash function evaluations and model the hash function as a random oracle: this technique is referred to as Fiat-Shamir with aborts.

The combination of the Fiat-Shamir heuristic and rejection sampling leads to several difficulties when analyzing the resulting signature scheme. Most analyses of Lyubashevsky's signatures consider a variant that we refer to as Fiat-Shamir with Bounded Aborts (FSwBA). In this variant, the number of loop iterations is a priori bounded by a parameter B of the scheme. If no non-aborting iteration is encountered within this bounded number B of loop iterations, the signing algorithm fails (the failure symbol $\perp$ is output). With FSwBA, the runtime analysis is trivial. In the security proof, the upper bound on the number of iterations is technically convenient as it provides a bound on how many random oracle values are being programmed by the challenger, which eases the analysis of the random oracle programming impact on the adversary's view. The most detailed security analyses are provided in [AFLT16] for the ROM, and in [KLS18] for the QROM. An alternative proof strategy in the QROM is suggested in [GHHM21], but not detailed. In concrete instantiations of Fiat-Shamir with aborts, such as the Dilithium signature scheme [DKL+18], the signing algorithm typically does not enforce any upper bound on the number of loop iterations. We call this variant Fiat-Shamir with Unbounded Aborts (FSwUA). It is more difficult to analyze, as arbitrarily many hash values may be programmed by the challenger in the security proof.

Contributions. Our first set of contributions relates to FSwBA. First, we explain below that all existing security analyses of FSwBA contain a subtle common flaw, with additional errors in the QROM analysis of [KLS18]. We then provide two security analyses of FSwBA in the QROM, the first one by correcting the one from [KLS18], and the second by adapting the approach suggested in [GHHM21]. As detailed below, it turns out that these QROM analyses are incomparable. In the process, we prove that the underlying Σ-protocol achieves a stronger notion of zero-knowledgeness than usually considered for Σ-protocols with aborts, which enables the proofs. Still for FSwBA, as far as we are aware of, there is no detailed correctness analysis in the literature: this is actually not trivial, and we provide a detailed correctness analysis.

Our second set of results concerns FSwUA. On the negative side, we exhibit an interactive proof system such that applying FSwUA to it leads to a signature scheme such that:

- for all signing keys, with non-zero probability over the random oracle randomness, signing loops forever for all messages; in particular, the expected signing runtime is infinite;
- with overwhelming probability over the random oracle randomness, for all messages and all signing keys, the expected runtime of signing over its own randomness is below a fixed polynomial.

This suggests a modification of the signing efficiency requirement, in which the runtime expectation is not taken over the randomness of the random oracle, but should be bounded by a polynomial with overwhelming probability over the randomness of the random oracle. On the positive side, we give analyses of correctness, signing efficiency (with respect to the modified definition) and security for FSwUA in the QROM (with a tighter reduction in the ROM).

Finally, as a side contribution, we generalize our analysis to rely on a Σ-protocol whose simulator's quality is measured in terms of the Rényi divergence (rather than the statistical distance) for non-aborting transcripts. As pointed out in [DFPS22], in the case of Lyubashevsky's signature with Gaussian distributions [Lyu12], when the signature is replaced with the non-aborting simulator in the security proof, the analysis based on the divergence provides security for a larger range of parameters. This allows one to decrease the standard deviation of the distribution in the signature, which in turn reduces the signature size by a small amount.

2   Technical Overview

We focus on analyzing the Fiat-Shamir with aborts transform in the context of digital signatures. Our techniques also allow to transform a constant-round public-coin interactive proof system into a non-interactive one, and most of our results carry over to this setup (a notable exception being the results exploiting the Rényi divergence simulation mentioned above). We specifically consider how this technique allows the challenger to simulate replies to sign queries without knowing the signing key (which is made possible by allowing the challenger to program the random oracle). More formally, we are interested in reducing the signature unforgeability under chosen message attacks (CMA) to its unforgeability under no-message attacks (NMA). How to obtain NMA security is beyond the scope of this work, and can be handled in different ways (see, e.g., [Lyu09, Lyu12, AFLT16, DFMS19]).

In order to fix notation, we refer to the prover's first message in the underlying Σ-protocol as the commitment w, and a transcript is a triple (w, c, z) where c is a uniformly random challenge. After applying the Fiat-Shamir transform, the challenge c is then replaced by a hash value $H(w\|\mu)$, with μ being the signed message. An adversary against the CMA security of a digital signature in the random oracle model is allowed to make two types of queries: sign queries and hash queries (the latter queries being classical in the ROM and in quantum superposition in the QROM). In the security analysis, we eventually want the challenger to be able to reply to the queries without relying on the signing key. For this purpose, we can let the challenger modify the way it replies to the queries, as long as the modifications are not visible to the adversary. The fact that the signing algorithm uses the hash function, which is controlled by the challenger, is handful for simulating signatures without knowing the signing key, but induces a difficulty: the challenger must reply to hash queries and sign queries consistently. In the case of Schnorr's signature, a sign query uses the hash function exactly once. However, in the Fiat-Shamir with Aborts variant, a sign query uses the hash function several times: the hash function is evaluated once in every loop iteration.

In what follows, we first describe flaws from existing analyses in the bounded abort setting, and then how we fix them. In the process, we introduce a stronger zero-knowledge definition for Σ-protocols with aborts, which allows to fix the analysis, and prove that existing protocols achieve this definition. We finally explain how our analysis extends to the case of unbounded aborts.

2.1   Flaws in Existing Analyses of FSwBA

An unsubstantiated intuition. We start by describing a first flaw appearing in all existing analyses. These analyses start as follows: in the genuine security experiment (denoted Game 0), all (successful or not) transcripts generated during a sign query use a challenge that is computed with the hash function. Then, a first hybrid (Game 1) changes the sign algorithm by sampling a uniformly random challenge and programming the hash function consistently with the successful proof transcript *only*. All proofs immediately conclude these two games are identical: the (unsubstantiated) intuition is that the adversary does not have access to the aborted transcripts, and hence programming these transcripts does not impact the adversary's view.

F1. Assume the challenger in the genuine CMA (or even CMA_1) security game answers a sign query μ using a sequence of commitments $w_1, w_2, \ldots$. Assume that rejecting is a deterministic function of w and c (this is for example the case for Lyubashevsky's signatures with the parameters considered in [AFLT16]). Then, as soon as w_1 fails to produce a valid transcript, the hash value $H(w_1 \| \mu)$ is fixed and the sign oracle can no longer return a valid signature which uses commitment w_1. This is not the case in Game 1, since the hash value $H(w_1 \| \mu)$ is not programmed by the failed attempt, and the sign query could return a signature (w_1, c', z') for $c' \neq c$.

FSwBA has been analyzed and used numerous times (we focus here on the most detailed analyses), yet the above flaw **F1** appears in [Lyu12, Lemma 5.3], [Lyu16, Lemma 4.1], [KLS18, Theorem 3.2], and [Kat21, Lemma 4.6]. It also appears in [AFLT16] though not in Game 1 but in Game 0: in the proof of [AFLT16, Theorem 1], the authors directly start with the above Game 1 rather than with the correct Game 0. Finally, the difficulty with the hash function inconsistencies seems identified in [ABB+17, Appendix B.4], but the authors do not handle the case of inconsistencies between different sign queries for the same message.

The fact that the adversary can make hash queries on superpositions of all inputs in the QROM makes it even more difficult to argue that the adversary cannot detect random oracle programmings, which induces additional errors.

Correlated challenges and implicit quantum sign queries in the QROM. To avoid the latter difficulty in the QROM, the reduction from [KLS18] is made history-free, i.e., the random oracle is never reprogrammed during the execution of the security game (see [BDF+11] for a general treatment of history-free reductions in the QROM). For this purpose, the authors let the hash function call the signing algorithm, to guarantee that the hash and sign queries are handled consistently. On the downside, any subsequent signing algorithm modification in the security proof is of a quantum nature, as the adversary can make quantum queries to the hash function. This leads the analysis to two additional errors.

Consider the CMA_1 security analysis [KLS18, Theorem 3.2]: as above, the reduction starts with Game 0, which is the genuine security experiment. In Game 1, on a hash query $(w\|\mu)$, the oracle calls a GetTrans function which runs the signing algorithm on input μ and checks if the commitment w of the *non-aborting* transcript matches the hash query. If the random oracle is called on that input (possibly as part of a quantum superposition), it is programmed to reply with the challenge programmed by the signing algorithm. This guarantees consistencies of hash values defined by hash queries and by sign queries. In addition, Game 1 replaces the Σ-protocol execution in the GetTrans function (called in both sign and hash queries) by the simulator. The authors bound the advantage loss of that game hop by $BQ_S\varepsilon_{zk}$, with B being the maximum number of loop iterations, Q_S the number of sign queries, and ε_{zk} the zero-knowledge error of the underlying interactive protocol.

As pinpointed above, a first flaw **F1** comes from the fact *only the non-aborting* challenge is programmed by GetTrans, but two additional flaws are induced by relying on the simulator in GetTrans.

F2. Recall that the zero-knowledge property of the underlying Σ-protocol is for a single execution of the protocol (as opposed to correlated executions). Hence, replacing executions which rely on challenges computed as hash values by simulated transcripts requires challenges to be statistically independent. This is only possible if the hash function is evaluated on distinct inputs $(w\|\mu)$, which is not guaranteed: there might be collisions on commitments w's used within a sign query for a message μ.

F3. Since the adversary can only make classical sign queries, it could seem that transitioning from real to simulated transcripts is required only for those that are generated by the sign queries (there are at most BQ_S of them, leading to the $BQ_S\varepsilon_{zk}$ term). However, the adversary can make quantum hash queries, and for consistency of hash evaluation, these queries make calls to the GetTrans function. Hence this transition has to be done for all possible sign queries (not only those that are actually made). In particular, even in the ROM, the reduction loss should already be $B(Q_S + Q_H)\varepsilon_{zk}$ as each sign query and hash query induces up to B simulated transcripts. In the QROM, the loss is even larger as the adversary can make Q_H quantum hash queries.

Flaws **F2** and **F3** appear in the QROM analyses of both [Kat21, Lemma 4.6] and [KLS18, Theorems 3.2 and 3.3].

2.2 Corrected Analyses of FSwBA

The security analysis in the ROM, which only suffers from **F1**, can be readily modified to handle this difficulty by bounding the probability the random oracle gets evaluated twice on a previously defined input. If the commitment has high min-entropy, this event happens with negligible probability. **F1** vanishes as the hash function is never evaluated twice on the same input. It would seem that the rest of the analysis goes through (e.g., following [AFLT16]), but this fix induces an additional problem described below.

We provide two different analyses in the QROM. The first one follows and fixes the [KLS18] analysis. The second one extends the adaptive reprogramming technique of [GHHM21] to Fiat-Shamir with aborts and achieves strong CMA security. When instantiated to the ROM, the latter analysis is arguably simpler than the one from [AFLT16], for which reason we will only describe this one.

Fixing the [KLS18] *analysis (up to the additional problem).* We deviate from the original analysis immediately after Game 0. We let the GetTrans function program the hash values not only for the non-aborting transcript, but also for all the intermediate *aborting* transcript. We further make the GetTrans function deterministic by deriving randomness from a random function. When a hash query is made on input $(w\|\mu)$, the GetTrans function is then called to check if signing μ defines a hash value for $(w\|\mu)$. All this avoids falling into **F1**.

Then, one would like to rely on simulated transcripts so that we can simulate the game without knowing the signing key. To avoid falling into **F2**, one then needs to prove that all challenges are independent. We define a hybrid game in which GetTrans outputs a special symbol if it calls conflicting hash inputs (i.e., uses twice the same commitment w inside the loop). Applying the One-Sided O2H Lemma [AHU19] combined with the high min-entropy of commitments then allows us to bound the distinguishing advantage of a (quantum) adversary between these two games by $(Q_S + Q_H)B/\sqrt{2^\alpha}$, with α denoting the min-entropy of commitments, Q_S, Q_H the number of sign and hash queries, and B the parameter bounding the number of loop iterations. Note that GetTrans is invoked by both hash and sign queries (hence the $Q_S + Q_H$ term). This solves **F2**: one can now replace real transcripts by simulated ones in GetTrans as all challenges are uniformly random and independent. Yet again, both hash and sign queries rely on GetTrans, which itself uses either actual or simulated transcripts. A similar argument as before, relying on Oracle-Indistinguishability [Zha12, Theorem 1.1] allows to bound the distinguishing advantage of a (quantum) adversary by $(Q_S + Q_H)^{3/2}/\sqrt{B \cdot \varepsilon_{zk}}$, handling the last error **F3**.

A security analysis in the QROM based on adaptive reprogramming. Independently, we provide a different security analysis based on the technique developed in [GHHM21]. In the latter, the authors study adaptive reprogramming in the QROM and exploit it to analyze the (no-abort) Fiat-Shamir heuristic. They suggest that the latter analysis can be extended to the Fiat-Shamir with aborts setting, and we provide such an analysis (see Theorem 4).

Adaptive reprogramming considers a setting in which a quantum adversary has access to a random oracle, and in addition can query a reprogramming oracle $\mathcal{O}$ with inputs μ. The oracle answers to such a query by sampling w from a target distribution (the commitment space in our case) and returning it to the adversary. In addition, the oracle either leaves the random oracle unchanged, or reprograms it on input $(w\|\mu)$. In the classical setting, it is clear that an adversary cannot tell whether $\mathcal{O}$ affects the random oracle unless it has already made the hash query $(w\|\mu)$. In [GHHM21], the authors provide a bound for the distinguishing advantage of a quantum adversary.

Adaptive reprogramming allows to immediately move from Game 0 to a Game 1 in which the GetTrans function, on input μ, samples fresh uniformly random and independent challenges c and reprograms the random oracle according to c on input $w\|\mu$. This immediately solves **F1** as it programs all intermediate values (even though some values can get programmed multiple times), as well as **F2** since challenges are now set to uniformly random and independent values thanks to reprogramming. Note that hash queries do not need to run GetTrans as adaptive reprogramming guarantees the adversary cannot find inconsistencies (which would allow to distinguish Games 0 and 1). It remains to replace real transcripts by simulated ones, which is easily argued with a security loss of $BQ_S\varepsilon_{zk}$, since only the (classical) sign queries rely on running the simulator. Doing so, we circumvent **F3**. One then needs to keep consistency in the hash values, which is done by keeping track of the last values reprogrammed by the (polynomial number of classical) sign queries.

Insufficiency of the usual simulators for Σ-protocols with aborts. While the above approaches seem sound, they induce an additional subtle problem: we now run all aborting and non-aborting executions of the underlying Σ-protocol at every step of the reduction, and in particular in the game hop replacing real transcripts by simulated ones. The no-abort Honest-Verifier Zero-Knowledge (naHVZK) property usually considered for Σ-protocols with aborts is insufficient to analyze this game hop. Rather than trying to rely on the prior naHVZK notion, we choose an alternative route and exploit a stronger Honest-Verifier Zero-Knowledge (HVZK) for Σ-protocols with aborts, which requires the simulator to be able to simulate both aborting and non-aborting transcripts. Equipped with this definition, the above proofs go through immediately.

There is still one major issue to solve: this definition of strong simulation is not known to be achieved by Σ-protocols involved in Lyubashevsky's signatures (which might be the reason for the existence of the naHVZK notion). We construct a simulator for this setting, which works as follows: With probability p, it generates a non-aborting transcript (using the well-known naHVZK simulator), with p being the known probability that a protocol iteration does not trigger an abort. Else, with probability $1 - p$, it returns a uniform commitment w (and $\perp$ for the z-part of the transcript). The main technicality is to show that uniform commitments are indeed indistinguishable from aborting transcript. Recall that the commitment w is of the form $\mathbf{A}\mathbf{y}$ for a public matrix $\mathbf{A}$ and a vector $\mathbf{y}$ sampled from a source distribution Q. If Q has high min-entropy, we use the fact that aborting does not decrease much the min-entropy of Q and use the leftover hash lemma to conclude that the protocol is *statistical* zero-knowledge. While this already handles many settings of Lyubashevsky's signature, we want the source distribution to have lower entropy in some cases. We prove that if the distribution Q is such that LWE is hard for noise distribution set to Q, the protocol is *computational* zero-knowledge, for a variant of computational zero-knowledgedness that is compatible with the Fiat-Shamir transform.

Correctness analysis of FSwBA signatures. In addition to these technical issues regarding the security analysis, it turns out that bounding the number of loop iterations and returning $\perp$ when the bound is reached makes the correctness analysis somewhat non-trivial. This is often brushed away in existing works, and we are not aware of a correct analysis. The goal is to provide a small upper bound on the probability that the signing algorithm outputs $\perp$. For this purpose, it is tempting to argue that at each loop iteration, the abort probability is the failure probability $\beta \in (0, 1)$ of the underlying proof system, and hence that the signing abort probability is β^B where B is the bound on the number of iterations. This is incorrect, as the executions of the underlying proof system are not statistically independent: all challenges are derived from the hash function. It hence seems unavoidable to assume the ROM not only for security but also for correctness, but this is not sufficient, as statistical dependencies between the loop iterations can stem from collisions between inputs of the hash function: if the hash inputs are the same in two iterations, the returned challenges are the same.

We provide a detailed proof of correctness. For this, we observe that the security analyses involves a game in which the signing loop iterations are statistically independent: the β^B bound above holds in these experiments. We then argue that the failure probability in the genuine execution is close to β^B, as otherwise we would be able to distinguish the genuine security experiment from the one in which the signing loop iterations are statistically independent. Our correctness analysis for FSwBA is actually a corollary of our (runtime) analysis of FSwUA, and is described in the corresponding section.

Wrapping up on FSwBA. We obtain several complete analyses with distinct security claims for signatures based on FSwBA, both in the ROM and the QROM. We provide an overview of our results in Table 1, using the same notation as above. The "reduction loss" is a bound on the difference of success probabilities of the adversary in the CMA and NMA security experiments. We assume the circuit model for quantum computations, except when mentioned otherwise. The table assumes that $Q_H \geq B \cdot Q_S$ (this assumption is justified by the fact that hash evaluations can be made without restriction whereas sign queries require interaction with the signer). Similarly, the zero-knowledge simulation time is neglected (unless it is very large, its contributions are typically dominated by the terms in the table). We also omit constant factors. Note that the reduction in the ROM simulates the random oracle using the lazy sampling method. However, the QROM reductions are relative to another random oracle that is accessible to the challenger (this assumption may be removed by relying on a quantum pseudorandom function [Zha12]). More detailed statements can be found in the referenced theorems.

Table 1. Comparison of the security analyses of FSwBA.

Analysis	Hash function	Reduction loss	Reduction runtime overhead
Adaptive reprogramming (Theorem 4)	ROM	$2^{-\alpha}BQ_SQ_H$ $+ \varepsilon_{zk}BQ_S$	$Q_H \log(Q_H)$
Adaptive reprogramming (Theorem 4)	QROM	$2^{-\alpha/2}BQ_SQ_H^{1/2}$ $+ \varepsilon_{zk}BQ_S$	$Q_H \log(BQ_S)$ with QRACM BQ_SQ_H without
History-free for CMA_1 security (Theorem 3)	QROM	$2^{-\alpha/2}BQ_H$ $+ \varepsilon_{zk}^{1/2}B^{1/2}Q_H^{3/2}$	BQ_H
History-free for CMA security [DFPS23, Theorem 10]	QROM	$2^{-\alpha/2}BQ_SQ_H$ $+ \varepsilon_{zk}^{1/2}B^{1/2}Q_H^{3/2}$	BQ_SQ_H

We observe that the QROM analyses are incomparable. In particular, the adaptive reprogramming technique from [GHHM21] is tight only when assuming quantum random access classical memory (QRACM), which is a stronger assumption than the quantum circuit model of computation. The history-free technique from [KLS18] is tight only when considering adversaries that may make at most one sign query for any message (CMA_1 security). This covers the deterministic version of the resulting signature, obtained by deriving the randomness from the message via a pseudo-random function evaluation. For CMA security, the reduction is not tight (even assuming QRACM) and the reduction loss is higher than the one obtained with the adaptive reprogramming technique.

2.3   Concrete Analysis of FSwUA

On the termination of FSwUA signatures. For FSwUA, we start by exhibiting an underlying identification scheme with the following peculiar property: for any execution of the key generation algorithm of the resulting signature, there exists a hash function such that the resulting signing algorithm loops forever on every input message. Yet, with overwhelming probability over the random choice of the hash function, the expected runtime is polynomially bounded. The scheme is a variant of Lyubashevsky's [Lyu09,Lyu12], with carefully crafted source and target distributions (we refer to [DFPS22] for a description of Lyubashevsky's signature with arbitrary source and target distributions). To make sure that every loop iteration always fails, we use a source and a target distribution that are uniform over some sets X_S and X_T, respectively, with $X_T \subseteq X_S$. The choice of uniform distributions leads to a deterministic rejection test: an iteration takes a uniform $\mathbf{y} \in X_S$ and maps it to a vector $\mathbf{z}$, and an abort occurs if $\mathbf{z} \notin X_T$. Going a little further into the details, the vector $\mathbf{z}$ is of the form $\mathbf{z} = \mathbf{y} + sk \cdot \mathbf{c}$, where the integer matrix sk is the signing key and $\mathbf{c}$ is the output of the hash function H on a function of $\mathbf{y}$ and the message. We want to design X_S and X_T such that: (1) for all sk, the probability over $\mathbf{y} \leftarrow U(X_S)$ and H that $\mathbf{z} = \mathbf{y} + sk \cdot \mathbf{c}$ belongs to X_T is at least a positive constant, and (2) for all sk, there exists an H such that for all $\mathbf{y}$ and message, the vector $\mathbf{z} = \mathbf{y} + sk \cdot \mathbf{c}$ does not belong to X_T.

The first condition forces us to set X_S not much larger than X_T. For the second condition, we design H so that any $\mathbf{y}$ is sent outside of X_T. As H depends on a function of $\mathbf{y}$, we first make sure that this function is injective, so that H is a function of $\mathbf{y}$ itself (else we would have to consider the set of predecessors and design H to jointly send them all outside of X_T). This injectivity is obtained by relying on the lossy version of Lyubashevsky's signature scheme [AFLT16]. Then for a vector $\mathbf{y}$, we design $\mathbf{c}$ so that $\mathbf{y} + sk \cdot \mathbf{c}$ is not in X_T and set $\mathbf{c}$ as the output of H on $\mathbf{y}$ and the message. For this purpose, we set X_S as a hyperball and X_t as an inner crust (a corona that almost aligns with the hyperball boundary). As hyperballs are concentrated on their surface, the volume ratio can be bounded by a positive constant even with a thin crust. Now, if $\mathbf{y} \in X_S \setminus X_T$, we set $\mathbf{c} = \mathbf{0}$ (for every message). If $\mathbf{y}$ belongs to X_T, we choose $\mathbf{y}' \in X_S \setminus X_T$ near $\mathbf{y}$ and define $\mathbf{c}$ such that $\mathbf{y} + sk \cdot \mathbf{c}$ is very close to $\mathbf{y}'$: for this purpose, it suffices to round $\mathbf{y}'$ to the lattice spanned by sk; by taking sk that is well-conditioned, we can guarantee that the rounded vector is close to $\mathbf{y}'$ and remains outside of X_T. As a result, all loop iterations of the resulting FSwUA signing algorithm fail.

The above counter-example is admittedly contrived, but illustrates the fact that specific difficulties arise when analyzing the unbounded version of Fiat-Shamir with aborts. In particular, this suggests to modify the requirement of signing runtime, so that it is authorized to take longer than desired, but only with small probability over the randomness of the random oracle (see Definition 9 for the formal requirement). We show that the signature obtained with the FSwUA transform indeed fulfills this requirement (in the random oracle model).

Security and correctness analyses of FSwUA signatures. We reduce the NMA security of FSwUA signatures to their CMA security, both in the ROM and the QROM. For this purpose, it is tempting to add a bound on the number of loop iterations, argue that the adversary cannot notice the difference, and then use the NMA security to CMA security reduction of FSwBA signatures. To prove that the adversary cannot notice the difference between the unbounded and bounded versions of the signing algorithm, one would argue that the probability of reaching that bound in at least one sign query is negligible, as the number of loop iterations follows a geometric law. But as discussed earlier, this is not true since there is a statistical dependency between different iterations of the rejection sampling. However, we show that the probability of the number of iterations until a success outcome be larger than B is small, over the randomness of the random oracle. This allows us to show the expected equivalence between FSwBA and FSwUA when the bound B is large, as an adversary will likely never see $\bot$ with the FSwBA variant. Using the same notations as before, the reduction loss of this step is bounded by $Q_S \cdot \beta^B + 2^{-\alpha/2} \cdot BQ_S \cdot \sqrt{Q_H}$ in the QROM and by $Q_S \cdot \beta^B + 2^{-\alpha} \cdot BQ_S Q_H$ in the ROM. (As above, these bounds assume that $Q_H \geq BQ_S$ and omit constant terms; we additionally assume that $\beta \in (0, 1)$ is a constant.)

We provide a correctness analysis of FSwUA signatures (in the ROM), which proceeds in a similar way. Assuming that the signature outputs a transcript, this transcript follows the same distribution as a transcript from the underlying identification protocol, i.e. the challenge is uniform over the challenge space. It may not be independent from previous signatures and failed iterations, but all that matters here is its marginal distribution. This lets us bound the correctness error of the signature as a function of the correctness error of the underlying identification protocol.

2.4 Related Works

The Fiat-Shamir with aborts paradigm [Lyu09, Lyu12] has been used too extensively to attempt a complete list of works whose provable security claims are impacted by the flaws we pointed at. The list notably includes the NIST-selected Dilithium signature scheme [DKL+18], whose provable security claim [DKL+18, Sect. 4.2] derives from [KLS18]. Our work provides fixes to the claims.

The difficulties encountered when analyzing Fiat-Shamir with aborts can be circumvented by modifying the scheme. For example, some works replace the rejection sampling used in Lyubashevsky's signatures by statistical flooding (see, e.g., [DPSZ12, Appendix A.1] in the context of zero-knowledge proofs, or [ASY22, Sect. 4] in the context of signatures). In [CLMQ21], the authors instantiate the hash function so that a proof can be obtained without the random oracle model. Another approach consists in committing to w rather than sending it. This idea is discussed in [BBE+18] and attributed therein to Vadim Lyubashevsky. All these proposals incur significant losses on signature sizes.

Our strong simulation has implications to masked instantiations of Lyubashevsky's signatures. For efficiency reasons, one does not want to mask the hash function evaluation. For this purpose, a heuristic assumption has been introduced in [BBE+18, BBE+19, MGTF19]: informally, it states that revealing the commitments of the aborted transcript does not hurt the security of the scheme. This assumption removes the need for masking the hash function since commitments are the only non-public information about the hash function evaluations (the message and the hash function are public). Our simulator shows that this heuristic assumption holds unconditionally for some parameter ranges.

A concurrent and independent work [BBD+23] also identifies flaw F1 in prior works on Fiat-Shamir with aborts. It fixes it while still relying on a zero-knowledge notion that considers only non-aborting transcripts. As in our approach based on adaptive reprogramming [GHHM21], their analysis uses reprogramming for both aborting and non-aborting transcripts. It differs in that it then undoes the reprogrammings for rejecting transcripts. This is not required in our case as our zero-knowledge notion captures aborting transcripts. We then show that this strengthened zero-knowledge requirement is achieved for the main application of Fiat-Shamir with aborts. We further identify and fix other difficulties with the Fiat-Shamir with aborts paradigm, notably with the history-free approach from [KLS18] and termination and correctness in the unbounded case. On the other hand, the concurrent work [BBD+23] additionally offers a fully mechanized security proof for Dilithium (in the ROM) using the EasyCrypt formal-verification platform.

3   Preliminaries

We use code-based games to write the proofs. We use capital letters with fraktur font (e.g., $\mathfrak{L}$) to denote the list of objects. We let $\mathsf{Coll} : \mathfrak{L} \mapsto \{0, 1\}$ be the function that takes as input a list and outputs 1 if and only if at least two of the elements of the list are equal. We sometimes abuse the notation and let $\mathsf{Coll}(\mathfrak{L})$ denote the event that it returns 1. We implicitly assume that all variables are parameterized by the security parameter λ. To denote that a function f (or a database) is reprogrammed at input x to the value y we use the notation $f^{x \mapsto y}$. All our logarithms are in base 2.

We provide reminders about probabilities, Rényi divergence, digital signatures, quantum computing in the full version [DFPS23, Appendix A].

3.1 Σ-Protocols

We start by recalling various definitions pertaining to Σ-protocols.

Definition 1 (Σ-Protocol with Aborts). *Let $\mathcal{X}$ and $\mathcal{Y}$ be two finite sets. A Σ-protocol for a relation $R \subseteq \mathcal{X} \times \mathcal{Y}$ with commitment set $\mathcal{W}$, challenge set $\mathcal{C}$ and response set $\mathcal{Z}$ is a 3-round interactive proof system between a prover written as $\mathsf{P} = (\mathsf{P}_1, \mathsf{P}_2)$ and a verifier $\mathsf{V} = (\mathsf{V}_1, \mathsf{V}_2)$ with the following specifications:*

- $\mathsf{P}_1 : (x, y) \to (w, st)$ *is a* PPT *algorithm that takes as input a pair of strings in $\mathcal{X} \times \mathcal{Y}$ and outputs a commitment $w \in \mathcal{W}$ and a state $st \in \{0, 1\}^*$;*
- $\mathsf{V}_1 : (x, w) \to c$ *is a* PPT *algorithm that takes as inputs a string $x \in \mathcal{X}$ and a commitment $w \in \mathcal{W}$ and outputs a challenge $c \in \mathcal{C}$;*
- $\mathsf{P}_2 : (x, y, w, c, st) \to z$ *is a* PPT *algorithm that takes as inputs a pair of strings in $\mathcal{X} \times \mathcal{Y}$, a commitment $w \in \mathcal{W}$, a challenge $c \in \mathcal{C}$, and a state st and outputs a response $z \in \mathcal{Z} \cup \{\bot\}$ (we say that P_2 aborts if it outputs $\bot$);*
- $\mathsf{V}_2 : (x, w, c, z) \to b \in \{0, 1\}$ *is a deterministic polynomial-time algorithm that takes as inputs a string $x \in \mathcal{X}$, a commitment $w \in \mathcal{W}$, a challenge $c \in \mathcal{C}$, and a response $z \in \mathcal{Z}$ and outputs a bit b which represents acceptance or rejection; in the case that $z = \bot$, it returns 0.*

A Σ-protocol is said to be public-coin if V_1 outputs a challenge string c that is uniformly sampled from the challenge space C, independently from its input.

Note that the above definition (and the following ones) is implicitly parameterized by the security parameter λ, that we omit for the sake of simplicity. Given a language $\mathcal{L} = \{x \in \mathcal{X} \mid \exists y \in \mathcal{Y} : (x, y) \in R\}$ for a relation $R \subseteq \mathcal{X} \times \mathcal{Y}$, we are interested in the following properties of a Σ-protocol.

Definition 2 (Correctness). *Let $\gamma, \beta > 0$. A Σ-protocol $((P_1, P_2), (V_1, V_2))$ is (γ, β)-correct if for every $x \in \mathcal{L}$ and valid witness $y \in \mathcal{Y}$ the following holds.*

- *If the response of the prover is not $\perp$, the verifier accepts with probability at least γ:*

$$\Pr\left[V_2(x, w, c, z) = 1 \;\middle|\; \begin{matrix} (w, st) \leftarrow P_1(x, y), \\ c \leftarrow V_1(x, w), z \leftarrow P_2(x, y, w, c, st), \\ z \neq \perp \end{matrix} \right] \geq \gamma.$$

- *The probability that the prover aborts is bounded by β:*

$$\Pr\left[z = \perp \;\middle|\; \begin{matrix} (w, st) \leftarrow P_1(x, y), \\ c \leftarrow V_1(x, w), z \leftarrow P_2(x, y, w, c, st) \end{matrix} \right] \leq \beta.$$

We also let β denote *the probability of aborting*. We are interested in the regime of parameters in which $\gamma \geq 1 - \lambda^{-\omega(1)}$ and $\beta \leq 1 - 1/\mathsf{poly}(\lambda)$. Note that by repeating the protocol $\mathsf{poly}(\lambda)$ times, the parameter β will be pushed toward 0, whereas γ will stay close to 1.

We refer to the following definition as the one that is usually used in the literature of Fiat-Shamir with aborts. Note that we will not use it. Later in Sect. 4, we will discuss our modifications.

Definition 3 (No-Abort Statistical Honest-Verifier Zero-Knowledge).
Let $\varepsilon_{zk}, T \geq 0$. A Σ-protocol is (ε_{zk}, T)-naHVZK if there exists a simulator Sim with runtime at most T, that given x, outputs a transcript (w, c, z) such that the distribution of (w, c, z) has statistical distance at most ε_{zk} from a honestly generated transcript (w', c', z') produced by the interaction conditioned on $z \neq \perp$.

If Σ is public-coin, then without loss of generality, the challenge c can be sampled uniformly from the challenge space C and passed over as input to the simulator Sim. In the rest of the paper, we limit ourselves to public-coin Σ-protocols.

For cryptographic purposes, one instantiates the Σ-protocol with hard samples. This notion is captured in the following definition.

Definition 4 (Identification Protocol). *An identification protocol is a Σ-protocol for an NP relation R, where the prover and verifier are dealt their statement and witness by a PPT instance generator Gen.*

A useful statistical property of a Σ-protocol is the min-entropy of the commitments. We borrow the following definition from [KLS18].

Definition 5 (Commitment Min-Entropy). *For $\alpha \geq 0$, we say that an identification scheme $((P_1, P_2), (V_1, V_2))$ with instance generator Gen has commitment min-entropy α if $H_\infty[w|(w, st) \leftarrow P_1(x, y)] \geq \alpha$, for all $(x, y) \leftarrow \mathsf{Gen}(1^\lambda)$.*

Note that we could accommodate our results to schemes for which the above holds only with overwhelming probability over the randomness of Gen.

3.2 Fiat-Shamir Transform

Let $\Sigma = ((P_1, P_2), (V_1, V_2))$ be an identification protocol with an instance generator Gen for a binary relation R. Further, let $H : \{0, 1\}^* \to \mathcal{C}$ be a hash function where $\mathcal{C}$ is the challenge space of Σ. Then, for every positive integer B, one can construct a signature scheme $\mathsf{SIG}_B = \mathsf{FS}_B[\Sigma, H]$ by applying the Fiat-Shamir transform with bounded aborts (FSwBA) as in Fig. 1. We are particularly interested in applying the Fiat-Shamir transform without imposing a bound on the number of iterations in the rejection sampling as it is the case for Dilithium [DKL+18], among other schemes. One can define the unbounded version $\mathsf{SIG}_\infty = \mathsf{FS}_\infty[\Sigma, H]$ of the Fiat-Shamir transform for a Σ-protocol Σ as in Fig. 1. Note that the signing algorithm of SIG_∞ may not be PPT as required in the usual definition (see the full version [DFPS23, Appendix A.3] for reminders on usual definitions). Ideally, it would still be expected polynomial-time.

$\mathsf{KeyGen}(1^\lambda)$:	$\mathsf{Sign}(sk, \mu)$:	$\mathsf{Ver}(vk, \mu, \sigma)$:
1: $(x, y) \leftarrow \mathsf{Gen}(1^\lambda)$	1: $\kappa := 1$	1: Parse $\sigma = (w, z)$
2: $(vk, sk) = (x, (x, y))$	2: **While** $z = \bot$ **and** $\kappa \leq B$	2: $c = H(w\|\mu)$
3: **return** (vk, sk)	3: $(w, st) \leftarrow P_1(sk)$	3: **return** $V_2(vk, w, c, z)$
	4: $c = H(w\|\mu)$	
	5: $z \leftarrow P_2(sk, w, c, st)$	
	6: $\kappa := \kappa + 1$	
	7: **if** $z = \bot$ **return** $\bot$	
	8: **return** $\sigma = (w, z)$	

Fig. 1. Signatures $\mathsf{SIG}_B = \mathsf{FS}_B[\Sigma, H]$ and $\mathsf{SIG}_\infty = \mathsf{FS}_\infty[\Sigma, H]$. The signature SIG_B uses blocks highlighted with the blue color, whereas SIG_∞ does not.

In this work we show that sUF-CMA security (and sometimes sUF-CMA$_1$) of such signatures can be reduced to their UF-NMA security. Here, we briefly recall two possible ways to reduce UF-NMA security to the security of the underlying Σ-protocol. For more details, we refer the reader to prior works (e.g., [Lyu09, Lyu12, AFLT16, DFMS19, LZ19]).

- In [AFLT16, KLS18], the authors consider *lossy identification schemes* in which there exists another instance generator function Gen_{ls} for the protocol that only outputs an instance x_{ls} without any witness. Moreover, its output distribution is computationally indistinguishable from the one of the real instance generator Gen. Further, it is said to be $\varepsilon_{\mathsf{ls}}$-sound if no cheating prover (even unbounded) can impersonate the real prover given x_{ls} as input and make the verifier to accept with probability more than $\varepsilon_{\mathsf{ls}}$. They reduce UF-NMA security of a signature based on the Fiat-Shamir transform to the $\varepsilon_{\mathsf{ls}}$-soundness of the underlying identification scheme and the indistinguishability of the outputs of Gen and $\mathsf{Gen}_{\mathsf{ls}}$.

- In [DFMS19,LZ19] and implicitly in [Lyu09,Lyu12], the authors reduce the UF-NMA security of a signature based on the Fiat-Shamir transform to the *proof of knowledge* property of the underlying Σ-protocol. Their reduction is less tight than the one of [KLS18].

3.3 Adaptive Reprogramming in the QROM

We rely on the following lemma for one of our analyses in the QROM. Consider the following decision game: Assume the hash function takes inputs of the form (x_1, x_2), and an adversary (with quantum access to the hash function) has access to a reprogramming oracle which can be queried with any value x_2. On a query x_2, the oracle samples a value x_1 and either leaves the hash function unchanged or reprograms it on input (x_1, x_2) to a uniformly random value y from its range. It may also maintain a state x'. Given (x_1, x'), the adversary's goal is to decide whether the oracle reprograms the hash function or not. The following lemma proves this game to be hard even for quantum adversaries. We remind a classical variant of this lemma in the full version [DFPS23, Lemma 12].

Lemma 1 (Adaptive Reprogramming [GHHM21, Proposition 2]). *Let* X_1, X_2, X' *and* Y *be finite sets, and let* D *be a distribution on* $X_1 \times X'$. *Let* $\mathcal{A}$ *be a distinguisher playing in the reprogramming game in Fig. 2 and making* q *quantum queries to the random oracle and* r *classical queries to the* Reprogram *function. Then*

$$\left| \Pr[1 \Leftarrow \mathsf{Reprogram}_0^{\mathcal{A}}] - \Pr[1 \Leftarrow \mathsf{Reprogram}_1^{\mathcal{A}}] \right| \leq \frac{3r}{2}\sqrt{q \cdot 2^{-\alpha}},$$

where α *is the min-entropy of the first component of* D.

Game $\mathsf{Reprogram}_b$:	Reprogram(x_2) :
1: $H_0 \leftarrow U(Y^{X_1 \times X_2})$	1: $(x_1, x') \leftarrow D$
2: $H_1 := H_0$	2: $y \leftarrow U(Y)$
3: $b' \leftarrow \mathcal{A}^{\lvert H_b \rangle,\ \mathsf{Reprogram}(\cdot)}$	3: $H_1 := H_1^{(x_1, x_2) \mapsto y}$
4: **return** b'	4: **return** (x_1, x')

Fig. 2. The reprogramming game.

4   A Simulator for Lyubashevsky's Σ-Protocol

As we discussed in the introduction, Definition 3 is not sufficient for our purposes. In this section, we strengthen it in both statistical and computational settings.

We consider the following statistical HVZK definition, which benefits from a simulator even for aborting transcripts of the Σ-protocol. One can see this modification as a return to the classic definition in the literature of the zero-knowlege interactive proof systems.

Definition 6 (Statistical Honest-Verifier Zero-Knowledge).   *Let ε_{zk}, $T \geq 0$. A Σ-protocol is (ε_{zk}, T)-HVZK if there exists a simulator* Sim *with runtime at most T, that given x, outputs a transcript (w, c, z) such that the distribution of (w, c, z) has statistical distance at most ε_{zk} from a honestly generated transcript (w', c', z') produced by the interaction. This includes aborting transcripts, i.e., those for which $z = \bot$.*

If Σ is public-coin, then without loss of generality, the challenge c can be sampled uniformly from the challenge space $\mathcal{C}$ and passed over as input to the simulator Sim.

A central application of the Fiat-Shamir with aborts paradigm is Lyubashevsky's signature scheme [Lyu09,Lyu12]. We show here that the underlying Σ-protocol satisfies the zero-knowledge property of Definition 6, i.e., admits an efficient simulator for all transcripts including the aborting ones.

Let us first recall the Σ-protocol, using the formalism from [DFPS22]. Let P and Q be two distributions over $\mathbb{Z}^m$: we will refer to Q as the source distribution, and to P as the target distribution. The relation R is parametrized by a matrix $\mathbf{A} \in \mathbb{Z}_q^{n \times m}$ which we assume to be in Hermite Normal Form, i.e., $\mathbf{A} = (\mathbf{I}_n | \mathbf{B})$ for some $\mathbf{B} \in \mathbb{Z}_q^{n \times (m-n)}$. It is also parameterized by some dimension k and norm bound $\beta_{\mathsf{SIS}} > 0$. The relation R is of the form:

$$R_{m,n,k,q,\beta_{\mathsf{SIS}}}(\mathbf{A}) = \left\{ (\mathbf{S}, \mathbf{T}) \in \mathbb{Z}^{m \times k} \times \mathbb{Z}_q^{n \times k} : \mathbf{AS} = \mathbf{T} \bmod q \wedge \max_{i \in [k]} \|\mathbf{s}_i\| \leq \beta_{\mathsf{SIS}} \right\}.$$

The Σ-protocol, with repetition parameter $M \geq 1$ and norm bound β_{SIS} is given in Fig. 3. We note that V_2 is not needed to discuss the zero-knowledge property of the protocol.

We consider the simulator Sim described in Fig. 4.

The proof that the simulation is correct in the non-aborting case is quite standard and derives from the rejection sampling. For the aborting case, our proof relies on the leftover hash lemma and requires the source distribution Q to have high min-entropy. The case of low min-entropy source distributions Q will be handled later on.

4.1   High Min-Entropy Source Distributions

We first consider the case where Q has high min-entropy. In that case, we obtain statistical zero-knowledgedness as per Definition 6.

$P_1(\mathbf{S})$:	$P_2(\mathbf{S}, \mathbf{c}, st)$:
1: $\mathbf{y} \leftarrow Q$	1: $\mathbf{z} := \mathbf{y} + \mathbf{Sc}$
2: $st := \mathbf{y}$	2: **with** probability $\min(P(\mathbf{z})/(M \cdot Q(\mathbf{y})), 1)$
3: $\mathbf{w} = \mathbf{Ay} \bmod q$	3: **return** $\mathbf{z}$
4: **return** $\mathbf{w}$	4: **else return** $\perp$
$V_1(\mathbf{T}, \mathbf{w})$:	$V_2(\mathbf{T}, (\mathbf{w}, \mathbf{c}, \mathbf{z}))$:
1: $\mathbf{c} \leftarrow U(\mathcal{C})$	1: **if** $\|\mathbf{z}\| \leq \beta_{\mathsf{SIS}}$ and $\mathbf{Az} = \mathbf{w} + \mathbf{Tc} \bmod q$
2: **return** $\mathbf{c}$	2: **return** Accept
	3: **return** Reject

Fig. 3. Lyubashevsky's identification protocol.

$\mathrm{Sim}(\mathbf{T}, \mathbf{c})$:
1: **with** probability $1/M$
2:     $\mathbf{z} \leftarrow P$
3:     $\mathbf{w} := \mathbf{Az} - \mathbf{Tc}$
4: **else**
5:     $\mathbf{w} \leftarrow U(\mathbb{Z}_q^n)$
6:     $\mathbf{z} := \perp$
7: **return** $(\mathbf{w}, \mathbf{z})$

Fig. 4. Simulator Sim of Lyubashevsky's Σ-protocol.

Theorem 1. *Let $m \geq n$ and k be positive integers, q prime, $\varepsilon, \beta_{\mathsf{SIS}} > 0$ and $\eta \in [0, 1/2]$. Assume that*

$$H_\infty(Q) \geq n \log q + \log\left(1 - \frac{1-\eta}{M}\right) + 2\log\frac{1}{\varepsilon}.$$

Let $(\mathbf{S}, \mathbf{T}) \in R_{m,n,k,q,\beta_{\mathsf{SIS}}}(\mathbf{A})$ for some $\mathbf{A} \leftarrow U(\mathbb{Z}_q^{n \times m})$. Assume that

$$\forall \mathbf{c} \in \mathcal{C} : \Pr_{\mathbf{z} \leftarrow P}\left[P(\mathbf{z}) \leq M \cdot Q(\mathbf{z} - \mathbf{Sc})\right] \geq 1 - \eta.$$

Then the distribution of the transcript $(\mathbf{w}, \mathbf{c}, \mathbf{z})$ generated by $\langle P(\mathbf{S}), V(\mathbf{T})\rangle$ is within statistical distance $\varepsilon + \eta(1 + 1/M)$ from the distribution of the triple $(\mathbf{w}, \mathbf{c}, \mathbf{z})$ obtained by sampling $\mathbf{c}$ uniformly in $\mathcal{C}$ and sampling $(\mathbf{w}, \mathbf{z}) \leftarrow \mathrm{Sim}(\mathbf{T}, \mathbf{c})$.

Observe that $\mathbf{c}$ is distributed uniformly in $\mathcal{C}$ in both genuine and simulated transcripts. It hence suffices to study the distribution of the rest of the transcript conditioned on the value of $\mathbf{c}$.

The first part of the following result derives from [DFPS22, Lemma 2.2], and the second part derives from the description of Sim. The claim ensures that the probabilities of the event $\mathbf{z} = \perp$ in the genuine and simulated transcripts are close-by.

Lemma 2. *For all $\mathbf{c}$ output by V_1, the probability (over the random coins of P_1 and P_2) that P_2 outputs $\perp$ belongs to $[1 - 1/M, 1 - (1 - \eta)/M]$. For all $\mathbf{c}$, the* *probability (over its random coins) that the output component* $\mathbf{z}$ *of* Sim *is equal to* $\perp$ *is* $1 - 1/M$.

We now consider the transcript distribution conditioned on the event $\mathbf{z} \neq \perp$.

Lemma 3. *Conditioned on* $\mathbf{z} \neq \perp$, *the distribution of the transcript* $(\mathbf{w}, \mathbf{c}, \mathbf{z})$ *generated by* (P, V) *is within statistical distance* η *from the simulated distribution.*

Proof. For all $\mathbf{c}$ and conditioned on $\mathbf{z} \neq \perp$, the distribution of $\mathbf{z}$ output by P_2 is within statistical distance η from P (see [DFPS22, Lemma 2.2]). The latter is exactly the distribution of $\mathbf{z}$ conditioned on $\mathbf{z} \neq \perp$.

To complete the proof of Lemma 3, we argue that when $\mathbf{z} \neq \perp$, the first coefficient of the triple is fully determined by the two others, and equal to $\mathbf{Az} - \mathbf{Tc}$ in both transcript and simulation. □

Finally, we consider the statistical distance of the distributions conditioned on $\mathbf{z} = \perp$. The following claim considers the distribution of the transcript conditioned on not outputting $\perp$.

Lemma 4. *Conditioned on* $\mathbf{z} = \perp$, *the distribution of the transcript* $(\mathbf{w}, \mathbf{c}, \mathbf{z})$ *generated by* (P, V) *is within statistical distance* ε *from the simulated distribution.*

Proof. It suffices to prove that for all $\mathbf{c}$ and conditioned on $\mathbf{z} = \perp$, the distribution of $\mathbf{w}$ in the transcript generated by (P, V) is statistically close to uniform over $\mathbb{Z}_q^n$. Thanks to the first claim above, we have:

$$H_\infty[\mathbf{y}|\mathbf{c} \wedge \mathbf{z} = \perp] \geq H_\infty[\mathbf{y}] - \log \Pr[\mathbf{z} = \perp|\mathbf{c}]$$
$$\geq H_\infty[\mathbf{y}] - \log\left(1 - \frac{1-\eta}{M}\right).$$

We conclude by using the leftover hash lemma (see, e.g. [DFPS23, Lemma 9]). □

Theorem 1 follows from the above lemmas by term collection. □

4.2   Low Min-Entropy Source Distributions

The above handles many settings of Lyubashevsky's signature, as the source distribution Q is often chosen to have high min-entropy so that the map $\mathbf{y} \mapsto \mathbf{Ay} \bmod q$ is (very) surjective. In some cases, however, it is chosen of lower entropy and the map $\mathbf{y} \mapsto \mathbf{Ay} \bmod q$ is very far from surjective. For example, this allows to avoid the forking lemma in the security proof [AFLT16], which both leads to a tight security proof and facilitates unforgeability proofs in the QROM. Our pathological construction from Sect. 6.1 also relies on this regime.

We explain how this can be handled, for some distributions. First, we consider computational zero-knowledgedness rather than statistical zero-knowledgedness.

As one needs to be able to replace real transcripts of (many) sign queries by simulated ones in the security proof, we consider a strong notion of computational zero-knowledgeness: computational indistinguishability is required to hold even when the distinguisher is given the witness (of course, the simulator does not use the witness). This definition is compatible with our Fiat-Shamir with aborts analyses. For example, in the analysis based on adaptive reprogramming (Sect. 5.2), transcripts can be replaced one at a time by simulated ones using a hybrid argument, since the witness allows to generate real signatures. In particular, our definition implies the notion of computational HVZK for multiple transcripts used in [GHHM21, Definition 2], which they use to argue that all transcripts can be replaced by simulated ones in a single step. Note that in all the analyses we consider in this work, when we use the zero-knowledge property, the witness y is available to the challenger.

Definition 7 (Strong Computational HVZK). *Let $\varepsilon_{zk}, T \geq 0$ with ε_{zk} a negligible function of the security parameter. A Σ-protocol $((\mathsf{P}_1, \mathsf{P}_2), (\mathsf{V}_1, \mathsf{V}_2))$ for a relation R is (ε_{zk}, T)-sc-HVZK if there exists a simulator Sim with runtime at most T such that for all polynomial-time algorithm $\mathcal{A}$ and all $(x, y) \in R$, the following advantage is $\leq \varepsilon_{zk}$:*

$$\mathrm{Adv}(\mathcal{A}) = \left| \Pr \left[\mathcal{A}((w, c, z), y) = 1 \,\middle|\, \begin{array}{l} (w, st) \leftarrow \mathsf{P}_1(x, y), \\ c \leftarrow \mathsf{V}_1(x, w), \\ z \leftarrow \mathsf{P}_2(x, y, c, w, st) \end{array} \right] \right.$$

$$\left. - \Pr \left[\mathcal{A}((w, c, z), y) = 1 \,\middle|\, (w, c, z) \leftarrow \mathsf{Sim}(x) \right] \right|.$$

One may consider classical or quantum adversaries $\mathcal{A}$.

As in the statistical case, if the Σ-protocol is public-coin, then without loss of generality, the challenge c can be sampled uniformly from the challenge space $\mathcal{C}$ and passed over as input to the simulator Sim. In the following, we use this formalism.

The computational assumption that we will rely on is the Learning With Errors problem [Reg09]. We use its knapsack form, introduced in [MM11].

Definition 8 (k-LWE). *Let $m \geq n \geq 1$, $q \geq 2$ and D a distribution over $\mathbb{Z}_q^m$. The search knapsack-LWE problem $\mathsf{sk\text{-}LWE}_{m,n,q,D}$ with parameters m, n, q, D consists in recovering $\mathbf{e}$ from $(\mathbf{A}, \mathbf{Ae})$, where $\mathbf{A} \leftarrow U(\mathbb{Z}_q^{m \times n})$ and $\mathbf{e} \leftarrow D$. The decision knapsack-LWE problem $\mathsf{dk\text{-}LWE}_{m,n,q,D}$ with parameters m, n, q, D consists in distinguishing between the distributions $(\mathbf{A}, \mathbf{Ae})$ and $(\mathbf{A}, \mathbf{u})$, where $\mathbf{A} \leftarrow U(\mathbb{Z}_q^{m \times n})$, $\mathbf{e} \leftarrow D$ and $\mathbf{u} \leftarrow U(\mathbb{Z}_q^n)$.*

We now argue that for some distributions Q, it is possible to prove computational zero-knowledgedness in the sense of Definition 7, with exactly the same simulator as above (Fig. 4).

Theorem 2. *Let $m \geq n$ and k be positive integers, $q \leq \text{poly}(m,n)$ prime and $\beta_{\text{SIS}} > 0$. Assume that the distribution Q is such that the* $\text{dk-LWE}_{m,n,q,Q}$ *problem is hard. Let $(\mathbf{S}, \mathbf{T}) \in R_{m,n,k,q,\beta_{\text{SIS}}}(\mathbf{A})$ for some $\mathbf{A} \leftarrow U(\mathbb{Z}_q^{n \times m})$. Assume that*

$$\forall \mathbf{c} \in \mathcal{C} : \Pr_{\mathbf{z} \leftarrow P} \left[P(\mathbf{z}) \leq M \cdot Q(\mathbf{z} - \mathbf{Sc}) \right] \geq 1 - \eta,$$

where $1 + 1/\text{poly}(m,n) \leq M \leq \text{poly}(m,n)$ and $\eta \geq 0$ is negligible.

Then the distribution of the transcript $(\mathbf{w}, \mathbf{c}, \mathbf{z})$ generated by $\langle P(\mathbf{S}), V(\mathbf{T}) \rangle$ is computationally indistinguishable from the distribution of the triple $(\mathbf{w}, \mathbf{c}, \mathbf{z})$ obtained by sampling $\mathbf{c}$ uniformly in $\mathcal{C}$ and sampling $(\mathbf{w}, \mathbf{z}) \leftarrow \text{Sim}(\mathbf{T}, \mathbf{c})$, even if the distinguisher is given $\mathbf{S}$.

The first two claims (Lemmas 2 and 3) of the proof of Theorem 1 still hold. It hence suffices to prove the computational indistinguishability of the genuine and simulated transcripts $(\mathbf{w}, \mathbf{c}, \mathbf{z})$ conditioned on $\mathbf{z} = \bot$.

We first show that the genuine distribution of $\mathbf{y}$ conditioned on $\mathbf{z}$ being rejected resembles the distribution Q of $\mathbf{y}$.

Lemma 5. *Assume that $M > 1$. Consider the execution $\langle P(\mathbf{S}), V(\mathbf{T}) \rangle$. Let $Q^\bot$ denote the distribution of $\mathbf{y}$ conditioned on $\mathbf{z} = \bot$. Then we have:*

$$R_\infty(Q^\bot \| Q) \leq \frac{M}{M - 1}.$$

Proof. For all $\mathbf{y}$, we have

$$Q^\bot(\mathbf{y}) = \frac{\Pr[\mathbf{y} \wedge \mathbf{z} = \bot]}{\Pr[\mathbf{z} = \bot]} \leq \frac{Q(\mathbf{y})}{\Pr[\mathbf{z} = \bot]}.$$

Lemma 2 ensures that the denominator is at least $1 - 1/M$. $\qquad\square$

The following result states that if $(\mathbf{A}, \mathbf{Ay})$ is pseudo-random for $\mathbf{y} \leftarrow D$, then so is it for $\mathbf{y} \leftarrow D'$ for any distribution D' such that $R_\infty(Q' \| Q)$ is polynomially bounded.

Lemma 6. *Let $m \geq n \geq 1$. Let $q \leq \text{poly}(m,n)$ prime. Let D and D' be two distributions over $\mathbb{Z}^m$ such that $R_\infty(D' \| D) \leq \text{poly}(m,n)$. Then $\text{dk-LWE}_{m,n,q,D}$ reduces to $\text{dk-LWE}_{m,n,q,D'}$.*

Proof. Note first that $\text{dk-LWE}_{m,n,q,D}$ reduces to $\text{sk-LWE}_{m,n,q,D}$. Also, as we have $R_\infty(D' \| D) \leq \text{poly}(m,n)$, by the probability preservation property (see e.g. [BLR+18, Lemma 2.7]), $\text{sk-LWE}_{m,n,q,D}$ reduces to $\text{sk-LWE}_{m,n,q,D'}$. Finally, by [MM11, Theorem 3.1], $\text{sk-LWE}_{m,n,q,D'}$ reduces to $\text{dk-LWE}_{m,n,q,D'}$. The composition of these reductions leads to the above claim. $\qquad\square$

Theorem 2 now follows from combining Lemmas 5, 6, 2 and 3. $\qquad\square$

5   ROM and QROM Analyses of FSwBA

In this section we discuss the security of the Fiat-Shamir transform with bounded aborts. We first prove the UF-CMA security of the signature in the QROM based on the flawed proof in [KLS18], and then in the sequel of the section we discuss the adaptive reprogramming techniques to prove the UF-CMA security in the QROM (and with tighter reductions in the ROM).

We further provide an analysis relying on the Rényi divergence instead of the statistical distance in the full version [DFPS23, Appendix B.2].

5.1   The History-Free Approach

Below, we reduce the (s)UF-CMA$_1$ security to its UF-NMA security using the statistical zero-knowledge property of the Σ-protocol. One can see this proof as a correction of [KLS18]. Due to space limitation, we detail the proof in the full version [DFPS23, Appendix B.1]. There, we also claim that the same approach applies to UF-CMA security.

Theorem 3. *Let* $\varepsilon_{zk}, \alpha, T_{\mathsf{Sim}} \geq 0$, $B \geq 0$ *and* H *and* G *hash functions modeled as random oracles. Assume that* $\Sigma = ((\mathsf{P}_1, \mathsf{P}_2), (\mathsf{V}_1, \mathsf{V}_2))$ *is an* $(\varepsilon_{zk}, T_{\mathsf{Sim}})$-HVZK *public-coin identification protocol, and that the commitment message of the prover has min-entropy* α. *For any quantum adversary* $\mathcal{A}$ *against* UF-CMA$_1$ *(or* sUF-CMA$_1$*) security of* $\mathsf{SIG}_B = \mathsf{FS}_B[\Sigma, H]$ *that issues at most* Q_H *quantum queries to the random oracle* H *and* Q_S *classical queries to the signing oracle, there exists a quantum adversary* $\mathcal{B}$ *against* UF-NMA *security of* SIG_B *with* $\mathsf{Time}(B) \approx \mathsf{Time}(A) + T_{\mathsf{Sim}} \cdot B \cdot (Q_S + Q_H)$ *such that*

$$\mathsf{Adv}^{\mathsf{(s)UF\text{-}CMA}_1}_{\mathsf{SIG}_B}(\mathcal{A}) \leq \mathsf{Adv}^{\mathsf{UF\text{-}NMA}}_{\mathsf{SIG}_B}(\mathcal{B}) + 2^{\frac{-\alpha+3}{2}} \cdot B \cdot (Q_S + Q_H)$$
$$+ 30\sqrt{\varepsilon_{zk} \cdot B} \cdot (Q_S + Q_H)^{\frac{3}{2}} .$$

Our reduction relies on $\mathcal{B}$ *having access to a private random oracle* H' *with the same domain and range as* H *that is not accessible by* $\mathcal{A}$.

The results also hold if we replace HVZK *by* sc-HVZK *and assume* ε_{zk} *to be negligible in the security parameter.*

Note that one could adjust the proof of the above statement (as well as those of the next statements) to replace access to the private random oracle by relying on a quantum pseudorandom function in the reduction [Zha12].

5.2   The Adaptive Reprogramming Approach

We show how to reduce UF-CMA security and sUF-CMA security of the signature to UF-NMA security, separately in the ROM and QROM. Our separate handling of the random oracle models enables us to obtain a tighter proof in the ROM compared to the lower bound that the QROM proof imposes on any ROM proof.

We use the similar frameworks for adaptive reprogramming ([DFPS23, Lemma 12] and Lemma 1) in the ROM and the QROM. Also, we note that our proof is crucially based on our new zero-knowledge simulator.

Theorem 4. *Let $\varepsilon_{zk}, \alpha, T_{\mathsf{Sim}} \geq 0$, $B \geq 0$ and H a hash function modeled as a random oracle. Assume that $\Sigma = ((\mathsf{P}_1, \mathsf{P}_2), (\mathsf{V}_1, \mathsf{V}_2))$ is a $(\varepsilon_{zk}, T_{\mathsf{Sim}})$-HVZK public-coin identification protocol, and that the prover has commitment min-entropy α. Let $\mathcal{A}$ be an adversary against* UF-CMA *security of* $\mathsf{SIG}_B = \mathsf{FS}_B[\Sigma, H]$ *that issues at most Q_H queries to the random oracle H and Q_S classical queries to the sigining oracle. Let $\mathsf{X} \in \{\mathsf{UF}, \mathsf{sUF}\}$; we define Δ_{X} as follows: $\Delta_{\mathsf{UF}} = 0$ and $\Delta_{\mathsf{sUF}} = BQ_S \cdot 2^{-\alpha}$.*

- *In the ROM, there exists an adversary $\mathcal{B}$ against* UF-NMA *security of* SIG_B *with runtime* $\mathsf{Time}(\mathcal{A}) + \mathcal{O}((T_{\mathsf{Sim}} \cdot B \cdot Q_S + Q_H) \log(B \cdot Q_S + Q_H))$ *such that*

$$\mathsf{Adv}_{\mathsf{SIG}_B}^{\mathsf{X\text{-}CMA}}(\mathcal{A}) \leq \mathsf{Adv}_{\mathsf{SIG}_B}^{\mathsf{UF\text{-}NMA}}(\mathcal{B}) + 2^{-\alpha} \cdot B \cdot Q_S \cdot (B \cdot Q_S + Q_H + 1)$$
$$+ \varepsilon_{zk} \cdot B \cdot Q_S + \Delta_{\mathsf{X}} \ .$$

- *In the QROM, there exists an adversary $\mathcal{B}$ against* UF-NMA *security of* SIG_B *such that*

$$\mathsf{Adv}_{\mathsf{SIG}_B}^{\mathsf{X\text{-}CMA}}(\mathcal{A}) \leq \mathsf{Adv}_{\mathsf{SIG}_B}^{\mathsf{UF\text{-}NMA}}(\mathcal{B}) + 2^{-\frac{\alpha}{2}} \cdot \frac{3B \cdot Q_S}{2} \cdot \sqrt{(B \cdot Q_S + Q_H + 1)}$$
$$+ \varepsilon_{zk} \cdot B \cdot Q_S + \Delta_{\mathsf{X}} \ .$$

Our reduction relies on $\mathcal{B}$ having access to a private random oracle H' with the same domain and range as H that is not accessible by $\mathcal{A}$. Furthermore, the runtime of $\mathcal{B}$ is $\mathsf{Time}(\mathcal{A}) + \mathcal{O}((T_{\mathsf{Sim}} \cdot B \cdot Q_S + Q_H) \log(B \cdot Q_S))$ *with QRACM, and* $\mathsf{Time}(\mathcal{A}) + \mathcal{O}((T_{\mathsf{Sim}} \cdot B \cdot Q_S + Q_H) \cdot (B \cdot Q_S))$ *without QRACM.*

The results also hold if we replace HVZK *by* sc-HVZK *and assume ε_{zk} to be negligible in the security parameter.*

Proof. The proof is based on a sequence of hybrid games.

Game G_0. The first game is the UF-CMA security game (Fig. 5).

Game G_1. In this game, the challenges of the transcripts are not computed by the random oracle anymore, but sampled independently and uniformly each time. Then, the random oracle is reprogrammed according to the new challenges as in Fig. 6.

To bound the distance between Game_0 and Game_1, we construct a wrapper $\mathcal{D}$ around $\mathcal{A}$ that uses $\mathcal{A}$ to solve a reprogramming game. It works as in Fig. 7.

Note that if $b = 0$ in Fig. 7, then $\mathcal{D}$ perfectly simulates G_0, and otherwise it perfectly simulates G_1. Therefore,

$$\left| \Pr[1 \Leftarrow G_0^{\mathcal{A}}] - \Pr[1 \Leftarrow G_1^{\mathcal{A}}] \right| \leq \left| \Pr[1 \Leftarrow \mathsf{Reprogram}_0^{\mathcal{D}}] - \Pr[1 \Leftarrow \mathsf{Reprogram}_1^{\mathcal{D}}] \right|.$$

During the game, distinguisher $\mathcal{D}$ makes $B \cdot Q_S$ reprogramming queries and $B \cdot Q_S + Q_H + 1$ random oracle queries. In the ROM, [DFPS23, Lemma 12] bounds

Game :	GetTrans(μ) :
1: $\mathcal{M} := \varnothing$	1: $\kappa := 0$
2: $(vk, sk) \leftarrow \mathsf{KeyGen}(1^\lambda)$	2: **while** $z = \bot$ and $\kappa \leq B$
3: $(\mu^*, \sigma^*) \leftarrow \mathcal{A}^{H,\ \mathsf{Sign}(sk, \cdot)}(vk)$	3: $\quad (w, st) \leftarrow \mathsf{P}_1(sk)$
4: Parse $\sigma^* = (w^*, z^*)$	4: $\quad c := H(w\|\mu)$
5: $c^* := H(w^*\|\mu^*)$	5: $\quad z \leftarrow \mathsf{P}_2(sk, w, c, st)$
6: **return** $[[\mu^* \notin \mathcal{M}]] \wedge \mathsf{V}_2(vk, w^*, c^*, z^*)$	6: $\quad \kappa := \kappa + 1$
	7: **return** (w, c, z)
Sign(sk, μ) :	
1: $\mathcal{M} := \mathcal{M} \cup \{\mu\}$	
2: $(w, c, z) \leftarrow \mathsf{GetTrans}(\mu)$	
3: **if** $z = \bot$ **return** $\bot$	
4: **return** $\sigma = (w, z)$	

Fig. 5. Game G_0

Game :	GetTrans(μ) :
1: $\mathcal{M} := \varnothing$	1: $\kappa := 0$
2: $(vk, sk) \leftarrow \mathsf{KeyGen}(1^\lambda)$	2: **while** $z = \bot$ and $\kappa \leq B$
3: $(\mu^*, \sigma^*) \leftarrow \mathcal{A}^{H,\ \mathsf{Sign}(sk, \cdot)}(vk)$	3: $\quad (w, st) \leftarrow \mathsf{P}_1(sk)$
4: Parse $\sigma^* = (w^*, z^*)$	4: $\quad c \leftarrow U(\mathcal{C})$
5: $c^* := H(w^*\|\mu^*)$	5: $\quad z \leftarrow \mathsf{P}_2(sk, w, c, st)$
6: **return** $[[\mu^* \notin \mathcal{M}]] \wedge \mathsf{V}_2(vk, w^*, c^*, z^*)$	6: $\quad H := H^{w\|\mu \mapsto c}$
	7: $\quad \kappa := \kappa + 1$
Sign(sk, μ) :	8: **return** (w, c, z)
1: $\mathcal{M} := \mathcal{M} \cup \{\mu\}$	
2: $(w, c, z) \leftarrow \mathsf{GetTrans}(\mu)$	
3: **if** $z = \bot$ **return** $\bot$	
4: **return** $\sigma = (w, z)$	

Fig. 6. Game G_1. The difference from G_0 is highlighted in blue.

the advantage of $\mathcal{D}$ by $B \cdot Q_S \cdot (B \cdot Q_S + Q_H + 1)2^{-\alpha}$. In the QROM, using Lemma 1, it follows that the advantage of $\mathcal{D}$ is bounded by

$$\frac{3B \cdot Q_S}{2} \cdot \sqrt{(B \cdot Q_S + Q_H + 1)2^{-\alpha}}.$$

Game G_2. Let Sim be the zero-knowledge simulator for Σ. In this game we modify $\mathsf{GetTrans}$ such that the transcripts are now produced by Sim and without the secret key. See Fig. 8.

We would like to bound the distance between games G_1 and G_2 using the zero-knowledge property. First we discuss the QROM case. Suppose that we are given a random oracle H' and $B \cdot Q_S$ transcripts that are either sampled honestly or sampled by the simulator. We use them to simulate G_1 or G_2, respectively. Note that in both games, after each transcript, the random oracle is reprogrammed according to the transcript. In order to simulate the reprogrammed

$\mathcal{D}^{H_b,\mathsf{Reprogram}}$:

1: $\mathcal{M} := \varnothing$
2: $(vk, sk) \leftarrow \mathsf{KeyGen}(1^\lambda)$
3: $(\mu^*, \sigma^*) \leftarrow \mathcal{A}^{H_b,\ \mathsf{Sign}(sk,\cdot)}(vk)$
4: Parse $\sigma^* = (w^*, z^*)$
5: $c^* := H_b(w^*\|\mu^*)$
6: **return** $[[\mu^* \notin \mathcal{M}]] \wedge \mathsf{V}_2(vk, w^*, c^*, z^*)$

$\mathsf{Reprogram}(\mu, sk)$:

1: $(w, st) \leftarrow \mathsf{P}_1(sk)$
2: $c \leftarrow U(\mathcal{C})$
3: $H_1 := H_1^{(w\|\mu) \mapsto c}$
4: **return** (w, st)

$\mathsf{Sign}(sk, \mu)$:

1: $\mathcal{M} := \mathcal{M} \cup \{\mu\}$
2: $\kappa := 0$
3: **while** $z = \bot$ **and** $\kappa \leq B$
4: $\quad (w, st) \leftarrow \mathsf{Reprogram}(\mu, sk)$
5: $\quad c := H_b(w\|\mu)$
6: $\quad z \leftarrow \mathsf{P}_2(sk, w, c, st)$
7: $\quad \kappa := \kappa + 1$
8: **if** $z = \bot$ **return** $\bot$
9: **return** $\sigma = (w, z)$

Fig. 7. The distinguisher $\mathcal{D}$.

Game :

1: $\mathcal{M} := \varnothing$
2: $(vk, sk) \leftarrow \mathsf{KeyGen}(1^\lambda)$
3: $(\mu^*, \sigma^*) \leftarrow \mathcal{A}^{H,\ \mathsf{Sign}(sk,\cdot)}(vk)$
4: Parse $\sigma^* = (w^*, z^*)$
5: $c^* := H(w^*\|\mu^*)$
6: **return** $[[\mu^* \notin \mathcal{M}]] \wedge \mathsf{V}_2(vk, w^*, c^*, z^*)$

$\mathsf{Sign}(sk, \mu)$:

1: $\mathcal{M} := \mathcal{M} \cup \{\mu\}$
2: $(w, c, z) \leftarrow \mathsf{GetTrans}(\mu)$
3: **if** $z = \bot$ **return** $\bot$
4: **return** $\sigma = (w, z)$

$\mathsf{GetTrans}(\mu)$:

1: $\kappa := 0$
2: **while** $z = \bot$ **and** $\kappa \leq B$
3: $\quad c \leftarrow U(\mathcal{C})$
4: $\quad \boxed{(w, z) \leftarrow \mathsf{Sim}(vk, c)}$
5: $\quad H := H^{w\|\mu \mapsto c}$
6: $\quad \kappa := \kappa + 1$
7: **return** (w, c, z)

Fig. 8. Game G_2. The difference from G_1 is highlighted in blue.

random oracle perfectly, we keep track of a list $\mathfrak{D}$ of the classical values in which the random oracle must be reprogrammed. We describe the details in Fig. 9.

Note that $\mathcal{C}$ can perfectly simulate G_1 or G_2 with its respective transcripts. Furthermore, it is given $B \cdot Q_S$ transcripts. By the statistical HVZK property of the Σ-protocol, it follows that

$$\left| \Pr[1 \Leftarrow G_1^\mathcal{A}] - \Pr[1 \Leftarrow G_2^\mathcal{A}] \right| \leq B \cdot Q_S \cdot \varepsilon_{zk}.$$

The ROM case is similar except that instead of using the private random oracle H' to simulate H, we use the lazy sampling method. The rest of the reduction is exactly the same as in Fig. 9. We obtain

$$\left| \Pr[1 \Leftarrow G_1^\mathcal{A}] - \Pr[1 \Leftarrow G_2^\mathcal{A}] \right| \leq B \cdot Q_S \cdot \varepsilon_{zk}.$$

$\mathcal{C}^{|H'\rangle}(\{w_{i,\kappa}, c_{i,\kappa}, z_{i,\kappa}\}_{i\in[Q_S], \kappa\in[B]})$:

1: $\mathcal{M} := \varnothing$
2: $i := 0$
3: $\mathfrak{D} := \varnothing$
4: $(vk, sk) \leftarrow \mathsf{KeyGen}(1^\lambda)$
5: $(\mu^*, \sigma^*) \leftarrow \mathcal{A}^{|H\rangle,\ \mathsf{Sign}(sk,\cdot)}(vk)$
6: Parse $\sigma^* = (w^*, z^*)$
7: $c^* := H_b(w^* \| \mu^*)$
8: **return** $[[\mu^* \notin \mathcal{M}]] \wedge V_2(vk, w^*, c^*, z^*)$

$H(w\|\mu)$:

1: **if** $\exists c$ such that $(w, \mu, c) \in \mathfrak{D}$
2:    **return** c
3: **return** $H'(w\|\mu)$

$\mathsf{Sign}(sk, \mu)$:

1: $\mathcal{M} := \mathcal{M} \cup \{\mu\}$
2: $i := i + 1$
3: $\kappa := 0$
4: **while** $z = \bot$ and $\kappa \leq B$
5:    $(w, c, z) = (w_{i,\kappa}, c_{i,\kappa}, z_{i,\kappa})$
6:    **if** $\exists c'$ such that $(w, \mu, c') \in \mathfrak{D}$
7:      $\mathfrak{D} := \mathfrak{D} \setminus (w, \mu, c')$
8:    $\mathfrak{D} := \mathfrak{D} \cup (w, \mu, c)$
9:    $\kappa := \kappa + 1$
10: **if** $z = \bot$ **return** $\bot$
11: **return** $\sigma = (w, z)$

Fig. 9. The distinguisher $\mathcal{C}$ for real and simulated transcripts of Σ based on $\mathcal{A}$.

Game G_3. In this game, we add one more statement to the winning conditions. Let $(\mu^*, (w^*, z^*))$ be the forgery. If the value $w^* \| \mu^*$ has been programmed in the random oracle H during the game, then we abort. The value $w^* \| \mu^*$ would be programmed during the game if the adversary has made a sign query with μ^*. As the winning condition in the UF-CMA game already requires a forgery for a message that has not been queried before, the adversary's view is identical to that of the previous one.

Game G_4. The signing algorithm does not use the signing key anymore and uses the zero-knowledge simulator to answer the sign queries. The last remaining technicality lies in how to simulate the random oracle. In the ROM, we use the lazy sampling method. At each query to the random oracle, we return a match if there exists any in the database, otherwise we return an element freshly sampled from the range of H and we add it in the database. In the QROM, we cannot simulate the random oracle with the lazy sampling method since the access to it is quantum. The challenger uses a private random oracle H' to simulate the hash queries of the adversary but also keeps a database of reprogrammed inputs. Whenever it receives a hash query, it first searches the database for a match and, if there is none, it returns the evaluation of the query with the private random oracle H'. We refer the reader to Fig. 10 for the details of this game. We note that this is only a syntactic modification since the reprogramming has already been carried out in G_1.

It remains to reduce G_4 to UF-NMA security. Using the UF-NMA game, one can perfectly simulate G_4 for the adversary. If the adversary $\mathcal{A}$ finds a forgery (μ^*, σ^*), then the random oracle has not been reprogrammed at this value during the course of G_4 since it has not been queried before. Hence, it would be a valid signature for the UF-NMA game.

To complete this proof, we provide a detailed runtime analysis as well as a proof of strong unforgeability in the full version [DFPS23]. $\qquad\qquad\square$

```
Game :                                          GetTrans(μ) :                      ▷ ROM
 1: M := ∅                                        1: κ := 0
 2: D := ∅                                        2: while z = ⊥ and κ ≤ B
 3: (vk, sk) ← KeyGen(1^λ)                        3:   c ← U(C)
 4: (μ*, σ*) ← A^{H, Sign(sk,·)}(vk)              4:   (w, z) ← Sim(vk, c)
 5: Parse σ* = (w*, z*)                           5:   if ∃c such that (w, μ, c') ∈ D
 6: c* := H(w*‖μ*)                                6:     Abort
 7: return  [[μ* ∉ M]] ∧ V_2(vk, w*, c*, z*)     7:   D := D ∪ {(w, μ, c)}
                                                  8:   κ := κ + 1
                                                  9: return  (w, c, z)
 H(w‖μ) :                            ▷ ROM
 1: if ∃c such that (w, μ, c) ∈ D
 2:   return c                                   GetTrans(μ) :                     ▷ QROM
 3: else                                          1: κ := 0
 4:   c ← U(C)                                     2: while z = ⊥ and κ ≤ B
 5:   D := D ∪ {(w, μ, c)}                         3:   c ← U(C)
 6: return  c                                      4:   (w, z) ← Sim(vk, c)
                                                   5:   if ∃c such that (w, μ, c') ∈ D
                                                   6:     D := D \ (w, μ, c')
 H(w‖μ) :                            ▷ QROM       7:     D := D ∪ {(w, μ, c)}
 1: if ∃c such that (w, μ, c) ∈ D                  8:   κ := κ + 1
 2:   return c                                      9: return  (w, c, z)
 3: else
 4: return  H'(w‖μ)
```

Fig. 10. Random oracle simulation in Game G_4.

6 Concrete Analysis of FSwUA: Negative Result

In the rest of the paper, we focus on analyzing formally signatures constructed from combining an identification protocol with the Fiat-Shamir with unbounded aborts paradigm. To the best of our knowledge, this is the first complete analysis of FSwUA.

In this first section, we exhibit a signature constructed using FS_∞ for which the signing runtime is infinite for an instantiation of the hash function H. Therefore, the expected runtime is also infinite and the standard definition of runtime must be changed. We propose minor updates to the signature definitions so that they support such pathological behaviors. Note that FSwUA is the main paradigm used in practice: there is no reason to add a bound for the number of loop iterations in the code if the algorithm never reaches it except with negligible probability, but the latter statement thus needs to be proven.

In Sect. 6.2, we will prove Fiat-Shamir with unbounded aborts does yield signatures (both in the ROM and QROM with tighter reductions in the ROM) which satisfy all correctness, runtime, and security requirements. Correctness of FSwBA is also addressed in Sect. 6.2 as a corollary of our analysis.

6.1   Infinite Signing Runtime in the Worst Case of FSwUA

We prove the following theorem in the full version [DFPS23].

Theorem 5. *There exist a parametrization of* $\text{dk-LWE}_{m,n,q,Q}$ *such that the following holds assuming the hardness of* $\text{dk-LWE}_{m,n,q,Q}$. *There exists a public-coin identification protocol* Σ *with instance generator* Gen *such that, with overwhelming probability over the randomness of* Gen, *there exists a hash function* H_{bad} *such that the signing algorithm of* $\text{SIG}_\infty := \text{FS}_\infty[\Sigma, H_{bad}]$ *on inputs the signing key and any message does not halt.*

The proof relies on constructing the appropriate identification protocol, and then identifying a specific bad instantiation for the hash function. The main idea is to instantiate Lyubashevsky's signature scheme with source distribution Q being the uniform distribution over a ball B and target distribution being the uniform distribution over a corona C, as illustrated in the full version [DFPS23]. For a keypair $\mathbf{A}, \mathbf{S}$, a loop iteration then samples $\mathbf{y} \leftarrow U(B)$, defines a commitment $\mathbf{w} \leftarrow \mathbf{Ay} \bmod q$, and returns $\mathbf{y} + \mathbf{Sc}$ with $\mathbf{c} \leftarrow H(\mathbf{Ay} \bmod q \| \mu)$, if and only if $\mathbf{y} + \mathbf{Sc} \in C$.

The cornerstone of our proof is to show that there exists a hash function H_{bad} such that, for every message μ and every $\mathbf{y}$, the challenge $\mathbf{c} = H(\mathbf{Ay} \bmod q \| \mu)$ is such that $\mathbf{y} + \mathbf{Sc} \notin C$. This implies that the signing algorithm of $\text{FS}_\infty[\Sigma, H_{bad}]$ never halts on any input message.

So far, this only exhibits a single bad choice for the hash function, while signatures based on FSwUA support messages of unbounded length. Hence, there are infinitely many possible hash functions (functions with domain $\mathcal{W} \times \{0, 1\}^*$ and range $\mathcal{C}$, with $\mathcal{W}$ being the commitment space). As a consequence, it is not immediate that a single bad hash function implies an infinite expected runtime for the signature scheme in the ROM, and one could think that simply considering the runtime when H is a random oracle could be sufficient to fix it.

Corollary 1. *We have* $\Pr_H[\forall w \in \mathcal{W}, H(w\|\mu) = H_{bad}(w\|\mu)] \geq |\mathcal{C}|^{-|\mathcal{W}|}$ *for any message* μ. *Therefore, the expected runtime of* $\text{Sign}(sk, \mu)$ *over the choice of the random oracle* H *is infinite.*

Our result relies on the hardness of the dk-LWE problem when the weight vector is sampled from the uniform distribution over a hyperball. This is an unusual distribution for dk-LWE. However, it can be checked that for appropriate parameters, the proof of [BLR+18, Sect. 5] that decision LWE is hard for a noise distribution that is uniform in a hypercube carries over to the hyperball setting.

6.2   Updated Signature Definition

As shown in Sect. 6.1, there are instances of identification protocols that yield signature schemes with infinite expected runtime of the signing algorithm. This requires relaxing the runtime requirement in the definition to be expected polynomial time with overwhelming probability over the choice of the hash function.

Yet, there is another subtlety doing so: in the security game, an adversary might make a sign query that never halts. In the case of the above construction, the challenger, which is unbounded, can still notice it as the commitment space is bounded and the rejection step is deterministic. Once all the potential commitments have failed to produce a valid signature, the challenger knows that it cannot answer the query. This is however not the case of every signature scheme. To take such event into account, we consider that an attacker automatically wins if the challenger takes more than T' time to answer a signature query, for some parameter T'. An alternative choice could be to consider that an adversary which makes a non-terminating sign query loses, since the challenger does not answer anymore. We prefer to add this parameter T' as this makes the definition stronger by further guaranteeing that an adversary cannot find a query which forces the signer to run for a long time, which could be desirable in practice as well.

We now state our updated definition for signatures. It is highly similar to the standard definition and we only highlight the differences.

Definition 9 (Modified Digital Signature in the ROM). *Let H be a random oracle to which all algorithms have oracle access. A signature scheme is a tuple (KeyGen, Sign, Verify) of algorithms with the following specifications. Everything is as in the standard definition, except for the runtime of Sign, which we define below, and a minor tweak in the security game.*

- *$\mathsf{Sign}^H : (sk, \mu) \to \sigma$ is a probabilistic algorithm that takes as inputs a signing key sk and a message $\mu \in \mathcal{M}$ and outputs a signature σ. We denote with $T_{\mathsf{Sign}^H(sk,\mu)}$ the runtime of $\mathsf{Sign}(sk,\mu)$.*

Let $\gamma > 0, T = \mathsf{poly}(\lambda)$ and $\varepsilon = \mathsf{negl}(\lambda)$. We say that the signature scheme is γ-correct if for any pair (vk, sk) in the range of KeyGen and μ,

$$\Pr[\mathsf{Verify}(vk, \mu, \mathsf{Sign}(sk, \mu)) = 1 \mid \mathsf{Sign}(sk, \mu) \text{ halts}] \geq \gamma,$$

and we say that it is (T, ε)-efficient if for any pair (vk, sk) in the range of KeyGen and μ,

$$\Pr_H[T_{\mathsf{Sign}^H(sk,\mu)} > T] < \varepsilon.$$

where both probabilities are taken over the random coins of the two algorithms and the random oracle.

In addition, we update the security game as follows. Let T' be another function of λ. We define T'-UF-CMA security exactly as the usual UF-CMA security, except that we further make the adversary win as soon as it makes a sign query for which the signing algorithm takes more than T' steps to halt.

Definition 9 does not forbid the situation described in Sect. 6.1 from occurring but guarantees that it should be hard to find non-halting queries.

Theorem 6 (Runtime). *Let $\gamma > 0, \beta \in (0, 1)$ and H a hash function modeled as a random oracle. Let $\Sigma = ((\mathsf{P}_1, \mathsf{P}_2), (\mathsf{V}_1, \mathsf{V}_2))$ be an identification protocol that* *is (γ, β)-correct and has commitment min-entropy α. Let* $\mathsf{SIG}_\infty = \mathsf{FS}_\infty[\Sigma, H]$. *Let $\mathcal{M}$ be the message space and* $I_{\mathsf{Sign}^H}(sk, \mu)$ *denote the random variable counting the number of iterations of the signing algorithm on input (sk, μ) using a random oracle H where $\mu \in \mathcal{M}$. It holds that for any $(vk, sk) \leftarrow \mathsf{KeyGen}(1^\lambda)$, any message $\mu \in \mathcal{M}$, and any integer i:*

$$\Pr_H(I_{\mathsf{Sign}^H}(sk, \mu) > i) \leq \beta^i + \frac{2^{-\alpha}}{(1 - \beta)^3}.$$

Assume that $\alpha = \omega(\log(\lambda))$. Setting $i = \omega(\log(\lambda)/\log(1/\beta))$ ensures that with overwhelming probability over the choice of H, signing runs in polynomial time. We note that this bound does not contradict the previous (negative) result. Indeed, it does not imply any statement on the finiteness of the expected value of T_{Sign^H}, which is infinite in the previous section.

We move on to checking that FSwUA satisfies the new γ-correctness property, assuming that the underlying identification protocol is (γ, β)-correct.

Theorem 7. *Let $\gamma > 0, \beta \in (0, 1)$ and let H denote a hash function modeled as a random oracle. Let $\Sigma = ((\mathsf{P}_1, \mathsf{P}_2), (\mathsf{V}_1, \mathsf{V}_2))$ be an identification protocol that is (γ, β)-correct. Let T denote the runtime of one interaction in the worst-case. Let $\alpha > 0$ be its commitment min-entropy. Let* $\mathsf{SIG}_\infty = \mathsf{FS}_\infty[\Sigma, H]$. *Then for any $i = \omega(\log(\lambda)/\log(1/\beta))$, it is γ-correct as well as $(iT, \beta^i + 2^{-\alpha}/(1 - \beta)^3)$-efficient.*

With FSwBA, the problem is reversed: bounding the runtime becomes easy, whereas proving the correctness becomes mildly more tedious, as one needs to check that $\perp$ is not output too often.

Theorem 8. *Let $\gamma > 0, \beta \in (0, 1)$ and $B > 0$. Let H be a hash function modeled a random oracle. Let $\Sigma = ((\mathsf{P}_1, \mathsf{P}_2), (\mathsf{V}_1, \mathsf{V}_2))$ be an identification protocol that is (γ, β)-correct and has commitment min-entropy α. Let* $\mathsf{SIG}_B = \mathsf{FS}_B[\Sigma, H]$. *Then, for any $(vk, sk) \leftarrow \mathsf{KeyGen}(1^\lambda)$ and any message $\mu \in \mathcal{M}$, we have*

$$\Pr[\mathsf{Verify}(vk, \mu, \mathsf{Sign}(sk, \mu)) = 1] \geq \gamma \cdot \left(1 - \beta^B - \frac{2^{-\alpha}}{(1 - \beta)^3}\right),$$

where the randomness is taken over H as well as the coins of Sign.

We finally prove the security of the unbounded version of the Fiat-Shamir transform in both ROM and QROM. We note that our proof in the ROM is tighter. We reduce the T'-UF-CMA security of the unbounded signature scheme to the UF-CMA security of the bounded one in the QROM.

Theorem 9. *Let $\alpha \geq 0, \beta \in (0, 1)$, and let H be a hash function modeled as a random oracle. Assume that $\Sigma = ((\mathsf{P}_1, \mathsf{P}_2), (\mathsf{V}_1, \mathsf{V}_2))$ is a (γ, β)-correct identification protocol, and that the commitment message of P_1 has min-entropy α. Let T denote the runtime of one iteration of the protocol with the hash function. Let $T' > BT$. For any arbitrary adversary $\mathcal{A}$ against T'-UF-CMA security of* $\mathsf{SIG}_\infty = \mathsf{FS}_\infty[\Sigma, H]$ *that issues at most Q_H queries to the random oracle H and Q_S classical queries to the signing oracle and for any fixed integer B,* *the same adversary* $\mathcal{A}$ *against* UF-CMA *security of* $\mathsf{SIG}_B = \mathsf{FS}_B[\Sigma, H]$ *is such that* $|\mathsf{Adv}_{\mathsf{SIG}_\infty}^{T'\text{-}\mathsf{UF}\text{-}\mathsf{CMA}}(\mathcal{A}) - \mathsf{Adv}_{\mathsf{SIG}_B}^{\mathsf{UF}\text{-}\mathsf{CMA}}(\mathcal{A})|$ *is bounded as*

$$
Q_S \cdot \beta^B + \frac{\beta^B \cdot 2^{-\alpha}}{(1-\beta)^3} + \begin{cases} 2^{-\alpha} \cdot B \cdot Q_S \cdot (B \cdot Q_S + Q_H + 1) & \text{in the ROM,} \\ 2^{-\frac{\alpha}{2}} \cdot \frac{3B \cdot Q_S}{2} \cdot \sqrt{(B \cdot Q_S + Q_H + 1)} & \text{in the QROM.} \end{cases}
$$

This also holds replacing UF-CMA *with* $\mathsf{UF\text{-}CMA_1}$ *or* sUF-CMA *security.*

Acknowledgments. We thank Andreas Hülsing, Chistian Majenz, and Thomas Prest for helpful discussions. This work was supported by the ANR Project ANR-21-ASTR-0016 AMIRAL, the France 2030 ANR Project ANR-22-PECY-003 SecureCompute, and the France 2030 ANR Project ANR-22-PETQ-0008 PQ-TLS.

References

ABB+17. Alkim, E., et al.: Revisiting TESLA in the quantum random oracle model. In: PQCrypto (2017)

AFLT16. Abdalla, M., Fouque, P.-A., Lyubashevsky, V., Tibouchi, M.: Tightly secure signatures from lossy identification schemes. J. Cryptol. (2016)

AHU19. Ambainis, A., Hamburg, M., Unruh, D.: Quantum security proofs using semi-classical oracles. In: CRYPTO (2019)

ASY22. Agrawal, S., Stehlé, D., Yadav, A.: Round-optimal lattice-based threshold signatures, revisited. In: ICALP (2022)

BBD+23. Barbosa, M., et al.: Fixing and mechanizing the security proof of Fiat-Shamir with aborts and Dilithium. In: CRYPTO (2023)

BBE+18. Barthe, G., et al.: Masking the GLP lattice-based signature scheme at any order. In: EUROCRYPT (2018)

BBE+19. Barthe, G., Belaïd, S., Espitau, T., Fouque, P.-A., Rossi, M., Tibouchi, M.: GALACTICS: gaussian sampling for lattice-based constant- time implementation of cryptographic signatures, revisited. In: CCS (2019)

BDF+11. Boneh, D., Dagdelen, Ö., Fischlin, M., Lehmann, A., Schaffner, C., Zhandry, M.: Random oracles in a quantum world. In: ASIACRYPT (2011)

BLR+18. Bai, S., Lepoint, T., Roux-Langlois, A., Sakzad, A., Stehlé, D., Steinfeld, R.: Improved security proofs in lattice-based cryptography: Using the Rényi divergence rather than the statistical distance. J. Cryptol. (2018)

CLMQ21. Chen, Y., Lombardi, A., Ma, F., Quach, W.: Does Fiat-Shamir require a cryptographic hash function? In: CRYPTO (2021)

DFMS19. Don, J., Fehr, S., Majenz, C., Schaffner, C.: Security of the Fiat-Shamir transformation in the quantum random-oracle model. In: CRYPTO (2019)

DFPS22. Devevey, J., Fawzi, O., Passelègue, A., Stehlé, D.: On rejection sampling in Lyubashevsky's signature scheme. In: ASIACRYPT (2022)

DFPS23. Devevey, J., Fallahpour, P., Passelègue, A., Stehlé, D.: A detailed analysis of fiat-shamir with aborts. Cryptology ePrint Archive, Paper 2023/245 (2023). https://eprint.iacr.org/2023/245

DKL+18. Ducas, L., et al.: CRYSTALS-dilithium: a lattice-based digital signature scheme. In: TCHES (2018)

DPSZ12. Damgård, I., Pastro, V., Smart, N.P., Zakarias, S.: Multiparty computation from somewhat homomorphic encryption. In: CRYPTO (2012)

FS86. Fiat, A., Shamir, A.: How to prove yourself: Practical solutions to identification and signature problems. In: CRYPTO (1986)

GHHM21. Grilo, A.B., Hövelmanns, K., Hülsing, A., Majenz, C.: Tight adaptive reprogramming in the QROM. In: ASIACRYPT (2021)

Kat21. Katsumata, S.: A new simple technique to bootstrap various lattice zero-knowledge proofs to QROM secure NIZKs. In: CRYPTO (2021)

KLS18. Kiltz, E., Lyubashevsky, V., Schaffner, C.: A concrete treatment of Fiat-Shamir signatures in the quantum random-oracle model. In: EUROCRYPT (2018)

Lyu09. Lyubashevsky, V.: Fiat-Shamir with aborts: Applications to lattice and factoring-based signatures. In: ASIACRYPT (2009)

Lyu12. Lyubashevsky, V.: Lattice signatures without trapdoors. In: EUROCRYPT (2012)

Lyu16. Lyubashevsky, V.: Digital signatures based on the hardness of ideal lattice problems in all rings. In: ASIACRYPT (2016)

LZ19. Liu, Q., Zhandry, M.: Revisiting post-quantum Fiat-Shamir. In: CRYPTO (2019)

MGTF19. Migliore, V., Gérard, B., Tibouchi, M., Fouque, P.-A.: Masking Dilithium - efficient implementation and side-channel evaluation. In: ACNS (2019)

MM11. Micciancio, D., Mol, P.: Pseudorandom knapsacks and the sample complexity of LWE search-to-decision reductions. In: CRYPTO (2011)

Reg09. Regev, O.: On lattices, learning with errors, random linear codes, and cryptography. J. ACM (2009)

Sch89. Schnorr, C.-P.: Efficient identification and signatures for smart cards (abstract). In: EUROCRYPT (1989)

Zha12. Zhandry, M.: How to construct quantum random functions. In: FOCS (2012)

Fixing and Mechanizing the Security Proof of Fiat-Shamir with Aborts and Dilithium

Manuel Barbosa[1]([✉])([iD]), Gilles Barthe[2]([iD]), Christian Doczkal[2]([iD]), Jelle Don[3],
Serge Fehr[3,4], Benjamin Grégoire[5]([iD]), Yu-Hsuan Huang[3], Andreas Hülsing[6]([iD]),
Yi Lee[2,7]([iD]), and Xiaodi Wu[7]([iD])

[1] University of Porto (FCUP) and INESC TEC, Porto, Portugal
mbb@fc.up.pt
[2] Max Planck Institute for Security and Privacy, Bochum, Germany
{gilles.barthe,christian.doczkal}@mpi-sp.org
[3] Centrum Wiskunde & Informatica, Amsterdam, The Netherlands
{jelle.don,serge.fehr,yhh}@cwi.nl
[4] Leiden University, Leiden, The Netherlands
[5] Inria Centre at Université Côte d'Azur, Valbonne, France
benjamin.gregoire@inria.fr
[6] Eindhoven University of Technology, Eindhoven, The Netherlands
andreas@huelsing.net
[7] University of Maryland, College Park, USA
{xiaodiwu,ylee1228}@umd.edu

Abstract. We extend and consolidate the security justification for the Dilithium signature scheme. In particular, we identify a subtle but crucial gap that appears in several ROM and QROM security proofs for signature schemes that are based on the Fiat-Shamir with aborts paradigm, including Dilithium. The gap lies in the CMA-to-NMA reduction and was uncovered when trying to formalize a variant of the QROM security proof by Kiltz, Lyubashevsky, and Schaffner (Eurocrypt 2018). The gap was confirmed by the authors, and there seems to be no simple patch for it. We provide new, fixed proofs for the affected CMA-to-NMA reduction, both for the ROM and the QROM, and we perform a concrete security analysis for the case of Dilithium to show that the claimed security level is still valid after addressing the gap. Furthermore, we offer a fully mechanized ROM proof for the CMA-security of Dilithium in the Easy-Crypt proof assistant. Our formalization includes several new tools and techniques of independent interest for future formal verification results.

1 Introduction

Modern cryptographic standards, including AES and SHA3, are often selected through open, multi-year cryptographic competitions. An important goal of these

Authors are listed in alphabetical order; see https://www.ams.org/profession/leaders/culture/JointResearchandItsPublicationfinal.pdf.

competitions is to increase confidence in the schemes selected for standardization. To this end, candidate schemes are exposed to scrutiny by the cryptography community. This scrutiny generally yields a combination of cryptanalytic attacks and provable security claims. The former leads to schemes being abandoned, narrowing the choice of candidates, while the latter plays a fundamental role in the selection of the remaining candidates. Overall, competitions increase confidence in selected standards. However, competitions are not infallible. In particular, flaws in candidate designs may go undetected by public scrutiny far into the standardization process. These "near misses" beg for complementary methods for validating provable security claims of widely used standards.

POST-QUANTUM CRYPTOGRAPHY AND DILITHIUM. In 2016, NIST initiated a competition for standardizing cryptographic algorithms that could withstand quantum adversaries. The competition recently reached an important milestone with the selection of four standards: one KEM (Kyber) and three signature algorithms (Dilithium, Falcon, SPHINCS+). These algorithms were chosen out of 69 candidates, some of which may still be selected during a fourth round. The selected candidates will form the backbone of quantum-resistant cryptography. Given the stakes, there is ample motivation for supporting all the selected candidates with computer-aided security proofs.

Dilithium [1,2] is a lattice-based digital signature based on the Fiat-Shamir with aborts (FSwA) paradigm introduced by Lyubashevsky [3,4]. Recall that the classic Fiat-Shamir (FS) paradigm transforms an interactive identification scheme (IDS) based on the standard commit-challenge-response structure into a digital signature scheme. The FS transform takes an IDS scheme ID and a hash function H (which is typically modelled as a random oracle) and sets the signature key pair to be that of ID. Then, to produce a signature on message m, the signer generates a first message w, locally sets the challenge to be $c := H(w, m)$ and completes the signature as $\sigma := (w, z)$, where z is the response generated by ID upon first message w and challenge c. A signature $\sigma = (w, z)$ is valid if $(w, H(w, m), z)$ is accepted by ID. The Fiat-Shamir with aborts (FSwA) paradigm extends the FS transform to allow for the response generation procedure to abort[1] — hence FS with aborts — which means that the signing algorithm must now execute the IDS repeatedly until a valid trace (w, c, z) is produced. We will denote this transformation by FSwA[ID, H].

The security of FSwA has been analyzed many times. In particular, the original analysis in [4] (in the ROM) concludes that the resulting signature scheme is secure down to the underlying lattice-based assumption. Later, Kiltz, Lyubashevsky, and Schaffner [5] (KLS) developed a modular framework that follows the structure of the FSwA transform and used it to extend the results of the security analysis to quantum attackers in the Quantum-accessible Random Oracle Model (QROM).

---

[1] This is necessary for a large class of lattice-based IDS, to avoid leaking the secret key via biased responses z.

COMPUTER-AIDED CRYPTOGRAPHY (CAC). CAC is an emerging approach that develops computer tools for building and independently verifying provable security claims [6]. CAC formal verification tools have been used to validate the security claims for a number of cryptographic primitives and protocols, and they have progressed to a point where they can be used to increase the level of assurance in standardisation processes. The most outstanding application of CAC to date is arguably the TLS (Transport Layer Security) protocol: the most recent version, TLS 1.3, was designed under the coordination of the IETF with the active involvement of formal verification experts, who used formal tools to unveil logical flaws in previous versions of TLS and intermediate designs, and to validate the security arguments [7–10].

In this paper we focus on EasyCrypt, a tool designed for machine-checking code-based computational security proofs, and hence ideally suited for formally verifying the security proofs for low-level primitives such as digital signature and encryption schemes. EasyCrypt permits stating and proving computational security goals using the same formalisms adopted in cryptographic papers. We report the results of our efforts to formally verify the security proof for the Dilithium signature scheme and provide further evidence that computer-aided cryptography permits guraranteeing the absence of design flaws in cryptographic standards to a much higher level of assurance than manual inspection.

Main Contributions. The main contributions of this paper are three-fold. First, we identify a subtle but crucial gap that appears in several ROM and QROM security proofs of Dilithium and other schemes based on FSwA, including [4] and [5]. This gap was uncovered when formalizing a variant of the proof in [5]. Second, we provide fixed proofs, both for the ROM and the QROM. Third, we fully mechanize the ROM proof in the EasyCrypt proof assistant. Our formalization includes several new tools and techniques of independent interest for future formal verification results.

We elaborate on these contributions below, but stress at this point two important take-aways: 1) our results extend and consolidate the security justification for the Dilithium signature scheme and 2) the gap in the proof would have been found earlier if any of the affected works, most prominently the Dilithium submission to the NIST post-quantum competition, had been subject to formal verification in the past.

THE GAP. The gap in the proof of FSwA occurs in the reduction from chosen message attacks (CMA) to no-message attacks (NMA). In this step, signature queries made by the considered CMA-attacker $A^{\text{Sign},H}$, which has access to a singing oracle and the random oracle, must be answered without knowledge of the secret key, replacing real signatures with fake ones produced by an Honest-Verifier Zero Knowledge (HVZK) simulator associated with the IDS. To ensure that the attacker cannot detect that it is being given fake signatures, it is also necessary to reprogram the random oracle to be consistent with the transcripts produced by the simulator. The crucial step boils down to replacing the oracle Sign by the oracle Trans (see Fig. 1), where Resp is an algorithm that may return ⊥.

Sign(m):
1: **repeat**
2:     $(w, \mathsf{st}) \leftarrow \mathsf{Com}(sk)$
3:     $c := H(w, m)$
4:     $z := \mathsf{Resp}(w, c, \mathsf{st})$
5: **until** $z \neq \perp$
6:
7: **return** (w, z)

Trans(m):
1: **repeat**
2:     $(w, \mathsf{st}) \leftarrow \mathsf{Com}(sk)$
3:     $c \leftarrow \mathsf{ChSet}$
4:     $z := \mathsf{Resp}(w, c, \mathsf{st})$
5: **until** $z \neq \perp$
6:     $H(w, m) := c$
7: **return** (w, z)

Fig. 1. Oracles Sign and Trans.

Clearly, the adversary $\mathcal{A}$ can attempt to guess w and query H on w before calling Sign/Trans, and then detect the inconsistency introduced by the reprogramming in case of Trans. However, even if the adversary makes no prior H-queries, the distribution of the random oracle changes, and this is where the gap lies. The reprogramming in Trans only reprograms the random oracle with accepting transcripts and thereby shifts the random oracle slightly towards pairs $((w, m), c)$ such that $\mathsf{Resp}(w, c, \mathsf{st}) \neq \perp$. Even though one expects this change in the distribution of the random oracle to be small, there is still a gap that needs to be properly bounded.

Both Lyubashevsky [4] and KLS [5] miss the loss incurred by the bias in H in their analysis. In [4] this is missed in the hop from the real signing oracle to Hybrid 1 in the proof of Lemma 5.3—note that the bound in [4] remains correct due to a loose analysis. In [5] the gap is missed in the game hop from G_0 to G_1 in the proof of Theorem 3.2. Moreover, this oversight is not a problem limited to [4] and [5], and it potentially affects all FS-based schemes involving rejection sampling. This includes a long list of works [2, 11–14] on lattice-based and isogeny-based signature schemes (and non-interactive proof systems) that need to be re-examined carefully.

BRIGDING THE GAP. Our second contribution is a new, fixed proof for the CMA-to-NMA reduction for FSwA in general, and for Dilithium in particular. We address both the ROM and the QROM case; in order to optimize the reduction loss, we use slightly different (lower level) hybrids for the two cases.[2]

In order to circumvent the gap (while keeping the reduction loss reasonable), we follow a rather different (but in some sense also more natural) proof strategy than [5]. We present a high-level outline of the proof (which is the same for ROM and QROM) in Sect. 3. The proof requires fine-grained control of the modifications to the random oracle, which we handle using nested hybrid arguments. In order to deal with QROM adversaries, we make use of the compressed-oracle technique [15]. However, special care has to be taken to deal with the potentially unbounded number of random oracle queries done by the signing procedure, as a result of the unbounded rejection sampling loop; moreover, this number depends on the choice of the message to be signed, which is under the adversary's control.

---

[2] We note that for simplicity, we consider ordinary unforgeability. It is not too hard to extend our results to *strong* unforgeability if the considered IDS satisfies the additional property of having computational unique-responses.

Result-wise, we note that our CMA-to-NMA reduction differs from the (flawed) one in [5] in that we can rely on a weaker variant of HVZK than in [5]. On the downside, the bound we obtain for the CMA-to-NMA reduction is worse than the one claimed in [5]. For this reason, we conclude in Sect. 7 with an analysis of the security loss incurred by our proof for concrete parameters — the analysis is close to that given in [5], but we improve the analysis of relevant entropy metrics — and confirm that the parameters in the Dilithium NIST submission [1] provide sufficient slack to accommodate the additional loss and still comfortably reach the claimed security for all considered NIST security levels (2, 3, and 5).

MACHINE-CHECKED PROOF. We mechanize the entire security proof of Dilithium in the ROM using EasyCrypt.[3] The formalization covers the fixed CMA-to-NMA reduction (Sect. 5), the correctness of an HVZK simulator for the IDS underlying Dilithium, and the reduction from NMA security to MLWE and SelfTargetMSIS. The latter two proofs largely follow the original proofs in [5] and are described in Sect. 6. These results guarantee the absence of additional gaps in the ROM proof and, due to their similarity, give high confidence that such gaps also do not exist in the QROM proof. In fact, in Sect. 3 we show that the two proofs have the same overall structure and that the only significant differences lie in how the probability of bad events is bounded in the ROM and the QROM.

The intricacy of the security proof, particularly the new CMA-to-NMA reduction, posed interesting challenges when formalizing the proof in EasyCrypt (even in the ROM). Indeed, the mechanized proof uses several tools that were not used in earlier mechanized cryptographic proofs.

- Proving an advantage bound that matches the pen-and-paper proof implies reasoning about the expected number of iterations of the unbounded rejection sampling loop in Dilithium. To do this, we make use of an expectation logic that was recently added to EasyCrypt to reason about the expected complexity of randomized programs [17]. The logic is based on the seminal work by Kozen [18].
- Some hybrid arguments in the proof modify the operation of the rejection sampling loop one iteration at the time, which means that the total number of hybrid steps is potentially infinite. In consequence, we need to prove the convergence of advantage expressions that result from putting together all the hybrid steps, as the number of hybrid steps goes to infinity.
- In addition to various minor additions to existing EasyCrypt libraries (e.g., for limits of sequences and sums, or for conditional sampling) we developed a new matrix library supporting variable-width matrices and vectors as well as block matrices.[4] For the application to Dilithium, we created a new library that refines the existing EasyCrypt support for abstract polynomial rings modulo an ideal. This was necessary to express and prove low-level properties that justify some of the optimizations in Dilithium.

---

[3] Support for QROM in EasyCrypt is still under active development [16], and the existing features do not yet allow to formally verify the QROM proof.

[4] This was done in collaboration with Oskar Goldhahn and has now been merged into the EasyCrypt standard library.

Altogether, the machine-checked security proof is about 6000 lines long. In addition, the generic library extensions also amount to several thousand lines. The EasyCrypt development, along with documentation on where to find the various theorem statements and how to automatically machine-check the proofs, is available at https://github.com/formosa-crypto/dilithium.

CONCURRENT WORK. Concurrent and independent work [19] partially overlaps with the results we present in this paper. Both our work and [19] identify the same gap in the CMA-to-NMA reduction that is present in prior works on Fiat-Shamir with aborts. Furthermore, both [19] and our work offer new, corrected CMA-to-NMA reductions (both in the ROM and QROM), where the high-level strategy to fix the previous proofs involves reprogramming the random oracle both on accepted and rejected transcripts. But then, the two works proceed differently. [19] considers an HVZK simulator for the underlying IDS that can be used simultaneously for reprogramming accepted and rejected transcripts; such a simulator is then constructed for a particular class of signatures. On the other hand, in this paper we introduce an additional hybrid step that removes the reprogrammings of the rejected transcripts, which allows us to rely on a weaker HVZK simulator that only needs to simulate accepting transcripts. Finally, beyond the above, [19] and our work include the following respective disjoint contributions: [19] identifies and discusses some further difficulties with the Fiat-Shamir with aborts paradigm, e.g., with the history-free approach from [5], and with termination and correctness in the unbounded case. On the other hand, we offer a fully mechanized security proof for Dilithium (for the classical ROM setting) using the EasyCrypt formal-verification platform.

Outline. We first explain the high-level structure of the CMA-to-NMA reduction (Sect. 3). We then show how we bound the critical game hops in the QROM proof (Sect. 4) and the mechanized ROM proof (Sect. 5). Based on this, we describe the mechanized security proof for Dilithium (Sect. 6). We conclude with a concrete analysis of the security loss for specific parameters (Sect. 7).

2 Preliminaries

We consider a signature scheme obtained by applying Fiat-Shamir with aborts (FSwA) to an interactive identification scheme (IDS) that follows the standard commit-challenge-response structure. The latter means that for a public/secret key pair (pk, sk), the scheme works in three flows: 1) the Prover generates a *first message* $(w, st) \leftarrow \mathsf{Com}(sk)$ (sometimes also called the *commitment*), and sends w to the Verifier; 2) the Verifier choses a random *challenge* $c \leftarrow C$ and sends it back to the Prover; 3) the Prover computes a *response* $z := \mathsf{Resp}(sk, w, c, st)$, which the Verifier checks using $\mathsf{Verify}(pk, w, c, z)$.[5] We write KeyGen for the algorithm that generates the key pair (pk, sk).

The Fiat-Shamir transformation turns such an IDS into a signature scheme by computing the challenge c as the hash of w and the to-be-singed message m.

---

[5] Throughout the paper, when clear from the context, we often omit the dependence on pk and sk in our notation.

We stress that by considering FSwA, we allow the IDS to abort, i.e., Resp to output $z = \bot$; in this case, the signing procedure will simply retry with a fresh new first message w until it succeeds (see Sign in Fig. 1 or 2). For a given key pair (pk, sk), we let the abort probability for w generated by Com and a random challenge c be

$$p_{(pk,sk)} := \Pr_{\substack{(w,\mathsf{st}) \leftarrow \mathsf{Com}(sk) \\ c \leftarrow C}} [\mathsf{Resp}(w, c, \mathsf{st}) = \bot].$$

The entropy of w will be an important parameter, implicitly captured by the guessing probability

$$\epsilon_{(pk,sk)} := \max_{w_0 \in W} \Pr_{(w,\mathsf{st}) \leftarrow \mathsf{Com}(sk)} [w = w_0]. \tag{1}$$

where W is the support set for IDS commitments. Finally, we require the IDS to satisfy the following honest-verifier zero-knowledge variant, which admits to simulate *accepted* transcripts.[6]

Definition 1. (Accepting Honest-verifier Zero-knowledge) An IDS as above is said to be acHVZK with simulation error ζ_{zk} if there exists a poly-time algorithm ZKSim that, when given the public key pk, outputs (w, c, z) with a distribution that has statistical distance at most ζ_{zk} from the distribution of a transcript (w, c, z) produced by an honest execution of the protocol *conditioned on $z \neq \bot$*.

We note that this is a different flavor of HVZK than naHVZK considered in [5], and it is weaker (at least in spirit). In [5] the simulator must match the full distribution of traces, which means that a (strict or expected) poly-time naHVZK simulator implies an *expected* poly-time simulator as we require it: the acHVZK simulator repeatedly runs the naHVZK simulator until a good trace is generated. Whether the acHVZK simulator is strict or expected poly-time will determine whether we require the computational hardness assumption to hold for strict or expected poly-time algorithms.[7] E.g., the scheme considered in [4] admits a strict poly-time acHVZK simulator, while for Dilithium we only know how to simulate accepted transcripts in expected poly-time.

3   Outline of the Proof

In this section, we provide a detailed account of how we closed the gap in the proof described in the introduction. We first give some intuition about the general proof strategy, and we pinpoint the main two technical steps of the proof, i.e., we isolate two quantities (corresponding to two distinguishing advantages for some game hops) that remain to be bounded. We then discuss the challenges

---

[6] For simplicity, and since this is sufficient for out main application (Dilithium), we consider statistical indistinguishability of the simulated transcript. Our results extend to a computational variant in the obvious way.

[7] Also note that, at the cost of an increased simulation error, an expected poly-time simulator can always be turned into a strict poly-time one by cutting the runtime.

in bounding these quantities, and we provide some intuition on how we solve them. The rigorous analyses of these quantities are then done in subsequent sections, separately for the QROM and the mechanized ROM proof.

Below, we consider an IDS as considered above, which satisfies Definition 1, and the goal is to show that EF-NMA security implies EF-CMA security for the signature scheme that is obtained from the IDS via FSwA.[8]

3.1 Proof Skeleton

We follow the common approach, which is to show that for any CMA attacker $\mathcal{A}^{\mathsf{Sign},H}$, which has access to a signing oracle Sign and the random oracle H, one can replace the signing oracle Sign by an oracle Sim that does not have the secret key, but instead produces a valid transcript by using the acHVZK-simulator and reprograms H to be consistent with the transcript (see the description of Sim in Fig. 2 below). Turning $\mathcal{A}^{\mathsf{Sim},H}$ into an NMA attacker $\mathcal{B}^H$ that does not ask signature queries (and does not reprogram H and produces forgeries consistent with H) is then a standard argument (discussed in more detail further down).

In order to show that replacing Sign by Sim has little effect, we introduce two hybrid oracles Prog and Trans, as specified in Fig. 2, and we show that

$$\mathcal{A}^{\mathsf{Sign},H} \approx \mathcal{A}^{\mathsf{Prog},H} \approx \mathcal{A}^{\mathsf{Trans},H} \approx \mathcal{A}^{\mathsf{Sim},H} .$$

The oracle Prog samples transcripts (w, c, z) of the IDS for randomly chosen challenges c and then reprograms H consistently (denoted $H(w, m) := c \leftarrow C$), both for rejected and accepted transcripts. We emphasize that, since the reprogramming happens independently of whether the transcript is accepted or not, there is no dependency between w and c, circumventing the issue in [5]. Intuitively, in order to notice the difference, $\mathcal{A}$ must have queried H on one of the points (w, m) before H gets reprogrammed on it; this is unlikely if w has high entropy.

The oracle Trans is as Prog, except that it only reprograms H on the final accepted transcript. This modification to the game introduces a bias in H towards accepting transcripts. However, this should remain unnoticed unless $\mathcal{A}$ queries such a pair (w, m) where Trans reprograms H yet Prog does not. Because w is chosen with high-entropy and not revealed to $\mathcal{A}$, this is unlikely to happen.

Finally, closeness of $\mathcal{A}^{\mathsf{Trans},H}$ and $\mathcal{A}^{\mathsf{Sim},H}$ follows by definition of the acHVZK property: for each of the calls $\mathcal{A}$ makes to Trans, replacing it by a call to Sim changes the output distribution of $\mathcal{A}$ by at most ζ_{zk}.

The key part of the proof is bounding the loss incurred by the hops to $\mathcal{A}^{\mathsf{Prog},H}$ and $\mathcal{A}^{\mathsf{Trans},H}$, which we will do separately for the QROM proof (Sect. 4) and the mechanized ROM proof (Sect. 5). Here, we rigorously define those quantities and explain the arguments that are common to both proofs.

For any $0 \leqslant \epsilon$ and $p < 1$, for any key pair (pk, sk) with $p_{(pk,sk)} \leqslant p$ and $\epsilon_{(pk,sk)} \leqslant \epsilon$, and for any choice of $q_S, q_H \in \mathbb{N}$, let the quantities $\Delta_{p,\epsilon}^{\mathsf{Sign} \rightarrow \mathsf{Prog}}(q_S, q_H)$

---

[8] The acronym EF-NMA (resp. EF-CMA) stands for existential unforgeability against no (resp. chosen) message attacks.

Sign(m):
1: **repeat**
2:     $(w, \mathsf{st}) \leftarrow \mathsf{Com}(sk)$
3:     $c := H(w, m)$
4:     $z := \mathsf{Resp}(w, c, \mathsf{st})$
5: **until** $z \neq \perp$
6: **return** (w, z)

Prog(m):
1: **repeat**
2:     $(w, \mathsf{st}) \leftarrow \mathsf{Com}(sk)$
3:     $H(w, m) := c \leftarrow C$
4:     $z := \mathsf{Resp}(w, c, \mathsf{st})$
5: **until** $z \neq \perp$
6: **return** (w, z)

Trans(m):
1: **repeat**
2:     $(w, \mathsf{st}) \leftarrow \mathsf{Com}(sk)$
3:     $c \leftarrow C$
4:     $z := \mathsf{Resp}(w, c, \mathsf{st})$
5: **until** $z \neq \perp$
6: $H(w, m) := c$
7: **return** (w, z)

Sim(m):
1: $(w, c, z) \leftarrow \mathsf{ZKSim}(pk)$
2: $H(w, m) := c$
3: **return** (w, z)

Fig. 2. Overview of the different oracles used for the hybrid proof.

and $\Delta^{\mathsf{Prog} \to \mathsf{Trans}}_{p,\epsilon}(q_S, q_H)$ be monotone in p and in ϵ, bounded from above by 1, and so that

$$\Delta^{\mathsf{Sign} \to \mathsf{Prog}}_{p,\epsilon}(q_S, q_H) \geq \left| \Pr\left[1 \leftarrow \mathcal{A}^{\mathsf{Sign}, H}\right] - \Pr\left[1 \leftarrow \mathcal{A}^{\mathsf{Prog}, H}\right] \right| \qquad \text{and}$$

$$\Delta^{\mathsf{Prog} \to \mathsf{Trans}}_{p,\epsilon}(q_S, q_H) \geq \left| \Pr\left[1 \leftarrow \mathcal{A}^{\mathsf{Prog}, H}\right] - \Pr\left[1 \leftarrow \mathcal{A}^{\mathsf{Trans}, H}\right] \right|$$

for any (classical or quantum) oracle algorithm $\mathcal{A}^{\mathsf{Sign}, H}$ that makes at most q_S classical calls to Sign and q_H (classical or quantum) calls to the random oracle H, and outputs a single bit at the end. We take it as understood here that Sign uses the considered fixed secret key sk for the public key pk given to $\mathcal{A}$, and the same for Prog and Trans.

Having control over these two parameters, we obtain the desired CMA-to-NMA reduction via the following result. We note that the statement holds both for *classical* and *quantum* $\mathcal{A}$, where the latter can make quantum queries to H (but still only classical queries to Sign), with $\mathcal{B}$ then also being classical or quantum, respectively. In order to deal with unlikely "bad" keys that give rise to values of $p_{(pk,sk)}$ and $\epsilon_{(pk,sk)}$ close to 1, which we need to avoid, the formal statement has a precondition that bounds these two quantities (in some ways) except with small probability.

Lemma 1. *Let $\epsilon \geq 0$ and $p < 1$, and let $\delta := \Pr[\neg \Gamma]$ for an event Γ for which*

$$\Pr[p_{(pk,sk)} \leq p \wedge \epsilon_{(pk,sk)} \leq \epsilon \mid \Gamma] = 1 \qquad (2)$$

where the randomness is over $(pk, sk) \leftarrow \mathsf{KeyGen}$. Let $\mathcal{A}^{\mathsf{Sign}, H}$ be a CMA attacker against $\mathsf{FSwA}[\mathsf{ID}, H]$ that makes q_S queries to the signing oracle Sign and q_H queries to the random oracle H. Then, there exists an NMA attacker $\mathcal{B}^H$ against $\mathsf{FSwA}[\mathsf{ID}, H]$ so that

$$\mathsf{Adv}^{\mathsf{EF\text{-}CMA}}(\mathcal{A}) \leq \mathsf{Adv}^{\mathsf{EF\text{-}NMA}}(\mathcal{B})$$
$$+ q_S \zeta_{zk} + \Delta^{\mathsf{Sign} \to \mathsf{Prog}}_{p,\epsilon}(q_S, q_H + 1) + \Delta^{\mathsf{Prog} \to \mathsf{Trans}}_{p,\epsilon}(q_S, q_H + 1) + \delta,$$

and with running time $\mathsf{TIME}(\mathcal{B}^H) \approx \mathsf{TIME}(\mathcal{A}) + q_S \mathsf{TIME}(\mathsf{ZKSim})$. *If* $\Delta_{p,\epsilon}^{\mathsf{Sign} \to \mathsf{Prog}}$
and $\Delta_{p,\epsilon}^{\mathsf{Prog} \to \mathsf{Trans}}$ *are concave as functions in* ϵ, *then (2) can be relaxed to*

$$\mathbb{E}[\epsilon_{(pk,sk)}|\Gamma] \leqslant \epsilon \qquad and \qquad \Pr[p_{(pk,sk)} \leqslant p \,|\, \Gamma] = 1\,.$$

See full version [20, Proof of Lemma 1] for the proof.

3.2 Challenges, and How We Solve Them

The challenges that arise in bounding $\Delta_{p,\epsilon}^{\mathsf{Sign} \to \mathsf{Prog}}$ and $\Delta_{p,\epsilon}^{\mathsf{Prog} \to \mathsf{Trans}}$ — and also our solutions — apply independently of whether $\mathcal{A}$ is classical or quantum. The case of a classical $\mathcal{A}$ is conceptually simpler in that we can see the random oracle as using standard lazy sampling and the elementary steps in the proof are argued using up-to-bad reasoning: we define a series of hybrids, where two consecutive games are identical until a *bad* event is triggered. This bad event typically corresponds to the adversary being able to observe a change in the distribution of a single value sampled by the random oracle. The proof then follows from proving an upper-bound on the probability of each bad event occurring and aggregating these bounds into a global advantage term.

In the case of a quantum $\mathcal{A}$, we resort to the compressed oracle technique, which can be understood as a quantum version of lazy sampling. In this setting, a *bad* event as above may then be defined via a *measurement* (we expand on this analogy in Sect. 4). Such a measurement typically disturbs the state, and thus the continuation of the experiment. However, thanks to the gentle-measurement lemma, if the probability of the event occurring is small (which follows from pretty much the same argument as classically) we immediately know that this disturbance is small as well. Thus, conceptually, there is no big difference in the argument for a classical and for a quantum $\mathcal{A}$. However, and interestingly, it turns out that in order to optimize the respective bounds on $\Delta_{p,\epsilon}^{\mathsf{Prog} \to \mathsf{Trans}}$, we have to use slightly different approaches in the ROM and in the QROM proofs.

We outline the proofs of the two non trivial hops next.

THE 'PROGRAM ALWAYS' GAME HOP.. To bound $\Delta_{p,\epsilon}^{\mathsf{Sign} \to \mathsf{Prog}}$, the game hop from $\mathcal{A}^{\mathsf{Sign},H}$ to $\mathcal{A}^{\mathsf{Prog},H}$ is broken down into multiple steps and substeps. At the top level, the q_S calls to Sign are replaced by calls to Prog *one by one*. For each such replacement, the challenge lies in the fact that there is no fixed upper bound on the number of loop iterations executed by the modified Sign oracle query, and thus on the number of reprogrammings that must be dealt with. Even worse, per-se, $\mathcal{A}$ could potentially affect the number of loop iterations by choosing m dependent on responses to prior H-queries. To deal with this, for each replacement of Sign by Prog, we do the replacement gradually by replacing the loop body in the query to Sign by the content of the loop body in Prog *one iteration at a time*. I.e., we consider the hybrid Hyb^k, which programs $H(w,m)$ to a fresh random c for the first k iterations of the loop and sets $c := H(w,m)$ for the remaining ones (see Fig. 3, middle). Thus, $\mathsf{Hyb}^0 = \mathsf{Sign}$ and $\mathsf{Hyb}^\infty = \mathsf{Prog}$.

An important observation at this point is that we can exploit that the probability of remaining in the loop becomes exponentially smaller for increasing k — i.e., Hyb^k and Hyb^{k+1} become harder to distinguish — because the iteration

Sign(m):
1: **repeat**
2:   $(w, \mathsf{st}) \leftarrow \mathsf{Com}(sk)$
3:   $c := H(w, m)$
4:   $z := \mathsf{Resp}(w, c, \mathsf{st})$
5: **until** $z \neq \bot$
6: **return** (w, z)

Hyb^k(m):
1: $i := 0$
2: **repeat**
3:   $(w, \mathsf{st}) \leftarrow \mathsf{Com}(sk)$
4:   **if** $i < k$ **then**
5:     $H(w, m) := c \leftarrow C$
6:   **else**
7:     $c := H(w, m)$
8:   $z := \mathsf{Resp}(w, c, \mathsf{st})$
9:   $i := i + 1$
10: **until** $z \neq \bot$
11: **return** (w, z)

Prog(m):
1: **repeat**
2:   $(w, \mathsf{st}) \leftarrow \mathsf{Com}(sk)$
3:   $H(w, m) := c \leftarrow C$
4:   $z := \mathsf{Resp}(w, c, \mathsf{st})$
5: **until** $z \neq \bot$
6: **return** (w, z)

Fig. 3. The oracles Sign (left) and Prog (right), and Hyb^k in-between (middle).

where they could differ is less likely to be reached. In particular, the probability that round k (counting from 0) is reached, which is the round where Hyb^k and Hyb^{k+1} differ, is p^k — we stress that we crucially exploit here that in the previous rounds the challenge c was chosen at random (and not computed via H); this ensures that $\mathcal{A}$ cannot influence this probability by choosing m one or another way. Furthermore, if this round is reached then $\mathcal{A}$ can notice the difference between the two hybrids only if it has made a prior H-query to the point (w, m) where Hyb^{k+1} reprograms H while Hyb^k does not.[9] However, since w has high min-entropy, this is unlikely to have occurred. Altogether, one replacement of Sign by Prog thus incurs an error that is bounded by an infinite geometric series, for which there is the high-school closed formula. Multiplying the result with q_S, to account for the q_S times we replace Sign by Prog, we then get the desired bound on $\Delta_{p,\epsilon}^{\mathsf{Sign} \to \mathsf{Prog}}$.

The quantum case is slightly trickier in that we cannot directly "inspect" prior H-queries to see if the point (w, m), where Hyb^{k+1} reprograms H while Hyb^k does not, has been queried before by $\mathcal{A}$. However, one can mimic this line of reasoning using the compressed oracle technique and doing a certain measurement, which is likely to give the desired outcome again due to the high entropy of w; furthermore, the gentle measurement lemma then ensures that the measurement introduces little disturbance. The quantitative difference to the classical case is that conditioned on reaching iteration k, the distinguishing advantage (essentially) gets a square-root, but of course the probability of reaching that iteration remains to be p^k, and so we end up with a similar, though slightly worse, infinite geometric series.

THE 'PROGRAM ONCE' GAME HOP. The bounding of $\Delta_{p,\epsilon}^{\mathsf{Prog} \to \mathsf{Trans}}$ is handled differently in the QROM and the ROM, in order to optimize the respective bounds. For the classical proof, the structure of the hybrids is the same as in the previous hop, in that we replace Prog by Trans *one by one*, and for each replacement we do it gradually *one iteration at a time*. This will then give rise to a similar infinite geometric series. The main difference to before is that if the crucial iteration

---

[9] Or, if H got reprogrammed on (m, w) already during a prior call to Prog.

(where one hybrid reprograms H at the point (m, w) and the other does not) is reached, then the reasoning for why the distinguishing advantage is small is different. Here, we rely on the fact that in order to notice the difference, $\mathcal{A}$ must make a future H-query to (m, w), but since w has high min-entropy *and* is not revealed to $\mathcal{A}$, this is unlikely to happen.

In principle, a similar strategy can be applied in the QROM setting. However, the "inspection" of future H-queries will require a measurement for every future H-query, which will lead to a unnecessarily large loss. Instead, we will do a slight detour involving a "clone" H' of H, and a variant of Prog (see Fig. 4) that also reprograms H', but only on the accepted (m, w), and then the hybrid works by replacing $\mathcal{A}$'s calls to H by calls to H' one by one.

The detailed bounds and proofs are given in Sects. 4 and 5.

4 Proof in the Quantum Random Oracle Model

Here, we provide the technical details of the CMA-to-NMA reduction for the considered signature scheme obtained via Fiat-Shamir with aborts, in the QROM. As explained in Sect. 3, this boils down to bounding $\Delta_{p,\epsilon}^{\text{Sign}\to\text{Prog}}$ and $\Delta_{p,\epsilon}^{\text{Prog}\to\text{Trans}}$, and applying Lemma 1.

We start by introducing some notation and recalling a couple of elementary concepts in the context of quantum information (Sect. 4.1), and by introducing an abstract distance measure for oracles (Def. 2 in Sect. 4.2) that captures the indistinguishability of two oracles in the QROM.

4.1 Preliminaries

Let ρ_{E} be a density operator. We can speak of a (classical) event Γ, if ρ_{E} decomposes into $\rho_{\mathsf{E}} = \Pr[\Gamma]\rho_{\mathsf{E}|\Gamma} + \Pr[\neg\Gamma]\rho_{\mathsf{E}|\neg\Gamma}$ for probabilities $\Pr[\Gamma]$ and $\Pr[\neg\Gamma]$ that add up to 1, and density operators $\rho_{\mathsf{E}|\Gamma}$ and $\rho_{\mathsf{E}|\neg\Gamma}$. In typical cases ρ_{E} is part of a bigger state $\rho_{X\mathsf{E}}$, where X is classical, and Γ is then obtained by requiring X to satisfy some property.

We will also consider events that are obtained by applying a measurement. Let ρ_{E} be a density operator and $\{P_\Gamma, P_{\neg\Gamma}\}$ a binary projective measurement, labeled by Γ and $\neg\Gamma$. By default, we then write Γ (and correspondingly for $\neg\Gamma$) for the event of observing the measurement outcome associated with P, i.e., $\Pr[\Gamma] = \text{tr}(P_\Gamma\rho_{\mathsf{E}})$, and we let $\tilde{\rho}_{\mathsf{E}|\Gamma} = \frac{1}{\Pr[\Gamma]}P_\Gamma\rho_{\mathsf{E}}P_\Gamma$ be the corresponding post-measurement state.

We use $\delta(\rho_{\mathsf{E}}, \rho_{\mathsf{E}'}) := \frac{1}{2}\|\rho_{\mathsf{E}} - \rho_{\mathsf{E}'}\|_1$ to denote the *trace distance* between density operators ρ_{E} and $\rho_{\mathsf{E}'}$. The trace distance forms an upper bound to the advantage of any quantum algorithm in distinguishing ρ_{E} from $\rho_{\mathsf{E}'}$.

Lemma 2 (Gentle Measurement Lemma). *Let ρ_{E} be a density operator and $\{P_\Gamma, P_{\neg\Gamma}\}$ a binary projective measurement. Then $\delta(\rho_{\mathsf{E}}, \tilde{\rho}_{\mathsf{E}|\Gamma}) \leqslant \sqrt{\Pr[\neg\Gamma]}$.*

4.2 Setting Up the Stage

As explained in Sect. 3, in order to control $\Delta_{p,\epsilon}^{\text{Sign}\to\text{Prog}}$ and $\Delta_{p,\epsilon}^{\text{Prog}\to\text{Trans}}$, we consider a hybrid argument where we repeatedly replace *one* oracle call to a certain oracle by another one. To smoothen the exposition, we introduce first an abstraction of this core problem, together with a metric that captures the figure of merit.

Replacing One Oracle by Another. We consider a quantum oracle algorithm $\mathcal{A}^{H,O_1,\ldots,O_r,\mathcal{O}}$ that makes oracle calls to a random function H (i.e., a random oracle) and to arbitrary but specified oracles $O_1,\ldots,O_r$, and it makes *one* call to an *unspecified* oracle $\mathcal{O}$ (though with a specified set $\mathcal{M}$ of possible inputs), and the goal will be to show that for two particular specifications O and O', the algorithm $\mathcal{A}$ will not notice the difference whether $\mathcal{O}$ is instantiated with O or with O', i.e., that $\Pr\left[1 \leftarrow \mathcal{A}^{H,O_1,\ldots,O_r,O}\right] \approx \Pr\left[1 \leftarrow \mathcal{A}^{H,O_1,\ldots,O_r,O'}\right]$.

Considering that $\mathcal{A}$ is a quantum algorithm, we allow the queries to the random oracle H to be in superposition; for the purpose of this work, the queries to all the other oracles are classical though.

Furthermore, we note that we allow the oracle instantiations $O_1,\ldots,O_r$, as well as O and O', to also have oracle (read) access to H, and even to have oracle *write* access, i.e., they may *reprogram* H at a chosen point to a chosen value. Formally, $O_1,\ldots,O_r,O,O'$ are classical, stateless, possibly randomized oracle algorithms, with oracle *read* and *write* access to H.[10]

Closeness of Oracles. In order to show indistinguishability of answering $\mathcal{A}$'s $\mathcal{O}$-query by O or O', it is sufficient to show that the output produced by $O(m)$ or $O'(m)$, together with H (which may also look different in one and the other case, due to possible different reprogramming), look alike to $\mathcal{A}$.

Using the compressed oracle technique, we can consider H to be obtained by measuring a certain quantum system D (the "compressed oracle"); namely, $H(x)$ can be obtained by measuring register D_x of D in the computational basis. Indeed the technique ensures existence of a system D, the state of which evolves (and gets entangled) upon random-oracle (superposition) queries, and that satisfies:

1. The random-oracle queries commute with measuring any of the registers of D in the computational basis. This includes reprogramming queries, which, on input (x,y) replaces the state of register D_x by $|y\rangle$.
2. After q (read or write) random-oracle queries, measuring all of D in the Fourier basis produces a function table that is $\hat{0}$ (sometimes denoted $\perp$) everywhere, except for up to q points. In particular, measuring all of D before any random-oracle query in the computational basis produces a uniformly random function (table) H.

The above considerations motivate to define the (parameterized) following metric, which then gives rise to the subsequent Theorem 1.

Definition 2. *For oracle instantiations O and O' of $\mathcal{O}$, and for $q \in \mathbb{N}$,*

$$d_q(O,O') := \max_{m,\rho_{\mathsf{DE}}} \delta\left(\rho_{O(m)\mathsf{HE}}, \rho_{O'(m)\mathsf{HE}}\right)$$

---

[10] We may actually allow $O_1,\ldots,O_r$, to be stateful, all having access to the same state, but for the propose of "switching" from O to O' for any $\mathcal{A}$, this state can always be maintained and provided by $\mathcal{A}$.

where the maximum is over all possible $m \in \mathcal{M}$ and over all states ρ_{DE} with the property that D behaves as in Item 2. above (for the considered q) upon measuring in the Fourier basis; furthermore, $\rho_{O(m)\mathsf{HE}}$ is obtained from m and ρ_{DE} by running O on input m, and by measuring all of D in the computational basis to obtain H, and the same for $\rho_{O'(m)\mathsf{HE}}$.

It is not too hard to argue that the maximum is indeed attained in the definition of d_q. Furthermore, $q' \geqslant q \Rightarrow d_{q'} \geqslant d_q$, and d_q satisfies the triangle inequality.

To help to understand the intuition for this metric, we point out that in the corresponding classical counter part, we would maximize over all query inputs m and over all possible lazy-sampled databases D that have at most q entries, and then compare the respective distributions of $(O(m), H)$ and $(O'(m), H)$, obtained by running O, respectively O', on m, and obtaining H by filling in all the empty places in (the possibly reprogrammed) database D by random values.

The following is straightforward to prove.

Theorem 1. *Consider a quantum oracle algorithm $\mathcal{A}^{H,O_1,\ldots,O_r,\mathcal{O}}$ for arbitrary but fixed oracle instantiations $O_1, \ldots, O_r$, and let O and O' be two possible instantiations for $\mathcal{O}$, as specified above. Recall that $\mathcal{A}$ is restricted to making one query to $\mathcal{O}$. Let Q be the number of oracle calls to H, made by $\mathcal{A}$ and $O_1, \ldots, O_r$, prior to $\mathcal{A}$'s oracle call to $\mathcal{O}$.[11] Then,*

$$\left| \Pr\left[1 \leftarrow \mathcal{A}^{H,O_1,\ldots,O_r,O}\right] - \Pr\left[1 \leftarrow \mathcal{A}^{H,O_1,\ldots,O_r,O'}\right] \right| \leqslant \mathbb{E}_Q[d_Q(O,O')].$$

As a toy example application, consider a quantum oracle algorithm $\mathcal{A}^{H,\mathcal{O}}$ that makes at most q_H queries to a random oracle H and $q_{\mathcal{O}}$ queries to a non-instantiated oracle $\mathcal{O}$. Let us assume that O and O' are instantiations of $\mathcal{O}$ that make no queries to H, and it holds that $d_q(O, O') \leqslant q_H \varepsilon$ for any q. Then, by repeated application of Theorem 1 in order to switch from O to O' one by one, we immediately obtain that $\left| \Pr\left[1 \leftarrow \mathcal{A}^{H,O}\right] - \Pr\left[1 \leftarrow \mathcal{A}^{H,O'}\right] \right| \leqslant q_H q_{\mathcal{O}} \varepsilon$.

Typical Strategies. There are two generic approaches to prove that $d_q(O, O')$ is small:

Strategy 1. Show the existence of a (classical) event Γ (Γ for "good" event) with the property that, for any m and ρ_{DE}, (1) the event Γ has the same probability $\Pr[\Gamma]$ of occurrence when running O and O', and (2) O and O' act identically conditioned on Γ, and thus the two states $\rho_{O(m)\mathsf{HE}|\Gamma}$ and $\rho_{O'(m)\mathsf{HE}|\Gamma}$ are identical. Indeed, in that case, by basic properties of the trace distance,

$$\delta\left(\rho_{O(m)\mathsf{HE}}, \rho_{O'(m)\mathsf{HE}}\right) \leqslant \Pr[\Gamma]\delta(\rho_{O(m)\mathsf{HE}|\Gamma}, \rho_{O'(m)\mathsf{HE}|\Gamma})$$
$$+ \Pr[\neg\Gamma]\delta(\rho_{O(m)\mathsf{HE}|\neg\Gamma}, \rho_{O'(m)\mathsf{HE}|\neg\Gamma}) \qquad (3)$$
$$\leqslant \Pr[\neg\Gamma]. \qquad (4)$$

---

[11] This includes calls to reprogram H.

Strategy 2. Show the existence of a binary projective measurement $\{P_\Gamma, P_{\neg\Gamma}\}$ on D and the internal state of the respective oracles, so that when applied during the run of the oracle, similarly to above, (i) the event Γ (of observing the measurement outcome associated with P_Γ) has the same probability $\Pr[\Gamma]$ of occurrence when running O and O', and (ii) O and O' act identically conditioned on Γ, and thus the two states $\tilde\rho_{O(m)HE|\Gamma}$ and $\tilde\rho_{O'(m)HE|\Gamma}$ are identical. Indeed, in that case, by triangle inequality,

$$\delta\big(\rho_{O(m)HE}, \rho_{O'(m)HE}\big) \leqslant \delta(\rho_{O(m)HE}, \tilde\rho_{O(m)HE|\Gamma})$$
$$+ \delta(\tilde\rho_{O(m)HE|\Gamma}, \tilde\rho_{O'(m)HE|\Gamma})$$
$$+ \delta(\tilde\rho_{O'(m)HE|\Gamma}, \rho_{O(m)HE}) \tag{5}$$
$$\leqslant 2\sqrt{\Pr[\neg\Gamma]} \tag{6}$$

where the final inequality is by applying the gentle measurement lemma twice.

This extends in the obvious way to a *classically-controlled* measurement, i.e., to a measurement that is only applied if a particular classical bit b is set, and such that (o) the classical bit b is set with the same probability when running O and O', (i) conditioned on b being set, the event Γ has the same probability $\Pr[\Gamma]$ of occurrence when running O and O', and (ii) O and O' act identically conditioned on b not being set, or conditioned on b set and Γ. The above bound then becomes

$$\delta\big(\rho_{O(m)HE}, \rho_{O'(m)HE}\big) \leqslant 2\Pr[b=1]\sqrt{\Pr[\neg\Gamma|b=1]}. \tag{7}$$

4.3 Core of the Proof

We need to bound the quantities $\Delta_{p,\epsilon}^{\mathsf{Sign}\to\mathsf{Prog}}(q_S, q_H)$ and $\Delta_{p,\epsilon}^{\mathsf{Prog}\to\mathsf{Trans}}(q_S, q_H)$. For that purpose, we consider a fixed key (pk, sk) for which $p_{(pk,sk)} \leqslant p$ and $\epsilon_{(pk,sk)} \leqslant \epsilon$, and we consider a quantum oracle algorithm $\mathcal{A}$ with a binary output, and which makes q_S classical queries to Sign and q_H quantum queries to the random oracle H. Our goal then is to bound the respective closeness of $\mathcal{A}^{\mathsf{Sign},H}$ and $\mathcal{A}^{\mathsf{Prog},H}$ and of $\mathcal{A}^{\mathsf{Prog},H}$ and $\mathcal{A}^{\mathsf{Trans},H}$; we do this below.

Closeness of $\mathcal{A}^{\mathsf{Sign},H}$ and $\mathcal{A}^{\mathsf{Prog},H}$. For the purpose of showing closeness of Sign and Prog, we introduce the following hybrid oracles. For every $k \in \mathbb{N}$, the oracle Hyb^k replaces the first k evaluations $c := H(w, m)$ in the loop of Sign to freshly reprogramming $H(w, m) := c \leftarrow C$, with the convention that $\mathsf{Hyb}^0 := \mathsf{Sign}$. In other words, Hyb^k acts like Prog for the first k iterations of the loop, and then like Sign for the remaining ones (if it is still looping then).

Lemma 3. $d_q(\mathsf{Hyb}^{k-1}, \mathsf{Hyb}^k) \leqslant 2p^{k-1}\sqrt{(q+k)\epsilon}$ *for every* $k \geqslant 1$.

The claim here is closely related to the *adaptive reprogramming* in [21]; however, there are some subtle technical differences (with the crucial reprogramming step being reached only with a certain probability, and with prior reprogrammings taking place). For this reason, and for consistency with the other parts of the proof, we prove Lemma 3 from scratch.

Proof. The oracle Hyb^{k-1} and Hyb^k only differ at the kth iteration, in which the former performs an evaluation $c := H(w, m)$, while the latter performs a fresh reprogramming $H(w, m) := c \leftarrow C$. We call this the crucial iteration.

We follow Strategy 2 and consider a binary projective measurement performed right before c is determined in the crucial iteration, classically controlled by the bit b that is set if the crucial iteration is executed (i.e., the loop has not stopped before). The measurement checks whether or not the sampled w in the crucial iteration is such that measuring $\mathsf{D}_{(w,m)}$ in the Fourier basis produces $\hat{0}$, and Γ is satisfied if this is the case (i.e., if (w, m) is not recorded in the database). Recall that in case the loop terminates prior to the crucial iteration, no measurement is performed.

Clearly, (o) b is set with the same probability when running Hyb^{k-1} and Hyb^k, (i) if the crucial iteration is reached then $\Pr[\Gamma]$ is the same when running Hyb^{k-1} and Hyb^k, and (ii) if the crucial iteration is reached and Γ is satisfied then, in both cases, c is uniformly random and $H(w, m)$ becomes c — in case of Hyb^k by construction, and in case of Hyb^{k-1} since c is then obtained by measuring the state $|\hat{0}\rangle$ of $\mathsf{D}_{(a,m)}$ in the computational basis — and thus Hyb^{k-1} and Hyb^k act identically. Hyb^{k-1} and Hyb^k obviously also behave the same if the crucial iteration is not reached. Thus, by Inequality (7), $d_q(\mathsf{Hyb}^{k-1}, \mathsf{Hyb}^k) \leq 2\Pr[b = 1]\sqrt{\Pr[\neg\Gamma|b=1]}$. It remains to control this latter term.

For $b = 1$ to happen, the loop must have entered the kth iteration, which happens with probability $\Pr[b = 1] = p^{k-1}$ because every previous transcript is freshly sampled.

Conditioned on $b = 1$ where the loop enters the kth iteration, the database records no more than $q + k$ non-$\hat{0}$ entries, and a is freshly sampled, and thus by Eq. (1) and union bound, we obtain $\Pr[\neg\Gamma|b = 1] \leq (q + k)\epsilon$. This concludes the proof. $\qquad\square$

Now applying Lemma 3 k times, together with the triangle inequality for d_q we obtain

$$d_q(\mathsf{Sign}, \mathsf{Hyb}^k) \leq \sum_{1 \leq i \leq k} 2p^{i-1}\sqrt{(q+i)\epsilon} \leq \frac{2\sqrt{\epsilon}}{1-p}(1-p)\sum_{i \geq 1} p^{i-1}\sqrt{(q+i)}$$

$$\leq \frac{2\sqrt{\epsilon}}{1-p}\sqrt{(1-p)\sum_{i \geq 1} p^{i-1}q + (1-p)\sum_{i \geq 1} p^{i-1}i} \leq \frac{2\sqrt{\epsilon}}{1-p}\sqrt{q + \frac{1}{(1-p)}}, \quad (8)$$

where the third inequality is Jensen's inequality (exploiting that, by the standard formula for a geometric series, $(1 - p)\sum_i p^{i-1} = 1$), and the last one follows by again applying the standard formula for a geometric series (noting that the second term is the derivative of a geometric series).

Next, we argue closeness of Hyb^k to Prog. Recall that Prog is obtained from Sign by replacing every evaluation $c := H(w, m)$ in the loop to a fresh reprogramming $H(w, m) := c \leftarrow C$, whereas Hyb^k does so only for the first k iterations.

Lemma 4. $d_q(\mathsf{Hyb}^k, \mathsf{Prog}) \leq p^k$ for every $k \in \mathbb{N}$.

Proof. We follow Strategy 1 and define the good event Γ where a non-abort response $z \neq \perp$ is output within the first k iterations in a call to $\mathsf{Hyb}^k/\mathsf{Prog}$. Indeed, (i) the probability $\Pr[\neg\Gamma]$ depends only on the first k iterations, hence it is the same in both oracles, and (ii) conditioned on Γ, the loop terminates within k iterations, so that both oracles behave identically. Since within each iteration the transcript (w, c, z) is freshly sampled, the probability that all k iterations yield $z = \perp$ is bounded by $\Pr[\neg\Gamma] \leqslant p^k$. Thus, by Inequality (4) we conclude that $d_q(\mathsf{Hyb}^k, \mathsf{Prog}) \leqslant \Pr[\neg\Gamma] \leqslant p^k$. $\qquad\square$

By combining Inequality (8) and Lemma 4, and letting k go to infinity, we obtain

$$d_q(\mathsf{Sign}, \mathsf{Prog}) \leqslant \frac{2\sqrt{\epsilon}}{1 - p} \sqrt{q + \frac{1}{1 - p}}.$$

Replacing every invocation of Sign in $\mathcal{A}^{\mathsf{Sign}, H}$ by Prog from left to right, and further taking into account that the expected number of read/write queries to H prior to every replacement is $\mathbb{E}[Q] \leqslant q_H + (q_S - 1)/(1 - p)$, we apply Theorem 1 q_S times and obtain

$$\left| \Pr\left[1 \leftarrow \mathcal{A}^{\mathsf{Sign}, H}\right] - \Pr\left[1 \leftarrow \mathcal{A}^{\mathsf{Prog}, H}\right] \right| \leqslant q_S \cdot \mathbb{E}_Q[d_Q(\mathsf{Sign}, \mathsf{Prog})]$$

$$\leqslant q_S \cdot \mathbb{E}_Q\left[\frac{2\sqrt{\epsilon}}{1 - p}\sqrt{Q + \frac{1}{1 - p}}\right] \leqslant \frac{2q_S\sqrt{\epsilon}}{1 - p}\sqrt{\mathbb{E}_Q[Q] + \frac{1}{1 - p}}$$

$$\leqslant \frac{2q_S\sqrt{\epsilon}}{1 - p}\sqrt{q_H + \frac{q_S}{1 - p}},$$

where the third inequality is by Jensen's inequality. This proves Corollary 1.

Corollary 1. $\left|\Pr\left[1 \leftarrow \mathcal{A}^{\mathsf{Sign}, H}\right] - \Pr\left[1 \leftarrow \mathcal{A}^{\mathsf{Prog}, H}\right]\right| \leqslant \frac{2q_S\sqrt{\epsilon}}{1-p}\sqrt{q_H + \frac{q_S}{1-p}}.$

Closeness of $\mathcal{A}^{\mathsf{Prog}, H}$ and $\mathcal{A}^{\mathsf{Trans}, H}$. For the purpose of showing closeness of $\mathcal{A}^{\mathsf{Prog}, H}$ and $\mathcal{A}^{\mathsf{Trans}, H}$, we introduce a second instantiation H' of the random oracle, which is set to be equal to H at the beginning, and we modify Prog to Prog' so as to also reprogram H', but only on the accepted transcript (see Fig. 4 middle). Looking ahead, we notice that this detour via Prog' and H' is not done in the ROM proof; there, we have a (more) direct argument to go from $\mathcal{A}^{\mathsf{Prog}, H}$ to $\mathcal{A}^{\mathsf{Trans}, H}$, very similar to the one going from $\mathcal{A}^{\mathsf{Sign}, H}$ to $\mathcal{A}^{\mathsf{Prog}, H}$. The reason we do it this way here is that we obtain a better bound than when trying to mimic the reasoning that is used in the ROM proof.

Since the adverary $\mathcal{A}$ in an execution of $\mathcal{A}^{\mathsf{Prog}, H}$ has its random-oracle queries answered by H, and $\mathcal{A}$ has no access to H', we obviously have that $\mathcal{A}^{\mathsf{Prog}, H} = \mathcal{A}^{\mathsf{Prog}', H}$. Similarly, $\mathcal{A}^{\mathsf{Prog}', H'} = \mathcal{A}^{\mathsf{Trans}, H}$. Thus, it remains to show closeness of $\mathcal{A}^{\mathsf{Prog}', H}$ and $\mathcal{A}^{\mathsf{Prog}', H'}$. Towards this goal, we first settle the following properties of an execution of Prog'.

Proposition 1. *For an arbitrary but fixed message m_0, let (w, c, z) be the first non-$\perp$ transcript produced in an invocation of $\mathsf{Prog}'(m_0)$, and let S' be the set of w's sampled in the loop for which $z = \perp$. Then the following holds.*

Prog(m):	Prog$'$(m):	Trans(m):
1: **repeat**	1: **repeat**	1: **repeat**
2: $(w, \mathsf{st}) \leftarrow \mathsf{Com}(sk)$	2: $(w, \mathsf{st}) \leftarrow \mathsf{Com}(sk)$	2: $(w, \mathsf{st}) \leftarrow \mathsf{Com}(sk)$
3: $H(w, m) := c \leftarrow C$	3: $H(w, m) := c \leftarrow C$	3: $c \leftarrow C$
4: $z := \mathsf{Resp}(w, c, \mathsf{st})$	4: $z := \mathsf{Resp}(w, c, \mathsf{st})$	4: $z := \mathsf{Resp}(w, c, \mathsf{st})$
5: **until** $z \neq \bot$	5: **until** $z \neq \bot$	5: **until** $z \neq \bot$
6: **return** (w, z)	6: $H'(w, m) := c$	6: $H(w, m) := c$
	7: **return** (w, z)	7: **return** (w, z)

Fig. 4. The oracles Prog, Prog$'$ and Trans.

- *The distribution of (S', w, c, z) is invariant to the choice of m_0.*   (9)
- *S' is statistically independent of (w, c, z).*   (10)
- *For every $w^0 \in A$, $\Pr[w^0 \in S'] \leq \frac{\epsilon}{1-p}$.*   (11)

Proof. Let $t_i = (w_i, c_i, z_i)$ be the transcript sampled in the i-th iteration of the loop. For the purpose of the analysis, we assume that t_i is sampled for *every* $i \in \mathbb{Z}_{>0}$, even if the loop stops before. Then, the t_i's are i.i.d. distributed, and S' equals $\{w_1, \ldots, w_{K-1}\}$, with K being minimal such that $z_K \neq \bot$ and $(w, c, z) = t_K$. As the sampling of (S', w, c, z) does not involve m_0 at all, Item (9) follows immediately.

For the analysis of Item (10), we consider the list $L := [t_1, \ldots, t_{K-1}]$; clearly showing independence of L and (w, c, z) implies independence of S' and (w, c, z). Further consider an arbitrary but fixed list $L^0 = [t_1^0, \ldots, t_{k-1}^0]$ of transcripts $t_i^0 = (w_i^0, c_i^0, z_i^0)$, and an arbitrary but fixed transcript $t^0 = (w^0, c^0, z^0)$. With the goal to show that

$$\Pr\left[L = L^0 \text{ and } (w, c, z) = t^0\right] = \Pr\left[L = L^0\right] \cdot \Pr\left[(w, c, z) = t^0\right], \quad (12)$$

we may assume $z_1^0 = \cdots = z_{k-1}^0 = \bot$ and $z^0 \neq \bot$, because otherwise both sides of Eq. (12) vanish trivially. But then, by definition of L and (w, c, z),

$$\Pr\left[L = L^0 \text{ and } (w, c, z) = t^0\right] = \Pr\left[\forall i < k : t_i = t_i^0 \text{ and } t_k = t^0\right]$$

$$= \Pr\left[\forall i < k : t_i = t_i^0 \text{ and } t_k = t^0 \text{ and } z_k \neq \bot\right]$$

$$= \Pr\left[\begin{matrix} z_k \neq \bot \\ \forall i < k : t_i = t_i^0 \end{matrix}\right] \cdot \Pr\left[t_k = t^0 \,\middle|\, \begin{matrix} z_k \neq \bot \\ \forall i < k : t_i = t_i^0 \end{matrix}\right]$$

$$= \Pr\left[\begin{matrix} z_k \neq \bot \\ \forall i < k : t_i = t_i^0 \end{matrix}\right] \cdot \Pr\left[t_k = t^0 \,\middle|\, z_k \neq \bot\right]$$

$$= \Pr\left[L = L^0\right] \cdot \Pr\left[t_k = t^0 \,\middle|\, z_k \neq \bot\right],$$

where the fourth equality is due to independence between $(t_1, \ldots, t_{k-1})$ and t_k. Furthermore, summing up both sides of the above equality over all choices of L^0, noting that $\Pr\left[t_k = t^0 \,\middle|\, z_k \neq \bot\right]$ does not depend on k (since the t_i's are i.i.d.), we immediately get that $\Pr\left[t_k = t^0 \middle| z_k \neq \perp\right] = \Pr\left[(w,c,z) = t^0\right]$, which shows Eq. (12) and thus Item (10).

Next, notice that $|L| \geq \ell$ implies $z_1 = \cdots = z_\ell = \perp$. Thus,

$$\Pr\left[a^0 \in S'\right] \leq \sum_{\ell \geq 1} \Pr\left[w_\ell = w^0 \text{ and } |L| \geq \ell\right]$$

$$\leq \sum_{\ell \geq 1} \Pr\left[w_\ell = w^0 \text{ and } z_1 = \cdots = z_{\ell-1} = \perp\right]$$

$$= \sum_{\ell \geq 1} \Pr\left[w_\ell = w^0\right] \cdot \Pr\left[z_1 = \cdots = z_{\ell-1} = \perp\right] \leq \sum_{\ell \geq 1} p^{\ell-1}\epsilon \leq \frac{\epsilon}{1-p},$$

where the equality holds due to the independence between a_ℓ and $(z_1, \ldots, z_{\ell-1})$. This concludes Item (11). $\qquad\square$

For this purpose, for every $0 \leq i \leq q_H$ we let $\mathcal{G}_i$ be the hybrid between $\mathcal{A}^{\mathsf{Prog}',H}$ and $\mathcal{A}^{\mathsf{Prog}',H'}$ that has the first i queries to the random oracle answered by H', and the remaining ones by H. Obviously, $\mathcal{G}_0 = \mathcal{A}^{\mathsf{Prog}',H}$, while $\mathcal{G}_{q_H} = \mathcal{A}^{\mathsf{Prog}',H'}$. Thus, considering an arbitrary but fixed $1 \leq i \leq q_H$ and setting $\mathcal{G} := \mathcal{G}_{i-1}$ and $\mathcal{G}' := \mathcal{G}_i$, it is sufficient to show that $\mathcal{G}$ and $\mathcal{G}'$ are close. This is indeed the case:

Lemma 5. $\left|\Pr[1 \leftarrow \mathcal{G}] - \Pr[1 \leftarrow \mathcal{G}']\right| \leq 2\sqrt{\frac{q_S\epsilon}{1-p}}$.

Proof. Below, we refer to the i-th query of $\mathcal{A}$ to the random oracle, i.e., the query on which $\mathcal{G}$ and $\mathcal{G}'$ differ, as the *crucial query*.

In the respective executions of $\mathcal{G}$ and $\mathcal{G}'$, we define S as the set of all the w's that Prog' sampled but for which $\mathsf{Resp}(w,c,\mathsf{st}) = \perp$, in all the invocations of Prog' before the crucial query. Thus, by construction, at the time of the crucial query, H and H' differ at most at the points in S. (They might agree on a point in S, if the freshly sampled value for H at this point equals the old value.)

For the sake of analysis, consider a binary projective measurement on the input query register for the crucial query, which measures whether or not the input (w,m) is such that $w \in S$. Let Γ be satisfied if $w \notin S$, and let $\tilde{\mathcal{G}}$ and $\tilde{\mathcal{G}}'$ be the two respective games obtained by performing this measurement. Since H and H' only differ at the places (w,m) where $w \in S$, conditioned on Γ, the two oracles behave identically, and thus do $\tilde{\mathcal{G}}$ and $\tilde{\mathcal{G}}'$. Furthermore, the probability $\Pr[\Gamma]$ is the same in both games.

Thus by a double application of the gentle measurement lemma, we have

$$|\Pr[1 \leftarrow \mathcal{G}] - \Pr[1 \leftarrow \mathcal{G}']| \leq |\Pr[1 \leftarrow \mathcal{G}] - \Pr[1 \leftarrow \tilde{\mathcal{G}}' \mid \Gamma]|$$

$$+ |\Pr[1 \leftarrow \tilde{\mathcal{G}}'|\Gamma] - \Pr[1 \leftarrow \tilde{\mathcal{G}} \mid \Gamma]|$$

$$+ |\Pr[1 \leftarrow \tilde{\mathcal{G}}|\Gamma] - \Pr[1 \leftarrow \mathcal{G}]|$$

$$\leq 2\sqrt{\Pr[\neg\Gamma]}.$$

Hence, it remains to bound the probability $\Pr[\neg\Gamma]$. The intuition is that S collects those w's that Prog dismisses; thus, $\mathcal{A}$ does not get to see them, so it is hard for him to find an element in S, hence Γ is satisfied most likely. However, turning this intuition into a rigorous argument is not fully straightforward, since the set S, as a random variable, has a somewhat odd distribution.

Let Q be the random variable indicating the number of queries made to Prog prior to the crucial query; we have with certainty that $Q \leqslant q_S$.

A crucial observation that holds for both $\mathcal{G}, \mathcal{G}'$ is that, conditioned on $Q = q$ for an arbitrary but fixed q, the set S equals $S_1' \cup \cdots \cup S_q'$ where every S_j' is the set S' that was produced in the jth query of Prog' as specified in Proposition 1. We note that, at the time the adversary $\mathcal{A}$ makes the crucial query, H has not been queried, and (w, c, z) in Proposition 1 is the only information that is dissipated to the adversary for every prior query to Prog'. It follows from Item (9) and Item (10) that every S_j' is independent from the view of adversary, and hence so is S.

Due to the independence, it suffices to bound $\Pr[w^0 \in S | Q = q]$ for every $w^0 \in W$. Then it follows from the union bound and Item (11) that

$$\Pr[w^0 \in S | Q = q] \leqslant \sum_{j \in [q]} \Pr[w^0 \in S_j'] \leqslant \frac{q_S \epsilon}{1 - p}.$$

Putting things together, the proof is concluded. $\square$

Corollary 2. $\left| \Pr\left[1 \leftarrow \mathcal{A}^{\mathsf{Prog}, H} \right] - \Pr\left[1 \leftarrow \mathcal{A}^{\mathsf{Trans}, H} \right] \right| \leqslant 2q_H \sqrt{\frac{q_S \epsilon}{1 - p}}$.

4.4 Wrapping Up

From the above it follows that

$$\Delta_{p, \epsilon}^{\mathsf{Sign\text{-}Prog}}(q_S, q_H) \leqslant \frac{2q_S \sqrt{\epsilon}}{1 - p} \sqrt{q_H + \frac{q_S}{1 - p}} \quad \text{and} \quad \Delta_{p, \epsilon}^{\mathsf{Prog\text{-}Trans}}(q_S, q_H) \leqslant 2q_H \sqrt{\frac{q_S \epsilon}{1 - p}}$$

and thus by Lemma 1, we obtain the following.

Theorem 2. *Let $\epsilon, p, \delta < 1$ be so that there exists an event Γ with $\Pr[\neg \Gamma] \leqslant \delta$, $\Pr[p_{(pk, sk)} \leqslant p \mid \Gamma] = 1$ and $\mathbb{E}[\epsilon_{(pk, sk)} \mid \Gamma] \leqslant \epsilon$ for $(pk, sk) \leftarrow \mathsf{KeyGen}$. Let $\mathcal{A}^{\mathsf{Sign}, H}$ be a quantum CMA attacker against $\mathsf{FSwA}[\mathsf{ID}, H]$ that makes q_S queries to the signing oracle Sign and q_H quantum queries to the random oracle H. Then, there exists a quantum NMA attacker $\mathcal{B}^H$ so that*

$$\mathsf{Adv}^{\mathsf{EF\text{-}CMA}}(\mathcal{A}) \leqslant \mathsf{Adv}^{\mathsf{EF\text{-}NMA}}(\mathcal{B})$$

$$+ \frac{2q_S \sqrt{\epsilon}}{1 - p} \sqrt{q_H + 1 + \frac{q_S}{1 - p}} + 2(q_H + 1) \sqrt{\frac{q_S \epsilon}{1 - p}} + q_S \zeta_{zk} + \delta$$

and with running time $\mathsf{TIME}(\mathcal{B}^H) \approx \mathsf{TIME}(\mathcal{A}) + q_S \mathsf{TIME}(\mathsf{ZKSim})$.

5   The Mechanized ROM Proof

We now describe the mechanized proof of the CMA-to-NMA reduction in the ROM. As argued in Sect. 3, the high-level structure is the same as in the QROM proof. We again want to instantiate Lemma 1. We assume query bounds q_S for signature queries and q_H for random oracle queries. In order to obtain the bound for the CMA-to-NMA reduction, we need to provide $\Delta_{p,\epsilon}^{\mathsf{Sign}\rightarrow\mathsf{Prog}}$ and $\Delta_{p,\epsilon}^{\mathsf{Prog}\rightarrow\mathsf{Trans}}$ and prove these bounds for an arbitrary (but fixed) key pair (pk, sk) such that $p_{(pk,sk)} \leqslant p$ and $\epsilon_{(pk,sk)} \leqslant \epsilon$. We set:

$$\Delta_{p,\epsilon}^{\mathsf{Sign}\rightarrow\mathsf{Prog}} := q_S\epsilon\left(\frac{q_S + 1}{2(1-p)^2} + \frac{q_H}{1-p}\right)$$

$$\Delta_{p,\epsilon}^{\mathsf{Prog}\rightarrow\mathsf{Trans}} := \frac{q_S q_H \epsilon}{1-p}$$

Applying some simplifications, this allows us to prove the following bound.

Theorem 3. *Let $\epsilon, p, \delta < 1$ be as in Theorem 2. Let $\mathcal{A}^{\mathsf{Sign},H}$ be a classical CMA attacker against $\mathsf{FSwA}[\mathsf{ID}, H]$ that makes q_S queries to the signing oracle Sign and q_H queries to the random oracle H. Then, there exists a classical NMA attacker $\mathcal{B}^H$ against $\mathsf{FSwA}[\mathsf{ID}, H]$ so that*

$$\mathsf{Adv}^{\mathsf{EF\text{-}CMA}}(\mathcal{A}) \leqslant \mathsf{Adv}^{\mathsf{EF\text{-}NMA}}(\mathcal{B}) + \frac{2q_S(q_H + 1)\epsilon}{(1-p)} + \frac{q_S\epsilon(q_S + 1)}{2(1-p)^2} + q_S\zeta_{zk} + \delta$$

and with running time $\mathsf{TIME}(\mathcal{B}^H) \approx \mathsf{TIME}(\mathcal{A}) + q_S\,\mathsf{TIME}(\mathsf{ZKSim})$.

Proof. It suffices to show that the bounds for $\Delta_{p,\epsilon}^{\mathsf{Sign}\rightarrow\mathsf{Prog}}$ and $\Delta_{p,\epsilon}^{\mathsf{Prog}\rightarrow\mathsf{Trans}}$ are indeed correct; the theorem then follows with Lemma 1. For $\Delta_{p,\epsilon}^{\mathsf{Sign}\rightarrow\mathsf{Prog}}$, as outlined in Sect. 3.2, we successively replace the individual loop iterations of the Sign oracle with iterations from the Prog oracle (cf. Hyb in Fig. 3). That is, we have q_S sequences of hybrid arguments (one for each query), each replacing one-by-one κ loop iterations (cf. Hyb in Fig. 3). After κ steps, we cut off the remaining loop for a loss of p^κ. This yields an intermediate game where $\mathcal{A}$ interacts with H and Prog^κ, the latter behaving like Prog but aborting after κ iterations. The final bound is then obtained as the limit when κ is increased to infinity (causing Prog^κ to become Prog). Consider the hybrid step where the queries 0 to $i-1$ are answered by Prog^κ, query i is answered by Hyb^j and all remaining queries are answered by Sign. We bound the loss of answering query i with Hyb^{j+1} instead. Assuming a lazy implementation of the random oracle, both games behave the same unless iteration j on query i is reached *and* the pair (w, m) is already in the (previously queried) domain of H. The probability of this "bad" event occurring can be bounded by

$$\delta_{i,j} := p^j\epsilon\left(\frac{i}{1-p} + q_H + j\right)$$

where the term in parentheses is an upper bound on the *expected* size of the (previously queried) domain of H at the point where the bad event might occur (i.e., iteration j of query i). In there, the term $\frac{i}{1-p}$ is the expected number of iterations of the i preceding calls. Summing the total loss over i and j we have

$$\sum_{i=0}^{q_S-1} \left(p^\kappa + \sum_{j=0}^{\kappa-1} \delta_{i,j} \right) \leqslant q_S \cdot p^\kappa + \Delta_{p,\epsilon}^{\mathsf{Sign}\rightarrow\mathsf{Prog}}$$

which converges to $\Delta_{p,\epsilon}^{\mathsf{Sign}\rightarrow\mathsf{Prog}}$ as κ is increased to infinity. For $\Delta_{p,\epsilon}^{\mathsf{Prog}\rightarrow\mathsf{Trans}}$ the structure of the hybrid argument is exactly the same, the difference lies in how the bad event is bounded. Let Hyb_2 be the analog to Hyb, replacing iterations of Prog with those of Trans, and consider the replacement of Hyb_2^j with Hyb_2^{j+1} on query i. The two games behave the same, unless (a) iteration j of query i is reached and unsuccessful and (b) the adversary queries H using the pair (w, m) at some (later) point in the game. The probability of (a) is bounded by p^j and the probability of b is at most $q_H \epsilon$. Summing and taking the limit as above yields $\Delta_{p,\epsilon}^{\mathsf{Prog}\rightarrow\mathsf{Trans}}$. $\qquad\square$

Remark 1. The theorem we formalized in EasyCrypt is slightly less general than Theorem 3. We only consider the case of a perfect simulator (i.e., $\zeta_{zk} = 0$), and we restrict to the case where the simulator is obtained by wrapping a simulator for a single run of the IDS in a while loop. These simplifications naturally match our application to Dilithium.

Mechanizing the proof of the aforementioned variant of Theorem 3 turned out to be challenging for a number of reasons. In the following, we briefly comment on the most important ones.

First and foremost, the analysis of the bad event used to establish the bound $\Delta_{p,\epsilon}^{\mathsf{Sign}\rightarrow\mathsf{Prog}}$ crucially relies on the ability to take into account the expected size of the domain of the random oracle at the point where the bad event can (potentially) occur. Even with the intermediate oracle Prog^κ, a worst-case assumption on the i preceding queries would give a term of $i \cdot \kappa$ instead of $\frac{i}{1-p}$, causing the sum to no longer converge as κ is increased to infinity. The expected-size analysis for the domain of the random oracle H is carried out using an expectation logic. This expectation logic is an adaptation of the seminal work by Kozen [18] and was recently added to EasyCrypt to reason about the expected complexity of randomized programs. Our work [17] provides the first application of this logic to cryptographic proofs.

Moreover, while the argument for $\Delta_{p,\epsilon}^{\mathsf{Prog}\rightarrow\mathsf{Trans}}$ is intuitively much simpler than the argument for $\Delta_{p,\epsilon}^{\mathsf{Sign}\rightarrow\mathsf{Prog}}$, the proof in EasyCrypt is almost as complex. Unlike for $\Delta_{p,\epsilon}^{\mathsf{Sign}\rightarrow\mathsf{Prog}}$, the bad event is not necessarily triggered during the critical iteration; it can be triggered whenever H is queried. In order to bound the probability of the bad event occurring, we exploit that—assuming that iteration j of query i is unsuccessful—the commitment w is never used. This allows us to bound the bad event by transforming the game into one where w is sampled *after* the adversary is finished. This is called an eager/lazy argument in EasyCrypt.

Lastly, the hybrid arguments for bounding $\Delta_{p,\epsilon}^{\mathsf{Sign}\rightarrow\mathsf{Prog}}$ and $\Delta_{p,\epsilon}^{\mathsf{Prog}\rightarrow\mathsf{Trans}}$ involve a complex interplay of up-to-bad reasoning, hybrid steps, and a limit construction that ultimately lets the number of hybrid steps approach infinity. To the best of our knowledge, such a construction has not been formalized in EasyCrypt before.

6 A Machine-Checked Security Proof for Dilithium

We now describe the machine-checked security proof for Dilithium. More precisely, we prove EF-CMA security of the "template scheme" from the specification document [1, Fig. 1] extended with public key compression. This is equivalent to Dilithium-QROM [5, Figure 17] with $\mathbf{A}$ and $\mathbf{y}$ sampled randomly (i.e., not generated from a seed) and with an unbounded loop for the signing procedure.

The overall structure of the machine-checked proof largely follows [5]. We first prove EF-NMA security by a reduction from MLWE and SelfTargetMSIS. We then express Dilithium as the FSwA transform of an IDS and provide an HVZK simulator for this IDS. This allows us to instantiate Theorem 3 and conclude EF-CMA security of Dilithium.

6.1 Dilithium Specification

Most of the operations in Dilithium operate on vectors and matrices over the rings $R := \mathbb{Z}[X]/(X^n + 1)$ and $R_q := \mathbb{F}_q[X]/(X^n + 1)$. The specification [1] sets n to 256 and q to the prime $8380417 = 2^{23} - 2^{13} + 1$. In addition, there are a number of supporting algorithms (e.g., highBits or makeHint) that deal with certain kinds of rounding.

While the specification is written for one (parametric) mathematical structure, the security proof of Dilithium only makes use of a select few properties of this structure. For the machine-checked security proof, we insert an extra layer of abstraction. We define an abstract theory defining an abstract ring type R_q together with the various (abstract) supporting algorithms and the properties relating them. We then carry out the entire security proof with respect to these abstract operations. We also prove that the polynomial ring from the specification can be used to implement all operations such that all axioms are satisfied. While this extra layer of abstraction does not remove any proof burden, it allows us to make explicit the minimal structure required to carry out the security proof and cleanly separate the arithmetic reasoning required to build the required structure from the more high-level parts of the security proof.

The supporting algorithms are as follows. In addition to L_1 and the L_∞ norms, written $\|_-\|_1$ and $\|_-\|_\infty$ respectively, we have two rounding functions. Intuitively, power2round(r, d) rounds to the nearest multiple of 2^d and removes trailing zeros. Similarly, highBits(r, α) round into α buckets of (roughly) equal size. We treat the result of highBits as an (abstract) bucket designation while lowBits(r, α) can be seen as the difference between r and the center of its designated bucket. Lastly, $h := \text{makeHint}(z, r, \alpha)$ creates a "hint" for useHint(h, r, α) to compute the high bits of $r + z$ without knowing z, provided z is small. All operations, except $\|_-\|_1$ and $\|_-\|_\infty$, are generalized pointwise to vectors R_q^k. The former is only used on R_q while for the latter the vector version is defined as $\|\mathbf{r}\|_\infty := \max_i \|\mathbf{r}_i\|_\infty$. Further, we write S_γ^l for the uniform distribution over R_q^l

keygen():

1: $\mathbf{A} \leftarrow R_q^{k \times l}$
2: $(\mathbf{s}_1, \mathbf{s}_2) \leftarrow S_\eta^l \times S_\eta^k$
3: $\mathbf{t} := \mathbf{As}_1 + \mathbf{s}_2$
4: $\mathbf{t}_1 := \mathsf{power2round}(\mathbf{t}, d)$
5: $\mathbf{t}_0 := \mathbf{t} - \mathbf{t}_1 \cdot 2^d$
6: $pk := (\mathbf{A}, \mathbf{t}_1)$
7: $sk := (\mathbf{A}, \mathbf{s}_1, \mathbf{s}_2, \mathbf{t}_0)$
8: **return** (pk, sk)

verify(pk, m, σ):

1: $(\mathbf{A}, \mathbf{t}_1) := pk$
2: $(c, (\mathbf{z}, \mathbf{h})) := \sigma$
3: $\mathbf{w}_1 := \mathsf{useHint}(\mathbf{h}, \mathbf{Az} - c\mathbf{t}_1 \cdot 2^d, 2\gamma_2)$
4: $c' := H(\mathbf{w}_1, m)$
5: **return** $\llbracket \ \|\mathbf{z}\|_\infty < \gamma_1 - \beta \wedge c = c' \ \rrbracket$.

sign(sk, m):

1: $(\mathbf{A}, \mathbf{s}_1, \mathbf{s}_2, \mathbf{t}_0) := sk$
2: $r := \bot$
3: **while** $r = \bot$ **do**
4: $\quad \mathbf{y} \leftarrow S_{\gamma_1 - 1}^l$
5: $\quad \mathbf{w} := \mathbf{Ay}$
6: $\quad w_1 := \mathsf{highBits}(\mathbf{w}, 2\gamma_2)$
7: $\quad c \in B_\tau := H(w_1, m)$
8: $\quad z := \mathbf{y} + c\mathbf{s}_1$
9: $\quad$ **if** $\|\mathbf{z}\|_\infty < \gamma_1 - \beta \wedge \|\mathsf{lowBits}(\mathbf{w} - c\mathbf{s}_2, 2\gamma_2)\|_\infty < \gamma_2 - \beta$ **then**
10: $\quad\quad \mathbf{h} := \mathsf{makeHint}(-c\mathbf{t}_0, \mathbf{w} - c\mathbf{s}_2 + c\mathbf{t}_0, 2\gamma_2)$
11: $\quad\quad r := (\mathbf{z}, \mathbf{h})$
12: **return** (c, r)

Fig. 5. The Dilithium signature scheme

conditioned on $\|\_\|_\infty \leqslant \gamma$. With the supporting algorithms in place, the Dilithium signature scheme is defined in Fig. 5.

While we present our results using a conventional mathematical presentation, the scheme and the security proof are completely formalized in EasyCrypt (see full version [20, Fig. 13]). Note that, in contrast to [5], we are working in a typed setting. In particular, the hash function (or random oracle) H takes pairs (w_1, m), where m is a message and $w : \mathsf{high}_{2\gamma_2}$, as arguments and outputs a uniformly random $c \in B_\tau$:

$$B_\tau := \{c \in R_q \mid \|c\|_\infty = 1 \text{ and } \|c\|_1 = \tau\}.$$

In addition to the parameters n and q internal to R_q, the scheme has a number of additional parameters: the size of $\mathbf{A}$ (i.e., $k \times l$) the coefficient ranges for $\mathbf{s}_1, \mathbf{s}_2$ (the interval $[-\eta, \eta]$) and $\mathbf{y}$ (the interval $[-\gamma_1 + 1, \gamma_1 - 1]$), the low-order rounding range ($\alpha := 2\gamma_2$), the number d of bits dropped from $\mathbf{t}$, and the number τ of $\pm 1's$ in c (cf. B_τ above). Further, there is the derived parameter $\beta := \tau \cdot \eta$.[12]

We now give some of the properties of R_q and the supporting algorithms that we require for the security proof. Let q and α be integers such that $2\alpha < q$, $q \equiv 1$ mod α and α is even. Further let $\mathbf{r}$ and $\mathbf{z}$ be vectors over R_q where $\|\mathbf{z}\|_\infty \leqslant \alpha/2$

---

[12] See [1] for a discussion on how these parameters are set in practice.

and let $\mathbf{h}$ be a vector of hints. We require:

$$\mathsf{useHint}(\mathsf{makeHint}(\mathbf{z},\mathbf{r},\alpha),\mathbf{r},\alpha) = \mathsf{highBits}(\mathbf{r}+\mathbf{z},\alpha)\,, \tag{13}$$

$$\|\mathbf{r} - \mathsf{shift}_\alpha(\mathsf{useHint}(\mathbf{h},\mathbf{r},\alpha))\|_\infty \leqslant \alpha+1\,, \tag{14}$$

$$\|\mathbf{r} - \mathsf{power2round}(\mathbf{r},d) \cdot 2^d\|_\infty \leqslant 2^{d-1}\,, \text{ and} \tag{15}$$

$$\mathsf{shift}_\alpha \text{ is injective.} \tag{16}$$

There are, of course, a number of additional properties we require (e.g., $0 \leqslant \|\mathbf{r}\|_\infty$, $\|\mathbf{ct}\|_\infty \leqslant \|\mathbf{c}\|_1 \cdot \|\mathbf{t}\|_\infty$, or the triangle inequality $\|\mathbf{u}+\mathbf{v}\|_\infty \leqslant \|\mathbf{u}\|_\infty + \|\mathbf{v}\|_\infty$). For the complete list we refer to the DRing theory (for the properties of R_q and the supporting algorithms) and the DVect theory for the lifting to vectors.

Even though verify only uses $\mathbf{A}$ and $\mathbf{t}_1$, the security proofs assume that the adversary knows $\mathbf{t}$, allowing it to derive both $\mathbf{t}_1$ and $\mathbf{t}_0$. In particular, the entirety of $\mathbf{t}$ is needed to define the HVZK simulator for the EF-CMA to EF-NMA reduction. Hence, the first step of the proof is to change the public key to $(\mathbf{A},\mathbf{t})$, the secret key to $(\mathbf{A},\mathbf{s}_1,\mathbf{s}_2)$, and adapt sign and verify to compute $\mathbf{t}_1$ and $\mathbf{t}_0$ as necessary. We call this scheme *Simplified Dilithium* (DilithiumS) and prove the following lemma showing that it is sufficient to establish security for this variant of the construction.

Lemma 6. *Let* $\mathcal{A}^{\mathsf{Sign},H}$ *be a CMA attacker against* Dilithium. *Then there exists an adversary* $\mathcal{B}^{\mathsf{Sign},H}$ *such that:* $\mathsf{Adv}^{\mathsf{EF\text{-}CMA}}_{\mathsf{Dilithium}}(\mathcal{A}) \leqslant \mathsf{Adv}^{\mathsf{EF\text{-}CMA}}_{\mathsf{DilithiumS}}(\mathcal{B})$ *Further,* $\mathsf{Time}(\mathcal{A}) \approx \mathsf{Time}(\mathcal{B})$.

6.2   Reduction to MLWE and SelfTargetMSIS

We now prove EF-NMA security of the simplified scheme. The reduction to MLWE and SelfTargetMSIS closely follows [1,5]. We first sketch the mathematical proof for the sake of completeness — we correct minor points with respect to the statements in [5] and [1] that became clear in the formal proof — and then comment on the formalization in EasyCrypt. We begin by recalling the MLWE and SelfTargetMSIS security assumptions for the ring R_q used by Dilithium.

Definition 3 (MLWE Assumption). *Let* m *and* k *be integers and let* $D : R_q \to [0,1]$ *be a distribution. The advantage of an algorithm* $\mathcal{A}$ *for solving the decisional* $\mathsf{MLWE}_{m,k,D}$ *problem over the ring* R_q *is:*

$$\mathsf{Adv}^{\mathsf{MLWE}}_{m,k,D}(\mathcal{A}) := \left| \Pr\left[\mathcal{A}(\mathbf{A},\mathbf{t}) = 1 \;\middle|\; \mathbf{A} \leftarrow R_q^{m\times k}; \mathbf{t} \leftarrow R_q^m \right] - \right.$$
$$\left. \Pr\left[\mathcal{A}(\mathbf{A},\mathbf{A}\mathbf{s}_1 + \mathbf{s}_2) = 1 \;\middle|\; \mathbf{A} \leftarrow R_q^{m\times k}; \mathbf{s}_1 \leftarrow D^k; \mathbf{s}_2 \leftarrow D^m \right] \right|.$$

Definition 4 (Self-target MSIS Assumption). *Let* m *and* k *be integers and let* $H : R_q^m \times M \to B_\tau$ *be a random oracle.*

$$\mathsf{Adv}^{\mathsf{SelfTargetMSIS}}_{H,m,k,\gamma} :=$$
$$\Pr\left[\begin{array}{c} \|\mathbf{r}\|_\infty \leqslant \gamma \\ H([\,\mathbf{I}_m \mid \mathbf{A}\,] \cdot \mathbf{r}, \mu) = \mathbf{r}[m+k-1] \end{array} \middle| \mathbf{A} \leftarrow R_q^{m\times k}; (\mathbf{r},\mu) \leftarrow \mathcal{A}^H(\mathbf{A}) \right].$$

keygen'():
1: $\mathbf{A} \leftarrow R_q^{k \times l}$
2: $\mathbf{t} \leftarrow R_q^k$
3: **return** $((\mathbf{A}, \mathbf{t}), \text{witness})$

$\mathcal{C}(\mathbf{A}' : R_q^{k \times l+1})$:
1: $(\mathbf{A}, \bar{\mathbf{t}}) := \mathbf{A}'$
2: $\mathbf{t} := -\bar{\mathbf{t}}$
3: $(m, (c, (\mathbf{z}, \mathbf{h}))) \leftarrow \mathcal{A}^{H'}(\mathbf{A}, \mathbf{t})$
4: $\mathbf{t}_1 := \text{power2round}(d, \mathbf{t})$
5: $\mathbf{r} := \mathbf{Az} - c\mathbf{t}_1 \cdot 2^d$
6: $\mathbf{u}_1 := \mathbf{r} - \text{shift}_\alpha(\text{useHint}(\mathbf{h}, \mathbf{r}, \alpha))$
7: $\mathbf{u}_2 := c(\mathbf{t} - \mathbf{t}_1 \cdot 2^d)$
8: **return** $((\mathbf{u}_1 - \mathbf{u}_2) \,|\, \mathbf{z} \,|\, [c])$

Fig. 6. Randomized keygen and reduction to SelfTargetMSIS

The goal of this section is then to prove the following lemma.

Lemma 7. *For every adversary $\mathcal{A}^{\text{Sign},H}$ breaking NMA security of simplified Dilithium, we can construct an MLWE adversary $\mathcal{B}$ and a SelfTargetMSIS adversary $\mathcal{C}$ such that:*

$$\text{Adv}^{\text{EF-NMA}}_{\text{DilithiumS}}(\mathcal{A}) \leqslant \text{Adv}^{\text{MLWE}}_{k,l,S_\eta}(\mathcal{B}) + \text{Adv}^{\text{SelfTargetMSIS}}_{G,k,l+1,\zeta}(\mathcal{C})$$

where $\zeta := \max\left\{\gamma_1 - \beta, 2\gamma_2 + 1 + \tau 2^{d-1}\right\}$ and $G : R_q \times \text{Msg} \to B_\tau$ is a random oracle. Further $\text{Time}(\mathcal{A}) \approx \text{Time}(\mathcal{B}) \approx \text{Time}(\mathcal{C})$.

Proof (Sketch). The proof consists of three steps. The first step is to replace keygen with a keygen', sampling $\mathbf{t}$ uniformly at random and returning an undefined (and unused) secret key (cf. Fig. 6). Taking $\mathcal{B}$ to be the remainder of the EF-NMA security game after key generation, the difference between the two games is exactly $\text{Adv}^{\text{MLWE}}_{k,l,R_q}(\mathcal{B})$. Next, we define an oracle $H'(\mathbf{w}_1, m) := G(\text{shift}_\alpha(\mathbf{w}_1), m)$. Since shift_α is injective and both H (used by our scheme) and G (the random oracle from the SelfTargetMSIS assumption) have as output distribution the uniform distribution over B_τ, replacing H by H' incurs no loss.

It remains to construct the reduction $\mathcal{C}$ that returns a valid solution for the SelfTargetMSIS problem whenever $\mathcal{A}^{H'}(\mathbf{A}, \mathbf{t})$ successfully forges a signature (for some $(\mathbf{A}, \mathbf{t})$ derived from the SelfTargetMSIS instance). Writing $|$ for vector concatenation, the reduction is given in Fig. 6. Given a SelfTargetMSIS instance $\mathbf{A}'$ with dimensions $k \times l + 1$, $\mathcal{C}$ splits off the last column, negates it, and passes the parts to the EF-NMA adversary. We have that the distribution of $(\mathbf{A}, \mathbf{t})$ is identical to the EF-NMA game (using keygen' for key generation). Now assume that $(m, (c, (\mathbf{z}, \mathbf{h})))$ passes verification with respect to H'. That is, we have:

1. $H'(\text{useHint}(\mathbf{h}, \mathbf{Az} - c\mathbf{t}_1 \cdot 2^d, \alpha), m) = c$
2. $\|\mathbf{z}\|_\infty < \gamma_1 - \beta$

Now with $\mathbf{r}' := ((\mathbf{u}_1 - \mathbf{u}_2) \,|\, \mathbf{z} \,|\, [c]) \in R_q^{k+l+1}$ as defined in $\mathcal{C}$, we have:

$$\begin{aligned} G([\mathbf{I}_k | \mathbf{A}'] \cdot \mathbf{r}', m) &= G([\mathbf{I}_k | \mathbf{A}| - \mathbf{t}] \cdot \mathbf{r}', m) \\ &= G(\mathbf{Az} - c\mathbf{t} + (\mathbf{u}_1 - \mathbf{u}_2), m) \\ &= H'(\text{useHint}(\mathbf{h}, \mathbf{Az} - c\mathbf{t}_1 \cdot 2^d, \alpha), m) \\ &= \mathbf{r}'[k + l]. \end{aligned}$$

Hence, $\mathbf{r}'$ satisfies the "self-target" condition and it remains to show $\|\mathbf{r}'\|_\infty \leqslant$ $\max\{\gamma_1 - \beta, 2\gamma_2 + 1 + \tau 2^{d-1}\}$. For $\mathbf{z}$ this follows by assumption, and for c we have $\|[c]\|_\infty = 1$. For $(\mathbf{u}_1 - \mathbf{u}_2)$, recalling that we set $\alpha = 2\gamma_2$, we have:

$$\|\mathbf{u}_1 - \mathbf{u}_2\|_\infty \leqslant \|\mathbf{u}_1\|_\infty + \|\mathbf{u}_2\|_\infty \leqslant 2\gamma_2 + 1 + \|c\|_1 \cdot \|\mathbf{t} - \mathbf{t}_1 \cdot 2^d\|_\infty \leqslant 2\gamma_2 + 1 + \tau 2^{d-1}$$

where the bound for $\mathbf{u}_1$ follows with Inequality (14) and the bound for $\mathbf{u}_2$ follows with Inequality (15). □

The main technical difficulty when formalizing the results in this section was to develop a matrix library that would support all the required operations. This was done in collaboration and is shared between several developments. In the mathematical presentation we have assumed tacitly that all matrix operations are carried out on matrices and vectors of compatible dimensions. In EasyCrypt, we use a matrix theory where operations are defined even if the dimensions do not match, with "undefined" behaviors chosen to simplify the equational theory. This does not cause any problems for matrices and vectors provided by the schemes or games. However, vectors given by the adversary (i.e., the $\mathbf{z}$ and $\mathbf{h}$ component of a signature) need to be checked for the correct length by the verify procedure (see full version [20, Fig. 13]).

6.3 The HVZK Simulator and EF-CMA Security

We now extend the security proof from EF-NMA to EF-CMA. This mainly amounts to instantiating Theorem 3. In order to do so, we need to express the simplified Dilithium scheme as the FSwA transform of an IDS and provide a HVZK simulator for this IDS. There are two minor technical complications. The first is that, in order to simplify the mechanization of the proof of Theorem 3, we restricted ourselves to IDS where Com, Resp, and Verify were given as operators (i.e., mathematical functions) rather than procedures (i.e., imperative code such as that given in Fig. 5). Now we have to "pay" for this simplification and show that our scheme can indeed be seen as the FS transform of such an operator-based IDS. The second complication is that Dilithium is actually based on a variant of the FS transform that is specific to commitment recoverable IDS, allowing to replace the commitment w with the (in practice much smaller) challenge c in the signature. The difference is mainly in verification as shown below (generic on the left, commitment recoverable on the right):

verify$(pk, m, \sigma = (w, z))$:   verify$(pk, m, \sigma = (c, z))$:
1: $c := \mathsf{H}(w, m)$ 1: $w := \mathsf{Recover}(pk, c, z)$
2: **return** $[\![\mathsf{Verify}(pk, w, c, z)]\!]$ 2: **return** $[\![\mathsf{Verify}(pk, w, c, z)]\!] \wedge [\![c = \mathsf{H}(w, m)]\!]$

The Recover function for Dilithium is

$$\mathsf{Recover}((\mathbf{A}, \mathbf{t}), c, (\mathbf{z}, \mathbf{h})) := \mathsf{useHint}(\mathbf{h}, \mathbf{A}\mathbf{z} - c \cdot \mathsf{power2round}(\mathbf{t}, d) \cdot 2^d).$$

For Sign (cf. Fig. 5), Lines 4–6 correspond to Com while Lines 8–11 correspond to Resp. Defining the remaining operators and proving that no context can distinguish the original scheme from the FSwA transform of the IDS is routine.

$\mathsf{Sim}(pk = (\mathbf{A}, \mathbf{t}))$:
1: $r := \bot$
2: $b \leftarrow D_z$
3: **if** b **then**
4:      $\mathbf{t}_0 := \mathbf{t} - \mathsf{power2round}(\mathbf{t}, d) \cdot 2^d$
5:      $c \leftarrow B_\tau$
6:      $\mathbf{z} \leftarrow S^l_{\gamma_1 - \beta - 1}$
7:      **if** $\|\mathsf{lowBits}(\mathbf{Az} - c\mathbf{t}, \alpha)\|_\infty < \gamma_2 - \beta$ **then**
8:          $h := \mathsf{makeHint}(-c\mathbf{t}_0, \mathbf{Az} - c\mathbf{t} + c\mathbf{t}_0))$
9:          $r := (\mathsf{Recover}(pk, c, \mathbf{z}), c, (z, h))$
10: **return** r.

Fig. 7. HVZK simulator

Proving EF-CMA security of the scheme obtained using the FSwA transform for commitment-recoverable IDS can trivially be reduced to proving EF-CMA security of the standard FSwA transform. However, the reduction requires an additional q_S random oracle queries to turn the signatures of the form (w, z), returned by the signing oracle, into signatures of the form (c, z) as expected by the adversary.

Now we define the HVZK Simulator for the IDS sketched above. We let D_z be the distribution that with probability $|S^l_{\gamma_1 - \beta - 1}|/|S^l_{\gamma_1 - 1}|$ returns true and otherwise returns false. The Sim in Fig. 7 is a minor variation of the one in [5, Figure 14]. The main difference is that we make explicit the use of Recover to satisfy the interface of Theorem 3. As mentioned earlier, executing Sim in a while loop until $z \neq \bot$ yields an acHVZK simulator.

Putting everything together, we obtain the security theorem for Dilithium as we have formalized it in EasyCrypt:

Theorem 4. *Let* Γ, δ, ϵ *and* $p_0 < 1$ *be such that* $\Pr_{A \leftarrow R_q^{k \times l}}[\neg \Gamma] \leqslant \delta$,

$$\mathbb{E}_{A \leftarrow R_q^{k \times l}} \left[\max_w \Pr_{\mathbf{y} \leftarrow S^l_{\gamma_1 - 1}} [\mathsf{highBits}(\mathbf{Ay}, 2\gamma_2) = w] \,\middle|\, \Gamma \right] \leqslant \epsilon, \text{ and}$$

$\Pr_{\mathbf{z} \leftarrow S^l_{\gamma_1 - \beta - 1}}[\|\mathsf{lowBits}(\mathbf{Az} - c\mathbf{t}, 2\gamma_2)\|_\infty \geqslant \gamma_2 - \beta] \leqslant p_0$ *for all* $\mathbf{A}$ *satisfying* Γ, *all* $c \in B_\tau$ *and all* $\mathbf{t} \in R_q^l$. *Then for every classical adversary* $\mathcal{A}^{\mathsf{Sign}, H}$ *making at most* q_S *signing queries and at most* q_H *random oracle queries and for the adversaries* $\mathcal{B}$ *(against* MLWE*) and the* $\mathcal{C}^G$ *(against* SelfTargetMSIS*) constructed in the proof of Lemma 7 we have:*

$$\mathsf{Adv}^{\mathsf{EF\text{-}CMA}}_{\mathsf{Dilithium}}(\mathcal{A}) \leqslant \mathsf{Adv}^{\mathsf{MLWE}}_{k,l,S_\eta}(\mathcal{B}) + \mathsf{Adv}^{\mathsf{SelfTargetMSIS}}_{G,k,l+1,\zeta}(\mathcal{C})$$
$$+ \frac{2q_S(q_H + q_S + 1)\epsilon}{1 - p} + \frac{q_S\epsilon(q_S + 1)}{2(1 - p)^2} + \delta$$

where $p := \dfrac{|S^l_{\gamma_1 - \beta - 1}|}{|S^l_{\gamma_1 - 1}|} p_0 + \left(1 - \dfrac{|S^l_{\gamma_1 - \beta - 1}|}{|S^l_{\gamma_1 - 1}|}\right)$ *and* $\zeta := \max\{\gamma_1 - \beta, 2\gamma_2 + 1 + \tau 2^{d-1}\}$.

We remark that we do not show in EasyCrypt that the execution times of $\mathcal{B}$ and $\mathcal{C}$ are close to the execution time of $\mathcal{A}$, but this can be checked by inspection. As a consequence, the formal statement needs to be with respect to specific reductions rather than existentially quantified adversaries (see full version [20, Fig. 14]).

7   Concrete Security Analysis

In the following, we quantify the security loss of our proof to analyze the impact on the concrete security of Dilithium. Our proof of security for Dilithium has the same overall structure as the one given in [5] regarding the reductions from the underlying computational assumptions MLWE and SelfTargetMSIS. Indeed, the bounds we establish for the advantage of both classical and quantum attackers differ from the original proofs only in the additive terms, which in our case are larger due to additional (Q)ROM reprogramming steps.

In the NIST submission [1, Sect. 6.2] the authors simplify the additive security loss as 2^{-254} — a conservative value — and claim that this bound is achieved for all of the parameter sets considered, based on the analysis performed in [5]. In what follows, we give more precise bounds for this additive loss according to our corrected proofs. We show that it is still low enough to comfortably meet the requirements of the relevant NIST security levels.

We recall the expressions for the security loss L in the ROM from Theorem 4, and its quantum counter part L^* obtained from Theorem 2, i.e.

$$L := \frac{2q_S(q_H + q_S + 1)\epsilon}{1 - p} + \frac{q_S\epsilon(q_S + 1)}{2(1 - p)^2} + \delta$$

and

$$L^* := \frac{2q_S\sqrt{\epsilon}}{1 - p}\sqrt{q_H + 1 + \frac{q_S}{1 - p}} + 2(q_H + 1)\sqrt{\frac{q_S\epsilon}{1 - p}} + \delta.$$

We present an extended analysis of the bounds on ϵ and δ for the different parameter settings for Dilithium (for the different NIST levels) in the full version [20, Appendix A] using a computer-aided analysis of the distribution of the rank of (the upper square part of) the matrix $\mathbf{A}$. We note that δ and ϵ are related and allow for different tradeoffs for fixed parameters which we did not fully exploit, yet. For the rejection probability p, we use the heuristic from [5] to treat lowBits($\mathbf{A}z - ct$) as uniformly random in $S_{\gamma_2-1}^k$. This gives rise to the following table.

	p	q_S	q_H	δ	ϵ	loss
NIST2	$\leqslant \frac{49}{64}$	2^{64}	2^{128}	2^{-209}	2^{-403}	$L \leqslant 2^{-206}$
				2^{-64}	2^{-446}	$L^* \leqslant 2^{-58}$
			2^{64}	2^{-265}	2^{-390}	$L \leqslant 2^{-257}$
				2^{-117}	2^{-428}	$L^* \leqslant 2^{-113}$
			1	2^{-265}	2^{-390}	$L \leqslant 2^{-257}$
				2^{-117}	2^{-428}	$L^* \leqslant 2^{-113}$
NIST3	$\leqslant \frac{103}{128}$	2^{64}	2^{192}	2^{-867}	2^{-1108}	$L \leqslant 2^{-847}$
				2^{-362}	2^{-1180}	$L^* \leqslant 2^{-360}$
NIST5	$\leqslant \frac{759}{1024}$	2^{64}	2^{256}	2^{-1268}	2^{-1584}	$L \leqslant 2^{-1260}$
				2^{-540}	2^{-1664}	$L^* \leqslant 2^{-538}$

Fig. 8. Concrete security loss of Dilithium from Theorems 2 (L^*) and 4 (L).

The take-away from our analysis is that the statistical additive loss remains sufficiently small for all scenarios and therefore the dominant terms for the security level will remain the bounds for MLWE and SelfTargetMSIS. To be more precise, the table says that an attacker doing q_H hash computations only gains an additive advantage of 2^{-58} in the worst case (quantum attack against level 2). For reference, NIST security level 2 corresponds to a setting where the expected cost of a successful attack should match that of a collision search in a generic 256-bit hash function. This is often estimated to be $256/3 \approx 86$. So, after 2^{86} quantum queries, we would expect to find a collision. In our case, even after 2^{128} quantum queries, the success probability is bounded by 2^{-58}. Actually, one number that may appear debatable (in the sense of really guaranteeing the claimed security) is the bound for level 2 after a single query of a success probability of 2^{-113}. This number is caused by the number of signing queries which dominates in this case. This implies that for this attack, the cost is also dominated by the signing queries (here 2^{64}). What the number says is that, if one could ignore the cost of the signing queries, then there would exist an attack with an expected cost of about 2^{113} which is just the number of hash queries. However, given that the cost of each of these attacks is at least 2^{64} the total attack cost is 2^{177}. Hence, for all the parameters there is a comfortable margin regarding the security loss induced by the reduction. Thereby the full security of Dilithium is still determined by the hardness of solving MLWE and SelfTargetMSIS.

Acknowledgments. Jelle Don is supported by the ERC-ADG project ALGSTR ONGCRYPTO (Project No. 740972). Benjamin Grégoire is supported by the Agence Nationale de la Recherche (French National Research Agency) as part of the France 2030 programme - ANR-22-PECY-0006. Yu-Hsuan Huang is supported by the Dutch Research Agenda (NWA) project HAPKIDO (Project No. NWA.1215.18.002), which is financed by the Dutch Research Council (NWO). Andreas Hülsing is supported by an NWO VIDI grant (Project No. VI.Vidi.193. 066). Xiaodi Wu is supported by AFOSR Young Investigator Program (YIP) Award (FA95502110094) and NSF CAREER Award (NSF-CCF-1942837).

References

1. Ducas, L., et al.: CRYSTALS-Dilithium - algorithm specifications and supporting documentation (version 3.1). Technical report (February 2021). Specification document
2. Ducas, L., et al.: CRYSTALS-Dilithium: A lattice-based digital signature scheme. IACR Trans. Cryptographic Hardware Embedded Syst., 238–268 (2018)
3. Lyubashevsky, V.: Fiat-shamir with aborts: applications to lattice and factoring-based signatures. In: Matsui, M. (ed.) ASIACRYPT 2009. LNCS, vol. 5912, pp. 598–616. Springer, Heidelberg (2009). https://doi.org/10.1007/978-3-642-10366-7_35
4. Lyubashevsky, V.: Lattice signatures without trapdoors. In: Pointcheval, D., Johansson, T. (eds.) EUROCRYPT 2012. LNCS, vol. 7237, pp. 738–755. Springer, Heidelberg (2012). https://doi.org/10.1007/978-3-642-29011-4_43
5. Kiltz, E., Lyubashevsky, V., Schaffner, C.: A concrete treatment of Fiat-Shamir signatures in the quantum random-oracle model. In: Nielsen, J.B., Rijmen, V. (eds.) EUROCRYPT 2018. LNCS, vol. 10822, pp. 552–586. Springer, Cham (2018). https://doi.org/10.1007/978-3-319-78372-7_18
6. Barbosa, M., et al.: Sok: Computer-aided cryptography. In: 42nd IEEE Symposium on Security and Privacy, SP 2021, San Francisco, CA, USA, 24–27 May 2021, pp. 777–795. IEEE (2021)
7. Bhargavan, K., Blanchet, B., Kobeissi, N.: Verified models and reference implementations for the TLS 1.3 standard candidate. In: IEEE Symposium on Security and Privacy (S&P), pp. 483–502. IEEE Computer Society (2017)
8. Delignat-Lavaud, A., et al.: Implementing and proving the TLS 1.3 record layer. In: IEEE Symposium on Security and Privacy (S&P), pp. 463–482. IEEE Computer Society (2017)
9. Cremers, C., Horvat, M., Scott, S., van der Merwe, T.: Automated analysis and verification of TLS 1.3: 0-rtt, resumption and delayed authentication. In: IEEE Symposium on Security and Privacy (S&P), pp. 470–485. IEEE Computer Society (2016)
10. Cremers, C., Horvat, M., Hoyland, J., Scott, S., van der Merwe, T.: A comprehensive symbolic analysis of TLS 1.3. In: ACM Conference on Computer and Communications Security (CCS), pp. 1773–1788. ACM (2017)
11. Lyubashevsky, V., Nguyen, N.K., Plancon, M.: Lattice-based zero-knowledge proofs and applications: Shorter, simpler, and more general. Cryptology ePrint Archive (2022)
12. De Feo, L., Galbraith, S.D.: SeaSign: compact isogeny signatures from class group actions. In: Ishai, Y., Rijmen, V. (eds.) EUROCRYPT 2019. LNCS, vol. 11478, pp. 759–789. Springer, Cham (2019). https://doi.org/10.1007/978-3-030-17659-4_26
13. Beullens, W., Katsumata, S., Pintore, F.: Calamari and Falafl: logarithmic (linkable) ring signatures from isogenies and lattices. In: Moriai, S., Wang, H. (eds.) ASIACRYPT 2020. LNCS, vol. 12492, pp. 464–492. Springer, Cham (2020). https://doi.org/10.1007/978-3-030-64834-3_16
14. Beullens, W., Dobson, S., Katsumata, S., Lai, Y.-F., Pintore, F.: Group signatures and more from isogenies and lattices: Generic, simple, and efficient. In: Annual International Conference on the Theory and Applications of Cryptographic Techniques, pp. 95–126. Springer (2022). https://doi.org/10.1007/s10623-023-01192-x
15. Zhandry, M.: How to record quantum queries, and applications to quantum indifferentiability. In: Boldyreva, A., Micciancio, D. (eds.) CRYPTO 2019. LNCS, vol.

11693, pp. 239–268. Springer, Cham (2019). https://doi.org/10.1007/978-3-030-26951-7_9

16. Barbosa, M.: EasyPQC: Verifying post-quantum cryptography. In: Proceedings of the 2021 ACM SIGSAC Conference on Computer and Communications Security, CCS 2021, pp. 2564–2586. Association for Computing Machinery, New York (2021)

17. Avanzini, M., Barthe, G., Grégoire, B., Moser, G., Vanoni, G.: A mechanisation of the complexity analysis of skiplists. Unpublished manuscript (2023)

18. Kozen, D.: A probabilistic pdl. In: Proceedings of the Fifteenth Annual ACM Symposium on Theory of Computing, STOC 1983, pp. 291–297. Association for Computing Machinery, New York (1983)

19. Devevey, J., Fallahpour, P., Passelègue, A., Stehlé, D.: A detailed analysis of Fiat-Shamir with aborts. Cryptology ePrint Archive, Paper 2023/245 (2023). https://eprint.iacr.org/2023/245

20. Barbosa, M.: Fixing and mechanizing the security proof of Fiat-Shamir with aborts and Dilithium. Cryptology ePrint Archive, Paper 2023/246 (2023). https://eprint.iacr.org/2023/246

21. Grilo, A.B., Hövelmanns, K., Hülsing, A., Majenz, C.: Tight adaptive reprogramming in the QROM. In: Tibouchi, M., Wang, H. (eds.) ASIACRYPT 2021. LNCS, vol. 13090, pp. 637–667. Springer, Cham (2021). https://doi.org/10.1007/978-3-030-92062-3_22

Compact Lattice Gadget and Its Applications to Hash-and-Sign Signatures

Yang Yu[1,2,3], Huiwen Jia[4,5(✉)], and Xiaoyun Wang[6,7,8]

[1] BNRist, Tsinghua University, Beijing, China
yu-yang@mail.tsinghua.edu.cn
[2] Zhongguancun Laboratory, Beijing, China
[3] National Financial Cryptography Research Center, Beijing, China
[4] School of Mathematics and Information Science, Key Laboratory of Information Security, Guangzhou University, Guangzhou, China
hwjia@gzhu.edu.cn
[5] Guangzhou Center for Applied Mathematics, Guangzhou University, Guangzhou, China
[6] Institute for Advanced Study, Tsinghua University, Beijing, China
xiaoyunwang@mail.tsinghua.edu.cn
[7] Key Laboratory of Cryptologic Technology and Information Security (Ministry of Education), Qingdao, China
[8] Shandong Institute of Blockchain, Jinan, China

Abstract. Lattice gadgets and the associated algorithms are the essential building blocks of lattice-based cryptography. In the past decade, they have been applied to build versatile and powerful cryptosystems. However, the practical optimizations and designs of gadget-based schemes generally lag their theoretical constructions. For example, the gadget-based signatures have elegant design and capability of extending to more advanced primitives, but they are far less efficient than other lattice-based signatures.

This work aims to improve the practicality of gadget-based cryptosystems, with a focus on hash-and-sign signatures. To this end, we develop a compact gadget framework in which the used gadget is a *square* matrix instead of the short and fat one used in previous constructions. To work with this compact gadget, we devise a specialized gadget sampler, called *semi-random sampler*, to compute the approximate preimage. It first *deterministically* computes the error and then randomly samples the preimage. We show that for uniformly random targets, the preimage and error distributions are simulatable without knowing the trapdoor. This ensures the security of the signature applications. Compared to the Gaussian-distributed errors in previous algorithms, the deterministic errors have a smaller size, which lead to a substantial gain in security and enables a practically working instantiation.

As the applications, we present two practically efficient gadget-based signature schemes based on NTRU and Ring-LWE respectively. The NTRU-based scheme offers comparable efficiency to Falcon and Mitaka and a simple implementation without the need of generating the NTRU trapdoor. The LWE-based scheme also achieves a desirable overall performance. It not only greatly outperforms the state-of-the-art LWE-based

H. Handschuh and A. Lysyanskaya (Eds.): CRYPTO 2023, LNCS 14085, pp. 390–420, 2023.
https://doi.org/10.1007/978-3-031-38554-4_13

hash-and-sign signatures, but also has an even smaller size than the LWE-based Fiat-Shamir signature scheme Dilithium. These results fill the long-term gap in practical gadget-based signatures.

1   Introduction

Lattice-based cryptography is a promising post-quantum cryptography family having attractive features in both theory and practice. It has been shown to provide powerful versatility leading to various advanced cryptosystems including fully homomorphic encryption [Gen09], attribute-based encryption [GVW13], group signatures [GKV10] and much more [GVW15, BVWW16, Agr17, PS19]. For the basic encryption and signatures, lattice-based schemes are the most practically efficient among post-quantum cryptosystems and three of four post-quantum algorithms selected by NIST for standardization are lattice-based: Kyber [SAB20] for public key encryption/KEMs; Dilithium [LDK22] and Falcon [PFH22] for digital signatures.

At the core of many lattice-based schemes is the so-called Ajtai's function $f_{\mathbf{A}}(\mathbf{x}) = \mathbf{A}\mathbf{x} \bmod Q$ where $\mathbf{A} \in \mathbb{Z}_Q^{n \times m}$ is a short and fat random matrix. Ajtai showed in his seminal work [Ajt96] that the inversion of $f_{\mathbf{A}}$, i.e. finding a short preimage $\mathbf{x}$, is as hard as some worst-case lattice problems. With a *lattice trapdoor* for $\mathbf{A}$, one can efficiently compute a short preimage. In some applications, e.g. signatures, the preimage distribution is required to be *simulatable* without knowing the trapdoor. This is essential for security: some early proposals [GGH97, HHP03] were indeed broken by statistical attacks [NR06, DN12, YD18], since the preimages leak information of the trapdoor. To get rid of such leaks, Gentry, Peikert and Vaikuntanathan proposed a provably secure trapdoor framework, known as the GPV framework [GPV08], in which the preimage is sampled from a distribution statistically close to some publicly known discrete Gaussian. In the past decade, the GPV framework has been continuously enriched by new Gaussian sampling algorithms and trapdoor constructions. This leads to a series of efficient instantiations that can be basically classified into two families: *NTRU trapdoor based* and *gadget based*.

NTRU Trapdoor Based GPV Instantiations. The NTRU trapdoor, that is a high-quality basis of the NTRU lattice, was originally used in [HHP03]. In [DLP14], Ducas, Lyubashevsky and Prest first discovered that the lengths of the NTRU trapdoors can be within a small constant factor of optimal by choosing proper parameters, which gives a compact instantiation of the GPV framework over NTRU lattices. As an application, they presented the first lattice-based identity-based encryption (IBE) scheme with practical parameters. This instantiation was further developed as the Falcon signature scheme by integrating the fast Fourier sampler [DP16]. Falcon is now selected by NIST for the post-quantum standardization, due to its good performance in terms of bandwidth and efficiency. However, the signing and key generation algorithms of Falcon are rather complex. Recently, Espitau et al. proposed a simplified variant of Falcon, called Mitaka [EFG22]. Mitaka uses the hybrid sampler [Pre15] for easier implementation at the cost of a substantial security loss. To mitigate the security loss, Mitaka adopts some techniques to improve the trapdoor quality, which further complicates the key generation. Overall, Falcon and Mitaka are currently the most efficient lattice-based signatures, but their complex algorithms may be difficult to implement in constrained environments. Furthermore, the security of NTRU is shown to be significantly reduced in the overstretched parameter regime [KF17, DvW21], thus the NTRU trapdoor based instantiations are mainly used in signature and IBE applications.

Gadget Based GPV Instantiations. The gadget based instantiation was first proposed by Micciancio and Peikert [MP12]. In the Micciancio-Peikert framework, the public matrix $\mathbf{A} = [\bar{\mathbf{A}} \mid \mathbf{G} - \bar{\mathbf{A}}\mathbf{R}]$ where the trapdoor $\mathbf{R}$ is a matrix with small entries and the *gadget* $\mathbf{G} = \mathbf{I}_n \otimes \mathbf{g}^t$ with $\mathbf{g} = (1, b, \cdots, b^{k-1}), k = \lceil \log_b(Q) \rceil$. The inversion of $f_\mathbf{A}$ is converted into the inversion of $f_\mathbf{G}$ with $\mathbf{R}$. The latter boils down to the Gaussian sampling over the lattice $\Lambda_Q^\perp(\mathbf{g}) = \{\mathbf{u} \mid \langle \mathbf{u}, \mathbf{g} \rangle = 0 \bmod Q\}$ that is easy and fast [MP12, GM18, ZY22]. Compared to the NTRU trapdoor based GPV instantiations, the gadget based framework offers significant advantages in terms of implementation and turns out to be extremely versatile for the constructions of advanced primitives. However, the gadget based schemes suffer from rather large preimage and public key sizes. To improve the practicality of gadget based schemes, Chen, Genise and Mukherjee introduced the notion of approximate trapdoor [CGM19] and proposed to use a truncated gadget $\mathbf{f} = (b^l, \cdots, b^{k-1})$ for the trapdoor construction. While the improvement is substantial, the size of their gadget-based signature scheme is still far larger than that of Falcon and Dilithium.

As seen above, both NTRU trapdoor based schemes and gadget based ones occupy fairly different positions in lattice-based cryptography, but they also have own limitations. Particularly, the practical designs of gadget-based cryptosystems still lag far behind their theoretical constructions. It is therefore important to improve the practical efficiency of gadget-based cryptosystems including the hash-and-sign signatures.

Our Contributions. We develop some new technique to reduce the size of the gadget-based schemes. Using our compact gadget, we propose two hash-and-sign signature schemes based on NTRU and Ring-LWE respectively. They both offer a desirable performance and an easy implementation. This fills the gap in practical gadget-based signatures.

Compact Gadget with Semi-random Sampler. In our construction, the used gadget is $\mathbf{P} \in \mathbb{Z}^{n \times n}$ along with $\mathbf{Q} \in \mathbb{Z}^{n \times n}$ such that $\mathbf{PQ} = Q \cdot \mathbf{I}_n$, and the trapdoor $\mathbf{T}$ for the public matrix $\mathbf{A} \in \mathbb{Z}_Q^{n \times m}$ satisfies $\mathbf{AT} = \mathbf{P} \bmod Q$. The main technique to enable this compact gadget is a new gadget sampler for approximate trapdoors, called *semi-random* sampler. Given the target $\mathbf{u}$, this sampler computes a short approximate preimage $\mathbf{x}$ such that $\mathbf{u} = \mathbf{Px} + \mathbf{e} \bmod Q$ with a short error $\mathbf{e}$. In our sampler, only the preimage is randomly generated and the error is fixed by the target, which is why we name "semi-random". More concretely, the semi-random sampler consists of two steps respectively performed over the lattices defined by $\mathbf{P}$ and $\mathbf{Q}$:

1. *Deterministic error decoding:* The sampler first computes an error $\mathbf{e}$ such that $\mathbf{u} - \mathbf{e} = \mathbf{Pc} \in \Lambda(\mathbf{P})$ with deterministic lattice decoding.
2. *Random preimage sampling:* Then the sampler generates a short preimage $\mathbf{x} \in \Lambda(\mathbf{Q}) + \mathbf{c}$ with Gaussian sampling.

It is easy to verify that $\mathbf{Px} = \mathbf{u} - \mathbf{e} \bmod Q$. Despite the deterministic errors, we show that the distribution of $(\mathbf{x}, \mathbf{e})$ is simulatable for *uniformly random targets*. This is sufficient for the applications of digital signatures.

Our general construction can be instantiated with various lattices $\Lambda(\mathbf{P})$ and $\Lambda(\mathbf{Q})$ with specialized decoding and sampling algorithms. This opens up interesting avenues in the designs of lattice trapdoors. This paper showcases the merit of our gadget construction with a natural and simple instantiation: $(\mathbf{P} = p\mathbf{I}_n, \mathbf{Q} = q\mathbf{I}_n)$. We now contrast this simple instantiation with the truncated gadget $\mathbf{I}_n \otimes (b^l, \cdots, b^{k-1})^t$ in [CGM19]. Indeed, the gadget in our instantiation has the same structure with the special case of [CGM19] in which $l = k - 1$, $b^l = p$ and $Q = b^{l+1}$, but the associated sampling algorithms in two cases are quite distinct, which yields the differences in size and efficiency (see Table 1). For uniformly random targets, the error in our gadget sampler is uniformly distributed over $\mathbb{Z}_p^n$ and the preimage is distributed as Gaussian of width $q \cdot \omega(\sqrt{\log n})$. Then the error size is $\approx \frac{p\sqrt{n}}{\sqrt{12}}$ and the preimage size is $\approx \frac{Q}{p} \cdot \omega(\sqrt{n \log n})$. When it comes to the case of [CGM19], the error and the preimage are distributed as Gaussian of width $\sigma\sqrt{\frac{b^{2l}-1}{b^2-1}}$ and σ respectively where $\sigma \geq \sqrt{b^2+1} \cdot \omega(\sqrt{\log n})$. Then the error size is $\approx p \cdot \omega(\sqrt{n \log n})$ and the preimage size is $\approx \frac{Q}{p} \cdot \omega(\sqrt{n \log n})$ when $b^l = p$ and $Q = b^{l+1}$. As a consequence, our technique reduces the error size by a factor of $\sqrt{12} \cdot \omega(\sqrt{\log n})$ while keeping the preimage size. This gives a noticeable gain in concrete security and enables a practically working instantiation with the compact gadget. In addition, our semi-random sampler only needs n times integer Gaussian sampling along with n times modulo operations, whereas the sampler in [CGM19] needs nk times integer Gaussian sampling along with $O(nk)$ additions and multiplications. Our sampler is therefore simpler and more efficient. To sum up, our technique substantially improves the practical performance of the gadget-based schemes.

Simpler NTRU-Based Hash-and-Sign Signatures. We use the new gadget algorithms to build a new NTRU-based hash-and-sign signature scheme ROBIN. It achieves high efficiency comparable to Falcon [PFH22] and Mitaka [EFG22] that are two representative NTRU trapdoor based signatures (see Table 2). The main advantage of ROBIN is its convenient implementation. Firstly, ROBIN uses one NTRU vector instead of a full NTRU trapdoor basis as the signing key, which avoids the highly complex key generation. Secondly, like most of gadget-based

Table 1. Comparisons with our gadget sampler with the special case of [CGM19] in which $l = k - 1$, $b^l = p$ and $Q = b^{l+1}$.

	preimage size	error size	#integer sampling
[CGM19]	$\frac{Q}{p} \cdot \omega(\sqrt{n \log n})$	$p \cdot \omega(\sqrt{n \log n})$	nk
This work	$\frac{Q}{p} \cdot \omega(\sqrt{n \log n})$	$\frac{p\sqrt{n}}{\sqrt{12}}$	n

signatures, the signing procedure of ROBIN has an online/offline structure and the online sampling only consists of $D_{8\mathbb{Z}+c,r}$ for $c = 0, 1, \cdots, 7$, which allows an easier and more efficient implementation and side-channel protection. Additionally, the whole ROBIN algorithm including key generation, signing and verification can be conveniently implemented without using floating-point arithmetic. Therefore, ROBIN can be seen as an attractive post-quantum signature scheme especially for constrained devices.

Table 2. Comparison between ROBIN with Falcon [PFH22] and Mitaka [EFG22] at NIST-I and NIST-V security levels.

	NIST-I level			NIST-V level		
	Falcon	Mitaka	ROBIN	Falcon	Mitaka	ROBIN
Sig. size (bytes)	643	807	992	1249	1376	1862
Pub. key size (bytes)	896	972	1227	1792	1792	2399

Shorter LWE-Based Hash-and-Sign Signatures. We also propose a Ring-LWE-based instantiation of signatures based on our gadget, called EAGLE. While EAGLE is less efficient than its NTRU-based counterpart ROBIN, it still has a desirable performance and a simple implementation. Compared to other LWE-based hash-and-sign signatures, EAGLE offers a significantly smaller bandwidth. Specifically, the signature (resp. public key) size of EAGLE is $\leq 55\%$ (resp. $\leq 35\%$) of that of the scheme from [CGM19] with refined parameters and security estimates for both 80-bits and 192-bits of security levels. In fact, EAGLE is even more compact than Dilithium that is a representative LWE-based Fiat-Shamir signature scheme: for 192-bits of security level, the signature size of EAGLE is smaller by $\approx 8\%$ compared with Dilithium. To the best of our knowledge, EAGLE is the first LWE-based hash-and-sign signature scheme of key and signature sizes on par or better than practical LWE-based Fiat-Shamir signatures.

Roadmap. We start in Sect. 2 with preliminary materials, followed by recalling the existing gadget trapdoors in Sect. 3. Section 4 introduces our new gadget and the corresponding approximate trapdoor framework. We present concrete NTRU-based and Ring-LWE-based hash-and-sign signatures instantiated with

Table 3. Comparison between EAGLE with [CGM19] at 80-bits and NIST-III (192-bits) security levels.

	80-bits security		NIST-III level	
	[CGM19]	EAGLE	[CGM19]	EAGLE
Sig. size (bytes)	2753	1406	7172	3052
Pub. key size (bytes)	2720	928	7712	1952

our compact gadget framework in Sect. 5 and Sect. 6 respectively. Finally, we conclude in Sect. 7.

2 Preliminaries

Notations. Let $\mathbb{R}$ and $\mathbb{Z}$ denote the set of real numbers and integers respectively. For a positive integer q, let $\mathbb{Z}_q = \{-\lfloor q/2 \rfloor, -\lfloor q/2 \rfloor + 1, \cdots, q - \lfloor q/2 \rfloor - 1\}$. For a real-valued function f and a countable set S, we write $f(S) = \sum_{x \in S} f(x)$ assuming this sum is absolutely convergent. We write $a \leftarrow D$ to represent the sample a drawn from the distribution D. For a finite set S, let $U(S)$ be the uniform distribution over S and $a \xleftarrow{\$} S$ denote the sample $a \leftarrow U(S)$.

2.1 Linear Algebra and Lattices

A vector is denoted by a bold lower case letter, e.g. $\mathbf{x} = (x_1, \ldots, x_n)$, and in column form. The concatenation of $\mathbf{x}_1, \mathbf{x}_2$ is denoted by $(\mathbf{x}_1, \mathbf{x}_2)$. Let $\langle \mathbf{x}, \mathbf{y} \rangle$ be the inner product of $\mathbf{x}, \mathbf{y} \in \mathbb{R}^n$ and $\|\mathbf{x}\| = \sqrt{\langle \mathbf{x}, \mathbf{x} \rangle}$ be the ℓ_2 norm of $\mathbf{x}$. A matrix is denoted by a bold upper case letter, e.g. $\mathbf{A} = [\mathbf{a}_1 \mid \cdots \mid \mathbf{a}_n]$, where $\mathbf{a}_i$ denotes the ith column of $\mathbf{A}$. Let $\widetilde{\mathbf{A}} = [\widetilde{\mathbf{a}_1} \mid \cdots \mid \widetilde{\mathbf{a}_n}]$ denote the Gram-Schmidt orthogonalization of $\mathbf{A}$. Let $\mathbf{A} \oplus \mathbf{B}$ denote the block diagonal concatenation of $\mathbf{A}$ and $\mathbf{B}$. The largest singular value of $\mathbf{A}$ is denoted by $s_1(\mathbf{A}) = \max_{\mathbf{x} \neq \mathbf{0}} \frac{\|\mathbf{A}\mathbf{x}\|}{\|\mathbf{x}\|}$. Let $\mathbf{A}^t$ be the transpose of $\mathbf{A}$.

We write $\Sigma \succ 0$, when a symmetric matrix $\Sigma \in \mathbb{R}^{m \times m}$ is positive definite, i.e. $\mathbf{x}^t \Sigma \mathbf{x} > 0$ for all nonzero $\mathbf{x} \in \mathbb{R}^m$. We write $\Sigma_1 \succ \Sigma_2$ if $\Sigma_1 - \Sigma_2 \succ 0$. For any scalar s, we write $\Sigma \succ s$ if $\Sigma - s \cdot \mathbf{I} \succ 0$. If $\Sigma = \mathbf{B}\mathbf{B}^t$, we call $\mathbf{B}$ a square root of Σ. We use $\sqrt{\Sigma}$ to denote any square root of Σ when the context permits it.

Given $\mathbf{B} = [\mathbf{b}_1 \mid \cdots \mid \mathbf{b}_n] \in \mathbb{R}^{m \times n}$ with each $\mathbf{b}_i$ linearly independent, the lattice generated by $\mathbf{B}$ is $\Lambda(\mathbf{B}) = \{\mathbf{B}\mathbf{z} \mid \mathbf{z} \in \mathbb{Z}^n\}$. The dimension of $\Lambda(\mathbf{B})$ is n and $\mathbf{B}$ is called a basis. Let $\Lambda^* = \{\mathbf{y} \in \text{span}(\Lambda) \mid \langle \mathbf{x}, \mathbf{y} \rangle \in \mathbb{Z}, \forall \mathbf{x} \in \Lambda\}$ be the dual lattice of a lattice Λ.

In lattice-based cryptography, the q-ary lattice is of special interest and defined for some $\mathbf{A} \in \mathbb{Z}_q^{n \times m}$ as

$$\Lambda_q^\perp(\mathbf{A}) = \{\mathbf{x} \in \mathbb{Z}^m : \mathbf{A}\mathbf{x} = \mathbf{0} \mod q\}.$$

The dimension of $\Lambda_q^\perp(\mathbf{A})$ is m and $(q \cdot \mathbb{Z})^m \subseteq \Lambda_q^\perp \subseteq \mathbb{Z}^m$. Each $\mathbf{u} \in \mathbb{Z}_q^n$ defines a lattice coset

$$\Lambda_{q,\mathbf{u}}^\perp(\mathbf{A}) = \{\mathbf{x} \in \mathbb{Z}^m : \mathbf{A}\mathbf{x} = \mathbf{u} \mod q\}.$$

Given a matrix $\mathbf{A} \in \mathbb{Z}_q^{n \times m}$, let $f_\mathbf{A}(\mathbf{x}) = \mathbf{A}\mathbf{x} \mod q$ be the associated Ajtai's function [Ajt96] where $\mathbf{x}$ is usually short. We simply denote by $f_\mathbf{A}^{-1}$ the inversion procedure, namely finding a short *preimage* $\mathbf{x}$.

2.2   Gaussians

The Gaussian function $\rho : \mathbb{R}^m \to (0,1]$ is defined as $\rho(\mathbf{x}) = \exp(-\pi \cdot \langle \mathbf{x}, \mathbf{x} \rangle)$. Applying a linear transformation given by an invertible matrix $\mathbf{B}$ yields

$$\rho_\mathbf{B}(\mathbf{x}) = \rho(\mathbf{B}^{-1}\mathbf{x}) = \exp(-\pi \cdot \mathbf{x}^t \Sigma^{-1} \mathbf{x}),$$

where $\Sigma = \mathbf{B}\mathbf{B}^t$. Since $\rho_\mathbf{B}$ is exactly determined by Σ, we also write it as $\rho_{\sqrt{\Sigma}}$. For a lattice Λ and $\mathbf{c} \in \mathrm{span}(\Lambda)$, the discrete Gaussian distribution $D_{\Lambda+\mathbf{c},\sqrt{\Sigma}}$ is defined as: for any $\mathbf{x} \in \Lambda + \mathbf{c}$,

$$D_{\Lambda+\mathbf{c},\sqrt{\Sigma}}(\mathbf{x}) = \frac{\rho_{\sqrt{\Sigma}}(\mathbf{x})}{\rho_{\sqrt{\Sigma}}(\Lambda + \mathbf{c})}.$$

Let $\eta_\epsilon(\Lambda) = \min\{s > 0 \mid \rho(s \cdot \Lambda^*) \leq 1 + \epsilon\}$ be the smoothing parameter with respect to a lattice Λ and $\epsilon \in (0,1)$. We write $\sqrt{\Sigma} \geq \eta_\epsilon(\Lambda)$, if $\rho_{\sqrt{\Sigma^{-1}}}(\Lambda^*) \leq 1 + \epsilon$.

Lemma 1 ([GPV08]). *Let Λ be an m-dimensional lattice with a basis $\mathbf{B}$, then $\eta_\epsilon(\Lambda) \leq \max_i \|\widetilde{\mathbf{b}}_i\| \cdot \sqrt{\log(2m(1+1/\epsilon))/\pi}$, where $\widetilde{\mathbf{b}}_i$ is the i-th vector of $\widetilde{\mathbf{B}}$.*

Lemma 2 ([MR07]). *Let Λ be a lattice, $\mathbf{c} \in \mathrm{span}(\Lambda)$. Then for any $\epsilon \in (0, \frac{1}{2})$ and $s \geq \eta_\epsilon(\Lambda)$, $\rho_s(\Lambda + \mathbf{c}) \in \left[\frac{1-\epsilon}{1+\epsilon}, 1\right] \rho_s(\Lambda)$.*

Lemma 3 ([GPV08], **Corollary 2.8**). *Let Λ, Λ' be two lattices such that $\Lambda' \subseteq \Lambda$. Let $s \geq \eta_\epsilon(\Lambda')$. Then for any $\epsilon \in (0, \frac{1}{2})$ and $\mathbf{c} \in \mathrm{span}(\Lambda)$, the distribution of $(D_{\Lambda+\mathbf{c},s} \mod \Lambda')$ is within statistical distance at most 2ϵ of $U(\Lambda \mod \Lambda')$.*

Theorem 1 ([GMPW20]). *For any $\epsilon \in [0,1)$ defining $\bar{\epsilon} = 2\epsilon/(1-\epsilon)$, a matrix $\mathbf{S}$ of full column rank, a lattice coset $A = \Lambda + \mathbf{a} \subset \mathrm{span}(\mathbf{S})$, and a matrix $\mathbf{T}$ such that $\ker(\mathbf{T})$ is a Λ-subspace and $\eta_\epsilon(\Lambda \cap \ker(\mathbf{T})) \leq \mathbf{S}$, we have*

$$\mathbf{T} \cdot D_{A,\mathbf{S}} \approx_{\bar{\epsilon}} D_{\mathbf{T}A,\mathbf{T}\mathbf{S}}.$$

2.3   The Ring $\mathbb{Z}[x]/(x^n \pm 1)$

We work with two polynomial rings in the paper. The first one is the convolution ring $\mathcal{R}_n^- = \mathbb{Z}[x]/(x^n - 1)$ where n is a prime. For any $a = \sum_{i=0}^{n-1} a_i x^i \in \mathcal{R}_n^-$, let $v(a) = (a_0, a_1 \cdots, a_{n-1})$ be its coefficient vector and the circulant matrix

$$\mathcal{M}(a) = \begin{bmatrix} a_0 & a_{n-1} & \cdots & a_1 \\ a_1 & a_0 & \cdots & a_2 \\ \vdots & \vdots & \vdots & \vdots \\ a_{n-1} & a_{n-2} & \cdots & a_0 \end{bmatrix} = [v(a), v(a \cdot x), \cdots, v(a \cdot x^{n-1})].$$

be its matrix form. The second ring in the paper is the power-of-2 cyclotomic ring, i.e. $\mathcal{R}_n^+ = \mathbb{Z}[x]/(x^n + 1)$ with n a power of 2. For $a = \sum_{i=0}^{n-1} a_i x^i \in \mathcal{R}_n^+$, its coefficient vector is also written as $v(a)$ and the matrix form becomes an anticirculant matrix

$$\mathcal{M}(a) = \begin{bmatrix} a_0 & -a_{n-1} & \cdots & -a_1 \\ a_1 & a_0 & \cdots & -a_2 \\ \vdots & \vdots & \vdots & \vdots \\ a_{n-1} & a_{n-2} & \cdots & a_0 \end{bmatrix} = [v(a), v(a \cdot x), \cdots, v(a \cdot x^{n-1})].$$

In the rest of the paper, we identify a with $v(a)$ when the context is clear.

Let $\bar{a} = a(x^{-1})$ for $a \in \mathcal{R}$, then $\bar{a} = a_0 + \sum_{i=1}^{n-1} a_{n-i} x^i$ when $\mathcal{R} = \mathcal{R}_n^-$ and $\bar{a} = a_0 - \sum_{i=1}^{n-1} a_{n-i} x^i$ when $\mathcal{R} = \mathcal{R}_n^+$. More generally, let $\sigma_k(a) = a(x^k)$ for $k \in \mathbb{Z}_n^*$. For both $\mathcal{R}_n^-$ and $\mathcal{R}_n^+$, the following properties hold:

- $\mathcal{M}(a) + \mathcal{M}(b) = \mathcal{M}(a + b)$
- $\mathcal{M}(a) \cdot \mathcal{M}(b) = \mathcal{M}(ab)$.
- $\mathcal{M}(\bar{a}) = \mathcal{M}(a)^t$

2.4   NTRU

The NTRU module determined by $h \in \mathcal{R}$ is given by

$$\Lambda_{NTRU}^h = \{(u, v) \in \mathcal{R}^2 : uh - v = 0 \mod Q\}.$$

Our NTRU-based scheme mainly uses $\mathcal{R} = \mathcal{R}_n^-$, and the NTRU module is seen as a lattice of dimension $2n$.

In typical NTRU-based cryptosystems, the secret key is composed of two short polynomials $f, g \in \mathcal{R}$, while the public key is $h = f^{-1}g \mod Q$. Then (f, g) is a short vector of Λ_{NTRU}^h. In addition, an *inhomogeneous* version of NTRU was introduced in [GGH19]. In this version, the public key $h = f^{-1}(g + e) \mod Q$ where e is a public constant. The corresponding problems are defined as follows.

Definition 1 (NTRU and inhomogeneous NTRU). *Let $\mathcal{R} = \mathbb{Z}[x]/(x^n - 1)$ with n a prime. Let $Q > 0$ be an integer and χ be a distribution over $\mathcal{R}$. Let D_χ (resp. $D_{\chi,e}$) be the distribution of the NTRU public key $h = f^{-1}g \mod Q$ (resp. $h = \frac{g+e}{f} \mod Q$) with $f, g \leftarrow \chi$.*

- $\mathsf{NTRU}_{\mathcal{R},Q,\chi}$: *Given $h \leftarrow D_\chi$, find short (f, g) such that $h = f^{-1}g \mod Q$.*
- $\mathsf{iNTRU}_{\mathcal{R},Q,\chi,e}$: *Given $h \leftarrow D_{\chi,e}$, find short (f, g) such that $h = \frac{g+e}{f} \mod Q$.*

2.5   LWE

The LWE (learning with errors) problem is defined as follows.

Definition 2 (LWE). *Let $n, m, Q > 0$ be integers and χ be a distribution over $\mathbb{Z}$. Given $\mathbf{s} \in \mathbb{Z}_Q^n$, let $A_{\mathbf{s},\chi}$ be the distribution of $(\mathbf{a}, b)$ where $\mathbf{a} \xleftarrow{\$} \mathbb{Z}_Q^n$ and $b = \langle \mathbf{a}, \mathbf{s} \rangle + e \mod Q$ with $e \leftarrow \chi$.*

– Decision-LWE$_{n,m,Q,\chi}$: *Given m independent samples from either $A_{\mathbf{s},\chi}$ with $\mathbf{s} \leftarrow \chi$ (fixed for all m samples) or $U(\mathbb{Z}_Q^n \times \mathbb{Z}_Q)$, distinguish which is the case.*
– Search-LWE$_{n,m,Q,\chi}$: *Given m independent samples from $A_{\mathbf{s},\chi}$ with $\mathbf{s} \leftarrow \chi$, find* $\mathbf{s}$.

To improve the efficiency and key sizes, some algebraic variants of LWE were proposed and used to build practical lattice-based cryptosystems. In this paper, we mainly use the ring variant proposed in [LPR10].

Definition 3 (Ring-LWE). *Let $\mathcal{R} = \mathbb{Z}[x]/(x^n + 1)$ with n a power of 2. Let $m, Q > 0$ be integers and χ be a distribution over $\mathcal{R}$. Let $\mathcal{R}_Q = \mathcal{R}/(Q \cdot \mathcal{R})$. Given $s \in \mathcal{R}_Q$, let $A_{s,\chi}$ be the distribution of (a, b) where $a \xleftarrow{\$} \mathcal{R}_Q$ and $b = as + e \bmod Q$ with $e \leftarrow \chi$.*

– Decision-RLWE$_{\mathcal{R},m,Q,\chi}$: *Given m independent samples from either $A_{s,\chi}$ with $s \leftarrow \chi$ (fixed for all m samples) or $U(\mathcal{R}_Q \times \mathcal{R}_Q)$, distinguish which is the case.*
– Search-RLWE$_{\mathcal{R},m,Q,\chi}$: *Given m independent samples from $A_{s,\chi}$ with $s \leftarrow \chi$, find s.*

2.6 SIS

We recall the SIS (short integer solution) problem and its inhomogeneous variant.

Definition 4 (SIS and inhomogeneous SIS). *Let $n, m, Q > 0$ be integers and $\beta > 0$.*

– SIS$_{n,m,Q,\beta}$: *Given a uniformly random $\mathbf{A} \in \mathbb{Z}_Q^{n \times m}$, find a non-zero integer vector $\mathbf{x}$ such that $\mathbf{Ax} = \mathbf{0} \bmod Q$ and $\|\mathbf{x}\| \leq \beta$.*
– ISIS$_{n,m,Q,\beta}$: *Given a uniformly random $\mathbf{A} \in \mathbb{Z}_Q^{n \times m}$ and $\mathbf{y} \in \mathbb{Z}_Q^n$, find a non-zero integer vector $\mathbf{x}$ such that $\mathbf{Ax} = \mathbf{y} \bmod Q$ and $\|\mathbf{x}\| \leq \beta$.*

The public matrix $\mathbf{A}$ in SIS and ISIS problems can be in the Hermite normal form (HNF), i.e. $\mathbf{A} = [\mathbf{I}_n \mid \mathbf{A}']$. This gives the HNF version of SIS problems, HNF.SIS and HNF.ISIS. Such variants are as hard as the standard version.

The ring variants of SIS and ISIS are immediate. We only show the definition of Ring-ISIS.

Definition 5 (Ring-ISIS, RISIS$_{\mathcal{R},m,Q,\beta}$). *Let $\mathcal{R} = \mathbb{Z}[x]/(x^n + 1)$ with n a power of 2. Let $m, Q > 0$ be integers and $\beta > 0$. Let $\mathcal{R}_Q = \mathcal{R}/(Q \cdot \mathcal{R})$. Given a uniformly random $\mathbf{A} \in \mathcal{R}_Q^m$ and $y \in \mathcal{R}_Q$, find a non-zero integer vector $\mathbf{x} \in \mathcal{R}^m$ such that $\mathbf{Ax} = y \bmod Q$ and $\|\mathbf{x}\| \leq \beta$.*

The approximate version of ISIS was introduced in [CGM19]. It can be immediately adapted to the ring version ApproxRISIS$_{\mathcal{R},m,Q,\alpha,\beta}$ and the HNF version HNF.ApproxISIS$_{\mathcal{R},m,Q,\alpha,\beta}$.

Definition 6 (Approximate ISIS, ApproxISIS$_{n,m,Q,\alpha,\beta}$). *Let $n, m, Q > 0$ be integers and $\beta > 0$. Given a uniformly random $\mathbf{A} \in \mathbb{Z}_Q^{n \times m}$ and a random $\mathbf{y} \in \mathbb{Z}_Q^n$, find an integer vector $\mathbf{x}$ such that $\mathbf{A}\mathbf{x} = \mathbf{y} - \mathbf{e} \bmod Q$ with $\|\mathbf{e}\| \leq \alpha$ and $\|\mathbf{x}\| \leq \beta$.*

We will also use an NTRU version of SIS. It is the underlying assumption of NTRU-based signatures [PFH22, EFG22, DDLL13]. The NTRU-SIS problem can be immediately adapted to the inhomogeneous version NTRUISIS$_{\mathcal{R},Q,\chi,\beta}$ and the approximate version ApproxNTRUISIS$_{\mathcal{R},Q,\chi,\alpha,\beta}$.

Definition 7 (NTRU-SIS, NTRUSIS$_{\mathcal{R},Q,\chi,\beta}$). *Let $\mathcal{R} = \mathbb{Z}[x]/(x^n - 1)$ with n a prime. Let $Q > 0$ be an integer, χ be a distribution over $\mathcal{R}$ and $\beta > 0$. Given a random NTRU public key h of either NTRU$_{\mathcal{R},Q,\chi}$ or iNTRU$_{\mathcal{R},Q,\chi,e}$, find a non-zero vector (x_0, x_1) such that $\|(x_0, x_1)\| \leq \beta$ and $x_0 + hx_1 = 0 \bmod Q$.*

3   Recall the Gadget Trapdoors

While Ajtai's function $f_{\mathbf{A}}$ is hard to invert for a random matrix $\mathbf{A}$, the inversion $f_{\mathbf{A}}^{-1}$ can be easily computed with a short trapdoor. The most famous and efficient lattice trapdoors are based on the lattice gadget framework developed in [MP12]. In a gadget trapdoor scheme, the inversion of $f_{\mathbf{A}}$ is converted into the gadget inversion, i.e. the inversion of $f_{\mathbf{G}}$ for a gadget matrix $\mathbf{G}$. The gadget inversion turns out to be highly simple and fast for some well-designed $\mathbf{G}$. For better completeness and contrast, let us briefly recall the classical gadget trapdoor from [MP12] and its approximate variant from [CGM19].

3.1   Exact Gadget Trapdoor from [MP12]

The earliest and most widely used gadget trapdoor is proposed by Micciancio and Peikert in [MP12]. In the Micciancio-Peikert trapdoor, the gadget matrix is $\mathbf{G} = \mathbf{I}_n \otimes \mathbf{g}^t \in \mathbb{Z}^{n \times m'}$ where $\mathbf{g} = (1, b, \cdots, b^{k-1})$, $k = \lceil \log_b(Q) \rceil$ and $m' = nk$. The public matrix is

$$\mathbf{A} = [\bar{\mathbf{A}} \mid \mathbf{G} - \bar{\mathbf{A}}\mathbf{R}] \in \mathbb{Z}_Q^{n \times m}$$

where $\bar{\mathbf{A}} \in \mathbb{Z}_Q^{n \times \bar{m}}$, $m = \bar{m} + m'$ and $\mathbf{R}$ is a secret matrix of small entries such that $\bar{\mathbf{A}}\mathbf{R}$ is either statistically near-uniform or computationally pseudorandom under certain assumptions. In this paper, we are interested in the pseudorandom case that offers better practicality due to the smaller dimension of $\mathbf{A}$.

Let $\mathbf{T} = \begin{bmatrix} \mathbf{R} \\ \mathbf{I} \end{bmatrix}$, then $\mathbf{A}\mathbf{T} = \mathbf{G} \bmod Q$. This linear relation gives a direct transformation from $f_{\mathbf{A}}^{-1}$ to the gadget inversion $f_{\mathbf{G}}^{-1}$: given a target $\mathbf{u} \in \mathbb{Z}_Q^n$, $\mathbf{x} = \mathbf{T}\mathbf{x}'$ is a short preimage of $f_{\mathbf{A}}^{-1}(\mathbf{u})$ when $\mathbf{x}'$ is a short preimage of $f_{\mathbf{G}}^{-1}(\mathbf{u})$. Many applications, e.g. digital signatures, also need the preimage distribution to be simulatable without using the trapdoor for *uniformly random* targets for security purpose. To this end, a common approach is to make the preimage distribution statistically close to some Gaussian independent of the trapdoor by adding some perturbation following the idea of [Pei10]. More concretely, the inversion $f_{\mathbf{A}}^{-1}(\mathbf{u})$ in the Micciancio-Peikert framework proceeds as follows:

1. *(Perturbation sampling)* Sample $\mathbf{p}$ from $D_{\mathbb{Z}^m, \sqrt{\Sigma_p}}$ where $\Sigma_p = s^2 \mathbf{I}_m - r^2 \mathbf{T}\mathbf{T}^t$
2. Compute $\mathbf{u}' = \mathbf{u} - \mathbf{A}\mathbf{p} \bmod Q$
3. *(Gadget sampling)* Sample $\mathbf{x}'$ from $D_{\Lambda^\perp_{Q,\mathbf{u}'}(\mathbf{G}), r}$
4. Output the preimage $\mathbf{x} = \mathbf{p} + \mathbf{T}\mathbf{x}' \bmod Q$

The required parameter conditions by the Gaussian sampling include $r \geq \eta_\epsilon(\Lambda^\perp_Q(\mathbf{G}))$ and $s \geq r \cdot s_1(\mathbf{T})$.

3.2   Approximate Gadget Trapdoor from [CGM19]

In [CGM19], Chen, Genise and Mukherjee introduced the notion of *approximate trapdoor*. Such a trapdoor allows to approximately invert Ajtai's function $f_\mathbf{A}$, i.e. to find a short preimage $\mathbf{x}$ of $f_\mathbf{A}^{-1}(\mathbf{u})$ such that $\mathbf{A}\mathbf{x} = \mathbf{u} - \mathbf{e} \bmod Q$ for some short $\mathbf{e}$. The vector $\mathbf{e}$ is termed *approximate error* or simply *error*. An approximate variant of the Micciancio-Peikert gadget trapdoor was given in [CGM19]. In the Chen-Genise-Mukherjee trapdoor, the gadget matrix is $\mathbf{F} = \mathbf{I}_n \otimes \mathbf{f}^t \in \mathbb{Z}^{n \times m'}$ where $\mathbf{f} = (b^l, b^{l+1}, \cdots, b^{k-1})$ is truncated from the gadget $\mathbf{g}$ in the exact case, and $m' = n(k - l)$. The public matrix accordingly becomes

$$\mathbf{A} = [\bar{\mathbf{A}} \mid \mathbf{F} - \bar{\mathbf{A}}\mathbf{R}] \in \mathbb{Z}_Q^{n \times m},$$

where $m = \bar{m} + m'$. Compared to the exact gadget, the approximate variant substantially reduces the dimension of $\mathbf{A}$ and thus leads to more practical hash-and-sign signatures.

Let $\mathbf{T} = \begin{bmatrix} \mathbf{R} \\ \mathbf{I} \end{bmatrix}$ and $\mathbf{D} = \mathbf{I}_n \otimes \mathbf{d}^t$ where $\mathbf{d} = (1, b, \cdots, b^{l-1})$. Then the exact gadget $\mathbf{G} = \mathbf{I}_n \otimes [\mathbf{d}^t \mid \mathbf{f}^t]$. The approximate inversion follows the spirit of transforming $f_\mathbf{A}^{-1}$ to the (approximate) gadget inversion. Given a target $\mathbf{u}$, it proceeds as follows:

1. *(Perturbation sampling)* Sample $\mathbf{p}$ from $D_{\mathbb{Z}^m, \sqrt{\Sigma_p}}$ where $\Sigma_p = s^2 \mathbf{I}_m - r^2 \mathbf{T}\mathbf{T}^t$
2. Compute $\mathbf{u}' = \mathbf{u} - \mathbf{A}\mathbf{p} \bmod Q$
3. *(Gadget sampling)* Sample $\mathbf{x}'$ from $D_{\Lambda^\perp_{Q,\mathbf{u}'}(\mathbf{G}), r}$
4. *(Preimage truncation)* Let $\mathbf{x}' = (\mathbf{x}'_1, \ldots, \mathbf{x}'_n)$ with $\mathbf{x}'_i \in \mathbb{Z}^k$. Set $\mathbf{x}''_i$ as the last $(k - l)$ entries of $\mathbf{x}'_i$ and $\mathbf{x}'' = (\mathbf{x}''_1, \ldots, \mathbf{x}''_n)$
5. Output the preimage $\mathbf{x} = \mathbf{p} + \mathbf{T}\mathbf{x}'' \bmod Q$

Let $\mathbf{x}' := (\mathbf{x}''', \mathbf{x}'')$, then the approximate error is

$$\mathbf{e} = \mathbf{u} - \mathbf{A}\mathbf{x} = \mathbf{u} - \mathbf{A}\mathbf{p} - \mathbf{F}\mathbf{x}'' = \mathbf{u}' - \mathbf{F}\mathbf{x}'' = \mathbf{D}\mathbf{x}''' \bmod Q.$$

For uniformly random $\mathbf{u}$, the distribution of $(\mathbf{u}, \mathbf{x}, \mathbf{e})$ can be simulated by sampling $\mathbf{x} \leftarrow D_{\mathbb{Z}^m, s}$ and $\mathbf{e} \leftarrow D_{\mathbb{Z}^n, r \cdot \|\mathbf{d}\|}$ and then setting $\mathbf{u} = \mathbf{A}\mathbf{x} + \mathbf{e} \bmod Q$. The required parameter conditions include $r \geq \eta_\epsilon(\Lambda^\perp_Q(\mathbf{G}))$ and $s \geq C \cdot r \cdot s_1(\mathbf{T})$ where C is a small constant for commonly-used trapdoors.

3.3   Equivalence Between Exact and Approximate Trapdoors

Recall that the approximate trapdoor allows to sample a short preimage $\mathbf{x}$ such that $\mathbf{A}\mathbf{x} + \mathbf{e} = \mathbf{u} \bmod Q$ with a short error $\mathbf{e}$. When $\mathbf{A} = [\mathbf{I}_n \mid \mathbf{A}']$, one can transform the approximate preimage $\mathbf{x} = (\mathbf{x}_0, \mathbf{x}_1)$ and the error $\mathbf{e}$ into an exact preimage $\mathbf{x}' = (\mathbf{x}_0 + \mathbf{e}, \mathbf{x}_1)$ such that $\mathbf{A}\mathbf{x}' = \mathbf{u} \bmod Q$. Hence the exact and approximate trapdoors are somewhat equivalent from an algorithmic aspect. This equivalence is characterized in the reduction form as follows.

Lemma 4 ([CGM19], Lemma 3.5, adapted). *For $n, m, Q \in \mathbb{Z}, \alpha, \beta \geq 0$*

- $\mathsf{HNF.ApproxISIS}_{n,m,Q,\alpha,\beta} \leq_p \mathsf{HNF.ISIS}_{n,m,Q,\beta}$ *for any $\alpha \geq 0$*
- $\mathsf{HNF.ISIS}_{n,m,Q,\alpha+\beta} \leq_p \mathsf{HNF.ApproxISIS}_{n,m,Q,\alpha,\beta}$

Remark 1. Lemma 4 simply takes $(\alpha + \beta)$ as the bound of the size of the exact preimage $\mathbf{x}' = (\mathbf{x}_0 + \mathbf{e}, \mathbf{x}_1)$. When it comes to concrete security estimate, this additive bound is loose and a more accurate approach is to estimate $\|\mathbf{x}_0 + \mathbf{e}\|$ and $\|\mathbf{x}_1\|$ separately. The term $\|\mathbf{x}_0 + \mathbf{e}\|$ can be estimated based on the Pythagorean additive property when $\mathbf{x}_0$ and $\mathbf{e}$ are Gaussian-like. Moerover, we consider the unbalanced sizes of $\mathbf{x}_0 + \mathbf{e}$ and $\mathbf{x}_1$ in later security estimates.

4   Compact Gadget for Approximate Trapdoor

We present a new gadget for approximate trapdoors in this section. In contrast with existing gadgets from [MP12,CGM19], our gadget matrix is of size only n-by-n, which allows more compact public keys and trapdoors. At the core of our construction is a new type of approximate gadget sampler that we term *semi-random* sampler. In this sampler, the preimage is randomly sampled, whereas the error is *deterministically fixed* by the target. While the semi-random sampler loses some randomness of the error part, the distributions of the preimages and the errors can be still simulatable for *uniformly random targets*. This suffices for the need of the application of hash-and-sign signatures.

4.1   Description of Our Gadget Trapdoor

This section gives a general description of our gadget trapdoor and the semi-random sampler. We believe that such a general description can guide further study of new gadget designs.

Let $\mathbf{P} \in \mathbb{Z}^{n \times n}$ denote the gadget matrix used in our trapdoor construction and $\mathbf{Q} \in \mathbb{Z}^{n \times n}$ such that

$$\mathbf{P}\mathbf{Q} = Q \cdot \mathbf{I}_n.$$

The public matrix is $\mathbf{A} \in \mathbb{Z}_Q^{n \times m}$ with $m > n$ and the approximate trapdoor for $\mathbf{A}$ is defined as a matrix $\mathbf{T} \in \mathbb{Z}^{m \times n}$ such that

$$\mathbf{A}\mathbf{T} = \mathbf{P} \quad \bmod Q.$$

Then the approximate trapdoor inversion is transformed to the approximate gadget inversion implemented by our semi-random sampler.

Remark 2. Our trapdoor can be instantiated under different assumptions:

– LWE-based: $\mathbf{A} = [\mathbf{I} \mid \bar{\mathbf{A}} \mid \mathbf{P} + \bar{\mathbf{A}}\mathbf{S} + \mathbf{E}]$ and $\mathbf{T} = [-\mathbf{E}^t \mid -\mathbf{S}^t \mid \mathbf{I}]^t$;
– NTRU-based: $\mathbf{A} = [\mathbf{I} \mid (\mathbf{P} - \mathbf{F}) \cdot \mathbf{G}^{-1}]$ and $\mathbf{T} = [\mathbf{F}^t \mid \mathbf{G}^t]^t$.

See Sects. 5 and 6 for more details.

Given a target $\mathbf{u}'$, the semi-random gadget sampler outputs a preimage $\mathbf{x}'$ such that $\mathbf{P}\mathbf{x}' = \mathbf{u}' - \mathbf{e} \bmod Q$ for some small error $\mathbf{e}$. It proceeds in two steps: (1) *deterministic error decoding* and (2) *random preimage sampling*. In the first step, the sampler computes the error $\mathbf{e}$ such that $\mathbf{u}' - \mathbf{e} = \mathbf{P}\mathbf{c} \in \Lambda(\mathbf{P})$. This can be done by lattice decoding algorithms, e.g. Babai's CVP algorithms [Bab86]. We denote by LatticeDecoder the deterministic lattice decoder and use it in a black-box way. Typically, the output errors are identical for all vectors in a coset $\mathbf{t} + \Lambda(\mathbf{P})$. We denote by $E(\mathbf{P})$ the set of all possible errors and write $\mathbf{e} = (\mathbf{u}' \bmod \Lambda(\mathbf{P}))$ the error for $\mathbf{u}'$. The next step is to sample the preimage $\mathbf{x}'$ from $D_{\Lambda(\mathbf{Q})+\mathbf{c},r}$. Let $\mathbf{x}' = \mathbf{Q}\mathbf{v} + \mathbf{c}$ for $\mathbf{v} \in \mathbb{Z}^n$. One can verify that

$$\mathbf{P}\mathbf{x}' = \mathbf{P}\mathbf{Q}\mathbf{v} + \mathbf{P}\mathbf{c} = \mathbf{u}' - \mathbf{e} \bmod Q. \tag{1}$$

A formal description is given in Algorithm 1.

Algorithm 1: ApproxGadget($\mathbf{u}', r, \mathbf{P}, \mathbf{Q}$)

Input: matrices $\mathbf{P}, \mathbf{Q} \in \mathbb{Z}^{n \times n}$ such that $\mathbf{P}\mathbf{Q} = Q \cdot \mathbf{I}_n$ and $r \geq \eta_\epsilon(\Lambda(\mathbf{Q}))$
Output: a sample $\mathbf{x}' \sim D_{\mathbb{Z}^n,r}$ conditioned on $\mathbf{P}\mathbf{x}' = \mathbf{u}' - \mathbf{e} \bmod Q$ and $\mathbf{e} \in E(\mathbf{P})$.
1: $(\mathbf{c}, \mathbf{e}) \leftarrow$ LatticeDecoder($\mathbf{u}', \mathbf{P}$) such that $\mathbf{c} \in \mathbb{Z}^n$ and $\mathbf{u}' - \mathbf{e} = \mathbf{P}\mathbf{c}$
2: $\mathbf{x}' \leftarrow D_{\Lambda(\mathbf{Q})+\mathbf{c},r}$
3: **return** $\mathbf{x}'$

The correctness of Algorithm 1 is shown in Lemma 5.

Lemma 5. *Algorithm 1 is correct. More precisely, let $\mathbf{P}, \mathbf{Q} \in \mathbb{Z}^{n \times n}$ such that $\mathbf{P}\mathbf{Q} = Q \cdot \mathbf{I}_n$ and $r \geq \eta_\epsilon(\Lambda(\mathbf{Q}))$. Then the output $\mathbf{x}'$ of ApproxGadget($\mathbf{u}', r, \mathbf{P}, \mathbf{Q}$) follows the distribution of $D_{\mathbb{Z}^n,r}$ conditioned on $\mathbf{P}\mathbf{x}' = \mathbf{u}' - \mathbf{e} \bmod Q$ with $\mathbf{e} \in E(\mathbf{P})$.*

Proof. Given $\mathbf{u}'$, there exists a unique error $\mathbf{e} = (\mathbf{u}' \bmod \Lambda(\mathbf{P}))$ satisfying $\mathbf{e} \in E(\mathbf{P})$ and $\mathbf{u}' - \mathbf{e} = \mathbf{P}\mathbf{c} \in \Lambda(\mathbf{P})$. For $\mathbf{x}'$ such that $\mathbf{P}\mathbf{x}' = \mathbf{u}' - \mathbf{e} \bmod Q$, let $\mathbf{P}\mathbf{x}' = \mathbf{u}' - \mathbf{e} + Q\mathbf{v}$, then $\mathbf{P}\mathbf{x}' = \mathbf{P}(\mathbf{c} + \mathbf{Q}\mathbf{v})$ and thus $\mathbf{x}' \in \Lambda(\mathbf{Q}) + \mathbf{c}$. For $\mathbf{x}' \in \Lambda(\mathbf{Q}) + \mathbf{c}$, let $\mathbf{x}' - \mathbf{c} = \mathbf{Q}\mathbf{v}$ for some $\mathbf{v} \in \mathbb{Z}^n$, then $\mathbf{P}\mathbf{x}' = \mathbf{u}' - \mathbf{e} \bmod Q$ as shown by Eq. (1). Therefore $\mathbf{P}\mathbf{x}' = \mathbf{u}' - \mathbf{e} \bmod Q$ holds if and only if $\mathbf{x}' \in \Lambda(\mathbf{Q}) + \mathbf{c}$. The proof is completed. $\qquad\square$

We now prove that for uniformly random $\mathbf{u}'$, the preimage and error distributions of ApproxGadget($\mathbf{u}', r, \mathbf{P}, \mathbf{Q}$) can be simulated.

Lemma 6. *Let* $\mathbf{P}, \mathbf{Q} \in \mathbb{Z}^{n \times n}$ *such that* $\mathbf{PQ} = Q \cdot \mathbf{I}_n$ *and* $r \geq \eta_\epsilon(\Lambda(\mathbf{Q}))$ *with some negligible* $\epsilon > 0$. *Let* $\chi_\mathbf{e}$ *be the distribution of* $(\mathbf{v} \bmod \Lambda(\mathbf{P})) \in E(\mathbf{P})$ *where* $\mathbf{v} \leftarrow U(\mathbb{Z}_Q^n)$. *Then the following two distributions are statistically close.*

1. *First sample* $\mathbf{u}' \leftarrow U(\mathbb{Z}_Q^n)$, *then sample* $\mathbf{x}' \leftarrow \mathsf{ApproxGadget}(\mathbf{u}', r, \mathbf{P}, \mathbf{Q})$, *compute* $\mathbf{e} = (\mathbf{u}' \bmod \Lambda(\mathbf{P}))$, *output* $(\mathbf{x}', \mathbf{u}', \mathbf{e})$;
2. *First sample* $\mathbf{e} \leftarrow \chi_\mathbf{e}$, *then sample* $\mathbf{x}' \leftarrow D_{\mathbb{Z}^n, r}$, *set* $\mathbf{u}' = \mathbf{e} + \mathbf{Px}' \bmod Q$, *output* $(\mathbf{x}', \mathbf{u}', \mathbf{e})$.

Proof. The supports of two distributions are identical as follows:

$$\{(\mathbf{x}', \mathbf{u}', \mathbf{e}) \in \mathbb{Z}^n \times \mathbb{Z}_Q^n \times E(\mathbf{P}) \mid \mathbf{u}' = \mathbf{e} + \mathbf{Px}' \bmod Q\}.$$

Distribution 1 outputs $(\mathbf{x}', \mathbf{u}', \mathbf{e})$ with probability

$$P_1[(\mathbf{x}', \mathbf{u}', \mathbf{e})] = \frac{1}{Q^n} P_1[\mathbf{x}'|\mathbf{u}'] = \frac{1}{Q^n} \cdot \frac{\rho_r(\mathbf{x}')}{\rho_r(\Lambda(\mathbf{Q}) + \mathbf{c})}$$

and Distribution 2 with

$$P_2[(\mathbf{x}', \mathbf{u}', \mathbf{e})] = \frac{1}{\det(\mathbf{P})} \cdot \frac{\rho_r(\mathbf{x}')}{\rho_r(\mathbb{Z}^n)} = \frac{\det(\mathbf{Q})}{Q^n} \cdot \frac{\rho_r(\mathbf{x}')}{\rho_r(\mathbb{Z}^n)}.$$

Since $r \geq \eta_\epsilon(\Lambda(\mathbf{Q}))$ and $\rho_r(\mathbb{Z}^n) = \sum_{\mathbf{c} \in \mathcal{P}(\mathbf{Q}) \cap \mathbb{Z}^n} \rho_r(\mathbf{c} + \Lambda(\mathbf{Q}))$, Lemma 2 shows

$$\rho_r(\Lambda(\mathbf{Q}) + \mathbf{c}) \in \left[\frac{1-\epsilon}{1+\epsilon}, \frac{1+\epsilon}{1-\epsilon}\right] \cdot \frac{\rho_r(\mathbb{Z}^n)}{\det(\mathbf{Q})}.$$

Hence $P_1[(\mathbf{x}', \mathbf{u}', \mathbf{e})] \in \left[\frac{1-\epsilon}{1+\epsilon}, \frac{1+\epsilon}{1-\epsilon}\right] \cdot P_2[(\mathbf{x}', \mathbf{u}', \mathbf{e})]$ and we complete the proof. $\square$

Algorithm 2 illustrates the approximate trapdoor inversion algorithm by using our gadget. The output preimage $\mathbf{x}$ satisfies that

$$\mathbf{Ax} = \mathbf{Px}' + \mathbf{Ap} = \mathbf{u}' - \mathbf{e} + \mathbf{Ap} = \mathbf{u} - \mathbf{e} \bmod Q.$$

Therefore the approximation error $\mathbf{e}$ in $\mathsf{ApproxPreSamp}(\mathbf{A}, \mathbf{T}, \mathbf{u}, r, s)$ is exactly the one in $\mathsf{ApproxGadget}(\mathbf{u}', r, \mathbf{P}, \mathbf{Q})$: for uniformly random $\mathbf{u}$, the error $\mathbf{e}$ follows the distribution $\chi_\mathbf{e}$ defined in Lemma 6.

Algorithm 2: $\mathsf{ApproxPreSamp}(\mathbf{A}, \mathbf{T}, \mathbf{u}, r, s)$

Input: $(\mathbf{A}, \mathbf{T}) \in \mathbb{Z}_Q^{n \times m} \times \mathbb{Z}^{m \times n}$ such that $\mathbf{AT} = \mathbf{P} \bmod Q$, a vector $\mathbf{u} \in \mathbb{Z}_Q^n$, $r \geq \eta_\epsilon(\Lambda(\mathbf{Q}))$ and $s^2 \mathbf{I}_m \succ r^2 \mathbf{TT}^t$.
Output: an approximate preimage $\mathbf{x}$ of $\mathbf{u}$ for $\mathbf{A}$.
1: $\mathbf{p} \leftarrow D_{\mathbb{Z}^m, \sqrt{\Sigma_p}}$ where $\Sigma_p = s^2 \mathbf{I}_m - r^2 \mathbf{TT}^t$
2: $\mathbf{u}' = \mathbf{u} - \mathbf{Ap} \bmod Q$
3: $\mathbf{x}' \leftarrow \mathsf{ApproxGadget}(\mathbf{u}', r, \mathbf{P}, \mathbf{Q})$
4: **return** $\mathbf{x} = \mathbf{p} + \mathbf{Tx}'$

Let $\mathbf{L} = [\mathbf{I}_m \mid \mathbf{T}]$. The next lemma characterizes the distribution of the linear transformation on the concatenation of $\mathbf{p} \leftarrow D_{\mathbb{Z}^m, \sqrt{\Sigma_p}}$ and $\mathbf{x}' \leftarrow D_{\mathbb{Z}^n, r}$, which represents the convolution step, i.e.,

$$\mathbf{x} = \mathbf{p} + \mathbf{T}\mathbf{x}' = \mathbf{L} \cdot (\mathbf{p}, \mathbf{x}').$$

Lemma 7. *Let $r \geq \eta_\epsilon(\mathbb{Z}^n)$. The distribution $\mathbf{L} \cdot D_{\mathbb{Z}^{m+n}, \sqrt{\Sigma_p \oplus r^2 \mathbf{I}_n}}$ is statistically close to $D_{\mathbb{Z}^m, s}$, if $s^2 \geq \left(r^2 + \eta_\epsilon(\mathbb{Z}^n)^2\right) \cdot \left(s_1(\mathbf{T})^2 + 1\right)$.*

Proof. Let $\Lambda_{\mathbf{L}} = \mathbb{Z}^{m+n} \cap \ker(\mathbf{L})$ that is an integer lattice. By Theorem 1, it suffices to show $\sqrt{\Sigma_p \oplus r^2 \mathbf{I}_n} \geq \eta_\epsilon(\Lambda_{\mathbf{L}})$. Let $\mathbf{B} = \begin{bmatrix} \mathbf{T} \\ -\mathbf{I}_n \end{bmatrix}$, then $\mathbf{B}$ is a basis of $\Lambda_{\mathbf{L}}$. The dual basis of $\mathbf{B}$ is

$$\mathbf{B}^* = \mathbf{B}(\mathbf{B}^t\mathbf{B})^{-1} = \begin{bmatrix} \mathbf{T} \\ -\mathbf{I}_n \end{bmatrix} \left(\mathbf{T}^t\mathbf{T} + \mathbf{I}_n\right)^{-1}.$$

According to the definition of smoothing parameter, we need to show

$$\sqrt{\Sigma_p \oplus r^2 \mathbf{I}_n} \geq \eta_\epsilon(\Lambda(\mathbf{B}))$$

i.e.,

$$(\mathbf{B}^*)^t(\Sigma_p \oplus r^2 \cdot \mathbf{I}_n)\mathbf{B}^* \succ \eta_\epsilon^2(\mathbb{Z}^n).$$

This reduces to showing

$$\left(\mathbf{T}^t\mathbf{T} + \mathbf{I}_n\right)^{-t} \cdot \left(s^2\mathbf{T}^t\mathbf{T} - r^2(\mathbf{T}^t\mathbf{T})^2 + r^2\mathbf{I}_n\right) \cdot \left(\mathbf{T}^t\mathbf{T} + \mathbf{I}_n\right)^{-1} \succ \eta_\epsilon^2(\mathbb{Z}^n).$$

Let $\mathbf{T}^t\mathbf{T} = \mathbf{U}\mathbf{V}\mathbf{U}^{-1}$ be the eigenvalue decomposition where $\mathbf{V} = \mathrm{diag}(\lambda_1, \ldots, \lambda_n)$ with λ_i being the eigenvalues. The left-hand side can be rewritten as

$$\mathbf{U}(\mathbf{V} + \mathbf{I}_n)^{-t} \left(s^2\mathbf{V} - r^2\mathbf{V}^2 + r^2\mathbf{I}_n\right) (\mathbf{V} + \mathbf{I}_n)^{-1}\mathbf{U}^{-1},$$

and we need to prove

$$\frac{s^2\lambda_i - r^2\lambda_i^2 + r^2}{(\lambda_i + 1)^2} \geq \eta_\epsilon^2(\mathbb{Z}^n),$$

i.e.

$$s^2 \geq (r^2 + \eta_\epsilon(\mathbb{Z}^n)^2) \cdot \lambda_i + 2 \cdot \eta_\epsilon(\mathbb{Z}^n)^2 + \frac{\eta_\epsilon(\mathbb{Z}^n)^2 - r^2}{\lambda_i}.$$

By some routine computation, one can check that this condition is satisfied when $r \geq \eta_\epsilon(\mathbb{Z}^n)$ and $\left(r^2 + \eta_\epsilon(\mathbb{Z}^n)^2\right) \cdot \left(s_1(\mathbf{T})^2 + 1\right)$. $\qquad\square$

We now prove that the preimage and error distributions are simulatable without knowing the trapdoor. This property is needed in most trapdoor based use cases. Our argument only holds for uniformly random $\mathbf{u}$ as in [CGM19].

Theorem 2. *Let* $\mathbf{P}, \mathbf{Q} \in \mathbb{Z}^{n \times n}$ *such that* $\mathbf{P}\mathbf{Q} = Q \cdot \mathbf{I}_n$. *Let* $(\mathbf{A}, \mathbf{T})$ *be a matrix-approximate trapdoor pair,* (r, s) *satisfying* $s^2 \geq \left(r^2 + \eta_\epsilon(\mathbb{Z}^n)^2\right) \cdot \left(s_1(\mathbf{T})^2 + 1\right)$ *and* $r \geq \eta_\epsilon(\Lambda(\mathbf{Q}))$. *Then the following two distributions are statistically indistinguishable:*

$$\left\{ (\mathbf{A}, \mathbf{x}, \mathbf{u}, \mathbf{e}) : \ \mathbf{u} \leftarrow U(\mathbb{Z}_Q^n), \ \mathbf{x} \leftarrow \mathsf{ApproxPreSamp}(\mathbf{A}, \mathbf{T}, \mathbf{u}, r, s), \ \mathbf{e} = \mathbf{u} - \mathbf{A}\mathbf{x} \bmod Q \right\}$$

$$\left\{ (\mathbf{A}, \mathbf{x}, \mathbf{u}, \mathbf{e}) : \ \mathbf{x} \leftarrow D_{\mathbb{Z}^m, s}, \ \mathbf{e} \leftarrow \chi_\mathbf{e}, \ \mathbf{u} = \mathbf{A}\mathbf{x} + \mathbf{e} \bmod Q \right\}.$$

Proof. Let

- $\mathbf{p} \leftarrow D_{\mathbb{Z}^m, \sqrt{\Sigma_p}}$ be a perturbation,
- $\mathbf{u} \in \mathbb{Z}_Q^n$ be the target of $\mathsf{ApproxPreSamp}(\mathbf{A}, \mathbf{T}, \mathbf{u}, r, s)$,
- $\mathbf{u}' = \mathbf{u} - \mathbf{A}\mathbf{p} \bmod Q$ be the target of $\mathsf{ApproxGadget}(\mathbf{u}', r, \mathbf{P}, \mathbf{Q})$,
- $\chi_\mathbf{e}$ be the distribution of $(\mathbf{v} \bmod \Lambda(\mathbf{P})) \in E(\mathbf{P})$ where $\mathbf{v} \leftarrow U(\mathbb{Z}_Q^n)$.

Real distribution: The real distribution of $(\mathbf{A}, \mathbf{x}, \mathbf{u}, \mathbf{e})$ is

$$\mathbf{A}, \mathbf{u} \leftarrow U(\mathbb{Z}_Q^n), \mathbf{p} \leftarrow D_{\mathbb{Z}^m, \sqrt{\Sigma_p}}, \mathbf{u}' = \mathbf{u} - \mathbf{A}\mathbf{p},$$

$$\mathbf{x}' \leftarrow \mathsf{ApproxGadget}(\mathbf{u}', r, \mathbf{P}, \mathbf{Q}), \mathbf{x} = \mathbf{p} + \mathbf{T}\mathbf{x}', \mathbf{e} = \mathbf{u} - \mathbf{A}\mathbf{x} \bmod Q.$$

Hybrid 1: Instead of sampling $\mathbf{u} \leftarrow U(\mathbb{Z}_Q^n)$, we sample $\mathbf{u}' \leftarrow U(\mathbb{Z}_Q^n)$ and $\mathbf{p} \leftarrow D_{\mathbb{Z}^m, \sqrt{\Sigma_p}}$, then compute $\mathbf{u} = \mathbf{u}' + \mathbf{A}\mathbf{p}$. We keep $(\mathbf{x}', \mathbf{x}, \mathbf{e})$ unchanged. Clearly, the real distribution and Hybrid 1 are the same.

Hybrid 2: Instead of sampling $\mathbf{u}', \mathbf{x}'$ and computing $\mathbf{e}$ as in Hybrid 1, we sample $\mathbf{x}' \leftarrow D_{\mathbb{Z}^n, r}$ and $\mathbf{e} \leftarrow \chi_\mathbf{e}$, then compute $\mathbf{u}' = \mathbf{P}\mathbf{x}' + \mathbf{e}$. All other terms $(\mathbf{p}, \mathbf{x}, \mathbf{u})$ remain unchanged. By Lemma 6, Hybrid 1 and Hybrid 2 are statistically close.

Hybrid 3: Instead of sampling $\mathbf{p}, \mathbf{x}'$ and computing $\mathbf{x} = \mathbf{p} + \mathbf{T}\mathbf{x}'$ in Hybrid 2, we sample directly $\mathbf{x} \leftarrow D_{\mathbb{Z}^m, s}$ and compute $\mathbf{u} = \mathbf{A}\mathbf{x} + \mathbf{e} \bmod Q$, where $\mathbf{e} \leftarrow \chi_\mathbf{e}$ is as before. Note that in Hybrid 2,

$$\mathbf{u} = \mathbf{u}' + \mathbf{A}\mathbf{p} = \mathbf{e} + \mathbf{P}\mathbf{x}' + \mathbf{A}\mathbf{p} = \mathbf{e} + \mathbf{A}(\mathbf{T}\mathbf{x}' + \mathbf{p}) = \mathbf{A}\mathbf{x} + \mathbf{e} \bmod Q$$

and $\mathbf{x} = \mathbf{p} + \mathbf{T}\mathbf{x}'$ follows the distribution $[\mathbf{I}_m \mid \mathbf{T}] \cdot D_{\mathbb{Z}^{m+n}, \sqrt{\Sigma_p \oplus r^2 \mathbf{I}_n}}$. By Lemma 7, Hybrid 3 and Hybrid 2 are statistically close. Now we complete the proof.   □

4.2   Simple Instantiation and Comparisons

Our new gadget trapdoor has a very simple instantiation by using

$$(\mathbf{P}, \mathbf{Q}) = (p\mathbf{I}_n, q\mathbf{I}_n)$$

where $p, q \in \mathbb{Z}$ such that $Q = pq$. In this case, $\mathsf{LatticeDecoder}$ is implemented by coefficient-wise mod p operations and $E(\mathbf{P}) = \mathbb{Z}_p^n$, $\chi_\mathbf{e} = U(\mathbb{Z}_p^n)$. Hence for

Table 4. Comparisons with the gadgets from [MP12] and [CGM19]. Here m' is the column number of the gadget matrix, $\mathbf{x}' \in \mathbb{Z}^{m'}$ is the preimage, $\mathbf{e} \in \mathbb{Z}^n$ is the error and $\eta = \eta_\epsilon(\mathbb{Z})$.

	Gadget	Q	m'	$\|\mathbf{x}'\|/\sqrt{m'}$	$\|\mathbf{e}\|/\sqrt{n}$
[MP12]	$\mathbf{I}_n \otimes \mathbf{g}^t,\ \mathbf{g} = (1, b, \cdots, b^{k-1})$	$(b^{k-1}, b^k]$	nk	$\approx \sqrt{(b^2+1)}\eta$	0
[CGM19]	$\mathbf{I}_n \otimes \mathbf{f}^t,\ \mathbf{f} = (b^l, \cdots, b^{k-1})$	$(b^{k-1}, b^k]$	$n(k-l)$	$\approx \sqrt{(b^2+1)}\eta$	$\approx b^l\eta$
This work	$p \cdot \mathbf{I}_n$	pq	n	$\approx q\eta$	$\approx \sqrt{\frac{p^2-1}{12}}$

uniformly random targets, the standard deviation of error coefficients is $\sqrt{\frac{p^2-1}{12}}$. Since $\eta_\epsilon(\Lambda(\mathbf{Q})) = q \cdot \eta_\epsilon(\mathbb{Z}^n)$, the preimage size is about $\sqrt{n} \cdot q \cdot \eta_\epsilon(\mathbb{Z}^n)$. Table 4 shows the comparisons between previous gadgets and ours.

The above instantiation of our approximate gadget offers significant advantages in terms of compactness, efficiency and parameter selection:

Compactness. Our gadget vector consists of only one entry, i.e. p, while to the best of our knowledge, the gadget from [CGM19] requires at least three entries in practical applications. As a direct consequence, the hash-and-sign signatures based on our gadget have much shorter key and signatures. The reduced trapdoor size also results in a smaller Gaussian width and thus supports a smaller modulus.

Efficiency. Due to the semi-random sampler, the error in this simple instantiation is deterministically generated by modulo, which is highly efficient in terms of speed and randomness. The preimage sampling boils down to only n times sampling of $D_{q\mathbb{Z}+c,r}$. By contrast, although [CGM19] proposed to replace the gadget $\mathbf{g} = (1, b, \cdots, b^k)$ with a truncated version $(b^l, \cdots, b^k)$, the gadget sampling is still performed over the gadget lattice defined by $\mathbf{g}$ and thus requires k times integer sampling. In addition, our gadget allows smaller trapdoors, which also reduces the cost of perturbation sampling.

Parameter Selection. As mentioned before, the modulus associated with our gadget is $Q = pq$ and the preimage and error sizes are linear in q and p respectively. This is convenient for flexible and tight parameter choices. However, for the gadget in [CGM19], its error size is roughly proportional to b^{l-1} and such an exponential growth heavily limits optimal parameter selection.

In the rest of the paper, we will use the above simple gadget instantiation to build hash-and-sign signatures. Nevertheless, the design space can be further expanded by taking some lattices with efficient decoding or sampling[1] into account. More practical instantiations definitely need much efforts. We leave this to future works.

---

[1] Such remarkable lattices are listed in [DvW22].

5 Efficient Hash-and-Sign Signatures over NTRU Lattices

This section presents an NTRU-based hash-and-sign signature scheme, named ROBIN, that is instantiated with the compact gadget in Sect. 4. ROBIN achieves good performance comparable to Falcon [PFH22] and its variant Mitaka [EFG22]. It also offers significant advantages from an implementation standpoint. Its signing procedure is considerably simpler and easier to implement without floating point arithmetic. Its secret key is one short vector instead of one short basis as in Falcon and Mitaka, which dramatically simplifies and accelerates the trapdoor generation. ROBIN can therefore be an attractive choice particularly in constrained environments.

5.1 Description of the ROBIN Signature Scheme

Parameters. The underlying NTRU is parameterized by the ring $\mathcal{R} = \mathcal{R}_n^- = \mathbb{Z}[x]/(x^n - 1)$ and the modulus Q. Let

$$\mathcal{T}(n,a,b) = \left\{ v \in \mathcal{R} \,\middle|\, \begin{array}{l} a \text{ coefficients equal to } 1; \\ v \text{ has exactly } b \text{ coefficients equal to } -1; \\ n - a - b \text{ coefficients equal to } 0. \end{array} \right\}.$$

The secret key (f, g) are uniformly sampled from $\mathcal{T}(n, a, b)$. The gadget matrix is $\mathbf{P} = p\mathbf{I}_n$ and the associated $\mathbf{Q} = q\mathbf{I}_n$ such that $pq = Q$. Let α be the parameter controlling the quality of the trapdoor such that

$$\sqrt{s_1\left(\mathcal{M}(f\bar{f} + g\bar{g})\right)} \leq \alpha\|(f,g)\| = \alpha\sqrt{2(a+b)}.$$

Let $\bar{r} = \eta_\epsilon(\mathbb{Z}^n)$ and $r \geq q\bar{r}$ be the width for the approximate gadget sampler. Let $s \geq \frac{\sqrt{1+q^2}}{q} r\alpha\sqrt{2(a+b)}$ be the width for approximate preimages. Let β be the acceptance bound of $\|(z_0 + e, \gamma z_1)\|$ where (z_0, z_1) is the approximate preimage, e is the approximate error and $\gamma = \frac{\sqrt{s^2+(p^2-1)/12}}{s}$ such that $\|z_0 + e\| \approx \gamma\|z_1\|$.

Key Generation. The key generation of ROBIN is very different from that of other NTRU-based hash-and-sign signatures Falcon and Mitaka. Instead, it is similar to that of BLISS [DDLL13] which is an NTRU-based Fiat-Shamir signature scheme. More concretely, ROBIN uses an inhomogeneous NTRU key pair in which the secret key is composed of two short polynomials (f, g) and the public key is $h = (p - g)/f \bmod Q$, then $hf + g = p \bmod Q$. In addition, we partially apply the techniques suggested in [EFG22] to get a high-quality trapdoor in a short time. The whole key generation is formally described in Algorithm 3.

Algorithm 3: Robin.KeyGen

Input: the ring $\mathcal{R} = \mathcal{R}_n^-$ with n a prime, $Q = pq$, $(a, b) \in \mathbb{Z}^2$ and $\alpha > 0$.
Output: public key $h \in \mathcal{R}/(Q \cdot \mathcal{R})$, secret key $(f, g) \in \mathcal{R}^2$

1: $f_1, \cdots, f_K, g_1, \cdots, g_K \xleftarrow{\$} \mathcal{T}(n, a, b)$ with $K = 5$
2: **for** $i = 1$ to K **do**
3:     **for** $j = 1$ to K **do**
4:         find $k \in \mathbb{Z}_n^*$ minimizing $s_1 \left(\mathcal{M} \left(f_i \bar{f}_i + \sigma_k(g_j) \overline{\sigma_k(g_j)} \right) \right)$
5:         $(f, g) \leftarrow (f_i, \sigma_k(g_j))$
6:         **if** $\sqrt{s_1 \left(\mathcal{M}(f\bar{f} + g\bar{g}) \right)} \leq \alpha\sqrt{2(a+b)}$ **then**
7:             $h \leftarrow (p - g)/f \bmod Q$
8:             return $(h, (f, g))$
9:         **end if**
10:    **end for**
11: **end for**
12: restart

Signing Procedure. Algorithm 4 shows the signing procedure that is in essence the approximate preimage sampling (Algorithm 2). Given the hashed message u, Algorithm 4 samples a preimage (z_0, z_1) such that $z_0 + hz_1 = u - e \bmod Q$ for small e. Only z_1 is used as the actual signature, as the short term $(z_0 + e) = u - hz_1 \bmod Q$ can be recovered during verification. We set the acceptance bound $\beta = 1.04 \cdot \mathbb{E}[\|(z_0 + e, \gamma z_1)\|]$. We experimentally verified that the restart happens with probability $\approx 1\%$ for this setting.

Algorithm 4: Robin.Sign

Input: a message msg, the NTRU key pair $(h, (f, g))$, $r \geq q\eta_\epsilon(\mathbb{Z}^n)$,

$\quad s \geq r\alpha\sqrt{2(a+b)}$, $\gamma = \frac{\sqrt{s^2 + (p^2 - 1)/12}}{s}$, $\beta > 0$.
Output: a signature (salt, z)

1: $\mathbf{A} \leftarrow [\mathbf{I}_n \mid \mathcal{M}(h)]$, $\mathbf{T} \leftarrow \begin{bmatrix} \mathcal{M}(g) \\ \mathcal{M}(f) \end{bmatrix}$
2: $\mathsf{salt} \xleftarrow{\$} \{0, 1\}^{320}$, $u \leftarrow \mathsf{H}(\mathsf{msg}, \mathsf{salt})$
3: $(z_0, z_1) \leftarrow \mathsf{ApproxPreSamp}(\mathbf{A}, \mathbf{T}, u, r, s)$
4: $e \leftarrow u - (z_0 + z_1 h) \bmod Q$
5: **if** $\|(z_0 + e, \gamma z_1)\| > \beta$ **then**
6:    restart
7: **end if**
8: return (salt, z_1)

Verification. The preimage $(z_0 + e, z_1)$ is short and $(z_0 + e) + hz_1 = u \bmod Q$. The verification is to check the shortness of $(u - hz_1, z_1)$. To balance the sizes of $u - hz_1 = z_0 + e$ and z_1, we scale z_1 by a factor $\gamma = \frac{\sqrt{s^2 + (p^2 - 1)/12}}{s}$ in the shortness check. A formal description is given in Algorithm 5.

Algorithm 5: Robin.Verify

Input: a signature (salt, z) of a message msg, the public key h,

$\gamma = \frac{\sqrt{s^2 + (p^2 - 1)/12}}{s}, \beta > 0$.

Output: Accept or Reject

1: $u \leftarrow \mathsf{H}(\mathsf{msg}, \mathsf{salt})$, $z' \leftarrow (u - hz) \bmod Q$
2: Accept if $\|(z', \gamma z)\| \leq \beta$, otherwise Reject

---

5.2 Security Analysis

We now give a security proof for ROBIN. To start with, we need some treatment on the scaling factor γ which modified the shortness condition for better concrete security. To this end, we introduce a variant of NTRU-SIS in the twisted norm as follows.

Definition 8 (NTRU-SIS in the twisted norm, $\mathsf{NTRUSIS}_{\mathcal{R},Q,\chi,\beta}^{\|\cdot\|_\gamma}$). *Let $\mathcal{R} = \mathbb{Z}[x]/(x^n - 1)$ with n a prime. Let $Q > 0$ be an integer, χ be a distribution over $\mathcal{R}$ and $\beta > 0$, $\gamma \geq 1$. Given a random NTRU public key h of either $\mathsf{NTRU}_{\mathcal{R},Q,\chi}$ or $\mathsf{iNTRU}_{\mathcal{R},Q,\chi,e}$, find a non-zero vector (x_0, x_1) such that $\|(x_0, \gamma x_1)\| \leq \beta$ and $x_0 + hx_1 = 0 \bmod Q$.*

It is easy to verify that

$$\mathsf{NTRUSIS}_{\mathcal{R},Q,\chi,\beta\gamma} \leq_p \mathsf{NTRUSIS}_{\mathcal{R},Q,\chi,\beta}^{\|\cdot\|_\gamma} \leq_p \mathsf{NTRUSIS}_{\mathcal{R},Q,\chi,\beta/\gamma},$$

which shows the equivalence between NTRU-SIS and its twisted-norm version.

To prove the strong EU-CMA security of ROBIN, we follow the same arguments for the GPV signatures [GPV08] and combine Theorem 2 showing that the preimage and error output by ApproxPreSamp is simulatable for uniformly random targets.

Theorem 3. *The ROBIN signature scheme is strongly existentially unforgeable under a chosen-message attack in the random oracle model assuming the hardness of $\mathsf{NTRUSIS}_{\mathcal{R},Q,\chi,2\beta}^{\|\cdot\|_\gamma}$.*

Proof. Suppose, for contradiction, that there is an adversary $\mathcal{A}$ that breaks the strong EU-CMA security of ROBIN with non-negligible probability ε. We construct a polynomial time algorithm $\mathcal{S}$ that solves $\mathsf{NTRUSIS}_{\mathcal{R},Q,\chi,2\beta}^{\|\cdot\|_\gamma}$ with probability close to ε. Given a random NTRU public key h, $\mathcal{S}$ runs $\mathcal{A}$ and simulates the random oracle H and signing oracle as follows:

- for the query to H on (salt, msg), if H(salt, msg) is not queried, then $\mathcal{S}$ samples $(\mathbf{z} = (z_0, z_1), e) \leftarrow D_{\mathbb{Z}^{2n},s} \times U(\mathbb{Z}_p^n)$, returns $u = z_0 + z_1 h + e \mod Q$ as the random oracle response and stores $((\text{salt}, \text{msg}), z_0, z_1, e, u)$. Otherwise $\mathcal{S}$ looks up $((\text{salt}, \text{msg}), z_0, z_1, e, u)$ and returns u to $\mathcal{A}$.
- for every signing query on msg, $\mathcal{S}$ samples salt $\xleftarrow{\$} \{0,1\}^{320}$, $(\mathbf{z} = (z_0, z_1), e) \leftarrow D_{\mathbb{Z}^{2n},s} \times U(\mathbb{Z}_p^n)$, then outputs (salt, z_1) to $\mathcal{A}$ as the signature, and stores $((\text{salt}, \text{msg}), z_0, z_1, e, u = z_0 + z_1 h + e \mod Q)$ in the random oracle storage.

Without loss of generality, assume that before outputting the signature forgery (salt^*, z_1) for the message msg^*, $\mathcal{A}$ queries H on $(\text{salt}^*, \text{msg}^*)$. Then $\mathcal{S}$ computes $z_0' = \text{H}(\text{salt}^*, \text{msg}^*) - z_1 h \mod Q$ and looks up $((\text{salt}^*, \text{msg}^*), z_0^*, z_1^*, e^*, u^*)$ in its local storage. Finally, $\mathcal{S}$ outputs $(z_0^* + e^* - z_0', z_1^* - z_1)$ as a solution.

By Theorem 2, the view of $\mathcal{A}$ in the real scheme is indistinguishable from the view provided by $\mathcal{S}$ except with negligible probability $Q_{sign}^2 / 2^{320}$, in which case repeated signature queries on the same message msg use the same salt. It remains to prove that $z_1^* \neq z_1$. In fact, if msg^* has been queried to the signing oracle before, then the above inequality holds by the definition of a successful forgery; if msg^* has not been queried to the signing oracle, then z_1 is with high min-entropy for appropriate parameters, so $z_1^* \neq z_1$ with overwhelming probability. $\qquad\square$

5.3   Concrete Parameters

We provide 3 parameter sets for ROBIN in Table 5 for the NIST security levels 1, 3 and 5 respectively. In all parameter sets, Q is a power of 2 and n is a prime such that the order of 2 in $\mathbb{Z}_n$ is either $n-1$ or $\frac{n-1}{2}$ as suggested in [HPS17]. Let $b = a - 1 = \lfloor \frac{n}{4} \rfloor$. We choose $\alpha \approx 1.7$ to guarantee the key generation terminate with a small number of trials. The parameter $\bar{r} = \eta_\epsilon(\mathbb{Z}^n)$ uses $\epsilon = 2^{-36}$ that suffices to ensure a security level ≤ 256 bits with up to 2^{64} signature queries as per [Pre17].

In Table 5, the numbers of signature sizes are made according to the entropy of the preimage. This can be efficiently obtained by using batch encoding with ANS (Asymmetric Numeral System) as in [ETWY22]. The concrete security is estimated by the usual cryptanalytic methods for lattice-based cryptography. Details are provided in the full version [YJW23].

Table 5. Suggested parameters for ROBIN.

	ROBIN-701	ROBIN-1061	ROBIN-1279
Target security level	NIST-I	NIST-III	NIST-V
n	701	1061	1279
(Q, p, q)	$(16384, 2048, 8)$	$(32768, 4096, 8)$	$(32768, 4096, 8)$
(a, b)	$(176, 175)$	$(266, 265)$	$(320, 319)$
α	1.65	1.7	1.75
r	10.22	10.28	10.31
s	449.8	573.8	650.4
γ	1.65	2.29	2.07
β	28928.7	62965.5	70983.7
Public key size (in bytes)	1227	1990	2399
Signature size (in bytes)	992	1527	1862
Key recovery security (C/Q)	116 / 105	181 / 165	228 / 207
Forgery security (C/Q)	130 / 118	214 / 195	264 / 240

5.4 Comparison with Falcon and Mitaka

Implementation. ROBIN has significant advantages from the implementation standpoint. First, ROBIN uses only one vector as the NTRU secret and avoids the notoriously complex NTRU trapdoor generation. This can be crucial to the implementations and the key storage, especially when the key management for the entire lifecycle is required (e.g. by the FIPS 140-2 [NIS]). Second, ROBIN has an online/offline structure as Mitaka, and its online operations are simple and fully over integers, which surpasses Mitaka. In particular, base samplings in the online phase are in the form $D_{q\mathbb{Z}+c,r}$ with $c \in \mathbb{Z}$. This is beneficial for further optimization and side-channel protections. Third, the offline sampling can also be implemented without resorting floating-point numbers by the technique in [DGPY20]. The integral implemenation seems more convenient compared to the integer version of Mitaka.

Performance. The size of ROBIN is comparable to that of Falcon and Mitaka: the total bandwidth (i.e. public key size + signature size) of ROBIN is larger by $\approx 40\%$ than that of Falcon and by $25\% - 35\%$ than that of Mitaka. Detailed comparisons are shown in Table 6.

6 Shorter LWE-Based Hash-and-Sign Signatures

The LWE-based hash-and-sign signatures are rarely seen as a competitive post-quantum candidate in contrast to their NTRU and Fiat-Shamir counterparts, mainly due to their large sizes. In this section, we fill the gap in practical LWE-based hash-and-sign signatures with a new scheme EAGLE. EAGLE is instantiated

Table 6. Comparisons in terms of sizes with Falcon and Mitaka. For a fair comparison, all signature sizes are estimated as per the entropic bound, which can be closely obtained by entropic encoding as shown in [ETWY22].

	Security level	Pub. Key size (in bytes)	Sig. size (in bytes)
Falcon-512	NIST-I	896	643
Mitaka-648	NIST-I	972	807
Robin-701	NIST-I	**1227**	**992**
Mitaka-864	NIST-III	1512	1148
Robin-1061	NIST-III	**1990**	**1527**
Falcon-1024	NIST-V	1792	1249
Mitaka-1024	NIST-V	1792	1376
Robin-1279	NIST-V	**2399**	**1862**

with our compact gadget and based on Ring-LWE. It achieves a desirable performance: EAGLE is substantially smaller than the state-of-the-art LWE-based hash-and-sign signatures [CGM19], and even smaller than the LWE-based Fiat-Shamir signature scheme Dilithium [LDK22]. While EAGLE is less efficient than the NTRU-based instantiation ROBIN, we believe it is of practical interest given the preference for using LWE to NTRU sometimes.

6.1   Description of the EAGLE Signature Scheme

Parameters. EAGLE is based on the Ring-LWE assumption over $\mathcal{R} = \mathcal{R}_n^+ = \mathbb{Z}[x]/(x^n + 1)$ with n a power of 2 and the modulus $Q = pq$. EAGLE uses the secret with a fixed hamming weight in $\mathcal{T}(n, a, b)$ (defined in Sect. 5.1), and let α be the parameter controlling the quality of the trapdoor such that $\sqrt{s_1\left(\mathcal{M}(f\bar{f} + g\bar{g})\right)} \leq \alpha\|(f, g)\| = \alpha\sqrt{2(a + b)}$. Let $\bar{r} = \eta_\epsilon(\mathbb{Z}^n)$ and $r \geq q\bar{r}$ be the width for the approximate gadget sampler. Let $s \geq \frac{\sqrt{1+q^2}}{q}r\alpha\sqrt{2(a + b)}$ be the width for approximate preimages. Let β be the acceptance bound of $\|(z_0 + e, \gamma z_1, \gamma z_2)\|$ where (z_0, z_1, z_2) is the approximate preimage, e is the approximate error and $\gamma = \frac{\sqrt{s^2 + (p^2 - 1)/12}}{s}$ such that $\|z_0 + e\| \approx \gamma\|z_1\| \approx \gamma\|z_2\|$.

Key Generation. The public key is essentially $(a, b = p - (af + g) \bmod Q)$ where a is uniformly random over $\mathcal{R}_Q = \mathcal{R}/(Q \cdot \mathcal{R})$ and $f, g \xleftarrow{\$} \mathcal{T}(n, a, b)$. The polynomial a is stored as a seed (of length 32 bytes), which halves the public key size. We apply the techniques in [EFG22] as in ROBIN to refine the quality of (f, g). A formal description of the key generation is given in Algorithm 6.

Signing Procedure. Given the hashed message u, the signing procedure shown in Algorithm 7 samples a short preimage (z_0, z_1, z_1) such that $z_0 + az_1 + bz_1 =$

Algorithm 6: Eagle.KeyGen

Input: the ring $\mathcal{R} = \mathcal{R}_n^+$ with n a power of 2, $Q = pq$, and $\alpha > 0$.
Output: public key (seed_a, b), secret key $(f, g) \in \mathcal{R}^2$

1: $\mathsf{seed}_a \overset{\$}{\leftarrow} \{0,1\}^{256}$, $a \leftarrow \mathsf{Expand}(\mathsf{seed}_a)$ {Expand maps a seed to an element in $\mathcal{R}$}
2: $f_1, \cdots, f_K, g_1, \cdots, g_K \overset{\$}{\leftarrow} \mathcal{T}(n, a, b)$ with $K = 5$
3: **for** $i = 1$ to K **do**
4:   **for** $j = 1$ to K **do**
5:     find $k \in \mathbb{Z}_n^*$ minimizing $s_1 \left(\mathcal{M} \left(f_i \bar{f}_i + \sigma_k(g_j) \overline{\sigma_k(g_j)} \right) \right)$
6:     $(f, g) \leftarrow (f_i, \sigma_k(g_j))$
7:     **if** $\sqrt{s_1 \left(\mathcal{M}(f\bar{f} + g\bar{g}) \right)} \le \alpha \sqrt{2(a + b)}$ **then**
8:       $b \leftarrow p - (af + g) \bmod Q$
9:       **return** $((\mathsf{seed}_a, b), (f, g))$
10:     **end if**
11:   **end for**
12: **end for**
13: restart

$u - e \bmod Q$ for a small e. Only (z_1, z_2) is used as the actual signature, as the short term $(z_0 + e) = u - az_1 - bz_2 \bmod Q$ can be recovered during verification. Again, the acceptance bound $\beta = 1.04 \cdot \mathbb{E}[\|\|(z_0 + e, \gamma z_1)\|\|]$, which makes the restart happen with low probability.

Verification. The preimage $(z_0 + e, z_1, z_2)$ is short and $(z_0 + e) + az_1 + bz_2 = u \bmod Q$. The verification is to check the shortness of $(u - az_1 - bz_2, z_1, z_2)$. A formal description is given in Algorithm 8.

Algorithm 7: Eagle.Sign

Input: a message msg and the key pair $((\mathsf{seed}_a, b), (f, g))$
Output: a signature $(\mathsf{salt}, (z_1, z_2))$

1: $a \leftarrow \mathsf{Expand}(\mathsf{seed}_a)$, $\mathsf{salt} \overset{\$}{\leftarrow} \{0,1\}^{320}$, $u \leftarrow \mathsf{H}(\mathsf{msg}, \mathsf{salt})$
2: $\mathbf{A} \leftarrow [\mathbf{I}_n \mid \mathcal{M}(a) \mid \mathcal{M}(b)]$, $\mathbf{T} \leftarrow \begin{bmatrix} \mathcal{M}(g) \\ \mathcal{M}(f) \\ \mathbf{I}_n \end{bmatrix}$
3: $(z_0, z_1, z_2) \leftarrow \mathsf{ApproxPreSamp}(\mathbf{A}, \mathbf{T}, u, r, s)$
4: $e \leftarrow u - (z_0 + az_1 + bz_2) \bmod Q$
5: **if** $\|(z_0 + e, \gamma z_1, \gamma z_2)\| > \beta$ **then**
6:   restart
7: **end if**
8: **return** $(\mathsf{salt}, (z_1, z_2))$

Algorithm 8: Eagle.Verify

Input: a signature $(\mathsf{salt}, (z_1, z_2))$ of a message msg, the public key (seed_a, b),
$\gamma = \frac{\sqrt{s^2 + (p^2 - 1)/12}}{s}$, $\beta > 0$.
Output: Accept or Reject
1: $u \leftarrow \mathsf{H}(\mathsf{msg}, \mathsf{salt})$, $a \leftarrow \mathsf{Expand}(\mathsf{seed}_a)$, $z' \leftarrow (u - az_1 - bz_2) \bmod Q$
2: Accept if $\|(z', \gamma z_1, \gamma z_2)\| \leq \beta$, otherwise Reject

---

6.2   Security Analysis

Similar to ROBIN, the security of EAGLE is based on a variant of Ring-SIS in
the twisted norm.

Definition 9 (Ring-SIS in the twisted norm, $\mathsf{RSIS}^{\|\cdot\|_\gamma}_{\mathcal{R},m,Q,\beta}$). *Let $\mathcal{R} =$
$\mathbb{Z}[x]/(x^n + 1)$ with n a power of 2. Let $m, Q > 0$ be integers and $\beta > 0$.
Let $\mathcal{R}_Q = \mathcal{R}/(Q \cdot \mathcal{R})$. Given a uniformly random $\mathbf{A} \in \mathcal{R}_Q^m$, find a non-zero
$\mathbf{x} = (x_0, \mathbf{x}_1) \in \mathcal{R} \times \mathcal{R}^{m-1}$ such that $\mathbf{A}\mathbf{x} = 0 \bmod Q$ and $\|(x_0, \gamma \mathbf{x}_1)\| \leq \beta$.*

Theorem 4 shows the strong EU-CMA security of EAGLE. We omit the proof,
as it follows the same argument with that of Theorem 3.

Theorem 4. *The EAGLE signature scheme is strongly existentially unforgeable
under a chosen-message attack in the random oracle model assuming the hard-
ness of $\mathsf{RSIS}^{\|\cdot\|_\gamma}_{\mathcal{R},m,Q,\beta}$ and $\mathsf{RLWE}_{\mathcal{R},1,Q,\chi}$ with $\chi = U(\mathcal{T}(n, a, b))$.*

6.3   Concrete Parameters

We provide 2 parameter sets for EAGLE in Table 7. The public key size is computed as $n \cdot \log_2(Q)/8 + 32$ and the signature size is estimated as the entropic
bound of the preimage plus 40 bytes for the salt. The details of concrete security
estimate is shown in the full version [YJW23].

6.4   Comparison with LWE-based Signatures

Thanks to the compact gadget, EAGLE has much better compactness than existing LWE-based hash-and-sign signatures. We first compare EAGLE with the
Ring-LWE-based construction from [CGM19]. For a fair comparison, we re-
parameterize the scheme in [CGM19] such that the used secret has the same
size with that in EAGLE and the overall size is nearly optimal for the target
security level. Nevertheless, for 80-bits (resp. 192-bits) of classical security level,
the bandwidth of EAGLE is only about $30 - 40\%$ of that of the instantiation
from [CGM19]. EAGLE is even smaller than Dilithium that is a representative LWE-based Fiat-Shamir signature scheme. Detailed numbers are shown in
Table 8.

Table 7. Suggested parameters for EAGLE.

	EAGLE-512	EAGLE-1024
Target security level	80-bit	NIST-III
n	512	1024
(Q, p, q)	$(16000, 2000, 8)$	$(32400, 2700, 12)$
(a, b)	$(128, 128)$	$(256, 256)$
α	1.7	1.7
r	10.17	15.42
s	394.2	841.5
γ	1.36	1.19
β	28493.5	66118.5
Public key size (in bytes)	928	1952
Signature size (in bytes)	1406	3052
Key recovery security (C/Q)	79 / 71	176 / 160
Forgery security (C/Q)	83 / 75	189 / 172

Table 8. Comparisons in terms of sizes with Dilithium [LDK22] and [CGM19]. The bit-security for Dilithium corresponds to the strongly-unforgeable version. The signature sizes for [CGM19] and EAGLE are estimated as per the entropic bound.

	Security (C/Q)	Pub. Key size (in bytes)	Sig. size (in bytes)
Dilithium 1⁻	89 / 81	992	1843
[CGM19]	79 / 71	2720	2753
EAGLE-512	79 / 71	928	1406
Dilithium 3	176 / 159	1952	3293
[CGM19]	180 / 164	7712	7172
EAGLE-1024	176 / 160	1952	3052

6.5 Comparison with ROBIN

As readers may have noticed, the Ring-LWE-based instantiation EAGLE is less efficient than the NTRU-based instantiation ROBIN in Sect. 5. For the NIST-III security level, while EAGLE and ROBIN have roughly the same public key size, the EAGLE signatures are about 2 times the size of ROBIN signatures. This is an inherent gap, as the signatures in NTRU-based schemes are one ring element whereas the signatures in LWE-based schemes require at least two ring elements to recover the preimage. In addition, the forgery security of EAGLE-1024 is lower than that of ROBIN-1061 by more than 20-bits, although the degrees of the used ring are close. The main cause is as follows. While the public matrix $\mathbf{A}$ in EAGLE is n-by-$3n$, the best forgery attack would only use its submatrix of size n-by-$2n$, which is the same with the case of ROBIN. In contrast to ROBIN, the acceptance bound of the EAGLE signature size is larger due to the wider $\mathbf{A}$. This lowers the forgery security.

Despite the worse performance than ROBIN, EAGLE still occupies a fairly important position within the practical design of lattice signatures. The underlying Ring-LWE assumption could receive some preference to NTRU, especially for more powerful applications with overstretched parameters. Furthermore, EAGLE can be more conveniently adapted to the unstructured setting, thanks to the absence of costly matrix inversions in the key generation. This may be a merit given the emphasis of post-quantum signatures not based on structured lattices raised by NIST[2].

7 Conclusion

We develop a new lattice gadget construction of better compactness than the state-of-the-art. The main technique is a novel approximate gadget sampler, called semi-random sampler, in which the approximate error is deterministically generated and the preimage distribution is still simulatable without using the trapdoor. As an application, we present two practical hash-and-sign signature schemes instantiated with our compact gadget respectively based on NTRU and Ring-LWE. Our NTRU-based instantiation ROBIN offers a quite simple implementation and high efficiency comparable to Falcon and Mitaka. This makes ROBIN an attractive post-quantum signature for constrained environments. Our Ring-LWE-based scheme EAGLE is significantly smaller than the one [CGM19] and even smaller than Dilithium. This demonstrates that LWE-based hash-and-sign signatures have much more potential than previously considered for practical applications.

7.1 Future Works

Our gadget framework actually supports diverse instantiations beyond the one used in ROBIN and EAGLE. It would be interesting to explore more efficient constructions by combining different gadget matrices, lattice decoders and Gaussian samplers. It is also worthy to develop more algorithms for our gadget and then to build a complete toolkit as in [GMP19].

Our gadget-based schemes are simpler than the NTRU trapdoor based ones and easily implemented fully over integers with the technique of [DGPY20]. We leave the optimized implementation and the provable side-channel protections as future works. In addition, our technique can be applied in advanced lattice cryptosystems. Evaluating its impact on the performance of advanced schemes needs a thorough investigation.

Our proposals of ROBIN and EAGLE do not fully integrate some recent techniques [JHT22, EFG22, ETWY22] to improve the performance and security, as

---

[2] https://csrc.nist.gov/csrc/media/Projects/pqc-dig-sig/documents/call-for-proposals-dig-sig-sept-2022.pdf.

we would like to focus more on the new gadget itself. Hence there shall be some room to improve the performance by adding these optimizations.

Acknowledgements. We would like to thank Léo Ducas and the anonymous reviewers for helpful comments and suggestions. This work is supported by the National Key Research and Development Program of China (Grant No. 2021YFB3100200), the National Natural Science Foundation of China (Grant No. 62102216, 12171114), the Mathematical Tianyuan Fund of the National Natural Science Foundation of China (Grant No. 12226006), the National Key Research and Development Program of China (Grant No. 2018YFA0704701), the Major Program of Guangdong Basic and Applied Research (Grant No. 2019B030302008), Major Scientific and Technological Innovation Project of Shandong Province, China (Grant No. 2019JZZY010133), Shandong Key Research and Development Program (Grant No. 2020ZLYS09) and National key research and development program(Grant No. 2022YFB2702804).

References

[Agr17] Agrawal, S.: Stronger security for reusable garbled circuits, general definitions and attacks. In: Katz, J., Shacham, H. (eds.) CRYPTO 2017. LNCS, vol. 10401, pp. 3–35. Springer, Cham (2017). https://doi.org/10.1007/978-3-319-63688-7_1

[Ajt96] Ajtai, M.: Generating hard instances of lattice problems. In: Proceedings of the Twenty-eighth Annual ACM Symposium on Theory of Computing, pp. 99–108 (1996)

[Bab86] Babai, L.: On lovász' lattice reduction and the nearest lattice point problem. Combinatorica **6**(1), 1–13 (1986)

[BVWW16] Brakerski, Z., Vaikuntanathan, V., Wee, H., Wichs, D.: Obfuscating conjunctions under entropic ring lwe. In: ITCS 2016, pp. 147–156 (2016)

[CGM19] Chen, Y., Genise, N., Mukherjee, P.: Approximate trapdoors for lattices and smaller hash-and-sign signatures. In: ASIACRYPT 2019, pp. 3–32 (2019). https://doi.org/10.1007/978-3-030-34618-8_1

[DDLL13] Ducas, L., Durmus, A., Lepoint, T., Lyubashevsky, V.: Lattice signatures and bimodal gaussians. In: Canetti, R., Garay, J.A. (eds.) CRYPTO 2013. LNCS, vol. 8042, pp. 40–56. Springer, Heidelberg (2013). https://doi.org/10.1007/978-3-642-40041-4_3

[DGPY20] Ducas, L., Galbraith, S., Prest, T., Yu, Y.: Integral matrix gram root and lattice gaussian sampling without floats. In: Canteaut, A., Ishai, Y. (eds.) EUROCRYPT 2020. LNCS, vol. 12106, pp. 608–637. Springer, Cham (2020). https://doi.org/10.1007/978-3-030-45724-2_21

[DLP14] Ducas, L., Lyubashevsky, V., Prest, T.: Efficient identity-based encryption over NTRU lattices. In: Sarkar, P., Iwata, T. (eds.) ASIACRYPT 2014. LNCS, vol. 8874, pp. 22–41. Springer, Heidelberg (2014). https://doi.org/10.1007/978-3-662-45608-8_2

[DN12] Ducas, L., Nguyen, P.Q.: learning a zonotope and more: Cryptanalysis of NTRUSign countermeasures. In: Wang, X., Sako, K. (eds.) ASIACRYPT 2012. LNCS, vol. 7658, pp. 433–450. Springer, Heidelberg (2012). https://doi.org/10.1007/978-3-642-34961-4_27

[DP16] Ducas, L., Prest, T.: Fast fourier orthogonalization. In: ISSAC 2016, pp. 191–198 (2016)

[DvW21]   Ducas, L., van Woerden, W.: NTRU fatigue: how stretched is over-stretched? In: Tibouchi, M., Wang, H. (eds.) ASIACRYPT 2021. LNCS, vol. 13093, pp. 3–32. Springer, Cham (2021). https://doi.org/10.1007/978-3-030-92068-5_1

[DvW22]   Ducas, L., van Woerden, W.: On the lattice isomorphism problem, quadratic forms, remarkable lattices, and cryptography. In: EUROCRYPT 2022, pp. 643–673 (2022). https://doi.org/10.1007/978-3-031-07082-2_23

[EFG22]   Espitau, T., et al.: MITAKA: a simpler, parallelizable. maskable variant of. In EUROCRYPT 2022, 222–253 (2022). https://doi.org/10.1007/978-3-031-07082-2_9

[ETWY22] Espitau, T., Tibouchi, M., Wallet, A., Yang, Yu.: Shorter hash-and-sign lattice-based signatures. In: CRYPTO 2022, pp. 245–275 (2022). https://doi.org/10.1007/978-3-031-15979-4_9

[Gen09]   Gentry, C.: Fully homomorphic encryption using ideal lattices. In: STOC 2009, pp. 169–178 (2009)

[GGH97]   Goldreich, O., Goldwasser, S., Halevi, S.: Public-key cryptosystems from lattice reduction problems. In: Kaliski, B.S. (ed.) CRYPTO 1997. LNCS, vol. 1294, pp. 112–131. Springer, Heidelberg (1997). https://doi.org/10.1007/BFb0052231

[GGH19]   Genise, N., Gentry, C., Halevi, S., Li, B., Micciancio, D.: Homomorphic encryption for finite automata. In: Galbraith, S.D., Moriai, S. (eds.) ASIACRYPT 2019. LNCS, vol. 11922, pp. 473–502. Springer, Cham (2019). https://doi.org/10.1007/978-3-030-34621-8_17

[GKV10]   Gordon, S.D., Katz, J., Vaikuntanathan, V.: A group signature scheme from lattice assumptions. In: Abe, M. (ed.) ASIACRYPT 2010. LNCS, vol. 6477, pp. 395–412. Springer, Heidelberg (2010). https://doi.org/10.1007/978-3-642-17373-8_23

[GM18]   Genise, N., Micciancio, D.: Faster gaussian sampling for trapdoor lattices with arbitrary modulus. In: Nielsen, J.B., Rijmen, V. (eds.) EUROCRYPT 2018. LNCS, vol. 10820, pp. 174–203. Springer, Cham (2018). https://doi.org/10.1007/978-3-319-78381-9_7

[GMP19]   Genise, N., Micciancio, D., Polyakov, Y.: Building an efficient lattice gadget toolkit: subgaussian sampling and more. In: Ishai, Y., Rijmen, V. (eds.) EUROCRYPT 2019. LNCS, vol. 11477, pp. 655–684. Springer, Cham (2019). https://doi.org/10.1007/978-3-030-17656-3_23

[GMPW20] Genise, N., Micciancio, D., Peikert, C., Walter, M.: Improved discrete gaussian and subgaussian analysis for lattice cryptography. In: Kiayias, A., Kohlweiss, M., Wallden, P., Zikas, V. (eds.) PKC 2020. LNCS, vol. 12110, pp. 623–651. Springer, Cham (2020). https://doi.org/10.1007/978-3-030-45374-9_21

[GPV08]   Gentry, C., Peikert, C., Vaikuntanathan, V.: Trapdoors for hard lattices and new cryptographic constructions. In STOC 2008, pp. 197–206 (2008)

[GVW13]   Gorbunov, S., Vaikuntanathan, V., Wee, H.: Attribute-based encryption for circuits. In: STOC 2013, pp. 545–554 (2013)

[GVW15]   Gorbunov, S., Vaikuntanathan, V., Wee, H.: Predicate encryption for circuits from LWE. In: Gennaro, R., Robshaw, M. (eds.) CRYPTO 2015. LNCS, vol. 9216, pp. 503–523. Springer, Heidelberg (2015). https://doi.org/10.1007/978-3-662-48000-7_25

[HHP03]   Hoffstein, J., Howgrave-Graham, N., Pipher, J., Silverman, J.H., Whyte, W.: NTRUSIGN: digital signatures using the NTRU lattice. In: CT-RSA 2003, pp. 122–140 (2003)

[HPS17] Hoffstein, J., Pipher, J., Schanck, J.M., Silverman, J.H., Whyte, W., Zhang, Z.: Choosing parameters for ntruencrypt. In: CT-RSA 2017, pp. 3–18 (2017)

[JHT22] Jia, H., Yupu, H., Tang, C.: Lattice-based hash-and-sign signatures using approximate trapdoor, revisited. IET Inf. Secur. **16**(1), 41–50 (2022)

[KF17] Kirchner, P., Fouque, P.-A.: Revisiting lattice attacks on overstretched NTRU parameters. In: Coron, J.-S., Nielsen, J.B. (eds.) EUROCRYPT 2017. LNCS, vol. 10210, pp. 3–26. Springer, Cham (2017). https://doi.org/10.1007/978-3-319-56620-7_1

[LDK22] Lyubashevsky, V.: Dilithium: Submission to the NIST's post-quantum cryptography standardization process (2022). https://csrc.nist.gov/Projects/post-quantum-cryptography/selected-algorithms-2022

[LPR10] Lyubashevsky, V., Peikert, C., Regev, O.: On ideal lattices and learning with errors over rings. In: Gilbert, H. (ed.) EUROCRYPT 2010. LNCS, vol. 6110, pp. 1–23. Springer, Heidelberg (2010). https://doi.org/10.1007/978-3-642-13190-5_1

[MP12] Micciancio, D., Peikert, C.: Trapdoors for lattices: simpler, tighter, faster, smaller. In: Pointcheval, D., Johansson, T. (eds.) EUROCRYPT 2012. LNCS, vol. 7237, pp. 700–718. Springer, Heidelberg (2012). https://doi.org/10.1007/978-3-642-29011-4_41

[MR07] Micciancio, D., Regev, O.: Worst-case to average-case reductions based on gaussian measures. SIAM J. Comput. **37**(1), 267–302 (2007)

[NIS] NIST. NIST: Security requirements for cryptographic modules. https://nvlpubs.nist.gov/nistpubs/FIPS/NIST.FIPS.140-2.pdf

[NR06] Nguyen, P.Q., Regev, O.: Learning a parallelepiped: cryptanalysis of GGH and NTRU signatures. In: Vaudenay, S. (ed.) EUROCRYPT 2006. LNCS, vol. 4004, pp. 271–288. Springer, Heidelberg (2006). https://doi.org/10.1007/11761679_17

[Pei10] Peikert, C.: An efficient and parallel gaussian sampler for lattices. In: Rabin, T. (ed.) CRYPTO 2010. LNCS, vol. 6223, pp. 80–97. Springer, Heidelberg (2010). https://doi.org/10.1007/978-3-642-14623-7_5

[PFH22] Prest, T.: Falcon: Submission to the NIST's post-quantum cryptography standardization process (2022). https://csrc.nist.gov/Projects/post-quantum-cryptography/selected-algorithms-2022

[Pre15] Prest, T.: Gaussian Sampling in Lattice-Based Cryptography. PhD thesis, PhD thesis, École Normale Supérieure Paris 2015 (2015)

[Pre17] Prest, T.: Sharper bounds in lattice-based cryptography using the Rényi divergence. In: Takagi, T., Peyrin, T. (eds.) ASIACRYPT 2017. LNCS, vol. 10624, pp. 347–374. Springer, Cham (2017). https://doi.org/10.1007/978-3-319-70694-8_13

[PS19] Peikert, C., Shiehian, S.: Noninteractive zero knowledge for NP from (Plain) learning with errors. In: Boldyreva, A., Micciancio, D. (eds.) CRYPTO 2019. LNCS, vol. 11692, pp. 89–114. Springer, Cham (2019). https://doi.org/10.1007/978-3-030-26948-7_4

[SAB20] Schwabe, P.: Kyber: Submission to the NIST's post-quantum cryptography standardization process (2020). https://csrc.nist.gov/Projects/post-quantum-cryptography/selected-algorithms-2022

[YD18] Yu, Y., Ducas, L.: Learning strikes again: the case of the DRS signature scheme. In: Peyrin, T., Galbraith, S. (eds.) ASIACRYPT 2018. LNCS, vol. 11273, pp. 525–543. Springer, Cham (2018). https://doi.org/10.1007/978-3-030-03329-3_18

[YJW23] Yu, Y., Jia, H., Wang, X.: Compact lattice gadget and its applications to hash-and-sign signatures. Cryptology ePrint Archive, Paper 2023/729 (2023). https://eprint.iacr.org/2023/729

[ZY22] Zhang, S., Yang, Y.: Towards a simpler lattice gadget toolkit. In: PKC 2022, pp. 498–520 (2022)

Machine-Checked Security for XMSS as in RFC 8391 and SPHINCS+

Manuel Barbosa[1]([⊠])(iD), François Dupressoir[2]([⊠])(iD), Benjamin Grégoire[3]([⊠])(iD), Andreas Hülsing[4]([⊠])(iD), Matthias Meijers[4]([⊠])(iD), and Pierre-Yves Strub[5]([⊠])(iD)

[1] University of Porto (FCUP) and INESC TEC, Porto, Portugal
[2] University of Bristol, Bristol, UK
[3] Université Côte d'Azur, Inria, Sophia Antipolis, France
[4] Eindhoven University of Technology, Eindhoven, The Netherlands
`fv-xmss@mmeijers.com`
[5] Meta, Paris, France

Abstract. This work presents a novel machine-checked tight security proof for XMSS—a stateful hash-based signature scheme that is (1) standardized in RFC 8391 and NIST SP 800-208, and (2) employed as a primary building block of SPHINCS+, one of the signature schemes recently selected for standardization as a result of NIST's post-quantum competition.

In 2020, Kudinov, Kiktenko, and Fedoro pointed out a flaw affecting the tight security proofs of SPHINCS+ and XMSS. For the case of SPHINCS+, this flaw was fixed in a subsequent tight security proof by Hülsing and Kudinov. Unfortunately, employing the fix from this proof to construct an analogous tight security proof for XMSS would merely demonstrate security with respect to an insufficient notion.

At the cost of modeling the message-hashing function as a random oracle, we complete the tight security proof for XMSS and formally verify it using the EasyCrypt proof assistant. (Note that this merely extends the use of the random oracle model, as this model is already required in other parts of the security analysis to justify the currently standardized parameter values). As part of this endeavor, we formally verify the crucial step common to the security proofs of SPHINCS+ and XMSS that was found to be flawed before, thereby confirming that the core of the aforementioned security proof by Hülsing and Kudinov is correct.

As this is the first work to formally verify proofs for hash-based signature schemes in EasyCrypt, we develop several novel libraries for the fundamental cryptographic concepts underlying such schemes—e.g., hash functions and digital signature schemes—establishing a common starting point for future formal verification efforts. These libraries will be particularly helpful in formally verifying proofs of other hash-based signature schemes such as LMS or SPHINCS+.

Keywords: XMSS · SPHINCS+ · EasyCrypt · Formal Verification · Machine-Checked Proofs · Computer-Aided Cryptography

H. Handschuh and A. Lysyanskaya (Eds.): CRYPTO 2023, LNCS 14085, pp. 421–454, 2023.
https://doi.org/10.1007/978-3-031-38554-4_14

1 Introduction

Quantum computers threaten the security of virtually all public-key cryptography deployed today [19]. Although it is still unclear if and when large-scale quantum computers will become operational, there is continuous progress [11] and the stakes are too high to risk not being prepared. For this reason, in late 2016, the National Institute of Standards and Technology (NIST) initiated a standardization process for post-quantum cryptography, i.e., classically computable cryptographic constructions that can withstand attacks by quantum-capable adversaries [20]. Nearly six years later, NIST finally announced the first four constructions to be standardized: the key encapsulation mechanism CRYSTALS-Kyber, and the digital signature schemes CRYSTALS-Dilithium, Falcon, and SPHINCS+ [21]. However, for early adopters, NIST published an initial standard (in 2020) describing the stateful hash-based signature schemes XMSS and LMS [8], both previously specified in Request For Comments (RFC) publications [12,18]. These schemes provide post-quantum secure signatures to users that can handle a secret state, i.e., a secret key that changes over time. Interestingly, these schemes share a lot of structure with each other and with SPHINCS+.

In 2020, Kudinov, Kiktenko, and Fedoro pointed out a flaw in the tight security proof of the Winternitz One-Time Signature Scheme (WOTS) [17], one of the main building blocks of XMSS and SPHINCS+. This flaw invalidated the tight security proof of XMSS [15], as well as that of SPHINCS+ [6]. (The non-tight security proofs were not affected by this flaw; however, these proofs could not justify practical parameters.) Regarding SPHINCS+, this flaw was fixed by explicitly specifying the particular variant of WOTS employed in SPHINCS+ (and XMSS), called WOTS-TW, and providing a new tight security proof for this variant [13]. This proof, however, only shows security of WOTS-TW against non-adaptive chosen-message attacks. For SPHINCS+, this turns out to be sufficient because it uses WOTS-TW exclusively to sign user-controlled data; nevertheless, for XMSS, this is not sufficient as it additionally uses WOTS-TW to sign data that might be controlled by an adversary. This leaves the security of XMSS an open question. Moreover, the fact that this flaw was only found after four years—during which the concerned schemes received quite some attention—questions the guarantees provided by the novel security proof for SPHINCS+.

Computer-Aided Cryptography. Hash-based signature schemes are not the only cryptographic constructions that have had flawed security proofs. Indeed, there exist numerous examples of proofs for cryptographic constructions that were widely considered to be correct after heavy scrutiny, but still turned out to be faulty. Furthermore, in some of these cases, the corresponding constructions were additionally shown to be insecure [16]. Often, the culprit in these situations is, at least partially, the sheer complexity of the cryptographic constructions and their proofs, as well as a lack of rigor in the exposition of the arguments in the proofs. Since post-quantum constructions and the corresponding proofs tend to be relatively complex—and in many cases based on relatively novel and lesser-studied concepts—additional care and rigor should be applied in their evaluation.

Naturally, in the six years leading up to the final announcement in NIST's standardization process, each one of the eventually selected constructions underwent extensive scrutiny by the cryptographic community and, potentially after some adaptations, gained sufficient trust to be chosen for standardization. (Certainly, the above-mentioned flaw invalidating the original security proof of SPHINCS$^+$ was discovered during this process.) Nevertheless, this does not exclude the possibility that the current beliefs regarding the security of these constructions may be wrong, even if the corresponding proofs are currently deemed correct.

In an attempt to address the complexity issues associated with devising and evaluating cryptographic constructions and their proofs, the field of computer-aided cryptography has produced a multitude of tools and frameworks aimed at reducing the manual effort required for the verification of cryptography and, ideally, reducing this effort to merely checking the security claims. Over the years, these tools and frameworks have been successfully applied in the construction and verification of increasingly intricate and important use cases. For instance, in no particular order, CertiCrypt has been used to formally verify the security of OAEP [5]; EasyCrypt has been used to formally verify the security and correctness of Saber's public-key encryption scheme [14]; Jasmin (in conjunction with EasyCrypt) has been used to construct and formally verify a functionally correct, constant-time, and efficient implementation of SHA-3 [1]; and Tamarin has been used to formally verify TLS 1.3 [9]. For a more comprehensive overview and discussion of computer-aided cryptography, refer to [2]. However, to the best of our knowledge, the security properties of the standardized post-quantum hash-based signature schemes have not been analyzed using computer-aided cryptography prior to this work.

Our Contribution. In this work, we face the challenge of reestablishing or increasing the trust in the security of (the parameter sets considered for) XMSS and SPHINCS$^+$. To this end, we give a new tight security proof for XMSS building on the analysis of [13] and, moreover, formally verify the entire proof. As the proof in [13], our proof bases security on the properties of several keyed and tweakable hash functions in the standard model (see Sect. 2 for definitions) and achieves a minimal security loss of $\log w$ bits (where w is the Winternitz parameter, often set to 16 or 256 in practice). By performing our proof in a modular manner, we independently verify the part of the proof that is shared with the proof for SPHINCS$^+$ presented in [13]. To complete the proof for XMSS, we need to handle the signing of arbitrary-length messages; for this to work, we have to model the message-compression function as a random oracle. Although this segment of the proof could be carried out in the Quantum-accessible Random Oracle Model (QROM) using [10], we restrict ourselves to the Random Oracle Model (ROM) due to the current limitations of the utilized tool. Nevertheless, we closely follow the proof of [10] to facilitate the lifting to the quantum setting as soon as the relevant shortcomings of the tool are overcome. It should be noted that in order to justify the currently standardized parameter values, the security analysis of XMSS already requires the (Q)ROM for matters other than the compression of messages [15]; hence, our work does not introduce the (Q)ROM but merely extends the use of it. More precisely, as discussed in [15], the (Q)ROM is already needed to argue that one can reduce the size of the public key by replacing a lengthy list of random values by a single public seed (that can be expanded to this list of random values using a public function). This use of the (Q)ROM is not explicit in this work as it is hidden behind the notion of tweakable hash functions.

We employ EasyCrypt, a tool predominantly designed for the formal verification of security properties through code-based, game-playing proofs in the computational model [4]. Since this is the first proper effort to verify hash-based signatures in EasyCrypt, our work includes several additions to the tool. In particular, we construct multiple comprehensive EasyCrypt libraries containing generic specifications of several fundamental cryptographic concepts underlying the schemes considered in this work. Specifically, we provide libraries for hash functions—both keyed and tweakable—and digital signature schemes— both stateless and stateful. As their content is specified generically, these libraries can be reused in any other context that considers these concepts. Although not presented here in detail, these libraries can be found in the code corresponding to this work or in the standard library of EasyCrypt.

Summarizing, the purpose of this work is to establish greater confidence in the security of XMSS and, by extension, SPHINCS$^+$. Additionally, this work aims to facilitate future formal verification efforts by providing generic libraries that are reusable in a plethora of contexts.

Future Work. In future work, we will expand this work in two complementary directions.

Extension to Quantum Setting. Our proof is formalized in the classical (i.e., non-quantum) setting. However, since most of contemporary interest in (standalone) XMSS is due to the scheme's claimed quantum-resistance, verifying whether this is actually veracious would be of significant value. In principle, the reasoning used throughout most of the formal verification still holds true in the quantum setting. However, handling of the message-compression step in the proof occurs in the ROM and, while this step can also be performed in the QROM, the necessary techniques [10] make use of advanced concepts such as compressed oracles [23]. At the time of writing, the quantum extension of EasyCrypt [3] does not yet support some of these necessary techniques, but ongoing work attempts to surmount this deficiency and lift the proof to the quantum setting.

Formal Verification of SPHINCS$^+$ and LMS. A significant portion of this work focuses on the security of the substructure of XMSS that it shares with LMS and SPHINCS$^+$. Indeed, given that our proof sticks to the abstraction of tweakable hash functions, a proof for LMS seems realizable by harnessing the foundations established in this work. Similarly, this work marks a significant milestone in formally verifying the security proof of SPHINCS$^+$. Building on the relevant results from this work, such a formal verification project seems feasible. Nevertheless, we note that this still requires significant additional effort due to the complexity of the SPHINCS$^+$ construction. For instance, among others, it requires the additional incorporation of FORS, the few-time signature scheme used in SPHINCS$^+$. In this context, because improper instantiations of the employed tweakable hash functions can lead to compromised security [22], another interesting avenue for future work is the validation of the constructions of tweakable hash functions from [6]. However, again, this necessitates an expansion of the current quantum extension of EasyCrypt.

Overview. The remainder of this paper is structured as follows. First, Sect. 2 introduces the primary concepts underlying the considered cryptographic constructions and their formal verification. Second, Sect. 3 presents a high-level overview of (the employed approach to) the formal verification. Finally, the remaining sections—Section 4, Sect. 5, and Sect. 6—discuss different parts of the formal verification in more detail.

2   Preliminaries

Below, we provide the background necessary for the remainder of the paper.

Keyed Hash Functions. A Keyed Hash Function (KHF) is a function KHF : $\mathcal{K} \times \mathcal{M} \to \mathcal{Y}$ where *key space* $\mathcal{K}$ denotes a set of keys, and *message space* $\mathcal{M}$ and *digest space* $\mathcal{Y}$ are sets of bitstrings. Often, $\mathcal{Y}$ constitutes the set of bitstrings of a certain length—that is, $\mathcal{Y} = \{0,1\}^n$ for some $n > 0$—and $\mathcal{M}$ constitutes the set of bitstrings of arbitrary length—that is, for potentially many different $n > 0$, $\{0,1\}^n \subseteq \mathcal{M}$. At times, instead of viewing a KHF as a single function, we interpret and refer to it as a family of hash functions that is indexed by keys from the key space. Indeed, each hash function in such a family has the message space as its domain and the digest space as its codomain.

Regarding KHFs, we are merely concerned with the *Collision Resistance* (CR) and *Pseudo-Random Function family* (PRF) properties. Intuitively, a KHF is collision-resistant if for a known, randomly selected hash function from the family defined by the KHF, it is computationally infeasible to compute two messages that map to the same digest; a KHF is a PRF if querying an unknown, randomly selected hash function from the family defined by the KHF is computationally indistinguishable from randomly sampling elements from the digest space. The CR and PRF properties for KHFs are formalized as the games in Fig. 1 and Fig. 2, respectively; the oracle employed in the PRF game is given in Fig. 3. Certainly, in the PRF game, the adversary merely gains access to the oracle's Query procedure.

Then, the advantage of any adversary $\mathcal{A}$ against CR is straightforwardly defined as follows.

$$\mathsf{Adv}^{\mathrm{CR}}_{\mathsf{KHF}}(\mathcal{A}) = \Pr\left[\mathrm{Game}^{\mathrm{CR}}_{\mathcal{A},\mathsf{KHF}} = 1\right]$$

$$\text{Game}_{\mathcal{A},\text{KHF}}^{\text{CR}}$$

1 : $k \leftarrow\!\!\$ \, \mathcal{U}(\mathcal{K})$
2 : $(x, x') \leftarrow \mathcal{A}.\text{Find}(k)$
3 : **return** $x \neq x' \wedge \text{KHF}(k, x) = \text{KHF}(k, x')$

Fig. 1. CR game for keyed hash functions.

$$\text{OPRF}_{\text{KHF}}$$

vars b, k, m

Init(bi)

1 : $b, m \leftarrow \text{bi}, \text{emptymap}$
2 : $k \leftarrow\!\!\$ \, \mathcal{U}(\mathcal{K})$

Query(x)

1 : **if** b **then**
2 :   **if** $m.[x] \neq \perp$ **then**
3 : $y \leftarrow\!\!\$ \, \mathcal{U}(\mathcal{Y})$
4 : $m.[x] \leftarrow y$
5 : $y \leftarrow m.[x]$
6 : **else**
7 : $y \leftarrow \text{KHF}(k, x)$
8 : **return** y

$$\text{Game}_{\mathcal{A},\text{KHF}}^{\text{PRF}}(b)$$

1 : $\text{OPRF}_{\text{KHF}}.\text{Init}(b)$
2 : $b' \leftarrow \mathcal{A}^{\text{OPRF}_{\text{KHF}}}.\text{Distinguish}()$
3 : **return** b'

Fig. 2. PRF game for keyed hash functions.

Fig. 3. Oracle employed in the PRF game for keyed hash functions.

Moreover, the advantage of any adversary $\mathcal{A}$ against PRF is defined as given below.

$$\text{Adv}_{\text{KHF}}^{\text{PRF}}(\mathcal{A}) = |\Pr[\text{Game}_{\mathcal{A},\text{KHF}}^{\text{PRF}}(0) = 1] - \Pr[\text{Game}_{\mathcal{A},\text{KHF}}^{\text{PRF}}(1) = 1]|$$

Tweakable Hash Functions. A Tweakable Hash Function (THF) is a function $\text{THF} : \mathcal{P} \times \mathcal{T} \times \mathcal{M} \to \mathcal{Y}$ where *(public) parameter space* $\mathcal{P}$ and *tweak space* $\mathcal{T}$ respectively denote a set of (public) parameters and a set of tweaks, and *message space* $\mathcal{M}$ and *digest space* $\mathcal{Y}$ are sets of bitstrings (corresponding to the same sets as the identically named sets in the definition of KHFs). THFs were first introduced in [6]. They form an extension of KHFs by allowing for the consideration of contextual data in the form of tweaks, i.e., elements from the tweak space.[1] Tweaks are predominantly used for the mitigation of multi-target attacks.

Alongside THFs, the authors of SPHINCS+ introduced the concept of collections of such functions, containing a single THF for each possible length of the input messages [6]. Such a collection can be viewed as the set $\text{THFC} = \{\text{THF}_\lambda :$

---

[1] The parameter space of THFs is analogous to the key space of KHFs.

$\mathcal{P} \times \mathcal{T} \times \mathcal{M}_\lambda \to \mathcal{Y}\}_{\lambda \in \Lambda}$ where Λ is the index set that contains all the possible lengths of input messages and $\mathcal{M}_\lambda$ is the set of bitstrings of length λ, i.e., $\mathcal{M}_\lambda = \{0,1\}^\lambda$.

The properties we consider for (collections of) THFs in this work are the *Single-function, Multi-target, Distinct-Tweak* versions of *UnDetectability* (SM-DT-UD-C); *Target-Collision Resistance* (SM-DT-TCR-C); and *PREimage resistance* (SM-DT-PRE-C) *of a THF as a member of a Collection*. These properties were first introduced in [13] for the purpose of recovering the tight security proof of SPHINCS+. For an extensive discussion and in-depth analysis of these properties, refer to [13]. As their names suggest, the THF properties we consider are rather similar in their formalizations. Namely, for each property, the formalization is approximately structured as follows. First, during initialization, a parameter used to index the THF collection is sampled uniformly at random. Then, both the *challenge oracle* and the *collection oracle* are initialized with the sampled parameter. The challenge oracle allows the adversary to adaptively define targets (through queries consisting of tweaks and, depending on the property, potentially messages or digests) and learn the (claimed) corresponding mappings under the considered THF. The collection oracle enables the adversary to adaptively query any THF from the considered collection without defining these queries as targets. After initialization, the target-selection stage commences. During this stage, the adversary has access to both oracles, specifying its targets by queries to the challenge oracle. Afterward, the attack stage begins. Here, the adversary is given the used parameter and is asked to provide a solution for (one of) the targets that it specified in the target-selection stage.

Certainly, the form that a solution takes depends on the considered game: For SM-DT-UD-C, a solution is a boolean b' indicating whether the adversary thinks the challenge oracle returned digest of uniformly random messages ($b' = \text{false}$) or uniformly distributed digests ($b' = \text{true}$); for SM-DT-TCR-C, a solution consists of an index i pointing to a target (tw, x), and a message x' that should map to the same digest as message x when using tweak tw; and for SM-DT-PRE-C, a solution consists of an index i pointing to a target (tw, y), and a message x that should map to y using tweak tw.

Finally, following the attack stage, success of the adversary is checked by validating both the provided solution and the adversary's behavior. The latter is necessary as the adversary is not allowed to (1) specify more than a certain number of tweaks, (2) use the same tweak for different targets, and (3) query the collection oracle with a tweak occurring in any of the targets; this concurs with the fact that XMSS and SPHINCS+ do not use the same tweak more than once. The games formalizing the considered THF properties are given in Fig. 4; the oracles provided to the adversary in these games are specified in Fig. 5 (SM-DT-UD-C challenge oracle), Fig. 6 (SM-DT-TCR-C challenge oracle), Fig. 7 (SM-DT-PRE-C challenge oracle), and Fig. 8 (collection oracle). Naturally, the adversary exclusively gains access to the Query procedures of the given oracles. Furthermore, in these games, t denotes the number of targets the adversary may specify, and VQS_t is a predicate that validates the adversary's behavior based on the lists of tweaks from the challenge and collection oracles. Then,

$\text{Game}^{\text{SM-DT-UD-C}}_{\mathcal{A},\text{THF},\text{THFC},t}(b)$	$\text{Game}^{\text{SM-DT-TCR-C}}_{\mathcal{A},\text{THF},\text{THFC},t}$	$\text{Game}^{\text{SM-DT-PRE-C}}_{\mathcal{A},\text{THF},\text{THFC},t}$
1 :	$p \leftarrow\!\!\$\, \mathcal{U}(\mathcal{P})$	
2 :	$\boxed{\text{OUD}_{\text{THF}}.\text{Init}(b,p)}$ $\boxed{\text{OTCR}_{\text{THF}}.\text{Init}(p)}$ $\boxed{\text{OPRE}_{\text{THF}}.\text{Init}(p)}$	
3 :	$\text{OC}_{\text{THFC}}.\text{Init}(p)$	
4 :	$\boxed{\mathcal{A}^{\text{OUD}_{\text{THF}},\text{OC}_{\text{THFC}}}.\text{Pick}()}$ $\boxed{\mathcal{A}^{\text{OTCR}_{\text{THF}},\text{OC}_{\text{THFC}}}.\text{Pick}()}$ $\boxed{\mathcal{A}^{\text{OTCR}_{\text{THF}},\text{OC}_{\text{THFC}}}.\text{Pick}()}$	
5 :	$\boxed{b' \leftarrow \mathcal{A}.\text{Distinguish}(p)}$ $\boxed{i,x' \leftarrow \mathcal{A}.\text{Find}(p)}$ $\boxed{i,x \leftarrow \mathcal{A}.\text{Find}(p)}$	
6 :	$\boxed{\text{Skip}}$ $\boxed{\text{tw},x \leftarrow \text{OTCR}.\mathscr{T}[i], \text{OTCR}.\mathscr{X}[i]}$ $\boxed{\text{tw},y \leftarrow \text{OPRE}.\mathscr{T}[i], \text{OPRE}.\mathscr{Y}[i]}$	
7 :	$\mathbf{return}\ b' \wedge \text{VQS}_t(\text{OUD}_{\text{THF}}.\mathscr{T}, \text{OC}_{\text{THFC}}.\mathscr{T})$	
	$\mathbf{return}\ x \neq x' \wedge \text{THF}(p,\text{tw},x) = \text{THF}(p,\text{tw},x') \wedge \text{VQS}_t(\text{OTCR}_{\text{THF}}.\mathscr{T}, \text{OC}_{\text{THFC}}.\mathscr{T})$	
	$\mathbf{return}\ \text{THF}(p,\text{tw},x) = y \wedge \text{VQS}_t(\text{OPRE}_{\text{THF}}.\mathscr{T}, \text{OC}_{\text{THFC}}.\mathscr{T})$	

Fig. 4. SM-DT-UD-C (blue boxes), SM-DT-TCR-C (yellow boxes), and SM-DT-PRE-C (green boxes) game for tweakable hash functions. Statements not within colored boxes are executed in every game. (Color figure online)

OUD$_{\text{THF}}$

vars $b, p, \mathscr{T}$

Init(bi, pi)

1 : $b, p, \mathscr{T} \leftarrow \text{bi, pi, }[\,]$

Query(tw)

1 : **if** b **then**

2 : $y \leftarrow\!\!\$\, \mathcal{U}(\mathcal{Y})$

3 : **else**

4 : $x \leftarrow\!\!\$\, \mathcal{U}(\mathcal{X})$

5 : $y \leftarrow \text{THF}(p,\text{tw},x)$

6 : $\mathscr{T} \leftarrow \mathscr{T}\ ||\ \text{tw}$

7 : **return** y

Fig. 5. Challenge oracle employed in SM-DT-UD-C game.

OTCR$_{\text{THF}}$

vars $p, \mathscr{T}, \mathscr{X}$

Init(pi)

1 : $p, \mathscr{T}, \mathscr{X} \leftarrow \text{pi, }[\,],[\,]$

Query(tw, x)

1 : $y \leftarrow \text{THF}(p,\text{tw},x)$

2 : $\mathscr{T}, \mathscr{X} \leftarrow \mathscr{T}\ ||\ \text{tw}, \mathscr{X}\ ||\ x$

3 : **return** y

Fig. 6. Challenge oracle employed in SM-DT-TCR-C game.

---

we respectively define the advantage of any adversary $\mathcal{A}$ against SM-DT-UD-C, SM-DT-TCR-C, and SM-DT-PRE-C as follows.

$$\text{Adv}^{\text{SM-DT-UD-C}}_{\text{THF},\text{THFC},t}(\mathcal{A}) = \Big| \Pr\big[\text{Game}^{\text{SM-DT-UD-C}}_{\mathcal{A},\text{THF},\text{THFC},t}(0) = 1\big]$$
$$- \Pr\big[\text{Game}^{\text{SM-DT-UD-C}}_{\mathcal{A},\text{THF},\text{THFC},t}(1) = 1\big]\Big|,$$
$$\text{Adv}^{\text{SM-DT-TCR-C}}_{\text{THF},\text{THFC},t}(\mathcal{A}) = \Pr\big[\text{Game}^{\text{SM-DT-TCR-C}}_{\mathcal{A},\text{THF},\text{THFC},t} = 1\big],\ \text{and}$$
$$\text{Adv}^{\text{SM-DT-PRE-C}}_{\text{THF},\text{THFC},t}(\mathcal{A}) = \Pr\big[\text{Game}^{\text{SM-DT-PRE-C}}_{\mathcal{A},\text{THF},\text{THFC},t} = 1\big]$$

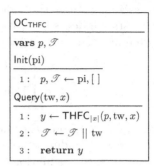

Fig. 7. Challenge oracle employed in SM-DT-PRE-C game.

Fig. 8. Collection oracle employed in games of properties for tweakable hash functions.

Addresses. XMSS—and, by extension, SPHINCS+—consists of multiple components; in each of these components, the same collection of THFs is employed. As such, to mitigate multi-target attacks, schemes such as XMSS and SPHINCS+ use a unique tweak for each THF call throughout the entire construction. For the generation of these tweaks, XMSS implements a particular addressing scheme. Although one could almost completely abstract this addressing scheme away in the analysis of XMSS and its components, we remain somewhat concrete as to keep the connection to the actual specification clear. In particular, XMSS employs addresses consisting of a fixed-length sequence of nonnegative integers indicating the location and purpose of the THF call in the virtual structure. Naturally, not all (fixed-length) sequences of nonnegative integers constitute valid addresses. Furthermore, when analyzing a specific component individually, some of the integers in the sequence may be irrelevant as they exclusively serve the purpose of achieving uniqueness when multiple instances of the same component are considered simultaneously.[2] For these reasons, in this paper, we use "address" to refer to a fixed-length sequence of nonnegative integers that constitutes (the relevant part of a) valid XMSS or SPHINCS+ address in the considered context. Further details regarding address validity will be provided, when relevant, throughout the paper.

(Tweakable Hash) Function Chains. Informally, a function chain is a sequence of values obtained by repeatedly applying a function on (a part of) its own output, starting with some given value as input. In the context of WOTS-TW, the chained function is a THF. In this chaining, the initially provided address is updated in each application of the THF as to ensure the

---

[2] For example, XMSS employs multiple instances of WOTS-TW, each of which is provided an address to perform its operations with. Since each instance manipulates and uses the same part of the provided address in an identical manner, XMSS ensures the part that is not considered by the WOTS-TW instances is different for each instance in order to still guarantee the uniqueness of the utilized addresses between instances.

address's uniqueness throughout. More precisely, given a function THF, parameter p, start index $s \in \mathbb{N}$, iteration counter $i \in \mathbb{N}$, message x, and address ad, the chaining function $\mathsf{Ch_{THF}}$ is recursively defined as follows.

$$\mathsf{Ch_{THF}}(p, \mathrm{ad}, s, i, x) = \begin{cases} x, & \text{if } i \leq 0 \\ \mathsf{THF}(p, \mathrm{ad}_{s+i-1}, \mathsf{Ch_{THF}}(p, \mathrm{ad}, s, i-1, x)), & \text{otherwise} \end{cases}$$

Here, ad_{s+i-1} denotes the address resulting from adjusting ad to be the unique address corresponding to the $s + i - 1$-th call to THF in the considered chain. Furthermore, this definition requires that the digest space of THF is contained in its message space; this is invariably the case for the THFs considered throughout this work. From this definition, we can derive the compositional property of chain functions that is represented by the following equality, where $i, j \in \mathbb{N}$, $0 \leq i$, $0 \leq j$, and the remaining values are as previously specified.

$$\mathsf{Ch_{THF}}(p, \mathrm{ad}, s + i, j, \mathsf{Ch_{THF}}(p, \mathrm{ad}, s, i, x)) = \mathsf{Ch_{THF}}(p, \mathrm{ad}, s, i + j, x)$$

Intuitively, this equality states that chaining i times starting from position s—thus ending in position $s + i$—and, subsequently, chaining j times from position $s + i$ is equal to chaining $i + j$ times starting from position s.

3   Approach

Our objectives in this work are basically twofold: First, we seek to formally verify the security property of XMSS as a standalone construction to increase the confidence in the security of this standardized scheme; second, we aim to formally verify the fix of the security proof of SPHINCS+ —and, implicitly, XMSS— presented in [13] as to validate the remediation of the flaw in the original proof and pave the way for a complete formal verification of SPHINCS+. Fortunately, when approached appropriately, the first objective can be achieved by extending (the results of) the second objective. In essence, this is because SPHINCS+ employs (a variant of) XMSS as building block.

On a high level, XMSS is a Merkle signature scheme; that is, it comprises a binary hash tree of height h that authenticates the public keys of 2^h key pairs from a One-Time Signature (OTS) scheme. As alluded to before, the OTS employed in XMSS is (a variant of) WOTS. To reduce the size of the secret key, the sequence of 2^h WOTS secret keys—that originally constitutes the secret key—is replaced by a single seed used to (re)generate a WOTS secret key from the sequence whenever required via a PRF. A message is signed by first signing it with a WOTS secret key and then generating the authentication information for the corresponding public key. All of the above is the same for XMSS as standalone and XMSS as building block of SPHINCS+.

There are two principal differences between XMSS as standalone and XMSS as used in SPHINCS+. Foremost, standalone XMSS compresses messages using randomized hashing before they are signed. In SPHINCS+, this is not necessary as messages signed by XMSS are public keys of other instances of signature schemes; these public keys already have the desired format. Second, the addresses in SPHINCS⁺ have a slightly different format than those of standalone XMSS; nevertheless, their properties are identical.

As in the novel tight security proof for SPHINCS⁺ [13], we describe XMSS using THFs whenever the input to the hash function includes an address (immediately giving rise to WOTS-TW [13] as the employed variant of WOTS), and base security on the properties of the utilized KHFs and THFs. That is, we formally verify that XMSS—both as standalone and as in SPHINCS⁺—is secure assuming that the employed KHFs and THFs have certain properties. This leads to a slightly more abstract description and result than for the "actual" standardized XMSS, where the utilized THFs are explicitly instantiated with KHFs (some of which are PRFs) [12]. Considering this slightly more abstract version of the standardized XMSS allows for a more natural way of achieving the above-mentioned objectives and makes the result more general, but precludes the security analysis of any concrete instantiations of the THFs (including the ones specified for XMSS in [12]). Henceforth, we refer to this slightly more abstract version of standalone XMSS as XMSS-TW; accordingly, we refer to XMSS as used in SPHINCS⁺ as fixed-length XMSS-TW.

The fixed-length XMSS-TW employed by SPHINCS⁺ does not achieve the standard Existential UnForgeability under adaptive Chosen-Message Attacks (EUF-CMA) security property that we typically expect standalone signature schemes, such as XMSS-TW, to possess. However, it does achieve the weaker Existential UnForgeability under Random Message Attacks (EUF-RMA) security property. Fortunately, because the difference between fixed-length XMSS-TW and (standalone) XMSS-TW can be seen as an instance of a particular transformation using the hash-then-sign paradigm, this weaker property of fixed-length XMSS is sufficient to show—in the ROM—that XMSS-TW satisfies the desired EUF-CMA security property.[3]

A high-level overview of (the proofs underlying) our formal verification, i.e., the relations between the different properties we formally verify, is given in Fig. 9. In this figure, each node signifies a property of a cryptographic construction or function: The initial lines state the considered construction or function; the last line states the considered property. Arrows denote the dependencies between properties; more precisely, the property of a cryptographic construction associated with a certain node is implied by—or, equivalently, can be reduced from—the conjunction of the properties of the cryptographic constructions and functions associated with the origin nodes of the incoming arrows.

The topmost node in Fig. 9 states the first objective of this work: The formal verification of the EUF-CMA security of XMSS-TW. Now, this construction uses randomized hash-then-sign; that is, it compresses arbitrary-length messages to fixed-length messages using a KHF indexed by a (pseudo)random value. This value is freshly generated for each message compression using another KHF indexed by

---

[3] Although one could consider the SEUF-CMA security notion for XMSS-TW (which is slightly stronger than EUF-CMA), we refrain from doing so because this would clutter the overall proof (and formal verification) without providing novel insights or being particularly relevant for most applications.

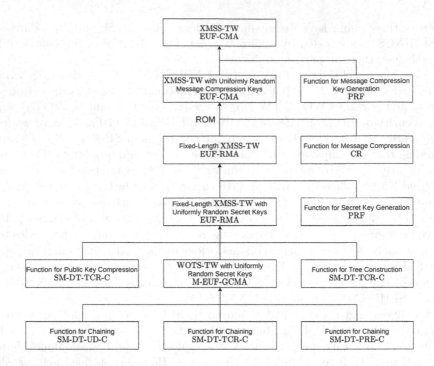

Fig. 9. Overview of the (dependencies between) properties formally verified in this work. Within each node, the last line states the considered property of the cryptographic construction or function specified on the preceding lines. Furthermore, the property of the cryptographic construction or function associated with a node is implied by—or, equivalently, can be reduced from—the conjunction of the properties of the cryptographic constructions and functions associated with the origin nodes of the incoming arrows.

a (secret) key that is randomly sampled during key generation. This latter KHF is required to be a PRF in order to successfully perform adaptive reprogramming in the ROM based on the entropy of the values produced by this KHF. Moreover, the former KHF is required to have CR. As shown in [7], one can construct a reduction from weaker properties, i.e., some form of target-collision resistance. However, this requires an unconventional (index-bound) model for stateful signature schemes and their security; we consider this out-of-scope for this work.

In Fig. 9, the two uppermost implications are related to the randomized hash-then-sign paradigm used in XMSS-TW. The latter of these implications is (partially) from the EUF-RMA property of fixed-length XMSS-TW which we, as the figure suggests, further deconstruct as follows. First, we demonstrate that this property is implied by the PRF property of the KHF employed in fixed-length XMSS-TW to generate secret keys and the EUF-RMA property of fixed-length XMSS-TW with uniformly random secret keys. Then, we show the EUF-RMA property of this variant of fixed-length XMSS-TW is implied by the SM-DT-TCR-C property of the two THFs used to construct the binary hash tree, and a variant of the EUF-CMA property specifically devised for WOTS-TW in [13]. However, instead of the original WOTS-TW—in which the secret key is generated via a PRF—we consider a version with uniformly random secret keys as a consequence of the PRF-related reduction for XMSS-TW mentioned above. Finally, we complete the second objective of this work—i.e, the formal verification of the fix of the security proof of SPHINCS$^+$ presented in [13]—by demonstrating that the SM-DT-UD-C, SM-DT-TCR-C, and SM-DT-PRE-C properties of the THF employed in WOTS-TW imply this dedicated variant of the EUF-CMA property.

After formally verifying each of the aforementioned implications, we combine the results to formally verify that the EUF-CMA security of XMSS-TW can exclusively be based on the properties of the employed THFs and KHFs (when the message-compression function is modeled as a random oracle), as desired.

In the subsequent sections, we discuss the formal verification process more thoroughly in a bottom-up manner; that is, we commence with WOTS-TW, proceed to fixed-length XMSS-TW, and finish with standalone XMSS-TW. Throughout this discussion, due to space considerations, we do not present any material directly from the produced formal verification artifacts. Instead, we go over the proofs that immediately underlie the formal verification in a manner that admits a near-direct translation to EasyCrypt and, hence, closely and accurately represents the formally verified material. Nonetheless, the produced formal verification artifacts can be found at https://github.com/MM45/FV-XMSS-EC.

4   WOTS-TW

The first explicit specification of (fixed-length) WOTS-TW was provided by Hülsing and Kudinov in their endeavor to recover the tight security proof of SPHINCS$^+$ [13]. As mentioned in the previous section, this original specification compresses the secret key via a PRF which, in our case, already happens on the level of XMSS-TW, leading to a variant of WOTS-TW that straightforwardly considers uniformly random secret keys. In the ensuing, we denote this variant by WOTS-TW$^\$$ (and use WOTS-TW to refer to the original version).

Before presenting the actual specification, we go over several preliminaries. Foremost, the construction is defined with respect to parameters n—the byte-length of (1) secret key, public key, and signature elements, and (2) messages—and w—the Winternitz parameter, i.e., the radix in which messages are encoded. From these parameters, the following constants are computed: $\text{len}_1 = \lceil \frac{8 \cdot n}{\log_2(w)} \rceil$ (number of w-ary digits necessary to represent any value of n bytes), $\text{len}_2 = \lfloor \log_w(\text{len}_1 \cdot (w - 1)) \rfloor + 1$ (number of w-ary digits required to represent any value in the range $[0, \text{len}_1 \cdot (w - 1)])$, and $\text{len} = \text{len}_1 + \text{len}_2$. In addition to these parameters and constants, WOTS-TW$^\$$ employs a THF with which it constructs function chains. Throughout the remainder, this THF and the corresponding chaining function are denoted by F and CF($:= \text{Ch}_\text{F}$), respectively. The message and digest space of F both equal $\{0, 1\}^{8 \cdot n}$. Moreover, the parameter and tweak space of F are respectively referred to as the *public seed space* $\mathcal{PS}$ and *address space* $\mathcal{AD}$. Certainly, since we primarily consider

WOTS-TW$^\$$ as a component of some greater structure such as (fixed-length) XMSS-TW or SPHINCS$^+$, these spaces may coincide with the corresponding spaces of the encompassing structure. In any case, we require the addresses to at least have a *chain index*—a nonnegative integer indicating the function chain in question—and a *hash index*—a nonnegative integer indicating the considered hash "iteration" within the function chain. As per the definition of a chaining function, the hash index is assumed to be updated internally by CF such that, even within a single chain, F is exclusively called with unique addresses. Besides these indices, the addresses may contain additional nonnegative integers that, for example, guarantee the uniqueness of the addresses between multiple instances of WOTS-TW$^\$$. As the concrete manifestation of such additional integers is irrelevant to the current analysis, we leave this unspecified here.

Algorithm 1 WOTS-TW$^\$$'s Public Key From Secret Key Algorithm

---

1: **procedure** WOTS-TW$^\$$.PkWotsFromSkWots(skWots, ps, ad)
2:      pkWots $\leftarrow$ [ ]
3:      **for** $i = 0, \ldots, \text{len} - 1$ **do**
4:          ad.chainIndex $\leftarrow i$
5:          pkWots $\leftarrow$ pkWots $\|$ CF(ps, ad, 0, $w - 1$, skWots[i])
6:      **return** pkWots

Algorithm 2 WOTS-TW$^\$$'s Public Key From Signature Algorithm

---

1: **procedure** WOTS-TW$^\$$.PkWotsFromSig(m, sig, ps, ad)
2:      em $\leftarrow$ EncodeMessageWots(m)
3:      pkWots $\leftarrow$ [ ]
4:      **for** $i = 0, \ldots, \text{len} - 1$ **do**
5:          ad.chainIndex $\leftarrow i$
6:          pkWots $\leftarrow$ pkWots $\|$ CF(ps, ad, em[i], $w - 1 - $ em[i], sig[i])
7:      **return** pkWots

In WOTS-TW$^\$$, secret keys, public keys, and signatures consist of a sequence of len bitstrings, each of length $8 \cdot n$. Intuitively, the construction of these artifacts goes as follows. First, a secret key sk $=$ sk$_0 \ldots$ sk$_{\text{len}-1}$ is sampled uniformly at random from its domain. Then, the corresponding public key is computed by applying the chaining function to each sk$_i$, $0 \leq i < \text{len}$, for $w - 1$ iterations. Given a message $m \in \{0, 1\}^{8 \cdot n}$, a signature is constructed by first encoding the message into a sequence of len w-ary digits. This encoding must have the property that, for any other message, it contains at least one digit that is strictly less than the digit at the same index of the encoding of this other message. Albeit the majority of WOTS-based constructions—among which WOTS-TW and, hence, WOTS-TW$^\$$—employ the same approach to encoding, we abstract away from the concrete approach and show that the results hold for any encoding with the foregoing property. Nevertheless, for completeness, we additionally demonstrate that the concrete encoding used by WOTS-TW possesses this property. Hereafter, we denote the operator performing the encoding by EncodeMessageWots. After encoding m into EncodeMessageWots(m) $= d_0 \ldots d_{\text{len}-1}$, the signature is obtained by applying the chaining function to sk$_i$ for d_i iterations, $0 \leq i < \text{len}$.

Notice that, from a message and its signature, the public key can be computed by completing the function chains. In fact, computing a public key in this manner and comparing it to the known public key is precisely how a signature is verified in WOTS-TW$^\$$.

Algorithm 3 WOTS-TW$^\$$'s Key Generation Algorithm

1: **procedure** WOTS-TW$^\$$.KeyGen(ps, ad)
2:     skWots $\leftarrow\$ \mathcal{U}((\{0,1\}^{8 \cdot n})^{\text{len}})$
3:     pkWots $\leftarrow$ WOTS-TW$^\$$.PkWotsFromSkWots(skWots, ps, ad)
4:     **return** pk := (pkWots, ps, ad), sk := (skWots, ps, ad)

Algorithm 4 WOTS-TW$^\$$'s Signing Algorithm

1: **procedure** WOTS-TW$^\$$.Sign(sk := (skWots, ps, ad), m)
2:     em $\leftarrow$ EncodeMessageWots(m)
3:     sig $\leftarrow$ [ ]
4:     **for** $i = 0, \ldots, \text{len} - 1$ **do**
5:        ad.chainIndex $\leftarrow i$
6:        sig $\leftarrow$ sig $\|$ CF(ps, ad, 0, em[i], skWots[i])
7:     **return** sig

Algorithm 5 WOTS-TW$^\$$'s Verification Algorithm

1: **procedure** WOTS-TW$^\$$.Verify(pk := (pkWots, ps, ad), m, sig)
2:     pkWots' $\leftarrow$ WOTS-TW$^\$$.PkWotsFromSig(m, sig, ps, ad)
3:     **return** pkWots' = pkWots

The specification of WOTS-TW$^\$$ is provided in Algorithm 1 through Algorithm 5. Here, the former two are auxiliary algorithms performing tasks necessary in both WOTS-TW$^\$$ and, as defined in the subsequent sections, (fixed-length) XMSS-TW; the latter three constitute the key generation, signature, and verification algorithms, respectively.

Security Property. For the security property of WOTS-TW$^\$$, we consider *Multi-instance Existential UnForgeability under Generic Chosen-Message Attack* (M-EUF-GCMA),[4] a variant of the EUF-CMA property that was specifically devised to recover the tight security proof of SPHINCS⁺ [13]. Intuitively, this property captures the feasibility of forging a signature for any of several WOTS-TW$^\$$ instances after obtaining a signature (and corresponding public key) on an adaptively chosen address-message pair for each considered instance. Crucially, the public key of a WOTS-TW$^\$$ instance is only given to the adversary after it issued the signature/challenge query for that instance. The forged signature should be valid with respect to the same address as the observed signature for that instance of WOTS-TW$^\$$. The game that formalizes this property, parameterized on the considered THF collection THFC and the number of WOTS-TW$^\$$ instances d, is given in Fig. 10; the oracles provided to the adversary in this game

---

[4] In [13], the authors introduce this property as D-EF-naCMA.

$$\text{Game}_{\mathcal{A},\text{WOTS-TW}^\$,\text{THFC},d}^{\text{M-EUF-GCMA}}$$

1: $\quad ps \leftarrow_\$ \mathcal{U}(\mathcal{PS})$

2: $\quad O_{\text{WOTS-TW}^\$}.\text{Init}(ps)$

3: $\quad OC_{\text{THFC}}.\text{Init}(ps)$

4: $\quad \mathcal{A}^{O_{\text{WOTS-TW}^\$},OC_{\text{THFC}}}.\text{Choose}()$

5: $\quad i, m', \text{sig}' \leftarrow \mathcal{A}.\text{Forge}(ps)$

6: $\quad ad, m, \text{pkWots} \leftarrow O_{\text{WOTS-TW}^\$}.\mathcal{A}[i], O_{\text{WOTS-TW}^\$}.\mathcal{M}[i], O_{\text{WOTS-TW}^\$}.\mathcal{P}[i]$

7: $\quad \text{isValid} \leftarrow \text{WOTS-TW}^\$.\text{Verify}((\text{pkWots}, ps, ad), m', \text{sig}')$

8: $\quad \text{isFresh} \leftarrow m \neq m'$

9: $\quad \textbf{return}\ \text{isValid} \wedge \text{isFresh} \wedge \text{VAD}_d(O_{\text{WOTS-TW}^\$}.\mathcal{A}, OC_{\text{THFC}}.\mathcal{A})$

Fig. 10. M-EUF-GCMA game for WOTS-TW$^\$$.

$O_{\text{WOTS-TW}^\$}$

vars $ps, \mathcal{A}, \mathcal{M}, \mathcal{P}$

Init (psi)

1: $\quad ps, \mathcal{A}, \mathcal{M}, \mathcal{P} \leftarrow psi, [\,], [\,], [\,]$

Query (ad, m)

1: $\quad \mathcal{A}, \mathcal{M} \leftarrow \mathcal{A} \parallel ad, \mathcal{M} \parallel m$

2: $\quad \text{skWots} \leftarrow_\$ \mathcal{U}((\{0,1\}^{8 \cdot n})^{\text{len}})$

3: $\quad \text{pkWots} \leftarrow [\,]$

4: $\quad \textbf{for}\ i = 0, \ldots, \text{len} - 1\ \textbf{do}$

5: $\quad\quad ad.\text{chainIndex} \leftarrow i$

6: $\quad\quad \text{pkWots} \leftarrow \text{pkWots} \parallel \text{CF}(ps, ad, 0, w - 1, \text{skWots}[i])$

7: $\quad \text{em} \leftarrow \text{EncodeMessageWots}(m)$

8: $\quad \text{sig} \leftarrow [\,]$

9: $\quad \textbf{for}\ i = 0, \ldots, \text{len} - 1\ \textbf{do}$

10: $\quad\quad ad.\text{chainIndex} \leftarrow i$

11: $\quad\quad \text{sig} \leftarrow \text{sig} \parallel \text{CF}(ps, ad, 0, \text{em}[i], \text{skWots}[i])$

12: $\quad \mathcal{P} \leftarrow \mathcal{P} \parallel \text{pkWots}$

13: $\quad \textbf{return}\ \text{pkWots}, \text{sig}$

Fig. 11. Signature/Challenge oracle employed in M-EUF-GCMA game for WOTS-TW$^\$$.

are specified in Fig. 11 (signature/challenge oracle) and Fig. 8 (collection oracle). As per usual, the adversary is merely given access to the Query procedures of these oracles.

Akin to the games formalizing the THF properties, $\text{Game}_{\mathcal{A},\text{WOTS-TW}^\$,\text{THFC},d}^{\text{M-EUF-GCMA}}$ is defined with respect to a two-stage adversary: In the first stage, this adversary is asked to select (up to) d target addresses, receiving corresponding signatures on chosen messages, while being able to query the considered (indexed) THF collection; in the second stage, given the public seed used to index F (in WOTS-TW$^\$$) and the considered THF collection, this adversary is asked to provide a signature on a fresh message that is valid with respect to one of the targets specified in the first stage. In the end, in addition to the legitimacy of the forgery, the adversary's behavior throughout the game is validated; this validation is performed by the $\mathsf{VAD}_d(\mathsf{O}_{\mathrm{WOTS\text{-}TW}^\$}.\mathcal{A}, \mathsf{OC}_{\mathsf{THFC}}.\mathcal{A})$ predicate, checking whether the number of specified target addresses was at most d, whether the target addresses were unique with respect to the part that can be used to differentiate between instances of WOTS-TW$^\$$—i.e., the part excluding the aforementioned chain index and hash index—and whether the target addresses were never used in queries to the collection oracle. Then, the advantage of any adversary $\mathcal{A}$ against M-EUF-GCMA (of WOTS-TW$^\$$) is defined as follows.

$$\mathsf{Adv}^{\mathrm{M\text{-}EUF\text{-}GCMA}}_{\mathrm{WOTS\text{-}TW}^\$,\mathsf{THFC},d}(\mathcal{A}) = \Pr\left[\mathsf{Game}^{\mathrm{M\text{-}EUF\text{-}GCMA}}_{\mathcal{A},\mathrm{WOTS\text{-}TW}^\$,\mathsf{THFC},d} = 1\right]$$

Formal Verification. We presently discuss the (proof of) the security statement for WOTS-TW$^\$$ that we formally verify in this work. As depicted in Fig. 9, we aim to demonstrate an implication from (the conjunction of) the SM-DT-UD-C, SM-DT-TCR-C, and SM-DT-PRE-C properties of F to the M-EUF-GCMA property of WOTS-TW$^\$$. More formally, the security theorem we prove is the following.

Security Theorem 1 (M-EUF-GCMA for WOTS-TW$^\$$). *For any adversary $\mathcal{A}$, there exist adversaries $\mathcal{B}_0$, $\mathcal{B}_1$, and $\mathcal{B}_2$—each with approximately the same running time as $\mathcal{A}$—such that the following inequality holds.*

$$\mathsf{Adv}^{\mathrm{M\text{-}EUF\text{-}GCMA}}_{\mathrm{WOTS\text{-}TW}^\$,\mathsf{FC},d}(\mathcal{A}) \leq (w-2) \cdot \mathsf{Adv}^{\mathrm{SM\text{-}DT\text{-}UD\text{-}C}}_{\mathsf{F},\mathsf{FC},t_{\mathrm{udf}}}(\mathcal{B}_0) + \mathsf{Adv}^{\mathrm{SM\text{-}DT\text{-}TCR\text{-}C}}_{\mathsf{F},\mathsf{FC},t_{\mathrm{tcrf}}}(\mathcal{B}_1)$$
$$+ \mathsf{Adv}^{\mathrm{SM\text{-}DT\text{-}PRE\text{-}C}}_{\mathsf{F},\mathsf{FC},t_{\mathrm{pref}}}(\mathcal{B}_2)$$

Here, FC denotes an arbitrary THF collection containing F, $d \geq 1$, $t_{\mathrm{udf}} = d \cdot \mathrm{len}$, $t_{\mathrm{tcrf}} = d \cdot \mathrm{len} \cdot w$, and $t_{\mathrm{pref}} = d \cdot \mathrm{len}$.

Conceptually, the formal verification of the above security theorem closely follows the original proof presented in [13]. Specifically, the formal verification considers a sequence of two games; in order, we denote these games by $\mathsf{Game}^0_{\mathcal{A}}$ and $\mathsf{Game}^1_{\mathcal{A}}$. Both of these games only differ from $\mathsf{Game}^{\mathrm{M\text{-}EUF\text{-}GCMA}}_{\mathcal{A},\mathrm{WOTS\text{-}TW}^\$,\mathsf{FC},d}$—and, hence, each other—with respect to the Query procedure of the challenge oracle provided to the adversary. As such, the ensuing exposition of the proof predominantly focuses on the challenge oracles instead of the games. The advantage of any adversary $\mathcal{A}$ playing in $\mathsf{Game}^i_{\mathcal{A}}$, $i \in \{0,1\}$, is defined similarly to $\mathsf{Adv}^{\mathrm{M\text{-}EUF\text{-}GCMA}}_{\mathrm{WOTS\text{-}TW}^\$,\mathsf{FC},d}(\mathcal{A})$; we refer to such an advantage as $\mathsf{Adv}^i(\mathcal{A})$. Imminently, we relate or bound (the differences between) advantages obtained in the games of the game sequence. Afterward, we combine the obtained results to acquire the aforementioned implication from the desired properties of F to the M-EUF-GCMA property of WOTS-TW$^\$$.

$O_0.\mathsf{Query}(\mathrm{ad}, m)$	$O_1.\mathsf{Query}(\mathrm{ad}, m)$

1 : $\mathscr{A}, \mathscr{M} \leftarrow \mathscr{A} \parallel \mathrm{ad}, \mathscr{M} \parallel m$

2 : $\mathrm{skWots} \leftarrow_\$ \mathcal{U}((\{0,1\}^{8 \cdot n})^{\mathrm{len}})$

3 : $\mathrm{em} \leftarrow \mathsf{EncodeMessageWots}(m)$

4 : $\mathrm{sig} \leftarrow [\,]$

5 : **for** $i = 0, \ldots, \mathrm{len} - 1$ **do**

6 : $\mathrm{ad.chainIndex} \leftarrow i$

7 : $\boxed{\mathrm{sig} \leftarrow \mathrm{sig} \parallel \mathsf{CF}(\mathrm{ps}, \mathrm{ad}, 0, \mathrm{em}[i], \mathrm{skWots}[i])}$

     $\boxed{\mathrm{sig} \leftarrow \mathrm{sig} \parallel (\mathrm{skWots}[i] \ \mathbf{if} \ \mathrm{em}[i] = 0 \ \mathbf{else} \ \mathsf{CF}(\mathrm{ps}, \mathrm{ad}, \mathrm{em}[i] - 1, 1, \mathrm{skWots}[i]))}$

8 : $\mathrm{pkWots} \leftarrow [\,]$

9 : **for** $i = 0, \ldots, \mathrm{len} - 1$ **do**

10 : $\mathrm{ad.chainIndex} \leftarrow i$

11 : $\mathrm{pkWots} \leftarrow \mathrm{pkWots} \parallel \mathsf{CF}(\mathrm{ps}, \mathrm{ad}, \mathrm{em}[i], w - 1 - \mathrm{em}[i], \mathrm{sig}[i])$

12 : $\mathscr{P} \leftarrow \mathscr{P} \parallel \mathrm{pkWots}$

13 : **return** $\mathrm{pkWots}, \mathrm{sig}$

Fig. 12. Query procedures of the challenge oracles employed in $\mathsf{Game}_{\mathcal{A}}^0$ (blue boxes) and $\mathsf{Game}_{\mathcal{A}}^1$ (yellow boxes). Statements not within colored boxes are executed in both procedures.

Relation Between $\mathsf{Adv}_{\mathrm{WOTS\text{-}TW^\$,FC},d}^{\mathrm{M\text{-}EUF\text{-}GCMA}}(\mathcal{A})$ *and* $\mathsf{Adv}^0(\mathcal{A})$. As hinted at above, the first game in the game sequence, $\mathsf{Game}_{\mathcal{A}}^0$, only differs from $\mathsf{Game}_{\mathcal{A},\mathrm{WOTS\text{-}TW^\$,FC},d}^{\mathrm{M\text{-}EUF\text{-}GCMA}}$ in the Query procedure of the challenge oracle. Namely, first, the order of the construction of the public key and signature is reversed; second, the public key is constructed by finishing the function chains based on the signature instead of computing the complete function chains based on the secret key. Figure 12 provides the specification of the resulting oracle procedure. Indeed, comparing $O_{\mathrm{WOTS\text{-}TW^\$}}.\mathsf{Query}$ and $O_0.\mathsf{Query}$, we see that the for-loops (and the preceding initialization of the variables used in these loops) concerning the computation of the public key pkWots and signature sig are swapped. Furthermore, rather than computing the i-th element of pkWots immediately as $\mathsf{CF}(\mathrm{ps}, \mathrm{ad}, 0, w - 1, \mathrm{skWots}[i])$, as $O_0.\mathsf{Query}$ does, $O_1.\mathsf{Query}$ computes it as $\mathsf{CF}(\mathrm{ps}, \mathrm{ad}, \mathrm{em}[i], w - 1 - \mathrm{em}[i], \mathrm{sig}[i])$, where $\mathrm{sig}[i]$ equals $\mathsf{CF}(\mathrm{ps}, \mathrm{ad}, 0, \mathrm{em}[i], \mathrm{skWots}[i])$. However, from the compositional property of chaining functions (see Sect. 2), it follows that $\mathsf{CF}(\mathrm{ps}, \mathrm{ad}, \mathrm{em}[i], w - 1 - \mathrm{em}[i], \mathsf{CF}(\mathrm{ps}, \mathrm{ad}, 0, \mathrm{em}[i], \mathrm{skWots}[i])) = \mathsf{CF}(\mathrm{ps}, \mathrm{ad}, 0, w - 1, \mathrm{skWots}[i])$; as such, the different computations of the public key are equivalent. Then, the two Query procedures and, in turn, $\mathsf{Game}_{\mathcal{A},\mathrm{WOTS\text{-}TW^\$,FC},d}^{\mathrm{M\text{-}EUF\text{-}GCMA}}$ and $\mathsf{Game}_{\mathcal{A}}^0$ are semantically equivalent. In consequence, we can derive the following result.

$$\forall_{\mathcal{A}} : \ \mathsf{Adv}_{\mathrm{WOTS\text{-}TW^\$,FC},d}^{\mathrm{M\text{-}EUF\text{-}GCMA}}(\mathcal{A}) = \mathsf{Adv}^0(\mathcal{A})$$

Bound on Difference Between $\mathsf{Adv}^0(\mathcal{A})$ *and* $\mathsf{Adv}^1(\mathcal{A})$. As $\mathsf{Game}_{\mathcal{A},\mathrm{WOTS\text{-}TW}^\$,\mathrm{FC},d}^{\mathrm{M\text{-}EUF\text{-}GCMA}}$ and $\mathsf{Game}_{\mathcal{A}}^0$, $\mathsf{Game}_{\mathcal{A}}^0$ and $\mathsf{Game}_{\mathcal{A}}^1$ exclusively differ in the Query procedure of their challenge oracles, the specifications of which are provided in Fig. 12. Collating these procedures, we see that their disparity solely concerns the generation of the signature: O_0.Query properly constructs the signature by applying the chaining function on each secret key element for the number of iterations indicated by the corresponding element of the encoded message; O_1.Query merely performs the final iteration of each of these applications of the chaining function. Here, remember that the chaining function essentially reduces to the identity function whenever the iteration counter is less than or equal to zero. As such, in both procedures, $\mathrm{sig}[i]$ equals $\mathrm{skWots}[i]$ if $\mathrm{em}[i] = 0$, where $0 \le i < \mathrm{len}$.

Considering their difference, distinguishing between $\mathsf{Game}_{\mathcal{A}}^0$ and $\mathsf{Game}_{\mathcal{A}}^1$ intuitively boils down to distinguishing between, for any message and address (and uniformly random public seed), the signature distribution resulting from applying the chaining function the appropriate number of times on the elements of a uniformly random secret key, and the distribution resulting from only applying the final iteration of the chaining function on the elements of a uniformly random secret key. Surely, these distributions should be computationally indistinguishable if, for any address (and uniformly random public seed), the output of the chaining function—when applied on a uniformly random value—remains computationally indistinguishable from a uniformly random value for up to $w - 2$ iterations. Namely, this would imply that, irrespective of the value of $\mathrm{em}[i]$, $\mathsf{CF}(\mathrm{ps}, \mathrm{ad}, 0, \mathrm{em}[i] - 1, \mathrm{skWots}[i])$ is computationally indistinguishable from $\mathrm{skWots}[i]$. Indeed, this is closely related to the SM-DT-UD-C property we assume F to possess; in fact, by means of a hybrid argument based on the number of omitted initial applications of F in a call to CF, we can reduce this property to distinguishing between $\mathsf{Game}_{\mathcal{A}}^0$ and $\mathsf{Game}_{\mathcal{A}}^1$. More precisely, given an adversary $\mathcal{A}$ playing in $\mathsf{Game}_{\mathcal{A}}^0$ and $\mathsf{Game}_{\mathcal{A}}^1$, we can construct a reduction adversary $\mathcal{R}^{\mathcal{A}}$ playing in $\mathsf{Game}_{\mathcal{R}^{\mathcal{A}},\mathrm{F},\mathrm{FC},t_{\mathrm{udf}}}^{\mathrm{SM\text{-}DT\text{-}UD\text{-}C}}(b)$ that samples $i \in [0, w - 3]$ uniformly at random, constructs either the i-th or $i + 1$-th hybrid—depending on whether its challenge oracle returns mappings of uniformly random values or returns uniformly random values, respectively—and employs $\mathcal{A}$ to determine which hybrid it is, thereby achieving a related advantage in its own game. As a result, abstracting away the particular reduction adversary, we obtain the following bound.

$$\forall_{\mathcal{A}} \exists_{\mathcal{B}_0} : |\mathsf{Adv}^0(\mathcal{A}) - \mathsf{Adv}^1(\mathcal{A})| \le (w - 2) \cdot \mathsf{Adv}_{\mathrm{F},\mathrm{FC},t_{\mathrm{udf}}}^{\mathrm{SM\text{-}DT\text{-}UD\text{-}C}}(\mathcal{B}_0)$$

Bound on $\mathsf{Adv}^1(\mathcal{A})$. In the situation where an adversary playing in $\mathsf{Game}_1^{\mathcal{A}}$ returns a valid forgery, it *must* be the case that this forgery allows for the extraction of a collision or a preimage for F. Namely, a forgery in $\mathsf{Game}_1^{\mathcal{A}}$ is a valid signature sig' on a fresh message m' under a previously established public key pkWots, address ad and public seed ps. That is, there already exists a valid signature sig on another message m (different from m') under this public key, address, and public seed. As m' and m are different, the message encoding guarantees that there exists an i, $0 \le i < \mathrm{len}$, such that $\mathrm{em}'[i] < \mathrm{em}[i]$ (where em' and em respectively denote the encodings of m' and m); consequently, for such an i, the verification algorithm performs more iterations of the chaining function on sig$'[i]$ than it performs on sig$[i]$. Nevertheless, since sig and sig$'$ are both valid under pkWots, both function chains must result in pkWots$[i]$. As such, we can distinguish two cases: CF(ps, ad, em$'[i]$, em$[i]$ − em$'[i]$, sig$'[i]$) $\neq$ sig$[i]$ and CF(ps, ad, em$'[i]$, em$[i]$ − em$'[i]$, sig$'[i]$) = sig$[i]$. In the former case, the value of the function chain of sig$'[i]$ at the same iteration as sig$[i]$ does not equal sig$[i]$. However, from both of these values, pkWots$[i]$ can be obtained by completing the function chains in an identical manner as, at this point, the same (number of) iterations remain for both function chains. Following, since at some point along the remainder of the function chains the output of F must become equal, the values in the function chains preceding these equal outputs constitute a collision for F. In the other case, the value of the function chain of sig$'[i]$ at the same iteration as sig$[i]$ does equal sig$[i]$. Then, the value in the function chain of sig$'[i]$ directly preceding the value at the same iteration as sig$[i]$ constitutes a preimage of sig$[i]$ under F.

In line with the above reasoning, we can construct reduction adversaries that are witnesses for the following bound.

$$\forall_{\mathcal{A}}\exists_{\mathcal{B}_1,\mathcal{B}_2} : \mathsf{Adv}^1(\mathcal{A}) \leq \mathsf{Adv}_{\mathsf{F},\mathsf{FC},t_{\mathrm{tcrf}}}^{\mathrm{SM\text{-}DT\text{-}TCR\text{-}C}}(\mathcal{B}_1) + \mathsf{Adv}_{\mathsf{F},\mathsf{FC},t_{\mathrm{pref}}}^{\mathrm{SM\text{-}DT\text{-}PRE\text{-}C}}(\mathcal{B}_2)$$

Final Result. Combining the foregoing results, we can derive Security Theorem 1 as follows.

$$\forall_{\mathcal{A}}\exists_{\mathcal{B}_0,\mathcal{B}_1,\mathcal{B}_2} : \mathsf{Adv}_{\mathrm{WOTS\text{-}TW}^\$,\mathsf{FC},d}^{\mathrm{M\text{-}EUF\text{-}GCMA}}(\mathcal{A}) = \mathsf{Adv}^0(\mathcal{A}) \leq$$

$$|\mathsf{Adv}^0(\mathcal{A}) - \mathsf{Adv}^1(\mathcal{A})| + \mathsf{Adv}^1(\mathcal{A}) \leq$$

$$(w - 2) \cdot \mathsf{Adv}_{\mathsf{F},\mathsf{FC},t_{\mathrm{udf}}}^{\mathrm{SM\text{-}DT\text{-}UD\text{-}C}}(\mathcal{B}_0) + \mathsf{Adv}_{\mathsf{F},\mathsf{FC},t_{\mathrm{tcrf}}}^{\mathrm{SM\text{-}DT\text{-}TCR\text{-}C}}(\mathcal{B}_1) + \mathsf{Adv}_{\mathsf{F},\mathsf{FC},t_{\mathrm{pref}}}^{\mathrm{SM\text{-}DT\text{-}PRE\text{-}C}}(\mathcal{B}_2)$$

Although no formal runtime analysis is provided, it is evident from the prior discussion (and from the EasyCrypt artifacts) that there exists $\mathcal{B}_0$, $\mathcal{B}_1$, and $\mathcal{B}_2$ that not only satisfy the above inequality, but also execute in approximately the same time as $\mathcal{A}$. This completes the formal verification of the fix of the security proof of SPHINCS[+] presented in [13].

5 Fixed-Length XMSS-TW

Fixed-length XMSS-TW builds on WOTS-TW and is a component of SPHINCS[+]. Conceptually, fixed-length XMSS-TW constitutes a binary hash tree, or Merkle tree, that employs WOTS-TW as its one-time signature scheme and exclusively processes messages of some fixed length; in fact, this fixed length matches the fixed length of the messages processed by WOTS-TW. As briefly elaborated on in Sect. 4, WOTS-TW only differs from WOTS-TW$^\$$ concerning the generation and handling of the secret keys. More precisely, rather than sampling the secret key uniformly at random and maintaining it in its entirety, WOTS-TW merely maintains a secret seed—an element from the *secret seed space $\mathcal{SS}$*—(re)generating the secret key via a PRF each time it is required.

For the purpose of (re)generating the secret key, WOTS-TW specifies an additional algorithm, provided in Algorithm 6. In this algorithm, SKWG is a KHF of which the key space and message space are instantiated with $\mathcal{SS}$ and $\mathcal{PS} \times \mathcal{AD}$, respectively. Then, the remainder of the algorithms of WOTS-TW are analogous to the algorithms of WOTS-TW$^\$$; as such, we refer to them using the same identifiers, yet preceded with WOTS-TW instead of WOTS-TW$^\$$.

Foremost, we go over several additional preliminaries. Besides the parameters required for WOTS-TW, fixed-length XMSS-TW is defined with respect to a parameter h that signifies the height of the tree. From h, since fixed-length XMSS-TW constitutes a Merkle tree, we can compute the number of leaves as $l = 2^h$. Furthermore, in addition to the THF employed in WOTS-TW, XMSS-TW utilizes two THFs: one for the compression of WOTS-TW public keys to leaves— denoted by PKCO—and one for the construction of the tree from the leaves— denoted by TRC. For both of these THFs, the parameter space and tweak space are, respectively, $\mathcal{PS}$ and $\mathcal{AD}$, identical to those of F. Nevertheless, as fixed-length XMSS-TW constitutes a larger structure than WOTS-TW, we require the addresses from $\mathcal{AD}$ to—on top of the previously introduced chain index and hash index required by WOTS-TW—contain a *type index*, *key pair index*, *tree height index*, and *tree breadth index*. These indices are nonnegative integers that, in order, indicate the considered type of operation (either function chaining, public key compression, or tree construction), the considered WOTS-TW key pair (or leaf), the height of the considered tree node, and the breadth of the considered tree node (at the height indicated by the tree height index). Here, the key pair index is only used for the function chaining and public key compression operations, and the tree height and tree breadth indices are only used for the tree construction operation; moreover, the chain and hash indices are only used for the function chaining operation.[5] Finally, besides these indices, the addresses may comprise other nonnegative integers that, e.g., guarantee the uniqueness of the addresses when (fixed-length) XMSS-TW is considered in an encompassing structure such as SPHINCS$^+$. As before, we leave these unspecified.

In fixed-length XMSS-TW, key pairs are, intuitively, constructed as follows. Foremost, a secret key is a four-tuple sk $= (i, \text{ss}, \text{ps}, \text{ad})$, where $i \in [0, l-1]$, ss $\in \mathcal{SS}$, ps $\in \mathcal{PS}$, and ad $\in \mathcal{AD}$. Here, i indicates which WOTS-TW key pair is supposed to be used for the construction of the next signature. Then, the public key associated with sk is produced by, first, generating a sequence of l WOTS-TW secret keys via SKWG. Subsequently, the corresponding sequence of WOTS-TW public keys is computed and, in turn, transformed into a sequence of leaves by means of PKCO. Now, this sequence of leaves uniquely defines a Merkle tree of which we can obtain the root by iteratively computing each of the tree's layers. Specifically, in the construction of the layer at height thi, the node at breadth tbi is computed from its children cl and cr as TRC(ps, ad$_{\text{thi,tbi}}$, cl $\parallel$ cr), where ad$_{\text{thi,tbi}}$ signifies the address resulting from modifying ad to be the unique address for the node at height thi and breadth tbi. After obtaining the root

---

[5] Consequently, in practice, it may be the case that, e.g., the chain index and the tree height index refer to the same location of an address.

rt, the public key is defined as the three-tuple pk = (rt, ps, ad). Henceforth, we
denote the operator that performs this root computation by RootFromLeaves.

Given a key pair (pk, sk) constructed as described above and a message
$m \in \{0,1\}^{8 \cdot n}$, signatures are, on a high level, created and verified as follows.
First, using the i-th WOTS-TW secret key from the aforementioned sequence
(recall that i is part of sk), a WOTS-TW signature sigWots on m is produced.
Next, a so-called *authentication path* is computed for the i-th leaf of the Merkle
tree. This path is a sequence of nodes that, in order, comprises the siblings of the
nodes on the path from the root to the i-th leaf. Hereafter, we denote the operator
that computes this authentication path by AuthPath. Given the authentication
path ap, the signature on m is the three-tuple sig = $(i, \text{sigWots}, \text{ap})$. Verification
of sig is performed by, first, computing the WOTS-TW public key pkWots corresponding to sigWots and compressing it to a leaf lf using PKCO. Afterward, a
candidate root value rt$'$ for the Merkle tree is computed from lf and ap. Indeed,
this is achieved by reconstructing the path from the i-th leaf to the root by using
lf and the sibling nodes in ap. For example, if the i-th leaf is a left child, the sec-
ond node on the path is reconstructed as $p_1 = \text{TRH}(\text{ps}, \text{ad}_{1,j}, \text{lf} \parallel \text{ap}[h-1])$, where
$j = \lfloor i/2 \rfloor$; then, if p_1 is a right child, the third node on the path is reconstructed
as $p_2 = \text{TRH}(\text{ps}, \text{ad}_{2,k}, \text{ap}[h-2] \parallel p_1)$, where $k = \lfloor j/2 \rfloor$; et cetera.[6] Throughout
the remainder, we denote the operator that performs this computation of a can-
didate root by RootFromAuthPath. Finally, if rt$'$ equals rt, verification succeeds;
otherwise, verification fails.

Algorithm 6 WOTS-TW's Secret Key Generation Algorithm

1: **procedure** WOTS-TW.SkWotsGen(ss, ps, ad)
2:      skWots ← [ ]
3:      **for** $i = 0, \ldots, \text{len} - 1$ **do**
4:          ad.chainIndex, ad.hashIndex ← $i, 0$
5:          skWots ← skWots $\parallel$ SKWG(ss, (ps, ad))
6:      **return** skWots

Algorithm 7 FL-XMSS-TW's Leaves From Secret Key Algorithm

1: **procedure** FL-XMSS-TW.LeavesFromSk(ss, ps, ad)
2:      leaves ← [ ]
3:      **for** $i = 0, \ldots, l - 1$ **do**
4:          ad.typeIndex, ad.keypairIndex ← chainType, i
5:          skWots ← WOTS-TW.SkWotsGen(ss, ps, ad)
6:          pkWots ← WOTS-TW.PkWotsFromSkWots(skWots, ps, ad)
7:          ad.typeIndex ← compressionType
8:          leaves ← leaves $\parallel$ PKCO(ps, ad, pkWots)
9:      **return** leaves

Following the above description, the specification of fixed-length XMSS-TW
is provided in Algorithm 7 through Algorithm 10. Here, the former is an auxiliary
algorithm for the construction of the leaves from the secret seed, public seed,

---

[6] Whether the nodes along the reconstructed path are left or right children can be
determined from the value of i.

and address of the secret key; the latter three constitute the actual key generation, signing, and verification algorithms, respectively. In these algorithms, and from this point onward, we explicitly refer to fixed-length XMSS-TW as FL-XMSS-TW to prevent potential ambiguity with (standalone) XMSS-TW.

Algorithm 8 FL-XMSS-TW's Key Generation Algorithm

1: **procedure** FL-XMSS-TW.KeyGen(ss, ps, ad)
2:    leaves ← FL-XMSS-TW.LeavesFromSk(ss, ps, ad)
3:    ad.typeIndex ← treeType
4:    rt ← RootFromLeaves(leaves, ps, ad)
5:    **return** pk := (rt, ps, ad), sk := (0, ss, ps, ad)

Algorithm 9 FL-XMSS-TW's Signing Algorithm

1: **procedure** FL-XMSS-TW.Sign(sk := (i, ss, ps, ad), m)
2:    ad.typeIndex, ad.keypairIndex ← chainType, i
3:    sigWots ← WOTS-TW.Sign((ss, ps, ad), m)
4:    leaves ← FL-XMSS-TW.LeavesFromSk(ss, ps, ad)
5:    ad.typeIndex ← treeType
6:    ap ← AuthPath(i, leaves, ps, ad)
7:    **return** sig := $(i, \text{sigWots}, \text{ap})$, sk := $(i + 1, ss, ps, ad)$

Algorithm 10 FL-XMSS-TW's Verification Algorithm

1: **procedure** FL-XMSS-TW.Verify(pk := (rt, ps, ad), m, sig := $(i, \text{sigWots}, \text{ap})$)
2:    ad.typeIndex, ad.keypairIndex ← chainType, i
3:    pkWots ← WOTS-TW.PkWotsFromSig(m, sigWots, ps, ad)
4:    ad.typeIndex ← compressionType
5:    lf ← PKCO(ps, ad, pkWots)
6:    rt$'$ ← RootFromAuthPath(i, lf, ap)
7:    **return** rt$'$ = rt

Security Property. As hinted at in Sect. 3, the security property we consider for FL-XMSS-TW is the EUF-RMA property. However, to be more precise, we actually consider a minor variant of this property that accounts for the fact that FL-XMSS-TW operates on an address that is provided by the environment and, besides having (valid values for) the previously described indices, may be arbitrarily structured.[7] Ensuring FL-XMSS-TW possesses the desired security property regardless of the additional components of the provided address, the variant of EUF-RMA we consider is defined with respect to a two-stage adversary that selects the address to be used in its first stage, and only attempts to provide a forgery in its second stage. Figure 13 provides the game formalizing this property. Then, the advantage of any adversary $\mathcal{A}$ against EUF-RMA (of

---

[7] For example, as previously mentioned, an address may contain additional indices that differentiate the context in an encompassing structure.

$$\text{Game}_{\mathcal{A},\text{FL-XMSS-TW}}^{\text{EUF-RMA}}$$

1 : $\text{ss} \leftarrow\!\!\$\ \mathcal{U}(\mathcal{SS})$

2 : $\text{ps} \leftarrow\!\!\$\ \mathcal{U}(\mathcal{PS})$

3 : $\text{ad} \leftarrow \mathcal{A}.\text{Choose}()$

4 : $\text{pk}, \text{sk} \leftarrow \text{FL-XMSS-TW}.\text{KeyGen}(\text{ss}, \text{ps}, \text{ad})$

5 : $\text{ms}, \text{sigs} \leftarrow [\ ], [\ ]$

6 : $\textbf{for } i = 0, \ldots, l - 1 \textbf{ do}$

7 : $m \leftarrow\!\!\$\ \mathcal{U}(\{0,1\}^{8 \cdot n})$

8 : $\text{sig}, \text{sk} \leftarrow \text{FL-XMSS-TW}.\text{Sign}(\text{sk}, m)$

9 : $\text{ms}, \text{sigs} \leftarrow \text{ms} \parallel m, \text{sigs} \parallel \text{sig}$

10 : $m', \text{sig}' \leftarrow \mathcal{A}.\text{Forge}(\text{pk}, \text{ms}, \text{sigs})$

11 : $\text{isValid} \leftarrow \text{FL-XMSS-TW}.\text{Verify}(\text{pk}, m', \text{sig})$

12 : $\text{isFresh} \leftarrow m' \notin \text{ms}$

13 : $\textbf{return } \text{isValid} \wedge \text{isFresh}$

Fig. 13. EUF-RMA game for FL-XMSS-TW.

FL-XMSS-TW) is defined as follows.

$$\text{Adv}_{\text{FL-XMSS-TW}}^{\text{EUF-RMA}}(\mathcal{A}) = \Pr\big[\text{Game}_{\mathcal{A},\text{FL-XMSS-TW}}^{\text{EUF-RMA}} = 1\big]$$

Formal Verification. We now go over the (proof of) the security statement concerning FL-XMSS-TW that we formally verify in this work. As illustrated in Fig. 9, we aim to show that the EUF-RMA property of FL-XMSS-TW is implied by the PRF property of SKWG, the M-EUF-GCMA property of WOTS-TW$^{\$}$, and the SM-DT-TCR-C property of PKCO and TRC. Specifically, we formally verify the following security theorem.

Security Theorem 2 (EUF-RMA for FL-XMSS-TW). *For any adversary $\mathcal{A}$, there exist adversaries $\mathcal{B}_0$, $\mathcal{B}_1$, $\mathcal{B}_2$, and $\mathcal{B}_3$—each with approximately the same running time as $\mathcal{A}$—such that the following inequality holds.*

$$\text{Adv}_{\text{FL-XMSS-TW}}^{\text{EUF-RMA}}(\mathcal{A}) \leq \text{Adv}_{\text{SKWG}}^{\text{PRF}}(\mathcal{B}_0) + \text{Adv}_{\text{WOTS-TW}^{\$},\text{THFC},l}^{\text{M-EUF-GCMA}}(\mathcal{B}_1)$$
$$+ \text{Adv}_{\text{PKCO},\text{THFC},l}^{\text{SM-DT-TCR-C}}(\mathcal{B}_2)$$
$$+ \text{Adv}_{\text{TRC},\text{THFC},l-1}^{\text{SM-DT-TCR-C}}(\mathcal{B}_3)$$

Here, THFC denotes an arbitrary THF collection containing F, PKCO, and TRC.

The formal verification of Theorem 2 proceeds as follows. Foremost, we consider FL-XMSS-TW$^{\$}$ instead of FL-XMSS-TW to obtain $\text{Game}_{\mathcal{A},\text{FL-XMSS-TW}^{\$}}^{\text{EUF-RMA}}$. Here, FL-XMSS-TW$^{\$}$ is analogous to WOTS-TW$^{\$}$ in that, rather than (re)generating the WOTS-TW secret keys via SKWG whenever necessary, it samples these keys uniformly at random and directly takes them as input whenever they are required. Alternatively stated, FL-XMSS-TW$^{\$}$ is obtained from FL-XMSS-TW by replacing the call to WOTS-TW.SkWotsGen in FL-XMSS-TW.LeavesFromSk with the appropriate sampling operation, and replacing the calls to the remaining WOTS-TW procedures with their WOTS-TW$^\$$ analogs. Given these differences, we reduce from the PRF property of SKWG to distinguishing between $\mathsf{Game}^{\text{EUF-RMA}}_{\mathcal{A},\text{FL-XMSS-TW}}$ and $\mathsf{Game}^{\text{EUF-RMA}}_{\mathcal{A},\text{FL-XMSS-TW}^\$}$. Afterward, considering the situation in which $\mathcal{A}$ returns a valid forgery in $\mathsf{Game}^{\text{EUF-RMA}}_{\mathcal{A},\text{FL-XMSS-TW}^\$}$, we perform a case analysis, allowing us to rephrase the corresponding probability as a sum of several terms. Subsequently, we bound each of these terms by providing a reduction from either the M-EUF-GCMA property of WOTS-TW$^\$$, or the SM-DT-TCR-C property of PKCO or TRC. Altogether, this suffices to derive the desired result.

Bound on Difference Between $\mathsf{Adv}^{\text{EUF-RMA}}_{\text{FL-XMSS-TW}}(\mathcal{A})$ *and* $\mathsf{Adv}^{\text{EUF-RMA}}_{\text{FL-XMSS-TW}^\$}(\mathcal{A})$. As alluded to above, the sole semantic difference between $\mathsf{Game}^{\text{EUF-RMA}}_{\mathcal{A},\text{FL-XMSS-TW}}$ and $\mathsf{Game}^{\text{EUF-RMA}}_{\mathcal{A},\text{FL-XMSS-TW}^\$}$ regards the manner in which the secret key is obtained: In FL-XMSS-TW, the secret key is (re)generated via SKWG each time it is required; in FL-XMSS-TW$^\$$, the secret key is sampled uniformly at random, maintained as is, and reused whenever it is required. Ergo, given an adversary $\mathcal{A}$ playing in these games, we can straightforwardly construct a reduction adversary $\mathcal{R}^{\mathcal{A}}$ achieving an advantage in $\mathsf{Game}^{\text{PRF}}_{\mathcal{R}^{\mathcal{A}},\text{SKWG}}(b)$ that equals the (absolute) difference between $\mathsf{Adv}^{\text{EUF-RMA}}_{\text{FL-XMSS-TW}}(\mathcal{A})$ and $\mathsf{Adv}^{\text{EUF-RMA}}_{\text{FL-XMSS-TW}^\$}(\mathcal{A})$. Generalizing this result, we acquire the following bound.

$$\forall_{\mathcal{A}} \exists_{\mathcal{B}_0} : |\mathsf{Adv}^{\text{EUF-RMA}}_{\text{FL-XMSS-TW}}(\mathcal{A}) - \mathsf{Adv}^{\text{EUF-RMA}}_{\text{FL-XMSS-TW}^\$}(\mathcal{A})| \leq \mathsf{Adv}^{\text{SKWG}}_{\text{PRF}}(\mathcal{B}_0)$$

Case Distinction for $\mathsf{Game}^{\text{EUF-RMA}}_{\mathcal{A},\text{FL-XMSS-TW}^\$} = 1$. Considering the situation where an adversary playing in $\mathsf{Game}^{\text{EUF-RMA}}_{\mathcal{A},\text{FL-XMSS-TW}^\$}$ provides a valid forgery, we can distinguish three (exhaustive) cases. Namely, a valid forgery in $\mathsf{Game}^{\text{EUF-RMA}}_{\mathcal{A},\text{FL-XMSS-TW}^\$}$ consists of a message m' and a signature $\text{sig}' = (i', \text{sigWots}', \text{ap}')$ such that m' is fresh and sig' is valid for m' under the considered public key $\text{pk} = (\text{rt}, \text{ps}, \text{ad})$. Now, recall that sig' being valid for m' under pk means that the candidate root rt' equals the actual root rt. As such, at a certain point along the computation of rt', the considered values should coincide with the corresponding values used in the computation of rt. Building on this observation, the first case we distinguish concerns pkWots', the WOTS-TW$^\$$ public key corresponding to $\text{sigWots}'$, coinciding with $\text{pkWots}_{i'}$, the i'-th WOTS-TW$^\$$ public key in the sequence used during key generation and, hence, the computation of rt. As per the verification procedure of WOTS-TW$^\$$, this means that $\text{sigWots}'$ is a valid signature for m' under $\text{pkWots}_{i'}$; since m' is fresh, it follows that m' and $\text{sigWots}'$ form a valid forgery for the WOTS-TW$^\$$ instance corresponding to the i'-th leaf of the Merkle tree. Henceforth, we denote the event that this first case occurs by E_F. Then, if pkWots' does not equal $\text{pkWots}_{i'}$, the second case we distinguish regards the leaves resulting from the compression of these WOTS-TW$^\$$ public keys coinciding. In this case, the inputs of PKCO are unequal yet map, under the same public seed and address, to the same output. Consequently, pkWots' and $\text{pkWots}_{i'}$ constitute a collision for PKCO. Hereafter, E_P signifies the event that this second case occurs. Lastly, if both of the preceding cases do not happen, it must be the case that, from a certain point onward, the reconstructed path coincides with the corresponding path through the original Merkle tree. Following, since the initial (few) nodes along the paths *do not* coincide, the first node for which the paths *do* coincide must be obtained by applying TRC, with the same public seed and address, on different inputs. As such, these inputs form a collision for TRC.

Formally, the foregoing can essentially be summarized by the following, where $G_{\mathcal{A}}$ serves as a shorthand for $\mathrm{Game}_{\mathcal{A},\mathrm{FL\text{-}XMSS\text{-}TW}^{\$}}^{\mathrm{EUF\text{-}RMA}}$.

$$\forall_{\mathcal{A}} : \Pr[G_{\mathcal{A}} = 1] =$$
$$\Pr[G_{\mathcal{A}} = 1 \wedge E_F] + \Pr[G_{\mathcal{A}} = 1 \wedge \neg E_F] =$$
$$\Pr[G_{\mathcal{A}} = 1 \wedge E_F] + \Pr[G_{\mathcal{A}} = 1 \wedge \neg E_F \wedge E_P] + \Pr[G_{\mathcal{A}} = 1 \wedge \neg E_F \wedge \neg E_P]$$

Bound on $\Pr\left[\mathrm{Game}_{\mathcal{A},\mathrm{FL\text{-}XMSS\text{-}TW}^{\$}}^{\mathrm{EUF\text{-}RMA}} = 1 \wedge E_F\right]$. For the case where the (valid) forgery returned by $\mathcal{A}$ in $\mathrm{Game}_{\mathcal{A},\mathrm{FL\text{-}XMSS\text{-}TW}^{\$}}^{\mathrm{EUF\text{-}RMA}}$ comprises a valid forgery for the indicated WOTS-TW$^{\$}$ instance, we can devise a reduction adversary $\mathcal{R}^{\mathcal{A}}$ playing in $\mathrm{Game}_{\mathcal{R}^{\mathcal{A}},\mathrm{F},\mathrm{THFC},l}^{\mathrm{M\text{-}EUF\text{-}GCMA}}$ as follows. Foremost, $\mathcal{R}^{\mathcal{A}}$ produces a sequence of l WOTS-TW$^{\$}$ signatures and public keys by repeatedly querying its challenge oracle on an appropriately updated address (based on the address obtained from $\mathcal{A}$) and a uniformly random message.[8] Then, utilizing the public seed provided in its second stage, the reduction adversary finishes the generation of, and provides $\mathcal{A}$ with, the FL-XMSS-TW$^{\$}$ signatures and public key corresponding to the previously produced sequence of WOTS-TW$^{\$}$ signatures and public keys. Finally, as soon as $\mathcal{A}$ returns a (valid) forgery—comprised of, say, message m' and signature $\mathrm{sig}' = (i', \mathrm{sigWots}', \mathrm{ap}')$—$\mathcal{R}^{\mathcal{A}}$ straightforwardly extracts and returns i', m', and $\mathrm{sigWots}'$.

Based on the above, we can derive the ensuing result.

$$\forall_{\mathcal{A}} \exists_{\mathcal{B}_1} : \Pr\left[\mathrm{Game}_{\mathcal{A},\mathrm{FL\text{-}XMSS\text{-}TW}^{\$}}^{\mathrm{EUF\text{-}RMA}} = 1 \wedge E_F\right] \leq \mathrm{Adv}_{\mathrm{WOTS\text{-}TW}^{\$},\mathrm{THFC},l}^{\mathrm{M\text{-}EUF\text{-}GCMA}}(\mathcal{B}_1)$$

Bound on $\Pr\left[\mathrm{Game}_{\mathcal{A},\mathrm{FL\text{-}XMSS\text{-}TW}^{\$}}^{\mathrm{EUF\text{-}RMA}} = 1 \wedge \neg E_F \wedge E_P\right]$. In the case that the (valid) forgery provided by $\mathcal{A}$ in $\mathrm{Game}_{\mathcal{A},\mathrm{FL\text{-}XMSS\text{-}TW}^{\$}}^{\mathrm{EUF\text{-}RMA}}$ does not contain a WOTS-TW$^{\$}$ forgery but does allow for the extraction of a collision for PKCO, we consider the ensuing reduction adversary $\mathcal{R}^{\mathcal{A}}$ playing in $\mathrm{Game}_{\mathcal{R}^{\mathcal{A}},\mathrm{PKCO},\mathrm{THFC},l}^{\mathrm{SM\text{-}DT\text{-}TCR\text{-}C}}$. First, $\mathcal{R}^{\mathcal{A}}$ samples a sequence of l WOTS-TW$^{\$}$ secret keys uniformly at random and, subsequently, computes the corresponding public keys by continually querying its collection oracle on a properly updated address (based on the address provided by $\mathcal{A}$) and a function chain element. Afterward, the reduction adversary produces the corresponding sequence of leaves through its challenge oracle, thereby specifying every WOTS-TW$^{\$}$ public key as a collision target.[9] Then,

---

[8] As such, it suffices to consider l simultaneous WOTS-TW$^{\$}$ instances and, accordingly, only allow l queries to the challenge oracle.

[9] Thus, allowing for at most l targets is sufficient, as this is precisely the number of considered WOTS-TW$^{\$}$ public keys.

employing the public seed provided in its second stage, $\mathcal{R}^{\mathcal{A}}$ constructs, and provides $\mathcal{A}$ with, the FL-XMSS-TW$^\$$ signatures (on uniformly random messages) and public key corresponding to the formerly obtained sequences. Lastly, when $\mathcal{A}$ returns a (valid) forgery—consisting of, say, message m' and signature sig$'$ = $(i', \text{sigWots}', \text{ap}')$—the reduction adversary computes the WOTS-TW$^\$$ public key corresponding to sigWots$'$ and returns it together with i'.

From the preceding, we can deduce the following bound.

$$\forall_{\mathcal{A}} \exists_{\mathcal{B}_2} : \Pr\left[\text{Game}_{\mathcal{A},\text{FL-XMSS-TW}^\$}^{\text{EUF-RMA}} = 1 \wedge \neg E_F \wedge E_P\right] \leq \text{Adv}_{\text{PKCO,THFC},l}^{\text{SM-DT-TCR-C}}(\mathcal{B}_2)$$

Bound on $\Pr\left[\text{Game}_{\mathcal{A},\text{FL-XMSS-TW}^\$}^{\text{EUF-RMA}} = 1 \wedge \neg E_F \wedge \neg E_P\right]$. In the final case, the (valid) forgery provided by $\mathcal{A}$ in $\text{Game}_{\mathcal{A},\text{FL-XMSS-TW}^\$}^{\text{EUF-RMA}}$ allows for the extraction of a collision for TRC; so, we consider a reduction adversary $\mathcal{R}^{\mathcal{A}}$ playing in $\text{Game}_{\mathcal{R}^{\mathcal{A}},\text{PKCO,THFC},l}^{\text{SM-DT-TCR-C}}$. In essence, this reduction adversary is fairly similar to the reduction adversary considered in the previous case. Namely, $\mathcal{R}^{\mathcal{A}}$ commences identically but produces the leaves by querying its collection oracle instead of its challenge oracle. Subsequently, the reduction adversary actually computes the corresponding FL-XMSS-TW$^\$$ public key via its challenge oracle; as such, it specifies all (concatenations of sibling) nodes in the entire Merkle tree as collision targets.[10] Then, in its second stage, $\mathcal{R}^{\mathcal{A}}$ produces the FL-XMSS-TW$^\$$ signatures (on uniformly random messages) corresponding to the previously obtained values and provides these signatures, together with the FL-XMSS-TW$^\$$ public key, to $\mathcal{A}$. Ultimately, whenever $\mathcal{A}$ returns a (valid) forgery, the reduction adversary computes the corresponding path and searches for the first node on this path that coincides with the corresponding node in the original Merkle tree. After finding this node, the reduction adversary returns (the concatenation of) its children and an integer j such that the j-th query to the challenge oracle contained the colliding value from the original Merkle tree.

Given the foregoing, we can derive the following result.

$$\forall_{\mathcal{A}} \exists_{\mathcal{B}_3} : \Pr\left[\text{Game}_{\mathcal{A},\text{FL-XMSS-TW}^\$}^{\text{EUF-RMA}} = 1 \wedge \neg E_F \wedge \neg E_P\right] \leq \text{Adv}_{\text{TRC,THFC},l-1}^{\text{SM-DT-TCR-C}}(\mathcal{B}_3)$$

Final Result. Aggregating the results established above, we can derive Security Theorem 2 as shown below. In this derivation, $G_{\mathcal{A}}$ denotes $\text{Game}_{\mathcal{A},\text{FL-XMSS-TW}^\$}^{\text{EUF-RMA}}$.

$$\forall_{\mathcal{A}} \exists_{\mathcal{B}_0, \mathcal{B}_1, \mathcal{B}_2, \mathcal{B}_3} : \text{Adv}_{\text{FL-XMSS-TW}}^{\text{EUF-RMA}}(\mathcal{A}) \leq$$
$$|\text{Adv}_{\text{FL-XMSS-TW}}^{\text{EUF-RMA}}(\mathcal{A}) - \text{Adv}_{\text{FL-XMSS-TW}^\$}^{\text{EUF-RMA}}(\mathcal{A})| + \text{Adv}_{\text{FL-XMSS-TW}^\$}^{\text{EUF-RMA}}(\mathcal{A}) \leq$$
$$\text{Adv}_{\text{PRF}}^{\text{SKWG}}(\mathcal{B}_0) + \text{Adv}_{\text{FL-XMSS-TW}^\$}^{\text{EUF-RMA}}(\mathcal{A}) =$$
$$\text{Adv}_{\text{PRF}}^{\text{SKWG}}(\mathcal{B}_0) + \Pr[G_{\mathcal{A}} = 1 \wedge E_F] + \Pr[G_{\mathcal{A}} = 1 \wedge \neg E_F \wedge E_P]$$
$$+ \Pr[G_{\mathcal{A}} = 1 \wedge \neg E_F \wedge \neg E_P] \leq$$

---

[10] Hence, allowing for at most $l-1$ targets is sufficient, since this is exactly the number of nodes in the Merkle tree (excluding the leaves).

$$\mathsf{Adv}_{\mathsf{PRF}}^{\mathsf{SKWG}}(\mathcal{B}_0) + \mathsf{Adv}_{\mathsf{WOTS\text{-}TW^\$,THFC},l}^{\mathsf{M\text{-}EUF\text{-}GCMA}}(\mathcal{B}_1) + \mathsf{Adv}_{\mathsf{PKCO,THFC},l}^{\mathsf{SM\text{-}DT\text{-}TCR\text{-}C}}(\mathcal{B}_2)$$
$$+ \mathsf{Adv}_{\mathsf{TRC,THFC},l-1}^{\mathsf{SM\text{-}DT\text{-}TCR\text{-}C}}(\mathcal{B}_3)$$

Once again, even though no formal runtime analysis is provided, it is clear from the preceding discussion (and from the EasyCrypt artifacts) that there exist $\mathcal{B}_0$, $\mathcal{B}_1$, $\mathcal{B}_2$, and $\mathcal{B}_3$ that not only satisfy the above inequality, but also terminate in approximately the same time as $\mathcal{A}$.

Here, we could trivially combine Security Theorem 1 and Security Theorem 2 to obtain a bound on $\mathsf{Adv}_{\mathsf{FL\text{-}XMSS\text{-}TW}}^{\mathsf{EUF\text{-}RMA}}(\mathcal{A})$ solely based on the properties of the employed KHFs and THFs.

6   XMSS-TW

XMSS-TW extends FL-XMSS-TW in a way that allows for the processing of arbitrary-length messages. In essence, the transformation from FL-XMSS-TW to XMSS-TW is an instance of the hash-then-sign paradigm. To this end, XMSS-TW employs two additional KHFs—MKG and MCO—to compress arbitrary-length messages before executing the relevant procedures of FL-XMSS-TW. More precisely, MKG is used to generate an indexing key for MCO; in turn, indexed on this key, MCO is used to compress the message. The specification of XMSS-TW is provided in Algorithm 11 (key generation), Algorithm 12 (signing), and Algorithm 13 (verification). Here, $\mathcal{MS}$ denotes the set of indexing keys for MKG, and ad_c signifies an arbitrary address that satisfies the requirements for addresses used in FL-XMSS-TW (see Sect. 5).

Algorithm 11 XMSS-TW's Key Generation Algorithm

1: **procedure** XMSS-TW.KeyGen()
2:    $\mathsf{ms} \leftarrow\!\!\$\ \mathcal{U}(\mathcal{MS})$
3:    $\mathsf{ss} \leftarrow\!\!\$\ \mathcal{U}(\mathcal{SS})$
4:    $\mathsf{ps} \leftarrow\!\!\$\ \mathcal{U}(\mathcal{PS})$
5:    $\mathsf{ad} \leftarrow \mathsf{ad}_c$
6:    $\mathsf{pk}, \_ \leftarrow \mathsf{FL\text{-}XMSS\text{-}TW.KeyGen}(\mathsf{ss}, \mathsf{ps}, \mathsf{ad})$
7:    **return** $\mathsf{pk} := (\mathsf{rt}, \mathsf{ps}, \mathsf{ad}), \mathsf{sk} := (\mathsf{ms}, 0, \mathsf{ss}, \mathsf{ps}, \mathsf{ad})$

Algorithm 12 XMSS-TW's Signing Algorithm

1: **procedure** XMSS-TW.Sign($\mathsf{sk} := (\mathsf{ms}, i, \mathsf{ss}, \mathsf{ps}, \mathsf{ad}), m$)
2:    $\mathsf{mk} \leftarrow \mathsf{MKG}(\mathsf{ms}, i)$
3:    $\mathsf{cm} \leftarrow \mathsf{MCO}(\mathsf{mk}, m)$
4:    $(i, \mathsf{sigWots}, \mathsf{ap}), \_ \leftarrow \mathsf{FL\text{-}XMSS\text{-}TW.Sign}((i, \mathsf{ss}, \mathsf{ps}, \mathsf{ad}), \mathsf{cm})$
5:    **return** $\mathsf{sig} := (\mathsf{mk}, i, \mathsf{sigWots}, \mathsf{ap}), \mathsf{sk} := (\mathsf{ms}, i+1, \mathsf{ss}, \mathsf{ps}, \mathsf{ad})$

Algorithm 13 XMSS-TW's Verification Algorithm

1: **procedure** XMSS-TW.Verify($\mathsf{pk} := (\mathsf{rt}, \mathsf{ps}, \mathsf{ad}), m, \mathsf{sig} := (\mathsf{mk}, i, \mathsf{sigWots}, \mathsf{ap})$)
2:    $\mathsf{cm} \leftarrow \mathsf{MCO}(\mathsf{mk}, m)$
3:    $\mathsf{ver} \leftarrow \mathsf{FL\text{-}XMSS\text{-}TW.Verify}(\mathsf{pk}, \mathsf{cm}, (i, \mathsf{sigWots}, \mathsf{ap}))$
4:    **return** ver

Game$_{\mathcal{A},\text{XMSS-TW}}^{\text{EUF-CMA}}$
1 : pk, sk $\leftarrow$ XMSS-TW.KeyGen()
2 : $O_{\text{XMSS-TW}}$.Init(sk)
3 : m', sig' $\leftarrow \mathcal{A}^{O_{\text{XMSS-TW}}}$.Forge(pk)
4 : isValid $\leftarrow$ XMSS-TW.Verify(pk, m', sig')
5 : isFresh $\leftarrow m' \notin O_{\text{XMSS-TW}}.\mathcal{M}$
6 : **return** isValid $\wedge$ isFresh $\wedge \, |O_{\text{XMSS-TW}}.\mathcal{M}| \leq l$

Fig. 14. EUF-CMA game for XMSS-TW.

$O_{\text{XMSS-TW}}$
vars sk, $\mathcal{M}$
Init(ski)
1 : sk, $\mathcal{M} \leftarrow$ ski, [ ]
Query(m)
1 : $\mathcal{M} \leftarrow \mathcal{M} \, || \, m$
2 : sig, sk $\leftarrow$ XMSS-TW.Sign(sk, m)
3 : **return** sig

Fig. 15. Signature oracle employed in EUF-CMA game for XMSS-TW.

Security Property. As for the majority of standalone signature schemes, we require XMSS-TW to possess the EUF-CMA security property. However, since XMSS-TW only allows for the signing of at most l signatures, we consider a bounded version of EUF-CMA. The game formalizing this property is provided in Fig. 14; the (signature) oracle given to the adversary in this game is specified in Fig. 15. As before, the adversary exclusively gains access to the oracle's Query procedure. Then, the advantage of any adversary $\mathcal{A}$ against EUF-CMA (of XMSS-TW) is defined as follows.

$$\text{Adv}_{\text{XMSS-TW}}^{\text{EUF-CMA}}(\mathcal{A}) = \Pr\left[\text{Game}_{\mathcal{A},\text{XMSS-TW}}^{\text{EUF-CMA}} = 1\right]$$

Formal Verification. Next, we cover the (proof of) the security statement concerning XMSS-TW that we formally verify in this work. As can be extracted from Fig. 9, we aim to demonstrate that the EUF-CMA property of XMSS-TW is implied by the PRF property of MKG, the CR property of MCO, and the EUF-RMA property of FL-XMSS-TW. More precisely, we formally verify the following security statement.

Security Theorem 3 (EUF-CMA for XMSS-TW). *Let MCO be a random oracle. Then, for any adversary $\mathcal{A}$, there exist adversaries $\mathcal{B}_0$, $\mathcal{B}_1$, and $\mathcal{B}_2$—each with approximately the same running time as $\mathcal{A}$—such that the following inequality holds.*

$$\text{Adv}_{\text{XMSS-TW}}^{\text{EUF-CMA}}(\mathcal{A}) \leq \text{Adv}_{\text{MKG}}^{\text{PRF}}(\mathcal{B}_0) + \text{Adv}_{\text{MCO}}^{\text{CR}}(\mathcal{B}_1) + \text{Adv}_{\text{FL-XMSS-TW}}^{\text{EUF-RMA}}(\mathcal{B}_2)$$
$$+ \frac{(q_M + q_S + 1) \cdot q_S}{|\mathcal{MS}|} + \frac{l}{2^{8 \cdot n}}$$

Here, q_M and q_S denote the number of queries that $\mathcal{A}$ issues to MCO and $O_{\text{XMSS-TW}}$, respectively.

Evidently, as MCO is assumed to be a random oracle, this security theorem—and, consequently, its formal verification—manifests itself in the ROM. Intuitively, this is required because, at some point, MCO needs to be adaptively reprogrammed in order to properly simulate the signature oracle. This reprogramming induces the additional $((q_M + q_S + 1) \cdot q_S)/|\mathcal{MS}|$ term in the bound. Furthermore, since MCO is considered to be a random oracle, the corresponding CR property essentially becomes a statistical bad event that occurs when two key-message pairs queried to the random oracle turn out to have the same output.

Loosely speaking, the formal verification of Security Theorem 3 proceeds as follows. Foremost, we change $\text{Game}_{\mathcal{A},\text{XMSS-TW}}^{\text{EUF-CMA}}$ to $\text{Game}_{\mathcal{A},\text{XMSS-TW}^{\$}}^{\text{EUF-CMA}}$; that is, we consider XMSS-TW$^{\$}$ instead of XMSS-TW. Here, XMSS-TW$^{\$}$ is nearly identical to XMSS-TW, merely replacing the call to MKG by a sampling from the appropriate uniform distribution; accordingly, XMSS-TW$^{\$}$ does not sample and maintain ms, i.e., the value from XMSS-TW that is exclusively used as input to MKG. As these constitute the sole differences, we can reduce the PRF property of MKG to distinguishing between $\text{Game}_{\mathcal{A},\text{XMSS-TW}}^{\text{EUF-CMA}}$ to $\text{Game}_{\mathcal{A},\text{XMSS-TW}^{\$}}^{\text{EUF-CMA}}$. Then, we separate the situation in which an adversary playing in $\text{Game}_{\mathcal{A},\text{XMSS-TW}^{\$}}^{\text{EUF-CMA}}$ returns a valid forgery into two cases. For both of these cases, we bound the probability via a reduction from either the CR property of MCO or the EUF-RMA property of FL-XMSS-TW. Here, the reduction from the EUF-RMA property of FL-XMSS-TW requires the consideration of a bad event that gives rise to the additional $l/2^{8 \cdot n}$ term in the security theorem. Collectively, this allows us to acquire the desired result.

Bound on Difference Between $\text{Adv}_{\text{XMSS-TW}}^{\text{EUF-CMA}}(\mathcal{A})$ *and* $\text{Adv}_{\text{XMSS-TW}^{\$}}^{\text{EUF-CMA}}(\mathcal{A})$. Considering the differences between XMSS-TW and XMSS-TW$^{\$}$ described above, we can—given an adversary $\mathcal{A}$ playing in $\text{Game}_{\mathcal{A},\text{XMSS-TW}}^{\text{EUF-CMA}}$ and $\text{Game}_{\mathcal{A},\text{XMSS-TW}^{\$}}^{\text{EUF-CMA}}$—straightforwardly construct a reduction adversary $\mathcal{R}^{\mathcal{A}}$ attaining an advantage in $\text{Game}_{\mathcal{R}^{\mathcal{A}},\text{MKG}}^{\text{PRF}}(b)$ that equals the (absolute) difference between $\text{Adv}_{\text{XMSS-TW}}^{\text{EUF-CMA}}(\mathcal{A})$ and $\text{Adv}_{\text{XMSS-TW}^{\$}}^{\text{EUF-CMA}}(\mathcal{A})$. In consequence, we obtain the following bound.

$$\forall_{\mathcal{A}} \exists_{\mathcal{B}_0} : |\text{Adv}_{\text{XMSS-TW}}^{\text{EUF-CMA}}(\mathcal{A}) - \text{Adv}_{\text{XMSS-TW}^{\$}}^{\text{EUF-CMA}}(\mathcal{A})| \leq \text{Adv}_{\text{MKG}}^{\text{PRF}}(\mathcal{B}_0)$$

Case Distinction for $\text{Game}_{\mathcal{A},\text{XMSS-TW}^{\$}}^{\text{EUF-CMA}} = 1$. In the situation where an adversary playing in $\text{Game}_{\mathcal{A},\text{XMSS-TW}^{\$}}^{\text{EUF-CMA}}$ provides a valid forgery—consisting of, say, message m' and signature $\text{sig}' = (\text{mk}', i', \text{sigWots}', \text{ap}')$—we distinguish two (exhaustive) cases: In the first case, the provided forgery allows for the extraction of a collision for MCO; in the second case, it does not. More precisely, in the first case, mk' and m' map to the same value under MCO as (at least) one of the pairs of values used during the signature queries of $\mathcal{A}$. Furthermore, in the second case, it is possible—by appropriately reprogramming MCO—to guarantee (up to some bad events) that the forgery for XMSS-TW$^{\$}$ contains a valid forgery for FL-XMSS-TW with respect to the EUF-RMA property. Hereafter, E_{COLL} represents the event that the forgery allows for the extraction of a collision for MCO in the above way.

Formally, the preceding can be summarized by the following equality, where $G_{\mathcal{A}}$ denotes $\text{Game}^{\text{EUF-CMA}}_{\mathcal{A},\text{XMSS-TW}^{\$}}$.

$$\forall_{\mathcal{A}} : \Pr[G_{\mathcal{A}} = 1] = \Pr[G_{\mathcal{A}} = 1 \wedge E_{\text{COLL}}] + \Pr[G_{\mathcal{A}} = 1 \wedge \neg E_{\text{COLL}}]$$

Bound on $\Pr\left[\text{Game}^{\text{EUF-CMA}}_{\mathcal{A},\text{XMSS-TW}^{\$}} = 1 \wedge E_{\text{COLL}}\right]$. In case the (valid) forgery provided by $\mathcal{A}$ in $\text{Game}^{\text{EUF-CMA}}_{\mathcal{A},\text{XMSS-TW}^{\$}}$ allows for the extraction of a collision for MCO in the previously described manner, we can trivially construct a reduction adversary $\mathcal{R}^{\mathcal{A}}$ playing in $\text{Game}^{\text{CR}}_{\mathcal{R}^{\mathcal{A}},\text{MCO}}$ that searches for the collision in the message compressions corresponding to $\mathcal{A}$'s signature queries and returns it. As a result, we can deduce the following bound.

$$\forall_{\mathcal{A}} \exists_{\mathcal{B}_1} : \Pr\left[\text{Game}^{\text{EUF-CMA}}_{\mathcal{A},\text{XMSS-TW}^{\$}} = 1 \wedge E_{\text{COLL}}\right] \leq \text{Adv}^{\text{CR}}_{\text{MCO}}(\mathcal{B}_1)$$

Bound on $\Pr\left[\text{Game}^{\text{EUF-CMA}}_{\mathcal{A},\text{XMSS-TW}^{\$}} = 1 \wedge \neg E_{\text{COLL}}\right]$. In case the (valid) forgery provided by $\mathcal{A}$ in $\text{Game}^{\text{EUF-CMA}}_{\mathcal{A},\text{XMSS-TW}^{\$}}$ does not allow for the extraction of a collision for MCO in the above manner, we can construct a reduction adversary $\mathcal{R}^{\mathcal{A}}$ playing in $\text{Game}^{\text{EUF-RMA}}_{\mathcal{R}^{\mathcal{A}},\text{FL-XMSS-TW}}$ that directly forwards each random oracle query, but reprograms MCO in every signature query. Specifically, when $\mathcal{A}$ issues the i-th signature query, the reduction adversary samples an indexing key for MCO uniformly at random and, subsequently, reprograms MCO to map this indexing key and the message from the signature query to the message of the i-th message-signature pair it received from its own game. Afterward, it returns the signature of the i-th message-signature pair, prepending the previously sampled indexing key. Indeed, $\mathcal{A}$ can only detect this reprogramming if it queried MCO on an indexing key and message *before* it issued a signature query with this same message in which, by pure chance, $\mathcal{R}^{\mathcal{A}}$ happened to sample the same indexing key. Thus, since $\mathcal{A}$ issues q_S signature queries—each of which has a probability of at most $\frac{1}{|\mathcal{MS}|}$ of coinciding with *any* of the up to q_M random oracle queries $\mathcal{A}$ issued before and *any* of the up to q_S previous reprogrammings as part of signature queries—the probability that $\mathcal{A}$ detects *any* reprogramming is at most $((q_M + q_S) \cdot q_S)/|\mathcal{MS}|$.[11] In the ensuing, we denote the event that detection occurs by E_{DR}. Then, if $\mathcal{A}$ does not detect any reprogramming, at some point it returns a (valid) forgery—comprised of, say, m' and $\text{sig}' = (\text{mk}', i', \text{sigWots}', \text{ap}')$—for XMSS-TW$^{\$}$ with respect to the EUF-CMA property. Certainly, provided that $\text{MCO}(\text{mk}', m')$ is still fresh in $\text{Game}^{\text{EUF-RMA}}_{\mathcal{R}^{\mathcal{A}},\text{FL-XMSS-TW}}$, $\text{MCO}(\text{mk}', m')$ and $(i', \text{sigWots}', \text{ap}')$ then constitute a valid forgery for FL-XMSS-TW with respect to the EUF-RMA property. Given that m' is fresh in $\text{Game}^{\text{EUF-CMA}}_{\mathcal{A},\text{XMSS-TW}^{\$}}$ and the forgery provided by $\mathcal{A}$ does not allow for the extraction of a collision for MCO in the previously discussed way, $\text{MCO}(\text{mk}', m')$ is fresh in $\text{Game}^{\text{EUF-RMA}}_{\mathcal{R}^{\mathcal{A}},\text{FL-XMSS-TW}}$ if

---

[11] In the final bound, we get an extra one in the numerator. This is merely a proof artifact caused by the reduction adversary having to make a final query to verify the forgery.

it does not equal any of the messages from the message-signature pairs (provided to $\mathcal{R}^{\mathcal{A}}$) that *were not* used in answering the signature queries of $\mathcal{A}$. As there are l message-signature pairs of which each message is independently sampled uniformly at random, the (bad) event that m' equals any of the messages from the unused pairs is at most $l/2^{8 \cdot n}$.

Based on the above, we can derive the following result. Here, $G_{\mathcal{A}}$ serves as a shorthand for $\mathrm{Game}_{\mathcal{A},\mathrm{XMSS\text{-}TW}^{\$}}^{\mathrm{EUF\text{-}CMA}}$.

$$\forall_{\mathcal{A}} \exists_{\mathcal{B}_2} : \Pr[G_{\mathcal{A}} = 1 \wedge \neg E_{\mathrm{COLL}}] =$$
$$\Pr[G_{\mathcal{A}} = 1 \wedge \neg E_{\mathrm{COLL}} \wedge E_{\mathrm{DR}}] + \Pr[G_{\mathcal{A}} = 1 \wedge \neg E_{\mathrm{COLL}} \wedge \neg E_{\mathrm{DR}}] \le$$
$$\frac{(q_M + q_S + 1) \cdot q_S}{|\mathcal{MS}|} + \mathrm{Adv}_{\mathrm{FL\text{-}XMSS\text{-}TW}}^{\mathrm{EUF\text{-}RMA}}(\mathcal{B}_2) + \frac{l}{2^{8 \cdot n}}$$

Final Result. Amalgamating the results obtained above, we can derive Security Theorem 3 as follows. In this derivation, $G_{\mathcal{A}}$ signifies $\mathrm{Game}_{\mathcal{A},\mathrm{XMSS\text{-}TW}^{\$}}^{\mathrm{EUF\text{-}CMA}}$.

$$\forall_{\mathcal{A}} \exists_{\mathcal{B}_0, \mathcal{B}_1, \mathcal{B}_2} : \mathrm{Adv}_{\mathrm{XMSS\text{-}TW}}^{\mathrm{EUF\text{-}CMA}}(\mathcal{A}) \le$$
$$|\mathrm{Adv}_{\mathrm{XMSS\text{-}TW}}^{\mathrm{EUF\text{-}CMA}}(\mathcal{A}) - \mathrm{Adv}_{\mathrm{XMSS\text{-}TW}^{\$}}^{\mathrm{EUF\text{-}CMA}}(\mathcal{A})| + \mathrm{Adv}_{\mathrm{XMSS\text{-}TW}^{\$}}^{\mathrm{EUF\text{-}CMA}}(\mathcal{A}) \le$$
$$\mathrm{Adv}_{\mathrm{MKG}}^{\mathrm{PRF}}(\mathcal{B}_0) + \mathrm{Adv}_{\mathrm{XMSS\text{-}TW}^{\$}}^{\mathrm{EUF\text{-}CMA}}(\mathcal{A}) =$$
$$\mathrm{Adv}_{\mathrm{MKG}}^{\mathrm{PRF}}(\mathcal{B}_0) + \Pr[G_{\mathcal{A}} = 1 \wedge E_{\mathrm{COLL}}] + \Pr[G_{\mathcal{A}} = 1 \wedge \neg E_{\mathrm{COLL}}] \le$$
$$\mathrm{Adv}_{\mathrm{MKG}}^{\mathrm{PRF}}(\mathcal{B}_0) + \mathrm{Adv}_{\mathrm{MCO}}^{\mathrm{CR}}(\mathcal{B}_1) + \mathrm{Adv}_{\mathrm{FL\text{-}XMSS\text{-}TW}}^{\mathrm{EUF\text{-}RMA}}(\mathcal{B}_2) + \frac{(q_M + q_S + 1) \cdot q_S}{|\mathcal{MS}|} + \frac{l}{2^{8 \cdot n}}$$

As for the preceding security theorems, even in the absence of a formal runtime analysis, it is evident from the foregoing discussion (and from the EasyCrypt artifacts) that there exist $\mathcal{B}_0$, $\mathcal{B}_1$, and $\mathcal{B}_2$ that not only satisfy the above inequality, but also execute in approximately the same time as $\mathcal{A}$.

At this point, we can straightforwardly combine Security Theorem 1, Security Theorem 2, and Security Theorem 3 to obtain a bound on $\mathrm{Adv}_{\mathrm{XMSS\text{-}TW}}^{\mathrm{EUF\text{-}CMA}}(\mathcal{A})$ that is exclusively based on the properties of the employed KHFs and THFs. This completes the formal verification of the security of XMSS-TW as a standalone construction.

Acknowledgments. Andreas Hülsing and Matthias Meijers are funded by an NWO VIDI grant (Project No. VI.Vidi.193.066). We thank the Formosa Crypto consortium for support and discussions.

References

1. Almeida, J.B., Baritel-Ruet, C., Barbosa, M., Barthe, G., Dupressoir, F., Grégoire, B., Laporte, V., Oliveira, T., Stoughton, A., Strub, P.-Y.: Machine-checked proofs for cryptographic standards: indifferentiability of sponge and secure high-assurance implementations of SHA-3. In: Cavallaro, L., Kinder, J., Wang, X., Katz, J. (eds.) ACM CCS 2019, pp. 1607–1622. ACM Press, Nov. (2019)

2. Barbosa, M., Barthe, G., Bhargavan, K., Blanchet, B., Cremers, C., Liao, K., Parno B.: SoK: computer-aided cryptography. In: 2021 IEEE Symposium on Security and Privacy (SP), pp. 777–795. IEEE Computer Society (2021)
3. Barbosa, M., Barthe, G., Fan, X., Grégoire, B., Hung, S.-H., Katz, J., Strub, P.-Y., Wu, X., Zhou, L.: EasyPQC: verifying post-quantum cryptography. In: Proceedings of the 2021 ACM SIGSAC Conference on Computer and Communications Security, CCS 2021, New York, NY, USA, pp. 2564–2586. Association for Computing Machinery (2021)
4. Barthe, G., Crespo, J.M., Grégoire, B., Kunz, C., Zanella Béguelin, S.: Computer-aided cryptographic proofs. In: Beringer, L., Felty, A. (eds.) ITP 2012. LNCS, vol. 7406, pp. 11–27. Springer, Heidelberg (2012). https://doi.org/10.1007/978-3-642-32347-8_2
5. Barthe, G., Grégoire, B., Lakhnech, Y., Zanella Béguelin, S.: Beyond provable security verifiable IND-CCA security of OAEP. In: Kiayias, A. (ed.) CT-RSA 2011. LNCS, vol. 6558, pp. 180–196. Springer, Heidelberg (2011). https://doi.org/10.1007/978-3-642-19074-2_13
6. Bernstein, D.J., Hülsing, A., Kölbl, S., Niederhagen, R., Rijneveld, J., Schwabe, P.: The SPHINCS$^+$ signature framework. In: Cavallaro, L., Kinder, J., Wang, X., Katz, J. (eds.) ACM CCS 2019, pp. 2129–2146. ACM Press (2019)
7. Bos, J.W., Hülsing, A., Renes, J., van Vredendaal, C.: Rapidly verifiable XMSS signatures. IACR TCHES 2021(1), 137–168 (2021). https://tches.iacr.org/index.php/TCHES/article/view/8730
8. Cooper, D., Apon, D., Dang, Q., Davidson, M., Dworkin, M., Miller, C.: Recommendation for stateful hash-based signature schemes (2020)
9. Cremers, C., Horvat, M., Hoyland, J., Scott, S., van der Merwe, T.: A comprehensive symbolic analysis of TLS 1.3. In: Thuraisingham, B.M., Evans, D., Malkin, T., Xu, D. (eds.) ACM CCS 2017, pp. 1773–1788. ACM Press (2017)
10. Grilo, A.B., Hövelmanns, K., Hülsing, A., Majenz, C.: Tight adaptive reprogramming in the QROM. In: Tibouchi, M., Wang, H. (eds.) ASIACRYPT 2021. LNCS, vol. 13090, pp. 637–667. Springer, Cham (2021). https://doi.org/10.1007/978-3-030-92062-3_22
11. Grumbling, E., Horowitz, M.: Quantum Computing: Progress and Prospects. National Academies of Sciences, Engineering, and Medicine. The National Academies Press, 1st edn. (2019)
12. Huelsing, A., Butin, D., Gazdag, S.-L., Rijneveld, J., Mohaisen, A.: XMSS: eXtended Merkle Signature Scheme. RFC 8391 (2018)
13. Hülsing, A., Kudinov, M.: Recovering the tight security proof of SPHINCS$^+$. In: Agrawal, S., Lin, D. (eds.) Advances in Cryptology - ASIACRYPT 2022, pp. 3–33. Springer, Cham (2022). https://doi.org/10.1007/978-3-031-22972-5_1
14. Hülsing, A., Meijers, M., Strub, P.-Y.: Formal verification of Saber's public-key encryption scheme in EasyCrypt. In: Dodis, Y., Shrimpton, T. (eds.) Advances in Cryptology - CRYPTO 2022, pp. 622–653. Springer, Cham (2022). https://doi.org/10.1007/978-3-031-15802-5_22
15. Hülsing, A., Rijneveld, J., Song, F.: Mitigating multi-target attacks in hash-based signatures. In: Cheng, C.-M., Chung, K.-M., Persiano, G., Yang, B.-Y. (eds.) PKC 2016. LNCS, vol. 9614, pp. 387–416. Springer, Heidelberg (2016). https://doi.org/10.1007/978-3-662-49384-7_15
16. Koblitz, N., Menezes, A.J.: Critical perspectives on provable security: fifteen years of "another look" papers. Adv. Math. Commun. 13(4), 517–558 (2019)

17. Kudinov, M., Kiktenko, E., Fedorov, A.: [pqc-forum] round 3 official comment: Sphincs+ (2020). https://csrc.nist.gov/CSRC/media/Projects/post-quantum-cryptography/documents/round-3/official-comments/Sphincs-Plus-round3-official-comment.pdf. Accessed 1 Feb 2022
18. McGrew, D., Curcio, M., Fluhrer, S.: Leighton-Micali Hash-Based Signatures. RFC 8554 (2019)
19. Mosca, M.: Cybersecurity in an era with quantum computers: will we be ready? IEEE Secur. Priv. **16**, 38–41 (2018)
20. NIST. National Institute for Standards and Technology. announcing request for nominations for public-key post-quantum cryptographic algorithms (2016). https://csrc.nist.gov/News/2016/Public-Key-Post-Quantum-Cryptographic-Algorithms
21. NIST. National Institute for Standards and Technology. PQC standardization process: Announcing four candidates to be standardized, plus fourth round candidates (2022). https://csrc.nist.gov/News/2022/pqc-candidates-to-be-standardized-and-round-4
22. Perlner, R., Kelsey, J., Cooper, D.: Breaking category five SPHINCS+ with SHA-256. In: Cheon, J.H., Johansson, T. (eds.) Post-Quantum Cryptography. pp, pp. 501–522. Springer, Cham (2022). https://doi.org/10.1007/978-3-031-17234-2_23
23. Zhandry, M.: How to record quantum queries, and applications to quantum indifferentiability. In: Boldyreva, A., Micciancio, D. (eds.) CRYPTO 2019. Part II, volume 11693 of LNCS, pp. 239–268. Springer, Heidelberg (2019). https://doi.org/10.1007/978-3-030-26951-7_9

Revisiting the Constant-Sum Winternitz One-Time Signature with Applications to SPHINCS+ and XMSS

Kaiyi Zhang[1], Hongrui Cui[1], and Yu Yu[1,2]($\boxtimes$)

[1] Department of Computer Science, Shanghai Jiao Tong University,
200240 Shanghai, China
{kzoacn,rickfreeman}@sjtu.edu.cn
[2] Shanghai Qi Zhi Institute, 200232 Shanghai, China
yuyu@yuyu.hk

Abstract. Hash-based signatures offer a conservative alternative to post-quantum signatures with arguably better-understood security than other post-quantum candidates. As a core building block of hash-based signatures, the efficiency of one-time signature (OTS) largely dominates that of hash-based signatures. The WOTS+ signature scheme (Africacrypt 2013) is the current state-of-the-art OTS adopted by the signature schemes standardized by NIST—XMSS, LMS, and SPHINCS+.

A natural question is whether there is (and how much) room left for improving one-time signatures (and thus standard hash-based signatures). In this paper, we show that WOTS+ one-time signature, when adopting the constant-sum encoding scheme (Bos and Chaum, Crypto 1992), is size-optimal not only under Winternitz's OTS framework, but also among all tree-based OTS designs. Moreover, we point out a flaw in the DAG-based OTS design previously shown to be size-optimal at Asiacrypt 1996, which makes the constant-sum WOTS+ the most size-efficient OTS to the best of our knowledge. Finally, we evaluate the performance of constant-sum WOTS+ integrated into the SPHINCS+ (CCS 2019) and XMSS (PQC 2011) signature schemes which exhibit certain degrees of improvement in both signing time and signature size.

Keywords: Hash-Based Signature · Post-Quantum Cryptography · SPHINCS+

1 Introduction

Hash-based signatures are one of the most promising candidates for (and perhaps the most conservative approach to) post-quantum digital signatures. An advantage of hash-based signatures is that its (classical as well as quantum) security strength is better understood (and easier to evaluate) than other candidates, by solely relying on the idealized hardness[1] of the cryptographic hash functions.

---

[1] The design philosophy of symmetric primitives (including hash functions) is that they should only admit generic attacks, otherwise the design is considered to be flawed.

© International Association for Cryptologic Research 2023
H. Handschuh and A. Lysyanskaya (Eds.): CRYPTO 2023, LNCS 14085, pp. 455–483, 2023.
https://doi.org/10.1007/978-3-031-38554-4_15

Lamport [28] and Rabin [36] proposed the first one-time signature (OTS) schemes that can be efficiently built from one-way functions (aka. the minimal assumption). The design was later made more efficient by Winternitz [30], Bos and Chaum [9], Vaudenay [41], and Hülsing's WOTS$^+$ scheme [22], which is the current state of the art. The subsequent work often adopts more complicated structures, and typically relies on hash functions with stronger assumptions.

Another line of works extends OTS to full-fledged signatures capable of signing multiple messages. In the context of hash-based signatures, the goals can be divided into *stateful* signatures and *stateless* ones, depending on whether or not the signer needs a state to keep track of signed messages. As far as *stateful* signatures are concerned, Merkle first proposed to sign multiple messages via a binary hash tree [31]. Merkle's original proposal was improved and optimized to become the eXtended Merkle Signature Scheme (XMSS) [23] and the Leighton-Micali Signature (LMS) [29], which are standardized by NIST [10] and IETF. As for stateless hash-based signatures, Goldreich proposed the first *stateless* construction [16,17], which removes the need for maintaining a local state but results in prohibitively large signatures. SPHINCS [4] offers a practical instantiation of the Goldreich-style stateless hash-based signature and serves as a basis for subsequent works, including Gravity-SPHINCS [2], SPHINCS-Simpira [18], and SPHINCS$^+$ [5]. Recently, SPHINCS$^+$ was selected as future standard signatures by the NIST PQC standardization process [39].

WOTS$^+$ and Hash-Based Signatures. The hash-based signatures to be standardized by NIST [5,23,29], whether stateless or stateful, all extensively rely on and invoke many times the WOTS$^+$ one-time signature as an important underlying building block. Therefore, improving the efficiency of WOTS$^+$ will bring about a corresponding increase in the resulting hash-based signature.

How WOTS$^+$ Encodes its Message. A line of works [9,11,26,34] focused on optimizing the message encoding scheme of the WOTS$^+$ in order to build more efficient OTS. The encoding problem in the Winternitz's OTS framework can be informally summarized as: every message m parsed as the base-w representation $m = (m_1, \ldots, m_{l_1}) \in \mathcal{M} \subseteq [w]^{l_1}$, where $[w] \stackrel{\text{def}}{=} \{0, 1, \ldots, w-1\}$, should be injectively mapped into codeword $(c_1, \ldots, c_{l_1+l_2}) \in \mathcal{C} \subseteq [w]^{l_1+l_2}$ such that there exist no distinct $(c_1, \ldots, c_{l_1+l_2})$, $(c'_1, \ldots, c'_{l_1+l_2}) \in \mathcal{C}$ satisfying $\forall i \in \{1, \ldots, l_1+l_2\}: c_i \leq c'_i$. Otherwise, it leads to a trivial forgery attack on the OTS scheme. Note that the encoding rate $(1 + l_2/l_1)$ translates to the average signature size per message bit[2]. The current WOTS$^+$ scheme [22] adopts a simple yet efficient encoding scheme by simply appending a checksum to the message, i.e., fix message space $\mathcal{M} = [w]^{l_1}$ and let the encoding be $(m_1, \ldots, m_{l_1}) \mapsto (m_1, \ldots, m_{l_1}, c)$, where the checksum $c = \sum_{i=1}^{l_1}(w - 1 - m_i)$ is represented in base-w as well. A natural idea to improve the encoding rate is to choose only those m with a fixed

---

[2] In fact, the average number of hash function evaluations during KeyGen is $(w - 1) \cdot (1 + l_2/l_1)$ (which is equal to the total number of hash function evaluations during Sign and Verify), and therefore the encoding rate is also related to computational efficiency, which is consistent with the experimental results in Sect. 5.

(constant) checksum value c (so that c doesn't need to appear in the codeword explicitly), i.e., let $\mathcal{C} = \{(m_1, \ldots, m_l) \in [w]^l : \sum_{i=1}^{l} m_i = s\} \subseteq [w]^l$ and construct an efficient encoding algorithm $\mathsf{Enc} : \mathcal{M} \to \mathcal{C}$, where the message space is maximized when $s = \lfloor \frac{l(w-1)}{2} \rfloor$ (among all possible values for s). This encoding is referred to as constant-sum encoding. Bos and Chaum [9] first proposed the constant-sum encoding in the binary setting (i.e., $w = 2$). Vaudenay [41] extended it to the arbitrary w setting but did not give an explicit encoding algorithm. Curz et al. [11] proposed a probabilistic encoding algorithm. More recently, Perin et al. [34] introduced an efficient deterministic encoding algorithm. Kudinov et al. [26] introduce an efficient encoding method (via rejection sampling) for constant-sum encoding, and integrated it into the SPHINCS$^+$ algorithm to achieve performance improvement.

Motivation. It is therefore natural to ask the following questions in the pursuit of more efficient digital signatures or in order to avoid further futile efforts.

Question 1: Does the constant-sum encoding already achieve the optimal encoding rate or is there a better encoding scheme in the WOTS$^+$ framework?

Question 2: Are there OTS schemes with better signature size and computational efficiency in a more general framework?

Our Contributions. We answer the first question affirmatively, and provide both positive and negative results for the second one.

- For Question 1, we show that the constant-sum encoding achieves the optimal encoding rate among all encoding schemes in Winternitz-style OTS framework. Following previous observation [6], we show this by first interpreting the problem of maximizing the message space (for fixed-length codewords) as an order-theoretic problem of finding the largest anti-chain in the induced partially ordered set. Then, using Dilworth's theorem, we show that the anti-chain size is maximized when the elements sum to half of the maximally allowable value, which corresponds to the constant-sum encoding.
- For Question 2, we first show that the DAG-based OTS design previously considered asymptotically optimal [7,13] contains a security flaw, which may lead to trivial forgery attacks. On the positive side, we show that the constant-sum WOTS$^+$ maximizes message space among all *tree-based* OTS schemes. We prove this result by adapting the technique of Bleichenbacher and Maurer [8] in the binary tree setting to the arbitrary tree structure.

We conclude that the constant-sum WOTS$^+$ scheme not only achieves optimal encoding rate in the WOTS$^+$ framework, but it also maximizes the message space among all tree-based OTS schemes. Further, after refuting the DAG-based designs [7,13,21] we're not aware of any other more size-efficient DAG-based design.

On the practical side, we replace the WOTS$^+$ component in SPHINCS$^+$ and XMSS with constant-sum WOTS$^+$ and evaluate the corresponding performance improvement[3]. For SPHINCS$^+$, by carefully adjusting the parameters, the resulting stateless signature scheme exhibits up to a 12.4% reduction in signature size compared to the size-optimized variant of SPHINCS$^+$ at the 128-bit security level. We note that our experiment takes into account the fix [24] of the latest attack [27]. For XMSS, we simply change the encoding scheme to constant-sum while keeping the original parameter sets, which results in up to a 1.78% reduction in signature size.

2 Preliminary

In this section, we define the notations, provide some basic background of order theory, and recall some previous constructions in the literature.

2.1 Notations

We use $[w] \stackrel{\text{def}}{=} \{0, 1, \ldots, w-1\}$ for $w \in \mathbb{N}^+$. We denote the i-th element of a vector v by v_i. By $\log(x)$ we refer to the binary logarithm, i.e., $\log_2(x)$. We denote the concatenation of strings (vectors) a and b by $a\|b$ or (a, b). For a set S, we denote the size of S and the power set of S by $|S|$ and $P(S)$ respectively. We let λ be the security parameter, and refer to a λ-bit value as a block. Let $H : \{0, 1\}^* \to \{0, 1\}^*$ be a hash function.

2.2 Preliminaries of Order Theory

Definition 1 (Poset). *A poset $(S, \leq)$ consists of a set S together with an anti-symmetric, transitive, and reflexive binary relation '$\leq$', according to which certain pairs $(x, y) \in S$ are comparable ($x \leq y$ or $y \leq x$).*

Note that a poset does not require all pairs in S to be comparable, and thus it is also known as a partially ordered set.

Definition 2 ((Anti)chain and decomposition). *A chain (resp., antichain) refers to a subset of a poset, for which every pair of elements is comparable (resp., incomparable). A chain decomposition is a partition of a poset into disjoint chains.*

Theorem 1 (Dilworth's theorem [12]). *For any finite poset S, the size of S's maximum antichain equals the size of S's minimum chain decomposition.*

---

[3] We dub the optimized SPHINCS$^+$ scheme as SPHINCS-α, and a self-contained description of that hash-based signature is available in [45]. We stress that the focus of this paper is one-time signatures and thus we do not include the additional details of SPHINCS-α other than the OTS component in this paper.

2.3   Hash-Based One-Time Signature

Here we recall the original construction of one-time signature by Lamport [28] and various optimizations that lead to the currently widely used WOTS$^+$ scheme [22].

Lamport One-Time Signature. Suppose the length of the message is λ, we describe the Lamport signature scheme as follows:

- **KeyGen**: On input 1^λ, for each $i \in \{1, \ldots, \lambda\}$ choose two uniform strings $x_{i,0}, x_{i,1} \leftarrow \{0, 1\}^\lambda$ and compute $y_{i,0} = \mathsf{H}(x_{i,0}), y_{i,1} = \mathsf{H}(x_{i,1})$. Define the public key as $\mathsf{pk} := \{(y_{i,0}, y_{i,1})\}_{i \in [1,\lambda]}$ and private key as $\mathsf{sk} := \{(x_{i,0}, x_{i,1})\}_{i \in [1,\lambda]}$.
- **Sign**: On input a private key sk and a message $m \in \{0, 1\}^\lambda$. Interpret m as a string of base-2 values $(m_1, m_2, \ldots, m_\lambda)$. Output the signature $\sigma = (x_{1,m_1}, \ldots, x_{\lambda,m_\lambda})$.
- **Verify**: On input a public key pk, a message $m \in \{0, 1\}^\lambda$ and a signature $\sigma = (x_1, x_2, \ldots, x_\lambda)$, output 1 iff $\mathsf{H}(x_i) = y_{i,m_i}$ for all $i \in [\lambda]$.

The above scheme can be proved secure if H is a one-way function [17]. Nevertheless, it can only sign one message since given two signatures an adversary can forge a new signature by reordering those preimages of hash values.

From OTS to General Signature. To enable signing multiple messages (of length λ), Goldreich [16] proposes to use a binary tree of depth λ where each node is associated with an OTS public/secret key pair and authenticates the public keys of its children nodes. Therefore, every message in $\{0, 1\}^\lambda$ can be signed by a unique OTS public key on the corresponding leaf node.

Nevertheless, generating this tree takes exponential time. Instead, we use a pseudorandom function to generate it "on-the-fly". That is, we use a pseudorandom function to compress all the randomness of the tree. To sign a message $m \in \{0, 1\}^\lambda$, the signer computes the path from the root to a leaf corresponding to the binary representation of m. For each node u in the path, the signer generates the node and its two children $u0, u1$ and add $\sigma_u = \mathrm{Sign}(sk_u, pk_{u0}||pk_{u1})$ to the final signature. To verify the signature, the verifier checks that each node except the root is correctly signed by its parent and that the path corresponds to the message m.

Improved OTS from Sperner Family. In Lamport's OTS scheme signing a λ-bit message takes λ hash blocks but message space can be enlarged in the following way. Briefly speaking, the Sperner family is defined by $\mathcal{S} = \{S : S \subseteq [n] \wedge |S| = \lfloor n/2 \rfloor\}$. It has some properties:

- $|\mathcal{S}| = \binom{n}{\lfloor n/2 \rfloor}$.
- It is (one of) the largest family in which no set contains any other set (in this family).

Let n be the smallest integer such that $\binom{n}{\lfloor n/2 \rfloor} \geq 2^\lambda$. Informally, the second property ensures that given any valid signature, it is computationally infeasible for any adversary to forge a new valid signature since signature patterns do not cover each other. We describe this improved OTS scheme below:

- **KeyGen**: On input 1^λ, for each $i \in [n]$ choose a uniform string $x_i \in \{0,1\}^\lambda$ and compute $y_i = \mathsf{H}(x_i)$. The public key and secret key are defined similarly to Lamport OTS.
- **Sign**: On input a private key sk and a message $m \in \{0,1\}^\lambda$. Encode m into $S \in \mathcal{S}$, output the signature $\sigma = \{x_i\}_{i \in S}$.
- **Verify**: On input a public key pk, a message $m \in \{0,1\}^\lambda$ and a signature σ, output 1 if $\mathsf{H}(x_i) = y_i$ for all $i \in S$.

Looking ahead to Sect. 3, we will see this encoding method is a special case of the constant-sum encoding method (for $w = 2$), where we show that the more general scheme achieves maximum message space, and provide an efficient encoding algorithm.

Winternitz One-Time Signature. Denote w as the Winternitz parameter. Let l be the number of blocks in an uncompressed WOTS$^+$ private key, public key, and signature, where

$$l = l_1 + l_2, l_1 = \left\lceil \frac{\lambda}{\log(w)} \right\rceil, l_2 = \left\lfloor \frac{\log(l_1(w-1))}{\log(w)} \right\rfloor + 1 .$$

Let $\mathsf{H}^a(x) \stackrel{\text{def}}{=} \mathsf{H}(\mathsf{H}^{a-1}(x))$ and $\mathsf{H}^0(x) = x$. We present WOTS$^+$ as follows:

- **KeyGen**: On input 1^λ, for each $i \in \{1, ..., l\}$ choose a uniform string $x_i \in \{0,1\}^\lambda$ and compute $y_i = \mathsf{H}^{w-1}(x_i)$. Define the public key and private key as $\mathsf{pk} := \mathsf{H}(y_1, \ldots, y_l)$ and $\mathsf{sk} := \{x_i\}_{i \in [1,l]}$.
- **Sign**: On input a private key sk and a message $m \in \{0,1\}^\lambda$. Encode m into its base-w representation $(m_1, \ldots, m_{l_1})$. Then compute the checksum $c = \sum_{i=1}^{l_1}(w - 1 - m_i)$ and represent c in base-w as $(c_1, \ldots, c_{l_2})$. Let $M = (m_1, \ldots, m_{l_1}, c_1, \ldots, c_{l_2})$. For each $i \in [l]$ output the signature $\sigma_i = \mathsf{H}^{M_i}(x_i)$.
- **Verify**: On input a public key pk, a message $m \in \{0,1\}^\lambda$ and a signature σ, output 1 if $\mathsf{H}(\mathsf{H}^{w-1-M_1}(\sigma_1), \ldots, \mathsf{H}^{w-1-M_l}(\sigma_l)) = \mathsf{pk}$.

The reason that the WOTS$^+$ (as well as other Winternitz-type OTS) scheme introduces the checksum is that in the absence of the checksum, the adversary can efficiently forge signatures given a single valid message/signature pair. That is, given (σ, m) he forges any m' satisfying $\forall i, m_i \leq m'_i$ by computing $\mathsf{H}^{m'_i}(\mathsf{sk}_i) = \mathsf{H}^{m'_i - m_i}(\mathsf{H}^{m_i}(\mathsf{sk}_i))$.

The checksum addresses the issue: an increase in any m_i leads to decreasing at least one c_i (recall $c = \sum_{i=1}^{l_1}(w - 1 - m_i)$). Therefore, the adversary cannot forge any (m', c') simultaneously satisfying both $m_i \leq m'_i$ and $c_i \leq c'_i$ for $i \in [l]$.

3 Constant-Sum WOTS$^+$

In this section, we recall the constant-sum encoding scheme and prove the size optimality of constant-sum in WOTS$^+$ using order theory.

3.1 Size-Optimal Encoding

More formally, the problem of constructing a one-time signature reduces to that of building an efficient encoding scheme $\mathsf{Enc} : \mathcal{M} \to \mathcal{C} \subseteq [w]^l$ for some incomparable codeword set $\mathcal{C}$ (see Definition 3). In the case of WOTS$^+$, the encoding function Enc simply appends the checksum to the original message. Note that WOTS$^+$ fixes the size of the message to l_1 (i.e., $\mathcal{M} = [w]^{l_1}$) and then constructs as small codewords as possible (minimizing $l - l_1$).

Definition 3 ((In)comparability). *For $c, c' \in [w]^l$, we denote by $c \leq c'$ if for every $i \in [l]$ we have $c_i \leq c_i'$. If $c \leq c'$ or $c' \leq c$ we say that c and c' comparable, or otherwise they are incomparable. A set $S \subseteq [w]^l$ is said to be incomparable (or called an "antichain" in order theory terminology) if any two elements of S are incomparable.*

We take a slightly different approach to encoding the messages. That is, we first fix the size of the codewords to l, $\mathcal{C} \subseteq [w]^l$, and strive to accommodate as large message space $\mathcal{M}$ as possible. Given that Enc is an injection it is essentially to maximize the size of $\mathcal{C} \subseteq [w]^l$. A natural approach is to encode the codewords such that all elements of every codeword sum to the same value, and therefore the checksum is not explicitly needed.

Theorem 2 ([9,41]). *For any $s \in [l(w-1)+1]$, $\mathcal{C}_s \stackrel{\text{def}}{=} \{c \in [w]^l : \sum_{i=1}^l c_i = s\}$ is incomparable.*

Proof: Suppose towards contradiction that $\mathcal{C}_s$ (for some fixed $s \in [l(w-1)+1]$) is not incomparable, then there exist distinct $c, c' \in \mathcal{C}_s$ s.t. $c \leq c'$. There must be an index j such that $c_j < c_j'$ (otherwise $c = c'$). However, due to equal sum $\sum_i c_i = \sum_i c_i'$ we have $\sum_{1 \leq i \leq l \wedge i \neq j}(c_i - c_i') > 0$, and there must exist some $1 \leq k \leq l$ such that $c_k > c_k'$, which is a contradiction to $c \leq c'$. ∎

Every $\mathcal{C}_s$ gives an encoding scheme but with different sizes. For $s = 0$ or $s = l(w-1)$, $\mathcal{C}_s$ consists of only a single codeword. We argue that the size of $\mathcal{C}_s$ reaches its maximal in the middle, i.e., when $s = \lfloor \frac{l(w-1)}{2} \rfloor$. One easily verifies that this holds in the binary case (i.e., $w = 2$) where $|\mathcal{C}_s| = \binom{l}{s}$. We note that this encoding method appears previously in the literature [9,41], and Perin et al. [34] proved that $|\mathcal{C}_s|$ reaches its maximum when $s = \lfloor \frac{l(w-1)}{2} \rfloor$. But to the best of our knowledge, we are the first to present a size-optimality proof over all encoding schemes in WOTS$^+$. In particular, we prove in Theorem 3 that the size of $\mathcal{C}_s$, when $s = \lfloor \frac{l(w-1)}{2} \rfloor$, is not only the largest in all $\mathcal{C}_s$ for $s \in [l(w-1)+1]$ but the largest among all valid sets of codewords.

Theorem 3 (Size-optimal encoding). *For every incomparable $C^* \in P([w]^l)$, it holds that*

$$|C^*| \leq |\mathcal{C}_{\lfloor \frac{l(w-1)}{2} \rfloor}| .$$

We defer its proof to Theorem 4, which rephrases Theorem 3 in the language of order theory. Prior to that, we discuss how to compute $|\mathcal{C}_s|$ by recursion, and give an explicit construction of encoding messages into $\mathcal{C}_s$ for $s = \lfloor \frac{l(w-1)}{2} \rfloor$. Hereafter, we denote such $\mathcal{C}_s$ with maximal size by $\mathcal{C}$ for brevity.

Counting the Size. Now we need to figure out the size of $\mathcal{C}$. As a special case, $|\mathcal{C}| = \binom{l}{\lfloor l/2 \rfloor}$ when $w = 2$. Fix w, let

$$D_{l,s} = |\{c \in [w]^l : \sum_{i=1}^{l} c_i = s\}| \ ,$$

we have their initial values

$$D_{0,0} = 1,$$
$$D_{0,s} = 0, \text{ for } s \in \{1, 2, \ldots, w-1\}$$
$$D_{l,s} = 0, \text{ for } 1 \leq l \in \mathbb{Z}, s \in \mathbb{Z}^- \ ,$$

and recurrence relation

$$D_{l,s} = \sum_{i=0}^{w-1} D_{l-1,s-i}, 2 \leq l \in \mathbb{Z}, s \in \{0, 1, \ldots, l(w-1)\} \ .$$

Note when $w = 2$, this method is equivalent to the recurrence relation of binomial coefficient, i.e., $\binom{l}{s} = \binom{l-1}{s-1} + \binom{l-1}{s}$.

Let us explain the recurrence relation. To compute $D_{l,s}$, consider the value of its last summand, which could be any value in $\{0, 1, \ldots, w-1\}$. If this value is set to i, the sum of the first $l-1$ elements must be $s-i$. Therefore, we notice that the problem "l elements with sum to s" into those "$l-1$ elements with sum to $s-i$". Thus we can simply count $D_{l,s}$ by accumulating $D_{l-1,s-i}$. Following this method, $D_{l,\lfloor l(w-1)/2 \rfloor}$ gives the size of $\mathcal{C}$.

We note that $D_{l,s}$ is also the s-th coefficient of $(1 + x + x^2 + \cdots + x^{w-1})^l$. Euler [15] has studied $w = 3, 4, 5$, known as trinomial, quadrinomial, and quintinomial coefficients respectively. The generalized form was studied in the literature, e.g., [1,3,42]. Actually, we can use an inclusion-exclusion argument to express it as a function of binomial coefficients [43]

$$D_{l,s} = \sum_{i=0}^{\lfloor s/w \rfloor} (-1)^i \binom{l}{i} \binom{s+l-iw-1}{l-1} \ .$$

The Encoding Algorithm. Now we make the construction explicit by giving an efficient encoding algorithm[4], which maps a message $x \in [|\mathcal{C}|]$ into an element in $\mathcal{C}$. We give the pseudocode of the encoding procedure in Algorithm 1.

Let us explain the encoding algorithm. As previously stated, the problem can be divided into several sub-problems by considering the value of the first element

---

[4] We note that a similar algorithm was previously proposed by Perin et al. [34] and we stress that the encoding algorithm is included for the sole purpose of completeness and it is not considered as part of our contributions.

Algorithm 1: Encode:$[|\mathcal{C}|] \to \mathcal{C}$.

Function Encode(x)

    Let v be an array of size l;

    $m \leftarrow \lfloor l(w-1)/2 \rfloor$;

    for $i \leftarrow l \ldots 1$ **do**

        for $j \leftarrow 0 \ldots \min(w-1, m)$ **do**

            if $x \geq D_{i-1,s-j}$ **then**

                $x \leftarrow x - D_{i-1,s-j}$;

            else

                $v_{l-i} \leftarrow j$;

                break;

        $m \leftarrow m - v_{l-i}$;

    return v;

---

v_{l-i}. To encode a natural number $x \in [0, D_{i,m})$, we can simply determine $v_{l-i} = j$ by seeking which j satisfies $x \in [\sum_{k<j} D_{i-1,m-k}, \sum_{k\leq j} D_{i-1,m-k})$. Once the value of v_{l-i} is determined, we proceed to the next terms until all elements are decided.

Now prove the encoding-rate optimality of the constant-sum scheme using order theory (recalled in Sect. 2.2), which has been shown to be closely related to the design of one-time signatures [6].

Theorem 4. *Let $S_l = ([w]^l, \leq)$ be a finite poset and $\mathcal{C} := \{\mathbf{c} \in S_l | \sum_{i=1}^{l} c_i = \lfloor l(w-1)/2 \rfloor$. Then $\mathcal{C}$ is the maximum antichain in S_l.*

Proof: According to Dilworth's theorem, we can prove that $\mathcal{C}$ is the maximum antichain of S_l by arguing that (1) $\mathcal{C}$ is an antichain and (2) we can find a chain decomposition whose size equals to $|\mathcal{C}|$. We have proved that $\mathcal{C}$ is an antichain in Theorem 2. It remains to construct the chain decomposition of size $|\mathcal{C}|$ as follows. Our proof can be viewed as a generalization of the proof of Sperner's theorem [38], which considers the special case for $w = 2$.

Consider poset $S_l = ([w]^l, \leq)$, and we denote its element by $\mathbf{c} := (c_1, ..., c_l) \in [w]^l$ and differentiate different elements using superscript. We slightly abuse the notation by $|(c_1, ..., c_n)| \stackrel{\text{def}}{=} c_1 + ... + c_n$.

We construct the chain decomposition for S_l by induction, where every chain $\mathbf{c}^1 \leq \ldots \leq \mathbf{c}^t$ satisfies the following two properties:

- $|\mathbf{c}^{i+1}| = |\mathbf{c}^i| + 1, \forall i \in \{1, 2, \ldots, t-1\}$,
- $|\mathbf{c}^1| + |\mathbf{c}^t| = l \cdot (w-1)$.

The case for $l = 1$ is trivial, i.e., $D_{1,\lfloor (w-1)/2 \rfloor} = 1$, which corresponds to the chain $(0) \leq (1) \leq \ldots \leq (w-1)$.

Assuming that we have a chain decomposition for S_{l-1} satisfying the above two properties, we proceed to the construction of a chain decomposition for S_l.

By the inductive assumption, we have the chain decomposition for S_{l-1} satisfying the two properties. For any chain $c^1 \leq c^2 \leq \ldots \leq c^t$ from the aforementioned decomposition of S_{l-1}, we build $k+1$ chains for S_l as follows, where $k = \min(w-1, t-1)$. That is, for every $j \in \{0, \ldots, k\}$ the j-th chain consists of:

$$(c^1, j) \leq \ldots \leq (c^{t-j}, j) \leq (c^{t-j}, j+1) \leq \ldots \leq (c^{t-j}, w-1) \ .$$

This yields the $k+1$ chains as shown in Fig. 1.

$$(c^1, 0) \leq \ldots \qquad \ldots \qquad \ldots \leq (c^t, 0) \leq \ldots \quad \leq (c^t, w-1)$$
$$\vdots \qquad \ldots \qquad \ldots \qquad \ldots \qquad \ldots \qquad \vdots$$
$$(c^1, k) \leq \ldots \leq (c^{t-k}, k) \leq \ldots \qquad \ldots \qquad \ldots \leq (c^{t-k}, w-1)$$

Fig. 1. A demonstration of how a chain from S_{l-1} is expanded into $k+1$ chains for S_l, where every row is an expanded chain. Note that it is not a rectangular matrix (every row has two fewer elements than the previous one).

It is easy to verify that $|(c^1, j)| + |(c^{t-j}, w-1)| = |(c^1, 0)| + j + |(c^t, 0)| - j + (w-1) = l(w-1)$, and every subsequent element increase the sum value of its predecessor by one. Namely, the two properties are preserved for all the constructed chains of S_n.

It remains to argue that all the chains constructed (from the decomposed chains of S_{l-1}) constitute a partition of $S_l := [w]^l$. That is, for every $c^i \in S_{l-1}$, each of its augmented elements $(c^i, 0), \ldots, (c^i, w-1)$ appears in the constructed chains exactly once. Note that every c^i belongs to exactly one of the decomposed chains of S_{l-1}, say $c^1 \leq \ldots \leq c^t$. We discuss the following cases.

Case $t \leq w$. We have $k = t - 1 \leq w - 1$. Viewing the elements in Fig. 1 as a matrix by filling the lower right corner with zeros, we have $[(c^i, 0), \ldots, (c^i, k+1-i)]$ appears as the first $(k+2-i)$ elements of the i-th column, and then $[(c^i, k+1-i), \ldots, (c^i, w-1)]^T$ as the last $(w+i-k-1)$ elements of the $(k+2-i)$-th row.

Case $t > w$. We have $k = w-1 < t-1$. If $1 \leq i \leq t-w+1$, then $[(c^i, 0), \ldots, (c^i, w-1)]$ appears as the i-th column in Fig. 1. Otherwise, it holds that $t - w + 1 < i \leq t$. $[(c^i, 0), \ldots, (c^i, t-i)]$ and $[(c^i, t-i), \ldots, (c^i, w-1)]^T$ are the first $t-i+1$ elements of the i-th column, and the last $(w+i-t)$ elements of the $(t-i+1)$-th row respectively.

Therefore, we have shown that for every $c \in [w]^{n-1}$, $(c, 0), \ldots, (c, w-1)$ appears exactly once in the newly constructed chains, namely, the chains constitutes as a chain decomposition for S_l. Finally, it remains to count the number of chains in the decomposition. The two properties guarantee that every chain contains exactly one element c^{mid} with $|c^{\text{mid}}| = \lfloor l(w-1)/2 \rfloor$ (i.e., $c^{\text{mid}} \in \mathcal{C}$). Thus, the size of chain decomposition is $|\mathcal{C}| = D_{l, \lfloor l(w-1)/2 \rfloor}$. This completes the proof that $\mathcal{C}$ is the maximum antichain. ■

3.2 Theoretical Performance

The constant-sum WOTS$^+$ has two advantages over the original WOTS$^+$.

- Constant computing time. The number of hash function calls is fixed, in contrast to possibly variable numbers for the signing and verification algorithm of WOTS$^+$. While no timing attacks are identified against the implementations of WOTS$^+$, stable computing time is always preferable (especially for signing algorithms whose computation involves a private key).
- Reduced signature size and hash calls. For instance, the SPHINCS$^+$-256s parameter set suggests $w = 16$ and $l = 67$. In constant-sum WOTS$^+$, for $w = 16$ we require $l = 66$, which reduces 1.5% in both running time (in terms of the expected number of hash function calls) and size. We refer to Table 1 for more details.

Table 1. Comparison of length l between WOTS$^+$ and constant-sum WOTS$^+$ for different values of Winternitz parameters w and security parameter λ ("CS" denotes constant-sum).

w	128-bit		192-bit		256-bit	
	WOTS$^+$	CS	WOTS$^+$	CS	WOTS$^+$	CS
8	46	45	67	66	90	88
16	35	34	51	50	67	66
24	31	30	45	44	59	58
32	28	27	42	40	55	53
40	27	26	39	38	52	50
48	25	25	37	36	48	48

Although the encoding algorithm of constant-sum WOTS$^+$ costs slightly more than the checksum method, it is less dominant compared to the number of hash function calls used in the signature scheme, which will be confirmed in the experiments.

4 Graph-Based One-Time Signature

In this section, we prove that the constant-sum WOTS$^+$ scheme achieves the maximum message space among all tree-based OTS with the same graph size. Moreover, we point out a flaw in the graph-based design previously considered optimal [7], which leaves the constant-sum WOTS$^+$ the most size-optimal among all existing schemes to the best of our knowledge. We begin by recalling the graph-based OTS notations and then present our proof.

4.1   DAG-Based One-Time Signature

Since Lamport introduced the construction of one-time signature based on one-way function [28], there have been various works improving the efficiency of such construction. The state-of-the-art analysis framework is by modeling the internal computation structure as a directed acyclic graph [6,13,21]. In this subsection, We recall the notations and definitions which mainly come from [6,13].

Without loss of generality, we consider DAGs with only one sink vertex r (i.e., with out-degree zero). Given a DAG $G = (V, E)$, the secret key vertices $SK \subseteq V$ are defined as the sets of vertices with in-degree zero and the public key vertex $PK \subseteq V$ is $\{r\}$ (i.e. the sink vertex). Let X be a subset of V. A vertex w is defined recursively to be computable from X if either $w \in X$ or all predecessors of w are computable from X. A set $Y \subseteq V$ is computable from X if any $y \in Y$ is computable from X.

A set $X \subseteq V$ is called verifiable if r is computable from X. A verifiable set X is minimal if no proper subset of X is verifiable.

We define the set of all minimal verifiable sets (MVSs) of a DAG G as G^*, and additionally define the following binary relation on G^*.

Definition 4. *Given a DAG $G = (V, E)$ and G^*, we define the relation $U \leq V$ for two verifiable sets $U, V \in G^*$ if U is computable from V.*

With the binary relation, the set G^* becomes a partially ordered set (poset). We additionally call the two verifiable sets $U, V \in G^*$ incomparable if neither $U \leq V$ nor $V \leq U$. The following lemma shows that any DAG with only one sink vertex implies a one-time signature scheme, which was proved in [13,21].

Lemma 1. *Given a DAG $G = (V, E)$ with only one sink vertex r and n source nodes $s_1, ..., s_n$, we can define the following one-time signature scheme. The secret key is a length-n vector of λ-bit blocks $\mathsf{sk}_1, ..., \mathsf{sk}_n$, each one corresponding to a source vertex. We recursively define $\mathsf{label}(u)$ of each vertex $u \in G$ as follows:*

- *If $u = s_i$ then $\mathsf{label}(u) = \mathsf{sk}_i$*
- *Otherwise, $\mathsf{label}(u) = \mathsf{H}(\mathsf{label}(u_1), ..., \mathsf{label}(u_k))$ where $u_1, ..., u_k$ are the predecessors of vertex u.*

The public key is $\mathsf{label}(r)$. Fix an antichain $\mathcal{A}$ of G^*, the message m in the message space $\mathcal{M} := \{0, ..., |\mathcal{A}| - 1\}$ is mapped to the m-th MVS in the antichain $\mathcal{A}$ (which is also referred to as the signature scheme). The properties of MVS guarantee that one can generate the labels of any verifiable sets in $\mathcal{A}$ from the source vertices (signing keys) and derive the label of the sink node (public key) from the labels of any verifiable sets.

We list a table below to show the relationship between a directed acyclic graph and its corresponding hash-based one-time signature scheme.

Table 2. The correspondence between concepts in DAG and those in OTS.

Concept in DAG	Concept in OTS
Sink Vertex r	Public Key
Source Vertices $s_1, \ldots, s_n$	Private Key
Antichain $\mathcal{A}$ of G^*	Message Space/Signature Scheme
MVS $c \in \mathcal{A}$	Signature Pattern
Max Size in $\mathcal{A}$	Maximum Signature Size
Graph Size $|G|$	Computational Cost

4.2 From Trees to Chains

In this section, we prove that with regard to the same tree size, the chain structure has the same performance as any tree structure. We prove this result by adapting the technique of Bleichenbacher and Maurer [8] in the binary tree setting to the arbitrary tree structure.

Theorem 5. *Let C_s denote a chain with size s. Let x be the root of a tree T, and $T_1, \ldots, T_n$ be the subtrees of T where $n \geq 1$. Then*

$$C_s^* \cong C_s$$

and

$$T^* \cong T_1^* \times \cdots \times T_n^* \cup \{x\}$$

Proof: It is easy to verify that $C_s^* \cong C_s$. For any $p \in T^*$, if $p \neq \{x\}$ then p can be split by each subtrees, thus $p \in T_1^* \times \cdots \times T_n^* \cup \{x\}$. If $p = \{x\}$ then $p \in T_1^* \times \cdots \times T_n^* \cup \{x\}$. p can not be $\{x\} \cup S$ for a non-empty set S because p is minimal. The arguments for the other direction is similar. Therefore $T^* \cong T_1^* \times \cdots \times T_n^* \cup \{x\}$.

Theorem 6. *Given a tree $T = (V, E)$ with associated signature scheme $\mathcal{S}$, we can construct another tree T' with associated signature scheme $\mathcal{S}'$, where the root of T' is the only node with indegree greater than 1, and $|\mathcal{S}'| \geq |\mathcal{S}|$.*

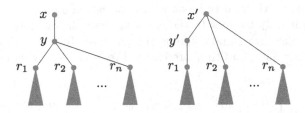

Fig. 2. The conversion process that moves the splitting point further to the top, where triangles denote subtrees.

Proof: Let y be a non-root node in T with indegree greater than 1. Denote x as its parent and $r_1, \ldots, r_n$ as its children for $n > 1$. And $z_1, \ldots, z_m$ be the children of x other than y for $m \geq 0$. We replace the tree $T[x]$ with $T[x']$, where we set the parent of $r_2, \ldots, r_n$ from y to x'. To simplify the expression, let T_r^* be $T^*[r_1] \times \cdots \times T^*[r_n]$ and T_z^* be $T^*[z_1] \times \cdots \times T^*[z_m]$. According to Theorem 5, we have

$$
\begin{aligned}
T^*[x] &= T^*[y] \times (T^*[z_1] \times \ldots T^*[z_m]) \cup \{x\} \\
&= (T^*[r_1] \times \cdots \times T^*[r_n] \cup \{y\}) \times (T^*[z_1] \times \cdots \times T^*[z_m]) \cup \{x\} \\
&= (T_r^* \cup \{y\}) \times T_z^* \cup \{x\}
\end{aligned}
$$

and

$$
\begin{aligned}
T^*[x'] &= (T^*[y'] \times T^*[r_2] \times \cdots \times T^*[r_n]) \times (T^*[z_1] \times \ldots T^*[z_m]) \cup \{x'\} \\
&= ((T^*[r_1] \cup \{y'\}) \times T^*[r_2] \times \cdots \times T^*[r_n]) \times T_z^* \cup \{x'\} \\
&= (T_r^* \cup \{y'\} \times T^*[r_2] \times \cdots \times T^*[r_n]) \times T_z^* \cup \{x'\}
\end{aligned}
$$

For any signature pattern $p \in T^*[x]$, if $y \in p$ then we replace y with $y', r_2 \ldots, r_n$ and map p to the resulting $p' \in T^*[x']$; If $p = \{x\}$ then we map p to the $\{x'\} \in T^*[x']$; Otherwise we map p directly to $T[x']$. According to the formulas above, the mapping is injective. Therefore the size of its associated signature scheme $\mathcal{S}'$ is always not less than the size of $\mathcal{S}$.

We repeat this transformation until there is only one node with indegree greater than one (i.e., the root), which completes the proof. ∎

Optimal Tree with Bounded Signature Size. The conversion above shows that the chain structure is never worse than any other tree structure of the same tree size. However, this conversion may increase the signature size. Table 3 lists the optimal tree for fixed tree size and signature size, found by brute-force search. All optimal trees listed in the table have a chain structure.

4.3   The Flaw of "The Best Known Graph" Construction

Bleichenbacher and Maurer [7] first proposed "The best-known graph" but didn't give an explicit encoding algorithm. Dods et al. [13] presented this construction in detail. We describe the construction and show that it is not a valid scheme.

The scheme is parameterized by an integer w and an integer B. The scheme consists of a set of B blocks, each block is a matrix of width w and height $w + 1$. There is also an additional 0-th block which consists of a single row of w entries. We use the term $z_{b,r,c}$ to refer to the entry in the r-th row and c-th column of the b-th block, where rows and columns are numbered from zero. The entries are assumed to hold values, and they are inferred from the following computational rule:

$$
z_{b,r,c} = \begin{cases}
\mathsf{H}(z_{b,r-1,c} \| z_{b-1,w,(c+r) \bmod w}) & r > 0 \text{ and } b > 1, \\
\mathsf{H}(z_{b,r-1,c} \| z_{b-1,0,(c+r) \bmod w}) & r > 0 \text{ and } b = 1, \\
x_{bw+c} & r = 0
\end{cases}
$$

Table 3. Optimal trees of small sizes, where the notations follow the conventions in [6]. Here C_s denotes a chain with size s, $[T_1, \ldots, T_n]$ denotes a tree constructed by connecting the roots of subtree $T_1, \ldots, T_n$ to a new root node. In this case, all subtrees are chains.

	Upper Bound of Signature Size		
Tree Size	2	3	4
6	$[C_2, C_3]$	$[C_2, C_3]$	$[C_2, C_3]$
7	$[C_3, C_3]$	$[C_3, C_3]$	$[C_3, C_3]$
8	$[C_3, C_4]$	$[C_2, C_2, C_3]$	$[C_2, C_2, C_3]$
9	$[C_4, C_4]$	$[C_2, C_3, C_3]$	$[C_2, C_3, C_3]$
10	$[C_4, C_5]$	$[C_3, C_3, C_3]$	$[C_3, C_3, C_3]$
11	$[C_5, C_5]$	$[C_3, C_3, C_4]$	$[C_2, C_2, C_3, C_3]$
12	$[C_5, C_6]$	$[C_3, C_4, C_4]$	$[C_2, C_3, C_3, C_3]$
13	$[C_6, C_6]$	$[C_4, C_4, C_4]$	$[C_3, C_3, C_3, C_3]$

To define a signature we first need to define a signature pattern. This is an ordered list of w numbers $p = (r_0, \ldots, r_{w-1})$, each $r_i \in \{0, \ldots, w\}$, i.e., one row per column. We select the set of patterns $\mathcal{S}$ such that

$$\bigcup_{i \in \{0, \ldots, w-1\}} \{i + j \bmod w : r_i \leq j < w\} = \{0, \ldots, w-1\}$$

As a toy example, when $w = 2$ the signature space consists 6 choices: $(0, 0)$, $(1, 0)$, $(2, 0)$, $(0, 2)$, $(0, 1)$, $(1, 1)$. We use $\mathcal{S}_i$ to denote the i-th element of $\mathcal{S}$ (e.g. $\mathcal{S}_0 = (0, 0), \mathcal{S}_3 = (0, 2)$ when $w = 2$), which is also a mapping from $\{0, \ldots, |\mathcal{S}| - 1\}$ to $\mathcal{S}$. We further define $wt(p) \overset{\text{def}}{=} \sum_{i=0}^{w-1} (w - r_i)$ for $p \in \mathcal{S}$. Note that $wt(p) < |\mathcal{S}|$.

The secret key consists of $N = (B+1)w$ values $x_0, \ldots, x_{N-1}$ which are placed in the bottom row of each block. The public key is $H(z_{B,w,0}||\cdots||z_{B,w,w-1})$, i.e. the hash of the values in the top row of the last block.

To sign a λ-bit message m, we first represent m in base-$|\mathcal{S}|$ $(m_1, \ldots, m_l)$ where $l = \lceil \lambda/\log_2 |\mathcal{S}| \rceil$. Then we compute the checksum in base-$|\mathcal{S}|$: i.e., $c = \sum_{i=1}^{l} wt(\mathcal{S}_{m_i}) = (c_1, \ldots, c_{l'})$ where $l' = \lceil 1 + \log_{|\mathcal{S}|} l \rceil$. Let $B = l + l'$, finally we encode $M = (m_1, \ldots, m_l, c_1, \ldots, c_{l'})$ to this graph which consists of B blocks.

The flaw is that the checksum works on Winternitz type structure but it does not generally work on every structure. We present two messages with their checksums respectively $(m, c), (m', c')$ that they are comparable.

Consider the simplest case: $w = 2$ and $l = l' = 1$. For $m = 0, c = 4$ we have $M = (0, 0, 0, 1)$. For $m' = 1, c' = 3$ we have $M' = (1, 0, 0, 2)$. They are comparable. In other words, if the signer signs the first message m, an adversary can easily forge a signature for message m'. We refer to Appendix B for more discussions.

5 Experiments

We replace the OTS component in the SPHINCS$^+$ and XMSS signature schemes with the constant-sum WOTS$^+$ and report the performance improvement.

5.1 Implementation

We adapt the respective official implementations on github [37,40] to ours [19, 44], where we reuse most of its basic modules such as hash functions, and implement from scratch only the newly added, i.e., the encoding algorithm. Notice that the latest implementation of SPHINCS$^+$ takes into consideration the flaw in the security reduction [24], and thus the comparison is fair and up-to-date.

We use the SPHINCS$^+$ implementation optimized with architecture-specific instructions such as AESNI or AVX2 [40]. The optimized SPHINCS$^+$ signature is called SPHINCS-α and its details are available in [45]. Since the XMSS team does not provide an official high-performance implementation, we resort to the reference code in [37]. In other words, we choose the best available implementation of the baseline schemes and plug in the constant-sum encoding, without additional engineering optimization.

Instantiation. For SPHINCS$^+$, we provide 12 combinations of parameter choices and instantiations. The classic security level includes 128, 192 or 256 bits. The hash functions can be shake256 [14] or sha2 [33] (we also use sha512 to avoid the attack on sha256 [35]). Following the decisions made by NIST [32], we remove haraka [25] and robust version from tweakable hash function. We also offer a small or fast option towards either small signatures or fast signature generation.

For XMSS, we select 41 sets of parameter choices[5] among which the security level can be 192, 256 or 512 bits. The hash function can be either sha2 series or shake series.

Parameter Sets. The parameter sets for SPHINCS$^+$ are re-tuned and listed in Table 4. Note "bitsec" represents the classic security level. Readers can also find the parameter estimation code in our open-source implementation. Please open para.ipynb in Jupyter Notebook with SageMath. The parameters for XMSS are chosen according to the original configuration and we refer the readers to the original publication [23] for the details.

We note that, unlike SPHINCS$^+$ which comes with fast and short variants, the IETF documentation of XMSS [23] does not explicitly specify the optimization direction for the XMSS scheme. Instead, it only lists out the parameters for different combinations of tree/hyper-tree depths (which determines the message space), hash functions (SHA2 or SHAKE), and security levels (256 or 512). Therefore, we simply replace WOTS$^+$ with the constant-sum variant and benchmark the performance. In general, we believe that it is possible to re-tune the

---

[5] We omit the parameter sets that lead to extremely high runtime to facilitate fast experiment.

Table 4. Parameter sets for the SPHINCS-α scheme.

Parameter Set	n	h	d	$\log t$	k	w	l	bitsec	sec level	sig bytes
sphincs-a-128s	16	63	9	13	12	73	22	128	I	6880
sphincs-a-128f	16	63	21	8	25	14	36	128	I	16720
sphincs-a-192s	24	63	9	14	17	77	32	192	III	14568
sphincs-a-192f	24	64	16	8	37	8	66	192	III	34896
sphincs-a-256s	32	66	11	13	23	79	42	255	V	27232
sphincs-a-256f	32	68	17	9	35	16	66	255	V	49312

parameters of XMSS in order to achieve a specific design goal (e.g., to achieve the smallest signature possible while keeping the verification and signing time below a certain threshold) for application-specific scenarios.

Table 5. Performance comparison between SPHINCS$^+$ and SPHINCS-α, with simple tweakable hash function instantiated with shake. Key generation, signing, and verification time are in terms of CPU cycles; the public key, secret key, and signature sizes are in bytes. All cycle counts are the median of 100 runs.

	SPHINCS$^+$				SPHINCS-α				Relative Change			
Param	KeyGen	Sign	Verify	Size	KeyGen	Sign	Verify	Size	KeyGen	Sign	Verify	Size
128f	1143558	26872236	2204802	17088	1036602	26635716	2028186	16720	−9.35%	−0.88%	−8.01%	−2.15%
192f	1662498	45405504	3003534	35664	2199276	45218790	1744038	34896	32.29%	−0.41%	−41.93%	−2.15%
256f	4327632	92059542	2967642	49856	4286574	91335474	3175290	49312	−0.95%	−0.79%	7.00%	−1.09%
128s	72597852	551233638	846486	7856	51421086	537033762	2689650	6880	−29.17%	−2.58%	217.74%	−12.42%
192s	105310692	1022229270	1201230	16224	78050718	988899534	3845970	14568	−25.89%	−3.26%	220.17%	−10.21%
256s	69033492	918473904	1701324	29792	52048332	764352612	6005448	27232	−24.60%	−16.78%	252.99%	−8.59%

Environment. We conduct our benchmarks on a Ubuntu 20.04 machine with Ryzen™ 5 3600 CPU and 16GB RAM, compiled with gcc-9.3.0 -O3 -march=native -fomit-frame-pointer -flto.

5.2 Performance

We report the performance of the improved schemes in this subsection. Instances that are optimized using architecture-specific instructions such as AVX2 are marked as avx2 otherwise they are marked as ref.

For SPHINCS$^+$, we show in Table 5 a tiny performance comparison. Table 7 and Table 8 give comprehensive performance summaries for all the parameter sets. As summarized in Table 9, the improved scheme reduces both signing time and signature size for most parameter sets. On the downside, we experience an up to 253% increase in verification time.

In general, we re-tune the parameters toward minimizing signature size (the short variant) or signing time (the fast variant), which showcases advantages over

SPHINCS$^+$ of the same security strength. Otherwise said, verification time is not the main factor taken into consideration as it is typically one order of magnitude smaller than the signing time. As a result, the verification time is increased for certain parameter choices. Nevertheless, we argue that for specific scenarios where verification time is critical, we can re-tune the parameters towards fast verification. This is also the reason behind the fluctuation of key generation time in Table 9.

For XMSS, we refer to Table 10 and Table 11 for comprehensive summaries of all parameter sets and to Table 12 for the summarized comparison. The improvement over XMSS is less significant (up to 1.78% saving in signature size) compared to that over SPHINCS$^+$, which may attribute to that we only replaced the encoding scheme without re-tuning the parameters.

Acknowledgement. Yu Yu was supported by the National Key Research and Development Program of China (Grant Nos. 2020YFA0309705) and the National Natural Science Foundation of China (Grant Nos. 62125204 and 92270201). This work was also supported in part by the National Key Research and Development Program of China (Grant 2018YFA0704701) and the Major Program of Guangdong Basic and Applied Research (Grant No. 2019B030302008). This work has been supported by the New Cornerstone Science Foundation through the XPLORER PRIZE.

A   An Example of Constant-Sum WOTS$^+$

In this section, we present a concrete example of constant-sum WOTS$^+$, including counting, encoding algorithm, and the optimality proof. In this example, we choose parameter $l = 3$ and $w = 4$, therefore the size of $\mathcal{C}$ is maximum when the constant-sum is $\lfloor l(w-1)/2 \rfloor = 4$. This example can be also generated from a Python code, which is open-sourced at [20].

Counting the Size. Recall that

$$D_{l,s} = |\{\mathbf{c} \in [w]^l : \sum_{i=1}^{l} c_i = s\}| \ ,$$

with their initial values

$$D_{0,0} = 1,$$
$$D_{0,s} = 0, \text{ for } s \in \{1, 2, \dots, w-1\}$$
$$D_{l,s} = 0, \text{ for } 1 \leq l \in \mathbb{Z}, s \in \mathbb{Z}^- \ ,$$

and recurrence relation

$$D_{l,s} = \sum_{i=0}^{w-1} D_{l-1,s-i}, 2 \leq l \in \mathbb{Z}, s \in \{0, 1, \dots, l(w-1)\} \ .$$

We can compute the table of D, Table 6.

Table 6. The table of D

l	s									
	0	1	2	3	4	5	6	7	8	9
0	1	0	0	0	0	0	0	0	0	0
1	1	1	1	1	1	0	0	0	0	0
2	1	2	3	4	3	2	1	0	0	0
3	1	3	6	10	12	12	10	6	3	1

The value of $D_{3,4}$ tells us that we have 12 different vectors such that the length of each is 3 and the sum of each is 4.

The Encoding Algorithm. Since we $D_{3,4} = 12$, we can encode at most 12 different messages, represented by $\{0, 1, \ldots, 11\}$. We show how to encode $x = 4$ to a constant-sum vector. Recall that for each loop, we determine $v_{l-i} = j$ by seeking which j satisfies $x \in [\sum_{k<j} D_{l-1,s-k}, \sum_{k\le j} D_{l-1,s-k})$.

- Initialization. Initially, we have $x = 4$ and $s = 4$.
- Loop 1. $D_{l,s} = D_{3,4} = 12 = 2 + 3 + 4 + 3 = D_{2,1} + D_{2,2} + D_{2,3} + D_{2,4}$ and $D_{2,4} \le x = 4 < D_{2,3} + D_{2,4}$. So we have $j = 1$. Update the variables to $v_1 = 1, s = 3, x = 1$.
- Loop 2. $D_{l,s} = D_{2,3} = 4 = 1 + 1 + 1 + 1 = D_{1,0} + D_{1,1} + D_{1,2} + D_{1,3}$ and $D_{1,3} \le x = 1 < D_{1,2} + D_{1,3}$. So we have $j = 1$. Update the variables to $v_2 = 1, s = 2, x = 0$.
- Loop 3. $D_{l,s} = D_{1,2} = 1 = 1 + 0 + 0 = D_{0,0} + D_{0,1} + D_{0,2}$ and $D_{0,1} + D_{0,2} + \le x = 0 < D_{0,0} + D_{0,1} + D_{0,2}$. So we have $j = 2$. Update the variables to $v_3 = 2, s = 0, x = 0$.
- Finally. We get $v = (1, 1, 2)$.

By executing the encoding algorithm, We can list those 12 vectors (in order): $\{(0, 1, 3), (0, 2, 2), (0, 3, 1), (1, 0, 3), (1, 1, 2), (1, 2, 1), (1, 3, 0), (2, 0, 2), (2, 1, 1), (2, 2, 0), (3, 0, 1), (3, 1, 0)\}$.

Optimality Proof

By Dilworth's theorem, the proof of optimality is also a construction of chain decomposition. We present an example here, which is computed in the way of the proof of Theorem 4.

- $l = 1$. This is a trivial case. We have only one chain $(0) \le (1) \le (2) \le (3)$.
- $l = 2$. We have 4 chains, they are:
  1. $(0, 0) \le (1, 0) \le (2, 0) \le (3, 0) \le (3, 1) \le (3, 2) \le (3, 3)$.
  2. $(0, 1) \le (1, 1) \le (2, 1) \le (2, 2) \le (2, 3)$.
  3. $(0, 2) \le (1, 2) \le (1, 3)$.
  4. $(0, 3)$.
- $l = 3$. We have 12 chains, they are:

1. $(0,0,0) \leq (1,0,0) \leq (2,0,0) \leq (3,0,0) \leq (3,1,0) \leq (3,2,0) \leq (3,3,0) \leq$
   $(3,3,1) \leq (3,3,2) \leq (3,3,3)$
2. $(0,0,1) \leq (1,0,1) \leq (2,0,1) \leq (3,0,1) \leq (3,1,1) \leq (3,2,1) \leq (3,2,2) \leq$
   $(3,2,3)$
3. $(0,0,2) \leq (1,0,2) \leq (2,0,2) \leq (3,0,2) \leq (3,1,2) \leq (3,1,3)$
4. $(0,0,3) \leq (1,0,3) \leq (2,0,3) \leq (3,0,3)$
5. $(0,1,0) \leq (1,1,0) \leq (2,1,0) \leq (2,2,0) \leq (2,3,0) \leq (2,3,1) \leq (2,3,2) \leq$
   $(2,3,3)$
6. $(0,1,1) \leq (1,1,1) \leq (2,1,1) \leq (2,2,1) \leq (2,2,2) \leq (2,2,3)$
7. $(0,1,2) \leq (1,1,2) \leq (2,1,2) \leq (2,1,3)$
8. $(0,1,3) \leq (1,1,3)$
9. $(0,2,0) \leq (1,2,0) \leq (1,3,0) \leq (1,3,1) \leq (1,3,2) \leq (1,3,3)$
10. $(0,2,1) \leq (1,2,1) \leq (1,2,2) \leq (1,2,3)$
11. $(0,2,2) \leq (0,2,3)$
12. $(0,3,0) \leq (0,3,1) \leq (0,3,2) \leq (0,3,3)$

The size of this chain decomposition meets the size of antichain $\mathcal{C}$. According to Dilworth's theorem, the antichain $\mathcal{C}$ is maximum.

B   On the Best Known Graph

We first correct a minor fault in the design of the weight function of [13]. The old weight function was $wt(p) = \sum_{i=0}^{w-1}(w+1-r_i)$. Since we know $r_i \in \{0,\ldots,w\}$, the range of the old weight function is $[w, w(w+1)]$. When $w = 2$, this range can not be fitted into $\{0,\ldots,|\mathcal{S}|-1\}$. Thus we make it into $wt(p) = \sum_{i=0}^{w-1}(w-r_i) \in [0, w^2]$, which is a more suitable choice.

For $l = l' = 1, w = 2$, we can have a correct construction if we reorder the mapping $\{\mathcal{S}_i\}$ to $(0,0), (1,0), (0,1), (1,1), (2,0), (0,2)$. ([13] does not specify the order that mapping integers to signature patterns.) This does not mean we fixed this construction. The key problem is we can not prove the pairs of the message and checksum (m, c) form an antichain in this graph. There may exist forgery attacks for larger l, l', w parameters.

There is a way to fix it by using "separate representation function encoding", purposed in [7], which can be viewed as a generalized checksum method. However, even if we use this new encoding, the performance of this graph-based is clearly worst than WOTS$^+$ (with checksum). Both two constructions require encoding checksum separately. For $w = 3$, the WOTS$^+$ fully utilized $(w+1)^w = 64$ message space while the graph-based has only $|\mathcal{S}| = 51$ choices.

C   More Detailed Comparisons

C.1   Comparison Between Original and Improved SPHINCS$^+$

We benchmarked the performance of the improved SPHINCS$^+$ under 24 parameter settings ($\{\text{shake256}, \text{sha256}\} \times \{128, 192, 256\} \times \{\text{fast}, \text{small}\} \times \{\text{ref}, \text{avx2}\}$). To facilitate a fair comparison, we tested our implementation (adapted from the SPHINCS$^+$ codes) along with the original SPHINCS$^+$. The test results are reported in Table 7 and Table 8 with a comparison in Table 9.

Table 7. Runtime benchmarks for SPHINCS$^+$. Key generation, signing, and verification time are in the number of cpu cycles; the public key, secret key, and signature size are in bytes. All cycle counts are the median of 100 runs.

Parameter Set	Impl.	KeyGen	Sign	Verify	Pk	Sk	Sig
sphincs-shake-128f	ref	7622514	178188408	10775124	32	64	17088
sphincs-shake-192f	ref	11240172	290022120	15972588	48	96	35664
sphincs-shake-256f	ref	29488050	593083386	15949980	64	128	49856
sphincs-shake-128s	ref	493648758	3747092580	3602178	32	64	7856
sphincs-shake-192s	ref	717515010	6427813662	5332932	48	96	16224
sphincs-shake-256s	ref	470748762	5584718124	7709508	64	128	29792
sphincs-sha2-128f	ref	4600566	107749800	6402438	32	64	17088
sphincs-sha2-192f	ref	6705198	181354752	9365400	48	96	35664
sphincs-sha2-256f	ref	17695728	362443014	9947394	64	128	49856
sphincs-sha2-128s	ref	294665274	2237140404	2282346	32	64	7856
sphincs-sha2-192s	ref	428811300	3954195432	3266478	48	96	16224
sphincs-sha2-256s	ref	283132530	3503794590	4785678	64	128	29792
sphincs-shake-128f	avx2	2494854	58500990	4063716	32	64	17088
sphincs-shake-192f	avx2	3541392	91863954	5919426	48	96	35664
sphincs-shake-256f	avx2	9676188	193273884	6019830	64	128	49856
sphincs-shake-128s	avx2	159844320	1210947264	1491894	32	64	7856
sphincs-shake-192s	avx2	233254134	2093058036	2165706	48	96	16224
sphincs-shake-256s	avx2	153274212	1799699922	3085776	64	128	29792
sphincs-sha2-128f	avx2	1143558	26872236	2204802	32	64	17088
sphincs-sha2-192f	avx2	1662498	45405504	3003534	48	96	35664
sphincs-sha2-256f	avx2	4327632	92059542	2967642	64	128	49856
sphincs-sha2-128s	avx2	72597852	551233638	846486	32	64	7856
sphincs-sha2-192s	avx2	105310692	1022229270	1201230	48	96	16224
sphincs-sha2-256s	avx2	69033492	918473904	1701324	64	128	29792

Table 8. Runtime benchmarks for SPHINCS-α. Key generation, signing, and verification time are in the number of cpu cycles; the public key, secret key, and signature size are in bytes. All cycle counts are the median of 100 runs.

Parameter Set	Impl.	KeyGen	Sign	Verify	Pk	Sk	Sig
sphincs-a-shake-128f	ref	6861114	176440590	9035874	32	64	16720
sphincs-a-shake-192f	ref	14555628	281397294	7353450	48	96	34896
sphincs-a-shake-256f	ref	29112588	586596492	15740802	64	128	49312
sphincs-a-shake-128s	ref	347407200	3628303722	12591234	32	64	6880
sphincs-a-shake-192s	ref	533064942	6209945190	19292382	48	96	14568
sphincs-a-shake-256s	ref	362125278	4942646316	31932360	64	128	27232
sphincs-a-sha2-128f	ref	4157334	106933014	5569452	32	64	16720
sphincs-a-sha2-192f	ref	8837622	173603070	4654278	48	96	34896
sphincs-a-sha2-256f	ref	17439858	357693966	9646776	64	128	49312
sphincs-a-sha2-128s	ref	208068264	2172320100	7584102	32	64	6880
sphincs-a-sha2-192s	ref	319426722	3827118258	11723508	48	96	14568
sphincs-a-sha2-256s	ref	215034228	3011033142	19147662	64	128	27232
sphincs-a-shake-128f	avx2	2218014	57069090	3558492	32	64	16720
sphincs-a-shake-192f	avx2	4614804	92073114	3028500	48	96	34896
sphincs-a-shake-256f	avx2	9563742	191187306	5983920	64	128	49312
sphincs-a-shake-128s	avx2	108983646	1139743980	4891482	32	64	6880
sphincs-a-shake-192s	avx2	171004500	1996754616	7254738	48	96	14568
sphincs-a-shake-256s	avx2	115604604	1582371720	11677806	64	128	27232
sphincs-a-sha2-128f	avx2	1036602	26635716	2028186	32	64	16720
sphincs-a-sha2-192f	avx2	2199276	45218790	1744038	48	96	34896
sphincs-a-sha2-256f	avx2	4286574	91335474	3175290	64	128	49312
sphincs-a-sha2-128s	avx2	51421086	537033762	2689650	32	64	6880
sphincs-a-sha2-192s	avx2	78050718	988899534	3845970	48	96	14568
sphincs-a-sha2-256s	avx2	52048332	764352612	6005448	64	128	27232

Table 9. Performance comparison between the original and improved SPHINCS$^+$ in terms of relative changes.

Parameter Set			Runtime			
SPHINCS$^+$	SPHINCS-α	Impl.	KeyGen	Sign	Verify	Sig Size
sphincs-shake-128f	sphincs-a-shake-128f	ref	−9.99%	−0.98%	−16.14%	−2.15%
sphincs-shake-192f	sphincs-a-shake-192f	ref	29.50%	−2.97%	−53.96%	−2.15%
sphincs-shake-256f	sphincs-a-shake-256f	ref	−1.27%	−1.09%	−1.31%	−1.09%
sphincs-shake-128s	sphincs-a-shake-128s	ref	−29.62%	−3.17%	249.55%	−12.42%
sphincs-shake-192s	sphincs-a-shake-192s	ref	−25.71%	−3.39%	261.76%	−10.21%
sphincs-shake-256s	sphincs-a-shake-256s	ref	−23.07%	−11.50%	314.19%	−8.59%
sphincs-sha2-128f	sphincs-a-sha2-128f	ref	−9.63%	−0.76%	−13.01%	−2.15%
sphincs-sha2-192f	sphincs-a-sha2-192f	ref	31.80%	−4.27%	−50.30%	−2.15%
sphincs-sha2-256f	sphincs-a-sha2-256f	ref	−1.45%	−1.31%	−3.02%	−1.09%
sphincs-sha2-128s	sphincs-a-sha2-128s	ref	−29.39%	−2.90%	232.29%	−12.42%
sphincs-sha2-192s	sphincs-a-sha2-192s	ref	−25.51%	−3.21%	258.90%	−10.21%
sphincs-sha2-256s	sphincs-a-sha2-256s	ref	−24.05%	−14.06%	300.10%	−8.59%
sphincs-shake-128f	sphincs-a-shake-128f	avx2	−11.10%	−2.45%	−12.43%	−2.15%
sphincs-shake-192f	sphincs-a-shake-192f	avx2	30.31%	0.23%	−48.84%	−2.15%
sphincs-shake-256f	sphincs-a-shake-256f	avx2	−1.16%	−1.08%	−0.60%	−1.09%
sphincs-shake-128s	sphincs-a-shake-128s	avx2	−31.82%	−5.88%	227.87%	−12.42%
sphincs-shake-192s	sphincs-a-shake-192s	avx2	−26.69%	−4.60%	234.98%	−10.21%
sphincs-shake-256s	sphincs-a-shake-256s	avx2	−24.58%	−12.08%	278.44%	−8.59%
sphincs-sha2-128f	sphincs-a-sha2-128f	avx2	−9.35%	−0.88%	−8.01%	−2.15%
sphincs-sha2-192f	sphincs-a-sha2-192f	avx2	32.29%	−0.41%	−41.93%	−2.15%
sphincs-sha2-256f	sphincs-a-sha2-256f	avx2	−0.95%	−0.79%	7.00%	−1.09%
sphincs-sha2-128s	sphincs-a-sha2-128s	avx2	−29.17%	−2.58%	217.74%	−12.42%
sphincs-sha2-192s	sphincs-a-sha2-192s	avx2	−25.89%	−3.26%	220.17%	−10.21%
sphincs-sha2-256s	sphincs-a-sha2-256s	avx2	−24.60%	−16.78%	252.99%	−8.59%

C.2   Comparison Between Original and Improved XMSS

We benchmarked the performance of the improved XMSS under selected parameter settings. To facilitate a fair comparison, we tested our implementation (adapted from the official repository) along with the original XMSS. The test results are reported in Table 10 and Table 11 with a comparison in Table 12.

Table 10. Runtime benchmarks for XMSSMT. Key generation, signing and verification time are in the number of cpu cycles; public key, secret key and signature size are in bytes. All cycle counts are the median of 16 runs.

Parameter Set	Runtime			Size		
	KeyGen	Sign	Verify	Pk	Sk	Sig
XMSSMT-SHA2-20/2-256	3127413888	3771702	1617156	64	5998	4963
XMSSMT-SHA2-20/4-256	222559560	6706008	3110238	64	10938	9251
XMSSMT-SHA2-40/4-256	6285411684	6830658	3247326	64	15252	9893
XMSSMT-SHA2-40/8-256	401766552	6904440	6711552	64	24516	18469
XMSSMT-SHA2-60/6-256	9494855496	10171836	5168160	64	24507	14824
XMSSMT-SHA2-60/12-256	631228644	6877116	9580554	64	38095	27688
XMSSMT-SHA2-20/2-512	21988477260	27152100	11814210	128	15822	18115
XMSSMT-SHA2-20/4-512	1398460644	47020626	22096512	128	33818	34883
XMSSMT-SHA2-40/4-512	43629570864	47908404	23528916	128	42164	36165
XMSSMT-SHA2-40/8-512	2805197148	47601774	45550674	128	76964	69701
XMSSMT-SHA2-60/6-512	65939229972	69142698	33890688	128	68507	54216
XMSSMT-SHA2-60/12-512	4155322500	47779668	68537412	128	120111	104520
XMSSMT-SHA2-20/2-192	2020361292	2466378	1176246	48	4182	2955
XMSSMT-SHA2-20/4-192	127543572	4318398	2133288	48	7138	5403
XMSSMT-SHA2-40/4-192	4053119040	4406868	2126394	48	10444	5885
XMSSMT-SHA2-40/8-192	256662108	4352274	4225824	48	15884	10781
XMSSMT-SHA2-60/6-192	6067543248	6375420	3298608	48	16707	8816
XMSSMT-SHA2-60/12-192	378984168	4349250	6459930	48	24631	16160
XMSSMT-SHAKE-20/2-256	11248052760	13700142	6175242	64	5998	4963
XMSSMT-SHAKE-20/4-256	710060580	24423426	11387034	64	10938	9251
XMSSMT-SHAKE-40/4-256	22458447756	24651684	11682468	64	15252	9893
XMSSMT-SHAKE-40/8-256	1439101980	24385518	23653764	64	24516	18469
XMSSMT-SHAKE-60/6-256	33696560700	35529246	16996320	64	24507	14824
XMSSMT-SHAKE-60/12-256	2150833356	24420024	36412686	64	38095	27688
XMSSMT-SHAKE-20/4-512	2455477200	83672478	40536054	128	33818	34883
XMSSMT-SHAKE-40/4-512	76825886112	84051144	40027680	128	42164	36165
XMSSMT-SHAKE-40/8-512	4869152712	83529522	78300342	128	76964	69701
XMSSMT-SHAKE-60/6-512	115072275744+11	121304394	60009516	128	68507	54216
XMSSMT-SHAKE-60/12-512	7279843032	83360394	120177378	128	120111	104520
XMSSMT-SHAKE256-20/2-256	10871025984	13265334	5549670	64	5998	4963
XMSSMT-SHAKE256-20/4-256	717916932	23495616	11077614	64	10938	9251
XMSSMT-SHAKE256-40/4-256	21817454832	23909310	12181104	64	15252	9893
XMSSMT-SHAKE256-40/8-256	1402673508	23652882	22820472	64	24516	18469
XMSSMT-SHAKE256-60/6-256	32735511720	34534476	18080442	64	24507	14824
XMSSMT-SHAKE256-60/12-256	2086527672	23456430	34476750	64	38095	27688
XMSSMT-SHAKE256-20/2-192	8045426736	9687330	4610826	48	4182	2955
XMSSMT-SHAKE256-20/4-192	527327388	17429292	8847306	48	7138	5403
XMSSMT-SHAKE256-40/4-192	16079381892	17519976	8559144	48	10444	5885
XMSSMT-SHAKE256-40/8-192	1035980136	17371080	17699076	48	15884	10781
XMSSMT-SHAKE256-60/6-192	24215925168	25526448	13124520	48	16707	8816
XMSSMT-SHAKE256-60/12-192	1525123404	17327790	25423218	48	24631	16160

Table 11. Runtime benchmarks for improved XMSSMT. Key generation, signing and verification time are in the number of cpu cycles; public key, secret key and signature size are in bytes. All cycle counts are the median of 16 runs.

Parameter Set	Runtime			Size		
	KeyGen	Sign	Verify	Pk	Sk	Sig
XMSSMT-i-SHA2-20/2-256	3118500216	3768984	1676682	64	5966	4899
XMSSMT-i-SHA2-20/4-256	205928460	6701778	3302856	64	10842	9123
XMSSMT-i-SHA2-40/4-256	6111330408	6775578	3367674	64	15156	9765
XMSSMT-i-SHA2-40/8-256	421704720	6636150	6578640	64	24292	18213
XMSSMT-i-SHA2-60/6-256	9212217048	9834372	5043978	64	24347	14632
XMSSMT-i-SHA2-60/12-256	590852376	6655554	9848970	64	37743	27304
XMSSMT-i-SHA2-20/2-512	21771015228	26223552	11456892	128	15758	17987
XMSSMT-i-SHA2-20/4-512	1444733100	47859624	22947750	128	33626	34627
XMSSMT-i-SHA2-40/4-512	43337753064	47542536	23114718	128	41972	35909
XMSSMT-i-SHA2-40/8-512	2891694348	47495754	46440648	128	76516	69189
XMSSMT-i-SHA2-60/6-512	65241573480	68704668	34608996	128	68187	53832
XMSSMT-i-SHA2-60/12-512	4197559644	47451924	69522930	128	119407	103752
XMSSMT-i-SHA2-20/2-192	1997951040	2467044	1099980	48	4158	2907
XMSSMT-i-SHA2-20/4-192	133595676	4259340	2137932	48	7066	5307
XMSSMT-i-SHA2-40/4-192	3993020136	4302990	2186424	48	10372	5789
XMSSMT-i-SHA2-40/8-192	270959364	4279050	4293126	48	15716	10589
XMSSMT-i-SHA2-60/6-192	5922093888	6206382	3251826	48	16587	8672
XMSSMT-i-SHA2-60/12-192	388450260	4318524	6467760	48	24367	15872
XMSSMT-i-SHAKE-20/2-256	10926481032	13278870	5770854	64	5966	4899
XMSSMT-i-SHAKE-20/4-256	722327868	23823738	11518020	64	10842	9123
XMSSMT-i-SHAKE-40/4-256	21800594664	23788656	11308122	64	15156	9765
XMSSMT-i-SHAKE-40/8-256	1422925776	23784876	22552668	64	24292	18213
XMSSMT-i-SHAKE-60/6-256	32771966400	34440912	17060670	64	24347	14632
XMSSMT-i-SHAKE-60/12-256	2132075484	23932764	33975306	64	37743	27304
XMSSMT-i-SHAKE-20/4-512	2481508404	83815794	39808368	128	33626	34627
XMSSMT-i-SHAKE-40/4-512	75490496244	82866564	39879108	128	41972	35909
XMSSMT-i-SHAKE-40/8-512	4944876840	83403126	79286958	128	76516	69189
XMSSMT-i-SHAKE-60/6-512	1.13728E+11	119970360	59860440	128	68187	53832
XMSSMT-i-SHAKE-60/12-512	7349705244	82872720	119115792	128	119407	103752
XMSSMT-i-SHAKE256-20/2-256	10433094588	12529494	5531094	64	5966	4899
XMSSMT-i-SHAKE256-20/4-256	698620392	22806234	11090754	64	10842	9123
XMSSMT-i-SHAKE256-40/4-256	20830958172	22584744	11067732	64	15156	9765
XMSSMT-i-SHAKE256-40/8-256	1357966188	22758804	22020138	64	24292	18213
XMSSMT-i-SHAKE256-60/6-256	31048091712	32707962	16657614	64	24347	14632
XMSSMT-i-SHAKE256-60/12-256	2019728664	22604778	32743098	64	37743	27304
XMSSMT-i-SHAKE256-20/2-192	7701230628	9301482	4125564	48	4158	2907
XMSSMT-i-SHAKE256-20/4-192	513443304	16590348	8076150	48	7066	5307
XMSSMT-i-SHAKE256-40/4-192	15321653784	16670448	8214084	48	10372	5789
XMSSMT-i-SHAKE256-40/8-192	979483644	16741926	16256556	48	15716	10589
XMSSMT-i-SHAKE256-60/6-192	22849024932	24038622	12288024	48	16587	8672
XMSSMT-i-SHAKE256-60/12-192	1470316644	16589088	24196410	48	24367	15872

Table 12. Performance comparison between the original and improved XMSS in terms of relative changes.

Parameter Set		Runtime			
Original	Improved	KeyGen	Sign	Verify	Sig Size
XMSSMT-SHA2-20/2-256	XMSSMT-i-SHA2-20/2-256	−0.29%	−1.29%	3.68%	−1.29%
XMSSMT-SHA2-20/4-256	XMSSMT-i-SHA2-20/4-256	−7.47%	−1.38%	6.19%	−1.38%
XMSSMT-SHA2-40/4-256	XMSSMT-i-SHA2-40/4-256	−2.77%	−1.29%	3.71%	−1.29%
XMSSMT-SHA2-40/8-256	XMSSMT-i-SHA2-40/8-256	4.96%	−1.39%	−1.98%	−1.39%
XMSSMT-SHA2-60/6-256	XMSSMT-i-SHA2-60/6-256	−2.98%	−1.30%	−2.40%	−1.30%
XMSSMT-SHA2-60/12-256	XMSSMT-i-SHA2-60/12-256	−6.40%	−1.39%	2.80%	−1.39%
XMSSMT-SHA2-20/2-512	XMSSMT-i-SHA2-20/2-512	−0.99%	−0.71%	−3.02%	−0.71%
XMSSMT-SHA2-20/4-512	XMSSMT-i-SHA2-20/4-512	3.31%	−0.73%	3.85%	−0.73%
XMSSMT-SHA2-40/4-512	XMSSMT-i-SHA2-40/4-512	−0.67%	−0.71%	−1.76%	−0.71%
XMSSMT-SHA2-40/8-512	XMSSMT-i-SHA2-40/8-512	3.08%	−0.73%	1.95%	−0.73%
XMSSMT-SHA2-60/6-512	XMSSMT-i-SHA2-60/6-512	−1.06%	−0.71%	2.12%	−0.71%
XMSSMT-SHA2-60/12-512	XMSSMT-i-SHA2-60/12-512	1.02%	−0.73%	1.44%	−0.73%
XMSSMT-SHA2-20/2-192	XMSSMT-i-SHA2-20/2-192	−1.11%	−1.62%	−6.48%	−1.62%
XMSSMT-SHA2-20/4-192	XMSSMT-i-SHA2-20/4-192	4.75%	−1.78%	0.22%	−1.78%
XMSSMT-SHA2-40/4-192	XMSSMT-i-SHA2-40/4-192	−1.48%	−1.63%	2.82%	−1.63%
XMSSMT-SHA2-40/8-192	XMSSMT-i-SHA2-40/8-192	5.57%	−1.78%	1.59%	−1.78%
XMSSMT-SHA2-60/6-192	XMSSMT-i-SHA2-60/6-192	−2.40%	−1.63%	−1.42%	−1.63%
XMSSMT-SHA2-60/12-192	XMSSMT-i-SHA2-60/12-192	2.50%	−1.78%	0.12%	−1.78%
XMSSMT-SHAKE-20/2-256	XMSSMT-i-SHAKE-20/2-256	−2.86%	−1.29%	−6.55%	−1.29%
XMSSMT-SHAKE-20/4-256	XMSSMT-i-SHAKE-20/4-256	1.73%	−1.38%	1.15%	−1.38%
XMSSMT-SHAKE-40/4-256	XMSSMT-i-SHAKE-40/4-256	−2.93%	−1.29%	−3.20%	−1.29%
XMSSMT-SHAKE-40/8-256	XMSSMT-i-SHAKE-40/8-256	−1.12%	−1.39%	−4.66%	−1.39%
XMSSMT-SHAKE-60/6-256	XMSSMT-i-SHAKE-60/6-256	−2.74%	−1.30%	0.38%	−1.30%
XMSSMT-SHAKE-60/12-256	XMSSMT-i-SHAKE-60/12-256	−0.87%	−1.39%	−6.69%	−1.39%
XMSSMT-SHAKE-20/4-512	XMSSMT-i-SHAKE-20/4-512	1.06%	−0.73%	−1.80%	−0.73%
XMSSMT-SHAKE-40/4-512	XMSSMT-i-SHAKE-40/4-512	−1.74%	−0.71%	−0.37%	−0.71%
XMSSMT-SHAKE-40/8-512	XMSSMT-i-SHAKE-40/8-512	1.56%	−0.73%	1.26%	−0.73%
XMSSMT-SHAKE-60/6-512	XMSSMT-i-SHAKE-60/6-512	−1.17%	−0.71%	−0.25%	−0.71%
XMSSMT-SHAKE-60/12-512	XMSSMT-i-SHAKE-60/12-512	0.96%	−0.73%	−0.88%	−0.73%
XMSSMT-SHAKE256-20/2-256	XMSSMT-i-SHAKE256-20/2-256	−4.03%	−1.29%	−0.33%	−1.29%
XMSSMT-SHAKE256-20/4-256	XMSSMT-i-SHAKE256-20/4-256	−2.69%	−1.38%	0.12%	−1.38%
XMSSMT-SHAKE256-40/4-256	XMSSMT-i-SHAKE256-40/4-256	−4.52%	−1.29%	−9.14%	−1.29%
XMSSMT-SHAKE256-40/8-256	XMSSMT-i-SHAKE256-40/8-256	−3.19%	−1.39%	−3.51%	−1.39%
XMSSMT-SHAKE256-60/6-256	XMSSMT-i-SHAKE256-60/6-256	−5.15%	−1.30%	−7.87%	−1.30%
XMSSMT-SHAKE256-60/12-256	XMSSMT-i-SHAKE256-60/12-256	−3.20%	−1.39%	−5.03%	−1.39%
XMSSMT-SHAKE256-20/2-192	XMSSMT-i-SHAKE256-20/2-192	−4.28%	−1.62%	−10.52%	−1.62%
XMSSMT-SHAKE256-20/4-192	XMSSMT-i-SHAKE256-20/4-192	−2.63%	−1.78%	−8.72%	−1.78%
XMSSMT-SHAKE256-40/4-192	XMSSMT-i-SHAKE256-40/4-192	−4.71%	−1.63%	−4.03%	−1.63%
XMSSMT-SHAKE256-40/8-192	XMSSMT-i-SHAKE256-40/8-192	−5.45%	−1.78%	−8.15%	−1.78%
XMSSMT-SHAKE256-60/6-192	XMSSMT-i-SHAKE256-60/6-192	−5.64%	−1.63%	−6.37%	−1.63%
XMSSMT-SHAKE256-60/12-192	XMSSMT-i-SHAKE256-60/12-192	−3.59%	−1.78%	−4.83%	−1.78%

References

1. André, D.: Mémoire sur les combinaisons régulières et leurs applications. In: Annales scientifiques de l'École Normale Supérieure, vol. 5, pp. 155–198 (1876)
2. Aumasson, J.-P., Endignoux, G.: Improving stateless hash-based signatures. In: Smart, N.P. (ed.) CT-RSA 2018. LNCS, vol. 10808, pp. 219–242. Springer, Cham (2018). https://doi.org/10.1007/978-3-319-76953-0_12
3. Belbachir, H., Igueroufa, O.: Congruence properties for Bi^s nomial coefficients and like extended Ram and Kummer theorems under suitable hypothesis. Mediterr. J. Math. **17**(1), 1–14 (2020)
4. Bernstein, D.J., et al.: SPHINCS: practical stateless hash-based signatures. In: Oswald, E., Fischlin, M. (eds.) EUROCRYPT 2015. LNCS, vol. 9056, pp. 368–397. Springer, Heidelberg (2015). https://doi.org/10.1007/978-3-662-46800-5_15
5. Bernstein, D.J., Hülsing, A., Kölbl, S., Niederhagen, R., Rijneveld, J., Schwabe, P.: The SPHINCS$^+$ signature framework. In: Cavallaro, L., Kinder, J., Wang, X., Katz, J. (eds.) ACM CCS 2019: 26th Conference on Computer and Communications Security, pp. 2129–2146. ACM Press (11–15 Nov 2019). https://doi.org/10.1145/3319535.3363229
6. Bleichenbacher, D., Maurer, U.M.: Directed Acyclic Graphs, One-way Functions and Digital Signatures. In: Desmedt, Y.G. (ed.) CRYPTO 1994. LNCS, vol. 839, pp. 75–82. Springer, Heidelberg (1994). https://doi.org/10.1007/3-540-48658-5_9
7. Bleichenbacher, D., Maurer, U.: On the efficiency of one-time digital signatures. In: Kim, K., Matsumoto, T. (eds.) ASIACRYPT 1996. LNCS, vol. 1163, pp. 145–158. Springer, Heidelberg (1996). https://doi.org/10.1007/BFb0034843
8. Bleichenbacher, D., Maurer, U.M.: Optimal tree-based one-time digital signature schemes. In: Puech, C., Reischuk, R. (eds.) STACS 1996. LNCS, vol. 1046, pp. 361–374. Springer, Heidelberg (1996). https://doi.org/10.1007/3-540-60922-9_30
9. Bos, J.N.E., Chaum, D.: Provably unforgeable signatures. In: Brickell, E.F. (ed.) CRYPTO 1992. LNCS, vol. 740, pp. 1–14. Springer, Heidelberg (1993). https://doi.org/10.1007/3-540-48071-4_1
10. Cooper, D.A., et al.: Recommendation for stateful hash-based signature schemes. NIST Spec. Publ. **800**, 208 (2020)
11. Cruz, J.P., Yatani, Y., Kaji, Y.: Constant-sum fingerprinting for Winternitz one-time signature. In: 2016 International Symposium on Information Theory and Its Applications (ISITA), pp. 703–707. IEEE (2016)
12. Dilworth, R.P.: A decomposition theorem for partially ordered sets. In: Classic Papers in Combinatorics, pp. 139–144. Springer (2009). https://doi.org/10.1007/978-1-4899-3558-8_1
13. Dods, C., Smart, N.P., Stam, M.: Hash based digital signature schemes. In: Smart, N.P. (ed.) 10th IMA International Conference on Cryptography and Coding. LNCS, vol. 3796, pp. 96–115. Springer, Heidelberg (19–21 Dec 2005). https://doi.org/10.1007/978-3-540-88702-7_3
14. Dworkin, M.: SHA-3 standard: Permutation-based hash and extendable-output functions (Aug 2015). https://doi.org/10.6028/NIST.FIPS.202
15. Euler, L.: De evolutione potestatis polynomialis cuiuscunque $(1 + x + x^2 + x^3 + x^4 + etc.)^n$. Nova Acta Academiae Scientiarum Imperialis Petropolitanae, pp. 47–57 (1801)
16. Goldreich, O.: Two remarks concerning the Goldwasser-Micali-Rivest signature scheme. In: Odlyzko, A.M. (ed.) CRYPTO 1986. LNCS, vol. 263, pp. 104–110. Springer, Heidelberg (1987). https://doi.org/10.1007/3-540-47721-7_8

17. Goldreich, O.: Foundations of Cryptography: Basic Applications, vol. 2. Cambridge University Press, Cambridge (2004)
18. Gueron, S., Mouha, N.: SPHINCS-simpira: Fast stateless hash-based signatures with post-quantum security. Cryptology ePrint Archive, Report 2017/645 (2017). http://eprint.iacr.org/2017/645
19. Hash Based Signature: XMSS-i. https://github.com/hashbasedsignature/xmss-i (2022)
20. Hash Based Signature: CSWOTS. https://github.com/hashbasedsignature/cswots (2023)
21. Hevia, A., Micciancio, D.: The provable security of graph-based one-time signatures and extensions to algebraic signature schemes. In: Zheng, Y. (ed.) ASIACRYPT 2002. LNCS, vol. 2501, pp. 379–396. Springer, Heidelberg (2002). https://doi.org/10.1007/3-540-36178-2_24
22. Hülsing, A.: W-OTS+ – shorter signatures for hash-based signature schemes. In: Youssef, A., Nitaj, A., Hassanien, A.E. (eds.) AFRICACRYPT 2013. LNCS, vol. 7918, pp. 173–188. Springer, Heidelberg (2013). https://doi.org/10.1007/978-3-642-38553-7_10
23. Hülsing, A., Butin, D., Gazdag, S.L., Rijneveld, J., Mohaisen, A.: XMSS: extended merkle signature scheme. In: RFC 8391. IRTF (2018)
24. Hülsing, A., Kudinov, M.: Recovering the tight security proof of SPHINCS+. Cryptology ePrint Archive, Paper 2022/346 (2022). https://eprint.iacr.org/2022/346
25. Kölbl, S., Lauridsen, M.M., Mendel, F., Rechberger, C.: Haraka v2 - Efficient short-input hashing for post-quantum applications. IACR Trans, Symmetric Cryptology **2016**(2), 1–29 (2016). https://doi.org/10.13154/tosc.v2016.i2.1-29, http://tosc.iacr.org/index.php/ToSC/article/view/563
26. Kudinov, M., Hülsing, A., Ronen, E., Yogev, E.: SPHINCS+C: Compressing SPHINCS+ with (almost) no cost. Cryptology ePrint Archive, Paper 2022/778 (2022). https://eprint.iacr.org/2022/778
27. Kudinov, M.A., Kiktenko, E.O., Fedorov, A.K.: Security analysis of the W-OTS+ signature scheme: Updating security bounds. Matematicheskie Voprosy Kriptografii [Mathematical Aspects of Cryptography] **12**(2), 129–145 (2021). https://doi.org/10.4213/mvk362
28. Lamport, L.: Constructing digital signatures from a one-way function. Technical Report SRI-CSL-98, SRI International Computer Science Laboratory (Oct 1979)
29. McGrew, D., Curcio, M., Fluhrer, S.: Leighton-Micali hash-based signatures. In: RFC 8554. IRTF (2019)
30. Merkle, R.C.: A digital signature based on a conventional encryption function. In: Pomerance, C. (ed.) CRYPTO 1987. LNCS, vol. 293, pp. 369–378. Springer, Heidelberg (1988). https://doi.org/10.1007/3-540-48184-2_32
31. Merkle, R.C.: A certified digital signature. In: Brassard, G. (ed.) CRYPTO 1989. LNCS, vol. 435, pp. 218–238. Springer, New York (1990). https://doi.org/10.1007/0-387-34805-0_21
32. Moody, D.: Parameter selection for the selected algorithms (2022). https://groups.google.com/a/list.nist.gov/g/pqc-forum/c/4MBurXr58Rs/m/lj4VRfAnFwAJ
33. National Institute of Standards and Technology: Secure hash standard (2015-08-04 2015). https://doi.org/10.6028/NIST.FIPS.180-4
34. Perin, L.P., Zambonin, G., Custódio, R., Moura, L., Panario, D.: Improved constant-sum encodings for hash-based signatures. J. Cryptogr. Eng. **11**, 329–351 (2021)

35. Perlner, R., Kelsey, J., Cooper, D.: Breaking category five SPHINCS+ with SHA-256. Cryptology ePrint Archive, Paper 2022/1061 (2022). https://eprint.iacr.org/2022/1061
36. Rabin, M.O.: Digitalized signatures. Foundations of secure computation, pp. 155–168 (1978)
37. Rijneveld, J., Hülsing, A., Cooper, D., Westerbaan, B.: The XMSS reference code (2022). https://github.com/XMSS/xmss-reference
38. Sperner, E.: Ein satz über untermengen einer endlichen menge. Math. Z. **27**(1), 544–548 (1928)
39. Team, TNP: PQC standardization process: Announcing four candidates to be standardized, plus fourth round candidates. NIST (2022). https://csrc.nist.gov/News/2022/pqc-candidates-to-be-standardized-and-round-4
40. The SPHINCS+ Team: The SPHINCS+ reference code, accompanying the submission to NIST's post-quantum cryptography project (2021). https://github.com/sphincs/sphincsplus
41. Vaudenay, S.: One-time identification with low memory. In: Camion, P., Charpin, P., Harari, S. (eds.) Eurocode '92. ICMS, vol. 339, pp. 217–228. Springer, Vienna (1993). https://doi.org/10.1007/978-3-7091-2786-5_19
42. Warnaar, S.O.: The Andrews-Gordon identities and q-multinomial coefficients. Commun. Math. Phys. **184**(1), 203–232 (1997)
43. Zare, D.: How to express $(1 + x + x^2 + \cdots + x^m)^n$ as a power series? Mathematics Stack Exchange, https://math.stackexchange.com/q/28861, (version: 2011-11-15)
44. Zhang, K.: sphincs-a (2023). https://github.com/kzoacn/sphincs-a
45. Zhang, K., Cui, H., Yu, Y.: SPHINCS-α: A compact stateless hash-based signature scheme. Cryptology ePrint Archive, Paper 2022/059 (2022). https://eprint.iacr.org/2022/059

Efficient Hybrid Exact/Relaxed Lattice Proofs and Applications to Rounding and VRFs

Muhammed F. Esgin[1,2(✉)], Ron Steinfeld[1], Dongxi Liu[2], and Sushmita Ruj[3]

[1] Monash University, Melbourne, Australia
muhammed.esgin@monash.edu
[2] CSIRO's Data61, Marsfield, Australia
[3] University of New South Wales, Sydney, Australia

Abstract. In this work, we study *hybrid exact/relaxed zero-knowledge proofs* from lattices, where the proved relation is exact in one part and relaxed in the other. Such proofs arise in important real-life applications such as those requiring verifiable PRF evaluation and have so far not received significant attention as a standalone problem.

We first introduce a general framework, LANES⁺, for realizing such hybrid proofs efficiently by combining standard *relaxed* proofs of knowledge RPoK and the LANES framework (due to a series of works in Crypto'20, Asiacrypt'20, ACM CCS'20). The latter framework is a powerful lattice-based proof system that can prove exact linear and multiplicative relations. The advantage of LANES⁺ is its ability to realize hybrid proofs more efficiently by exploiting RPoK for the high-dimensional part of the secret witness while leaving a low-dimensional secret witness part for the exact proof that is proven at a significantly lower cost via LANES. Thanks to the flexibility of LANES⁺, other exact proof systems can also be supported.

We apply our LANES⁺ framework to construct substantially shorter proofs of rounding, which is a central tool for *verifiable* deterministic lattice-based cryptography. Based on our rounding proof, we then design an efficient long-term verifiable random function (VRF), named LaV. LaV leads to the shortest VRF outputs among the proposals of standard (i.e., long-term and stateless) VRFs based on quantum-safe assumptions. Of independent interest, we also present generalized results for challenge difference invertibility, a fundamental soundness security requirement for many proof systems.

Keywords: Lattice · Zero-Knowledge Proofs · Post-Quantum · Learning with Rounding · Verifiable Random Function

1 Introduction

Zero-knowledge proofs are fundamental tools for construction of privacy-preserving cryptographic protocols. Constructing such protocols with security against quantum attacks is an active research area, with lattice-based techniques a leading candidate. In such lattice-based privacy-preserving protocols,

© International Association for Cryptologic Research 2023
H. Handschuh and A. Lysyanskaya (Eds.): CRYPTO 2023, LNCS 14085, pp. 484–517, 2023.
https://doi.org/10.1007/978-3-031-38554-4_16

the desired protocol functionality boils down to constructing a zero-knowledge protocol for proving a relation of the form

$$\mathbf{Ar} + \mathbf{Bm} = \mathbf{t}, \tag{1}$$

over the underlying ring $\mathcal{R}_{q,d}$ (which may be $\mathbb{Z}_q$ or a d-dimensional polynomial ring modulo an integer q). In the above expression, $\mathbf{A}, \mathbf{B}$ are public matrices, $\mathbf{t}$ is a public vector and $(\mathbf{r}, \mathbf{m})$ is a pair of secret vectors constituting the prover's witness in the zero-knowledge proof, having *small* coordinates in some sets S_1, S_2 (e.g., $S_i = \{-1, 0, 1\}$). The witness vectors may also be required to satisfy additional constraints (e.g., linear relations). When the zero-knowledge protocol proves knowledge of such a witness satisfying (1) exactly and with coordinates guaranteed to be in the set S_i, it is said to be an *exact* proof. There is a line of work on constructing such exact lattice-based proofs, from long Stern-type [53] proofs [41], to more compact algebraic proofs [12,55], culminating in the state-of-the-art, which we call the LANES framework, consisting of the combination of techniques developed in [3, 24, 46] (the LANES acronym we use is derived from the initials of the authors of those latter works). However, even the state-of-the-art LANES framework for exact lattice-based proofs often results in relatively long proofs in practice. In contrast, some cryptographic functionalities, such as plain signatures [21, 42, 43], ring signatures and applications [26, 28, 29, 48] and group signatures [20, 28, 29], have been shown to be realizable more compactly without resorting to exact proofs, replacing them with significantly shorter *relaxed (approximate) proofs of knowledge* RPoK, i.e., proofs of relations of the form

$$\mathbf{Ar}' + \mathbf{Bm}' = \bar{c}\mathbf{t}, \tag{2}$$

for a short "relaxation factor" $\bar{c} \in \mathcal{R}_{q,d}$, and also allowing some slack in the set S_i in which the coordinates of the witness vector $(\mathbf{r}', \mathbf{m}')$ are proved to be in.

In this paper, we focus on important cryptographic functionalities for which *exact* proofs are required for proving the well-formedness of *part* of the witness. In such *hybrid exact/relaxed proof* applications, it is crucial that the proof is exact for the portion $\mathbf{m}$ of the witness $(\mathbf{r}, \mathbf{m})$, in the sense that the coordinates of $\mathbf{m}$ are proved to exactly belong in some set S_i (and satisfy the appropriate additional, e.g., linear constraints), but the coordinates of $\mathbf{r}$ may have some soundness slack, and the relation to be satisfied is of the form

$$\mathbf{Ar}' + \bar{c}\mathbf{Bm} = \bar{c}\mathbf{t}. \tag{3}$$

Note that if $\bar{c}$ is invertible in $\mathcal{R}_{q,d}$, then (3) can be re-written as $\mathbf{Ar} + \mathbf{Bm} = \mathbf{t}$ for $\mathbf{r} := \mathbf{r}'/\bar{c}$ so that it is exact for the $\mathbf{Bm}$ term while the relaxation factor $\bar{c}$ only affects the $\mathbf{r} = \mathbf{r}'/\bar{c}$ witness part (we remark that when the real witness $\mathbf{r}$ has unconstrained coordinates, this actually becomes an exact proof with extracted witness $\mathbf{r} = \mathbf{r}'/\bar{c}$; the relaxation factor only comes in when we require $\mathbf{r}$ to be short). Unfortunately, a limitation of the LANES framework for exact proofs is that it is not flexible enough to support such hybrid exact/relaxed relations *efficiently*. Namely, when using LANES for such hybrid relations, one is forced to prove an exact relation for the *whole* witness $(\mathbf{r}, \mathbf{m})$, which leads to long proofs, as the length of the LANES proof is proportional to the total length of the witness (we discuss this more precisely in 'Technical Overview' section). On the other hand, compact relaxed proofs alone cannot be used due to the exact proof requirement on the **m** part of the witness.

A case in point of hybrid exact/relaxed relation that forms the central motivation of this paper is that of *rounding proofs*. Given a public matrix $\mathbf{A}$ and a vector $\mathbf{t}$ over $\mathbb{Z}_q$, and a rounding modulus p, a rounding proof proves knowledge of a secret vector $\mathbf{s}$ such that $\mathbf{t} = \lfloor \mathbf{As} \rceil_p := \lfloor \frac{p}{q} \cdot \mathbf{As} \rceil$, where the rounding is done coefficient-wise. Rounding proofs come up in protocols that prove the well-formedness of lattice-based Pseudo-Random Functions (PRFs) based on the Learning with Rounding (LWR) problem introduced in [6] and several LWR-based constructions of PRFs are known [5,6,11]. Proofs of correct PRF evaluation have applications in Verifiable Random Functions (VRFs) as constructed in this paper, along with privacy-preserving de-centralized e-cash systems [9,18,34], stateful anonymous credentials [19], n-times periodic anonymous authentication [14], traceable ring signatures [30], anonymous survey systems [35], password-protected secret sharing [36] and unlinkable pseudonyms for distributed databases [15] as stated in [41]. For $p \mid q$, the rounding relation $\mathbf{t} = \lfloor \mathbf{As} \rceil_p$ can be written in the form $\frac{q}{p}\mathbf{t} = \mathbf{As} - \mathbf{e}$, where $\mathbf{e} \in [0, q/p - 1]^m$ is the rounding error. This has the form of (1), where the witness consists of $(\mathbf{s}, \mathbf{e})$. In rounding proofs, it is crucial that the proof is exact for the $\mathbf{e}$ part to ensure that its coordinates are in $[0, q/p - 1]$ for the correct rounding relation, whereas it turns out to be fine for applications to relax the proof requirement for the $\mathbf{s}$ portion of the witness. For example, a set of standard LWR samples does not require the secret $\mathbf{s}$ to be short. In typical applications, the dimension of the relaxed portion $\mathbf{s}$ of the witness is dictated by security constraints of the LWR problem, and is much longer than the dimension of the exact portion of the witness $\mathbf{e}$. Therefore, rounding proofs are a typical example of hybrid exact/relaxed proofs where the inflexibility limitation of the plain LANES framework would lead to long proofs, despite the short dimension of the exact portion of the witness.

The main application of rounding proofs we focus on in this paper is to the construction of lattice-based long-term (stateless) *Verifiable Random Functions* (VRFs). A VRF is a type of pseudorandom function whose output is both authenticated and publicly verifiable [50]. VRFs based on quantum-insecure assumptions have been used in practice, for example, in the DNSSEC protocol [32], WhatsApp's key transparency protocol [40], and in blockchain Proof-of-Stake consensus protocols [17,31,37]. Existing quantum-safe VRF constructions, on the other hand, fall into two classes. The first class are constructions in the standard model [10,33,54], which are relatively inefficient in practice but avoid the use of a common reference string or random oracle. The second class are constructions in the random oracle model [13,23,55]. The latter constructions are more practically oriented, but are limited due to the lack of compact rounding proofs or other reasons as discuss below. The lattice-based VRF construction sketched in [55] uses inefficient exact proofs of rounding that have lengths in the order of MBs. Even if improved using the LANES framework, such exact rounding proofs would typically still be quite long, in the order of 100 KB[1]. The lattice-based VRF construction in [23]

---

[1] Even the optimized proof of 1024-dimensional LWE samples with *ternary* secret and error (i.e., $\mathbf{s}, \mathbf{e} \in \{-1, 0, 1\}^{1024}$) in [47] is at 33 KB. The magnitude of rounding error coefficients needs to be bigger for a VRF to circumvent algebraic attacks.

Table 1. Comparison of (plausibly) post-quantum practical VRFs. ✓ means the property is partially satisfied. 'Key Hom.' means the underlying PRF is (approximately) 'key homomorphic'. For the communication size (Comm. Size) of LB-VRF, we consider the sum of proof size, VRF value and public key since the construction is one-time.

	Comm. Size	Key Hom.	Long Term	Stateless	Low Storage & Fast Keygen	Security
X-VRF [13]	3 KB	✗	✓	✗	✗	Hash
LB-VRF [23]	8.34 KB	✓	✗	✓	✓	Lattice
SL-VRF [13]	40 KB	✗	✓	✓	✓	Hash
LaV (this work)	10.3 KB	✓	✓	✓	✓	Lattice

is compact (with proof sizes around 5–8 KB) but, to avoid the need for rounding proofs, it leaks an exact linear relation on the secret key with each VRF evaluation, which limits the number of times it can be evaluated to a small value (typically 1–5 evaluations), i.e., the construction in [23] is a *few-time* VRF rather than a full-fledged (practically unlimited-time) VRF as we construct in this paper.

In the application of VRF to Algorand's blockchain protocol, the few-time limitation on the VRF of [23] introduces modifications and additional overheads to the Algorand consensus protocol, in order to periodically refresh the VRF keys of the users [23]. Other applications of VRFs, such as the DNSSEC protocol [32], inherently require a long-term VRF. The authors of [23] stated that the main bottleneck to constructing an efficient long-term lattice-based VRF is the lack of an efficient rounding proof. We address this open problem in this paper.

Two VRF constructions based on symmetric-key primitives are given in [13], but also suffer from significant practical limitations. The first construction in [13], called X-VRF, achieves compact proofs (around 3 KB) but suffers from a *stateful* VRF algorithm and a key generation time and prover storage cost that increases in proportion to the number of allowed VRF evaluations (e.g., leading to days long key generation times for 2^{27} VRF evaluations). The second construction in [13], called SL-VRF, avoids stateful evaluation and long setup and memory costs, but suffers from long proofs in the order of 40KB (see Table 1).

Another significant consideration for higher-level applications of VRFs (or correct PRF evaluation proofs) is (an approximate) *key-homomorphism* of the underlying PRF (i.e., $\mathsf{PRF}_{\mathsf{sk}_0}(m) + \mathsf{PRF}_{\mathsf{sk}_1}(m) \approx \mathsf{PRF}_{\mathsf{sk}_0+\mathsf{sk}_1}(m)$), as this is an important property for various applications such as anonymous e-cash, distributed PRFs, symmetric-key proxy re-encryption and updatable encryption. The symmetric-key based proposals in [13] do not offer key-homomorphism.

1.1 Our Contributions

LANES+ framework: Compact Hybrid Exact/Relaxed Proofs. We introduce a novel general framework called LANES+ for constructing compact proofs for hybrid exact/relaxed relations, addressing the limitations of the LANES framework. LANES+ combines the best of LANES and Relaxed Proofs of Knowledge (RPoK) to achieve much shorter proofs than LANES when the exact part of the witness is short compared to the full length of the witness. The LANES+ framework proves relations of the form (3) and supports additional exact linear relations and polynomial constraints on the exact part $\mathbf{m}$ of the witness. Our LANES$^+$ framework is flexible enough to support different exact proof systems, including a concurrent work [44] as discussed further in Sect. 1.2.

Compact Lattice-Based Rounding Proofs. We present an efficient instantiation of our LANES$^+$ framework applied to the design of compact rounding proofs for cryptographic protocols based on the LWR problem. Our rounding proof is substantially shorter than prior proposals [41,55] as they require communication in the order of MBs. We believe our compact rounding proof techniques will find future applications for the design of efficient correct PRF evaluation proofs in lattice-based privacy-preserving protocols such as anonymous e-cash [41]. We leave the application of our techniques to anonymous e-cash as future work.

LaV: Compact (Long-Term) Lattice-Based VRF. To demonstrate the utility of our new techniques, we present an efficient application of our LANES$^+$-based rounding proofs to the construction of a compact (long-term) lattice VRF, called LaV. Our construction is the *first practical* lattice-based VRF supporting practically unrestricted number (2^{128}) of VRF evaluations. For typical parameters, LaV achieves a VRF output size of about 10.3 KB, which is about 1.24× overhead over the communication size needed in [23], while allowing for an arbitrary number of VRF evaluations (versus the 1–5 evaluation limitation of [23]). In Table 1, we provide a comparison between practical post-quantum VRF proposals.

To support our new VRF construction and rounding proofs, we also introduce another technical contribution of potential independent interest as below.

Generalization of Challenge Difference Invertibility Bounds. RPoK part of our LANES$^+$ protocol requires the invertibility of challenge differences in the underlying polynomial ring and it is important for the practical efficiency of LaV that $\dim(\mathcal{R}_{q,d}) = d$ is small (e.g., $d = 32$). The latter requirement forces the protocol challenge c to have relatively large coefficients. To support this, we generalize the challenge difference invertibility bounds from [3,28], which apply only to *ternary* challenge coordinates. In particular, we derive bounds for challenges with coefficients of infinity norm γ for any $\gamma \geq 1$. These generalized results are used to optimize the length of our rounding proofs in LaV, and we believe they will find further applications in future lattice proof systems. In general, compared to prior results applicable for $\gamma > 1$ such as [49], our new results allow to use a smaller modulus q and/or a highly-splitting ring $\mathcal{R}_{q,d}$.

1.2   Technical Overview

LANES$^+$ Framework. We first explain in more detail the inflexibility limitations of the LANES framework. We recall that LANES uses a commitment scheme defined over a cyclotomic polynomial ring $\mathcal{R}_{q,\hat{d}} := \mathbb{Z}_q[X]/(X^{\hat{d}} + 1)$ where $\hat{d}$ is a power of 2 and q is chosen so that $\mathcal{R}_{q,\hat{d}}$ splits into l subrings via the Chinese Remainder Theorem (CRT). We also use $\mathcal{R}_{q,d}$ to denote the ring where operations external to LANES are performed. In the following, for a vector $\mathbf{x} \in \mathcal{R}_{q,d}^n$, $\vec{\mathbf{x}} \in \mathbb{Z}_q^{dn}$ denotes the (concatenated) coefficient vector of $\mathbf{x}$ over $\mathbb{Z}_q$. In general, we will write $\vec{x}$ to denote vectors over $\mathbb{Z}_q$ and $\mathbf{x}$ to denote vectors over $\mathcal{R}_{q,d}$.

Due to the way relations are proved in LANES, one cannot reduce the proof size by exploiting the *partial* exactness of the relation so that a relaxed proof of knowledge can be leveraged for the relaxed relation part. We elaborate more on this further below once we set out our target problem next.

Recall that the most common relations in lattice-based cryptography are of the form (1). We call $\mathbf{m}$ as "message" and $\mathbf{r}$ as "randomness" for ease of reference. As far as our framework is concerned, the distinction is merely that $\mathbf{m}$ is the secret vector part that goes into LANES, while $\mathbf{r}$ is the remaining part.

It is a common requirement to prove not just that (1) holds, but also that the message and/or the randomness satisfy certain properties (such as having small coefficients). Now suppose that we want to prove such a common relation along with some arbitrary linear relation $\mathbf{G}_1\overrightarrow{\mathbf{m}} = \mathbf{G}_2\overrightarrow{v}$ for $(\mathbf{G}_1, \mathbf{G}_2, \overrightarrow{v})$ defined over $\mathbb{Z}_q$. First note that revealing $\overrightarrow{v}$ or $\mathbf{G}_1\overrightarrow{\mathbf{m}}$ in many cases would leak secret information (for example, when $\overrightarrow{v}$ is the binary decomposition of $\overrightarrow{\mathbf{m}}$). Hence, they need to be part of the prover's witness. Now, the way to prove these relations in LANES would be to write all of the relations in the following form

$$\underbrace{\begin{pmatrix} \mathsf{Rot}(\mathbf{A}) & \mathsf{Rot}(\mathbf{B}) & 0 \\ 0 & \mathbf{G}_1 & -\mathbf{G}_2 \end{pmatrix}}_{=:\mathbf{L}} \cdot \underbrace{\begin{pmatrix} \overrightarrow{\mathbf{r}} \\ \overrightarrow{\mathbf{m}} \\ \overrightarrow{v} \end{pmatrix}}_{=:\overrightarrow{x}} = \underbrace{\begin{pmatrix} \overrightarrow{t} \\ \overrightarrow{0} \end{pmatrix}}_{=:\overrightarrow{t}}, \tag{4}$$

where $\mathsf{Rot}(\cdot)$ denotes the representative matrix of its input over $\mathbb{Z}_q$, and just prove this linear relation (along with additional multiplicative relations). However, the drawback of this approach is that the secret witness dimension here is $\dim(\overrightarrow{x}) = \dim(\overrightarrow{\mathbf{r}}) + \dim(\overrightarrow{\mathbf{m}}) + \dim(\overrightarrow{v})$. In many cases, the dimension of the randomness $\overrightarrow{\mathbf{r}}$ is lower-bounded by the security requirements (such as hiding and pseudorandomness) and thus cannot be very small. Indeed, there are applications where the dimension of the message $\overrightarrow{\mathbf{m}}$ is much smaller than that of the randomness, i.e., $\dim(\overrightarrow{\mathbf{m}}) \ll \dim(\overrightarrow{\mathbf{r}})$. Consider, for example, the case when we want to prove knowledge of a *single* LWR sample. Here, $\mathbf{r}$ being the secret key would typically have $\dim(\overrightarrow{\mathbf{r}}) \geq 1024$ while $\mathbf{m}$ being the rounding error would just have $\dim(\overrightarrow{\mathbf{m}}) = 1$. Since the size of a LANES proof output scales linearly in the dimension of the witness (see (12) in Sect. 2.4), it may not be ideal in such applications to use the LANES framework directly.

To get around the above efficiency challenge, we introduce a hybrid framework that allows to combine a RPoK with LANES. Particularly, our goal is to prove the relation in (1) using very efficient RPoK (as those used in ordinary signatures) shown in Algorithm 1 and exploit LANES to prove the remaining linear (and multiplicative) relation (i.e., $\mathbf{G}_1\overrightarrow{\mathbf{m}} = \mathbf{G}_2\overrightarrow{v}$). This way, we will be combining the best of two worlds by (i) proving the (often low-dimensional) $\mathbf{G}_1\overrightarrow{\mathbf{m}} = \mathbf{G}_2\overrightarrow{v}$ linear relation *exactly* (via LANES), and (ii) using the efficient relaxed proofs whenever possible for the high-dimensional relations as in (1). A technical challenge here is that LANES protocol does not involve a masked opening of its input message (i.e., $\mathbf{m}$), preventing the utilization of standard EQ or AND protocol compositions that use the same masked opening in multiple proof parts.

Algorithm 1. Standard Lattice-based Relaxed Proof of Knowledge (RPoK)

1: **procedure** RPoK$((\mathbf{A}, \mathbf{B}, \mathbf{t}); (\mathbf{r}, \mathbf{m}))$:
2:     Sample short rand. masking $\mathbf{y}$
3:     Sample message masking $\mathbf{u}$
4:     $\mathbf{w} = \mathbf{A}\mathbf{y} + \mathbf{B}\mathbf{u}$ over $\mathcal{R}_{q,d}$
5:     $c \leftarrow \mathcal{H}(\mathbf{A}, \mathbf{B}, \mathbf{t}, \mathbf{w})$ for a hash $\mathcal{H}$
6:     $\mathbf{z} = \mathbf{y} + c \cdot \mathbf{r}$
7:     $\mathbf{f} = \mathbf{u} + c \cdot \mathbf{m}$
8:     Rejection samp. on $\mathbf{z}$ (and $\mathbf{f}$ if req.)
9:     **return** proof $\pi = (c, \mathbf{z}, \mathbf{f})$
10: **end procedure**

11: **procedure** Verify$((\mathbf{A}, \mathbf{B}, \mathbf{t}), \pi)$:
12:     Parse $\pi = (c, \mathbf{z}, \mathbf{f})$
13:     If $\mathbf{z}$ (and $\mathbf{f}$) is not sufficiently short,
            return 0
14:     $\mathbf{w}' = \mathbf{A}\mathbf{z} + \mathbf{B}\mathbf{f} - c\mathbf{t}$ over $\mathcal{R}_{q,d}$
15:     If $c \neq \mathcal{H}(\mathbf{A}, \mathbf{B}, \mathbf{t}, \mathbf{w}')$, **return** 0
16:     **return** 1
17: **end procedure**

Using a standard rewinding argument, we can show that RPoK in Algorithm 1 proves knowledge of $(\bar{c}, \bar{\mathbf{z}}, \bar{\mathbf{f}})$ with short $(\bar{c}, \bar{\mathbf{z}})$ (and possibly short $\bar{\mathbf{f}}$) such that

$$\mathbf{A}\bar{\mathbf{z}} + \mathbf{B}\bar{\mathbf{f}} = \bar{c}\mathbf{t}, \tag{5}$$

where $\bar{c}, \bar{\mathbf{z}}, \bar{\mathbf{f}}$ are the differences of rewinded protocol outputs $(c, \mathbf{z}, \mathbf{f})$ and $(c', \mathbf{z}', \mathbf{f}')$. From Algorithm 1, we can see that the masked message opening in RPoK is $\mathbf{f} = \mathbf{u} + c \cdot \mathbf{m}$. We exploit this to make a connection between the two proof parts (RPoK and LANES). Particularly, we prove via LANES that $\overrightarrow{\mathbf{f}} = \overrightarrow{\mathbf{u}} + \mathsf{Rot}(c) \cdot \overrightarrow{\mathbf{m}}$ over $\mathbb{Z}_q$, ensuring that $\mathbf{f}$ is indeed of the desired form, along with the low-dimensional linear relation $\mathbf{G}_1\overrightarrow{\mathbf{m}} = \mathbf{G}_2\overrightarrow{v}$ and any other polynomial constraints on the coordinates of $\overrightarrow{\mathbf{m}}$. From the LANES witness extractor, a similar relation holds for the rewinded transcript such that $\overrightarrow{\mathbf{f}'} = \overrightarrow{\mathbf{u}} + \mathsf{Rot}(c') \cdot \overrightarrow{\mathbf{m}}$ with the same $(\overrightarrow{\mathbf{u}}, \overrightarrow{\mathbf{m}})$ by the binding of the LANES commitment. This gives that $\overrightarrow{\mathbf{f}} - \overrightarrow{\mathbf{f}'} = \mathsf{Rot}(\bar{c}) \cdot \overrightarrow{\mathbf{m}}$, and thus $\bar{\mathbf{f}} = \bar{c}\mathbf{m}$ over $\mathcal{R}_{q,d}$. Plugging this in (5) gives the desired hybrid relation in (3) with $\mathbf{r}' = \bar{\mathbf{z}}$. With this approach, $\mathbf{r}$ is never involved in the LANES part and we can guarantee the use of the same witness $\overrightarrow{\mathbf{m}}$ in both LANES and RPoK.

Overall, the goal of LANES$^+$ is to prove knowledge of a tuple $(\bar{c}, \mathbf{m}, \mathbf{r}, \overrightarrow{v}) \in \mathcal{L}^+(\mathsf{mp}, \mathsf{ulp})$ (i.e., $(\mathsf{ck}, (\mathsf{mp}, \mathsf{ulp}), (\bar{c}, \mathbf{m}, \mathbf{r}, \overrightarrow{v})) \in R_{\mathsf{LANES+}}$) such that

$$\mathcal{L}^+(\mathsf{mp}, \mathsf{ulp}) = \left\{ (\bar{c}, \mathbf{m}, \mathbf{r}, \overrightarrow{v}) : \begin{array}{c} \mathbf{t} = \mathbf{A}\mathbf{r} + \mathbf{B}\mathbf{m} \text{ over } \mathcal{R}_{q,d} \wedge \mathbf{G}_1\overrightarrow{\mathbf{m}} = \mathbf{G}_2\overrightarrow{v} \bmod q \\ \wedge P(\overrightarrow{\mathbf{m}}, \overrightarrow{v}) = 0 \bmod q \ \forall P \in \mathsf{mp} \wedge \\ \|\bar{c}\mathbf{r}\|_\infty \leq \gamma_r \wedge \|\bar{c}\|_\infty \leq \gamma_c \text{ for } \gamma_r, \gamma_c \ll q \in \mathbb{Z}^+ \end{array} \right\},$$

where mp is a set of multivariate polynomials in the coordinates of $(\overrightarrow{\mathbf{m}}, \overrightarrow{v})^2$ over $\mathbb{Z}_q$ (for example, enforcing the smallness of the witness coefficients via $P_i(\overrightarrow{\mathbf{m}}, \overrightarrow{v}) = v_i(v_i - 1)$ for $\overrightarrow{v} = (v_0, v_1, \dots)$), ulp $= ((\mathbf{A}, \mathbf{B}, \mathbf{t}), (\mathbf{G}_1, \mathbf{G}_2))$ is the collection of linear relations and γ_r, γ_c are some public norm-bounds. Note that the above language does not necessarily require $\mathbf{r}$ to be short, but $\bar{c}\mathbf{r}$ is short. Furthermore, the relation in (1) and the operations in LANES are not necessarily defined over the same polynomial ring. Particularly, LANES works internally

---

[2] The polynomials need to obey certain restrictions depending on the structure of the underlying ring $\mathcal{R}_{q,d}$, which is explained formally in Sect. 2.4.

over $\mathcal{R}_{q,\hat{d}}$ and proves relations over $\mathbb{Z}_q$, while (1) is over $\mathcal{R}_{q,d}$. In many cases, the relation proved by LANES is in fact over the integers (without mod q) and in those cases, we can use different moduli for the two rings $\mathcal{R}_{q,d}$ and $\mathcal{R}_{q,\hat{d}}$. This gives a lot of flexibility in choosing parameters and is critical for our rounding and VRF applications because the rounding/VRF relation requires a composite modulus while LANES works with a prime modulus.

Comparison with Concurrent Work. We further note that an approach from a concurrent and independent work [45] may also be adapted to solve our target problem. As we discuss next, our approach has the following advantages over a potential adaptation of [45] to our setting: (i) efficient and simple support for different system moduli, and (ii) better efficiency for applications with an expanding matrix $\mathbf{B}$. To use the techniques in [45] in our setting, one can use the term $\mathbf{w} := \mathbf{A}\mathbf{y}$ as a witness for LANES[3] and prove the relation $\mathbf{A}\mathbf{z} + c \cdot \mathbf{B}\mathbf{m} = \mathbf{w} + c \cdot \mathbf{t}$ via LANES. In this case, it is difficult to use different moduli for the LANES proof and the main relation $\mathbf{A}\mathbf{r} + \mathbf{B}\mathbf{m} = \mathbf{t}$ because the main relation is being proven by LANES. It may be possible to overcome this by proving a relation of the form $\mathbf{A}\mathbf{z} + c \cdot \mathbf{B}\mathbf{m} = \mathbf{w} + c \cdot \mathbf{t} + v \cdot q$ over $\mathbb{Z}$ (without mod q) with LANES. This requires the LANES modulus to be significantly bigger, for example exceeding $\|v \cdot q\|_{\infty}$, which leads to a longer LANES output, larger communication and a more complicated protocol overall. Furthermore, since the LANES witness in a possible approach based on [45] is $(\mathbf{m}, \mathbf{w})$, the proof length will grow linearly with $\dim(\mathbf{w}) = \dim(\mathbf{t})$. Although our framework focuses on the case where $\mathbf{m}$ is small dimensional, we do not necessarily require/assume $\dim(\mathbf{t})$ to be small. For example, when $\mathbf{B}$ is an expanding matrix, we would have $\dim(\mathbf{t}) > \dim(\mathbf{m})$, implying a lower communication cost in our approach. Such expanding matrices are used in different contexts, for example, where a 'gadget' vector/matrix $\mathbf{G}$ multiplies a *scalar* message m, and hence, $\dim(\mathbf{G}m) \gg \dim(m) = 1$.

Thanks to the flexibility of our LANES$^+$ framework, we can support other exact proof systems. Particularly, another concurrent and independent work [44] recently introduced a new exact proof system, that we call the LNP22 proof. Much like LANES, the LNP22 proof is also a commit-and-prove protocol. Since our LANES$^+$ framework makes black-box use of LANES, we can easily adapt LANES$^+$ to work with the LNP22 proof, where the commit-and-prove functionalities of LANES would be replaced with those of the LNP22 proof. However, for our focus of *small* dimensional message vectors, we found that LANES still produces shorter proofs than the LNP22 proof. Particularly, in consultation with Nguyen [51] (an author of [44]), we looked at the LNP22 proof size of the exact proof component needed for our VRF application and found it to be 11.2 KB. This is larger than our 7.1 KB proof size using LANES (see Sect. 6.5). More generally, Nguyen [51] confirmed that the LNP22 proof size lowerbound is at least 10 KB for any useful application. Therefore, for our focus applications with small-dimensional messages in this work, LANES is a better exact proof option than the LNP22 proof. However, for medium-sized message vectors, equipping

---

[3] Note that in this case, we need to hide $\mathbf{w} := \mathbf{A}\mathbf{y}$. Otherwise, everyone could compute $\mathbf{t} - \mathbf{w} = \mathbf{B}\mathbf{m}$, which leaks information on the secret $\mathbf{m}$.

LANES$^+$ with the LNP22 proof as discussed above may result in smaller proof sizes, extending the advantage of LANES$^+$ to a wider application domain.

Rounding Proof Technique. As explained above, our proof of rounding applies our LANES$^+$ framework to the rounding relation $\mathbf{t} = \lfloor \mathbf{Cs} \rfloor_p$ written in the form $\frac{q}{p}\mathbf{t} = \mathbf{Cs} - \mathbf{e}$, where $\mathbf{e} \in [0, q/p-1]^m$ is the rounding error vector and $\mathbf{C}$ is a matrix. Here, we invoke our LANES$^+$ proof with the witness $(\mathbf{m}, \mathbf{r}, \overrightarrow{v}) = (\mathbf{e}, \mathbf{s}, \overrightarrow{b})$, where $\mathbf{e}$ is the (typically short) part of the witness for which the exact proof is needed, $\mathbf{s}$ is the longer part of the witness for which a relaxed proof is sufficient, and $\overrightarrow{b}$ is a β-ary digit decomposition of $\mathbf{e}$ for some small β chosen to optimise the proof length. The main LANES$^+$ matrices are set as $(\mathbf{A}, \mathbf{B}) = (\mathbf{C}, -\mathbf{I})$ to enforce the rounding relation between $\mathbf{s}$ and $\mathbf{e}$, while the LANES$^+$ exact linear relation matrices are set as $(\mathbf{G}_1, \mathbf{G}_2) = (\mathbf{I}, \mathbf{G}_\beta)$, where $\mathbf{G}_\beta$ denotes the β-ary digit reconstruction gadget matrix (having powers of β along its rows) to enforce the β-ary reconstruction relation $\overrightarrow{e} = \mathbf{G}_\beta \overrightarrow{b}$. We set the LANES$^+$ exact polynomial constraint $P(b_i) = \prod_{j \in [\beta]}(b_i - j) = 0$ to enforce the range $[0, \beta - 1]$ for the β-ary digits of $\mathbf{e}$ encoded as the coordinates b_i of $\overrightarrow{b}$. Consequently, the proof length of our call to LANES inside LANES$^+$ depends only on the length of the (short) witness part $\mathbf{e}$ and β, and not on the long witness part $\mathbf{s}$.

Generic Folklore VRF Construction and LaV. A natural way to construct a VRF is to combine a PRF function with a NIZK proof of correct PRF evaluation. In more detail, the VRF public key is a PRF output $\mathsf{pk} = \mathsf{PRF}_{\mathsf{sk}}(0)$ under a VRF/PRF secret key sk. To evaluate the VRF on a message m using secret key sk, we compute $v = \mathsf{PRF}_{\mathsf{sk}}(\mathsf{m})$ as the VRF value. Then, a NIZK proof, π, is generated to prove the well-formedness of values pk and v under the same secret key sk. Here, the pseudorandomness property of PRF is used to provide the VRF pseudorandomness. For the uniqueness of the VRF, we require the PRF to satisfy additional key-homomorphism (as defined in the introduction) and key-binding properties, where the latter ensures that if $\mathsf{PRF}_{\mathsf{sk}_0}(\mathsf{m}) = \mathsf{PRF}_{\mathsf{sk}_1}(\mathsf{m})$, then $\mathsf{sk}_0 = \mathsf{sk}_1$. The soundness of NIZK Π also contributes to uniqueness by ensuring that v is the only output that can pass the NIZK verification test.

We remark that this folklore VRF approach was informally sketched, e.g., in [10, Sect. 1.2]. As discussed in the full version of this work [25], ECVRF [52] and LB-VRF [23] are examples of this paradigm. Our instantiation LaV in this work uses $\mathsf{PRF}_{\mathsf{sk}}(\mathsf{m}) := \lfloor \mathbf{A} \cdot \mathsf{sk} \rfloor_p = \mathbf{v}$ with $\mathbf{A} \leftarrow \mathcal{G}(\mathsf{m})$ for a random oracle $\mathcal{G}$ (where the PRF enjoys an approximate key homomorphism property), based on the Module LWR (MLWR) assumption.

In the context of LaV, the exact guarantee for the rounding error $\mathbf{e}$ in our LANES$^+$-based roundness proof NIZK is essential to guarantee the uniqueness of the VRF (as otherwise the adversary could pass the NIZK verification test with multiple errors $\mathbf{e}$ and break VRF uniqueness). LaV optimizes this generic construction by shrinking the vector $\mathbf{v}$ from a full PRF output to a portion of it (one ring element), and relaxing the NIZK requirement so it does not need to prove exact well-formedness of pk; a relaxed proof is sufficient. This is crucial to the efficiency of LaV as it allows us to use our LANES$^+$ framework as the NIZK Π, without including the long secret key sk in the underlying LANES exact proof.

2   Preliminaries

We use $[n] = \{0, \ldots, n-1\}$ for $n \in \mathbb{Z}^+$ and $\mathbb{Z}_q = [-(q-1)/2, (q-1)/2]$ for an odd modulus q. We utilize polynomial rings of the form $\mathcal{R}_{q,d} = \mathbb{Z}_q[X]/(X^d + 1)$ for power-of-2 d and modulus $q \geq 2$. For a positive integer $c \leq q/2$, $\mathbb{S}_{c,d}$ denotes the set of polynomials in $\mathcal{R}_{q,d}$ with infinity norm at most c (w.r.t. the monomial (coefficient) basis). For a vector $\mathbf{x} \in \mathcal{R}_{q,d}^n$, $\overrightarrow{\mathbf{x}} \in \mathbb{Z}_q^{dn}$ denotes the (concatenated) coefficient vector of $\mathbf{x}$. In general, we will write $\overrightarrow{x}$ to denote vectors over $\mathbb{Z}_q$ and $\mathbf{x}$ to denote vectors over $\mathcal{R}_{q,d}$. We write $\lfloor \overrightarrow{x} \rfloor_p$ to denote $\lfloor \frac{p}{q} \cdot \overrightarrow{x} \rfloor$ for $\overrightarrow{x} \in \mathbb{Z}_q^m$, where the rounding is done coordinate-wise. The same notation extends analogously to vectors over $\mathcal{R}_{q,d}$ by applying the rounding to the coefficient vector. In this paper, we use the rounding down operation, but our results easily extend to the rounding up or to the closest integer operations. For an element of and a matrix over $\mathcal{R}_{q,d}$, we write $\mathsf{Rot}(f)$ and $\mathsf{Rot}(\mathbf{A})$, respectively, to denote its representative matrix over $\mathbb{Z}_q$. For vectors $\overrightarrow{x}$ and $\overrightarrow{y}$ over $\mathbb{Z}_q$, $\overrightarrow{x} \circ \overrightarrow{y}$ denotes coordinate-wise multiplication. We use $\bigcirc$ to denote coordinate-wise multiplication over a set of elements. $\mathsf{HW}(f)$ denotes the Hamming weight of the coefficient vector of $f \in \mathcal{R}_{q,d}$, and $\mathbb{D}_{\sigma,d}$ denotes the d-dimensional discrete Gaussian distribution with standard deviation σ and center 0. Due to limited space, some preliminaries including formal VRF definitions, MSIS/MLWR definitions, and rejection sampling are deferred to the full version of this work [25].

The following fact plays an important role in our rounding proof and VRF.

Fact 1 (adapted from [41]). *Let $\overrightarrow{u} \in \mathbb{Z}_q^n$ and $\overrightarrow{v} \in \mathbb{Z}_p^n$ for $q > p$, where p divides q. Then, $\overrightarrow{v} = \lfloor \overrightarrow{u} \rfloor_p$ if and only if there exists $\overrightarrow{e} \in \mathbb{Z}^n$ such that $\overrightarrow{e} \in [q/p]^n$ and $\overrightarrow{e} = \overrightarrow{u} - \frac{q}{p} \cdot \overrightarrow{v} \pmod{q}$.*

2.1   NIZK and Commit-and-Prove Protocols

We define a commit-and-prove (CP) protocol [16,38] similar to the descriptions provided in [22]. Particularly, let ck, x and w denote a commitment key, a statement and a witness, respectively. Further, let $R_\mathcal{L}$ be a polynomial-time verifiable relation containing tuples (ck, x, w). We define a language $\mathcal{L}_{\mathsf{ck}}$ as the set of statements for which there exists a witness w with $(\mathsf{ck}, x, w) \in R_\mathcal{L}$. In general, a CP protocol allows one to commit to a sequence of messages $m = (m_1, \ldots, m_N)$ for $N \geq 1$ and prove certain statements about the committed messages. For a commitment output, we will have a pair $(t; t')$ of public-secret outputs, where the latter needs to be retained by the prover for further steps.

Formally, a commit-and-prove protocol consists of four polynomial time algorithms $\Pi = (\Pi.\mathsf{Gen}, \Pi.\mathsf{Com}, \Pi.\mathsf{Prove}, \Pi.\mathsf{Ver})$ as follows.

$\mathsf{pp} \leftarrow \Pi.\mathsf{Gen}(1^\lambda)$: On input a security parameter λ, generate a commitment key ck, which also specifies a message space $\mathcal{S}_M$, a randomness space $\mathcal{S}_R$ and a commitment space $\mathcal{S}_C$. Generate further system parameters pp', if needed, and output $\mathsf{pp} = (\mathsf{ck}, \mathsf{pp}')$

$(t; t') \leftarrow \Pi.\mathsf{Com}_{\mathsf{pp}}(m; r)$: On input public parameters pp containing a commitment key ck, a message $m \in \mathcal{S}_M$ and a randomness $r \in \mathcal{S}_R$, output a commitment $t \in \mathcal{S}_C$ along with its secret opening t'.

$\pi \leftarrow \Pi.\mathsf{Prove}_{\mathsf{pp}}(x, (t; t'))$: On input a statement x and commitment output pair $(t; t')$, output a proof π.

$0/1 \leftarrow \Pi.\mathsf{Ver}_{\mathsf{pp}}(x, t, \pi)$: On input a statement x, a commitment t and a proof π, output 1 if the proof is accepted. Otherwise, output 0.

If a set of messages are committed in sequence, then we write $(\overrightarrow{t}; \overrightarrow{t'}) \leftarrow \Pi.\mathsf{Com}_{\mathsf{pp}}(\overrightarrow{m}; \overrightarrow{r})$ to denote $(t_i, t'_i) \leftarrow \Pi.\mathsf{Com}_{\mathsf{pp}}(m_i; r_i)$ where $\overrightarrow{m} = (m_1, \ldots, m_N)$, $\overrightarrow{r} = (r_1, \ldots, r_N)$, $\overrightarrow{t} = (t_1, \ldots, t_N)$ and $\overrightarrow{t'} = (t'_1, \ldots, t'_N)$. We next provide the properties of a CP protocol, which are similar to those in [22,47].

Definition 1 (Correctness). *A commit-and-prove protocol* $\Pi = (\Pi.\mathsf{Gen}, \Pi.\mathsf{Com}, \Pi.\mathsf{Prove}, \Pi.\mathsf{Ver})$ *has statistical correctness if the following probability is negligible in* λ *for all adversaries* $\mathcal{A}$

$$\Pr \left[\begin{array}{l} \mathsf{pp} \leftarrow \Pi.\mathsf{Gen}(1^\lambda); (x, \overrightarrow{m}, \overrightarrow{r}) \leftarrow \mathcal{A}(\mathsf{pp}); \\ (\overrightarrow{t}; \overrightarrow{t'}) \leftarrow \Pi.\mathsf{Com}_{\mathsf{pp}}(\overrightarrow{m}; \overrightarrow{r}); \\ \pi \leftarrow \Pi.\mathsf{Prove}_{\mathsf{pp}}(x, (\overrightarrow{t}; \overrightarrow{t'})) \end{array} : \Pi.\mathsf{Ver}_{\mathsf{pp}}(x, \overrightarrow{t}, \pi) = 0 \right],$$

where $\mathcal{A}$ *outputs* $\overrightarrow{m} \in \mathcal{S}_M^N$ *and* $\overrightarrow{r} \in \mathcal{S}_R^N$ *for some* $N \geq 1$ *with* $(ck, x, \overrightarrow{m}) \in R_{\mathcal{L}}$.

Since our protocols rely on LANES, we define simulatability as in [47], where the randomness for the commitment is sampled properly (from χ) as it would be in the real-world protocol.

Definition 2 (Simulatability). *A commit-and-prove protocol* $\Pi = (\Pi.\mathsf{Gen}, \Pi.\mathsf{Com}, \Pi.\mathsf{Prove}, \Pi.\mathsf{Ver})$ *is simulatable if for all PPT adversaries* $\mathcal{A}$, *there exist PPT simulators* SimC *and* SimP *such that the following holds*

$$\Pr \left[\begin{array}{l} \mathsf{pp} = (ck, \mathsf{pp}') \leftarrow \Pi.\mathsf{Gen}(1^\lambda); (x, \overrightarrow{m}) \leftarrow \mathcal{A}(\mathsf{pp}); \\ \overrightarrow{r} \leftarrow \chi^N; (\overrightarrow{t}, \overrightarrow{t'}) \leftarrow \Pi.\mathsf{Com}_{\mathsf{pp}}(\overrightarrow{m}; \overrightarrow{r}); \\ \pi \leftarrow \Pi.\mathsf{Prove}_{\mathsf{pp}}(x, (\overrightarrow{t}; \overrightarrow{t'})) \end{array} : \begin{array}{l} (ck, x, \overrightarrow{m}) \in R_{\mathcal{L}} \\ \wedge \mathcal{A}(\overrightarrow{t}, \pi) = 1 \end{array} \right]$$

$$\approx \Pr \left[\begin{array}{l} \mathsf{pp} = (ck, \mathsf{pp}') \leftarrow \Pi.\mathsf{Gen}(1^\lambda); (x, \overrightarrow{m}) \leftarrow \mathcal{A}(\mathsf{pp}); \\ \overrightarrow{t} \leftarrow \mathsf{SimC}_{\mathsf{pp}}(x); \\ \pi \leftarrow \mathsf{SimP}_{\mathsf{pp}}(x, \overrightarrow{t}) \end{array} : \begin{array}{l} (ck, x, \overrightarrow{m}) \in R_{\mathcal{L}} \\ \wedge \mathcal{A}(\overrightarrow{t}, \pi) = 1 \end{array} \right],$$

where χ *is a probability distribution on* $\mathcal{S}_R$.

Definition 3 (Knowledge Soundness). *A commit-and-prove protocol* $\Pi = (\Pi.\mathsf{Gen}, \Pi.\mathsf{Com}, \Pi.\mathsf{Prove}, \Pi.\mathsf{Ver})$ *satisfies knowledge soundness if for all PPT adversaries* $\mathcal{A}$, *there exists an expected polynomial time extractor* $\mathcal{E}$ *such that the following probability is negligible in* λ

$$\Pr \left[\begin{array}{l} \mathsf{pp} = (ck, \mathsf{pp}') \leftarrow \Pi.\mathsf{Gen}(1^\lambda); \\ (x, \overrightarrow{t}, \pi) \leftarrow \mathcal{A}(\mathsf{pp}; \rho); \\ (\overrightarrow{m}^*; \overrightarrow{r}^*) \leftarrow \mathcal{E}(\mathsf{pp}, \rho) \end{array} : \begin{array}{l} \Pi.\mathsf{Ver}_{\mathsf{pp}}(x, \overrightarrow{t}, \pi) = 1 \wedge \\ \left((ck, x, \overrightarrow{m}) \notin R_{\mathcal{L}} \vee \Pi.\mathsf{Com}_{\mathsf{pp}}(\overrightarrow{m}^*; \overrightarrow{r}^*) \neq \overrightarrow{t} \right) \end{array} \right],$$

where $\mathcal{E}$ *outputs* $\overrightarrow{m}^* \in \mathcal{S}_M^N$ *and* $\overrightarrow{r}^* \in \mathcal{S}_R^N$ *for some* $N \geq 1$.

Our soundness definition is similar to the special soundness of Sigma protocols since our application protocols in this work are of the form of a Sigma protocol, but made non-interactive using the Fiat-Shamir transformation. LANES protocol has actually 5 moves with an additional 'randomization' move, but still relies on the standard rewinding arguments for soundness. When proving knowledge soundness of our proposals, we will similarly use standard rewinding arguments where the extractor rewinds the adversary to a specific point and, e.g., provides a different random oracle output.

For efficient lattice-based proofs, it is necessary to relax the soundness requirement and have $(\mathsf{ck}, x, \vec{m}) \in \bar{R}_{\mathcal{L}}$ for $R_{\mathcal{L}} \subseteq \bar{R}_{\mathcal{L}}$. We adopt the same relaxation as in many prior works, e.g., [26, 27, 47]. Therefore, while correctness and simulatability are defined w.r.t. to a *base* relation $R_{\mathcal{L}}$, the soundness only guarantees the extraction of a witness for an *extended* relation $\bar{R}_{\mathcal{L}}$. An honest prover's witness is in $R_{\mathcal{L}}$ (i.e., an honest run of Π uses a witness from $R_{\mathcal{L}}$).

As discussed in [22], a CP protocol is a generalization of a standard non-interactive zero-knowledge (NIZK) proof, where the same commitment outputs can be used across multiple NIZKs. Therefore, when considering a NIZK, we use the same syntax above while omitting $\Pi.\mathsf{Com}$, the commitment key ck in the elements of $R_{\mathcal{L}}$ and the commitment output t (and t') in $\Pi.\mathsf{Prove}$ and $\Pi.\mathsf{Ver}$.

2.2   Desired PRF Properties

A Pseudorandom Function (PRF) is a function that maps an input message m to a random-looking output v under a secret key sk, i.e., $v = \mathsf{PRF}_{\mathsf{sk}}(\mathsf{m})$. We denote the key space by $\mathcal{K}$, and output space by $\mathcal{T}$. We require a PRF to satisfy the standard pseudorandomness property where no polynomial-time adversary having adaptive oracle access to the PRF function can distinguish PRF outputs (under a random key) from independent uniformly random elements in $\mathcal{T}$ with an advantage non-negligible in the security parameter λ. We let κ be the number of oracle queries allowed in the pseudorandomness game. We sometimes write κ-pseudorandomness to explicitly denote the number of PRF oracle queries allowed in the pseudorandomness game. Some prior VRF constructions such as [23] only allow a small κ value. As our lattice-based PRF in this work satisfies the standard pseudorandomness and allows for up to $\kappa = 2^{\lambda}$ evaluations (where $\lambda = 128$ for our parameter settings, see Sect. 6), it results in a standard VRF construction. For the folklore VRF construction based on a PRF, we additionally require the following PRF properties. We note that these properties are defined w.r.t. an *extended key space* $\mathcal{K}'$ to accommodate for the relaxed soundness of efficient lattice-based proofs.

Key-Binding. A PRF is *statistically key-binding w.r.t. extended key space $\mathcal{K}'$* with $\mathcal{K} \subseteq \mathcal{K}'$ if the following probability over the randomness of an adversary $\mathcal{A}$ is negligible

$$\Pr\left[(\mathsf{m}, k_0, k_1) \leftarrow \mathcal{A} : k_1 \neq k_0 \in \mathcal{K}' \wedge \mathsf{PRF}_{k_1}(\mathsf{m}) = \mathsf{PRF}_{k_0}(\mathsf{m}) \right].$$

If the adversary $\mathcal{A}$ is assumed to be PPT, then the PRF is said to be *computationally key-binding*.

Additive Key-Homomorphism. The extended key space $\mathcal{K}'$ is a subset of a module with operations $(+, \cdot)$ over some underlying commutative scalar ring $\mathfrak{R}$, the output space $\mathcal{T}$ is a subset of a module with operations $(\oplus, \otimes)$ over $\mathfrak{R}$, and there exists a 'homomorphism' space $S \subseteq \mathfrak{R}$ of scalars such that for any keys $k_0, k_1 \in \mathcal{K}'$, message m and scalar $\alpha \in S$, we have $\mathsf{PRF}_{\alpha \cdot k_0 + k_1}(\mathsf{m}) = \alpha \otimes \mathsf{PRF}_{k_0}(\mathsf{m}) \oplus \mathsf{PRF}_{k_1}(\mathsf{m})$.

2.3 Folklore VRF from PRF and NIZK

We now present the folklore approach to constructing a VRF based on a PRF and a NIZK proof. Our treatment is a bit more general than the traditional idea to accommodate for the relaxations in efficient lattice-based NIZKs. We note that our PRF and NIZK instantiations in this work are in the random oracle model. We also remark that the PRF in this section can also be viewed as a commitment scheme by interpreting $\mathsf{PRF}_k(\mathsf{m}) = \mathsf{Com}_{\mathsf{ck}}(k)$, where $\mathsf{ck} \leftarrow \mathcal{G}(\mathsf{m})$ for a random oracle $\mathcal{G}$ mapping messages to commitment keys and the key k serves as the commitment randomness.

Let PRF be a PRF defined as in Sect. 2.2 and Π be a NIZK, proving the following relation

$$R_{\mathrm{vrf}} = \left\{ ((\mathsf{m}, \mathsf{pk}, v), (f, k)) \; : \; \begin{array}{c} f \otimes \mathsf{pk} = \mathsf{PRF}_k(0) \wedge f \otimes v = \mathsf{PRF}_k(\mathsf{m}) \\ \wedge f \in F \wedge f' \cdot k \in \mathcal{K}' \quad \forall f' \in F \end{array} \right\}, \quad (6)$$

for a message m, a public key pk, a PRF output v, and a set $F \subseteq \mathfrak{R}$ of "relaxation factors". To allow for the use of *efficient* lattice-based zero-knowledge proofs, it is necessary to relax the relation guaranteed by the NIZK and, therefore, we introduce a *relaxation factor* f. For standard NIZKs outside of the lattice setting, we simply have $f = 1$ (and $F = \{1\}$), but efficient proofs in the lattice setting have a *soundness gap*, where the proved relation has the additional relaxation factor while an *honest* prover would simply use $f = 1$. Hence, we allow the existence of such a relaxation factor as, e.g., in [26,27]. We show in the uniqueness proof of the VRF how to handle this relaxation (see Theorem 1). We next describe the generic VRF construction.

V.ParamGen$(1^\lambda, \mathsf{PRF}, \Pi)$: Generate NIZK public parameters $\mathsf{pp} \leftarrow \Pi.\mathsf{Gen}(1^\lambda)$, and output pp.

V.KeyGen(pp): Sample a randomness $k \xleftarrow{\$} \mathcal{K}$ and compute $\mathsf{pk} \leftarrow \mathsf{PRF}_k(0)$. Return $(\mathsf{pk}, \mathsf{sk})$ for $\mathsf{sk} = k$.

V.Eval$_{\mathsf{pp}}(\mathsf{pk}, \mathsf{sk}, \mathsf{m})$: Given the message m, together with the key pair pk and $\mathsf{sk} = k$, proceed as follows:
  – Compute $v \leftarrow \mathsf{PRF}_k(\mathsf{m})$.
  – Run the NIZK proof system to generate a proof for the relation in (6).

$$\pi \leftarrow \Pi.\mathsf{Prove}_{\mathsf{pp}}((\mathsf{m}, \mathsf{pk}, v), (v; k)).$$

  – Output v as the VRF value and π as the proof.

V.Verify$_{\mathsf{pp}}(\mathsf{pk}, \mathsf{m}, v, \pi)$: This algorithm verifies the VRF value v as below.
  – Return $\Pi.\mathsf{Ver}_{\mathsf{pp}}(\mathsf{m}, \mathsf{pk}, v, \pi)$.

The full version of this work [25] discusses some of the example instantiations in the literature.

Security Analysis. We prove that the above VRF framework satisfies uniqueness (defined in the full version of this work [25]), and also state pseudorandomness requirements. The proof of pseudorandomness follows from simulatability of Π and pseudorandomness of PRF as detailed in the full version of this work [25].

Theorem 1. *If the NIZK proof Π is statistically (resp. computationally) sound, the PRF PRF is statistically (resp. computationally) key-binding with respect to extended key space $\mathcal{K}'$ and additively key-homomorphic, the set of relaxation factors F is a subset of the homomorphism space (i.e., $F \subseteq S$), and any element of F is invertible in $\mathfrak{R}$, then the generic VRF constructed over (PRF, Π) in Sect. 2.3 satisfies unconditional (resp. computational) uniqueness.*

Proof. Suppose that an adversary $\mathcal{A}$ produces $(\mathsf{m}, \mathsf{pk}, v_1, \pi_1, v_2, \pi_2)$ such that $\mathsf{V.Verify}_{\mathsf{pp}}(\mathsf{pk}, \mathsf{m}, v_1, \pi_1) = \mathsf{V.Verify}_{\mathsf{pp}}(\mathsf{pk}, \mathsf{m}, v_2, \pi_2) = 1$. We want to show that $v_1 = v_2$.

Now, we use the extractor $\mathcal{E}$ of Π to extract (f_1^*, k_1^*) and (f_2^*, k_2^*) such that $((\mathsf{m}, \mathsf{pk}, v_1), (f_1^*, k_1^*)) \in R_{\mathsf{vrf}}$ and $((\mathsf{m}, \mathsf{pk}, v_2), (f_2^*, k_2^*)) \in R_{\mathsf{vrf}}$. If Π is *computationally* sound, then the extraction works against a PPT $\mathcal{A}$ (except for a negligible probability). Then, we get the following expressions

$$f_1^* \otimes \mathsf{pk} = \mathsf{PRF}_{k_1^*}(0) \implies f_2^* \otimes f_1^* \otimes \mathsf{pk} = \mathsf{PRF}_{f_2^* \cdot k_1^*}(0), \tag{7}$$

$$f_1^* \otimes v_1 = \mathsf{PRF}_{k_1^*}(\mathsf{m}), \tag{8}$$

$$f_2^* \otimes \mathsf{pk} = \mathsf{PRF}_{k_2^*}(0) \implies f_1^* \otimes f_2^* \otimes \mathsf{pk} = \mathsf{PRF}_{f_1^* \cdot k_2^*}(0), \tag{9}$$

$$f_2^* \otimes v_2 = \mathsf{PRF}_{k_2^*}(\mathsf{m}). \tag{10}$$

By the statistical (resp. computational) key-binding property of PRF, $\mathfrak{R}$ being commutative, and (7) and (9), we must have $f_2^* \cdot k_1^* = f_1^* \cdot k_2^*$ over $\mathfrak{R}$ against the (resp. PPT) adversary $\mathcal{A}$ except for a negligible probability.

Then, by (8) and (10), and the key-homomorphism of PRF, we get

$$f_2^* \otimes f_1^* \otimes v_1 = \mathsf{PRF}_{f_2^* \cdot k_1^*}(\mathsf{m}) = \mathsf{PRF}_{f_1^* \cdot k_2^*}(\mathsf{m}) = f_1^* \otimes f_2^* \otimes v_2,$$

where the middle equality follows from the fact that $f_2^* \cdot k_1^* = f_1^* \cdot k_2^*$ over $\mathfrak{R}$. Hence, we get $f_2^* \otimes f_1^* \otimes v_1 = f_1^* \otimes f_2^* \otimes v_2$, and thus $v_1 = v_2$ by the relaxation factor invertibility property. $\qquad\qquad\square$

Remark 1. Note in the above uniqueness proof that, the key-binding property of the PRF is only applied on pk, and not on (v_1, v_2). Hence, it is in fact sufficient if v is generated via a weaker PRF evaluation *without* a key-binding property, which is one of the optimizations we employ in LaV in Sect. 6.3.

Theorem 2. *If the PRF PRF has κ-pseudorandomness for $\kappa \geq 1$, and Π is simulatable, then the generic VRF constructed over (PRF, Π) in Sect. 2.3 is κ-pseudorandom.*

2.4   LANES Framework

In this section, we recall the LANES framework [3,24,46] without going into its technical details as we will use it as a black-box. Our description is similar to that in [46]. The framework allows one to prove (unstructured) linear and multiplicative relations over $\mathbb{Z}_q$ about a committed message without leaking the secret message information. The zero-knowledge proof is performed over a polynomial ring $\mathcal{R}_{q,d} = \mathbb{Z}_q[X]/(X^d + 1)$ for a power-of-2 d while allowing $\mathcal{R}_{q,d}$ to split into l sub-rings for a parameter $2 \leq l \leq d$ by choosing a prime modulus q with $q \equiv 2l + 1 \pmod{4l}$. We stress here that even though the proof is performed over $\mathcal{R}_{q,d}$, the proved relations hold over $\mathbb{Z}_q$.[4] Suppose that the prover $\mathcal{P}$ has a vector $\overrightarrow{m} = (\overrightarrow{m}_1, \ldots, \overrightarrow{m}_N)$ with $\overrightarrow{m}_i \in \mathbb{Z}_q^l$ for $N \geq 1$ and wants to prove the satisfiability of a public set, mp, of polynomials in N variables (for multiplicative proof) $P_i : (\mathbb{Z}_q^l)^N \to \mathbb{Z}_q^{\gamma_i l}$ with maximal degree α and $\gamma_i \geq 1$, where addition and multiplication are done component-wise. Further, we let $\mathsf{ulp} = (\mathbf{A}, \overrightarrow{u}) \in \mathbb{Z}_q^{vl \times Nl} \times \mathbb{Z}_q^{vl}$ denote the public statement of the linear relation the prover wants to prove (i.e., $\mathbf{A}\overrightarrow{m} = \overrightarrow{u}$). One simply pads zero rows, if needed, to make sure that the number of rows of $\mathbf{A}$ is a multiple of l. We also define k as the smallest positive integer such that $q^{-kd/l}$ is negligible.

Overall, the LANES framework proves knowledge of $\overrightarrow{m} \in \mathcal{L}(\mathsf{mp}, \mathsf{ulp})$ for

$$\mathcal{L}(\mathsf{mp}, \mathsf{ulp}) = \left\{ \overrightarrow{m} \in \mathbb{Z}_q^{Nl} : \forall P \in \mathsf{mp},\, P(\overrightarrow{m}) = \overrightarrow{0} \bmod q \wedge \mathbf{A}\overrightarrow{m} = \overrightarrow{u} \bmod q \right\}.$$

That is, the target relation R_{LANES} for a commitment key ck is the following

$$(\mathsf{ck}, (\mathsf{mp}, \mathsf{ulp}), \overrightarrow{m}) \in R_{\mathsf{LANES}} \iff \overrightarrow{m} \in \mathcal{L}(\mathsf{mp}, \mathsf{ulp}). \tag{11}$$

Let us present LANES as a CP protocol as described in Sect. 2.1, where the commitment scheme is instantiated using the BDLOP commitment [7].

$\mathsf{pp} \leftarrow \mathsf{LANES.Gen}(1^\lambda)$: generate a commitment key ck for the BDLOP commitment, specifying the message, randomness and commitment spaces. Generate further systems parameters pp', if needed. Output $\mathsf{pp} = (\mathsf{ck}, \mathsf{pp}')$.

$(t; t') \leftarrow \mathsf{LANES.Com}_{\mathsf{pp}}(\overrightarrow{m})$: sample a randomness $\mathbf{r} \in \mathbb{S}_1^{n+\ell+N+\alpha}$ for the BDLOP commitment and commit to the message $\hat{\mathbf{m}} = (\hat{\mathbf{m}}_1, \ldots, \hat{\mathbf{m}}_N) \in \mathcal{R}_{q,d}^N$ where $\hat{\mathbf{m}}_i$ is the polynomial in $\mathcal{R}_{q,d}$ whose CRT coefficient vector is $\overrightarrow{m}_i$ for $i = 1, \ldots, N$. Output the commitment t and the secret state information t'.

$\pi \leftarrow \mathsf{LANES.Prove}_{\mathsf{pp}}((\mathsf{mp}, \mathsf{ulp}), (t; t'))$: run a NIZK proof (see, e.g., [46, Fig. 8]) to prove relation (11) for $\overrightarrow{m}$. Output a proof π.

$0/1 \leftarrow \mathsf{LANES.Ver}_{\mathsf{pp}}((\mathsf{mp}, \mathsf{ulp}), t, \pi)$: Check that π is a valid proof of knowledge for the relation (11).

The LANES output (t, π) requires (without compression) a total communication of $(n + N + \alpha + 1)d \log q + k \cdot (n + \ell + N + \alpha)d \log(12\mathfrak{s})$ bits, where $\mathfrak{s}$ denotes the standard deviation of the discrete Gaussian distribution that the masked randomness follows. Note that the communication size only depends

---

[4] We note here that for $l < d$, the proved relations actually hold over $\mathbb{F}_{q^{d/l}}$. However, with a shortness proof of the form $P_i(x) = \prod_{j \in [\beta]}(x - j)$ for some $\beta < q \in \mathbb{Z}^+$, the proved relation is restricted to $\mathbb{Z}_q \subseteq \mathbb{F}_{q^{d/l}}$. This is explained further in [24, App. A]. We have such a shortness proof for all of our applications in this work, and therefore, our description is focused on $\mathbb{Z}_q$.

on the maximal polynomial degree α, not the individual degrees of P_i's. With the compression techniques in [4, 21] and considering the entropy of the discrete Gaussian (instead of a worst-case tail bound), the output size can be reduced to about (neglecting the size of very small "hints")

$$nd(\log q - D) + (N + \alpha + 1)d \log q + k \cdot (\ell + N + \alpha)d \log(4.13 \cdot \mathfrak{s}) \quad \text{bits,} \quad (12)$$

where D denotes the number of least significant bits dropped from commitment (a.k.a. *commitment compression*). A typical choice of D is around 13. The constant 4.13 is the result of our empirical tests that showed the entropy of a discrete Gaussian variable with standard deviation $\mathfrak{s}$ is very close to $\log(4.13 \cdot \mathfrak{s})$ for a wide range of parameters. A reasonable choice of the standard deviation would be $\mathfrak{s} \approx w\sqrt{k(\ell + N + \alpha)d}$ when using the optimized rejection sampling in [47], where w is an upper-bound on the ℓ_1-norm of the challenge c used in the protocol (see, e.g., the fourth move of [24, Fig. 3]). Alternatively, we can use the very recent results of [39] to set $\mathfrak{s} \approx 2\sqrt{2}w\mathfrak{s}_0$ for $\mathfrak{s}_0 = \sqrt{\ln(2d(1 + 1/\varepsilon))}/\pi$ with, e.g., $\varepsilon = 2^{-100}$. The advantages in the latter case are (i) $\mathfrak{s}$ is independent of the (dimension) parameters (k, ℓ, N, α, d), (ii) no rejection sampling (inside LANES) is needed, and (iii) the security argument relies on the standard MLWE assumption (instead of the "Extended-MLWE" assumption in [47]).

It is important to note that the commitment phase LANES.Com does not rely on the multiplicative-linear relations (mp, ulp), which we will exploit in Sect. 4. The soundness and zero-knowledge/simulatability properties of this framework were established in [3, 24, 46] and we refer the reader to them for more details.

A classical use-case of LANES is to prove knowledge of a message $\overrightarrow{m}$ with small coordinates, say in $[0, T - 1]$ with $T < q$, that also satisfies a linear relation $\mathbf{A}\overrightarrow{m} = \overrightarrow{u}$.[5] Using base-$\beta$ integer decomposition (a.k.a. 'gadget') matrices, the latter relation can easily be transformed into an equivalent relation $\mathbf{A}'\overrightarrow{m}' = \overrightarrow{u}$, where $T = \beta^r$ and $\overrightarrow{m}'$ is r times bigger than $\overrightarrow{m}$ (i.e., $\dim(\overrightarrow{m}') = r \cdot \dim(\overrightarrow{m})$). In this case, it is sufficient to prove that $m_i(m_i - 1) \cdots (m_i - (\beta - 1)) = 0$ for each coordinate m_i of $\overrightarrow{m}'$. This is a multiplicative relation of degree $\alpha = \beta$ that will contribute to mp. Looking now at the proof length in (12), for such protocols, the LANES framework performs the best by choosing α that minimizes $\dim(\overrightarrow{m}') + \alpha = N \cdot r + \alpha = N \cdot \log_\alpha(T) + \alpha$.

In the rest of the paper, we will use hatted notations like $\hat{d}, \hat{q}$ to distinguish the parameters of LANES from the rest of the protocol (if they are indeed different).

3   Generalized Challenge Difference Invertibility Results

In this section, we generalize recent results [3, 28] on invertibility of challenge differences in polynomial rings based on Fourier analysis. Our generalization

---

[5] We note here that one does not necessarily need to consider positive ranges $[0, T-1]$. It is straightforward to "shift" the range to support a more general range $[a, b]$ with $a \leq b \in \mathbb{Z}$. For example, proving knowledge of $\overrightarrow{m} \in [a, b]^N$ with $\mathbf{A}\overrightarrow{m} = \overrightarrow{u}$ is equivalent to proving knowledge of $\overrightarrow{m}' \in [0, b - a]^N$ such that $\mathbf{A}\overrightarrow{m}' = \overrightarrow{u}'$ for $\overrightarrow{u}' := \overrightarrow{u} - \mathbf{A}\overrightarrow{a}^N$ and $\overrightarrow{a}^N := (a, \dots, a) \in \mathbb{Z}^N$. Hence, the important part is the width, T, of the range.

extends the *Partition-and-Sample* (PaS) challenge distribution of [28] and the results of [3] to allow challenge polynomials of infinity norm γ for any $\gamma \geq 1$, extending the case $\gamma = 1$ in [3,28]. We require the $\gamma > 1$ case for our efficient VRF construction in Sect. 6.

Let $l \leq d$ be powers of 2 and $q \equiv 2l+1 \pmod{4l}$ and $\delta := d/l$. Fix a primitive $2l$'th root of unity ζ in $\mathbb{Z}_q$. Then, the polynomial $X^d + 1$ factors into l irreducible polynomials $g_i(X) := X^\delta + \zeta_i$ modulo q, where for $i \in [l]$, $\zeta_i := \zeta^{2i+1}$ are the primitive $(2l)$-th roots of unity in $\mathbb{Z}_q$.

For $a(X) \in \mathcal{R}_{q,d}$ and $i \in [l]$, we denote by $a\{i\}(X) := a(X) \bmod g_i(X)$ the i'th CRT slot of $a(X)$. Let $\mathbb{S}_{\gamma,d}^{(\delta)}$ be the set of polynomials in $\mathbb{S}_{\gamma,d}$ of the form $f(X) = f_0 + f_\delta X^\delta + \cdots + f_{(l-1)\delta} X^{(l-1)\delta}$. Our bounds apply to the challenge set $\mathcal{C}$, defined as

$$\mathcal{C} = \left\{ \tilde{c}_0 + \tilde{c}_1 X + \cdots + \tilde{c}_{\delta-1} X^{\delta-1} : \tilde{c}_i \in \mathbb{S}_{\gamma,d}^{(\delta)} \wedge \mathsf{HW}(\tilde{c}_i) \leq \tilde{w} \right\}. \quad (13)$$

Note that challenges $c(X) = \sum_{k=0}^{\delta-1} \tilde{c}_i(X) X^k$ in $\mathcal{C}$ have total Hamming weight $w \leq \delta\tilde{w}$ with non-zero coefficients in $[-\gamma, +\gamma]$, and the coefficient index set $S_k := \{j \in [d] : j = k \bmod \delta\}$ appearing in $\tilde{c}_k(X)$ has weight $\leq \tilde{w}$ for each $k \in [\delta]$. We consider the challenge probability distribution $\mathfrak{C}$ on $\mathcal{C}$ defined as follows: for each $k \in [\delta]$, we choose a uniformly random subset $T_k \subset S_k$ of size $|T_k| = \tilde{w}$ and independently sample each challenge coefficient in T_k to be zero with probability p_z and uniformly random on $[-\gamma, +\gamma] \setminus 0$ with probability $1 - p_z$.

Lemma 1 (Generalization of [28, Lemma 1] and [3, Lemma 3.3]). *Let P_2 denote the probability distribution of the coefficient $\tilde{c}_{i,k}$ of X^k in the i'th CRT slot $c\{i\} = c(X) \bmod g_i(X)$ of a challenge $c(X)$ sampled from the distribution $\mathfrak{C}$ on $\mathcal{C}$ defined above. Then, for $\eta := \frac{l^{\tilde{w}}(l-\tilde{w})!}{l!}$ and all $i \in [l]$ and $k \in [\delta]$, we have:*

$$\max_y P_2(y) \leq \min(M_2, N_2), \quad (14)$$

$$M_2 := \frac{\eta}{q} \left(1 + 2l \sum_{j \in \mathbb{Z}_q^* / <\zeta_i>} |\hat{\mu}(j)|^{\tilde{w}} \right), \quad (15)$$

$$N_2 := \frac{1}{q} \left(1 + 2l \sum_{j \in \mathbb{Z}_q^* / <\zeta_i>} |\hat{P}_2(j)| \right), \quad (16)$$

and for $j \in \mathbb{Z}_q^* / <\zeta_i>$, we define

$$\hat{\mu}(j) := \frac{1}{l} \sum_{k \in [l]} \hat{\mu}_k(j), \quad (17)$$

$$\hat{P}_2(j) := \frac{1}{\binom{l}{\tilde{w}}} \sum_{S \subset [l], |S| = \tilde{w}} \prod_{k \in S} \hat{\mu}_k(j), \quad (18)$$

$$\hat{\mu}_k(j) := p_z + \frac{1 - p_z}{\gamma} \sum_{b \in [1,\gamma]} \cos(2\pi j b \zeta_i^k / q). \quad (19)$$

Table 2. Sample challenge space parameters and challenge difference invertibility bounds over $\mathcal{R}_{q,d}$. Here, q and γ are minimised subject to challenge invertibility probability bound $p_{\mathrm{inv}} \leq 2^{-90}$ computed using Corollary 1.

q	d	l	$\tilde{w}$	γ	$\log_2 p_{\mathrm{inv}}$	$|\mathcal{C}|$
61	32	2	2	16	-91.5	2^{160}
13	64	2	2	2	-99	2^{128}

The proof of the above lemma is provided in the full version of this work [25]. Using the independence of the δ coefficients of each CRT slot, and the fact that a challenge difference $c(X) - c'(X)$ is non-invertible in $\mathcal{R}_{q,d}$ if and only if one of its CRT slots is 0, we immediately get the following corollary.

Corollary 1 (Generalization of [28, Corollary 1]). *Let $c(X), c'(X)$ denote a pair of challenges independently sampled from distribution $\mathfrak{C}$. The probability that $c(X) - c'(X)$ is not invertible in $\mathcal{R}_{q,d}$ is upper bounded by $p_{\mathrm{inv}} := l \min(M_2, N_2)^{\delta}$, where M_2, N_2 are the bounds from Lemma 1.*

We remark that as in [28], we can split the computation of the invertibility bound of Corollary 1 into two phases. In the longer pre-computation step that does not depend on w, we compute a table of $\hat{\mu}$ and in the faster post-computation step, we compute the bound M_2 using this table. The computation time cost $O(q/l)$ of our post-computation step is similar to that in [28]. However, our table pre-computation step computation time cost is $O(\gamma q/l)$, which is $O(\gamma)$ times larger than the table computation time in [28] in the case $\gamma = 1$. Table 2 shows the resulting computed bounds for two sets of challenge space parameter choices. Our actual optimised VRF parameter set in Sect. 6.5 uses the parameters in the first row of the table ($d = 32$).

4   LANES$^+$: a Framework for Hybrid Exact/Relaxed Lattice-Based Proofs

We recall from Sect. 1.2, that the goal of LANES$^+$ is to prove knowledge of a tuple $(\bar{c}, \mathbf{m}, \mathbf{r}, \overrightarrow{v}) \in \mathcal{L}^+(\mathsf{mp}, \mathsf{ulp})$ (i.e., $(\mathsf{ck}, (\mathsf{mp}, \mathsf{ulp}), (\bar{c}, \mathbf{m}, \mathbf{r}, \overrightarrow{v})) \in R_{\mathsf{LANES}+}$) such that

$$\mathcal{L}^+(\mathsf{mp}, \mathsf{ulp}) = \left\{ (\bar{c}, \mathbf{m}, \mathbf{r}, \overrightarrow{v}) : \begin{array}{l} \mathbf{t} = \mathbf{Ar} + \mathbf{Bm} \text{ over } \mathcal{R}_{q,d} \wedge \mathbf{G}_1 \overrightarrow{\mathbf{m}} = \mathbf{G}_2 \overrightarrow{v} \bmod q \\ \wedge P(\overrightarrow{\mathbf{m}}, \overrightarrow{v}) = 0 \bmod q \; \forall P \in \mathsf{mp} \wedge \\ \|\bar{c}\mathbf{r}\|_{\infty} \leq \gamma_r \wedge \|\bar{c}\|_{\infty} \leq \gamma_c \text{ for } \gamma_r, \gamma_c \ll q \in \mathbb{Z}^+ \end{array} \right\}.$$
(20)

where $\mathsf{ulp} = ((\mathbf{A}, \mathbf{B}, \mathbf{t}), (\mathbf{G}_1, \mathbf{G}_2))$ and mp is a set of polynomials over $\mathbb{Z}_q$ as in Sect. 2.4. By setting $d = 1$, the whole relation becomes over $\mathbb{Z}_q$. Hence, there is no loss of generality and we stick to the naming 'unstructured' linear relation for $(\mathbf{A}, \mathbf{B}, \mathbf{t})$. Often the relation is over a polynomial ring for better efficiency.

As discussed in Sect. 1.2, the approach of LANES$^+$ to proving the hybrid exact/relaxed relation (20) is to use an efficient RPoK to prove the (typically) high-dimensional relation $\mathbf{t} = \mathbf{Ar} + \mathbf{Bm}$, and use the costly exact LANES framework only to prove the (typically) low-dimensional relations $\mathbf{G}_1 \overrightarrow{\mathbf{m}} = \mathbf{G}_2 \overrightarrow{v} \bmod q$

Algorithm 2. LANES$^+$: Framework for Hybrid Exact/Relaxed Proofs

---

1: **procedure** LANES$^+$.Gen(1^λ)
2:      Pick $\mathcal{H} : \{0,1\}^* \to \mathcal{C} \subseteq \mathcal{R}_{q,d}$
3:      $\mathsf{pp}_L \leftarrow$ LANES.Gen(1^λ)
4:      **return** $\mathsf{pp} = (\mathsf{pp}_L, \mathcal{H})$
5: **end procedure**

6: **procedure** LANES$^+$.Com$_{\mathsf{pp}}(\mathbf{m}, \mathbf{r}, \overrightarrow{v})$ ▷ $(\mathbf{m}, \overrightarrow{v}) \in \mathcal{R}^V_{q,d} \times \mathbb{Z}^{Ml}_q$ and $\mathbf{G}_1 \overrightarrow{\mathbf{m}} = \mathbf{G}_2 \overrightarrow{v}$
7:      Set public params $\eta, \eta_m, \phi, \phi_m$ s.t. $\eta \geq \|c\mathbf{r}\|$ and $\eta_m \geq \|c\mathbf{m}\|$ for any $c \in \mathcal{C}$
8:      Sample msg masking $\mathbf{u} \xleftarrow{\$} \mathbb{D}^V_{\phi_m \eta_m, d}$ if flag$_{\mathsf{rs}} =$ true; otherwise $\mathbf{u} \xleftarrow{\$} \mathcal{R}^V_{q,d}$
9:      $\overrightarrow{s} = (\overrightarrow{\mathbf{u}}, \overrightarrow{\mathbf{m}}, \overrightarrow{v}) \in \mathbb{Z}^{2Vd+Ml}_q$
10:     $(t_L; t'_L) \leftarrow$ LANES.Com$_{\mathsf{pp}_L}(\overrightarrow{s})$
11:     **return** $(t; t') = (t_L; (t'_L, \mathbf{m}, \mathbf{r}, \overrightarrow{v}, \mathbf{u}))$ ▷ t is public and t' is secret
12: **end procedure**

13: **procedure** LANES$^+$.Prove$_{\mathsf{pp}}((\mathsf{mp}, \mathsf{ulp}), (t; t'); \rho)$ ▷ ρ is optional; only used as $\mathcal{H}$ input
14:     Parse $(t; t') = (t_L; (t'_L, \mathbf{m}, \mathbf{r}, \overrightarrow{v}, \mathbf{u}))$
15:     Sample short randomness masking $\mathbf{y} \xleftarrow{\$} \mathbb{D}^{\dim(\mathbf{r})}_{\phi \eta, d}$
16:     Compute $\mathbf{w} = \mathbf{A}\mathbf{y} + \mathbf{B}\mathbf{u}$
17:     $c \leftarrow \mathcal{H}(\mathsf{pp}, \mathsf{mp}, \mathsf{ulp}, t, \mathbf{w}; \rho)$
18:     $\mathbf{z} = \mathbf{y} + c \cdot \mathbf{r}$
19:     $\mathbf{f} = \mathbf{u} + c \cdot \mathbf{m} \in \mathcal{R}^V_{q,d}$
20:     Restart if Rej$(\mathbf{z}, c\mathbf{r}, \phi, \eta)$
21:     Restart if flag$_{\mathsf{rs}} =$ true and Rej$(\mathbf{f}, c\mathbf{m}, \phi_m, \eta_m)$
22:     $\mathsf{ulp}' = \left(\mathbf{L}, \begin{pmatrix} \overrightarrow{\mathbf{f}} \\ \overrightarrow{0} \end{pmatrix} \right)$ where $\mathbf{L} := \begin{pmatrix} \mathbf{I}_{Vd} \, \mathbf{I}_V \otimes \mathrm{Rot}(c) & \mathbf{0} \\ \mathbf{0} & \mathbf{G}_1 & -\mathbf{G}_2 \end{pmatrix}$
23:     $\pi_L \leftarrow$ LANES.Prove$_{\mathsf{pp}_L}((\mathsf{mp}, \mathsf{ulp}'), (t_L; t'_L))$
24:     **return** the proof $\pi = (\pi_L, \hat{\pi})$ with $\hat{\pi} = (c, \mathbf{z}, \mathbf{f})$
25: **end procedure**

26: **procedure** LANES$^+$.Ver$_{\mathsf{pp}}((\mathsf{mp}, \mathsf{ulp}), t, \pi; \rho)$ ▷ ρ is an optional argument
27:     Parse $\pi = (\pi_L, (c, \mathbf{z}, \mathbf{f}))$
28:     If $\|\mathbf{z}\|_\infty > 6\phi\eta$ or (flag$_{\mathsf{rs}} =$ true and $\|\mathbf{f}\|_\infty > 6\phi_m\eta_m$), **return** 0
29:     Compute $\mathbf{w}' = \mathbf{A}\mathbf{z} + \mathbf{B}\mathbf{f} - c\mathbf{t}$
30:     If $c \neq \mathcal{H}(\mathsf{pp}, \mathsf{mp}, \mathsf{ulp}, t, \mathbf{w}'; \rho)$, **return** 0
31:     Set ulp' as in LANES$^+$.Prove
32:     **return** LANES.Ver$_{\mathsf{pp}_L}((\mathsf{mp}, \mathsf{ulp}'), t_L, \pi_L)$
33: **end procedure**

---

and $P(\overrightarrow{\mathbf{m}}, \overrightarrow{v}) = 0 \bmod q$, along with the well-formedness of the RPoK masked message relation $\mathbf{f} = \mathbf{u} + c\mathbf{m}$ that links the RPoK and LANES proofs.

We provide the full LANES$^+$ protocol as a commit-and-prove protocol in Algorithm 2, where $\mathsf{ulp} = ((\mathbf{A}, \mathbf{B}, \mathbf{t}), (\mathbf{G}_1, \mathbf{G}_2))$ as before. We write the steps relating to LANES in purple colour to make it easy to distinguish them from RPoK steps. The flag flag$_{\mathsf{rs}}$ is used to specify if a rejection sampling on $\mathbf{m}$ is done.

4.1 Security Analysis

The analysis of our LANES$^+$ framework is fairly intuitive. Correctness follows straightforwardly from the completeness of a standard RPoK and the correctness of LANES. The simulatability (or zero-knowledge) property follows from the simulatability properties of a standard RPoK and LANES. The more difficult part is the soundness, which we look at more closely next.

Theorem 3. LANES$^+$ *protocol in Algorithm 2 is*

1. *correct if* LANES *is correct,*
2. *simulatable if* LANES *is simulatable, and*
3. *knowledge sound if* LANES *is knowledge sound and any non-zero difference of challenges in* $\mathcal{C}$ *is invertible in* $\mathcal{R}_{q,d}$.

Proof. The correctness of LANES$^+$ follows straightforwardly. The simulation of LANES$^+$ output $(t_L, (\pi_L, \hat{\pi}))$ also follows via standard arguments as discussed next. By assumption, LANES is simulatable and thus (t_L, π_L) can be simulated using the simulator of LANES, given the public input $(\mathbf{f}, c)$ to the LANES prove algorithm. Here, $\mathbf{f}$ and c must be simulated first using the simulator for the remaining proof part $\hat{\pi} = (c, \mathbf{z}, \mathbf{f})$, which follows from the rejection sampling. In particular, if the 'uniform' rejection sampling in [42] is used for $\mathbf{z}$ (and $\mathbf{f}$), then simulation of $\mathbf{z}$ (and $\mathbf{f}$) is done by sampling each coefficient from a known uniform distribution. If the 'Gaussian' rejection sampling in [43] is used for $\mathbf{z}$ (and $\mathbf{f}$), which is what is described in Algorithm 2, then simulation of $\mathbf{z}$ (and $\mathbf{f}$) is done by sampling each coefficient from a known discrete Gaussian distribution (i.e., $\mathbf{z} \xleftarrow{\$} \mathbb{D}_{\phi\eta,d}^{\dim(\mathbf{r})}$ and $\mathbf{u} \xleftarrow{\$} \mathbb{D}_{\phi_m\eta_m,d}^{V}$). If no rejection sampling is used, then each coordinate in $\mathbf{f}$ are simply sampled as a uniformly random element of $\mathcal{R}_{q,d}$. The simulator picks $c \xleftarrow{\$} \mathcal{C}$ and then programs the random oracle $\mathcal{H}$ such that $\mathcal{H}(\mathsf{pp}, \mathsf{mp}, \mathsf{ulp}, t_L, \mathbf{Az} + \mathbf{Bf} - ct; \rho) = c$. This concludes the simulatability proof.

We now investigate soundness, which is the more critical property. Using a standard rewinding argument (e.g., [8]), we get two accepting protocol outputs $\pi = (\pi_L, (c, \mathbf{z}, \mathbf{f}))$ and $\pi' = (\pi_L', (c', \mathbf{z}', \mathbf{f}'))$ for $c \neq c'$ w.r.t. the same hash input $(\mathsf{pp}, \mathsf{mp}, \mathsf{ulp}, t, \mathbf{w}; \rho)$. From the verification Step 29, we have

$$\bar{c}t = \mathbf{A}\bar{\mathbf{z}} + \mathbf{B}\bar{\mathbf{f}} \text{ over } \mathcal{R}_{q,d}, \tag{21}$$

where $\bar{c} := c - c'$, $\bar{\mathbf{z}} := \mathbf{z} - \mathbf{z}'$ and $\bar{\mathbf{f}} := \mathbf{f} - \mathbf{f}'$. Note that $\|\bar{\mathbf{z}}\|_\infty \leq 12\phi\eta$ and $\|\bar{\mathbf{f}}\|_\infty \leq 12\phi_m\eta_m$ (if $\mathsf{flag}_{\mathsf{rs}} = \mathsf{true}$) by Step 28.

Now, we will use the extractor $\mathcal{E}_0$ of LANES, which itself also relies on a standard rewinding, as in [24, Theorem 4.1] to extract a witness $\vec{s}^*$. First, it is important to observe that the commitment phase LANES.Com is performed *before* the challenge computation at Step 17. The special soundness of LANES requires this commitment to be binding and thus a PPT adversary cannot find two distinct openings. As a result, when running $\mathcal{E}_0$ on both sets of transcripts w.r.t. c and c', the commitment opening returned by $\mathcal{E}_0$ will be the same for both cases, except with negligible probability.

With the above in mind, we use $\mathcal{E}_0$ to extract a witness $\overrightarrow{s}^* := (\overrightarrow{u}^*, \overrightarrow{m}^*, \overrightarrow{v}^*) \in$
$\mathbb{Z}_q^{2Vd+Ml}$ for $\mathsf{ulp} = \left(\mathbf{L}, \begin{pmatrix} \overrightarrow{\mathbf{f}} \\ \overrightarrow{0} \end{pmatrix} \right)$ where $\mathbf{L} := \begin{pmatrix} \mathbf{I}_{Vd} \, \mathbf{I}_V \otimes \mathsf{Rot}(c) & \mathbf{0} \\ \mathbf{0} & \mathbf{G}_1 & -\mathbf{G}_2 \end{pmatrix}$ such that

$$P(\overrightarrow{s}^*) = 0 \bmod q \quad \text{for all } P \in \mathsf{mp}, \text{ and} \tag{22}$$

$$\mathbf{L} \cdot \begin{pmatrix} \overrightarrow{u}^* \\ \overrightarrow{m}^* \\ \overrightarrow{v}^* \end{pmatrix} = \begin{pmatrix} \overrightarrow{\mathbf{f}} \\ \overrightarrow{0} \end{pmatrix} \bmod q, \tag{23}$$

which is equivalent to

$$\mathbf{f} = \mathbf{u}^* + c \cdot \mathbf{m}^* \text{ over } \mathcal{R}_{q,d}, \text{ and} \tag{24}$$

$$\mathbf{G}_1 \overrightarrow{m}^* = \mathbf{G}_2 \overrightarrow{v}^* \text{ over } \mathbb{Z}_q, \tag{25}$$

where $\mathbf{u}^*$ and $\mathbf{m}^*$ are the vectors of polynomials in $\mathcal{R}_{q,d}$ corresponding to $\overrightarrow{u}^*$ and $\overrightarrow{m}^*$, respectively (i.e., $\mathbf{u}^* = \overrightarrow{u}^*$ and $\mathbf{m}^* = \overrightarrow{m}^*$).

From the above discussion for the same witness $\overrightarrow{s}^* = (\overrightarrow{u}^*, \overrightarrow{m}^*, \overrightarrow{v}^*)$, we similarly use $\mathcal{E}_0$ to obtain

$$\mathbf{f}' = \mathbf{u}^* + c' \cdot \mathbf{m}^* \text{ over } \mathcal{R}_{q,d}. \tag{26}$$

Plugging (24) and (26) into (21), we get

$$\bar{c}\mathbf{t} = \mathbf{A}\bar{\mathbf{z}} + \bar{c}\mathbf{B}\mathbf{m}^* \text{ over } \mathcal{R}_{q,d}, \tag{27}$$

for $\overrightarrow{s}^* = (\overrightarrow{u}^*, \overrightarrow{m}^*, \overrightarrow{v}^*)$ and $\overrightarrow{m}^* = \overrightarrow{m}^*$. By assumption, $\bar{c}$ is invertible in $\mathcal{R}_{q,d}$, and hence the extractor can compute $\mathbf{r}^* := \bar{\mathbf{z}}/\bar{c} \bmod q$ such that (20) holds w.r.t. $(\bar{c}, \mathbf{m}^*, \mathbf{r}^*, \overrightarrow{v})$. This concludes the proof. $\qquad\square$

Remark 2. Note that the extracted randomness $\mathbf{r}^*$ in the proof of Theorem 3 is not proven to be short, but this is not needed for our applications. In our rounding proof and VRF applications, the shortness proof will be done using LANES for the message part, which will correspond to an error term. Moreover, we do also prove a relaxed relation as in (27), where the randomness $\bar{\mathbf{z}}$ is short.

Remark 3 (Using different system moduli). Suppose that we want to use different moduli, e.g., $\hat{q}$ in LANES and q in RPoK. To achieve this, we need to focus on the components that are used both in LANES and RPoK. In particular, we need to assume the following

1. $\|\overrightarrow{s}^*\|_\infty < \hat{q}/2$,
2. q is large enough that $\mathbf{f} = \mathbf{u} + c\mathbf{m}$ holds without mod q, (i.e. $\|\mathbf{f}\|_\infty < q/2$),
3. $\|\mathbf{f}\|_\infty, \|c\mathbf{m}^*\|_\infty < \hat{q}/4$,
4. $\hat{q}$ is large enough that $\mathbf{G}_1 \overrightarrow{m} = \mathbf{G}_2 \overrightarrow{v}$ holds without mod $\hat{q}$.

With the above assumptions, the witness $\overrightarrow{s} = (\overrightarrow{\mathbf{u}}, \overrightarrow{\mathbf{m}}, \overrightarrow{v})$ of LANES is a vector over $\mathbb{Z}$ with coordinates in $[-(\hat{q}-1)/2, (\hat{q}-1)/2]$, and hence can be seen as $\mathbb{Z}_{\hat{q}}$ elements without any change. Also, no coefficient of the expression $\mathbf{f} = \mathbf{u} + c\mathbf{m}$

exceeds q or $\hat{q}$, and it can be proven without any change in the two proof parts. Particularly, LANES will prove that $\overrightarrow{\mathbf{f}} = \overrightarrow{u}^* + \mathbf{I}_V \otimes \mathsf{Rot}(c) \cdot \overrightarrow{m}^* \bmod \hat{q}$ and $\overrightarrow{\mathbf{f'}} = \overrightarrow{u}^* + \mathbf{I}_V \otimes \mathsf{Rot}(c') \cdot \overrightarrow{m}^* \bmod \hat{q}$. Hence, $\overrightarrow{\mathbf{f}} - \overrightarrow{\mathbf{f'}} = \mathbf{I}_V \otimes (\mathsf{Rot}(c) - \mathsf{Rot}(c')) \cdot \overrightarrow{m}^* \bmod \hat{q}$. By the above infinity-norm assumptions, we get $\overrightarrow{\mathbf{f}} - \overrightarrow{\mathbf{f'}} = \mathbf{I}_V \otimes (\mathsf{Rot}(c) - \mathsf{Rot}(c')) \cdot \overrightarrow{m}^*$ over $\mathbb{Z}$, which implies that $\bar{\mathbf{f}} = \bar{c}\mathbf{m}^*$ over $\mathcal{R}_d := \mathbb{Z}[X]/(X^d + 1)$ (without mod q or $\hat{q}$), as needed. Finally, the linear relation proven by LANES now holds over the ring $\mathcal{R}_d$ and hence it also holds over the ring $\mathcal{R}_{q,d}$ (with mod q).

The above assumptions in Remark 3 naturally hold for our application to VRFs because the message $\mathbf{m}$ will be an error term with coefficients much less than q and $\hat{q}$. Hence, we can also easily construct $\mathbf{f}$ via rejection sampling to make sure that it has relatively small coefficients. The linear relation $(\mathbf{G}_1, \mathbf{G}_2)$ will represent an integer decomposition of the error coefficients and hence $\mathbf{G}_1\overrightarrow{\mathbf{m}} = \mathbf{G}_2\overrightarrow{v}$ will readily hold over $\mathbb{Z}$. As a result, we will have more flexibility in choosing concrete parameters in our application without imposing aggressive conditions.

The total average number of repetitions for LANES$^+$ will be about $\mu(\phi) \cdot \mu(\phi_m) \cdot M_L$ (and $\mu(\phi) \cdot M_L$ if no rejection sampling is done for $\mathbf{m}$), where M_L denotes the average number of repetitions in LANES and $\mu(\phi) = e^{12/\phi + 1/(2\phi^2)}$. Recall that $M_L = 1$ if the results of [39] are used.

5   Proof of Rounding

In this section, we describe our protocol that allows proving knowledge of a vector satisfying a rounding relation of the form

$$R_{\mathrm{rnd}} = \left\{ ((\mathbf{B}, \mathbf{v}); \mathbf{s}) \; : \; \mathbf{s} \in \mathcal{R}_{q,d}^m \wedge \mathbf{v} = \lfloor \mathbf{Bs} \rceil_p \bmod p \right\}. \tag{28}$$

In the rest of the paper, q is assumed to be a multiple of p so that we can use Fact 1. Typical applications would require that $(\mathbf{B}, \mathbf{v})$ does not leak information about $\mathbf{s}$ since otherwise it may not make sense to prove the rounding relation in zero-knowledge. However, we do not necessarily assume $\mathbf{B}$ to be binding.

The proof relies on the observation in Fact 1. Particularly, given public $(\mathbf{B}, \mathbf{v})$, the prover proves knowledge of $(\mathbf{s}, \mathbf{e})$ satisfying the following relation

$$R'_{\mathrm{rnd}} = \left\{ ((\mathbf{B}, \mathbf{v}); (\mathbf{s}, \mathbf{e})) : \mathbf{s} \in \mathcal{R}_{q,d}^m \wedge \mathbf{e} = \mathbf{Bs} - \frac{q}{p}\mathbf{v} \bmod q \wedge \overrightarrow{\mathbf{e}} \in [q/p]^{Vd} \right\}, \tag{29}$$

which is equivalent to proving (28). To prove this relation, we make use of LANES$^+$ such that the knowledge of $\mathbf{s}$ is proven efficiently via RPoK while having small coefficients for $\mathbf{e}$ is proven via LANES. Note that we do not necessarily need to prove that $\mathbf{s}$ is short and hence an RPoK is an ideal solution for that part. However, LANES$^+$ already proves knowledge of an f such that $f \cdot \mathbf{s}$ is short (which is not made explicit in the above relation). Now, we set $q/p = \beta^r$ and run the commitment step of LANES$^+$ with input $(\mathbf{e}, \mathbf{s}, \overrightarrow{b})$, where $\overrightarrow{b}$ denotes the base-β representation of the coefficient vector of $\mathbf{e}$. We can then prove in

Algorithm 3. Proof of Correct Rounding

1: **procedure** R.Gen(1^λ)
2:    **return** pp $\leftarrow$ LANES$^+$.Gen(1^λ)
3: **end procedure**

4: **procedure** R.Prove(pp, $(\mathbf{B}, \mathbf{v}), \mathbf{s}; \rho$)   ▷ ρ is an optional argument
5:    $\mathbf{e} = \mathbf{Bs} - \frac{q}{p} \cdot \mathbf{v}$
6:    Set (β, r) s.t. $q/p = \beta^r$
7:    Compute $\overrightarrow{b} \in \mathbb{Z}^{dVr}$ as the base-β digits of the coefficients in $\mathbf{e}$
8:    $P(\overrightarrow{e}, \overrightarrow{b}) = \bigcirc_{i \in [\beta]} (\overrightarrow{b} - \overrightarrow{i})$ for $\overrightarrow{i} := (i, \ldots, i)$, where $\bigcirc$ denotes coordinate-wise multiplication over a set of elements
9:    mp $:= \{P\}$
10:    $\mathbf{G} = \mathbf{I}_{Vd} \otimes \mathbf{g}$ with $\mathbf{g} = (1, \beta, \ldots, \beta^{r-1})$ ▷ $\overrightarrow{e} = \mathbf{G}\overrightarrow{b}$
11:    ulp $= \left(\left(\mathbf{B}, -\mathbf{I}_{Vd}, \frac{q}{p}\mathbf{v} \right), (\mathbf{I}_{Vd}, \mathbf{G}) \right)$
12:    $(t; t') \leftarrow$ LANES$^+$.Com$_{pp}$($\mathbf{e}, \mathbf{s}, \overrightarrow{b}$)
13:    $\pi \leftarrow$ LANES$^+$.Prove$_{pp}$((mp, ulp), $(t; t'); \rho$)
14:    **return** (t, π)
15: **end procedure**

16: **procedure** R.Ver(pp, $(\mathbf{B}, \mathbf{v}), (t_L, \pi); \rho$)   ▷ ρ is an optional argument
17:    Set mp and ulp as in R.Prove
18:    **return** LANES$^+$.Ver$_{pp}$((mp, ulp), $t, \pi; \rho$)
19: **end procedure**

LANES that the coordinates of $\overrightarrow{b}$ are in $[\beta]$ using a multiplicative relation of the form $b_i(b_i - 1) \cdots (b_i - (\beta - 1)) = 0$ and also prove that they re-construct the coefficients of $\mathbf{e}$ via a linear relation such that the coefficients remain in the desired range. As a result, we prove (29), and hence (28). The full rounding protocol is presented in Algorithm 3.

In certain cases (as our VRF application), we may not be able to set $q/p = \beta^r$ for $2 \leq \beta < q$, e.g., since q/p needs to be prime. In such cases, we can set $\beta^r \geq q$, which raises the issue that proof of being in the range $[\beta^r]$ is not equivalent to that of being in $[q/p]$. However, we can get around it by proving that certain digits in the decomposition satisfy a lower-order multiplicative relation of the form $P_a(X) = X \cdot (X - 1) \cdots (X - a) = 0$ for $a \leq \beta - 1$ so that reconstructed integer coefficients of $\mathbf{e}$ are really in $[q/p]$, not $[\beta^r]$. This is possible in LANES as long as the digits satisfying the $P_a(X)$ for the same a are packed within the same ring element of $\mathcal{R}_{\hat{q},\hat{d}}$. As discussed in Sect. 2.4, the communication size of LANES only depends on the maximal degree $\alpha = \beta$.

It is easy to see that the size of a proof output $\sigma = (t, \pi) = (t_L, (\pi_L, c, \mathbf{z}, \mathbf{f}))$ for Algorithm 3 can be approximated by (ignoring the very small size of c)

$$|\sigma| \approx \underbrace{|t_L| + |\pi_L|}_{\text{size of LANES}} + \underbrace{|\mathbf{z}| + |\mathbf{f}|}_{\text{size of RPoK}} . \tag{30}$$

The advantage of our proof comes from (i) minimizing the entropy of the secret witness of LANES, and (ii) exploiting the efficient lattice-based RPoK for the high-entropy secret witness part. Particularly, the dimension over $\mathbb{Z}$ of the secret witness $\overrightarrow{s}$ in LANES is equal to $2Vd + Vdr = Vd(2 + r)$. In the case of a single module LWR sample, we have $V = 1$. We can also reasonably assume that $d \leq \hat{d}$, where $\hat{d} = 128$ in LANES is the default choice. Let us take $d = 32$ as in the concrete parameters of our VRF proposal. Finally, if we take $q/p = 2^4$ and $\beta = 4$ as an example, then we end up with $r = 2$. Hence, $\dim(\overrightarrow{s}) = Vd(2+r) = 128$. On the other hand, if we directly apply the LANES framework to prove knowledge of a single module LWR sample (i.e., $(\mathbf{s}, e)$ such that $\frac{q}{p}v = \langle \mathbf{b}, \mathbf{s} \rangle + e$), we would have the same cost for decomposition of the error e plus the much bigger dimension of $\overrightarrow{s}$ compared to $\dim(\overrightarrow{e}) = d$. In practice, we would likely need $\dim(\overrightarrow{s}) \geq 1024$, hence the total dimension of the secret witness in LANES would be 1088 using the same $(V, d, r) = (1, 32, 2)$, which pushes LANES to its less efficient realm where multiple proof responses need to be sent.

Theorem 4. *Assume that* LANES$^+$ *is correct, simulatable and knowledge sound as in Theorem 3, and uses a prime modulus $\hat{q}$ for* LANES *and another modulus q for* RPoK *with $p \mid q$. Further assume that any non-zero difference of challenges in $\mathcal{C}$ is invertible in $\mathcal{R}_{q,d}$ and that the assumptions in Remark 3 hold. Then, the protocol in Algorithm 3 is correct, simulatable and sound w.r.t. the relation in* (28).

Proof (Theorem 4). Correctness and simulatability properties follow from correctness and simulatability of LANES$^+$.

For the knowledge soundness, running the extractor $\mathcal{E}_L$ of LANES$^+$ as in the proof of Theorem 3, we obtain $(\mathbf{e}^*, \mathbf{s}^*, \overrightarrow{b^*})$ such that

$$\frac{q}{p} \cdot \mathbf{v} = \mathbf{B}\mathbf{s}^* - \mathbf{e}^* \text{ over } \mathcal{R}_{q,d}, \tag{31}$$

$$\overrightarrow{e^*} = \mathbf{G}\overrightarrow{b^*} \bmod \hat{q}, \text{ and} \tag{32}$$

$$\bigcirc_{i \in [\beta]} (\overrightarrow{b} - \overrightarrow{i}) = 0 \bmod \hat{q} \text{ for } \overrightarrow{i} := (i, \ldots, i). \tag{33}$$

Since $\hat{q}$ is prime by assumption, (33) implies that $\overrightarrow{b^*} \in [\beta]^{Vdr}$. Then, by the structure of $\mathbf{G}$, (32) gives that $\overrightarrow{e^*} \in [q/p]^{Vd}$. Since $\mathbf{v} \in \mathcal{R}^V_{p,d}$, we conclude that $\mathbf{v} = \lfloor \mathbf{B}\mathbf{s}^* \rceil_p$ by Fact 1. $\qquad\square$

6   LaV: Our Efficient Long-Term Lattice-Based VRF

In this section, we first describe our concrete instantiations of the PRF and the NIZK from lattices to realize the general VRF framework from Sect. 2.3. Then, we optimize over this proposal and describe our final VRF scheme, LaV.

6.1   Instantiation of the PRF

We describe our MLWR-based PRF below that is parametrized by η with $q > \eta \geq 1$. The PRF is then defined as

$$\mathsf{PRF}_k(\mathsf{m}) = \lfloor \mathbf{A}\mathbf{r} \rceil_p, \text{ where } \mathbf{A} \leftarrow \mathcal{G}(\mathsf{m}) \text{ and } k = \mathbf{r}, \tag{34}$$

for a short vector $\mathbf{r} \in \mathcal{K} := \mathbb{S}_{\eta,d}^{\ell}$ and a random oracle $\mathcal{G} : \{0,1\}^* \to \mathcal{R}_{q,d}^{n \times \ell}$. The output space is therefore $\mathcal{T} = \mathcal{R}_{q,d}^n$. We also define an extended key space of our PRF as in Sect. 2.2. In particular, for some parameter $\eta_1 \geq \eta$, the extended key space of the PRF is $\mathbb{S}_{\eta_1,d}^{\ell}$, which may be larger than the key space $\mathbb{S}_{\eta,d}^{\ell}$ for honest PRF executions. This property is useful for efficient lattice-based zero-knowledge proofs, and we want to make sure that the PRF is key-binding for the extended key space (which includes the key space).

Lemma 2. *The PRF defined above is computationally key-binding w.r.t. the extended key space* $\mathbb{S}_{\eta_1,d}^{\ell}$ *(see Sect. 2.2) if* $\mathsf{MSIS}_{n,d,n+\ell,q,\beta_{\mathsf{SIS}}}^{\infty}$ *is hard for* $\beta_{\mathsf{SIS}} = \max\{2\eta_1, 2q/p\}$. *It also satisfies computational* κ*-pseudorandomness (see Sect. 2.2) if* $\mathsf{MLWR}_{\ell,d,n\kappa,q,p,\eta}$ *is hard and p divides q.*

The proof of the above lemma follows standard MSIS/MLWR-based security arguments and is provided in the full version of this work [25].

6.2 Instantiation of the NIZK

We first define the set of relaxation factors as $F := \{c - c' : c, c' \in \mathcal{C} \wedge c \neq c'\}$ for $\mathcal{C}$ defined in (13). For the invertibility of relaxation factors, we rely on our results from Sect. 3 and set the parameters accordingly. We define $\zeta := 2w\gamma$ with $w = \delta\tilde{w}$. Then, we say that $(f, \mathbf{r})$ is a valid opening of a PRF output $\mathbf{v}$ if, for some parameter $\bar{\eta} < q$,

- $\|\mathbf{r}\|_\infty \leq \bar{\eta}$, $\|f\|_1 \leq \zeta$ with $f \in F$, and
- $\mathbf{v} = \lfloor \mathbf{A}(\mathbf{r}/f) \rceil_p$, where division is done mod q.

We require the NIZK to prove knowledge of such a valid opening and also set $\eta_1 = \zeta\bar{\eta}$ so that $f' \cdot \mathbf{r}$ falls in the extended key space for any $f' \in F$. Now, let $\mathbf{A} \leftarrow \mathcal{G}(0)$ and $\mathbf{B} \leftarrow \mathcal{G}(\mathsf{m})$ be two matrices output by a random oracle $\mathcal{G}$. Denote $\mathsf{pk} = \mathbf{t}$ as the public key and $v = \mathbf{v}$ as the VRF value. Recall that we are interested in proving (6), which corresponds to proving the following relation for our concrete PRF instantiation

$$R_{\mathrm{lbvrf}} = \left\{ ((\mathbf{A}, \mathbf{B}, \mathbf{t}, \mathbf{v}), (f, \mathbf{r})) : \begin{array}{c} \mathbf{t} = \lfloor \mathbf{A}(\mathbf{r}/f) \rceil_p \wedge \mathbf{v} = \lfloor \mathbf{B}(\mathbf{r}/f) \rceil_p \\ \wedge \|f\|_1 \leq \zeta \wedge \|\mathbf{r}\|_\infty \leq \bar{\eta} \end{array} \right\}. \quad (35)$$

The above itself is equivalent to proving the following $\begin{pmatrix} \mathbf{t} \\ \mathbf{v} \end{pmatrix} = \left\lfloor \begin{pmatrix} \mathbf{A} \\ \mathbf{B} \end{pmatrix} (\mathbf{r}/f) \right\rceil_p$, which can be easily done using our rounding proof from Sect. 5. So, the NIZK for the above rounding relation together with the PRF from Sect. 6.1 is enough to instantiate the generic VRF proposal from Sect. 2.3. However, the scheme in this case is sub-optimal and, in the next section, we introduce a more efficient protocol that leads to our final long-term VRF proposal, LaV.

We remark that our MLWR-based PRF satisfies an approximate variant of additive key-homomorphism (as also observed in [11]) which suffices for the VRF uniqueness argument in the proof of Theorem 1 to go through, exploiting the fact that the key-binding property of our PRF also holds up to some approximation error in the PRF output. In more detail, observe that a PRF output $\mathbf{v}$ with a relaxed opening $(f, \mathbf{r})$ satisfies $\frac{q}{p} \cdot \mathbf{v} = \mathbf{A}\mathbf{r}/f - \mathbf{e} \bmod q$ where $\mathbf{e}$ is the rounding error. In this case, for small scaling factor α, we have $\alpha \cdot \frac{q}{p} \cdot \mathbf{v} = \mathbf{A}\alpha\mathbf{r}/f - \alpha\mathbf{e}$ which is approximately a PRF evaluation under $\alpha\mathbf{r}$ up to small error $\alpha\mathbf{e}$. The binding-based argument used in the proof of Theorem 1 still holds for our PRF in the presence of such small errors using an MSIS-based argument with respect to the matrix $[\, \mathbf{I}_n \,\|\, \mathbf{A} \,]$ as discussed in Sect. 6.4.

6.3   Final Unrolled VRF Scheme

We employ several optimizations over the general VRF framework instantiation. First, one can observe that a user is bound to a particular opening $(f, \mathbf{r})$ by the opening proof of the public key $\mathsf{pk} = \mathbf{t}$ (see Remark 1). Therefore, the VRF value $\mathbf{v}$ need not be a full-sized PRF output and we shrink it to a single $\mathcal{R}_{q,d}$ element. That is, we set $v = \lfloor \langle \mathbf{b}, \mathbf{s} \rangle \rceil_p$ for a user secret key $\mathsf{sk} = \mathbf{s}$ and $\mathbf{b} \leftarrow \mathcal{G}(\mathsf{m})$.

The second optimization arises from the fact that we do not need to prove the well-formedness of the public key *exactly*, and can just bind the user to a *short* secret key $\mathsf{sk}' = (\mathbf{s}', \mathbf{e}')$ such that $\bar{c} \cdot \frac{q}{p}\mathbf{t} = \mathbf{A}\mathbf{s}' - \mathbf{e}'$ for a relaxation factor $\bar{c}$ using a RPoK. From an MSIS-based binding argument, it is computationally hard to find another triple $(\bar{c}_1, \mathbf{s}'_1, \mathbf{e}'_1)$ such that $\bar{c}_1 \cdot \frac{q}{p}\mathbf{t} = \mathbf{A}\mathbf{s}'_1 - \mathbf{e}'_1$ with $\mathbf{s}'_1/\bar{c}_1 \neq \mathbf{s}'/\bar{c}$. Hence, proving that $v = \lfloor \langle \mathbf{b}, \mathbf{s}'/\bar{c} \rangle \rceil_p$ is sufficient to ensure uniqueness. This is further discussed in Sect. 6.4.

Lastly, we make use of the Bai-Galbraith compression technique [4] at Step 26 of LaV.Eval. In Algorithm 4, we describe the full LaV VRF scheme, where the challenge space $\mathcal{C}$ is instantiated as in (13) and $[\![\mathbf{x}]\!]_K$ denotes dropping $K \geq 1$ least-significant bits of each coefficient in $\mathbf{x}$. For simplicity, we sample the matrix $\mathbf{A}$ at random in Step 4, instead of generating it via a random oracle.

Remark 4. The NIZK proof in LaV.Eval can also be seen as executing LANES$^+$ with $\mathsf{ulp} = ((\mathbf{A}', \mathbf{b}', \mathbf{t}'), (\mathbf{I}_d, \mathbf{G}))$ where $\mathbf{G}$ is the integer reconstruction matrix for e' as in R.Prove, $\mathbf{A}' = \begin{pmatrix} \mathbf{A} & -\mathbf{I}_n \\ \mathbf{b}^\top & \mathbf{0}^\top \end{pmatrix}$, $\mathbf{b}' = \begin{pmatrix} \mathbf{0} \\ -1 \end{pmatrix}$, and $\mathbf{t}' = \begin{pmatrix} \frac{q}{p} \cdot \mathbf{t} \\ \frac{q}{p} \cdot v \end{pmatrix}$. The secret witness for LANES$^+$ (i.e., input of LANES$^+$.Com) is then $\left(\begin{pmatrix} \mathbf{s} \\ \mathbf{e} \end{pmatrix}, e', \vec{b} \right)$, where $\vec{b}$ is the base-β decomposition of the coefficients of e'.

The total average number of restarts in LaV is approximately equal to $\mu(\phi) \cdot \mu(\phi_m) \cdot \exp(1) \cdot M_L$ for $2^K \approx w\gamma \cdot q/p \cdot nd$, where M_L denotes the average number of repetitions in LANES and $\mu(\phi) = e^{12/\phi + 1/(2\phi^2)}$. Recall that $M_L = 1$ if we use the results of [39] in LANES since that approach does not require rejection sampling. We can perform a single rejection sampling on the concatenated vector $(\mathbf{z}, \mathbf{f})$ if $\mathcal{B} \approx q/p$. In this case, we would have $\phi_m = \phi$ and the total average number of repetitions $\approx \mu(\phi) \cdot \exp(1) \cdot M_L$.

We list in Assumption 1, the assumptions needed to establish a secure VRF from Algorithm 4. We refer to each requirement in Assumption 1 as 'Sub-Assumption i'. We discuss in Sect. 6.4 that our optimizations do not harm the security of LaV.

Algorithm 4. LaV : Our long-term lattice-based VRF construction

1: **procedure** LaV.ParamGen(1^λ)	14: $v = \lfloor \langle \mathbf{b}, \mathbf{s} \rangle \rfloor_p$ and $e' = \langle \mathbf{b}, \mathbf{s} \rangle - \frac{q}{p}v$
2: $\mathsf{pp}' \leftarrow$ R.Gen(1^λ)	15: Sample $\mathbf{y}$ for Step 15 of Alg. 2
3: Pick random $\mathcal{G} : \{0,1\}^* \rightarrow \mathcal{R}_{q,d}^\ell$	16: $\mathbf{w}_2 = [\![\mathbf{Ay}]\!]_K$ for $2^K \approx w\gamma \cdot q/p \cdot nd$
4: $\mathbf{A} \xleftarrow{\$} \mathcal{R}_{q,d}^{n \times \ell}$	17: $(t, \pi) \leftarrow$ R.Prove($\mathsf{pp}', (\mathbf{b}, v), \mathbf{s}; \mathbf{w}_2$)
5: **return** $\mathsf{pp} = (\mathsf{pp}', \mathbf{A}, \mathcal{G})$	18: Parse $\pi = (\pi_L, (c, \mathbf{z}, \mathbf{f}))$
6: **end procedure**	19: $\hat{\mathbf{w}}_2 = \mathbf{Az} - c \cdot \frac{q}{p}\mathbf{t} \bmod 2^K$
	20: **if** $\|\hat{\mathbf{w}}_2\|_\infty > 2^{K-t} - w\gamma\frac{q}{p}$, **then** Restart
7: **procedure** LaV.KeyGen(pp)	21: **return** VRF value v and proof $\sigma = (t, \pi)$
8: $\mathbf{s} \xleftarrow{\$} \mathbb{S}_{B,d}^\ell$	22: **end procedure**
9: $\mathbf{t} = \lfloor \mathbf{As} \rfloor_p$	
10: **return** $(\mathsf{pk}, \mathsf{sk}) = (\mathbf{t}, \mathbf{s})$	23: **procedure** LaV.Verify$_{\mathsf{pp}}$($\mathsf{pk}, \mathsf{m}, v, \sigma$)
11: **end procedure**	24: Parse $\sigma = (t, (\pi_L, (c, \mathbf{z}, \mathbf{f})))$
	25: $\mathbf{b} \leftarrow \mathcal{G}(\mathsf{m})$ and let $\mathbf{t} = \mathsf{pk}$
	26: $\mathbf{w}_2' = [\![\mathbf{Az} - c \cdot \frac{q}{p}\mathbf{t}]\!]_K$
12: **procedure** LaV.Eval$_{\mathsf{pp}}$($\mathsf{pk}, \mathsf{sk}, \mathsf{m}$)	27: **return** R.Ver($\mathsf{pp}', (\mathbf{b}, v), \sigma; \mathbf{w}_2'$)
13: $\mathbf{b} \leftarrow \mathcal{G}(\mathsf{m})$ and let $\mathbf{t} = \mathsf{pk}$	28: **end procedure**

Assumption 1. *We assume the following to establish security of* LaV *with (at most)* κ *evaluations per key pair.*

1. *Any non-zero difference of challenges in* $\mathcal{C}$ *is invertible in* $\mathcal{R}_{q,d}$.
2. $\hat{q} > \max\{24\phi_m\eta_m, w\gamma\beta^r\}$ *and* $q > 12\phi_m\eta_m$ *(these assumptions ensure that those in Remark 3 are satisfied).*
3. $q > \beta_{\mathrm{SIS}}$ *and* $\mathsf{MSIS}_{n,d,n+\ell,q,\beta_{\mathrm{SIS}}}^\infty$ *for* $\beta_{\mathrm{SIS}} = 4w\gamma \cdot \max\{12\phi\eta, 2^K\}$ *is hard.*
4. $\mathsf{MLWR}_{\ell,d,n+\kappa,q,p,\mathcal{B}}$ *is hard.*
5. *Internal parameters for* LANES *are set properly.*

6.4   Security Discussion of LaV

As we have already formally proved the security of the generic VRF construction in Sect. 2.3 and the required properties of the concrete lattice-based instantiation, we now discuss the impact of our optimizations.

Assume that a user creates at most κ VRF outputs per key pair. Since the underlying NIZK used in LaV.Eval is zero-knowledge (or simulatable), for pseudorandomness, it is sufficient to consider the information leaked by the public key pk and the VRF values v_i's for $1 \le i \le \kappa$. The difference of Algorithm 4 from the generic approach is that each VRF output leaks a single MLWR sample rather than n samples. As a result, in LaV, $n + \kappa$ MLWR samples are produced after κ VRF outputs. Hence, it is sufficient to assume Sub-Assumption 4.

For the uniqueness property of LaV, the intuition is that we do not need to prove the well-formedness of the public key *exactly*, and can just bind the user to a *short* secret key $\mathsf{sk}' = (\mathbf{s}', \mathbf{e}')$ such that $\bar{c} \cdot \frac{q}{p}\mathbf{t} = \mathbf{As}' - \mathbf{e}' \bmod q$ for a relaxation factor $\bar{c}$ using a RPoK. Let us discuss the uniqueness of LaV in more detail.

Uniqueness of LaV. Let $(v, (t, (\pi_L, (c, \mathbf{z}, \mathbf{f}))))$ and $(v', (t', (\pi'_L, (c', \mathbf{z}', \mathbf{f}'))))$ be two valid VRF outputs for the same message m and public key $\mathsf{pk} = t$. We want to show that $v = v'$. Similar to [23], we use a double rewinding argument.

Rewind 1: We rewind w.r.t. to the first output and obtain another accepting output $(v, (t, (\pi_L^{(0)}, (c^{(0)}, \mathbf{z}^{(0)}, \mathbf{f}^{(0)}))))$. Define $\bar{\mathbf{z}} := \mathbf{z} - \mathbf{z}^{(0)}$, and $\bar{c} := c - c^{(0)}$. Then, by Step 26 of LaV.Verify (note that $\mathbf{w}'_2$ goes as an input to the random oracle $\mathcal{H}$ and thus must not change between rewindings), we get

$$[\![\mathbf{A}\mathbf{z} - c \cdot \frac{q}{p}\mathbf{t}]\!]_K = [\![\mathbf{A}\mathbf{z}^{(0)} - c^{(0)} \cdot \frac{q}{p}\mathbf{t}]\!]_K \tag{36}$$

$$\Longleftrightarrow \qquad \bar{c} \cdot \frac{q}{p}\mathbf{t} = \mathbf{A}\bar{\mathbf{z}} - \bar{\mathbf{e}} =: \mathbf{A}' \cdot \bar{\mathbf{s}} \pmod{q}, \tag{37}$$

for some $\bar{\mathbf{e}}$ with $\|\bar{\mathbf{e}}\|_\infty \leq 2^K$, $\bar{\mathbf{s}} := \begin{pmatrix} \bar{\mathbf{z}} \\ \bar{\mathbf{e}} \end{pmatrix}$ and $\mathbf{A}' := [\mathbf{A} \| -\mathbf{I}_n]$. Note that $\|\bar{\mathbf{s}}\|_\infty \leq \max\{12\phi\eta, 2^K\}$.

Rewind 2: We do a similar rewinding w.r.t. to the second output and obtain the following

$$\bar{c}' \cdot \frac{q}{p}\mathbf{t} = \mathbf{A}' \cdot \bar{\mathbf{s}}' \pmod{q}. \tag{38}$$

Again, we have $\|\bar{\mathbf{s}}'\|_\infty \leq \max\{12\phi\eta, 2^K\}$. Multiplying (37) by $\bar{c}'$ and (38) by $\bar{c}$ to equalize the left-hand sides of both expressions, and then subtracting the results, we get

$$\mathbf{A}' \cdot (\bar{c}'\bar{\mathbf{s}} - \bar{c}\bar{\mathbf{s}}') = \mathbf{0} \pmod{q}. \tag{39}$$

Observe that $\|\bar{c}'\bar{\mathbf{s}} - \bar{c}\bar{\mathbf{s}}'\|_\infty \leq 4w\gamma \cdot \max\{12\phi\eta, 2^K\} =: \beta_{\mathsf{SIS}}$. By the hardness of MSIS^∞ in Sub-Assumption 3, we conclude that

$$\bar{c}'\bar{\mathbf{s}} = \bar{c}\bar{\mathbf{s}}'. \tag{40}$$

Note that q must be strictly bigger than $\beta_{\mathsf{SIS}} > \|\bar{c}'\bar{\mathbf{s}}\|_\infty, \|\bar{c}\bar{\mathbf{s}}'\|_\infty$ to ensure MSIS^∞ hardness. Hence, the above equality holds without mod q.

Now, by the soundness of R.Prove, we have that $v = \lfloor\langle\mathbf{b}, \mathbf{s}^*\rangle\rfloor_p$ and $v' = \lfloor\langle\mathbf{b}, \mathbf{s}'^*\rangle\rfloor_p$, where $\mathbf{s}^* := \bar{\mathbf{z}}/\bar{c} \bmod q$ and $\mathbf{s}'^* := \bar{\mathbf{z}}'/\bar{c}' \bmod q$ as shown at the end of the soundness proof of Theorem 3. Since $\bar{c}' \cdot \bar{\mathbf{z}} = \bar{c} \cdot \bar{\mathbf{z}}' \bmod q$ by (40), we can use the fact that $\bar{c}, \bar{c}'$ are invertible mod q to conclude that $\bar{\mathbf{z}}/\bar{c} = \bar{\mathbf{z}}'/\bar{c}' \bmod q$ and hence $\mathbf{s}^* = \mathbf{s}'^*$ and $v = v'$.

6.5 Parameter Setting

As noted as a footnote in Sect. 2.4, it is easy to shift the range for the NIZK proof so that it is centred at zero. Hence, we can apply it (for free in communication) so that the error e' has coefficients in $\left[-\frac{q}{2p}, \frac{q}{2p}\right) \cap \mathbb{Z}$ to save a factor 2 when bounding $\|e'\|_\infty$. In MSIS and MLWE/MLWR problems, it is also often the case that the solution coefficients are centred at zero. Hence, we assume the same shifting of the range when estimating their hardness.

Setting Parameters External to LANES. One of the most critical assumptions that restrict our choice of parameters is Sub-Assumption 1. This is because we need q to be composite so that $p \mid q$ and we can use Fact 1. If we have $q = q_0 \cdot p$ for prime values q_0 and p, then $\mathcal{R}_{q,d} \cong \mathcal{R}_{q_0,d} \times \mathcal{R}_{p,d}$ does not split further w.r.t. the integer modulus q. As a result, Sub-Assumption 1 is satisfied if and only if challenge differences are invertible in $\mathcal{R}_{q_0,d}$ and $\mathcal{R}_{p,d}$. That is, we need to guarantee the results from Sect. 3 in both $\mathcal{R}_{q_0,d}$ and $\mathcal{R}_{p,d}$. Since we want to minimize q_0 to reduce the entropy of the input message, e', for LANES, this task itself reduces to focusing on $\mathcal{R}_{q_0,d}$. As a result, we looked at the smallest d we can set while satisfying Sub-Assumption 1 and found that $d = 32$ is the best choice. Otherwise, we need $q_0 > 2^{12}$, which is quite large. Hence, we choose $d = 32$ first.

Having fixed $d = 32$, the smallest $q_0 = q/p$ while satisfying Sub-Assumption 1 is $q_0 = 61$ from the results of Sect. 3. In this case, the assumption holds with probability at least $1 - 2^{-91.5}$. We also set $(w, \gamma) = (32, 16)$ from the results in Table 2, where $w = \delta\tilde{w} = 16 \cdot 2$ is the full weight of a challenge in (13).

Now, since $q_0 = q/p$ is prime, we cannot exactly have $q_0 = q/p = \beta^r$ for $2 \leq \beta < q_0$. Instead, we choose $(\beta, r) = (3, 4)$ such that $\beta^r \geq q/p$. As discussed before in Sect. 5, this choice is still fine. In particular, our choice of parameters for LANES have $l = 32 = d$ as the optimal option to minimize LANES communication size. Now, let $\vec{e'} = (e_0, \ldots, e_{d-1})$ and $e_i = (e_{i,0}, \ldots, e_{i,r-1})$ in base β. Then, since $l = d$, we can store in each ring element $\hat{m}_i \in \mathcal{R}_{\hat{q},\hat{d}}$ exactly $l = d$ values using the CRT slots. Particularly, we can set $\hat{m}_i = \mathsf{CRT}^{-1}(e_{0,i}, \ldots, e_{d-1,i})$, storing the i-th digit of the integers in the same ring element. Now, instead of proving that $\hat{m}_i \cdot (\hat{m}_i - 1) \cdots (\hat{m}_i - (\beta - 1)) = 0$ for all $i \in [r]$ in the multiplicative proof of LANES, we can instead prove that $\hat{m}_i \cdot (\hat{m}_i - 1) \cdots (\hat{m}_i - a) = 0$ for some $a \leq \beta - 1$ and a specific set of indices i to make sure that the integer reconstruction from the digits does not exceed q/p.

We also set $\phi = \phi_m = 12$ as a typical choice and $\mathcal{B} = 1$ to minimize the communication size. In terms of (η, η_m) (the ℓ_2-norm bounds in Algorithm 2), they are computed as $\eta = w\gamma\mathcal{B}\sqrt{ld}$ and $\eta_m = w\gamma\lfloor q_0/2 \rfloor \sqrt{d}$ (recall that the coefficients of e' are centred at zero and hence $\|e'\|_\infty \leq \lfloor q_0/2 \rfloor$).

Finally, we look at the practical MSIS/MLWR requirements against known attacks to set the module ranks n and ℓ (for MSIS$^\infty$ and MLWR, respectively) and the modulus $q = q_0 \cdot p$. When estimating the security of these problems against lattice attacks, we consider the "root Hermite factor (RHF)", a common metric used to measure the practical hardness of MSIS and MLWE/MLWR problems, and aim for RHF ≈ 1.0045 as in, e.g., [3,24,29,46]. For MSIS$^\infty$, we used "Asymmetric-MSIS" scripts of [28] and found that setting $n = 48$ and $q \approx 2^{37}$ (i.e., $p \approx 2^{31}$) leads to a RHF of 1.0045. Since challenge difference invertibility requirement is satisfied for a much smaller modulus $q_0 \ll p$, finding a suitable prime p is easy.

For MLWR with $(d, q, p, \mathcal{B}) \approx (32, 2^{37}, 2^{31}, 1)$, we set $\ell = 40$ to achieve a root Hermite Factor ≈ 1.0045 against lattice attacks, estimated using the LWE estimator [2] BKZ quantum sieve model for LWE with a ternary coordinate secret distribution. We also estimated using the LWE estimator the complexity of algebraic Gröbner Base (GB) attacks against MLWR with $\kappa + n$ samples over $\mathcal{R}_{q,d}$, assuming semi-regularity of the system, based on the model in [1]. The system of equations in the nd secret coordinates over $\mathbb{Z}_q$ includes $d(\kappa + n)$ equations of degree $q_0 = 61$ (the rounding error interval size) and also nd equations of degree $2\mathcal{B} + 1 = 3$ (the secret coordinate interval size). However, with our parameter set $(d, q, p, \mathcal{B}) \approx (32, 2^{37}, 2^{31}, 1)$ the estimated GB attack complexity always exceeded the lattice attack complexity, for any number of MLWR samples $\kappa \leq 2^{128}$, indicating that the LaV VRF with our parameter set is secure against known attacks with an essentially unbounded number of outputs.

Setting Internal Parameters for LANES. One of the advantages of our proposal is that we have the flexibility to minimize the dimension (and entropy) of the input message for LANES so as to push it towards its more efficient realm. In particular, from the above setting of $\beta = 3$, we get the maximal polynomial degree in mp as $\alpha = \beta = 3$. Furthermore, we can use the *partition-and-sample* technique in [28] (i.e., $\gamma = 1$ case of the results in Sect. 3) to have $\mathcal{R}_{\hat{q},\hat{d}}$ split into $l = 32$ factors with $\hat{d} = 128$ while also keeping the ℓ_1-norm of the challenge c_L used in LANES (see the fourth move of [24, Fig. 3]) small. In this case, we can set $k = 1$ and the challenge differences will be invertible with overwhelming probability. Particularly, we set $\|c_L\|_1 \leq \hat{w} = 44$, which leads to a challenge space of size about 2^{152} for LANES. With the choice of $(d, l, r) = (32, 32, 4)$, we end up with $N = d(2 + r)/l = 6$ as the input message dimension over $\mathbb{Z}_{\hat{q}}^l$.

Then, using the "Hint-MLWE" approach of [39], we looked at the possible choices of $(\log \hat{q}, \hat{n}, \hat{\ell})$ for LANES with our small-dimensional input message and found that choosing $(\log \hat{q}, \hat{n}, \hat{\ell}) = (26, 6, 7)$ leads to a RHF ≈ 1.0045, which is similar to the choices in [3, 24, 46]. Since we do not have any additional condition (over those needed in LANES) on the shape of $\hat{q}$, it can be set as a suitable prime with $\hat{q} \equiv 2l + 1 \pmod{4l}$. Note also that both moduli q and $\hat{q}$ are sufficiently large to satisfy Sub-Assumption 2. We also assume that $D = 13$ for commitment compression in LANES ([24, 46] use $D = 14$).

The above parameter setting for LANES leads to a total communication size of $|t_L| + |\pi_L| \approx 7.1$ KB (using (12) with $\mathfrak{s} \approx 2\sqrt{2}w\mathfrak{s}_0$ defined in Sect. 2.4) for the LANES part of LaV output.

Overall, the above parameter setting leads to 3.18 KB for RPoK, and the total proof size of LaV is $|\sigma| \approx 10.27$ KB. The VRF value v is 124 bytes and the public key size is about 5.81 KB. One could apply the public key compression technique in Dilithium [21] to reduce the public key size further (which may come at a cost in proof size). Since communication of a public key in (long-term) VRF is often a one-time task, we consider the proof cost as the major factor.

Acknowledgements. This research was supported in part by ARC Discovery Project grants DP180102199 and DP220101234.

References

1. Albrecht, M.R., Cid, C., Faugère, J., Fitzpatrick, R., Perret, L.: Algebraic algorithms for LWE problems. ACM Commun. Comput. Algebra **49**(2), 62 (2015)
2. Albrecht, M.R., Player, R., Scott, S.: On the concrete hardness of learning with errors. J. Math. Cryptol. **9**(3), 169–203 (2015). https://bitbucket.org/malb/lwe-estimator/src/master/
3. Attema, T., Lyubashevsky, V., Seiler, G.: Practical product proofs for lattice commitments. In: Micciancio, D., Ristenpart, T. (eds.) CRYPTO 2020. LNCS, vol. 12171, pp. 470–499. Springer, Cham (2020). https://doi.org/10.1007/978-3-030-56880-1_17
4. Bai, S., Galbraith, S.D.: An improved compression technique for signatures based on learning with errors. In: Benaloh, J. (ed.) CT-RSA 2014. LNCS, vol. 8366, pp. 28–47. Springer, Cham (2014). https://doi.org/10.1007/978-3-319-04852-9_2
5. Banerjee, A., Peikert, C.: New and improved key-homomorphic pseudorandom functions. In: Garay, J.A., Gennaro, R. (eds.) CRYPTO 2014. LNCS, vol. 8616, pp. 353–370. Springer, Heidelberg (2014). https://doi.org/10.1007/978-3-662-44371-2_20
6. Banerjee, A., Peikert, C., Rosen, A.: Pseudorandom functions and lattices. In: Pointcheval, D., Johansson, T. (eds.) EUROCRYPT 2012. LNCS, vol. 7237, pp. 719–737. Springer, Heidelberg (2012). https://doi.org/10.1007/978-3-642-29011-4_42
7. Baum, C., Damgård, I., Lyubashevsky, V., Oechsner, S., Peikert, C.: More efficient commitments from structured lattice assumptions. In: Catalano, D., De Prisco, R. (eds.) SCN 2018. LNCS, vol. 11035, pp. 368–385. Springer, Cham (2018). https://doi.org/10.1007/978-3-319-98113-0_20
8. Bellare, M., Neven, G.: Multi-signatures in the plain public-key model and a general forking lemma. In: ACM CCS, pp. 390–399. ACM (2006)
9. Ben-Sasson, E., et al.: Zerocash: Decentralized anonymous payments from bitcoin. In: IEEE Symposium on Security and Privacy, pp. 459–474. IEEE Computer Society (2014)
10. Bitansky, N.: Verifiable random functions from non-interactive witness-indistinguishable proofs. J. Cryptol. **33**(2), 459–493 (2020)
11. Boneh, D., Lewi, K., Montgomery, H., Raghunathan, A.: Key homomorphic PRFs and their applications. In: Canetti, R., Garay, J.A. (eds.) CRYPTO 2013. LNCS, vol. 8042, pp. 410–428. Springer, Heidelberg (2013). https://doi.org/10.1007/978-3-642-40041-4_23
12. Bootle, J., Lyubashevsky, V., Seiler, G.: Algebraic techniques for short(er) exact lattice-based zero-knowledge proofs. In: Boldyreva, A., Micciancio, D. (eds.) CRYPTO 2019. LNCS, vol. 11692, pp. 176–202. Springer, Cham (2019). https://doi.org/10.1007/978-3-030-26948-7_7
13. Buser, M., et al.: Post-quantum verifiable random function from symmetric primitives in pos blockchain. IACR Cryptology ePrint Archive, Paper 2021/302 (2021)
14. Camenisch, J., Hohenberger, S., Kohlweiss, M., Lysyanskaya, A., Meyerovich, M.: How to win the clonewars: efficient periodic n-times anonymous authentication. In: ACM CCS, pp. 201–210. ACM (2006)
15. Camenisch, J., Lehmann, A.: (Un)linkable pseudonyms for governmental databases. In: ACM CCS, pp. 1467–1479. ACM (2015)
16. Canetti, R., Lindell, Y., Ostrovsky, R., Sahai, A.: Universally composable two-party and multi-party secure computation. In: STOC, pp. 494–503. ACM (2002)

17. Chen, J., Micali, S.: Algorand: a secure and efficient distributed ledger. Theor. Comput. Sci. **777**, 155–183 (2019)
18. Chiesa, A., Green, M., Liu, J., Miao, P., Miers, I., Mishra, P.: Decentralized anonymous micropayments. In: Coron, J.-S., Nielsen, J.B. (eds.) EUROCRYPT 2017. LNCS, vol. 10211, pp. 609–642. Springer, Cham (2017). https://doi.org/10.1007/978-3-319-56614-6_21
19. Coull, S., Green, M., Hohenberger, S.: Controlling access to an oblivious database using stateful anonymous credentials. In: Jarecki, S., Tsudik, G. (eds.) PKC 2009. LNCS, vol. 5443, pp. 501–520. Springer, Heidelberg (2009). https://doi.org/10.1007/978-3-642-00468-1_28
20. del Pino, R., Lyubashevsky, V., Seiler, G.: Lattice-based group signatures and zero-knowledge proofs of automorphism stability. In: ACM CCS, pp. 574–591. ACM (2018)
21. Ducas, L., Lepoint, T., Lyubashevsky, V., Schwabe, P., Seiler, G., Stehlé, D.: CRYSTALS-Dilithium: digital signatures from module lattices. In: CHES, vol. 2018, January 2018
22. Escala, A., Groth, J.: Fine-tuning Groth-Sahai proofs. In: Krawczyk, H. (ed.) PKC 2014. LNCS, vol. 8383, pp. 630–649. Springer, Heidelberg (2014). https://doi.org/10.1007/978-3-642-54631-0_36
23. Esgin, M.F., et al.: Practical post-quantum few-time verifiable random function with applications to Algorand. In: Borisov, N., Diaz, C. (eds.) FC 2021. LNCS, vol. 12675, pp. 560–578. Springer, Heidelberg (2021). https://doi.org/10.1007/978-3-662-64331-0_29
24. Esgin, M.F., Nguyen, N.K., Seiler, G.: Practical exact proofs from lattices: new techniques to exploit fully-splitting rings. In: Moriai, S., Wang, H. (eds.) ASIACRYPT 2020. LNCS, vol. 12492, pp. 259–288. Springer, Cham (2020). https://doi.org/10.1007/978-3-030-64834-3_9
25. Esgin, M.F., Steinfeld, R., Liu, D., Ruj, S.: Efficient hybrid exact/relaxed lattice proofs and applications to rounding and VRFs. Cryptology ePrint Archive, Paper 2022/141 (2022). https://eprint.iacr.org/2022/141
26. Esgin, M.F., Steinfeld, R., Liu, J.K., Liu, D.: Lattice-based zero-knowledge proofs: new techniques for shorter and faster constructions and applications. In: Boldyreva, A., Micciancio, D. (eds.) CRYPTO 2019. LNCS, vol. 11692, pp. 115–146. Springer, Cham (2019). https://doi.org/10.1007/978-3-030-26948-7_5
27. Esgin, M.F., Steinfeld, R., Sakzad, A., Liu, J.K., Liu, D.: Short lattice-based one-out-of-many proofs and applications to ring signatures. In: Deng, R.H., Gauthier-Umaña, V., Ochoa, M., Yung, M. (eds.) ACNS 2019. LNCS, vol. 11464, pp. 67–88. Springer, Cham (2019). https://doi.org/10.1007/978-3-030-21568-2_4
28. Esgin, M.F., Steinfeld, R., Zhao, R.K.: MatRiCT$^+$: more efficient post-quantum private blockchain payments. In: IEEE Symposium on Security and Privacy (S&P), pp. 1281–1298. IEEE (2022). (Full version at ia.cr/2021/545)
29. Esgin, M.F., Zhao, R.K., Steinfeld, R., Liu, J.K., Liu, D.: MatRiCT: efficient, scalable and post-quantum blockchain confidential transactions protocol. In: ACM CCS, pp. 567–584. ACM (2019)
30. Fujisaki, E., Suzuki, K.: Traceable ring signature. In: Okamoto, T., Wang, X. (eds.) PKC 2007. LNCS, vol. 4450, pp. 181–200. Springer, Heidelberg (2007). https://doi.org/10.1007/978-3-540-71677-8_13
31. Gilad, Y., Hemo, R., Micali, S., Vlachos, G., Zeldovich, N.: Algorand: Scaling Byzantine Agreements for cryptocurrencies. In: SOSP, pp. 51–68. ACM (2017)

32. Goldberg, S., Naor, M., Papadopoulos, D., Reyzin, L., Vasant, S., Ziv, A.: NSEC5: provably preventing DNSSEC zone enumeration. In: NDSS. The Internet Society (2015)
33. Goyal, R., Hohenberger, S., Koppula, V., Waters, B.: A generic approach to constructing and proving verifiable random functions. In: Kalai, Y., Reyzin, L. (eds.) TCC 2017. LNCS, vol. 10678, pp. 537–566. Springer, Cham (2017). https://doi.org/10.1007/978-3-319-70503-3_18
34. Green, M., Miers, I.: Bolt: anonymous payment channels for decentralized currencies. In: ACM CCS, pp. 473–489. ACM (2017)
35. Hohenberger, S., Myers, S.A., Pass, R., Shelat, A.: ANONIZE: a large-scale anonymous survey system. In: IEEE Symposium on Security and Privacy, pp. 375–389. IEEE Computer Society (2014)
36. Jarecki, S., Kiayias, A., Krawczyk, H.: Round-optimal password-protected secret sharing and T-PAKE in the password-only model. In: Sarkar, P., Iwata, T. (eds.) ASIACRYPT 2014. LNCS, vol. 8874, pp. 233–253. Springer, Heidelberg (2014). https://doi.org/10.1007/978-3-662-45608-8_13
37. Kiayias, A., Russell, A., David, B., Oliynykov, R.: Ouroboros: a provably secure proof-of-stake blockchain protocol. In: Katz, J., Shacham, H. (eds.) CRYPTO 2017. LNCS, vol. 10401, pp. 357–388. Springer, Cham (2017). https://doi.org/10.1007/978-3-319-63688-7_12
38. Kilian, J.: Uses of Randomness in Algorithms and Protocols. MIT Press (1990)
39. Kim, D., Lee, D., Seo, J., Song, Y.: Toward practical lattice-based proof of knowledge from Hint-MLWE. Cryptology ePrint Archive, Paper 2023/623 (2023). https://eprint.iacr.org/2023/623
40. Lawlor, S., Lewi, K.: Deploying key transparency at WhatsApp. https://engineering.fb.com/2023/04/13/security/whatsapp-key-transparency/. Accessed 16 May 2023
41. Libert, B., Ling, S., Nguyen, K., Wang, H.: Zero-knowledge arguments for lattice-based PRFs and applications to e-cash. In: Takagi, T., Peyrin, T. (eds.) ASIACRYPT 2017. LNCS, vol. 10626, pp. 304–335. Springer, Cham (2017). https://doi.org/10.1007/978-3-319-70700-6_11
42. Lyubashevsky, V.: Fiat-Shamir with aborts: applications to lattice and factoring-based signatures. In: Matsui, M. (ed.) ASIACRYPT 2009. LNCS, vol. 5912, pp. 598–616. Springer, Heidelberg (2009). https://doi.org/10.1007/978-3-642-10366-7_35
43. Lyubashevsky, V.: Lattice signatures without trapdoors. In: Pointcheval, D., Johansson, T. (eds.) EUROCRYPT 2012. LNCS, vol. 7237, pp. 738–755. Springer, Heidelberg (2012). https://doi.org/10.1007/978-3-642-29011-4_43
44. Lyubashevsky, V., Nguyen, N.K., Plançon, M.: Lattice-based zero-knowledge proofs and applications: shorter, simpler, and more general. In: Dodis, Y., Shrimpton, T. (eds.) Advances in Cryptology, CRYPTO 2022. LNCS, vol. 13508, pp. 71–101. Springer, Cham (2022). https://doi.org/10.1007/978-3-031-15979-4_3
45. Lyubashevsky, V., Nguyen, N.K., Plancon, M., Seiler, G.: Shorter lattice-based group signatures via "almost free" encryption and other optimizations. In: Tibouchi, M., Wang, H. (eds.) ASIACRYPT 2021. LNCS, vol. 13093, pp. 218–248. Springer, Cham (2021). https://doi.org/10.1007/978-3-030-92068-5_8

46. Lyubashevsky, V., Nguyen, N.K., Seiler, G.: Practical lattice-based zero-knowledge proofs for integer relations. In: ACM CCS, pp. 1051–1070. ACM (2020)
47. Lyubashevsky, V., Nguyen, N.K., Seiler, G.: Shorter lattice-based zero-knowledge proofs via one-time commitments. In: Garay, J.A. (ed.) PKC 2021. LNCS, vol. 12710, pp. 215–241. Springer, Cham (2021). https://doi.org/10.1007/978-3-030-75245-3_9
48. Lyubashevsky, V., Nguyen, N.K., Seiler, G.: SMILE: set membership from ideal lattices with applications to ring signatures and confidential transactions. In: Malkin, T., Peikert, C. (eds.) CRYPTO 2021. LNCS, vol. 12826, pp. 611–640. Springer, Cham (2021). https://doi.org/10.1007/978-3-030-84245-1_21
49. Lyubashevsky, V., Seiler, G.: Short, invertible elements in partially splitting cyclotomic rings and applications to lattice-based zero-knowledge proofs. In: Nielsen, J.B., Rijmen, V. (eds.) EUROCRYPT 2018. LNCS, vol. 10820, pp. 204–224. Springer, Cham (2018). https://doi.org/10.1007/978-3-319-78381-9_8
50. Micali, S., Rabin, M.O., Vadhan, S.P.: Verifiable random functions. In: FOCS, pp. 120–130. IEEE Computer Society (1999)
51. Nguyen, N.K.: Private communication (2022)
52. Papadopoulos, D., et al.: Making NSEC5 practical for DNSSEC. Cryptology ePrint Archive, Report 2017/099 (2017). https://eprint.iacr.org/2017/099
53. Stern, J.: A new identification scheme based on syndrome decoding. In: Stinson, D.R. (ed.) CRYPTO 1993. LNCS, vol. 773, pp. 13–21. Springer, Heidelberg (1994). https://doi.org/10.1007/3-540-48329-2_2
54. Yamada, S.: Asymptotically compact adaptively secure lattice ibes and verifiable random functions via generalized partitioning techniques. In: Katz, J., Shacham, H. (eds.) CRYPTO 2017. LNCS, vol. 10403, pp. 161–193. Springer, Cham (2017). https://doi.org/10.1007/978-3-319-63697-9_6
55. Yang, R., Au, M.H., Zhang, Z., Xu, Q., Yu, Z., Whyte, W.: Efficient lattice-based zero-knowledge arguments with standard soundness: construction and applications. In: Boldyreva, A., Micciancio, D. (eds.) CRYPTO 2019. LNCS, vol. 11692, pp. 147–175. Springer, Cham (2019). https://doi.org/10.1007/978-3-030-26948-7_6

LaBRADOR: Compact Proofs for R1CS
from Module-SIS

Ward Beullens[✉] and Gregor Seiler

IBM Research Europe, Zurich, Switzerland
ward@beullens.com

Abstract. The most compact quantum-safe proof systems for large circuits are PCP-type systems such as Ligero, Aurora, and Shockwave, that only use weak cryptographic assumptions, namely hash functions modeled as random oracles. One would expect that by allowing for stronger assumptions, such as the hardness of Module-SIS, it should be possible to design more compact proof systems. But alas, despite considerable progress in lattice-based proofs, no such proof system was known so far. We rectify this situation by introducing a Lattice-Based Recursively Amortized Demonstration Of R1CS (LaBRADOR), with more compact proof sizes than known hash-based proof systems. At the 128 bits security level, LaBRADOR proves knowledge of a solution for an R1CS mod $2^{64} + 1$ with 2^{20} constraints, with a proof size of only 58 KB, an order of magnitude more compact than previous quantum-safe proofs.

1 Introduction

A (publicly-verifiable) system for proving arbitrary binary or arithmetic circuits is a very versatile cryptographic tool that is useful for the construction of many advanced protocols, e.g. in the areas of privacy-preserving cryptography, blockchain systems, and outsourced computation. The presentation of circuit satisfaction problems as rank-one constraint systems (R1CS) provides a convenient abstraction that simplifies proof systems and their comparison. The proof size is often of central importance because the proof needs to be transmitted over a network or stored on a blockchain.

Since many classical cryptographic algorithms will become insecure when large fault-tolerant quantum computers are built, it is important to develop efficient quantum-safe alternatives. Lattice-based cryptography has been very successful at providing quantum-safe basic primitives such as encryption and signature schemes. Lattice-based primitives offer practical output sizes and execution runtimes that are often faster than their classical counterparts, which makes them suitable as drop-in replacements for the classical algorithms. The same can not yet be said for more advanced protocols, and in particular lattice-based proof systems. The (plausibly) quantum-safe proof systems with the most

This work is supported by the EU H2020 ERC Project 101002845 PLAZA. Ward Beullens holds Junior Post-Doctoral fellowship 1S95620N from the Research Foundation Flanders (FWO).

H. Handschuh and A. Lysyanskaya (Eds.): CRYPTO 2023, LNCS 14085, pp. 518–548, 2023.
https://doi.org/10.1007/978-3-031-38554-4_17

compact proof sizes for moderate to large statements are hash-based PCP-type systems such as Ligero [AHIV17], Aurora [BCR+19], and Brakedown [GLS+21]. Their proof sizes scale sublinearly or even poly-logarithmically with the witness size. There are several lattice-based sublinear-size proof systems [BBC+18, BLNS20, ACL+22] but, even though they rely on much stronger cryptographic assumptions, they are only somewhat practical at best, and can still not compete with the concretely small proof size of the poly-logarithmic PCP-type systems.

Nevertheless, there has been steady progress in practical lattice-based zero-knowledge proof systems, e.g. [ESLL19, ALS20, ENS20, LNP22]. The proof sizes of these systems scale linearly with the witness size, so even though they are efficient for proving small statements, they become inefficient for proving larger statements. The concrete proof size for proving a representative reference statement has been reduced from 3.8 MB in 2017 to 14 KB in 2022 [LNP22]. This has been achieved with a combination of (1) adapting techniques from non-lattice systems to the lattice setting; (2) finding ways around the unique lattice complications surrounding the requirement that certain vectors have to be short both in the honest execution as well as in the extraction from a prover algorithm; (3) developing new ways to exploit the algebraic structure of (cyclotomic) polynomial rings; and (4) optimizing the techniques and parameters in the resulting huge design space. The somewhat practical sublinear-size proof system from [NS22] leverages and improves the insights and techniques developed for linear-size systems, in combination with new techniques that allowed for sublinear scaling.

Contributions. This work introduces a Lattice-Based Recursively Amortized Demonstration Of R1CS (LaBRADOR). LaBRADOR is the first lattice-based proof system that closes the proof-size gap with PCP-type systems and, in fact, improves upon them by a large margin. LaBRADOR builds upon and improves the set of techniques for practical lattice-based proof systems, and uses recursion to achieve very compact proof sizes. For the range of R1CS sizes that is relevant in practice, the proof size is dominated by the cost of the last step of the recursion, which is independent of the size of the R1CS instance. This means the proof size is almost constant in this range.

Concrete Sizes. The concrete proof sizes for our protocol are very compact. To prove knowledge of a solution for an R1CS modulo $2^{64} + 1$ with a number of constraints ranging from 2^{10} to 2^{20}, our proof size varies from 47 KB to 58 KB, which is much better than existing post-quantum approaches, especially at the high end of this range. Figure 1 compares our proof sizes with those of Aurora [BCR+19] and Ligero [AHIV17], obtained by running the open source `libiop` implementation, for a field with 64 bits, zero-knowledge disabled, and a soundness error of 2^{-125}, configured to provide provable security. We also compare to Brakedown and Shockwave, using the numbers in [GLS+21], for a field size of 256 bits and 2^{-128} soundness error. We remark that one can run Aurora with certain heuristics to significantly improve the proof size at the expense of provable security. Our proof sizes are still smaller than those of optimistic versions of Aurora. Our proof sizes are more than two and three orders of magnitude more compact than those of [NS22] and k-R-ISIS [ACL+22] respectively. But unlike our work, the proofs from k-R-ISIS have the advantage that the verification time is sublinear in n.

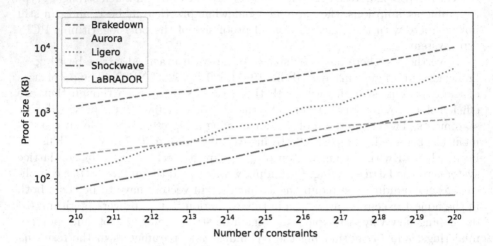

Fig. 1. Proof sizes of LaBRADOR compared to other SNARKs, for R1CS with a number of constraints varying from 2^{10} to 2^{20}. The data can be found in Table 1.

Zero-Knowledge Property. The zero-knowledge property is not crucial for sublinear-size proof systems and there are interesting applications for proof systems without zero-knowledge when the proof size is concretely smaller than the witness size. Moreover, achieving zero-knowledge can simply be done by designing a simple linear-sized shim protocol that masks the input witness. The shim can then be composed with our non-zero-knowledge proof system such that the composition is still zero-knowledge and the proof size not much larger than from our system alone. For these reasons we disregard the zero-knowledge property in this work. In all our comparisons to other proof systems we always use the variants that are also not zero-knowledge.

1.1   Technical Overview

Dot Product Constraints. Our main result is a compact proof of knowledge of a short solution $\vec{s} = \vec{s}_1, \ldots, \vec{s}_r \in \mathcal{R}_q^{n \times r}$ for a system of arbitrarily many dot product constraints, i.e. constraints of the form

$$f(\vec{s}) = \sum_{1 \le i,j \le r} \mathbf{a}_{ij} \langle \vec{s}_i, \vec{s}_j \rangle + \sum_{i=1}^{r} \langle \vec{\varphi}_i, \vec{s}_i \rangle + \mathbf{b} = 0\,,$$

where $\mathbf{a}_{ij}, \mathbf{b} \in \mathcal{R}_q = \mathbb{Z}_q[X]/(X^d + 1)$ and $\vec{\varphi}_i \in \mathcal{R}_q^n$. We also allow for dot product constraints where we only require that the constant term of $f(\vec{s})$ is zero. In Sect. 7

we show that these dot product constraint systems are at least as powerful as R1CSs because proving knowledge of a solution for an R1CS reduces efficiently to proving knowledge of a short solution to a related dot product constraint system.

Recursive Composition. Inspired by bulletproof-style arguments [BCC+16, BBB+18], we want to design a proof of knowledge of a short solution $\vec{s}^{(0)}$ for a dot product constraint system $\mathcal{F}^{(0)}$, such that the proof consists of a short part $\pi^{(1)}$, and a potentially larger part $\vec{s}^{(1)}$, where the proof is valid if $\vec{s}^{(1)}$ is itself a short solution to a new dot product constraint system $\mathcal{F}^{(1)}$, which can be deduced from $\mathcal{F}^{(0)}$ and $\pi^{(1)}$. We also want that $\vec{s}^{(1)}$ is more compact than the original solution $\vec{s}^{(0)}$. If we have such a proof system we can recursively apply it to get very compact proofs: we iteratively use the proof system on input $(\mathcal{F}^{(i)}, \vec{s}^{(i)})$ to produce the next proof $(\pi^{(i+1)}, \vec{s}^{(i+1)})$, where $\vec{s}^{(i+1)}$ is a short solution for some system $\mathcal{F}^{(i+1)}$. We do this until we reach some $\vec{s}^I$ that is short enough so that it can be sent to the verifier, along with all the short proof pieces $\pi^{(1)}, \ldots, \pi^{(I)}$. The verifier then recomputes $\mathcal{F}^{(I)}$ from $\mathcal{F}^{(0)}$ and $\pi^{(1)}, \ldots, \pi^{(I)}$, and only verifies that $\vec{s}^{(i+1)}$ is a short solution to $\mathcal{F}^I$. We prove (with some generality) that this kind of composition preserves soundness.

Amortization. Much like the work of Nguyen and Seiler [NS22], we achieve a sublinear proof size by splitting up the witness in multiple parts $\vec{s} = \vec{s}_1, \ldots, \vec{s}_r$ (potentially splitting into more parts than in the dot product constraint system we are trying to prove), sending commitments $\vec{t}_i = \mathbf{A}\vec{s}_i$ for each of the parts and doing an amortized proof of knowledge of openings. To do the amortized proof, the verifier chooses some challenges c_i, and the prover sends $\vec{z} = \sum c_i \vec{s}_i$. The verifier checks that $\vec{z}$ has small ℓ_2-norm, and that and that $\mathbf{A}\vec{z} = \sum_i c_i \vec{t}_i$. At the cost of sending $O(r^2)$ so-called garbage terms and doing some checks, we can augment the proof to also prove that the openings to the $\vec{t}_i$ commitments satisfy the dot-product relations. Since the r parts of $\vec{s}^{(i)}$ are folded into $\vec{z}$, the witness gets shorter by a factor r', although the size of the coefficients goes up by a factor $\sqrt{r\tau}$, where τ is the ℓ_2-norm of challenges $\{c_i\}_{i \in [r]}$. To prevent the coefficients from growing indefinitely, we decompose $\vec{z} = \vec{z}_0 + b\vec{z}_1$ and set $\vec{s}^{(i+1)} = \vec{z}_0 \| \vec{z}_1$ instead.

Proving Smallness. The amortized proof proves knowledge of an opening of the commitment that satisfies the dot product constraint system, but it does not yet prove that the solution has small ℓ_2-norm. To do this, we use an improved version of the modular Johnson-Lindenstrauss lemma of [GHL21]. This lemma essentially says that random linear projections preserve the ℓ_2-norm quite well (up to some scaling factor). This means that instead of checking the ℓ_2-norm of $\vec{s}$ directly, we can let the verifier choose a random projection $\Pi : \mathbb{Z}_q^{dn} \to \mathbb{Z}_q^{256}$, drawn from a certain distribution D. The prover then sends $p = \Pi\vec{s} \bmod q$ to the verifier and proves that p was computed correctly. With our distribution the ℓ_2-norm of $\Pi\vec{s} \bmod q$ is larger than $\sqrt{30} \|\vec{s}\|_2$ with overwhelming probability, and smaller than $\sqrt{128} \|\vec{s}\|_2$ with probability close to $1/2$. So if $\|p\|_2$ is small, then $\|\vec{s}\|_2$ must have been small as well. The gap between the ℓ_2-norm that is proven, and the ℓ_2-norm of the real witness is only a factor $\sqrt{128/30} \approx 2.07$. Proving that p was computed correctly comes for free because $p = \Pi\vec{s} \bmod q$ is just 256 additional (constant terms of) dot product constraints, which we can simply add to the list of constraints.

Outer Commitments. So far, the i-th iteration of the base protocol reduces the size of the witness by roughly a factor $r^{(i)}/2$, but it requires communicating a proof $\pi^{(i)}$ that consists of the $r^{(i)}$ Ajtai commitments $\vec{t}_i$ and $O(r'^2)$ garbage terms, so a priori we cannot use large $r^{(i)}$ without blowing up the proof size. An important optimization is that instead of sending the commitments $\vec{t}_i$ and the garbage terms, the prover just sends a short commitment $\vec{u}_1$ to the $\vec{t}_i$ and a subset of the garbage terms, and later in the protocol a second short commitment $\vec{u}_2$ to the remaining garbage terms. Then we just include $\vec{t}_i$ and the garbage terms in $\vec{s}^{(i+1)}$. We call the $\vec{u}_i$ the outer commitment, and the $\vec{t}_i$ the inner commitments. This optimization allows us to move material from $\pi^{(i+1)}$ to $\vec{s}^{(i+1)}$, which is very beneficial for the proof size of the overall protocol because all the material in $\vec{s}^{(i+1)}$ will be shrunk in the subsequent iterations. This optimization allows us to pick a much larger $r'^{(i)}$. Asymptotically, $r'^{(i)} = O(|\vec{s}^{(i)}|^{1/3})$ is optimal, which means that the size of the witness goes from $|\vec{s}^{(i)}|$ to $O(|\vec{s}^{(i)}|^{2/3})$ with each iteration of the protocol. Therefore, we need only $O(\log \log n)$ iterations of the base protocol. In practice, using 6 or 7 iterations gives the best results.

Relation to Prior Work. This work is based on the lattice techniques for proving algebraic and norm constraints on integer vectors stemming mainly from [ALS20, ENS20, LNP22]. The latter protocols have linear-sized outputs. In order to achieve sublinear output scaling we use the amortization technique [BBC+18, NS22] together with a recursive composition strategy. This is similar to Bulletproofs [BBB+18]. Since lattice commitments are linear, and we prove linear constraints it is possible to efficiently prove knowledge of an opening of a lattice commitment. This allows us to improve over a naive adaptation of the Bulletproof strategy in mainly three ways. Firstly, we can use a simpler folding strategy with fewer garbage commitments ("cross commitments"). More concretely, in Bulletproofs the bilinearity of commitments is used to fold the commitment messages as well as the commitment keys – resulting in quadratic verification equations. This also directly proves the original commitments, but since we don't need this we can get away with linear verification equations. Secondly, instead of sending the garbage terms we only send short committments to them, and we efficiently prove knowledge of an opening to these commitments in the next step of the recursion. This allows us to split the witness into more parts, and reduces the number of iterations from $\log n$ to $\log \log n$. Thirdly, we use Johnson-Lindenstrauss projections for proving the ℓ_2-norm in each iteration of our protocol in a way that doesn't lead to an accumulation of the norm slack over the recursion, which preevious lattice-based instantiations of Bulletproofs have suffered from. Finally, a key contribution of our work is the parameter setting. Due to the recursive nature of the protocol, the parameter space is exponentially larger compared to typical lattice-based protocols and finding good parameterizations is a highly non-trivial task.

There have been previous proposals for sublinear-sized lattice-based proof systems in the literature, e.g. [BBC+18, BLNS20, ACK21, ACL+22]. These protocols have either not been parameterized or are not practically efficient. And we believe that it us unlikely that the protocols admit efficient parameterizations. Since this work is about practical proof systems we consider them outside of the scope of this work.

2   Preliminaries

Notation. Let q be a modulus, and let $\mathbb{Z}_q$ be the ring of integers mod q. We denote by $\vec{a} \in \mathbb{Z}_q^m$ a vector of length m, and by $a_i \in \mathbb{Z}_q$ the i-th entry of $\vec{a}$. We denote matrices $A \in \mathbb{Z}_q^{m \times n}$ by capital letters. Let d be a power of two, and let $\mathcal{R}$ and $\mathcal{R}_q$ be the rings $\mathbb{Z}[X]/(X^d + 1)$ and $\mathbb{Z}_q[X]/(X^d + 1)$ respectively, where q, d are such that $X^d + 1$ splits in two irreducible factors mod q. We denote elements of $\mathcal{R}$ and $\mathcal{R}_q$ by boldface letters such as $\mathbf{f}$, and vectors of ring elements by $\vec{\mathbf{a}}$. If $\mathbf{f} = a_0 + a_1 X + \cdots + a_{n-1} X^{n-1} \in R_n$, then we denote by $\mathsf{ct}(\mathbf{f})$ the constant term of $\mathbf{f}$, i.e., $\mathsf{ct}(\mathbf{f}) = a_0$. If $\vec{\mathbf{a}} \in \mathcal{R}_q^n$ is a vector of ring elements then we denote the i-th entry of $\vec{\mathbf{a}}$ by $\mathbf{a}_i \in \mathcal{R}$, and we denote by $\vec{s} \in \mathbb{Z}_q^{dn}$ (lowercase) the vector obtained by concatenating the coefficients of all the entries of $\vec{\mathbf{s}}$. We denote matrices $\mathbf{A} \in \mathcal{R}_q^{m \times n}$ by boldface capital letters. If $\vec{\mathbf{a}} \in \mathcal{R}_q^{n_a}$ and $\vec{\mathbf{b}} \in \mathcal{R}_q^{n_b}$ are vectors, we denote by $\vec{\mathbf{a}} \| \vec{\mathbf{b}} \in \mathcal{R}_q^{n_a + n_b}$ the vector obtained by concatenating $\vec{\mathbf{a}}$ and $\vec{\mathbf{b}}$. We denote the set of integers $\{1, \ldots, k\}$ by $[k]$.

For an interactive protocol $\Pi = (\mathcal{P}, \mathcal{V})$ between two algorithms $\mathcal{P}$ and $\mathcal{V}$ we write $\langle \mathcal{P}(a), \mathcal{V}(b) \rangle$ to denote the random variable describing the output of $\mathcal{V}$ after jointly running $\mathcal{P}$ and $\mathcal{V}$ where $\mathcal{P}$ is given a as input and $\mathcal{V}$ is given b as input.

Challenge Space. Throughout the paper we let $\mathcal{C} \subset \mathcal{R}$ be a challenge space, such that $\mathbf{c}_1 - \mathbf{c}_2$ is invertible for any pair of distinct $\mathbf{c}_1, \mathbf{c}_2$ in $\mathcal{C}$, and such that $\|\mathbf{c}\|_2 \leq \tau$ and $\|\mathbf{c}\|_{\mathsf{op}} \leq T$ for all $\mathbf{c} \in \mathcal{C}$, for some constants $\tau, T \in \mathbb{R}$, where

$$\|\mathbf{c}\|_{\mathsf{op}} = \sup_{\mathbf{r} \in \mathcal{R}} \frac{\|\mathbf{cr}\|_2}{\|\mathbf{r}\|_2},$$

is the operator norm of $\mathbf{c}$.

In our concrete instantiations we use the ring $\mathcal{R} = \mathbb{Z}_q[X]/(X^{64} + 1)$, and as challenges we use ring elements with 23 zero coefficients, 31 coefficient that are ± 1, and 10 coefficients that are ± 2. There are more than 2^{128} such elements. All these polynomials have l_2-norm 71 and we use rejection sampling to restrict to challenges with operator norm at most 15. (On average we need to sample roughly 6 elements before we sample an element $\mathbf{c}$ with operator $\|\mathbf{c}\|_{\mathsf{op}} < 15$.) Differences of distinct challenges are invertible according to [LS18, Corollary 1.2].

Weak Commitment Openings. In the analysis of our protocols, we need the notion of a weak commitment opening stemming from [ALS20, Section 4]. Given an Ajtai commitment $\vec{t} = A\vec{s} \in \mathcal{R}_q^\kappa$, a weak opening of norm β is a vector $\vec{s}^*$

together with a challenge difference $\bar{c} \in \mathcal{C} - \mathcal{C}$ such that $\vec{t} = A\vec{s}^*$ and $\|\bar{c}\vec{s}^*\| \leq \beta$. The commitment $\vec{t}$ is binding for weak openings of norm β if Module-SIS is hard for rank κ and norm $4T\beta$. If Module-SIS is hard for norm 2β, then the commitment is binding for weak openings with the same challenge difference $\bar{c}$.

The Conjugation Automorphism σ_{-1}. For proving dot products $\langle \vec{a}, \vec{b} \rangle$ between coefficient vectors $\vec{a}, \vec{b} \in \mathbb{Z}_q^{nd}$ corresponding to polynomial vectors $\vec{a}, \vec{b} \in \mathcal{R}_q^n$, we use the observation that $\langle \vec{a}, \vec{b} \rangle = \mathsf{ct}\left(\langle \sigma_{-1}(\vec{a}), \vec{b} \rangle \right)$ for the automorphism $\sigma_{-1} \in \mathsf{Aut}(\mathcal{R}_q)$ defined by $\sigma_{-1}(X) = X^{-1}$ that corresponds to -1 under $\mathsf{Aut}(\mathcal{R}_q) \cong \mathbb{Z}_{2d}^{\times}$. This was introduced in [LNP22], and the constant coefficient as a handle on dot products in [ENS20].

3   Composing Proofs of Knowledge

In this section, we define proofs-of-knowledge and proof-of-knowledge reductions, and we prove that composing proof-of-knowledge reductions preserves soundness.

Definition 3.1 (multi-round public-coin interactive proofs). *A public-coin interactive proof $\Pi = (\mathcal{P}, \mathcal{V})$ is a protocol between a prover $\mathcal{P}$ and a verifier $\mathcal{V}$, where the prover takes as input (x, w), and the verifier gets x as input. The prover and verifier take turns sending messages, and the prover sends the last message. Finally the verifier outputs $V(x, c_1, \ldots, c_k, z_1, \ldots, z_{k'}) \in \{\mathsf{accept}, \mathsf{reject}\}$, where V is a verification predicate, $z_1, \ldots, z_{k'}$ are the messages sent by the prover, and $c_1, \ldots, c_k$ are the messages sent by the verifier. Moreover, the verifier chooses its i-th message c_i uniformly at random from some challenge set $\mathcal{C}_i$ for all $i \in [k]$.*

Definition 3.2 (completeness). *We say that an interactive protocol $\Pi = (\mathcal{P}, \mathcal{V})$ is a complete proof of knowledge for relation R with failure probability ϵ if for all $(x, w) \in R$, we have*

$$\Pr[\langle \mathcal{P}(x, w), \mathcal{V}(x) \rangle = \mathsf{accept}] \geq 1 - \epsilon.$$

Definition 3.3 (knowledge soundness). *We say that an interactive protocol $\Pi = (\mathcal{P}, \mathcal{V})$ is a knowledge-sound proof of knowledge for a relation R with soundness error κ if there exists an oracle algorithm $\mathcal{E}$ (called the extractor), that runs in expected polynomial time such that for all $(x, w) \in R$, and all provers $\mathcal{P}^*$ we have*

$$\Pr[(x, w') \in R \mid w' \leftarrow \mathcal{E}^{\mathcal{P}^*}(x)] \geq \epsilon(\mathcal{P}^*, x) - \kappa,$$

where $\epsilon(\mathcal{P}^*, x)$ is the success probability of the prover $\mathcal{P}^*$ for the statement x, which is defined as

$$\epsilon(\mathcal{P}^*, x) = \Pr[\langle \mathcal{P}^*(), \mathcal{V}(x) \rangle = \mathsf{accept}].$$

Remark 3.4. Note that it makes sense for a proof system to be complete with regards to a relation R, and knowledge-sound for a different relation R' (usually $R \subset R'$). This is often the case for efficient lattice-based proofs.

An alternative definition for knowledge soundness says that there is an extractor which outputs a witness with probability 1, but which is allowed to run in expected time $O(\text{poly}(|x|)/(\epsilon(\mathcal{P}^*, x) - \kappa))$. Bellare and Goldreich showed that both definitions are equivalent for NP relations [BG92], so we will use both definitions interchangeably. It is well known (see, e.g., [AF21] for a proof) that to prove knowledge soundness it suffices to construct an extractor for deterministic provers.

Definition 3.5 (proof-of-knowledge reduction). *We say a proof of knowledge $\Pi = (\mathcal{P}, \mathcal{V})$ for a relation R_1 is a reduction from R_1 to R_2 if the verification predicate of $\mathcal{V}$ "factors through R_2", by which we mean that :*

- *The last message sent by $\mathcal{P}$ is a tuple (z'_k, w_2), and*
- *there exists an efficient algorithm $\tilde{\mathcal{V}}$ such that*

$$\mathcal{V} \text{ accepts the transcript } (x_1, c_1, \ldots, c_k, z_1, \ldots, z_{k'}, w_2)$$
$$\Longleftrightarrow$$
$$(\tilde{\mathcal{V}}(x_1, c_1, \ldots, c_k, z_1, \ldots, z_{k'}), w_2) \in R_2$$

Definition 3.6 (Composition of reductions). *Let $\Pi_{12} = (\mathcal{P}_{12}, \mathcal{V}_{12})$ be a proof-of-knowledge reduction from R_1 to R_2 and let $\Pi_2 = (\mathcal{P}_2, \mathcal{V}_2)$ be a proof of knowledge for R_2. We define the composition $\Pi_2 \circ \Pi_{12}$ as the interactive protocol $(\mathcal{P}, \mathcal{V})$, where $\mathcal{P}(x_1, w_1)$ and $\mathcal{V}(x_1)$ run $\mathcal{P}_{12}(x_1, w_1)$ and $\mathcal{V}_{12}(x_1)$, except that instead of sending w_2 and letting the verifier check that $(x_2, w_2) \in R_2$ for the new statement $x_2 \leftarrow \tilde{\mathcal{V}}(x_1, c_1, \ldots, c_k, z_1, \ldots, z_{k'})$, $\mathcal{P}$ and $\mathcal{V}$ run $\mathcal{P}_2(x_2, w_2)$ and $\mathcal{V}_2(x_2)$. The composed verifier $\mathcal{V}(x_1)$ accepts if and only if $\mathcal{V}_2(x_2)$ accepts.*

Lemma 3.7 (Composition preserves knowledge soundness). *Let Π_{12} and Π_2 be proof systems as in Definition 3.6. If Π_{12} and Π_2 are knowledge sound with soundness error κ_{12} and κ_2 respectively, then their composition $\Pi_2 \circ \Pi_{12}$ is a knowledge-sound proof of knowledge for R_1 with soundness error $\kappa_{12} + \kappa_2$. Concretely, given extractors $\mathcal{E}_{12}$ and $\mathcal{E}_2$ for Π_{12} and Π_2 respectively, we construct an extractor $\mathcal{E}_1$ for the composed proof system. If $\mathcal{E}_{12}$ and $\mathcal{E}_2$ run in expected time T_{12} and T_2 respectively and if $\mathcal{E}_{12}$ makes at most Q queries to the prover oracle, then $\mathcal{E}_1$ runs in expected time $O(T_{12} + QT_2)$.*

Proof. Let $\mathcal{E}_{12}$ and $\mathcal{E}_2$ be extractors for Π_{12} and Π_2 respectively. We construct an extractor $\mathcal{E}_1$ for the composed proof system. The main idea is that, when $\mathcal{E}_1$ is given access to a prover $\mathcal{P}_1^*$ for the composed proof system $\Pi_2 \circ \Pi_{12}$, it first uses $\mathcal{E}_2$ and $\mathcal{P}_1^*$ to construct an efficient prover $\mathcal{P}_{12}^*$ for the reduction Π_{12}, and then $\mathcal{E}_1$ extracts a witness from $\mathcal{P}_{12}^*$ using $\mathcal{E}_{12}$.

The new prover $\mathcal{P}_{12}^*$ for Π_{12}, which makes use of rewindable oracle access to $\mathcal{P}_1^*$, is defined as follows. First, $\mathcal{P}_{12}^*$ runs $\mathcal{P}_1^*$, forwards the prover messages $z_1, \ldots, z_{k'}$ from $\mathcal{P}_1^*$ to $\mathcal{V}_{12}$, and forwards the challenges $c_1, \cdots, c_k$ from $\mathcal{V}_{12}$ back to $\mathcal{P}_1^*$. This continues until $\mathcal{P}_1^*$ outputs $z_{k'}$. Now, to finish the proof, $\mathcal{P}_{12}^*$ needs to find w_2 such that $(x_2, w_2) \in R_2$, where $x_2 = \tilde{\mathcal{V}}(x_1, c_1, \ldots, c_k, z_1, \ldots, z_{k'})$. To do this $\mathcal{P}_{12}^*$ runs $\mathcal{E}_2$ on input x_2. Each time $\mathcal{E}_2$ makes a query to its prover oracle,

$\mathcal{P}_{12}^*$ prepends the challenges $c_1, \ldots, c_k$ of the first part of the protocol to the query and forwards it to $\mathcal{P}_1^*$. When $\mathcal{E}_2$ finishes and outputs a potential witness w_2, then $\mathcal{P}_{12}^*$ outputs (z_k', w_2) as its final message, and $\mathcal{V}_{12}$ will accept the proof if and only if $(x_2, w_2) \in R_2$.

Conditioned on each set of challenges $(c_1, \ldots, c_k)$ being sent by $\mathcal{V}_{12}$, the success probability of our prover $\mathcal{P}_{12}^*$ is equal to the probability that $\mathcal{E}_2(x_2)^{\mathcal{P}_1^*(c_1, \ldots, c_k, \cdot)}$ outputs a valid witness for x_1, which is at least $\epsilon(\mathcal{P}_1^*(c_1, \ldots, c_k, \cdot), x_2) - \kappa_2$. Taking the average over all possible sets of challenges $(c_1, \ldots, c_k)$ we get that $\epsilon(\mathcal{P}_{12}^*, x_1)$ is at least $\epsilon(\mathcal{P}_1^*, x_1) - \kappa_2$.

Now we define the extractor $\mathcal{E}_1$ for the composed proof protocol $\Pi_2 \circ \Pi_{12}$. When given input x_1, $\mathcal{E}_1(x_1)$ just runs the extractor $\mathcal{E}_{12}(x_1)$, and answers all the prover queries as if $\mathcal{E}_{12}(x_1)$ interacts with our prover $\mathcal{P}_{12}^*$ from the previous paragraphs. When $\mathcal{E}_{12}$ outputs a witness w_1, $\mathcal{E}_1$ finishes and also outputs w_1. If the expected runtime of $\mathcal{E}_{12}$ and $\mathcal{E}_2$ is T_{12} and T_2 respectively, and if $\mathcal{E}_{12}$ makes Q queries to the prover oracle, then the expected runtime of $\mathcal{E}_1$ is $O(T_{12} + QT_2)$, because running $\mathcal{E}_1$ requires in expectation T_{12} time, and answering $\mathcal{E}_{12}$'s prover oracle queries takes in expectation $O(QT_2)$ time, because each query is answered by running $\mathcal{E}_2$.

Now we only have to prove that $\mathcal{E}_1(x_1)^{\mathcal{P}_1^*}$ outputs a valid witness with probability at least $\epsilon(\mathcal{P}_1^*, x_1) - \kappa_2 - \kappa_{12}$. Since $\mathcal{E}_1$ simply simulates a run of $\mathcal{E}_{12}^{\mathcal{P}_{12}^*}(x_1)$ and outputs the same witness, the success probability of $\mathcal{E}_1(x_1)^{\mathcal{P}_1^*}$ is equal to the success probability of $\mathcal{E}_{12}^{\mathcal{P}_{12}^*}(x_1)$ which is at least

$$\epsilon(\mathcal{P}_{12}^*, x_1) - \kappa_{12} \geq \epsilon(\mathcal{P}_1^*, x_1) - \kappa_{12} - \kappa_2.$$

$\square$

It follows from this lemma that for any integer k, the composition of k proof-of-knowledge reductions with soundness errors $\kappa_1, \ldots, \kappa_k$ is sound with soundness error $\kappa_1 + \cdots + \kappa_k$. Recursive proofs such as bulletproof-type systems and our LaBRADOR proof system can be seen as the repeated composition of a base proof-of-knowledge reduction from a relation $\mathcal{R}$ to itself. Even though the number of repetitions k usually increases with the size of the witness and is not bounded by a constant, we can in some cases still prove the soundness of the recursive protocol:

Corollary 3.8. *Suppose Π is a proof-of-knowledge reduction from a relation $\mathcal{R}$ to itself. Suppose there exists constants $\alpha < 1$ and C, such that for all statement-witness pairs (x, w), where the size of the statement x is larger than C the proof-of-knowledge reduction Π reduces proving knowledge of $(x, w) \in R$ to proving knowledge of a witness for a new statement x' such that $|x'| < \alpha|x|$. Then we can define a recursive proof protocol Π^* that iteratively applies Π until the size of the statement is smaller than C, and then sends a witness w_k for the final statement x_k to the verifier, who checks that $(x_k, w_k) \in \mathcal{R}$ directly.*

If the base protocol Π is knowledge-sound with soundness error κ, with the additional property that there exists a constant β such that the extractor makes at most $\beta|x|/|x'|$ queries to the prover oracle, for $|x| > C$. Then Π^* is knowledge-sound with soundness error $\lceil -\log_\alpha(|x|/C) \rceil \kappa$.

Proof. Since the base protocol is repeated at most $k = \lceil -\log_\alpha(|x|/C) \rceil$ times, the extractor from the proof of lemma 3.7 has a success probability of at least $\epsilon(\mathcal{P}^*) - k\kappa$, as desired. We only have to prove that the extractor runs in polynomial time. Let $p(|x|) = c|x|^d$ be a polynomial that bounds the expected running time of the base extractor, and let $T(|x|)$ be the expected running time of the recursive extractor. Let $x^{(i)}$ be statement to be proven in the i-th recursion, with $x^{(k+1)}$ being the last statement. Then, by Lemma 3.7, we have

$$
\begin{aligned}
T(|x^{(1)}|) &\le p(|x^{(1)}|) + Q^{(1)}T(|x^{(1)}|) \\
&\le p(|x^{(1)}|) + Q^{(1)}p(|x^{(2)}|) + Q^{(1)}Q^{(2)}T(|x^{(3)}|) \\
&\le \quad \cdots \\
&\le p(|x^{(1)}|) + Q^{(1)}p(|x^{(2)}|) + \cdots + Q^{(1)} \cdot \cdots \cdot Q^{(k)}p(|x^{(k+1)}|) , \quad (1)
\end{aligned}
$$

where $Q^{(i)}$ is the number of prover queries that the base extractor makes for the reduction from $x^{(i)}$ to $x^{(i+1)}$. Note that, because of the assumption that $Q^{(i)} \le \beta|x^{(i)}|/|x^{(i+1)}|$, we have that $Q^{(1)} \cdot Q^{(2)} \cdot \ldots \cdot Q^{(\ell)} \le \beta^\ell |x^{(1)}|/|x^{(\ell)}|$. The right-hand side of (1) has $k = O(\log|x|)$ terms, and each term is bounded by $\beta^k \cdot |x| \cdot p(|x|)$, so the total runtime of the recursive extractor is $O(\log|x|) \cdot \beta^{O(\log(|x|))} \cdot |x| \cdot p(|x|)$, which is indeed polynomial in $|x|$. $\square$

4   Modular Johnson-Lindenstrauss Lemma

In our proof system, we need to prove knowledge of a long vector $\vec{w} \in \mathbb{Z}^d$ with small ℓ_2-norm. Revealing the entire vector so that the verifier can check that it has small ℓ_2-norm would be very costly, so we rely on a version of the Johnson-Lindenstrauss lemma to reduce the dimensionality. The intuition is that random linear projections almost preserve the ℓ_2-norm. So, instead of revealing $\vec{w}$ we let the verifier sample a random linear map $\Pi : \mathbb{Z}^d \to \mathbb{Z}^{256}$, where the entries of Π are independent and equal to $-1, 0,$ or 1 with probabilities $1/4, 1/2,$ and $1/4$ respectively. The prover then only reveals $\Pi\vec{w}$, which is much more compact than the long vector $\vec{w}$. One can check that the average of $\|\Pi\vec{w}\|_2$ is $\sqrt{128}\|\vec{w}\|_2$, and Gentry, Halevi, and Lyubashevsky argue that regardless of the vector $\vec{w}$, with overwhelming probability, the ℓ_2-norm cannot be much higher or lower [GHL21].

Lemma 4.1 (Corollary 3.2, [GHL21]). *Let* C *be a distribution on* $\{-1, 0, 1\}$ *with* $\Pr[\mathsf{C} = 0] = 1/2$, *and* $\Pr[\mathsf{C} = 1] = \Pr[\mathsf{C} = -1] = 1/4$, *then for every vector* $\vec{w} \in \mathbb{Z}^d$ *we have*

$$
\Pr_{\vec{\pi} \leftarrow \mathsf{C}^d}[|\langle \vec{\pi}, \vec{w}\rangle| > \quad 9.5\|\vec{w}\|_2] \lesssim 2^{-141}
$$

$$
\Pr_{\Pi \leftarrow \mathsf{C}^{256 \times d}}[\|\Pi\vec{w}\|_2 < \quad \sqrt{30}\|\vec{w}\|_2] \lesssim 2^{-128}
$$

$$
\Pr_{\Pi \leftarrow \mathsf{C}^{256 \times d}}[\|\Pi\vec{w}\|_2 > \sqrt{337}\|\vec{w}\|_2] \lesssim 2^{-128}
$$

Therefore, the prover can send $\Pi\vec{w}$, and prove that it is computed correctly. Then, if the verifier sees that $\|\Pi\vec{w}\|_2 \leq \sqrt{30}b$ for some bound b, then he is convinced that $\|\vec{w}\|_2$ is at most b. One caveat is that the prover only proves that $\Pi\vec{w}$ is correct mod q, which might mess up the soundness because $\|\Pi\vec{w} \mod q\|_2$ could be smaller than $\|\Pi\vec{w}\|_2$. Gentry, Halevi, and Lyubashevsky prove that, despite the potential reduction mod q, the proof strategy is still sound, on the condition that $b < q/45d$. They use a 256-bit prime q, so this restriction is not a problem for them. However, for efficiency reasons we want to use a small modulus q (e.g. $q \approx 2^{32}$), so we strengthen their result to only require $b < q/125$ instead. We believe this lemma could be useful for future works in lattice-based proof systems. Its proof relies on the Berry-Esseen Theorem [Ber41, Ess42], and is given in the full version of the paper.

Lemma 4.2 (strengthening of Corollary 3.3, [GHL21]). *Let $q \in \mathbb{N}$, and let C be the distribution from Lemma 4.1, then for every vector $\vec{w} \in [\pm q/2]^d$ with $\|\vec{w}\|_2 \geq b$ for some bound $b \leq q/125$, we have*

$$\Pr_{\Pi \leftarrow \mathsf{C}^{256 \times d}} \left[\|\Pi\vec{w} \mod q\|_2 < \sqrt{30}b \right] \lesssim 2^{-128}.$$

5 Protocol

5.1 Principal Relation

We define the principal relation R for our proof system. The relation is parameterized by a rank $n \geq 1$, a multiplicity $r \geq 1$, and a norm bound $\beta > 0$. It consists of short solutions to dot product constraints over $\mathcal{R}_q$ that can be proven efficiently with lattice techniques. Concretely, a statement consists of a family $\mathcal{F} = (f^{(k)} \mid k = 1, \ldots, K)$ of quadratic dot product functions $f \colon \mathcal{R}_q^n \times \cdots \times \mathcal{R}_q^n \to \mathcal{R}_q$ (r times) of the form

$$f(\vec{s}_1, \ldots, \vec{s}_r) = \sum_{i,j=1}^{r} a_{ij}\langle\vec{s}_i, \vec{s}_j\rangle + \sum_{i=1}^{r}\langle\vec{\varphi}_i, \vec{s}_i\rangle - b,$$

where $a_{i,j}, b \in \mathcal{R}_q$ and $\vec{\varphi}_i \in \mathcal{R}_q^n$. The matrix (a_{ij}) can be assumed to be symmetric without loss of generality, i.e. $a_{ij} = a_{ji}$. Sometimes we are only interested in the constant polynomial coefficient of a function f. For such a function all the higher coefficients of the polynomial b are irrelevant so we do not include them in the statement. This saves space, especially when there are many such functions. We collect these functions in a second family $\mathcal{F}' = (f'^{(l)} \mid l = 1, \ldots, L)$ in a statement for the relation $\mathcal{R}$. Now, a witness consists of r vectors $\vec{s}_1, \ldots, \vec{s}_r \in \mathcal{R}_q^n$ such that $f(\vec{s}_1, \ldots, \vec{s}_r) = 0$ for all $f \in \mathcal{F}$, $\mathsf{ct}(f'(\vec{s}_1, \ldots, \vec{s}_r)) = 0$ for all $f' \in \mathcal{F}'$, and $\sum_{i=1}^{r} \|\vec{s}_i\|_2^2 \leq \beta^2$. In symbols,

$$\mathcal{R} = \left\{ ((\mathcal{F}, \mathcal{F}', \beta), (\vec{s}_1, \ldots, \vec{s}_r)) \;\middle|\; \begin{array}{l} f(\vec{s}_1, \ldots, \vec{s}_r) = 0 \quad \forall f \in \mathcal{F}, \\ \mathsf{ct}(f'(\vec{s}_1, \ldots, \vec{s}_r)) = 0 \quad \forall f' \in \mathcal{F}', \\ \displaystyle\sum_{i=1}^{r} \|\vec{s}_i\|_2^2 \leq \beta^2 \end{array} \right\}.$$

We reduce R1CS to this relation R in Sect. 7. In this section, we construct an interactive proof for $\mathcal{R}$ with very compact proof sizes. Our proof introduces a small amount of slack, which means that it does not exactly prove knowledge of a solution with norm bound β, but only a solution with a norm bound that is slightly bigger, approximately by a factor of two. This does not pose a problem for our reduction from R1CS.

5.2 Main Protocol

Our main protocol is an interactive proof for the principal relation R that works by committing to the witness vectors, replacing the norm statement with a Johnson-Lindenstrauss projection, aggregating the dot product functions, and amortizing over the witness vectors.

Committing. In the first step of the protocol the prover commits to the vectors $\vec{s}_i$ by computing Ajtai commitments

$$\vec{t}_i = \boldsymbol{A}\vec{s}_i \in \mathcal{R}_q^\kappa.$$

We have that $\|\vec{s}_i\| \leq \beta$, but the commitments must tolerate some slack. Especially because they need to be binding with respect to weak openings extracted from an amortized opening. We handle this in the security analysis of the protocol.

Sending all the $\vec{t}_i$ would be costly. Therefore the prover again commits to them in a single Ajtai commitment $\vec{u}_1$ and only sends $\vec{u}_1$. This allows to only send the $\vec{t}_i$ as part of the prover's last message and thus push the $\vec{t}_i$ to the target relation of the protocol, which can be proven recursively with little cost. The $\vec{t}_i$ have coefficients that are arbitrary modulo q. So they need to be decomposed into $t_1 \geq 2$ parts with respect to a small base b_1 before committing. That is, one writes $\vec{t}_i = \vec{t}_i^{(0)} + \vec{t}_i^{(1)}b_1 + \cdots + \vec{t}_i^{(t_1-1)}b_1^{t_1-1}$ where centered representatives modulo b_1 are used, i.e. $\|\vec{t}_i^{(k)}\|_\infty \leq b_1/2$. Now let $\vec{t} \in \mathcal{R}_q^{rt_1\kappa}$ be a concatenation of all the decomposition parts $\vec{t}_i^{(k)}$. Then we get the Ajtai commitment

$$\vec{u}_1 = \boldsymbol{B}\vec{t} \in \mathcal{R}_q^{\kappa_1}, \quad \text{with} \quad \|\vec{t}\| \leq \gamma_1. \tag{2}$$

We say that $\vec{u}_1$ is an *outer* commitment, and $\vec{t}_i$, $i = 1, \ldots, r$, are the *inner* commitments. The decomposition parameters t_1, b_1 and the norm bound γ_1 are discussed in Subsect. 5.4.

Projecting. Now, the norm statement in the relation R can be replaced by a Johnson-Lindenstrauss projection. So the verifier sends random matrices $\Pi_i \in \{-1, 0, 1\}^{256 \times nd}$ for $i = 1, \ldots, r$. Then the prover sends the projection $\vec{p} = \sum_{i=1}^r \Pi_i \vec{s}_i$. The verifier checks that $\|\vec{p}\| \leq \sqrt{128}\beta$. This is true with probability $1/2$, but the prover can request projection matrices until it is the case. Moreover, it implies with overwhelming probability that $\sum_{i=1}^r \|\vec{s}_i\|^2 \leq (128/30)\beta^2$. Here the slack of a factor of $\sqrt{128/30} \approx 2$ is introduced. For proving correct projection, we write $\vec{p} = \sum_i \Pi_i \vec{s}_i$ as dot product constraints on the polynomial vectors $\vec{s}_i$. Let $\vec{\pi}_i^{(j)}$ be the jth row of Π_i for $j = 1, \ldots, 256$. Then for each $j = 1, \ldots, 256$ define the dot product function

$$\sum_{i=1}^{r} \langle \sigma_{-1}(\vec{\pi}_i^{(j)}), \vec{s}_i \rangle - p_j \, .$$

These functions do not vanish in $\mathcal{R}_q$ but have zero constant coefficients. So they are of the form of the functions in the family $\mathcal{F}'$.

Aggregating. In the first aggregation step, the above functions for proving the JL projection and the functions in $\mathcal{F}'$ are aggregated to only $\lceil 128/\log q \rceil$ functions with zero constant coefficients by linear combining all functions with uniformly random challenges from $\mathbb{Z}_q$. This preserves the zero constant coefficients. So the verifier sends $\vec{\psi}^{(k)} \overset{\$}{\leftarrow} (\mathbb{Z}_q)^L$ and $\vec{\omega}^{(k)} \in (\mathbb{Z}_q)^{256}$ for $k = 1, \ldots, \lceil 128/\log q \rceil$, where $L = |\mathcal{F}'|$. The prover computes

$$f''^{(k)}(\vec{s}_1, \ldots, \vec{s}_r) = \sum_{l=1}^{L} \psi_l^{(k)} f'^{(l)}(\vec{s}_1, \ldots, \vec{s}_r) + \sum_{j=1}^{256} \omega_j^{(k)} (\langle \sigma_{-1}(\vec{\pi}_i^{(j)}), \vec{s}_i \rangle - p_j)$$

$$= \sum_{i,j=1}^{r} a''^{(k)} \langle \vec{s}_i, \vec{s}_j \rangle + \sum_{i=1}^{r} \langle \vec{\varphi}_i''^{(k)}, \vec{s}_i \rangle - b_0''^{(k)} \, ,$$

where $b_0''^{(k)} = \sum_l \psi_l^{(k)} b_0'^{(l)} + \langle \vec{\omega}^{(k)}, \vec{p} \rangle$. Then the prover extends these integers to full polynomials $b''^{(k)}$ so that the new functions $f''^{(k)}$ become completely vanishing and of the same type as the functions in $\mathcal{F}$. The prover sends the $b''^{(k)}$ and the verifier checks that their constant coefficients are correct.

In the second step, we aggregate all functions in $\mathcal{F}$ together with the new functions. The verifier sends $K + \lceil 128/\log q \rceil$ random challenge polynomials $\vec{\alpha} \overset{\$}{\leftarrow} \mathcal{R}_q^K$ and $\vec{\beta} \overset{\$}{\leftarrow} \mathcal{R}_q^{\lceil 128/\log q \rceil}$, where $K = |\mathcal{F}|$. Then, define

$$F(\vec{s}_1, \ldots, \vec{s}_r) = \sum_{k=1}^{K} \alpha_k f^{(k)}(\vec{s}_1, \ldots, \vec{s}_r) + \sum_{k=1}^{\lceil 128/\log q \rceil} \beta_k f''^{(k)}$$

$$= \sum_{i,j=1}^{r} a_{ij} \langle \vec{s}_i, \vec{s}_j \rangle + \sum_{i=1}^{r} \langle \vec{\varphi}_i, \vec{s}_i \rangle - b \, .$$

Amortizing. Finally, we amortize over the $\vec{s}_i$. This means that instead of opening the individual inner commitments $\vec{t}_i$ by sending all the $\vec{s}_i$, the prover opens a random linear-combination $\vec{z} = c_1 \vec{t}_1 + \cdots + c_r \vec{t}_r$ with challenge polynomials $c_i \in \mathcal{C} \subset \mathcal{R}_q$ chosen by the verifier. The verifier checks that

$$A\vec{z} = \sum_{i=1}^{r} c_i \vec{t}_i \in \mathcal{R}_q^\kappa \quad \text{and} \quad \|\vec{z}\| \leq \gamma \, . \tag{3}$$

The aggregated dot product constraint $F(\vec{s}_1, \ldots, \vec{s}_r) = \mathbf{0}$ is proven probabilistically using the amortized opening $\vec{z}$. This works by proving

$$\langle \vec{z}, \vec{z} \rangle = \sum_{i,j=1}^{r} g_{ij} c_i c_j, \quad \sum_{i=1}^{r} \langle \vec{\varphi}_i, \vec{z} \rangle c_i = \sum_{i,j=1}^{r} h_{ij} c_i c_j,$$

$$\sum_{i,j=1}^{r} a_{ij} g_{ij} + \sum_{i=1}^{r} h_{ii} - b = 0, \tag{4}$$

where $\vec{\varphi}_i \in \mathcal{R}_q^n$ are vectors independent of the challenges c_i, and the g_{ij}, h_{ij} are garbage polynomials that are also independent of the c_i. If $\vec{z} = c_1 \vec{s}_1 + \cdots + c_r \vec{s}_r$, then these equations together imply with low soundness error that

$$F(\vec{s}_1, \ldots, \vec{s}_r) = \sum_{i,j=1}^{r} a_{ij} \langle \vec{s}_i, \vec{s}_j \rangle + \sum_{i=1}^{r} \langle \vec{\varphi}_i, \vec{s}_i \rangle - b = 0.$$

Moreover, the garbage matrices (g_{ij}) and (h_{ij}) can assumed to be symmetric.

This strategy is implemented in the protocol in the following way. The prover computes the garbage polynomials

$$g_{ij} = \langle \vec{s}_i, \vec{s}_j \rangle \quad \text{and} \quad h_{ij} = \frac{1}{2} \left(\langle \vec{\varphi}_i, \vec{s}_j \rangle + \langle \vec{\varphi}_j, \vec{s}_i \rangle \right)$$

for $i, j = 1, \ldots, r$. Then, similarly to the inner commitments $\vec{t}_i$, the prover does not directly send the garbage polynomials but produces an outer commitment to them. Here the h_{ij} are again arbitrary modulo q and hence will be decomposed into t_1 parts modulo b_1. On the other hand, the remaining garbage polynomials g_{ij} are short modulo q. Nevertheless, they are decomposed into $t_2 \geq 2$ parts with respect to a base b_2 to reduce their width further. Let $\vec{g} \in \mathcal{R}_q^{t_2(r^2+r)/2}$ and $\vec{h} \in \mathcal{R}_q^{t_1(r^2+r)/2}$ be vectors containing all the decomposition parts of all the garbage polynomials. Then the second outer commitment is given by

$$\vec{u}_2 = C\vec{g} + D\vec{h} \in \mathcal{R}_q^{\kappa_2} \quad \text{with} \quad \sqrt{\|\vec{g}\|^2 + \|\vec{h}\|^2} \leq \gamma_2. \tag{5}$$

We note that the garbage polynomials g_{ij} are independent of all challenges, not just the c_i. Therefore the prover can compute them already at the very beginning of the protocol and include them in the first outer commitment $\vec{u}_1$. This change allows for a slightly better security proof.

Finally, the verifier sends the r challenge polynomials $c_1, \ldots, c_r \xleftarrow{\$} \mathcal{C}$, and the prover replies with the amortized opening $\vec{z} = c_1 \vec{s}_1 + \cdots + c_r \vec{s}_r$ and the outer commitment openings $\vec{t}, \vec{g}, \vec{h}$. The amortized opening is such that $\|\vec{z}\| \leq \gamma$.

Verifying. The verifier checks that $\vec{z}$ is an amortized opening with challenges c_i for the inner commitments defined by $\vec{t}$, and that $\vec{t}$ and $\vec{g}, \vec{h}$ are openings for the outer commitments. That is, he checks (2), (3), (5). Moreover, the verifier checks the dot product equations (4) where the vectors $\vec{\varphi}_i$, matrix (a_{ij}), and polynomial b are those defining the aggregated function F.

5.3   Recursion and Decomposition

The target relation of our main protocol is almost another instance of the dot product constraint relation R. Indeed, the witness as given by the last prover message consists of four vectors $\vec{z}, \vec{t}, \vec{g}, \vec{h}$ that must only fulfill equations of dot product type and norm checks in (2), (3), (4), (5). The only difference is that there are three separate norm checks instead of a single global one. But those checks only serve to ensure that the outer and inner commitments are binding. So, when we consolidate the three checks into

$$\|\vec{z}\|^2 + \|\vec{t}\|^2 + \|\vec{g}\|^2 + \|\vec{h}\|^2 \leq \gamma^2 + \gamma_1^2 + \gamma_2^2,$$

we obtain a protocol that is sound for a suitable choice of the commitment ranks κ, κ_1 and κ_2, and whose target relation is exactly another instance of R. A different approach would be to generalize R by allowing several norm checks, which could be handled in the protocol with several parallel Johnson-Lindenstrauss projections.

It now follows that the protocol can be recursed to further reduce the proof size. See Sect. 3 for details and specifically Lemma 3.7 for how this affects the soundness error. The protocol relies on amortization to achieve small proof sizes, so before directly recursing the protocol on the target relation we first decrease the rank and increase the multiplicity by decomposing the witness vectors and rewriting the target relation using the decomposed vectors. We also reduce the width of the masked opening $\vec{z}$ and decompose it into two additive parts by reducing modulo a base b.

We start by slightly simplifying the target relation. Notice that all Eqs. (2)-(5) except the norm checks are linear in the witness vectors $\vec{t}, \vec{g}, \vec{h}$. So we may concatenate

$$\vec{v} = \vec{t} \parallel \vec{g} \parallel \vec{h} \in R_q^m.$$

Then we can write all equations as linear dot product equations in the single vector $\vec{v} \in R_q^m$, where $m = rt_1\kappa + (t_1 + t_2)(r^2 + r)/2$. The global norm check becomes $\|\vec{z}\|^2 + \|\vec{v}\|^2 \leq \gamma^2 + \gamma_1^2 + \gamma_2^2$.

Decomposing the witness. If we would naively recurse our proof protocol and repeatedly fold the witness, then the coefficients of $\vec{z}$ would quickly blow up. Therefore, we decompose $\vec{z}$ into 2 additive parts by reducing the coefficients of $\vec{z}$ modulo a base $b \geq 2$; that is, we write $\vec{z} = \vec{z}^{(0)} + b\vec{z}^{(1)}$ with centered representatives modulo b. The quadratic dot product $\langle \vec{z}, \vec{z} \rangle$ in Eq. (4) transforms to $\langle \vec{z}^{(0)}, \vec{z}^{(0)} \rangle + 2b\langle \vec{z}^{(1)}, \vec{z}^{(0)} \rangle + b^2\langle \vec{z}^{(1)}, \vec{z}^{(1)} \rangle$. There is no need to decompose $\vec{v}$ since its width is controlled in the preceding execution of the protocol. So the reduction of $\vec{z}$ can be anticipated and the decomposition bases b_1 and b_2 chosen such that $b \approx b_1 \approx b_2$. The final norm check we will use is

$$\|\vec{z}^{(0)}\|^2 + \|\vec{z}^{(1)}\|^2 + \|\vec{v}\|^2 \leq \frac{2}{b^2}\gamma^2 + \gamma_1^2 + \gamma_2^2 = (\beta')^2. \tag{6}$$

This implies $\|\vec{z}\| = \|\vec{z}^{(0)} + b\vec{z}^{(1)}\| \leq (1 + b)\beta'$.

Next, to prepare for the next iteration of our protocol, we write the vectors $\vec{z}^{(0)}, \vec{z}^{(1)} \in \mathcal{R}_q^n$ as a concatenation of $\nu \geq 1$ vectors $\vec{s}_i' \in \mathcal{R}_q^{\lceil n/\nu \rceil}$, i.e., $\vec{z}^{(0)} = \vec{s}_1' \parallel \cdots \parallel \vec{s}_\nu'$, $\vec{z}^{(1)} = \vec{s}_{\nu+1}' \parallel \cdots \parallel \vec{s}_{2\nu}'$, and similarly we write $\vec{v} = \vec{s}_{2\nu+1}' \parallel \cdots \parallel \vec{s}_{2\nu+\mu}'$ as a concatenation of μ vectors $\vec{s}_i' \in \mathcal{R}_q^{\lceil m/\mu \rceil}$. We then zero-pad all $\vec{s}_i'$ to have length $n' = \max\{\lceil n/\nu \rceil, \lceil m/\mu \rceil\}$. To avoid padding too much, we choose the parameters such that $\frac{n}{\nu} \approx \frac{m}{\mu}$. So, we now have $r' = 2\nu + \mu$ vectors $\vec{s}_i'$ of rank n'.

Now, observe that the final verification equations are the norm check (6), and $\kappa + \kappa_1 + \kappa_2 + 3$ dot product constraints, i.e., equations that can be written in the form,

$$g^{(k)}(\vec{s}_1, \ldots, \vec{s}_{r'}) = \sum_{i,j=1}^{r'} a_{ij}^{(k)} \langle \vec{s}_i, \vec{s}_j \rangle + \sum_{i=1}^{r'} \langle \vec{\varphi}_i^{(k)}, \vec{s}_i \rangle - b^{(k)} = 0 \qquad (7)$$

for $k = 1, \ldots, \kappa + \kappa_1 + \kappa_2 + 3 = K'$. The matrices $(a_{ij}^{(k)})$ are symmetric and tridiagonal, i.e. $a_{ij} = a_{ji}$, and $a_{ij} = 0$ for $|i - j| > 1$. Furthermore, $a_{ij}^{(k)} = 0$ unless $i, j \leq 2\nu$.

We let $\mathcal{G} = \{g^{(k)} \mid k = 1, \ldots, K'\}$ be the new family of dot product constraints. Then the verifier accepts if and only $\|\vec{p}\| < \sqrt{128}\beta$, $b_0''^{(k)}$ is correct, and $((\mathcal{G}, \{\}, \beta'), (\vec{s}_i')_{i \in [r']})$ is in R with parameters n', r', β', so we can indeed compose the protocol with itself recursively.

We have now finished the description of our protocol. It is completely presented in Fig. 2, which includes the consolidated norm statement (6) from this section (Fig. 3).

5.4   Norm Bounds and Decomposition Parameters

We now study the norm bound β' of the target relation that is derived from the bounds $\gamma, \gamma_1, \gamma_2$ on $\vec{z}, \vec{t} \parallel \vec{g}$ and $\vec{h}$, respectively. The bounds γ_1 and γ_2 are in turn derived from the decomposition parameters. The goal of the analysis is to choose bounds that are as small as possible while still being feasible in the honest execution of the protocol. Our analysis is heuristic, rather than worst-case, whenever this is allowed by the security proof. Although we have observed experimentally that our heuristics are highly accurate, it could happen that during an execution of the protocol some quantities are larger than predicted by our analysis. This does not affect the soundness of our proof and only potentially affects the proof size or prover runtime. For security, we need that the commitments are binding with respect to the lengths of the vectors that actually appear in an execution of the protocol. If the vectors turn out longer than expected the prover needs to either restart the protocol until the vectors are short enough, or increase the commitment parameters dynamically to ensure the commitments are binding.

$\underline{\text{Prover } \mathcal{P}}$ 　　　　　　　　　　　　　　　　　　　　　　　　$\underline{\text{Verifier } \mathcal{V}}$

$\vec{s}_1, \ldots, \vec{s}_r \in \mathcal{R}_q^n, \ \sum_{i=1}^{r} \|\vec{s}_i\|_2^2 \le \beta^2$ 　　　　　　　　　　$\vec{\varphi}_i^{(k)}, a_{ij}^{(k)}, b^{(k)}$

$b^{(k)} = \sum_{i,j=1}^{r} a_{ij}^{(k)} \langle \vec{s}_i, \vec{s}_j \rangle + \sum_{i=1}^{r} \langle \vec{\varphi}_i^{(k)}, \vec{s}_i \rangle, \ k \in [K]$ 　　$\vec{\varphi}_i'^{(l)}, a_{ij}'^{(l)}, b_0'^{(l)}$

$b'^{(l)} = \sum_{i,j=1}^{r} a_{ij}'^{(l)} \langle \vec{s}_i, \vec{s}_j \rangle + \sum_{i=1}^{r} \langle \vec{\varphi}_i'^{(l)}, \vec{s}_i \rangle, \ l \in [L]$

$\vec{t}_i = A\vec{s}_i = \vec{t}_i^{(0)} + \cdots + \vec{t}_i^{(t_1-1)} b_1^{t_1-1}$

$g_{ij} = \langle \vec{s}_i, \vec{s}_j \rangle = g_{ij}^{(0)} + \cdots + g_{ij}^{(t_2-1)} b_2^{t_2-1}$

$\vec{u}_1 = \sum_{i=1}^{r} \sum_{k=0}^{t_1-1} B_{ik} \vec{t}_i^{(k)} + \sum_{i \le j} \sum_{k=0}^{t_2-1} C_{ijk} g_{ij}^{(k)}$ 　　　$\xrightarrow{\quad \vec{u}_1 \quad}$

　　　　　　　　　　　　　　　　$\xleftarrow{\quad \Pi_i = (\vec{\pi}_i^{(j)})_j \quad}$ 　$\Pi_i \xleftarrow{\$} \chi^{256 \times nd}$

$p_j = \sum_{i=1}^{r} \langle \vec{\pi}_i^{(j)}, \vec{s}_i \rangle$ 　　　　　　　　$\xrightarrow{\quad \vec{p} = (p_j) \quad}$ 　$\|\vec{p}\| \overset{?}{\le} \sqrt{128}\beta$

　　　　　　　　　　　　　　　　　　　　　　$\vec{\psi}^{(k)} \xleftarrow{\$} (\mathbb{Z}_q)^L$

$a_{ij}''^{(k)} = \sum_{l=1}^{L} \psi_l^{(k)} a_{ij}'^{(l)}$ 　　　　　　$\xleftarrow{\quad \vec{\psi}^{(k)}, \vec{\omega}^{(k)} \quad}$ 　$\vec{\omega}^{(k)} \xleftarrow{\$} (\mathbb{Z}_q)^{256}$

$\vec{\varphi}_i''^{(k)} = \sum_{l=1}^{L} \psi_l^{(k)} \vec{\varphi}_i'^{(l)} + \sum_{j=1}^{256} \omega_j^{(k)} \sigma_{-1}(\vec{\pi}_i^{(j)})$

$b''^{(k)} = \sum_{i,j=1}^{r} a_{ij}''^{(k)} \langle \vec{s}_i, \vec{s}_j \rangle + \sum_{i=1}^{r} \langle \vec{\varphi}_i''^{(k)}, \vec{s}_i \rangle$ 　　$\xrightarrow{\quad b''^{(k)} \quad}$ 　$b_0''^{(k)} \overset{?}{=} \langle \vec{\omega}^{(k)}, \vec{p} \rangle$

　　　　　　　　　　　　　　　　　　　　　　　$+ \sum_{l=1}^{L} \psi_l^{(k)} b_0'^{(l)}$

　　　　　　　　　　　　　　　　　　　　　　$\vec{\alpha} \xleftarrow{\$} \mathcal{R}_q^K$

$\vec{\varphi}_i = \sum_{k=1}^{K} \alpha_k \vec{\varphi}_i^{(k)} + \sum_{k=1}^{\lceil 128/\log q \rceil} \beta_k \vec{\varphi}_i''^{(k)}$ 　　$\xleftarrow{\quad \vec{\alpha}, \vec{\beta} \quad}$ 　$\vec{\beta} \xleftarrow{\$} \mathcal{R}_q^{\lceil 128/\log q \rceil}$

$h_{ij} = \frac{1}{2}(\langle \vec{\varphi}_i, \vec{s}_j \rangle + \langle \vec{\varphi}_j, \vec{s}_i \rangle)$

　　$= h_{ij}^{(0)} + \cdots + h_{ij}^{(t_1-1)} b_1^{t_1-1}$

$\vec{u}_2 = \sum_{i \le j} \sum_{k=0}^{t_1-1} D_{ijk} h_{ij}^{(k)}$ 　　　　　　$\xrightarrow{\quad \vec{u}_2 \quad}$

　　　　　　　　　　　　　　　　　　$\xleftarrow{\quad c_i \quad}$ 　$c_i \xleftarrow{\$} \mathcal{C}$

$\vec{z} = c_1 \vec{s}_1 + \cdots + c_r \vec{s}_r$ 　　　　$\xrightarrow{\quad \vec{z}, \vec{t}_i, g_{ij}, h_{ij} \quad}$ 　$\text{VERIFY}(\text{st}, \text{tr})$

Fig. 2. Our main Protocol. The common reference string consists of the commitment matrices $A \in \mathcal{R}_q^{\kappa \times n}$, $B_{ik} \in \mathcal{R}_q^{\kappa_1 \times \kappa}$ for $1 \le i \le r$, $0 \le k \le t_1 - 1$, $C_{ijk} \in \mathcal{R}_q^{\kappa_2 \times 1}$ for $1 \le i \le j \le r$, $0 \le k \le t_2 - 1$, and $D_{ijk} \in \mathcal{R}_q^{\kappa_2 \times 1}$ for $1 \le i \le j \le r$, $0 \le k \le t_1 - 1$.

VERIFY$(\mathsf{st}, \mathsf{tr})$

01 $\mathsf{st} = (\vec{\varphi}_i^{(k)}, a_{ij}^{(k)}, b^{(k)}, \vec{\varphi}_i'^{(l)}, a_{ij}'^{(l)}, b_0'^{(l)})$

02 $\mathsf{tr} = (\vec{u}_1, \vec{\pi}_i^{(j)}, \vec{p}, \vec{\psi}^{(k)}, \vec{\omega}^{(k)}, b''^{(k)}, \vec{\alpha}, \vec{\beta}, \vec{u}_2, c_i, \vec{z}, \vec{t}_i, g_{ij}, h_{ij})$

03 $a_{ij}''^{(k)} = \sum_{l=1}^{L} \psi_l^{(k)} a_{ij}'^{(l)}$

04 $\vec{\varphi}_i''^{(k)} = \sum_{l=1}^{L} \psi_l^{(k)} \vec{\varphi}_i'^{(l)} + \sum_{j=1}^{256} \omega_j^{(k)} \sigma_{-1}(\vec{\pi}_i^{(j)})$

05 $a_{ij} = \sum_{k=1}^{K} \alpha_k a_{ij}^{(k)} + \sum_{k=1}^{\lceil 128/\log q \rceil} \beta_k a_{ij}''^{(k)}$

06 $\vec{\varphi}_i = \sum_{k=1}^{K} \alpha_k \vec{\varphi}_i^{(k)} + \sum_{k=1}^{\lceil 128/\log q \rceil} \beta_k \vec{\varphi}_i''^{(k)}$

07 $b = \sum_{k=1}^{K} \alpha_k b^{(k)} + \sum_{k=1}^{\lceil 128/\log q \rceil} \beta_k b''^{(k)}$

08 $g_{ij} \stackrel{?}{=} g_{ji}$

09 $h_{ij} \stackrel{?}{=} h_{ji}$

10 $\vec{z} = \vec{z}^{(0)} + \vec{z}^{(1)} b, \quad \|\vec{z}^{(0)}\|_\infty \le \frac{b}{2}$

11 $\vec{t}_i = \vec{t}_i^{(0)} + \cdots + \vec{t}_i^{(t_1-1)} b_1^{t_1-1}, \quad \|\vec{t}_i^{(k)}\|_\infty \le \frac{b_1}{2}, \, k \le t_1 - 2$

12 $g_{ij} = g_{ij}^{(0)} + \cdots + g_{ij}^{(t_2-1)} b_2^{t_2-1}, \quad \|g_{ij}^{(k)}\|_\infty \le \frac{b_2}{2}, \, k = 0 \le t_2 - 2$

13 $h_{ij} = h_{ij}^{(0)} + \cdots + h_{ij}^{(t_1-1)} b_1^{t_1-1}, \quad \|h_{ij}^{(k)}\|_\infty \le \frac{b_1}{2}, \, k \le t_1 - 2$

14 $\sum_{i=0}^{1} \|\vec{z}^{(i)}\|^2 + \sum_{i=1}^{r} \sum_{k=0}^{t_1-1} \|\vec{t}_i^{(k)}\|^2 + \sum_{i,j=1}^{r} \sum_{k=0}^{t_2-1} \|g_{ij}^{(k)}\|^2 + \sum_{i,j=1}^{r} \sum_{k=0}^{t_1-1} \|h_{ij}^{(k)}\|^2$
$\stackrel{?}{\le} (\beta')^2$

15 $A\vec{z} \stackrel{?}{=} c_1 \vec{t}_1 + \cdots + c_r \vec{t}_r$

16 $\langle \vec{z}, \vec{z} \rangle \stackrel{?}{=} \sum_{i,j=1}^{r} g_{ij} c_i c_j$

17 $\sum_{i=1}^{r} \langle \vec{\varphi}_i, \vec{z} \rangle c_i \stackrel{?}{=} \sum_{i,j=1}^{r} h_{ij} c_i c_j$

18 $\sum_{i,j=1}^{r} a_{ij} g_{ij} + \sum_{i=1}^{r} h_{ii} - b \stackrel{?}{=} 0$

19 $\vec{u}_1 \stackrel{?}{=} \sum_{i=1}^{r} \sum_{k=0}^{t_1-1} B_{ik} \vec{t}_i^{(k)} + \sum_{1 \le i \le j \le r} \sum_{k=0}^{t_2-1} C_{ijk} g_{ij}^{(k)}$

20 $\vec{u}_2 \stackrel{?}{=} \sum_{1 \le i \le j \le r} \sum_{k=0}^{t_1-1} D_{ijk} h_{ij}^{(k)}$

Fig. 3. Verification algorithm for Fig. 2. The algorithm checks that the last prover message is a witness for the target relation, which is an instance of the principal relation from Subsect. 5.1. In particular, the algorithm uses the consolidated norm check in Line 14 as discussed in Subsect. 5.3. The other checks in Lines 15–20 are of dot product type.

Assume that the $\mathbb{Z}_q$-coefficients of the vectors $\vec{s}_i$ have standard deviation $\mathfrak{s} = \beta/\sqrt{rnd}$. Then each $\mathbb{Z}_q$-coefficient of $\vec{z}$ is the sum of rd coefficients from the $\vec{s}_i$, each multiplied with a challenge coefficient. The sum of the coefficients of a challenge polynomial has variance τ. So we can model the coefficients of $\vec{z} = \sum_i c_i \vec{s}_i$ as Gaussian with standard deviation $\mathfrak{s}\sqrt{r\tau}$.

Before the next recursion level the vector $\vec{z}$ is usually decomposed into two parts by reducing it modulo a base b. The coefficients of the low part are uniformly random modulo b and hence have standard deviation essentially $b/\sqrt{12}$. The coefficients of the high part are still Gaussian with standard deviation $\mathfrak{s}\sqrt{r\tau}/b$. If

$$b = \left\lfloor \sqrt{\sqrt{12r\tau}\mathfrak{s}} \right\rceil,$$

then the low and high coefficients have about the same standard deviation $\mathfrak{s}' = b/\sqrt{12} \approx \mathfrak{s}\sqrt{r\tau}/b$. This determines how the inner commitments and garbage matrices are decomposed at the current level for producing the outer commitments. Indeed, as already explained, the coefficients of $\vec{t}, \vec{g}, \vec{h}$ should all have standard deviation similar to $\mathfrak{s}'$ since together with the parts of $\vec{z}$ they are going to form the new $\vec{s}_i$. Recall that in the uniformly random case of $\vec{t}$ and $\vec{h}$, one wants to decompose into $t_1 \geq 2$ parts. The minimal base for this is $b_1 = \lceil q^{1/t_1} \rceil$. We want $b_1 \approx b$, and therefore set

$$t_1 = \left\lfloor \frac{\log q}{\log b} \right\rceil.$$

In the Gaussian case of $\vec{g}$ we first need to analyze the standard deviation of the garbage polynomials $g_{ij} = \langle \vec{s}_i, \vec{s}_j \rangle$. For $i \neq j$, each $\mathbb{Z}_q$-coefficient of g_{ij} is the sum of nd products of two coefficients with standard deviation $\mathfrak{s}$. Therefore, we model the coefficients of $\vec{g}_{ij}$ as Gaussian with standard deviation $\sqrt{nd}\mathfrak{s}^2$. On the other hand, for $i = j$, each coefficient is essentially twice the sum of $nd/2$ products of two coefficients with standard deviation $\mathfrak{s}$. Hence, in this case, we model the coefficients as Gaussian with standard deviation $\sqrt{2nd}\mathfrak{s}^2$. If they are decomposed into t_2 parts modulo b_2, then the $t_2 - 1$ low parts are uniform with standard deviation $b_2/\sqrt{12}$ and the high part is Gaussian with standard deviation $\sqrt{2nd}\mathfrak{s}^2/b_2^{t_2-1}$. So we want $b_2 = \left\lfloor (\sqrt{24nd}\mathfrak{s}^2)^{1/t_2} \right\rceil$. We also want $b_2 \approx b$ and thus

$$t_2 = \left\lfloor \frac{\log(\sqrt{24nd}\mathfrak{s}^2)}{\log b} \right\rceil.$$

Now we turn to the norms. The coefficients of $\vec{z}$ are not independent but we found experimentally that the ℓ_2-norm is nonetheless around $\mathfrak{s}\sqrt{r\tau nd} = \beta\sqrt{\tau}$. The same holds for the other vectors $\vec{t}$ and $\vec{g} \parallel \vec{h}$. We therefore use the following norm bounds

$$\gamma = \beta\sqrt{\tau},$$

$$\gamma_1 = \sqrt{\frac{b_1^2 t_1}{12} r\kappa d + \frac{b_2^2 t_2}{12} \frac{r^2 + r}{2} d},$$

$$\gamma_2 = \sqrt{\frac{b_1^2 t_1}{12} \frac{r^2 + r}{2} d},$$

$$\beta' = \sqrt{\frac{2}{b^2}\gamma^2 + \gamma_1^2 + \gamma_2^2}.$$

5.5   Security Analysis

For the completeness of the protocol in Fig. 2, one can observe as usual that the verification equations defining the target relation are fulfilled in an honest execution of the protocol. The norm check is also satisfied according to our heuristic analysis from Subsect. 5.4. The more interesting part is proving the knowledge soundness of our protocol, under the assumed hardness of Module-SIS. Our result is given in Theorem 5.1, and the proof can be found in the full version of the paper.

Theorem 5.1. *Let $\mathcal{C}$ be the challenge space $\mathcal{C} \subset \mathcal{R}_q$ from Sect. 2 consisting of polynomials with ℓ_2-norm τ and operator norm T. Suppose that Module-SIS is hard for rank $\kappa_1 = \kappa_2$ and norm $2\beta'$, and also hard for rank κ and norm $\max(8T(b+1)\beta', 2(b+1)\beta' + 4T\sqrt{128/30}\beta)$. Further suppose that $\beta \leq \sqrt{30/128}q/125$. Then the protocol in Fig. 2 is a knowledge-sound proof for relation R with soundness error $\varepsilon_0 = 2^{-125}$ and norm slack $\sqrt{128/30} \approx 2$, i.e. the extractor is only guaranteed to output a witness with norm at most $\sqrt{128/30}\beta$.*

Remark 5.2. The norm bounds for the hardness of Module-SIS in the Theorem are relative to the norm bound β' in the target relation, i.e. a bound on the vectors revealed by the prover in his last message. If the protocol is recursed so that the verifier can not directly check the norm, but instead only gets a proof for it with slack $\sqrt{128/30}$, then the bounds for the Module-SIS hardness must also be increased by this factor.

5.6   No Outer Commitments and Fewer Garbage Polynomials

In the last level of the recursion, there is no point in producing the outer commitments as their openings are going to be sent at the end of the protocol. Moreover, not committing to the garbage polynomials allows us to use interaction as in [NS22] to reduce the number of garbage polynomials. We now explain this modification for the garbage polynomials h_{ij} in the verification equation $\sum_i \langle \vec{\varphi}_i, \vec{z} \rangle c_i = \sum_{i,j} h_{ij} c_i c_j$. The r challenges c_i are spread out over $2r$ rounds where the prover and verifier alternate between sending garbage polynomials and challenges. In this way the garbage polynomials in the $(2i-1)$th round can depend on the challenges $c_1, \ldots, c_{i-1}$. This in turn allows us to combine many of the previous garbage polynomials in a single polynomial if it is not necessary to separate between them. In round $2i - 1$, $i \geq 1$, the prover sends

$$h_{2i-1} = \sum_{1 \leq j < i} \left(\langle \vec{\varphi}_j, \vec{s}_i \rangle + \langle \vec{\varphi}_i, \vec{s}_j \rangle \right) c_j,$$

$$h_{2i} = \langle \vec{\varphi}_i, \vec{s}_i \rangle.$$

The verifier sends the ith challenge c_i in round $2i$. The verification equation becomes

$$\sum_{i=1}^{r} \langle \vec{\varphi}_i, \vec{z} \rangle c_i = \sum_{i=1}^{r} \left(h_{2i-1} c_i + h_{2i} c_i^2 \right).$$

So there are merely $2r - 1$ (non-zero) garbage polynomials instead of $(r^2 + r)/2$ before. This still proves $h_{2i} = \langle \vec{\varphi}_i, \vec{\varphi}_i \rangle$ with soundness error $2r/2^{128}$. The verifier is only interested in these diagonal terms as only those are needed for the verification equation $\sum_{i,j} a_{ij} g_{ij} + \sum_i h_{2i} = b$. The prover can not use later garbage terms to correct any error since in the verification equation the garbage terms are being multiplied by random challenges not known when he needs to send the the garbage terms. Any potential correction gets distorted by the random challenges. See [NS22, Lemma 2] for a formal treatment. The same technique can be applied to the other challenge polynomials g_{ij}. In the last iteration of the main protocol the target relation of the previous iteration of the main protocol is proven. The corresponding instance of the principal relation R has multiplicity $r = \nu + \mu$ because we choose not to decompose $\vec{z}$ before the last round of the protocol. Therefore, the only nonzero a_{ij} in all dot product functions have $i = j \leq \nu$. Indeed, the only quadratic function is for proving $\langle \vec{z}, \vec{z} \rangle = \sum_{i,j} g_{ij} c_i c_j$ from the previous iteration of the main protocol. Hence, the verifier is only interested in the g_{ii} for $i = 1, \ldots, \nu$. By reordering the challenges in the protocol we can now use the verification equation

$$\langle \vec{z}, \vec{z} \rangle = g_0 + \sum_{i=1}^{\nu} (g_{2i-1} c_i + g_{2i} c_i^2)$$

with only $2\nu + 1$ garbage terms.

5.7   Proof Size

The size of the non-interactive variant (via Fiat-Shamir) of the main protocol is given by the size of the outer commitments $\vec{u}_1, \vec{u}_2$, the Johnson-Lindenstrauss projection $\vec{p}$, and the $\lceil 128/\log q \rceil$ polynomials $b''^{(k)}$ for proving the partial functions $\mathcal{F}'$ and the JL projection. For computing the size of $\vec{p}$ we model the vector as Gaussian distributed with standard deviation $\beta\sqrt{1/2}$. Then using standard tail bounds we assume that each coefficient can be encoded using $\log(12\beta/\sqrt{2})$ bits. Alternatively, one can directly compute the entropy of the Gaussian coefficients. The last prover message only needs to be counted once for the last iteration of the protocol. The challenges can all be expanded from short 128-bit seeds. So, this yields the following proof size in bits:

$$\underbrace{(\kappa_1 + \kappa_2) d \log q}_{\text{Outer commitments}} + \underbrace{256 \log(12\beta/\sqrt{2})}_{\text{JL projection}} + \underbrace{\left\lceil \frac{128}{\log q} \right\rceil d \log q}_{\text{JL proof}} + \underbrace{4 \cdot 128}_{\text{Challenges}} .$$

The last prover message consisting of masked opening $\vec{z}$, inner commitments $\vec{t}_i$, and garbage polynomials g_{ij}, h_{ij} has size

$$\underbrace{nd \log \left(12\beta\sqrt{\tau/nd} \right)}_{\vec{z}} + \underbrace{r\kappa d \log q}_{\vec{t}_i} + \underbrace{\frac{r^2 + r}{2} d \log \left(12\sqrt{2/(r^2 nd)} \beta^2 \right)}_{g_{ij}} + \underbrace{\frac{r^2 + r}{2} d \log q}_{h_{ij}} .$$

Optimizing the Recursion Strategy. As explained, for small proof sizes we want to recurse the protocol several times. Essentially until the size of the last prover message is not anymore bigger than an optimal proof for it. The central goal of the recursion is to reduce the witness rank n. This is achieved in each recursion level by the decomposition of the masked opening $\vec{z}$ into ν parts in the construction of the target relation for the next level, c.f. Subsect. 5.3. Here it is important to find a good trade-off between a small ν that does not reduce the rank by much and hence results in more recursion levels, and a large ν that results in a large number of garbage polynomials in the next level. Recall that there are $r^2 + r$ garbage polynomials in the next level for $r = 2\nu + \mu$. The garbage polynomials (and inner commitments) are expanded so that they become approximately as wide as the (reduced) masked opening. So the vectors $\vec{z}^{(0)} \parallel \vec{z}^{(1)}$ and $\vec{v} = \vec{t} \parallel \vec{g} \parallel \vec{h}$ of rank $2n$ and m, respectively, are similarly wide. Then the amortization at the next level is as effective as possible. But there is only one global norm check for the two vectors so we also want their norm to be similar; that is, $2n \approx m$. We choose ν at each level such that this is the case.

6   Adding Zero-Knowledge

We now discuss in more detail how to augment our protocol to also achieve the zero-knowledge property. As mentioned in the introduction, an easy way to do this is to prepend a simple shim protocol that proves the input relation in zero-knowledge. Then the correct verification of the shim, i.e. its output relation, can be proven with the protocol from this work. The shim can essentially be any zero-knowledge proof system that does not need to have sublinear proof size. But we want that the part of its proof without the last message from the prover, i.e. without the witness for the output relation, is small so that using the protocol for adding zero-knowledge to the protocol from this work does not blow up the proof size. On the contrary, the size of the output witness can be much larger than the size of the input witness. This does not pose a problem because the proof size of the protocol from this work is dominated by the essentially constant cost of the last iteration and so a larger witness does not increase the proof size by much.

It is most natural to use a linear-sized lattice-based protocol of the type in [ENS20, LNP22] for the shim, as these protocols share the algebraic setup and many techniques with the protocol from this work. Moreover, proving correct verification then consists of verifying polynomial equations of dot-product type together with a norm-constraint. So, the verification circuit will directly give an instance of our principal relation.

An alternative approach to zero-knowledge is to defer the computationally expensive masking of the witness to after several iterations of our main protocol or even fully to the end of the protocol where the witness is small. So then one appends a zero-knowledge shim after our protocol. But one needs to blind the outer commitments in the foregoing iterations by adding some LWE randomness in each commitment and also needs to avoid sending the Johnson-Lindenstrauss projections in the clear by for example also blinding them. Finally, the resulting target relation can then again be proven with essentially any zero-knowledge proof system, e.g. [ENS20, LNP22]. If one does not care about quantum security, then the zero-knowledge proof system for the target relation can even be a (pairing-based) SNARK, which will only have a proof size of around 1 Kilobyte. In this way one can still profit from the high computational efficiency of our prover algorithm.

Example. For concreteness we computed parameters for adding zero-knowledge to our example application of proving binary R1CS with 2^{20} constraints. The prime modulus q of 32 bits that we use in our protocol instantiations without zero-knowledge is too small to mask the witness at the beginning of the protocol. The masked opening would not allow for SIS-hardness for the inner commitments. Instead of increasing q we defer the masking to after several iterations of the main protocol, as explained. This does not result in an optimal proof size though, and a larger q would be advantageous. We modified the main protocol for the initial iterations as follows. In order to blind the outer commitments, we added randomness to their openings. We chose the standard deviation of the randomness to be similar to the standard deviation of the existing opening; that is, similar to the standard deviation of the witness of the target relation. Then we computed the required dimensions so that the commitments are indistinguishable from random under Module-LWE. We also added additional LWE errors in the first outer commitment that are used for masking the polynomials $b''(k)$ in the style of BDLOP commitments. For blinding the Johnson-Lindenstrauss projection $\vec{p}$ we added a Gaussian mask, c.f. [LNP22, Section 5.1]. This increases the slack of the ℓ_2-norm proof from $\sqrt{128/30}$ to $2\sqrt{128 \cdot 256/26}$. The mask is also committed-to in the first outer commitment. The modified main protocol is executed three times in the proof for R1CS with $k = 2^{20}$ where the output witnesses are decomposed in rank in 3, 2, and 1 parts, respectively. The three iterations are followed by a simple zero-knowledge proof of the target relation. Here we don't use amortization and instead commit to the concatenation $\vec{s} = \vec{s}_1 \parallel \cdots \parallel \vec{s}_n$ of the witness vectors in a single inner commitment. Additionally, there is a second inner commitment to a random masking vector $\vec{y}$. Here, the inner commitments must be hiding, so their openings include LWE randomness. The prover eventually opens the commitments with a masked opening $\vec{z} = \vec{y} + c\vec{s}$. In order to prove the relation constraints, the protocol also involves garbage polynomials. The garbage polynomials for the linear relation parts are blinded using BDLOP and the ones for the quadratic parts are expanded and included in the inner commitment to $\vec{s}$. For the ℓ_2-norm proof we also use a masked Johnson-Lindenstrauss projection as before. We also put the inner commitments and the (masked) linear garbage polynomials into outer commitments. The outer commitments don't have to be hiding and only serve to decrease the proof size. The cost of this zero-knowledge protocol is about equal to one iteration of the (modified) main protocol; namely 4.53 KB. After this zero knowledge proof we continue with 5 iterations of the original main protocol where we do not need to care about zero-knowledge anymore. The total zero-knowledge proof size for binary R1CS with $k = 2^{20}$ turns out to be 60.33 KB, compared to 49.02 KB without zero-knowledge. Next to the additional zero-knowledge proof, the increase in proof size also mainly comes from one more execution of the main protocol compared to the case without zero-knowledge. This can likely be avoided by using an amortizing protocol for the zero-knowlege proof that does not blow up the relation parameters as much. We leave this and the task of computing parameters for the other strategy with increased q to future work.

7 Proving R1CS

In this section, we show how to reduce rank-1 constraint systems to our dot product constraint systems.

Definition 7.1 (rank-1 constraint system (R1CS)). *A rank-1 constraint system of k constraints in n variables consists of three matrices $\mathcal{A}, \mathcal{B}, \mathcal{C} \in \mathbb{Z}_N^{k \times n}$ modulo an integer N. We say a vector $\vec{w} \in \mathbb{Z}_N^n$ satisfies the system if $\mathcal{A}\vec{w} \circ \mathcal{B}\vec{w} = \mathcal{C}\vec{w}$, where $\circ$ denotes the component-wise product, i.e. $(\vec{a} \circ \vec{b})_i = a_i b_i$. This defines the R1CS relation mod N as follows*

$$R_{R1CS} = \left\{ ((\mathcal{A}, \mathcal{B}, \mathcal{C}), (\vec{w})) \ \middle| \ \begin{array}{c} \mathcal{A}, \mathcal{B}, \mathcal{C} \in \mathbb{Z}_N^{k \times n} \\ \vec{w} \in \mathbb{Z}_N^n \\ \mathcal{A}\vec{w} \circ \mathcal{B}\vec{w} = \mathcal{C}\vec{w} \end{array} \right\}.$$

Binary R1CS

We first give an efficient reduction from R_{R1CS} to R, for binary $R1CS$ (i.e., $N = 2$). We can compose this reduction with our proof system from Sect. 5 to efficiently prove binary $R1CS$. Padding with zeros if necessary, we can assume that the number of constraints and the number of variables are multiples of d, the dimension of $\mathcal{R}$. The reduction works as follows. The prover sends a commitment $\vec{t} = A(\vec{a}||\vec{b}||\vec{c}||\vec{w})$, where $\vec{w}$ is the R1CS witness, and $\vec{a} = \mathcal{A}\vec{w}, \vec{b} = \mathcal{B}\vec{w}, \vec{c} = \mathcal{C}\vec{w}$. Then we prove knowledge of an opening $(\vec{a}, \vec{b}, \vec{c}, \vec{w})$ to the commitment $\vec{t}$, such that indeed $\vec{a} = \mathcal{A}\vec{w} \mod 2, \vec{b} = \mathcal{B}\vec{w} \mod 2, \vec{c} = \mathcal{C}\vec{w} \mod 2$, such that the coefficients of $\vec{a}, \vec{b}, \vec{c}, \vec{w}$ are binary, and such that $\vec{a} \circ \vec{b} = \vec{c}$. These are proven as follows:

- To prove that the coefficients of $\vec{a}$ are binary, the prover proves knowledge of $\tilde{\vec{a}}$ such that $\tilde{\vec{a}} = \sigma_{-1}(\vec{a})$, and such that the constant term of $\langle \vec{a}, \tilde{\vec{a}} - \mathbf{1} \rangle$ is zero. This constant term is equal to $\sum_i \vec{a}_i(\vec{a}_i - 1) \mod q$. The prover also proves that $\||\vec{a}||\tilde{\vec{a}}||\vec{b}||\tilde{\vec{b}}||\vec{c}||\tilde{\vec{c}}||\vec{w}||\tilde{\vec{w}}\|_2 < \sqrt{q}$, which implies that $\sum_i \vec{a}_i(\vec{a}_i - 1)$ is zero over the integers, meaning that $\vec{a}$ indeed has binary coefficients. This follows from $\sum_i a_i(a_i - 1) \leq 2 \|\vec{a}\|_2^2 = \|\vec{a}||\tilde{\vec{a}}\|_2^2 < q$. If $n + 3k < 15q/128$ the l_2-norm of $\vec{a}||\tilde{\vec{a}}||\vec{b}||\tilde{\vec{b}}||\vec{c}||\tilde{\vec{c}}||\vec{w}||\tilde{\vec{w}}$ is smaller than $\sqrt{q}$ by at least the slack factor $\sqrt{128/30}$, so we can prove this with the main protocol of Sect. 5. The main protocol also supports supports $\mathbb{Z}_q$-linear equations such as $\tilde{\vec{a}} = \sigma_{-1}(\vec{a})$, constant terms of inner-product relations over $\mathcal{R}_q$ such as $\langle \vec{a}, \tilde{\vec{a}} - \mathbf{a} \rangle$. Proving that the coefficients of $\vec{b}, \vec{c}$, and $\vec{w}$ are binary is handled in the same way.

- To prove that $\vec{a} \circ \vec{b} = \vec{c}$, we use the observation that for integers $a, b, c \in \{0, 1\}$ we have $ab = c$ if and only if $a + b - 2c \in \{0, 1\}$. A similar observation was used in [GOS12]. So the prover just has to prove that $\vec{a} + \vec{b} - 2\vec{c}$ has binary coefficients, which he does by proving that the constant term of $\langle \vec{a} + \vec{b} - 2\vec{c}, \tilde{\vec{a}} + \tilde{\vec{b}} - 2\tilde{\vec{c}} - 1 \rangle$ is zero mod q, which implies it is zero over the integers, because $\sum_i (a_i + b_i - 2c_i)(a_i + b_i - 2c_i - 1) \le 6k < q$.

- Rather than proving the $3k$ linear relations $\vec{a}' = \mathcal{A}\vec{w}', \vec{b}' = \mathcal{B}\vec{w}', \vec{c}' = \mathcal{C}\vec{w}'$ modulo 2 separately, we use the usual technique of first combining them into fewer relations. To do this, the verifier chooses, l $\mathbb{F}_2$-linear combinations of the equations at random, and then the prover proves that only these l equations are satisfied. This results in a soundness error of 2^{-l}. Concretely, the verifier sends $\{\vec{\alpha}_i, \vec{\beta}_i, \vec{\gamma}_i\}_{i \in [l]}$, the binary coefficients of the l linear combinations. The prover and the verifier both compute

$$\vec{\delta}_i = \mathrm{Lift}(\alpha_i \mathcal{A}^\mathsf{T} + \beta_i \mathcal{B}^\mathsf{T} + \gamma_i \mathcal{C}^\mathsf{T} \mod 2) \in \mathbb{Z}_q^{dn}$$

such that

$$\langle \alpha_i, \vec{a} - \mathcal{A}\vec{w} \rangle + \langle \beta_i, \vec{b} - \mathcal{B}\vec{w} \rangle + \langle \gamma_i, \vec{c} - \mathcal{C}\vec{w} \rangle$$
$$= \langle \alpha_i, \vec{a} \rangle + \langle \beta_i, \vec{b} \rangle + \langle \gamma_i, \vec{c} \rangle - \langle \delta_i, \vec{w} \rangle \mod 2$$

The prover responds with $g_i = \langle \alpha_i, \vec{a} \rangle + \langle \beta_i, \vec{b} \rangle + \langle \gamma_i, \vec{c} \rangle - \langle \delta_i, \vec{w} \rangle \in \mathbb{Z}_q$ for all i in $[l]$. Note that there cannot be an overflow mod q, if we assume $n + 3k < q$, and we prove that $\vec{a}, \vec{b}, \vec{c}, \vec{w}$ have binary coefficients. The verifier checks that the g_i are indeed 0 mod 2. Then it is proven that the g_i are computed correctly mod q, which can be delegated to the protocol of Sect. 5 because these are a small number of $\mathbb{Z}_q$-linear equations on the coefficient vectors of the witness.

The full protocol is given in Fig. 4, where with some abuse of notation we define two sets of inner product functions over $\mathcal{R}_q$. (where $\mathbb{Z}_q$-linear functions f should be interpreted as the unique $\mathcal{R}_q$-linear function f' such that $\mathrm{ct}(f') = f$.)

$$\mathcal{F}_1 = \{A(\vec{a}\|\vec{b}\|\vec{c}\|\vec{w}) - \vec{t}\}$$
$$\mathcal{F}_2 = \{\tilde{\vec{a}} = \sigma_{-1}(\vec{a}), \quad \tilde{\vec{b}} = \sigma_{-1}(\vec{b}), \quad \tilde{\vec{c}} = \sigma_{-1}(\vec{c}), \quad \tilde{\vec{w}} = \sigma_{-1}(\vec{w}),$$
$$\langle \vec{a}, \tilde{\vec{a}} - 1_{k/d} \rangle, \quad \langle \vec{b}, \tilde{\vec{b}} - 1_{k/d} \rangle,$$
$$\langle \vec{c}, \tilde{\vec{c}} - 1_{k/d} \rangle, \quad \langle \vec{w}, \tilde{\vec{w}} - 1_{n/d} \rangle,$$
$$\langle \vec{a} + \vec{b} - 2\vec{c}, \tilde{\vec{a}} + \tilde{\vec{b}} - 2\tilde{\vec{c}} - 1 \rangle\}$$
$$\cup \{\langle \alpha_i, \vec{a} \rangle + \langle \beta_i, \vec{b} \rangle + \langle \gamma_i, \vec{c} \rangle - \langle \delta_i, \vec{w} \rangle - g_i\}_{i \in [\lambda]} .$$

Theorem 7.2. *If $n + 3k < q$ and $6k < q$, then the proof of knowledge reduction of Fig. 4 is computationally knowledge-sound with soundness error 2^{-l}, under the assumption that $\mathsf{MSIS}_{m,2n+6k}$ is hard with an l_∞-norm bound of 1. Moreover, if $n + 3k < 15q/128$, then there is enough slack to compose the reduction with the main protocol of Sect. 5.*

R1CS modulo $2^d + 1$

We now give a way to prove knowledge of a witness for an R1CS instance modulo $2^d + 1$. We use the ring morphism of evaluating at $X = 2$

$$\varphi : \mathcal{R} \to \mathbb{Z}_{2^d+1} : \sum_{i=0}^{d-1} a_i X^i \mapsto \sum_{i=0}^{d-1} a_i 2^i \mod 2^d + 1 .$$

Using the non-adjacent form [Rei60], we can encode each element $a \in \mathbb{Z}_{2^d+1}$ as an element $Enc(a) \in \mathcal{R}_q$ with coefficients in $\{-1, 0, 1\}$ and with l_2-norm at most $\sqrt{d/2}$, such that $\varphi(\text{Lift}(Enc(a))) = a$. We then have $\varphi(\text{Lift}(Enc(a)Enc(b))) = ab \mod 2^d + 1$, as long as no overflow mod q happens in the multiplication of the encodings.

In our proof system for R1CS mod $2^d + 1$, the prover commits to small encodings of $\mathcal{A}\vec{w}, \mathcal{B}\vec{w}, \mathcal{C}\vec{w}$, and $\vec{w}$ in $\mathcal{R}_q$, and proves knowledge of an opening with

Prover $\mathcal{P}$		Verifier $\mathcal{V}$
Inputs:		
$\vec{w} \in \{0,1\}^n$		$\mathcal{A}, \mathcal{B}, \mathcal{C} \in \{0,1\}^{k \times n} \subset \mathbb{Z}_q^{k \times n}$
		$A \in \mathcal{R}_q^{m/d \times (3k+n)/d}$
$\vec{\mathbf{a}} \leftarrow \text{Lift}(\mathcal{A}\vec{w} \mod 2) \in \{0,1\}^k$		
$\vec{\mathbf{b}} \leftarrow \text{Lift}(\mathcal{B}\vec{w} \mod 2) \in \{0,1\}^k$		
$\vec{\mathbf{c}} \leftarrow \text{Lift}(\mathcal{C}\vec{w} \mod 2) \in \{0,1\}^k$		
$\vec{\mathbf{t}} = A(\vec{\mathbf{a}}\|\vec{\mathbf{b}}\|\vec{\mathbf{c}}\|\vec{\mathbf{w}}) \mod q$		
	$\xrightarrow{\quad\vec{\mathbf{t}}\quad}$	
	$\xleftarrow{\{\vec{\alpha}_i, \vec{\beta}_i, \vec{\gamma}_i\}_{i \in [\lambda]}}$	$\vec{\alpha}_i, \vec{\beta}_i, \vec{\gamma}_i \xleftarrow{\$} \{0,1\}^k$
$\forall i \in [\lambda]:$		
$\vec{\delta}_i \leftarrow \text{Lift}(\alpha_i \mathcal{A}^\mathsf{T} + \beta_i \mathcal{B}^\mathsf{T} + \gamma_i \mathcal{C}^\mathsf{T} \mod 2)$		
$g_i \leftarrow \langle \vec{\alpha}_i, \vec{a} \rangle + \langle \vec{\beta}_i, \vec{b} \rangle + \langle \vec{\gamma}_i, \vec{c} \rangle - \langle \vec{\delta}_i, \vec{w} \rangle$	$\xrightarrow{\{g_i\}_{i \in [\lambda]}}$	$\mathcal{V}$ rejects if g_i
		is odd for some i
$\tilde{\mathbf{a}}, \tilde{\mathbf{b}} \leftarrow \sigma_{-1}(\vec{\mathbf{a}}), \sigma_{-1}(\vec{\mathbf{b}})$		
$\tilde{\mathbf{c}}, \tilde{\mathbf{w}} \leftarrow \sigma_{-1}(\vec{\mathbf{c}}), \sigma_{-1}(\vec{\mathbf{w}})$		
$\vec{\mathbf{r}} = (\vec{\mathbf{a}}, \vec{\mathbf{b}}, \vec{\mathbf{c}}, \vec{\mathbf{w}}, \tilde{\mathbf{a}}, \tilde{\mathbf{b}}, \tilde{\mathbf{c}}, \tilde{\mathbf{w}})$	$\xrightarrow{\quad\vec{\mathbf{r}}\quad}$	$\mathcal{V}$ accepts if and only if:
		$((\mathcal{F}_1, \mathcal{F}_2, \sqrt{q}), \vec{\mathbf{r}}) \in R$

Fig. 4. Proof of knowledge reduction from binary R1CS to R.

l_2-norm $< \beta$ (where β is small enough to ensure the commitment is binding under MSIS) that encodes $\vec{a}, \vec{b}, \vec{c}, \vec{w} \in \mathbb{Z}_{2^d+1}$ that is well-formed (meaning that $\vec{a} = \mathcal{A}\vec{w}$, etc.), and which additionally satisfies the quadratic constraints $\vec{a} \circ \vec{b} = \vec{c}$. The strategy to prove the quadratic constraints is to let the verifier send l challenge vectors $\varphi_i \in \mathbb{Z}_{d^2+1}^k$, and let the prover prove that $\langle \varphi_i, \vec{a} \circ \vec{b} - \vec{c} \rangle = 0$ for all $i \in [l]$. This has soundness error p^{-l}, where p is the smallest prime factor of $2^d + 1$. For example, the smallest prime factor of $2^{64} + 1$ is 18 bits long, so we can choose $l = \lceil 128/18 \rceil = 8$ to get a negligible soundness error[1]. To prove $\langle \varphi_i, \vec{a} \circ \vec{b} - \vec{c} \rangle = 0$ mod $2^d + 1$, the prover computes $\vec{d_i} = \varphi_i \circ \vec{a}$ for all $i \in [l]$ and commits to small encoding of these in $\mathcal{R}_q$. Then the prover proves knowledge of a short opening that encodes $\vec{d_i}$ such that $\varphi_i \circ \vec{a} = \vec{d_i}$, and $\langle \vec{d_i}, \mathcal{B}\vec{w} \rangle = \langle \varphi_i, \mathcal{C}\vec{w} \rangle$.

The relations $\mathcal{A}\vec{w} - \vec{a} = 0, \mathcal{B}\vec{w} - \vec{b} = 0, \mathcal{C}\vec{w} - \vec{c} = 0, \varphi_i \circ \vec{a} - \vec{d_i} = 0, \langle \vec{d_i}, \vec{b} \rangle - \langle \varphi_i, \vec{c} \rangle = 0$ mod $X - 2$ are all linear relations or dot product relations. We let the verifier send l sets of challenges in $\mathbb{Z}_{2^d+1}$ to aggregate the equations into l linear combinations. This aggregation step also has a soundness error of p^{-l}, where p is the largest prime factor of $2^d + 1$. Concretely, the verifier sends a challenge vectors $c^{(i)} = (\alpha^{(i)}, \beta^{(i)}, \gamma^{(i)}, \delta_1^{(i)}, \ldots, \delta_l^{(i)}) \in \mathbb{Z}_{2^d+1}^{k \times l+3}$, which defines the l linear combinations

$$f_i(\vec{a}, \vec{b}, \vec{c}, \vec{w}, \{\vec{d_i}\}) := \langle \alpha^{(i)}, \mathcal{A}\vec{w} - \vec{a} \rangle + \langle \beta^{(i)}, \mathcal{B}\vec{w} - \vec{b} \rangle + \langle \gamma^{(i)}, \mathcal{C}\vec{w} - \vec{c} \rangle$$
$$+ \langle \vec{d_i}, \vec{b} \rangle - \langle \varphi_i, \vec{c} \rangle + \sum_{j=1}^{l} \langle \delta_j^{(i)}, \varphi_i \circ \vec{a} - \vec{d_i} \rangle.$$

Let $\mathbf{\vec{a}}, \mathbf{\vec{b}}, \mathbf{\vec{c}}, \mathbf{\vec{w}}$ and the $\mathbf{\vec{d}_i}$ be the short encodings of $\vec{a}, \vec{b}, \vec{c}, \vec{w}$ and the $\vec{d_i}$ respectively, and let $\tilde{f}_i(\mathbf{\vec{a}}, \mathbf{\vec{b}}, \mathbf{\vec{c}}, \mathbf{\vec{w}}, \{\mathbf{\vec{d}_i}\})$ be the dot product function over $\mathcal{R}_q$ obtained by replacing all the coefficients of $f_i(\vec{a}, \vec{b}, \vec{c}, \{\vec{d_i}\})$ by short encodings in $\mathcal{R}_q$. The prover computes $\mathbf{g}_i = \tilde{f}_i(\mathbf{\vec{a}}, \mathbf{\vec{b}}, \mathbf{\vec{c}}, \mathbf{\vec{w}}, \{\mathbf{\vec{d}_i}\})$ for all $i \in [l]$ over the ring $\mathcal{R}_q$ (where we are guaranteed no overflows mod q occur if $\sqrt{(n + (3+l)k)d}\beta + \beta^2/2 < q$), sends the $\mathbf{g}_i$ to the verifier, and proves that they are computed correctly using our main protocol. The verifier checks that the main proof was valid and that the $\mathbf{g}_i$ are indeed zero mod $X - 2$. The protocol is displayed in Fig. 5.

Theorem 7.3. *Let $\beta \in \mathbb{R}$ such that $\sqrt{(n + (3+l)k)d/2}\beta + \beta^2/2 < q$, then the protocol from Fig. 5 is a computationally sound proof of knowledge with soundness error $2p^{-l}$, where p is the smallest prime factor of $2^d + 1$, under the assumption that $\mathsf{MSIS}_{m,n+3k}$ and $\mathsf{MSIS}_{md,lk}$ are hard with an l_2-norm bound of β. If $(n + (3+l)k)d < 0.3q$, then we can put $\beta = \sqrt{128/30}\sqrt{(n + (3+l)k)d/2}$ to have enough slack to compose the proof with the main protocol from Sect. 5.*

---

[1] In 1855, Thomas Clausens mentioned in a letter to Gauss that he managed to factorize $2^{64} + 1$ into its prime factors 274177 and 67280421310721, adding that the latter was probably the largest prime number known at the moment [Bie64].

Prover $\mathcal{P}$		Verifier $\mathcal{V}$
Inputs:		
$\vec{w} \in \mathbb{Z}_{2^d+1}$		$\mathcal{A}, \mathcal{B}, \mathcal{C} \in \mathbb{Z}_{2^d+1}^{k \times n}$
		$A \in \mathcal{R}_q^{m \times (3k+n)}$
		$B \in \mathcal{R}_q^{m_d \times (lk)}$

$\vec{\mathbf{a}} \leftarrow Enc(\mathcal{A}\vec{w})$		
$\vec{\mathbf{b}} \leftarrow Enc(\mathcal{B}\vec{w})$		
$\vec{\mathbf{c}} \leftarrow Enc(\mathcal{C}\vec{w})$		
$\vec{\mathbf{w}} \leftarrow Enc(\vec{w})$		
$\vec{\mathbf{t}} = A(\vec{\mathbf{a}}\|\vec{\mathbf{b}}\|\vec{\mathbf{c}}\|\vec{\mathbf{w}}) \mod q$	$\xrightarrow{\quad \vec{\mathbf{t}} \quad}$	
	$\xleftarrow{\{\vec{\varphi}_i\}_{i \in [l]}}$	$\forall i \in [l] : \vec{\varphi}_i \xleftarrow{\$} \mathbb{Z}_{2^d+1}^k$
$\forall i \in [l] : \vec{\mathbf{d}}_i \leftarrow Enc(\varphi_i \circ \mathcal{A}\vec{w})$		
$\vec{\mathbf{t}}_d = B(\vec{\mathbf{d}}_1\|\dots\|\vec{\mathbf{d}}_l)$	$\xrightarrow{\quad \vec{\mathbf{t}}_d \quad}$	
	$\xleftarrow{\{c^{(i)}\}_{i \in [l]}}$	$\forall i \in [l] : c^{(i)} \leftarrow \mathbb{Z}_{2^d+1}^{k(l+3)+l}$
$\forall j \in [l]:$		
$\mathbf{g}_j \leftarrow \tilde{f}_j(\vec{\mathbf{a}}, \vec{\mathbf{b}}, \vec{\mathbf{c}}, \vec{\mathbf{w}}, \{\vec{\mathbf{d}}_i\})$	$\xrightarrow{\{\mathbf{g}_j\}_{j \in [l]}}$	$\mathcal{V}$ rejects if $\mathbf{g}_j$ is not
		divisible by $X - 2$
		for some $j \in [l]$
$\vec{\mathbf{r}} = (\vec{\mathbf{a}}, \vec{\mathbf{b}}, \vec{\mathbf{c}}, \vec{\mathbf{w}}, \{\vec{\mathbf{d}}_i\}_{i \in [l]})$	$\xrightarrow{\quad \vec{\mathbf{r}} \quad}$	$\mathcal{V}$ accepts if and only if:
		$(((\{\tilde{f}_j\}_{j \in [l]}, \{\}, \beta), \vec{\mathbf{r}}) \in R$

Fig. 5. Proof of knowledge reduction from R1CS mod $2^d + 1$ to R.

7.1 Proof Sizes of Our Protocol for R1CS

We now compute proof sizes for R1CS using the protocol from Sect. 7 followed by several recursive iterations of the main protocol from Sect. 5 where the last execution uses the variant without outer commitments and fewer garbage polynomials. The amortized opening $\vec{z}$ is always reduced in width ($b \geq 2$) except in the second to last execution. This minimizes the number of garbage terms going to be sent in the very last execution. We use the ring $\mathbb{Z}_q[X]/(X^d + 1)$ with degree $d = 64$ and modulus $q \approx 2^{32}$ splitting into two prime ideals of degree $d/2$, and the challenge space $\mathcal{C} \subset \mathcal{R}_q$ from Sect. 2 consisting of challenges with ℓ_2-norm τ and operator norm T. The commitment ranks κ, κ_1 and κ_2 are computed in each level so that Module-SIS meets our desired security level of 128 bits for the norm bounds in Theorem 5.1. More precisely, we estimate the hardness of Module-SIS using the Core-SVP methodology [ADPS16] with the BDGL sieve [BDGL16]. The various other system parameters are computed as described in Sect. 5. Table 1 contains the proof sizes of the comparison of our proof of R1CS mod $2^{64} + 1$ with other SNARKs in the literature, as discussed in the introduction and displayed in Fig. 1. Table 2 contains the proof sizes for binary R1CS with the number of constraints k varying between 2^{20} and 2^{25}, and $n = k$.

Table 1. Proof sizes in kilobytes for R1CS with a varying number of constraints.

Proof system	2^{10}	2^{11}	2^{12}	2^{13}	2^{14}	2^{15}	2^{16}	2^{17}	2^{18}	2^{19}	2^{20}
Brakedown	1279	1597	1974	2200	2710	3165	3926	4824	6122	7899	10230
Aurora	235	278	323	376	420	461	519	664	720	766	831
Ligero	135	180	299	364	615	721	1239	1415	2461	2797	4905
Shockwave	72	95	122	160	210	284	386	523	721	990	1384
LaBRADOR	47	47	49	51	52	52	54	54	57	57	58

Table 2. Proof sizes in kilobytes for binary R1CS with a varying number of constraints.

No. of constraints	2^{20}	2^{21}	2^{22}	2^{23}	2^{24}	2^{25}
Proof Size	49.02	49.37	51.47	51.6	52.7	53.84

Acknowledgements. We thank Vadim Lyubashevsky and Khan Nguyen for helpfull discussions. We also thank Thomas Attema for pointing out that the proof of lemma 3.7 in an earlier version of this paper was more complex than it needed to be.

References

[ACK21] Attema, T., Cramer, R., Kohl, L.: A compressed ς-protocol theory for lattices. In: Malkin, T., Peikert, C. (eds.) CRYPTO 2021. LNCS, vol. 12826, pp. 549–579. Springer, Cham (2021). https://doi.org/10.1007/978-3-030-84245-1_19

[ACL+22] Albrecht, M.R., Cini, V., Lai, R.W.F., Malavolta, G., Thyagarajan, S.A.K.: Lattice-based snarks: Publicly verifiable, preprocessing, and recursively composable. IACR Cryptol. ePrint Arch., p. 941 (2022)

[ADPS16] Alkim, E., Ducas, L., Pöppelmann, T., Schwabe, P.: Post-quantum key exchange - a new hope. In: USENIX Security Symposium, pp. 327–343. USENIX Association (2016)

[AF21] Attema, T., Fehr, S.: Parallel repetition of $(k_1, \ldots, k_\mu)$-special-sound multiround interactive proofs. Cryptology ePrint Archive, Paper 2021/1259 (2021). https://eprint.iacr.org/2021/1259

[AHIV17] Ames, S., Hazay, C., Ishai, Y., Venkitasubramaniam, M.: Ligero: lightweight sublinear arguments without a trusted setup. In: CCS, pp. 2087–2104. ACM (2017)

[ALS20] Attema, T., Lyubashevsky, V., Seiler, G.: Practical product proofs for lattice commitments. In: Micciancio, D., Ristenpart, T. (eds.) CRYPTO 2020. LNCS, vol. 12171, pp. 470–499. Springer, Cham (2020). https://doi.org/10.1007/978-3-030-56880-1_17

[BBB+18] Bünz, B., Bootle, J., Boneh, D., Poelstra, A., Wuille, P., Maxwell, G.: Bulletproofs: short proofs for confidential transactions and more. In: IEEE Symposium on Security and Privacy, pp. 315–334. IEEE Computer Society (2018)

[BBC+18] Baum, C., Bootle, J., Cerulli, A., del Pino, R., Groth, J., Lyubashevsky, V.: Sub-linear lattice-based zero-knowledge arguments for arithmetic circuits. In: Shacham, H., Boldyreva, A. (eds.) CRYPTO 2018. LNCS, vol. 10992, pp. 669–699. Springer, Cham (2018). https://doi.org/10.1007/978-3-319-96881-0_23

[BCC+16] Bootle, J., Cerulli, A., Chaidos, P., Groth, J., Petit, C.: Efficient zero-knowledge arguments for arithmetic circuits in the discrete log setting. In: Fischlin, M., Coron, J.-S. (eds.) EUROCRYPT 2016. LNCS, vol. 9666, pp. 327–357. Springer, Heidelberg (2016). https://doi.org/10.1007/978-3-662-49896-5_12

[BCR+19] Ben-Sasson, E., Chiesa, A., Riabzev, M., Spooner, N., Virza, M., Ward, N.P.: Aurora: transparent succinct arguments for R1CS. In: Ishai, Y., Rijmen, V. (eds.) EUROCRYPT 2019. LNCS, vol. 11476, pp. 103–128. Springer, Cham (2019). https://doi.org/10.1007/978-3-030-17653-2_4

[BDGL16] Becker, A., Ducas, L., Gama, N., Laarhoven, T.: New directions in nearest neighbor searching with applications to lattice sieving. In: SODA, pp. 10–24. SIAM (2016)

[Ber41] Berry, A.C.: The accuracy of the gaussian approximation to the sum of independent variates. Trans. Am. Math. Soc. **49**(1), 122–136 (1941)

[BG92] Bellare, M., Goldreich, O.: On defining proofs of knowledge. In: Brickell, E.F. (ed.) CRYPTO 1992. LNCS, vol. 740, pp. 390–420. Springer, Heidelberg (1993). https://doi.org/10.1007/3-540-48071-4_28

[Bie64] Biermann, K.R.: Thomas clausen, mathematiker und astronom. **1964**(216), 159–198 (1964)

[BLNS20] Bootle, J., Lyubashevsky, V., Nguyen, N.K., Seiler, G.: A non-PCP approach to succinct quantum-safe zero-knowledge. In: Micciancio, D., Ristenpart, T. (eds.) CRYPTO 2020. LNCS, vol. 12171, pp. 441–469. Springer, Cham (2020). https://doi.org/10.1007/978-3-030-56880-1_16

[ENS20] Esgin, M.F., Nguyen, N.K., Seiler, G.: Practical exact proofs from lattices: new techniques to exploit fully-splitting rings. In: Moriai, S., Wang, H. (eds.) ASIACRYPT 2020. LNCS, vol. 12492, pp. 259–288. Springer, Cham (2020). https://doi.org/10.1007/978-3-030-64834-3_9

[ESLL19] Esgin, M.F., Steinfeld, R., Liu, J.K., Liu, D.: Lattice-based zero-knowledge proofs: new techniques for shorter and faster constructions and applications. In: Boldyreva, A., Micciancio, D. (eds.) CRYPTO 2019. LNCS, vol. 11692, pp. 115–146. Springer, Cham (2019). https://doi.org/10.1007/978-3-030-26948-7_5

[Ess42] Esseen, C.-G.: On the liapunoff limit of error in the theory of probability. Arkiv för Matematik, Astronomi och Fysik. **28**, 1–19 (1942)

[GHL21] Gentry, C., Halevi, S., Lyubashevsky, V.: Practical non-interactive publicly verifiable secret sharing with thousands of parties. IACR Cryptol. ePrint Arch., p. 1397 (2021)

[GLS+21] Golovnev, A., Lee, J., Setty, S.T.V., Thaler, J., Wahby, R.S.: Brakedown: linear-time and post-quantum snarks for R1CS. IACR Cryptol. ePrint Arch., p. 1043 (2021)

[GOS12] Groth, J., Ostrovsky, R., Sahai, A.: New techniques for noninteractive zero-knowledge. J. ACM (JACM) **59**(3), 1–35 (2012)

[LNP22] Lyubashevsky, V., Nguyen, N.K., Plançon, M.: Lattice-based zero-knowledge proofs and applications: Shorter, simpler, and more general. IACR Cryptol. ePrint Arch., p. 284 (2022)

[LS18] Lyubashevsky, V., Seiler, G.: Short, invertible elements in partially splitting cyclotomic rings and applications to lattice-based zero-knowledge proofs. In: Nielsen, J.B., Rijmen, V. (eds.) EUROCRYPT 2018. LNCS, vol. 10820, pp. 204–224. Springer, Cham (2018). https://doi.org/10.1007/978-3-319-78381-9_8

[NS22] Nguyen, N.K., Seiler, G.: Practical sublinear proofs for R1CS from lattices. In: CRYPTO (2), volume 13508 of Lecture Notes in Computer Science, pp. 133–162. Springer, Heidelberg (2022)

[Rei60] Reitwiesner, W.G.: Binary arithmetic. Adv. Comput. **1**, 231–308 (1960)

Toward Practical Lattice-Based Proof of Knowledge from Hint-MLWE

Duhyeong Kim[1]📷, Dongwon Lee[2]📷, Jinyeong Seo[2]📷, and Yongsoo Song[2](✉)📷

[1] Intel Labs, Hillsboro, OR, USA
`duhyeong.kim@intel.com`
[2] Seoul National University, Seoul, South Korea
`{dongwonlee95,jinyeong.seo,y.song}@snu.ac.kr`

Abstract. In the last decade, zero-knowledge proof of knowledge protocols have been extensively studied to achieve active security of various cryptographic protocols. However, the existing solutions simply seek zero-knowledge for both message and randomness, which is an overkill in many applications since protocols may remain secure even if some information about randomness is leaked to the adversary.

We develop this idea to improve the state-of-the-art proof of knowledge protocols for RLWE-based public-key encryption and BDLOP commitment schemes. In a nutshell, we present new proof of knowledge protocols without using noise flooding or rejection sampling which are provably secure under a computational hardness assumption, called Hint-MLWE. We also show an efficient reduction from Hint-MLWE to the standard MLWE assumption.

Our approach enjoys the best of two worlds because it has no computational overhead from repetition (abort) and achieves a polynomial overhead between the honest and proven languages. We prove this claim by demonstrating concrete parameters and compare with previous results. Finally, we explain how our idea can be further applied to other proof of knowledge providing advanced functionality.

Keywords: Zero-knowledge · Proof of Plaintext Knowledge · BDLOP · Hint-MLWE

1 Introduction

In the last decade, lattice cryptography has emerged as one of the most promising foundations due to its versatility and robustness against quantum attacks. In particular, it has wide applications in the construction of cryptographic primitives such as homomorphic encryption (e.g. [11,12]) and commitment schemes (e.g. [9,25]), whose security relies on the hardness of the Learning with Errors (LWE) [34] and the Short Integer Solution (SIS) [2] problems. Furthermore, these primitives serve as fundamental building blocks for privacy-preserving protocols, including multi-party computation [5,16], group signature [26], and ring signature [29] schemes.

© International Association for Cryptologic Research 2023
H. Handschuh and A. Lysyanskaya (Eds.): CRYPTO 2023, LNCS 14085, pp. 549–580, 2023.
https://doi.org/10.1007/978-3-031-38554-4_18

When constructing such protocols, the usual strategy is to initially design a protocol in the semi-honest model and then compile it into an adaptively secure version that provides security against adaptive adversaries. During the compilation step, zero-knowledge proof of knowledge are typically utilized to prove the well-formedness of ciphertexts or commitments, without revealing any secret information about the randomness $\mathbf{r}$, which is used to generate them. This can be achieved using sigma protocols, where the prover generates a mask $\mathbf{y}$, receives a challenge γ from the verifier, and then sends a response $\mathbf{z} = \mathbf{y} + \gamma \cdot \mathbf{r}$ to the verifier. Since $\mathbf{z}$ potentially leaks partial information about $\mathbf{r}$, two major methodologies, namely noise flooding [5] and rejection sampling [23], are used to ensure the zero-knowledge property of $\mathbf{z}$.

First, the noise flooding technique samples $\mathbf{y}$ from an exponentially large distribution to fully hide the information of $\gamma \cdot \mathbf{r}$. On the other hand, the rejection sampling makes the random variable $\mathbf{z}$ independent to $\mathbf{r}$ by manipulating its probability distribution. This technique has an advantage in that the size of masking $\|\mathbf{y}\|_2$ is relatively small, but instead can abort the protocol repeatedly until generating an accepting transcript. Both methods commonly aim to prevent any information leakage on the randomness of the input ciphertext/commitment, which results in the semantic security of the protocol including the zero-knowledge of the message.

This work starts from the observation that the previous approach can be an overkill since it provides zero-knowledge for both message and randomness, while the primary goal of the zero-knowledge proof is mostly to ensure that there is no information leakage on the message from the transcripts. In other words, we do not always have to achieve the zero-knowledge for randomness, but it is allowed to reveal some information about it as long as the message privacy is guaranteed.

1.1 Our Contribution

The existing lattice-based proof techniques, such as noise flooding and rejection sampling, employ statistical analysis to ensure that a transcript includes no information of both message and randomness. In contrast, we present a novel approach that allows a proof of knowledge to leak some information on the randomness used in encryption or commitment.

A natural question is how this information leakage of randomness affects the security of proof of knowledge protocols. We first analyze the conditional probability distribution of randomness given such partial information. Specifically, we show that if both a randomness $\mathbf{r}$ and a masking $\mathbf{y}$ are sampled from discrete Gaussians, then the distribution of $\mathbf{r}$ conditioned on $\mathbf{y} + \gamma \cdot \mathbf{r}$ also follows a discrete Gaussian distribution. At a high level, we conclude that the real transcript of a proof of knowledge protocol can be simulated when the underlying scheme relies on the hardness of MLWE based on discrete Gaussian distributions, even if it includes non-negligible information on the randomness.

We apply this idea to a Proof of Plaintext Knowledge (PPK) protocol for the public-key encryption scheme [11, 19], a Proof of Opening Knowledge (POK) protocol for the BDLOP commitment scheme [9] and its applications [6,18] whose semantic security or hiding property rely on hardness of MLWE. As a result, we show that it is possible to build secure PPK and POK protocols without noise flooding or rejection sampling while achieving a polynomial overhead between the honest and proven languages. Finally, we present concrete parameter sets to convince that our method outperforms the state-of-the-art results.

1.2 Technical Overview

In this section, we briefly explain that transcripts of our proof of knowledge protocols can be interpreted as an MLWE instance with *hints* on the secret and errors. Then, we demonstrate security proofs based on a new variant of MLWE, named as *Hint-MLWE*. Finally, we discuss how MLWE can be reduced to Hint-MLWE under *discrete Gaussian* setting, and demonstrate our improvements on the parameter size.

PPK for RLWE-Based Public-Key Encryption. For a public key pk, let $\mathsf{Enc}_{\mathsf{pk}}(m, \mathbf{r})$ be a ciphertext which we want to prove the plaintext knowledge where m and $\mathbf{r}$ denote the message and encryption randomness, respectively. Then, the transcript of the PPK protocol consists of a ciphertext $\mathbf{c} = \mathsf{Enc}_{\mathsf{pk}}(m, \mathbf{r})$, random ciphertexts $\mathsf{Enc}_{\mathsf{pk}}(u_i, \mathbf{y}_i)$, challenges γ_i and responses $(v_i, \mathbf{z}_i) = (u_i, \mathbf{y}_i) + \gamma_i \cdot (m, \mathbf{r})$ for $0 \le i < \ell$ and we need to show that it does not leak any information about m. Since $\mathsf{Enc}_{\mathsf{pk}}(u_i, \mathbf{y}_i) = \mathsf{Enc}_{\mathsf{pk}}(v_i, \mathbf{z}_i) - \gamma_i \cdot \mathbf{c}$, it suffices to show that the following is simulatable for given challenges $\gamma_0, \ldots, \gamma_{\ell-1}$ and a public key pk:

$$\left(\mathsf{Enc}_{\mathsf{pk}}(m, \mathbf{r}), (v_0, \mathbf{z}_0), \ldots, (v_{\ell-1}, \mathbf{z}_{\ell-1})\right).$$

Similar to Chen et al. [14], our protocol is based on the BFV scheme [11,19] with a plaintext modulus p and a ciphertext modulus q such that $p \mid q$. Recall that $\mathsf{Enc}_{\mathsf{pk}}(m, \mathbf{r}) = r_2 \cdot \mathbf{p} + ((q/p) \cdot m + r_0, r_1)$ for a public key $\mathsf{pk} = \mathbf{p} \in R_q^2$ and an encryption randomness $\mathbf{r} = (r_0, r_1, r_2) \in R^3$. Then, the transcript of PPK described above can be viewed as the following tuples:

$$\left(r_2 \cdot \mathbf{p} + ((q/p) \cdot m + r_0, r_1)\right) \qquad \text{(Ciphertext)}$$
$$(\mathbf{y}_0 + \gamma_0 \cdot \mathbf{r}, \ldots, \mathbf{y}_{\ell-1} + \gamma_{\ell-1} \cdot \mathbf{r}) \qquad \text{(Hints on the randomness } \mathbf{r})$$

POK for BDLOP Commitment. For a commitment key $\mathsf{ck} = (\mathbf{B}_0, \mathbf{B}_1)$ consisting of two matrices over R_q, the commitment of a message $\mathbf{m}$ is defined as $\mathsf{Com}_{\mathsf{ck}}(\mathbf{m}, \mathbf{r}) = (\mathbf{B}_0\mathbf{r}, \mathbf{B}_1\mathbf{r}+\mathbf{m})$ for a commitment randomness $\mathbf{r}$, which we want to prove the opening knowledge. The transcript of the POK protocol consists of a commitment $\mathsf{Com}_{\mathsf{ck}}(\mathbf{m}, \mathbf{r})$, $\mathbf{w} = \mathbf{B}_0\mathbf{y}$ for a random masking $\mathbf{y}$, a challenge γ and the response $\mathbf{z} = \mathbf{y} + \gamma \cdot \mathbf{r}$. Similar to the case of PPK, we need to show that the tuple $\left(\mathbf{B}, \mathbf{B}\mathbf{r} + \begin{bmatrix} \mathbf{0} \\ \mathbf{m} \end{bmatrix}, \mathbf{y} + \gamma \cdot \mathbf{r}\right)$ for $\mathbf{B} = \begin{bmatrix} \mathbf{B}_0 \\ \mathbf{B}_1 \end{bmatrix}$ leaks no information about $\mathbf{m}$.

In BDLOP, a commitment key is written as $\mathbf{B} = \mathbf{R} \cdot [\mathbf{I} \,|\, \mathbf{A}]$ for some invertible matrix $\mathbf{R}$ and a matrix $\mathbf{A}$. Therefore, it suffices to show that the tuple $\left(\mathbf{A}, [\mathbf{I} \,|\, \mathbf{A}]\mathbf{r} + \mathbf{R}^{-1} \cdot \begin{bmatrix} \mathbf{0} \\ \mathbf{m} \end{bmatrix}, \mathbf{y} + \gamma \cdot \mathbf{r}\right)$ can be simulated without the message $\mathbf{m}$.

Security Reduction from Hint-MLWE. For the security proof, we define a variant of Module-LWE (MLWE), which we call *Hint-MLWE*, and prove the security of our protocols under the hardness assumption of Hint-MLWE. To be precise, the Hint-MLWE problem gives MLWE samples $(\mathbf{A}, [\mathbf{I} \,|\, \mathbf{A}]\mathbf{r})$ with a bounded number of hints on the secret and errors as $(\mathbf{y}_0 + \gamma_0 \cdot \mathbf{r}, \ldots, \mathbf{y}_{\ell-1} + \gamma_{\ell-1} \cdot \mathbf{r})$ where $\mathbf{A} \leftarrow \mathcal{U}(R_q^{m \times d})$, $\mathbf{r} \leftarrow \chi, \mathbf{y}_i \leftarrow \xi$ for some distributions χ, ξ over R^{d+m}, and $\gamma_0, \ldots, \gamma_{\ell-1}$ are chosen from some distribution $\mathcal{C}$ over R^ℓ. The Hint-MLWE assumption implies that it is hard to distinguish between the MLWE samples and the uniform samples $(\mathbf{a}, \mathbf{b})$ for $\mathbf{b} \leftarrow \mathcal{U}(R_q^m)$ even if the hints on the secret and error are given.

We can directly apply the Hint-MLWE assumption to show the security of our protocols: For PPK, regarding $(\mathbf{p}, r_2 \cdot \mathbf{p} + (r_0, r_1))$ as two RLWE samples, the Hint-RLWE assumption[1] implies that one cannot distinguish this tuple from $(\mathbf{p}, \mathbf{b})$ for $\mathbf{b} \leftarrow \mathcal{U}(R_q^2)$ even when some hints on $\mathbf{r}$ are given. Similarly for POK, the tuple $(\mathbf{A}, [\mathbf{I} \,|\, \mathbf{A}]\mathbf{r}, \mathbf{y} + \gamma \cdot \mathbf{r})$ is computationally indistinguishable with $(\mathbf{A}, \mathbf{u}, \mathbf{y} + \gamma \cdot \mathbf{r})$ for a uniform random $\mathbf{u}$ under the Hint-MLWE assumption.

Hardness of Hint-MLWE. We prove that there exists an efficient reduction from standard MLWE to Hint-MLWE under a discrete Gaussian setting. Roughly speaking, if χ and ξ are discrete Gaussian distributions with parameters σ_1 and σ_2 respectively, then Hint-MLWE is no easier than the MLWE problem of parameter $\sigma > 0$ such that $\frac{1}{\sigma^2} = 2(\frac{1}{\sigma_1^2} + \frac{B}{\sigma_2^2})$ for some constant $B > 0$ determined by the challenge distribution $\mathcal{C}$.

To be precise, we analyze the *conditional* distribution of the secret $\mathbf{r}$ for given hints $\mathbf{y}_0 + \gamma_0 \cdot \mathbf{r}, \ldots, \mathbf{y}_{\ell-1} + \gamma_{\ell-1} \cdot \mathbf{r}$ and show that it is still a discrete Gaussian distribution $(D_{\mathbb{Z}^n, \sqrt{2}\sigma, \mathbf{c}})^d$ with width parameter $\sqrt{2}\sigma$ and some center $\mathbf{c}$ which is determined by challenges γ_i and hints $\mathbf{y}_i + \gamma_i \cdot \mathbf{r}$. This implies that the joint distribution of $(\mathbf{r}, \mathbf{y}_0 + \gamma_0 \cdot \mathbf{r}, \ldots, \mathbf{y}_{\ell-1} + \gamma_{\ell-1} \cdot \mathbf{r})$ is essentially identical to that of $(\hat{\mathbf{r}}, \mathbf{y}_0 + \gamma_0 \cdot \mathbf{r}, \ldots, \mathbf{y}_{\ell-1} + \gamma_{\ell-1} \cdot \mathbf{r})$ where $\hat{\mathbf{r}} \leftarrow (D_{\mathbb{Z}^n, \sqrt{2}\sigma, \mathbf{c}})^d$. From this observation, the reduction from MLWE to Hint-MLWE is done at a high level as following: Let $(\mathbf{A}, \mathbf{b}) = (\mathbf{A}, [\mathbf{I} \,|\, \mathbf{A}]\mathbf{r}')$ be a given MLWE instance where $\mathbf{r}' \leftarrow (D_{\mathbb{Z}^n, \sigma, 0})^d$. We sample the hints $\mathbf{y}_i + \gamma_i \cdot \mathbf{r}$ *first* and use them to generate $\mathbf{t} \leftarrow (D_{\mathbb{Z}^n, \sigma, \mathbf{c}})^d$. Then, the output of the reduction is $(\mathbf{A}, \mathbf{b} + [\mathbf{I} \,|\, \mathbf{A}]\mathbf{t}, \mathbf{y}_0 + \gamma_0 \cdot \mathbf{r}, \ldots, \mathbf{y}_{\ell-1} + \gamma_{\ell-1} \cdot \mathbf{r})$. Note that the distribution of $\mathbf{r}' + \mathbf{t}$ is statistically indistinguishable to that of $\hat{\mathbf{r}}$ under a certain condition on σ, and hence we finally obtain the Hint-MLWE instance $(\mathbf{A}, [\mathbf{I} \,|\, \mathbf{A}]\mathbf{r}, \mathbf{y}_0 + \gamma_0 \cdot \mathbf{r}, \ldots, \mathbf{y}_{\ell-1} + \gamma_{\ell-1} \cdot \mathbf{r})$.

Performance Improvements. Our result has several advantages over the existing solutions such as noise flooding and rejection sampling in terms of both parameter size and computational cost. Under the MLWE assumption of parameter $\sigma > 0$, the noise flooding technique requires σ_2 to be exponentially large compared to σ. On the other hand, the rejection sampling method may take smaller parameters $\sigma_1 = \sigma$ and $\sigma_2 = O(\sqrt{\ell nd} \cdot \sigma)$, but it requires several repetitions to obtain valid proofs.

---

[1] Note that we can naturally define the Hint-RLWE problem as a special case ($d = 1$) of Hint-MLWE.

Our security reduction implies that it is sufficient to set $\sigma_1 = O(\sigma)$ and $\sigma_2 = O(\sqrt{\ell}\sigma)$. To be precise, while the rejection sampling requires σ_2 to be proportional to the *2-norm* of $\gamma_i \cdot \mathbf{r}$, our method enables to set σ_2 proportional to its *infinity-norm*, and hence there exists the gap $O(\sqrt{nd})$ on the size σ_2 of the masking vectors between our method and rejection sampling. As a result, our method offers more compact parameters, which is reduced by a factor of $O(\sqrt{nd})$ compared to the rejection sampling, without requiring any repetitions.

1.3 Related Work

Lattice-Based Proof Systems. In the last few years, there have been active researches in the field of lattice-based proof systems. In particular, the BDLOP commitment scheme [9] has paved the way for efficient lattice-based proof techniques for multiplicative relations [6], linear relations [18], and integer relations [27], offering viable proof sizes for practical applications. These proof techniques have been successfully employed in the construction of efficient group signature schemes [26] and ring signature schemes [29]. In order to enhance the efficiency of BDLOP, a recent work [25] introduces the ABDLOP commitment scheme, which combines the Ajtai commitment scheme [2] with BDLOP. This work takes advantage of the intrinsic property of the Ajtai commitment scheme, allowing for amortized commitments, and results in smaller proof sizes, which can be considered as an orthogonal approach to ours. Based on this work, more compact lattice-based group and ring signature schemes [24] have also been proposed.

LWE with Side Information. In the previous literature, several variants of LWE with different forms of side information have been proposed. In [4,32], a variant called extended-LWE was firstly proposed which gives a hint on LWE secret and error vectors in a form of a "noisy" inner product, i.e., $(\mathbf{A}, [\mathbf{I} \,|\mathbf{A}]\mathbf{r}, \langle \mathbf{r}, \mathbf{z} \rangle + f)$ for a small integer f and given small vectors $\mathbf{z}$, with a reduction from standard LWE. Later, extended-LWE has been modified in various forms according to its usage. In [13], for example, the noisy hint was substituted by the "exact" inner product (*i.e.,* $f = 0$), and the problem was generalized into the multi-secret version, which was used to prove the hardness of LWE with a binary secret. Recently, Lyubashevsky et al. [28] observe that the forementioned type of side information can improve the efficiency of the rejection sampling method. Their method specifically reveals the sign value of $\langle \mathbf{z}, \mathbf{r} \rangle$, leading to a more efficient rejection sampling process with smaller parameter sizes. The security of their method is based on a variant of extended-LWE and has been proven to be secure for the plain LWE case.[2]

The Hint-LWE problem was firstly defined in [15,22], which publishes a hint on the LWE error with *additive* Gaussian noise, i.e., $(\mathbf{A}, \mathbf{As}+\mathbf{e}, \mathbf{e}+\mathbf{f})$ for a small vector $\mathbf{f}$. The main differences between the Hint-LWE problems in [22] and our paper are as followings: (1) We consider *multiple* hints on *both* LWE secret and error, while [22] only considers a single hint on LWE error, (2) We also consider

---

[2] In [28], the authors applied their method to MLWE cases to instantiate new POK protocol, but they only provided the proof for plain LWE cases.

the *multiplication of challenges* to the LWE secret and error in the hints while [22] did not, (3) We prove the hardness of Hint-LWE under *discrete* Gaussian setting while [22] uses continuous Gaussian (Hence, [22] is not able to consider the hint on LWE secret which should be discrete). A multi-secret version was considered in [22], but we note that our Hint-LWE problem can also be naturally generalized to the multi-secret version.

Alternatives to Rejection Sampling. There has been another direction of research [1,7] that constructs efficient lattice-based signatures without the use of rejection sampling or noise flooding. These works share the same motivation as ours, which is to investigate how partial information leakage in the transcript affects the security of the signature schemes. Instead of using statistical distance, these studies use Rényi divergence to quantify the difference between the real and simulated transcripts, and show that the resulting Rényi divergence does not compromise the unforgeability of the proposed signature scheme. Although the Rényi-divergence-based analysis offers provable security for the signature scheme, it does not inherently provide simulation-based security unless an additional assumption known as public sampleability [7] is fulfilled. This inhibits its black-box usage in the construction of secure protocols compared to noise flooding or rejection sampling.

2   Preliminaries

2.1   Notation

We use bold lower-case and upper-case letters to denote column vectors, and matrices respectively. For a positive integer q, we use $\mathbb{Z} \cap (-q/2, q/2]$ as a representative set of $\mathbb{Z}_q$, and denote by $[a]_q$ the reduction of a modulo q.

Let n be a power of two and q be an integer. We denote by $R = \mathbb{Z}[X]/(X^n+1)$ the ring of integers of the $2n$-th cyclotomic field and $R_q = \mathbb{Z}_q[X]/(X^n + 1)$ the residue ring of R modulo q. For a polynomial $f = \sum_{i=0}^{n-1} f_i X^i \in R$, the ℓ^p $(p \geq 1)$ and ℓ^∞ norms are defined as follows:

$$\|f\|_p := \sqrt[p]{\sum_{i=0}^{n-1} |f_i|^p}, \qquad \|f\|_\infty := \max_{0 \leq i < n} |f_i|$$

For a vector of polynomials $\mathbf{f} = (f^{(0)}, \ldots, f^{(m-1)}) \in R^m$, we write

$$\|\mathbf{f}\|_p := \sqrt[p]{\sum_{i=0}^{m-1} \|f^{(i)}\|_p^p}, \qquad \|\mathbf{f}\|_\infty := \max_{0 \leq i < m} \left\|f^{(i)}\right\|_\infty$$

For a polynomial $c \in R$, we denote the vector of its coefficients by a bold letter $\mathbf{c}$ and the corresponding negacyclic matrix by $\mathbf{M}(c)$. For a matrix $\mathbf{A} \in \mathbb{R}^{m \times n}$, we denote the matrix norm of $\mathbf{A}$ by $\|\mathbf{A}\|_2 := \max_{0 \neq \mathbf{x} \in \mathbb{R}^n} \frac{\|\mathbf{Ax}\|_2}{\|\mathbf{x}\|_2}$.

We denoted the largest and the smallest singular value of a real-value matrix $\mathbf{A}$ by $\sigma_{\max}(\mathbf{A})$ and $\sigma_{\min}(\mathbf{A})$, respectively.

2.2 Probability Distributions

We denote sampling x from the distribution $\mathcal{D}$ by $x \leftarrow \mathcal{D}$. For distributions $\mathcal{D}_1$ and $\mathcal{D}_2$ over a countable set S (e.g. $\mathbb{Z}^n$), the statistical distance of $\mathcal{D}_1$ and $\mathcal{D}_2$ is defined as $\frac{1}{2} \cdot \sum_{x \in S} |\mathcal{D}_1(x) - \mathcal{D}_2(x)| \in [0,1]$. We denote the uniform distribution over S by $\mathcal{U}(S)$ when S is finite.

We define the n-dimensional spherical Gaussian function $\rho_{\mathbf{c}} : \mathbb{R}^n \to (0,1]$ centered at $\mathbf{c} \in \mathbb{R}^n$ as $\rho_{\mathbf{c}}(\mathbf{x}) := \exp(-\pi \cdot (\mathbf{x} - \mathbf{c})^\top (\mathbf{x} - \mathbf{c}))$. In general, for a positive definite matrix $\mathbf{\Sigma} \in \mathbb{R}^{n \times n}$, we define the elliptical Gaussian function $\rho_{\mathbf{c},\sqrt{\mathbf{\Sigma}}} : \mathbb{R}^n \to (0,1]$ as $\rho_{\mathbf{c},\sqrt{\mathbf{\Sigma}}}(\mathbf{x}) := \exp(-\pi \cdot (\mathbf{x} - \mathbf{c})^\top \mathbf{\Sigma}^{-1}(\mathbf{x} - \mathbf{c}))$.

Let $\Lambda \subseteq \mathbb{R}^n$ be a lattice and $\mathbf{v} \in \mathbb{R}^n$. The discrete Gaussian distribution $\mathcal{D}_{\mathbf{v}+\Lambda,\mathbf{c},\sqrt{\mathbf{\Sigma}}}$ is defined as a distribution over the coset $\mathbf{v} + \Lambda$, whose probability mass function is $\mathcal{D}_{\mathbf{v}+\Lambda,\mathbf{c},\sqrt{\mathbf{\Sigma}}}(\mathbf{x}) = \rho_{\mathbf{c},\sqrt{\mathbf{\Sigma}}}(\mathbf{x})/\rho_{\mathbf{c},\sqrt{\mathbf{\Sigma}}}(\mathbf{v} + \Lambda)$ for $\mathbf{x} \in \mathbf{v} + \Lambda$ where $\rho_{\mathbf{c},\sqrt{\mathbf{\Sigma}}}(\mathbf{v} + \Lambda) := \sum_{\mathbf{y} \in \mathbf{v}+\Lambda} \rho_{\mathbf{c},\sqrt{\mathbf{\Sigma}}}(\mathbf{y}) < \infty$. Note that $\mathcal{D}_{\mathbf{v}+\Lambda,\mathbf{c},\sqrt{\mathbf{\Sigma}}}$ is identical to the distribution of $\mathbf{c} + \mathbf{x}$ where $\mathbf{x} \leftarrow \mathcal{D}_{(\mathbf{v}-\mathbf{c})+\Lambda,0,\sqrt{\mathbf{\Sigma}}}$. When $\mathbf{c} = \mathbf{0}$, then we omit $\mathbf{c}$ in the subscripts of both ρ and $\mathcal{D}$. When $\mathbf{\Sigma} = \sigma^2 \cdot \mathbf{I}_n$ for $\sigma > 0$ where $\mathbf{I}_n$ is the $(n \times n)$ identity matrix, then we substitute $\sqrt{\mathbf{\Sigma}}$ by σ in the subscript and refer to σ as the width parameter of $\mathcal{D}_{\Lambda,\mathbf{c},\sigma}$. We denote by $x \leftarrow \mathcal{D}_{\mathbb{Z}^n,\sigma}$ for $x \in R$ when we sample its corresponding coefficient vector $\mathbf{x}$ from $\mathcal{D}_{\mathbb{Z}^n,\sigma}$.

2.3 Module SIS/LWE

Definition 1. *Let m,d be positive integers, and $0 < \beta < q$. Then, the goal of the Module-SIS (MSIS) problem is to find, for a given matrix $\mathbf{A} \leftarrow \mathcal{U}(R_q^{m \times d})$, $\mathbf{x} \in R_q^d$ such that $\mathbf{Ax} = \mathbf{0} \pmod{q}$ and $\|\mathbf{x}\|_2 \leq \beta$. We say that a PPT adversary $\mathcal{A}$ has advantages ε in solving $\mathsf{MSIS}_{R,d,m,q,\beta}$ if*

$$\Pr\left[\|\mathbf{x}\|_2 < \beta \wedge \mathbf{Ax} = \mathbf{0} \pmod{q} \mid \mathbf{A} \leftarrow \mathcal{U}(R_q^{m \times d}); \mathbf{x} \leftarrow \mathcal{A}(\mathbf{A})\right] \geq \varepsilon.$$

Definition 2. *Let d,m,q be positive integers, and χ be a distribution over R^{d+m}. Then, the goal of the Module-LWE (MLWE) problem is to distinguish $(\mathbf{A}, \mathbf{u})$ from $(\mathbf{A}, [\mathbf{I}_m \mid \mathbf{A}]\mathbf{r})$ for $\mathbf{A} \leftarrow \mathcal{U}(R_q^{m \times d})$, $\mathbf{u} \leftarrow \mathcal{U}(R_q^m)$, and $\mathbf{r} \leftarrow \chi$. We say that a PPT adversary $\mathcal{A}$ has advantages ε in solving $\mathsf{MLWE}_{R,d,m,q,\chi}$ if*

$$|\Pr\left[b = 1 \mid \mathbf{A} \leftarrow \mathcal{U}(R_q^{m \times d}); \mathbf{r} \leftarrow \chi; b \leftarrow \mathcal{A}(\mathbf{A}, [\mathbf{I}_m \mid \mathbf{A}]\mathbf{r})\right]$$
$$- \Pr\left[b = 1 \mid (\mathbf{A}, \mathbf{u}) \leftarrow \mathcal{U}(R_q^{m \times d} \times R_q^m); b \leftarrow \mathcal{A}(\mathbf{A}, \mathbf{u})\right]| \geq \varepsilon.$$

The MLWE problem with $d = 1$ is called the Ring-LWE problem and denoted by $\mathsf{RLWE}_{R,m,q,\chi}$.

2.4 RLWE-Based Public-Key Encryption

We describe the BFV scheme [11,19], which is a standard RLWE-based public-key encryption with homomorphic property, to describe our PPK protocol.

- $\mathsf{Setup}(1^\lambda)$: Given a security parameter λ, outputs the parameter set $\mathsf{pp} = (R, q, p, \chi)$ where χ is a distribution over R^2, and p, q are odd integers such that $p \mid q$.

  The parameters p, q do not need to satisfy $p \mid q$ in general, but Chen et al. [14] introduced this condition to simplify the proof of plaintext knowledge. We make the same assumption to take its advantage in the protocol construction. The scaling factor will be denoted by $\Delta := q/p \in \mathbb{Z}$.

- $\mathsf{Gen}(\mathsf{pp})$: Given a public parameter $\mathsf{pp} = (R, q, p, \chi)$, sample a secret key $s \leftarrow \chi$. Sample $a \leftarrow \mathcal{U}(R_q)$ and $e \leftarrow \chi$. Set a public key pk as $\mathbf{p} = (b, a) \in R_q^2$ where $b = -as + e \pmod{q}$.

- $\mathsf{Enc}_{\mathsf{pk}}(m, \mathbf{r})$: For a public key $\mathsf{pk} = \mathbf{p}$, a message $m \in R_p$, and an encryption randomness $\mathbf{r} = (r_0, r_1, r_2) \in R^3$, output the ciphertext $\mathbf{c} = r_2 \cdot \mathbf{p} + (r_0 + \Delta \cdot m, r_1) \pmod{q}$.

- $\mathsf{Dec}(s, \mathbf{c})$: For a secret key s and a ciphertext $\mathbf{c} = (c_0, c_1) \in R_q^2$, output $m = \lfloor \Delta^{-1} \cdot (c_0 + c_1 \cdot s) \rceil \pmod{p}$.

The encryption randomness $\mathbf{r}$ is generally chosen to be small so that the decryption works correctly. Note that the additive homomorphism holds for both message and randomness: For messages $m_1, m_2 \in R_p$, $\gamma \in R$, and randomnesses $\mathbf{r}_1, \mathbf{r}_2 \in R^3$, it holds that

$$\mathsf{Enc}_{\mathsf{pk}}(m_1, \mathbf{r}_1) + \gamma \cdot \mathsf{Enc}_{\mathsf{pk}}(m_2, \mathbf{r}_2) = \mathsf{Enc}_{\mathsf{pk}}(m_1 + \gamma \cdot m_2, \mathbf{r}_1 + \gamma \cdot \mathbf{r}_2) \pmod{q}.$$

2.5   Lattice-Based Commitment Scheme

We first recall the definition of commitment scheme.

Definition 3 (Commitment Scheme). *A commitment scheme consists of the following three algorithms:*

- $\mathsf{Gen}(1^\lambda)$: *Given a security parameter λ, it generates a commitment key ck.*
- $\mathsf{Com}_{\mathsf{ck}}(m, r)$: *Given a commitment key ck, a message m, and randomness r, it outputs a commitment c.*
- $\mathsf{Open}_{\mathsf{ck}}(c, m, r)$: *Given a commitment c, a message m, and randomness r, it outputs either 0 or 1.*

where Gen is probabilistic and $\mathsf{Com}, \mathsf{Open}$ are deterministic. Let $\mathcal{R}$ be a distribution for randomness. Then a commitment scheme $(\mathsf{Gen}, \mathsf{Com}, \mathsf{Open})$ is said to be secure if it satisfies the following properties:

- **Hiding:** *For all PPT adversaries $\mathcal{A}$, the following advantage is negligible:*

$$\left| \Pr\left[b = b' \;\middle|\; \begin{array}{l} \mathsf{ck} \leftarrow \mathsf{Gen}(1^\lambda); (m_0, m_1) \leftarrow \mathcal{A}(\mathsf{ck}); r \leftarrow \mathcal{R}; \\ b \leftarrow \mathcal{U}(\{0,1\}); c = \mathsf{Com}_{\mathsf{ck}}(m_b, r); b' \leftarrow \mathcal{A}(\mathsf{ck}, c); \end{array} \right] - \frac{1}{2} \right|.$$

- **Binding:** *For all PPT adversaries $\mathcal{A}$, the following probability is negligible:*

$$\Pr\left[(\mathsf{Open}_{\mathsf{ck}}(c, m, r) = \mathsf{Open}_{\mathsf{ck}}(c, m', r') = 1) \wedge (m \neq m') \;\middle|\; \begin{array}{l} \mathsf{ck} \leftarrow \mathsf{Gen}(1^\lambda); \\ (c, m, r, m', r') \leftarrow \mathcal{A}(\mathsf{ck}) \end{array} \right].$$

Below, we present the BDLOP commitment scheme, whose binding and hiding properties rely on the hardness of $\mathsf{MSIS}_{R,\mu+\nu+k,\mu,q,\beta_{\mathsf{BDLOP}}}$ and $\mathsf{MLWE}_{R,\nu,q,\chi}$, respectively, where χ is a distribution for commitment randomness. We refer the reader to [9] for more details.

- $\mathsf{BDLOP.Gen}(1^\lambda)$: Given a security parameter λ, it outputs a commitment key $\mathsf{ck} = (\mathbf{B}_0, \mathbf{B}_1)$ which are generated as follows:
    - $\mathbf{B}_0 = [\mathbf{I}_\mu \mid \mathbf{B}_0'] \in R_q^{\mu \times (\mu+\nu+k)}$ where $\mathbf{B}_0' \leftarrow \mathcal{U}(R_q^{\mu \times (\nu+k)})$.
    - $\mathbf{B}_1 = [\mathbf{0}^{k \times \mu} \mid \mathbf{I}_k \mid \mathbf{B}_1'] \in R_q^{k \times (\mu+\nu+k)}$ where $\mathbf{B}_1' \leftarrow \mathcal{U}(R_q^{k \times \nu})$.
- $\mathsf{BDLOP.Com}_{\mathsf{ck}}(\mathbf{m}, \mathbf{r})$: Given a commitment key ck, a message $\mathbf{m} \in R_q^k$, and randomness $\mathbf{r} \in R^{\mu+\nu+k}$, it outputs $\mathbf{c} = (\mathbf{c}_0, \mathbf{c}_1)$ where $\mathbf{c}_0 = \mathbf{B}_0\mathbf{r} \pmod{q}$ and $\mathbf{c}_1 = \mathbf{B}_1\mathbf{r} + \mathbf{m} \pmod{q}$.
- $\mathsf{BDLOP.Open}_{\mathsf{ck}}(\mathbf{c}, \mathbf{m}, \mathbf{r})$: Given a commitment $\mathbf{c} = (\mathbf{c}_0, \mathbf{c}_1)$, a message $\mathbf{m}$, and randomness $\mathbf{r}$, it outputs 1 if and only if $\mathbf{c} = \mathsf{BDLOP.Com}_{\mathsf{ck}}(\mathbf{m}, \mathbf{r})$ and $\|\mathbf{r}\|_2 \leq \beta_{\mathsf{BDLOP}}$.

In [9], there is a weaker version of opening algorithm supporting for efficient proof of opening knowledge, which we will describe in Sect. 5.1. The commitment scheme also satisfy the additive homomorphism for both message and randomness as well as the BFV scheme.

2.6 Proof of Knowledge and Simulatability

In this subsection, we present a new approach to building a secure proof-of-knowledge protocol. The conventional construction involves a zero-knowledge proof for the prover's secret input and randomness used in generating statements to be proved. However, our new definition primarily relies on the idea that the leakage of some information on randomness does not lead to an attack against the prover's secret input, which is formally described below.

Definition 4. *Let $\mathbf{L}, \mathbf{L}'$ be NP-languages satisfying $\mathbf{L} \subseteq \mathbf{L}'$. Let $\mathbf{R}, \mathbf{R}'$ be witness relations for $\mathbf{L}$ and $\mathbf{L}'$ respectively i.e., $(t \in \mathbf{L} \Leftrightarrow \exists w \ (t, w) \in \mathbf{R})$ and $(t \in \mathbf{L}' \Leftrightarrow \exists w' \ (t, w') \in \mathbf{R}')$. Let $(\mathcal{P}, \mathcal{V})$ be an interactive protocol where $\mathcal{P}$ takes a secret input m and a public parameter pp as input, and $\mathcal{V}$ only takes a public parameter pp as input. Then $(\mathcal{P}, \mathcal{V})$ is called a secure proof-of-knowledge protocol for the languages $(\mathbf{L}, \mathbf{L}')$ if and only if it satisfies the followings:*

- *Two Phases: The protocol consists of the following phases.*
    - *Generate-phase: In generate-phase, the prover first samples randomness r, and then generates a statement t with x and r. At the end of the phase, it sends the statement t to the verifier $\mathcal{V}$.*
    - *Prove-phase: In prove-phase, the prover and the verifier take (pp, t, x, r) and (pp, t) as input respectively. Then, they interact each other to prove that $t \in \mathbf{L}'$. At the end of the phase, the verifier outputs either 0 or 1.*
    We refer the sequence of messages exchanged between $\mathcal{P}$ and $\mathcal{V}$ during the generate-phase and the prove-phase as the transcript, and denote it by $\mathrm{Tr}(\mathcal{P}(\mathsf{pp}, x), \mathcal{V}(\mathsf{pp}))$.

- **Completeness:** *If $\mathcal{P}$ generates a statement $t \in \mathbf{L}$ in the generate-phase, the prove-phase ends with 1 except for negligible probability.*
- **Knowledge Soundness:** *If there exists an adversarial prover $\mathcal{P}^*$ which makes the verifier outputs 1 at the prove-phase with non-negligible probability, then there exists an efficient algorithm $\mathcal{E}$, called an extractor, which, given black-box access to $\mathcal{P}^*$, outputs w' such that $(t, w') \in \mathbf{R}'$ with non-negligible probability.*
- **Simulatability:** *There exists a PPT algorithm $\mathcal{S}$, called a simulator, whose input is pp and output is tr which is computationally indistinguishable from the transcript from the honest prover $\mathcal{P}$ and verifier $\mathcal{V}$, for any secret input x. In other words, for all PPT algorithm $\mathcal{A}$, the following advantage is negligible:*

$$\left| \Pr\left[b = 1 \,\middle|\, \begin{array}{l} x \leftarrow \mathcal{A}(\mathsf{pp}); \ \mathsf{tr} \leftarrow \mathrm{Tr}(\mathcal{P}(\mathsf{pp},x),\mathcal{V}(\mathsf{pp})); \\ b \leftarrow \mathcal{A}(\mathsf{pp},\mathsf{tr}) \end{array} \right] - \Pr\left[b = 1 \,\middle|\, \begin{array}{l} x \leftarrow \mathcal{A}(\mathsf{pp}); \ \mathsf{tr} \leftarrow \mathcal{S}(\mathsf{pp}); \\ b \leftarrow \mathcal{A}(\mathsf{pp},\mathsf{tr}); \end{array} \right] \right|$$

In this definition, we reformulate zero-knowledge condition on the prover's secret input by simulatability. The main difference between our simulatability property and the conventional zero-knowledge proof is whether randomness is perfectly hidden together or not. Since the essential purpose of secure proof-of-knowledge protocol is to hide the prover's secret input rather than a randomness, it suffices to satisfy our simulatability property for the desired security requirement. It is worth noting that similar approaches have been considered in [17,28].

Our definition utilizes two languages $\mathbf{L} \subseteq \mathbf{L}'$, called the honest and proven languages respectively, to address common scenarios in lattice-based construction. There have been studies, such as [10,30], which reduce the communication cost by weakening extractors' power in the knowledge soundness property. Since our instantiations of proof-of-knowledge in this paper also employ these methods, our definition makes use of two languages to cover these cases. The gap between $\mathbf{L}$ and $\mathbf{L}'$ is often referred as *soundness slack*.

2.7 Useful Lemmas

Lemma 1 ([23, Lemma 4.4]). *For any $k > 0$, $\Pr\left[\|\mathbf{x}\|_\infty < k\sigma \mid \mathbf{x} \leftarrow \mathcal{D}_{\mathbb{Z}^n,\sigma}\right] > 1 - 2n \cdot \exp(-\pi k^2)$.*

Lemma 2 ([6, Lemma 2.5]). *$\Pr\left[\|\mathbf{x}\|_2 < \sigma\sqrt{n/\pi} \mid \mathbf{x} \leftarrow \mathcal{D}_{\mathbb{Z}^n,\sigma}\right] > 1 - 2^{-n/8}$.*

Lemma 3 (Simplified Convolution Lemma [33]). *Let Σ_1, Σ_2 be positive definite matrices such that $\Sigma_3^{-1} := \Sigma_1^{-1} + \Sigma_2^{-1}$ satisfies $\sqrt{\Sigma_3} \geq \eta_\varepsilon(\mathbb{Z}^n)$ for $0 < \varepsilon < 1/2$. Then for an arbitrary $\mathbf{c} \in \mathbb{Z}^n$, the distribution*

$$\left\{ \mathbf{x}_1 + \mathbf{x}_2 \mid \mathbf{x}_1 \leftarrow \mathcal{D}_{\mathbb{Z}^n,\sqrt{\Sigma_1}}, \ \mathbf{x}_2 \leftarrow \mathcal{D}_{\mathbb{Z}^n,\mathbf{c},\sqrt{\Sigma_2}} \right\}$$

is within statistical distance 2ε of $\mathcal{D}_{\mathbb{Z}^n,\mathbf{c},\sqrt{\Sigma_1+\Sigma_2}}$.

Definition 5 (Smoothing parameter [31]). *For an n-dimensional lattice Λ and positive real $\varepsilon > 0$, the smoothing parameter $\eta_\varepsilon(\Lambda)$ is the smallest s such that $\rho_{1/s}(\Lambda^* \backslash \{\mathbf{0}\}) \leq \varepsilon$.*

Definition 6 ([33, **Definition 2.3**]). *Let* $\boldsymbol{\Sigma}$ *be a positive-definite matrix. We say that* $\sqrt{\boldsymbol{\Sigma}} \geq \eta_\varepsilon(\Lambda)$ *if* $\eta_\varepsilon(\sqrt{\boldsymbol{\Sigma}}^{-1} \cdot \Lambda) \leq 1$, *i.e.,* $\rho\left(\sqrt{\boldsymbol{\Sigma}}^\top \cdot \Lambda^* \backslash \{\mathbf{0}\}\right) \leq \varepsilon$.

Lemma 4 ([31, **Lemma 3.3**]). *For any* n-*dimensional lattice* Λ *and* $\varepsilon > 0$,

$$\eta_\varepsilon(\Lambda) \leq \sqrt{\frac{\ln(2n(1 + 1/\varepsilon))}{\pi}} \cdot \lambda_n(\Lambda)$$

where $\lambda_n(\Lambda)$ *is the smallest real number* $r > 0$ *such that* $\dim(\mathrm{span}(\Lambda \cap r\mathcal{B})) = n$ *and* $\mathcal{B}$ *is the* n-*dimensional unit ball centered at the origin.*

Lemma 5. *For a positive-definite matrix* $\boldsymbol{\Sigma}$, $\sqrt{\boldsymbol{\Sigma}} \geq \eta_\varepsilon(\Lambda)$ *if* $\left\|\boldsymbol{\Sigma}^{-1}\right\|_2 \leq \eta_\varepsilon(\Lambda)^{-2}$.

Proof. Note that the matrix norm equals to the largest singular value, and hence $\sqrt{\sigma_{\min}(\boldsymbol{\Sigma})} = 1/\sqrt{\sigma_{\max}(\boldsymbol{\Sigma}^{-1})} = 1/\sqrt{\|\boldsymbol{\Sigma}^{-1}\|_2} \geq \eta_\varepsilon(\Lambda)$. Therefore, it holds that $\sum_{\mathbf{x} \in \Lambda^* \backslash \{\mathbf{0}\}} \exp\left(-\pi\sigma_{\min}(\boldsymbol{\Sigma}) \cdot \mathbf{x}^\top \mathbf{x}\right) \leq \varepsilon$ by Def. 5.

Since $\boldsymbol{\Sigma}$ is positive-definite, it holds that $\mathbf{x}^\top \boldsymbol{\Sigma} \mathbf{x} \geq \sigma_{\min}(\boldsymbol{\Sigma}) \cdot \mathbf{x}^\top \mathbf{x}$ for any $\mathbf{x} \in \Lambda^*$, and we obtain

$$\sum_{\mathbf{x} \in \Lambda^* \backslash \{\mathbf{0}\}} \exp(-\pi \cdot \mathbf{x}^\top \boldsymbol{\Sigma} \mathbf{x}) \leq \sum_{\mathbf{x} \in \Lambda^* \backslash \{\mathbf{0}\}} \exp\left(-\pi\sigma_{\min}(\boldsymbol{\Sigma}) \cdot \mathbf{x}^\top \mathbf{x}\right) \leq \varepsilon,$$

which implies $\eta_\varepsilon(\sqrt{\boldsymbol{\Sigma}}^{-1} \cdot \Lambda) \leq 1$. $\qquad\square$

Lemma 6 ([10, **Lemma 3.1**]). *Let* n *be a power of two, and let* $0 \leq i, j < 2n$ *such that* $i \neq j$. *Then,* $2(X^i - X^j)^{-1}$ *is an element of* R *such that*

$$\left\|2(X^i - X^j)^{-1}\right\|_\infty \leq 1,$$

where the inverse of $(X^i - X^j)$ *is taken over the field* $\mathbb{Q}[X]/(X^n + 1)$.

3   Hint-MLWE

In this section, we introduce a variant of the MLWE problem called *Hint-MLWE*. The Hint-MLWE problem is inspired by the structure of transcripts generated by lattice-based proof of knowledge protocols. They often include partial information about secret values such as the MLWE secret and the errors in MLWE instances, which are obtained by adding random errors to them. Since these 'hints' on the secret values may affect the security of MLWE, noise flooding or rejection sampling have utilized to ensure that no useful information is leaked from a transcript.

Apart from these previous approaches, we aim to precisely measure how much information on the secret values can be leaked from a transcript and its impact on the security of the protocol. In this context, we come up with the Hint-MLWE problem where the adversary is given the MLWE problem with some hints about secrets and errors. As expected, this problem is useful for proving the security of proof-of-knowledge protocols which we will deal with in Sect. 4 and 5.

To return, we will show that our goal can be achieved if both the secret values and the errors for generating hints are drawn from (discrete) Gaussian distributions by precisely analyzing the conditional distribution of the secret values for given hints. We start by giving a formal definition of the Hint-MLWE problem.

Definition 7 (The Hint-MLWE Problem). *Let d, m, ℓ be positive integers, χ, ξ be distributions over R^{d+m}, and $\mathcal{C}$ be a distribution over R^ℓ. The Hint-MLWE problem, denoted by $\mathsf{HintMLWE}_{R,d,m,q,\chi}^{\ell,\xi,\mathcal{C}}$, asks an adversary $\mathcal{A}$ to distinguish the following two cases:*

1. $\left(\mathbf{A}, [\mathbf{I}_m | \mathbf{A}] \mathbf{r}, \gamma_0, \dots, \gamma_{\ell-1}, \mathbf{z}_0, \dots, \mathbf{z}_{\ell-1} \right)$ *for* $\mathbf{A} \leftarrow \mathcal{U}(R_q^{m \times d})$, $\mathbf{r} \leftarrow \chi$, $\mathbf{y}_i \leftarrow \xi$, $(\gamma_0, \dots, \gamma_{\ell-1}) \leftarrow \mathcal{C}$, *and* $\mathbf{z}_i = \gamma_i \cdot \mathbf{r} + \mathbf{y}_i$ *for* $0 \le i < \ell$.

2. $\left(\mathbf{A}, \mathbf{u}, \gamma_0, \dots, \gamma_{\ell-1}, \mathbf{z}_0, \dots, \mathbf{z}_{\ell-1} \right)$ *for* $\mathbf{A} \leftarrow \mathcal{U}(R_q^{m \times d})$, $\mathbf{u} \leftarrow \mathcal{U}(R_q^m)$, $\mathbf{r} \leftarrow \chi$, $\mathbf{y}_i \leftarrow \xi$, $(\gamma_0, \dots, \gamma_{\ell-1}) \leftarrow \mathcal{C}$, *and* $\mathbf{z}_i = \gamma_i \cdot \mathbf{r} + \mathbf{y}_i$ *for* $0 \le i < \ell$.

We call the $d = 1$ case of Hint-MLWE as the Hint-RLWE problem and denote it by $\mathsf{HintRLWE}_{R,m,q,\chi}^{\ell,\xi,\mathcal{C}}$.

We often refer $(\mathbf{z}_0, \dots, \mathbf{z}_{\ell-1})$ as hints since it contains partial information about the secret $\mathbf{r}$. When χ and ξ are spherical discrete Gaussian distributions, we replace them with their width parameters in the Hint-MLWE notation for simplicity.

Below, we present the key lemma for proving the hardness of the Hint-MLWE problem when the secret and errors are sampled from discrete Gaussian distributions. At a high level, the lemma states that the conditional distribution of r given $(\gamma_0 \cdot r + y_0 \dots, \gamma_{\ell-1} \cdot r + y_{\ell-1})$ follows a (possibly not balanced) discrete Gaussian distribution again. Namely, the distribution of the first component of r given $z_i = \gamma_i \cdot r + y_i$ can be expressed as the Gaussian distribution over $\mathbb{Z}^n$ with suitable parameters.

Lemma 7. *Let $\ell > 0$ be an integer and $\sigma_1, \sigma_2 > 0$ be reals. For $\gamma_0, \dots, \gamma_{\ell-1} \in R$, let $\mathbf{\Gamma}_i$ be the negacyclic matrix corresponding to γ_i and $\mathbf{\Sigma}_0 := (\frac{1}{\sigma_1^2} \cdot \mathbf{I} + \frac{1}{\sigma_2^2} \cdot \sum_{i=0}^{\ell-1} \mathbf{\Gamma}_i^\top \mathbf{\Gamma}_i)^{-1}$. Then, the following two distributions over $R^{\ell+1}$ are statistically identical:*

$$\left\{ (r, z_0, \dots, z_{\ell-1}) \mid r \leftarrow \mathcal{D}_{\mathbb{Z}^n, \sigma_1}, \ y_i \leftarrow \mathcal{D}_{\mathbb{Z}^n, \sigma_2}, \ z_i = \gamma_i \cdot r + y_i \right\}$$

$$\left\{ (\hat{r}, z_0, \dots, z_{\ell-1}) \ \middle| \ \begin{matrix} r \leftarrow \mathcal{D}_{\mathbb{Z}^n, \sigma_1}, \ y_i \leftarrow \mathcal{D}_{\mathbb{Z}^n, \sigma_2}, \ z_i = \gamma_i \cdot r + y_i, \\ \mathbf{c} = \frac{1}{\sigma_2^2} \mathbf{\Sigma}_0 \cdot \sum_{i=0}^{\ell-1} \mathbf{\Gamma}_i^\top \mathbf{z}_i, \ \hat{r} \leftarrow \mathcal{D}_{\mathbb{Z}^n, \mathbf{c}, \sqrt{\mathbf{\Sigma}_0}} \end{matrix} \right\}$$

Proof. We claim that two random variables have the same probability mass function. The probability that the first random variable outputs $(v, w_0, \ldots, w_{\ell-1}) \in R^{\ell+1}$ can be written as following:

$$\Pr\left[r = v, \ \gamma_i \cdot r + y_i = w_i \mid r \leftarrow \mathcal{D}_{\mathbb{Z}^n, \sigma_1}, y_i \leftarrow \mathcal{D}_{\mathbb{Z}^n, \sigma_2}\right]$$

$$= \mathcal{D}_{\mathbb{Z}^n, \sigma_1}(\mathbf{v}) \cdot \prod_{i=0}^{\ell-1} \mathcal{D}_{\mathbb{Z}^n, \sigma_2}(\mathbf{w}_i - \mathbf{\Gamma}_i \mathbf{v})$$

$$\propto \exp\left[-\pi\left(\frac{1}{\sigma_1^2} \cdot \mathbf{v}^\top \mathbf{v} + \frac{1}{\sigma_2^2} \cdot \sum_{i=0}^{\ell-1} (\mathbf{w}_i - \mathbf{\Gamma}_i \mathbf{v})^\top (\mathbf{w}_i - \mathbf{\Gamma}_i \mathbf{v})\right)\right]$$

$$= \exp\left[-\pi\left((\mathbf{v} - \mathbf{c})^\top \mathbf{\Sigma}_0^{-1}(\mathbf{v} - \mathbf{c}) - \mathbf{c}^\top \mathbf{\Sigma}_0^{-1} \mathbf{c} + \frac{1}{\sigma_2^2} \cdot \sum_{i=0}^{\ell-1} \mathbf{w}_i^\top \mathbf{w}_i\right)\right]$$

where $\mathbf{c} = \frac{1}{\sigma_2^2} \mathbf{\Sigma}_0 \cdot \sum_{i=0}^{\ell-1} \mathbf{\Gamma}_i^\top \mathbf{w}_i$.

Hence, the conditional probability $\Pr\left[r = v \mid \gamma_i \cdot r + y_i = w_i\right]$ is proportional to $\exp\left[-\pi(\mathbf{v} - \mathbf{c})^\top \mathbf{\Sigma}_0^{-1}(\mathbf{v} - \mathbf{c})\right]$ for any $w_1, \ldots, w_\ell \in R$, which implies

$$\Pr\left[r = v \mid \gamma_i \cdot r + y_i = w_i\right] \equiv \rho_{\sqrt{\mathbf{\Sigma}_0}}(\mathbf{v} - \mathbf{c}) \equiv \Pr\left[\hat{r} = v \mid \gamma_i \cdot r + y_i = w_i\right].$$

Therefore, the given two distributions are statistically identical. □

Based on the above lemma, we prove the hardness of Hint-MLWE under the MLWE assumption when the secret and errors are sampled from discrete Gaussian distributions.

Theorem 1 (Hardness of Hint-MLWE). *Let d, k, m, q, ℓ be positive integers and $\mathcal{C}$ be a distribution over R^ℓ. Let $B > 0$ be a real number which satisfies $\sum_{j=0}^{\ell-1} \|\gamma_j\|_1^2 \leq B$ for any possible $(\gamma_0, \ldots, \gamma_{\ell-1})$ sampled from $\mathcal{C}$. For $\sigma_1, \sigma_2 > 0$, let $\sigma > 0$ be a real number defined as $\frac{1}{\sigma^2} = 2\left(\frac{1}{\sigma_1^2} + \frac{B}{\sigma_2^2}\right)$. If $\sigma \geq \sqrt{2} \cdot \eta_\varepsilon(\mathbb{Z}^n)$ for $0 < \varepsilon \leq 1/2$, then there exists an efficient reduction from $\mathsf{MLWE}_{R,d,m,q,\sigma}$ to $\mathsf{HintMLWE}_{R,d,m,q,\sigma_1}^{\ell,\sigma_2,\mathcal{C}}$ that reduces the advantage by at most $(d + m) \cdot 2\varepsilon$.*

Proof. Let $(\gamma_0, \ldots, \gamma_{\ell-1}) \leftarrow \mathcal{C}$, and let $\mathbf{\Sigma}_0 = (\sigma_1^{-2} \cdot \mathbf{I}_n + \sigma_2^{-2} \cdot \sum_{j=0}^{\ell-1} \mathbf{\Gamma}_j^\top \mathbf{\Gamma}_j)^{-1}$ where $\mathbf{\Gamma}_j := \mathbf{M}(\gamma_j)$ is the corresponding negacyclic matrix of γ_j for $0 \leq j < \ell$.

Let $(\mathbf{A}, \mathbf{b}) \in R_q^{m \times d} \times R_q^m$ be given $\mathsf{MLWE}_{R,d,m,q,\sigma}$ instance. Our reduction starts by sampling some polynomials in R:

$$r_i \leftarrow \mathcal{D}_{\mathbb{Z}^n, \sigma_1}, \ y_{i,j} \leftarrow \mathcal{D}_{\mathbb{Z}^n, \sigma_2} \text{ for } 0 \leq i < d + m, \text{ and } 0 \leq j < \ell$$

$$t_i \leftarrow \mathcal{D}_{\mathbb{Z}^n, \mathbf{c}_i, \sqrt{\mathbf{\Sigma}_0 - \sigma^2 \cdot \mathbf{I}_n}} \text{ for } \mathbf{c}_i = \frac{1}{\sigma_2^2} \mathbf{\Sigma}_0 \cdot \sum_{j=0}^{\ell-1} \mathbf{\Gamma}_j^\top (\mathbf{\Gamma}_j \mathbf{r}_i + \mathbf{y}_{i,j}) \text{ and } 0 \leq i < d + m$$

We write $(r_0, \ldots, r_{d+m-1})$, $(y_0, \ldots, y_{d+m-1})$, and $(t_0, \ldots, t_{d+m-1})$ as $\mathbf{r}$, $\mathbf{y}$, and $\mathbf{t}$ respectively. Note that $\mathbf{\Sigma}_0 - \sigma^2 \cdot \mathbf{I}_n$ is positive-definite, since the smallest singular value of $\mathbf{\Sigma}_0$ is $\left(\sigma_1^{-2} + \sigma_2^{-2} \cdot \left\|\sum_{j=0}^{\ell-1} \mathbf{\Gamma}_j^\top \mathbf{\Gamma}_j\right\|_2\right)^{-1} \geq (\sigma_1^{-2} + \sigma_2^{-2} \cdot$

$B)^{-1} = 2\sigma^2 > \sigma^2$, where the first inequality is derived from $\left\| \sum_{j=0}^{\ell-1} \Gamma_j^\top \Gamma_j \right\|_2 \leq$
$\sum_{j=0}^{\ell-1} \left\| \Gamma_j^\top \Gamma_j \right\|_2 \leq \sum_{j=0}^{\ell-1} \left\| \gamma_j \right\|_1^2 \leq B$.

Then, we use the sampled polynomials to transform the given MLWE instance $(\mathbf{A}, \mathbf{b})$ into $\left(\mathbf{A}, \ \mathbf{b} + [\mathbf{I}_m \,|\mathbf{A}]\mathbf{t}, \ \gamma_0, \ldots, \gamma_{\ell-1}, \ \mathbf{z}_0, \ldots, \mathbf{z}_{\ell-1} \right)$ where $\mathbf{z}_j = \gamma_j \cdot \mathbf{r} + \mathbf{y}_j$ for $0 \leq j < \ell$, which are the output of the reduction.

We first assume that $\mathbf{b} = [\mathbf{I}_m \,|\mathbf{A}]\mathbf{r}'$ for $\mathbf{r}' \leftarrow \mathcal{D}_{\mathbb{Z}^n, \sigma}^{d+m}$. Then, we have $\mathbf{b} + [\mathbf{I}_m \,|\mathbf{A}]\mathbf{t} = [\mathbf{I}_m \,|\mathbf{A}](\mathbf{r}' + \mathbf{t})$ where $\mathbf{r}' + \mathbf{t}$ follows the distributions $\prod_{i=0}^{d+m-1}(\mathcal{D}_{\mathbb{Z}^n, \sigma} + \mathcal{D}_{\mathbb{Z}^n, \mathbf{c}_i, \sqrt{\Sigma_0 - \sigma^2 \cdot \mathbf{I}_n}})$.

Now we show that $\sqrt{\Sigma_3} \geq \eta_\varepsilon(\mathbb{Z}^n)$ where $\Sigma_3^{-1} := \sigma^{-2} \cdot \mathbf{I}_n + (\Sigma_0 - \sigma^2 \cdot \mathbf{I}_n)^{-1}$. By Lemma 5, it is enough to show that $\left\| \Sigma_3^{-1} \right\|_2 \leq \eta_\varepsilon(\mathbb{Z}^n)^{-2}$. Recall that the smallest singular value of $\Sigma_0 - \sigma^2 \cdot \mathbf{I}_n$ is at least σ^2 as discussed above. Therefore, it holds that

$$\left\| \Sigma_3^{-1} \right\|_2 = \sigma^{-2} + \left\| (\Sigma_0 - \sigma^2 \cdot \mathbf{I}_n)^{-1} \right\|_2 \leq \sigma^{-2} + \sigma^{-2} = 2\sigma^{-2} \leq \eta_\varepsilon(\mathbb{Z}^n)^{-2}.$$

By Lemma 3, the distributions $\mathcal{D}_{\mathbb{Z}^n, \sigma} + \mathcal{D}_{\mathbb{Z}^n, \mathbf{c}_i, \sqrt{\Sigma_0 - \sigma^2 \mathbf{I}_n}}$ are within the statistical distance 2ε of $\mathcal{D}_{\mathbb{Z}^n, \mathbf{c}_i, \sqrt{\Sigma_0}}$. Therefore, the distribution of

$$\left(\mathbf{A}, \ \mathbf{b} + [\mathbf{I}_m \,|\mathbf{A}]\mathbf{t}, \ \gamma_0, \ldots, \gamma_{\ell-1}, \ \mathbf{z}_0, \ldots, \mathbf{z}_{\ell-1} \right)$$

is within statistical distance $(d + m) \cdot 2\varepsilon$ of

$$\left(\mathbf{A}, \ [\mathbf{I}_m \,|\mathbf{A}]\hat{\mathbf{r}}, \ \gamma_0, \ldots, \gamma_{\ell-1}, \ \mathbf{z}_0, \ldots, \mathbf{z}_{\ell-1} \right) \text{ for } \hat{\mathbf{r}} \leftarrow \prod_{i=0}^{d+m-1} \mathcal{D}_{\mathbb{Z}^n, \mathbf{c}_i, \sqrt{\Sigma_0}}.$$

As the last step, we apply Lemma 7 on $(\hat{\mathbf{r}}, \mathbf{z}_0, \ldots, \mathbf{z}_{\ell-1})$, then its distribution is identical to that of $(\mathbf{r}, \mathbf{z}_0, \ldots, \mathbf{z}_{\ell-1})$. As a result, the distribution of $\left(\mathbf{A}, \ [\mathbf{I}_m \,|\mathbf{A}]\hat{\mathbf{r}}, \ \gamma_0, \ldots, \gamma_{\ell-1}, \ \mathbf{z}_0, \ldots, \mathbf{z}_{\ell-1} \right)$ is identical to that of $\left(\mathbf{A}, \ [\mathbf{I}_m \,|\mathbf{A}]\mathbf{r}, \right.$
$\left. \gamma_0, \ldots, \gamma_{\ell-1}, \ \mathbf{z}_0, \ldots, \mathbf{z}_{\ell-1} \right)$, which exactly follows the distribution of samples from $\mathsf{HintMLWE}_{R,d,m,q,\sigma_1}^{\ell, \sigma_2, \mathcal{C}}$.

If $\mathbf{b} \leftarrow \mathcal{U}(R_q^m)$, then $\left(\mathbf{A}, \ \mathbf{b} + [\mathbf{I}_m \,|\mathbf{A}]\mathbf{t}, \ \gamma_0, \ldots, \gamma_{\ell-1}, \ \mathbf{z}_0, \ldots, \mathbf{z}_{\ell-1} \right)$ follows the same distribution with $\left(\mathbf{A}, \ \mathbf{u}, \ \gamma_0, \ldots, \gamma_{\ell-1}, \ \mathbf{z}_0, \ldots, \mathbf{z}_{\ell-1} \right)$ where $\mathbf{u} \leftarrow \mathcal{U}(R_q^m)$.

Therefore, the reduction is correct and reduces the advantage at most $(d + m) \cdot 2\varepsilon$. $\qquad \square$

Comparison to Previous Approaches. To illustrate the differences between our method and two previous approaches, rejection sampling and noise flooding, we analyze the ratio between the bound for the masking vector and the MLWE secret multiplied by the challenges, i.e., $\|\mathbf{y}_i\|_\infty$ and $\|\gamma_i \cdot \mathbf{r}\|_\infty$. Let T_∞ and T_2 be upper bounds on the size of $\gamma_i \cdot \mathbf{r}$ in terms of ℓ^∞ norm and ℓ^2 norm, respectively. In noise flooding [5,8], $\|\mathbf{y}_i\|_\infty$ is set to be exponentially larger than T_∞. Rejection sampling [23,28] does not require such exponential factor, but it should set $\|\mathbf{y}_i\|_\infty$ proportional to the ℓ^2 norm $T_2 = O(\sqrt{nd} \cdot T_\infty)$ and requires the number of repetitions to be exponential to ℓ. One can alternatively set $\|\mathbf{y}_i\|_\infty = O(\sqrt{\ell nd} \cdot T_\infty)$ to avoid such exponentially large number of repetitions.

On the other hand, our method allows us to set $\|\mathbf{y}_i\|_\infty = O(\sqrt{\ell} \cdot T_\infty)$, not proportional to T_2, while maintaining a similar security level of the underlying MLWE assumption. To be precise, the existing proof of knowledge protocols based on the previous approaches assume the hardness of $\mathsf{MLWE}_{R,d,m,q,\sigma_1}$, while our new constructions based on Hint-MLWE, which will be introduced in following sections, assume the hardness of $\mathsf{MLWE}_{R,d,m,q,\sigma}$. Here, we note that we are able to set $\sigma_1 = 2\sigma$ and $\sigma_2 = 2\sqrt{B}\sigma$ so that they satisfy the condition of Theorem 1, and then there is only a single bit difference on σ_1 and σ. Hence, by increasing the modulus q by one bit, we can achieve almost the same level of security when applying our Hint-MLWE method instead of previous methods.

4 Proof of Plaintext Knowledge for RLWE-Based Public-Key Encryption

The Proof of Plaintext Knowledge (PPK) protocol is frequently used to attain active security in the constructions of secure multiparty computation protocols [5,16]. To be precise, the prover would like to send a ciphertext $\mathbf{c}$ to the verifier and convince the verifier that $\mathbf{c}$ is well-formed while revealing no information about the underlying message m.

One can formalize the functionality of PPK protocol using the framework of the secure proof of knowledge protocol in Sect. 2.6. Let $(\mathsf{Gen}, \mathsf{Enc}, \mathsf{Dec})$ be a public-key encryption scheme, and pk be a public key for Enc. Then, the public parameter corresponds to pk, the secret input is the prover's message m, and the honest language $\mathbf{L}$ and the proven language $\mathbf{L}'$ are the set of honestly generated ciphertexts and the set of accepted ciphertexts respectively. In the generation phase, the prover samples encryption randomness $\mathbf{r}$ and generates a ciphertext by $\mathbf{c} = \mathsf{Enc}_{\mathsf{pk}}(m, \mathbf{r})$. In the proof phase, the verifier checks whether $\mathbf{c}$ is valid or not. If it outputs 1, it is the case that $\mathbf{c} \in \mathbf{L}'$.

The completeness ensures that an honestly generated ciphertext $\mathbf{c} \in \mathbf{L}$ always passes the proof phase except for negligible probability. The soundness ensures that if the prove-phase ends with 1, then $\mathbf{c} \in \mathbf{L}'$ and the prover knows encryption randomness $\mathbf{r}$ and message m except for negligible probability. Finally, the simulatability ensures that a verifier cannot know the underlying message m from the transcript between the honest prover and verifier. Thus, the construction of PPK protocol based on the proof-of-knowledge framework fulfills all the required functionality.

4.1   PPK Based on Hint-RLWE

Now, we provide a concrete instantiation of PPK protocol for the BFV scheme [11,19]. The main objective of the PPK protocol is to convince the verifier that a ciphertext is generated with small randomness. For $\mathsf{pp} = \mathsf{Setup}(1^\lambda)$; $\mathsf{pk} \leftarrow \mathsf{Gen}(\mathsf{pp})$, we first define the witness relationship $\mathbf{R}_{\mathsf{PPK}}$ and $\mathbf{R}'_{\mathsf{PPK}}$ as follows:

$$\mathbf{R}_{\mathsf{PPK}} = \{(m, \mathbf{r}, \mathbf{c}) \mid \mathsf{Enc}_{\mathsf{pk}}(m, 2\mathbf{r}) = \mathbf{c} \wedge \|\mathbf{r}\|_\infty \le \beta\},$$
$$\mathbf{R}'_{\mathsf{PPK}} = \{(m, \mathbf{r}, \mathbf{c}) \mid \mathsf{Enc}_{\mathsf{pk}}(m, \mathbf{r}) = \mathbf{c} \wedge \|\mathbf{r}\|_\infty \le \beta'\},$$

Then, $(m, \mathbf{r})$ can be viewed as a witness for the statement about $\mathbf{c}$. The honest language $\mathbf{L}_{\mathsf{PPK}}$ and the proven language $\mathbf{L}'_{\mathsf{PPK}}$ are defined as follows:

$$\mathbf{L}_{\mathsf{PPK}} = \left\{\mathbf{c} \in R_q^2 \mid \exists (m, \mathbf{r}) \in R_p \times R^3 \text{ s.t. } (m, \mathbf{r}, \mathbf{c}) \in \mathbf{R}_{\mathsf{PPK}}\right\},$$
$$\mathbf{L}'_{\mathsf{PPK}} = \left\{\mathbf{c} \in R_q^2 \mid \exists (m, \mathbf{r}) \in R_p \times R^3 \text{ s.t. } (m, \mathbf{r}, \mathbf{c}) \in \mathbf{R}'_{\mathsf{PPK}}\right\}.$$

In Fig. 1, we describe the PPK protocol Π_{PPK} for the BFV scheme whose security relies on the hardness of (Hint)RLWE. We remark that an encryption randomness $\mathbf{r}$ is multiplied by 2 in $\mathbf{R}_{\mathsf{PPK}}$ for the honest language due to the weakened knowledge extractor. In the soundness proof, we show that a knowledge extractor can obtain $(X^i - X^j) \cdot (m, \mathbf{r})$ for some $i \ne j$. Since $(X^i - X^j)^{-1} \notin R$ and $2(X^i - X^j)^{-1} \in R$ by Lemma 6, we can finally get $(2m, 2\mathbf{r})$ rather than $(m, \mathbf{r})$. The prior work [8] had the same issue, but it resolved the problem by changing the proven language of PPK. To be precise, the previous PPK protocol does not guarantee the validity of $\mathbf{c}$, but the validity of $2\mathbf{c}$ instead. However, this approach induces another issue that $2\mathbf{c}$ is an encryption of $2m$, not m. Hence, we tweak the relation $\mathbf{R}_{\mathsf{PPK}}$ of the honest prover so that we can guarantee that the ciphertext $\mathbf{c}$ itself is a valid encryption of m in the proven language.

Since the membership decision for $\mathbf{R}_{\mathsf{PPK}}$ and $\mathbf{R}'_{\mathsf{PPK}}$ can be done in polynomial time, both $\mathbf{L}_{\mathsf{PPK}}$ and $\mathbf{L}'_{\mathsf{PPK}}$ are NP-languages. The bounds β_i and β'_i are parameters that will be determined later after $\mathcal{P}$ and $\mathcal{V}$ are designated.

Theorem 2. *Let ℓ be a positive integer, $\sigma_1, \sigma_2 > 0$ and $\kappa = \sqrt{\ln(2n/\varepsilon)/\pi}$ for a negligible $\varepsilon > 0$. Let $\mathsf{pp} = (R, q, p, \chi) \leftarrow \mathsf{Setup}(1^\lambda)$, $\mathsf{pk} \leftarrow \mathsf{Gen}(\mathsf{pp})$, $C = \{X^j : 0 \le j < 2n\}$, $\beta = \kappa\sigma_1$, and $\beta' = 2n\kappa(\sigma_1 + \sigma_2)$. If $(2n)^{-\ell}$ is negligible, then Π_{PPK} is a secure proof-of-knowledge protocol for the pair of NP-languages $(\mathbf{L}_{\mathsf{PPK}}, \mathbf{L}'_{\mathsf{PPK}})$ under the hardness assumption of $\mathsf{RLWE}_{R,1,q,\chi}$ and $\mathsf{HintRLWE}_{R,2,q,\sigma_1}^{\ell,\sigma_2,\mathcal{U}(C^\ell)}$.*

Proof. We show the completeness, knowledge soundness, and simulatability of Π_{PPK} as below.

Completeness: Suppose that both prover and verifier honestly follow the protocol. Then, the ciphertext $\mathbf{c}$ generated by the prover satisfies the honest language $\mathbf{L}_{\mathsf{PPK}}$ since $\|\mathbf{r}\|_\infty < \beta$ except for a negligible probability ε from Cor. 1. The equality $\mathsf{Enc}_{\mathsf{pk}}(v_i, \mathbf{z}_i) = \mathbf{w}_i + \gamma_i \cdot \mathbf{c}$ follows from the fact that $v_i = u_i + \gamma_i \cdot m$ and $\mathbf{z}_i = \mathbf{y}_i + \gamma_i \cdot \mathbf{r}$. It remains to show that $\|\mathbf{z}_i\|_\infty < (1 + \sigma_2/\sigma_1) \cdot \beta$ for $0 \le i < \ell$.

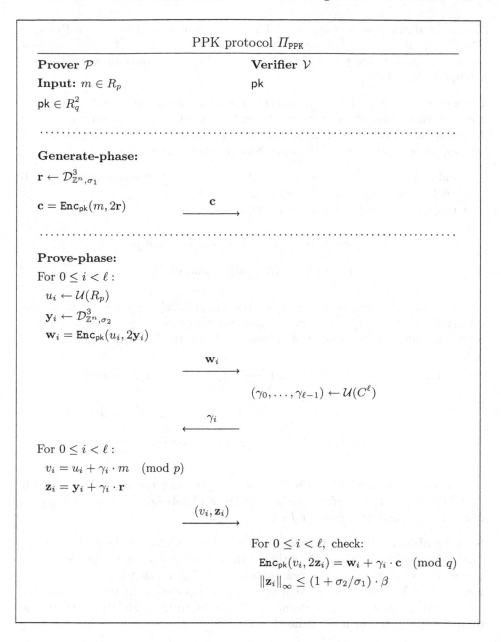

Fig. 1. Our PPK protocol for the BFV scheme.

Let $\mathbf{z}_i = (z_i^{(0)}, z_i^{(1)}, z_i^{(2)})$. From the definition, $z_i^{(j)}$ follows the distribution $\mathcal{D}_{\mathbb{Z}^n,\sigma_1} + \gamma_i \cdot \mathcal{D}_{\mathbb{Z}^n,\sigma_2}$ for $0 \leq j < 3$. Note that $\gamma_i \cdot \mathcal{D}_{\mathbb{Z}^n,\sigma_2}$ is statistically identical to $\mathcal{D}_{\mathbb{Z}^n,\sigma_2}$ regardless of γ_i, as γ_i is a monomial with the leading coefficient 1 and

$D_{\mathbb{Z}^n, \sigma_2}$ is spherical with center zero. Then, $z_i^{(j)}$ follows the distribution $D_{\mathbb{Z}^n, \sigma_1} + D_{\mathbb{Z}^n, \sigma_2}$ for all $0 \le i < \ell$, which is bounded by $(1 + \sigma_2/\sigma_1) \cdot \beta = (\sigma_1 + \sigma_2) \cdot \kappa$ with an overwhelming probability. Therefore, the verifier outputs 1 except for a negligible probability.

Soundness: Since the soundness error $(2n)^{-\ell}$ is negligible, it suffices to show the existence of an efficient knowledge extractor which can generate a witness from two accepting transcripts $(\mathbf{c}, \mathbf{w}_i, \gamma_i, (v_i, \mathbf{z}_i))$ and $(\mathbf{c}, \mathbf{w}_i, \gamma_i', (v_i', \mathbf{z}_i'))$ such that $\gamma_i \ne \gamma_i'$ for some $0 \le i < \ell$. We define an extractor $\mathcal{E}$ as follows:

1. Find an index i such that $\gamma_i \ne \gamma_i'$, and set $\bar{\gamma}_i = \gamma_i - \gamma_i'$. It is shown in Lemma 6 that $2\bar{\gamma}_i^{-1}$ is an element of R with $\left\| 2\bar{\gamma}_i^{-1} \right\|_\infty \le 1$.
2. Compute and output $(m, \mathbf{r})$ as follows:

$$m = \frac{p+1}{2} \cdot (2\bar{\gamma}_i^{-1}) \cdot (v_i - v_i') \pmod{p}$$

$$\mathbf{r} = (2\bar{\gamma}_i^{-1}) \cdot (\mathbf{z}_i - \mathbf{z}_i') \pmod{q}$$

From $\text{Enc}_{\mathsf{pk}}(v_i, 2\mathbf{z}_i) = \mathbf{w}_i + \gamma_i \cdot \mathbf{c}$ and $\text{Enc}_{\mathsf{pk}}(v_i', 2\mathbf{z}_i') = \mathbf{w}_i + \gamma_i' \cdot \mathbf{c}$, we get $\text{Enc}_{\mathsf{pk}}(v_i - v_i', 2(\mathbf{z}_i - \mathbf{z}_i')) = \bar{\gamma}_i \cdot \mathbf{c}$. We also note that $\frac{p+1}{2} = \frac{q+1}{2} \pmod{p}$ if p and q are odd integers such that $p \mid q$. Then, we obtain the following equality:

$$\text{Enc}_{\mathsf{pk}}(m, \mathbf{r}) = (2\bar{\gamma}_i^{-1}) \cdot \text{Enc}_{\mathsf{pk}} \left(\frac{p+1}{2}(v_i - v_i'), \mathbf{z}_i - \mathbf{z}_i' \right) \pmod{q}$$

$$= (2\bar{\gamma}_i^{-1}) \cdot \frac{q+1}{2} \cdot \text{Enc}_{\mathsf{pk}}(v_i - v_i', 2(\mathbf{z}_i - \mathbf{z}_i')) \pmod{q}$$

$$= (2\bar{\gamma}_i^{-1}) \cdot \frac{q+1}{2} \cdot \bar{\gamma}_i \cdot \mathbf{c} = \mathbf{c} \pmod{q}.$$

Meanwhile, we get $\left\| \mathbf{r} \right\|_\infty \le n \cdot \left\| \mathbf{z}_i - \mathbf{z}_i' \right\|_\infty \le \beta'$ since $\mathbf{r} = 2\bar{\gamma}_i^{-1} \cdot (\mathbf{z}_i - \mathbf{z}_i') \in R$ and $\left\| 2\bar{\gamma}_i^{-1} \right\|_\infty \le 1$. Therefore, the output $(m, \mathbf{r}, \mathbf{c})$ satisfies the relation $\mathbf{R}_{\mathsf{PPK}}'$, so $\mathcal{E}$ is an knowledge extractor for Π_{PPK}.

Simulatability. We show that $\mathcal{S}_{\mathsf{PPK}}$ in Fig 2 is a simulator for the protocol Π_{PPK}. Let $\mathcal{D}_0(m)$ and $\mathcal{D}_1$ be the distribution of the transcripts generated by the honest prover and verifier of Π_{PPK} for each message $m \in R_p$ and that generated by $\mathcal{S}_{\mathsf{PPK}}$, respectively. We prove these distributions are computationally indistinguishable by the hybrid argument: Let $\mathcal{H}_0(m) = \mathcal{D}_0(m)$, $\mathcal{H}_1(m)$, $\mathcal{H}_2$ and $\mathcal{H}_3 = \mathcal{D}_1$ be the distributions of tr which are defined as follows:

$\mathcal{H}_0(m)$: tr $\leftarrow \text{Tr}(\mathcal{P}(\mathsf{pk}, m), \mathcal{V}(\mathsf{pk}))$ for pp $= \text{Setup}(1^\lambda)$; pk $\leftarrow \text{Gen}(\mathsf{pp})$ and given $m \in R_p$.

$\mathcal{H}_1(m)$: tr $\leftarrow \text{Tr}(\mathcal{P}(\mathsf{pk}, m), \mathcal{V}(\mathsf{pk}))$ for pk $\leftarrow \mathcal{U}(R_q^2)$ and given $m \in R_p$.

$\mathcal{H}_2$: tr $\leftarrow \mathcal{S}_{\mathsf{PPK}}(\mathsf{pk})$ for pk $\leftarrow \mathcal{U}(R_q^2)$.

$\mathcal{H}_3$: tr $\leftarrow \mathcal{S}_{\mathsf{PPK}}(\mathsf{pk})$ for pp $= \text{Setup}(1^\lambda)$; pk $\leftarrow \text{Gen}(\mathsf{pp})$.

Simulator $\mathcal{S}_{\mathsf{PPK}}$

Input

$\mathsf{pk} \in R_q^2$

---

1. Sample $\mathbf{c} \leftarrow \mathcal{U}(R_q^2)$ and $(\gamma_0, \ldots, \gamma_{\ell-1}) \leftarrow \mathcal{U}(C^\ell)$.
2. Sample $\mathbf{r} \leftarrow \mathcal{D}_{\mathbb{Z}^n, \sigma_1}^3$.
3. Sample $\mathbf{y}_i \leftarrow \mathcal{D}_{\mathbb{Z}^n, \sigma_2}^3$, and compute $\mathbf{z}_i = \mathbf{y}_i + \gamma_i \cdot \mathbf{r}$ for $0 \leq i < \ell$.
4. Sample $v_i \leftarrow \mathcal{U}(R_p)$, and compute $\mathbf{w}_i = \mathsf{Enc}_{\mathsf{pk}}(v_i, 2\mathbf{z}_i) - \gamma_i \cdot \mathbf{c} \pmod{q}$ for $0 \leq i < \ell$.
5. Output $\mathsf{tr} = (\mathbf{c}, (\mathbf{w}_i, \gamma_i, (v_i, \mathbf{z}_i))_{0 \leq i < \ell})$.

Fig. 2. Simulator for Π_{PPK}.

Claim 1: $\mathcal{H}_0(m)$ and $\mathcal{H}_1(m)$ are computationally indistinguishable for any message $m \in R_p$ under the hardness assumption of $\mathsf{RLWE}_{R,1,q,\chi}$.

For a given RLWE sample pk, one can pick any message $m \in R_p$ and generate the transcript $\mathsf{tr} \leftarrow \mathsf{Tr}(\mathcal{P}(m, \mathsf{pk}), \mathcal{V}(\mathsf{pk}))$. When pk is sampled from the RLWE distribution (resp. the uniform distribution), then tr follows $\mathcal{H}_0(m)$ (resp. $\mathcal{H}_1$). Therefore, $\mathcal{H}_0(m)$ and $\mathcal{H}_1$ are computationally indistinguishable if $\mathsf{RLWE}_{R,1,q,\chi}$ is hard.

Claim 2: $\mathcal{H}_1(m)$ and $\mathcal{H}_2$ are computationally indistinguishable for any message $m \in R_p$ under the hardness assumption of $\mathsf{HintRLWE}_{R,2,q,\sigma_1}^{\ell,\sigma_2,\mathcal{U}(C^\ell)}$.

Let $\mathcal{A}$ be an algorithm that distinguishes $\mathcal{H}_1(m)$ and $\mathcal{H}_2$ with an advantage ε' for a message $m \in R_p$. Then, we can construct an algorithm $\mathcal{B}$ solving $\mathsf{HintRLWE}_{R,2,q,\sigma_1}^{\ell,\sigma_2,\mathcal{U}(C^\ell)}$ by exploiting $\mathcal{A}$.

The algorithm $\mathcal{B}$ first receives a sample $\left(\mathbf{a}, \mathbf{b}, \gamma_0, \ldots, \gamma_{\ell-1}, \mathbf{z}_0, \ldots, \mathbf{z}_{\ell-1} \right)$ from the Hint-RLWE challenger. Let $\mathsf{pk} = \mathbf{a}$, $\mathbf{c} = 2 \cdot \mathbf{b} + ((q/p)m, 0) \pmod{q}$, $v_i := u_i + \gamma_i \cdot m \pmod{p}$ for $u_i \leftarrow \mathcal{U}(R_p)$, and $\mathbf{w}_i := \mathsf{Enc}_{\mathsf{pk}}(v_i, 2\mathbf{z}_i) - \gamma_i \cdot \mathbf{c}$ $\pmod{q}$ for $0 \leq i < \ell$. The algorithm $\mathcal{B}$ runs $\mathcal{A}(\mathsf{pk}, \mathsf{tr})$ for the transcript $\mathsf{tr} := (\mathbf{c}, (\mathbf{w}_i, \gamma_i, (v_i, \mathbf{z}_i))_{0 \leq i < \ell})$, and it outputs the response from $\mathcal{A}$.

If $\mathbf{b} = [\mathbf{I}_2 | \mathbf{a}]\mathbf{r}$ where $\mathbf{r} \leftarrow \mathcal{D}_{\mathbb{Z}^n, \sigma_1}^3$, $\mathbf{y}_i \leftarrow \mathcal{D}_{\mathbb{Z}^n, \sigma_2}^3$, $\mathbf{z}_i = \gamma_i \cdot \mathbf{r} + \mathbf{y}_i$ for $0 \leq i < \ell$. Then, $\mathbf{c} = \mathsf{Enc}_{\mathsf{pk}}(m, 2\mathbf{r})$ holds. Moreover, it holds that $\mathbf{w}_i = \mathsf{Enc}_{\mathsf{pk}}(u_i, 2\mathbf{y}_i)$ since $p \mid q$. Therefore, tr follows the distribution $\mathcal{H}_1(m)$. Otherwise, if $\mathbf{b}$ is sampled from $\mathcal{U}(R_q^2)$, $\mathbf{c}$ and v_i become uniform over R_q^2 and R_p, respectively. Therefore, tr follows the distribution $\mathcal{H}_2$.

Thus, the algorithm $\mathcal{B}$ solves $\mathsf{HintRLWE}_{R,2,q,\sigma_1}^{\ell,\sigma_2,\mathcal{U}(C^\ell)}$ with the same advantage ε', and ε' should be negligible by the hardness assumption, and therefore $\mathcal{H}_1(m)$ and $\mathcal{H}_2$ are computationally indistinguishable for any message $m \in R_p$.

Claim 3: $\mathcal{H}_2$ and $\mathcal{H}_3$ are computationally indistinguishable under the hardness assumption of $\mathsf{RLWE}_{R,1,q,\chi}$.

For a given RLWE sample pk, one can generate the transcript $\mathsf{tr} \leftarrow \mathcal{S}_{\mathsf{PPK}}(\mathsf{pk})$. When pk is sampled from the RLWE distribution (resp. the uniform distribution), then tr follows $\mathcal{H}_2$ (resp. $\mathcal{H}_3$). Therefore, if one can distinguish $\mathcal{H}_2$ and $\mathcal{H}_3$ with advantage $\varepsilon' > 0$, then it can also solve $\mathsf{RLWE}_{R,1,q,\chi}$ with advantage ε'.

By Claim 1,2 and 3, the distributions $\mathcal{H}_0(m)$ and $\mathcal{H}_3$ are computationally indistinguishable for any message $m \in R_p$, and hence Π_{PPK} is simulatable assuming that $\mathsf{RLWE}_{R,1,q,\chi}$ and $\mathsf{HintRLWE}_{R,2,q,\sigma_1}^{\ell,\sigma_2,\mathcal{U}(C^\ell)}$ are hard to solve. Thus, the completeness, knowledge soundness, and simulatability of Π_{PPK} are completely proved. $\qquad\square$

Soundness Slack. In the previous work [8], the value β'/β is used to describe soundness slack between $\mathbf{L}_{\mathsf{PPK}}$ and $\mathbf{L}'_{\mathsf{PPK}}$. This measurement correctly captures the intuition of soundness slack since it represents an overhead derived from the noise flooding. However, this context does not perfectly fit with our case since the security of our protocol eventually depends on $\kappa\sigma$ (rather than $\beta = \kappa\sigma_1$) if we reduce the hardness of Hint-RLWE from RLWE. Thus we use the quantity $\beta'/\kappa\sigma = \frac{2n(\sigma_1+\sigma_2)}{\sigma}$ as an alternative measurement for soundness slack in our protocol since it precisely describes how much cost is incurred to achieve the security against a malicious adversary.

Parameter Setting. We explain a methodology to choose optimal parameter sets for Π_{PPK} following the conditions of Thms 1 and 2. We denote by λ_{Snd} and λ_{ZK} the security parameters of soundness and simulatability of our protocol, respectively. The soundness security stands for the soundness error of the protocol so it is determined by the size of the challenge space. The zero-knowledge security is originally intended to denote a statistical distance between the simulator and real accepting conversation because simulators in the previous studies [8,20] are based on statistical indistinguishability. Since our simulator is based on computational indistinguishability, we only account for statistical advantage for λ_{ZK} neglecting computational ones.

We now set the parameters k, ℓ, σ_1, and σ_2 for given λ_{Snd} and λ_{ZK}. We first consider the soundness security. We set $\ell = \lceil \lambda_{\mathsf{Snd}} / \log 2n \rceil$ so that $(2n)^{-\ell} \leq 2^{-\lambda_{\mathsf{Snd}}}$ holds. Then, we set the parameters σ_1, σ_2 which are related to the zero-knowledge security λ_{ZK}. Note that indistinguishability for $\mathcal{S}_{\mathsf{PPK}}$ comes from computational hardness of $\mathsf{RLWE}_{R,1,q,\chi}$ and $\mathsf{HintRLWE}_{R,2,q,\sigma_1}^{\ell,\sigma_2,\mathcal{U}(C^\ell)}$. Since we use standard HE parameter sets presented in [3] for $\mathsf{RLWE}_{R,1,q,\chi}$, it is computationally hard. The upper bound B of $\sum_{j=0}^{\ell-1} \|\gamma_j\|_1^2$ can be set to ℓ since the challenges γ_j are all monic monomials. Then, by Theorem 1, the hardness of $\mathsf{HintRLWE}_{R,2,q,\sigma_1}^{\ell,\sigma_2,\mathcal{U}(C^\ell)}$ is reduced from $\mathsf{RLWE}_{R,2,q,\sigma}$ with loss of advantage at most 6ε where $\frac{1}{\sigma^2} = 2(\frac{1}{\sigma_1^2} + \frac{\ell}{\sigma_2^2})$, and $\varepsilon > 0$ is some value satisfying $\sigma \geq \sqrt{2} \cdot \eta_\varepsilon(\mathbb{Z}^n)$.

Thus, it suffices to consider the hardness of $\mathsf{RLWE}_{R,1,q,\chi}$ and the advantage 6ε occurred during reduction for the zero-knowledge security λ_{ZK}. We set $\varepsilon =$

$2^{-\lambda_{\mathsf{ZK}}}/6$ and $\sigma = \sqrt{2} \cdot \sqrt{\frac{\ln(2n(1+1/\varepsilon))}{\pi}} \simeq \sqrt{2} \cdot \sqrt{\frac{\lambda_{\mathsf{ZK}}+\ln(12n)}{\pi}}$ so that $\sigma \geq \sqrt{2} \cdot \eta_\varepsilon(\mathbb{Z}^n)$ for given λ_{ZK}. Note that standard HE parameters presented in [3] use $3.2 \cdot \sqrt{2\pi}$ as width parameter for error distribution of RLWE. Since the value of σ is larger than that value for $\lambda_{\mathsf{ZK}} = 128$, it does not affect on the hardness assumption of RLWE with our parameter.

Note that the soundness slack of our protocol is determined by $\sigma_1 + \sigma_2$ when σ is fixed. Hence, we aim to choose σ_1 and σ_2 so that the soundness slack is minimized for given σ. It is easy to show that the best parameters are such that $\sigma_1 = \sqrt{\ell^{\frac{1}{3}} + 1} \cdot \sigma$, $\sigma_2 = \ell^{\frac{1}{3}} \cdot \sigma_1$ and Therefore, the soundness slack of our protocol is calculated as $2n(\sigma_1 + \sigma_2)/\sigma = 2n(1 + \ell^{\frac{1}{3}})^{\frac{3}{2}}$.

Finally, we set the parameter κ which is related to the completeness. If we set $\kappa = \sqrt{\ln(2n/\varepsilon)/\pi}$ for a negligible ε', a honestly generated conversation gets accepted with an overwhelming probability by Theorem 2.

4.2 Extension to Multi-prover PPK

Among versatile applications of PPK protocol, we focus on its usage on the SPDZ multi-party computation (MPC) protocol [16] which utilizes somewhat homomorphic encryption (HE). To achieve active security, SPDZ runs a zero-knowledge PPK protocol for HE ciphertexts so that they are ensured to be honestly generated.

There have been several follow-up studies [8,20] that improve the efficiency of the PPK protocol in SPDZ. The current state-of-the-art PPK protocol for SPDZ is called k-prover PPK protocol [8], which consists of k parties who play roles of both prover and verifier. In this protocol, all parties verify the validity of a single (accumulated) ciphertext instead of verifying multiple ciphertexts by repeatedly running Π_{PPK} for each party. This reduces the computational cost of verification by a factor of k. However, for this purpose, all parties must be online to jointly generate a shared challenge. Therefore, the noise flooding method is enforced to achieve zero-knowledge since the rejection sampling method would lead to a slowdown due to potentially having to rerun the protocol multiple times [8]. Hence, it achieves a faster verification procedure at the expense of increased communication cost due to the larger ciphertext size resulting from the noise flooding method.

We note that our PPK protocol can be naturally extended to the k-prover case, as described in the full version of this paper [21, Appx. A]. Compared to the previous work, which uses the noise flooding, our method significantly reduces soundness slack, which incurs a smaller ciphertext size and reduced communication cost. Additionally, we note that the previous work was based on the BGV scheme [12], but we use BFV as a substitute.

Parameter Setting. A parameter setting for the k-party PPK protocol for BFV can be done in a similar manner. The only difference is that the bounds β and β' become k times larger since each party adds k commitments or responses during the prove-phase, but it does not affect the soundness slack as both of them get increased by the same factor. As a result, the soundness slack is still $2n(1 + \ell^{\frac{1}{3}})^{\frac{3}{2}}$. In asymptotic scale, the soundness slack for our PPK protocol is $2n(1 + \ell^{\frac{1}{3}})^{\frac{3}{2}} = O(n \cdot \sqrt{\ell}) = O(n \cdot \sqrt{\lambda_{\mathsf{Snd}}/\log n})$ since $\ell = O(\lambda_{\mathsf{Snd}}/\log n)$. Meanwhile, the soundness slack in the previous PPK protocol [8] accompanies the exponential factor $2^{\lambda_{\mathsf{ZK}}}$ which comes from the noise flooding technique.

5   Proof of Opening Knowledge for BDLOP

The commitment scheme has been used extensively as a core building block of various cryptographic schemes (e.g. [26,27,29]). In these applications, the Proof of Opening Knowledge (POK) protocol is usually incorporated together to ensure the security against active adversaries. While the existing constructions of POK rely on zero-knowledge proofs for both input message and commitment randomness, we aim to construct a more efficient POK protocol that allows us to leak partial information of the randomness while still guaranteeing the full message privacy.

Such POK protocol can be implemented using the secure proof-of-knowledge framework in Sect. 2.6. Let (Gen, Com, Open) be a commitment scheme, and ck be a commitment key generated by Gen. Then, the public parameter pp is ck, the secret input x is the prover's message m, and the honest language $\mathbf{L}$ and the proven language $\mathbf{L}'$ are the set of honestly generated commitments and the set of accepted commitments, respectively. Then, the completeness guarantees that the prove-phase ends with 1 if the commitment $c \in \mathbf{L}$. The soundness guarantees that if the prove-phase ends with 1, then $c \in \mathbf{L}'$ and the prover knows randomness r and message m used for generating the commitment c. Finally, the simulatability guarantees that the transcript between the prover and the verifier does not leak any information about input message m.

In the rest of this section, we present a concrete instantiation of the POK protocol for the BDLOP commitment scheme [9] based on the hardness assumption of Hint-MLWE, and we provide a concrete parameter set of our POK protocol with a comparison to prior work. It is worth noting that our POK protocol is free from aborting, contrary to previous constructions in [9,28] using rejection sampling. This work also answers the open questions stated in [28], whether it would be possible to achieve any security proof for POK without rejection.

5.1   POK Without Abort Based on Hint-MLWE

In this subsection, we propose a POK protocol for the BDLOP commitment scheme [9], which is one of the most widely used building blocks for lattice-based cryptographic primitives [26,29]. While our protocol leaks some information about commitment randomness, it still satisfies security conditions to be a key ingredient for the construction of the advanced proof techniques such as proofs for product relation [6] and proofs for linear relation [18]. We discuss how our POK protocol can be extended to cover these applications in the next subsection.

We first recall soundness slack that arises in lattice-based proof-of-knowledge construction. The BDLOP scheme follows the proof style presented in [30], so a knowledge extractor can only obtain a witness of the form $(\bar{\gamma} \cdot \mathbf{m}, \mathbf{r})$, where $\bar{\gamma}$ is an element from the difference set $\bar{C} := \{\gamma - \gamma' \mid \gamma, \gamma' \in C\}$ given a challenge set C. Hence, it requires a weakened version of the opening algorithm to accommodate soundness slack. Below, we present the weakened opening algorithm for BDLOP.

- $\texttt{BDLOP.WeakOpen}_{\text{ck}}(\mathbf{c}, \mathbf{m}, \mathbf{r}, \bar{\gamma})$: Given a commitment $\mathbf{c} = (\mathbf{c}_0, \mathbf{c}_1)$, a message $\mathbf{m} \in R_q^k$, randomness $\mathbf{r} \in R^{\mu+\nu+k}$, and an element $\bar{\gamma} \in \bar{C}$, it outputs 1 if and only if $\bar{\gamma} \cdot \mathbf{c} = \texttt{BDLOP.Com}_{\text{ck}}(\bar{\gamma} \cdot \mathbf{m}, \mathbf{r})$ and $\|\mathbf{r}\|_2 < 2\beta'_{\text{BDLOP}}$.

Then, the witness relations for POK are defined as follows:

$$\mathbf{R}_{\text{Open}} := \{(\mathbf{c}, \mathbf{m}, \mathbf{r}) \mid \texttt{BDLOP.Open}_{\text{ck}}(\mathbf{c}, \mathbf{m}, \mathbf{r}) = 1\}$$

$$\mathbf{R}'_{\text{Open}} := \{(\mathbf{c}, \mathbf{m}, \mathbf{r}, \bar{\gamma}) \mid \texttt{BDLOP.WeakOpen}_{\text{ck}}(\mathbf{c}, \mathbf{m}, \mathbf{r}, \bar{\gamma}) = 1\}$$

where $\text{ck} \leftarrow \texttt{BDLOP.Gen}(1^\lambda)$. We note that $(\mathbf{m}, \mathbf{r}, \bar{\gamma})$ serves the role of witness in $\mathbf{R}'_{\text{Open}}$. The corresponding honest/proven languages are defined as follows:

$$\mathbf{L}_{\text{Open}} := \{\mathbf{c} \in R_q^{\mu+k} \mid \exists (\mathbf{m}, \mathbf{r})\ (\mathbf{c}, \mathbf{m}, \mathbf{r}) \in \mathbf{R}_{\text{BDLOP}}\}$$

$$\mathbf{L}'_{\text{Open}} := \{\mathbf{c} \in R_q^{\mu+k} \mid \exists (\mathbf{m}, \mathbf{r}, \bar{\gamma})\ (\mathbf{c}, \mathbf{m}, \mathbf{r}, \bar{\gamma}) \in \mathbf{R}'_{\text{BDLOP}}\}$$

In Fig. 3, we describe our new POK protocol Π_{Open} for the BDLOP commitment scheme. We assume that q is a prime integer satisfying $q = 5 \pmod 8$, and $C := \{\gamma \in R \mid \|\gamma\|_1 = \kappa \wedge \|\gamma\|_\infty \leq 1\}$, the set of polynomials with ternary coefficients in $\{0, \pm 1\}$ and hamming weight $\kappa > 0$. Then, it is known that every element of $\bar{C}$ except 0 is invertible in R_q [30, Cor. 1.2].

We formulate the security of Π_{Open} for the BDLOP commmitment scheme as the following theorem. Then, the binding property depends on the hardness of $\mathsf{MSIS}_{R,\mu+\nu+k,\mu,q,8\kappa\beta'_{\text{BDLOP}}}$ under the weakened opening algorithm as in the prior work [9].

Theorem 3. *Let ν, μ, k, q be positive integers, $\sigma_1, \sigma_2 > 0$, $\beta'_{\text{BDLOP}} = (\kappa\sigma_1 + \sigma_2)\sqrt{(\mu+\nu+k)n/\pi}$, and $\text{ck} \leftarrow \texttt{BDLOP.Gen}(1^\lambda)$. If $\binom{n}{\kappa}^{-1} \cdot 2^{-\kappa}$ and $2^{-(\mu+\nu+k)n/8}$ are negligible, then Π_{Open} is a secure proof-of-knowledge protocol for $(\mathbf{L}_{\text{Open}}, \mathbf{L}'_{\text{Open}})$ under the hardness assumption of $\mathsf{HintMLWE}_{R,\nu,\mu+k,q,\sigma_1}^{1,\sigma_2,\mathcal{U}(C)}$.*

Proof. We show the completeness, soundness and simulatability of Π_{Open}.

Completeness: Suppose that both the prover and the verifier are honest. Since the relation $\mathbf{B}_0\mathbf{z} = \mathbf{w} + \gamma \cdot \mathbf{c}_0 \pmod q$ always holds, we only need to check the condition $\|\mathbf{z}\|_2 < \beta'_{\text{BDLOP}} = (\kappa\sigma_1 + \sigma_2)\sqrt{(\mu+\nu+k)n/\pi}$. By Lemma 2, we have $\|\mathbf{r}\|_2 < \sigma_1\sqrt{(\mu+\nu+k)n/\pi}$ and $\|\mathbf{y}\|_2 < \sigma_2\sqrt{(\mu+\nu+k)n/\pi}$ with probability larger than $1 - 2^{-(\mu+\nu+k)n/8}$. Then, we obtain $\|\mathbf{z}\|_2 = \|\mathbf{y} + \gamma \cdot \mathbf{r}\|_2 < (\kappa\sigma_1 + \sigma_2)\sqrt{(\mu+\nu+k)n/\pi}$ with probability larger than $(1 - 2^{-(\mu+\nu+k)n/8})^2$ as $\|\gamma\|_1 = \kappa$.

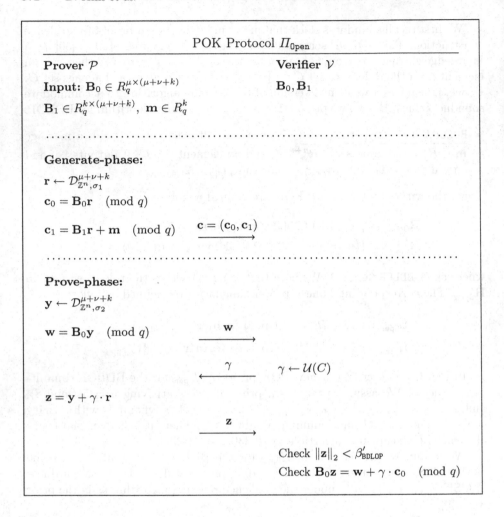

Fig. 3. The POK protocol for BDLOP.

Therefore, the verifier outputs 1 except for negligible probability since the value $2^{-(\mu+\nu+k)n/8}$ is negligible.

Soundness: Since the soundness error $1/|C| = \frac{1}{\binom{n}{\kappa} \cdot 2^{\kappa}}$ is negligible, it suffices to show the existence of efficient knowledge extractor for $\mathbf{R}'_{\text{BDLOP}}$. Consider two accepting transcripts generated by a cheating prover, denoted as $(\mathbf{w}, \gamma, \mathbf{z})$ and $(\mathbf{w}, \gamma', \mathbf{z}')$ where $\bar{\gamma} = \gamma - \gamma'$ is nonzero. Then, $\bar{\gamma}$ is invertible in R_q and $\mathbf{r} = \mathbf{z} - \mathbf{z}'$, $\mathbf{m} = \mathbf{c}_1 - \bar{\gamma}^{-1} \cdot \mathbf{B}_1\mathbf{r} \pmod{q}$, and $\bar{\gamma}$ become a witness for $\mathbf{c}$ in the relation $\mathbf{R}'_{\text{0pen}}$. For a more detailed analysis, we refer to [9].

Simulatability: In Fig. 4, we describe a simulator $\mathcal{S}_{\text{0pen}}$ for Π_{0pen}. Let $\mathcal{D}_0(m)$ and $\mathcal{D}_1$ be the distributions of the transcript tr generated by an honest prover and

---

Simulator $\mathcal{S}_{\text{Open}}$

Input

$\mathbf{B}_0 \in R_q^{\mu \times (\mu+\nu+k)}, \mathbf{B}_1 \in R_q^{k \times (\mu+\nu+k)}$

---

1. Sample $\mathbf{u} \leftarrow \mathcal{U}(R_q^{\mu+k}), \mathbf{V} \leftarrow \mathcal{U}(R_q^{\mu \times k})$ and $\gamma \leftarrow \mathcal{U}(C)$.
2. Sample $\mathbf{r} \leftarrow \mathcal{D}_{\mathbb{Z}^n,\sigma_1}^{\mu+\nu+k}$ and $\mathbf{y} \leftarrow \mathcal{D}_{\mathbb{Z}^n,\sigma_2}^{\mu+\nu+k}$.
3. Compute $\mathbf{c} = \begin{bmatrix} \mathbf{I}_\mu & \mathbf{V} \\ \mathbf{0}^{k \times \mu} & \mathbf{I}_k \end{bmatrix} \mathbf{u} \pmod{q}$ and parse $\mathbf{c} = \begin{bmatrix} \mathbf{c}_0 \\ \mathbf{c}_1 \end{bmatrix}$ for $\mathbf{c}_0 \in R_q^\mu, \mathbf{c}_1 \in R_q^k$.
4. Compute $\mathbf{z} = \mathbf{y} + \gamma \cdot \mathbf{r}$, and $\mathbf{w} = \mathbf{B}_0 \mathbf{z} - \gamma \cdot \mathbf{c}_0 \pmod{q}$.
5. Output $(\mathbf{c}, \mathbf{w}, \gamma, \mathbf{z})$.

Fig. 4. Simulator for Π_{Open}.

verifier for a message $\mathbf{m} \in R_q^k$ and that generated by the simulator, respectively, which are defined as follows:

$\mathcal{D}_0(\mathbf{m})$: $\mathsf{tr} \leftarrow \mathsf{Tr}(\mathcal{P}(\mathsf{ck}, \mathbf{m}), \mathcal{V}(\mathsf{ck}))$ for $\mathsf{ck} \leftarrow \mathsf{BDLOP.Gen}(1^\lambda)$ and given $\mathbf{m} \in R_q^k$

$\mathcal{D}_1$: $\mathsf{tr} \leftarrow \mathcal{S}_{\text{Open}}(\mathsf{ck})$ for $\mathsf{ck} \leftarrow \mathsf{BDLOP.Gen}(1^\lambda)$

Assume that there exists an algorithm $\mathcal{A}$ that distinguishes the distributions $\mathcal{D}_0(\mathbf{m})$ and $\mathcal{D}_1$ with advantage $\varepsilon > 0$ for a message $\mathbf{m} \in R_q^k$. Then, we can construct an efficient algorithm $\mathcal{B}$ for $\mathsf{HintMLWE}_{R,\nu,\mu+k,q,\sigma_1}^{1,\sigma_2,\mathcal{U}(C)}$ using $\mathcal{A}$ which works as follows:

1. Receive a Hint-MLWE instance $(\mathbf{A}, \mathbf{u}, \gamma, \mathbf{z})$ from a Hint-MLWE challenger. Write $\mathbf{z} = \begin{bmatrix} \mathbf{z}_0 \\ \mathbf{z}_1 \end{bmatrix} \in R^{\mu+\nu+k}$ and parse $\mathbf{A} = \begin{bmatrix} \mathbf{A}_0 \\ \mathbf{A}_1 \end{bmatrix}$ for $\mathbf{A}_0 \in R_q^{\mu \times \nu}$ and $\mathbf{A}_1 \in R_q^{k \times \nu}$.
2. Sample $\mathbf{V} \leftarrow \mathcal{U}(R_q^{\mu \times k})$. Set $\mathbf{B}_0 = \begin{bmatrix} \mathbf{I}_\mu \mid \mathbf{V} \mid \mathbf{A}_0 + \mathbf{V}\mathbf{A}_1 \end{bmatrix} \in R_q^{\mu \times (\mu+\nu+k)}$, $\mathbf{B}_1 = \begin{bmatrix} \mathbf{0}^{k \times \mu} \mid \mathbf{I}_k \mid \mathbf{A}_1 \end{bmatrix} \in R_q^{k \times (\mu+\nu+k)}$, and compute $\mathbf{c} = \begin{bmatrix} \mathbf{I}_\mu & \mathbf{V} \\ \mathbf{0}^{k \times \mu} & \mathbf{I}_k \end{bmatrix} \mathbf{u} + \begin{bmatrix} \mathbf{0} \\ \mathbf{m} \end{bmatrix}$ $\pmod{q}$. Parse $\mathbf{c} = \begin{bmatrix} \mathbf{c}_0 \\ \mathbf{c}_1 \end{bmatrix}$ for $\mathbf{c}_0 \in R_q^\mu, \mathbf{c}_1 \in R_q^k$.
3. Compute $\mathbf{w} = \mathbf{B}_0 \mathbf{z} - \gamma \cdot \mathbf{c}_0 \pmod{q}$, and set $\mathsf{tr} = (\mathbf{c}, \mathbf{w}, \gamma, \mathbf{z})$, $\mathsf{ck} = (\mathbf{B}_0, \mathbf{B}_1)$.
4. Send tr to $\mathcal{A}$, receive a response $b = \mathcal{A}(\mathsf{tr})$, and output b.

We first note that ck always follows the identical distribution with a sample from $\mathsf{BDLOP.Gen}(1^\lambda)$. If $\mathbf{u} = \begin{bmatrix} \mathbf{I}_{\mu+k} \ \mathbf{A} \end{bmatrix} \mathbf{r}$ for $\mathbf{r} \leftarrow \mathcal{D}_{\mathbb{Z}^n,\sigma_1}^{\mu+\nu+k}$, then it holds that

$$\mathbf{c} = \begin{bmatrix} \mathbf{I}_\mu & \mathbf{V} \\ \mathbf{0}^{k \times \mu} & \mathbf{I}_k \end{bmatrix} \begin{bmatrix} \mathbf{I}_{\mu+k} \ \mathbf{A} \end{bmatrix} \mathbf{r} + \begin{bmatrix} \mathbf{0} \\ \mathbf{m} \end{bmatrix} = \begin{bmatrix} \mathbf{B}_0 \\ \mathbf{B}_1 \end{bmatrix} \mathbf{r} + \begin{bmatrix} \mathbf{0} \\ \mathbf{m} \end{bmatrix} \pmod{q}.$$

By the definition of Hint-MLWE, we can rewrite $\mathbf{z}$ as $\mathbf{z} = \mathbf{y} + \gamma \cdot \mathbf{r}$ for some $\mathbf{r} \leftarrow \mathcal{D}_{\mathbb{Z}^n,\sigma_1}^{\mu+\nu+k}$ and $\mathbf{y} \leftarrow \mathcal{D}_{\mathbb{Z}^n,\sigma_2}^{\mu+\nu+k}$. Then, we can also check that

$$\mathbf{w} = \mathbf{B}_0(\mathbf{y} + \gamma \cdot \mathbf{r}) - \gamma \cdot \mathbf{B}_0 \mathbf{r} = \mathbf{B}_0 \mathbf{y} \pmod{q}$$

Therefore, the distribution of tr is identical to $\mathcal{D}_0(\mathbf{m})$.

On the other hand, if $\mathbf{u} \leftarrow \mathcal{U}(R_q^{\mu+k})$, all the variables are defined just as same with $\mathcal{S}_{\mathsf{Open}}$ except $\mathbf{c}$ due to the addition of $\begin{bmatrix} \mathbf{0} \\ \mathbf{m} \end{bmatrix}$.

Since $\begin{bmatrix} \mathbf{I}_\mu & \mathbf{V} \\ \mathbf{0}^{k\times\mu} & \mathbf{I}_k \end{bmatrix}$ is invertible over $R_q^{(\mu+k)\times(\mu+k)}$, $\begin{bmatrix} \mathbf{I}_\mu & \mathbf{V} \\ \mathbf{0}^{k\times\mu} & \mathbf{I}_k \end{bmatrix} \mathbf{u}$ is also uniform over $R_q^{\mu+k}$, and hence the distribution of $\mathbf{c}$ is identical to that sampled from $\mathcal{S}_{\mathsf{Open}}$. Therefore, the distribution of tr is identical to $\mathcal{D}_1$.

Thus, the adversary $\mathcal{B}$ has the same advantage ε as $\mathcal{A}$ in distinguishing the Hint-MLWE instance. As a result, distributions $\mathcal{D}_0(\mathbf{m})$ and $\mathcal{D}_1$ are computationally indistinguishable for any message $\mathbf{m} \in R_q^k$ if HintMLWE$_{R,\nu,\mu+k,q,\sigma_1}^{1,\sigma_2,\mathcal{U}(C)}$ is hard, which implies the simulatability of our Π_{Open}. □

Parameter Setting. We now present the method for setting parameters in our POK protocol. The binding property of the commitment scheme is based on the hardness of MSIS$_{R,\mu+\nu+k,\mu,q,8\kappa\beta'_{\mathsf{BDLOP}}}$, which is identical to the previous construction in [9]. Meanwhile, the simulatability of our POK protocol is based on the HintMLWE$_{R,\nu,\mu+k,q,\sigma_1}^{1,\sigma_2,\mathcal{U}(C)}$ assumption. Thus, the parameters must be chosen in such a way that all three problems remain computationally hard.

We note that C is a distributions over R^ℓ where each element γ_j satisfies $\|\gamma_j\|_\infty = 1$ and $\|\gamma_j\|_1 = \kappa$ for some integer κ. Then, the bound B for $\sum_{j=0}^{\ell-1} \|\gamma_j\|_1^2$ can be set to $\ell\kappa^2$. Therefore, we can reduce the hardness of HintMLWE$_{R,\nu,\mu+k,q,\sigma_1}^{1,\sigma_2,\mathcal{U}(C)}$ from MLWE$_{R,\nu,\mu+k,q,\sigma}$ where $1/\sigma^2 = 2(1/\sigma_1^2 + \kappa^2/\sigma_2^2)$. To this end, $\sigma \geq \sqrt{2} \cdot \eta_\varepsilon(\mathbb{Z}^n)$ should hold for some negligible $\varepsilon > 0$. Then, we only need to consider the hardness of MLWE$_{R,\nu,\mu+k,q,\sigma}$ when setting the parameters for simulatability. Recall that the upper bound of $\|\mathbf{z}\|_2$ is $\beta'_{\mathsf{BDLOP}} = (\kappa\sigma_1 + \sigma_2)\sqrt{(\mu+\nu+k)n/\pi}$. Thus, we choose σ_1 and σ_2 which minimizes $\kappa\sigma_1 + \sigma_2$ under the constraints $1/\sigma^2 = 2(1/\sigma_1^2 + \kappa^2/\sigma_2^2)$, $\sigma \geq \sqrt{2} \cdot \eta_\varepsilon(\mathbb{Z}^n)$.

In Table 1, we present concrete parameters which are calculated according to the aforementioned method. We measure the hardness of MSIS and MLWE in terms of the root Hermite factor δ, targeting for $\delta \approx 1.0043$ which gives 128-bit security. We first set $q \approx 2^{32}$ and $n = 2^7$ as presented in [28] and then adjust the MSIS rank μ and the MLWE rank ν. We also set $\kappa = 32$ to achieve a negligible soundness error $1/|C| = \binom{n}{\kappa}^{-1} \cdot 2^{-\kappa} < 2^{-128}$. We set $\sigma = \sqrt{2} \cdot \sqrt{\frac{\ln(2n(1+1/\varepsilon))}{\pi}}$ so that the condition $\sigma \geq \sqrt{2} \cdot \eta_\varepsilon(\mathbb{Z}^n)$ holds by Lemma 4.

Comparison to Rejection Sampling. In the previous work [9,28], the rejection sampling method is used to attain zero-knowledge or simulatability. Although it reduces the soundness slack significantly, it introduces additional computational overheads due to repetition. To provide comparison with our work, we also calculate concrete parameters in Table 1 which are obtained by using the rejection sampling method in [23,28]. We follow the notation from [28] where $\mathtt{Rej}_0$ and $\mathtt{Rej}_1$ refer to the rejection sampling methods presented in [23] and its improved version, respectively. In [28], they set randomness distribution to be $\mathcal{U}(\{-1,0,1\}^n)$ and the number of rejections $M = 6$. Then, $\mathtt{Rej}_0$ and $\mathtt{Rej}_1$ output $\mathbf{z}$ whose distribution is statistically close to $\mathcal{D}_{\mathbb{Z}^n,\tau_0}^{\mu+\nu+k}$ and $\mathcal{D}_{\mathbb{Z}^n,\tau_1}^{\mu+\nu+k}$, respectively, where $\tau_0 = 16.89 \cdot \kappa\sqrt{(\mu+\nu+k)n}$ and $\tau_1 = 1.69 \cdot \kappa\sqrt{(\mu+\nu+k)n}$.[3] Thus, their bound β_i of $\|\mathbf{z}\|_2$ is determined as $\beta_i = \tau_i \cdot \sqrt{(\nu+\mu+k)n/\pi}$ by Lemma 2.

Simulatability of $\mathtt{Rej}_0$ can be obtained by constructing the simulator that has a negligible statistical distance to the distribution of real transcripts, but the simulator for $\mathtt{Rej}_1$ requires additional assumption called Extended-MLWE [28] to achieve indistinguishability since it leaks some information on commitment randomness. We remark that the hardness of the Extended-MLWE problem has been proven only for the non-algebraic setting. In contrast, simulatability for our method depends on the Hint-MLWE problem, and its hardness can be reduced from the MLWE problem by Theorem 1.

We now compare the parameters with ours (Table 1). Note that ν is determined by the hardness of $\mathsf{MLWE}_{R,\nu,\mu+k,q,\chi_{ter}}$ where $\chi_{ter} = \mathcal{U}(\{-1,0,1\}^n)$. As a result, ν needs to be at least 10 for both $\mathtt{Rej}_0$ and $\mathtt{Rej}_1$ to attain root Hermite factor $\delta \approx 1.0043$, assuming the Extended-MLWE problem is as hard as the MLWE problem. However, our method enables us to set $\nu = 9$ due to the larger upper bound on the commitment randomness $\mathbf{r}$. It is worth noting that both $\mathtt{Rej}_0$ and $\mathtt{Rej}_1$ have an upper bound on the ratio $\|\mathbf{y}\|_2/\|\gamma\mathbf{r}\|_2$ in terms of the rejection rate, and therefore they try to set $\|\mathbf{r}\|_2$ as small as possible. However, our method is free from this restriction.

Note that μ is determined by the hardness of $\mathsf{MSIS}_{R,\mu+\nu+k,\mu,q,8\kappa\beta_i}$ for $\mathtt{Rej}_i$. As a result, μ should be at least 7 for $\mathtt{Rej}_0$ to attain root Hermite factor $\delta \approx 1.0043$. In case of $\mathtt{Rej}_1$, it reduces μ to 6 due to having a smaller width parameter. Meanwhile, it suffices to set $\mu = 5$ in our case. Therefore, our method gives smaller μ, ν values compared to the prior work under the same security level. Additionally, our method reduces computational overheads since it does not require any repetitions (rejections) to achieve simulatability.

5.2 Optimizations and Extensions

In the realm of lattice-based cryptography, there are several applications of the BDLOP commitment scheme such as proofs for integral relation [27], group signature [26] and ring signature [29]. In these applications, advanced proof techniques from [6,18] are employed to verify additional conditions for the input message. These conditions vary depending on applications, but they all stem from the core property of the BDLOP scheme: computational binding.

---

[3] Since the Gaussian function in [28] is defined as $\rho(\mathbf{x}) = \exp(-1/2 \cdot \mathbf{x}^\top \mathbf{x})$, we multiplied a factor of $\sqrt{2\pi}$ to those presented in [28].

Table 1. Parameters of each POK for BDLOP ($q \approx 2^{32}, n = 2^7, \kappa = 32, k = 1$)

	Rej_0	Rej_1	**Ours**
μ (MSIS rank)	7	6	**5**
ν (MLWE rank)	10	10	**9**
Repetition	6	6	–
Simulatability	–	Ext-MLWE	**MLWE**

In this subsection, we briefly describe how our POK protocol can be further extended to advanced proof systems for product relation [6] and for linear relation over $\mathbb{Z}_q$ [18].

Modification in Challenge Set. In recent applications of BDLOP, the modulus q is often set to be $q = 2n+1 \pmod{4n}$ to obtain the isomorphism $R_q \simeq \mathbb{Z}_q^n$. However, this approach has a disadvantage in that some elements of $\bar{C}$ are not invertible in R_q. To cope with this issue, a new challenge distribution $\mathcal{C}$ over $\{\gamma \in R \mid \|\gamma\|_\infty \leq 1\}$ was proposed in [6] where each coefficient is sampled independently from $-1, 0, 1$ with probability $1/2$ for 0 and $1/4$ for each -1 and 1. It has been shown in [6] that the POK protocol using the new challenge distribution $\mathcal{C}$ attains a soundness error of approximately q^{-1}.

The simulatability still holds for this case by simply substituting $\mathcal{U}(C)$ with $\mathcal{C}$ in Theorem 3. Since a sample $\gamma \leftarrow \mathcal{C}$ satisfies $\|\gamma\|_\infty \leq 1$ and $\|\gamma\|_1 \leq n$, the parameter setting procedure for this case is equal to that in Sect. 5.1 except $\kappa = n$.

Boosting Soundness. As mentioned earlier, the new challenge distribution provides a soundness error of q^{-1}, which is non-negligible in most applications where $q \approx 2^{32}$. To reduce the soundness error further (i.e., $q^{-\ell}$), an optimization technique [6] that amplifies a single challenge into multiple challenges via automorphisms is often used. In this case, the prover sends multiple responses $\mathbf{z}_i = \mathbf{y}_i + \varphi^i(\gamma) \cdot \mathbf{r}$ for $0 \leq i < \ell$ where $\varphi(X) = X^{2n/\ell+1}$, and the verifier checks if $\|\mathbf{z}_i\|_2 < \beta'_{\text{BDLOP}}$ and $\mathbf{B}_0\mathbf{z}_i = \mathbf{w}_i + \varphi^i(\gamma) \cdot \mathbf{c}_0 \pmod{q}$ for $0 \leq i < \ell$.

A further improvement [27, Appx. A.6] was proposed to reduce the size of transcripts by expressing $(\varphi^i(\gamma))_{0 \leq i < \ell}$ as a linear combination of the parsed polynomials $\gamma_i = \sum_{j=0}^{n/\ell-1} \gamma^{(j\ell+i)} X^{j\ell}$ for $0 \leq i < \ell$ of $\gamma = \sum_{j=0}^{n-1} \gamma^{(j)} X^j$. In this case, the prover sends $\mathbf{w}'_i = \mathbf{B}_0\mathbf{y}'_i$ and $\mathbf{z}'_i = \mathbf{y}'_i + \gamma_i \cdot \mathbf{r}$ for $\mathbf{y}'_i \leftarrow \mathcal{D}_{\mathbb{Z}^n, \sigma_1}^{\mu+\nu+k}$ and verifier checks if $\mathbf{B}_0\mathbf{z}'_i = \mathbf{w}'_i + \gamma_i \cdot \mathbf{c}_0$ for $0 \leq i < \ell$. Then, by computing $\mathbf{y}_i = \sum_{j=0}^{\ell-1} \varphi^i(X^j)\mathbf{y}'_j$, $\mathbf{z}_i = \sum_{j=0}^{\ell-1} \varphi^i(X^j)\mathbf{z}'_j$, and $\mathbf{w}_i = \sum_{j=0}^{\ell-1} \varphi^i(X^j)\mathbf{w}'_j$ for $0 \leq i < \ell$, one can reconstruct the relations $\mathbf{z}_i = \mathbf{y}_i + \varphi^i(\gamma) \cdot \mathbf{r}$ and $\mathbf{B}_0\mathbf{z}_i = \mathbf{w}_i + \varphi^i(\gamma) \cdot \mathbf{c}_0$. Thus, the soundness property is still maintained. Since $\|\gamma_i\|_1 \leq n/\ell$ while $\|\varphi^{(i)}(\gamma)\|_1 \leq n$, it results in smaller size of responses.

Adopting these optimizations, the transcript now contains multiple responses $\mathbf{z}'_i$ for $0 \leq i < \ell$, which increases the number of hints from 1 to ℓ in

Table 2. Parameters for proof of knowledge of a ternary solution of linear equation over $\mathbb{Z}_q$ $(q \approx 2^{32}, n = 2^7, \ell = 4, k = 19)$

	[18]	[28]	**Ours**
μ (MSIS rank)	9	8	**7**
ν (MLWE rank)	10	10	**9**
Repetition	18	6	–
Simulatability	–	Ext-MLWE	**MLWE**

terms of Hint-MLWE. Let $\mathcal{C}'$ be the distribution of $(\gamma_0, \dots, \gamma_{\ell-1})$ where $\gamma_i = \sum_{j=0}^{n/\ell-1} \gamma^{(j\ell+i)} X^{j\ell}$ for $\gamma = \sum_{j=0}^{n-1} \gamma^{(j)} X^j \leftarrow \mathcal{C}$. Then, the simulatability holds under the hardness assumption of $\text{HintMLWE}_{R,\nu,\mu+k,q,\sigma_1}^{\ell,\sigma_2,\mathcal{C}'}$. Meanwhile, the upper bound of $\|\mathbf{z}_i\|_2$ becomes $\beta'_{\text{BDLOP}} = (n\sigma_1 + \sqrt{\ell}\sigma_2)\sqrt{(\mu+\nu+k)n/\pi}$ since $\mathbf{y}_i = \sum_{j=0}^{\ell-1} \varphi^i(X^j) \mathbf{y}'_j$ follows $\sum_{j=0}^{\ell-1} \mathcal{D}_{\mathbb{Z}^n,\sigma_2}^{\mu+\nu+k}$, which is statistically close to $\mathcal{D}_{\mathbb{Z}^n,\sqrt{\ell}\sigma_2}^{\mu+\nu+k}$ assuming the convolution lemma (Lemma 3).

Applications. We first discuss the simulatability for advanced BDLOP-based proof systems: proof of multiplicative relation [6, Fig. 4] and proof of knowledge for a (ternary) solution to a linear Eq. [18, Fig. 1 and Fig. 3]. We present new simulatability proofs of these protocols without abortion under the Hint-MLWE assumption in the full version of this paper [21, Appx. B].

To summarize briefly, in those protocols the elements of the transcripts are fully simulatable except for $\mathbf{c}$ and $\mathbf{z}_i$ since they are sampled independently from the commitment randomness $\mathbf{r}$. Therefore, it suffices to consider the simulatability of $\mathbf{c}$ and $\mathbf{z}_i$, and it can be shown using the same methodology to Theorem 3, together with the aforementioned modifications. As a result, one can construct simulators for both protocols in a similar way to $\mathcal{S}_{\text{Open}}$. Note that our new simulatability proofs for the advanced BDLOP-based proof systems are valid only for non-aborting transcripts, which is the same restriction for zero-knowledge proofs in the previous work [6,18].

As a benchmark, we present parameters for the protocol in [18, Fig. 3] in Table 2, which proves knowledge for a ternary solution of a linear equation over $\mathbb{Z}_q$. In [18], a rejection sampling method whose output follows uniform distribution is used. Meanwhile, [28] uses the improved version of the rejection sampling method, Rej_1, so that it managed to reduce the parameter μ by 1.

For the parameters in our method, the binding property depends on the hardness of $\text{MSIS}_{R,\mu+\nu+k,\mu,q,8n\beta'_{\text{BDLOP}}}$. For the simulatability, it depends on the hardness of $\text{HintMLWE}_{R,\nu,\mu+k,q,\sigma_1}^{\ell,\sigma_2,\mathcal{C}'}$. We choose σ_1, σ_2 which minimizes $\beta'_{\text{BDLOP}} = (n\sigma_1 + \sqrt{\ell}\sigma_2)\sqrt{(\mu+\nu+k)n/\pi}$ under the constraints $1/\sigma^2 = 2(1/\sigma_1^2 + \ell \cdot (n/\ell)^2/\sigma_2^2)$, and $\sigma \geq \sqrt{2} \cdot \eta_\varepsilon(\mathbb{Z}^n)$. As a result, our method reduces both parameter μ and ν to 7 and 9, respectively. We also note that our method does not require any repetition, so it indeed reduces computation overheads.

Acknowledgement. This work was supported by Samsung Research Funding & Incubation Center of Samsung Electronics under Project Number SRFC-TB2103-01. We would like to thank the anonymous CRYPTO 2023 reviewers and Damien Stehlé for the useful comments and discussions.

References

1. Agrawal, S., Stehlé, D., Yadav, A.: Round-Optimal Lattice-Based Threshold Signatures, Revisited. In: 49th International Colloquium on Automata, Languages, and Programming (ICALP 2022). Leibniz International Proceedings in Informatics (LIPIcs), vol. 229, pp. 8:1–8:20 (2022)
2. Ajtai, M.: Generating hard instances of lattice problems. In: Proceedings of the Twenty-eighth Annual ACM Symposium on Theory Of Computing, pp. 99–108 (1996)
3. Albrecht, M., et al.: Homomorphic encryption standard. In: Lauter, K., Dai, W., Laine, K. (eds.) Protecting Privacy through Homomorphic Encryption, pp. 31–62. Springer, Cham (2021). https://doi.org/10.1007/978-3-030-77287-1_2
4. Alperin-Sheriff, J., Peikert, C.: Circular and KDM security for identity-based encryption. In: Fischlin, M., Buchmann, J., Manulis, M. (eds.) PKC 2012. LNCS, vol. 7293, pp. 334–352. Springer, Heidelberg (2012). https://doi.org/10.1007/978-3-642-30057-8_20
5. Asharov, G., Jain, A., López-Alt, A., Tromer, E., Vaikuntanathan, V., Wichs, D.: Multiparty computation with low communication, computation and interaction via threshold FHE. In: Pointcheval, D., Johansson, T. (eds.) EUROCRYPT 2012. LNCS, vol. 7237, pp. 483–501. Springer, Heidelberg (2012). https://doi.org/10.1007/978-3-642-29011-4_29
6. Attema, T., Lyubashevsky, V., Seiler, G.: Practical product proofs for lattice commitments. In: Micciancio, D., Ristenpart, T. (eds.) CRYPTO 2020. LNCS, vol. 12171, pp. 470–499. Springer, Cham (2020). https://doi.org/10.1007/978-3-030-56880-1_17
7. Bai, S., Lepoint, T., Roux-Langlois, A., Sakzad, A., Stehlé, D., Steinfeld, R.: Improved security proofs in lattice-based cryptography: using the rényi divergence rather than the statistical distance. J. Cryptol. **31**, 610–640 (2018)
8. Baum, C., Cozzo, D., Smart, N.P.: Using TopGear in overdrive: a more efficient ZKPoK for SPDZ. In: Paterson, K.G., Stebila, D. (eds.) SAC 2019. LNCS, vol. 11959, pp. 274–302. Springer, Cham (2020). https://doi.org/10.1007/978-3-030-38471-5_12
9. Baum, C., Damgård, I., Lyubashevsky, V., Oechsner, S., Peikert, C.: More efficient commitments from structured lattice assumptions. In: Catalano, D., De Prisco, R. (eds.) SCN 2018. LNCS, vol. 11035, pp. 368–385. Springer, Cham (2018). https://doi.org/10.1007/978-3-319-98113-0_20
10. Benhamouda, F., Camenisch, J., Krenn, S., Lyubashevsky, V., Neven, G.: Better zero-knowledge proofs for lattice encryption and their application to group signatures. In: Sarkar, P., Iwata, T. (eds.) ASIACRYPT 2014. LNCS, vol. 8873, pp. 551–572. Springer, Heidelberg (2014). https://doi.org/10.1007/978-3-662-45611-8_29
11. Brakerski, Z.: Fully homomorphic encryption without modulus switching from classical GapSVP. In: Safavi-Naini, R., Canetti, R. (eds.) CRYPTO 2012. LNCS, vol. 7417, pp. 868–886. Springer, Heidelberg (2012). https://doi.org/10.1007/978-3-642-32009-5_50

12. Brakerski, Z., Gentry, C., Vaikuntanathan, V.: (leveled) fully homomorphic encryption without bootstrapping. ACM Trans. Comput. Theor. (TOCT) 6(3), 1–36 (2014)
13. Brakerski, Z., Langlois, A., Peikert, C., Regev, O., Stehlé, D.: Classical hardness of learning with errors. In: Proceedings of the Forty-fifth Annual ACM Symposium On Theory Of Computing, pp. 575–584 (2013)
14. Chen, H., Kim, M., Razenshteyn, I., Rotaru, D., Song, Y., Wagh, S.: Maliciously secure matrix multiplication with applications to private deep learning. In: Moriai, S., Wang, H. (eds.) ASIACRYPT 2020. LNCS, vol. 12493, pp. 31–59. Springer, Cham (2020). https://doi.org/10.1007/978-3-030-64840-4_2
15. Cheon, J.H., Kim, D., Kim, D., Lee, J., Shin, J., Song, Y.: Lattice-based secure biometric authentication for hamming distance. In: Baek, J., Ruj, S. (eds.) ACISP 2021. LNCS, vol. 13083, pp. 653–672. Springer, Cham (2021). https://doi.org/10.1007/978-3-030-90567-5_33
16. Damgård, I., Pastro, V., Smart, N., Zakarias, S.: Multiparty computation from somewhat homomorphic encryption. In: Safavi-Naini, R., Canetti, R. (eds.) CRYPTO 2012. LNCS, vol. 7417, pp. 643–662. Springer, Heidelberg (2012). https://doi.org/10.1007/978-3-642-32009-5_38
17. Escala, A., Groth, J.: Fine-tuning groth-sahai proofs. In: Krawczyk, H. (ed.) PKC 2014. LNCS, vol. 8383, pp. 630–649. Springer, Heidelberg (2014). https://doi.org/10.1007/978-3-642-54631-0_36
18. Esgin, M.F., Nguyen, N.K., Seiler, G.: Practical exact proofs from lattices: new techniques to exploit fully-splitting rings. In: Moriai, S., Wang, H. (eds.) ASIACRYPT 2020. LNCS, vol. 12492, pp. 259–288. Springer, Cham (2020). https://doi.org/10.1007/978-3-030-64834-3_9
19. Fan, J., Vercauteren, F.: Somewhat practical fully homomorphic encryption. Cryptology ePrint Archive (2012)
20. Keller, M., Pastro, V., Rotaru, D.: Overdrive: making SPDZ great again. In: Nielsen, J.B., Rijmen, V. (eds.) EUROCRYPT 2018. LNCS, vol. 10822, pp. 158–189. Springer, Cham (2018). https://doi.org/10.1007/978-3-319-78372-7_6
21. Kim, D., Lee, D., Seo, J., Song, Y.: Toward practical lattice-based proof of knowledge from hint-mlwe. Cryptology ePrint Archive, Paper 2023/623 (2023). https://eprint.iacr.org/2023/623
22. Lee, J., Kim, D., Kim, D., Song, Y., Shin, J., Cheon, J.H.: Instant privacy-preserving biometric authentication for hamming distance. Cryptology ePrint Archive, Paper 2018/1214 (2018), https://eprint.iacr.org/2018/1214
23. Lyubashevsky, V.: Lattice signatures without trapdoors. In: Pointcheval, D., Johansson, T. (eds.) EUROCRYPT 2012. LNCS, vol. 7237, pp. 738–755. Springer, Heidelberg (2012). https://doi.org/10.1007/978-3-642-29011-4_43
24. Lyubashevsky, V., Nguyen, N.K.: Bloom: Bimodal lattice one-out-of-many proofs and applications. In: Advances in Cryptology-ASIACRYPT 2022: 28th International Conference on the Theory and Application of Cryptology and Information Security, Taipei, Taiwan, December 5–9, 2022, Proceedings, Part IV. pp. 95–125. Springer (2023). https://doi.org/10.1007/978-3-031-22972-5_4
25. Lyubashevsky, V., Nguyen, N.K., Plançon, M.: Lattice-based zero-knowledge proofs and applications: shorter, simpler, and more general. In: Advances in Cryptology-CRYPTO 2022: 42nd Annual International Cryptology Conference, CRYPTO 2022, Santa Barbara, CA, USA, August 15–18, 2022, Proceedings, Part II. pp. 71–101. Springer (2022). https://doi.org/10.1007/978-3-031-15979-4_3

26. Lyubashevsky, V., Nguyen, N.K., Plancon, M., Seiler, G.: Shorter lattice-based group signatures via "almost free" encryption and other optimizations. In: Tibouchi, M., Wang, H. (eds.) ASIACRYPT 2021. LNCS, vol. 13093, pp. 218–248. Springer, Cham (2021). https://doi.org/10.1007/978-3-030-92068-5_8

27. Lyubashevsky, V., Nguyen, N.K., Seiler, G.: Practical lattice-based zero-knowledge proofs for integer relations. In: Proceedings of the 2020 ACM SIGSAC Conference On Computer And Communications Security, pp. 1051–1070 (2020)

28. Lyubashevsky, V., Nguyen, N.K., Seiler, G.: Shorter lattice-based zero-knowledge proofs via one-time commitments. In: Garay, J.A. (ed.) PKC 2021. LNCS, vol. 12710, pp. 215–241. Springer, Cham (2021). https://doi.org/10.1007/978-3-030-75245-3_9

29. Lyubashevsky, V., Nguyen, N.K., Seiler, G.: SMILE: set membership from ideal lattices with applications to ring signatures and confidential transactions. In: Malkin, T., Peikert, C. (eds.) CRYPTO 2021. LNCS, vol. 12826, pp. 611–640. Springer, Cham (2021). https://doi.org/10.1007/978-3-030-84245-1_21

30. Lyubashevsky, V., Seiler, G.: Short, invertible elements in partially splitting cyclotomic rings and applications to lattice-based zero-knowledge proofs. In: Nielsen, J.B., Rijmen, V. (eds.) EUROCRYPT 2018. LNCS, vol. 10820, pp. 204–224. Springer, Cham (2018). https://doi.org/10.1007/978-3-319-78381-9_8

31. Micciancio, D., Regev, O.: Worst-case to average-case reductions based on gaussian measures. SIAM J. Comput. **37**(1), 267–302 (2007)

32. O'Neill, A., Peikert, C., Waters, B.: Bi-deniable public-key encryption. In: Rogaway, P. (ed.) CRYPTO 2011. LNCS, vol. 6841, pp. 525–542. Springer, Heidelberg (2011). https://doi.org/10.1007/978-3-642-22792-9_30

33. Peikert, C.: An efficient and parallel gaussian sampler for lattices. In: Rabin, T. (ed.) CRYPTO 2010. LNCS, vol. 6223, pp. 80–97. Springer, Heidelberg (2010). https://doi.org/10.1007/978-3-642-14623-7_5

34. Regev, O.: On lattices, learning with errors, random linear codes, and cryptography. J. ACM (JACM) **56**(6), 1–40 (2009)

Publicly Verifiable Zero-Knowledge and Post-Quantum Signatures from VOLE-in-the-Head

Carsten Baum[1,2]($\boxtimes$), Lennart Braun[1], Cyprien Delpech de Saint Guilhem[3], Michael Klooß[4], Emmanuela Orsini[5], Lawrence Roy[1], and Peter Scholl[1]

[1] Aarhus University, Aarhus, Denmark
[2] Technical University of Denmark, Kongens Lyngby, Denmark
cabau@dtu.dk
[3] imec-COSIC, KU Leuven, Leuven, Belgium
[4] Aalto University, Espoo, Finland
[5] Bocconi University, Milan, Italy

Abstract. We present a new method for transforming zero-knowledge protocols in the designated verifier setting into public-coin protocols, which can be made non-interactive and publicly verifiable. Our transformation applies to a large class of ZK protocols based on oblivious transfer. In particular, we show that it can be applied to recent, fast protocols based on *vector oblivious linear evaluation* (VOLE), with a technique we call *VOLE-in-the-head*, upgrading these protocols to support public verifiability. Our resulting ZK protocols have linear proof size, and are simpler, smaller and faster than related approaches based on MPC-in-the-head.

To build VOLE-in-the-head while supporting both binary circuits and large finite fields, we develop several new technical tools. One of these is a new proof of security for the SoftSpokenOT protocol (Crypto 2022), which generalizes it to produce certain types of VOLE correlations over large fields. Secondly, we present a new ZK protocol that is tailored to take advantage of this form of VOLE, which leads to a publicly verifiable VOLE-in-the-head protocol with only 2x more communication than the best, designated-verifier VOLE-based protocols.

We analyze the soundness of our approach when made non-interactive using the Fiat-Shamir transform, using round-by-round soundness. As an application of the resulting NIZK, we present FAEST, a post-quantum signature scheme based on AES. FAEST is the first AES-based signature scheme to be smaller than SPHINCS+, with signature sizes between 5.6 and 6.6kB at the 128-bit security level. Compared with the smallest version of SPHINCS+ (7.9kB), FAEST verification is slower, but the signing times are between 8x and 40x faster.

1 Introduction

Zero-knowledge (ZK) proofs allow a prover to convince a verifier of the truth of a statement, without revealing any further information. Since their inception in

Michael Klooß: Research was conducted at Karlsruhe Institute of Technology.

H. Handschuh and A. Lysyanskaya (Eds.): CRYPTO 2023, LNCS 14085, pp. 581–615, 2023.
https://doi.org/10.1007/978-3-031-38554-4_19

1985 [30], ZK proofs have become an essential part of a cryptographer's toolbox, being used for a range of applications including CCA-secure encryption, digital signatures, anonymous credentials, anonymous cryptocurrencies and more.

MPC-in-the-Head (MPCitH) is a method of using secure multi-party computation (MPC) protocols to build efficient ZK proof systems [33]. The idea is for the prover to emulate, in its head, the execution of an MPC protocol related to the statement being proven. The verifier then checks parts of this execution in order to verify the truth of the statement. MPCitH proofs can be based on relatively simple MPC protocols, which often allows them to be very efficient in terms of computational complexity [8,21,29,37]. MPCitH proofs are also public-coin[1], so can be easily made non-interactive (hence, publicly verifiable) using the Fiat-Shamir transform.

The main drawback of many MPCitH protocols is that their proof size scales linearly with the size of the (Boolean or arithmetic) circuit representation of the statement being proven. In practice, however, improvements that lowered the constants in linear-size proofs [31,36] have allowed MPCitH to shine in settings where a small prover runtime is critical, and/or when proving statements of small-to-medium sized circuits, where the linear proof size may not have a big impact. Another advantage is that MPCitH protocols are usually based on standard, symmetric cryptography, which can easily be made secure against quantum adversaries. This has led to them being used for post-quantum digital signature schemes such as Picnic [17] and follow-up constructions [6,26,36]. These are non-interactive ZK proofs (NIZKs), where the verification key of the signature is the output y of a one-way function f while the secret the prover shows knowledge of is an input x such that $y = f(x)$. These signatures can be particularly efficient if f has a nice circuit representation that is efficient to evaluate in MPCitH [6,20,26].

One exception to the linear proof size is Ligero [3]. For a circuit C, Ligero achieves $O(\sqrt{|C|})$ proof size by building upon an actively secure, honest-majority MPC protocol. A major downside of Ligero is that the computational costs of the prover and verifier are higher, due to the need for many Reed-Solomon encoding operations and consistency checks, as well as the fact that addition gates are no longer "free" (unlike in most other MPCitH protocols). Ligero also has an inherent "startup cost", so that its proof size only drops below the size of linear proofs [8,21,29,37] if $|C|$ is large enough.

VOLE-Based ZK. Another approach to prover-efficient, linear-sized ZK is to use vector oblivious linear evaluation (VOLE), a tool which has recently seen a lot of progress [13,44]. VOLE-based proofs use preprocessed random VOLE correlations to implement highly efficient proofs with a commit-and-prove type structure, where VOLE is used to commit to the witness, and then relations are proven about the commitments using information-theoretic techniques [5,7,22,44,45,47]. These proofs communicate as little as 1 field element per multiplication gate and are computationally very efficient. They also

---

[1] Meaning that the verifier's messages are always sampled uniformly at random.

Table 1. Comparison of linear-size zero-knowledge proof systems

Protocol	Field*	Model	Comm./gate†	Assumption
VOLE-ZK [47]‡	$\mathbb{F}_2$	deg-d constraints	1	LPN
VOLE-ZK [22,47]‡	$\mathbb{F}_p$	deg-d constraints	1	LPN
Limbo [21]	$\mathbb{F}_2$	Circuits (free XOR)	42 (11)	Hash
Limbo [21]	$\mathbb{F}_p$	Circuits (free add)	40 (11)	Hash
VOLE-in-the-head (full v.)	$\mathbb{F}_2$	deg-d constraints	16 (5)	Hash
VOLE-in-the-head (§5.1)	$\mathbb{F}_p$	deg-d constraints	3 (2)	Hash

* $p \approx 2^{64}$
† Soundness error at most 2^{-128} (2^{-40}). Cost is average number of field elements sent per AND/mult. gate, for a circuit with 2^{20} such gates.
‡ Designated-verifier only

permit optimizations such as efficient verification of low-degree polynomials [47] or disjunctions [7].

The main disadvantage of all these protocols is that they are inherently designated verifier proofs. This is because they require the verifier to keep a secret state, namely his parts of the VOLE correlation, to ensure soundness.

Succinct ZK. ZK proofs can be done with poly-logarithmic or even constant size, using techniques such as SNARKs [28] and STARKs [9]. Later works obtain succinct proofs with a linear prover runtime [12,46], however, the hidden constants are fairly large, meaning that in practice, the prover in these constructions is usually slower than MPCitH. In this work, we instead focus on proofs with a fast prover runtime that only achieve low communication for small-to-medium sized statements.

1.1 Our Contributions

We present *VOLE-in-the-head*, a new approach to building efficient ZK. Like MPCitH, VOLE-in-the-head proofs are based on standard symmetric cryptographic primitives and are publicly verifiable. At the same time, they inherit the simplicity and expressiveness of VOLE-based protocols, which allows them to be much smaller and faster than previous MPC-in-the-head methods.

From OT/VOLE-Based ZK to Public Verifiability. We start by presenting a simple compiler that takes a ZK protocol in the OT-hybrid model and converts it into a publicly verifiable protocol. We then extend this to compile ZK protocols in the VOLE-hybrid model, by giving a suitable VOLE based on OT. Unfortunately, our approach is not compatible with previous LPN-based VOLE protocols [13,14,44], since we require the prover to play the role of the OT sender, while in LPN-based VOLE, the prover is the OT receiver. We instead adapt the VOLE protocol from SoftSpokenOT [43], where the VOLE sender is also the OT sender. This protocol is restricted to VOLEs where the sender's message is over a small field. To allow for more general ZK, we give a generalized version of the protocol that (with some constraints) works over large fields; to prove this secure, we devise a new proof strategy for SoftSpokenOT.

Instantiations and Concrete Efficiency. We give two main instantiations of our compiler, using VOLE-based ZK. The first is a variant of the QuickSilver protocol [47] using (subfield) VOLE over $\mathbb{F}_2$, aimed at Boolean computations. We tweak QuickSilver to allow mixing constraints over $\mathbb{F}_2$ and any extension field $\mathbb{F}_{2^k}$, which is particularly useful for AES. As shown in Table 1, the communication cost of the protocol is as small as 5 bits per AND gate (or, when proving low-degree relations, per bit of the witness) with 40-bit statistical security. The runtime of the prover should be at least as fast as QuickSilver; the only difference is that instead of LPN-based VOLE, we use VOLE-in-the-head based on SoftSpokenOT; despite the higher communication, this is computationally cheaper than LPN-based methods [43].

Our second instantiation is designed for proving statements in $\mathbb{F}_{p^k}$ when p^k is large. This case is more challenging, due to some subtle issues and limitations of our VOLE protocol over large fields. For κ-bit security and a finite field of size $\geq 2^\kappa$, the resulting protocol has roughly $2\times$ the communication cost of the best designated-verifier VOLE-based protocol.

Application: Post-Quantum Signatures from AES. As an example application, we present a new post-quantum signature scheme based on proving knowledge of an AES pre-image, called FAEST. FAEST significantly outperforms prior AES-based signatures [6,36], while obtaining signature sizes under 7kB. We also compare FAEST to other efficient post-quantum schemes, showing that it achieves the smallest signature size, other than better prover running time, among all the schemes based on symmetric primitives and code-based assumptions, while SPHINCS+ [32] still has better verification time.

1.2   Technical Overview

We now give a more detailed overview of our techniques.

Compiling OT-Based Zero-Knowledge Proofs. At the heart of our approach is a compiler that starts with a ZK protocol based on oblivious transfer (OT) — where the prover is the OT sender and verifier is the receiver — and converts it into a publicly verifiable one. If the ZK protocol satisfies a natural public-coin type property, this is easily done by replacing the oblivious transfer with the prover committing to its OT messages; at the end of the proof, the verifier simply sends its OT choices in the clear to the prover, who opens the corresponding commitments. When using standard 1-out-of-2 OT, this approach (which is similar to e.g. MPC-in-the-head [33] and homomorphic commitments [16]) does not seem enough to transform ZK based on VOLE, because it is not compatible with efficient, LPN-based VOLE used in these ZK constructions: in these, the prover plays the role of the OT receiver and not the sender.

We therefore present a generalized version of the compiler, which starts with a ZK protocol based on $(N-1)$-out-of-N OT (all-but-one OT) on random strings, for some parameter N. By having the prover commit to a key for a puncturable PRF that defines N pseudorandom strings, the prover can later reveal all-but-one of these with only $O(\log N)$ communication by opening a punctured key.

Fiat–Shamir and Signatures. We show how to apply the notion of round-by-round soundness [15,18] to our compiled protocols when made non-interactive using the Fiat-Shamir transformation. To this end, we interpret our interactive protocol as an IOP (only for soundness, not for SHVZK), by treating the (malicious) prover's OT inputs as PCP-strings and the verifier's OT choices as queries to the PCP oracles. This allows also to build a Picnic-like post-quantum signature scheme based on AES.

Using VOLE Instead of OT. VOLE can be viewed as an arithmetic form of OT, where one party, who we call the prover $\mathcal{P}$, learns a pair $\mathbf{u} \in \mathbb{F}_p^\ell, \mathbf{v} \in \mathbb{F}_{p^k}^\ell$, while the verifier $\mathcal{V}$ learns a random $\Delta \in \mathbb{F}_{p^k}$ and $\mathbf{q} = \mathbf{u}\Delta + \mathbf{v} \in \mathbb{F}_{p^k}^\ell$. VOLE is used in ZK proofs as a kind of linear homomorphic commitment; $\mathcal{P}$ is committed to the vector $\mathbf{u}$ towards the verifier, and cannot open any component of $\mathbf{u}$ to a different value without guessing Δ. Note that $\mathbf{u}$ can be chosen in a small subfield $\mathbb{F}_p$, while Δ is in an extension $\mathbb{F}_{p^k}$, giving soundness error p^{-k}.

Our goal is to find a suitable VOLE protocol based on $(N-1)$-out-of-N OT, so we can use our compiler to transform VOLE-based ZK. We adapt the construction of [43], which is based on the observation that if $N = p^k$, then a single $(N-1)$-out-of-N OT can be converted into a VOLE correlation. Let $t_0, \ldots, t_{N-1} \in \mathbb{F}_p$ be the messages held by $\mathcal{P}$, and let $\Delta \in [1..N]$ be a random index chosen by $\mathcal{V}$, who then learns t_x for all $x \neq \Delta$. The idea is that Δ can be viewed as the secret in a VOLE correlation, given by:

$$q = \sum_{x \in \mathbb{F}_{p^k} \setminus \{\Delta\}} t_x(\Delta - x) = \sum_{x \in \mathbb{F}_{p^k}} t_x(\Delta - x) = \sum_{x \in \mathbb{F}_{p^k}} t_x \Delta + \sum_{x \in \mathbb{F}_{p^k}} t_x(-x) = u\Delta + v$$

$\mathcal{P}$ can compute u and v, while $\mathcal{V}$ gets $q = \Delta u + v$. This approach is only efficient when p^k is small; however, as long as p is small, it can be extended to handle arbitrarily large p^k with a little extra communication. We can directly combine this VOLE protocol with our OT-based compiler to get publicly verifiable ZK. We call this technique *VOLE-in-the-head*.

This approach for small p is loosely connected to MPCitH approaches like KKW [37] and Limbo [21]. We can view the OT setup as splitting the secret u into N shares r_i, where the verifier learns all-but-one of the shares. The key difference is that, instead of evaluating the circuit on all N sets of shares using MPC, we compress the shares into a VOLE (-in-the-head) correlation. Then, by adopting the simple multiplication checks of VOLE-based proofs, the circuit verification procedure becomes much simpler than MPCitH checks, in terms of both communication and computation.

Handling Large Fields. Unfortunately, the above method is limited to proving constraints over small finite fields, since the VOLE from [43] requires $O(p)$ computation. To circumvent this, we first observe that the VOLE idea can easily support any large field $\mathbb{F}_p$, under the constraint that the sender's secret Δ is sampled from a small subset of $S_\Delta \subseteq \mathbb{F}_p$.

One remaining issue is that even though we can now use a large field, Δ has low entropy, which means the ZK protocol will have a large soundness error. We fix this by using an *encoded* form of VOLE, called subspace VOLE, where $\mathcal{P}$'s input $\mathbf{u}$ is committed as

$$\mathbf{q} = \mathcal{C}(\mathbf{u}) * \Delta + \mathbf{v}$$

for some linear code $\mathcal{C}$. Here, Δ is a vector of length $n_\mathcal{C}$ field elements and $*$ is the component-wise product. If the code has minimum distance $d_\mathcal{C}$ and the $n_\mathcal{C}$ VOLE secrets are independent (one for each symbol of $\mathcal{C}(\mathbf{u})$), then to open to a different codeword $\mathcal{C}(\mathbf{u}')$, a malicious $\mathcal{P}$ must guess $d_\mathcal{C}$ entries of Δ instead of just one.

On its own, this type of subspace VOLE is incompatible with the standard VOLE used in previous ZK protocols. We therefore present a new ZK protocol based on subspace VOLE, with around $2\times$ overhead on standard VOLE-based protocols over large fields. Our protocol is based on a simple code-switching technique, which translates a vector that is committed under subspace VOLE, into one committed under (standard) VOLE-in-the-head. Using our compiler, we can replace subspace VOLE with VOLE-in-the-head, obtaining a publicly verifiable protocol.

Consistency Checking. While adjusting the VOLE to handle large fields $\mathbb{F}_p$, with $S_\Delta \subseteq \mathbb{F}_p$, is straightforward, we still need a consistency check to argue that subspace VOLE is secure against a malicious prover. Proving security of this consistency check is *not* straightforward, requiring a new analysis of the SoftSpokenOT consistency check. SoftSpokenOT makes much use of Δ being uniform in a linear space, making the distribution invariant under invertible linear transformations. This invariance no longer holds when Δ is sampled from an arbitrary subset S_Δ.

Another difficulty is proving that the consistency check works together with both the Fiat–Shamir transformation and the commitment-based "OT"s. The verifier's choice of a hash function for the consistency check and its revelation of Δ at the end must take place in two separate rounds, and a tight bound for Fiat–Shamir requires these rounds to be analyzed separately from each other. However, combining these bounds together is essential to the proof in SoftSpokenOT, as attackers can trade off success probability between these two rounds.

We address both these issues by giving a column-by-column analysis of the security, in the style of [40] (but without the issue in its proof), rather than the linear subspaces style of [43]. By defining it on columns, we do not need S_Δ to form a linear subspace; we only need each entry Δ_i to be independently random. To fix the Fiat–Shamir analysis, we first define a property defined on subsets of columns the prover's secret $\mathbf{U}$, and show that if the property is preserved by the hash function then the protocol secure. We then bound the probability that this property is not preserved by the hash function, independently from Δ.

2 Preliminaries

Here we recall some preliminaries that will be useful in the rest of the paper.

Basic Notation. The security parameter is denoted by λ, and given as an implicit input to all algorithms; all other parameters in our schemes are viewed as functions of λ. A function f which satisfies $\lim_{\lambda \to \infty} \mathsf{negl}(\lambda) \cdot \lambda^c = 0$ for any constant c is called negligible, and we use $\mathsf{negl}(\lambda)$ to denote such a function. We write $\mathsf{AdvDist}_{\mathcal{D}}^{X,Y}$ for the distinguishing advantage of algorithm $\mathcal{D}$ for probability ensembles $(X_{\lambda,z})$, $(Y_{\lambda,z})$, i.e. $\mathsf{AdvDist}_{\mathcal{D}}^{X,Y} = \Pr[\mathcal{D}(1^\lambda, z, X_{\lambda,z}) = 1] - \Pr[\mathcal{D}(1^\lambda, z, Y_{\lambda,z}) = 1]$.

Given two machines, A, B, we let $B^A(x)$ denote the output of machine B on input x and given oracle access to A.

For a set S, we denote by $s \leftarrow S$ the process of sampling s from S uniformly at random. For $n \in \mathbb{N}$, we denote by $[n]$ the set $\{1, \ldots, n\}$; for $a, b \in \mathbb{N}$ with $a \leq b$, we use $[a..b] = \{a, \ldots, b\}$ and $[a..b) = \{a, \ldots, b-1\}$.

We use bold lower-case letters for column vectors and bold upper-case letters for matrices. We denote the ith row (resp. column) of a matrix $\mathbf{A}$ by $\mathbf{A}_i$ (resp. $\mathbf{A}^i$), by $\mathbf{A}_{[a..b]}$ (resp. $\mathbf{A}^{[a..b]}$) the submatrix of $\mathbf{A}$ containing rows (resp. columns) a through b; we denote by x_i the i-th component of vector $\mathbf{x}$ and $\mathbf{x}_{[a..b]}$ the vector of components $x_a, \ldots, x_b$. Given a vector $\mathbf{x}$, we denote by $\mathsf{diag}(\mathbf{x})$ the diagonal matrix having $\mathbf{x}$ on the diagonal.

Linear Codes. An $[n_\mathcal{C}, k_\mathcal{C}, d_\mathcal{C}]_p$ linear code $\mathcal{C}$ over $\mathbb{F}_p$ is a $k_\mathcal{C}$-dimensional subspace of $\mathbb{F}_p^{n_\mathcal{C}}$, where $n_\mathcal{C}$ is the length and $d_\mathcal{C}$ the minimum distance of the code, i.e., the minimum Hamming distance between any two codewords. A matrix $\mathbf{G}_\mathcal{C} \in \mathbb{F}_p^{k_\mathcal{C} \times n_\mathcal{C}}$ is a generator matrix for $\mathcal{C}$ if its rows are a basis for $\mathcal{C}$ as a linear subspace, that is $\mathcal{C} = \{\mathbf{x}^T \mathbf{G}_\mathcal{C} : \mathbf{x} \in \mathbb{F}_p^{k_\mathcal{C}}\}$. We denote $\mathcal{C}(\mathbf{x}) = \mathbf{x}^T \mathbf{G}_\mathcal{C}$. We let $\mathbf{T}_\mathcal{C} \in \mathbb{F}_p^{n_\mathcal{C} \times n_\mathcal{C}}$ contain $\mathbf{G}_\mathcal{C}$ in its first $k_\mathcal{C}$ rows, with the remaining rows chosen linearly independently, so that $\mathbf{T}_\mathcal{C}$ is invertible and forms a basis of $\mathbb{F}_p^{n_\mathcal{C} \times n_\mathcal{C}}$. We recall that a code $\mathcal{C}$ is systematic if it has a generator matrix $\mathbf{G}_\mathcal{C}$ of the form $[\mathbf{A} \,|\, \mathbf{I}_{k_\mathcal{C}}]$, where $\mathbf{I}_{k_\mathcal{C}}$ is the $k_\mathcal{C} \times k_\mathcal{C}$ identity matrix.

Given a matrix $\mathbf{A} \in \mathbb{F}_p^{n \times k_\mathcal{C}}$ and an $[n_\mathcal{C}, k_\mathcal{C}, d_\mathcal{C}]_p$ linear code $\mathcal{C}$, by abuse of notation, we will write $\mathcal{C}(\mathbf{A})$ to denote the $n \times n_\mathcal{C}$ matrix whose rows are the encoding $\mathcal{C}(\mathbf{A}_i)$, $i \in [n]$, of $\mathbf{A}$'s rows, i.e., $\mathcal{C}(\mathbf{A}) = \mathbf{A} \cdot \mathbf{G}_\mathcal{C}$.

Universal Hash Functions. Several of our protocols take advantage of linear structure to perform a consistency check, where a number of equations are checked at once by taking a random linear combination. For such checks, it is often more efficient to use a linear universal hash function rather then taking a truly random linear combination.

Definition 1. *A linear ε-almost universal family of hashes is a family of matrices $\mathcal{H} \subseteq \mathbb{F}_q^{r \times \ell}$ such that for any nonzero $\mathbf{v} \in \mathbb{F}_q^\ell$,*

$$\Pr_{\mathbf{H} \leftarrow \mathcal{H}}[\mathbf{H}\mathbf{v} = 0] \le \varepsilon.$$

We also borrow the notion of a $\mathbb{F}_p^\ell$-hiding hash from [43].

Definition 2. *Let p and $q = p^k$ be prime powers. A matrix $\mathbf{H} \in \mathbb{F}_q^{r \times (\ell+h)}$ is $\mathbb{F}_p^\ell$-hiding if the distribution of $\mathbf{H}\mathbf{v}$ is independent from $\mathbf{v}_{[1..\ell]}$ when $\mathbf{v} \leftarrow \mathbb{F}_p^{\ell+h}$. Equivalently, if $\mathbf{H}' \in \mathbb{F}_p^{rk \times (\ell+h)}$ is $\mathbf{H}$ reinterpreted as a $\mathbb{F}_p$-linear map, then the column space of $\mathbf{H}'$ must equal the column space of $\mathbf{H}'_{[\ell+1..\ell+h]}$. A hash family $\mathcal{H} \subseteq \mathbb{F}_q^{r \times (\ell+h)}$ is $\mathbb{F}_p^\ell$-hiding if every $\mathbf{H} \in \mathcal{H}$ is $\mathbb{F}_p^\ell$-hiding.*

2.1 Zero-Knowledge Proofs of Knowledge

We define zero-knowledge proof systems in the combined common reference string (CRS) and random oracle (RO) model, short CRS+RO model. Our definition roughly corresponds to real-ideal multi-use zero-knowledge proofs of knowledge definitions, i.e. our definitions are sequentially composable.

An *interactive zero-knowledge proof system* Π for NP-relation $\mathcal{R}$ is a tuple $\Pi = (\mathsf{Setup}, \mathcal{P}, \mathcal{V})$ of PPT algorithms, the setup algorithm Setup which generates the CRS, the prover $\mathcal{P}$ and the verifier $\mathcal{V}$.

- $\mathsf{Setup}^H(1^\lambda) \to crs$: Given the security parameter, output a CRS.
- $\mathcal{P}^H(crs, \mathbb{x}, \mathbb{w})$ and $\mathcal{V}^H(crs, \mathbb{x})$ interact on common input $\mathbb{x}$. The prover's private input is $\mathbb{w}$ such that $(\mathbb{x}, \mathbb{w}) \in \mathcal{R}$. The verifier outputs a bit b indicating whether it accepts (1) or rejects (0). The prover has no output.

Note that all algorithms have access to crs and the random oracle(s), usually denoted H. Thus, we consider these as implicit inputs in the rest of the paper. We write $\mathsf{tr} \leftarrow \langle \mathcal{P}^H(x), \mathcal{V}^H(y) \rangle$ for the *transcript* of an interaction where $\mathcal{P}$ (resp. $\mathcal{V}$) has input x (resp. y) and *implicit input* crs and access to H. We also write $b = \langle \mathcal{P}^H(x), \mathcal{V}^H(y) \rangle$ for the verifier's output. A proof system is *public-coin* if the verifier's messages are parts of its random tape and it outputs $b = \mathsf{Verify}^H(crs, \mathbb{x}, \mathsf{tr})$ for a PPT algorithm Verify.

For concreteness, we provide explicit definitions of zero-knowledge and knowledge soundness in the combined CRS and RO model. In particular, our definitions allow CRS and RO dependent statements and are sequentially composable.

For these properties in the $\mathcal{F}_{\text{OT-}\bar{1}}$-hybrid or $\mathcal{F}_{\text{VOLE}}$-hybrid model,[2] we instead use the standard real-ideal notion of zero-knowledge proofs of knowledge. Most of these formal definitions are deferred to the full version.

Remark 1. Since CRS and RO are only used to "realize" $\mathcal{F}_{\text{OT-}\bar{1}}$ in our compiler, but not our VOLE (Sect. 4) or ZK proofs Sect. 5, we need not consider combinations of CRS+RO model with $\mathcal{F}_{\text{OT-}\bar{1}}$-hybrid models, etc.

Since the notions are less common, we define public-coin and special honest-verifier ZK the $\mathcal{F}_{\text{OT-}\bar{1}}^{N,\ell}$-hybrid model here. See Fig. 1 for the $\mathcal{F}_{\text{OT-}\bar{1}}^{N,\ell}$-functionality.

Definition 3 (Public-coin verifier). *A public-coin verifier $\mathcal{V}$ in the $\mathcal{F}_{\text{OT-}\bar{1}}$-hybrid model sends parts of its random tape as messages to the prover or as choices to $\mathcal{F}_{\text{OT-}\bar{1}}$. The output is computed via a function $\mathsf{Verify}(\mathsf{view}_\mathcal{V})$ depending on verifier's view at the end of the protocol.*

Definition 4 (SHVZK). *Let $\Pi = (\mathcal{P}, \mathcal{V})$ be a public-coin proof system in the $\mathcal{F}_{\text{OT-}\bar{1}}^{N,\ell}$-hybrid model. A semi-honest public-coin verifier $\hat{\mathcal{V}} = (\mathcal{V}, \mathcal{V}'')$ for Π acts as follows.*

- *$\hat{\mathcal{V}}$ treats its auxiliary input as its random tape and splits into two parts r', r''.*
- *To handle all "normal" protocol messages, $\hat{\mathcal{V}}$ executes the honest verifier $\mathcal{V}(\varkappa; r')$ with r' as random tape.*
- *To handle the requests of $\mathcal{F}_{\text{OT-}\bar{1}}^{N,\ell}$ for corrupt verifiers, $\hat{\mathcal{V}}$ executes algorithm $\mathcal{V}''(\mathsf{view}; r'')$ which decides how to program the $\mathcal{F}_{\text{OT-}\bar{1}}^{N,\ell}$ outputs F^i to the prover, given the view view of $\mathcal{V}$ above and random tape r''.*

A protocol in the $\mathcal{F}_{\text{OT-}\bar{1}}^{N,\ell}$-hybrid model is special honest-verifier zero-knowledge (SHVZK), if for every PPT semi-honest verifier $\hat{\mathcal{V}}$ as specified above, a straight-line zero-knowledge simulator $\mathcal{S}$ exists such that $\mathsf{AdvZK}_{\hat{\mathcal{V}}}^{\Pi,\mathcal{S}}(\lambda)$ is negligible, where the advantage is defined as usual.

2.2 Polynomial Constraint Systems

Our ZK protocols can prove NP relations defined by a set of degree-d constraints on a witness. This is a natural generalization of the standard models of arithmetic circuits and rank-1 constraint systems (R1CS). A statement $\varkappa$ for an NP relation R is defined by a set of t degree-d polynomials $f_i \in \mathbb{F}_{p^k}[X_1, \ldots, X_\ell]_{\leq d}$, for $i \in [t]$. The witness is a vector $\mathsf{w} \in \mathbb{F}_p^\ell$, where

$$(\varkappa, \mathsf{w}) \in R \Leftrightarrow f_i(\mathsf{w}) = 0, \forall i \in [t]$$

Note that even though the constraints are defined over an extension field $\mathbb{F}_{p^k}$, the witness is a vector over $\mathbb{F}_p$, embedded into $\mathbb{F}_{p^k}$ in the natural way.

---

[2] We use standard notions of hybrid models, see for example [38]. That is, we consider access to an (unbounded) number of instances (or sessions), distinguished of the hybrid functionality, which are distinguished by an identifier *sid*. Both CRS and RO model can be viewed as hybrid models as well, although we do not do this (and limit the CRS and RO to a single one in our protocols).

2.3   Random Vector Commitment Schemes

We define vector commitments w.r.t. common reference strings (CRS) and random oracles (RO), so as to cover the plain model, CRS model, RO model, and CRS plus RO model simultaneously.

Informally, a vector commitment scheme is a two-phase protocol between two PPT machines, a *sender* and a *receiver*. In the first phase, also called *commitment phase*, it enables the sender to commit to a vector of messages while keeping it secret; in the second phase, called *decommitment phase*, a subset of indices of the commitment is opened. The commitment scheme satisfies two main properties: the *binding property* ensures that the sender cannot open the commitment in two different ways; the *hiding property* guarantees that the commit phase does not reveal any information about the committed message before opening and that messages at *unopened indices* are hidden, even after opening a subset of indices.

Definition 5 (VC). *Let H be a random oracle. A (non-interactive) vector commitment scheme VC (with message space $\mathcal{M}$) in the CRS+RO model is defined by the following PPT algorithms:*

- $\mathsf{Setup}^H(1^\lambda, N) \to \mathsf{crs}$: *Given security parameter λ and vector length $N = \mathrm{poly}(\lambda)$ as input, output a commitment key crs.*
- $\mathsf{Commit}^H_{\mathsf{crs}}() \to (\mathsf{com}, \mathsf{decom}, (m_1, \ldots, m_N))$: *Given crs as input, output a commitment com with opening information decom for messages $(m_1, \ldots, m_N) \in \mathcal{M}^N$.*
- $\mathsf{Open}^H_{\mathsf{crs}}(\mathsf{decom}, I)$: *On input crs, opening decom and a subset $I \subseteq [N]$ of indices, output an opening decom_I for I.*
- $\mathsf{Verify}^H_{\mathsf{crs}}(\mathsf{com}, \mathsf{decom}_I, I) \to \{(m_i)_{i \in I}\} \cup \{\bot\}$: *Given crs, a commitment com, an opening decom for a subset I as well as the subset I, either output the messages $(m_i)_{i \in I}$ at indices I (accept the opening) or $\bot$ (reject the opening).*

As indicated, all algorithms have access to the random oracle H.

If in the definition above, instead of general $I \subseteq [N]$ only $I \in \mathcal{I}$ is allowed (otherwise, algorithms output $\bot$), then VC is restricted to $\mathcal{I}$-openings, where $\mathcal{I}$ is a fixed subset of $[N]$. If $\mathcal{I} = \{[N] \setminus \{i\} \mid i \in [N]\}$, then VC has *all-but-one* openings. We will explicitly state definitions for general VC, but they apply to VCs with $\mathcal{I}$-opening verbatim.

Remark 2. Our definition of VC is a *random* vector commitment scheme. By making the message vector an input to Commit instead of an output, one obtains the more common notion of (vector) commitments. However, our restricted definition is sufficient for our construction and has simpler security notions.

Definition 6 (Correctness). *A vector commitment scheme VC is (perfectly) correct if for all $N = \mathrm{poly}(\lambda)$, all oracles H and all $\lambda \in \mathbb{N}$:*

$$\forall \, \mathsf{crs} \leftarrow \mathsf{Setup}^H(1^\lambda, N), \; \forall \, (\mathsf{com}, \mathsf{decom}, (m_1, \ldots, m_N)) \leftarrow \mathsf{Commit}^H_{\mathsf{crs}}()$$

$$\forall \, I \subseteq [N], \; \forall \, \mathsf{decom}_I \leftarrow \mathsf{Open}^H_{\mathsf{crs}}(\mathsf{decom}, I) : \mathsf{Verify}^H_{\mathsf{crs}}(\mathsf{com}, \mathsf{decom}_I, I) = (m_i)_{i \in I}$$

Definition 7 (Extractable-Binding). *Let* VC *be a vector commitment in the CRS+RO-model with RO H. Let* (TSetup, Ext) *be PPT algorithms such that:*

- TSetup$^H(1^\lambda, N) \to$ (crs, td): *Given security parameter λ and vector length N, output a commitment key* crs *and a trapdoor* td.
- Ext(td, Q, com) $\to (m_i)_{i \in [N]}$: *Given the trapdoor* td, *a set of query-response pairs of random oracle queries, and a commitment* com, *output the committed messages. (*Ext *may output $m_i = \bot$, e.g. if committed value at index i is invalid.)*

For any $N = $ poly(λ), define the straightline extractable-binding game for VC *and stateful adversary $\mathcal{A}$ as follows:*

1. (crs, td) $\leftarrow$ TSetup$^H(1^\lambda, N)$
2. com $\leftarrow \mathcal{A}^H(1^\lambda, $ crs$)$
3. $(m_1^*, \ldots, m_N^*) = $ Ext(td, Q, com), *where Q is the set $\{(x_i, H(x_i))\}$ of query-response pairs of queries $\mathcal{A}$ made to H.*
4. $((m_i)_{i \in I}, \text{decom}_I, I) \leftarrow \mathcal{A}^H(\text{open})$
5. *Output 1 (success) if* Verify$_{\text{crs}}^H($com, decom$_I, I) = (m_i)_{i \in I}$ *but $m_i \neq m_i^*$ for any $i \in I$. Else output 0 (failure).*

We say VC *is straightline extractable w.r.t.* (TSetup, Ext) *if*

1. $\{$crs $\mid$ crs $\leftarrow$ Setup$^H(1^\lambda, N)\}$ *and* $\{$crs $\mid$ (crs, td) $\leftarrow$ TSetup$^H(1^\lambda, N)\}$ *are computationally indistinguishable for any $N = $ poly(λ). We denote the advantage of a distinguisher $\mathcal{A}$ by* AdvDist$_{\mathcal{A}}^{\text{Setup, TSetup}}$.
2. *Any PPT adversary $\mathcal{A}$ has negligible probability to win the extractable binding game. We denote the advantage, i.e. probability to win, by* AdvEB$_{\mathcal{A}}^{\text{VC}}$.

The definition of the hiding property for VC forces all unopened components of the message vector to be independent uniform (pseudo-)random elements.

Definition 8 (Hiding (real-or-random)). *Let* VC *be a vector commitment scheme in the CRS+RO-model with random oracle H. The adaptive hiding experiment for* VC *with $N = $ poly(λ) and stateful $\mathcal{A}$ is defined as follows.*

1. crs $\leftarrow$ Setup$^H(1^\lambda, N)$, $b^* \leftarrow \{0, 1\}$
2. (com, decom, $(m_1^*, \ldots, m_N^*)) \leftarrow$ Commit$_{\text{crs}}^H()$
3. $I \leftarrow \mathcal{A}^H(1^\lambda, $ crs, com$)$
4. decom$_I \leftarrow$ Open$_{\text{crs}}($decom, $I)$
5. $m_i \leftarrow m_i^*$ *for $i \in I$.*
6. *For $i \notin I$ set $m_i \leftarrow \begin{cases} m_i^* & \text{if } b^* = 0 \\ \text{random from } \mathcal{M} & \text{if } b^* = 1 \end{cases}$*
7. $b \leftarrow \mathcal{A}((m_i)_{i \in [N]}, \text{decom}_I)$.
8. *Output 1 (success) if $b = b^*$, else 0 (failure).*

In the selective hiding experiment, $\mathcal{A}$ must choose I prior to receiving com, *i.e. steps 2 and 3 are swapped but $\mathcal{A}$ still learns* crs.

The advantage AdvSelHide$_{\mathcal{A}}^{\text{VC}}$ *(resp.* AdvAdpHide$_{\mathcal{A}}^{\text{VC}}$*) of an adversary $\mathcal{A}$ is defined by* Pr$[\mathcal{A}$ wins$] - \frac{1}{2}$ *in the selective (resp. adaptive) hiding experiment. We say* VC *is selectively (resp. adaptively) hiding if every PPT adversary $\mathcal{A}$ has negligible advantage.*

2.4   Extractable Functions

In analogy to extractable commitments, we define extractable function families.

Definition 9. *A* function *(family)* in *the* CRS+RO *model is a tuple* (Setup, Eval) *of PPT algorithms where*

- Setup$^H(1^\lambda) \to crs$: *Given the security parameter* λ *generate a CRS crs.*
- Eval$^H_{crs}(x) \to y$: *Given a CRS crs and input* $x \in \mathcal{X}_{crs}$, *output* y. *Here,* $\mathcal{X}_{crs}$ *is the efficiently recognizable domain of* Eval$_{crs}$.

In the rest of this work, we will usually write F instead of (Setup, Eval) and F(x) instead of F.Eval$_{crs}(x)$. The definition of a *(straightline) extractable* function (family) (Setup, Eval) is analogous to extractable VC. Again, there is a pair (TSetup, Ext) of trapdoor setup and straightline extractor algorithms. The adversary's goal is to find a value y such that the extracted preimage x' differs from the preimage x which the adversary provides. (That is essentially the same as extractable binding, but with preimages instead of decommitments.) We refer to the full version for more formal definitions.

3   Compiling $\binom{N}{N-1}$-OT-Based Zero-Knowledge Protocols

We begin by constructing a compiler that replaces random OT instances with random vector commitments VC, where all but one committed (random) value is opened to the verifier. This will later allow us to design our protocols in the (more natural) random OT-hybrid model. Moreover, we believe that presenting this compilation step separately is of independent interest.

Towards achieving this, we first construct an efficient VC construction using a tree PRG, similar to prior works such as [6,37]. We then describe which properties a protocol must have such that our compiler can be applied and specify which flavor of OT it must use. We then describe the compiler, which directly replaces every call to an Oblivious Transfer instance to an appropriate VC instance instead, and show that the resulting protocol is still a ZKPoK.

3.1   Tree-PRG Vector Commitments

We now give a VC construction with all-but-one openings, which we later directly use in our compiler. VC will make commitments to N random seeds, where $N-1$ are later opened. Towards optimizing openings, we generate the seeds via a GGM tree of length-doubling PRGs, similarly to previous works [6,37].

Let PRG: $\{0,1\}^\lambda \to \{0,1\}^{2\lambda}$ be a PRG, H: $\{0,1\}^* \to \{0,1\}^{2\lambda}$ be a collision-resistant hash function (CRHF), G: $\{0,1\}^\lambda \to \{0,1\}^\lambda \times \{0,1\}^{2\lambda}$ be a PRG and CRHF and $N = 2^d$. We define the scheme VC$_{\mathsf{GGM}}$ below. If H and G are instantiated as (independent) random oracles, then VC$_{\mathsf{GGM}}$ is (secure) in the RO model (without CRS). If H is replaced by the identity function and G is an injective trapdoor function, then VC$_{\mathsf{GGM}}$ is (secure) in the CRS model.

- $\mathsf{Setup}^H(1^\lambda, N = 2^d)$:
  1. Compute $\mathsf{crs_G} \leftarrow \mathsf{G.Setup}(1^\lambda)$ resp. $\mathsf{crs_H} \leftarrow \mathsf{H.Setup}(1^\lambda)$.
  2. Define $\mathsf{crs} = (\lambda, d, \mathsf{crs_G}, \mathsf{crs_H})$, which is implicitly input to all other algorithms. Moreover, $\mathsf{crs_G}$ (resp. $\mathsf{crs_H}$) are implicit inputs to G, (resp. H).
- $\mathsf{Commit}()$:
  1. Sample $k \leftarrow \{0,1\}^\lambda$ and let $k_0^0 \leftarrow k$
  2. For each level $i \in [d]$, for $j \in [0..2^{i-1})$, compute $(k_{2j}^i, k_{2j+1}^i) \leftarrow \mathsf{PRG}(k_j^{i-1})$
  3. Let $(\mathsf{sd}_0, \dots, \mathsf{sd}_{N-1}) \leftarrow (k_0^d, \dots, k_{N-1}^d)$
  4. Compute $(m_i, \overline{\mathsf{com}}_i) \leftarrow \mathsf{G}(\mathsf{sd}_i)$, for $i \in [0..N)$
  5. Compute $h \leftarrow \mathsf{H}(\overline{\mathsf{com}}_0, \dots, \overline{\mathsf{com}}_{N-1})$
  6. Output the commitment $\mathsf{com} = h$, the opening $\mathsf{decom} = k$ and the messages $(m_0, \dots, m_{N-1})$
- $\mathsf{Open}(\mathsf{decom} = k, I = [0..N) \setminus \{j^*\})$: (where $j^* \in [0..N)$):
  1. Write $j^* = \sum_{i=0}^{d-1} 2^i b_i$, for $b_i \in \{0,1\}$
  2. Define the prefixes of j^* as $j^*|_i \leftarrow \sum_{k=0}^{i-1} 2^k b_k$ for $i \in [1..d]$
  3. Recompute k_j^i, for $i \in [d]$ and $j \in [0..2^i)$ as in Commit
  4. Output the opening information $\mathsf{decom}_I = (\overline{\mathsf{com}}_{j^*}, \{k_{2j^*|_i + \overline{b}_i}^i\}_{i \in [d]})$
- $\mathsf{Verify}(\mathsf{com} = (h), \mathsf{decom}_I = (\overline{\mathsf{com}}_{j^*}, \{k_{2j^*|_i + \overline{b}_i}^i\}_{i \in [d]}), I = [0..N) \setminus \{j^*\})$:
  1. Recompute sd_i from decom_I, for $i \neq j^*$, and compute $(m_i', \overline{\mathsf{com}}_i') \leftarrow \mathsf{G}(\mathsf{sd}_i)$
  2. Let $\overline{\mathsf{com}}'_{j^*} = \overline{\mathsf{com}}_{j^*}$
  3. If $h \neq \mathsf{H}(\overline{\mathsf{com}}'_0, \dots, \overline{\mathsf{com}}'_{N-1})$ output $\bot$. Otherwise output $(m_i')_{i \in I}$

We denote the above (all-but-one) vector commitment scheme by $\mathsf{VC_{GGM}}$. Clearly, $\mathsf{VC_{GGM}}$ is perfectly complete. We prove that it is extractable-binding and hiding in the two lemmas below. Note that we use 1-based indexing in the definition of $\mathsf{VC_{GGM}}$, because it is more suitable here than the 1-based indexing used in general VC definitions.

Remark 3 (Optimizations). Instead of hashing the $\overline{\mathsf{com}}_i$'s, they could be sent in the clear as well. However, for the equality check in Verify, a (extractable) collision-resistant hash function H is sufficient. If multiple $\mathsf{VC_{GGM}}$ commitments are made in parallel, one can hash the all $\overline{\mathsf{com}}_i^{(j)}$ where j ranges over the parallel instances, or hash the hashes com^i, further reducing communication.

Lemma 1. *Decompose* $\mathsf{G}: \{0,1\}^\lambda \to \{0,1\}^\lambda \times \{0,1\}^{2\lambda}$ *along the outputs into* $(\mathsf{G}_1, \mathsf{G}_2)$, *such that* $\mathsf{G}(x) = (\mathsf{G}_1(x), \mathsf{G}_2(x))$. *Suppose* G_2 *and* H *are straightline extractable. Then* $\mathsf{VC_{GGM}}$ *is straightline extractable-binding. More concretely, for any adversaries* $\mathcal{D}$, $\mathcal{A}$ *there exist adversaries* $\mathcal{D}_\mathsf{G}$, $\mathcal{D}_\mathsf{H}$, *resp.* $\mathcal{A}_\mathsf{G}$, $\mathcal{A}_\mathsf{H}$ *with roughly the same running time as* $\mathcal{D}$ *resp.* $\mathcal{A}$, *such that*

$$\mathsf{AdvDist}_\mathcal{D}^{\mathsf{VC_{GGM}.Setup}, \mathsf{VC_{GGM}.TSetup}} \leq \mathsf{AdvDist}_{\mathcal{D}_\mathsf{G}}^{\mathsf{G.Setup}, \mathsf{G.TSetup}} + \mathsf{AdvDist}_{\mathcal{D}_\mathsf{H}}^{\mathsf{H.Setup}, \mathsf{H.TSetup}}$$

$$\mathsf{AdvEB}_\mathcal{A}^{\mathsf{VC_{GGM}}} \leq N \cdot \mathsf{AdvExt}_{\mathcal{A}_\mathsf{G}}^{\mathsf{G}} + \mathsf{AdvExt}_{\mathcal{A}_\mathsf{H}}^{\mathsf{H}}$$

where $N = 2^d$ *is the vector length of* $\mathsf{VC_{GGM}}$.

Proof (Sketch). The extraction algorithms (TSetup, Ext) are defined in the obvious way: TSetup uses the trapdoor setups for G (i.e. G_2) and H. Given a commitment com $= h$, Ext first extracts the preimage $(\overline{\text{com}}_0, \ldots, \overline{\text{com}}_{N-1})$ of h under H, and then extracts preimages sd_i for each of the $\overline{\text{com}}_i$ under G_2. Now, we derive the claimed advantages.

For indistinguishability of the setup, first replace the honest setup of G with the trapdoor setup, and then do the same for H. These are direct reductions.

For extractability, observe that the extractor Ext of VC_GGM only fails if:

- Extracting H for com $= h$ yielded $(\overline{\text{com}}_0, \ldots, \overline{\text{com}}_{N-1})$ (or $\perp$), but the adversary presented a (different) preimage during an opening of com.
- Extracting G_2 for some $\overline{\text{com}}_i$ yielded sd_i (or $\perp$), but the adversary presented a (different) preimage during an opening of com.

In both cases, the reduction to the extractable-binding property of H (resp. G_2) is a straightforward (hybrid/guessing) argument.   □

Lemma 2. *Suppose PRG and G are PRGs. Then VC_GGM is all-but-one selectively hiding. More precisely, for any adversary $\mathcal{A}$ there exist adversaries $\mathcal{A}_\text{PRG}$, $\mathcal{A}_\text{G}$, with roughly the same running time as $\mathcal{A}$, such that $\text{AdvSelHide}_{\mathcal{A}_\text{PRG}}^{\text{VC}_\text{GGM}} \leq d \cdot \text{AdvPRG}_{\mathcal{A}_\text{PRG}}^{\text{PRG}} + \text{AdvPRG}_{\mathcal{A}_\text{G}}^{\text{G}}$, where $N = 2^d$.*

Proof (Sketch). In the all-but-one selective hiding experiment, the adversary's index vector $I = [N] \setminus i$ is chosen prior to commitment generation. Using knowledge of i, we can rely on the GGM construction being a secure puncturable PRF [11]. The respective security reduction replaces PRG calls along the path of i to the root of the GGM construction by true randomness. This is possible since only the seeds for the co-path nodes for i are given out as part of the commitment. Hence, a hybrid with $d = \log(N)$ steps replaces sd_i by a truly random output. In a final step, using that G is a PRG, and $G(\text{sd}_i)$ is a PRG output where sd_i is truly random and unknown to the adversary, we can replace the committed value m_i by a truly random committed value.   □

3.2   The Compiler

We now present our compiler, which takes ZKPoKs in the $\mathcal{F}_\text{OT-1}$-hybrid model which satisfy certain properties and replaces the $\mathcal{F}_\text{OT-1}$ calls with VC instances. The $\mathcal{F}_\text{OT-1}$ functionality is given in Fig. 1. Intuitively, our compiler uses the same approach as [16], that is, it replaces OTs by mere commitments.

To receive an OT output, the compiled verifier reveals its choice bit to the prover, which then opens the commitments as appropriate. Clearly, this limits the protocols which can be securely compiled. Namely, the verifier's actions should not depend on any intermediate OT outputs, so that all choice bit queries can be delayed to the very end of the protocol, as part of a final verification step. (Otherwise, a malicious prover would gain the power to make its responses

---

Functionality $\mathcal{F}_{\mathsf{OT}\text{-}\bar{1}}^{N,\ell}$

The functionality interacts with a sender $\mathcal{P}$, a receiver $\mathcal{V}$ and an adversary $\mathcal{A}$ which may corrupt either of the parties.

It is parametrized by integers N (number of choices) and ℓ (number of parallel instances).

1. Upon receiving (init) from $\mathcal{P}$: For $i \in [\ell]$
   - Sample $F^i \leftarrow (\{0,1\}^\lambda)^{[N]}$.
   - If $\mathcal{P}$ is corrupted, receive $F^i \in (\{0,1\}^\lambda)^{[N]}$ from $\mathcal{A}$.
   - If $\mathcal{V}$ is corrupted, receive $x^i \in [N]$, $F^{i,*} \in (\{0,1\}^\lambda)^{[N]\setminus\{x^i\}}$ from $\mathcal{A}$ and set $F^i(x) = F^{i,*}(x)$ for all $x \in [N] \setminus \{x^i\}$, $i \in [\ell]$.
2. Send $F^1, \ldots, F^\ell$ to $\mathcal{P}$ and (done) to $\mathcal{V}$.
3. Upon receiving (get, $(x^1, \ldots, x^\ell)$) from $\mathcal{V}$, send $((F^i(x))_{x \neq x^i})_{i=1,\ldots,\ell}$ to $\mathcal{V}$.

Fig. 1. $\mathcal{F}_{\mathsf{OT}\text{-}\bar{1}}^{N,\ell}$ functionality adapted from SoftSpokenOT [43]

dependent on choice bits, making typical protocols completely insecure[3].) To formalize this protocol structure, we use a functionality $\mathcal{F}_{\mathsf{OT}\text{-}\bar{1}}$ which outputs done to the OT receiver when inputs are provided by the OT sender, instead of the value. Only later, by sending get to $\mathcal{F}_{\mathsf{OT}\text{-}\bar{1}}$, the actual value can be obtained by the OT receiver.

Definition 10. *A ZKPoK $(\mathcal{P}, \mathcal{V})$ in the $\mathcal{F}_{\mathsf{OT}\text{-}\bar{1}}$-hybrid model is OT-admissible, if the following holds:*

1. *The prover $\mathcal{P}$ always plays the role of the sender in $\mathcal{F}_{\mathsf{OT}\text{-}\bar{1}}$.*
2. *The verifier $\mathcal{V}$ can be split into two phases $\mathcal{V}_1, \mathcal{V}_2$, where:*
   - *$\mathcal{V}_1(inputs)$ never sends get to $\mathcal{F}_{\mathsf{OT}\text{-}\bar{1}}$ (and outputs a state state for $\mathcal{V}_2$).*
   - *$\mathcal{V}_2(\mathsf{state})$ only sends get to $\mathcal{F}_{\mathsf{OT}\text{-}\bar{1}}$ (and outputs the verdict).*

Compiler. We describe the compiler under the assumption that the prover (resp. verifier) never sends multiple messages/choice bits or get to the same $\mathcal{F}_{\mathsf{OT}\text{-}\bar{1}}^{N,\ell}$ instance, as they would be ignored by $\mathcal{F}_{\mathsf{OT}\text{-}\bar{1}}^{N,\ell}$ (and hence may be ignored by the compiler). By O2C[Π], we denote the result of protocol compilation, where Π is an interactive proof system in the $\mathcal{F}_{\mathsf{OT}\text{-}\bar{1}}^{N,\ell}$-hybrid model. We also write $(\mathcal{P}^*, \mathcal{V}^*) := \mathsf{O2C}[(\mathcal{P}, \mathcal{V})]$ to denote the compiled prover and verifier. We make the assumption that each $\mathcal{F}_{\mathsf{OT}\text{-}\bar{1}}^{N,\ell}$ instance has a unique identifier *sid*.

Changes to any setup.

1. A trusted entity securely runs crs $\leftarrow$ VC.Setup($1^\lambda, N$) and sends it to $\mathcal{P}^*, \mathcal{V}^*$.
2. Additionally, run any setup that the original protocol may require.

---

[3] As an example, MPC-in-the-head approaches [34,35] leaking their watch-lists during execution allow a cheating prover to specifically maul unopened parties.

The compiled prover $\mathcal{P}^*$.

- Let $\mathcal{P}^*$ run a copy of $\mathcal{P}$ and forward all messages of $\mathcal{P}$, except for messages to/from $\mathcal{F}_{\mathsf{OT}\text{-}\bar{1}}^{N,\ell}$-instances.
- When $\mathcal{P}$ would send (init) to $\mathcal{F}_{\mathsf{OT}\text{-}\bar{1}}^{N,\ell}$ with identifier sid, $\mathcal{P}^*$ instead first runs $(\mathsf{com}_{sid}^i, \mathsf{decom}_{sid}^i, (m_1^i, \ldots, m_N^i)) = \mathsf{Commit}()$ for $i \in [\ell]$ and returns the functions $(F^i)_{i \in [\ell]}$ to $\mathcal{P}$ where $F^i(x) = m_x^i$. Then $\mathcal{P}^*$ sends $(sid, \mathsf{init}, (\mathsf{com}_{sid}^i)_{i \in \ell})$ to $\mathcal{V}^*$.
- Upon receiving $(sid, \mathsf{get}, (x^1, \ldots, x^\ell))$ from $\mathcal{V}^*$, with $x^i \in [N]$, $i \in [\ell]$, compute $\mathsf{decom}_{sid,x}^i = \mathsf{Open}(\mathsf{decom}_{sid}^i, [N] \setminus \{x^i\})$ and send $(sid, \mathsf{get}, (\mathsf{decom}_{sid,x}^i)_{i \in [\ell]})$ to $\mathcal{V}^*$.

Changes to the verifier $\mathcal{V}$.

- Let $\mathcal{V}^*$ run a copy of $\mathcal{V}$ and forward the messages of $\mathcal{V}$, except for messages to/from $\mathcal{F}_{\mathsf{OT}\text{-}\bar{1}}^{N,\ell}$-instances.
- Upon receiving $(sid, \mathsf{init}, (\mathsf{com}^i)_{i \in [\ell]})$ from $\mathcal{P}^*$, store com^i as com_{sid}^i. Then pass (done) on to the simulated $\mathcal{V}$ in place of $\mathcal{F}_{\mathsf{OT}\text{-}\bar{1}}^{N,\ell}$ with identifier sid.
- Upon $\mathcal{V}$ sending $(\mathsf{get}, (x_{sid}^i)_{i \in [\ell]})$ to $\mathcal{F}_{\mathsf{OT}\text{-}\bar{1}}^{N,\ell}$ with identifier sid, send $(sid, \mathsf{get}, (x_{sid}^i)_{i \in [\ell]})$ to $\mathcal{P}^*$.
- Upon receiving $(sid, \mathsf{get}, (\mathsf{decom}_{sid,x}^i)_{i \in [\ell]})$, for $i \in [\ell]$ compute messages $\mathsf{out}^i \leftarrow \mathsf{Verify}(\mathsf{com}_{sid}^i, \mathsf{decom}_{sid,x}^i, [N] \setminus \{x_{sid}^i\})$. If $\mathsf{out}^i = \bot$ for any $i \in [\ell]$ then reject. Else, output $\mathsf{out}^i = (m_x^i)_{x \in [N] \setminus \{x_{sid}^i\}}$ as the function values of F to $\mathcal{V}$.

Remark 4. The compiler O2C preserves public-coin verifiers.

Remark 5 (Public-coin $\implies$ OT-admissible). Any public-coin verifier is automatically OT-admissible. To see this, observe that a public-coin verifier by definition chooses challenges which are independent of the OT outputs, hence any call to get can be delayed until the final response is received, and then all OT outputs are gathered for $\mathsf{Verify}(\mathsf{view}_{\mathcal{V}})$. Clearly, this "modification" does not affect $\mathcal{V}$'s visible behaviour in any way.

Security of the Compiler for Interactive Protocols. For interactive zero-knowledge protocols Π in the $\mathcal{F}_{\mathsf{OT}\text{-}\bar{1}}^{N,\ell}$-hybrid model, our compiler is able to translate them into protocols with almost identical security parameters for SHVZK[4] and knowledge soundness, essentially by replacing $\mathcal{F}_{\mathsf{OT}\text{-}\bar{1}}^{N,\ell}$ instances with vector commitments (in the CRS and/or RO model).

Lemma 3. *Suppose the commitment scheme* VC *used in* O2C *is complete, straightline extractable-binding and real-or-random hiding in the CRS+RO model. Let Π be an OT-admissible proof system. Then, in the CRS+RO model, O2C[Π], when compiled with* VC *as specified above, satisfies the following properties.*

---

[4] We note that a modification of the compiler, which additionally forces the verifier to commit to its OT choices (with an extractable-binding commitment scheme), yields full zero-knowledge. However, this modification does not preserve public-coin.

– *Completeness, if Π is complete.*
– *Public-coin, if Π is public-coin.*
– *Knowledge soundness, with asymptotic error $\kappa + \mathsf{negl}(\lambda)$, if Π has a black-box knowledge extractor $\mathcal{E}_\Pi$ with knowledge error κ.*
– *SHVZK, if Π has a blackbox SHVZK simulator $\mathcal{S}_\Pi$.*

Moreover, if Π has a straightline extractor above, so has $\mathsf{O2C}[\Pi]$.

We give a short proof sketch. For a detailed proof, see the full version.

Proof (Sketch). Completeness follows easily. For extraction we take a malicious prover $\hat{\mathcal{P}}^*$ for $\mathsf{O2C}[\Pi]$ and turn it into a malicious prover $\hat{\mathcal{P}}$ for Π as follows. Whenever $\hat{\mathcal{P}}^*$ sends VC commitments, the extractor $\mathcal{E}$ uses the VC extractor to obtain the committed values, i.e. the random OT values. It then provides these inputs as the malicious prover $\hat{\mathcal{P}}$ to $\mathcal{E}_\Pi$. Moreover, $\mathcal{E}$ forwards get queries to $\hat{\mathcal{P}}^*$ and checks the decommitment. Output of the $\mathcal{F}_{\mathsf{OT}\text{-}\bar{1}}^{N,\ell}$-functionality is only delivered if the decommitments were valid. It is rather straightforward to reduce an extraction failure of $\mathcal{E}$ to either an extraction failure of $\mathcal{E}_\Pi$, which happens with probability at most $\kappa + \mathsf{negl}'(\lambda)$, or an extractable-binding attack against VC (adding another $\mathsf{negl}''(\lambda)$).

For SHVZK, the idea is similar. We explain the changes from real protocol to simulation in the following. The real protocol $\mathsf{O2C}[\Pi]$ uses VC to derive the committed OT inputs. In a first step, using knowledge of the verifier's OT challenges, we use the selective hiding property of VC to replace the hidden $F^i(x^i)$ by truly random values via a hybrid argument. Next, we map the honest verifier $\mathcal{V}^*$ of $\mathsf{O2C}[\Pi]$ to a semi-honest verifier $\hat{\mathcal{V}}$ for Π (according to Definition 4). To do so, observe that $\hat{\mathcal{V}}$ is allowed to program the outputs $F^i(x)$ of $\mathcal{F}_{\mathsf{OT}\text{-}\bar{1}}^{N,\ell}$ for all non-chosen inputs $x \neq x^i$, and $F^i(x^i)$ is chosen randomly. Thus, we let $\hat{\mathcal{V}}$ program $F^i(x)$ for $x \neq x^i$ to the opened values of the VC commitments. Consequently, execution and output of $\hat{\mathcal{V}}$ corresponds exactly to the previous step. By assumption, there is a SHVZK simulator for $\hat{\mathcal{V}}$. The simulator $\mathcal{S}$ for $\mathsf{O2C}[\Pi]$ now merely translates the simulated view of Π (which is independent of w) to a view of $\mathsf{O2C}[\Pi]$. □

3.3 NIZK via the Fiat–Shamir Transformation

If Π is a public-coin proof system in the $\mathcal{F}_{\mathsf{OT}\text{-}\bar{1}}^{N,\ell}$-hybrid model, then the Fiat–Shamir transformation, denoted $\mathsf{FS}^{H_{\mathsf{FS}}}$ when used with a random oracle H_{FS}, can be applied on top of the compiled protocol $\mathsf{O2C}^{H_{\mathsf{O2C}}}[\Pi]$ (which uses an independent random oracle H_{O2C}). The resulting proof system $\mathsf{FS}^{H_{\mathsf{FS}}} \circ \mathsf{O2C}^{H_{\mathsf{O2C}}}[\Pi]$ is then non-interactive and zero-knowledge if Π is SHVZK.

It is well-known that the Fiat–Shamir transformation does, in general, not preserve (knowledge) soundness. Consequently, stronger properties are required, such as state-restoration (knowledge) soundness [10], round-by-round (knowledge) soundness [15,18], or special soundness [4,19,41].

In the full version, we define a notion of round-by-round knowledge soundness [15] which is applicable to our protocols (presented in Sect. 5). For simplicity and compatibility, we define our notion of round-by-round knowledge soundness in the IOP setting, as in [18]. It requires that extraction must succeed, unless so-called *bad challenges* occur. Thus, to bound the advantage of an adversary (against a Fiat–Shamir-compiled protocol), it now suffices to bound the probability of such bad challenges occurring. To formally define our notion, we interpret the interactive protocol Π as an IOP (only for soundness, not for SHVZK), by treating the (malicious) prover's OT inputs as PCP-strings and the verifier's OT choices as queries to the PCP oracles. It is then rather straightforward to identify the "bad challenges" in our protocols, and thus obtaining knowledge soundness in the ROM for $\mathsf{FS} \circ \mathsf{O2C}[\Pi]$ if O2C is instantiated with VC that is straightline extractable-binding and real-or-random hiding.

The proof idea for the knowledge-soundness property is then as follows: We use straightline extraction to translate the attack on $\mathsf{FS} \circ \mathsf{O2C}[\Pi]$ into an attack on a Fiat–Shamir-compiled IOP corresponding to Π. Then, we use round-by-round knowledge soundness to bound the prover's success probability for attacking the IOP protocol. A detailed discussion can be found in in the full version.

4   Generalized Subspace VOLE Protocol

The VOLE protocols presented in SoftSpokenOT [43] achieve subspace VOLE over a polynomial-order field $\mathbb{F}_q$. Here, we generalize to exponentially large fields $\mathbb{F}_q$, with the limitation that the receiver's secret Δ must be sampled from a subset $S_\Delta \subseteq \mathbb{F}_q^{n_C}$, such that the projected set S_Δ^i, which contains the i-th coordinate of every element of S_Δ, has polynomial size. We also reorder the operations so that the protocols fit the (get), (init) model required for ZKP compilation (Definition 10). The subspace VOLE functionality we realize is in Fig. 2.

4.1   VOLE with Small-Domain Δ

The first step is to construct VOLE (that is, subspace VOLE where $n_C = k_C = 1$) from oblivious transfer. In Fig. 3, we've adapted the small field VOLE from SoftSpokenOT to work over an arbitrary field $\mathbb{F}_q$, as long as Δ is sampled from a polynomial-sized subset S_Δ. The security proof requires very few changes, so we have deferred it to the appendix.

Functionality $\mathcal{F}_{\text{sVOLE}}^{p,q,S_\Delta,\mathcal{C},\ell,\mathcal{L}}$

The functionality interacts with a sender $\mathcal{P}$, a receiver $\mathcal{V}$ and an adversary $\mathcal{A}$. It is parametrized by integers ℓ and p,q, such that $q = p^k$, as well as an $[n_{\mathcal{C}}, k_{\mathcal{C}}, d_{\mathcal{C}}]_p$ linear code $\mathcal{C}$ over $\mathbb{F}_p$ and a generator matrix $\mathbf{G}_{\mathcal{C}} \in \mathbb{F}_p^{k_{\mathcal{C}} \times n_{\mathcal{C}}}$ for $\mathcal{C}$.

1. Upon receiving (init) from $\mathcal{P}$ and $\mathcal{V}$, sample $\mathbf{U} \leftarrow \mathbb{F}_p^{\ell \times k_{\mathcal{C}}}$, $\mathbf{V} \leftarrow \mathbb{F}_q^{\ell \times n_{\mathcal{C}}}$ and $\Delta \leftarrow S_\Delta \subseteq \mathbb{F}_q^{n_{\mathcal{C}}}$ and set $\mathbf{Q} := \mathbf{V} + \mathbf{U}\mathbf{G}_{\mathcal{C}}\text{diag}(\Delta)$.
   - If $\mathcal{P}$ is corrupt, receive $\mathbf{U}, \mathbf{V}$ from $\mathcal{A}$, and recompute $\mathbf{Q}$ as above.
   - If $\mathcal{V}$ is corrupt, receive $\Delta, \mathbf{Q}$ from $\mathcal{A}$ and compute $\mathbf{V} := \mathbf{Q} - \mathbf{U}\mathbf{G}_{\mathcal{C}}\text{diag}(\Delta)$.
   - Send $(\mathbf{U}, \mathbf{V})$ to $\mathcal{P}$.
   - If $\mathcal{P}$ is corrupt, receive a leakage query $L \in \mathcal{L}$ from $\mathcal{A}$.
2. Upon receiving (get) from $\mathcal{V}$, if $\Delta \notin L$, send (check-failed) to $\mathcal{V}$ and abort. Otherwise, send $(\Delta, \mathbf{Q})$ to $\mathcal{V}$.

Fig. 2. Subspace VOLE functionality adapted from SoftSpokenOT [43]

Protocol $\Pi_{\text{small-VOLE}}^{p,q,S_\Delta,\ell}$

Requires $S_\Delta = \{f_1, \ldots, f_N\} \subseteq \mathbb{F}_q$, where $N = |S_\Delta| = \text{poly}(\lambda)$. Also requires $S_\Delta \setminus \{f_1\}$ to span $\mathbb{F}_q$, viewed as a vector space over $\mathbb{F}_p$. Let $\text{PRG} : \{0,1\}^\lambda \to \mathbb{F}_p^\ell$ be a PRG.

On (init), $\mathcal{P}$ does as follows:

1. Call $\mathcal{F}_{\text{OT-}\bar{1}}^{N,1}$ with (init), and receive the messages $s_1, \ldots, s_N \in \{0,1\}^\lambda$.
2. For $i \in [N]$, let $\mathbf{t}_{f_i} = \text{PRG}(s_i)$.
3. Compute and output $\mathbf{u} := \sum_{x \in S_\Delta} \mathbf{t}_x$ and $\mathbf{v} := -\sum_{x \in S_\Delta} \mathbf{t}_x x$.

On (init), $\mathcal{V}$ passes the (init) message on to $\mathcal{F}_{\text{OT-}\bar{1}}^{N,1}$.

On (get), $\mathcal{V}$ does as follows:

1. Sample $j \leftarrow [N]$, and let $\Delta = f_j$.
2. Call $\mathcal{F}_{\text{OT-}\bar{1}}^{N,1}$ with input (get, j), and receive s_i for $i \in [N] \setminus \{j\}$.
3. For $i \in [N] \setminus \{j\}$, let $\mathbf{t}_{f_i} := \text{PRG}(s_i)$.
4. Compute $\mathbf{q} := \sum_{x \in S_\Delta \setminus \{\Delta\}} \mathbf{t}_x(\Delta - x)$.
5. Output $(\Delta, \mathbf{q})$.

Fig. 3. VOLE protocol in the (init), (get) model, with Δ from a small domain S_Δ. Note that we notate the subspace VOLE here with vectors $\mathbf{u}$ instead of matrices $\mathbf{U}$, because they all only have 1 column.

Theorem 1. *The protocol $\Pi_{\text{small-VOLE}}^{p,q,S_\Delta,\ell}$ in Fig. 3 securely realizes $\mathcal{F}_{\text{sVOLE}}^{p,q,S_\Delta,\mathbb{F}_p,\ell,\{2^{S_\Delta}\}}$ in the $\mathcal{F}_{\text{OT-}\bar{1}}^{N,1}$-hybrid model, with malicious security.[5]*

Proof. See the full version.

---

[5] Note that setting $\mathcal{L} = \{2^{S_\Delta}\}$ is equivalent to no leakage, i.e., not allowing a corrupt $\mathcal{P}$ to perform a selective failure attack.

Protocol $\Pi_{\text{VOLE}}^{p,q,S_\Delta,\mathcal{C},\ell}$

$\mathcal{H} \subseteq \mathbb{F}_q^{r \times (\ell+h)}$ is a family of ℓ-hiding, ε-universal linear hash functions.
$\mathcal{L}$ must contain all single variable constraints: $\{\Delta \in S_\Delta \mid \Delta_i = y\} \in \mathcal{L}, \forall i, y$.

On (init), $\mathcal{P}$ and $\mathcal{V}$ run the following protocol:

1. $\mathcal{P}$ & $\mathcal{V}$: Send (init) to $\mathcal{F}_{\text{sVOLE}}^{p,q,S_\Delta,\mathbb{F}_p^{n_\mathcal{C}},\ell+h,\{2^{S_\Delta}\}}$.
2. $\mathcal{P}$: Receive $\mathbf{U}' \in \mathbb{F}_p^{(\ell+h) \times n_\mathcal{C}}$ and $\mathbf{V} \in \mathbb{F}_q^{(\ell+h) \times n_\mathcal{C}}$ from $\mathcal{F}_{\text{sVOLE}}^{p,q,S_\Delta,\mathbb{F}_p^{n_\mathcal{C}},\ell+h,\{2^{S_\Delta}\}}$.
3. $\mathcal{P}$: Compute $[\mathbf{U} \, \mathbf{C}] := \mathbf{U}'\mathbf{T}_\mathcal{C}^{-1}$ and send the correction $\mathbf{C} \in \mathbb{F}_q^{(\ell+h) \times (n_\mathcal{C} - k_\mathcal{C})}$.
4. $\mathcal{P}$: Output $(\mathbf{U}_{[1..\ell]}, \mathbf{V}_{[1..\ell]})$.
5. $\mathcal{V}$: Sample and send a uniformly random challenge $\mathbf{H} \leftarrow \mathcal{H}$.
6. $\mathcal{P}$: Send $\widetilde{\mathbf{U}} := \mathbf{H}\mathbf{U}$ and $\widetilde{\mathbf{V}} := \mathbf{H}\mathbf{V}$.

On (get), $\mathcal{V}$ does as follows:

1. Send (get) to $\mathcal{F}_{\text{sVOLE}}^{p,q,S_\Delta,\mathbb{F}_p^{n_\mathcal{C}},\ell+h,\{2^{S_\Delta}\}}$, and receive $\Delta \in S_\Delta$ and $\mathbf{Q}' = \mathbf{U}'\Delta + \mathbf{V}$.
2. Compute $\mathbf{Q} := \mathbf{Q}' - [0 \, \mathbf{C}]\mathbf{T}_\mathcal{C}\text{diag}(\Delta)$.
3. Abort if $\widetilde{\mathbf{V}} \neq \mathbf{H}\mathbf{Q} - \widetilde{\mathbf{U}}\mathbf{G}_\mathcal{C}\text{diag}(\Delta)$.
4. Output $(\Delta, \mathbf{Q}_{[1..\ell]})$.

Fig. 4. Subspace VOLE protocol in the (init), (get) model, with each Δ_i from a small domain S_Δ.

4.2 Subspace VOLE with Small-Domain Δ

From $\mathbb{F}_p$ subspace VOLE to $\mathbb{F}_p^n$. Suppose $S_\Delta = S_\Delta^1 \times \cdots \times S_\Delta^n$, where each $S_\Delta^i \subseteq \mathbb{F}_q$. By running n parallel instances of $\mathcal{F}_{\text{sVOLE}}^{p,q,S_\Delta^i,\mathbb{F}_p,\ell,\{2^{S_\Delta^i}\}}$, we can obtain a single instance of subspace[6] VOLE for S_Δ, where the vectors $\mathbf{u} \in \mathbb{F}_q^\ell, \mathbf{v} \in \mathbb{F}_q^\ell, \mathbf{q} \in \mathbb{F}_q^\ell$ have been stacked into matrices $\mathbf{U} \in \mathbb{F}_p^{\ell \times n}, \mathbf{V} \in \mathbb{F}_q^{\ell \times n}, \mathbf{Q} \in \mathbb{F}_q^{\ell \times n}$. This is exactly the functionality $\mathcal{F}_{\text{sVOLE}}^{p,q,S_\Delta,\mathbb{F}_p^n,\ell,\{2^{S_\Delta}\}}$. We skip the trivial security proof for this transformation.

From $\mathbb{F}_p^n$ VOLE to $\mathcal{C}$ subspace VOLE. However, we want to construct an *actual* subspace VOLE, where the rows of $\mathbf{U}$ can be constrained to lie in the subspace defined by an arbitrary linear code $\mathcal{C}$. When $\mathcal{P}$ is honest this is easily achieved with derandomization, but $\mathcal{P}$ could lie, leading to rows of $\mathbf{U}$ that are not in $\mathcal{C}$.

In Fig. 4, we adapt the SoftSpokenOT consistency check to our problem, rearranging the protocol to fit the (init), (get) model, and restricting Δ to be sampled from a subset $S_\Delta \subseteq \mathbb{F}_q^{n_\mathcal{C}}$. We've made two changes that drastically change the proof of security for malicious $\mathcal{V}$: first, Δ is sampled from an arbitrary set S_Δ, while SoftSpokenOT's analysis requires that Δ be uniform in a linear space, because it makes much use of Δ's distribution being invariant under invertible linear transformations.

---

[6] In this case, the "subspace" is just the whole vector space $\mathbb{F}_p^n$.

Second, we want our bound to be compatible with Fiat–Shamir, which lets the adversary restart the proof between sampling $\mathbf{H}$ and the consistency check as many times as it wants. This means that our analysis of the hash $\mathbf{H}$ must be independent of Δ, so we give a bad event for $\mathbf{H}$ and show that it's unlikely on its own, whether or not the adversary succeeds in guessing (part of) Δ. These two changes unfortunately make our bound looser than SoftSpokenOT's, but it is good enough to be practically useful.

Theorem 2. *The protocol* $\Pi_{\mathsf{small\text{-}VOLE}}^{p,q,S_\Delta,\mathcal{C},\ell}$ *in Fig. 4 securely realizes* $\mathcal{F}_{\mathsf{sVOLE}}^{p,q,S_\Delta,\mathcal{C},\ell,\mathcal{L}}$ *using* $\mathcal{F}_{\mathsf{sVOLE}}^{p,q,S_\Delta,\mathbb{F}_p^{n_\mathcal{C}},\ell+h,\{2^{S_\Delta}\}}$. *The distinguisher has advantage at most* $\varepsilon\binom{n_\mathcal{C}}{k_\mathcal{C}+1}$. *This advantage comes from a single bad event in the malicious* $\mathcal{P}$ *case that is decided once* $\mathbf{H}$ *is sampled.*

Proof. By comparing with the SoftSpokenOT subspace VOLE, notice that the adversary can only gain an additional advantage when $\mathcal{V}$ is honest. Indeed, when $\mathcal{V}$ is malicious, the underlying $\mathcal{F}_{\mathsf{sVOLE}}$ functionality lets the adversary choose Δ however it wants, so it makes no difference what distribution an honest $\mathcal{V}$ would sample Δ from.

Both Honest. This case follows easily from SoftSpokenOT's security proof, because the only change is to Δ's distribution. Δ is passed straight through from the underlying $\mathcal{F}_{\mathsf{sVOLE}}$ functionality, so our protocol's distribution is identical to conditioning SoftSpokenOT on Δ being in S_Δ. Because SoftSpokenOT is perfectly secure in the honest–honest case (in the $\mathcal{F}_{\mathsf{sVOLE}}$-hybrid model), our protocol then realizes $\mathcal{F}_{\mathsf{sVOLE}}^{p,q,\mathbb{F}_q^{n_\mathcal{C}},\mathcal{C},\ell,\mathcal{L}}$, but with the distribution conditioned on $\Delta \in S_\Delta$. This conditioned distribution is exactly the same as $\mathcal{F}_{\mathsf{sVOLE}}^{p,q,S_\Delta,\mathcal{C},\ell,\mathcal{L}}$.

Malicious $\mathcal{P}$. While our consistency-checking protocol is most directly based on SoftSpokenOT, for this case our simulator and proof also take inspiration from OOS [40]. In particular, our proof is based on erasure decoding, like with OOS. SoftSpokenOT pointed out an error in OOS's proof, so to use their proof technique we will need to patch this error. We will use a union bound to fix the problem, which is why our security bound is considerably looser than OOS's.

We present the simulator in Fig. 5. The simulator first extracts $\mathbf{U}''$, the derandomization of $\mathbf{U}'$, and samples a challenge $\mathbf{H}$. Based on $\mathbf{U}''$, $\mathbf{H}$, and the errors $(\tilde{\mathbf{U}}, \tilde{\mathbf{V}})$ in the adversary's consistency check messages $(\tilde{\mathbf{U}}, \tilde{\mathbf{V}})$, we can rewrite the consistency check as follows.

$$\tilde{\mathbf{V}} = \mathbf{HQ} - \tilde{\mathbf{U}}\mathbf{G}_\mathcal{C}\mathrm{diag}(\Delta)$$
$$\tilde{\mathbf{V}} = \mathbf{HV} + \mathbf{HU}''\mathrm{diag}(\Delta) - \tilde{\mathbf{U}}\mathbf{G}_\mathcal{C}\mathrm{diag}(\Delta)$$
$$-\bar{\mathbf{V}} = \bar{\mathbf{U}}\,\mathrm{diag}(\Delta)$$

From this equation, the simulator extracts guesses Δ_i^* for Δ_i for all i in a subset G of the columns. The consistency check is equivalent to the correctness of these guesses.

The guessed columns G represent lies that the adversary has made while derandomizing $\mathbf{U}$. The simulator attempts to extract $\mathcal{P}$'s real output $\mathbf{U}^*$ by erasure decoding $\mathbf{U}''$ using only the columns that are not in G, hoping that these

---

On (init) sent to $\mathcal{F}_{\text{sVOLE}}^{p,q,S_\Delta,\mathbb{F}_p^{n_C},\ell+h,\{2^{S_\Delta}\}}$:

1. Receive $\mathbf{U}', \mathbf{V}$ from $\mathcal{A}$ and send them to $\mathcal{P}$.
2. Receive $\mathbf{C}$ from $\mathcal{P}$.
3. Compute the derandomization $\mathbf{U}'' := \mathbf{U}' - [0\,\mathbf{C}]\mathbf{T}_{\mathcal{C}}$. We have:

$$\begin{aligned}
\mathbf{Q} &= \mathbf{Q}' - [0\,\mathbf{C}]\mathbf{T}_{\mathcal{C}}\text{diag}(\Delta) \\
&= \mathbf{V} + \mathbf{U}'\text{diag}(\Delta) - [0\,\mathbf{C}]\mathbf{T}_{\mathcal{C}}\text{diag}(\Delta) \\
&= \mathbf{V} + \mathbf{U}''\text{diag}(\Delta).
\end{aligned}$$

4. Sample and send a uniformly random challenge $\mathbf{H} \leftarrow \mathcal{H}$ to $\mathcal{P}$.
5. Receive the response $\widetilde{\mathbf{U}}$ and $\widetilde{\mathbf{V}}$ from $\mathcal{P}$.
6. Compute the response errors: $\bar{\mathbf{U}} := \mathbf{H}\mathbf{U}'' - \widetilde{\mathbf{U}}\mathbf{G}_{\mathcal{C}}$ and $\bar{\mathbf{V}} := \mathbf{H}\mathbf{V} - \widetilde{\mathbf{V}}$.
7. The consistency checking equation is $-\bar{\mathbf{V}} = \bar{\mathbf{U}}\,\text{diag}(\Delta)$. Abort if no solutions for Δ exist. Otherwise, there exists a set G of guessed columns (the nonzero columns of $\bar{\mathbf{U}}$) and values Δ_i^* such that the solution set is $\{\Delta \in S_\Delta \mid \forall i \in G. \Delta_i = \Delta_i^*\}$.
8. Decode $\mathbf{U}''_{-G}$ with $\mathcal{C}_{-G}$ to get $\mathbf{U}^* \in \mathbb{F}_p^{\ell \times k_C}$, aborting if any row of $\mathbf{U}''_{-G}$ isn't in $\mathcal{C}_{-G}$.
9. Recover $\mathbf{V}^* := \mathbf{V} + (\mathbf{U}'' - \mathbf{U}^*\mathbf{G}_{\mathcal{C}})\text{diag}(\Delta^*)$ from the adversary's guesses. We have $\mathbf{V}^* = \mathbf{V} + \mathbf{U}''\text{diag}(\Delta) - \mathbf{U}^*\mathbf{G}_{\mathcal{C}}\text{diag}(\Delta) = \mathbf{Q} - \mathbf{U}^*\mathbf{G}_{\mathcal{C}}\text{diag}(\Delta)$ if the consistency check passes, because $\mathbf{U}'' - \mathbf{U}^*\mathbf{G}_{\mathcal{C}}$ is zero except for the columns in G, and $\Delta_i = \Delta_i^*$ for $i \in G$.
10. Send $\{\Delta \in S_\Delta \mid \forall i \in G. \Delta_i = \Delta_i^*\}$ to $\mathcal{L}$ to $\mathcal{F}_{\text{sVOLE}}^{p,q,S_\Delta,\mathcal{C},\ell,\mathcal{L}}$.
11. Send $\mathbf{U}^*_{[1..\ell]}, \mathbf{V}^*_{[1..\ell]}$ to $\mathcal{F}_{\text{sVOLE}}^{p,q,S_\Delta,\mathcal{C},\ell,\mathcal{L}}$.

Fig. 5. Simulator for $\Pi_{\text{small-VOLE}}^{p,q,S_\Delta,\mathcal{C},\ell}$ with malicious $\mathcal{P}$.

---

columns represent the truth about $\mathbf{U}$, as the erasure removes the lies present in the consistency check. That is, let $\mathcal{C}_{-G}$ be the punctured code created by removing all columns in G from $\mathcal{C}$, and let $\mathbf{U}''_{-G}$ be the corresponding punctured matrix. If $|G| \geq d_{\mathcal{C}}$, then $\mathcal{C}_{-G}$ may have 0 minimum distance, which means that decoding isn't unique; it is sufficient to pick an arbitrary decoding. The simulator can then extract the $\mathcal{P}$'s other real output $\mathbf{V}^*$ as $\mathbf{V} + (\mathbf{U}'' - \mathbf{U}^*\mathbf{G}_{\mathcal{C}})\text{diag}(\Delta^*)$, using that $\mathbf{U}''$ must match $\mathbf{U}^*\mathbf{G}_{\mathcal{C}}$ on all columns that were not erased, and that $\Delta_i = \Delta_i^*$ for the erased columns $i \in G$. If this all works, the simulation is perfect – the consistency check is correctly represented by the leakage test, and $(\mathbf{U}^*, \mathbf{V}^*, \mathbf{Q}, \Delta)$ satisfy the subspace VOLE correlation.

The flaw is that some lies might not be present in the consistency check. That is, there may be some row of $\mathbf{U}''_{-G}$ that isn't in $\mathcal{C}_{-G}$, making the erasure decoding fail. The simulator aborts in this case. Next we present a bad event that must occur for the erasure decoding to fail, and then bound it's probability. This bad event is described in terms of the set of all circuits $\mathcal{C}$ in the matroid represented by the columns of $\mathbf{G}_{\mathcal{C}}$. Recall that the definition of a circuit in a matroid is a set c that is linearly dependent, and is minimal in the sense that all proper subsets are independent. That is, $\mathcal{C}$ is the collection of all subsets c of columns of $\mathbf{G}_{\mathcal{C}}$ such that c is linearly dependent, but every $c' \subsetneq c$ is linearly independent.

Bad Event: For all $c \in \mathcal{C}$, all rows of $\mathbf{U}''_c$ must be in $\mathcal{C}_c$ (the punctured code containing only the columns in c) if and only if the rows of $\mathbf{HU}''_c$ are all in $\mathcal{C}_c$. The bad event triggers if this does not hold.

The simulator fails if a row $\mathbf{u}_{-G}$ of $\mathbf{U}''_{-G}$ is not in $\mathcal{C}_{-G}$. For this to occur, there must be some vector $\mathbf{p}_{-G}$ in column space of the parity check matrix $\mathbf{P}_{\mathcal{C}_{-G}}$ of $\mathcal{C}_{-G}$ (equivalently, $\mathbf{p}_{-G}$ is in the null space of $\mathbf{G}_{\mathcal{C}_{-G}}$) such that $\mathbf{u}_{-G} \cdot \mathbf{p}_{-G} \neq 0$. Out of all such $\mathbf{p}_{-G}$, pick a maximally sparse $\mathbf{p}_{-G}$, minimizing the number of nonzero entries. The set c of nonzero entries of $\mathbf{p}_{-G}$ forms a circuit in $\mathcal{C}$. The parity check matrix $\mathbf{P}_{\mathcal{C}_c}$ of $\mathcal{C}_c$ is then $\mathbf{p}_c$. We have $\mathbf{u}_c \cdot \mathbf{p}_c = \mathbf{u}_{-G} \cdot \mathbf{p}_{-G} \neq 0$, yet $\mathbf{HU}''_c \mathbf{p}_c = \mathbf{HU}''_{-G} \mathbf{p}_{-G} = 0$, because the rows of $\mathbf{HU}''_{-G}$ are in $\mathcal{C}_{-G}$. Therefore, the rows of $\mathbf{HU}''_c$ are in $\mathcal{C}_c$, but the rows of $\mathbf{U}''_c$ are not all in $\mathcal{C}_c$, so the bad event must trigger.

Next, we bound the probability of the bad event occurring for any fixed $c \in \mathcal{C}$. Let $\mathbf{p}_c \in \mathbb{F}_p^{|c|}$ be the parity check matrix of $\mathcal{C}_c$, i.e., a vector such that $\mathbf{u}_c \in \mathcal{C}_c$ if and only if $\mathbf{u}_c \cdot \mathbf{p}_c = 0$. Then all rows of $\mathbf{U}''_c$ are in $\mathcal{C}_c$ if and only if $\mathbf{U}''_c \mathbf{p}_c = 0$, and similarly all rows of $\mathbf{HU}''_c$ are all in $\mathcal{C}_c$ if and only if $\mathbf{HU}''_c \mathbf{p}_c = 0$. The first clearly implies the second, so we only need to bound the probability that $\mathbf{U}''_c \mathbf{u}_p \neq 0$ but $\mathbf{HU}''_c \mathbf{p}_c = 0$. Since $\mathbf{H}$ is sampled from an ε-almost universal family, if $\mathbf{U}''_c \mathbf{p}_c \neq 0$ we have that $\Pr[\mathbf{HU}''_c \mathbf{p}_c = 0] \leq \varepsilon$.

Finally, $|\mathcal{C}| \leq \binom{n_C}{k_C+1}$ [24, Theorem 2.1], so a union bound shows that the bad event occurs with probability at most $\varepsilon \binom{n_C}{k_C+1}$.

5 Zero-Knowledge from Generalized Subspace VOLE

We give two instantiations of the compiler from Sect. 3, by presenting two public coin, interactive ZK protocols in the $\mathcal{F}_{\mathsf{sVOLE}}$-hybrid model. The first one allows to prove statements over large fields using the generalized subspace VOLE given in Sect. 4. We start by describing a general ZK protocol for degree-2 relations, $\Pi^t_{\mathsf{2D-LC}}$, as specified in Fig. 6 and, in the full version, we show how to generalize it to any degree-d polynomials, for small d.

Our second protocol, $\Pi^t_{\mathsf{2D-Rep}}$, can be seen as a variant of the QuickSilver protocol [47] and is more tailored for proving statements over small fields. It permits to prove degree-2 constraints over any extension field $\mathbb{F}_{2^r}$. The protocol is described in the full version and its security is stated in Theorem 4.

5.1 ZK for Degree-2 Relations from Generalized sVOLE

Our 7-round ZK protocol for degree-2 relations allows for circuit satisfiability over any large field, while also cheaply proving useful operations like inner products, without unrolling them to a circuit. We highlight that the protocol uses subspace VOLE for a general code, rather than the trivial 1-dimensional code $\mathbb{F}_p$ (or the repetition code) used in previous VOLE-based ZK constructions [7,47]. The main challenge here is that, while VOLE with the repetition code can be

---

Protocol $\Pi^t_{\text{2D-LC}}$

The protocol is parametrized by an $[n_\mathcal{C}, k_\mathcal{C}, d_\mathcal{C}]_p$ linear code $\mathcal{C}$, set $S_\Delta = (S'_\Delta)^{n_\mathcal{C}} \subset \mathbb{F}_p^{n_\mathcal{C}}$ and a leakage space $\mathcal{L}$ (used in $\mathcal{F}_{\text{sVOLE}}$). INPUTS: Both parties hold a set of polynomials $f_i \in \mathbb{F}_p[X_1, \ldots, X_{k_\mathcal{C}\ell}]_{\leq 2}$, $i \in [t]$. $\mathcal{P}$ also holds a witness $\mathbf{w} \in \mathbb{F}_p^{k_\mathcal{C}\ell}$ such that $f_i(\mathbf{w}) = 0$, for all $i \in [t]$.

Round 1. $\mathcal{P}$ does as follows:
1. $\mathcal{P}$ and $\mathcal{V}$ call $\mathcal{F}_{\text{sVOLE}}^{p,p,S_\Delta,\mathcal{C},2\ell+1,\mathcal{L}}$, $\mathcal{P}$ receives $\mathbf{U} \in \mathbb{F}_p^{(2\ell+2)\times k_\mathcal{C}}, \mathbf{V} \in \mathbb{F}_p^{(2\ell+2)\times n_\mathcal{C}}$, while $\mathcal{V}$ gets the message done.
2. $\mathcal{P}$ sets $\mathbf{V}_1 = \mathbf{V}_{[1..\ell+1]}$, $\mathbf{V}_2 = \mathbf{V}_{[\ell+2..2\ell+2]}$ and $\mathbf{R} = \mathbf{U}_{[\ell+2..2\ell+2]}$
3. $\mathcal{P}$ commits to its witness by sending $\mathbf{D} = \mathbf{W} - \mathbf{U}_{[1..\ell]}$.

Round 2. $\mathcal{V}$ samples $\chi \leftarrow \mathbb{F}_p^t$ and sends it to $\mathcal{P}$.

Round 3. $\mathcal{P}$ proceeds as follows.
1. For each $i \in [t]$, compute

$$g_i(Y) := \sum_{h \in [0,2]} f_{i,h}(\mathbf{r}_1 + \mathbf{w}_1 \cdot Y, \ldots, \mathbf{r}_\ell + \mathbf{w}_\ell \cdot Y) \cdot Y^{2-h}$$
$$= \sum_{h \in [0,1]} A_{i,h} \cdot Y^h$$

2. Compute $\widetilde{\mathbf{b}} = \sum_{i \in [t]} \chi_i \cdot A_{i,0} + \mathbf{r}_{\ell+1}$ and $\widetilde{\mathbf{a}} = \sum_{i \in [t]} \chi_i \cdot A_{i,1} + \mathbf{u}_{1,\ell+1}$, where $\mathbf{u}_{1,i}$ is the ith row of $\mathbf{U}$.
3. Send $(\widetilde{\mathbf{b}}, \widetilde{\mathbf{a}})$ to $\mathcal{V}$.

Round 4. $\mathcal{V}$ samples $\Delta' \leftarrow \mathbb{F}_p$ and sends it to the prover.

Round 5. $\mathcal{P}$ sends $\mathbf{S} = \mathbf{R} + \mathbf{U}_{[1..\ell+1]} \cdot \Delta' \in \mathbb{F}_p^{(\ell+1)\times n_\mathcal{C}}$ to $\mathcal{V}$

Round 6. $\mathcal{V}$ samples $\eta \leftarrow \mathbb{F}_p^{\ell+1}$ and sends it to $\mathcal{P}$

Round 7. $\mathcal{P}$ computes $\widetilde{\mathbf{v}} = \eta^\top (\mathbf{V}_2 + \mathbf{V}_1 \cdot \Delta')$ and sends it to $\mathcal{V}$.

Verification. $\mathcal{V}$ runs the following checks.
1. *Check the constraints:*
   - Compute $\mathbf{S}' = \mathbf{S} + \begin{bmatrix} \mathbf{D} \\ 0 \end{bmatrix} \cdot \Delta' = \mathbf{R} + \begin{bmatrix} \mathbf{W} \\ \mathbf{u}_{\ell+1} \end{bmatrix} \cdot \Delta'$.
   - For each $i \in [t]$, compute

$$\mathbf{c}_i(Y) = \sum_{h \in [0,2]} f_{i,h}(\mathbf{s}'_1, \ldots, \mathbf{s}'_\ell) \cdot Y^{2-h}.$$

   - Let $\widetilde{\mathbf{s}} = \sum_{i \in [t]} \chi_i \cdot \mathbf{c}_i(\Delta') + \mathbf{s}'_{\ell+1}$.
   - Check that $\widetilde{\mathbf{s}} = \widetilde{\mathbf{b}} + \widetilde{\mathbf{a}} \cdot \Delta'$.
2. *Check the opening of $\mathbf{S}$:*
   - Call $\mathcal{F}_{\text{sVOLE}}^{p,p,S_\Delta,\mathcal{C},2\ell+1,\mathcal{L}}$ on input (get) and obtain $\Delta \in S_\Delta$ and $\mathbf{Q} \in \mathbb{F}_p^{(2\ell+2)\times n_\mathcal{C}}$ such that $\mathbf{Q} = \mathbf{V} + \mathcal{C}(\mathbf{U}) \cdot \text{diag}(\Delta)$
   - Set $\mathbf{Q}_1 = \mathbf{Q}_{[1..\ell+1]}$ and $\mathbf{Q}_2 = \mathbf{Q}_{[\ell+2..2\ell+2]}$.
   - Check that

$$\eta^\top (\mathbf{Q}_2 + \mathbf{Q}_1 \cdot \Delta') = \widetilde{\mathbf{v}} + \eta^\top \cdot \mathcal{C}(\mathbf{S}) \cdot \text{diag}(\Delta)$$

Fig. 6. ZK for Arbitrary Degree-2 Relation

viewed as a linearly homomorphic commitment scheme for messages in $\mathbb{F}_p$, with a general code, we only get a restricted form of homomorphic commitment to vectors in $\mathbb{F}_p^{k_\mathcal{C}}$, where linear operations must be applied across the vectors.

We let $\mathcal{C}$ be an $[n_\mathcal{C}, k_\mathcal{C}, d_\mathcal{C}]_p$ linear code with large enough distance, which for simplicity is given in systematic form. We assume the witness $\mathbf{w}$ can be divided into ℓ vectors $(\mathbf{w}_1, \ldots, \mathbf{w}_\ell) \in (\mathbb{F}_p^{k_\mathcal{C}})^\ell$, where we also write $\mathbf{w} \in \mathbb{F}_p^{k_\mathcal{C}\ell}$ to mean the concatenation of these vectors. Let $\mathbb{F}_p[X]_{\leq 2} := \mathbb{F}_p[X_1, \ldots, X_{k_\mathcal{C}\ell}]_{\leq 2}$ be the set of polynomials over $\mathbb{F}_p$ in $k_\mathcal{C}\ell$ variables with degree at most 2. Notice each $f_i \in \mathbb{F}_p[X]_{\leq 2}$ can be written as $f_i = f_{i,0} + f_{i,1} + f_{i,2}$ such that $\deg(f_{i,h}) = h$. The prover $\mathcal{P}$ wants to prove that $f_i(\mathbf{w}) = 0$, for $i \in [t]$. Here we consider the case where p is large.

The intuition of the scheme is as follows. Let S'_Δ be a polynomially sized subset of $\mathbb{F}_p$ and $S_\Delta = (S'_\Delta)^{n_\mathcal{C}}$. First, both $\mathcal{P}$ and $\mathcal{V}$ call the subspace VOLE functionality $\mathcal{F}_{\mathsf{sVOLE}}^{p,\mathcal{C},S_\Delta,2\ell+2,\mathcal{L}}$, so that $\mathcal{P}$ receives the matrices $\mathbf{U} \in \mathbb{F}_p^{(2\ell+2) \times k_\mathcal{C}}, \mathbf{V} \in \mathbb{F}_p^{(2\ell+2) \times n_\mathcal{C}}$, while the verifier $\mathcal{V}$ gets the notification done. Let $\mathbf{W}$ be the $\ell \times k_\mathcal{C}$ matrix whose ith are $\mathbf{w}_i$. The idea is to use the first $\ell + 1$ rows of the output of the ideal functionality to commit to the witness, and the remaining $\ell + 1$ rows as auxiliary random commitments. More precisely, we split the matrices as

$$\mathbf{V} = \begin{pmatrix} \mathbf{V}_1 \\ \mathbf{V}_2 \end{pmatrix} \quad \text{and} \quad \mathbf{U} = \begin{pmatrix} \mathbf{U}_1 \\ \mathbf{R} \end{pmatrix},$$

where each sub-matrix consists of $\ell + 1$ rows. Hence, $\mathcal{P}$ commits to the witness by sending $\mathbf{D} = \mathbf{W} - \mathbf{U}_{1,[1..\ell]}$.

The idea is that $\mathcal{P}$ will run a VOLE-based ZK proof "in-the-head", as if $\mathbf{U}_1$ and $\mathbf{R}$ were a set of VOLE outputs where $\mathcal{V}$ held $\mathbf{S} = \mathbf{R}_1 + \mathbf{U}_1 \cdot \Delta'$ for some random $\Delta' \in \mathbb{F}_p$. Even though $\mathcal{V}$ does not (yet) have $\mathbf{S}$, it can send a random challenge for the proof and get the prover's response. We then have $\mathcal{V}$ send a random Δ', and have $\mathcal{P}$ open $\mathbf{S}$ so that $\mathcal{V}$ can check the proof. $\mathcal{V}$ can verify that $\mathbf{S}$ was opened reliably using the original subspace VOLE instance — if $\mathcal{P}$ tries to cheat, it must guess at least $d_\mathcal{C}$ entries of the secret $\Delta \in S_\Delta$.

The underlying VOLE-based proof that is run in-head is essentially the same as the protocol for proving degree-2 constraints from QuickSilver [47], and can be seen in round 3 (for $\mathcal{P}$) and the first part of round 7 (for $\mathcal{V}$). Once $\mathcal{P}$ receives the random challenge $\chi \leftarrow \mathbb{F}_p^t$ it computes:

$$g_i(Y) = \sum_{h \in [0,2]} f_{i,h}(\mathbf{r}_1 + \mathbf{w}_1 \cdot Y, \ldots, \mathbf{r}_\ell + \mathbf{w}_\ell \cdot Y) \cdot Y^{2-h}$$

$$= \sum_{h \in [0,2]} f_{i,h}(\mathbf{w}_1, \ldots, \mathbf{w}_\ell) \cdot Y^2 + \sum_{h \in [0,1]} A_{i,h} \cdot Y^h$$

$$= f_i(\mathbf{w}_1, \ldots, \mathbf{w}_\ell) \cdot Y^2 + \sum_{h \in [0,1]} A_{i,h} \cdot Y^h,$$

where $A_{i,h} \in \mathbb{F}_p^{k_\mathcal{C}}$ is the aggregated coefficient of Y^h. The key observation is that, if the prover $\mathcal{P}$ is honest, then $f_i(\mathbf{w}_1, \ldots, \mathbf{w}_\ell) = 0$ and $g_i(Y) = \sum_{h \in [0,1]} A_{i,h} \cdot Y^h$.

Using the challenge χ, $\mathcal{P}$ computes and sends to $\mathcal{V}$

$$\widetilde{\mathbf{a}} = \sum_{i \in [t]} \chi_i \cdot A_{i,1} + \mathbf{u}_{1,\ell+1} \qquad \widetilde{\mathbf{b}} = \sum_{i \in [t]} \chi_i \cdot A_{i,0} + \mathbf{r}_{\ell+1},$$

where $\mathbf{u}_{\ell+1}$ and $\mathbf{r}_{\ell+1}$ are extra rows of the original VOLE output used to mask the check values.

Next, $\mathcal{V}$ sends a challenge $\Delta' \in \mathbb{F}_p$ to $\mathcal{P}$, who opens the matrix $\mathbf{S} = \mathbf{R} + \mathbf{U}_{[1..\ell+1]} \cdot \Delta'$. This will be used as $\mathcal{V}$'s "VOLE-in-the-head" output, to check the QuickSilver proof values just sent by $\mathcal{P}$. First, though, it needs $\mathcal{P}$ to prove that $\mathbf{S}$ was sent correctly. To do this, $\mathcal{V}$ sends the last challenge $\boldsymbol{\eta} \leftarrow \mathbb{F}_p^{\ell+1}$, and gets $\widetilde{\mathbf{v}} = \boldsymbol{\eta}^\top (\mathbf{V}_2 + \mathbf{V}_1 \cdot \Delta')$ in response.[7] This is later verified in the second part of round 7, once $\mathcal{V}$ learns the subspace VOLE output $\mathbf{Q} = \mathbf{V} + \mathcal{C}(\mathbf{U}) \cdot \mathrm{diag}(\Delta)$. $\mathcal{V}$ can then use this to check the subspace VOLE relation between $\widetilde{\mathbf{v}}$ and $\boldsymbol{\eta}^\top \mathcal{C}(\mathbf{S})$, ensuring that $\mathbf{S}$ was correctly sent.

In the first part of the verification, $\mathcal{V}$ first computes

$$\mathbf{S}' = \mathbf{S} + \begin{bmatrix} \mathbf{D} \\ \mathbf{0} \end{bmatrix} \cdot \Delta',$$

to adjust its subspace VOLE output to be a valid commitment to the prover's input $\mathbf{W}$. It then uses the rows of $\mathbf{S}'$ to compute polynomials $c_i(Y)$, similarly to the prover's polynomials $g_i(Y)$. These are used to check the constraints, by taking a linear combination and verifying that they form a valid VOLE correlation.

We can formally prove the result below (See the full version for the proof).

Theorem 3. *The protocol Π_{2D-LC}^t (Fig. 6) is a SHVZKPoK for arbitrary degree-2 relations with soundness error $3/p + 2|S'_\Delta|^{-d_C}$ in the $\mathcal{F}_{sVOLE}^{p,S_\Delta,\mathcal{C},2(\ell+2),\mathcal{L}}$-hybrid model.*

Communication cost. In Π_{2D-LC}^t, given in Fig. 6, other than the cost of the sVOLE step, the prover has to send the initial commitment, consisting of a matrix in $\mathbb{F}_p^{\ell \times k_C}$, then two vectors in $\mathbb{F}_p^{k_C}$, one vectors in $\mathbb{F}_p^{n_C}$ and finally a matrix in $\mathbb{F}_q^{\ell \times k_C}$. Summing up the cost is

$$\mathsf{CommCost}_{\Pi_{2D-LC}^t} = \mathsf{CommCost}_{sVOLE} + (2\ell + 2) \cdot \left(k_C \cdot \log_2 p \right) + n_C \cdot \log_2 p.$$

Note that is roughly 2 times the cost of QuickSilver and other VOLE-based protocols in the designated-verifier setting. Using our protocol from Sect. 4, $\mathsf{CommCost}_{sVOLE}$ is dominated by $\ell \cdot (n_C - k_C)$ field elements, so this part is sublinear in the witness length ($\ell \cdot k_C$) if $\mathcal{C}$ has a good enough rate.

---

[7] The challenge $\boldsymbol{\eta}$ is only used to save communication. $\mathcal{P}$ could instead directly send $\mathbf{V}_2 + \mathbf{V}_1 \cdot \Delta$ for $\mathcal{V}$ to check.

5.2   ZK for Degree-2 from Small-Sized sVOLE

For small fields, the previous protocol would not perform so well, since we'd need many repetitions to achieve a good soundness error. Instead, a better approach is to adopt the QuickSilver protocol [47] with subspace VOLE based on the $[\tau, 1, \tau]$ repetition code. This avoids the need for the code-switching step of the previous protocol, with the additional Δ' challenge, since the ZK proof can be done directly on repetition coded VOLE.

To help with our AES use-case, we generalize QuickSilver slightly to allow for proving constraints over an extension field $\mathbb{F}_{p^k}$, even when the witness is committed over $\mathbb{F}_p$. We refer the reader to the full version for a complete description of the protocol and proof of the following theorem.

Theorem 4. *The protocol $\Pi_{2D\text{-Rep}}^t$ is a SHVZKPoK for arbitrary degree-2 relations with soundness error $1/p^{r\tau} + 2|S_\Delta|^{-1}$ in the $\mathcal{F}_{sVOLE}^{p,q,\tau,\ell+\tau r}$-hybrid model.*

We can extend both $\Pi_{2D\text{-LC}}^t$ and $\Pi_{2D\text{-Rep}}^t$ to handle degree-d relations, for small d, with the technique mentioned above and described in the full version.

6   FAEST: AES-Based Signature

We can use our non-interactive zero-knowledge protocol, obtained by applying the methodology described in Sect. 3.3 with the ZK scheme from small-sized subspace VOLE of Sect. 5.2 to build a Picnic-like post-quantum signature scheme based on AES.

More precisely, given a block cipher E, AES in our case, we define a family of one-way functions (OWF) $\{f_x\}$ such that $f_x(k) = E_k(x)$, where $E_k(x)$ denotes the encryption of x under the key k. In this way, the private key k and public values (x, y), with x sampled uniformly at random and $y = E_k(x)$, define the OWF relation $((x, y), k) \in R \iff E_k(x) = y$. Hence, a signature on a message μ is generated by binding μ with a non-interactive zero-knowledge proof of knowledge of k.

Recent works, starting with [17,29], have used this approach to build efficient post-quantum secure signatures from MPCitH-based non-interactive zero-knowledge schemes [33]. One such scheme is Picnic [17,37] which is a third-round alternate candidate for the NIST post-quantum standardization process. While Picnic relies on the LowMC block cipher [2] as the underlying OWF, a non-standard assumption, more recent works replaced LowMC with AES [20] or other well-studied problems such as the syndrome decoding (SD) [27].

Another scheme solely based on symmetric-key primitives is SPHINCS+ [32] which is one of three recently standardized by NIST, while the other two, Falcon [42] and Dilithium [39] are based on public-key lattice problems.

In the rest of this section, we first describe our signature scheme, FAEST, in more detail and then compare it to other post-quantum secure schemes.

6.1   The **FAEST** Signature Scheme

The main tool to build our signature scheme is a NIZK scheme, Π_{FAEST}, obtained by applying the Fiat–Shamir transform as described in Sect. 3.3 to the QuickSilver-style protocol $\Pi_{\mathsf{2D\text{-}Rep\text{-}OT}}$ set in the $\mathcal{F}_{\mathsf{OT\text{-}\bar{1}}}$-hybrid model, given by composing $\Pi^t_{\mathsf{2D\text{-}Rep}}$ of the full version with $\Pi^{p,q,S_\Delta,\mathcal{C},\ell}_{\mathsf{small\text{-}VOLE}}$ of Fig. 4, where $S_\Delta = \mathbb{F}_q$, $q = p^r$, $\mathcal{C} = \mathcal{C}_{\mathsf{Rep}} = [\tau, 1, \tau]$ and $\mathcal{H}$ is an ε-universal hash family such that $\varepsilon\binom{\tau}{2} \leq 2/p^{r\tau}$. In particular, we prove the following result.

Theorem 5. *The Π_{FAEST} protocol, defined as*

$$\Pi_{\mathsf{FAEST}} = \mathsf{FS}^{H_{\mathsf{FS}}}[\mathsf{O2C}^{H_{\mathsf{O2C}}}[\Pi_{\mathsf{2D\text{-}Rep\text{-}OT}}]],$$

is a zero-knowledge non-interactive proof system in the CRS+RO model with knowledge error

$$2 \cdot (Q_{\mathsf{FS}} + Q_{\mathsf{Verify}}) \cdot \frac{2}{p^{r\tau}} + M \cdot (Q_{\mathsf{FS}} + Q_{\mathsf{Verify}}) \cdot \mathsf{AdvEB}^{\mathsf{VC}}_{\mathcal{A}'}[Q_{H_{\mathsf{O2C}}}]$$
$$+ \mathsf{AdvDist}^{\mathsf{VC.Setup},\mathsf{VC.TSetup}}_{\mathcal{D}},$$

where M is an upper bound on the number of VC commitments sent during a run of $\mathsf{O2C}[\Pi_{\mathsf{2D\text{-}Rep\text{-}OT}}]$.

Proof. We apply our Fiat–Shamir security Lemma from the full version to the composed protocol $\Pi_{\mathsf{2D\text{-}Rep\text{-}OT}}$ in the $\mathcal{F}_{\mathsf{OT\text{-}\bar{1}}}$-hybrid model. First, by looking at the init phase of $\Pi_{\mathsf{small\text{-}VOLE}}$, we see that the sending of $\widetilde{\mathbf{U}}$ and $\widetilde{\mathbf{V}}$ by the prover can be combined with the sending of $\mathbf{d}$ from $\Pi^t_{\mathsf{2D\text{-}Rep}}$. The combined protocol $\Pi_{\mathsf{2D\text{-}Rep\text{-}OT}}$ therefore contains a total of $\mu = 2$ verifier messages and runs in a total of $2\mu+1 = 5$ rounds. Next, we analyse the round-by-round knowledge error κ of $\Pi_{\mathsf{2D\text{-}Rep\text{-}OT}}$.

1. When the prover sends the correction $\mathbf{C}$ in $\Pi_{\mathsf{small\text{-}VOLE}}$, the probability that applying the universal hash $\mathbf{H} \leftarrow \mathcal{H}$ hides any cheating in $\mathbf{U}$ and $\mathbf{V}$ is $\varepsilon\binom{\tau}{2}$, where $\mathcal{H}$ is ε-universal.
2. Similarly, when the prover sends the correction $\mathbf{d}$ in $\Pi^t_{\mathsf{2D\text{-}Rep}}$, the probability that the random challenges χ_i hide a non-zero result of the constraint system is $1/p^{r\tau}$.
3. Given the responses $\tilde{a}, \tilde{b}$ for $\Pi^t_{\mathsf{2D\text{-}Rep}}$ and $\widetilde{\mathbf{U}}\widetilde{\mathbf{V}}$ for $\Pi_{\mathsf{small\text{-}VOLE}}$, the probability that the implicit challenge Δ hides errors in both of these at the same time is upper-bounded by the probability it hides errors in $\tilde{a}, \tilde{b}$ and is therefore at most $2/p^{r\tau}$.

Since $\mathcal{H}$ is such that $\varepsilon\binom{\tau}{2} \leq 2/p^{r\tau}$, this gives $\kappa = 2/p^{r\tau}$ as round-by-round knowledge error.

Finally, since both $\Pi_{\mathsf{small\text{-}VOLE}}$ and $\Pi^t_{\mathsf{2D\text{-}Rep}}$ are SHVZK, then the FS-transformed compiled protocol is indeed a NIZK in the programmable ROM.   □

To implement the signature scheme FAEST, we expressed the AES-128 algorithm, including its key schedule, as a set of $200°$-2 constraints over an extension $\mathbb{F}_{q^\tau}$ of $\mathbb{F}_{2^8}$. Since the AES S-box is a field inversion over $\mathbb{F}_{2^8}$ (for non-zero inputs), each constraint checks that the output of each inversion is the valid inverse of a linear combination of the outputs of the previous layer, where this linear combination represents the AES linear layer.

6.2 Implementation

We implemented FAEST in Rust for AES-128 using $\mathbb{F}_{2^{128}}$ as well as the fields $\mathbb{F}_q$ with $q = 2^7, \ldots, 2^{11}$. In the implementation we used AES in counter mode and ChaCha20 as PRGs and the Blake3 hash and extendable output function. We ran our experiments on an Intel Core i9-9900 CPU. For comparison, we also benchmarked Limbo [21] and SPHINCS+ [32] on the same hardware. The runtimes and signatures sizes for FAEST are given in Table 2.

Table 2. Runtimes for signing and verification as well as signature sizes for FAEST with AES-128 and $\lambda = 128$.

q	$t_{\mathcal{P}}$ in ms	$t_{\mathcal{V}}$ in ms	$|\mathsf{sign}|$ in B
2^7	2.631253318	2.430684966	7506
2^8	2.278704158	2.108979367	6583
2^9	4.302648306	3.951969049	6435
2^{10}	6.447418942	5.940921486	5803
2^{11}	11.053304612	10.183919884	5559

Varying the field size parameter q gives a trade-off between computation time and signature size: With larger q the signature size shrinks, but both the signer and the verifier need to perform computation linear in q. The fastest instantiation with about 2.2 ms for signing and verification is obtained by setting $q = 2^8$, which also exploits that an $\mathbb{F}_q$ element fits exactly into a byte.

6.3 Comparison with Other PQ Signatures

We focus on MPCitH protocols based on AES or code-based assumptions which we recall below.

AES-based MPCitH Signature Schemes. While AES is the first natural choice as block cipher in MPCitH schemes, it leads to large signatures since the AES circuit over $\mathbb{F}_2$ is far more complex than LowMC in term of non-linear AND gates. In BBQ [20], it was proposed to evaluate AES directly on $\mathbb{F}_{2^8}$ instead, such that the only non-linear operation remaining are the S-box inversions; this reduced the

Table 3. Comparison of timings and signature sizes at the 128-bit security level for some standardized schemes from the NIST PQC standardization project, new alternatives and the designs explored in this work. The results for **FAEST**, Limbo [21], and SPHINCS+ [32] were obtained on the system described in Sect. 6.2. The other numbers are taken from [27,36].

Scheme	t_P (ms)	t_V (ms)	|sign| (B)	Assumption
SDitH [27] (fast)	13.40	12.70	17 866	SD $\mathbb{F}_2$
SDitH [27] (short)	64.20	60.70	12 102	SD $\mathbb{F}_2$
SDitH [27] (fast)	6.40	5.90	12 115	SD $\mathbb{F}_{256}$
SDitH [27] (short)	29.50	27.10	8 481	SD $\mathbb{F}_{256}$
BN++Rain$_4$ [36] (fast)	2.52	2.36	5 536	Rain$_4$
BN++Rain$_4$ [36] (short)	4.79	4.53	4 992	Rain$_4$
Helium+AES [36] (fast)	9.87	9.60	11 420	Hash/AES
Helium+AES [36] (short)	16.53	16.47	9 888	Hash/AES
Limbo [21] (fast)	2.61	2.25	23 264	Hash/AES
Limbo [21] (short)	24.51	21.82	13 316	Hash/AES
SPHINCS+-SHA2 [32] (fast)	4.40	0.40	17 088	Hash
SPHINCS+-SHA2 [32] (short)	88.21	0.15	7 856	Hash
Falcon-512 [42]	0.12	0.03	666	Lattice
Dilithium2 [39]	0.06	0.03	2 420	Lattice
FAEST (**this work**, fast, $q = 2^8$)	2.28	2.11	6 583	Hash/AES
FAEST (**this work**, short, $q = 2^{11}$)	11.05	10.18	5 559	Hash/AES

proof size by about 40%. Further improvements were introduced in Banquet [6], Limbo [21] and the Helium proof system [36]. We report in Table 3 runtimes of Limbo [21], as well as the numbers for the AES-based scheme Helium+AES from [36], which outperforms Limbo. With **FAEST**, we managed to obtain signatures that are around 2× smaller then the fast version of Helium+AES, while having comparable runtimes for signing and verification. Compared with the short variant of Helium+AES, our two **FAEST** variants both perform faster and have around 35–45% smaller signatures.

Non-Standard Variants of AES [23]. To reduce the size of AES-based signatures, Dobraunig et al. proposed new methods which also improved the overall performance of signature and verification [23]. Their approach differs from previous ones mainly with their use of different OWF that are more ZK-friendly. First, they show how to safely remove the key-schedule from the MPC protocol using the single-key Even-Mansour (EM) scheme [25], effectively reducing the number of S-boxes from 200 to 160 for AES-128. Secondly, they propose a different variant of AES with larger S-boxes (LSAES), which is more amenable to zero-knowledge schemes over large fields. Finally, they describe a new OWF, Rain, specifically tailored for MPCitH schemes, which combines both the EM and LSAES tricks mentioned above and additionally modifies the AES linear layers. These techniques were also incorporated into subsequent improvements on the zero-knowledge side [36] (building on [8]), and led to signatures as small as 5kB, with a conservative 4-round version of Rain. In Table 3, we show timings from [36] for BN++Rain, a signature based on the 4-round version of Rain.

In parameter settings with a similar signature size, FAEST seems to perform several times slower than using Rain, while using the standard AES. However, the runtimes were obtained on different hardware, which prohibits an exact comparison. We could also use these alternative OWFs in FAEST — we estimate that Even-Mansour-based AES could reduce sizes by 10–15%, while using Rain could give a 30–40% reduction, giving smaller signatures than BN++Rain$_4$.

Code-Based MPCitH Schemes. In a recent work, Feneuil et al. proposed an MPCitH-based signature scheme where the 5-round ZK protocol is a PoK of a vector x such that $y = Hx$, where x is a vector with Hamming weight $wt(x)$ less than a fixed t [27]. The resulting scheme, in addition to being competitive with SPHINCS+, outperforms all the known code-based signatures. Another very recent work, [1], presents a new approach to amplify the soundness of MPCitH protocols. When applied to build code-based signature schemes, it shows concrete improvement over [27] in running time. In Table 3, we also include the scheme of Feneuil et al., reporting directly the estimations given in their paper [27]. Compared to this scheme, we achieve both smaller signature sizes and faster running time.

Acknowledgments. The work of Michael Klooß was supported by KASTEL Security Research Labs and by Helsinki Institute for Information Technology HIIT. Carsten Baum, Lennart Braun, Cyprien Delpech de Saint Guilhem, Emmmanuela Orsini, Lawrence Roy and Peter Scholl have been supported by the Defense Advanced Research Projects Agency (DARPA) under Contract No. HR001120C0085. Any opinions, findings and conclusions or recommendations expressed in this material are those of the author(s) and do not necessarily reflect the views of any of the funders. The U.S. Government is authorized to reproduce and distribute reprints for governmental purposes notwithstanding any copyright annotation therein. Lennart Braun has been further supported by the European Research Council (ERC) under the European Unions's Horizon 2020 research and innovation programme under grant agreement No 803096 (SPEC). Cyprien Delpech de Saint Guilhem is a Junior FWO Postdoctoral Fellow under project 1266123N and was also supported by CyberSecurity Research Flanders with reference number VR20192203 Peter Scholl was also supported by the Aarhus University Research Foundation, and the Independent Research Fund Denmark under project number 0165-00107B (C3PO).

References

1. Aguilar-Melchor, C., Gama, N., Howe, J., Hülsing, A., Joseph, D., Yue, D.: The return of the sdith. Cryptology ePrint Archive, Paper 2022/1645 (2022). https://eprint.iacr.org/2022/1645
2. Albrecht, M.R., Rechberger, C., Schneider, T., Tiessen, T., Zohner, M.: Ciphers for MPC and FHE. In: Oswald, E., Fischlin, M. (eds.) EUROCRYPT 2015. LNCS, vol. 9056, pp. 430–454. Springer, Heidelberg (2015). https://doi.org/10.1007/978-3-662-46800-5_17

3. Ames, S., Hazay, C., Ishai, Y., Venkitasubramaniam, M.: Ligero: Lightweight sub-linear arguments without a trusted setup. In: Thuraisingham, B.M., Evans, D., Malkin, T., Xu, D. (eds.) ACM CCS 2017, pp. 2087–2104. ACM Press (Oct / Nov 2017). https://doi.org/10.1145/3133956.3134104

4. Attema, T., Fehr, S., Klooß, M.: Fiat-shamir transformation of multi-round inter-active proofs. In: Kiltz, E., Vaikuntanathan, V. (eds.) TCC 2022, Part I. LNCS, vol. 13747, pp. 113–142. Springer, Heidelberg (Nov 2022). https://doi.org/10.1007/978-3-031-22318-1_5

5. Baum, C., Braun, L., Munch-Hansen, A., Scholl, P.: Moz$\mathbb{Z}_{2^k}$arella: Efficient vector-OLE and zero-knowledge proofs over $\mathbb{Z}_{2^k}$. In: Dodis, Y., Shrimpton, T. (eds.) CRYPTO 2022, Part IV. LNCS, vol. 13510, pp. 329–358. Springer, Heidelberg (Aug 2022). https://doi.org/10.1007/978-3-031-15985-5_12

6. Baum, C., de Saint Guilhem, C.D., Kales, D., Orsini, E., Scholl, P., Zaverucha, G.: Banquet: short and fast signatures from AES. In: Garay, J.A. (ed.) PKC 2021. LNCS, vol. 12710, pp. 266–297. Springer, Cham (2021). https://doi.org/10.1007/978-3-030-75245-3_11

7. Baum, C., Malozemoff, A.J., Rosen, M.B., Scholl, P.: Mac′n′Cheese: zero-knowledge proofs for boolean and arithmetic circuits with nested disjunctions. In: Malkin, T., Peikert, C. (eds.) CRYPTO 2021. LNCS, vol. 12828, pp. 92–122. Springer, Cham (2021). https://doi.org/10.1007/978-3-030-84259-8_4

8. Baum, C., Nof, A.: Concretely-efficient zero-knowledge arguments for arithmetic circuits and their application to lattice-based cryptography. In: Kiayias, A., Kohlweiss, M., Wallden, P., Zikas, V. (eds.) PKC 2020. LNCS, vol. 12110, pp. 495–526. Springer, Cham (2020). https://doi.org/10.1007/978-3-030-45374-9_17

9. Ben-Sasson, E., et al.: Computational integrity with a public random string from quasi-linear PCPs. In: Coron, J.-S., Nielsen, J.B. (eds.) EUROCRYPT 2017. LNCS, vol. 10212, pp. 551–579. Springer, Cham (2017). https://doi.org/10.1007/978-3-319-56617-7_19

10. Ben-Sasson, E., Chiesa, A., Spooner, N.: Interactive oracle proofs. In: Hirt, M., Smith, A. (eds.) TCC 2016. LNCS, vol. 9986, pp. 31–60. Springer, Heidelberg (2016). https://doi.org/10.1007/978-3-662-53644-5_2

11. Boneh, D., Waters, B.: Constrained Pseudorandom Functions and Their Appli-cations. In: Sako, K., Sarkar, P. (eds.) ASIACRYPT 2013. LNCS, vol. 8270, pp. 280–300. Springer, Heidelberg (2013). https://doi.org/10.1007/978-3-642-42045-0_15

12. Bootle, J., Chiesa, A., Groth, J.: Linear-time arguments with sublinear verification from tensor codes. In: Pass, R., Pietrzak, K. (eds.) TCC 2020. LNCS, vol. 12551, pp. 19–46. Springer, Cham (2020). https://doi.org/10.1007/978-3-030-64378-2_2

13. Boyle, E., Couteau, G., Gilboa, N., Ishai, Y.: Compressing vector OLE. In: Lie, D., Mannan, M., Backes, M., Wang, X. (eds.) ACM CCS 2018, pp. 896–912. ACM Press (Oct 2018). https://doi.org/10.1145/3243734.3243868

14. Boyle, E., et al.: Efficient two-round OT extension and silent non-interactive secure computation. In: Cavallaro, L., Kinder, J., Wang, X., Katz, J. (eds.) ACM CCS 2019, pp. 291–308. ACM Press (Nov 2019). https://doi.org/10.1145/3319535.3354255

15. Canetti, R., et al.: Fiat-Shamir: from practice to theory. In: Charikar, M., Cohen, E. (eds.) 51st ACM STOC, pp. 1082–1090. ACM Press (Jun 2019). https://doi.org/10.1145/3313276.3316380

16. Cascudo, I., Damgård, I., David, B., Döttling, N., Dowsley, R., Giacomelli, I.: Effi-cient UC commitment extension with homomorphism for free (and applications).

In: Galbraith, S.D., Moriai, S. (eds.) ASIACRYPT 2019. LNCS, vol. 11922, pp. 606–635. Springer, Cham (2019). https://doi.org/10.1007/978-3-030-34621-8_22

17. Chase, M., et al.: Post-quantum zero-knowledge and signatures from symmetric-key primitives. In: Thuraisingham, B.M., Evans, D., Malkin, T., Xu, D. (eds.) ACM CCS 2017, pp. 1825–1842. ACM Press (Oct / Nov 2017). https://doi.org/10.1145/3133956.3133997

18. Chiesa, A., Manohar, P., Spooner, N.: Succinct arguments in the quantum random oracle model. In: Hofheinz, D., Rosen, A. (eds.) TCC 2019. LNCS, vol. 11892, pp. 1–29. Springer, Cham (2019). https://doi.org/10.1007/978-3-030-36033-7_1

19. Cramer, R., Damgård, I., Schoenmakers, B.: Proofs of partial knowledge and simplified design of witness hiding protocols. In: Desmedt, Y.G. (ed.) CRYPTO 1994. LNCS, vol. 839, pp. 174–187. Springer, Heidelberg (1994). https://doi.org/10.1007/3-540-48658-5_19

20. de Saint Guilhem, C.D., De Meyer, L., Orsini, E., Smart, N.P.: BBQ: using AES in picnic signatures. In: Paterson, K.G., Stebila, D. (eds.) SAC 2019. LNCS, vol. 11959, pp. 669–692. Springer, Cham (2020). https://doi.org/10.1007/978-3-030-38471-5_27

21. de Saint Guilhem, C., Orsini, E., Tanguy, T.: Limbo: Efficient zero-knowledge MPCitH-based arguments. In: Vigna, G., Shi, E. (eds.) ACM CCS 2021, pp. 3022–3036. ACM Press (Nov 2021). https://doi.org/10.1145/3460120.3484595

22. Dittmer, S., Ishai, Y., Ostrovsky, R.: Line-point zero knowledge and its applications. In: 2nd Conference on Information-Theoretic Cryptography (ITC 2021). Schloss Dagstuhl-Leibniz-Zentrum für Informatik (2021)

23. Dobraunig, C., Kales, D., Rechberger, C., Schofnegger, M., Zaverucha, G.: Shorter signatures based on tailor-made minimalist symmetric-key crypto. In: Yin, H., Stavrou, A., Cremers, C., Shi, E. (eds.) ACM CCS 2022, pp. 843–857. ACM Press (Nov 2022). https://doi.org/10.1145/3548606.3559353

24. Dósa, G., Szalkai, I., Laflamme, C.: The maximum and minimum number of circuits and bases of matroids. Pure Math. Appl. 15(4), 383–392 (2004), https://math.uni-pannon.hu/~szalkai/Szalkai-2006-DosaGy-PUMA.pdf

25. Dunkelman, O., Keller, N., Shamir, A.: Minimalism in cryptography: the even-mansour scheme revisited. In: Pointcheval, D., Johansson, T. (eds.) EUROCRYPT 2012. LNCS, vol. 7237, pp. 336–354. Springer, Heidelberg (2012). https://doi.org/10.1007/978-3-642-29011-4_21

26. Feneuil, T., Joux, A., Rivain, M.: Syndrome decoding in the head: Shorter signatures from zero-knowledge proofs. Cryptology ePrint Archive, Report 2022/188 (2022). https://eprint.iacr.org/2022/188

27. Feneuil, T., Joux, A., Rivain, M.: Syndrome decoding in the head: Shorter signatures from zero-knowledge proofs. In: Dodis, Y., Shrimpton, T. (eds.) CRYPTO 2022, Part II. LNCS, vol. 13508, pp. 541–572. Springer, Heidelberg (Aug 2022). https://doi.org/10.1007/978-3-031-15979-4_19

28. Gennaro, R., Gentry, C., Parno, B., Raykova, M.: Quadratic span programs and succinct NIZKs without PCPs. In: Johansson, T., Nguyen, P.Q. (eds.) EUROCRYPT 2013. LNCS, vol. 7881, pp. 626–645. Springer, Heidelberg (2013). https://doi.org/10.1007/978-3-642-38348-9_37

29. Giacomelli, I., Madsen, J., Orlandi, C.: ZKBoo: Faster zero-knowledge for Boolean circuits. In: Holz, T., Savage, S. (eds.) USENIX Security 2016, pp. 1069–1083. USENIX Association (Aug 2016)

30. Goldwasser, S., Micali, S., Rackoff, C.: The knowledge complexity of interactive proof-systems (extended abstract). In: 17th ACM STOC, pp. 291–304. ACM Press (May 1985). https://doi.org/10.1145/22145.22178

31. Gvili, Y., Ha, J., Scheffler, S., Varia, M., Yang, Z., Zhang, X.: TurboIKOS: improved non-interactive zero knowledge and post-quantum signatures. In: Sako, K., Tippenhauer, N.O. (eds.) ACNS 2021. LNCS, vol. 12727, pp. 365–395. Springer, Cham (2021). https://doi.org/10.1007/978-3-030-78375-4_15
32. Hulsing, A., et al.: SPHINCS+. Tech. rep., National Institute of Standards and Technology (2022), available at https://csrc.nist.gov/Projects/post-quantum-cryptography/selected-algorithms-2022
33. Ishai, Y., Kushilevitz, E., Ostrovsky, R., Sahai, A.: Zero-knowledge from secure multiparty computation. In: Johnson, D.S., Feige, U. (eds.) 39th ACM STOC, pp. 21–30. ACM Press (Jun 2007). https://doi.org/10.1145/1250790.1250794
34. Ishai, Y., Kushilevitz, E., Ostrovsky, R., Sahai, A.: Cryptography with constant computational overhead. In: Ladner, R.E., Dwork, C. (eds.) 40th ACM STOC, pp. 433–442. ACM Press (May 2008). https://doi.org/10.1145/1374376.1374438
35. Ishai, Y., Prabhakaran, M., Sahai, A.: Founding cryptography on oblivious transfer – efficiently. In: Wagner, D. (ed.) CRYPTO 2008. LNCS, vol. 5157, pp. 572–591. Springer, Heidelberg (2008). https://doi.org/10.1007/978-3-540-85174-5_32
36. Kales, D., Zaverucha, G.: Efficient lifting for shorter zero-knowledge proofs and post-quantum signatures. Cryptology ePrint Archive, Report 2022/588 (2022). https://eprint.iacr.org/2022/588
37. Katz, J., Kolesnikov, V., Wang, X.: Improved non-interactive zero knowledge with applications to post-quantum signatures. In: Lie, D., Mannan, M., Backes, M., Wang, X. (eds.) ACM CCS 2018, pp. 525–537. ACM Press (Oct 2018). https://doi.org/10.1145/3243734.3243805
38. Lindell, Y.: How to simulate it – a tutorial on the simulation proof technique. In: Tutorials on the Foundations of Cryptography. ISC, pp. 277–346. Springer, Cham (2017). https://doi.org/10.1007/978-3-319-57048-8_6
39. Lyubashevsky, V., et al.: CRYSTALS-DILITHIUM. Tech. rep., National Institute of Standards and Technology (2022), available at https://csrc.nist.gov/Projects/post-quantum-cryptography/selected-algorithms-2022
40. Orrù, M., Orsini, E., Scholl, P.: Actively secure 1-out-of-N OT extension with application to private set intersection. In: Handschuh, H. (ed.) CT-RSA 2017. LNCS, vol. 10159, pp. 381–396. Springer, Cham (2017). https://doi.org/10.1007/978-3-319-52153-4_22
41. Pointcheval, D., Stern, J.: Security proofs for signature schemes. In: Maurer, U. (ed.) EUROCRYPT 1996. LNCS, vol. 1070, pp. 387–398. Springer, Heidelberg (1996). https://doi.org/10.1007/3-540-68339-9_33
42. Prest, T., et al.: FALCON. Tech. rep., National Institute of Standards and Technology (2022). https://csrc.nist.gov/Projects/post-quantum-cryptography/selected-algorithms-2022
43. Roy, L.: SoftSpokenOT: Quieter OT extension from small-field silent VOLE in the minicrypt model. In: Dodis, Y., Shrimpton, T. (eds.) CRYPTO 2022, Part I. LNCS, vol. 13507, pp. 657–687. Springer, Heidelberg (Aug 2022). https://doi.org/10.1007/978-3-031-15802-5_23
44. Weng, C., Yang, K., Katz, J., Wang, X.: Wolverine: Fast, scalable, and communication-efficient zero-knowledge proofs for boolean and arithmetic circuits. In: 2021 IEEE Symposium on Security and Privacy, pp. 1074–1091. IEEE Computer Society Press (May 2021). https://doi.org/10.1109/SP40001.2021.00056
45. Weng, C., Yang, K., Yang, Z., Xie, X., Wang, X.: AntMan: Interactive zero-knowledge proofs with sublinear communication. In: Yin, H., Stavrou, A., Cremers, C., Shi, E. (eds.) ACM CCS 2022, pp. 2901–2914. ACM Press (Nov 2022). https://doi.org/10.1145/3548606.3560667

46. Xie, T., Zhang, Y., Song, D.: Orion: Zero knowledge proof with linear prover time. In: Dodis, Y., Shrimpton, T. (eds.) CRYPTO 2022, Part IV. LNCS, vol. 13510, pp. 299–328. Springer, Heidelberg (Aug 2022). https://doi.org/10.1007/978-3-031-15985-5_11

47. Yang, K., Sarkar, P., Weng, C., Wang, X.: QuickSilver: Efficient and affordable zero-knowledge proofs for circuits and polynomials over any field. In: Vigna, G., Shi, E. (eds.) ACM CCS 2021, pp. 2986–3001. ACM Press (Nov 2021). https://doi.org/10.1145/3460120.3484556

Lattice-Based Authenticated Key Exchange with Tight Security

Jiaxin Pan[1]([✉])[iD], Benedikt Wagner[2,3][iD], and Runzhi Zeng[1][iD]

[1] Department of Mathematical Sciences, NTNU – Norwegian University of Science and Technology, Trondheim, Norway
{jiaxin.pan,runzhi.zeng}@ntnu.no
[2] CISPA Helmholtz Center for Information Security, Saarbrücken, Germany
benedikt.wagner@cispa.de
[3] Saarland University, Saarbrücken, Germany

Abstract. We construct the first tightly secure authenticated key exchange (AKE) protocol from lattices. Known tight constructions are all based on Diffie-Hellman-like assumptions. Thus, our protocol is the *first* construction with tight security from a post-quantum assumption.

Our AKE protocol is constructed tightly from a new security notion for key encapsulation mechanisms (KEMs), called one-way security against checkable chosen-ciphertext attacks (OW-ChCCA). We show how an OW-ChCCA secure KEM can be tightly constructed based on the Learning With Errors assumption, leading to the desired AKE protocol. To show the usefulness of OW-ChCCA security beyond AKE, we use it to construct the *first* tightly bilateral selective-opening (BiSO) secure PKE. BiSO security is a stronger selective-opening notion proposed by Lai et al. (ASIACRYPT 2021).

Keywords: Authenticated key exchange · lattices · tight security · selective-opening security · random oracle

1 Introduction

Authenticated key exchange (AKE) protocols enable two parties to securely exchange a session key and establish a secure channel. As a crucial building block for secure communication, its security needs to be carefully proven. Compared to many other cryptographic primitives, security proofs of AKE protocols are often very complicated, mostly because an active adversary against an AKE protocol has very strong yet realistic capabilities. For instance, it can control the communication in public networks and arbitrarily modify messages transferred there. Furthermore, it can corrupt parties' secret keys, reveal session keys or even internal states, while adaptively attacking other "fresh" sessions in a meaningful

The work of Pan and Zeng is supported by the Research Council of Norway under Project No. 324235. Parts of the work were done while the second author was visiting NTNU. The visit was supported by the same project.

H. Handschuh and A. Lysyanskaya (Eds.): CRYPTO 2023, LNCS 14085, pp. 616–647, 2023.
https://doi.org/10.1007/978-3-031-38554-4_20

manner. These capabilities are formally captured by security models, such as the Bellare-Rogaway [4] and the (extended) Canetti-Krawczyk [7, 24] models.

TIGHTNESS. The strong and complex security requirements do not only make it difficult to prove AKE security, but also introduce a large security loss. The security loss quantitatively measures the gap between the concrete security of a cryptographic protocol and the hardness of the underlying assumption. More precisely, in the security proof, we show that the underlying assumption P implies the security of a cryptographic protocol Π, and establish a relation $\varepsilon_\Pi \leq \ell \cdot \varepsilon_P$ between the advantage of attacking Π and breaking P, where ℓ is called the security loss. We call a proof *tight*, when ℓ is a small constant *independent* of parameters unknown at deployment time such as numbers of parties, protocol sessions, signatures, etc. We do not distinguish full tightness (i.e., ℓ being a small constant) and almost tightness (i.e., ℓ being linearly dependent on the security parameter). Instead, we are precise with the concrete security loss.

Unfortunately, most of existing AKE protocol are non-tight and, in particular, come with a security loss significantly larger than for other primitives. More precisely, such a protocol often loses a *quadratic* factor in the number of all sessions established in the protocol's lifetime, while a non-tight signature scheme may only lose a linear factor in the number of all issued signatures. Considering today's massive amount of TLS connections, this quadratic security loss is too large to be compensated in practice, since increasing parameters may lead to an intolerable performance overhead. Even if increasing security parameters is an option, it is impossible to correctly guess parameters such as the number of all protocol sessions, since they are unknown at the time of deployment. If our estimation is too small, the provided security guarantee is not backed by the security proof. If our estimation is too large, we end up with an unnecessarily inefficient implementation.

As a result, tightly secure AKE protocols have become an active area recently. Results include feasibility [3, 15, 26], practical constructions [14, 18], and concrete analysis of deployed protocols [10, 11, 30]. All these works require techniques based on variants of the Diffie-Hellman assumption. Currently, there is no tightly secure AKE protocol based on a post-quantum assumption.

OUR GOAL. Our goal is to construct a lattice-based AKE protocol with tight security. We consider a multi-challenge setting defined by the "Single-Bit-Guess" (SBG) security model, where an adversary is given multiple challenge session keys and all the challenge keys are either real or random depending on a single bit. Another multi-challenge notion is the "Multi-Bit-Guess" (MBG) model where the distribution of each session key is decided by a different random bit. As pointed out by Jager et al. [18], the SBG model is more meaningful than the MBG model, and it can be composed tightly with symmetric primitives to yield a secure channel, while this is not known for the MBG model.

LIMITATIONS OF EXISTING APPROACHES. We survey existing approaches in tightly secure AKE in the SBG model and their limitations in achieving our goal:

Strong DH-Based Approaches. Diemert and Jager [11] and, independently, Davis and Günther [10] gave tight security proofs of the three-message TLS 1.3 handshake AKE protocol with explicit authentication. The two-message protocol of Pan et al. [30] also falls into this category. All their protocols are (or are similar to) signed Diffie-Hellman protocol and their tight security proofs are all based on the Strong Diffie-Hellman (StDH) assumption [1] and the multi-user security of digital signatures. First of all, we do not have a StDH-like assumption in the lattice setting. This seems inherent, since the gap between decisional and computational variants of an assumption does not exist for lattices. For instance, the decisional Learning With Errors (LWE) assumption [34] is equivalent to its computational version. Secondly, the signature scheme of Pan and Wagner [31] is the only known lattice-based scheme with tight multi-user security. Although its signature size is compact and independent of the message length, it is still not efficient, due to the use of OR-proof techniques. The inefficiency of signature schemes can make the resulting AKE protocols impractical.

HPS-Based Approaches. Jager et al. [18] proposed a very efficient tightly secure AKE protocol in the SBG model. Moreover, its security model supports internal state reveals from the adversary. Their construction follows the generic "KEM-to-AKE" transformation [17] with a multi-receiver non-committing key encapsulation mechanism (KEM), and this KEM is only known to be constructed tightly based on the number-theoretic hash proof systems (HPS). A follow-up work of Han et al. [15] also relies on number-theoretic HPS and a multi-user secure signature scheme. Both works require tight random self-reducibility of the subset membership problem in the HPS.

Existing lattice-based HPS [5, 20, 35] do not have suitable properties to tightly implement frameworks in [15, 18]. For instance, frameworks in [15, 18] require tight random self-reducibility, but constructions in [20, 35] do not have this property, since their language instances are associated with some labels and cannot be easily re-randomized. Another undesirable property is the approximate correctness of the lattice-based HPS. Similar to the password-based AKE [5, 20, 35], it is highly non-trivial whether approximate HPS can be fit in the AKE frameworks as in [15, 18]. Finally, existing lattice-based HPS are very inefficient. For instance, the construction in [5] has only one-bit hash values, and extending it to many-bit, which is necessary for security, requires expanding the public key per portion to the number of hash bits. The resulting AKE protocol is very inefficient. For Han et al.'s protocol, the efficiency is even worse, due to the inefficiency of Pan-Wagner's signature scheme.

1.1 Our Contributions

We construct the first tightly secure lattice-based AKE protocol in the random oracle model (ROM). Its security is based on the decisional Learning With Errors (LWE) assumption with security loss that is independent of parameters such as the number of users or protocol sessions. Our protocol is a two-pass implicit AKE, and it does not require any signature. We use the multi-challenge AKE security model as in [18], namely, it considers the SBG security and allows an adversary to adaptively corrupt long-term secret keys, reveal session keys and internal states, and make multiple TEST queries whose outputs are the non-comprised session keys or random keys. This model captures key compromise impersonation and reflection attacks, and weak forward secrecy, which is the strongest forward secrecy a two-pass implicit AKE protocol can have [22].

TIGHT AKE FROM ONE-WAY CHECKABLE CCA SECURITY. Our approach is modular, summarized in Fig. 2. To enable tight security from lattices, we introduce a new security notion for KEMs, called one-way checkable security against chosen-ciphertext attacks (OW-ChCCA) in the multi-user, multi-challenge setting. This new notion is sufficient to construct a tightly secure AKE protocol, and can be constructed efficiently and tightly from the LWE assumption. In a nutshell, it is a multi-user, multi-challenge enhancement of one-way security against plaintext-checkable attacks (OW-PCA) [29]. More precisely, in our OW-ChCCA security, adversaries are given multiple challenge ciphertexts and multiple users' public keys. Adversaries can check whether a pair of encapsulated key and ciphertext is valid wrt some user via a CHECK oracle, and are allowed to corrupt some of the user secret keys. Different to OW-PCA, an adversary can additionally decapsulate any ciphertexts, including the challenge ciphertexts. This decapsulation is stronger than the decapsulation of the standard CCA notion where only non-challenge ciphertexts can be decapsulated. To highlight this capability, we model decapsulating challenge ciphertexts as an additional oracle REVEAL in our definition. Our OW-ChCCA security guarantees that it is still hard for such an adversary to decapsulate the remaining ciphertexts on its own.

We propose two different approaches to construct tightly secure AKE protocols from an OW-ChCCA KEM in the ROM. Our first approach (cf. Sect. 4.1) is a generic construction of AKE protocols directly from an OW-ChCCA secure KEM. Our second approach (cf. Sect. 5.1) is to firstly show that our OW-ChCCA security tightly implies a non-committing KEM (NCKEM) as defined in [18]. Then via the generic transformation in [18], this yields a tight AKE protocol. This is less direct than our first approach, and each user needs to do some additional hashing, compared to the first approach, due to the "OW-ChCCA-to-NCKEM" transformation. Figure 1 gives an overview of these two approaches.

Our motivation of OW-ChCCA is to "outsource" all necessary properties for tight AKE into a notion for KEMs. We think that this is easier than directly constructing a tightly secure AKE. Conceptually, AKE is quite a complex primitive, as it is interactive and adversaries can inject new messages adaptively. If we directly construct a tightly secure AKE from lattices, it would be very difficult to start, since there are many corner cases we need to handle because of the complex adversary strategy (which is reflected by the freshness definition). Our OW-ChCCA notion simplifies this complex task. Moreover, we think that OW-ChCCA is more natural and easier to understand than NCKEM as in [18]. For instance, the NCKEM is defined wrt. a random oracle per user.

Party P_i : $(\mathsf{pk}_i, \mathsf{sk}_i)$ **Party P_j : $(\mathsf{pk}_j, \mathsf{sk}_j)$**

$(\widetilde{\mathsf{pk}}, \widetilde{\mathsf{sk}}) \leftarrow \mathsf{KG}_0(1^\lambda)$

$(\mathsf{ct}_j, \mathsf{K}_j) \leftarrow \mathsf{Encaps}_1(\mathsf{pk}_j)$

$\xrightarrow{\quad (\widetilde{\mathsf{pk}}, \mathsf{ct}_j) \quad}$

$(\widetilde{\mathsf{ct}}, \widetilde{\mathsf{K}}) \leftarrow \mathsf{Encaps}_0(\widetilde{\mathsf{pk}})$

$\mathsf{K}_j := \mathsf{Decaps}_1(\mathsf{sk}_j, \mathsf{ct}_j)$

$\xleftarrow{\quad (\widetilde{\mathsf{ct}}, \mathsf{ct}_i) \quad}$ $(\mathsf{ct}_i, \mathsf{K}_i) \leftarrow \mathsf{Encaps}_1(\mathsf{pk}_i)$

$\widetilde{\mathsf{K}} := \mathsf{Decaps}_0(\widetilde{\mathsf{sk}}, \widetilde{\mathsf{ct}})$ $\mathsf{ctxt} := (\mathsf{pk}_i, \mathsf{pk}_j, \widetilde{\mathsf{pk}}, \mathsf{ct}_i, \mathsf{ct}_j, \widetilde{\mathsf{ct}})$

$\mathsf{K}_i := \mathsf{Decaps}_1(\mathsf{sk}_i, \mathsf{ct}_i)$ $\mathsf{SK} := \mathsf{H}(\mathsf{ctxt}, \mathsf{K}_i', \mathsf{K}_j', \widetilde{\mathsf{K}}')$

$\mathsf{ctxt} := (\mathsf{pk}_i, \mathsf{pk}_j, \widetilde{\mathsf{pk}}, \mathsf{ct}_i, \mathsf{ct}_j, \widetilde{\mathsf{ct}})$

$\mathsf{SK} := \mathsf{H}(\mathsf{ctxt}, \mathsf{K}_i', \mathsf{K}_j', \widetilde{\mathsf{K}}')$

$\mathsf{K}_i' := \mathsf{K}_i, \mathsf{K}_i' := \mathsf{H}'(\mathsf{pk}_i, \mathsf{ct}_i, \mathsf{K}_i)$

$\mathsf{K}_j' := \mathsf{K}_j, \mathsf{K}_j' := \mathsf{H}'(\mathsf{pk}_j, \mathsf{ct}_j, \mathsf{K}_j)$

$\widetilde{\mathsf{K}}' := \widetilde{\mathsf{K}}, \widetilde{\mathsf{K}}' := \mathsf{H}'(\widetilde{\mathsf{pk}}, \widetilde{\mathsf{ct}}, \widetilde{\mathsf{K}})$

Fig. 1. Our two approaches of constructing tightly secure AKE protocols between two parties from OW-ChCCA secure KEMs, $\mathsf{KEM}_1 = (\mathsf{Setup}_1, \mathsf{KG}_1, \mathsf{Encaps}_1, \mathsf{Decaps}_1)$ and $\mathsf{KEM}_0 = (\mathsf{Setup}_0, \mathsf{KG}_0, \mathsf{Encaps}_0, \mathsf{Decaps}_0)$. Our two approaches only differ on how the final session keys are derived. We mark the difference in our second approach with gray. H and H' are two independent hash functions.

OW-ChCCA FROM LWE, TIGHTLY. Our second step is constructing an efficient OW-ChCCA secure KEM tightly from the LWE assumption in the ROM. The technical challenge is to design a scheme such that its security reduction can tightly embed the LWE problem challenge, while being able to respond all oracle queries defined by OW-ChCCA, in particular, the secret key corruption (CORR) and challenge ciphertext decapsulation (REVEAL). Our construction has a novel use of the Naor-Yung (NY) double encryption [28] and the lossy LWE approach as in [19,25] to resolve this. Different to the NY encryption, we do not require non-interactive zero-knowledge proofs by using random oracles and carefully programming them. Our concrete scheme and proof are rather technical. We refer to Sect. 3.2 for more discussion. Additionally, our idea can be implemented using the Matrix Decisional Diffie-Hellman (MDDH) assumption [12], which is a generalization of the (standard) DDH assumption, and we construct a OW-ChCCA KEM from MDDH[1].

EFFICIENCY OF OUR LATTICE-BASED AKE. Asymptotically, our ciphertext is at most twice as long as that of plain Regev's KEM [34]. This carries to our AKE protocol. We argue that such a price is worthy of paying, since it provides stronger theoretically sound security guarantees. A common construction for AKE from lattices is using the generic construction based on a passively

---

[1] We believe that the MDDH-based construction in [18] can also satisfy our notion. As it does not satisfy the deterministic ciphertext derivation property that we need for SIM-BiSO-CCA security, we decided not to present it.

secure KEM as in [17]. Due to the guessing proof strategy, it has a security loss $O((N+S)S \cdot T)$ in the multi-TEST setting[2], where N, S, and T are the numbers of users, total sessions, and TEST sessions, respectively. We assume $S \approx T$, since an adversary can ask TEST queries for some constant fraction of the total sessions. With real-world scenarios, (N, S) can easily reach $(2^{16}, 2^{16})$ (which is the "small-to-medium" scale as in [9,14]). This means the resulting non-tight AKE (implementing with 128-bit secure Regev's KEM) has 80-bit security supported by the non-tight proof, while ours still has 120-bit security. In the truly large scale with $(N, S) = (2^{32}, 2^{32})$, the non-tight protocol has 32-bit security, while ours still has 120-bit security. 80-bit or 32-bit security is not a secure margin against today's computers.

BEYOND AKE: TIGHT BILATERAL SELECTIVE-OPENING SECURITY. We show that our KEM security notion is useful beyond AKE protocols. One of the examples is simulation-based bilateral selective-opening (SIM-BiSO-CCA) security [23] for public-key encryption (PKE) schemes. Combining our OW-ChCCA KEM with a one-time pad and a message authentication code, we construct the *first* tightly SIM-BiSO-CCA secure PKE that can be instantiated based on the LWE or MDDH assumption. Informally, selective-opening (SO) security captures the fact that adversaries can learn some randomness used in the encryption algorithm, and bilateral SO security additionally allows user secret key corruptions and is stronger than SO security. SIM-BiSO-CCA formalizes this in a simulation-based manner. This security notion is motivated by some real-world scenarios, where it is expensive to erase cryptographic secrets and adversaries can learn senders' encryption randomness and receivers' secret keys. Currently, the only known SIM-BiSO-CCA PKE is a non-tight scheme in the ROM [23].

(TIGHT) RELATIONS TO OTHER KEM NOTIONS. We first observe that by a guessing strategy one can show the standard IND-CCA security non-tightly implies OW-ChCCA with a loss of $O(N \cdot C)$, where N and C are numbers of users and ciphertexts, respectively. We also show that, by hashing its encapsulated key, a OW-ChCCA secure KEM is tightly indistinguishable against enhanced chosen-ciphertext attacks (IND-ECCA) in the ROM. IND-ECCA is a notion proposed by Han et al. [16] to rule out constructing tightly secure AKE from many well-known KEMs in the standard model. Our work bypasses their impossibility result using random oracles. Although an IND-ECCA KEM contains necessary requirements of a secure AKE protocol, there is no formal proof showing that an IND-ECCA KEM tightly implies an AKE. Since IND-ECCA implies the standard IND-CCA security, our OW-ChCCA tightly implies the standard IND-CCA security in the ROM. Combining with our previous discussion, this shows that our OW-ChCCA notion is the core for tight security of different KEM notions, PKE, and AKE. Figure 2 summarizes all our contributions and implications in this paper.

---

[2] This security loss can be derived as in [17, Theorem 3] by ignoring the quantum RO and the additive negligible terms. The single-to-multi-challenge reduction introduces the multiplicative term T.

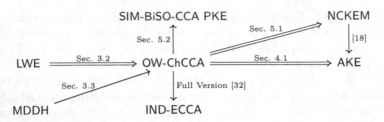

Fig. 2. Overview of our contributions. All implications are tight, and they are all new and proposed in this paper except for NCKEM → AKE. We highlight those key implications for a tightly secure lattice-based AKE with double arrows, "⇒".

OPEN PROBLEMS. We initiate the first step in constructing efficient lattice-based tightly secure AKE protocols. There are several interesting directions to explore. One of them is to construct a OW-ChCCA secure KEM with shorter ciphertexts from lattices, which will lead to more efficient tightly secure AKE. Although we consider an AKE from post-quantum assumptions in this paper, we are interested in "lifting" our results to the quantum random oracle model. Finally, we are interested in constructing tightly secure lattice-based AKE in the non-programmable random oracle model or even the standard model.

MORE POST-QUANTUM AKE. We note that the isogeny-based protocol of de Kock et al. in [21] is not tight based on a variant of the Commutative Supersingular Isogeny Diffie-Hellman (CSIDH) assumption [8] and loses a factor in the number of users. Such a non-tight factor is optimal and unavoidable.

2   Preliminaries

A (probabilistic) algorithm $\mathcal{A}$ is PPT, if its running time (denoted by $\mathbf{T}(\mathcal{A})$) can be bounded by a polynomial in its input length. A function $f : \mathbb{N} \to \mathbb{R}$ with input λ is negligible in λ if $f \in \lambda^{-\omega(1)}$. The term negl denotes a negligible function. A function of the form $1 - \text{negl}(\lambda)$ is said to be overwhelming. Let $\mathcal{A}$ be an algorithm. We write $y \leftarrow \mathcal{A}(x)$ to indicate that y is set to the output of $\mathcal{A}$ in input x with freshly sampled random coins. We write $y := \mathcal{A}(x; \tau)$ to make these coins τ explicit. We write $y \in \mathcal{A}(x)$ to state that y is a potential output (i.e. there are random coins) of $\mathcal{A}$ in input x. For distribution D, we write $x \leftarrow D$ if x is sampled according to D. We write $x \xleftarrow{\$} S$ if x is sampled uniformly from a finite set S. We use the notation $[L] := \{1, \ldots, L\}$ for the first L natural numbers. We use both verbal descriptions and pseudocode to describe games. For that, we make the convention that all variables are initialized to 0, ⊥ or ∅, depending on the data type. Also, when we say that the game aborts, this means that the entire game terminates. This is different from the case where an algorithm or oracle outputs ⊥, in which the game continues. If $\mathbf{G}$ is a game, the notation $\mathbf{G} \Rightarrow b$ indicates that $\mathbf{G}$ outputs b. For all security notions in the multi-user setting, we implicitly assume that the number of users N is polynomially bounded in λ.

<u>KEY ENCAPSULATION MECHANISMS.</u> We recall the syntax of key encapsulation mechanisms, and give a definition of ciphertext entropy. As introducing a new security notion is part of our contribution, we do not define security here.

Definition 1 (Key Encapsulation Mechanism). *A key encapsulation mechanism is a tuple of algorithms* KEM = (Setup, Gen, Encap, Decap) *where* Setup, Gen, Encap *are PPT and* Decap *is deterministic:*

- Setup(1^λ) → par *takes as input the security parameter* 1^λ, *and outputs global system parameters* par. *We assume that* par *implicitly define ciphertext space* $\mathcal{C} = \mathcal{C}_{\mathsf{par}}$, *key space* $\mathcal{K} = \mathcal{K}_{\mathsf{par}}$, *and public key space* $\mathcal{P} = \mathcal{P}_{\mathsf{par}}$.
- Gen(par) → (pk, sk) *takes as input parameters* par, *and outputs a public key* pk ∈ $\mathcal{P}$ *and a secret key* sk.
- Encap(pk) → (ct, K) *takes as input a public key* pk ∈ $\mathcal{P}$, *and outputs a ciphertext* ct ∈ $\mathcal{C}$, *and a key* K ∈ $\mathcal{K}$.
- Decap(sk, ct) → K *is deterministic, takes as input a secret key* sk *and a ciphertext* ct ∈ $\mathcal{C}$, *and outputs a key* K ∈ $\mathcal{K} \cup \{\bot\}$.

We say that KEM *is* ρ-correct, *if for every* par ∈ Setup(1^λ), *the following probability is at least* ρ:

$$\Pr\left[K = K' \mid (\mathsf{pk}, \mathsf{sk}) \leftarrow \mathsf{Gen}(\mathsf{par}), (\mathsf{ct}, K) \leftarrow \mathsf{Encap}(\mathsf{pk}), K' \leftarrow \mathsf{Decap}(\mathsf{sk}, \mathsf{ct})\right].$$

For some constructions, we may require that the scheme has high public key or ciphertext entropy. We give formal definitions of these natural notions in our full version [32].

<u>BACKGROUND ON LATTICES.</u> Let Λ be an m-dimensional lattice, i.e. a discrete additive subgroup of $\mathbb{R}^m$. For $s > 0$, we define $D_{\Lambda,s}$ to be the distribution proportional to $\rho_s(\mathbf{x}) := \exp(-\pi \|\mathbf{x}\|^2 / s^2)$ restricted to Λ. The distribution $D_{\Lambda,s}$ is called the discrete Gaussian distribution with parameter s over Λ. Further, we make the convention that elements in $\mathbb{Z}_q$ are represented by their representative from $\{-(q-1)/2, \ldots, (q-1)/2\}$ (if q is odd) or $\{-q/2+1, \ldots, q/2\}$ (if q is even). We use some standard facts about discrete Gaussians, see [13, 27].

Lemma 1. *Let* $n, m \in \mathbb{N}$. *Let* q *be a prime at least polynomial in* n *and* $m \geq 2n \log q$. *Consider any* $\omega(\sqrt{\log m})$ *function and* $s \geq \omega(\sqrt{\log m})$. *Then for all but a negligible (in* n) *fraction of all* $\mathbf{A} \in \mathbb{Z}_q^{n \times m}$ *the following distribution is statistically close to uniform over* $\mathbb{Z}_q^n$: $\{\mathbf{Ae} \mid \mathbf{e} \leftarrow D_{\mathbb{Z}^m, s}\}$.

Lemma 2. *Consider any* $\omega(\sqrt{\log m})$ *function and* $s \geq \omega(\sqrt{\log m})$. *Then we have*

$$\Pr\left[\|\mathbf{x}\| > s\sqrt{m} \mid \mathbf{x} \leftarrow D_{\mathbb{Z},s}^m\right] \leq 2^{-m+1}.$$

We also use the following lemma about the lossiness of a certain matrix distribution, following [2, 19]. It lower bounds the so called "smooth average min-entropy" $\tilde{H}_\infty(\cdot|\cdot)$ [19].

Lemma 3. *Let n, k, m, q, η be positive integers, $\beta, \alpha' > 0$ such that $\alpha' \geq \beta \eta n m q$. Let χ be a distribution such that $\Pr\left[|x| \geq \beta q \mid x \leftarrow \chi\right] \leq \mathsf{negl}(\lambda)$. Let $\mathbf{s}$ be uniformly distributed over $[-\eta, \eta]^n$, and $\mathbf{e}$ be distributed according to $D_{\mathbb{Z}, \alpha'}^m$. Let $\mathbf{A} := \bar{\mathbf{A}} \mathbf{C} + \mathbf{F}$ for*

$$\bar{\mathbf{A}} \xleftarrow{\$} \mathbb{Z}_q^{n \times k}, \quad \mathbf{C} \xleftarrow{\$} \mathbb{Z}_q^{k \times m}, \quad \mathbf{F} \leftarrow \chi^{n \times m}.$$

Then, for any $\epsilon \geq 2^{-\lambda}$, we have

$$\tilde{H}_\infty^\epsilon\left(\mathbf{s} \mid \mathbf{A}^t \mathbf{s} + \mathbf{e}\right) \geq H_\infty\left(\mathbf{s}\right) - (k + 2\lambda) \log q - \mathsf{negl}(\lambda).$$

We make use of the generalized leftover hash lemma, taken from [19].

Lemma 4. *Let $\mathcal{H} := \{h_k : \mathcal{X} \to \mathcal{Y}\}_k$ be a universal family of hash functions, where keys k are distributed according to a distribution K. Let U denote a random variable distributed uniformly over $\mathcal{Y}$. Let X be random variable with values in $\mathcal{X}$ and I be any random variable. Let $\epsilon \geq 0$. Then, the statistical distance between $(K, h_K(X), I)$ and (K, U, I) is at most*

$$2\epsilon + \frac{1}{2}\sqrt{2^{-\tilde{H}_\infty^\epsilon(X|I)} \cdot |\mathcal{Y}|}.$$

Our construction relies on the well-known LWE assumption [6, 33, 34].

Definition 2 (LWE Assumption). *Let $n = n(\lambda) \in \mathbb{N}$, $m = m(n) \in \mathbb{N}$, $q = q(n)$ be prime number and $\chi = \chi(n)$ be a distribution over $\mathbb{Z}$. We say that the LWE $_{n,m,q,\chi}$ assumption holds, if for every PPT algorithm $\mathcal{B}$ the following advantage is negligible in λ:*

$$\mathsf{Adv}_{\mathcal{B}}^{\mathsf{LWE}\ n,m,q,\chi}(\lambda) := \left| \Pr\left[\mathcal{B}(\mathbf{A}, \mathbf{b}) = 1 \mid \mathbf{A} \xleftarrow{\$} \mathbb{Z}_q^{n \times m}, \mathbf{b} \xleftarrow{\$} \mathbb{Z}_q^m \right] \right.$$
$$\left. - \Pr\left[\mathcal{B}(\mathbf{A}, \mathbf{A}^t \mathbf{s} + \mathbf{e}) = 1 \mid \mathbf{A} \xleftarrow{\$} \mathbb{Z}_q^{n \times m}, \mathbf{s} \xleftarrow{\$} \mathbb{Z}_q^n, \mathbf{e} \leftarrow \chi^m \right] \right|.$$

3   One-Way Checkable CCA Security

We first propose a new security notion for key encapsulation mechanisms (KEM), One-Way Checkable Security against Chosen-Ciphertext Attacks (OW-ChCCA). Then we realize this notion with lattices in a tight way.

3.1   Definition of OW-ChCCA Security

Before we formalize our notion for KEMs, we give some intuitions behind it. At a very high level, our OW-ChCCA security can be seen as an extension of OW-PCA security [29]. Our goal here is to formalize the "minimal" requirements on KEM for constructing tightly secure AKE. We first observe that an indistinguishability notion, such as IND-CPA, is not necessary for AKE, and the weaker, one-way notion (namely, decapsulating the challenge ciphertexts) is sufficient. This is because the AKE session keys are often derived from the corresponding KEM key using a hash function which is modeled as a random oracle (RO). By searching the RO-history, it can be shown that a one-way notion tightly implies the corresponding IND one.

To tightly use a one-way notion in our security reduction without guessing, we still need to identify the correct key-ciphertext pairs. Thus, we provide an oracle to check if a key-ciphertext pair is valid, which essentially results in the OW-PCA notion for KEMs. However, OW-PCA is not sufficient to get authenticated key exchange tightly. At a high level, an AKE adversary can adaptively attack multiple sessions and forces the reduction to guess which are the challenge sessions (aka. TEST sessions). This will lead to a large security loss. We therefore add additional adversary capabilities (i.e. oracles) to KEM's OW-PCA security to resolve this

- The adversary can get multiple challenge ciphertexts.
- The adversary has access to a decapsulation oracle, which is used for non-challenge ciphertexts.
- The adversary can adaptively decapsulate some challenge ciphertexts. This allows the AKE security reduction to answer session key reveals for sessions that possibly contain challenge KEM ciphertexts. An AKE adversary can force this happen.
- The adversary can adaptively corrupt users' their secret key. This corresponds to long-term secret key corruptions in the AKE protocol.

We formalize the OW-ChCCA security for KEMs as follows:

Definition 3 (OW-ChCCA Security). *Let* KEM = (Setup, Gen, Encap, Decap) *be a key encapsulation mechanism and consider the game* OW-ChCCA *defined in Fig. 3. We say that* KEM *is* OW-ChCCA *secure, if for all PPT adversaries* $\mathcal{A}$, *the following advantage is negligible:*

$$\mathsf{Adv}_{\mathcal{A},\mathsf{KEM}}^{\mathsf{OW\text{-}ChCCA}}(\lambda) := \Pr\left[\mathsf{OW\text{-}ChCCA}_{\mathsf{KEM}}^{\mathcal{A}}(\lambda) \Rightarrow 1\right].$$

For our construction of SIM-BiSO-CCA secure encryption in Sect. 5.2, we require that KEM has deterministic ciphertext derivation:

Definition 4 (Deterministic Ciphertext Derivation). *Let* KEM = (Setup, Gen, Encap, Decap) *be a key encapsulation mechanism with key space* $\mathcal{K}$. *We say that* KEM *has deterministic ciphertext derivation, if there is a deterministic algorithm* $\widehat{\mathsf{Encap}}$, *such that for all* par $\in$ Setup(1^λ) *and all* (pk, sk) $\in$ Gen(par), *the following two distributions are equivalent*

$$\{(\mathsf{ct}, K) \mid K \xleftarrow{\$} \mathcal{K}, \ \mathsf{ct} := \widehat{\mathsf{Encap}}(\mathsf{pk}, K)\} \ and \ \{(\mathsf{ct}, K) \leftarrow \mathsf{Encap}(\mathsf{pk})\}.$$

3.2 Construction from Lattices

We construct $\mathsf{KEM}_{\mathsf{LWE}}$ that is tightly OW-ChCCA secure under the LWE assumption. Our scheme is described in Fig. 4. It uses algorithms SampleD and Round:

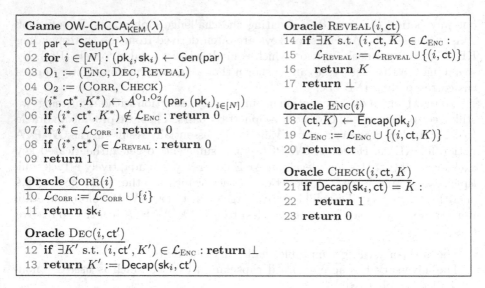

Fig. 3. The game OW-ChCCA for a key encapsulation mechanism KEM := (Setup, Gen, Encap, Decap).

- SampleD$(m, \alpha'; \rho) \rightarrow \mathbf{e}$: Sample Gaussian $\mathbf{e} \leftarrow D^m_{\mathbb{Z}, \alpha'}$ using random coins $\rho \in \{0, 1\}^\lambda$.
- Round$(\mathbf{t}) \rightarrow \mathbf{h}$: Do componentwise rounding of $\mathbf{t} \in \mathbb{Z}_q^\lambda$ to get $\mathbf{h} \in \{0, 1\}^\lambda$, i.e. for all $i \in [\lambda]$, we have $\mathbf{h}_i = 0$ if $\mathbf{t}_i$ is closer to 0 than to $\lfloor q/2 \rceil$, and $\mathbf{h}_i = 1$ otherwise.

Our scheme is parameterized by matrix dimensions $n, m, k \in \mathbb{N}$, a modulus $q \in \mathbb{N}$, and (Gaussian) widths $\alpha, \alpha', \gamma, \eta > 0$. The scheme also makes use of random oracles $\mathsf{H}: \{0, 1\}^* \rightarrow \{0, 1\}^\lambda$ and $\mathsf{G}: \{0, 1\}^* \rightarrow [-\eta, \eta]^n \times \{0, 1\}^\lambda \times \{0, 1\}^\lambda \times \{0, 1\}^\lambda$. For our analysis, the parameters have to satisfy the following conditions.

- For Lemma 1: q prime, $m \geq 2n \log q$, $\alpha \geq \omega(\sqrt{\log m})$
- For Lemma 2: $\alpha, \alpha' \geq \omega(\sqrt{\log m})$
- For Lemmata 3 and 4: $n \log(2\eta + 1) - (k + 3\lambda) \log q \geq \lambda \log q + \Omega(n)$ and $\alpha' \geq \beta \eta n m q$; we use $\beta q = n$ in Lemma 3.
- For correctness: $4\alpha'\alpha m < q$.

For example, given λ, we could conservatively use the following parameter setting.

$$n := 70\lambda \quad n^6 < q \leq n^7, \quad \eta := \sqrt{n}, \quad \gamma := \sqrt{n},$$
$$k := \lambda, \quad m := 2n \log q, \quad \alpha := \sqrt{n}, \quad \alpha' := n^{2.5} m.$$

Correctness follows from standard calculations, and we postpone it to our full version [32]. Further, it can easily be seen that $\mathsf{KEM_{LWE}}$ has deterministic ciphertext derivation.

Before going into the security analysis, we give an overview of the rationale behind our construction, omitting LWE specific details. First, recall that in the

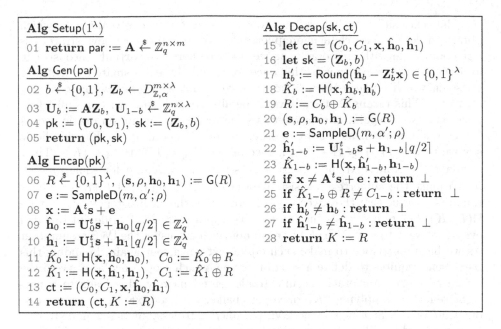

Fig. 4. The key encapsulation mechanism $\mathsf{KEM}_{\mathsf{LWE}} = (\mathsf{Setup}, \mathsf{Gen}, \mathsf{Encap}, \mathsf{Decap})$, where $\mathsf{H}: \{0,1\}^* \to \{0,1\}^\lambda$ and $\mathsf{G}: \{0,1\}^* \to [-\eta,\eta]^n \times \{0,1\}^\lambda \times \{0,1\}^\lambda \times \{0,1\}^\lambda$ are random oracles. To save space, one could set $\mathbf{A} := \mathsf{H}^*(0)$ for a random oracle $\mathsf{H}^*: \{0,1\}^* \to \mathbb{Z}_q^{n \times m}$.

security proof, we need to simulate a corruption oracle, returning secret keys sk_i for user i. To do this without using non-tight guessing arguments, we have to know a secret key for each user. As we still need to embed our LWE challenge in the challenge ciphertexts, we should not be able to decrypt them. We can solve this first dilemma by splitting the ciphertext into two parts $\mathsf{ct} = (\mathsf{ct}_0, \mathsf{ct}_1)$, and having two potential secret keys sk_0 and sk_1, where ct_b allows to recover the encapsulation key K using secret key sk_b. Then, for each user i, we hold sk_{i,b_i} for a random bit b_i. Now, the strategy is to use LWE to modify ct_{1-b_i}. Let us call such modified ciphertext parts inconsistent. Finally, we argue that the adversary does not learn b_i for uncorrupted users, and then we switch roles of b_i and $1 - b_i$ to apply the same argument. This overall strategy can be implemented, if we only have to provide a corruption oracle. However, once we need to simulate a decapsulation oracle, the situation becomes a bit more tricky. Namely, we have to guarantee that decapsulation (simulated using sk_{i,b_i}) does not reveal information about b_i. We solve this challenge by deterministically deriving the ciphertext parts $\mathsf{ct}_0, \mathsf{ct}_1$ from the encapsulated key K. Ciphertext parts could have roughly the form $\mathsf{ct}_b = K \oplus F_b(K)$ for some deterministic F_b. During decapsulation, we recompute $\mathsf{ct}_0, \mathsf{ct}_1$ from K, and only accept K if this recomputation is consistent. A careful analysis shows that this hides all information about b_i. We can also implement a check oracle now using the deterministic functions F_0, F_1. On the other hand, applying changes to $\mathsf{ct}_{1-b_i} = K \oplus F_{1-b_i}(K)$ may lead to circular security problems. At a high level, we solve this issue by implementing the functions F_b using a random oracle.

The next challenge that we have to solve arises from the reveal oracle, which allows to decapsulate challenge ciphertexts. We see that our above strategy is not compatible with this oracle, as we make ciphertexts partially inconsistent, and the adversary can notice this once we reveal the encapsulated key. Again, guessing which ciphertexts will be revealed is not an option without loosing tightness. This means that we have to be able to make inconsistent ciphertext parts consistent again, once a query to the reveal or corruption oracle occurs. We carefully implement this by another use of a random oracle. For simplicity, say we replace $F_b(\cdot)$ by $H(F_b(\cdot))$, i.e. we have $ct_{1-b_i} = K \oplus H(F_{1-b_i}(K))$. Then, to make the ciphertext inconsistent, we set $ct_{1-b_i} = K \oplus \hat{h}$ for some random $\hat{h}$. To make the ciphertext consistent later on, we program $H(F_b(K)) := \hat{h}$. It remains to argue that the adversary can not detect the inconsistency by querying $H(F_b(K))$ before it queries the reveal or corruption oracle. To rule out this bad event, we want to switch $F_b(K)$ to a random element using the LWE assumption. As we have no chance to make such ciphertext consistent again, bounding this bad event requires to define a separate game, which stops once a query to the reveal or corruption oracle occurs. Implemented naively, this leads to a non-tight reduction, applying LWE once per challenge ciphertext. However, it turns out that we can first switch the LWE parameters to lossy mode, as done in [19], and then analyze all of these separate games in a purely statistical way. There is a complex interplay between all of these challenges and potential solutions, and the formal proof requires heavy use of delayed analysis.

Theorem 1. *Let* $H: \{0,1\}^* \to \{0,1\}^\lambda$ *and* $G: \{0,1\}^* \to [-\eta, \eta]^n \times \{0,1\}^\lambda \times \{0,1\}^\lambda \times \{0,1\}^\lambda$ *be random oracles. If the* LWE $_{k,m,q,D_{\mathbb{Z},\gamma}}$ *assumption holds, then the scheme* KEM_{LWE} *is* OW-ChCCA *secure.*

Concretely, for any PPT algorithm $\mathcal{A}$ *there is a PPT algorithm* $\mathcal{B}$ *with* $\mathbf{T}(\mathcal{A}) \approx \mathbf{T}(\mathcal{B})$ *and*

$$\mathsf{Adv}^{OW\text{-}ChCCA}_{\mathcal{A}, KEM_{LWE}}(\lambda) \leq 6n \cdot \mathsf{Adv}^{LWE\ k,m,q,D_{\mathbb{Z},\gamma}}_{\mathcal{B}}(\lambda) + \mathsf{negl}(\lambda).$$

Proof. Let $\mathcal{A}$ be a PPT algorithm and $KEM := KEM_{LWE}$. We show the claim using a sequence of games $\mathbf{G}_i$ for $i \in \{0, \ldots, 6\}$. To simplify notation, we define

$$\mathsf{Adv}_i := \Pr[\mathbf{G}_i \Rightarrow 1], \text{ for } i \in \{0, \ldots, 6\}.$$

Let us first give an informal overview of the proof strategy. We define $\mathbf{G}_0 := \text{OW-ChCCA}^{\mathcal{A}}_{KEM}(\lambda)$ and introduce changes to game $\mathbf{G}_0$ until we end up at game $\mathbf{G}_3$. For this one, we argue that the probability that $\mathbf{G}_3$ outputs 1 is negligible. Games $\mathbf{G}_i$ for $i \geq 4$ are only needed in Lemmata 6 and 7, which are used to bound the difference between $\mathbf{G}_0$ and $\mathbf{G}_3$ using a delayed analysis technique. We will now give the details of the proof. The games are formally presented in Figs. 5 and 6.

Game $\mathbf{G}_0$: We define $\mathbf{G}_0$ as the real OW-ChCCA game. That is, we set $\mathbf{G}_0 :=$ OW-ChCCA$_{\mathsf{KEM}}^{\mathcal{A}}(\lambda)$. To fix some notation, we recall how this game works. First, the game samples $\mathsf{par} := \mathbf{A} \overset{\$}{\leftarrow} \mathbb{Z}_q^{n \times m}$. Then, for each $i \in [N]$, it computes public keys and secret keys $(\mathsf{pk}_i, \mathsf{sk}_i)$ as follows: It samples a bit $b_i \overset{\$}{\leftarrow} \{0,1\}$, it samples a matrix $\mathbf{Z}_{i,b_i}$ as in the scheme, and sets $\mathbf{U}_{i,b_i} := \mathbf{A}\mathbf{Z}_{i,b_i}$. Then, it samples $\mathbf{U}_{i,1-b_i}$ uniformly at random as in the scheme. The public key is $\mathsf{pk}_i := (\mathbf{U}_{i,0}, \mathbf{U}_{i,1})$, and the secret key is $\mathsf{sk}_i := (\mathbf{Z}_{i,b_i}, b_i)$. Then, adversary $\mathcal{A}$ gets all public keys and par as input. Further, it gets access to oracles ENC, DEC, REVEAL, CORR, CHECK, as well as random oracles H, G. The game simulates random oracles H, G in a lazy manner, using maps h and g that map the inputs of H, G to the outputs of H, G, respectively. We denote the number of queries to H, G, and ENC by $Q_{\mathsf{H}}, Q_{\mathsf{G}}$, and Q_{E}, respectively. In the end, $\mathcal{A}$ outputs $(i^*, \mathsf{ct}^*, K^*)$. The game outputs 1, if ct^* has been output by ENC(i^*), where it was computed together with K^*, the adversary $\mathcal{A}$ never queried CORR(i^*), and never queried REVEAL(i^*, ct^*). By definition, we have

$$\mathsf{Adv}_0 = \Pr\left[\text{OW-ChCCA}_{\mathsf{KEM}}^{\mathcal{A}}(\lambda) \Rightarrow 1\right].$$

Game $\mathbf{G}_1$: In game $\mathbf{G}_1$, we introduce a bad event badR, and abort the game if badR occurs. To define the event, consider a query of the form ENC(i). Recall that in such a query, the game samples $R \overset{\$}{\leftarrow} \{0,1\}^{\lambda}$ and derives values $\mathbf{s}, \mathbf{e}, \mathbf{h}_0, \mathbf{h}_1$ from it using random oracle G. These are then used to define a ciphertext ct. We say that the bad event badR occurs, if one of the following holds:

- At this point, $\mathcal{A}$ already queried $\mathsf{G}(R)$, or
- at some later point, before any query of the form CORR(i) or REVEAL(i, ct) for these i, ct, $\mathcal{A}$ queries $\mathsf{G}(R)$. Note that this also includes indirect queries made by oracles DEC, CHECK.

In the code, we model this using a list $\mathcal{L}_R$ that contains the tuples (i, ct, R). The tuples are added in the query ENC(i) and removed in queries CORR(i) or REVEAL(i, ct). In each random oracle query $\mathsf{G}(R)$, we check if such a tuple is currently in the list and set $\mathsf{badR} := 1$ in this case.

As the ciphertext ct still contains information about R (namely, in C_0, C_1), we do not bound the probability of badR, but instead delay its analysis. We have

$$|\mathsf{Adv}_0 - \mathsf{Adv}_1| \leq \Pr[\mathsf{badR} \text{ in } \mathbf{G}_1].$$

Game $\mathbf{G}_2$: In game $\mathbf{G}_2$, we change how the matrix $\mathbf{A}$ is generated. Recall that before, it is generated as $\mathbf{A} \overset{\$}{\leftarrow} \mathbb{Z}_q^{n \times m}$. In game $\mathbf{G}_2$, we instead generate it as $\mathbf{A} := \bar{\mathbf{A}}\mathbf{C} + \mathbf{F}$ for $\bar{\mathbf{A}} \overset{\$}{\leftarrow} \mathbb{Z}_q^{n \times k}$, $\mathbf{C} \overset{\$}{\leftarrow} \mathbb{Z}_q^{k \times m}$, and $\mathbf{F} \leftarrow D_{\mathbb{Z},\gamma}^{n \times m}$. It is easy to see that we can bound the difference between $\mathbf{G}_1$ and $\mathbf{G}_2$, by n applications (one for each row of $\mathbf{A}$) of LWE $_{k,m,q,D_{\mathbb{Z},\gamma}}$, or equivalently, an n-fold LWE assumption. The corresponding reduction $\mathcal{B}$ gets $\mathbf{A}, \mathbf{C}$ as input, and uses $\mathsf{par} := \mathbf{A}$. Then, it simulates $\mathbf{G}_1$, and outputs whatever the game outputs. It follows that

$$|\mathsf{Adv}_1 - \mathsf{Adv}_2| \leq n \cdot \mathsf{Adv}_{\mathcal{B}}^{\mathsf{LWE}\ k,m,q,D_{\mathbb{Z},\gamma}}(\lambda).$$

Game G_0-G_6

```
01  par := A ←$ Z_q^{n×m}                                                    // G_0-G_1,G_4-G_6
02  Ā ←$ Z_q^{n×k},  C ←$ Z_q^{k×m},  F ← D_{Z,γ}^{n×m},  par := A := ĀC + F   // G_2-G_3
03  for i ∈ [N] :
04      b_i ←$ {0,1},  Z_{i,b_i} ← D_{Z,α}^{m×λ},  U_{i,b_i} := AZ_{i,b_i}
05      Z_{i,1-b_i} ← D_{Z,α}^{m×λ},  U_{i,1-b_i} := AZ_{i,1-b_i}            // G_5-G_6
06      U_{i,1-b_i} ←$ Z_q^{n×λ}                                            // G_0-G_4
07      let Z_{i,b_i} = [z_1 | · · · | z_λ]                                  // G_6
08      if ∃j ∈ [λ] s.t. ‖z_j‖ > α√m :  abort                              // G_6
09      let Z_{i,1-b_i} = [z_1 | · · · | z_λ]                                // G_6
10      if ∃j ∈ [λ] s.t. ‖z_j‖ > α√m :  abort                              // G_6
11      pk_i := (U_{i,0}, U_{i,1}),  sk_i := (Z_{i,b_i}, b_i)
12  (i*, ct*, K*) ← A^{ENC,DEC,REVEAL,CORR,CHECK,H,G}(par, (pk_i)_{i∈[N]})
13  if (i*, ct*, K*) ∉ L_ENC ∨ i* ∈ L_CORR ∨ (i*, ct*) ∈ L_REVEAL :  return 0
14  return 1
```

Oracle $\text{ENC}(i)$

```
15  R ←$ {0,1}^λ
16  if g[R] ≠ ⊥ : badR := 1,  abort                                        // G_1-G_6
17  (s, ρ, h_0, h_1) := G(R),  e ← SampleD(m, α'; ρ)
18  x := A^t s + e,  ĥ_0 := U_{i,0}^t s + h_0⌊q/2⌉,  ĥ_1 := U_{i,1}^t s + h_1⌊q/2⌉
19  qry_0 := (x, ĥ_0, h_0),  qry_1 := (x, ĥ_1, h_1)
20  if h[qry_{b_i}] ≠ ⊥ :  badK1 := 1,  abort                              // G_3-G_6
21  if h[qry_{1-b_i}] ≠ ⊥ :  badK0 := 1,  abort                            // G_3-G_6
22  K̂_0 := H(x, ĥ_0, h_0),  K̂_1 := H(x, ĥ_1, h_1)
23  C_0 := K̂_0 ⊕ R,  C_1 := K̂_1 ⊕ R
24  ct := (C_0, C_1, x, ĥ_0, ĥ_1)
25  L_R := L_R ∪ {(R, i, ct)}                                              // G_1-G_6
26  L_{K,0} := L_{K,0} ∪ {(qry_{1-b_i}, i, ct)}                            // G_3-G_6
27  L_{K,1} := L_{K,1} ∪ {(qry_{b_i}, i, ct)}                              // G_3-G_6
28  L_ENC := L_ENC ∪ {(i, ct, K := R)}
29  return ct
```

Fig. 5. The games G_0–G_6 in the proof of Theorem 1. Oracles DEC and CHECK are as in the real games. The remaining oracles are given in Fig. 6. Highlighted lines are only executed in the corresponding games.

We can also give a similar reduction, that only outputs 1 if and only if event badR occurs, which can be checked efficiently. This implies that

$$|\Pr[\text{badR in } G_1] - \Pr[\text{badR in } G_2]| \le n \cdot \mathsf{Adv}_{\mathcal{B}}^{\mathsf{LWE}\, k,m,q,D_{Z,γ}}(λ).$$

Game G_3: In game G_3, we introduce another bad event badK := badK0∨badK1, and let the game abort if it occurs. This event is very similar to event badR. Namely, we consider a query of the form $\text{ENC}(i)$. Recall that in this query, values $x, ĥ_0, h_0$ and $ĥ_1, h_1$ are defined. Then, the oracle sets $K̂_0 := H(x, ĥ_0, h_0)$

Oracle $\mathrm{REVEAL}(i, \mathsf{ct})$	
01 **if** $\exists K$ s.t. $(i, \mathsf{ct}', K) \in \mathcal{L}_{\mathrm{ENC}}$:	
02 $\quad \mathcal{L}_{\mathrm{REVEAL}} := \mathcal{L}_{\mathrm{REVEAL}} \cup \{(i, \mathsf{ct})\}$	
03 $\quad \mathcal{L}_R := \mathcal{L}_R \setminus \{(R, i', \mathsf{ct}') \in \mathcal{L}_R \mid (i', \mathsf{ct}') = (i, \mathsf{ct})\}$	$/\!/\mathbf{G_1}\text{-}\mathbf{G_6}$
04 $\quad \mathcal{L}_{K,0} := \mathcal{L}_{K,0} \setminus \{(\mathsf{qry}, i', \mathsf{ct}) \in \mathcal{L}_{K,0} \mid (i', \mathsf{ct}') = (i, \mathsf{ct})\}$	$/\!/\mathbf{G_3}\text{-}\mathbf{G_6}$
05 $\quad \mathcal{L}_{K,1} := \mathcal{L}_{K,1} \setminus \{(\mathsf{qry}, i', \mathsf{ct}) \in \mathcal{L}_{K,1} \mid (i', \mathsf{ct}') = (i, \mathsf{ct})\}$	$/\!/\mathbf{G_3}\text{-}\mathbf{G_6}$
06 $\quad$ **return** K	
07 **return** $\perp$	
Oracle $\mathrm{CORR}(i)$	
08 $\mathcal{L}_{\mathrm{CORR}} := \mathcal{L}_{\mathrm{CORR}} \cup \{i\}$	
09 $\mathcal{L}_R := \mathcal{L}_R \setminus \{(R, i', \mathsf{ct}) \in \mathcal{L}_R \mid i' = i\}$	$/\!/\mathbf{G_1}\text{-}\mathbf{G_6}$
10 $\mathcal{L}_{K,0} := \mathcal{L}_{K,0} \setminus \{(\mathsf{qry}, i', \mathsf{ct}) \in \mathcal{L}_{K,0} \mid i' = i\}$	$/\!/\mathbf{G_3}\text{-}\mathbf{G_6}$
11 $\mathcal{L}_{K,1} := \mathcal{L}_{K,1} \setminus \{(\mathsf{qry}, i', \mathsf{ct}) \in \mathcal{L}_{K,1} \mid i' = i\}$	$/\!/\mathbf{G_3}\text{-}\mathbf{G_6}$
12 **return** sk_i	
Oracle $\mathsf{H}(\mathbf{x}', \hat{\mathbf{h}}, \mathbf{h})$	
13 $\mathsf{qry} := (\mathbf{x}', \hat{\mathbf{h}}, \mathbf{h})$	$/\!/\mathbf{G_3}\text{-}\mathbf{G_6}$
14 **if** $\exists i, \mathsf{ct}$ s.t. $(\mathsf{qry}, i, \mathsf{ct}) \in \mathcal{L}_{K,0}$: $\mathsf{badK0} := 1$, **abort**	$/\!/\mathbf{G_3}\text{-}\mathbf{G_6}$
15 **if** $\exists i, \mathsf{ct}$ s.t. $(\mathsf{qry}, i, \mathsf{ct}) \in \mathcal{L}_{K,1}$: $\mathsf{badK1} := 1$, **abort**	$/\!/\mathbf{G_3}\text{-}\mathbf{G_6}$
16 **if** $h[\mathbf{x}', \hat{\mathbf{h}}, \mathbf{h}] = \perp$: $h[\mathbf{x}', \hat{\mathbf{h}}, \mathbf{h}] \overset{\$}{\leftarrow} \{0,1\}^\lambda$	
17 **if** $\exists (\mathbf{x}'', \hat{\mathbf{h}}', \mathbf{h}') \neq \mathsf{qry}$ s.t. $h[\mathbf{x}'', \hat{\mathbf{h}}', \mathbf{h}'] = h[\mathbf{x}', \hat{\mathbf{h}}, \mathbf{h}]$: **abort**	$/\!/\mathbf{G_6}$
18 **return** $h[\mathbf{x}', \hat{\mathbf{h}}, \mathbf{h}]$	
Oracle $\mathsf{G}(R')$	
19 **if** $\exists i, \mathsf{ct}$ s.t. $(R', i, \mathsf{ct}) \in \mathcal{L}_R$: $\mathsf{badR} := 1$, **abort**	$/\!/\mathbf{G_1}\text{-}\mathbf{G_6}$
20 **if** $g[R'] = \perp$:	
21 $\quad (\mathbf{s}, \rho, \mathbf{h}_0, \mathbf{h}_1) \overset{\$}{\leftarrow} \mathbb{Z}_q^n \times (\{0,1\}^\lambda)^3$	
22 $\quad$ **if** $\|\mathsf{SampleD}(m, \alpha'; \rho)\| > \alpha'\sqrt{m}$: **abort**	$/\!/\mathbf{G_6}$
23 $\quad g[R'] := (\mathbf{s}, \rho, \mathbf{h}_0, \mathbf{h}_1)$	
24 **return** $g[R']$	

Fig. 6. The oracles in the proof of Theorem 1. The rest of the games is given in Fig. 5. Highlighted lines are only executed in the corresponding games.

and $\hat{K}_1 := \mathsf{H}(\mathbf{x}, \hat{\mathbf{h}}_1, \mathbf{h}_1)$. Later, a ciphertext ct is returned to $\mathcal{A}$. We say that the event $\mathsf{badK0}$ occurs, if one of the following holds:

- At this point, $\mathcal{A}$ already queried $\mathsf{H}(\mathbf{x}, \hat{\mathbf{h}}_{1-b_i}, \mathbf{h}_{1-b_i})$, or
- at some later point, before any query of the form $\mathrm{CORR}(i)$ or $\mathrm{REVEAL}(i, \mathsf{ct})$ for these i, ct, $\mathcal{A}$ queries $\mathsf{H}(\mathbf{x}, \hat{\mathbf{h}}_{1-b_i}, \mathbf{h}_{1-b_i})$.

Similarly, we say that the event $\mathsf{badK1}$ occurs, if one of the following holds:

- At this point, $\mathcal{A}$ already queried $\mathsf{H}(\mathbf{x}, \hat{\mathbf{h}}_{b_i}, \mathbf{h}_{b_i})$, or
- at some later point, before any query of the form $\mathrm{CORR}(i)$ or $\mathrm{REVEAL}(i, \mathsf{ct})$ for these i, ct, $\mathcal{A}$ queries $\mathsf{H}(\mathbf{x}, \hat{\mathbf{h}}_{b_i}, \mathbf{h}_{b_i})$.

As for event badR, this also includes indirect queries made by oracles DEC, CHECK. Similar to event badR, we formally model these two events via lists

$\mathcal{L}_{K,0}$ and $\mathcal{L}_{K,1}$, where $\mathcal{L}_{K,0}$ is associated to event badK0 and $\mathcal{L}_{K,1}$ is associated to event badK1. Also, note that although we defined the events with respect to bit b_i, their symmetry ensures that there is no additional information about b_i given to $\mathcal{A}$. Clearly, we have

$$|\Pr[\text{badR in } \mathbf{G}_2] - \Pr[\text{badR in } \mathbf{G}_3]| \leq \Pr[\text{badK in } \mathbf{G}_3]$$

and

$$|\mathsf{Adv}_2 - \mathsf{Adv}_3| \leq \Pr[\text{badK in } \mathbf{G}_3]$$
$$\leq \Pr[\text{badK0 in } \mathbf{G}_3] + \Pr[\text{badK1 in } \mathbf{G}_3].$$

We upper bound these probabilities in Lemma 6 and Lemma 7. Also, we upper bound the probability of badR in $\mathbf{G}_3$ in Lemma 5.

Further, we claim that the probability that $\mathbf{G}_3$ outputs 1 is negligible. To see this, consider the final output $(i^*, \mathsf{ct}^*, K^*)$ of $\mathcal{A}$. If the game outputs 1, then ct^* has been output by $\mathrm{ENC}(i^*)$, and $K^* = R$, where R has been sampled in the query $\mathrm{ENC}(i^*)$ that returned ct^*. Further, if the game outputs 1, then the events badR and badK did not occur. The game can only output if $\mathcal{A}$ never queried $\mathrm{CORR}(i^*)$, and never queried $\mathrm{REVEAL}(i^*, \mathsf{ct}^*)$, and therefore we know that $\mathcal{A}$ never queried $\mathsf{G}(R)$ and never queried $\mathsf{H}(\mathbf{x}, \hat{\mathbf{h}}_{b_i}, \mathbf{h}_{b_i})$ or $\mathsf{H}(\mathbf{x}, \hat{\mathbf{h}}_{1-b_i}, \mathbf{h}_{1-b_i})$, where the values $\mathbf{x}, \hat{\mathbf{h}}_0, \hat{\mathbf{h}}_1, \mathbf{h}_0, \mathbf{h}_1$ have been defined in the query $\mathrm{ENC}(i^*)$ that returned ct^*. This means that the ciphertext ct^* information-theoretically hides the value R, and R is distributed uniformly at random from $\mathcal{A}$'s point of view. Thus, the probability that $K^* = R$ is at most $2^{-\lambda}$, and we get

$$\mathsf{Adv}_3 \leq \frac{Q_\mathsf{E}}{2^\lambda}.$$

In summary, we can upper bound Adv_0 by

$$\Pr[\text{badR in } \mathbf{G}_1] + n \cdot \mathsf{Adv}_{\mathcal{B}}^{\mathsf{LWE}\ k,m,q,D_{\mathbb{Z},\gamma}}(\lambda) + \Pr[\text{badK in } \mathbf{G}_3] + \frac{Q_\mathsf{E}}{2^\lambda}$$

$$\leq \ \Pr[\text{badR in } \mathbf{G}_3] + 2n \cdot \mathsf{Adv}_{\mathcal{B}}^{\mathsf{LWE}\ k,m,q,D_{\mathbb{Z},\gamma}}(\lambda) + 2 \cdot \Pr[\text{badK1 in } \mathbf{G}_3] + \mathsf{negl}(\lambda)$$

$$\leq \ 2n \cdot \mathsf{Adv}_{\mathcal{B}}^{\mathsf{LWE}\ k,m,q,D_{\mathbb{Z},\gamma}}(\lambda) + 2 \cdot \Pr[\text{badK1 in } \mathbf{G}_3] + \mathsf{negl}(\lambda)$$

$$\leq \ 2n \cdot \mathsf{Adv}_{\mathcal{B}}^{\mathsf{LWE}\ k,m,q,D_{\mathbb{Z},\gamma}}(\lambda) + 2 \left(2n \cdot \mathsf{Adv}_{\mathcal{B}}^{\mathsf{LWE}\ k,m,q,D_{\mathbb{Z},\gamma}}(\lambda) + \mathsf{negl}(\lambda) \right) + \mathsf{negl}(\lambda)$$

$$\leq \ 6n \cdot \mathsf{Adv}_{\mathcal{B}}^{\mathsf{LWE}\ k,m,q,D_{\mathbb{Z},\gamma}}(\lambda) + \mathsf{negl}(\lambda).$$

$\square$

Lemma 5. *With assumptions from the proof of Theorem 1, we have*

$$\Pr[\text{badR } in \ G_3] \leq \frac{2Q_\mathsf{E}Q_\mathsf{G}}{2^\lambda} \leq \mathsf{negl}(\lambda).$$

The proof of the lemma is postponed to our full version [32].

Lemma 6. *With assumptions from the proof of Theorem 1, we have*

$$\Pr\left[\mathsf{badKO} \text{ in } \mathbf{G}_3\right] \leq \mathsf{negl}(\lambda).$$

Proof. First, we write the event badKO as

$$\mathsf{badKO} = \bigvee_{j \in [Q_E]} \mathsf{badKO}_j,$$

where Q_E is the number of $\mathcal{A}$'s queries to ENC and badKO_j denotes the event that badKO_j occurs for the entry $(\mathsf{qry}, i, \mathsf{ct})$ that is inserted into list $\mathcal{L}_{K,0}$ in the jth query to oracle ENC. We bound the probability of each badKO_j separately, and conclude with a union bound.

To this end, fix $j \in [Q_E]$. We define a new game $\mathbf{G}'_j$, which is defined to be as game $\mathbf{G}_3$, but with the following change: Consider the jth query to oracle ENC. Assume that in this query an entry $(\mathsf{qry}, i, \mathsf{ct})$ is inserted into list $\mathcal{L}_{K,0}$. Game $\mathbf{G}'_j$ immediately outputs 1 as soon as badKO_j occurs, i.e. if either $\mathsf{H}(\mathsf{qry})$ is already defined before the query, or $\mathsf{H}(\mathsf{qry})$ is queried before queries $\mathrm{CORR}(i)$ or $\mathrm{REVEAL}(i, \mathsf{ct})$. Also, if badKO_j can no longer occur (i.e. $\mathcal{A}$ queries $\mathrm{CORR}(i)$ or $\mathrm{REVEAL}(i, \mathsf{ct})$), the game immediately outputs 0. Note that until game $\mathbf{G}'_j$ outputs something, the view of $\mathcal{A}$ is identical to its view in $\mathbf{G}_3$. This implies that

$$\Pr\left[\mathsf{badKO}_j \text{ in } \mathbf{G}_3\right] = \Pr\left[\mathbf{G}'_j \Rightarrow 1\right].$$

Next, we change $\mathbf{G}'_j$ into $\mathbf{G}''_j$. In this game, consider the jth query to oracle ENC again. Recall that in this oracle query, a vector $\hat{\mathbf{h}}_{1-b_i}$ is defined via

$$\hat{\mathbf{h}}_{1-b_i} := \mathbf{U}^t_{i,1-b_i}\mathbf{s} + \mathbf{h}_{1-b_i}\lfloor q/2 \rceil.$$

In this game, we instead sample $\hat{\mathbf{h}}_{1-b_i} \xleftarrow{\$} \mathbb{Z}_q^\lambda$. We argue that the games are statistically close by using the generalized leftover hash lemma (Lemma 4), where the hash function is given by $\mathbf{s} \mapsto \mathbf{U}^t_{i,1-b_i}\mathbf{s}$. Note that $\mathbf{U}_{i,1-b_i}$ is sampled uniformly at random in $\mathbf{G}'_j$, and therefore this constitutes a universal family of hash functions. To use the generalized leftover hash lemma, we first need to lower bound the entropy of $\mathbf{s}$. To this end, we make use of Lemma 3.

Observe that in the jth query to oracle ENC, the only information (apart from $\mathbf{U}^t_{i,1-b_i}\mathbf{s}$) that $\mathcal{A}$ gets is $\mathbf{x}$ and $\hat{\mathbf{h}}_{b_i}$. Let $\epsilon = 2^{-\lambda}$. Then, we can use Lemma 3 (note that $\mathbf{A}$ has the correct form $\bar{\mathbf{A}}\mathbf{C} + \mathbf{F}$) to get

$$\tilde{H}^\epsilon_\infty\left(\mathbf{s}\big|\mathbf{x}, \hat{\mathbf{h}}_{b_i}\right) \geq \tilde{H}^\epsilon_\infty\left(\mathbf{s}|\mathbf{x}\right) - \lambda \log q$$

$$= \tilde{H}^\epsilon_\infty\left(\mathbf{s}|\mathbf{A}^t\mathbf{s} + \mathbf{e}\right) - \lambda \log q \geq H_\infty\left(\mathbf{s}\right) - (k + 3\lambda)\log q - \mathsf{negl}(\lambda)$$

$$= n \log(2\eta + 1) - (k + 3\lambda)\log q - \mathsf{negl}(\lambda) \geq \lambda \log q + \Omega(n).$$

For the last inequality, we used our assumption about the parameters. Now, we can use Lemma 4 with $\epsilon = 2^{-\lambda}$ and $\mathcal{Y} := \mathbb{Z}_q^{\lambda}$, and get that the statistical distance is at most

$$2\epsilon + \frac{1}{2}\sqrt{2^{-\tilde{H}_{\infty}^{\epsilon}(\mathbf{s}|\mathbf{x}, \hat{\mathbf{h}}_{b_i})} \cdot |\mathcal{Y}|} \leq 2^{-\lambda+1} + \frac{1}{2}\sqrt{2^{-\lambda \log q - \Omega(n) + \lambda \log q}} \leq \mathsf{negl}(\lambda).$$

Thus, we have
$$\left| \Pr\left[\mathbf{G}_j' \Rightarrow 1\right] - \Pr\left[\mathbf{G}_j'' \Rightarrow 1\right] \right| \leq \mathsf{negl}(\lambda).$$

Remark. The subtlety in the above argument is that oracles DEC and CHECK depend on the secret key. As the secret key is statistically independent of the value $\mathbf{s}$, the argument goes through even if the adversary had the secret key. However, this only holds under the assumption that event badR does not occur, as otherwise decrypting and reencrypting (and therefore querying $\mathsf{G}(R)$) would reveal $\mathbf{s}$.

Finally, we bound the probability that $\mathbf{G}_j''$ outputs 1. Recall that in the jth query to oracle ENC, the value $\mathbf{h}_{1-b_i}$ is part of the output of $\mathsf{G}(R)$. As we assume that badR does not occur, this means that during the query, this is a fresh value sampled uniformly at random. Also, our previous change removed all information about $\mathbf{h}_{1-b_i}$ from the response of oracle ENC. Thus, this value is uniformly random from $\mathcal{A}$'s view for the entire game. As it is part of the random oracle query qry that triggers event badK0$_j$ and lets the game output 1, we can use a union bound over all random oracle queries and get

$$\Pr\left[\mathbf{G}_j'' \Rightarrow 1\right] \leq \frac{Q_{\mathsf{H}}}{2^{\lambda}} \leq \mathsf{negl}(\lambda).$$

$\square$

Lemma 7. *With assumptions from the proof of Theorem 1, there is a PPT algorithm $\mathcal{B}$ with $\mathbf{T}(\mathcal{B}) \approx \mathbf{T}(\mathcal{A})$ and*

$$\Pr\left[\mathsf{badK1} \ in \ G_3\right] \leq 2n \cdot \mathsf{Adv}_{\mathcal{B}}^{\mathsf{LWE} \ k,m,q,D_{\mathbb{Z},\gamma}}(\lambda) + \mathsf{negl}(\lambda).$$

Proof. To bound the probability, we introduce games $\mathbf{G}_4, \mathbf{G}_5$ and $\mathbf{G}_6$. We argue that the probability of badK1 does not change significantly from $\mathbf{G}_3$ to $\mathbf{G}_6$. In game $\mathbf{G}_6$, we use Lemma 8 to argue that the view of $\mathcal{A}$ is independent of the bit b_i as long as the events badK0 and badK1 can occur. This will imply that the probabilities of badK0 and badK1 are the same in $\mathbf{G}_6$. Therefore, we can just bound the probability of badK0 in $\mathbf{G}_6$. This can easily be done by going back to game $\mathbf{G}_3$ and using Lemma 6. We will now proceed in more detail.

Game $\mathbf{G}_4$: Game $\mathbf{G}_4$ is as $\mathbf{G}_3$, but we change how par $:= \mathbf{A}$ is sampled. Concretely, we revert the change from $\mathbf{G}_1$ to $\mathbf{G}_2$ and sample $\mathbf{A} \xleftarrow{\$} \mathbb{Z}_q^{n \times m}$. As from

$\mathbf{G}_1$ to $\mathbf{G}_2$, it follows that

$$|\Pr\left[\mathsf{badK1\ in\ }\mathbf{G}_{3,}\right] - \Pr\left[\mathsf{badK1\ in\ }\mathbf{G}_4\right]| \leq n \cdot \mathsf{Adv}_{\mathcal{B}}^{\mathsf{LWE}\ k,m,q,D_{\mathbb{Z},\gamma}}(\lambda),$$

$$|\Pr\left[\mathsf{badK0\ in\ }\mathbf{G}_3\right] - \Pr\left[\mathsf{badK0\ in\ }\mathbf{G}_4\right]| \leq n \cdot \mathsf{Adv}_{\mathcal{B}}^{\mathsf{LWE}\ k,m,q,D_{\mathbb{Z},\gamma}}(\lambda).$$

Game $\mathbf{G}_5$: Game $\mathbf{G}_5$ is as $\mathbf{G}_4$, but we change how the matrices $\mathbf{U}_{i,1-b_i}$ are defined for all $i \in [N]$. Recall that before, these are sampled uniformly at random from $\mathbb{Z}_q^{n \times \lambda}$. In $\mathbf{G}_5$, we first sample $\mathbf{Z}_{i,1-b_i} \leftarrow D_{\mathbb{Z},\alpha}^{m \times \lambda}$ and then set $\mathbf{U}_{i,1-b_i} := \mathbf{A}\mathbf{Z}_{i,1-b_i}$. By Lemma 1, the distributions of these matrices are statistically close to uniform. Thus we get

$$|\Pr\left[\mathsf{badK1\ in\ }\mathbf{G}_4\right] - \Pr\left[\mathsf{badK1\ in\ }\mathbf{G}_5\right]| \leq \mathsf{negl}(\lambda),$$

$$|\Pr\left[\mathsf{badK0\ in\ }\mathbf{G}_4\right] - \Pr\left[\mathsf{badK0\ in\ }\mathbf{G}_5\right]| \leq \mathsf{negl}(\lambda).$$

Game $\mathbf{G}_6$: Game $\mathbf{G}_6$ is as $\mathbf{G}_5$, but we add additional bad events, that let the game abort. Namely, the game aborts as soon as one of the following occurs:

- For some $i \in [N]$, one of the columns $\mathbf{z}$ of $\mathbf{Z}_{i,0}$ or $\mathbf{Z}_{i,1}$ satisfies $\|\mathbf{z}\| > \alpha\sqrt{m}$.
- For some random oracle query $\mathsf{G}(R)$ that returns $(\mathbf{s}, \rho, \mathbf{h}_0, \mathbf{h}_1)$, it holds that $\|\mathsf{SampleD}(m, \alpha'; \rho)\| > \alpha'\sqrt{m}$.
- There is a collision in random oracle H.

By Lemma 2, the first two events occur only with negligible probability. As hash values for H are sampled uniformly at random from $\{0,1\}^\lambda$, the third event also occurs only with negligible probability. It follows that

$$|\Pr\left[\mathsf{badK1\ in\ }\mathbf{G}_5\right] - \Pr\left[\mathsf{badK1\ in\ }\mathbf{G}_6\right]| \leq \mathsf{negl}(\lambda),$$

$$|\Pr\left[\mathsf{badK0\ in\ }\mathbf{G}_5\right] - \Pr\left[\mathsf{badK0\ in\ }\mathbf{G}_6\right]| \leq \mathsf{negl}(\lambda).$$

Finally, we claim that

$$\Pr\left[\mathsf{badK1\ in\ }\mathbf{G}_6\right] = \Pr\left[\mathsf{badK0\ in\ }\mathbf{G}_6\right].$$

Note that once we showed this, the statement follows.

It remains to show the claim. First, fix a point in the execution of the game, and let $\mathcal{I} \subseteq [N]$ denote the set of indices $i \in [N]$, for which $\mathcal{A}$ did not yet query $\mathrm{CORR}(i)$ at this point. Note that the events $\mathsf{badK0}$ and $\mathsf{K1}$ can only occur for indices in $\mathcal{I}$. We claim that the view of $\mathcal{A}$ at this point does not depend on the bits b_i for $i \in \mathcal{I}$. This is because the public keys itself do not reveal b_i (because both $\mathbf{U}_{i,0}$ and $\mathbf{U}_{i,1}$ have the same distribution), the queries to ENC and REVEAL do not reveal b_i, and, by Lemma 8, queries to DEC and CHECK do not reveal b_i. Second, note that the events $\mathsf{badK0}, \mathsf{badK1}$ are exactly the same, except for the lists $\mathcal{L}_{K,0}$ and $\mathcal{L}_{K,1}$ that appear in their definition. Also, the lists only differ depending on the bit b_i. As $\mathcal{A}$ has no information about b_i, and the events $\mathsf{badK0}$ and $\mathsf{badK1}$ occur with equal probability. $\qquad\square$

Lemma 8. *Let $4\alpha\alpha'm < q$. Let $\mathbf{Z}_0, \mathbf{Z}_1 \in \mathbb{Z}_q^{m\times\lambda}$ such that $\|\mathbf{z}_{b,i}\| \leq \alpha\sqrt{m}$ for all $i \in [\lambda], b \in \{0,1\}$, where $\mathbf{z}_{b,i}$ denotes column i of $\mathbf{Z}_b$. Let $\mathsf{par} := \mathbf{A} \in \mathbb{Z}_q^{n\times m}$ and $\mathbf{U}_0 := \mathbf{A}\mathbf{Z}_0$, $\mathbf{U}_1 := \mathbf{A}\mathbf{Z}_1$. Assume that for all outputs $(\mathbf{s}, \rho, \mathbf{h}_0, \mathbf{h}_1)$ of G and $\mathbf{e} \leftarrow \mathsf{SampleD}(m, \alpha'; \rho)$ it holds that $\|\mathbf{e}\| \leq \alpha'\sqrt{m}$. Further, assume that for each $x \neq x' \in \{0,1\}^*$ we have $\mathsf{H}(x) \neq \mathsf{H}(x')$. Then, for each $\mathsf{ct} = (C_0, C_1, \mathbf{x}, \hat{\mathbf{h}}_0, \hat{\mathbf{h}}_1) \in \{0,1\}^\lambda \times \{0,1\}^\lambda \times \mathbb{Z}_q^m \times \mathbb{Z}_q^\lambda \times \mathbb{Z}_q^\lambda$ it holds that $\mathsf{Decap}((\mathbf{Z}_0, 0), \mathsf{ct}) = \mathsf{Decap}((\mathbf{Z}_1, 1), \mathsf{ct})$.*

The proof of the lemma is postponed to our full version [32].

3.3   Construction from Matrix Decisional Diffie-Hellman

We construct an OW-ChCCA secure key encapsulation mechanism based on the (matrix) decisional Diffie-Hellman assumption [12], which has deterministic ciphertext derivation. The construction mimics our lattice-based construction. We postpone the formal description and details to our full version [32].

4   AKE from OW-ChCCA Secure KEMs

A two-message AKE protocol $\mathsf{AKE} := (\mathsf{Setup}', \mathsf{KG}', \mathsf{Init}, \mathsf{Der}_\mathsf{R}, \mathsf{Der}_\mathsf{I})$ consists of five algorithms. The setup algorithm Setup', on input security parameter 1^λ, outputs global AKE system parameters par'. KG' takes the system parameters par' as input and outputs a long-term key pair $(\mathsf{pk}', \mathsf{sk}')$ for one party.

Let P_i and P_j as two parties and $(\mathsf{pk}'_i, \mathsf{sk}'_i)$ and $(\mathsf{pk}'_j, \mathsf{sk}'_j)$ be the long-term key pair of P_i and P_j, respectively. Figure 7 shows how P_i, (as initiator) establish a shared key with P_j (as responder). To initialize the session with P_j, P_i runs the initialization algorithm Init, which takes $\mathsf{sk}'_i, \mathsf{pk}'_j$ as inputs and outputs a protocol message M_i and session state st, and then P_i sends M_i to P_j. On receiving M_i, P_j runs the responder's derivation algorithm Der_R, which takes $\mathsf{sk}'_j, \mathsf{pk}'_i$, and the received message M_i as input, to generate a responded message M_j and a session key SK_j. P_j sends M_j to P_i. Finally, on receiving M_j, P_i runs the initiator's derivation algorithm Der_I which inputs $\mathsf{sk}'_i, \mathsf{pk}'_j$, the received message M_j, and the session state st generated before, to generate a session key sk'_i. In two-message AKE protocols, the responder does not need to save session state since it can compute the session key right after receiving the initiator's message.

Party P_i : $(\mathsf{pk}'_i, \mathsf{sk}'_i)$		**Party P_j : $(\mathsf{pk}'_j, \mathsf{sk}'_j)$**
$(\mathsf{M}_i, \mathsf{st}) \leftarrow \mathsf{Init}(\mathsf{sk}'_i, \mathsf{pk}'_j)$		
$\quad\quad\Big\downarrow \mathsf{st}$	$\xrightarrow{\quad\mathsf{M}_i\quad}$ $\xleftarrow{\quad\mathsf{M}_j\quad}$	$(\mathsf{M}_j, \mathsf{SK}_j) \leftarrow \mathsf{Der}_\mathsf{R}(\mathsf{sk}'_j, \mathsf{pk}'_i, \mathsf{M}_i)$
$\mathsf{SK}_i \leftarrow \mathsf{Der}_\mathsf{I}(\mathsf{sk}'_i, \mathsf{pk}'_j, \mathsf{M}_j, \mathsf{st})$		

Fig. 7. Illustration for a two-pass AKE protocol execution between party P_i and P_j.

We define the correctness of AKE protocols, stating that an honestly execution between two parties P_i and P_j as in Fig. 7 will produce the same session key $\mathsf{SK}_i = \mathsf{SK}_j$.

Definition 5 (AKE Correctness). *Let* $\mathsf{AKE} := (\mathsf{Setup}', \mathsf{KG}', \mathsf{Init}, \mathsf{Der_R}, \mathsf{Der_I})$ *be a AKE protocol. We say* AKE *is* ρ-*correct, if for any AKE system parameter* $\mathsf{par}' \leftarrow \mathsf{Setup}'(1^\lambda)$, *any* $(\mathsf{pk}'_i, \mathsf{sk}'_i) \leftarrow \mathsf{KG}'(\mathsf{par}')$, $(\mathsf{pk}'_j, \mathsf{sk}'_j) \leftarrow \mathsf{KG}'(\mathsf{par}')$, *the following probability is at least* ρ.

$$\Pr\left[\mathsf{SK}_j = \mathsf{SK}_i \,\middle|\, \begin{array}{c} (\mathsf{M}_i, \mathsf{st}) \leftarrow \mathsf{Init}(\mathsf{sk}'_i, \mathsf{pk}'_j) \\ (\mathsf{M}_j, \mathsf{SK}_j) \leftarrow \mathsf{Der_R}(\mathsf{sk}'_j, \mathsf{pk}'_i, \mathsf{M}_i) \\ \mathsf{SK}_i \leftarrow \mathsf{Der_I}(\mathsf{sk}'_i, \mathsf{pk}'_j, \mathsf{M}_j, \mathsf{st}) \end{array}\right]$$

AKE SECURITY MODEL. Following [18], we define a game-based AKE security model using pseudocode. We use the weak forward secrecy model wFS-St in [18] which captures some attacks against AKE such as key-compromise-impersonation (KCI) and maximal-exposure (MEX) and considers weak forward security. Details of wFS-St model are shown in our full version [32].

4.1 Our AKE Protocol

Let $\mathsf{KEM}_1 = (\mathsf{Setup}_1, \mathsf{KG}_1, \mathsf{Encaps}_1, \mathsf{Decaps}_1)$ and $\mathsf{KEM}_0 = (\mathsf{Setup}_0, \mathsf{KG}_0, \mathsf{Encaps}_0, \mathsf{Decaps}_0)$ be two KEM schemes. We construct our direct two-message AKE protocol $\mathsf{AKE} = (\mathsf{Setup}', \mathsf{KG}', \mathsf{Init}, \mathsf{Der_R}, \mathsf{Der_I})$ as shown in Fig. 8, where $H : \{0,1\}^* \to \mathcal{SK}$ is a hash function which is used to derive the session key, and $G : \{0,1\}^\kappa \times \{0,1\}^\kappa \to \{0,1\}^d$ is a hash function which outputs a one-time key to encrypt state. We assume that any unencrypted state, $\mathsf{st}' = (\widetilde{\mathsf{pk}}, \widetilde{\mathsf{sk}}, \mathsf{ct}_j, \mathsf{K}_j)$ as in Fig. 8 can be encoded as a d-bit string.

In Sect. 5.1 we show that an OW-ChCCA secure KEM gives us a tight non-committing KEM. By the work of Jager et al. [18], this will give us a tightly secure AKE indirectly. This is our second approach in constructing tightly secure AKE, and it is indirect. The only difference between our direct protocol AKE and our indirect one $\mathsf{AKE_{in}}$ is the session key derivation as described in the caption of Fig. 8.

CORRECTNESS. The correctness of our AKE protocol is dependent on KEM_1 or KEM_0. Suppose that KEM_1 is $(1 - \delta_1)$-correct and KEM_0 is $(1 - \delta_0)$-correct (cf. Definition 1). In our protocol (Fig. 8), each session includes two KEM_1 ciphertexts and one KEM_0 ciphertext. By the union bound, the probability that for honest matching sessions sID and sID', they do not produce the same key is at most $2\delta_1 + \delta_0$, so we have the following lemma.

Lemma 9. *If* KEM_1 *is* $(1 - \delta_1)$-*correct and* KEM_0 *is* $(1 - \delta_0)$-*correct, then the AKE protocol* AKE *in Fig. 8 is* $(1 - 2\delta_1 - \delta_0)$-*correct.*

SECURITY. Theorem 2 shows that if KEM_1 and KEM_0 are OW-ChCCA , and G and H are modeled as random oracles, then AKE is tightly wFS-St secure. We postpone the proof of Theorem 2 to our full version [32].

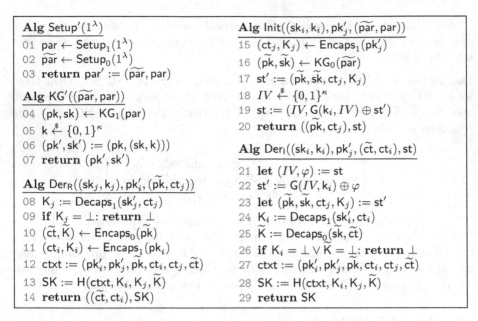

Fig. 8. Our direct AKE protocol AKE. Lines with purple are used to achieve security against internal states reveal by encrypting state st'. The only difference in our indirect AKE protocol AKE_{in} is that session keys in Lines 13 and 28 are computed as $\mathsf{SK} := \mathsf{H}(\mathsf{ctxt}, \mathsf{H}'(\mathsf{pk}_i, \mathsf{ct}_i, \mathsf{K}_i), \mathsf{H}'(\mathsf{pk}_j, \mathsf{ct}_j, \mathsf{K}_j), \mathsf{H}'(\widetilde{\mathsf{pk}}, \widetilde{\mathsf{ct}}, \widetilde{\mathsf{K}}))$ where H' is a different hash function.

Theorem 2. *Let* $\mathsf{H} : \{0,1\}^* \to \mathcal{SK}$ *and* $\mathsf{G} : \{0,1\}^\kappa \times \{0,1\}^\kappa \to \{0,1\}^d$ *be random oracles. If* KEM_1 *is* $(1 - \delta_1)$-*correct for* $\delta_1 = \mathsf{negl}(\lambda)$ *and* $\mathsf{OW\text{-}ChCCA}$ *secure with* $\gamma_1 = \omega(\log(\lambda))$ *bits ciphertext entropy and* $\mu_1 = \omega(\log(\lambda))$ *bits public key entropy, and* KEM_0 *is* $(1 - \delta_0)$-*correct for* $\delta_0 = \mathsf{negl}(\lambda)$ *and* $\mathsf{OW\text{-}ChCCA}$ *secure with* $\gamma_0 = \omega(\log(\lambda))$ *bits ciphertext entropy and* $\mu_0 = \omega(\log(\lambda))$ *bits public key entropy, then the AKE protocol* AKE *in Fig. 8 is* wFS-St *secure.*

For any PPT adversary $\mathcal{A}$ *against* wFS-St *security of* AKE, *there are PPT algorithm* $\mathcal{B}_1$ *and* $\mathcal{B}_0$ *with* $\mathbf{T}(\mathcal{A}) \approx \mathbf{T}(\mathcal{B}_1)$ *and* $\mathbf{T}(\mathcal{A}) \approx \mathbf{T}(\mathcal{B}_0)$ *and*

$$\mathsf{Adv}^{\mathsf{wFS\text{-}St}}_{\mathcal{A},\mathsf{AKE}}(\lambda) \leq 2\mathsf{Adv}^{\mathsf{OW\text{-}ChCCA}}_{\mathcal{B}_1,\mathsf{KEM}_1}(\lambda) + 2\mathsf{Adv}^{\mathsf{OW\text{-}ChCCA}}_{\mathcal{B}_0,\mathsf{KEM}_0}(\lambda)$$

$$+ 2\delta_1 + 2\delta_0 + \frac{(N+1) \cdot S \cdot Q_{\mathsf{G}}}{2^{\kappa-1}} + \frac{2(Q_{\mathsf{H}}^2 + S^2)}{|\mathcal{SK}|}$$

$$+ 2S \cdot (Q_{\mathsf{H}} + S) \cdot \left(\frac{1}{2^{\gamma_1}} + \frac{1}{2^{\gamma_0}} + \frac{1}{2^{\mu_0}} \right) + \frac{Q_{\mathsf{G}}^2 + N^2 + S^2}{2^{d-1}},$$

where Q_{G} *and* Q_{H} *are the numbers of queries to* G *and* H, *respectively.* N *and* S *are numbers of parties and sessions in the* wFS-St *security game, respectively.*

5   Further Applications of OW-ChCCA Security

We propose further applications of OW-ChCCA security. Namely, from an OW-ChCCA secure key encapsulation mechanism, we can tightly construct the following schemes:

- A non-committing key encapsulation mechanism, which implies a tightly secure AKE by [18]. The resulting AKE protocol, $\mathsf{AKE_{in}}$, is described as in Fig. 8;
- A public-key encryption scheme with simulation-based bi-selective opening security;
- A key encapsulation mechanism with enhanced CCA security [16]. Since it is not the main result of our paper, we postpone this application to our full version [32].

5.1   Non-committing Key Encapsulation Mechanism

<u>DEFINITION.</u> We recall the definition of non-committing key encapsulation mechanisms (KEM) [18].

Definition 6 (N-Receiver Non-Committing KEM). *Let* $\mathsf{KEM} = (\mathsf{Setup}, \mathsf{Gen}, \mathsf{Encap}, \mathsf{Decap})$ *be a key encapsulation mechanism which is relative to a simulator* $\mathsf{Sim} = (\mathsf{SimGen}, \mathsf{SimEncaps}, \mathsf{SimHash})$. *We define games* $\mathsf{NC_{real}}$ *and* $\mathsf{NC_{sim}}$ *as in Fig. 9. The simulator* Sim *is only used in* $\mathsf{NC_{sim}}$. *We say* KEM *is* NC-CCA *secure, if for all PPT adversaries* $\mathcal{A}$, $\mathcal{A}$*'s advantage is negligible:*

$$\mathsf{Adv}^{\mathsf{NC\text{-}CCA}}_{\mathsf{KEM},\mathsf{Sim},\mathcal{A}}(\lambda) := \left| \Pr\left[\mathsf{NC}^{\mathcal{A}}_{\mathsf{real}}(\lambda) \Rightarrow 1\right] - \Pr\left[\mathsf{NC}^{\mathcal{A}}_{\mathsf{sim}}(\lambda) \Rightarrow 1\right] \right|$$

<u>CONSTRUCTION.</u> In Fig. 10, we transform a OW-ChCCA secure $\mathsf{KEM_0} = (\mathsf{Setup_0}, \mathsf{Gen_0}, \mathsf{Encaps_0}, \mathsf{Decaps_0})$ into a NC-CCA secure KEM scheme $\mathsf{KEM} = (\mathsf{Setup}, \mathsf{Gen}, \mathsf{Encaps}, \mathsf{Decaps})$ using a random oracle $\mathsf{H} \colon \{0,1\}^* \to \{0,1\}^\kappa$, where $\kappa = \omega(\log(\lambda))$ is the key length of KEM. Following the definition in [18], Encaps and Decaps are associated with H. Namely, different users have access to different random oracles.

Theorem 3. *Let N be the number of users and let H_i for $i \in [N]$ be random oracles. If $\mathsf{KEM_0}$ is OW-ChCCA secure, $(1 - \delta_0)$-correct for $\delta_0 = \mathsf{negl}(\lambda)$, and has $\gamma_0 = \omega(\log(\lambda))$ bits of ciphertext entropy, then KEM is NC-CCA secure.*

Concretely, for any PPT algorithm $\mathcal{A}$, there is a PPT algorithm $\mathcal{B}$ such that $\mathbf{T}(\mathcal{A}) \approx \mathbf{T}(\mathcal{B})$ and

$$\mathsf{Adv}^{\mathsf{NC\text{-}CCA}}_{\mathsf{KEM},\mathsf{Sim},\mathcal{A}}(\lambda) \leq 2 \cdot \mathsf{Adv}^{\mathsf{OW\text{-}ChCCA}}_{\mathcal{B},\mathsf{KEM_0}}(\lambda) + 3\delta_0 + \frac{Q_\mathsf{H}^2 + Q_\mathsf{E}^2}{2^{\kappa-1}} + \frac{NQ_\mathsf{E}(Q_\mathsf{H} + 2Q_\mathsf{D})}{2^{\gamma_0}},$$

where Q_D, Q_E, and Q_H are the numbers of $\mathcal{A}$'s queries to DECAPS, ENCAPS, *and* $\{\mathsf{H}_i\}_{i \in [N]}$, *respectively, and $\mathcal{B}$ also queries* ENC Q_E *times.*

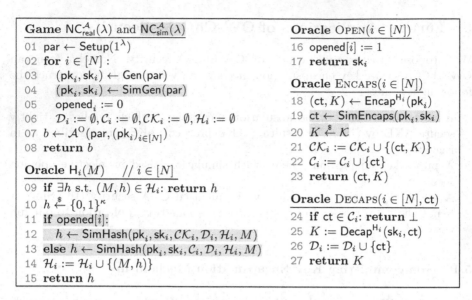

Fig. 9. $NC_{real}^{\mathcal{A}}(\lambda)$ and $NC_{sim}^{\mathcal{A}}(\lambda)$ for an adversary $\mathcal{A}$ and KEM = (Setup, Gen, Encap, Decap) with simulation processes (SimGen, SimEncaps, SimHash). Algorithms Encap and Decap have oracle access to H, but not SimEncaps. $\mathcal{A}$ has access to $O := \{H_1, ..., H_N,$ Encaps, Decaps, Open$\}$. Highlighted lines are only executed in $NC_{sim}^{\mathcal{A}}(\lambda)$.

Proof. Let $\mathcal{A}$ be an adversary against KEM in the $NC_{real}^{KEM}(\lambda)$ game, where N is the number of users. Each user $i \in [N]$ is associated with public key pk_i. We prove Theorem 3 with games as defined in Fig. 11 and Fig. 12.

Game G_0: This game is the same as $NC_{real}^{KEM}(\lambda)$, except that we exclude the collision among the outputs of H_i for all $i \in [N]$, and assume that challenge ciphertexts generated in Encaps are never been issued to Decaps before (i.e., if Encaps(i) outputs a ciphertext ct, then ct $\notin \mathcal{D}_i$). If such a collision happens at any time, then we abort the game. We do not explicitly define such events in the code for readability. By a union bound and the ciphertext entropy of KEM_0, we have

$$\left| \Pr\left[NC_{real}^{KEM,\mathcal{A}}(\lambda) \Rightarrow 1 \right] - \Pr\left[G_0^{\mathcal{A}} \Rightarrow 1 \right] \right| \leq \frac{Q_H^2 + Q_E^2}{2^\kappa} + \frac{NQ_EQ_D}{2^{\gamma_0}}.$$

Game G_1: We modify the generation of challenge keys and simulation of $\{H_i\}_{i \in [N]}$. In Encaps(i), we generate the key K by independent uniform sampling from the key space $\{0,1\}^\kappa$ (Line 20), and record (ct, ψ, K) in a list $\mathcal{CK}_i^{ow}$ (Line 21). When the adversary queries H_i on (ct, ψ), if (ct, ψ) is generated in Encaps(i), then we return K where $(ct, \psi, K) \in \mathcal{CK}_i^{ow}$ (Lines 27 to 28).

This modification does not change the view of $\mathcal{A}$ unless Encaps(i) generates some (ct, ψ) that $\mathcal{A}$ queried H_i on (ct, ψ). By the ciphertext entropy of KEM_0, we have

$$\left| \Pr\left[G_0^{\mathcal{A}} \Rightarrow 1 \right] - \Pr\left[G_1^{\mathcal{A}} \Rightarrow 1 \right] \right| \leq \frac{NQ_EQ_H}{2^{\gamma_0}}.$$

Alg $\mathsf{Encaps}^\mathsf{H}(\mathsf{pk})$	**Alg** $\mathsf{SimEncaps}(\mathsf{pk},\mathsf{sk})$
01 $(\mathsf{ct},\psi) \leftarrow \mathsf{Encaps}_0(\mathsf{pk})$	07 $(\mathsf{ct},\psi) \leftarrow \mathsf{Encaps}_0(\mathsf{pk})$
02 **return** $(\mathsf{ct}, K := \mathsf{H}(\mathsf{ct},\psi))$	08 **return** ct
Alg $\mathsf{Decaps}^\mathsf{H}(\mathsf{sk},\mathsf{ct})$	**Alg** $\mathsf{SimHash}(\mathsf{pk},\mathsf{sk},\mathcal{E}_i,\mathcal{D}_i,\mathcal{H}_i, M = (\mathsf{ct},\psi))$
03 $\psi' := \mathsf{Decaps}_0(\mathsf{sk},\mathsf{ct})$	09 **if** $\exists K$ s.t. $(\mathsf{ct}, K) \in \mathcal{E}_i \wedge \mathsf{Decaps}_0(\mathsf{sk},\mathsf{ct}) = \psi$:
04 **if** $\psi' = \bot : K' := \bot$	10 $\quad h := K$
05 **else** $K' := \mathsf{H}(\mathsf{ct},\psi')$	11 **else** $: h \xleftarrow{\$} \{0,1\}^\kappa$
06 **return** K'	12 **return** h

Fig. 10. Key encapsulation mechanism $\mathsf{KEM} = (\mathsf{Setup}, \mathsf{Gen}, \mathsf{Encaps}, \mathsf{Decaps})$ based on a KEM scheme $\mathsf{KEM}_0 = (\mathsf{Setup}_0, \mathsf{Gen}_0, \mathsf{Encaps}_0, \mathsf{Decaps}_0)$ and random oracle H, where $\mathsf{Setup} = \mathsf{Setup}_0$ and $\mathsf{Gen} = \mathsf{Gen}_0$. $\mathsf{Sim} = (\mathsf{SimGen}, \mathsf{SimEncaps}, \mathsf{SimHash})$ is a simulator of KEM, where $\mathsf{SimGen} = \mathsf{Gen}$. $\mathcal{E}_i$ is either $\mathcal{C}_i$ or $\mathcal{CK}_i$. $\mathcal{H}_i$ is a list that records the RO queries to H_i.

Game $\mathbf{G}_2$: We introduce an abort rule in H_i and modify the simulation of H_i for each $i \in [N]$:

- If $\mathcal{A}$ queries H_i on (ct,ψ), where ct is a challenge ciphertext wrt pk_i, ψ is the KEM_0 key of ct, and user i is not opened ($\mathsf{opened}[i] = 0$), then the game aborts (Lines 29 to 31). Let bad^ow be the event that $\mathcal{A}$ issued such queries to H_i for some $i \in [N]$.
- When $\mathcal{A}$ queries H_i on (ct,ψ), if user i is opened ($\mathsf{opened}[i] = 1$) and ψ is the KEM_0 key of ct, then we return K where (ct, K) is recorded in $\mathcal{CK}_i$ (Lines 32 to 35).

We claim that if bad^ow does not happen, then the view of $\mathcal{A}$ in $\mathbf{G}_1$ is the same as in $\mathbf{G}_2$. Suppose that bad^ow does not happen in $\mathbf{G}_1$. For any unopened user i, $\mathcal{A}$ never queries the hash input (ct,ψ) of the challenge keys of user i, which means that $\mathsf{H}_i(\mathsf{ct},\psi)$ will never be defined and the code in Lines 27 to 28 will never be executed (until user i is opened). That is, the code in Lines 27 to 28 is executed only if user i is opened. By definition of $\mathcal{CK}_i^\mathsf{ow}$, $(\mathsf{ct},\psi,K) \in \mathcal{CK}^\mathsf{ow}$ is equivalent to $(\mathsf{ct}, K') \in \mathcal{CK}_i \wedge \mathsf{Decaps}_0(\mathsf{sk}_i,\mathsf{ct}) = \psi$. So, the code in Lines 32 to 35 is a rephrasing of Lines 27 to 28. Lemma 10 bounds the difference between $\mathbf{G}_1$ with $\mathbf{G}_2$. For readability, we postpone the proof of Lemma 10 and continue the proof of Theorem 3.

Lemma 10. *With the notation and assumptions from the proof of Theorem 3, there is a PPT algorithm $\mathcal{B}$ with $\mathbf{T}(\mathcal{B}) \approx \mathbf{T}(\mathcal{A})$ and*

$$\left| \Pr\left[G_1^\mathcal{A} \Rightarrow 1 \right] - \Pr\left[G_2^\mathcal{A} \Rightarrow 1 \right] \right| \leq \Pr[\mathsf{bad}^\mathsf{ow}] \leq \mathsf{Adv}_{\mathcal{B},\mathsf{KEM}_0}^{\mathsf{OW\text{-}ChCCA}}(\lambda) + \delta_0,$$

where $\mathcal{B}$ is a PPT algorithm with $\mathbf{T}(\mathcal{B}) \approx \mathbf{T}(\mathcal{A})$.

Game $\mathbf{G}_3$: We undo the abort rules defined in $\mathbf{G}_2$. The difference between $\mathbf{G}_2$ with $\mathbf{G}_3$ is that if $\mathcal{A}$ triggers such abort events, $\mathbf{G}_3$ will not abort. So, by Lemma

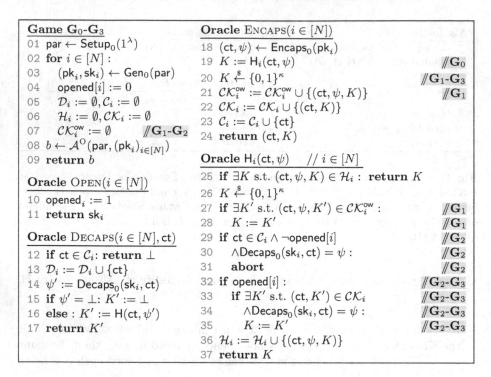

Fig. 11. The games G_0-G_3 in the proof of Theorem 3. Lines with highlighted comments are only executed in the corresponding games.

10, we have

$$\left| \Pr\left[G_2^{\mathcal{A}} \Rightarrow 1 \right] - \Pr\left[G_3^{\mathcal{A}} \Rightarrow 1 \right] \right| \leq \mathsf{Adv}_{\mathcal{B},\mathsf{KEM}_0}^{\mathsf{OW\text{-}ChCCA}}(\lambda) + \delta_0,$$

Game G_4: We rewrite the code of G_3 in Fig. 12 to follow the syntax of the game $\mathsf{NC}_{\mathsf{sim}}^{\mathcal{A}}(\lambda)$ (Fig. 9). Specifically, in G_4, key pairs $\{(\mathsf{pk}_i, \mathsf{sk}_i)\}_{i \in [N]}$ are generated by SimGen (which is the same as Gen), challenge ciphertexts are generated by $\mathsf{SimEncaps}$ (Fig. 10), and we use $\mathsf{SimHash}$ to handle queries to random oracles $\{\mathsf{H}_i\}_{i \in [N]}$ (Fig. 10).

One can check that G_4 is equivalent to G_3, and is the same as the game $\mathsf{NC}_{\mathsf{sim}}^{\mathcal{A}}(\lambda)$. Note that at the start of the proof we assume that there is no collision among the outputs of H_i for all $i \in [N]$ and challenge ciphertexts generated in $\mathrm{ENCAPS}(i)$ are never been issued to $\mathrm{DECAPS}(i)$ before for all i. We have

$$\left| \Pr\left[G_4^{\mathcal{A}} \Rightarrow 1 \right] - \Pr\left[\mathsf{NC}_{\mathsf{sim}}^{\mathcal{A}}(\lambda) \Rightarrow 1 \right] \right| \leq \frac{Q_{\mathsf{H}}^2 + Q_{\mathsf{E}}^2}{2^\kappa} + \frac{N Q_{\mathsf{E}} Q_{\mathsf{D}}}{2^{\gamma_0}}.$$

By combining all the probability bounds, we obtain the statement.   □

Proof (of Lemma 10). To bound $\Pr[\mathsf{bad}^{\mathsf{ow}}]$, we construct an adversary $\mathcal{B}$ that simulates G_2 (Fig. 11) for $\mathcal{A}$ and against OW-ChCCA security of KEM_0. By

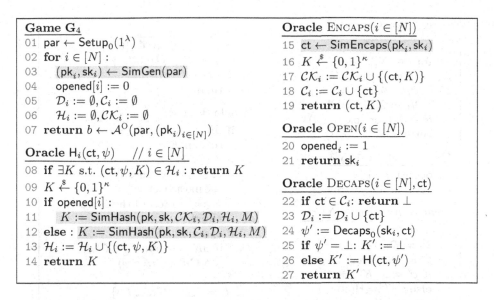

Fig. 12. Game $\mathbf{G}_4$ in the proof of Theorem 3. The differences to $\mathbf{G}_3$ are highlighted.

Definition 3 and Fig. 3, $\mathcal{B}$ is given parameters par, N public keys, and oracle accesses to ENC, DEC, CORR, CHECK. Reduction $\mathcal{B}$ is given in Fig. 13.

In Fig. 13, the simulations of DECAPS and OPEN are straightforward. In ENCAPS(i), $\mathcal{B}$ generates challenge ciphertext by querying ENC(i). Since $\mathcal{B}$ does not know the KEM_0 keys of challenge ciphertexts generated via ENC(i) and sk_i before $\mathcal{A}$ opens party i's secret key, to simulate $\mathbf{G}_2$, $\mathcal{B}$ uses the CHECK oracle to determine whether $\mathsf{Decaps}_0(\mathsf{sk}_i, \mathsf{ct}) = \psi$ or not.

If $\mathsf{bad}^{\mathsf{ow}}$ happens, which means that $\mathcal{A}$ queries H_i on (ct, ψ) where ψ is the KEM_0 key of a challenge ciphertext ct wrt pk_i and party i is unopened, then by the simulation of H_i in Fig. 13, $\mathcal{B}$ can detect such query and get the KEM_0 key of the challenge ciphertext ct. Therefore, if $\mathsf{bad}^{\mathsf{ow}}$ happens, $\mathcal{B}$ finally outputs ψ^* such that ψ^* is the one-way solution of some challenge ciphertext ct wrt pk_i and $\mathcal{B}$ never issue CORR(i). By Definition 3 and Fig. 3, $\mathcal{B}$ wins the OW-ChCCA$_{\mathsf{KEM}}(\lambda)$ game. Note that we also need to count in the correctness bound of KEM_0, since KEM_0 is imperfect, $(\mathsf{ct}, \psi) \leftarrow \mathsf{Encaps}_0(\mathsf{pk}_i)$ does not always imply $\psi = \mathsf{Decaps}_0(\mathsf{sk}_i, \mathsf{ct})$. By the argument of $\mathbf{G}_2$ in the proof of Theorem 3, we have

$$\left| \Pr\left[\mathbf{G}_1^{\mathcal{A}} \Rightarrow 1\right] - \Pr\left[\mathbf{G}_2^{\mathcal{A}} \Rightarrow 1\right] \right| \leq \Pr[\mathsf{bad}^{\mathsf{ow}}] \leq \mathsf{Adv}_{\mathcal{B},\mathsf{KEM}_0}^{\mathsf{OW\text{-}ChCCA}}(\lambda) + \epsilon_0.$$

$\square$

5.2 From OW-ChCCA to SIM-BiSO-CCA

We construct a bilateral selective-opening (i.e., SIM-BiSO-CCA) secure public-key encryption tightly from any OW-ChCCA KEM with deterministic ciphertext

$\mathcal{B}^{\text{ENC,DEC,CORR,CHECK}}(\text{par},(\text{pk}_i)_{i\in[N]})$	Oracle ENCAPS($i \in [N]$)
01 $\psi^* := \bot$	16 ct $\leftarrow$ ENC(i), $K \xleftarrow{\$} \{0,1\}^\kappa$
02 for $i \in [N]$:	17 $\mathcal{CK}_i := \mathcal{CK}_i \cup \{(\text{ct}, K)\}$
03 opened[i] := 0	18 $\mathcal{C}_i := \mathcal{C}_i \cup \{\text{ct}\}$
04 $\mathcal{D}_i := \emptyset, \mathcal{C}_i := \emptyset$	19 return (ct, K)
05 $\mathcal{H}_i := \emptyset, \mathcal{CK}_i := \emptyset$	
06 $b \leftarrow \mathcal{A}^O(\text{par},(\text{pk}_i)_{i\in[N]})$	Oracle H$_i$(ct, ψ) // $i \in [N]$
07 return ψ^*	20 if $\exists K$ s.t. (ct, ψ, K) $\in \mathcal{H}_i$:
	21 return K
Oracle OPEN($i \in [N]$)	22 $K \xleftarrow{\$} \{0,1\}^\kappa$
08 opened$_i$:= 1	23 if ct $\in \mathcal{C}_i \wedge \neg$opened[$i$]
09 return sk$_i$:= CORR(i)	24 $\wedge$ CHECK(i, ct, ψ) :
	25 $\psi^* := \psi$ //record the solution
Oracle DECAPS($i \in [N]$, ct)	26 abort and return ψ^*
10 if ct $\in \mathcal{C}_i$: return $\bot$	27 if opened[i] :
11 $\mathcal{D}_i := \mathcal{D}_i \cup \{\text{ct}\}$	28 if $\exists K'$ s.t. (ct, K') $\in \mathcal{CK}_i$
12 $\psi' := $ DEC(i, ct)	29 $\wedge$ CHECK(i, ct, ψ)
13 if $\psi' = \bot$: $K' := \bot$	30 $K := K'$
14 else : $K' := $ H(ct, ψ')	31 $\mathcal{H}_i := \mathcal{H}_i \cup \{(\text{ct}, \psi, K)\}$
15 return K'	32 return K

Fig. 13. The reduction $\mathcal{B}$ in the proof of Lemma 10. It uses the oracles (highlighted) provided by game OW-ChCCA$_{\text{KEM}}(\lambda)$ to simulate $\mathbf{G_4}$.

Alg Enc(pk, m)	Alg Dec(sk, ct = (ct$_0$, ct$_1$, ct$_2$))
01 (ct$_0$, K) $\leftarrow$ Encap(pk)	05 $K := $ Decap(sk, ct$_0$)
02 ($k^{(e)}, k^{(m)}$) := H(ct$_0$, K)	06 ($k^{(e)}, k^{(m)}$) := H(ct$_0$, K)
03 ct$_1$:= $k^{(e)} \oplus$ m, ct$_2$:= G($k^{(m)}$, ct$_1$)	07 if G($k^{(m)}$, ct$_1$) $\neq$ ct$_2$: return $\bot$
04 return ct := (ct$_0$, ct$_1$, ct$_2$)	08 return m := ct$_1 \oplus k^{(e)}$

Fig. 14. PKE $=$ (Setup, Gen, Enc, Dec) from KEM $=$ (Setup, Gen, Encap, Decap). H: $\{0,1\}^* \to \{0,1\}^\lambda \times \{0,1\}^\lambda$ and G: $\{0,1\}^* \to \{0,1\}^\lambda$ are random oracles. Setup and key generation algorithms in PKE are the same as those in KEM.

derivation. With KEMs in Sect. 3, we obtain the *first* tightly SIM-BiSO-CCA secure public-key encryption scheme. SIM-BiSO-CCA security [23] is a stronger simulation-based security notion for PKE in the multi-user setting. It models selective-opening attacks on both sender and receiver sides. Concreteley, in this notion, the adversary can learn some senders' plaintexts and the randomness used for encryption and corrupt some receivers' secret keys. SIM-BiSO-CCA security guarantees that such an adversary should not learn more than these. The formal definitions of PKE and SIM-BiSO-CCA security are given in our full version [32].

Let KEM $=$ (Setup, Gen, Encap, Decap) be a KEM. We construct PKE $=$ (Setup, Gen, Enc, Dec) in Fig. 14 using random oracles H: $\{0,1\}^* \to \{0,1\}^\lambda \times$ $\{0,1\}^\lambda$ and G: $\{0,1\}^* \to \{0,1\}^\lambda$. We show that if KEM is OW-ChCCA secure and has deterministic ciphertext derivation, then PKE is tightly SIM-BiSO-CCA secure. The formal statement and proof are postponed to our full version [32].

References

1. Abdalla, M., Bellare, M., Rogaway, P.: The oracle Diffie-Hellman assumptions and an analysis of DHIES. In: Naccache, D. (ed.) CT-RSA 2001. LNCS, vol. 2020, pp. 143–158. Springer, Heidelberg (2001). https://doi.org/10.1007/3-540-45353-9_12
2. Alwen, J., Krenn, S., Pietrzak, K., Wichs, D.: Learning with rounding, revisited - new reduction, properties and applications. In: Canetti, R., Garay, J.A. (eds.) CRYPTO 2013, Part I. LNCS, vol. 8042, pp. 57–74. Springer, Heidelberg (2013). https://doi.org/10.1007/978-3-642-40041-4_4
3. Bader, C., Hofheinz, D., Jager, T., Kiltz, E., Li, Y.: Tightly-secure authenticated key exchange. In: Dodis, Y., Nielsen, J.B. (eds.) TCC 2015, Part I. LNCS, vol. 9014, pp. 629–658. Springer, Heidelberg (2015). https://doi.org/10.1007/978-3-662-46494-6_26
4. Bellare, M., Rogaway, P.: Entity authentication and key distribution. In: Stinson, D.R. (ed.) CRYPTO 1993. LNCS, vol. 773, pp. 232–249. Springer, Heidelberg (1994). https://doi.org/10.1007/3-540-48329-2_21
5. Benhamouda, F., Blazy, O., Ducas, L., Quach, W.: Hash proof systems over lattices revisited. In: Abdalla, M., Dahab, R. (eds.) PKC 2018, Part II. LNCS, vol. 10770, pp. 644–674. Springer, Heidelberg (2018). https://doi.org/10.1007/978-3-319-76581-5_22
6. Brakerski, Z., Langlois, A., Peikert, C., Regev, O., Stehlé, D.: Classical hardness of learning with errors. In: Boneh, D., Roughgarden, T., Feigenbaum, J. (eds.) 45th ACM STOC, pp. 575–584. ACM Press, June 2013. https://doi.org/10.1145/2488608.2488680
7. Canetti, R., Krawczyk, H.: Analysis of key-exchange protocols and their use for building secure channels. In: Pfitzmann, B. (ed.) EUROCRYPT 2001. LNCS, vol. 2045, pp. 453–474. Springer, Heidelberg (2001). https://doi.org/10.1007/3-540-44987-6_28
8. Castryck, W., Lange, T., Martindale, C., Panny, L., Renes, J.: CSIDH: an efficient post-quantum commutative group action. In: Peyrin, T., Galbraith, S. (eds.) ASIACRYPT 2018, Part III. LNCS, vol. 11274, pp. 395–427. Springer, Heidelberg (2018). https://doi.org/10.1007/978-3-030-03332-3_15
9. Cohn-Gordon, K., Cremers, C., Gjøsteen, K., Jacobsen, H., Jager, T.: Highly efficient key exchange protocols with optimal tightness. In: Boldyreva, A., Micciancio, D. (eds.) CRYPTO 2019, Part III. LNCS, vol. 11694, pp. 767–797. Springer, Heidelberg (2019). https://doi.org/10.1007/978-3-030-26954-8_25
10. Davis, H., Günther, F.: Tighter proofs for the SIGMA and TLS 1.3 key exchange protocols. In: Sako, K., Tippenhauer, N.O. (eds.) ACNS 21, Part II. LNCS, vol. 12727, pp. 448–479. Springer, Heidelberg (2021). https://doi.org/10.1007/978-3-030-78375-4_18
11. Diemert, D., Jager, T.: On the tight security of TLS 1.3: theoretically sound cryptographic parameters for real-world deployments. J. Cryptol. **34**(3), 30 (2021). https://doi.org/10.1007/s00145-021-09388-x

12. Escala, A., Herold, G., Kiltz, E., Ràfols, C., Villar, J.: An algebraic framework for Diffie-Hellman assumptions. In: Canetti, R., Garay, J.A. (eds.) CRYPTO 2013, Part II. LNCS, vol. 8043, pp. 129–147. Springer, Heidelberg (2013). https://doi.org/10.1007/978-3-642-40084-1_8
13. Gentry, C., Peikert, C., Vaikuntanathan, V.: Trapdoors for hard lattices and new cryptographic constructions. Cryptology ePrint Archive, Report 2007/432 (2007). https://eprint.iacr.org/2007/432
14. Gjøsteen, K., Jager, T.: Practical and tightly-secure digital signatures and authenticated key exchange. In: Shacham, H., Boldyreva, A. (eds.) CRYPTO 2018, Part II. LNCS, vol. 10992, pp. 95–125. Springer, Heidelberg (2018). https://doi.org/10.1007/978-3-319-96881-0_4
15. Han, S., et al.: Authenticated key exchange and signatures with tight security in the standard model. In: Malkin, T., Peikert, C. (eds.) CRYPTO 2021, Part IV. LNCS, vol. 12828, pp. 670–700. Springer, Heidelberg, Virtual Event (2021). https://doi.org/10.1007/978-3-030-84259-8_23
16. Han, S., Liu, S., Gu, D.: Key encapsulation mechanism with tight enhanced security in the multi-user setting: impossibility result and optimal tightness. In: Tibouchi, M., Wang, H. (eds.) ASIACRYPT 2021, Part II. LNCS, vol. 13091, pp. 483–513. Springer, Heidelberg (2021). https://doi.org/10.1007/978-3-030-92075-3_17
17. Hövelmanns, K., Kiltz, E., Schäge, S., Unruh, D.: Generic authenticated key exchange in the quantum random oracle model. In: Kiayias, A., Kohlweiss, M., Wallden, P., Zikas, V. (eds.) PKC 2020, Part II. LNCS, vol. 12111, pp. 389–422. Springer, Heidelberg (2020). https://doi.org/10.1007/978-3-030-45388-6_14
18. Jager, T., Kiltz, E., Riepel, D., Schäge, S.: Tightly-secure authenticated key exchange, revisited. In: Canteaut, A., Standaert, F.X. (eds.) EUROCRYPT 2021, Part I. LNCS, vol. 12696, pp. 117–146. Springer, Heidelberg (2021). https://doi.org/10.1007/978-3-030-77870-5_5
19. Katsumata, S., Yamada, S., Yamakawa, T.: Tighter security proofs for GPV-IBE in the quantum random oracle model. In: Peyrin, T., Galbraith, S. (eds.) ASIACRYPT 2018, Part II. LNCS, vol. 11273, pp. 253–282. Springer, Heidelberg (2018). https://doi.org/10.1007/978-3-030-03329-3_9
20. Katz, J., Vaikuntanathan, V.: Smooth projective hashing and password-based authenticated key exchange from lattices. In: Matsui, M. (ed.) ASIACRYPT 2009. LNCS, vol. 5912, pp. 636–652. Springer, Heidelberg (2009). https://doi.org/10.1007/978-3-642-10366-7_37
21. de Kock, B., Gjøsteen, K., Veroni, M.: Practical isogeny-based key-exchange with optimal tightness. In: Dunkelman, O., Jacobson Jr., M.J., O'Flynn, C. (eds.) Selected Areas in Cryptography, pp. 451–479. Springer, Cham (2021). https://doi.org/10.1007/978-3-030-81652-0_18
22. Krawczyk, H.: HMQV: a high-performance secure Diffie-Hellman protocol. In: Shoup, V. (ed.) CRYPTO 2005. LNCS, vol. 3621, pp. 546–566. Springer, Heidelberg (2005). https://doi.org/10.1007/11535218_33
23. Lai, J., Yang, R., Huang, Z., Weng, J.: Simulation-based bi-selective opening security for public key encryption. In: Tibouchi, M., Wang, H. (eds.) ASIACRYPT 2021, Part II. LNCS, vol. 13091, pp. 456–482. Springer, Heidelberg (2021). https://doi.org/10.1007/978-3-030-92075-3_16
24. LaMacchia, B.A., Lauter, K., Mityagin, A.: Stronger security of authenticated key exchange. In: Susilo, W., Liu, J.K., Mu, Y. (eds.) ProvSec 2007. LNCS, vol. 4784, pp. 1–16. Springer, Heidelberg (2007). https://doi.org/10.1007/978-3-540-75670-5_1

25. Libert, B., Sakzad, A., Stehlé, D., Steinfeld, R.: All-but-many lossy trapdoor functions and selective opening chosen-ciphertext security from LWE. In: Katz, J., Shacham, H. (eds.) CRYPTO 2017, Part III. LNCS, vol. 10403, pp. 332–364. Springer, Heidelberg (2017). https://doi.org/10.1007/978-3-319-63697-9_12

26. Liu, X., Liu, S., Gu, D., Weng, J.: Two-pass authenticated key exchange with explicit authentication and tight security. In: Moriai, S., Wang, H. (eds.) ASIACRYPT 2020, Part II. LNCS, vol. 12492, pp. 785–814. Springer, Heidelberg (2020). https://doi.org/10.1007/978-3-030-64834-3_27

27. Micciancio, D., Regev, O.: Worst-case to average-case reductions based on Gaussian measures. In: 45th FOCS, pp. 372–381. IEEE Computer Society Press, October 2004. https://doi.org/10.1109/FOCS.2004.72

28. Naor, M., Yung, M.: Public-key cryptosystems provably secure against chosen ciphertext attacks. In: 22nd ACM STOC, pp. 427–437. ACM Press, May 1990. https://doi.org/10.1145/100216.100273

29. Okamoto, T., Pointcheval, D.: REACT: rapid Enhanced-security asymmetric cryptosystem transform. In: Naccache, D. (ed.) CT-RSA 2001. LNCS, vol. 2020, pp. 159–175. Springer, Heidelberg (2001). https://doi.org/10.1007/3-540-45353-9_13

30. Pan, J., Qian, C., Ringerud, M.: Signed Diffie-Hellman key exchange with tight security. In: Paterson, K.G. (ed.) CT-RSA 2021. LNCS, vol. 12704, pp. 201–226. Springer, Heidelberg (2021). https://doi.org/10.1007/978-3-030-75539-3_9

31. Pan, J., Wagner, B.: Lattice-based signatures with tight adaptive corruptions and more. In: Hanaoka, G., Shikata, J., Watanabe, Y. (eds.) PKC 2022, Part II. LNCS, vol. 13178, pp. 347–378. Springer, Heidelberg (2022). https://doi.org/10.1007/978-3-030-97131-1_12

32. Pan, J., Wagner, B., Zeng, R.: Lattice-based authenticated key exchange with tight security. Cryptology ePrint Archive, Paper 2023/823 (2023). https://eprint.iacr.org/2023/823

33. Peikert, C.: Public-key cryptosystems from the worst-case shortest vector problem: extended abstract. In: Mitzenmacher, M. (ed.) 41st ACM STOC, pp. 333–342. ACM Press, May/June 2009. https://doi.org/10.1145/1536414.1536461

34. Regev, O.: On lattices, learning with errors, random linear codes, and cryptography. In: Gabow, H.N., Fagin, R. (eds.) 37th ACM STOC, pp. 84–93. ACM Press, May 2005. https://doi.org/10.1145/1060590.1060603

35. Zhang, J., Yu, Y.: Two-round PAKE from approximate SPH and instantiations from lattices. In: Takagi, T., Peyrin, T. (eds.) ASIACRYPT 2017, Part III. LNCS, vol. 10626, pp. 37–67. Springer, Heidelberg (2017). https://doi.org/10.1007/978-3-319-70700-6_2

Error Correction and Ciphertext Quantization in Lattice Cryptography

Daniele Micciancio[ID] and Mark Schultz-Wu[✉][ID]

UC San Diego, La Jolla, USA
{daniele,mdschultz}@eng.ucsd.edu

Abstract. Recent work in the design of rate $1 - o(1)$ lattice-based cryptosystems have used two distinct design paradigms, namely replacing the noise-tolerant encoding $m \mapsto (q/2)m$ present in many lattice-based cryptosystems with a more efficient encoding, and post-processing traditional lattice-based ciphertexts with a lossy compression algorithm, using a technique very similar to the technique of "vector quantization" within coding theory.

We introduce a framework for the design of lattice-based encryption that captures both of these paradigms, and prove information-theoretic rate bounds within this framework. These bounds separate the settings of trivial and non-trivial quantization, and show the impossibility of rate $1 - o(1)$ encryption using both trivial quantization and polynomial modulus. They furthermore put strong limits on the rate of constructions that utilize lattices built by tensoring a lattice of small dimension with $\mathbb{Z}^k$, which is ubiquitous in the literature. We additionally introduce a new cryptosystem, that matches the rate of the highest-rate currently known scheme, while encoding messages with a "gadget", which may be useful for constructions of Fully Homomorphic Encryption.

1 Introduction

Lattice-based cryptography has many advantages over traditional number-theoretic encryption, from conjectured security against quantum attacks, to the ability to perform arbitrary computations over encrypted data, while at the same time enjoying very fast (quasi-linear time) encryption and decryption operations. This is much better than the cubic running time of the modular exponentiation typically used in constructions based on number theory. However, there is one aspect for which lattice-based constructions have always lagged behind number-theoretic ones: key and ciphertext *sizes*. In fact, early proposals of encryption schemes based on lattices suffered from a very poor *rate*, meaning the ratio of the size of a plaintext to the size of a ciphertext was very small.

Improving the rate of encryption schemes is an important and well-studied problem, and a problem with a well-understood solution: hybrid encryption. By using public-key encryption on a fixed size, randomly chosen symmetric key, and

Research supported in part by Samsung, Intel and NSF Award 1936703. Any opinions, findings, and conclusions or recommendations expressed in this material are those of the author(s) and do not necessarily reflect the views of the National Science Foundation.

H. Handschuh and A. Lysanskaya (Eds.): CRYPTO 2023, LNCS 14085, pp. 648–681, 2023.
https://doi.org/10.1007/978-3-031-38554-4_21

then using this key to encrypt the actual message using a much more efficient block cipher, the cost of the public-key operation (both in terms of running time and rate) can be amortized over a large payload. However, by using hybrid encryption one loses one of the main attractions of lattice-based cryptography: the ability to compute on encrypted data, as data is now encrypted using a block cipher with no useful homomorphic properties. Homomorphically decrypting AES or other "FHE-friendly" block ciphers [2,3], addresses this problem, but only partially: it allows one to move data from AES (or another symmetric encryption scheme) to lattice-based cryptography and then perform homomorphic computations on it. The reverse step, e.g. converting the FHE ciphertext back to a space-efficient symmetric ciphertext, is an open problem and would seem to require the symmetric cryptosystem to be fully homomorphic. This has motivated the study of lattice-based encryption schemes with better rate, leading to two constructions of lattice-based homomorphic encryption schemes with rate asymptotically close to 1 [6,18]. In this paper we present a unified study of high-rate lattice-based encryption schemes, presenting a general framework that parameterizes LWE-based (Learning With Error) encryption with two coding-theoretic objects we call *lattice codes*. The simplest lattice-based encryption scheme (originally proposed by Regev [32]), combines an LWE sample with simple scaling and rounding operations. Here, we replace these scalar operations with two arbitrary lattice codes, one used for error-correction (generalizing scaling), and one used for quantization (generalizing rounding). We then show that known constructions of rate $1 - o(1)$ encryption [6,18] can be described as instances of our general constructions for particular choices of lattice codes, and prove upper and lower bounds on the rate achievable in this framework. Analysis of these schemes in our framework highlights inefficiencies in many current constructions, which we fix to attain asymptotic (rate) improvements.

Organization: The rest of this paper is organized as follows. In the rest of the introduction we provide more details on our technical contributions and related work. In Sect. 2 we present background information on error-correcting codes needed to describe and analyze our construction. In Sect. 3 we present our generalized encryption framework. In Sect. 4 we show how previous constructions can be obtained as special cases of our framework simply by properly choosing a pair of error correcting codes, and also present a construction combining the desirable properties of [18] and [6]. In Sect. 5 we present impossibility results that limit the rate achievable using common subcases of our generalized construction. In Sect. 6, we give concluding thoughts, and present some open problems.

1.1 Our Contributions

There is a well-known strategy for building (private-key) encryption from LWE, namely

- start with an LWE sample $(\mathbf{A}, \mathbf{b} := \mathbf{A}\mathbf{s} + \mathbf{e})$, and
- add an encoding of the message $\mathsf{encode}(\mathbf{m})$ to the second component.

Provided one can later recover the message $\mathbf{m}$ from the noisy encoding $\mathsf{encode}(\mathbf{m}) + \mathbf{e}$, this suffices to build private-key encryption.

Given the ciphertext $(\mathbf{A}, \mathbf{b} := \mathbf{As} + \mathsf{encode}(\mathbf{m}) + \mathbf{e})$, how might we compress it? The matrix $\mathbf{A}$ is itself uniformly random, and can be easily compressed using standard techniques[1]. Therefore, we focus on compressing $\mathbf{b}$. This is pseudo-random under the LWE assumption, so we must appeal to some form of *lossy* compression. As the ciphertext already contains a form of error-correction, it can plausibly correct some additional noise.

We leverage a form of compression commonly known as *vector quantization*, where one maps a vector $\mathbf{v} \in \mathbb{R}^m$ to some discrete subset, say $\mathbb{Z}^m$, or more generally a lattice. We use this methodology to quantize $\mathbf{b}$ to a nearby lattice point $\lfloor \mathbf{b} \rceil_L \in L$, where $\lfloor \cdot \rceil_L : \mathbb{R}^m \to L$ is a generalized form of rounding, for example by solving the closest vector problem. Provided the sum of the quantization error $[\mathbf{b}]_Q := \mathbf{b} - \lfloor \mathbf{b} \rceil_Q$ and LWE error $\mathbf{e}$ can be corrected by the error-correcting code, our scheme will decrypt correctly, i.e. we will have successfully compressed an LWE ciphertext.

The above describes how our framework leverages two codes E, Q, for error-correction and quantization respectively. Concretely, the quantized LWE encryption scheme using E and Q (which we call $\mathsf{LWE}^{n,q}_{\chi_{\mathsf{sk}}, \chi_e}[E, Q]$) encrypts by computing

$$\mathsf{Enc}_{\mathbf{s}}(\mathbf{m}) := (\mathbf{A}, \lfloor \mathbf{As} + \mathbf{e} + \mathsf{encode}_E(\mathbf{m}) \rceil_Q), \tag{1}$$

where $\mathbf{A} \leftarrow \mathbb{Z}_q^{n \times m}$, and $\mathbf{e} \leftarrow \chi_e^m$ for an error distribution χ_e. This is a mild modification of (standard) LWE-based encryption (see Definition 11 for details). Despite the simplicity of this approach, our framework is

- broad,
- modular, and
- necessary to achieve high rate.

We discuss all of these points next.

Breadth: Our framework includes all forms of error-correction and vector quantization that are expressible in terms of *lattice codes* (Definition 1), which are the reduction of a q-ary lattice L modulo q. Equivalently, they are discrete subgroups $L_q := (L \bmod q) \subseteq \mathbb{R}^m/q\mathbb{Z}^m$. For any such subgroup, there are (many) fundamental domains $\mathcal{V}_L$ such that $L_q + \mathcal{V}_L = \mathbb{R}^m/q\mathbb{Z}^m$ is a partition. A lattice code can be thought of as the choice of a pair $(L_q, \mathcal{V}_L)$, along with algorithms to efficiently decompose $\mathbb{R}^m/q\mathbb{Z}^m \to (L_q, \mathcal{V}_L)$. This includes most techniques of decoding a point $\mathbf{x} \in \mathbb{R}^m$ to $\lfloor x \rceil \in L$, say by solving the closest vector problem exactly, or approximately via techniques such as Babai's Nearest Planes [4].

---

[1] In theory, the same $\mathbf{A}$ can be reused with many different $\mathbf{s}_i$, making the amortized cost of $\mathbf{A}$ arbitrarily small. In practice, $\mathbf{A}$ is often replaced with a short seed that is deterministically expanded to $\mathbf{A}$. This is process is not fully justified theoretically, but it is easily proved secure in the random oracle model.

In Sect. 4, we instantiate our framework with many different non-trivial LWE-based encryption schemes. In particular, we show that all existing rate $1 - o(1)$ encryption schemes [6,18] fit into our framework. Beside the schemes that we explicitly analyze, our framework additionally includes any scheme that encodes messages into a lattice for error correction (of which there are many [18,31–33]). All known cryptosystems which quantize ciphertexts are expressible in our framework, although this is a much shorter list (containing solely [6][2], and schemes which quantize via rounding each coordinate independently, which are common in practice [12,14]).

Moreover, we demonstrate the ease of working in our framework by "quantizing" several pre-existing cryptosystems. One such construction combines the desirable properties of [6,18], namely it encodes messages under a "gadget" lattice (similar to [18]), but attains the same (quasi-optimal) rate as [6].

Modular: Our framework separates the coding-theoretic analysis from the cryptographic analysis of encryption schemes. The cryptographic analysis of schemes in our framework is somewhat basic. We establish in Theorem 3 that $\mathsf{LWE}^{n,q}_{\chi_{\mathsf{sk}},\chi_e}[E,Q]$ is RND-CPA-secure[3] (but potentially incorrect) for any choice of E, Q via a simple argument.

The coding-theoretic analysis is similarly straightforward. We express the rate of our cryptosystem in terms of a simple function of the LWE modulus q, dimension m, and volumes $\det E$ and $\det Q$ of the fundamental domains of E, Q.

Correctness analysis requires some knowledge about the shape of these fundamental domains, although we find that it is enough to know their packing and covering radii in the ℓ_2 and ℓ_∞ norms. This analysis frequently highlights inefficiencies in the choice E, Q of codes a cryptosystem (implicitly) uses. Most commonly, the quantizer Q can be replaced with a sparser quantizer Q' without (asymptotically) impacting the correctness of the cryptosystem. We make this modification in several cases, and often find asymptotic improvements. We summarize the results of our analysis in Table 1. Our optimizations tend to improve constructions from rate $1 - f(m)$ to $1 - \frac{f(m)}{\log_2 m}$, i.e. improve on known constructions by a logarithmic factor in the dimension. We discuss the reason for these small improvements shortly.

---

[2] We defer discussion of how one can realize this work in our framework to Sect. 4.3.

[3] This is a stronger notion of security than IND-CPA-security, where one requires ciphertexts be pseudorandom, see Definition 9.

Table 1. The E, Q that we study the Quantized Encryption schemes $\mathsf{LWE}^{n,q}_{\chi_{sk},\chi_e}[E, Q]$ in Sect. 4, where $\mathbf{g}^t_p = (1, p, p^2, \ldots, p^{\ell-1})$ for $\ell = \lceil \log_p q \rceil$, $\mathbf{u}^t_m = (1, 1, \ldots, 1)^t \in \mathbb{R}^m$, and k is a free parameter, typically set to some small polynomial in n. Note that the various parameters p, q, m, k may be required to satisfy certain divisibility constraints, see details in Sect. 4. The rates are computed assuming Gaussian parameter $\sigma = \Theta(\sqrt{n})$, secret key length $n = \Theta(m)$, ciphertext dimension m, and decryption failure rate $\delta = \exp(-n)$. The quality of a gadget (defined in [17]) directly controls noise growth of scalar multiplications (and any operations that use scalar multiplication as a subroutine) in "Gadget-based" FHE constructions, i.e. smaller quality parameter leads to lower noise growth FHE constructions. Note that gadget encryption is also closely related to GSW-based encryption, see [28].

Name	E	Q	Rate	Gadget Quality of E	Source
Regev	$(q/p)\mathbb{Z}^m$	$\mathbb{Z}^m$	$1 - O(1)$	N/A	[32]
Quantized Regev	$(q/p)\mathbb{Z}^m$	$k\mathbb{Z}^m$	$1 - O\left(\frac{1}{\log_2 \frac{q}{k}}\right)$	N/A	Corollary 3
GH	$\Lambda^\perp_q(\mathbf{g}^t_p) \otimes \mathbb{Z}^{m/\ell}$	$\mathbb{Z}^m$	$1 - O(1)$	$O(q/p)$	[18]
Quantized GH	$\Lambda^\perp_q(\mathbf{g}^t_p) \otimes \mathbb{Z}^{m/\ell}$	$k\mathbb{Z}^m$	$1 - O\left(\frac{1}{\log_2 \frac{q}{k}}\right)$	$O(q/p)$	Sect. 4
BDGM	$(q/p)\mathbb{Z}^m$	$\Lambda_{q/p}(\mathbf{u}^t_m)$	$1 - O\left(\frac{\log_2(m\sigma)}{m\log_2 p}\right)$	N/A	[6]
Gadget	$\Lambda_q(\mathbf{g}^t_p) \otimes \mathbb{Z}^{m/\ell}$	$\mathbb{Z}^m$	$1 - O(1)$	$O(p)$	[28]
Quantized Gadget	$\Lambda_q(\mathbf{g}^t_p) \otimes \mathbb{Z}^{m/\ell}$	$\Lambda_{q/p}(\mathbf{u}^t_m)$	$1 - O\left(\frac{\log_2(m\sigma)}{m\log_2 p}\right)$	$O(p)$	Corollary 6

Necessary: Our framework allows us to derive (strong) coding-theoretic bounds on the rate of $\mathsf{LWE}^{n,q}_{\chi_{sk},\chi_e}[E, Q]$, for broad classes of E, Q. Our bounds are on the *rate* of $\mathsf{LWE}^{n,q}_{\chi_{sk},\chi_e}[E, Q]$, namely we show it can be at most $1 - f(n, q, m, \sigma, \delta)$ for explicit functions $f(\cdot)$ of the scheme parameters. Under the assumption that $\mathsf{LWE}^{n,q}_{\chi_{sk},\chi_e}[E, Q]$ meets some notion of correctness (described next), we show universal rate bounds of the above form in the settings of

- **Trivial Quantization**: Arbitrary E, with $Q = \mathbb{Z}^m$, and
- **Small Quantization**: Arbitrary E, with $\sqrt[m]{\det Q} \leq O(\sigma)$ of the same size as the LWE error.

We investigate two correctness notions, namely

- **Bounded Noise**: decryption failure rate $\delta = 0$, with respect to bounded noise of the same size (with high probability) as Gaussian noise of parameter σ (in an ℓ_2 ball of radius $\sqrt{m}\sigma$), and
- **Unbounded Noise**: decryption failure rate $\delta > 0$, with respect to arbitrary (concentrated) noise of variance σ^2.

For the first correctness notion, we proceed via "packing bounds", while in the second we proceed via "anti-concentration bounds". Throughout, we state the interesting consequences of our bounds for the case of q polynomially large, see Sect. 5 for full statements.

Our first set of bounds are in the bounded noise model. In this setting, the assumption $\delta = 0$ implies that E_q is a *packing* of $\mathbb{R}^m_q$, meaning that for $\mathcal{S}$ the support of the noise (either solely the LWE error, or the sum of the LWE and quantization error), the sets $\{v + \mathcal{S}\}_{v \in E_q}$ are all disjoint, i.e. one can always (uniquely) decode the noisy encoded points $v + \mathcal{S}$ back to $v \in E_q$.

Under the assumption E_q is a packing, we follow a standard volume-based argument (called the *sphere packing* or *Hamming* bound, depending on the context) to obtain an inequality between our parameters of interest. Instantiating this argument in the setting of trivial quantization $Q = \mathbb{Z}^m$ leads to the following bound (Theorem 4).

Bound 1. For any lattice code E, $\mathsf{LWE}_{\chi_{sk},\chi_e}^{n,q}[E, \mathbb{Z}^m]$ has rate at most $1 - \Omega(1)$, i.e. rate $1 - o(1)$ encryption is impossible.

This rules out the *a priori* appealing possibility of achieving high-rate encryption by solely optimizing over the error-correcting code E, and motivates investigating further techniques (e.g. quantization).

To handle non-trivial quantization, we require a heuristic assumption (Heuristic 1) that the LWE noise and quantization noise are independent, though we can remove this heuristic for a mild modification of our framework (Sect. 3.2). Our next bound (Theorem 5) then proceeds in essentially the same way, albeit in the case of small quantization, where the set $\mathcal{S}$ is more complicated.

Bound 2. Under a heuristic assumption, for any lattice codes E, Q, if there exists $\epsilon > 0$ such that $\sqrt[m]{\det Q} = \sigma^{1-\epsilon}$, then $\mathsf{LWE}_{\chi_{sk},\chi_e}^{n,q}[E, Q]$ has rate $1 - \Omega(1)$, i.e. rate $1 - o(1)$ encryption is impossible. If instead $\sqrt[m]{\det Q} \leq O(\sigma)$, then rate $1 - o\left(\frac{1}{\log_2 q}\right)$ encryption is impossible.

Therefore, in the bounded error model, quantization is necessary to achieve rate $1 - o(1)$ encryption from polynomial modulus. One can further show the aforementioned bounds are tight by repeating the analysis of Corollary 3 in this noise model, though we omit this analysis for brevity.

Our remaining bounds are in the more general setting of δ-correct encryption (for $\delta > 0$) with respect to what is known as *log-concave* noise. We include a brief primer on these random variables in Sect. 2.5, but for now simply state they include (continuous variants of) all of the noise distributions relevant to public-key lattice-based cryptography, and admit anti-concentration bounds of the form we will require.

The anti-concentration techniques yield bounds with more technical caveats (so *weaker* than the bounded noise model), although one of the bounds is "dimension dependent", which we leverage to give a *stronger* bound than any of our results in the bounded noise model.

Recall that to prove correctness of cryptographic constructions, one often upper bounds the decryption failure rate using concentration inequalities. To prove impossibility results in this noise model, we *lower bound* the decryption failure rate using *anti-concentration* inequalities (Proposition 6), i.e. upper bounds (rather than lower) on how likely it is for a random variable to be close to any particular point (such as its mean).

Our first bound is again for the case of no trivial quantization.

Bound 3. For any lattice code E, either

- the rate of $\mathsf{LWE}^{n,q}_{\chi_{sk},\chi_e}[E, \mathbb{Z}^m]$ is $1 - \Omega(1)$, i.e. not rate $1 - o(1)$, or
- the normalized covering radius satisfies $\overline{R}_E = \Omega(m)$.

While this bound is weaker than its analogue in the bounded noise model, we expect this to be a proof artifact — it would be quite peculiar if the way to achieve rate $1 - o(1)$ encryption was to use codes E for error-correction that are very bad *quantizers*[4]. Note that this result does suffice to rule out rate $1 - o(1)$ encryption from a class of *a priori* interesting codes (Corollary 8), namely codes E that are nearly optimal for *both* error-correction and quantization. Such codes are known to exist via randomized constructions, and are nearly optimal in many (non-cryptographic) settings.

Our next bound (Theorem 7) again extends our prior bound to the case of $\sqrt[m]{\det Q} \leq O(\sigma)$.

Bound 4. Under a heuristic assumption, for any lattice codes E, Q with $\sqrt[m]{\det Q} \leq O(\sigma)$, the rate of $\mathsf{LWE}^{n,q}_{\chi_{sk},\chi_e}[E, Q]$ is at most

$$1 - \Omega\left(\frac{1}{m \log_2(q/\sigma)}\right). \tag{2}$$

This bound is tight up to the $\log_2(q/\sigma)$ factor. Note that this bound explicitly depends on the dimension m, instead of solely σ, q. This is significant, due to a simple result (Lemma 7) showing that the rates of $\mathsf{LWE}^{n,q}_{\chi_{sk},\chi_e}[E, Q]$ and $\mathsf{LWE}^{n,q}_{\chi_{sk},\chi_e}[E \otimes \mathbb{Z}^k, Q \otimes \mathbb{Z}^k]$ are equal[5] for any k. As one can see from Table 1, lattices of this form (for large $k = O(m/\log_2 m)$) are incredibly common in practice. All constructions we are aware of (except for [6]) can be instantiated in our framework using lattices of this type. As a result, one gets a refinement of Bound 4 in this exceedingly common setting.

Bound 5. Under a heuristic assumption, for any lattice codes $E = E' \otimes \mathbb{Z}^{m/\log_2 m}, Q = Q' \otimes \mathbb{Z}^{m/\log_2 m}$ with $\sqrt[m]{\det Q} \leq O(\sigma)$, the rate of $\mathsf{LWE}^{n,q}_{\chi_{sk},\chi_e}[E, Q]$ is at most

$$1 - \Omega\left(\frac{1}{(\log_2 m) \log_2(q/\sigma)}\right).$$

While this is still theoretically rate $1 - o(1)$, practically (for cryptographically relevant dimensions) the convergence is slow. This can be readily observed via concrete comparisons (Fig. 1), where we find a practical gap between cryptosystems that satisfy the preconditions of Bound 5 (all of which are rate ≤ 0.9) and those that do not (of rate ≈ 1).

---

[4] For an indication of how bad $\overline{R}_E = \Omega(m)$ is, the most trivial lattice $\overline{R}_{\mathbb{Z}^m} = \Theta(\sqrt{m})$ is within a constant factor of being an optimal quantizer.

[5] There is a mild caveat that various parameters q, n, δ, σ may (implicitly) depend on $m = \dim E = \dim Q$, and these must be taken to be the same size for both instantiations. This will not impact the conclusions we draw from this bound.

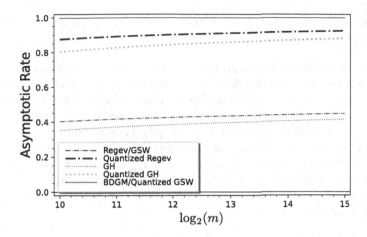

Fig. 1. The rate of the various cryptosystems $\mathsf{LWE}^{n,q}_{\chi_{sk},\chi_e}[E,Q]$, for the codes E,Q in Table 1. Throughout, we assume that $q \leq m^2$, $m = n$, $\delta = \exp(-128)$, $\sigma = 2\sqrt{n}$, and then optimize p and k to attain as high rate as possible for $m \in [2^{10}, 2^{15}]$, the range of dimensions included in the Homomorphic Encryption Standard [1].

Fortunately, one can get around this (exponentially) stronger bound by appealing to lattices without this special structure, such as the quantizer $\Lambda_{q/p}(\mathbf{u}^t_m)$ of [6]. As already summarized in Table 1, we find that the pre-existing scheme of [6] is within an $O(\log_2 m)$ factor of optimal, i.e. beats Bound 5 by a significant margin. We then reuse the quantizer $\Lambda_{q/p}(\mathbf{u}^t_m)$ to quantize messages encoded with a "gadget" $\Lambda_q(\mathbf{g}^t_p) \otimes \mathbb{Z}^{m/\ell}$ (similarly to [18], though with a different "gadget" that does not require super-polynomial moduli q), while attaining the same (much higher) rate as [6]. We view this construction as simultaneously achieving the best properties of both of [6,18] at no cost[6].

Optimal Decoding for the Quantizer of [6]: Independently of the rest of our work, we give an (optimal) $O(m \log_2 q)$ complexity algorithm (Corollary 1) to solve the closest vector problem on the lattice $\Lambda_q(\mathbf{u}^t_m)$, via a simple reduction to a $O(m \log_2 q)$-time CVP algorithm for the scaled root lattice qA^*_{m-1} [26]. We expect this CVP algorithm to be broadly applicable, due to this quantizer leading to constructions that do not satisfy the preconditions of Bound 5. While $\Lambda_q(\mathbf{u}^t_m)$ is used for quantization in [6], a formal decoding algorithm was not given (instead they focused on bounding the ℓ_∞ covering radius of $\mathcal{V}_{\Lambda_{q/p}(\mathbf{u}^t_m)}$). From the description in [6], there is an obvious sorting-based algorithm of complexity $\Theta(m(\log_2 m)(\log_2 q))$, i.e. slightly slower than our optimal algorithm. Our algorithm also has the benefit of having a simple to analyze distribution of quan-

---

[6] There may be some poly-logarithmic encoding/decoding cost, but in practice this seems small compared to computing the matrix-vector multiplication as part of LWE-based encryption.

tization errors, namely for many distributions of random inputs[7] it is uniform over an explicit convex body[8].

Log-Concavity of Distributions Relevant to Lattice-based Cryptography: As mentioned before, we leverage the class of *log-concave* random variables. Much of our analysis can be done by simply quoting standard references regarding this topic (for example [34]). To justify the claim that our lower-bounds apply to all noise distributions one encounters in public-key (algebraically-unstructured) lattice-based cryptography, we additionally require that $\langle e, e' \rangle$ is log-concave (for e, e' independent Gaussians) as well as $\langle e, e_K \rangle$ is log-concave (for e Gaussian, e_K uniform over a convex body K). We establish these results in Sect. 2.5, though for simplicity of presentation we focus on the case of private-key encryption in the main body of our paper.

1.2   Related Work

Our framework is similar to those of [33], which parametrizes the design of lattice-based KEMs via two nested[9] (lattice-based) error-correcting codes. Despite these similarities, [33] does not include bounds on constructions built within their framework, and moreover only considers instantiations with $E = E' \otimes \mathbb{Z}^k \subseteq Q' \otimes \mathbb{Z}^k = Q$ sharing a common low-dimensional structure with $\dim E' = \dim Q' = 8$, which by Bound 5 leads to constructions of severely limited rate.

The framework that has the most similar methods to ours is the framework for the construction of lattice-based KEMs of [22]. They parameterize the construction of lattice-based KEMs via novel primitives they call *Key Consensus* and *Asymmetric Key Consensus (AKC)*, and prove inequalities similar to our rate bounds in this setting. In comparison to our work, they require the assumption of perfect correctness ($\delta = 0$), and solely prove impossibility results in the setting of *single dimension* lattices. This leads them to suggest lattices of the form $Q = Q' \otimes \mathbb{Z}^k$ for $\dim Q' = O(1)$ as "optimal", which (again by Bound 5) is the opposite of what we find.

There is a relatively large body of work that (essentially) quantizes with $Q = c\mathbb{Z}^m$ a scaled integer lattice, dating back to Peikert's work quantizing LWE-based encryption [29], as well as cryptosystems based on the Learning with Rounding problem [5, 12]. Additionally, the "modulus switching" technique [7, 8] used in the Fully Homomorphic Encryption literature can be viewed from this perspective.

The work of [19] similarly obtains bounds on (public-key) constructions achievable from LWE with polynomially-large modulus, although they show the impossibility of *non-interactive* key exchange, rather than bounds on the rate of constructions.

---

[7] In particular, this holds for what are known as *modulo uniform* distributions, see Chap. 4 of [35].

[8] This is $\mathcal{V}_{\Lambda_{q/p}(\mathbf{u}_m^\ell)}$, which by Lemma 2 is the Minkowski sum of a (scaled) permutahedron and an interval.

[9] Note that our framework does not require a nesting assumption.

Finally, our work is closely related to the currently-known rate $1-o(1)$ lattice-based encryption schemes [6,18], as a large motivation for our work was to find a way to formally compare the techniques underlying their design.

2   Preliminaries

We write $x \leftarrow \chi$ for the operation of choosing x at random with distribution χ. If S is a finite set, then $x \leftarrow S$ chooses x at random from S with uniform distribution. We write $[\mathbf{A}, \mathbf{B}]$ for horizontal concatenation of matrices, and $(\mathbf{A}, \mathbf{B}) = [\mathbf{A}^t, \mathbf{B}^t]^t$ for vertical concatenation. We write $f(X) = \{f(x) \colon x \in X\}$ for the image of a set $X \subseteq A$ under a function $f \colon A \to B$, and $X + Y = \{x + y \mid x \in X, y \in Y\}$ for the (Minkowski) sum of two subsets $X, Y \subseteq A$ of an abelian group $(A, +, 0)$. We will write $r \cdot \mathcal{B}_n$ for the Euclidean ball of radius r, centered at 0, and $r \cdot \mathcal{B}_n^{(\infty)} = [-r, r)^n$ for the ℓ_∞ ball of radius r. We will write $r \cdot \mathcal{B}_n^{(p)}$ to uniformly refer to either of these objects (but omit p for the more common Euclidean case).

2.1   Lattices

A *lattice* is a discrete subgroup $L \subseteq \mathbb{R}^n$. The *rank* of a lattice is the dimension of the $\mathbb{R}$-subspace that it spans. Any rank k lattice can be written as $\mathbf{B}\mathbb{Z}^k$, where $\mathbf{B} \in \mathbb{R}^{n \times k}$ is a *basis* of its linear span. A lattice is called *full-rank* if its rank equals its dimension. Associated with any lattice L is its *dual lattice* $L^* = \{\mathbf{x} \in \text{span}_{\mathbb{R}}(L) \mid \forall \mathbf{v} \in L, \langle \mathbf{x}, \mathbf{v} \rangle \in \mathbb{Z}\}$. The *determinant* of a lattice $L = \mathbf{B}\mathbb{Z}^k$ is the k-dimensional volume of its fundamental region $\mathbf{B}[0, 1)^k$. The determinant does not depend on the choice of the basis $\mathbf{B}$, and can be efficiently computed as $\det(L) = \sqrt{\det \mathbf{B}^t \mathbf{B}}$, where $\det \mathbf{B}^t \mathbf{B}$ is the matrix determinant of $\mathbf{B}^t \mathbf{B} \in \mathbb{R}^{k \times k}$.

We say that L is a q-ary lattice if $q\mathbb{Z}^m \subseteq L$, i.e., L is periodic modulo q. Notice that q-ary lattices are always full rank, and the vectors of a q-ary lattice do not necessarily have integer coordinates. There are two standard q-ary integer lattices associated to any matrix $\mathbf{A} \in \mathbb{Z}_q^{n \times m}$:

$$\Lambda_q^\perp(\mathbf{A}) = \{\mathbf{x} \in \mathbb{Z}^m \mid \mathbf{A}\mathbf{x} \equiv 0 \bmod q\},$$
$$\Lambda_q(\mathbf{A}) = \{\mathbf{y} \in \mathbb{Z}^m \mid \exists \mathbf{x} \in \mathbb{Z}_q^m \text{ s.t. } \mathbf{A}^t\mathbf{x} = \mathbf{y} \bmod q\}.$$

These lattices are scaled duals of each other, meaning $\Lambda_q(\mathbf{A})^* = \frac{1}{q}\Lambda_q^\perp(\mathbf{A})$. For a q-ary lattice, we define the scaled dual as $L^\perp = qL^*$, which is such that $\Lambda_q(\mathbf{A})^\perp = \Lambda_q^\perp(\mathbf{A})$. We say that a matrix $\mathbf{A} \in \mathbb{Z}_q^{n \times m}$ is *primitive* if $\mathbf{A}\mathbb{Z}_q^m = \mathbb{Z}_q^n$, i.e. it is a surjection. For primitive matrices $\mathbf{A}$, $\det(\Lambda_q(\mathbf{A})) = q^{m-n}$ and $\det(\Lambda_q^\perp(\mathbf{A})) = q^n$.

We say that two full-rank lattices L, L' are *nested* if $L' \subseteq L$. Given nested lattices $L' \subseteq L$, the quotient L/L' forms a group of size $\frac{\det L'}{\det L} \in \mathbb{N}$, and therefore $\det(L)$ divides $\det(L')$. Any two lattices $L \subset \mathbb{R}^n$ and $L' \subset \mathbb{R}^{n'}$, can be combined into the *direct sum* $L \oplus L' \subset \mathbb{R}^{n+n'}$, and the *tensor product* $L \otimes L' \subset \mathbb{R}^{n \cdot n'}$. The direct sum is simply the Cartesian product of the two lattices $L \oplus L' = L \times L'$, obtained by concatenating vectors from L and L'. If $\mathbf{A}$ and $\mathbf{B}$ are bases of L and L', then the tensor product $L \otimes L'$ is the lattice with basis $\mathbf{A} \otimes \mathbf{B}$ given by the Kronecker product of $\mathbf{A}$ and $\mathbf{B}$, i.e., the block matrix obtained replacing each entry $a_{i,j}$ of $\mathbf{A}$ with the block $a_{i,j} \cdot \mathbf{B}$. The tensor product $L \otimes L'$ satisfies $\det(L \otimes L') = \det(L')^n \cdot \det(L)^{n'}$. The k-fold direct sum of a lattice $L^{\oplus k} = \oplus_{i=1}^{k} L$ can be equivalently expressed as the tensor product $L^{\oplus k} = \mathbb{Z}^k \otimes L$.

2.2 Convex Bodies

We say a set $K \subseteq \mathbb{R}^n$ is *convex* if, for any $\mathbf{x}, \mathbf{y} \in K$, and $t \in [0,1]$, $(1-t)\mathbf{x}+t\mathbf{y} \in K$. We furthermore say K is *symmetric* if $\mathbf{x} \in K \iff -\mathbf{x} \in K$. Associated with any convex symmetric set K is a *norm* $\|\mathbf{x}\|_K = \inf\{t > 0 \mid \mathbf{x}/t \in K\}$. For such K, we define the ℓ_p-*packing radius* $r_K^{(p)}$ to be the maximal r such that $r \cdot \mathcal{B}_n^{(p)} \subseteq K$. Similarly, we define the ℓ_p-*covering radius* $R_K^{(p)}$ to be the minimal R such that $K \subseteq R \cdot \mathcal{B}_n^{(p)}$. Again, when p is omitted, we mean $p = 2$. For a pair of convex symmetric sets K, K', we write $\|K'\|_K := \sup_{\mathbf{x} \in K'} \|\mathbf{x}\|_K$. We will need the following bounds, which are straightforward to derive.

Lemma 1. *Let K, K' be convex symmetric sets in $\mathbb{R}^n$. Then*

1. *if $K \subseteq K'$, then for all $\mathbf{x} \in \mathbb{R}^n$, $\|\mathbf{x}\|_K \geq \|\mathbf{x}\|_{K'}$,*
2. *if $s > 0$, then for all $\mathbf{x} \in \mathbb{R}^n$, $\|\mathbf{x}\|_{sK} = \frac{1}{s}\|\mathbf{x}\|_K$, and*
3. *$\|K'\|_K \in \left[\dfrac{R_{K'}^{(p)}}{R_K^{(p)}}, \dfrac{R_{K'}^{(p)}}{r_K^{(p)}} \right]$.*

2.3 Lattice Codes

Applications of lattices often require not only a lattice L, but also an efficient algorithm to map arbitrary vectors $\mathbf{x} \in \mathbb{R}^n$ to a nearby lattice point.

Definition 1. *A* lattice code *$(L, \lfloor \cdot \rceil)$ is a lattice $L \subset \mathbb{R}^n$ together with a round-ing algorithm $\lfloor \cdot \rceil : \mathsf{span}_{\mathbb{R}}(L) \to L$ such that $\lfloor \mathbf{0} \rceil = \mathbf{0}$ and $\lfloor \mathbf{x} + \mathbf{v} \rceil = \lfloor \mathbf{x} \rceil + \mathbf{v}$ for all $\mathbf{x} \in \mathsf{span}_{\mathbb{R}}(L)$ and $\mathbf{v} \in L$.*

We will be primarily interested in q-ary lattice codes, i.e., lattice codes $(L, \lfloor \cdot \rceil)$ such that L is a q-ary (but not necessarily integer) lattice. For any q-ary lattice code $L \subset \mathbb{R}^n$, we can take the quotients of L and $\mathbb{R}^n$ modulo the additive subgroup $q\mathbb{Z}^n$, and define the *codebook* $L_q = L/q\mathbb{Z}^n$, and *ambient torus* $\mathbb{R}_q^n = (\mathbb{R}/q\mathbb{Z})^n \equiv \mathbb{R}^n/q\mathbb{Z}^n$. Elements of the codebook L_q are called *codewords*, and can be represented as vectors $L \cap [0, q)^n$ with (not necessarily integer) coordinates in the range $[0, q)$. Given a $\mathbb{Z}$-basis of the lattice $\mathbf{B}$, one can moreover represent these codewords as integer via the encoding function $\mathsf{encode}_L(\mathbf{m}) := \mathbf{B}\mathbf{m} \bmod q$, and decoding function $\mathsf{decode}_L(\mathbf{c}) := \mathbf{B}^{-1} \lfloor \mathbf{c} \rceil_L \bmod q$. The codebook L_q is a subgroup of the ambient torus $\mathbb{R}_q^n$, and the rounding function $\lfloor \cdot \rceil : \mathbb{R}^n \to L$ induces a well-defined map $\mathbb{R}_q^n \to L_q$ from the ambient torus to the codebook.

Notice that the codebook L_q is a finite set of size $|L_q| = \frac{q^n}{\det(L)}$, so codewords can be represented with $\lceil \log_2 |L_q| \rceil \approx n \log q - \log \det(L)$ bits.

For any lattice code $(L, \lfloor \cdot \rceil_L)$, we define the fundamental decoding region $\mathcal{V}_L = \{\mathbf{x} \in \mathbb{R}^n \colon \lfloor \mathbf{x} \rceil_L = \mathbf{0}\}$, i.e., the set of all points that decode to $\mathbf{0}$. When $\lfloor \cdot \rceil$ is the CVP rounding function, $\mathcal{V}_{\mathsf{CVP}_L}$ is called the *Voronoi cell* of the lattice. The reduction of a point $\mathbf{x} \in \mathbb{R}^n$ modulo a lattice code $(L, \lfloor \cdot \rceil_L)$ is defined as $[\mathbf{x}]_L = \mathbf{x} - \lfloor \mathbf{x} \rceil_L$, so that every point in space can be (uniquely) written as the sum $\mathbf{x} = \lfloor \mathbf{x} \rceil_L + [\mathbf{x}]_L$ of a lattice point $\lfloor \mathbf{x} \rceil_L \in L$ and a rounding error $[\mathbf{x}]_L \in \mathcal{V}_L$ in the fundamental decoding region. Notice that the rounding error depends not only on the lattice L but also on the rounding function $\lfloor \cdot \rceil$ of the lattice code.

Throughout, we will assume that $\mathcal{V}_L$ is a convex symmetric set. When the choice of $\lfloor \cdot \rceil$ is unambiguous, we will refer to the norm $\|\cdot\|_L := \|\cdot\|_{\mathcal{V}_L}$, packing radius $r_L^{(p)} := r_{\mathcal{V}_L}^{(p)}$, and covering radius $R_L^{(p)} := R_{\mathcal{V}_L}^{(p)}$ of L. Note that when $\lfloor \cdot \rceil$ solves CVP on L, the parameters r_L and R_L are the familiar lattice parameters $\lambda_1(L)/2$ and $\rho(L)$. When discussing bounds on the packing/covering radii, we will find it useful to work with normalized (to be invariant to scaling $L \mapsto cL$) versions of these quantities $\overline{r} = (\det L)^{-1/n} r$ and $\overline{R} = (\det L)^{-1/n} R$.

Some Explicit Lattice Codes. We briefly summarize some explicit lattice codes we will use in our work, namely the lattice codes (implicitly) used in previous high-rate constructions of LWE-based encryption [6,18] (we justify this claim in Sect. 4).

Definition 2 (Primal Gadget Lattice). *For* $p, q \in \mathbb{N}$, *let* $\mathbf{g}_p = (1, p, p^2, \ldots, p^{\lceil \log_p q \rceil - 1})$ *be the base-p "gadget vector". The primal gadget lattice is the lattice* $\Lambda_q(\mathbf{g}_p^t)$.

Proposition 1. *Let* $q = p^\ell$. *Then the fundamental region when decoding with Babai's nearest planes* $\mathcal{V}_{\Lambda_q^\perp(\mathbf{g}_p^t)}^{\mathsf{babai}} = \frac{q}{2p} \cdot \mathcal{B}_\ell^{(\infty)}$, *and* $\det \Lambda_q(\mathbf{g}_p^t) = q^{\ell-1}$. *Moreover,* $\det \Lambda_q(\mathbf{g}_p^t) \otimes \mathbb{Z}^{m/\ell} = \det((q/p)\mathbb{Z}^m)$.

Proof. The fundamental region statement is from [27, Section 4], and the determinant calculation is straightforward. □

Definition 3 (Dual Gadget Lattice). *For* $p, q \in \mathbb{N}$, *let* $\mathbf{g}_p = (1, p, p^2, \ldots, p^{\lceil \log_p q \rceil - 1})$ *be the base-p "gadget vector". The dual gadget lattice is the lattice* $\Lambda_q^\perp(\mathbf{g}_p^t)$.

Proposition 2. *Let* $p < q$, *and let* $\ell = \lceil \log_p q \rceil$. *Then there exists a decoding algorithms for* $\Lambda_q^\perp(\mathbf{g}_p^t)$ *that satisfy*

- *when* $q = p^\ell$, $r_K^{(\infty)} \geq p/2$,
- *when* $q = p^\ell - 1$, $r_K^{(\infty)} \geq (p-1)/2$,
- *when* $q \in \mathbb{N}$, $r_K^{(\infty)} \geq \frac{(p-1)}{2} \frac{q}{p^\ell}$.

Proof. The case of $q = p^\ell$ follows from [27]. The case of $q = p^\ell - 1$ follows from [18] (we show that their "nearly square gadget matrix" is the dual gadget lattice in Sect. 4.2). The case of arbitrary q is implicit in [17] (it follows from standard analysis of a decoding algorithm they suggest). We provide this standard analysis below.

Let $S_q = [\mathbf{b}_0, \ldots, \mathbf{b}_{\ell-2}, \mathbf{q}]$ be the typical basis of $\Lambda_q^\perp(\mathbf{g}_p^t)$, where $\mathbf{b}_i = p\mathbf{e}_i - \mathbf{e}_{i+1}$, and $\mathbf{q} = (q_0, \ldots, q_{\ell-1})$ are the base-p digits of q. We abuse notation and state that $q = p^\ell$ has base-p decomposition of $(0, 0, \ldots, 0, p)$. The authors of [17] note that S_q admits a factorization as $S_q = S_{p^\ell} D_q$ where $D_q = [\mathbf{e}_0, \ldots, \mathbf{e}_{\ell-2}, \mathbf{d}_{p,q}]$ for the vector $\mathbf{d}_{p,q}$ with coefficients $\langle \mathbf{e}_i, \mathbf{d}_{p,q} \rangle = \frac{q \bmod p^{i+1}}{p^{i+1}}$. They then suggest using the decoder

$$\mathsf{decode}(x) = S_{p^\ell} \mathsf{decode}_{D_q \mathbb{Z}^\ell}(S_{p^\ell}^{-1} x), \tag{3}$$

where one decodes $D_q \mathbb{Z}^\ell$ using Babai's Nearest Planes. This has fundamental region that contains $\frac{q}{p^\ell}[-1/2, 1/2)^\ell$, and therefore the decoder of Eq. (3) has fundamental region that contains $S_{p^\ell} \frac{q}{p^\ell}[-1/2, 1/2)^\ell$. One can readily compute that this set contains $(p-1)\frac{q}{p^\ell}[-1/2, 1/2)^\ell$.

We omit the computation of the determinant, as it is straightforward. □

The next lattice belongs to parameterized family of lattices (for $\mathbf{u}_m^t = (1, 1, \ldots, 1) \in \mathbb{R}^m$) $\Lambda_q(\mathbf{u}_m^t)$ that we call the *Dual of Davenport's Lattice*. Well-known special cases are

- $q = 1$, where it is simply $\mathbb{Z}^m$, and
- $q = 2$, where it is a scaling of D_m^*, the dual of the standard $D_m = \Lambda_2(\mathbf{u}_m^t)$ root lattice.

The generalization to $m > 2$ has been implicit in many works, namely constructing explicit efficient coverings of $\mathbb{R}^m$ [11, Chapter 2, Sect. 1.3] [13], constructing efficient decoding algorithms for certain lattices [15], and constructing rate $1 - o(1)$ fully homomorphic encryption [6].

Definition 4 (Scaled Dual of Davenport's Lattice). *Let $m, q \in \mathbb{N}$. The scaled dual of Davenport's lattice $\Lambda_q(\mathbf{u}_m^t)$ is the lattice $\Lambda_q(\mathbf{u}_m^t) = q\mathbb{Z}^m + \mathbb{Z} \cdot \mathbf{u}_m$, where $\mathbf{u}_m$ is the all-ones vector of length m.*

Definition 5 (A_{m-1}^* Lattice). *For any $m \in \mathbb{N}$, the A_{m-1}^* lattice is defined to be the projection of $\mathbb{Z}^m$ perpendicular to the vector $\mathbf{u}_m$.*

When $m \mid q$, this lattice admits a simple orthogonal decomposition in terms of the root lattice A_{m-1}^*, which admits an $O(m)$-arithmetic operation CVP algorithm [26].

Lemma 2. *Provided $m \mid q$, $\Lambda_q(\mathbf{u}_m^t) = qA_{m-1}^* + \mathbb{Z} \cdot \mathbf{u}_m$, where $\langle qA_{m-1}^*, \mathbb{Z} \cdot \mathbf{u}_m \rangle = \{0\}$.*

Proof. As A^*_{m-1} is defined to be a projection orthogonal to $\mathbf{u}_m$, the last condition is immediate. One can check that $qA^*_{m-1}, \mathbf{u}_m$ are the projections of $\Lambda_q(\mathbf{u}^t_m)$ onto the subspaces perpendicular to and parallel to $\mathbf{u}_m$, respectively, so $qA^*_{m-1} + \mathbf{u}_m \supseteq \Lambda_q(\mathbf{u}^t_m)$. For the other direction, note that $\mathbf{u}_m \subseteq \Lambda_q(\mathbf{u}^t_m)$, as $\Lambda_q(\mathbf{u}^t_m) = q\mathbb{Z}^n + \mathbb{Z} \cdot \mathbf{u}_m$. The equality then immediately follows by [25, Proposition 1.1.6], which implies that the indicies of

- the intersection of $\Lambda_q(\mathbf{u}^t_m) \cap \mathbb{R} \cdot \mathbf{u}_m$ within the projection of $\Lambda_q(\mathbf{u}^t_m)$ onto $\mathbb{R} \cdot \mathbf{u}_m$, and
- the index of $\Lambda_q(\mathbf{u}^t_m)$ within $qA^*_{m-1} + \mathbb{Z} \cdot \mathbf{u}_m$,

are equal. As it is clear that the first index is 1, we have that $\Lambda_q(\mathbf{u}^t_m) = qA^*_{m-1} + \mathbb{Z} \cdot \mathbf{u}_m$. $\qquad\square$

This same argument works for $m \nmid q$, though the indices mentioned in the proof are not all equal to 1. It is fairly straightforward to verify that they are instead equal to $\frac{m}{\gcd(q,m)}$, so one gets an $O(m^2)$-arithmetic operation CVP algorithm for $\Lambda_q(\mathbf{u}^t_m)$ in general. This parameter setting does not appear to be useful for our setting though, as it is unclear how to get any useful information about the shape of the Voronoi cell of the lattice in general.

Proposition 3. *Let $m \mid q$. Then $R^{(\infty)}_{\Lambda_q(\mathbf{u}^t_m)} = \frac{q}{2}\left(1 - \frac{1}{m}\right) + \frac{1}{2}$, and $\det \Lambda_q(\mathbf{u}^t_m) = q^{m-1}$.*

Proof. The orthogonal decomposition implies that $\mathcal{V}_{\Lambda_q(\mathbf{u}^t_m)} = \mathcal{V}_{qA^*_{m-1}} + \mathcal{V}_{\mathbb{Z}\cdot\mathbf{u}_m}$. Applying triangle inequality, we can reduce computing $R^{(\infty)}_{\Lambda_q(\mathbf{u}^t_m)}$ to computing both $R^{(\infty)}_{qA^*_{m-1}}$ and $R^{(\infty)}_{\mathbb{Z}\cdot\mathbf{u}_m}$. The first is straightforward to compute given the explicit expression (found in [11, Chapter 4, Sect. 6.6]) for $\mathcal{V}_{A^*_{m-1}}$, namely as the convex hull of all coordinate permutations of the explicit vector $\mathbf{v} = \frac{1}{2m}(-m+1, -m+3, \ldots, m-3, m-1)$. The second is straightforward to compute as $1/2$.

Finally, to compute the determinant, note that the lattice may be generated by the $m+1$ vectors $[\mathbf{u}_m, q\mathbf{e}_1, \ldots, q\mathbf{e}_m]$, and that any single vector $q\mathbf{e}_i$ can easily be written as a linear combination of the other vectors in this generating set. It follows that $[q\mathbf{e}_1, q\mathbf{e}_2, \ldots, q\mathbf{e}_{m-1}, \mathbf{u}_m]$ is a triangular basis, and $\det \Lambda_q(\mathbf{u}^t_m) = q^{m-1}$.

$\qquad\square$

Corollary 1. *If $m \mid q$, one can solve CVP on $\Lambda_q(\mathbf{u}^t_m)$ in $O(m \log_2 q)$ time.*

Proof. Project parallel/perpendicular to $\mathbf{u}_n$, then use the known $O(m)$-arithmetic operation CVP algorithms on qA^*_{m-1} [26] and $\mathbb{Z} \cdot \mathbf{u}_m$. There is an additional $O(\log_2 q)$ overhead as the algorithm of [26] costs arithmetic operations at unit cost. $\qquad\square$

2.4   Bounds on Lattice Parameters

For any lattice L, the best normalized packing and covering radii are achieved by the CVP rounding algorithm, giving $\overline{r}_L$ and $\overline{R}_L$. For any m, let $\overline{r}_m = \sup_L \overline{r}_L$ and $\overline{R}_m = \inf_L \overline{R}_L$ be the optimal normalized radii over all lattices L of rank m. It is known that $\overline{r}_m = \Theta(\sqrt{m})$, and $\overline{R}_m = \Theta(\sqrt{m})$ (see Chaps. 1 and 2 of [11]). It is additionally known that in each dimension m, there are lattices $L \subseteq \mathbb{R}^m$ that (nearly) simultaneously achieve these bounds, meaning such that $\overline{R}_L / \overline{r}_L \leq 2 + o(1)$, see [9].

2.5   Probability

We define the Gaussian kernel to be $\rho_\sigma(x) = \exp(-x^2/2\sigma^2)$. Let $\mathcal{N}(0, \sigma^2 I_n)$ be the multivariate (continuous) Gaussian, with probability density function $f_\sigma(\mathbf{x}) = \frac{1}{\sqrt{(2\pi\sigma^2)^n}} \rho_\sigma(\|\mathbf{x}\|_2)$. We say that a random vector is *isotropic* if it is mean zero and has identity covariance matrix.

We will require the class of *log-concave* random variables.

Definition 6. *Let X be a random variable with pdf $p(x)$. We say that X is log-concave if $p(x) = \exp(-V(x))$ for $V(x)$ a convex function.*

We briefly summarize (from [34]) the properties this class of random variables satisfies.

Proposition 4. *Let $\mathbf{x}, \mathbf{x}' \in \mathbb{R}^n$ be log-concave and independent. Let $\mathbf{A} \in \mathbb{R}^{m \times n}$ be any linear transformation. Then $\mathbf{x} + \mathbf{x}'$ and $\mathbf{A}\mathbf{x}$ are log-concave.*

Standard examples of log-concave random variables are Gaussians, and uniform random variables on convex sets K. We establish log concavity of a few other distributions relevant to lattice-based cryptography at the end of this subsection.

Log-concave random variables are known to have strong concentration properties (they are "sub-exponential"). We use the following concentration bound mostly for simplicity of exposition — one can obtain tighter bounds by treating the cases of the $\|\cdot\|_2$ and $\|\cdot\|_\infty$ norms separately, though as we mention later (Sect. 4) this never impacts our (asymptotic) results.

Proposition 5 (Theorem 11 of [24]). *For any L-Lipschitz function $g \in \mathbb{R}^n$, if $\mathbf{x}$ is an isotropic log-concave random variable, then $\Pr[|g(\mathbf{x}) - \mathbb{E}[g(\mathbf{x})] > Lt|] \leq \exp(-\Omega(t\psi_n^{-1}))$.*

Here, ψ_n is *KLS constant*, which is (under the celebrated *KLS conjecture*) $O(1)$ as $n \to \infty$. The current best bound known is $\psi_n = O(\sqrt{\log n})$ [23]. In the rest of our work we will write $\exp(-\tilde{\Omega}(t))$, where this is understood to mean $\exp(-\Omega(t/\sqrt{\log n}))$.

Corollary 2. *If* $\mathbf{x}$ *is a log-concave random variable in* $\mathbb{R}^n$ *with covariance matrix* Σ, *then for* $p \in \{2, \infty\}$

$$\Pr[\|\mathbf{x}\|_p > \sqrt{\mathsf{Tr}(\Sigma)}(t + \sqrt{n})] \leq \exp(-\tilde{\Omega}(t)). \tag{4}$$

Proof. Note that $\Sigma^{-1/2}\mathbf{x}$ is isotropic, so we will apply the previous proposition to this random variable and $g(\mathbf{x}) = \|\Sigma^{1/2}\mathbf{x}\|_p$. For the ℓ_2 norm, the Lipschitz constant is the ℓ_2 to ℓ_2 operator norm, i.e. the maximum singular value of $\Sigma^{1/2}$, which is at most $\sqrt{\mathsf{Tr}(\Sigma)}$. For the ℓ_∞ norm, the Lipschitz constant is the ℓ_∞-ℓ_2 operator norm, i.e. the maximum ℓ_2 norm of a column of $\Sigma^{1/2}$. Note that each element of the main diagonal of Σ is the (squared) ℓ_2 norm of a column of Σ, so again we get that $\sqrt{\mathsf{Tr}(\Sigma)}$ bounds the Lipschitz constant.

We therefore have reduced to bounding $\mathbb{E}[g(\mathbf{x})]$ in both cases. For the ℓ_2 norm, by Jenson's inequality, we have that $\mathbb{E}[\|\mathbf{x}\|_2]^2 \leq \mathbb{E}[\|\mathbf{x}\|_2^2] = \mathsf{Tr}(\Sigma)$. For the ℓ_∞ norm, we apply the bound $\mathbb{E}[\|\mathbf{x}\|_\infty] \leq \mathbb{E}[\|\mathbf{x}\|_2] \leq \sqrt{\mathsf{Tr}(\Sigma)}$. □

We next introduce our *anti-concentration* inequality, which (in a general form) holds for arbitrary polynomials in log-concave random variables. For $t \in \mathbb{R}$ we apply it to the degree-2 polynomial $\|\mathbf{x}\|_2^2 - t$.

Proposition 6 (Theorem 8 of [10]). *If* $\mathbf{x}$ *is a log-concave random variable on* $\mathbb{R}^n$ *with covariance matrix* Σ, *then for every* $\epsilon > 0$,

$$\Pr[|\|X\|_2 - t| \leq \epsilon] \leq O\left(\frac{\epsilon}{\sqrt{\mathsf{Tr}(\Sigma)}}\right). \tag{5}$$

We end the sub-section by establishing log-concavity of some distributions of cryptographic interest.

Lemma 3. *Let* $\mathbf{e}_i \sim \mathcal{N}(0, \sigma_i^2 I_n)$ *for* $i \in \{0, 1\}$. *Then the distribution of* $\langle \mathbf{e}_0, \mathbf{e}_1 \rangle$ *is log-concave if* $n \geq 2$.

Proof. By [16, Eq. 2.15], one has that $\langle \mathbf{e}_0, \mathbf{e}_1 \rangle = \frac{\sigma_0 \sigma_1}{2}(V - V')$ as distributions, where V, V' are independent $\chi^2_{(n)}$ random variables. One can easily verify (by directly examining the pdf) that a $\chi^2_{(n)}$ random variable is log-concave if $n \geq 2$. By closure of log concavity under independent sums, the claimed result follows. □

Theorem 1. *Let* $n \geq 8$, *and let* K *be a bounded measurable subset of* $\mathbb{R}^n$. *Let* $\mathbf{x} \sim \mathcal{N}(0, \sigma^2 I_n)$, *and let* $\mathbf{y} \sim K$ *be independent from* $\mathbf{x}$. *Then* $\langle \mathbf{x}, \mathbf{y} \rangle$ *is log-concave.*

Note that by applying orthogonal transformations to both $\mathbf{x}, \mathbf{y}$, this implies log concavity in the more general case of $\mathbf{x} \sim \mathcal{N}(0, \Sigma)$.

Proof. One can verify that univariate $p(x)$ is log-concave if

$$\forall x : p(x)p''(x) \leq (p'(x))^2. \tag{6}$$

We will explicitly compute the pdf of $\langle \mathbf{x}, \mathbf{y} \rangle$, and show that it satisfies this inequality. Note that by the law of total probability

$$
\begin{aligned}
\mu(A) := \Pr[\langle \mathbf{x}, \mathbf{y} \rangle \in A] &= \int_{\mathbb{R}^n} \Pr[\langle \mathbf{x}, \mathbf{y} \rangle \in A \mid \mathbf{y} = \mathbf{z}] \Pr[\mathbf{y} = \mathbf{z}] d\mathbf{z} \\
&= \int_{\mathbb{R}^n} \left(\int_A \sqrt{2\pi\sigma^2 \|\mathbf{z}\|_2^2}^{-1} \exp\left(-\frac{x^2}{2\sigma^2\|\mathbf{z}\|_2^2}\right) dx \right) \mathrm{vol}(K)^{-1}\chi_K(\mathbf{z}) d\mathbf{z} \\
&= \int_A \left(\mathrm{vol}(K)^{-1} \int_K \sqrt{2\pi\sigma^2\|\mathbf{z}\|_2^2}^{-1} \exp\left(-\frac{x^2}{2\sigma^2\|\mathbf{z}\|_2^2}\right) \right) dx,
\end{aligned}
$$

where in the last step we applied Fubini's theorem and simplified. If we define $f(x, y^2) = \mathrm{vol}(K)^{-1}\sqrt{2\pi\sigma^2 y^2}^{-1} \exp\left(-\frac{x^2}{2\sigma^2 y^2}\right)$, it follows that the density is $p(x) = \int_K f(x, \|\mathbf{z}\|_2^2) d\mathbf{z}$.

To compute the derivatives $p'(x), p''(x)$, we need to interchange differentiation and integration a few times, which we do via the (measure-theoretic) Leibniz Integral rule. Before discussing this, we compute that $\partial_x f(x, y^2) = -\frac{x}{\sigma^2 y^2} f(x, y^2)$, $\partial_x^2 f(x, y^2) = \left(\frac{x^2}{\sigma^4 y^4} - \frac{1}{\sigma^2 y^2}\right) f(x, y^2)$, $\partial_x^3 f(x, y^2) = -\left(\frac{x^3}{\sigma^6 y^6} - \frac{3x}{\sigma^4 y^4}\right) f(x, y^2)$. Our applications of the Leibniz integral rule will require all of these functions (as well as $f(x, y^2)$ itself) to be integrable for all x. The largest singularity occurs when $x = 0$, where $\partial_x^3 f = O(y^{-7})$. As switching to spherical coordinates introduces a multiplicative factor y^{n-1}, provided $n \geq 8$ we can switch to spherical coordinates to get an integrand with no singularity, and show convergence. Note that this step is additionally where we require K to be bounded and measurable, as otherwise $\int_{\mathbb{R}^n} f(x, \|\mathbf{z}\|_2^2) d\mathbf{z} = \infty$ for the same reason that $\int_{\mathbb{R}^n} \|\mathbf{z}\|_2^2 d\mathbf{z} = \infty$. As the other preconditions of Leibniz are straightforward to verify, we omit them.

We next note that one can write

$$
\mathbb{E}_{\mathbf{x}}[f(\mathbf{x})]\mathbb{E}_{\mathbf{x}}[g(\mathbf{x})] = \mathbb{E}_{\mathbf{x},\mathbf{y}}\left[\frac{f(\mathbf{x})g(\mathbf{y}) + f(\mathbf{y})g(\mathbf{x})}{2}\right], \tag{7}
$$

where $\mathbf{y}$ is an i.i.d. copy of $\mathbf{x}$. It follows that

$$
(p'(x))^2 = \mathbb{E}_{\mathbf{z},\mathbf{z}'}\left[\frac{x^2}{\sigma^4}\|\mathbf{z}\|_2^{-2}\|\mathbf{z}'\|_2^{-2} f(x, \|\mathbf{z}\|_2^2) f(x, \|\mathbf{z}'\|_2^2)\right], \tag{8}
$$

and

$$
p(x)p''(x) = \mathbb{E}_{\mathbf{z},\mathbf{z}'}\left[\left(\frac{x^2}{\sigma^4}\left(\frac{\|\mathbf{z}\|_2^{-4} + \|\mathbf{z}'\|_2^{-4}}{2}\right) - \frac{1}{\sigma^2}\left(\frac{\|\mathbf{z}\|_2^{-2} + \|\mathbf{z}'\|_2^{-2}}{2}\right)\right) f(x, \|\mathbf{z}\|_2^2) f(x, \|\mathbf{z}'\|_2^2)\right]. \tag{9}
$$

Therefore establishing the inequality $(p'(x))^2 \geq p''(x)p(x)$ reduces to showing that some explicit integral is non-negative. Note that $f(x, \|\mathbf{z}\|_2^2) \geq 0$ by inspection. We therefore reduce to showing that the integrand

$$
\frac{x^2}{\sigma^4}\|\mathbf{z}\|_2^{-2}\|\mathbf{z}'\|_2^{-2} - \left(\frac{x^2}{\sigma^4}\left(\frac{\|\mathbf{z}\|_2^{-4} + \|\mathbf{z}'\|_2^{-4}}{2}\right) - \frac{1}{\sigma^2}\left(\frac{\|\mathbf{z}\|_2^{-2} + \|\mathbf{z}'\|_2^{-2}}{2}\right)\right) \geq 0. \tag{10}
$$

This itself follows from the bound $x^{-2}y^{-2} \geq \frac{x^{-4}+y^{-4}}{2}$, valid for any positive x, y, which in the more familiar form $\left(\frac{x^{-4}+y^{-4}}{2}\right)^{-1} \leq x^2y^2$ is simply the inequality between the Harmonic and Geometric means, applied to (x^4, y^4).

2.6   The Learning with Errors Problem

Much of lattice cryptography relies on the hardness of the *learning with errors* problem.

Definition 7 (LWE problem). *Let* $m = n^{O(1)}$, *and let* $q \in [n^{O(1)}, 2^{O(n)}]$. *Let* χ_{sk} *be a distribution on* $\mathbb{Z}_q$, *and* χ_e *be a distribution on* $\mathbb{R}_q$. *The Learning with Errors problem* $\mathsf{LWE}^{n,q}_{\chi_{sk}, \chi_e}$ *is to distinguish the distribution* $(\mathbf{A}, \mathbf{As} + \mathbf{e})$ *from* $(\mathbf{A}, \mathbf{u})$, *where* $\mathbf{A} \leftarrow \mathbb{Z}_q^{n \times m}$, $\mathbf{s} \leftarrow \chi_{sk}^n$, *and* $\mathbf{e} \leftarrow \chi_e^m$, *and* $\mathbf{u} \leftarrow \mathbb{R}_q^m$.

We rely on LWE where $\mathbf{e} \leftarrow \chi_e$ and $\mathbf{u} \leftarrow \mathbb{R}_q^m$ are *real* random variables (modulo q) to simplify our analysis. We omit the inclusion of m in the notation $\mathsf{LWE}^{n,q}_{\chi_{sk}, \chi_e}$, as it has minimal impact on the hardness of the problem. The primary justification for the hardness of $\mathsf{LWE}^{n,q}_{\chi_{sk}, \chi_e}$ is that it admits reductions from worst-case hard lattice problems, initially due to Regev [32].

Theorem 2. *For any* $m = n^{O(1)}$, *any modulus* $q \leq 2^{n^{O(1)}}$, *let* χ_e *be any (discretized) Gaussian distribution* χ *of parameter* $\sigma \geq 2\sqrt{n}$, *and* χ_{sk} *be the uniform distribution on* $\mathbb{Z}_q$. *Then solving the decision* $\mathsf{LWE}^{n,q}_{\chi_{sk}, \chi_e}$ *problem is at least as hard as quantumly solving* GapSVP_γ *and* SIVP_γ *on arbitrary* n-*dimensional lattices, where* $\gamma = \tilde{O}(nq/\sigma)$.

This work will not need definitions of of GapSVP_γ and SIVP_γ. We call attention to the approximation factor $\gamma = \tilde{O}(nq/\sigma)$, which controls the hardness of the problem, and depends on the "modulus to noise" ratio q/σ. The Gaussian parameter can often be set to a fixed polynomial $\sigma = 2\sqrt{n}$, so that larger values of q result in constructions that are both less efficient and less secure. Of particular interest will be the cases of *polynomial* $q/\sigma = n^{O(1)}$, and *superpolynomial* $q/\sigma = n^{\omega(1)}$ modulus to noise ratio.

2.7   Cryptographic Primitives

We will use the standard notion of IND-CPA security, as well as a less standard notion (that is better suited to lattice-based primitives) known as RND-CPA.

Definition 8 (IND-CPA). *An encryption scheme* (KGen, Enc, Dec) *is said to be* indistinguishable under chosen plaintext attack *if any efficient (probabilistic polynomial-time) adversary* $\mathcal{A}$ *can only achieve at most negligible advantage in the following game, parameterized by a bit* $b \in \{0, 1\}$:

1. $k \leftarrow \mathsf{KGen}(1^n)$,
2. $b' \leftarrow \mathcal{A}^{O_b(\cdot, \cdot)}$, *where* $O_b(m_0, m_1) = \mathsf{Enc}_k(m_b)$.

The adversary's advantage is defined to be $\mathsf{Adv}(\mathcal{A}) = |\Pr[b' = 1 \mid b = 0] - \Pr[b' = 1 \mid b = 1]|$.

Definition 9 (RND-CPA). *An encryption scheme* (KGen, Enc, Dec) *is said to be* pseudorandom under chosen plaintext attack *if any efficient (probabilistic polynomial-time) adversary* $\mathcal{A}$ *can only achieve at most negligible advantage in the following game, parameterized by a bit* $b \in \{0, 1\}$:

1. $k \leftarrow \mathsf{KGen}(1^n)$,
2. $b' \leftarrow \mathcal{A}^{O_b(\cdot)}$, *where* $O_b(m)$ *returns either*
   - $b = 0$: *an encryption* $\mathsf{Enc}_k(m)$ *of the message* m *under the key* k, *or*
   - $b = 1$: *a sample from a distribution that has support* $\{\mathsf{Enc}_k(m) \mid k \in \mathsf{supp}(\mathsf{KGen}(1^n)), m \in \mathcal{M}\}$.

The adversary's advantage is defined to be $\mathsf{Adv}(\mathcal{A}) = |\Pr[b' = 1 \mid b = 0] - \Pr[b' = 1 \mid b = 1]|$.

Note that the distribution in the $b = 1$ case is not dependent on k, m. A straightforward hybrid argument shows that RND-CPA-security implies IND-CPA-security, although the reverse implication does not hold[10]. We use the (standard) correctness notion of [20], specialized to the setting of private-key encryption.

Definition 10 (δ-Correctness). *A private-key encryption scheme* (KGen, Enc, Dec) *is said to be* δ*-correct if* $\mathbb{E}_{\mathsf{sk} \leftarrow \mathsf{KGen}(1^n)}[\max_{m \in \mathcal{M}}[\Pr[\mathsf{Dec}_{\mathsf{sk}}(c) \neq m \mid c \leftarrow \mathsf{Enc}_{\mathsf{sk}}(m)]]] \leq \delta$.

3 The Encryption Framework

We next present and analyze a secret-key encryption framework. This is done for simplicity of presentation, as the main complication of the public-key setting is a more complex (but, by our results of Sect. 2.5, still log-concave) noise distribution.

To prove bounds in some framework, one must first

- define a sensible *rate* for the framework, and
- define a *ciphertext error distribution* for the framework.

We do this for our secret-key framework in this section. We additionally show cryptographic security of constructions in our framework, although this is relatively straightforward.

---

[10] Take an IND-CPA-secure cryptosystem, and modify encryption to output $\mathsf{Enc}_k(m) \| H(k)$ for a hash function $H(\cdot)$, modeled as a random oracle. As k is not consistent between queries to $O_1(\cdot)$, there is a simple RND-CPA distinguisher, but the construction is still IND-CPA-secure.

KGen(1^n)	Encs(m)	Decs($\mathbf{A}, \mathbf{c}$)
$\mathbf{s} \leftarrow \chi_{\text{sk}}^n$	$\mathbf{A} \leftarrow \mathbb{Z}_q^{n \times m}$	return decode$_E(\mathbf{c} - \mathbf{As})$
return s	$\mathbf{e} \leftarrow \chi_e^m$	
	$\mathbf{b} = \mathbf{As} + \mathbf{e} + \text{encode}_E(\mathbf{m})$	
	return $(\mathbf{A}, \lfloor \mathbf{b} \rceil_Q)$	

Fig. 2. Quantized Encryption $\text{LWE}_{\chi_{\text{sk}}, \chi_e}^{n,q}[E, Q]$, defined relative to lattice codes $(E, \lfloor \cdot \rceil_E), (Q, \lfloor \cdot \rceil_Q)$.

Definition 11 (Quantized LWE Encryption). *Let* $(E, \lfloor \cdot \rceil_E), (Q, \lfloor \cdot \rceil_Q)$ *be lattice codes in* $\mathbb{R}_q^m$. *Let* χ_{sk} *be a distribution on* $\mathbb{Z}_q$, *and let* χ_e *be a distribution on* $\mathbb{R}_q$. *The Quantized LWE Encryption Scheme* $\text{LWE}_{\chi_{\text{sk}}, \chi_e}^{n,q}[E, Q]$ *is given by* (KGen, Enc, Dec), *as defined in Fig. 2.*

Definition 12. *Let* $(E, \lfloor \cdot \rceil_E), (Q, \lfloor \cdot \rceil_Q)$ *be lattice codes in* $\mathbb{R}_q^m$. *Let* χ_{sk} *be a distribution on* $\mathbb{Z}_q$, *and* χ_e *be a distribution on* $\mathbb{R}_q$. *We say the* asymptotic rate of $\text{LWE}_{\chi_{\text{sk}}, \chi_e}^{n,q}[E, Q]$ *is the quantity*

$$\frac{\log_2 |E/q\mathbb{Z}^m|}{\log_2 |Q/q\mathbb{Z}^m|} = 1 - \frac{\log_2 \frac{\det E}{\det Q}}{\log_2 \frac{q^m}{\det Q}}. \tag{11}$$

This expression for rate does not include the cost of transmitting $\mathbf{A}$, as there are many ways to reduce (or amortize) this cost, such as appealing to algebraically structured forms of $\text{LWE}_{\chi_{\text{sk}}, \chi_e}$, amortizing the cost of $\mathbf{A}$ across many (independent) communication sessions, or transmitting a short seed $s \in \{0, 1\}^n$, which one deterministically expands with an extendable output function. In settings where these optimizations are not available (say if one wants to incorporate the cost of transmission of an LWE public key that will be used a single time), one should of course modify the rate to match the particular setting of interest.

We next define the *ciphertext error distribution* of $\text{LWE}_{\chi_{\text{sk}}, \chi_e}^{n,q}[E, Q]$. This is the distribution that E must correct for decryption to succeed.

Lemma 4. *Let* $(E, \lfloor \cdot \rceil_E), (Q, \lfloor \cdot \rceil_Q)$ *be lattice codes in* $\mathbb{R}_q^m$. *Let* χ_{sk} *be a distribution on* $\mathbb{Z}_q$, *and* χ_e *be a distribution on* $\mathbb{R}_q$. *Let* $\mathbf{A} \leftarrow \mathbb{Z}_q^{n \times m}$, $\mathbf{e} \leftarrow \chi_e^m$, $\mathbf{s} \leftarrow \chi_{\text{sk}}^n$, *and* $\mathbf{b} = \mathbf{As} + \text{encode}_E(\mathbf{m}) + \mathbf{e}$. *Then*

$$\text{Dec}_{\mathbf{s}}(\text{Enc}_{\mathbf{s}}(\mathbf{m})) = \mathbf{m} \iff \mathbf{e} - [\mathbf{b}]_Q \in \mathcal{V}_E. \tag{12}$$

Proof. We have that

$$\text{Dec}_{\mathbf{s}}(\text{Enc}_{\mathbf{s}})(\mathbf{m}) = \text{decode}_E(\lfloor \mathbf{b} \rceil_Q - \mathbf{As})$$
$$= \text{decode}_E(\mathbf{b} - [\mathbf{b}]_Q - \mathbf{As})$$
$$= \mathbf{m} + \text{decode}_E(\mathbf{e} - [\mathbf{b}]_Q).$$

$\square$

In principle the ciphertext error distribution may depend on $\mathbf{m}$. This and other annoyances (namely that $[\mathbf{b}]_Q$ and $\mathbf{e}$ may be dependent) lead us to introduce the following heuristic description of the ciphertext error distribution.

Heuristic 1. Let $(Q, \lfloor \cdot \rceil)$ be a lattice code, $\mathbf{m}$ be any message, $\mathbf{c} \in \mathcal{V}_Q$, $\mathbf{s} \leftarrow \chi_{sk}^n$, $\mathbf{A} \leftarrow \mathbb{Z}_q^{n \times m}$, and $\mathbf{e} \leftarrow \chi_e^m$. Then the error $\mathbf{e} - [\mathbf{As} + \mathbf{e} + \mathsf{encode}_E(\mathbf{m})]$ is distributed as $\mathbf{e} - \mathbf{u}$, where $\mathbf{u} \leftarrow \mathcal{V}_Q$ is independent from $\mathbf{e}$.

We present a modification of our cryptosystem in Sect. 3.2 that has the same rate as $\mathsf{LWE}_{\chi_{sk}, \chi_e}^{n,q}[E, Q]$, which (provably) has the above ciphertext error distribution.

We next derive a bound on δ in terms of the scheme parameters. Curiously, we get a better bound if we first separate-off the (bounded) quantization error and apply a *worst-case* bound over this quantity, rather than naively applying Corollary 2.

Lemma 5. Let $(E, \lfloor \cdot \rceil_E), (Q, \lfloor \cdot \rceil_Q)$ be lattice codes in $\mathbb{R}_q^m$. Let χ_{sk} be a distribution on $\mathbb{Z}_q$, and χ_e be a distribution on $\mathbb{R}_q$. If $\Sigma_{\mathbf{e}}$ is the covariance matrix of $\mathbf{e} \leftarrow \chi_e^m$, $\mathbf{u} \leftarrow \mathcal{V}_Q$, then if for some $p \in \{2, \infty\}$, $r_E^{(p)} > \sqrt{\mathsf{Tr}(\Sigma_{\mathbf{e}})} \left(\tilde{O}(\ln(1/\delta)) + \sqrt{m} \right) + R_Q^{(p)}$, it follows that $\mathsf{LWE}_{\chi_{sk}, \chi_e}^{n,q}[E, Q]$ is δ-correct.

Proof. We have that $\delta = \Pr[\|\mathbf{e}^t - \mathbf{u}^t\|_E > 1] \le \Pr[\|\mathbf{e}^t\|_E > 1 - \|\mathbf{u}^t\|_E]$. By definition we have that $r_E^{(p)} \cdot \mathcal{B}_m^{(p)} \subseteq \mathcal{V}_E$, and therefore for any $\mathbf{x}$, $\|\mathbf{x}\|_E \le \frac{1}{r_E^{(p)}} \|\mathbf{x}\|_p$. It follows that $\delta \le \Pr[\|\mathbf{e}^t\|_p > r_E^{(p)} - R_Q^{(p)}]$. Under the assumed bound on $r_E^{(p)}$, our claim follows by Corollary 2. $\qquad\square$

3.1   Cryptographic Properties of $\mathsf{LWE}_{\chi_{sk}, \chi_e}^{n,q}[E, Q]$

We next establish RND-CPA security under the $\mathsf{LWE}_{\chi_{sk}, \chi_e}$ assumption. Note that we require no assumptions[11] on E, Q.

Theorem 3. $\mathsf{LWE}_{\chi_{sk}, \chi_e}^{n,q}[E, Q]$ *is* RND-CPA-*secure under the* $\mathsf{LWE}_{\chi_{sk}, \chi_e}$ *assumption.*

Proof. Given an adversary that breaks RND-CPA-security of $\mathsf{LWE}_{\chi_{sk}, \chi_e}$, we describe how to break the decisional $\mathsf{LWE}_{\chi_{sk}, \chi_e}$ assumption. Let $O_b(\cdot)$ be an oracle that either returns samples from (when $b = 0$) $(\mathbf{A}, \mathbf{As} + \mathbf{e})$, or (when $b = 1$) $(\mathbf{A}, \mathbf{u}) \leftarrow \mathbb{Z}_q^{n \times m} \times \mathbb{R}_q^m$. Construct an encryption oracle that encrypts $\mathbf{m}$ by

- sampling $(\mathbf{A}, \mathbf{b}) \leftarrow O_b(\cdot)$, and
- returning $(\mathbf{A}, \lfloor \mathbf{b} + \mathsf{encode}_E(\mathbf{m}) \rceil_Q)$.

---

[11] Part of this claim is an artifact of us using LWE samples with pseudorandom component $\mathbf{b} \in \mathbb{R}_q^m$. If we replace this with $\mathbb{Z}_q^m$, one can establish security if either $E_q \subseteq \mathbb{Z}_q^m$ or $Q_q \subseteq \mathbb{Z}_q^m$. This is still a relatively minor assumption, as it still implies security for E, Q sharing no common structure.

When $b = 0$, this is exactly the oracle $O_0(\mathbf{m})$ of the RND-CPA game. When $b = 1$, we will show that it is a random ciphertext. Note that $\mathbf{v} := \mathbf{u} + \mathsf{encode}_E(\mathbf{m})$ is the sum of a uniformly random element $\mathbf{u}$ of a group $\mathbb{R}_q^m$ along with an independent element of that group. By a standard argument analogous to the security of the one-time pad, $\mathbf{v}$ is itself uniform over $\mathbb{R}_q^m$, and independent of $\mathsf{encode}_E(\mathbf{m})$. Finally, for uniform $\mathbf{v}$, it is straightforward to see (as $q\mathbb{Z}^m \subseteq Q$) that $\lfloor \mathbf{v} \rceil_Q$ is uniform, finishing the proof. $\square$

We briefly remark that one could also achieve security of our cryptosystem using a "LWR-type" assumption, namely that $(\mathbf{A}, \lfloor \mathbf{As} \rceil_Q)$ is pseudorandom. This recovers the LWR assumption when Q is a scaling of $\mathbb{Z}^m$.

3.2   Quantized LWE Encryption with a Dither

$\mathsf{KGen}(1^n)$	$\mathsf{Enc_s(m)}$	$\mathsf{Dec_s(A, c, v)}$
$\mathbf{s} \leftarrow_\$ \chi_{\mathsf{sk}}^n$	$\mathbf{A} \leftarrow \mathbb{Z}_q^{n \times m}$	return $\mathsf{decode}_E(\mathbf{c} + \mathbf{v} - \mathbf{As})$
return $\mathbf{s}$	$\mathbf{e} \leftarrow_\$ \chi_e^m$	
	$\mathbf{b} = \mathbf{As} + \mathbf{e} + \mathsf{encode}_E(\mathbf{m})$	
	$\mathbf{v} \leftarrow \mathcal{V}_Q$	
	return $(\mathbf{A}, \lfloor \mathbf{b} - \mathbf{v} \rceil_Q, \mathbf{v})$	

Fig. 3. Dithered Quantized Encryption $\mathsf{DithLWE}_{\chi_{\mathsf{sk}}, \chi_e}^{n,q}[E, Q]$, defined relative to lattice codes $(E, \lfloor \cdot \rceil_E), (Q, \lfloor \cdot \rceil_Q)$. Sampling from $\mathcal{V}_Q$ can be done efficiently via sampling $\mathbf{v} \leftarrow [0, q)^m$, and then computing $[\mathbf{v}]_Q$.

We next describe a variant of quantized LWE for which Heuristic 1 holds. This utilizes what is known as the *subtractive dither* in coding theory, see Chap. 4 of [35] for more details. Security of our construction easily follows under the same conditions (and proof) of Theorem 3. We omit reproducing this proof for brevity, and instead show that the analogue of Heuristic 1 holds for $\mathsf{DithLWE}_{\chi_{\mathsf{sk}}, \chi_e}^{n,q}[E, Q]$ (Fig. 3).

Lemma 6. *Let $(E, \lfloor \cdot \rceil_E), (Q, \lfloor \cdot \rceil_Q)$ be lattice codes in $\mathbb{R}_q^m$. Then the ciphertext error distribution of $\mathsf{DithLWE}_{\chi_{\mathsf{sk}}, \chi_e}^{n,q}[E, Q]$ satisfies Heuristic 1.*

Proof. For any message $\mathbf{m}$, we can compute that

$$\mathsf{Dec_s(Enc_s(m))} = \mathsf{decode}_E(\lfloor \mathbf{b} - \mathbf{v} \rceil_Q + \mathbf{v} - \mathbf{As})$$
$$= \mathsf{decode}_E(\mathbf{b} - \mathbf{v} - [\mathbf{b} - \mathbf{v}]_Q + \mathbf{v} - \mathbf{As})$$
$$= \mathbf{m} + \mathsf{decode}_E(\mathbf{e} - [\mathbf{b} - \mathbf{v}]_Q).$$

Now, as $\mathbf{v}$ is uniform over $\mathcal{V}_Q$, we have that $[\mathbf{b} - \mathbf{v}]_Q$ is uniform over $\mathcal{V}_Q$ as well, and independent of $\mathbf{b}$ (and therefore $\mathbf{e}$). It follows that $\mathsf{Dec_s(Enc_s(m))} = \mathbf{m}$, unless $\mathbf{e} - \mathbf{u} \notin \mathcal{V}_E$, for an independent uniform random variable $\mathbf{u} = [\mathbf{b} - \mathbf{v}]_Q$. $\square$

We next argue that in practice, $\mathsf{LWE}^{n,q}_{\chi_{sk},\chi_e}[E,Q]$ and $\mathsf{DithLWE}^{n,q}_{\chi_{sk},\chi_e}[E,Q]$ have the same rate. Recall that we do not explicitly include the random matrix $\mathbf{A} \in \mathbb{Z}_q^{n \times m}$ in our computations of rate. One justification for this was that typically, $\mathbf{A}$ itself is not transmitted, and instead a short seed $s \in \{0,1\}^n$ is transmitted, which is then expanded into $\mathbf{A} := H(s)$ using an extendable output function $H(\cdot)$. If this (common) optimization is used, one can simply generate $\mathbf{v}$ in this same manner, so $\mathbf{v}$ does not need to be explicitly included in ciphertexts.

4   Constructions of Quantized LWE Encryption

We next describe the rate achievable by several instantiations (parameterized by lattice codes E, Q) of our framework. The following choice of parameters will be used to enable uniform rate comparisons.

Definition 13. *We say the* standard choice of parameters *are the choice of* $\delta = \exp(-n)$, $\sigma = 2\sqrt{n}$, *and* $m = O(n)$.

4.1   Quantizing Regev's Encryption

We first analyze a quantized variant Regev's initial cryptosystem [32] in our framework, namely $\mathsf{LWE}^{n,q}_{\chi_{sk},\chi_e}[(q/p)\mathbb{Z}^m, k\mathbb{Z}^m]$ for $k \in \mathbb{N}$. Regev's initial scheme corresponds to the cryptosystem with no quantization ($k = 1$). We will later optimize over the choice of k to attain a rate $1 - o(1)$ cryptosystem from polynomial modulus.

Definition 14 (Regev Encryption). *Let* $p, q, k \in \mathbb{N}$. *Regev Encryption is the Quantized LWE encryption scheme* $\mathsf{LWE}^{n,q}_{\chi_{sk},\chi_e}[(q/p)\mathbb{Z}^m, k\mathbb{Z}^m]$.

Corollary 3. *Let* $p < q$, *and* $k \in \mathbb{N}$. *Then for any* $\delta > 0$, *provided* $\frac{q}{2p} > \tilde{\Omega}(n^{3/2}\sqrt{n + k^2})$, *one can parameterize Regev encryption to be* δ-*correct under the standard choice of parameters and of asymptotic rate at least*

$$1 - O\left(\frac{\log_2(n^2/k)}{\log_2(q/k)}\right). \tag{13}$$

We highlight three main takeaways from this example, namely that

1. for trivial quantization ($k = 1$), it is asymptotic rate $1 - \Theta(1)$, i.e. asymptotic rate $1 - \Omega(1)$ from polynomial modulus,
2. for non-trivial quantization ($k = \Omega(n^2)$), it is asymptotic rate $1 - o(1)$ from polynomial modulus, and
3. no parameterization (with polynomially-large q) can achieve asymptotic rate better than $1 - o\left(\frac{1}{\log_2 n}\right)$.

Proof. We get by Lemma 5 that this cryptosystem is δ-correct under the standard choice of parameters provided

$$\frac{q}{2p} > \tilde{\Omega}\left(n^{3/2}\sigma\right) + k. \tag{14}$$

Choosing q/p at most a constant-factor larger than this, we get a scheme of asymptotic rate

$$1 - O\left(\frac{\log_2(n^2/k)}{\log_2(q/k)}\right) \tag{15}$$

$\square$

We briefly comment on the tightness of our bounds. Prior analysis of ours (not included in this work) that appealed to Gaussian-specific bounds[12] to optimize Eq. (14) yielded a different bound on q/p, namely the bound

$$\frac{q}{2p} > \sqrt{2}\sigma(\sqrt{\log_2 m} + \sqrt{\ln n}) + k, \tag{16}$$

i.e. with no implicit constants[13], and a bound of $q/2p > \Omega(n)$ rather than $q/2p > \tilde{\Omega}(n^2)$. This yields a scheme of asymptotic rate $1 - O\left(\frac{\log_2(n/k)}{\log_2(q/k)}\right)$. We say this to highlight that the more general log-concave analysis (compared to the Gaussian analysis, only relevant for private-key encryption) does result in *some* loss, but only impacts the three points we highlighted above via requiring a larger parameter $k = \Omega(n^2)$.

4.2 Quantizing the Cryptosystem of [18]

To demonstrate the breadth of our framework, we next show that it contains the high-rate cryptosystems of [18]. This work proposed two high-rate cryptosystems, namely

- **Section** 4.1: an (unquantized) form of what we call Regev encryption, and
- **Section** 4.2: an (unquantized) form of encryption that uses a lattice generated by a "nearly square gadget matrix" H for error-correction.

As we have already analyzed the first construction, we focus on the second construction in this sub-section. [18] constructs the matrix H as the kernel modulo q of an explicit matrix[14] $F' \otimes I_k$, where (for $q = p^\ell - 1$)

$$F' = \begin{pmatrix} p^{\ell-1} & 1 & \cdots & p^{\ell-2} \\ p^{\ell-2} & p^{\ell-1} & & p^{\ell-3} \\ \vdots & \vdots & \ddots & \vdots \\ 1 & p & \cdots & p^{\ell-1} \end{pmatrix}. \tag{17}$$

---

[12] To handle the (bounded) uniform component $\mathbf{u}$, we appealed to worst-case bounds on its size.

[13] For this reason, we use this tighter (yet standard) analysis to compute the curves in Fig. 1.

[14] The matrix we copy down is actually the transpose of the matrix of [18], as we have different conventions for whether lattices are generated by rows/columns of their basis.

One can verify that F' is precisely what one gets when reducing the collection of $\ell + 1$ vectors given by $[\mathbf{g}_p, q\mathbf{e}_1, \ldots, q\mathbf{e}_\ell]$ to a basis, i.e. is a basis of the lattice $\Lambda_q(\mathbf{g}_p^t)$. It then follows that the desired matrix H is a basis for the lattice $\Lambda_q^\perp(\mathbf{g}_p^t) \otimes \mathbb{Z}^k$ for some k, as we claimed in Table 1.

Definition 15 (Gentry-Halevi Encryption, [18]). *For $p, q \in \mathbb{N}$, the Gentry-Halevi Encryption scheme is the Quantized LWE encryption scheme* $\mathsf{LWE}_{\chi_{sk}, \chi_e}^{n,q} [\Lambda_q^\perp(\mathbf{g}_p^t) \otimes \mathbb{Z}^{m/\lceil \log_p q \rceil}, k\mathbb{Z}^m]$.

Corollary 4. *Let $p < q$, and let $\ell = \lceil \log_p q \rceil$. Assume that $q/p^\ell = O(1)$ with respect to p. Then provided $p > \tilde{\Omega}(n^2) + k$, one can parameterize Gentry-Halevi Encryption to be δ-correct under the standard choice of parameters, and of asymptotic rate at least*

$$1 - O\left(\frac{\log_2(n^2/k)}{\log_2(q/k)}\right). \tag{18}$$

Proof. By Lemma 5, this is δ-correct provided $\frac{q}{p^\ell} \frac{(p-1)}{2} > \sqrt{n}\sigma(\tilde{\Omega}(n) + \sqrt{m}) + k$. Under the standard choice of parameters (and assuming $\frac{q}{p^\ell} = O(1)$, independently of p), we get that it suffices to take $p > \tilde{\Omega}(n^2) + k$. This yields a cryptosystem of rate

$$1 - O\left(\frac{\log_2(p/k)}{\log_2(q/k)}\right) = 1 - O\left(\frac{\log_2(n^2/k)}{\log_2(q/k)}\right). \tag{19}$$

$\square$

Note that for large-enough $k = \Omega(n^2)$ this is asymptotic rate $1 - o(1)$ from polynomial modulus, while [18] required super-polynomial modulus to attain rate $1 - o(1)$.

4.3   Optimizing the Quantized Cryptosystem of [6]

We next consider the only cryptosystem in the literature that uses a quantizer that is not of the form $\mathbb{Z}^{m/k} \otimes Q'$, namely the cryptosystem of [6], which the authors of that work refer to as "linearly homomorphic encryption with ciphertext shrinking". We claim this defines exactly the cryptosystem $\mathsf{LWE}_{\chi_{sk}, \chi_e}^{n,q} [(q/2)\mathbb{Z}^m, \Lambda_{q/2}(\mathbf{u}_m^t)]$. As this equivalence is not obvious, we briefly recall their construction.

The construction starts with an (unquantized) Regev ciphertext $(\mathbf{A}, \mathbf{As}+\mathbf{e}+(q/2)m)$. It then shows (existentially) that one can find a scalar $r \in \mathbb{Z}_q$ such that the pair $(\mathbf{w} := \mathsf{decode}_{(q/2)\mathbb{Z}^m}(\mathbf{c}_2 + r \cdot \mathbf{u}_m^t), r) \in \mathbb{Z}_2^m \times \mathbb{Z}_q$ suffice for decryption. We view this pair $(\mathbf{w}, r)$ as defining an element of the lattice $\Lambda_{q/2}(\mathbf{u}_m^t) = (q/2)\mathbb{Z}^m + \mathbb{Z} \cdot \mathbf{u}_m$ via the obvious mapping $(\mathbf{w}, r) \mapsto (q/2)\mathbf{w} + r \cdot \mathbf{u}_m$. Note that this mapping is almost a bijection[15]. Under this identification, the pair $(\mathbf{w}, r)$ is simply equal

---

[15] When working modulo q, it is instead a bijection between $\mathbb{Z}_2^m \times \mathbb{Z}_{q/2}$ and our lattice, rather than $\mathbb{Z}_2^m \times \mathbb{Z}_q$ and our lattice. This extra bit in the r component can be removed from [6], i.e. it is not a difference between our schemes. While saving 1 bit does not matter much, for $p \neq 2$ one will save $\log_2 p$ bits, which can start to matter for $p = \omega(1)$.

to decode$_{\Lambda_{q/2}(\mathbf{u}_m^t)}(\mathbf{c_2})$ (for a decoding algorithm which need not solve CVP on $\Lambda_{q/2}(\mathbf{u}_m^t)$). If one then attempts to decrypt this ciphertext (using the decryption formula of our work), we have that

$$\text{decode}_{(q/2)\mathbb{Z}^m}(\text{encode}_{\Lambda_{q/2}(\mathbf{u}_m^t)}((\mathbf{w},r)) - \mathbf{As}) = \text{decode}_{(q/2)\mathbb{Z}^m}((q/2)\mathbf{w} + r \cdot \mathbf{u}_m - \mathbf{As})$$
$$= \mathbf{w} + \text{decode}_{(q/2)\mathbb{Z}^m}(r \cdot \mathbf{u}_m - \mathbf{As})$$
$$= \text{decode}_{(q/2)\mathbb{Z}^m}(\mathbf{c_2} + r \cdot \mathbf{u}_m)$$
$$- \text{decode}_{(q/2)\mathbb{Z}^m}(\mathbf{As} - r \cdot \mathbf{u}_m).$$

This is precisely the decryption formula that [6] proposed for their cryptosystem, and therefore their "linearly homomorphic encryption with ciphertext shrinking" is precisely our cryptosystem $\text{LWE}_{\chi_{sk},\chi_e}^{n,q}[(q/2)\mathbb{Z}^m, \Lambda_{q/2}(\mathbf{u}_m^t)]$.

We next analyze this construction in our framework, again for a parameterized (by k) family of quantizers that reduces to the cryptosystem of [6] when $k = 1$. The family we choose is given by $k\Lambda_{q/(kp)}(\mathbf{u}_m^t) = (q/p)\mathbb{Z}^m + k\mathbf{u}_m^t \cdot \mathbb{Z}$, i.e. we only sparsify the quantizer in a single dimension (parallel to $\mathbf{u}_m^t$). This yields a *much* smaller (non-asymptotic) improvement. We include this more general analysis so we can refer to it during the conclusion.

Our analysis is done where one decodes with respect to the CVP algorithm (Corollary 1) we have previously derived for this lattice.

Definition 16 (Modified BDGM Encryption). *Let $p, q, k \in \mathbb{N}$. The Modified BDGM Cryptosystem is* $\text{LWE}_{\chi_{sk},\chi_e}^{n,q}[(q/p)\mathbb{Z}^m, k\Lambda_{q/(kp)}(\mathbf{u}_m^t)]$.

Corollary 5. *For any $\delta > 0$, let k be such that $kp \mid q$ and $m \mid q/(kp)$. Then one can parameterize the Modified BDGM Cryptosystem under the standard parameters to be δ-correct, and of asymptotic rate at least*

$$1 - O\left(\frac{\log_2(\frac{n^{5/2}}{k})}{m\log_2 p}\right). \tag{20}$$

Proof. Note that by Proposition 3 we have that $R_{k\Lambda_{q/(kp)}(\mathbf{u}_m^t)}^{(\infty)} \leq \frac{q}{2p}\left(1 - \frac{1}{m}\right) + \frac{k}{2}$. By Lemma 5, we have that this cryptosystem is δ-correct provided

$$\frac{q}{2p} > \sqrt{m}\sigma(\tilde{O}(\ln(1/\delta)) + \sqrt{m}) + \frac{q}{2p}\left(1 - \frac{1}{m}\right) + \frac{k}{2}, \tag{21}$$

Under standard parameters, this follows provided $q/p \geq \tilde{\Omega}(n^{5/2}) + kn$. Choosing q/p that is at most a constant factor larger than this, we get (as $\det k\Lambda_{q/(kp)}(\mathbf{u}_m^t) = k(q/p)^{m-1}$) that the asymptotic rate is at least

$$1 - \frac{\log_2 q/kp}{\log_2(q/kp)p^m} \geq 1 - \frac{1}{1 + m\frac{\log_2 p}{\log_2 q/kp}} \geq 1 - O\left(\frac{\log_2(\frac{n^{5/2}}{k})}{m\log_2 p}\right). \tag{22}$$

$\square$

We comment the loss in Eq. (21) (compared to a Gaussian analysis) is smaller for this scheme — we require $q/p = \tilde{\Omega}(n^{5/2}) + kn$ rather than $q/p > \Omega(n^2) + kn$.

4.4 Novel Quantized "Gadget" Encryption

We next describe $\mathsf{LWE}^{n,q}_{\chi_{\mathsf{sk}},\chi_e}[\Lambda_q(\mathbf{g}^t_p)\otimes\mathbb{Z}^{m/\ell}, \Lambda_{q/p}(\mathbf{u}^t_m)]$, which combines the quantizer of [6] with the (standard) gadget $\Lambda_q(\mathbf{g}^t_p)\otimes\mathbb{Z}^{m/\ell}$. We find this combination has the exact same rate as [6], while still encoding under an error-correcting code that is a gadget, i.e. we combine the relative strengths of both known constructions of high-rate encryption [6,18].

Definition 17. *Let* $p, q, k \in \mathbb{N}$. *The Quantized Gadget Cryptosystem is* $\mathsf{LWE}_{\chi_{\mathsf{sk}},\chi_e}[\Lambda_q(\mathbf{g}^t_p)\otimes\mathbb{Z}^{m/\ell}, k\Lambda_{q/(kp)}(\mathbf{u}^t_m)]$.

Corollary 6. *For any* $\delta > 0$, *let* k *be such that* $kp \mid q$ *and* $m \mid q/(kp)$. *Let* $q = p^\ell$ *for some* $\ell > 0$. *Then one can parameterize the Quantized Gadget cryptosystem under the standard parameters to be* δ-*correct, and of asymptotic rate at least*

$$1 - O\left(\frac{\log_2(\frac{n^{5/2}}{k})}{m\log_2 p}\right). \tag{23}$$

Proof. Note that the proof of Corollary 5 only depends on $E = (q/p)\mathbb{Z}^m$ through $\mathcal{V}_E$ and $\det E$, and that by Proposition 1 these quantities are equal for $(q/p)\mathbb{Z}^m$ and $\Lambda_q(\mathbf{g}^t_p)\otimes\mathbb{Z}^{m/\ell}$.

5 Rate Impossibility Results

We next establish rate upper bounds (i.e. impossibility) results in two separate noise models, namely that of perfectly correct encryption (with respect to bounded noise), and that of δ-correct encryption (with respect to log-concave noise).

5.1 Bounded Noise Model

Recall that (with high probability), a Gaussian $\mathbf{e} \leftarrow \chi_e$ concentrates tightly within a ball of radius $\sigma\sqrt{m}$. We first assume that $\|\mathbf{e}\|_2 \leq \sigma\sqrt{m}$ (say by replacing χ_e^m with a Gaussian that is truncated to be contained in this set), and bound the rate of quantized encryption that has $\delta = 0$, i.e. no decryption failures. This setting is amenable to strong packing arguments.

Theorem 4. *Let* $(E, \lfloor\cdot\rceil)$ *be a lattice code in* $\mathbb{R}^m$. *Let* χ_e *be a distribution such that* $\mathrm{supp}(\chi_e^m) = \sqrt{m}\sigma\cdot\mathcal{B}_m$. *Then, if* $\mathsf{LWE}^{n,q}_{\chi_{\mathsf{sk}},\chi_e}[E, \mathbb{Z}^m]$ *is 0-correct, it has asymptotic rate at most* $1 - \Omega\left(\frac{\log_2(\sqrt{m}\sigma)}{\log_2 q}\right)$, *i.e. asymptotic rate* $1 - o(1)$ *encryption from polynomial modulus is impossible.*

Proof. For $\mathsf{LWE}^{n,q}_{\chi_{\mathsf{sk}},\chi_e}[E, Q]$ to be perfectly correct, we need that $\delta = \mathrm{Pr}_{\mathbf{e},\mathbf{b}}[\mathbf{e} - [\mathbf{b}]_Q \notin \mathcal{V}_E] = 0$. As we have that $Q = \mathbb{Z}^m$, we have that $[\mathbf{b}]_Q \in [-1/2, 1/2)^m$, and our condition reduces to $\mathrm{Pr}_{\mathbf{e}}[\mathbf{e} + [\mathbf{b}]_Q \notin \mathcal{V}_E] = 0$, or equivalently $\mathrm{Pr}_{\mathbf{e}}[\mathbf{e} +$

$[-1/2, 1/2)^m \subseteq \mathcal{V}_E] = 1$, i.e. $\mathsf{supp}(\chi_e^m) \subseteq \mathsf{supp}(\chi_e^m) + [-1/2, 1/2)^m = \sqrt{m}\sigma \cdot \mathcal{B}_m + [-1/2, 1/2)^m \subseteq \mathcal{V}_E$.

Now, as $E_q + \mathcal{V}_E = \mathbb{R}_q^m$ is a partition, we have that $E_q + \sqrt{m}\sigma \cdot \mathcal{B}_m \subseteq \mathbb{R}_q^m$ is a packing, meaning the sets $\{e + \sqrt{m}\sigma \cdot \mathcal{B}_m\}_{e \in E_q}$ are disjoint. Taking volumes of both sides, we have that

$$\mathsf{vol}(E_q + \mathsf{supp}(\chi_e^m)) \overset{1}{=} |E_q|\mathsf{vol}(\sqrt{m}\sigma \cdot \mathcal{B}_m) \leq q^m = \mathsf{vol}(\mathbb{R}_q^m), \qquad (24)$$

where (1) easily follows from the aforementioned disjointness condition.

Now, we have that $|E_q| = \frac{q^m}{\det E}$. Rearranging, we get that $\det E \geq \mathsf{vol}(\sqrt{m}\sigma \cdot \mathcal{B}_m)$. Stirling's approximation gives that $\mathsf{vol}(\sqrt{m}\sigma \cdot \mathcal{B}_m) \approx \frac{1}{\sqrt{m\pi}}\left(\frac{2\pi e}{m}\right)^{m/2}(\sqrt{m}\sigma)^m$. Finally, we have that the asymptotic rate is

$$R = 1 - \frac{\log_2 \frac{\det E}{\det \mathbb{Z}^m}}{\log_2 \frac{q^m}{\det \mathbb{Z}^m}} = 1 - \frac{\log_2 \det E}{m \log_2 q} \leq 1 - \Omega\left(\frac{\log_2(\sqrt{m}\sigma)}{\log_2 q}\right). \qquad (25)$$

$\square$

For our next result, we need the Brunn-Minkowski inequality.

Proposition 7 (Brunn-Minkowski). *Let A, B be non-empty compact subsets of $\mathbb{R}^m$. Then $\sqrt[m]{\mathsf{vol}(A+B)} \geq \sqrt[m]{\mathsf{vol}(A)} + \sqrt[m]{\mathsf{vol}(B)}$.*

Theorem 5. *Let $(E, \lfloor \cdot \rceil_E)$, and $(Q, \lfloor \cdot \rceil_Q)$ be lattice codes in $\mathbb{R}^m$. Let χ_e be a distribution such that $\mathsf{supp}(\chi_e^m) = \sqrt{m}\sigma \cdot \mathcal{B}_m$. Assume that Heuristic 1 holds. Then, if $\mathsf{LWE}_{\chi_{sk}, \chi_e}^{n,q}[E, Q]$ is 0-correct, it has asymptotic rate at most*

$$1 - \frac{\log_2(1 + \frac{\sqrt{2\pi e}\sigma}{\sqrt[m]{\det Q}})}{\log_2 \frac{q}{\sqrt[m]{\det Q}}}. \qquad (26)$$

Proof. For $\mathsf{LWE}_{\chi_{sk}, \chi_e}^{n,q}[E, Q]$ to be perfectly correct, we need that $\delta = \mathsf{Pr}_{e, b}[e - [b]_Q \notin \mathcal{V}_E] = 0$. Equivalently, we need that $\mathsf{Pr}_{e, b}[e - [b]_Q \in \mathcal{V}_E] = 1$. Under Heuristic 1, we have that the random variable $e - [b]_Q$ has support $\mathsf{supp}(\chi_e^m) + (-\mathcal{V}_Q)$. Note that $\mathcal{V}_Q$ is centrally symmetric, so $-\mathcal{V}_Q = \mathcal{V}_Q$. We therefore have that $\mathsf{LWE}_{\chi_{sk}, \chi_e}^{n,q}[E, Q]$ is 0-correct if and only if $\sqrt{m}\sigma \cdot \mathcal{B}_m + \mathcal{V}_Q \subseteq \mathcal{V}_E$.

Now, as $E_q + \mathcal{V}_E = \mathbb{R}_q^m$ is a partition, we have that $E_q + (\sqrt{m}\sigma \cdot \mathcal{B}_m + \mathcal{V}_Q) \subseteq \mathbb{R}_q^m$ is a packing, i.e. the sets $\{e + (\sqrt{m}\sigma \cdot \mathcal{B}_m + \mathcal{V}_Q)\}_{e \in E_q}$ are disjoint. Taking volumes, we have that

$$\mathsf{vol}(E_q + (\sqrt{m}\sigma \cdot \mathcal{B}_m + \mathcal{V}_Q)) = |E_q|\mathsf{vol}(\sqrt{m}\sigma \cdot \mathcal{B}_m + \mathcal{V}_Q) \leq q^m = \mathsf{vol}(\mathbb{R}_q^m). \quad (27)$$

As $|E_q| = \frac{q^m}{\det E}$, this inequality is equivalent to $\sqrt[m]{\det E} \geq \sqrt[m]{\mathsf{vol}(\sqrt{m}\sigma \cdot \mathcal{B}_m + \mathcal{V}_Q)}$. Applying the Brunn-Minkowski inequality and Stirling's Approximation, we get that

$$\sqrt[m]{\det E} \geq \sqrt{2\pi e}\sigma + \sqrt[m]{\det Q}. \qquad (28)$$

This immediately implies that the asymptotic rate is

$$R = 1 - \frac{\log_2 \frac{\det E}{\det Q}}{\log_2 \frac{q^m}{\det Q}} = 1 - \frac{\log_2(1 + \frac{\sqrt{2\pi e}\sigma}{\sqrt[m]{\det Q}})}{\log_2 \frac{q}{\sqrt[m]{\det Q}}}. \tag{29}$$

$\square$

Note that the upper bound becomes $1 - o\left(\frac{1}{\log_2 \frac{q}{\sigma}}\right)$ if $\sqrt[m]{\det Q} \approx \sigma$, i.e. rate $1 - o(1)$ encryption is no longer impossible provided one quantizes even a relatively small amount.

5.2   Results for Unbounded Errors

We next return to the setting of χ_e an arbitrary log-concave distribution, and bounding δ-correct encryption for $\delta > 0$. Here, we rely on the anti-concentration inequality of Proposition 6, rather than the prior packing arguments. We first give a bound that is mostly useful in the case of trivial quantization, i.e. where $Q = \mathbb{Z}^m$.

Theorem 6. *Let $\epsilon > 0$. Let $(E, \lfloor \cdot \rceil_E), (Q, \lfloor \cdot \rceil_Q)$ be any lattice codes in $\mathbb{R}^m$. Let the ciphertext error distribution has covariance matrix Σ. If* $\mathsf{LWE}^{n,q}_{\chi_{\mathrm{sk}},\chi_e}[E, Q]$ *is δ-correct, then the asymptotic rate of* $\mathsf{LWE}_{\chi_{\mathrm{sk}},\chi_e}[E, Q]$ *is at most*

$$1 - \frac{\log_2 \Omega\left(\frac{\sqrt{\mathsf{Tr}(\Sigma)}}{\overline{R}_E}\right)}{\log_2 q/\sqrt[m]{\det Q}} + o(1). \tag{30}$$

Proof. We have that

$$1 - \delta \leq \Pr_e[\|\mathbf{e}\|_E \leq 1] \leq \Pr_e[\|\mathbf{e}\|_2 \leq R_E] \leq O\left(\frac{R_E}{\sqrt{\mathsf{Tr}(\Sigma)}}\right).$$

The first inequality is from Lemma 1, and the second from Proposition 6. We then easily get the bound $\sqrt[m]{\det E} \geq \Omega\left(\frac{1-\delta}{\overline{R}_E}\sqrt{\mathsf{Tr}(\Sigma)}\right)$, and the asymptotic rate is

$$R = 1 - \frac{\log_2 \sqrt[m]{\det E}}{\log_2 q/\sqrt[m]{\det Q}} \leq 1 - \frac{\log_2 \Omega\left(\frac{\sqrt{\mathsf{Tr}(\Sigma)(1-\delta)}}{\overline{R}_E}\right)}{\log_2 q/\sqrt[m]{\det Q}}, \tag{31}$$

Finally, we separate off the $1 - \delta$ term, and note that $-\log_2(1 - \delta)/\log_2 q$ is easily $o(1)$ to get the claimed result. $\square$

The presence of $\overline{R}_E$ in this bound is peculiar, and we cannot remove it by appealing to a universal upper bound on $\overline{R}_E$ (no such bound exists, even if we restrict $\mathcal{V}_E$ to be the Voronoi cell of a lattice). If we assume $\overline{R}_E$ is not too large (either absolutely, or in comparison to $\overline{r}_E$), we can prove impossibility of rate $1 - o(1)$ encryption.

Corollary 7. *Let $\epsilon > 0$, and let $(E, \lfloor \cdot \rceil_E)$ be a lattice code in $\mathbb{R}^m$. If either*

- $\overline{R}_E \leq O(m^{1-\epsilon})$, *or*
- $\overline{R}_E / \overline{r}_E \leq O(m^{1/2-\epsilon})$,

and q is polynomially large, then $\mathsf{LWE}^{n,q}_{\chi_{sk},\chi_e}[E, \mathbb{Z}^m]$ is of rate $1 - \Omega(1)$, i.e. under these conditions rate $1 - o(1)$ encryption is impossible.

Proof. We show that the second condition implies the first. This is simple, as the bound $\overline{r}_E \leq O(m^{1/2})$ implies that $\overline{R}_E \leq O(\overline{r}_E m^{1/2-\epsilon}) \leq O(m^{1-\epsilon})$. Next, note that by Theorem 6, we have that the asymptotic rate is at most

$$1 - \frac{\log_2 \Omega\left(\frac{\sqrt{m}\sigma}{m^{1-\epsilon}}\right)}{\log_2 q} + o(1) = 1 - \epsilon \frac{\log_2 \Omega(m)}{\log_2 q} - \frac{\log_2 \frac{\sigma}{\sqrt{m}}}{\log_2 q} + o(1). \tag{32}$$

As q is polynomially large, this suffices for the claimed result. $\qquad\square$

Corollary 8. *There exist lattice codes E with $\overline{r}_E \geq \Omega(\sqrt{m})$, i.e. within a constant factor of optimal, such that $\mathsf{LWE}^{n,q}_{\chi_{sk},\chi_e}[E, \mathbb{Z}^m]$ is of rate $1 - \Omega(1)$.*

Proof. Choose E with $\frac{\overline{R}_E}{\overline{r}_E} \leq 2 + o(1)$, which are known to exist [9], and then apply Corollary 7. $\qquad\square$

Therefore, any result establishing rate $1 - o(1)$ encryption from $Q = \mathbb{Z}^m$ and $q = n^{O(1)}$ must do more than simply appeal to the packing radius $\overline{r}_E = \Theta(\sqrt{m})$ being nearly optimal.

We next extend our bound on $\mathsf{LWE}^{n,q}_{\chi_{sk},\chi_e}[E, Q]$ for ciphertext error distribution the sum of a log-concave random variable and $\mathbf{u} \leftarrow \mathcal{V}_Q$ uniform, in a similar way to how we got sharper upper bounds on δ by considering this special case.

Theorem 7. *Let $(E, \lfloor \cdot \rceil_E), (Q, \lfloor \cdot \rceil_Q)$ be lattice codes in $\mathbb{R}^m$, and assume that $\mathsf{LWE}^{n,q}_{\chi_{sk},\chi_e}[E, Q]$ is δ-correct. Assume that Heuristic 1 holds, i.e. one can write the ciphertext error distribution as the independent sum of a log-concave random variable (with covariance matrix Σ) and $\mathbf{u} \leftarrow \mathcal{V}_Q$. Then $\mathsf{LWE}^{n,q}_{\chi_{sk},\chi_e}[E, Q]$ is of asymptotic rate at most*

$$1 - \frac{\log_2 \Omega\left(\frac{\sqrt{m}\sigma}{R_Q}\right)}{m \log_2 \frac{q}{\sqrt[m]{\det Q}}} + o(1). \tag{33}$$

Proof. Throughout, let $p(x)$ be the density of the log-concave random variable $\mathbf{e}$. By the law of total probability, we have that

$$\Pr[\mathbf{e} - \mathbf{u} \in \mathcal{V}_E] = \frac{1}{\det Q} \int_{\mathcal{V}_Q} \int_{\mathcal{V}_E} p(\mathbf{e} - \mathbf{x}) d\mathbf{e} d\mathbf{x}$$

$$\leq \frac{1}{\det Q} \int_{\mathcal{V}_E} \Pr[\|\mathbf{e} - \mathbf{x}\|_2 \leq R_Q] d\mathbf{e}$$

$$\leq O\left(\frac{\det E}{\det Q} \frac{R_Q}{\sqrt{\mathsf{Tr}(\Sigma)}}\right),$$

where the first inequality is the containment $\mathcal{V}_Q \subseteq R_Q \cdot \mathcal{B}_n$ (as well as Fubini's theorem), and the second inequality is Proposition 6. It follows that the asymptotic rate is

$$1 - \frac{\log_2 \Omega\left(\frac{\mathrm{Tr}(\Sigma)}{R_Q}\right)}{\log_2 |Q/q\mathbb{Z}^m|} - \frac{\log_2(1-\delta)}{\log_2 |Q/q\mathbb{Z}^m|}. \tag{34}$$

We finish by applying the same bound to $1 - \delta$ as we did in Theorem 6.   □

Corollary 9. *Let* $(E, \lfloor\cdot\rceil_E), (Q, \lfloor\cdot\rceil_Q)$ *be lattice codes in* $\mathbb{R}^m$, *and let* $\epsilon > 0$. *Assume the validity of Heuristic 1. If* $\overline{R}_Q \leq O(\sqrt{m})$ *is within a constant factor of optimal, then the asymptotic rate of* $\mathsf{LWE}^{n,q}_{\chi_{\mathsf{sk}}, \chi_e}[E, Q]$ *is at most*

$$1 - \frac{\log_2 \Omega\left(\frac{\sigma}{\sqrt[m]{\det Q}}\right)}{m \log_2 \frac{q}{\sqrt[m]{\det Q}}} + o(1). \tag{35}$$

In particular, if $\sqrt[m]{\det Q} \leq O(\sigma)$, *this quantity is at most* $1 - \Omega\left(\frac{1}{m \log_2 \frac{q}{\sigma}}\right) + o(1)$.

Proof. This follows directly from plugging the bounds we assume into Theorem 7.   □

Note that, as our modification of BDGM encryption (Corollary 5) and the Quantized Gadget cryptosystem (Corollary 6) have rate $1 - O\left(\frac{1}{m}\right)$, under the standard choice of parameters this bound is tight up to an $O(\log_2 m)$ factor for quantizers with $\sqrt[m]{\det Q} \leq O(\sigma)$.

5.3 Exponentially Stronger Bounds Against a Common Design Paradigm

We finish by showing that the bound Corollary 9 can be significantly strengthened when restricting to $\mathsf{LWE}^{n,q}_{\chi_{\mathsf{sk}}, \chi_e}[E, Q]$ where $E = \mathbb{Z}^{m/\dim E'} \otimes E'$, $Q = \mathbb{Z}^{m/\dim E'} \otimes Q'$ are the direct sum of m/k identical (smaller) codes for $k = \dim E' = \dim Q'$. In what follows we *solely* change the dimension, and keep the other parameters q, δ, σ, n fixed.

Lemma 7. *Let* $E = \mathbb{Z}^{m/k} \otimes E'$, *and* $Q = \mathbb{Z}^{m/k} \otimes Q'$, *where* E', Q' *are* k-*dimensional lattice codes. Then the asymptotic rate of* $\mathsf{LWE}^{n,q}_{\chi_{\mathsf{sk}}, \chi_e}[E, Q]$ *is equal to the asymptotic rate of* $\mathsf{LWE}^{n,q}_{\chi_{\mathsf{sk}}, \chi_e}[E', Q']$.

Proof. Note that $\det E = (\det E')^{m/k}$, and similarly for $\det Q$. We then have that the asymptotic rate is

$$\frac{\log_2 \frac{q^m}{\det E}}{\log_2 \frac{q^m}{\det Q}} = \frac{\log_2 \frac{q^m}{(\det E')^{m/k}}}{\log_2 \frac{q^m}{(\det Q')^{m/k}}} = \frac{\log_2 \frac{q^k}{\det E'}}{\log_2 \frac{q^k}{\det Q'}}. \tag{36}$$

□

Corollary 10. *Let* $(E', \lfloor \cdot \rceil_{E'}), (Q', \lfloor \cdot \rceil_{Q'})$ *be lattice codes in* $\mathbb{R}^k$, *let* $k \mid m$, *and let* $\epsilon > 0$. *Assume the validity of Heuristic 1. If* $\overline{R}_{Q'} \leq O(\sqrt{k})$ *is within a constant factor of optimal, then the asymptotic rate of* $\mathsf{LWE}^{n,q}_{\chi_{sk}, \chi_e}[\mathbb{Z}^{m/k} \otimes E', \mathbb{Z}^{m/k} \otimes Q']$ *is at most*

$$1 - \frac{\log_2 \Omega \left(\frac{\sigma}{\sqrt[k]{\det Q}} \right)}{k \log_2 \frac{q}{\sqrt[k]{\det Q}}} + o(1). \tag{37}$$

In particular, if $\sqrt[k]{\det Q'} \leq O(\sigma)$, *this quantity is at most* $1 - \Omega \left(\frac{1}{k \log_2 \frac{q}{\sigma}} \right) + o(1)$.

Proof. Use Corollary 9 to bound the rate of $\mathsf{LWE}^{n,q}_{\chi_{sk}, \chi_e}[E', Q']$. By Lemma 7, this implies the same bound for $\mathsf{LWE}^{n,q}_{\chi_{sk}, \chi_e}[\mathbb{Z}^{m/k} \otimes E', \mathbb{Z}^{m/k} \otimes Q']$. $\qquad\square$

Note that in the literature, k is typically at most $O(\log_2 m)$, so this bound is exponentially stronger than Corollary 9 in this common setting.

6 Conclusion and Open Problems

Conclusion. We propose a framework that reduces the design of LWE-based encryption to a handful of coding-theoretic choices. We then prove bounds on any instantiation of this framework, and find that a preexisting cryptosystem in the literature [6] is within an $O(\log_2 m)$ factor of optimal rate. We additionally prove bounds against the common situation of building lattices for error-correction and quantization by setting $L = \bigoplus_{i=1}^{m/\log_2 m} L'$ for $\dim L' = \Theta(\log_2 m)$. We establish exponentially stronger bounds against this setting, which we validate via practical rate computations.

Open Problems. We find an $O(\log_2 m)$ gap between the best-known construction and our bound for any construction. This gap is surprisingly significant — if there exists a construction meeting our bound, it implies constant (independent of the amount of data to transmit) overhead lattice-based encryption, i.e. a lattice-based cryptosystem that is similar to (standard) hybrid encryption. Does such a cryptosystem exist, or can one establish the impossibility of such a construction? Note that our cryptosystem $\mathsf{LWE}^{n,q}_{\chi_{sk}, \chi_e}[(q/p)\mathbb{Z}^m, k\Lambda_{q/(kp)}(\mathbf{u}^t_m)]$ gets quite close. If we did not have the divisibility requirement $m \mid q/(kp)$, it would suffice to close the gap itself. Can this requirement be removed? Finally, our work suggests the quantizer $\Lambda_{q/p}(\mathbf{u}^t_m)$ is much better than $k\mathbb{Z}^m$, which is implicitly used to define the LWR assumption. Can one obtain secure and practical LWR-type constructions using this quantizer?

References

1. Albrecht, M., et al.: Homomorphic encryption security standard. HomomorphicEn-cryption.org, Toronto, Canada, Technical report (2018)

2. Albrecht, M., Grassi, L., Rechberger, C., Roy, A., Tiessen, T.: MiMC: efficient encryption and cryptographic hashing with minimal multiplicative complexity. In: Cheon, J.H., Takagi, T. (eds.) ASIACRYPT 2016. LNCS, vol. 10031, pp. 191–219. Springer, Heidelberg (2016). https://doi.org/10.1007/978-3-662-53887-6_7
3. Ashur, T., Mahzoun, M., Toprakhisar, D.: Chaghri - a FHE-friendly block cipher. In: Yin, H., Stavrou, A., Cremers, C., Shi, E. (eds.) ACM CCS 2022: 29th Conference on Computer and Communications Security, Los Angeles, CA, USA, 7–11 November 2022, pp. 139–150. ACM Press (2022)
4. Babai, L.: On lovász'lattice reduction and the nearest lattice point problem. Combinatorica **6**(1), 1–13 (1986)
5. Banerjee, A., Peikert, C., Rosen, A.: Pseudorandom functions and lattices. In: Pointcheval and Johansson [30], pp. 719–737 (2012)
6. Brakerski, Z., Döttling,N., Garg, S., Malavolta, G.: Leveraging linear decryption: rate-1 fully-homomorphic encryption and time-lock puzzles. In: Hofheinz and Rosen [21], pp. 407–437 (2019)
7. Brakerski, Z., Gentry, C., Vaikuntanathan, V.: (Leveled) fully homomorphic encryption without bootstrapping. In: Goldwasser, S. (ed.) ITCS 2012: 3rd Innovations in Theoretical Computer Science, Cambridge, MA, USA, 8–10 January 2012, pp. 309–325. Association for Computing Machinery (2022)
8. Brakerski, Z., Vaikuntanathan, V.: Efficient fully homomorphic encryption from (standard) LWE. In: Ostrovsky, R. (ed.) 52nd Annual Symposium on Foundations of Computer Science, Palm Springs, CA, USA, 22–25 October 2011, pp. 97–106. IEEE Computer Society Press (2011)
9. Butler, G.: Simultaneous packing and covering in euclidean space. Proc. Lond. Math. Soc. **3**(4), 721–735 (1972)
10. Carbery, A., Wright, J.: Distributional and l-q norm inequalities for polynomials over convex bodies in r-n. Math. Res. Lett. **8**, 233–248 (2001)
11. Conway, J.H., Sloane, N.J.A.: Sphere Packings, Lattices and Groups, volume 290 of Grundlehren der mathematischen Wissenschaften. Springer, New York (1999). https://doi.org/10.1007/978-1-4757-6568-7
12. D'Anvers, J.-P., Karmakar, A., Sinha Roy, S., Vercauteren, F.: Saber: module-LWR based key exchange, CPA-secure encryption and CCA-secure KEM. In: Joux, A., Nitaj, A., Rachidi, T. (eds.) AFRICACRYPT 2018. LNCS, vol. 10831, pp. 282–305. Springer, Cham (2018). https://doi.org/10.1007/978-3-319-89339-6_16
13. Davenport, H.: The covering of space by spheres. Rendiconti del Circolo Matematico di Palermo **1**(1), 92–107 (1952)
14. Ducas, L., et al. CRYSTALS-Dilithium: a lattice-based digital signature scheme. IACR Trans. Cryptogr. Hardw. Embed. Syst. **2018**(1), 238–268 (2018). https://tches.iacr.org/index.php/TCHES/article/view/839
15. Ducas, L., van Woerden, W.P.: The closest vector problem in tensored root lattices of type a and in their duals. Des. Codes Cryptogr. **86**, 137–150 (2018)
16. Gaunt, R.E.: The basic distributional theory for the product of zero mean correlated normal random variables. Statistica Neerlandica (2022)
17. Genise, N., Micciancio, D., Polyakov, Y.: Building an efficient lattice gadget toolkit: subgaussian sampling and more. In: Ishai, Y., Rijmen, V. (eds.) EUROCRYPT 2019. LNCS, vol. 11477, pp. 655–684. Springer, Cham (2019). https://doi.org/10.1007/978-3-030-17656-3_23
18. Gentry, C., Halevi, S.: Compressible FHE with applications to PIR. In: Hofheinz and Rosen [21], pp. 438–464 (2019)
19. Guo, S., Kamath, P., Rosen, A., Sotiraki, K.: Limits on the efficiency of (ring) LWE-based non-interactive key exchange. J. Cryptol. **35**(1), 1 (2022)

20. Hofheinz, D., Hövelmanns, K., Kiltz, E.: A modular analysis of the fujisaki-okamoto transformation. In: Kalai, Y., Reyzin, L. (eds.) TCC 2017. LNCS, vol. 10677, pp. 341–371. Springer, Cham (2017). https://doi.org/10.1007/978-3-319-70500-2_12
21. Hofheinz, D., Rosen, A. (eds.): TCC 2019. LNCS, vol. 11891. Springer, Cham (2019). https://doi.org/10.1007/978-3-030-36030-6
22. Jin, Z., Zhao, Y.: Generic and practical key establishment from lattice. In: Deng, R.H., Gauthier-Umaña, V., Ochoa, M., Yung, M. (eds.) ACNS 2019. LNCS, vol. 11464, pp. 302–322. Springer, Cham (2019). https://doi.org/10.1007/978-3-030-21568-2_15
23. Klartag, B.: Logarithmic bounds for isoperimetry and slices of convex sets (2023)
24. Lee, Y.T., Vempala, S.S.: The kannan-lovász-simonovits conjecture. Curr. Dev. Math. **2017**(1), 1–36 (2017)
25. Martinet, J.: Perfect Lattices in Euclidean Spaces, vol. 327 of Grundlehren der mathematischen Wissenschaften. Springer, Heidelberg (2003). https://doi.org/10.1007/978-3-662-05167-2
26. McKilliam, R.G., Smith, W.D., Clarkson, I.V.L.: Linear-time nearest point algorithms for coxeter lattices. IEEE Trans. Inf. Theory **56**(3), 1015–1022 (2010)
27. Micciancio, D., Peikert, C.: Trapdoors for lattices: simpler, tighter, faster, smaller. In: Pointcheval and Johansson [30], pp. 700–718 (2012)
28. Micciancio, D., Polyakov, Y.: Bootstrapping in fhew-like cryptosystems. In: Proceedings of the 9th on Workshop on Encrypted Computing & Applied Homomorphic Cryptography, pp. 17–28 (2021)
29. Peikert, C.: Public-key cryptosystems from the worst-case shortest vector problem: extended abstract. In: Mitzenmacher, M. (ed.) 41st Annual ACM Symposium on Theory of Computing, Bethesda, MD, USA, 31 May–2 June 2009, pp. 333–342. ACM Press (2009)
30. Pointcheval, D., Johansson, T. (eds.): EUROCRYPT 2012. LNCS, vol. 7237. Springer, Heidelberg (2012). https://doi.org/10.1007/978-3-642-29011-4
31. Poppelen, A.V.: Cryptographic Decoding of the Leech Lattice. Master's thesis, Utrecht University (2016). https://studenttheses.uu.nl/handle/20.500.12932/24606
32. Regev, O.: On lattices, learning with errors, random linear codes, and cryptography. In: Gabow, H.N., Fagin, R. (eds.) 37th Annual ACM Symposium on Theory of Computing, pp. 84–93, Baltimore, MA, USA, 22–24 May 2005. ACM Press (2005)
33. Saliba, C., Luzzi, L., Ling, C.: A reconciliation approach to key generation based on module-lwe. In: 2021 IEEE International Symposium on Information Theory (ISIT), pp. 1636–1641 (2021)
34. Saumard, A., Wellner, J.A.: Log-concavity and strong log-concavity: a review. Stat. Surv. **8**, 45 (2014)
35. Zamir, R., Nazer, B., Kochman, Y., Bistritz, I.: Lattice Coding for Signals and Networks: A Structured Coding Approach to Quantization, Modulation and Multiuser Information Theory. Cambridge University Press, Cambridge (2014)

Almost Tight Multi-user Security Under Adaptive Corruptions from LWE in the Standard Model

Shuai Han[1,2] , Shengli Liu[1,2(✉)] , Zhedong Wang[1,2], and Dawu Gu[1]

[1] School of Electronic Information and Electrical Engineering,
Shanghai Jiao Tong University, Shanghai 200240, China
{dalen17,slliu,wzdstill,dwgu}@sjtu.edu.cn
[2] State Key Laboratory of Cryptology, P.O. Box 5159, Beijing 100878, China

Abstract. In this work, we construct the *first* digital signature (SIG) and public-key encryption (PKE) schemes with almost tight multi-user security under adaptive corruptions based on the learning-with-errors (LWE) assumption in the standard model. Our PKE scheme achieves almost tight IND-CCA security and our SIG scheme achieves almost tight strong EUF-CMA security, both in the multi-user setting with adaptive corruptions. The security loss is quadratic in the security parameter λ, and independent of the number of users, signatures or ciphertexts. Previously, such schemes were only known to exist under number-theoretic assumptions or in classical random oracle model, thus vulnerable to quantum adversaries.

To obtain our schemes from LWE, we propose new frameworks for constructing SIG and PKE with a core technical tool named *probabilistic* quasi-adaptive hash proof system (pr-QA-HPS). As a new variant of HPS, our pr-QA-HPS provides *probabilistic* public and private evaluation modes that may toss coins. This is in stark contrast to the traditional HPS [Cramer and Shoup, Eurocrypt 2002] and existing variants like approximate HPS [Katz and Vaikuntanathan, Asiacrypt 2009], whose public and private evaluations are deterministic in their inputs. Moreover, we formalize a new property called evaluation indistinguishability by requiring statistical indistinguishability of the two probabilistic evaluation modes, even in the presence of the secret key. The evaluation indistinguishability, as well as other nice properties resulting from the probabilistic features of pr-QA-HPS, are crucial for the multi-user security proof of our frameworks under adaptive corruptions.

As for instantiations, we construct pr-QA-HPS from the LWE assumption and prove its properties with almost tight reductions, which admit almost tightly secure LWE-based SIG and PKE schemes under our frameworks. Along the way, we also provide new almost-tight reductions from LWE to multi-secret LWE, which may be of independent interest.

1 Introduction

Tight Security. In modern cryptography, the security of cryptographic primitives like digital signatures (SIG) and public-key encryptions (PKE) is established

H. Handschuh and A. Lysyanskaya (Eds.): CRYPTO 2023, LNCS 14085, pp. 682–715, 2023.
https://doi.org/10.1007/978-3-031-38554-4_22

by security reductions. Roughly speaking, a reduction turns an efficient adversary $\mathcal{A}$ breaking the security of the considered scheme with running time $t_{\mathcal{A}}$ and advantage $\epsilon_{\mathcal{A}}$ into an efficient algorithm $\mathcal{B}$ solving some computationally hard problem with running time $t_{\mathcal{B}}$ and advantage $\epsilon_{\mathcal{B}}$, and establishes a relation $\epsilon_{\mathcal{A}}/t_{\mathcal{A}} \leq \ell \cdot \epsilon_{\mathcal{B}}/t_{\mathcal{B}}$, where ℓ is called the *security loss* factor.

Usually, ℓ is a large polynomial in the number of users, signatures and/or ciphertexts in a deployed system. When instantiating the scheme in a theoretically sound manner, we have to compensate the security loss ℓ by increasing key lengths, group sizes or vector dimensions of the scheme. However, it might not be clear at the time of deployment that how many users will be involved and how many signatures or ciphertexts will be generated in the lifetime of the cryptographic system. If the estimation is too small, the provided security guarantee will not be backed by the security proof. Therefore, it is desirable that ℓ is a small constant or a small polynomial in the security parameter λ. Such a security reduction is called a *tight* one or an *almost tight* one. We do not distinguish tightness and almost tightness, but we will detail the security loss in the security theorems and scheme comparisons to reflect almost tightness.

Multi-user Security under Adaptive Corruptions (MU^c). The standard security notion for SIG is existential unforgeability under chosen-message attacks (EUF-CMA) and that for PKE is indistinguishability under chosen-plaintext/ciph- ertext attacks (IND-CPA/CCA). Both of the security notions are defined in a single-user setting. However, in practice, SIG and PKE are usually deployed in multi-user (and multi-challenge for PKE) settings, and leave more opportunities to adversaries implementing new attacks. An important attack is *user corruption* in that the adversary takes full control of some users and of course their secret keys. This happens since some adversary may snatch secrets from some user by system hacking or from key exposure due to the user's bad key management. Therefore, it is reasonable for us to consider EUF-CMA and IND-CPA/CCA securities in the multi-user (and multi-challenge) setting under adaptive corruptions [6,31], denoted by MU^c-CMA and MUMC^c-CPA/CCA, respectively. For ease of exposition, we also refer to them in a unified way as the MU^c security.

Apart from the motivations for the security itself, another important reason for considering MU^c security is that it captures the actual security requirements of many cryptosystems that use SIG and/or PKE as building blocks. A well-known example is authenticated key exchange (AKE) protocols which use SIG to authenticate protocol transcripts and use key encapsulation mechanism (KEM) or PKE to encapsulate elements contributing to session keys. Standard AKE security models, such as the Bellare-Rogaway [9] and the (extended) Canetti-Krawczyk [16,30] models, are in multi-user settings and allow adversaries to corrupt secret keys of some users. In particular, Bader et al. [6] present the first tightly MU^c-CMA secure SIG and tightly MUMC^c-CPA secure KEM (and PKE), and use them to construct the first tightly secure AKE protocol. Another example is signcryption, which can be built from SIG and PKE in various ways like "Encrypt-then-Sign", "Sign-then-Encrypt" and "Encrypt-and-Sign" [3]. The insider security model, which is concluded by Badertscher et al. [8] as the standard for signcryption and followed up by Bellare and Stepanovs [10], is also in multi-user settings and allows adaptive corruptions. In such scenarios, $\mathsf{MU^c}$-CMA security for SIG and $\mathsf{MUMC^c}$-CPA/CCA security for PKE play central roles. Tight $\mathsf{MU^c}$ security of SIG and PKE would lead to tight security of the applied cryptosystems.

On Achieving Tight $\mathsf{MU^c}$ Security. Due to their importance, SIG and PKE with tight $\mathsf{MU^c}$ security have become an active area recently, including impossibility results [7,36] and feasibility constructions [6,18,22–24,31,37].

On the one hand, it is quite challenging to construct SIG and PKE with tight $\mathsf{MU^c}$ security. In general, single-user security can only non-tightly imply $\mathsf{MU^c}$ security by a guessing strategy, which incurs a security loss linear in the number of users. As shown by Bader et al. [7], it is even impossible to achieve tight $\mathsf{MU^c}$-CMA and tight $\mathsf{MUMC^c}$-CPA/CCA securities if the relation between public key and secret key satisfies certain properties, which are satisfied by many existing SIG and PKE schemes. Alternatively, if the signing algorithm of SIG is deterministic, tight $\mathsf{MU^c}$-CMA security is also impossible to achieve [36].

On the other hand, there are very few SIG and PKE constructions in the literature proved to have tight $\mathsf{MU^c}$ security, even in the random oracle (RO) model. To the best of our knowledge, SIG schemes in [6,18,22–24,37] and PKE schemes in [6,24,31] are the only ones with tight $\mathsf{MU^c}$ security. Almost all of them base their security on number-theoretic assumptions, such as the Diffie-Hellman assumptions in cyclic groups or ϕ-hiding assumptions, which lead to insecurity in the presence of powerful quantum adversaries. The only exception is the SIG scheme of Pan and Wagner [18], which can be instantiated under either the learning-with-errors (LWE) or isogeny-based assumptions. However, their tight $\mathsf{MU^c}$-CMA security proof is based on the classical RO model, and it is left as an open problem in [18] to extend their approach in the quantum RO model, or even in the standard model. As for PKE, there is currently no construction with tight $\mathsf{MUMC^c}$-CCA security based on post-quantum assumptions, no matter in the RO model or in the standard model. This raises the following question:

Can we construct SIG and PKE schemes with tight $\mathsf{MU^c}$ security based on post-quantum assumptions (such as LWE) in the standard model?

Our Contributions. In this work, we answer the above question affirmatively.

- We present the *first* SIG and PKE schemes whose $\mathsf{MU^c}$ security can be almost tightly reduced to the LWE assumptions in the standard model. The security loss is quadratic in the security parameter λ. Our PKE scheme achieves almost tight $\mathsf{MUMC^c}$-CCA security, and our SIG scheme achieves almost tight $\mathsf{MU^c}$-CMA security with *strong* existential unforgeability, denoted by *strong* $\mathsf{MU^c}$-CMA security, which even guarantees the hardness for adversary to forge a new signature for an already signed message.
- We obtain our schemes by proposing new frameworks for tightly $\mathsf{MU^c}$ secure SIG and PKE. The core technical tool in our frameworks is a new variant of hash proof system (HPS) named *probabilistic* quasi-adaptive HPS

(pr-QA-HPS), with new properties resulting from its probabilistic features. We instantiate pr-QA-HPS from the LWE assumption and prove its properties with almost tight reductions, which is crucial for the almost tight $\mathsf{MU^c}$ security of the resulting SIG and PKE schemes.

- Along the way, we also provide new almost-tight reductions from LWE to multi-secret LWE, which serves as pivots for the almost tight $\mathsf{MU^c}$ security of our SIG and PKE schemes.

Technical Overview. In a recent work, Han, Liu and Gu [24] provided nice solutions to almost tightly $\mathsf{MU^c}$ secure SIG and PKE in the standard model, with the help of quasi-adaptive HPS (QA-HPS). Here "quasi-adaptive" means that the projection key of HPS may depend on the language for which HPS hash values are generated. Note that their frameworks apply only when QA-HPS has exact correctness and their framework for SIG also requires QA-HPS to be publicly verifiable. For the LWE-based cases, however, their frameworks (named HLG frameworks) do not work any more, because of the following obstacles.

- **Obstacle 1: There is no LWE-based QA-HPS with exact correctness.** It is not an easy task to instantiate (traditional) HPS under LWE, as there are many subtleties regarding the correctness (aka projectiveness) of HPS, let alone QA-HPS. Loosely speaking, HPS has two evaluation modes for computing HPS hash values, a public mode Pub using a projection key and a private mode Priv using a secret key. The (exact) correctness requires that the two evaluation models result in the same value for element in the language. Due to the noise inherent in LWE, it is hard (and even seems impossible) to achieve exact correctness. Instead, there are several attempts in the literature [11,21,27,29,43] to instantiate HPS under LWE by relaxing the exact correctness to *approximate correctness*, i.e., requiring only that the two evaluation models result in sufficiently close values. We refer to such HPS as *approximate HPS*. This is sufficient for the purpose of [11,27,29,43], but it is insufficient for the HLG framework [24] in proving $\mathsf{MU^c}$ security. Similar to the Cramer-Shoup argument [17], the computations of HPS hash value need to be switched from one mode (e.g., the real scheme uses the public mode) to the other mode (e.g., the security proof uses the private mode), without being noticed by the adversary. However, in the $\mathsf{MU^c}$ security proof, the adversary can first see the evaluated hash value, then ask to corrupt the user and obtain its secret key. With the secret key, the adversary is able to recompute the hash value in the private mode and compare it with the obtained hash value. Thus, any difference between the evaluated hash values in the two modes will be caught by the adversary.

- **Obstacle 2: There is no LWE-based QA-HPS with public verification.** In the HLG framework, in order to construct $\mathsf{MU^c}$-CMA secure SIG, the QA-HPS is required to support public verification of hash values given an extra verification key. Such QA-HPS is termed as *publicly-verifiable QA-HPS* (PV-QA-HPS) in [24]. PV-QA-HPS is necessary for the public verification of their SIG [24], but it only has instantiations over pairing groups, as it relies on the pairing operations to accomplish the public verifiability of hash values.

In the LWE setting, there is no counterpart to pairing operations, so it is hard to obtain PV-QA-HPS and the HLG framework does not apply.

To circumvent the above obstacles, we propose the concept of *probabilistic QA-HPS* and new approaches to tight MU^{c} security with the help of pr-QA-HPS.

(1) Probabilistic QA-HPS (pr-QA-HPS) from LWE. Recall that QA-HPS $= (\alpha(\cdot), \mathsf{Pub}, \mathsf{Priv})$ for NP-language $\mathcal{L} \subseteq \mathcal{X}$ is associated with a subset membership problem (SMP) so that $\{c \leftarrow_\$ \mathcal{L}\} \overset{c}{\approx} \{c \leftarrow_\$ \mathcal{X}\}$. Its projection function $\alpha(\cdot)$ maps a secret key sk to a projection key $pk = \alpha(sk)$, its public evaluation algorithm $\mathsf{Pub}(pk, c, w)$ computes the hash value $\Lambda_{sk}(c)$ for $c \in \mathcal{L}$ with witness w, and its private evaluation algorithm $\mathsf{Priv}(sk, c)$ computes the hash value $\Lambda_{sk}(c)$ for $c \in \mathcal{X}$. The (exact) correctness asks that $\mathsf{Pub}(pk, c, w) = \mathsf{Priv}(sk, c) = \Lambda_{sk}(c)$ for all $c \in \mathcal{L}$ with witness w.

Now we consider the LWE case. All the LWE samples for matrix $\mathbf{A} \in \mathbb{Z}_q^{n \times m}$ and error bound B constitute an NP-language

$$\mathcal{L}_{\mathbf{A}} := \{\mathbf{c} = \mathbf{A}^\top \mathbf{s} + \mathbf{e} \mid \mathbf{s} \in \mathbb{Z}_q^n, \mathbf{e} \in [-B, B]^m\}. \tag{1}$$

Then the LWE problem just serves as the SMP for $\mathcal{L}_{\mathbf{A}}$. Now we define $sk = \mathbf{k} \in \{0,1\}^m$, $pk = \mathbf{p} = \mathbf{A}\mathbf{k}$ and the hash value of instance $\mathbf{c} \in \mathbb{Z}_q^m$ is $\Lambda_{\mathbf{k}}(\mathbf{c}) := \mathbf{c}^\top \mathbf{k} \in \mathbb{Z}_q$. However, with $pk = \mathbf{p}$ and witness $(\mathbf{s}, \mathbf{e})$, public evaluation can only obtain a value like $\mathbf{s}^\top \mathbf{p} = \mathbf{s}^\top(\mathbf{A}\mathbf{k})$, which is hardly equal but close to $\Lambda_{\mathbf{k}}(\mathbf{c}) = \mathbf{c}^\top \mathbf{k} = (\mathbf{s}^\top \mathbf{A} + \mathbf{e}^\top)\mathbf{k}$.

To circumvent the problem of lacking exact correctness, we put forward a new variant of QA-HPS, called *probabilistic QA-HPS* (pr-QA-HPS). In stark contrast to the traditional HPS [17] and variants like approximate HPS [29] or QA-HPS [25], whose public and private modes are deterministic in their inputs, our pr-QA-HPS has *probabilistic* public and private modes (denoted by prPub and prPriv, respectively), the outputs of which are probabilistic distributions over the hash value space. Instead of requiring exact correctness, we require the statistical indistinguishability of the two probabilistic evaluation modes, *even in the presence of the secret key*. We formalize this as the property of *evaluation indistinguishability*. See Definition 7 in Sect. 3 for the formal definition.

The property of evaluation indistinguishability enables the switch of evaluation mode from one to the other in a statistically indistinguishable way, even in the view of adversaries who can implement corruption attacks and obtain the secret key, thus serving well for our MU^{c} security proof, as shown later.

Below we give an overview of our LWE-based pr-QA-HPS. Let B and B' be error bounds satisfying $B' \geq mB \cdot 2^{\omega(\log \lambda)}$ with λ the security parameter.

- The secret key is $sk = \mathbf{k} \in \{0,1\}^m$, and for language $\mathcal{L}_{\mathbf{A}} = \{\mathbf{c} = \mathbf{A}^\top \mathbf{s} + \mathbf{e} \mid \mathbf{s} \in \mathbb{Z}_q^n, \mathbf{e} \in [-B, B]^m\}$, the projection key is $pk = \mathbf{p} = \mathbf{A}\mathbf{k} \in \mathbb{Z}_q^n$.
- The hash value of an instance $\mathbf{c} \in \mathbb{Z}_q^m$ is defined by $\Lambda_{\mathbf{k}}(\mathbf{c}) := \mathbf{c}^\top \mathbf{k} \in \mathbb{Z}_q$.
- For an instance $\mathbf{c} = \mathbf{A}^\top \mathbf{s} + \mathbf{e}$ in the language $\mathcal{L}_{\mathbf{A}}$, the *probabilistic* public evaluation mode prPub generates a hash value by first sampling a random

value $e' \leftarrow_\$ [-B', B']$ uniformly, then computing $\mathbf{s}^\top \mathbf{p} + e'$ using the projection key $pk = \mathbf{p}$ and the witness $\mathbf{s}$ for $\mathbf{c} \in \mathcal{L}_\mathbf{A}$. Namely,

$$\mathbf{s}^\top \mathbf{p} + e' \leftarrow_\$ \mathsf{prPub}(\mathbf{p}, \mathbf{c}, \mathbf{s}) \quad \text{with} \quad e' \leftarrow_\$ [-B', B']. \tag{2}$$

- For an instance $\mathbf{c} \in \mathbb{Z}_q^m$ (no matter in $\mathcal{L}_\mathbf{A}$ or not), the *probabilistic* private evaluation mode prPriv generates a hash value by first sampling a random value $e' \leftarrow_\$ [-B', B']$ uniformly, then computing $\mathbf{c}^\top \mathbf{k} + e'$ using the secret key $sk = \mathbf{k}$. Namely,

$$\mathbf{c}^\top \mathbf{k} + e' \leftarrow_\$ \mathsf{prPriv}(\mathbf{k}, \mathbf{c}) \quad \text{with} \quad e' \leftarrow_\$ [-B', B']. \tag{3}$$

That is to say, the HPS hash function $\Lambda_\mathbf{k}$ is still deterministic, while there are two probabilistic ways to evaluate it. Our LWE-based pr-QA-HPS has evaluation indistinguishability, since the bigger noise e' smudges the small error to make the statistical distance between the two probabilistic modes negligibly small:

$$\Delta(\mathbf{s}^\top \mathbf{p} + e', \mathbf{c}^\top \mathbf{k} + e') = \Delta(\mathbf{s}^\top \mathbf{A}\mathbf{k} + e', \mathbf{s}^\top \mathbf{A}\mathbf{k} + \mathbf{e}^\top \mathbf{k} + e') \leq mB/B' \leq 2^{-\omega(\log \lambda)}.$$

(2) New Framework for Constructing SIG with pr-QA-HPS (from LWE). In the HLG framework for SIG, QA-HPS is required to support public verification of hash values with an extra verification key (i.e., the so-called *publicly-verifiable* QA-HPS), since a QA-HPS hash value is part of the signature. However, in order to instantiate such QA-HPS, they rely on the pairing operations, which have no counterpart in the LWE setting.

In our case, it seems very hard to define an extra verification key vk for our aforementioned LWE-based pr-QA-HPS, so that the correctness of hash values in (2) or (3) can be publicly checked with vk.[1]

To circumvent the problem, we propose a new framework for SIG. Instead of requiring the public verifiability of hash values from QA-HPS, we resort to tag-based quasi-adaptive non-interactive zero-knowledge argument (QA-NIZK) [28] and augment the HPS hash value verification to QA-NIZK. Meanwhile, we also make use of dual-mode commitment, which has two computationally indistinguishable modes (i.e., a binding mode and a hiding mode), to bind the signing key and the verification key of SIG.

Below is our new framework for SIG from pr-QA-HPS $= (\alpha(\cdot), \mathsf{prPub}, \mathsf{prPriv})$, dual-mode commitment Com and QA-NIZK $= (\mathsf{Prove}, \mathsf{Vrfy})$, where QA-NIZK is for the language $\mathcal{L}_{\mathsf{QANIZK}} :=$

$$\left\{ (\mathbf{c}, vk, d) \mid \exists (\mathbf{k}, r, e' \in [-B', B']), \text{s.t.} \, \mathbf{c} \in \mathcal{L}_\mathbf{A} \wedge vk = \mathsf{Com}(\mathbf{k}; r) \wedge d = \mathbf{c}^\top \mathbf{k} + e' \right\}. \tag{4}$$

- The signing key $sigk = (\mathbf{k}, r)$ contains the secret key $\mathbf{k}$ of pr-QA-HPS and random coins r, and the verification key is the commitment $vk = \mathsf{Com}(\mathbf{k}; r)$.

---

[1] Of course, we cannot simply set sk to vk, since vk is public and the properties of (pr-)QA-HPS should not be harmed in the presence of vk.

– The signature for message m is given by $\sigma :=$

$$(\mathbf{c} \leftarrow_\$ \mathcal{L}_\mathbf{A}, \ d \leftarrow_\$ \mathsf{prPriv}(\mathbf{k}, \mathbf{c}), \ \pi \leftarrow_\$ \mathsf{Prove}(\mathsf{tag} = m, (\mathbf{c}, vk, d), (\mathbf{k}, r, e')) \ ).$$

– The verification of $(m, \sigma = (\mathbf{c}, d, \pi))$ is just the QA-NIZK verification.

Now we roughly sketch the proving idea for the strong MU^c-CMA security of our SIG. We aim to show that the fresh message-signature pair $(m^*, \sigma^* = (\mathbf{c}^*, d^*, \pi^*))$ forged by the adversary hardly passes the verification of QA-NIZK, even if the adversary can query messages for signatures via a signing oracle and corrupt the signing keys of some users.

- To generate signature $\sigma = (\mathbf{c}, d, \pi)$ for message m, the signing oracle invokes the simulator of QA-NIZK using a simulation trapdoor, instead of invoking algorithm Prove using the witness $(\mathbf{k}, r, e')$, to generate the proof π. This change is indistinguishable due to the zero-knowledge of QA-NIZK.
- To generate signature $\sigma = (\mathbf{c}, d, \pi)$ for message m, the signing oracle switches the language from $\mathcal{L}_\mathbf{A}$ to $\mathcal{L}_{\mathbf{A}_0}$, where $\mathbf{A}$ and $\mathbf{A}_0$ are uniformly and independently chosen. That is, it samples $\mathbf{c} \leftarrow_\$ \mathcal{L}_{\mathbf{A}_0}$ instead of $\mathbf{c} \leftarrow_\$ \mathcal{L}_\mathbf{A}$. Note that $\mathcal{L}_\mathbf{A}$ is still used to determine the language $\mathcal{L}_{\mathsf{QANIZK}}$ in (4). By the LWE assumption, $(\mathbf{A}, \mathbf{A}^\top \mathbf{s} + \mathbf{e}) \overset{c}{\approx} (\mathbf{A}, \mathbf{u} \leftarrow_\$ \mathbb{Z}_q^m) \overset{c}{\approx} (\mathbf{A}, \mathbf{A}_0^\top \mathbf{s} + \mathbf{e})$, so this change is indistinguishable.
  Consequently, by the evaluation indistinguishability of pr-QA-HPS, the generation of $d \leftarrow_\$ \mathsf{prPriv}(\mathbf{k}, \mathbf{c})$ can be changed to $d \leftarrow_\$ \mathsf{prPub}(p_0 = \mathbf{A}_0\mathbf{k}, \mathbf{c}, \mathbf{s})$, where $\mathbf{s}$ is the witness for $\mathbf{c} = \mathbf{A}_0^\top \mathbf{s} + \mathbf{e} \in \mathcal{L}_{\mathbf{A}_0}$. This holds even if the adversary corrupts the user and obtains its signing key $\mathbf{k}$.
- The binding property of commitment makes sure that the unbounded simulation-soundness (USS) of QA-NIZK applies to the forged signature $\sigma^* = (\mathbf{c}^*, d^*, \pi^*)$. So a successful forgery for a target user must satisfy that $\mathbf{c}^* \in \mathcal{L}_\mathbf{A}$ and d^* lies close to $\mathbf{c}^{*\top}\mathbf{k} = (\mathbf{s}^{*\top}\mathbf{A} + \mathbf{e}^{*\top})\mathbf{k}$, where $(\mathbf{s}^*, \mathbf{e}^*)$ is the witness for $\mathbf{c}^* = \mathbf{A}^\top \mathbf{s}^* + \mathbf{e}^* \in \mathcal{L}_\mathbf{A}$ and $\mathbf{k}$ is the signing key of the target user.
- The dual-mode commitment is switched to the hiding mode, then vk does not leak information about the secret key $\mathbf{k}$. Now all information about $\mathbf{k}$ learned by the adversary is bounded by $\mathbf{A}_0\mathbf{k}$, if the adversary never corrupts the target user to obtain its signing key $\mathbf{k}$. When $m = 2n \log q + \omega(\log \lambda)$, there is still $n \log q + \omega(\log \lambda)$ bits of information left in $\mathbf{k}$. Taking $\mathbf{A}$ as an extractor, then $\mathbf{A}\mathbf{k}$ is statistically close to the uniform distribution (this is characterized as the $\langle \mathcal{L}_{\mathbf{A}_0}, \mathcal{L}_\mathbf{A} \rangle$-one-time-extracting property of pr-QA-HPS). As a result, the adversary can hardly forge a d^* such that d^* lies close to $\mathbf{c}^{*\top}\mathbf{k} = \mathbf{s}^{*\top}\mathbf{A}\mathbf{k} + \mathbf{e}^{*\top}\mathbf{k}$.[2] Then strong MU^c-CMA security follows.

Overall, the strong MU^c-CMA security proof is accomplished by the evaluation indistinguishability & $\langle \mathcal{L}_{\mathbf{A}_0}, \mathcal{L}_\mathbf{A} \rangle$-one-time-extracting property of pr-QA-HPS, SMP, zero-knowledge & USS of QA-NIZK, and indistinguishability of binding and hiding modes of commitment. Due to the nice properties of pr-QA-HPS,

---

[2] The bad case that $\mathbf{s}^* = \mathbf{0}$ has been excluded in the language $\mathcal{L}_\mathbf{A}$, see Footnote 6 for more details. We forgo making this explicit for the sake of simplicity.

we stress that all reduction algorithms can generate the signing keys of all users themselves, and hence can deal with adaptive corruptions by the adversary.

(3) Extending the HLG Framework for Constructing PKE with pr-QA-HPS (from LWE). The HLG framework for PKE needs the exact correctness of QA-HPS. To circumvent the obstacle in the LWE setting, we extend their framework by replacing QA-HPS with our pr-QA-HPS and augmenting error-correction code ECC = (Encode, Decode) to deal with the LWE errors. Below is our extended framework.

- The secret key of PKE is just the secret key $sk = \mathbf{k}$ of pr-QA-HPS, and the public key is the projection key $pk = \mathbf{p} = \mathbf{Ak}$.
- The encryption of message m results in the ciphertext $ct :=$

$$(\mathbf{c} \leftarrow_{\$} \mathcal{L}_\mathbf{A}, \ d \leftarrow_{\$} \mathsf{prPub}(\mathbf{p}, \mathbf{c}, \mathbf{s}) + \mathsf{Encode}(m), \ \pi \leftarrow_{\$} \mathsf{Prove}(tag, \mathbf{c}, (\mathbf{s}, \mathbf{e})) \ ),$$

  where tag is a collision-resistant hashing of (pk, d) and QA-NIZK = (Prove, Vrfy) is for the language $\mathcal{L}_\mathbf{A}$ in (1).
- The decryption of $ct = (\mathbf{c}, d, \pi)$ needs a successful verification of π by Vrfy and then the computation of $m := \mathsf{Decode}(d - \mathsf{prPriv}(\mathbf{k}, \mathbf{c}))$.

Now we sketch the proving idea for the MUMC$^\mathsf{c}$-CCA security of our PKE. We aim to show that the multiple challenge ciphertexts (may under different public keys) $\{ct^* = (\mathbf{c}^*, d^*, \pi^*)\}$ for plaintexts $\{m_0\}$ are indistinguishable from those for $\{m_1\}$, even if the adversary has access to a decryption oracle and can corrupt the secret keys of some users (but not those for the challenge ciphertexts).

- To generate challenge ciphertexts $\{ct^* = (\mathbf{c}^*, d^*, \pi^*)\}$ for plaintexts $\{m_b\}$ with $b \in \{0, 1\}$, the encryption oracle switches public evaluation $\mathsf{prPub}(\mathbf{p}, \mathbf{c}^*, \mathbf{s}^*)$ to the private one $\mathsf{prPriv}(\mathbf{k}, \mathbf{c}^*)$ for the computation of d^*, so

$$d^* \leftarrow_{\$} \mathsf{prPriv}(\mathbf{k}, \mathbf{c}^*) + \mathsf{Encode}(m_b) = \mathbf{c}^{*\top}\mathbf{k} + e' + \mathsf{Encode}(m_b). \tag{5}$$

  Clearly pr-QA-HPS ensures the evaluation indistinguishability. Then the witness for $\mathbf{c}^* \in \mathcal{L}_\mathbf{A}$ is not needed any more, and the proof π^* can be computed by the simulator of QA-NIZK, instead of algorithm Prove. This change is indistinguishable due to the zero-knowledge of QA-NIZK.
- To generate challenge ciphertexts $\{ct^* = (\mathbf{c}^*, d^*, \pi^*)\}$, the encryption oracle switches the language from $\mathcal{L}_\mathbf{A}$ to $\mathcal{L}_{\mathbf{A}_0}$. That is, it samples $\mathbf{c}^* \leftarrow_{\$} \mathcal{L}_{\mathbf{A}_0}$ instead of $\mathbf{c}^* \leftarrow_{\$} \mathcal{L}_\mathbf{A}$. By the LWE assumption, $\{\mathbf{A}^\top\mathbf{s}^* + \mathbf{e}^*\} \overset{c}{\approx} \{\mathbf{u} \leftarrow_{\$} \mathbb{Z}_q^m\} \overset{c}{\approx} \{\mathbf{A}_0^\top\mathbf{s}^* + \mathbf{e}^*\}$, so this change is indistinguishable.
  Consequently, for $\mathbf{c}^* = \mathbf{A}_0^\top\mathbf{s}^* + \mathbf{e}^* \in \mathcal{L}_{\mathbf{A}_0}$, (5) can be changed to

$$d^* \leftarrow_{\$} \mathsf{prPub}(\mathbf{p}_0 = \mathbf{A}_0\mathbf{k}, \mathbf{c}^*, \mathbf{s}^*) + \mathsf{Encode}(m_b) = \mathbf{s}^{*\top}\mathbf{A}_0\mathbf{k} + e' + \mathsf{Encode}(m_b)$$

  due to the evaluation indistinguishability of pr-QA-HPS.
- To decrypt a ciphertext $ct = (\mathbf{c}, d, \pi)$, the decryption oracle rejects ct if $\mathbf{c} \notin \mathcal{L}_\mathbf{A}$. This change is indistinguishable, since π hardly passes the verification

of QA-NIZK when $c \notin \mathcal{L}_A$, thanks to the USS of QA-NIZK. Then due to the evaluation indistinguishability of pr-QA-HPS, the decryption of $ct = (\mathbf{c}, d, \pi)$ with $\mathbf{c} \in \mathcal{L}_A$ can be done with prPub so that

$$m := \mathsf{Decode}(d - \mathsf{prPub}(\mathbf{p}, \mathbf{c}, \mathbf{s})) = \mathsf{Decode}(d - \mathbf{s}^\top \mathbf{A} \mathbf{k} - e'). \quad (6)$$

- Now for any user i, let its secret key be $\mathbf{k}^{(i)}$. The public key and decryption oracle only leak $\mathbf{A}\mathbf{k}^{(i)}$ via $pk^{(i)} = \mathbf{p}^{(i)} = \mathbf{A}\mathbf{k}^{(i)}$ and (6). When $m = 2n \log q + \omega(\log \lambda)$, there is still $n \log q + \omega(\log \lambda)$ bits of information left in $\mathbf{k}^{(i)}$. Taking $\mathbf{A}_0$ as an extractor, then $\mathbf{A}_0 \mathbf{k}^{(i)}$ is uniform (this is characterized by the $\langle \mathcal{L}_A, \mathcal{L}_{A_0} \rangle$-*key switching* property of pr-QA-HPS). So when computing ct^*, we have

$$(\mathbf{c}^{*\top} = \mathbf{s}^{*\top} \mathbf{A}_0 + \mathbf{e}^{*\top}, \mathbf{s}^{*\top} \mathbf{A}_0 \mathbf{k}^{(i)} + e') \stackrel{s}{\approx} \mathbf{s}^{*\top} (\mathbf{A}_0 | \mathbf{a}^{(i)}) + (\mathbf{e}^{*\top} | e') \stackrel{c}{\approx} \mathbf{u}^{(i)},$$

where $\mathbf{a}^{(i)} \leftarrow_{\$} \mathbb{Z}_q^n$, $\mathbf{u}^{(i)} \leftarrow_{\$} \mathbb{Z}_q^{m+1}$, and the last step is due to the LWE assumption. Therefore, we can use a random element, instead of $\mathsf{prPub}(\mathbf{p}_0, \mathbf{c}^*, \mathbf{s}^*)$, to perfectly hide m_b in d^* (this is characterized by the $\mathcal{L}_{A_0}$-*multi-key multi-extracting* property of pr-QA-HPS), and the MUMC^c-CCA security follows.

Overall, the MUMC^c-CCA security proof is accomplished by the evaluation indistinguishability & $\langle \mathcal{L}_A, \mathcal{L}_{A_0} \rangle$-key switching & $\mathcal{L}_{A_0}$-multi-key multi-extracting property of pr-QA-HPS, SMP, zero-knowledge & USS of QA-NIZK. Due to the nice properties of pr-QA-HPS, all reduction algorithms can generate the secret keys of all users themselves, and hence can deal with adaptive corruptions.

(4) Almost Tight MU^c Security from Reduction for Multi-secret LWE. In the MU^c security model for SIG/PKE, there are multiple signing queries/multiple challenge ciphertexts. Therefore, we need multi-fold SMP requiring that

$$(\mathbf{A}, \mathbf{SA} + \mathbf{E}) \stackrel{c}{\approx} (\mathbf{A}, \mathbf{U}) \quad (7)$$

with $\mathbf{A} \leftarrow_{\$} \mathbb{Z}_q^{n \times m}$, $\mathbf{S} \leftarrow_{\$} \mathbb{Z}_q^{Q \times n}$ and $\mathbf{U} \leftarrow_{\$} \mathbb{Z}_q^{Q \times m}$, which is in fact the *multi-secret LWE*. We show that the LWE assumption almost tightly implies multi-secret LWE, i.e., (7). The idea is inspired by [2]. Firstly, $\mathbf{A}$ can be divided into the first column $\mathbf{A}_1 \in \mathbb{Z}_q^n$ and the rest, which is denoted by $\mathbf{A}_2 \in \mathbb{Z}_q^{n \times (m-1)}$. Then $\mathbf{A}_2$ can be sampled with a lossy sampler $\mathbf{A}_2 := \mathbf{CB} + \mathbf{F}$, where $\mathbf{C} \leftarrow_{\$} \mathbb{Z}_q^{n \times \ell}, \mathbf{B} \leftarrow_{\$} \mathbb{Z}_q^{\ell \times (m-1)}$, $\mathbf{F} \in \mathbb{Z}_q^{n \times (m-1)}$ follows the error distribution and $\ell < n$. This change is indistinguishable based on the LWE assumption, with a reduction loss n by a standard hybrid argument. With a lossy $\mathbf{A}_2$, $\mathbf{SA}_2$ does not leak too much information about $\mathbf{S}$. Then the uniformly random $\mathbf{A}_1$ functions as an extractor so that $\mathbf{SA}_1$ is uniformly distributed. Consequently, the first column of $\mathbf{SA} + \mathbf{E}$ can be replaced with a uniform column. Column by column, $\mathbf{SA} + \mathbf{E}$ can be replaced with a uniform matrix, and thus (7) follows. Overall, there are totally m steps and each step loses a factor n, so the overall loss factor is $O(mn)$. Thus it is an almost tight reduction from LWE to multi-secret LWE.

In Sect. 5, we give a fine-grained almost tight reduction, with loss factor further decreased to $O(cn)$ ($c < m$), which can be as small as $O(\lambda^2)$.

Instantiation of Our Frameworks. In addition to our LWE-based pr-QA-HPS described earlier, we also need tightly secure dual-mode commitment and QA-NIZK from LWE to obtain tightly MU^c secure SIG and PKE schemes via our frameworks. For the dual-mode commitment scheme, we instantiate it by adapting the Regev's PKE scheme [42]. As for QA-NIZK, we instantiate it based on the recent advances in LWE-based NIZK in the standard model [15,32,40]. In particular, we follow one of the most efficient paradigms for LWE-based NIZK to date, which is due to Libert et al. [32], and construct tightly-secure QA-NIZK based on LWE directly for the languages defined in (4) for SIG and (1) for PKE respectively, bypassing a heavy reduction to an NP-complete problem [15,40]. To this end, we first construct trapdoor Σ-protocols based on LWE, then compile them via the tightness-preserving transformation proposed by Libert et al. [32] to obtain tightly-secure QA-NIZKs. See Subsect. 6.4 for more details.

To deal with the LWE errors, all the building blocks pr-QA-HPS, dual-mode commitment and QA-NIZK must support *gap language* (i.e., a pair of languages $\mathcal{L} \subseteq \widetilde{\mathcal{L}}$). For simplicity, we do not make this explicit in our overview and refer to the main body for more details.

On Efficiency of Our Schemes. Finally, we discuss the efficiency of our LWE-based SIG and PKE schemes with tight MU^c security. For our SIG, the verification key is a single matrix[3], the secret key consists of a bit-string plus a matrix, and the signature is made up of a single vector and a QA-NIZK proof. For our PKE, the public key is a single vector, the secret key is a single bit-string, and the ciphertext is made up of a single vector and a QA-NIZK proof.

Although we instantiate LWE-based QA-NIZK following one of the most efficient paradigm to date by Libert et al. [32], it is not quite practical at the moment. Consequently, our tightly MU^c secure SIG and PKE schemes may not be as efficient as the existing LWE-based SIG (e.g., [12,13,20,35]) and PKE schemes (e.g., [35,38,41]) in the standard model, almost all of which do not have tight reductions even in the single-user setting. However, we stress that the main purpose of this work is taking the first theoretical step to study whether tightly MU^c security from LWE in the standard model is possible and how to achieve it. We believe that our ideas may open the door to further improvements, e.g., by improving the efficiency of LWE-based QA-NIZK.

Furthermore, similar to [24], we note that we can obtain more cryptographic primitives with tight MU^c security from our SIG and PKE schemes, including signcryption (SC), message authentication code (MAC) and authenticated encryption (AE) schemes.

2   Preliminaries

Notations. Let $\lambda \in \mathbb{N}$ denote the security parameter throughout the paper, and all algorithms, distributions, functions and adversaries take 1^λ as an implicit

---

[3] Here we do not count the public parameters in the verification key, as it can be shared among all users. The same applies to the public key of PKE.

input. Let $\emptyset$ denote the empty set. If x is defined by y or the value of y is assigned to x, we write $x := y$. For $i \in \mathbb{N}$, define $[i] := \{1, 2, ..., i\}$. For a set $\mathcal{X}$, denote by $x \leftarrow_{s} \mathcal{X}$ the procedure of sampling x from $\mathcal{X}$ uniformly at random. If $\mathcal{X}$ is distribution, $x \leftarrow_{s} \mathcal{X}$ means that x is sampled according to $\mathcal{X}$. We use $y \leftarrow_{s} \mathcal{A}(x)$ to define the random variable y obtained by executing algorithm $\mathcal{A}$ on input x. We use $y \in \mathcal{A}(x)$ to indicate that y lies in the support of $\mathcal{A}(x)$. If $\mathcal{A}$ is deterministic we write $y \leftarrow \mathcal{A}(x)$. We also use $y \leftarrow \mathcal{A}(x; r)$ to make explicit the random coins r used in the probabilistic computation. Denote by $\mathbf{T}(\mathcal{A})$ the running time of $\mathcal{A}$. "PPT" abbreviates probabilistic polynomial-time. Denote by poly some polynomial function and negl some negligible function.

For distributions X, Y, Z, let $\Delta(X, Y) := \frac{1}{2} \cdot \sum_{x} |\Pr[X = x] - \Pr[Y = x]|$ denote the statistical distance between X and Y, $\Delta(X, Y | Z)$ a shorthand for $\Delta((X, Z), (Y, Z))$, and $\widetilde{\mathbf{H}}_{\infty}(X | Y) := -\log\left(\mathbb{E}_{y \leftarrow_{s} Y}\left[\max_{x} \Pr[X = x | Y = y]\right]\right)$ the average min-entropy of X conditioned on Y. If $\Delta(X, Y) \leq \mathsf{negl}(\lambda)$, we say that X and Y are statistically indistinguishable (close), and denote it by $X \overset{s}{\approx} Y$. If $|\Pr[\mathcal{D}(X) = 1] - \Pr[\mathcal{D}(Y) = 1]| \leq \mathsf{negl}(\lambda)$ for all PPT distinguishers $\mathcal{D}$, we say that X and Y are computationally indistinguishable, and denote it by $X \overset{c}{\approx} Y$. For a metric space $\mathcal{M}$ with metric dist, we use $\mathsf{Ball}_{\varepsilon}(m) := \{m' \in \mathcal{M} \mid \mathsf{dist}(m, m') \leq \varepsilon\}$ to denote the ball centered at $m \in \mathcal{M}$ of radius $\varepsilon > 0$. We use lower-case bold letters (like $\mathbf{v}$) to denote column vectors and upper-case bold letters (like $\mathbf{A}$) to denote matrices. For a vector $\mathbf{v}$, we let $\|\mathbf{v}\|$ (resp., $\|\mathbf{v}\|_{\infty}$) denote its ℓ_2 (resp., infinity) norm. For a matrix $\mathbf{A}$, we define $\|\mathbf{A}\|$ (resp., $\|\mathbf{A}\|_{\infty}$) as the largest ℓ_2 (resp., infinity) norm of $\mathbf{A}$'s rows. A distribution χ is B-bounded if its support is limited to $[-B, B]$. Let $\mathbb{Z}_q$ be the ring of integers modulo q, and its elements are represented by the integers in $(-q/2, q/2]$.

Lemma 1 ([19]). *Let X, Y, Z be three (possibly correlated) random variables. If Z has at most 2^{λ} possible values, then $\widetilde{\mathbf{H}}_{\infty}(X | (Y, Z)) \geq \widetilde{\mathbf{H}}_{\infty}(X | Y) - \lambda$.*

Due to space limitations, we present additional preliminaries in the full version [26], including the syntax of digital signature (SIG) and its strong $\mathsf{MU^c\text{-}CMA}$ security, the syntax of public-key encryption (PKE) and its $\mathsf{MUMC^c\text{-}CCA}$ security, the syntax of tag-based quasi-adaptive non-interactive zero-knowledge argument (QA-NIZK) for gap language and its zero-knowledge and unbounded simulation-soundness (USS), the definition of collision-resistant hash functions, and the definition of error-correcting codes.

2.1 Gap Language Distribution

In this work, we consider *gap* languages (i.e., a pair of NP-languages $\mathcal{L} \subseteq \widetilde{\mathcal{L}}$) and formalize a collection of gap languages as a gap language distribution.

Definition 1 (Gap Language Distribution). *A gap language distribution $\mathscr{L}$ is a probability distribution that outputs a language parameter ρ as well as a trapdoor td_{ρ} in polynomial time. The language parameter ρ publicly defines a gap language $\mathcal{GL}_{\rho} = (\mathcal{L}_{\rho}, \widetilde{\mathcal{L}}_{\rho})$ satisfying $\mathcal{L}_{\rho} \subseteq \widetilde{\mathcal{L}}_{\rho} \subseteq \mathcal{X}$, with $\mathcal{X}$ the universe.*

Moreover, $\mathscr{L}$ is associated with three PPT algorithms (Sample$_\mathcal{L}$, Sample$_\mathcal{X}$, Check$_{\widetilde{\mathcal{L}}}$): *Sample$_\mathcal{L}(\rho)$ samples an instance x from $\mathcal{L}_\rho$ together with a witness w; Sample$_\mathcal{X}$ samples an instance x from $\mathcal{X}$; Check$_{\widetilde{\mathcal{L}}}(\rho, td_\rho, x)$ is a deterministic algorithm that outputs a decision bit about whether x is in $\widetilde{\mathcal{L}}_\rho$, with the help of td_ρ. We require that for all $(\rho, td_\rho) \in \mathscr{L}$ and $x \in \mathcal{X}$, Check$_{\widetilde{\mathcal{L}}}(\rho, td_\rho, x) = 1$ holds if and only if $x \in \widetilde{\mathcal{L}}_\rho$. For simplicity, we will slightly abuse notations "$x \leftarrow_\$ \mathcal{L}_\rho$" and "$x \leftarrow_\$ \mathcal{X}$" to denote sampling x according to Sample$_\mathcal{L}(\rho)$ and Sample$_\mathcal{X}$, respectively.*

A gap language distribution $\mathscr{L}$ is associated with a subset membership problem (SMP), which asks whether an element is randomly chosen from $\mathcal{L}_\rho$ or $\mathcal{X}$. SMP can be extended to multi-fold SMP by considering multiple elements.

Definition 2 (SMP). *The subset membership problem (SMP) related to $\mathscr{L}$ is hard, if for any PPT adversary $\mathcal{A}$, it holds that $\mathsf{Adv}^{\mathsf{smp}}_{\mathscr{L},\mathcal{A}}(\lambda) := |\Pr[\mathcal{A}(\rho, x) = 1] - \Pr[\mathcal{A}(\rho, x') = 1]| \leq \mathsf{negl}(\lambda)$, where $(\rho, td_\rho) \leftarrow_\$ \mathscr{L}$, $x \leftarrow_\$ \mathcal{L}_\rho$ and $x' \leftarrow_\$ \mathcal{X}$.*

Definition 3 (Multi-fold SMP). *The multi-fold SMP related to $\mathscr{L}$ is hard, if for any PPT adversary $\mathcal{A}$ and any polynomial $Q = \mathsf{poly}(\lambda)$, it holds that $\mathsf{Adv}^{\mathsf{msmp}}_{\mathscr{L},\mathcal{A},Q}(\lambda) := |\Pr[\mathcal{A}(\rho, \{x_j\}_{j \in [Q]}) = 1] - \Pr[\mathcal{A}(\rho, \{x'_j\}_{j \in [Q]}) = 1]| \leq \mathsf{negl}(\lambda)$, where $(\rho, td_\rho) \leftarrow_\$ \mathscr{L}$, $x_1, ..., x_Q \leftarrow_\$ \mathcal{L}_\rho$ and $x'_1, ..., x'_Q \leftarrow_\$ \mathcal{X}$.*

Multi-fold SMP can generally be reduced to SMP with a security loss of the number of folds. In this work, we will instantiate gap language distributions based on LWE and show an almost tight reduction from SMP to multi-fold SMP.

2.2 Commitment Scheme

A dual-mode commitment scheme has two indistinguishable parameter generation modes, i.e., a binding mode and a hiding mode. Below we propose a new variant called dual-mode *gap* commitment scheme, by requiring the hiding property hold for messages in a message space $\mathcal{M}$ but the binding property hold for messages in a possibly larger message space $\widetilde{\mathcal{M}}$.

Definition 4 (Dual-Mode Gap Commitment Scheme). *A dual-mode gap commitment scheme* CMT = (BSetup, HSetup, Com) *consists of PPT algorithms:*

- pp$_\mathsf{CMT}$ $\leftarrow_\$$ BSetup/HSetup: *The binding-mode/hiding-mode setup algorithm outputs a public parameter* pp$_\mathsf{CMT}$, *which implicitly defines two message spaces $\mathcal{M} \subseteq \widetilde{\mathcal{M}}$ and two randomness spaces $\mathcal{R} \subseteq \widetilde{\mathcal{R}}$.*
- com $\leftarrow$ Com(pp$_\mathsf{CMT}$, $m; r$): *Taking as input* pp$_\mathsf{CMT}$, *a message $m \in \widetilde{\mathcal{M}}$ and a randomness $r \in \mathcal{R}$, the committing algorithm outputs a commitment* com.

Moreover, there exist negligible functions $\varepsilon_{\mathsf{binding}}$ and $\varepsilon_{\mathsf{hiding}}$ (in λ), such that the following properties hold:

- **Parameter Indistinguishability:** *For any PPT $\mathcal{A}$, it holds that*

$$\mathsf{Adv}^{\mathsf{para\text{-}ind}}_{\mathsf{CMT},\mathcal{A}}(\lambda) := |\Pr[\mathcal{A}(\mathsf{pp}_\mathsf{CMT}) = 1 \mid \mathsf{pp}_\mathsf{CMT} \leftarrow_\$ \mathsf{BSetup}]$$
$$- \Pr[\mathcal{A}(\mathsf{pp}_\mathsf{CMT}) = 1 \mid \mathsf{pp}_\mathsf{CMT} \leftarrow_\$ \mathsf{HSetup}]| \leq \mathsf{negl}(\lambda).$$

- $\varepsilon_{\text{binding}}$-**Statistical Binding for $\widetilde{\mathcal{M}}$ under BSetup:** *It holds that*

$$\Pr\left[\text{pp}_{\text{CMT}} \leftarrow_{\$} \text{BSetup} : \begin{array}{c} \exists\ m \neq m' \in \widetilde{\mathcal{M}}, r, r' \in \widetilde{\mathcal{R}}, \\ s.t.\ \text{Com}(\text{pp}_{\text{CMT}}, m; r) = \text{Com}(\text{pp}_{\text{CMT}}, m'; r') \end{array}\right] \leq \varepsilon_{\text{binding}}.$$

- $\varepsilon_{\text{hiding}}$-**Statistical Hiding for $\mathcal{M}$ under HSetup:** *It holds that*

$$\max_{m_0, m_1 \in \mathcal{M}} \Delta((\text{pp}_{\text{CMT}}, \text{Com}(\text{pp}_{\text{CMT}}, m_0; r)), (\text{pp}_{\text{CMT}}, \text{Com}(\text{pp}_{\text{CMT}}, m_1; r))) \leq \varepsilon_{\text{hiding}},$$

where the probability is over $\text{pp}_{\text{CMT}} \leftarrow_{\$} \text{HSetup}$ *and* $r \leftarrow_{\$} \mathcal{R}$.

2.3 Lattice Backgrounds

For $\sigma > 0$ and $\mathbf{c} \in \mathbb{R}^n$, we define the Gaussian function on $\mathbb{R}^n$ centered at $\mathbf{c}$ with parameter σ by $\rho_{\sigma,\mathbf{c}}(\mathbf{x}) := e^{-\pi \|\mathbf{x}-\mathbf{c}\|^2/\sigma^2}$. The *discrete Gaussian distribution* $D_{\Lambda,\sigma,\mathbf{c}}$ over an n-dimensional lattice $\Lambda \subseteq \mathbb{R}^n$ is defined by $D_{\Lambda,\sigma,\mathbf{c}}(\mathbf{x}) := \rho_{\sigma,\mathbf{c}}(\mathbf{x})/\rho_{\sigma,\mathbf{c}}(\Lambda)$ for any lattice vector $\mathbf{x} \in \Lambda$, where $\rho_{\sigma,\mathbf{c}}(\Lambda) := \sum_{\mathbf{z} \in \Lambda} \rho_{\sigma,\mathbf{c}}(\mathbf{z})$. The subscript $\mathbf{c}$ is taken to be $\mathbf{0}$ when omitted.

We will use the following variant of the leftover hash lemma.

Lemma 2 (Particular case of [34, Lemma 2.3]). *Let $n, m, q \in \mathbb{N}$ be integers and $\epsilon \in (0, 1)$. Suppose $\mathbf{s}$ is chosen from some distribution over $\mathbb{Z}_q^m$ and $\mathbf{A} \leftarrow_{\$} \mathbb{Z}_q^{n \times m}$, $\mathbf{u} \leftarrow_{\$} \mathbb{Z}_q^n$ are chosen independently of $\mathbf{s}$ from uniform distribution. Furthermore let Y be a random-variable (possibly) correlated with $\mathbf{s}$.*

- *If q is a prime, and $\widetilde{\mathbf{H}}_\infty(\mathbf{s} \bmod q | Y) \geq n \log q + 2 \log\left(\frac{1}{\epsilon}\right)$. Then we have: $\Delta((\mathbf{A}, \mathbf{As}), (\mathbf{A}, \mathbf{u}) | Y) \leq \epsilon$.*
- *If q is a composite number, and $\widetilde{\mathbf{H}}_\infty(\mathbf{s} \bmod p | Y) \geq 2n \log q + 2 \log\left(\frac{1}{\epsilon}\right)$ for any q's prime factor p. Then we have: $\Delta((\mathbf{A}, \mathbf{As}), (\mathbf{A}, \mathbf{u}) | Y) \leq \epsilon$.*

Definition 5 (LWE Assumption [42]). *Let $n, m, q \in \mathbb{N}$, and χ be a distribution over $\mathbb{Z}_q$. The $\text{LWE}_{n,q,\chi,m}$-assumption holds, if for any PPT adversary $\mathcal{A}$, it holds that $\text{Adv}_{[n,q,\chi,m],\mathcal{A}}^{\text{LWE}}(\lambda) := \big| \Pr[\mathcal{A}(\mathbf{A}, \mathbf{s}^\top \mathbf{A} + \mathbf{e}^\top) = 1] - \Pr[\mathcal{A}(\mathbf{A}, \mathbf{u}^\top) = 1] \big| \leq \text{negl}(\lambda)$, where $\mathbf{A} \leftarrow_{\$} \mathbb{Z}_q^{n \times m}$, $\mathbf{s} \leftarrow_{\$} \mathbb{Z}_q^n$, $\mathbf{e} \leftarrow_{\$} \chi^m$ and $\mathbf{u} \leftarrow_{\$} \mathbb{Z}_q^m$.*

Definition 6 (Multi-secret LWE Assumption). *Let $n, m, q, Q \in \mathbb{N}$, and χ be a distribution over $\mathbb{Z}_q$. The $Q\text{-LWE}_{n,q,\chi,m}$-assumption holds, if for any PPT $\mathcal{A}$ it holds that $\text{Adv}_{[n,q,\chi,m],\mathcal{A}}^{Q\text{-LWE}}(\lambda) := \big| \Pr[\mathcal{A}(\mathbf{A}, \mathbf{SA} + \mathbf{E}) = 1] - \Pr[\mathcal{A}(\mathbf{A}, \mathbf{U}) = 1] \big| \leq \text{negl}(\lambda)$, where $\mathbf{A} \leftarrow_{\$} \mathbb{Z}_q^{n \times m}$, $\mathbf{S} \leftarrow_{\$} \mathbb{Z}_q^{Q \times n}$, $\mathbf{E} \leftarrow_{\$} \chi^{Q \times m}$ and $\mathbf{U} \leftarrow_{\$} \mathbb{Z}_q^{Q \times m}$.*

A simple hybrid argument can show that $\text{Adv}_{[n,q,\chi,m]}^{Q\text{-LWE}}(\lambda) \leq Q \cdot \text{Adv}_{[n,q,\chi,m]}^{\text{LWE}}(\lambda)$. However, the security loss factor depends on the number of the secrets. In this paper, we will show an almost tight security reduction from LWE to multi-secret Q-LWE (see Theorem 3 in Sect. 5).

In [1,35], an algorithm named TrapGen is proposed to sample a "nearly" uniform random matrix $\mathbf{A}$ along with a low-norm trapdoor matrix $\mathbf{T_A}$ such that $\mathbf{A} \cdot \mathbf{T_A} = \mathbf{0}$ (cf. Lemma 3). Meanwhile, another algorithm called Invert is proposed to make use of $\mathbf{T_A}$ to invert an LWE sample $(\mathbf{A}, \mathbf{s}^\top \mathbf{A} + \mathbf{e}^\top)$ to obtain $\mathbf{s}$ and $\mathbf{e}$ (cf. Lemma 4).

Lemma 3 ([1,35]). *There exists a PPT algorithm* TrapGen *that takes as input positive integers* n, q $(q \geq 2)$ *and a sufficiently large* $m = O(n \log q)$, *outputs a matrix* $\mathbf{A} \in \mathbb{Z}_q^{n \times m}$ *and a trapdoor matrix* $\mathbf{T_A} \in \mathbb{Z}_q^{m \times m}$ *such that* $\mathbf{A}$ *is statistically close to the uniform distribution,* $\mathbf{A} \cdot \mathbf{T_A} = \mathbf{0}$, *and* $\|\mathbf{T_A}\| = O(\sqrt{n \log q})$.

Lemma 4 ([35, **Theorem 5.4**]). *There exists a deterministic polynomial-time algorithm* Invert *that takes as inputs the trapdoor information* $\mathbf{T_A}$[4] *and a vector* $\mathbf{s}^\top \mathbf{A} + \mathbf{e}^\top$ *with* $\mathbf{s} \in \mathbb{Z}_q^n$ *and* $\|\mathbf{e}\| \leq q/(10\sqrt{m})$, *and outputs* $\mathbf{s}$ *and* $\mathbf{e}$.

We recall the tail bound about the discrete Gaussian distributions over $\mathbb{Z}^m$.

Lemma 5 (**Tail Bound** [33]). *For any* $t > 0$, *we have* $\Pr_{x \leftarrow_\$ D_{\mathbb{Z},\sigma}}\left[|x| \geq t \cdot \sigma\right] \leq 2e^{-\frac{t^2}{2}}$ *and* $\Pr_{\mathbf{x} \leftarrow_\$ D_{\mathbb{Z}^m,\sigma}}\left[\|\mathbf{x}\| \geq \|\mathbf{x}\|_\infty \geq t \cdot \sigma\sqrt{m}\right] \leq t^m \cdot e^{\frac{m}{2}(1-t^2)}$.

In particular, for $t \geq \omega(\sqrt{\log \lambda})$, *the probability that* $|x| \geq t \cdot \sigma$ *and* $\|\mathbf{x}\| \geq \|\mathbf{x}\|_\infty \geq t \cdot \sigma\sqrt{m}$ *is negligible.*

The next smudging lemma shows that a uniform distribution over a sufficiently large interval $[-B', B']$ can swallow any distribution over a small interval $[-B, B]$ and yield a nearly uniform distribution over $[-B', B']$.

Lemma 6 (**Smudging Lemma,** [5, **Lemma 1**]). *Let* B, B' *be positive integers, and* $e \in [-B, B]$ *a fixed integer. Then for a uniformly chosen* $e' \leftarrow_\$ [-B', B']$, *it holds that* $\Delta(e + e', e') = B/B'$.

3 Probabilistic QA-HPS

Hash proof system (HPS) was proposed by Cramer and Shoup [17], and turned out to be a powerful tool in a wide range of applications. Han et al. [24,25] generalized HPS in a quasi-adaptive setting, termed as *Quasi-Adaptive HPS* (QA-HPS), by allowing the projection key to depend on the specific language $\mathcal{L}_\rho$ for which hash values are computed.

In this section, we propose a new primitive called *Probabilistic QA-HPS* (pr-QA-HPS), by further generalizing QA-HPS in two aspects. Firstly, pr-QA-HPS has *probabilistic* public and private evaluation algorithms (denoted by prPub and prPriv) that may toss coins. In other words, the outputs of prPub and prPriv are probabilistic distributions over the hash value space. Regarding correctness, instead of requiring exact correctness as for (QA-)HPS, we require an approximate correctness for pr-QA-HPS. Moreover, we require a statistical indistinguishability of the two probabilistic evaluation algorithms. Secondly, pr-QA-HPS is defined for a *gap* language distribution. Some properties of

---

[4] More precisely, the trapdoor information is not $\mathbf{T_A}$ itself, but some sensitive information used to generate $\mathbf{T_A}$. Here we abuse them for simplicity.

pr-QA-HPS, e.g., the evaluation indistinguishability in Definition 7 and the one-time extracting in Definition 11, require the underlying language distribution to be a gap one.

Firstly, we present the syntax of probabilistic QA-HPS.

Definition 7 (Probabilistic QA-HPS). *A probabilistic QA-HPS (pr-QA-HPS) scheme* $\mathsf{prQAHPS} = (\mathsf{Setup}_{\mathsf{HPS}}, \alpha_{(.)}, \mathsf{prPub}, \mathsf{prPriv})$ *for a gap language distribution $\mathscr{L}$ consists of four PPT algorithms:*

- $\mathsf{pp}_{\mathsf{HPS}} \leftarrow_{\$} \mathsf{Setup}_{\mathsf{HPS}}$: *The setup algorithm outputs a public parameter $\mathsf{pp}_{\mathsf{HPS}}$, which serves as an implicit input of other algorithms. $\mathsf{pp}_{\mathsf{HPS}}$ implicitly defines a hashing key space $\mathcal{SK}$, a hash value space $\mathcal{HV}$, and a family of hash functions $\Lambda_{(.)} : \mathcal{X} \longrightarrow \mathcal{HV}$ indexed by hashing keys $sk \in \mathcal{SK}$, where $\mathcal{X}$ is the universe for languages output by $\mathscr{L}$.*
  We require that $\Lambda_{(.)}$ is efficiently computable and there are PPT algorithms for sampling $sk \leftarrow_{\$} \mathcal{SK}$ uniformly and sampling $hv \leftarrow_{\$} \mathcal{HV}$ uniformly. We also require the hash value space $\mathcal{HV}$ to be a metric space.
- $pk_\rho \leftarrow \alpha_\rho(sk)$: *On input a hashing key $sk \in \mathcal{SK}$, the deterministic projection algorithm indexed by language parameter ρ outputs a projection key pk_ρ.*
- $hv \leftarrow_{\$} \mathsf{prPub}(pk_\rho, x, w)$: *Taking as input a projection key $pk_\rho = \alpha_\rho(sk)$ specified by ρ, an instance $x \in \widetilde{\mathcal{L}}_\rho$ and a witness w for $x \in \widetilde{\mathcal{L}}_\rho$, the probabilistic public evaluation algorithm outputs a hash value $hv \in \mathcal{HV}$.*
- $hv \leftarrow_{\$} \mathsf{prPriv}(sk, x)$: *On input a hashing key $sk \in \mathcal{SK}$ and an instance $x \in \mathcal{X}$, the probabilistic private evaluation algorithm outputs a hash value $hv \in \mathcal{HV}$.*

Moreover, there exist negligible functions $\varepsilon_{\mathsf{prPub}}$, $\varepsilon_{\mathsf{prPriv}}$ and $\varepsilon_{\mathsf{evalnd}}$ (in λ), such that the following properties hold:

- $(\varepsilon_{\mathsf{prPub}}, \varepsilon_{\mathsf{prPriv}})$-**Approximate Correctness for $\mathcal{L}_\rho$:** *For all $(\rho, td_\rho) \in \mathscr{L}$, $\mathsf{pp}_{\mathsf{HPS}} \in \mathsf{Setup}_{\mathsf{HPS}}$, $sk \in \mathcal{SK}$, $x \in \mathcal{L}_\rho$ with witness w, and $pk_\rho := \alpha_\rho(sk)$, it holds that* $\Pr[hv \leftarrow_{\$} \mathsf{prPub}(pk_\rho, x, w) : hv \in \mathsf{Ball}_{\varepsilon_{\mathsf{prPub}}}(\Lambda_{sk}(x))] = 1$

$$\text{and} \quad \Pr[hv \leftarrow_{\$} \mathsf{prPriv}(sk, x) : hv \in \mathsf{Ball}_{\varepsilon_{\mathsf{prPriv}}}(\Lambda_{sk}(x))] = 1.$$

  Here $hv \in \mathsf{Ball}_{\varepsilon_{\mathsf{prPub}}}(\Lambda_{sk}(x))$ (resp., $hv \in \mathsf{Ball}_{\varepsilon_{\mathsf{prPriv}}}(\Lambda_{sk}(x))$) means that hv is within distance at most $\varepsilon_{\mathsf{prPub}}$ (resp., $\varepsilon_{\mathsf{prPriv}}$) of the real hash value $\Lambda_{sk}(x)$.
- $\varepsilon_{\mathsf{evalnd}}$-**Evaluation Indistinguishability for $\widetilde{\mathcal{L}}_\rho$:** *For all $(\rho, td_\rho) \in \mathscr{L}$, $\mathsf{pp}_{\mathsf{HPS}} \in \mathsf{Setup}_{\mathsf{HPS}}$, $sk \in \mathcal{SK}$, $x \in \widetilde{\mathcal{L}}_\rho$ with witness w, and $pk_\rho := \alpha_\rho(sk)$, it holds that*
$$\Delta(\mathsf{prPub}(pk_\rho, x, w), \mathsf{prPriv}(sk, x)) \leq \varepsilon_{\mathsf{evalnd}},$$

  where the probability is only over the inner coin tosses of prPub and prPriv.

Note that the approximate correctness is required to hold for instances in $\mathcal{L}_\rho$, while the evaluation indistinguishability is required to hold for instances in $\widetilde{\mathcal{L}}_\rho$. Moreover, we can naturally define pr-QA-HPS for two gap language distributions

$\mathscr{L}$ and $\mathscr{L}_0$, by requiring the above two properties to hold not only for language parameters ρ output by $\mathscr{L}$, but also for language parameters ρ_0 output by $\mathscr{L}_0$.

Next, we recall and adapt some useful properties defined in [24,25] for QA-HPS to our pr-QA-HPS. We start by recalling a statistical property called $\langle\mathscr{L},\mathscr{L}_0\rangle$-*key-switching* from [25], parameterized by two gap language distributions $\mathscr{L}$ and $\mathscr{L}_0$. Informally speaking, it stipulates that in the presence of a projection key $\alpha_\rho(sk)$ w.r.t. a language parameter ρ output by $\mathscr{L}$, the projection key $\alpha_{\rho_0}(sk)$ w.r.t. another language parameter ρ_0 output by $\mathscr{L}_0$ can be switched to $\alpha_{\rho_0}(sk')$ for an independent sk'.

Definition 8 ($\langle\mathscr{L},\mathscr{L}_0\rangle$-Key-Switching). *Let $\mathscr{L}$ and $\mathscr{L}_0$ be two gap language distributions. A pr-QA-HPS scheme* prQAHPS *supports $\langle\mathscr{L},\mathscr{L}_0\rangle$-key-switching, if for any (possibly unbounded) adversary $\mathcal{A}$, it holds that*

$$\epsilon_{\mathsf{prQAHPS},\mathcal{A}}^{\langle\mathscr{L},\mathscr{L}_0\rangle\text{-ks}} := \big| \Pr[\mathcal{A}(\mathsf{pp_{HPS}},\rho,\rho_0,\alpha_\rho(sk),\alpha_{\rho_0}(sk)) = 1]$$
$$- \Pr[\mathcal{A}(\mathsf{pp_{HPS}},\rho,\rho_0,\alpha_\rho(sk),\alpha_{\rho_0}(sk')) = 1]\big| \leq \mathsf{negl}(\lambda),$$

where $\mathsf{pp_{HPS}} \leftarrow_\$ \mathsf{Setup_{HPS}}$, $(\rho,td_\rho) \leftarrow_\$ \mathscr{L}$, $(\rho_0,td_{\rho_0}) \leftarrow_\$ \mathscr{L}_0$, *and* $sk,sk' \leftarrow_\$ \mathcal{SK}$.

We recall another statistical property from [24], called *projection key diversity (PK-diversity)*, which expresses statistical collision resistance of projection keys under different hashing keys.

Definition 9 (PK-Diversity). *A pr-QA-HPS scheme* prQAHPS *for $\mathscr{L}$ has projection key diversity (PK-diversity), if* $\epsilon_{\mathsf{prQAHPS}}^{\mathsf{pk\text{-}div}} := \Pr[\alpha_\rho(sk) = \alpha_\rho(sk')] \leq \mathsf{negl}(\lambda)$, *where* $(\rho,td_\rho) \leftarrow_\$ \mathscr{L}$, $\mathsf{pp_{HPS}} \leftarrow_\$ \mathsf{Setup_{HPS}}$ *and* $sk,sk' \leftarrow_\$ \mathcal{SK}$.

In [24,25], a computational property called $\mathscr{L}_0$-*multi-key-multi-extracting* is defined for QA-HPS, which demands the pseudorandomness of multiple hash values $\{\Lambda_{sk_i}(x_j)\}_{i,j}$ for multiple instances $\{x_j \leftarrow_\$ \mathcal{L}_{\rho_0}\}_j$ (where $\rho_0 \in \mathscr{L}_0$) under multiple keys $\{sk_i \leftarrow_\$ \mathcal{SK}\}_i$.

Below we adapt the property to pr-QA-HPS, by requiring the pseudorandomness of $\{\mathsf{prPriv}(sk_i,x_{i,j})\}_{i,j}$ for multiple instances $\{x_{i,j} \leftarrow_\$ \mathcal{L}_{\rho_0}\}_{i,j}$ under multiple keys $\{sk_i \leftarrow_\$ \mathcal{SK}\}_i$.

Definition 10 ($\mathscr{L}_0$-Multi-Key-Multi-Extracting). *A pr-QA-HPS scheme* prQAHPS *supports $\mathscr{L}_0$-multi-key-multi-extracting, if for any PPT adversary $\mathcal{A}$, any polynomial N and any polynomial Q, it holds that*

$$\mathsf{Adv}_{\mathsf{prQAHPS},\mathcal{A},N,Q}^{\mathscr{L}_0\text{-mk-mext}}(\lambda) := \big| \Pr[\mathcal{A}(\mathsf{pp_{HPS}},\rho_0,\{x_{i,j},\mathsf{prPriv}(sk_i,x_{i,j})\}_{i\in[N],j\in[Q]}) = 1]$$
$$- \Pr[\mathcal{A}(\mathsf{pp_{HPS}},\rho_0,\{x_{i,j},hv_{i,j}\}_{i\in[N],j\in[Q]}) = 1]\big| \leq \mathsf{negl}(\lambda),$$

where $\mathsf{pp_{HPS}} \leftarrow_\$ \mathsf{Setup_{HPS}}$, $(\rho_0,td_{\rho_0}) \leftarrow_\$ \mathscr{L}_0$, $sk_1,...,sk_N \leftarrow_\$ \mathcal{SK}$, $x_{1,1},...,x_{N,Q} \leftarrow_\$ \mathcal{L}_{\rho_0}$ *and* $hv_{1,1},...,hv_{N,Q} \leftarrow_\$ \mathcal{HV}$.

In [24], a statistical property called $\langle \mathscr{L}_0, \mathscr{L} \rangle$-$one$-$time(OT)$-$extracting$ is defined for QA-HPS. Informally speaking, it demands high min-entropy of $\Lambda_{sk}(x)$ for *any* $x \in \mathcal{L}_\rho$ with ρ output by $\mathscr{L}$, when sk is uniformly chosen from $\mathcal{SK}$, even in the presence of a projection key $\alpha_{\rho_0}(sk)$ w.r.t. ρ_0 output by $\mathscr{L}_0$. This min-entropy makes sure that any (unbounded) adversary is unable to guess the correct hash value $\Lambda_{sk}(x)$.

Below we generalize it to ε_{ext}-$\langle \mathscr{L}_0, \mathscr{L} \rangle$-OT-Extracting for pr-QA-HPS, where $\varepsilon_{\text{ext}} \geq 0$, by stipulating the hardness even for *any* $x \in \widetilde{\mathcal{L}}_\rho$ and even for finding a hash value hv close to $\Lambda_{sk}(x)$, i.e., finding $hv \in \mathsf{Ball}_{\varepsilon_{\text{ext}}}(\Lambda_{sk}(x))$.

Definition 11 (ε_{ext}-$\langle \mathscr{L}_0, \mathscr{L} \rangle$-OT-Extracting). *Let $\mathscr{L}_0$ and $\mathscr{L}$ be a pair of language distributions. A pr-QA-HPS scheme prQAHPS supports ε_{ext}-$\langle \mathscr{L}_0, \mathscr{L} \rangle$-OT-extracting, if for any (possibly unbounded) adversary $\mathcal{A}$, it holds that*
$$\varepsilon_{\text{prQAHPS},\mathcal{A}}^{\varepsilon_{\text{ext}}-\langle \mathscr{L}_0, \mathscr{L} \rangle\text{-otext}}$$
$$:= \Pr \left[\begin{array}{l} \mathsf{pp}_{\text{HPS}} \leftarrow_{\$} \mathsf{Setup}_{\text{HPS}}, (\rho_0, td_{\rho_0}) \leftarrow_{\$} \mathscr{L}_0, \\ (\rho, td_\rho) \leftarrow_{\$} \mathscr{L}, sk \leftarrow_{\$} \mathcal{SK}, \\ (x^*, hv^*) \leftarrow_{\$} \mathcal{A}(\mathsf{pp}_{\text{HPS}}, \rho_0, \rho, \alpha_{\rho_0}(sk)) \end{array} : \begin{array}{l} x^* \in \widetilde{\mathcal{L}}_\rho \wedge \\ \\ hv^* \in \mathsf{Ball}_{\varepsilon_{\text{ext}}}(\Lambda_{sk}(x^*)) \end{array} \right] \leq \mathsf{negl}(\lambda).$$

4 Generic Constructions of SIG and PKE with Tight MU^c Security from Probabilistic QA-HPS

Recently, Han et al. [24] proposed generic constructions of digital signature (SIG) and public-key encryption (PKE) with tight MU^c security from QA-HPS and QA-NIZK. In this section, we propose a new generic SIG construction and extend their PKE construction, by using our probabilistic QA-HPS formalized in Sect. 3 as a central building block instead of QA-HPS, allowing instantiations from the LWE assumptions as shown later.

More precisely, we present our constructions of SIG with tight strong MU^c-CMA security in Subsect. 4.1 and PKE with tight MUMC^c-CCA security in Subsect. 4.2.

4.1 Generic Construction of SIG with Tight Strong MU^c-CMA Security

We present our generic construction of strongly MU^c-CMA secure SIG. Let $\mathcal{M}$ be an arbitrary message space. The underlying building blocks are as follows.

- Two gap language distributions $\mathscr{L}$ and $\mathscr{L}_0$, both of which have hard SMPs.
- A probabilistic prQAHPS = $(\mathsf{Setup}_{\text{HPS}}, \alpha_{(\cdot)}, \mathsf{prPub}, \mathsf{prPriv})$ for both $\mathscr{L}$ and $\mathscr{L}_0$ with hashing key space $\mathcal{SK}$, satisfying $(\varepsilon_{\text{prPub}}, \varepsilon_{\text{prPriv}})$-approximate correctness and ε_{ext}-$\langle \mathscr{L}_0, \mathscr{L} \rangle$-OT-extracting with $\varepsilon_{\text{prPriv}} \leq \varepsilon_{\text{ext}}$.
- A dual-mode gap commitment scheme CMT = $(\mathsf{BSetup}, \mathsf{HSetup}, \mathsf{Com})$ with message spaces $\mathcal{M}_{\text{CMT}} := \mathcal{SK} \subseteq \widetilde{\mathcal{SK}}$ and randomness spaces $\mathcal{R} \subseteq \widetilde{\mathcal{R}}$.
- A tag-based QANIZK = $(\mathsf{CRSGen}, \mathsf{Prove}, \mathsf{Vrfy}_{\text{NIZK}}, \mathsf{SimGen}, \mathsf{Sim})$ for the gap language $\mathcal{GL}_{\rho'}^{(\text{QANIZK})} = (\mathcal{L}_{\rho'}^{(\text{QANIZK})}, \widetilde{\mathcal{L}}_{\rho'}^{(\text{QANIZK})})$ defined in Fig. 1, with tag space $\mathcal{T}$. It is clear to see that $\mathcal{L}_{\rho'}^{(\text{QANIZK})} \subseteq \widetilde{\mathcal{L}}_{\rho'}^{(\text{QANIZK})}$ since $\mathcal{L}_\rho \subseteq \widetilde{\mathcal{L}}_\rho$, $\mathcal{SK} \subseteq \widetilde{\mathcal{SK}}$, $\mathcal{R} \subseteq \widetilde{\mathcal{R}}$ and $\varepsilon_{\text{prPriv}} \leq \varepsilon_{\text{ext}}$.

- A family of collision-resistant hash functions $\mathcal{H} = \{H : \mathcal{M} \longrightarrow \mathcal{T}\}$.

Our generic construction of $\mathsf{SIG} = (\mathsf{Setup}_{\mathsf{SIG}}, \mathsf{Gen}, \mathsf{Sign}, \mathsf{Vrfy}_{\mathsf{SIG}})$ is shown in Fig. 1. It is easy to see that the correctness of SIG follows from the $(\varepsilon_{\mathsf{prPub}}, \varepsilon_{\mathsf{prPriv}})$-approximate correctness of $\mathsf{prQAHPS}$ and the completeness of QANIZK, since d generated by $d \leftarrow_\$ \mathsf{prPriv}(sk, x)$ always satisfies $d \in \mathsf{Ball}_{\varepsilon_{\mathsf{prPriv}}}(\Lambda_{sk}(x))$.

$\mathsf{pp}_{\mathsf{SIG}} \leftarrow_\$ \mathsf{Setup}_{\mathsf{SIG}}$:
$(\rho, td_\rho) \leftarrow_\$ \mathscr{L}$, $\mathsf{pp}_{\mathsf{HPS}} \leftarrow_\$ \mathsf{Setup}_{\mathsf{HPS}}$, $\mathsf{pp}_{\mathsf{CMT}} \leftarrow_\$ \mathsf{BSetup}$.
$\rho' := (\rho, \mathsf{pp}_{\mathsf{HPS}}, \mathsf{pp}_{\mathsf{CMT}})$ defines a gap language $\mathcal{GL}_{\rho'}^{(\mathsf{QANIZK})} = (\mathcal{L}_{\rho'}^{(\mathsf{QANIZK})}, \widetilde{\mathcal{L}}_{\rho'}^{(\mathsf{QANIZK})})$, where

$$\mathcal{L}_{\rho'}^{(\mathsf{QANIZK})} := \left\{ (x, vk, d) \,\middle|\, \exists\,(w, sk \in \mathcal{SK}, r \in \mathcal{R}), \quad \text{s.t.} \quad \begin{array}{l} x \in \mathcal{L}_\rho \text{ with witness } w \\ \wedge\, vk = \mathsf{Com}(\mathsf{pp}_{\mathsf{CMT}}, sk; r) \\ \wedge\, d \in \mathsf{Ball}_{\varepsilon_{\mathsf{prPriv}}}(\Lambda_{sk}(x)) \end{array} \right\},$$

$$\widetilde{\mathcal{L}}_{\rho'}^{(\mathsf{QANIZK})} := \left\{ (x, vk, d) \,\middle|\, \exists\,(w, sk \in \widetilde{\mathcal{SK}}, r \in \widetilde{\mathcal{R}}), \quad \text{s.t.} \quad \begin{array}{l} x \in \widetilde{\mathcal{L}}_\rho \text{ with witness } w \\ \wedge\, vk = \mathsf{Com}(\mathsf{pp}_{\mathsf{CMT}}, sk; r) \\ \wedge\, d \in \mathsf{Ball}_{\varepsilon_{\mathsf{ext}}}(\Lambda_{sk}(x)) \end{array} \right\}.$$

$\mathsf{crs} \leftarrow_\$ \mathsf{CRSGen}(\rho')$. $H \leftarrow_\$ \mathcal{H}$.
Return $\mathsf{pp}_{\mathsf{SIG}} := (\rho, \mathsf{pp}_{\mathsf{HPS}}, \mathsf{pp}_{\mathsf{CMT}}, \mathsf{crs}, H)$.

$(vk, sigk) \leftarrow_\$ \mathsf{Gen}(\mathsf{pp}_{\mathsf{SIG}})$:	$\sigma \leftarrow_\$ \mathsf{Sign}(sigk = (sk, r), m)$:	$0/1 \leftarrow \mathsf{Vrfy}_{\mathsf{SIG}}(vk, m, \sigma)$:
$sk \leftarrow_\$ \mathcal{SK}$, $r \leftarrow_\$ \mathcal{R}$.	$x \leftarrow_\$ \mathcal{L}_\rho$ with witness w.	Parse $\sigma = (x, d, \pi)$.
$vk := \mathsf{Com}(\mathsf{pp}_{\mathsf{CMT}}, sk; r)$.	$d \leftarrow_\$ \mathsf{prPriv}(sk, x)$.	$\tau := H(m) \in \mathcal{T}$.
Return $(vk, sigk := (sk, r))$.	$vk := \mathsf{Com}(\mathsf{pp}_{\mathsf{CMT}}, sk; r)$.	If $\mathsf{Vrfy}_{\mathsf{NIZK}}(\mathsf{crs}, \tau, (x, vk, d), \pi) = 1$:
	$\tau := H(m) \in \mathcal{T}$.	Return 1.
	$\pi \leftarrow_\$ \mathsf{Prove}(\mathsf{crs}, \tau, (x, vk, d), (w, sk, r))$.	Else: Return 0.
	Return $\sigma := (x, d, \pi)$.	

Fig. 1. Generic construction of $\mathsf{SIG} = (\mathsf{Setup}_{\mathsf{SIG}}, \mathsf{Gen}, \mathsf{Sign}, \mathsf{Vrfy}_{\mathsf{SIG}})$ from prQAHPS, CMT, tag-based QANIZK and $\mathcal{H}$. The message space is $\mathcal{M}$.

Next, we show the strong $\mathsf{MU^c}$-CMA security of SIG via the following theorem.

Theorem 1 (Strong $\mathsf{MU^c}$-CMA Security of SIG). *Assume that (i) $\mathscr{L}$ and $\mathscr{L}_0$ have hard SMPs, (ii) prQAHPS is a probabilistic QA-HPS for both $\mathscr{L}$ and $\mathscr{L}_0$, having $(\varepsilon_{\mathsf{prPub}}, \varepsilon_{\mathsf{prPriv}})$-approximate correctness, $\varepsilon_{\mathsf{evalnd}}$-evaluation indistinguishability, and supporting $\varepsilon_{\mathsf{ext}}$-$\langle \mathscr{L}_0, \mathscr{L} \rangle$-OT-extracting, where $\varepsilon_{\mathsf{ext}} \geq \varepsilon_{\mathsf{prPriv}}$, (iii) CMT is a dual-mode gap commitment scheme that is $\varepsilon_{\mathsf{binding}}$-statistical binding and $\varepsilon_{\mathsf{hiding}}$-statistical hiding, (iv) QANIZK is a tag-based QA-NIZK for the gap language $\mathcal{GL}_{\rho'}^{(\mathsf{QANIZK})}$ defined in Fig. 1, satisfying both zero-knowledge and unbounded simulation-soundness, (iv) $\mathcal{H}$ is collision-resistant. Then the proposed SIG scheme in Fig. 1 is strongly $\mathsf{MU^c}$-CMA secure.*

Concretely, for any number N of users and any adversary $\mathcal{A}$ making at most Q_s times of $\mathcal{O}_{\mathsf{SIGN}}$ queries, there exist adversaries $\mathcal{B}_1, \cdots, \mathcal{B}_7$, s.t. $\mathbf{T}(\mathcal{B}_1) \approx \cdots \approx \mathbf{T}(\mathcal{B}_6) \approx \mathbf{T}(\mathcal{A}) + (N + Q_s) \cdot \mathsf{poly}(\lambda)$, with $\mathsf{poly}(\lambda)$ independent of $\mathbf{T}(\mathcal{A})$, and

$$\mathsf{Adv}_{\mathsf{SIG}, \mathcal{A}, N}^{\mathsf{str\text{-}cma\text{-}c}}(\lambda) \leq \mathsf{Adv}_{\mathsf{QANIZK}, \mathcal{B}_1}^{\mathsf{zk}}(\lambda) + \mathsf{Adv}_{\mathcal{H}, \mathcal{B}_2}^{\mathsf{cr}}(\lambda) + \mathsf{Adv}_{\mathscr{L}, \mathcal{B}_3, Q_s}^{\mathsf{msmp}}(\lambda) + \mathsf{Adv}_{\mathscr{L}_0, \mathcal{B}_4, Q_s}^{\mathsf{msmp}}(\lambda)$$

$$+ \mathsf{Adv}_{\mathsf{QANIZK}, \mathcal{B}_5}^{\mathsf{uss}}(\lambda) + \mathsf{Adv}_{\mathsf{CMT}, \mathcal{B}_6}^{\mathsf{para\text{-}ind}}(\lambda) + statist.\ loss,$$

where statist. loss $= 2 \cdot \varepsilon_{\mathsf{binding}} + Q_s \cdot \varepsilon_{\mathsf{evalnd}} + N \cdot \epsilon_{\mathsf{prQAHPS}, \mathcal{B}_7}^{\varepsilon_{\mathsf{ext}}\text{-}\langle \mathscr{L}_0, \mathscr{L} \rangle\text{-otext}} + \varepsilon_{\mathsf{hiding}} + \frac{N(N-1)}{2}/|\mathcal{SK}|$.

We refer to Sect. 1 for an overview of the proof. Due to space limitations, we postpone the formal proof to the full version [26]. Here we provide the game sequence G_0-G_7 used in the formal proof in Table 1. According to Theorem 1, SIG has tight strong MU^c-CMA security as long as both the multi-fold SMPs related to $\mathcal{L}$ and $\mathcal{L}_0$ have tight reductions (e.g., to the LWE assumptions), and CMT and QANIZK are tightly secure.

Table 1. Brief Description of Games G_0-G_7 for the strong MU^c-CMA security proof of SIG. Here column "$\mathcal{O}_{\text{SIGN}}$" suggests how a signature $\sigma = (x, d, \pi)$ is generated: sub-column "x from" refers to the language from which x is chosen; sub-column "d using" indicates the keys that are used in the computation of d; sub-column "π via" indicates the way (**Prove** or **Sim**) that π is computed. Column "$\mathcal{O}_{\text{COR}}$" shows the key returned by $\mathcal{O}_{\text{COR}}$. Column "Win's additional check for forgery $(i^*, m^*, \sigma^* = (x^*, d^*, \pi^*))$)" describes the additional check that $\mathcal{A}$'s forgery wins, besides the routine check $i^* \notin \mathcal{Q}_{\text{COR}} \wedge (i^*, m^*, \sigma^*) \notin \mathcal{Q}_{\text{SIGN}} \wedge \text{Vrfy}_{\text{NIZK}}(\text{crs}, \tau^*, (x^*, vk_{i^*}, d^*), \pi^*) = 1$, where $\tau^* := H(m^*)$.

	$\mathcal{O}_{\text{SIGN}}(i,m)$			$\mathcal{O}_{\text{COR}}(i)$	Win's additional check for forgery $(i^*, m^*, \sigma^* = (x^*, d^*, \pi^*))$	Remark/Assumption
	x from	d using	π via			
G_0	$\mathcal{L}_\rho$	sk_i	Prove	sk_i		The strong MU^c-CMA experiment
G_1	$\mathcal{L}_\rho$	sk_i	Prove	sk_i		Abort if verification keys collide: by *statistical binding* of CMT under BSetup & secret keys hardly collide
G_2	$\mathcal{L}_\rho$	sk_i	Sim	sk_i		By *zero-knowledge* of QANIZK
G_3	$\mathcal{L}_\rho$	sk_i	Sim	sk_i	$(\tau^*, (x^*, vk_{i^*}, d^*), \pi^*) \notin \mathcal{Q}_{\text{SIM}}$	By *collision-resistance* of $\mathcal{H}$
G_4	$\mathcal{L}_{\rho_0}$	sk_i	Sim	sk_i	$(\tau^*, (x^*, vk_{i^*}, d^*), \pi^*) \notin \mathcal{Q}_{\text{SIM}}$	By *multi-fold SMP* of $\mathcal{L}$ and $\mathcal{L}_0$
G_5	$\mathcal{L}_{\rho_0}$	sk_i	Sim	sk_i	$(\tau^*, (x^*, vk_{i^*}, d^*), \pi^*) \notin \mathcal{Q}_{\text{SIM}}$, $x^* \in \widetilde{\mathcal{L}}_\rho,\ d^* \in \text{Ball}_{\varepsilon_{\text{ext}}}(\Lambda_{sk_{i^*}}(x^*))$	By *USS* of QANIZK & *statistical binding* of CMT under BSetup
G_6	$\mathcal{L}_{\rho_0}$	$\alpha_{\rho_0}(sk_i)$	Sim	sk_i	$(\tau^*, (x^*, vk_{i^*}, d^*), \pi^*) \notin \mathcal{Q}_{\text{SIM}}$, $x^* \in \widetilde{\mathcal{L}}_\rho,\ d^* \in \text{Ball}_{\varepsilon_{\text{ext}}}(\Lambda_{sk_{i^*}}(x^*))$	By *evaluation indistinguishability* of prQAHPS
G_7	$\mathcal{L}_{\rho_0}$	$\alpha_{\rho_0}(sk_i)$	Sim	sk_i	$(\tau^*, (x^*, vk_{i^*}, d^*), \pi^*) \notin \mathcal{Q}_{\text{SIM}}$, $x^* \in \widetilde{\mathcal{L}}_\rho,\ d^* \in \text{Ball}_{\varepsilon_{\text{ext}}}(\Lambda_{sk_{i^*}}(x^*))$	Change to $\text{pp}_{\text{CMT}} \leftarrow_{\$} \text{HSetup}$: by *parameter indistinguishability* of CMT; $\Pr[\text{Win}] = \text{negl}$ in G_7: by ε_{ext}-$\langle \mathcal{L}_0, \mathcal{L} \rangle$-*OT-extracting* of prQAHPS & *statistical hiding* of CMT under HSetup

4.2   Generic Construction of PKE with Tight MUMC^c-CCA Security

We present our generic construction of MUMC^c-CCA secure PKE. Let $\mathcal{M}$ be an arbitrary message space. The underlying building blocks are as follows.

- Two gap language distributions $\mathcal{L}$ and $\mathcal{L}_0$, both of which have hard SMPs.
- A probabilistic $\text{prQAHPS} = (\text{Setup}_{\text{HPS}}, \alpha_{(\cdot)}, \text{prPub}, \text{prPriv})$ for both $\mathcal{L}$ and $\mathcal{L}_0$ with hashing key space $\mathcal{SK}$, projection key space $\mathcal{PK}$ and hash value space $\mathcal{HV}$, satisfying $(\varepsilon_{\text{prPub}}, \varepsilon_{\text{prPriv}})$-approximate correctness. We require $\mathcal{HV}$ to be an (additive) group.
- A tag-based $\text{QANIZK} = (\text{CRSGen}, \text{Prove}, \text{Vrfy}_{\text{NIZK}}, \text{SimGen}, \text{Sim})$ for the gap language $\mathcal{GL}_\rho = (\mathcal{L}_\rho, \widetilde{\mathcal{L}}_\rho)$ generated by $\mathcal{L}$, with tag space $\mathcal{T}$.
- A family of collision-resistant hash functions $\mathcal{H} = \{H : \mathcal{PK} \times \mathcal{HV} \longrightarrow \mathcal{T}\}$.

- An error-correcting code $\mathsf{ECC} = (\mathsf{Encode}, \mathsf{Decode})$ from $\mathcal{M}$ to $\mathcal{HV}$, which is able to correct $(\varepsilon_{\mathsf{prPub}} + \varepsilon_{\mathsf{prPriv}})$ errors efficiently.

Our generic construction of $\mathsf{PKE} = (\mathsf{Setup}_{\mathsf{PKE}}, \mathsf{Gen}, \mathsf{Enc}, \mathsf{Dec})$ is shown in Fig. 2. It is easy to check that the correctness of PKE follows from the $(\varepsilon_{\mathsf{prPub}}, \varepsilon_{\mathsf{prPriv}})$-approximate correctness of $\mathsf{prQAHPS}$, the $(\varepsilon_{\mathsf{prPub}} + \varepsilon_{\mathsf{prPriv}})$-correctness of ECC and the completeness of QANIZK: (1) by the $(\varepsilon_{\mathsf{prPub}}, \varepsilon_{\mathsf{prPriv}})$-approximate correctness of $\mathsf{prQAHPS}$, the hv generated by $hv \leftarrow_{\$} \mathsf{prPub}(pk, x, w)$ in Enc and the hv' generated by $hv' \leftarrow_{\$} \mathsf{prPriv}(sk, x)$ in Dec are within distance at most $(\varepsilon_{\mathsf{prPub}} + \varepsilon_{\mathsf{prPriv}})$, i.e., $hv' \in \mathsf{Ball}_{\varepsilon_{\mathsf{prPub}} + \varepsilon_{\mathsf{prPriv}}}(hv)$, (2) then $d - hv' = hv - hv' + \mathsf{Encode}(m) \in \mathsf{Ball}_{\varepsilon_{\mathsf{prPub}} + \varepsilon_{\mathsf{prPriv}}}(\mathsf{Encode}(m))$, and by the $(\varepsilon_{\mathsf{prPub}} + \varepsilon_{\mathsf{prPriv}})$-correctness of ECC, it follows that $\mathsf{Decode}(d - hv') = \mathsf{Decode}(hv - hv' + \mathsf{Encode}(m)) = m$.

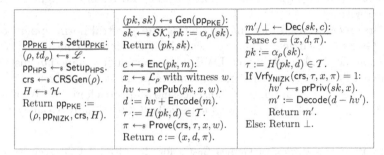

Fig. 2. Generic construction of $\mathsf{PKE} = (\mathsf{Setup}_{\mathsf{PKE}}, \mathsf{Gen}, \mathsf{Enc}, \mathsf{Dec})$ from $\mathsf{prQAHPS}$, tag-based QANIZK, $\mathcal{H}$ and ECC. The message space is $\mathcal{M}$.

Next, we show the $\mathsf{MUMC}^c\text{-}\mathsf{CCA}$ security of PKE via the following theorem.

Theorem 2 ($\mathsf{MUMC}^c\text{-}\mathsf{CCA}$ Security of PKE). *Assume that (i) $\mathscr{L}$ and $\mathscr{L}_0$ have hard SMPs, (ii) $\mathsf{prQAHPS}$ is a probabilistic QA-HPS for both $\mathscr{L}$ and $\mathscr{L}_0$, having $\varepsilon_{\mathsf{evalnd}}$-evaluation indistinguishability, PK-diversity, and supporting both $\langle \mathscr{L}, \mathscr{L}_0 \rangle$-key-switching and $\mathscr{L}_0$-multi-key-multi-extracting, (iii) QANIZK is a tag-based QA-NIZK for the gap language $\mathcal{GL}_\rho = (\mathcal{L}_\rho, \widetilde{\mathcal{L}}_\rho)$ generated by $\mathscr{L}$, satisfying both zero-knowledge and unbounded simulation-soundness, (iv) $\mathcal{H}$ is collision-resistant. Then the proposed PKE scheme in Fig. 2 is $\mathsf{MUMC}^c\text{-}\mathsf{CCA}$ secure.*

Concretely, for any number N of users and any adversary $\mathcal{A}$ who makes at most Q_e times of $\mathcal{O}_{\mathrm{ENC}}$ queries and Q_d times of $\mathcal{O}_{\mathrm{DEC}}$ queries, there exist adversaries $\mathcal{B}_1, \cdots, \mathcal{B}_7$, such that $\mathbf{T}(\mathcal{B}_1) \approx \cdots \approx \mathbf{T}(\mathcal{B}_6) \approx \mathbf{T}(\mathcal{A}) + (N + Q_e + Q_d) \cdot \mathsf{poly}(\lambda)$, with $\mathsf{poly}(\lambda)$ independent of $\mathbf{T}(\mathcal{A})$, and

$$\mathsf{Adv}^{\mathsf{cca\text{-}c}}_{\mathsf{PKE}, \mathcal{A}, N}(\lambda) \leq \mathsf{Adv}^{\mathsf{zk}}_{\mathsf{QANIZK}, \mathcal{B}_1}(\lambda) + \mathsf{Adv}^{\mathsf{cr}}_{\mathcal{H}, \mathcal{B}_2}(\lambda) + \mathsf{Adv}^{\mathsf{msmp}}_{\mathscr{L}, \mathcal{B}_3, Q_e}(\lambda) + \mathsf{Adv}^{\mathsf{msmp}}_{\mathscr{L}_0, \mathcal{B}_4, Q_e}(\lambda)$$
$$+ \mathsf{Adv}^{\mathsf{uss}}_{\mathsf{QANIZK}, \mathcal{B}_5}(\lambda) + \mathsf{Adv}^{\mathscr{L}_0\text{-}\mathsf{mk\text{-}mext}}_{\mathsf{prQAHPS}, \mathcal{B}_6, N, Q_e}(\lambda) + \mathit{statist.\ loss},$$

where $\mathit{statist.\ loss} = \frac{N(N-1)}{2} \cdot \epsilon^{\mathsf{pk\text{-}div}}_{\mathsf{prQAHPS}} + (3Q_e + 2Q_d) \cdot \varepsilon_{\mathsf{evalnd}} + N \cdot \epsilon^{\langle \mathscr{L}, \mathscr{L}_0 \rangle\text{-}\mathsf{ks}}_{\mathsf{prQAHPS}, \mathcal{B}_7}.$

We refer to Sect. 1 for an overview of the proof. Due to space limitations, we postpone the formal proof to the full version [26]. Here we provide the game sequence G_0-G_9 used in the formal proof in Table 2. According to Theorem 2, PKE has tight MUMC^c-CCA security as long as both the multi-fold SMPs related to $\mathscr{L}$ and $\mathscr{L}_0$ have tight reductions, prQAHPS has tight $\mathscr{L}_0$-multi-key-multi-extracting, and QANIZK is tightly secure.

5   Tighter Reduction from LWE to Multi-secret LWE

In this section, we will show an almost tight reduction from LWE to multi-secret LWE, which supports the almost tight security of our LWE-based instantiations as shown later in Sect. 6. We note that similar results could be derived from [2]. Nevertheless, our proof is simpler, more flexible and results in tighter reduction compared with [2].

We first recall a useful lemma presenting the spectral norm upper bound of discrete Gaussian matrices. Then we recall the definitions of continuous Gaussian distribution D_σ and multi-secret LWE with continuous Gaussian distribution D_σ, which will serve as an intermediate assumption in our reduction to obtain better parameters by applying the noise lossiness approach in [14]. We also recall the randomized rounding technique due to Peikert [39]. Finally we show Theorem

Table 2. Brief Description of Games G_0-G_9 for the MUMC^c-CCA security proof of PKE. Here column "$\mathcal{O}_{\mathrm{ENC}}$" suggests how a challenge ciphertext $c^* = (x^*, d^*, \pi^*)$ is generated: sub-column "x^* from" refers to the language from which x^* is chosen; sub-column "hv^* using" indicates the keys that are used in the computation of hv^*; sub-column "π^* via" indicates the way (Prove or Sim) that π^* is computed. Column "$\mathcal{O}_{\mathrm{DEC}}$" suggests how a decryption query $(i, c = (x, d, \pi))$ is answered: sub-column "additional check" describes the additional check made by $\mathcal{O}_{\mathrm{DEC}}$ besides the routine check $(i, c) \notin \mathcal{Q}_{\mathrm{ENC}} \wedge \mathsf{Vrfy}_{\mathrm{NIZK}}(\mathsf{crs}, \tau, x, \pi) = 1$, where $\tau := H(pk_i, d)$; $\mathcal{O}_{\mathrm{DEC}}$ outputs $\perp$ if the check fails; sub-column "hv' using" indicates the keys that are used in the computation of hv'. Column "$\mathcal{O}_{\mathrm{COR}}$" shows the key returned by $\mathcal{O}_{\mathrm{COR}}$. Recall that it is not allowed to query $\mathcal{O}_{\mathrm{ENC}}$ and $\mathcal{O}_{\mathrm{COR}}$ for a same user index i.

	$\mathcal{O}_{\mathrm{ENC}}(i^*, m_0, m_1)$			$\mathcal{O}_{\mathrm{DEC}}(i, c)$		$\mathcal{O}_{\mathrm{COR}}(i)$	Remark/Assumption
	x^* from	hv^* using	π^* via	additional check	hv' using		
G_0	$\mathcal{L}_\rho$	pk_{i^*}	Prove		sk_i	sk_i	The MUMC^c-CCA security experiment
G_1	$\mathcal{L}_\rho$	pk_{i^*}	Prove		sk_i	sk_i	Abort if public keys collide: by *PK-diversity* of prQAHPS
G_2	$\mathcal{L}_\rho$	sk_{i^*}	Sim		sk_i	sk_i	By *evaluation indistinguishability* of prQAHPS & *zero-knowledge* of QANIZK
G_3	$\mathcal{L}_\rho$	sk_{i^*}	Sim	$(\tau, x, \pi) \notin \mathcal{Q}_{\mathrm{SIM}}$	sk_i	sk_i	By *collision-resistance* of $\mathcal{H}$
G_4	$\mathcal{L}_{\rho_0}$	sk_{i^*}	Sim	$(\tau, x, \pi) \notin \mathcal{Q}_{\mathrm{SIM}}$	sk_i	sk_i	By *multi-fold SMP* of $\mathscr{L}$ & $\mathscr{L}_0$
G_5	$\mathcal{L}_{\rho_0}$	sk_{i^*}	Sim	$(\tau, x, \pi) \notin \mathcal{Q}_{\mathrm{SIM}}, x \in \tilde{\mathcal{L}}_\rho$	sk_i	sk_i	By *USS* of QANIZK
G_6	$\mathcal{L}_{\rho_0}$	$\alpha_\rho(sk_{i^*})$	Sim	$(\tau, x, \pi) \notin \mathcal{Q}_{\mathrm{SIM}}, x \in \tilde{\mathcal{L}}_\rho$	$\alpha_\rho(sk_i)$	sk_i	By *evaluation indistinguishability* of prQAHPS
$\{G_{7.\eta}\}_{\eta \in [N]}$	$\mathcal{L}_{\rho_0}$	$\alpha_{\rho_0}(sk'_{i^*})$, if $i^* \leq \eta$ $\alpha_{\rho_0}(sk_{i^*})$, if $i^* > \eta$	Sim	$(\tau, x, \pi) \notin \mathcal{Q}_{\mathrm{SIM}}, x \in \tilde{\mathcal{L}}_\rho$	$\alpha_\rho(sk_i)$	sk_i	By $(\mathscr{L}, \mathscr{L}_0)$-*key-switching* of prQAHPS
$G_{7.N}$	$\mathcal{L}_{\rho_0}$	$\alpha_{\rho_0}(sk'_{i^*})$	Sim	$(\tau, x, \pi) \notin \mathcal{Q}_{\mathrm{SIM}}, x \in \tilde{\mathcal{L}}_\rho$	$\alpha_\rho(sk_i)$	sk_i	—
G_8	$\mathcal{L}_{\rho_0}$	sk'_{i^*}	Sim	$(\tau, x, \pi) \notin \mathcal{Q}_{\mathrm{SIM}}, x \in \tilde{\mathcal{L}}_\rho$	sk_i	sk_i	By *evaluation indistinguishability* of prQAHPS
G_9	$\mathcal{L}_{\rho_0}$	= rand	Sim	$(\tau, x, \pi) \notin \mathcal{Q}_{\mathrm{SIM}}, x \in \tilde{\mathcal{L}}_\rho$	sk_i	sk_i	By $\mathscr{L}_0$-*multi-key-multi-extracting* of prQAHPS $\Pr[\mathsf{Win}] = \frac{1}{2}$ in G_9

3 that addresses the almost tight reduction from LWE to Multi-secret LWE for prime modulus. We also extend the result for composite modulus in the full version [26].

Lemma 7 ([35, **Lemma 2.8, 2.9**]). *Let* $\mathbf{F} \leftarrow_\$ D_{\mathbb{Z},\gamma}^{n \times m}$ *and* $m \geq n$. *Then with all but* 2^{-m} *probability it holds that the spectral norm* $\sigma_\mathbf{F}$ *of* $\mathbf{F}$ *satisfies* $\sigma_\mathbf{F} \leq \gamma \cdot C \cdot \sqrt{m}$ *where* C *is a global constant.*

Definition 12 (Multi-secret LWE Assumption with Continuous Gaussian [14]). *For* $\sigma > 0$, *the continuous Gaussian distribution* D_σ *over* $\mathbb{R}$ *centered at* 0 *is defined by the probability density function* $D_\sigma(x) := \rho_\sigma(x)/\rho_\sigma(\mathbb{R})$ *for any* $x \in \mathbb{R}$, *where* $\rho_\sigma(x) := e^{-\pi x^2/\sigma^2}$ *and* $\rho_\sigma(\mathbb{R}) := \int_\mathbb{R} \rho_\sigma(z) dz = \sigma$.

Let $n, m, q, Q \in \mathbb{N}$. *The* $Q\text{-LWE}_{n,q,D_\sigma,m}$-*assumption holds, if for any PPT* $\mathcal{A}$ *it holds that* $\mathsf{Adv}_{[n,q,D_\sigma,m],\mathcal{A}}^{Q\text{-LWE}}(\lambda) := \big| \Pr[\mathcal{A}(\mathbf{A}, \mathbf{SA} + \mathbf{E}) = 1] - \Pr[\mathcal{A}(\mathbf{A}, \mathbf{U} + \mathbf{E}) = 1] \big| \leq \mathsf{negl}(\lambda)$, *where* $\mathbf{A} \leftarrow_\$ \mathbb{Z}_q^{n \times m}$, $\mathbf{S} \leftarrow_\$ \mathbb{Z}_q^{Q \times n}$, $\mathbf{E} \leftarrow_\$ D_\sigma^{Q \times m}$ *and* $\mathbf{U} \leftarrow_\$ \mathbb{Z}_q^{Q \times m}$.

Lemma 8 (Particular case of [39, **Theorem 3.1**]). *Let* $\sigma > 0$ *and* $r \geq \sqrt{\lambda}$. *For* $e \leftarrow_\$ D_\sigma$ *and* $v \leftarrow_\$ D_{\mathbb{Z}-e,r}$, *the distribution of* $e + v$ *is statistically close to* $D_{\mathbb{Z},\sqrt{\sigma^2+r^2}}$, *with statistical distance at most* $2^{-\lambda}$.

Theorem 3 (LWE $\Rightarrow$ Multi-secret LWE with Prime Modulus). *Let* $n, m, \ell, q \in \mathbb{N}$, *and* q *be a prime. Let* $\sigma, \sigma_0, \sigma_1, r, \gamma > 0$ *such that* $\sigma = \sqrt{\sigma_0^2 + r^2}$, $\sigma_0 > \gamma \cdot C \cdot \sqrt{m} \cdot \sigma_1$, $\frac{q}{\sigma_1} \geq \sqrt{\frac{\ln(4n)}{\pi}}$ *and* $r \geq \sqrt{\lambda}$, *where* C *is the global constant from Lemma 7. For any adversary* $\mathcal{A}$, *there exists an adversary* $\mathcal{B}$, *such that* $\mathbf{T}(\mathcal{B}) \approx \mathbf{T}(\mathcal{A}) + Q \cdot \mathsf{poly}(\lambda)$ *with* $\mathsf{poly}(\lambda)$ *independent of* $\mathbf{T}(\mathcal{A})$, *and* $\mathsf{Adv}_{[n,q,D_{\mathbb{Z},\sigma},m],\mathcal{A}}^{Q\text{-LWE}}(\lambda) \leq 2cn \cdot \mathsf{Adv}_{[\ell,q,D_{\mathbb{Z},\gamma},m],\mathcal{B}}^{\text{LWE}}(\lambda) + \frac{Q(m+c+1)}{2^\lambda}$, *where* c *is an integer such that*

$$m' = \lfloor \tfrac{m}{c} \rfloor \quad and \quad n \geq (m' \log q + \ell \log q + 2\lambda + 1)/\log(\sigma_1). \tag{8}$$

Proof sketch. We will use the multi-secret LWE with continuous Gaussian D_{σ_0} defined in Definition 12 as an intermediate assumption, and show that there exists an adversary $\mathcal{B}'$ such that $\mathbf{T}(\mathcal{B}) \approx \mathbf{T}(\mathcal{B}') + Q \cdot \mathsf{poly}'(\lambda) \approx \mathbf{T}(\mathcal{A}) + Q \cdot \mathsf{poly}(\lambda)$ and

$$\mathsf{Adv}_{[n,q,D_{\mathbb{Z},\sigma},m],\mathcal{A}}^{Q\text{-LWE}}(\lambda) \leq \mathsf{Adv}_{[n,q,D_{\sigma_0},m],\mathcal{B}'}^{Q\text{-LWE}}(\lambda) + \frac{Qm}{2^\lambda}, \tag{9}$$

$$\mathsf{Adv}_{[n,q,D_{\sigma_0},m],\mathcal{B}'}^{Q\text{-LWE}}(\lambda) \leq 2cn \cdot \mathsf{Adv}_{[\ell,q,D_{\mathbb{Z},\gamma},m],\mathcal{B}}^{\text{LWE}}(\lambda) + \frac{Q(c+1)}{2^\lambda}. \tag{10}$$

Then Theorem 3 follows directly from (9) and (10).

To prove (9), we construct $\mathcal{B}'$ to break the $Q\text{-LWE}_{n,q,D_{\sigma_0},m}$-assumption by invoking $\mathcal{A}$. Given a challenge $(\mathbf{A}, \mathbf{B})$, $\mathcal{B}'$ wants to distinguish $\mathbf{B} = \mathbf{SA} + \mathbf{E}$ from $\mathbf{B} = \mathbf{U} + \mathbf{E}$, where $\mathbf{A} \leftarrow_\$ \mathbb{Z}_q^{n \times m}$, $\mathbf{S} \leftarrow_\$ \mathbb{Z}_q^{Q \times n}$, $\mathbf{E} \leftarrow_\$ D_{\sigma_0}^{Q \times m}$ and $\mathbf{U} \leftarrow_\$ \mathbb{Z}_q^{Q \times m}$. To decide which case it is, $\mathcal{B}'$ parses $\mathbf{B} = (b_{i,j})_{i \in [Q], j \in [m]}$, samples $v_{i,j} \leftarrow_\$ D_{\mathbb{Z}-b_{i,j},r}$ for all $i \in [Q], j \in [m]$, sets $\mathbf{B}' := (b_{i,j} + v_{i,j})_{i \in [Q], j \in [m]}$, feeds $(\mathbf{A}, \mathbf{B}')$ to $\mathcal{A}$, and returns whatever $\mathcal{A}$ outputs. We analyze the advantage of $\mathcal{B}'$.

In the case $\mathbf{B} = \mathbf{SA} + \mathbf{E}$. We parse $\mathbf{SA} = (t_{i,j})_{i\in[Q],j\in[m]}$ and $\mathbf{E} = (e_{i,j})_{i\in[Q],j\in[m]}$. Then we have $b_{i,j} = t_{i,j} + e_{i,j}$ and $\mathbf{B}' = (t_{i,j} + e_{i,j} + v_{i,j})_{i\in[Q],j\in[m]} = \mathbf{SA} + (e_{i,j} + v_{i,j})_{i\in[Q],j\in[m]}$. Since $t_{i,j} \in \mathbb{Z}$, $v_{i,j}$ follows the distribution $D_{\mathbb{Z}-b_{i,j},r} = D_{\mathbb{Z}-t_{i,j}-e_{i,j},r} = D_{\mathbb{Z}-e_{i,j},r}$. Then together with the fact that $e_{i,j}$ follows D_{σ_0}, by Lemma 8, the distribution of $e_{i,j} + v_{i,j}$ is within statistical distance $2^{-\lambda}$ of $D_{\mathbb{Z},\sigma} = D_{\mathbb{Z},\sqrt{\sigma^2+r^2}}$. Let $\mathbf{E}' := (e_{i,j}+v_{i,j})_{i\in[Q],j\in[m]}$. Then $\mathbf{B}' = \mathbf{SA} + \mathbf{E}'$ with $\mathbf{E}' = (e_{i,j} + v_{i,j})_{i\in[Q],j\in[m]}$ following a distribution statistically close to $D_{\mathbb{Z},\sigma}^{Q\times m}$, with statistical distance at most $Qm/2^{\lambda}$.

In the case $\mathbf{B} = \mathbf{U} + \mathbf{E}$. Similar to the above analysis, we can get that $\mathbf{B}' = \mathbf{U} + \mathbf{E}'$ with $\mathbf{E}' = (e_{i,j} + v_{i,j})_{i\in[Q],j\in[m]}$ distributed over $\mathbb{Z}_q^{Q\times m}$. Since $\mathbf{U}$ is uniformly distributed over $\mathbb{Z}_q^{Q\times m}$ and independent of $\mathbf{E}'$, $\mathbf{B}' = \mathbf{U} + \mathbf{E}'$ is also uniformly distributed over $\mathbb{Z}_q^{Q\times m}$.

Thus, $\mathcal{B}'$ successfully distinguishes $\mathbf{B} = \mathbf{SA} + \mathbf{E}$ from $\mathbf{B} = \mathbf{U} + \mathbf{E}$ as long as $\mathcal{A}$ can distinguish $\mathbf{B}' = \mathbf{SA}+\mathbf{E}'$ (with $\mathbf{E}'$ nearly following $D_{\mathbb{Z},\sigma}^{Q\times m}$) from the uniform distribution, i.e., breaking the $Q\text{-LWE}_{n,q,D_{\mathbb{Z},\sigma},m}$-assumption. This proves (9).

Next we turn to the proof of (10). Due to space limitations, the formal proof of (10) is postponed to the full version [26]. Here we describe the main ideas behind the proof. We aim to prove that the $Q\text{-LWE}_{n,q,D_{\sigma_0},m}$-assumption holds, i.e.,

$$(\mathbf{A}, \ \mathbf{SA} + \mathbf{E}) \overset{c}{\approx} (\mathbf{A}, \ \mathbf{U} + \mathbf{E}), \tag{11}$$

based on the $\text{LWE}_{\ell,q,D_{\mathbb{Z},\gamma},m}$-assumption, and determine the security loss factor. Here $\mathbf{A} \leftarrow_\$ \mathbb{Z}_q^{n\times m}$, $\mathbf{S} \leftarrow_\$ \mathbb{Z}_q^{Q\times n}$, $\mathbf{E} \leftarrow_\$ D_{\sigma_0}^{Q\times m}$ and $\mathbf{U} \leftarrow_\$ \mathbb{Z}_q^{Q\times m}$.

In the first step, we break $\mathbf{A} \in \mathbb{Z}_q^{n\times m}$ into $(\mathbf{A}_1|\bar{\mathbf{A}}_1) \in \mathbb{Z}_q^{n\times m'} \times \mathbb{Z}_q^{n\times(m-m')}$ and $\mathbf{E} \in D_{\sigma_0}^{Q\times m}$ into $(\mathbf{E}_1|\bar{\mathbf{E}}_1) \in D_{\sigma_0}^{Q\times m'} \times D_{\sigma_0}^{Q\times(m-m')}$, where the block $\mathbf{A}_1$ contains the first m' columns of $\mathbf{A}$. Then we change $\bar{\mathbf{A}}_1$ into a lossy one $\tilde{\mathbf{A}}_1 = \mathbf{CB} + \mathbf{F}$, where $\mathbf{C} \leftarrow_\$ \mathbb{Z}_q^{n\times\ell}, \mathbf{B} \leftarrow_\$ \mathbb{Z}_q^{\ell\times(m-m')}$ and $\mathbf{F} \in \mathbb{Z}_q^{n\times(m-m')}$ follows the error distribution $D_{\mathbb{Z},\gamma}^{n\times(m-m')}$. This change is indistinguishable due to the n-secret $\text{LWE}_{\ell,q,D_{\mathbb{Z},\gamma},m-m'}$-assumption. Therefore,

$$(\mathbf{A}, \mathbf{SA} + \mathbf{E}) = ((\mathbf{A}_1|\bar{\mathbf{A}}_1), (\mathbf{SA}_1 + \mathbf{E}_1)|\mathbf{S}\bar{\mathbf{A}}_1 + \bar{\mathbf{E}}_1) \overset{c}{\approx} ((\mathbf{A}_1|\tilde{\mathbf{A}}_1), (\mathbf{SA}_1 + \mathbf{E}_1|\mathbf{S}\tilde{\mathbf{A}}_1 + \bar{\mathbf{E}}_1))$$

but it incurs a loss factor of n since hybrid arguments yield $\text{Adv}_{[\ell,q,D_{\mathbb{Z},\gamma},m-m']}^{n\text{-LWE}}(\lambda) \leq n \cdot \text{Adv}_{[\ell,q,D_{\mathbb{Z},\gamma},m-m']}^{\text{LWE}}(\lambda) \leq n \cdot \text{Adv}_{[\ell,q,D_{\mathbb{Z},\gamma},m]}^{\text{LWE}}(\lambda)$. Now given a lossy $\tilde{\mathbf{A}}_1$, the information of $\mathbf{S}$ leaked by $\mathbf{S}\tilde{\mathbf{A}}_1$ is bounded. By taking $\mathbf{A}_1$ as extractor, we can extract the remaining entropy of $\mathbf{S}$, and result in $\mathbf{SA}_1 \overset{s}{\approx} \mathbf{U}_1$, where $\mathbf{U}_1 \leftarrow_\$ \mathbb{Z}_q^{Q\times m'}$. So we have

$$((\mathbf{A}_1|\tilde{\mathbf{A}}_1), (\mathbf{SA}_1 + \mathbf{E}_1|\mathbf{S}\tilde{\mathbf{A}}_1 + \bar{\mathbf{E}}_1)) \overset{s}{\approx} ((\mathbf{A}_1|\tilde{\mathbf{A}}_1), (\mathbf{U}_1 + \mathbf{E}_1|\mathbf{S}\tilde{\mathbf{A}}_1 + \bar{\mathbf{E}}_1)).$$

Next, we change the lossy $\tilde{\mathbf{A}}_1$ back to uniform $\bar{\mathbf{A}}_1$, and have

$$((\mathbf{A}_1|\tilde{\mathbf{A}}_1), (\mathbf{U}_1 + \mathbf{E}_1|\mathbf{S}\tilde{\mathbf{A}}_1 + \bar{\mathbf{E}}_1)) \overset{c}{\approx} ((\mathbf{A}_1|\bar{\mathbf{A}}_1), (\mathbf{U}_1 + \mathbf{E}_1|\mathbf{S}\bar{\mathbf{A}}_1 + \bar{\mathbf{E}}_1)).$$

Then we have loss factor n again.

In the second step, we break $\mathbf{A} = (\mathbf{A}_1|\bar{\mathbf{A}}_1)$ further into $(\mathbf{A}_1|\mathbf{A}_2|\bar{\mathbf{A}}_2) \in \mathbb{Z}_q^{n \times m'} \times \mathbb{Z}_q^{n \times m'} \times \mathbb{Z}_q^{n \times (m - 2m')}$ and $\mathbf{E} = (\mathbf{E}_1|\bar{\mathbf{E}}_1)$ into $(\mathbf{E}_1|\mathbf{E}_2|\bar{\mathbf{E}}_2) \in D_{\sigma_0}^{Q \times m'} \times D_{\sigma_0}^{Q \times m'} \times D_{\sigma_0}^{Q \times (m - 2m')}$, where the block $\mathbf{A}_2$ contains the second m' columns of $\mathbf{A}$. Then we change $\bar{\mathbf{A}}_2$ to a lossy one $\tilde{\mathbf{A}}_2$ and have

$$((\mathbf{A}_1|\bar{\mathbf{A}}_1),(\mathbf{U}_1 + \mathbf{E}_1|\mathbf{S}\bar{\mathbf{A}}_1 + \bar{\mathbf{E}}_1)) = ((\mathbf{A}_1|\mathbf{A}_2|\bar{\mathbf{A}}_2),(\mathbf{U}_1 + \mathbf{E}_1|\mathbf{S}\mathbf{A}_2 + \mathbf{E}_2|\mathbf{S}\bar{\mathbf{A}}_2 + \bar{\mathbf{E}}_2))$$
$$\overset{c}{\approx} ((\mathbf{A}_1|\mathbf{A}_2|\tilde{\mathbf{A}}_2),(\mathbf{U}_1 + \mathbf{E}_1|\mathbf{S}\mathbf{A}_2 + \mathbf{E}_2|\mathbf{S}\tilde{\mathbf{A}}_2 + \bar{\mathbf{E}}_2))$$

with a lossy factor n. With a similar argument, the uniform $\mathbf{A}_2$ can extract the remaining entropy of $\mathbf{S}$ so that $\mathbf{S}\mathbf{A}_2 \overset{s}{\approx} \mathbf{U}_2$, where $\mathbf{U}_2 \leftarrow_\$ \mathbb{Z}_q^{Q \times m'}$. So

$$((\mathbf{A}_1|\mathbf{A}_2|\tilde{\mathbf{A}}_2),(\mathbf{U}_1 + \mathbf{E}_1|\mathbf{S}\mathbf{A}_2 + \mathbf{E}_2|\mathbf{S}\tilde{\mathbf{A}}_2 + \bar{\mathbf{E}}_2)) \overset{s}{\approx} ((\mathbf{A}_1|\mathbf{A}_2|\tilde{\mathbf{A}}_2),(\mathbf{U}_1 + \mathbf{E}_1|\mathbf{U}_2 + \mathbf{E}_2|\mathbf{S}\tilde{\mathbf{A}}_2 + \bar{\mathbf{E}}_2)).$$

Changing lossy $\tilde{\mathbf{A}}_2$ back to uniform $\bar{\mathbf{A}}_2$ yields

$$((\mathbf{A}_1|\mathbf{A}_2|\tilde{\mathbf{A}}_2),(\mathbf{U}_1 + \mathbf{E}_1|\mathbf{U}_2 + \mathbf{E}_2|\mathbf{S}\tilde{\mathbf{A}}_2 + \bar{\mathbf{E}}_2)) \overset{c}{\approx} ((\mathbf{A}_1|\mathbf{A}_2|\bar{\mathbf{A}}_2),(\mathbf{U}_1 + \mathbf{E}_1|\mathbf{U}_2 + \mathbf{E}_2|\mathbf{S}\bar{\mathbf{A}}_2 + \bar{\mathbf{E}}_2))$$

with a price of another loss factor n.

Overall, with at most $c \approx \frac{m}{m'}$ steps, we can prove (11) with a loss factor of $2cn$. It should be noted that we analyze the entropy of $\mathbf{S}$ with the so-called "lossiness approach" in [14], which results in more flexible parameters. This finishes the proof sketch of (10), and we refer to the full version [26] for the formal proof.

Finally, taking (9) and (10) together, Theorem 3 holds. $\square$

Some Useful Setting of Parameters. Our reduction holds for a wide range of parameters. Here we describe two settings of parameters in Table 3, both of which satisfy the constrains in the statements of Theorem 3.

Table 3. Parameter setting for Theorem 3, where C denotes the global constant in Lemma 7.

Parameters	n	m	ℓ	q	c	σ_1	γ	σ_0	r	σ
Setting I	36λ	72λ	λ	λ^6	40	$\sqrt{\lambda}$	$12\sqrt{\lambda}$	$102C\lambda^{1.5}$	$\sqrt{205}C\lambda^{1.5}$	$103C\lambda^{1.5}$
Setting II	4λ	λ^2	λ	$2^{2\sqrt{\lambda}}$	2λ	$2^{\sqrt{\lambda}}$	λ	$\frac{\sqrt{2}}{2}\lambda^{2.5}2^{\sqrt{\lambda}}$	$\frac{\sqrt{2}}{2}\lambda^{2.5}2^{\sqrt{\lambda}}$	$\lambda^{2.5}2^{\sqrt{\lambda}}$

Setting I in Table 3 allows a constant factor c, resulting in a loss factor as small as $O(\lambda)$. In many applications, more constrains of parameter setting are considered. For example, the number of LWE samples m should be set as $O(n \log q)$ when applying the leftover hash lemma (i.e., Lemma 2), and the modulus q should be set as $2^{\omega(\log \lambda)}$ when we use smudging lemma (i.e., Lemma 6). Setting II in Table 3 also takes these additional constrains into account. In this setting, the factor c can be set as $O(\lambda)$, resulting in a loss factor of $O(\lambda^2)$.

Remark 1 (Comparison with the almost tight reduction in [2]). If we use techniques in [2], we can also obtain an almost tight reduction from LWE to multi-secret LWE. However, the loss factor would be $O(mn)$, as shown in the technical overview in Sect. 1 of our paper.

In contrast, our reduction in the proof of Theorem 3 is fine-grained and tighter, where the loss factor is $O(cn)$ with $c \leq m$. In fact, due to the flexible setting of σ_1, we can always set $\log(\sigma_1) = O(\log q)$. Then the parameter c can be set as small as $O(\frac{m}{n})$ to satisfy the constrain $n \geq O((\frac{m}{c}\log q + \ell \log q)/\log(\sigma_1))$. Consequently, the loss factor of our reduction can be as small as $O(cn) = O(m)$, saving a factor at least $O(n)$ compared with [2]'s reduction loss factor.

For example, in Setting I and Setting II in Table 3, their loss factor should be $O(\lambda^2)$ and $O(\lambda^3)$ respectively, while ours are $O(\lambda)$ and $O(\lambda^2)$ respectively.

6 Instantiation from LWE

In this section, we instantiate our generic SIG and PKE constructions proposed in Sect. 4 from the LWE assumptions. More precisely, we will show how to instantiate the underlying building blocks, including gap language distributions in Subsect. 6.1, probabilistic QA-HPS in Subsect. 6.2, dual-mode gap commitment in Subsect. 6.3 and compatible tag-based QA-NIZK in Subsect. 6.4.

For simplicity, all instantiations in this section take LWE-related public parameters $\mathsf{pp_{LWE}} = (n, m, \ell, q, \sigma, \gamma, \chi, B, \tilde{B}, B', \tilde{B}', \zeta, \zeta')$ as *implicit input*, where $n, m, \ell, q, \sigma, \gamma$ are parameters satisfying the constrains in Theorem 3, χ is the discrete Gaussian distribution $D_{\mathbb{Z},\sigma}$ as described in Theorem 3, $B, \tilde{B}, B', \tilde{B}' \in \mathbb{N}$ are error bounds such that χ is B-bounded, and ζ, ζ' are parameters for Gaussians. (Some instantiations use only part of $\mathsf{pp_{LWE}}$.) According to Lemma 5 (the tail bound), $\chi = D_{\mathbb{Z},\sigma}$ is $\sqrt{\lambda} \cdot \sigma$-bounded, except with exponentially small probability $2^{-\lambda}$,[5] so we can set $B = \sqrt{\lambda} \cdot \sigma$. The requirements for these parameters will be stated in the following theorems, and the concrete choices satisfying all requirements will be suggested in Table 4 in Subsect. 6.5.

6.1 Gap Language Distributions from LWE

Let $\mathsf{pp_{LWE}} = (n, m, \ell, q, \sigma, \gamma, \chi, B, \tilde{B}, \cdots)$ be the LWE-related public parameters that serve as implicit input to all algorithms and satisfy $B < \tilde{B} < q/(10m)$ and χ a B-bounded distribution. Our LWE-based gap language distribution $\mathscr{L}$ samples a language parameter ρ and its trapdoor td_ρ as follows.

- $\mathscr{L}$ invokes $(\mathbf{A}, \mathbf{T_A}) \leftarrow_\$ \mathsf{TrapGen}(n, q, m)$ (cf. Lemma 3) and outputs $(\rho := \mathbf{A} \in \mathbb{Z}_q^{n \times m}, td_\rho := \mathbf{T_A} \in \mathbb{Z}_q^{m \times m})$.

---

[5] We will not mention this exponentially small probability hereafter for simplicity, and take for granted that χ is B-bounded.

According to Lemma 3, $\mathbf{A}$ is almost uniform over $\mathbb{Z}_q^{n \times m}$ and $\|\mathbf{T_A}\|_\infty = O(\sqrt{n \log q})$. The language parameter $\rho = \mathbf{A}$ determines a gap language $\mathcal{GL}_\mathbf{A} = (\mathcal{L}_\mathbf{A}, \widetilde{\mathcal{L}}_\mathbf{A})$, where $\mathcal{L}_\mathbf{A}$ and $\widetilde{\mathcal{L}}_\mathbf{A}$ define "nearly" linear subspaces as follows[6]

$$\mathcal{L}_\mathbf{A} := \left\{ \mathbf{c} \in \mathbb{Z}_q^m \,\middle|\, \exists\, \mathbf{s} \in \mathbb{Z}_q^n \setminus \{\mathbf{0}\}, \mathbf{e} \in [-B, B]^m, \text{ s.t. } \mathbf{c}^\top = \mathbf{s}^\top \cdot \mathbf{A} + \mathbf{e}^\top \right\},$$

$$\widetilde{\mathcal{L}}_\mathbf{A} := \left\{ \mathbf{c} \in \mathbb{Z}_q^m \,\middle|\, \exists\, \mathbf{s} \in \mathbb{Z}_q^n \setminus \{\mathbf{0}\}, \mathbf{e} \in [-\tilde{B}, \tilde{B}]^m, \text{ s.t. } \mathbf{c}^\top = \mathbf{s}^\top \cdot \mathbf{A} + \mathbf{e}^\top \right\}.$$

Clearly, $\mathcal{L}_\mathbf{A} \subseteq \widetilde{\mathcal{L}}_\mathbf{A}$ and both of them are contained in the universal set $\mathcal{X} := \mathbb{Z}_q^m$. The associated algorithms $(\mathsf{Sample}_\mathcal{L}, \mathsf{Sample}_\mathcal{X}, \mathsf{Check}_{\widetilde{\mathcal{L}}})$ are defined as follows.

- $(\mathbf{c}, w_\mathbf{c}) \leftarrow_\$ \mathsf{Sample}_\mathcal{L}(\rho = \mathbf{A})$: It chooses $\mathbf{s} \leftarrow_\$ \mathbb{Z}_q^n$, $\mathbf{e} \leftarrow_\$ \chi^m$, computes $\mathbf{c}^\top = \mathbf{s}^\top \cdot \mathbf{A} + \mathbf{e}^\top$, and returns the instance $\mathbf{c}$ with its witness $w_\mathbf{c} := (\mathbf{s}, \mathbf{e})$.
- $\mathbf{c} \leftarrow_\$ \mathsf{Sample}_\mathcal{X}$: It outputs a uniformly chosen $\mathbf{c} \leftarrow_\$ \mathbb{Z}_q^m$.
- $0/1 \leftarrow \mathsf{Check}_{\widetilde{\mathcal{L}}}(\rho = \mathbf{A}, td_\rho = \mathbf{T_A}, \mathbf{c})$: It invokes $(\mathbf{s}, \mathbf{e}) \leftarrow \mathsf{Invert}(\mathbf{T_A}, \mathbf{c})$ (cf. Lemma 4), and outputs 1 if $\mathbf{e} \in [-\tilde{B}, \tilde{B}]^m$ and 0 otherwise.

Given that $\mathbf{e} \in [-\tilde{B}, \tilde{B}]^m$ and $\tilde{B} < q/(10m)$, we have $\|\mathbf{e}\| \le \sqrt{m}\tilde{B} \le q/(10\sqrt{m})$. Then according to Lemma 4, $\mathsf{Check}_{\widetilde{\mathcal{L}}}(\rho, td_\rho, \mathbf{c})$ outputs 1 iff $\mathbf{c} \in \widetilde{\mathcal{L}}_\mathbf{A}$.

The subset membership problem (SMP) for $\mathscr{L}$ is exactly the $\mathsf{LWE}_{n,q,\chi,m}$ problem, and the multi-fold SMP is just the multi-secret $\mathsf{LWE}_{n,q,\chi,m}$ problem. Since we set $\chi = D_{\mathbb{Z},\sigma}$, by the almost tight reduction from LWE to multi-secret LWE in Sect. 5, i.e., Theorem 3, we have the following lemma.

Lemma 9 ($\mathsf{LWE}_{\ell,q,D_{\mathbb{Z},\gamma},m} \Rightarrow$ Multi-fold SMP for $\mathscr{L}$). *Let $\chi = D_{\mathbb{Z},\sigma}$ in $\mathsf{Sample}_\mathcal{L}$. For any adversary $\mathcal{A}$, there exists an adversary $\mathcal{B}$ such that $\mathbf{T}(\mathcal{B}) \approx \mathbf{T}(\mathcal{A}) + Q \cdot \mathsf{poly}(\lambda)$ with $\mathsf{poly}(\lambda)$ independent of $\mathbf{T}(\mathcal{A})$, and $\mathsf{Adv}_{\mathscr{L},\mathcal{A},Q}^{\mathsf{msmp}}(\lambda) \le 2cn \cdot \mathsf{Adv}_{[\ell,q,D_{\mathbb{Z},\gamma},m],\mathcal{B}}^{\mathsf{LWE}}(\lambda) + \frac{Q(m+c+1)}{2^\lambda}$, where $\chi = D_{\mathbb{Z},\sigma}$ and $D_{\mathbb{Z},\gamma}$ are the discrete Gaussian distributions as described in Theorem 3, and c is an integer satisfying (8).*

6.2   Probabilistic QA-HPS from LWE

In this subsection, we instantiate probabilistic QA-HPS from the LWE assumption. Let $\mathsf{pp}_{\mathsf{LWE}} = (n, m, \ell, q, \sigma, \gamma, \chi, B, \tilde{B}, B', \cdots)$ be the LWE-related public parameters that serve as implicit input to all algorithms. Let both $\mathscr{L}$ and $\mathscr{L}_0$ be the gap language distribution specified in Subsect. 6.1. Here we use two distributions $\mathscr{L}$ and $\mathscr{L}_0$ to indicate the independence of them. We present our LWE-based scheme $\mathsf{prQAHPS}_{\mathsf{LWE}} = (\mathsf{Setup}_{\mathsf{HPS}}, \alpha_{(\cdot)}, \mathsf{prPub}, \mathsf{prPriv})$ for $\mathscr{L}$ in Fig. 3. The hash value space $\mathcal{HV} = \mathbb{Z}_q$ is a metric space with metric $\mathsf{dist}(hv, hv') := |hv - hv'|$ for $hv, hv' \in \mathbb{Z}_q$. Then $\mathsf{Ball}_\varepsilon(hv) := \{hv' \in \mathbb{Z}_q \mid |hv - hv'| \le \varepsilon\}$.

---

[6] For technical reasons (concretely, for the $\varepsilon_{\mathsf{ext}}$-$\langle \mathscr{L}_0, \mathscr{L} \rangle$-OT-extracting property of the pr-QA-HPS scheme constructed later), the vector $\mathbf{0}$ must be excluded from the set $\mathbb{Z}_q^n$ that $\mathbf{s}$ is chosen from. For simplicity, we forgo making this explicit in the sequel.

Firstly we prove that $\mathsf{prQAHPS}_{\mathsf{LWE}}$ is a pr-QA-HPS scheme in Theorem 4.

$\mathsf{pp}_{\mathsf{HPS}} \leftarrow_s \mathsf{Setup}_{\mathsf{HPS}}$: Return $\mathsf{pp}_{\mathsf{HPS}} := \mathsf{pp}_{\mathsf{LWE}}$, which implicitly defines $\quad (\mathcal{SK} := \{0,1\}^m,\ \mathcal{HV} := \mathbb{Z}_q,\ \Lambda_{(\cdot)})$, where $\Lambda_{sk}(\mathbf{c}) := \mathbf{c}^\top \cdot \mathbf{k} \in \mathbb{Z}_q$ $\quad$ for $sk = \mathbf{k} \in \mathcal{SK}$ and $\mathbf{c} \in \mathcal{X} = \mathbb{Z}_q^m$.	$hv \leftarrow_s \mathsf{prPub}(pk_\rho, \mathbf{c}, w_{\mathbf{c}} = (\mathbf{s}, \mathbf{e}))$, where $\mathbf{c} \in \tilde{\mathcal{L}}_\rho$ for $\rho = \mathbf{A}$: $\ \ /\!/ \mathbf{c}^\top = \mathbf{s}^\top \cdot \mathbf{A} + \mathbf{e}^\top$ Parse $pk_\rho = \mathbf{p} \in \mathbb{Z}_q^n$. $e' \leftarrow_s [-B', B']$. Return $hv := \mathbf{s}^\top \cdot \mathbf{p} + e' \in \mathbb{Z}_q$.
$pk_\rho \leftarrow \alpha_\rho(sk)$, where $\rho = \mathbf{A} \in \mathbb{Z}_q^{n \times m}$: Parse $sk = \mathbf{k} \in \{0,1\}^m$. $\mathbf{p} := \mathbf{A} \cdot \mathbf{k} \in \mathbb{Z}_q^n$. Return $pk_\rho := \mathbf{p}$.	$hv \leftarrow_s \mathsf{prPriv}(sk, \mathbf{c} \in \mathcal{X})$: Parse $sk = \mathbf{k} \in \{0,1\}^m$. $e' \leftarrow_s [-B', B']$. Return $hv := \mathbf{c}^\top \cdot \mathbf{k} + e' \in \mathbb{Z}_q$.

Fig. 3. The probabilistic QA-HPS scheme $\mathsf{prQAHPS}_{\mathsf{LWE}}$ from LWE.

Theorem 4. *The* $\mathsf{prQAHPS}_{\mathsf{LWE}}$ *proposed in Fig. 3 is a pr-QA-HPS scheme that has* $(\varepsilon_{\mathsf{prPub}}, \varepsilon_{\mathsf{prPriv}})$*-approximate correctness and* $\varepsilon_{\mathsf{evalnd}}$*-evaluation indistinguishability with* $\varepsilon_{\mathsf{prPub}} = B' + mB$, $\varepsilon_{\mathsf{prPriv}} = B'$ *and* $\varepsilon_{\mathsf{evalnd}} = m\tilde{B}/B'$.

See the technical overview in Sect. 1 for a proof sketch of Theorem 4. Due to space limitations, we postpone the proof to the full version [26].

Through the following theorems, we show the $\langle \mathcal{L}, \mathcal{L}_0 \rangle$-key-switching, PK-diversity and $\mathcal{L}_0$-multi-key-multi-extracting of $\mathsf{prQAHPS}_{\mathsf{LWE}}$, as needed for the MUMC^{c}-CCA security of our PKE in Subsect. 4.2 (cf. Theorem 2), then show the $\varepsilon_{\mathsf{ext}}$-$\langle \mathcal{L}_0, \mathcal{L} \rangle$-OT-extracting of $\mathsf{prQAHPS}_{\mathsf{LWE}}$, where $\varepsilon_{\mathsf{ext}} \geq \varepsilon_{\mathsf{prPriv}}$, as needed for the strong MU^{c}-CMA security of our SIG in Subsect. 4.1 (cf. Theorem 1).

Due to space limitations, we postpone the proofs of these theorems to the full version [26]. The high-level ideas behind the proofs are implicitly contained in the security proof sketches for our SIG and PKE schemes using LWE-based pr-QA-HPS as a building block in Sect. 1.

Theorem 5 ($\langle \mathcal{L}, \mathcal{L}_0 \rangle$**-Key-Switching of** $\mathsf{prQAHPS}_{\mathsf{LWE}}$**).** *Let* $m > 3n \log q + 2(\lambda + 1)$. *The proposed* $\mathsf{prQAHPS}_{\mathsf{LWE}}$ *in Fig. 3 supports* $\langle \mathcal{L}, \mathcal{L}_0 \rangle$*-key-switching with* $\epsilon_{\mathsf{prQAHPS}, \mathcal{A}}^{\langle \mathcal{L}, \mathcal{L}_0 \rangle\text{-}ks} \leq 2^{-\lambda}$ *for any (possibly unbounded) adversary* $\mathcal{A}$.

Theorem 6 (PK-Diversity of $\mathsf{prQAHPS}_{\mathsf{LWE}}$**).** *The proposed* $\mathsf{prQAHPS}_{\mathsf{LWE}}$ *in Fig. 3 has PK-diversity with* $\epsilon_{\mathsf{prQAHPS}}^{\mathsf{pk\text{-}div}} = 2^{-m} + q^{-n}$.

Theorem 7 (Almost Tight $\mathcal{L}_0$**-Multi-Key-Multi-Extracting of** $\mathsf{prQAHPS}_{\mathsf{LWE}}$**).** *Let* $m > 2n \log q + 2\lambda$. *If the* $\mathsf{LWE}_{\ell, q, D_{\mathbb{Z}, \gamma}, m}$ *assumptions hold, then the proposed* $\mathsf{prQAHPS}_{\mathsf{LWE}}$ *in Fig. 3 supports* $\mathcal{L}_0$*-multi-key-multi-extracting. Concretely, for any adversary* $\mathcal{A}$, *any* N *and any* Q, *there exist adversaries* $\mathcal{B}_1$ *and* $\mathcal{B}_2$, *such that* $\mathbf{T}(\mathcal{B}_1) \approx \mathbf{T}(\mathcal{B}_2) \approx \mathbf{T}(\mathcal{A}) + NQ \cdot \mathsf{poly}(\lambda)$ *with* $\mathsf{poly}(\lambda)$ *independent of* $\mathbf{T}(\mathcal{A})$, *and* $\mathsf{Adv}_{\mathsf{prQAHPS}, \mathcal{A}, N, Q}^{\mathcal{L}_0\text{-}mk\text{-}mext}(\lambda) \leq 2cn \cdot \mathsf{Adv}_{[\ell, q, D_{\mathbb{Z}, \gamma}, m], \mathcal{B}_1}^{\mathsf{LWE}}(\lambda) + 2cn \cdot \mathsf{Adv}_{[\ell, q, D_{\mathbb{Z}, \gamma}, m], \mathcal{B}_2}^{\mathsf{LWE}}(\lambda) + \frac{2NQ(m+c+2)+N}{2^\lambda} + NQ \cdot (m+1)B/B'$, *where* c *is an integer satisfying (8).*

Theorem 8 ($\varepsilon_{\mathsf{ext}}$-$\langle \mathscr{L}_0, \mathscr{L} \rangle$-**OT-Extracting of** $\mathsf{prQAHPS_{LWE}}$). *Let* $\varepsilon_{\mathsf{ext}} \geq \varepsilon_{\mathsf{prPriv}}$, $m > 3n \log q + 2\lambda$ *and* q *be a prime. The proposed* $\mathsf{prQAHPS_{LWE}}$ *in Fig. 3 supports* $\varepsilon_{\mathsf{ext}}$-$\langle \mathscr{L}_0, \mathscr{L} \rangle$-*OT-extracting with* $\epsilon_{\mathsf{prQAHPS},\mathcal{A}}^{\varepsilon_{\mathsf{ext}}-\langle \mathscr{L}_0, \mathscr{L} \rangle\text{-otext}} \leq 2^{-\lambda} + m\tilde{B}/B' + (2\varepsilon_{\mathsf{ext}} + 2B' + 1)/q$ *for any (possibly unbounded) adversary* $\mathcal{A}$.

6.3 Commitment Scheme from LWE

Let $\mathsf{pp_{LWE}} = (n, m, \ell, q, \sigma, \gamma, \chi, B, \tilde{B}, \cdots)$ be the LWE-related public parameters that serve as implicit input to all algorithms. We present our LWE-based dual-mode gap commitment scheme $\mathsf{CMT_{LWE}} = (\mathsf{BSetup}, \mathsf{HSetup}, \mathsf{Com})$ in Fig. 4, with two message spaces $\mathcal{M} = \{0,1\}^m \subseteq \widetilde{\mathcal{M}} = [-\tilde{B}, \tilde{B}]^m$ and two randomness spaces $\mathcal{R} = \{0,1\}^{m \times m} \subseteq \widetilde{\mathcal{R}} = [-\tilde{B}, \tilde{B}]^{m \times m}$. The scheme uses a modulus q^2.

$\mathsf{pp_{CMT}} \leftarrow_\$ \mathsf{BSetup}$: //Binding mode	$\mathsf{pp_{CMT}} \leftarrow_\$ \mathsf{HSetup}$: //Hiding mode
$\overline{\mathbf{X}} \leftarrow_\$ \mathbb{Z}_{q^2}^{n \times m}$.	$\mathbf{X} \leftarrow_\$ \mathbb{Z}_{q^2}^{(n+1) \times m}$.
$\mathbf{s} \leftarrow_\$ \mathbb{Z}_{q^2}^n,\ \mathbf{e} \leftarrow_\$ \chi^m$.	Return $\mathsf{pp_{CMT}} := \mathbf{X}$.
$\mathbf{b}^\top := \mathbf{s}^\top \overline{\mathbf{X}} + \mathbf{e}^\top \bmod q^2$.	$\mathsf{com} \leftarrow \mathsf{Com}(\mathsf{pp_{CMT}} = \mathbf{X}, \mathbf{m}; \mathbf{R})$: //$\mathbf{m} \in [-\tilde{B}, \tilde{B}]^m$, $\mathbf{R} \in [-\tilde{B}, \tilde{B}]^{m \times m}$
$\mathbf{X} := \left(\frac{\overline{\mathbf{X}}}{\mathbf{b}^\top} \right) \in \mathbb{Z}_{q^2}^{(n+1) \times m}$.	$\mathsf{com} := \mathbf{X} \cdot \mathbf{R} + \left(\begin{smallmatrix} \mathbf{0} \\ q \cdot \mathbf{m}^\top \end{smallmatrix} \right) \in \mathbb{Z}_{q^2}^{(n+1) \times m}$. //Here $\mathbf{0}$ is an $n \times m$ zero matrix
Return $\mathsf{pp_{CMT}} := \mathbf{X}$.	Return com.

Fig. 4. The dual-mode gap commitment scheme $\mathsf{CMT_{LWE}}$ from LWE.

This commitment scheme is essentially adapted from the Regev's PKE scheme [42]. Here, the public parameter in the binding mode is just the public key of Regev's scheme, while the committing algorithm is just Regev encryption algorithm. The decryption correctness of Regev's PKE guarantees the property of statistical binding. According to the LWE assumption, the public key of Regev's scheme is computationally indistinguishable from a uniform matrix, which serves as the public parameter in the hiding mode. The statistical hiding property in the hiding mode relies on the fact that a uniform matrix is a good extractor (cf. Lemma 2). Formally, we have the following theorem with proof appeared in the full version [26].

Theorem 9. *Let* $q > 2mB\tilde{B}$ *and* $m > 4(n+1) \log q + 2(\lambda+1)$. *If the* $\mathsf{LWE}_{n,q^2,\chi,m}$ *assumption holds, then the proposed* $\mathsf{CMT_{LWE}}$ *in Fig. 4 is a dual-mode gap commitment scheme that has* $\varepsilon_{\mathsf{binding}}$-*statistical binding and* $\varepsilon_{\mathsf{hiding}}$-*statistical hiding with* $\varepsilon_{\mathsf{binding}} = 0$ *and* $\varepsilon_{\mathsf{hiding}} = m \cdot 2^{-\lambda}$. *Moreover, for any adversary* $\mathcal{A}$, *there exists an adversary* $\mathcal{B}$ *s.t.* $\mathbf{T}(\mathcal{B}) \approx \mathbf{T}(\mathcal{A})$ *and* $\mathsf{Adv}_{\mathsf{CMT},\mathcal{A}}^{\mathsf{para\text{-}ind}}(\lambda) \leq \mathsf{Adv}_{[n,q^2,\chi,m],\mathcal{B}}^{\mathsf{LWE}}(\lambda)$.

6.4 QA-NIZK from LWE

In this subsection, we instantiate tag-based QA-NIZK for gap language based on the LWE assumptions. We will follow the generic transformation proposed by Libert et al. in [32, Subsect. 4.2] that compiles any trapdoor Σ-protocol for gap language into tag-based QA-NIZK for the same gap language, and moreover, the transformation is tightness-preserving, i.e., the resulting tag-based QA-NIZK has tight zero-knowledge and tight USS as long as the building blocks are tightly secure. The formal definitions of the building blocks including trapdoor Σ-protocol are provided in the full version [26] due to space limitations. Therefore, all we need to do is to instantiate trapdoor Σ-protocol for gap language from LWE.

The Gap Language for QA-NIZK. Note that the gap languages needed in our generic SIG and PKE constructions are different. More precisely, for the SIG construction in Subsect. 4.1, the gap language is the $\mathcal{GL}_{\rho'}^{(\mathsf{QANIZK})} = (\mathcal{L}_{\rho'}^{(\mathsf{QANIZK})}, \widetilde{\mathcal{L}}_{\rho'}^{(\mathsf{QANIZK})})$ defined in Fig. 1, which is determined by the gap language distribution $\mathscr{L}$, the pr-QA-HPS scheme prQAHPS and the commitment scheme CMT, while for the PKE construction in Subsect. 4.2, the gap language is exactly the $\mathcal{GL}_\rho = (\mathcal{L}_\rho, \widetilde{\mathcal{L}}_\rho)$ generated by $\mathscr{L}$, as defined in Subsect. 6.1.

We make the gap language $\mathcal{GL}_{\rho'}^{(\mathsf{QANIZK})} = (\mathcal{L}_{\rho'}^{(\mathsf{QANIZK})}, \widetilde{\mathcal{L}}_{\rho'}^{(\mathsf{QANIZK})})$ concrete by instantiating it with our LWE-based $\mathscr{L}$ in Subsect. 6.1, prQAHPS$_{\mathsf{LWE}}$ in Subsect. 6.2 and CMT$_{\mathsf{LWE}}$ in Subsect. 6.3. Let $\mathsf{pp}_{\mathsf{LWE}} = (n, m, \ell, q, \sigma, \gamma, \chi, B, \tilde{B}, B', \tilde{B}', \cdots)$ be the LWE-related public parameters that serve as implicit input to all algorithms, where $B < \tilde{B}$ and $B' < \tilde{B}'$. More precisely, let $\rho = \mathbf{A} \in \mathbb{Z}_q^{n \times m}$ be a language parameter output by $\mathscr{L}$, and let $\mathsf{pp}_{\mathsf{CMT}} = \mathbf{X} \in \mathbb{Z}_{q^2}^{(n+1) \times m}$ be a parameter generated by BSetup. Then according to Fig. 1, we have $\rho' = (\mathbf{A}, \mathbf{X})$ and the gap language $\mathcal{GL}_{\rho'}^{(\mathsf{QANIZK})}$ is instantiated as follows:

$$\mathcal{L}_{\rho'}^{(\mathsf{QANIZK})} = \left\{ (\mathbf{c}, vk, d) \;\middle|\; \begin{array}{cc} \exists\, (\mathbf{s} \in \mathbb{Z}_q^n, \mathbf{e} \in [-B, B]^m, & \mathbf{c}^\top = \mathbf{s}^\top \cdot \mathbf{A} + \mathbf{e}^\top \\ \mathbf{R} \in \{0,1\}^{m \times m}, \mathbf{k} \in \{0,1\}^m, \text{ s.t. } & \wedge\, vk = \mathbf{X} \cdot \mathbf{R} + \binom{0}{q \cdot \mathbf{k}^\top} \\ e' \in [-B', B']) & \wedge\, d = \mathbf{c}^\top \cdot \mathbf{k} + e' \end{array} \right\}, \quad (12)$$

$$\widetilde{\mathcal{L}}_{\rho'}^{(\mathsf{QANIZK})} = \left\{ (\mathbf{c}, vk, d) \;\middle|\; \begin{array}{cc} \exists\, (\mathbf{s} \in \mathbb{Z}_q^n, \mathbf{e} \in [-\tilde{B}, \tilde{B}]^m, & \mathbf{c}^\top = \mathbf{s}^\top \cdot \mathbf{A} + \mathbf{e}^\top \\ \mathbf{R} \in [-\tilde{B}, \tilde{B}]^{m \times m}, \mathbf{k} \in [-\tilde{B}, \tilde{B}]^m, \text{ s.t. } & \wedge\, vk = \mathbf{X} \cdot \mathbf{R} + \binom{0}{q \cdot \mathbf{k}^\top} \\ e' \in [-\tilde{B}', \tilde{B}']) & \wedge\, d = \mathbf{c}^\top \cdot \mathbf{k} + e' \end{array} \right\}. \quad (13)$$

The Trapdoor Σ-protocol from LWE. Observe that no matter the gap language $\mathcal{GL}_{\rho'}^{(\mathsf{QANIZK})} = (\mathcal{L}_{\rho'}^{(\mathsf{QANIZK})}, \widetilde{\mathcal{L}}_{\rho'}^{(\mathsf{QANIZK})})$ defined in (12) and (13) or the gap language $\mathcal{GL}_\rho = (\mathcal{L}_\rho, \widetilde{\mathcal{L}}_\rho)$ defined in Subsect. 6.1, both of them are defined with linear equations, i.e., the instance is linear in the witness, and parts of the witness are bounded. To build trapdoor Σ-protocol for these gap languages, we are inspired by the trapdoor Σ-protocol for ACPS ciphertexts [4] with tight security constructed by Libert et al. in [32, Sect. 5], where the gap languages defined by ACPS ciphertexts enjoy similar properties described as above.

Roughly speaking, our trapdoor Σ-protocol for $\mathcal{GL}_{\rho'}^{(\mathsf{QANIZK})}$ works as follows. To prove $(\mathbf{c}, vk, d) \in \mathcal{L}_{\rho'}^{(\mathsf{QANIZK})}$ with the help of a witness $(\mathbf{s}, \mathbf{e}, \mathbf{R}, \mathbf{k}, e')$, the prover first generates a fresh instance $(\mathbf{c}_0, vk_0, d_0)$ by sampling witness $(\mathbf{s}_0, \mathbf{e}_0, \mathbf{R}_0, \mathbf{k}_0, e'_0)$ appropriately and sends it to the verifier, then the verifier chooses a challenge $\mathsf{ch} \in \{0, 1\}$ uniformly at random. According to the linear properties, the "mixed" $(\mathbf{s}_0 + \mathsf{ch} \cdot \mathbf{s}, \mathbf{e}_0 + \mathsf{ch} \cdot \mathbf{e}, \mathbf{R}_0 + \mathsf{ch} \cdot \mathbf{R}, \mathbf{k}_0 + \mathsf{ch} \cdot \mathbf{k}, e_0' + \mathsf{ch} \cdot e')$ is also a witness for the "mixed" instance $(\mathbf{c}_0 + \mathsf{ch} \cdot \mathbf{c}, vk_0 + \mathsf{ch} \cdot vk, d_0 + \mathsf{ch} \cdot d)$ to satisfy the equations in (12) and (13). Therefore, the prover sends the "mixed" witness to the verifier, and the verifier checks the equations in (12) and (13) for the "mixed" instance and witness and also checks whether the corresponding parts of the "mixed" witness (namely $\mathbf{e}_0 + \mathsf{ch} \cdot \mathbf{e}, \mathbf{R}_0 + \mathsf{ch} \cdot \mathbf{R}, \mathbf{k}_0 + \mathsf{ch} \cdot \mathbf{k}, e_0' + \mathsf{ch} \cdot e')$ are bounded.

The trapdoor Σ-protocol for the gap language $\mathcal{GL}_\rho = (\mathcal{L}_\rho, \widetilde{\mathcal{L}}_\rho)$ is a simplified version of that for $\mathcal{GL}_{\rho'}^{(\mathsf{QANIZK})} = (\mathcal{L}_{\rho'}^{(\mathsf{QANIZK})}, \widetilde{\mathcal{L}}_{\rho'}^{(\mathsf{QANIZK})})$, since $\mathcal{GL}_\rho$ is much simpler.

Due to space limitations, we put the formal descriptions of the LWE-based trapdoor Σ-protocols and its security proof in the full version [26].

The QA-NIZK from LWE. Finally, by compiling the LWE-based trapdoor Σ-protocols via the generic transformation proposed by Libert et al. in [32, Subsect. 4.2], we are able to obtain tag-based QA-NIZK schemes for the gap language $\mathcal{GL}_{\rho'}^{(\mathsf{QANIZK})} = (\mathcal{L}_{\rho'}^{(\mathsf{QANIZK})}, \widetilde{\mathcal{L}}_{\rho'}^{(\mathsf{QANIZK})})$ and $\mathcal{GL}_\rho = (\mathcal{L}_\rho, \widetilde{\mathcal{L}}_\rho)$ from the LWE assumptions, serving as building blocks for our SIG and PKE constructions.

For completeness, in the full version [26], we first recall the generic transformation in [32, Subsect. 4.2], then describe how to compile our LWE-based trapdoor Σ-protocols into tag-based QA-NIZK schemes for gap languages. Especially, we obtain the following corollary in the full version [26].

Corollary 1 (Almost Tight Security of LWE-based QA-NIZK). *We obtain a tag-based QA-NIZK scheme for the gap language* $\mathcal{GL}_{\rho'}^{(\mathsf{QANIZK})} = (\mathcal{L}_{\rho'}^{(\mathsf{QANIZK})}, \widetilde{\mathcal{L}}_{\rho'}^{(\mathsf{QANIZK})})$ *specified by (12) and (13) and a tag-based QA-NIZK scheme for the gap language* $\mathcal{GL}_\rho = (\mathcal{L}_\rho, \widetilde{\mathcal{L}}_\rho)$ *specified in Subsect. 6.1, both of which have almost tight zero-knowledge and USS based on the LWE assumption.*

Concretely, the advantage of zero-knowledge for any (even all powerful) adversary $\mathcal{A}'$ is given by $\mathsf{Adv}_{\mathsf{QANIZK}, \mathcal{A}'}^{\mathsf{zk}}(\lambda) \leq 2^{-\Omega(\lambda)}$. *Meanwhile, the advantage of USS for any PPT adversary $\mathcal{A}$ is given by*

$$\mathsf{Adv}_{\mathsf{QANIZK}, \mathcal{A}}^{\mathsf{uss}}(\lambda) \leq \mathsf{Adv}_{[n,q,m,\beta], \mathcal{B}_1}^{\mathsf{SIS}}(\lambda) + 2\lambda^2 \cdot \mathsf{Adv}_{[\lambda,q,\chi,m], \mathcal{B}_2}^{\mathsf{LWE}}(\lambda) + 2^{-\Omega(\lambda)},$$

where PPT algorithms $\mathcal{B}_1$ and $\mathcal{B}_2$ run in about the same time as $\mathcal{A}$.

6.5 Setting the Parameters

We give a suggestion for parameters $\mathsf{pp}_{\mathsf{LWE}} = (n, m, \ell, q, \sigma, \gamma, \chi, B, \tilde{B}, B', \tilde{B}', \zeta, \zeta')$ in Table 4, so that all conditions of the theorems in the section can be met. Moreover, our parameter suggestion in Table 4 corresponds to the parameter Setting II in Table 3, thus the conditions in Theorem 3 (almost tight reduction from LWE to multi-secret LWE) are also satisfied. By instantiating our generic constructions in Sect. 4 with the LWE-based building blocks proposed in this section, we obtain LWE-based SIG and PKE schemes with almost tight strong MU^{c}-CMA and MUMC^{c}-CCA security, respectively. Under the parameters in Table 4, the security loss factor of our schemes is $O(\lambda^2)$.

Table 4. Parameter setting, where λ denotes the security parameter.

Parameters	n	m	ℓ	q	σ	γ	χ
Setting	4λ	λ^2	λ	$2^{2\sqrt{\lambda}}$	$\lambda^{2.5} \cdot 2^{\sqrt{\lambda}}$	λ	$D_{\mathbb{Z},\lambda^{2.5} \cdot 2^{\sqrt{\lambda}}}$

Parameters	B	$\tilde{B}$	B'	$\tilde{B}'$	ζ	ζ'
Setting	$\lambda^3 \cdot 2^{\sqrt{\lambda}}$	$\lambda^6 \cdot 2^{\sqrt{\lambda}}$	$2^{1.5\sqrt{\lambda}}$	$\lambda \cdot 2^{1.5\sqrt{\lambda}}$	$\lambda^{4.5} \cdot 2^{\sqrt{\lambda}}$	$\sqrt{\lambda} \cdot 2^{1.5\sqrt{\lambda}}$

Acknowledgments. We would like to thank the reviewers for their valuable comments. Shuai Han and Shengli Liu were partially supported by Guangdong Major Project of Basic and Applied Basic Research (2019B030302008), National Natural Science Foundation of China (Grant Nos. 62002223, 61925207), the National Key R&D Program of China under Grant 2022YFB2701503, Shanghai Sailing Program (20YF1421100), and Young Elite Scientists Sponsorship Program by China Association for Science and Technology (YESS20200185). Zhedong Wang was partially supported by National Natural Science Foundation of China (Grant No. 62202305), Young Elite Scientists Sponsorship Program by China Association for Science and Technology (YESS20220150) and Shanghai Pujiang Program under Grant 22PJ1407700. Dawu Gu was partially supported by the National Key R&D Program of China under Grant 2020YFA0712302.

References

1. Ajtai, M.: Generating hard instances of lattice problems (extended abstract). In: 28th ACM STOC, pp. 99–108. ACM Press (May 1996)
2. Alwen, J., Krenn, S., Pietrzak, K., Wichs, D.: Learning with rounding, revisited. In: Canetti, R., Garay, J.A. (eds.) CRYPTO 2013. LNCS, vol. 8042, pp. 57–74. Springer, Heidelberg (2013). https://doi.org/10.1007/978-3-642-40041-4_4
3. An, J.H., Dodis, Y., Rabin, T.: On the security of joint signature and encryption. In: Knudsen, L.R. (ed.) EUROCRYPT 2002. LNCS, vol. 2332, pp. 83–107. Springer, Heidelberg (2002). https://doi.org/10.1007/3-540-46035-7_6
4. Applebaum, B., Cash, D., Peikert, C., Sahai, A.: Fast cryptographic primitives and circular-secure encryption based on hard learning problems. In: Halevi, S. (ed.) CRYPTO 2009. LNCS, vol. 5677, pp. 595–618. Springer, Heidelberg (2009). https://doi.org/10.1007/978-3-642-03356-8_35
5. Asharov, G., Jain, A., López-Alt, A., Tromer, E., Vaikuntanathan, V., Wichs, D.: Multiparty computation with low communication, computation and interaction via threshold FHE. In: Pointcheval, D., Johansson, T. (eds.) EUROCRYPT 2012. LNCS, vol. 7237, pp. 483–501. Springer, Heidelberg (2012). https://doi.org/10.1007/978-3-642-29011-4_29
6. Bader, C., Hofheinz, D., Jager, T., Kiltz, E., Li, Y.: Tightly-secure authenticated key exchange. In: Dodis, Y., Nielsen, J.B. (eds.) TCC 2015. LNCS, vol. 9014, pp. 629–658. Springer, Heidelberg (2015). https://doi.org/10.1007/978-3-662-46494-6_26

7. Bader, C., Jager, T., Li, Y., Schäge, S.: On the impossibility of tight cryptographic reductions. In: Fischlin, M., Coron, J.-S. (eds.) EUROCRYPT 2016. LNCS, vol. 9666, pp. 273–304. Springer, Heidelberg (2016). https://doi.org/10.1007/978-3-662-49896-5_10

8. Badertscher, C., Banfi, F., Maurer, U.: A constructive perspective on signcryption security. In: Catalano, D., De Prisco, R. (eds.) SCN 2018. LNCS, vol. 11035, pp. 102–120. Springer, Cham (2018). https://doi.org/10.1007/978-3-319-98113-0_6

9. Bellare, M., Rogaway, P.: Entity authentication and key distribution. In: Stinson, D.R. (ed.) CRYPTO 1993. LNCS, vol. 773, pp. 232–249. Springer, Heidelberg (1994). https://doi.org/10.1007/3-540-48329-2_21

10. Bellare, M., Stepanovs, I.: Security under message-derived keys: signcryption in imessage. In: Canteaut, A., Ishai, Y. (eds.) EUROCRYPT 2020. LNCS, vol. 12107, pp. 507–537. Springer, Cham (2020). https://doi.org/10.1007/978-3-030-45727-3_17

11. Benhamouda, F., Blazy, O., Ducas, L., Quach, W.: Hash proof systems over lattices revisited. In: Abdalla, M., Dahab, R. (eds.) PKC 2018. LNCS, vol. 10770, pp. 644–674. Springer, Cham (2018). https://doi.org/10.1007/978-3-319-76581-5_22

12. Böhl, F., Hofheinz, D., Jager, T., Koch, J., Seo, J.H., Striecks, C.: Practical signatures from standard assumptions. In: Johansson, T., Nguyen, P.Q. (eds.) EUROCRYPT 2013. LNCS, vol. 7881, pp. 461–485. Springer, Heidelberg (2013). https://doi.org/10.1007/978-3-642-38348-9_28

13. Boyen, X.: Lattice mixing and vanishing trapdoors: a framework for fully secure short signatures and more. In: Nguyen, P.Q., Pointcheval, D. (eds.) PKC 2010. LNCS, vol. 6056, pp. 499–517. Springer, Heidelberg (2010). https://doi.org/10.1007/978-3-642-13013-7_29

14. Brakerski, Z., Döttling, N.: Hardness of LWE on general entropic distributions. In: Canteaut, A., Ishai, Y. (eds.) EUROCRYPT 2020. LNCS, vol. 12106, pp. 551–575. Springer, Cham (2020). https://doi.org/10.1007/978-3-030-45724-2_19

15. Canetti, R., et al.: Fiat-Shamir: from practice to theory. In: Charikar, M., Cohen, E. (eds.) 51st ACM STOC, pp. 1082–1090. ACM Press (Jun 2019)

16. Canetti, R., Krawczyk, H.: Analysis of key-exchange protocols and their use for building secure channels. In: Pfitzmann, B. (ed.) EUROCRYPT 2001. LNCS, vol. 2045, pp. 453–474. Springer, Heidelberg (2001). https://doi.org/10.1007/3-540-44987-6_28

17. Cramer, R., Shoup, V.: Universal hash proofs and a paradigm for adaptive chosen ciphertext secure public-key encryption. In: Knudsen, L.R. (ed.) EUROCRYPT 2002. LNCS, vol. 2332, pp. 45–64. Springer, Heidelberg (2002). https://doi.org/10.1007/3-540-46035-7_4

18. Diemert, D., Gellert, K., Jager, T., Lyu, L.: More efficient digital signatures with tight multi-user security. In: Garay, J.A. (ed.) PKC 2021. LNCS, vol. 12711, pp. 1–31. Springer, Cham (2021). https://doi.org/10.1007/978-3-030-75248-4_1

19. Dodis, Y., Ostrovsky, R., Reyzin, L., Smith, A.D.: Fuzzy extractors: How to generate strong keys from biometrics and other noisy data. SIAM J. Comput. 38(1), 97–139 (2008)

20. Ducas, L., Micciancio, D.: Improved short lattice signatures in the standard model. In: Garay, J.A., Gennaro, R. (eds.) CRYPTO 2014. LNCS, vol. 8616, pp. 335–352. Springer, Heidelberg (2014). https://doi.org/10.1007/978-3-662-44371-2_19

21. Gennaro, R., Lindell, Y.: A framework for password-based authenticated key exchange. ACM Trans. Inform. Syst. Sec. 9(2), 181–234 (2006)

22. Gjøsteen, K., Jager, T.: Practical and tightly-secure digital signatures and authenticated key exchange. In: Shacham, H., Boldyreva, A. (eds.) CRYPTO 2018. LNCS, vol. 10992, pp. 95–125. Springer, Cham (2018). https://doi.org/10.1007/978-3-319-96881-0_4

23. Han, S., et al.: Authenticated key exchange and signatures with tight security in the standard model. In: Malkin, T., Peikert, C. (eds.) CRYPTO 2021. LNCS, vol. 12828, pp. 670–700. Springer, Cham (2021). https://doi.org/10.1007/978-3-030-84259-8_23

24. Han, S., Liu, S., Gu, D.: Almost tight multi-user security under adaptive corruptions & leakages in the standard model. In: Hazay, C., Stam, M. (eds.) EUROCRYPT 2023, Part III. LNCS, vol. 14006, pp. 132–162. Springer, Heidelberg (Apr 2023). https://doi.org/10.1007/978-3-031-30620-4_5

25. Han, S., Liu, S., Lyu, L., Gu, D.: Tight leakage-resilient CCA-security from quasi-adaptive hash proof system. In: Boldyreva, A., Micciancio, D. (eds.) CRYPTO 2019. LNCS, vol. 11693, pp. 417–447. Springer, Cham (2019). https://doi.org/10.1007/978-3-030-26951-7_15

26. Han, S., Liu, S., Wang, Z., Gu, D.: Almost tight multi-user security under adaptive corruptions from LWE in the standard model. Cryptology ePrint Archive, 2023 (2023)

27. Jiang, S., Gong, G., He, J., Nguyen, K., Wang, H.: PAKEs: new framework, new techniques and more efficient lattice-based constructions in the standard model. In: Kiayias, A., Kohlweiss, M., Wallden, P., Zikas, V. (eds.) PKC 2020. LNCS, vol. 12110, pp. 396–427. Springer, Cham (2020). https://doi.org/10.1007/978-3-030-45374-9_14

28. Jutla, C.S., Roy, A.: Shorter quasi-adaptive NIZK proofs for linear subspaces. In: Sako, K., Sarkar, P. (eds.) ASIACRYPT 2013. LNCS, vol. 8269, pp. 1–20. Springer, Heidelberg (2013). https://doi.org/10.1007/978-3-642-42033-7_1

29. Katz, J., Vaikuntanathan, V.: Smooth projective hashing and password-based authenticated key exchange from lattices. In: Matsui, M. (ed.) ASIACRYPT 2009. LNCS, vol. 5912, pp. 636–652. Springer, Heidelberg (2009). https://doi.org/10.1007/978-3-642-10366-7_37

30. LaMacchia, B.A., Lauter, K., Mityagin, A.: Stronger security of authenticated key exchange. In: Susilo, W., Liu, J.K., Mu, Y. (eds.) ProvSec 2007. LNCS, vol. 4784, pp. 1–16. Springer, Heidelberg (Nov 2007). https://doi.org/10.1007/978-3-540-75670-5_1

31. Lee, Y., Lee, D.H., Park, J.H.: Tightly CCA-secure encryption scheme in a multi-user setting with corruptions. Des. Codes Crypt. 88(11), 2433–2452 (2020). https://doi.org/10.1007/s10623-020-00794-z

32. Libert, B., Nguyen, K., Passelègue, A., Titiu, R.: Simulation-sound arguments for LWE and applications to KDM-CCA2 security. In: Moriai, S., Wang, H. (eds.) ASIACRYPT 2020. LNCS, vol. 12491, pp. 128–158. Springer, Cham (2020). https://doi.org/10.1007/978-3-030-64837-4_5

33. Lyubashevsky, V.: Lattice signatures without trapdoors. In: Pointcheval, D., Johansson, T. (eds.) EUROCRYPT 2012. LNCS, vol. 7237, pp. 738–755. Springer, Heidelberg (2012). https://doi.org/10.1007/978-3-642-29011-4_43

34. Micciancio, D., Mol, P.: Pseudorandom knapsacks and the sample complexity of LWE search-to-decision reductions. In: Rogaway, P. (ed.) CRYPTO 2011. LNCS, vol. 6841, pp. 465–484. Springer, Heidelberg (2011). https://doi.org/10.1007/978-3-642-22792-9_26

35. Micciancio, D., Peikert, C.: Trapdoors for lattices: simpler, tighter, faster, smaller. In: Pointcheval, D., Johansson, T. (eds.) EUROCRYPT 2012. LNCS, vol. 7237, pp. 700–718. Springer, Heidelberg (2012). https://doi.org/10.1007/978-3-642-29011-4_41

36. Morgan, A., Pass, R., Shi, E.: On the adaptive security of MACs and PRFs. In: Moriai, S., Wang, H. (eds.) ASIACRYPT 2020. LNCS, vol. 12491, pp. 724–753. Springer, Cham (2020). https://doi.org/10.1007/978-3-030-64837-4_24

37. Pan, J., Wagner, B.: Lattice-based signatures with tight adaptive corruptions and more. In: Hanaoka, G., Shikata, J., Watanabe, Y. (eds.) PKC 2022, pp. 347–378 (2022)

38. Peikert, C.: Public-key cryptosystems from the worst-case shortest vector problem: extended abstract. In: Mitzenmacher, M. (ed.) 41st ACM STOC, pp. 333–342. ACM Press (May / Jun 2009)

39. Peikert, C.: An efficient and parallel gaussian sampler for lattices. In: Rabin, T. (ed.) CRYPTO 2010. LNCS, vol. 6223, pp. 80–97. Springer, Heidelberg (2010). https://doi.org/10.1007/978-3-642-14623-7_5

40. Peikert, C., Shiehian, S.: Noninteractive zero knowledge for NP from (Plain) learning with errors. In: Boldyreva, A., Micciancio, D. (eds.) CRYPTO 2019. LNCS, vol. 11692, pp. 89–114. Springer, Cham (2019). https://doi.org/10.1007/978-3-030-26948-7_4

41. Peikert, C., Waters, B.: Lossy trapdoor functions and their applications. In: Ladner, R.E., Dwork, C. (eds.) 40th ACM STOC, pp. 187–196. ACM Press (May 2008)

42. Regev, O.: On lattices, learning with errors, random linear codes, and cryptography. In: Gabow, H.N., Fagin, R. (eds.) 37th ACM STOC, pp. 84–93. ACM Press (May 2005)

43. Zhang, J., Yu, Y.: Two-round PAKE from approximate SPH and instantiations from lattices. In: Takagi, T., Peyrin, T. (eds.) ASIACRYPT 2017, Part III. LNCS, vol. 10626, pp. 37–67. Springer, Heidelberg (Dec (2017). https://doi.org/10.1007/978-3-319-70700-6_2

DualMS: Efficient Lattice-Based Two-Round Multi-signature with Trapdoor-Free Simulation

Yanbo Chen[✉][iD]

University of Ottawa, Ottawa, Canada
ychen918@uottawa.ca

Abstract. A multi-signature scheme allows multiple signers to jointly sign a common message. In recent years, two lattice-based two-round multi-signature schemes based on Dilithium-G were proposed: DOTT by Damgård, Orlandi, Takahashi, and Tibouchi (PKC'21) and MuSig-L by Boschini, Takahashi, and Tibouchi (Crypto'22).

In this work, we propose a new lattice-based two-round multi-signature scheme called DualMS. Compared to DOTT, DualMS is likely to significantly reduce signature size, since it replaces an opening to a homomorphic trapdoor commitment with a Dilithium-G response in the signature. Compared to MuSig-L, concrete parameters show that DualMS has smaller public keys, signatures, and lower communication, while the first round cannot be preprocessed offline as in MuSig-L.

The main reason behind such improvements is a trapdoor-free "dual signing simulation" of our scheme. Signature simulation of DualMS is virtually identical the normal signing procedure and does not use lattice trapdoors like DOTT and MuSig-L.

Keywords: Multi-signature · Dilithium · Fiat-Shamir with aborts · Lattice · Post-quantum

1 Introduction

A multi-signature scheme [23] allows a group of signers, each with its own individual key pair, to run an interactive protocol to sign a common message. All signers authenticate the message together by producing one multi-signature, which should take much smaller space than a bunch of individual signatures. In recent years, multi-signatures have found some real-world applications in blockchain and crypto-currency.

Multi-signatures Based on Schnorr Signatures. An important line of research is multi-signatures based on Schnorr signatures. Bellare and Neven [5] made an early major step. They proposed a provably secure scheme in the *plain public-key model*, where each signer just publishes their public key in clear without

Part of this work done while at the Chinese University of Hong Kong. The author was supported by Hong Kong RGC GRF grant CUHK14207721.

© International Association for Cryptologic Research 2023
H. Handschuh and A. Lysyanskaya (Eds.): CRYPTO 2023, LNCS 14085, pp. 716–747, 2023.
https://doi.org/10.1007/978-3-031-38554-4_23

any dedicated interactive key generation or proof of possession [40]. Their signing protocol has three rounds of interaction. Since then, a number of two-round schemes were proposed [2,30,31,41]. Unfortunately, it was pointed out that these schemes are vulnerable to concurrent attacks [6,13]. After that, a number of provably secure two-round schemes against concurrent attacks were proposed [1,4,13,35,36,38,42]. Maxwell et al. [31] raised the idea of *key aggregation*. In a scheme that supports key aggregation, the public keys of signers can be non-interactively aggregated, and the verifier only needs the aggregated key in verification. While multi-signatures already save space for signatures, this property further reduces storage and communication for public keys. Most subsequent proposals support key aggregation.

Lattice-Based Multi-signatures. In recent years, some lattice-based multi-signature schemes were proposed. The earliest schemes [7,16,19,20,29] are at least three-round. Moreover, the security proofs of [16,19,29] are incomplete, observed by [12]. The only two lattice-based two-round proposals so far are DOTT given by Damgård, Orlandi, Takahashi, and Tibouchi [11,12] and MuSig-L recently by Boschini, Takahashi, and Tibouchi [8]. All schemes we mentioned above are based on the Fiat-Shamir with aborts (FSwA) paradigm [25,26], and they make use of many insights from Schnorr-based schemes. For example, [9,29] use similar techniques to Schnorr-based schemes to support key aggregation in lattice setting. Recently, Fleischhacker et al. [18] proposed a non-interactive and concretely efficient scheme, but it only works in the synchronized model. In that setting, each signer can only produce one signature per time step, and only signatures produced in the same time step and on the same message can be aggregated.

Existing Two-Round Lattice-Based Multi-signature Schemes. In this work, we focus on lattice-based multi-signatures in the general setting (rather than restricted settings like the synchronized model). Existing two-round schemes, DOTT and MuSig-L, are both based on the non-optimized version of Dilithium-G [15], a FSwA signature scheme based on module SIS (MSIS) and LWE (MLWE). A Dilithium-G signature contains a relatively small challenge and a Gaussian distributed response that dominates the signature size.

DOTT is the first lattice-based two-round scheme. However, signature size of DOTT is relatively large. It takes homomorphic trapdoor commitment schemes as a building block, and its signature contains an opening to such a commitment in addition to a normal Dilithium-G signature. In the instantiations of such commitment schemes based on MSIS and MLWE [12,22,24], the size of an opening is likely much larger than a Dilithium-G signature.

Compared to DOTT, signatures in MuSig-L are in the original form of Dilithium-G and do not contain extra openings. Moreover, its first round can be preprocessed offline before knowing the message to sign. However, the Gaussian width of the response in the signature is much larger, which somehow blows up the whole scheme and in particular, increases the public-key and signature size. MuSig-L also has much higher communication complexity than DOTT in typical parameter settings.

1.1   Our Contribution

In this work, we propose a lattice-based two-round multi-signature scheme, DualMS. Following DOTT and MuSig-L, DualMS is based on Dilithium-G [15]. A DualMS signature contains two responses instead of only one in Dilithium-G. Compared to DOTT signature, we replace the opening with a response and thus are likely to have much smaller signatures.

Compared to MuSig-L, DualMS has smaller public keys and signatures in our sample parameters. Aiming at about 128-bit security level, public-key size + signature size of DualMS and MuSig-L are approximately 27 kB vs. 124 kB with at most 32 signers and 41 kB vs. 139 kB with at most 1024 signers. Moreover, the communication of DualMS is smaller by an order of magnitude in such parameter settings.

Our scheme supports key aggregation using common techniques. We prove its security against concurrent attacks, in the plain public-key model and the random oracle model (ROM), based on MLWE and MSIS.

Underlying our result is a "dual signing simulation" technique that simulates multi-signatures in the security proof without trapdoors. In the rest of this section, we will review the trapdoor-based simulation techniques of DOTT and MuSig-L, explain how they affect the performance of the schemes, and provide an overview of our scheme and simulation.

1.2   Simulation in Prior Works

Straight-Line Simulation. Let us consider multi-signatures based on Fiat-Shamir paradigm [17] or FSwA. To produce an individual signature in such a scheme, a signer first generates a random commitment, then hashes the commitment and the message to obtain a challenge, and finally gives a response to the challenge. A basic framework for multi-signature is as follows. The signers first take a round of interaction to exchange their individual commitments. They aggregate their commitments and hash the aggregated one to derive a common challenge or a bunch of per-signer challenges. After separately responding to the challenge(s), they exchange their responses in another round of interaction to finally compute an aggregated response. With fewer than two rounds of "exchange and aggregate", the size of multi-signature grows linearly with the number of signers.

However, this basic framework is not enough to construct a provably secure scheme. In the security proof, the reduction needs to simulate the signing procedure without the secret key. In the case of individual signatures, the reduction is allowed to generate the commitment, the challenge, and the response in any order. As long as it eventually outputs a valid signature, the order of simulation is hidden in a black box. Let us take Schnorr signature as an example. On input a challenge c, the reduction first samples a response z. Then it computes the commitment $R := g^z / X^c$, where g is the generator and X is the public key, and programs c into the random oracle. On the contrary, the order matters in the setting of multi-signatures. To play the part of an honest signer, the reduction has to give a commitment in the first round of interaction. At that time the challenge has not been determined yet, because it depends on those commitments given by other signers who are acted by the adversary. The reduction needs to output a correct response later when a challenge is decided. The standard simulation technique for Schnorr signatures does not work here, because the commitment R is decided after knowing c and z. This is an important observation: when we design a multi-signature scheme, we should intentionally enable such "simulation in order" or so-called *straight-line simulation*.

Trapdoor-Based Simulation Techniques of Existing Schemes. We observe that DOTT and MuSig-L both rely on trapdoor sampling [21,32] to enable straight-line simulation.

Let us first recall the underlying individual signature scheme, Dilithium-G. The scheme works over polynomial rings $R = \mathbb{Z}[X]/(f(X))$ and $R_q = \mathbb{Z}_q[X]/(f(X))$. In Dilithium-G, the secret key is a short vector $\mathbf{s} \in R^{l+k}$. The public key consists of a matrix $\mathbf{A} \in R_q^{k \times l}$ and a vector $\mathbf{t} := \bar{\mathbf{A}}\mathbf{s} \in R_q^k$ where $\bar{\mathbf{A}} := [\mathbf{A}|\mathbf{I}]$. To sign message μ, the signer first samples a masking vector $\mathbf{y} \in R^{l+k}$ from a discrete Gaussian distribution and computes a commitment $\mathbf{w} := \bar{\mathbf{A}}\mathbf{y} \in R_q^k$. It hashes $\mathbf{t}$, μ, and $\mathbf{w}$ to obtain a challenge $c := \mathsf{H}_{\mathrm{sig}}(\mathbf{t}, \mu, \mathbf{w})$ which is a small polynomial. It computes its response as $\mathbf{z} := \mathbf{y} + c\mathbf{s}$. Then it performs a rejection sampling: it aborts and restarts with some probability depending on $\mathbf{z}$ and $c\mathbf{s}$. As a result, the distribution of the final output $\mathbf{z}$ is independent of $\mathbf{s}$, which protects the secrecy of $\mathbf{s}$. The signature consists of challenge c and response $\mathbf{z}$. To verify it, the verifier recovers the commitment by $\mathbf{w} := \bar{\mathbf{A}}\mathbf{z} - c\mathbf{t}$ and checks whether $c = \mathsf{H}_{\mathrm{sig}}(\mathbf{t}, \mu, \mathbf{w})$.

DOTT follows the structure of mBCJ [2,13]. They utilize a homomorphic trapdoor commitment scheme to enable straight-line simulation. In the first round, each signer broadcasts nonce[1] $\mathbf{w}$ committed rather than in clear. The homomorphic property allows the signers to aggregate the commitments. In the second round, each signer opens its commitment in addition to broadcasts response $\mathbf{z}$. The reduction does not have to really decide $\mathbf{w}$ when it outputs the commitment in the first round. The trapdoor property allows it to open the commitment as any $\mathbf{w}$ of its choice later. It runs the standard simulation algorithm once the challenge is determined. In the second round, it opens its commitment as the nonce it obtains from the simulation. The authors proposed their scheme using a homomorphic trapdoor commitment scheme as a building block, while previously known instantiations of lattice based trapdoor commitment [22,24] and their own instantiation [12] all rely on trapdoor sampling.

MuSig-L uses a similar structure to DWMS [1] and MuSig2 [35], with a very different simulation technique. The signers exchange multiple pre-commitments in the first round. The actual individual commitment of each signer is a linear combination of its pre-commitments with coefficients derived from a hash function. In [9], the pre-commitment vectors $\mathbf{w}_1, \ldots, \mathbf{w}_m$ form a matrix

---

[1] "Commitment" appears both in the context of Fiat-Shamir signatures and commitment schemes. To avoid ambiguity, here we use "nonce" to indicate the commitment $\mathbf{w}$ in signatures.

$\mathbf{W} = [\mathbf{w}_1, \ldots, \mathbf{w}_m]$. The reduction generates a trapdoor of the matrix so that it can sample a Gaussian preimage $\mathbf{b}$ satisfying $\mathbf{W}\mathbf{b} = \mathbf{w}'$ for any $\mathbf{w}'$. The reduction obtains a commitment $\mathbf{w}'$ when it runs the standard simulation. It then samples a preimage $\mathbf{b}$ and programs $\mathbf{b}$ into the random oracle as the coefficients of linear combination. Here trapdoor sampling allows the reduction to linearly combine $\mathbf{W}$ into any commitment of its choice and thus also delays the decision of the real commitment.

Performance of Existing Schemes. Now let us look at how the use of trapdoor sampling affects the performance of DOTT and MuSig-L. In Dilithium-G, a signature consists of a challenge and a response. The challenge is relatively small. The response $\mathbf{z}$ is a $(l + k)$-dimensional Gaussian distributed vector, where we typically set the $l \leq k$. In DOTT, a signature additionally contains an opening to a homomorphic trapdoor commitment to the k-dimensional nonce $\mathbf{w}$. In the instantiation of [12], the opening is a preimage given by trapdoor sampling of [32]. The trapdoor sampling requires a wide $k \times m$ matrix $\mathbf{W}$ with $m \approx k \log q$, where q is the modulus. The Gaussian widths of $\mathbf{z}$ and the preimage are not hugely different, and they only affect signature size by a logarithmic factor. On the other hand, the dimension $m \approx k \log q$ of a preimage is much larger than $\mathbf{z}$. Thus, the extra opening is notably larger than the original Dilithium-G signature.

In MuSig-L, each signer broadcasts a matrix $\mathbf{W}$ that enables trapdoor sampling instead of a single commitment vector. This increases the communication complexity by roughly $k \log q$ times. Moreover, pre-commitments $\mathbf{W}$ are commitments to Gaussian vectors, and they are combined with coefficients $\mathbf{b}$ which are again Gaussian. Both distributions need to have large enough Gaussian width to support their simulation technique. This significantly increases the Gaussian width of response $\mathbf{z}$ and affects signature size. Other parameters also have to grow to keep signature forgery hard, again increasing public-key and signature size.

1.3   Overview of Our Scheme

Observing the inefficiency of existing schemes caused by trapdoor sampling in simulation, our idea is to construct a scheme with trapdoor-free simulation. First let us look at a variant scheme of Dilithium-G. Now the secret key contains another short vector $\bar{\mathbf{u}} \in R^{l'+k}$, and the public key contains an additional matrix $\mathbf{B} \in R_q^{k \times l'}$. We also have $\mathbf{t} := \bar{\mathbf{A}}\mathbf{s} + \bar{\mathbf{B}}\bar{\mathbf{u}}$ with $\bar{\mathbf{B}} := [\mathbf{B}|\mathbf{I}]$. The signer samples two masking vectors $\mathbf{y}$ and $\mathbf{p}$ and computes the commitment $\mathbf{w} := \bar{\mathbf{A}}\mathbf{y} + \bar{\mathbf{B}}\mathbf{p}$. It computes two responses $\mathbf{z} := \mathbf{y} + c\mathbf{s}$ and $\mathbf{r} := \mathbf{p} + c\bar{\mathbf{u}}$ and performs rejection sampling separately. The signature consists of c, $\mathbf{z}$, and $\mathbf{r}$, and the verifier can recover the commitment by $\mathbf{w} := \bar{\mathbf{A}}\mathbf{z} + \bar{\mathbf{B}}\mathbf{r} - c\mathbf{t}$. This variant scheme can be viewed as a lattice-based analogue of Okamoto signature [37]. Knowing any short enough $\mathbf{s}$ and $\bar{\mathbf{u}}$ satisfying $\bar{\mathbf{A}}\mathbf{s} + \bar{\mathbf{B}}\bar{\mathbf{u}} = \mathbf{t}$ is sufficient to produce a signature. In particular, the signer can set $\mathbf{s} = \mathbf{0}$ or $\bar{\mathbf{u}} = \mathbf{0}$.

In our protocol, matrix $\mathbf{B}$ is derived by hashing the aggregated public key and message μ. The signer signs in the special case of $\bar{\mathbf{u}} = \mathbf{0}$. When signing a common message μ, the signers derive the same matrix $\mathbf{B}$. Thus, the signers can exchange their commitment $\mathbf{w}$ and responses $\mathbf{z}$ and $\mathbf{r}$ and aggregate them by summing them up. This will give a correct multi-signature by linearity. More precisely, the signers obtain a common challenge c and takes $a_i c$ as their individual challenge where a_i is the key aggregation coefficient derived from a hash function. Then it holds that

$$\tilde{\mathbf{w}} = \bar{\mathbf{A}}\tilde{\mathbf{z}} + \bar{\mathbf{B}}\tilde{\mathbf{r}} - c\tilde{\mathbf{t}},$$

where $\tilde{\mathbf{w}} = \sum_{i=1}^{n} \mathbf{w}_i$, $\tilde{\mathbf{z}} = \sum_{i=1}^{n} \mathbf{z}_i$, $\tilde{\mathbf{r}} = \sum_{i=1}^{n} \mathbf{r}_i$, and $\tilde{\mathbf{t}} = \sum_{i=1}^{n} a_i \mathbf{t}_i$ are the aggregated commitment/responses/public key.

In the security proof, the reduction can generate $\mathbf{B}$ together with a dual secret key $\bar{\mathbf{u}}$ satisfying $\bar{\mathbf{B}}\bar{\mathbf{u}} = \mathbf{t}$. Thus, it can perform straight-line simulation by signing in the special case of $\mathbf{s} = \mathbf{0}$. To generate a random $\mathbf{B}$ with dual secret key $\bar{\mathbf{u}}$, the reduction samples short vector $\mathbf{u} \in R^{l'-1+k}$ and lets $\mathbf{B} := [\mathbf{b}|\hat{\mathbf{B}}]$ with random chosen $\hat{\mathbf{B}}$ and $\mathbf{b} := \mathbf{t} - [\hat{\mathbf{B}}|\mathbf{I}]\mathbf{u}$. It follows that

$$\bar{\mathbf{B}} \begin{bmatrix} 1 \\ \mathbf{u} \end{bmatrix} = [\mathbf{b}|\hat{\mathbf{B}}|\mathbf{I}] \begin{bmatrix} 1 \\ \mathbf{u} \end{bmatrix} = \mathbf{b} + [\hat{\mathbf{B}}|\mathbf{I}]\mathbf{u} = \mathbf{t}.$$

Therefore, it can take $[1, \mathbf{u}^\mathsf{T}]^\mathsf{T}$ as the dual secret key $\bar{\mathbf{u}}$. Matrix $\mathbf{B}$ generated in this way is computationally indistinguishable from a uniformly random one based on MLWE.

While DOTT follows the structure of mBCJ [2,13], and MuSig-L follows the structure of DWMS [1] and MuSig2 [35], our DualMS has an analogous structure to HBMS proposed by Bellare and Dai [4]. Nevertheless, the simulation techniques of the two schemes are noticeably different. Their reduction generates the hash-derived generator h (corresponding to $\mathbf{B}$) as a random combination of the common generator g (corresponding to $\mathbf{A}$) and public key X (corresponding to $\mathbf{t}$), and it gives two responses by solving two linear equations. However, in the lattice setting, solving random equations will unlikely give short responses. Thus, our "dual signing simulation" is crucial for a lattice-based scheme. Generation and indistinguishability of the dual key are also more indirect in lattice setting than discrete-logarithm setting.

In the formal specification of our scheme, we apply a simple and effective optimization. Note that $\mathbf{z}$ and $\mathbf{r}$ both contain an MLWE error term that will be multiplied by $\mathbf{I}$ in matrices $\bar{\mathbf{A}}$ and $\bar{\mathbf{B}}$ in the verification. Simply adding up two error terms can significantly reduce the signature size.

2   Preliminaries

Notation. For a positive number n, $[n]$ denotes $\{1, \ldots, n\}$. If x is a variable, then $y := x$ denotes that we assign the value of x to y. If D is a distribution, then $y \leftarrow D$ denotes that we sample y from D. If S is a set, then $y \leftarrow_\$ S$ denotes that we uniformly sample y from S. If f is a real-value function and S is a set, then $f(S)$ denotes $\sum_{x \in S} f(x)$.

2.1   Polynomial Rings and Discrete Gaussian Distribution

In this paper, most operations work over polynomial rings $R = \mathbb{Z}[X]/(f(X))$ and $R_q = \mathbb{Z}_q[X]/(f(X))$, where $f(X) = X^N + 1$ with N a power of two is the $2N$-th cyclotomic polynomial, and q is a prime that satisfies $q = 5 \mod 8$. Elements over the latter ring have coefficients between $-(q-1)/2$ and $(q-1)/2$. The L^p-norm for a vector of ring elements $\mathbf{v} = [\sum_{i=0}^{N-1} v_{1,i} X^i, \dots, \sum_{i=0}^{N-1} v_{m,i} X^i]^\mathsf{T} \in R^m$ is defined as

$$\|\mathbf{v}\|_p = \|[v_{1,0}, \dots, v_{1,N-1}, \dots, v_{m,0}, \dots, v_{m,N-1}]\|_p.$$

We need the following lemma about invertibility over R_q.

Lemma 1 ([27], Lemma 2.2). *Let $N > 1$ be a power of 2 and q a prime congruent to 5 mod 8. The ring R_q has exactly $2q^{N/2} - 1$ elements without an inverse. Moreover, every non-zero polynomial $a \in R_q$ with $\|a\|_\infty < \sqrt{q}/2$ has an inverse.*

We define the key set $S_\eta \subset R$ as

$$S_\eta = \{x \in R : \|x\|_\infty \le \eta\}$$

and the challenge set $C = C_\kappa \subset R$ as

$$C = \{c \in R : \|c\|_\infty = 1 \wedge \|c\|_1 = \kappa\}.$$

By Lemma 1, $c - c'$ has an inverse for any $c, c' \in C$ and $c \ne c'$.

The discrete Gaussian distribution over R^m is defined as follows.

Definition 2 (Discrete Gaussian Distribution over R^m). *For $\mathbf{x} \in R^m$, the Gaussian function of parameter $\mathbf{v} \in R^m$ and $s \in \mathbb{R}$ is defined as $\rho_{\mathbf{v},s}(\mathbf{x}) = \exp(-\pi \|\mathbf{x} - \mathbf{v}\|_2^2 / s^2)$. The discrete Gaussian distribution $D_{\mathbf{v},s}^m$ centered at $\mathbf{v}$ is defined as*

$$D_{\mathbf{v},s}^m(\mathbf{x}) = \frac{\rho_{\mathbf{v},s}(\mathbf{x})}{\rho_{\mathbf{v},s}(R^m)}.$$

In this paper, we omit the subscript $\mathbf{v}$ when $\mathbf{v} = \mathbf{0}$. For any $\epsilon > 0$, the *smoothing parameter* $\eta_\epsilon(\Lambda)$ [34] of lattice Λ is defined as the smallest $s > 0$ such that $\rho_{1/s}(\Lambda^* \setminus \{\mathbf{0}\}) \le \epsilon$, where Λ^* is the dual lattice of Λ. By lemma 3.2 of [34], $\eta_\epsilon(R^m) \le \sqrt{Nm}$ where $\epsilon = 2^{-Nm}$. The parameter s that we use in this paper exceeds $\eta_\epsilon(R^m)$ by a factor at least $\sqrt{2}$. In this setting, the following lemma holds, which is a special case of lemma 3.3 in [33]. We need the lemma to understand the distribution of the response in our multi-signature, which is the sum of individual responses.

Lemma 3. *Suppose $s \ge \sqrt{2} \cdot \eta_\epsilon(R^m)$ with a negligible ϵ. Let $\mathbf{x}_i$ for $i \in [n]$ be independent samples from $D_{s_i}^m$. Then the distribution of $\mathbf{x} = \sum_{i=1}^n \mathbf{x}_i$ is statistically close to D_s^m with $s = \sqrt{\sum_{i=1}^n s_i^2}$.*

The next two lemmas are important for Fiat-Shamir with aborts. Both of them are adapted from [26] by [12].

Lemma 4 ([26]). *For any $\gamma > 1$,*

$$\Pr\left[\|\mathbf{z}\|_2 > \gamma(s/\sqrt{2\pi})\sqrt{mN} : \mathbf{z} \leftarrow D_s^m\right] < \gamma^{mN} e^{mN(1-\gamma^2)/2}.$$

Lemma 5 ([26]). *Fix some t such that $t = \omega(\sqrt{\log(mN)})$ and $t = o(\log(mN))$. For any $\mathbf{v} \in R^m$, if $s \geq \sqrt{2\pi}\alpha\|\mathbf{v}\|_2$ for any positive α, then*

$$\Pr\left[M \cdot D_{\mathbf{v},s}^m(\mathbf{z}) \geq D_s^m(\mathbf{z}) : \mathbf{z} \leftarrow D_s^m\right] \geq 1 - \epsilon,$$

where $M = e^{t/\alpha + 1/(2\alpha^2)}$ and $\epsilon = 2e^{-t^2/2}$.

The following regularity result adapted from [28] gives the minimum Gaussian width of $\mathbf{x}$ to make $[\mathbf{A}|\mathbf{I}]\mathbf{x}$ statistically close to the uniform distribution.

Lemma 6 ([28]). *For positive integers k and l, suppose $m = l + k \leq \mathsf{poly}(N)$. let $\bar{\mathbf{A}} = [\mathbf{A}|\mathbf{I}] \in R_q^{k \times m}$, where $\mathbf{A}$ is uniformly distributed over $R_q^{k \times l}$. Then with probability $1 - 2^{-\Omega(N)}$ over the choice of $\mathbf{A}$, the distribution of $\bar{\mathbf{A}}\mathbf{x} \in R_q^k$, where $\mathbf{x} \leftarrow D_s^m$ with parameter $s > 2N \cdot q^{k/m+2/(Nm)}$, satisfies that the probability of each of the q^{Nk} possible outcomes is in the interval $(1 \pm 2^{-\Omega(N)})q^{-Nk}$. In particular, it is with statistical distance $2^{-\Omega(N)}$ of the uniform distribution over R_q^k.*

2.2   Assumptions

We restate the standard lattice hard problems, module short integer solution (MSIS) (in Hermite Normal Form) and learning with error (MLWE).

Definition 7 ($\mathsf{MSIS}_{q,k,l,\beta}$ problem). *The advantage of algorithm $\mathcal{A}$ against the $\mathsf{MSIS}_{q,k,l,\beta}$ problem is defined as*

$$\mathbf{Adv}_{\mathsf{MSIS}_{q,k,l,\beta}}(\mathcal{A})$$
$$= \Pr\left[[\mathbf{A}|\mathbf{I}] \cdot \mathbf{x} = \mathbf{0} \wedge 0 < \|\mathbf{x}\|_2 \leq \beta : \mathbf{A} \leftarrow_\$ R_q^{k \times l}; \mathbf{x} \leftarrow \mathcal{A}(\mathbf{A}) \in R_q^{l+k}\right].$$

Definition 8 ($\mathsf{MLWE}_{q,k,l,\eta}$ problem). *The advantage of algorithm $\mathcal{A}$ against the $\mathsf{MLWE}_{q,k,l,\eta}$ problem is defined as*

$$\mathbf{Adv}_{\mathsf{MLWE}_{q,k,l,\eta}}(\mathcal{A}) = \Pr\left[\mathcal{A}(\mathbf{A},\mathbf{t}) = 1 : \mathbf{A} \leftarrow_\$ R_q^{k \times l}; \mathbf{s} \leftarrow_\$ S_\eta^{l+k}; \mathbf{t} := [\mathbf{A}|\mathbf{I}] \cdot \mathbf{s}\right]$$
$$- \Pr\left[\mathcal{A}(\mathbf{A},\mathbf{t}) = 1 : (\mathbf{A},\mathbf{t}) \leftarrow_\$ R_q^{k \times l} \times R_q^k\right].$$

2.3 Two-Round Multi-signatures with Key Aggregation

Our definition of multi-signature schemes follows [35]. The definition specially considers those signing protocols with the following features: 1) the signers interact with each other by broadcasting protocol messages round by round, 2) the round number is two, and 3) the final multi-signature is simply an aggregation of all second-round protocol messages. We regard the second-round protocol message as the individual signature of each signer. We describe the signing protocol as three algorithms Sign_1, Sign_2, and SAgg corresponding to three stages. They are locally run by each signer. The signers exchange their protocol messages between these stages. Algorithms Sign_1 and Sign_2 output a protocol message (for Sign_2 it is an individual signature) for the signer to broadcast, and Sign_2 and SAgg takes as inputs protocol messages from other signers. A multi-signature is finally output by SAgg. The signers keep states between Sign_1 and Sign_2, while SAgg does not take any secret state. Hence, any designated aggregator who collects the signatures can run SAgg to produce the multi-signature. The property of key-aggregation [31] allows to non-interactively aggregate public keys using a key aggregation algorithm KAgg. The verification algorithm takes as inputs an aggregated key instead of a list of individual keys.

Definition 9 (Two-round multi-signatures with key aggregation). *A two-round multi-signature scheme* MS *with key aggregation consists of algorithms with syntax defined as follows:*

- $\mathsf{Setup}() \to \mathsf{pp}$*: The parameter generation algorithm outputs a set of public parameters* pp*. Throughout, we assume* pp *is given as an implicit input to all other algorithms.*
- $\mathsf{KGen}() \to (\mathsf{sk}, \mathsf{pk})$*: The key generation algorithm outputs a secret key* sk *and a public key* pk*.*
- $\mathsf{KAgg}(L) \to \mathsf{apk}$*: The deterministic key aggregation algorithm takes as inputs a set of public keys* $L = \{\mathsf{pk}_1, \ldots, \mathsf{pk}_n\}$ *and outputs an aggregated public key* apk*.*
- $\mathsf{Sign}_1(\mathsf{sk}_1, L, \mu) \to (\mathsf{st}_1, \mathsf{msg}_1)$*: The first-stage signing algorithm takes as inputs a secret key* sk_1*, a set of public keys* $L = \{\mathsf{pk}_1, \ldots, \mathsf{pk}_n\}$*, and a message* μ *and outputs a state* st_1 *and a protocol message* msg_1*.*
- $\mathsf{Sign}_2(\mathsf{st}_1, \{\mathsf{msg}_2, \ldots, \mathsf{msg}_n\}) \to \sigma_1$*: The second-stage signing algorithm takes as inputs a state* st_1 *and a set of protocol messages* $\{\mathsf{msg}_2, \ldots, \mathsf{msg}_n\}$ *and outputs an individual signature* σ_1*.*
- $\mathsf{SAgg}(\{\sigma_1, \ldots, \sigma_n\}) \to \tilde{\sigma}$*: The signature aggregation (also the third-stage signing algorithm) takes as inputs a set of individual signatures* $\{\sigma_1, \ldots, \sigma_n\}$ *and outputs a multi-signature* $\tilde{\sigma}$*.*
- $\mathsf{Vf}(\mathsf{apk}, \mu, \tilde{\sigma}) \to 0/1$*: The deterministic verification algorithm takes as inputs an aggregated public key* apk*, a message* μ*, and a multi-signature* $\tilde{\sigma}$ *and outputs 0 or 1.*

Definition 10 (ε-completeness). *Let algorithm* Sign *be as described in Fig. 1. A two-round multi-signature scheme* MS *with key aggregation is said to be* ε-*complete if fixing any positive integer* n*, any* $\mathsf{pp} \in \mathsf{Setup}()$*, any* $(\mathsf{sk}_i, \mathsf{pk}_i) \in \mathsf{KGen}()$ *for* $i \in [n]$*, and any* $\mu \in \{0, 1\}^*$*,*

> $\mathsf{Sign}(\{(\mathsf{sk}_1, \mathsf{pk}_1), \ldots, (\mathsf{sk}_n, \mathsf{pk}_n)\}, \mu)$
>
> ---
>
> $L := \{\mathsf{pk}_1, \ldots, \mathsf{pk}_n\}$
> **for** $i \in [n]$ **do** $(\mathsf{st}_i, \mathsf{msg}_i) \leftarrow \mathsf{Sign}_1(\mathsf{sk}_i, L, \mu)$
> **for** $i \in [n]$ **do** $\sigma_i \leftarrow \mathsf{Sign}_2(\mathsf{st}_i, \{\mathsf{msg}_j\}_{j \in [n] \setminus \{i\}})$
> $\tilde{\sigma} := \mathsf{SAgg}(\{\sigma_1, \ldots, \sigma_n\})$
> **return** $\tilde{\sigma}$

Fig. 1. Algorithm Sign that defines completeness.

$$\Pr[\mathsf{Vf}(\mathsf{KAgg}(L), \mu, \tilde{\sigma}) = 1 : \tilde{\sigma} \leftarrow \mathsf{Sign}(\{(\mathsf{sk}_1, \mathsf{pk}_1), \ldots, (\mathsf{sk}_n, \mathsf{pk}_n)\}, \mu)] \geq \varepsilon,$$

where $L = \{\mathsf{pk}_1, \ldots, \mathsf{pk}_n\}$.

Below we define the unforgeability of a multi-signature scheme. In the security game, adversary $\mathcal{A}$ is given a target public key pk_1. Its goal is to forge a multi-signature under a public-key list L^* of its choice while required to contain pk_1. In a chosen-message attack game, $\mathcal{A}$ can concurrently launch many signing sessions with an honest signer having public key pk_1. In each session, $\mathcal{A}$ plays the part of all other signers, with public keys of its choices. To formalize the chosen-message attack, $\mathcal{A}$ has the access to two signing oracles $\textsc{Sign}_1$ and $\textsc{Sign}_2$, corresponding to the first and the second stages of the signing protocol. $\textsc{Sign}_1$ takes necessary inputs for launching a signing session, i.e., a public key list and a message to sign. It returns the first-round protocol message of the honest signer. $\textsc{Sign}_2$ takes as inputs the first-round protocol messages from other signers and outputs the individual signature of the honest signer. States are kept between $\textsc{Sign}_1$ and $\textsc{Sign}_2$. When $\mathcal{A}$ calls $\textsc{Sign}_2$, it is required to specify a session ID sid to indicate which session it wants to proceed. Since SAgg involves no secret state, there is no need for a corresponding oracle. Note that in the setting of multi-signatures, $\mathcal{A}$ can win by forging a signature it has queried under different public-key lists from L^*.

Definition 11 (Unforgeablility against chosen-message/key-only attack). *The advantage of adversary $\mathcal{A}$ against the unforgeability against chosen-message attack (UF-CMA) of a multi-signature scheme* MS *in the ROM is defined as*

$$\mathbf{Adv}_{\mathsf{MS}}^{\mathsf{UF\text{-}CMA}}(\mathcal{A}) = \Pr[\mathsf{UF\text{-}CMA}_{\mathsf{MS}}(\mathcal{A}) = 1],$$

where the game UF-CMA$_{\mathsf{MS}}$ *is described in Fig. 2. The unforgeability against key-only attack (UF-KOA) is defined the same as UF-CMA except that $\mathcal{A}$ does not have the access to* $\textsc{Sign}_1$ *and* $\textsc{Sign}_2$.

UF-CMA$_{\text{MS}}(\mathcal{A})$	SIGN$_1(\{\text{pk}_2,\ldots,\text{pk}_n\},\mu)$
pp $\leftarrow$ Setup()	ctr $:=$ ctr $+ 1$
$(\text{sk}_1,\text{pk}_1) \leftarrow$ KGen()	sid $:=$ ctr; $\mathcal{S} := \mathcal{S} \cup \{\text{sid}\}$
ctr $:= 0$	$L := \{\text{pk}_1,\ldots,\text{pk}_n\}$
$\mathcal{S} := \emptyset;\ \mathcal{Q} := \emptyset$	$\mathcal{Q} := \mathcal{Q} \cup \{(L,\mu)\}$
$(L^*,\mu^*,\tilde{\sigma}^*) \leftarrow \mathcal{A}^{\text{SIGN}_1,\text{SIGN}_2,\text{H}}(\text{pp},\text{pk}_1)$	$(\text{msg}_1,\text{st}_{\text{sid}}) \leftarrow \text{Sign}_1(\text{sk}_1,L,\mu)$
if $(\text{pk}_1 \notin L^*) \vee (L^*,\mu^*) \in \mathcal{Q}$ then	return msg$_1$
return 0	
return Vf(KAgg$(L^*),\mu^*,\tilde{\sigma}^*)$	SIGN$_2(\text{sid},\{\text{msg}_2,\ldots,\text{msg}_n\})$
	if sid $\notin \mathcal{S}$ then return $\perp$
	$\sigma_1 \leftarrow \text{Sign}_2(\text{st}_{\text{sid}},\{\text{msg}_2,\ldots,\text{msg}_n\})$
	$\mathcal{S} := \mathcal{S} \setminus \{\text{sid}\}$
	return σ_1

Fig. 2. The UF-CMA security game against multi-signature scheme MS in the ROM, where H denotes the random oracle.

3 Our **DualMS** Scheme

3.1 Scheme Description

Figure 3 describes our DualMS scheme. The parameters are listed in Table 1. We explain our construction as below.

Setup, Key Generation, and Key Aggregation. In the setup stage, a matrix $\bar{\mathbf{A}} := [\mathbf{A}|\mathbf{I}] \in R_q^{k \times (l+k)}$ is generated as a public parameter with $\mathbf{A}$ uniformly chosen from $R_q^{k \times l}$. The secret key $\mathbf{s}$ of each signer is a short vector uniformly chosen from S_η^{l+k}. Recall that η is the maximum L^∞-norm. The public key is $\mathbf{t} := \bar{\mathbf{A}}\mathbf{s}$. Note that $\mathbf{A}$ and $\mathbf{t}$ constitute a MLWE sample, which ensures the secrecy of $\mathbf{s}$. The key aggregation algorithm aggregates a list of public keys $L = \{\mathbf{t}_1,\ldots,\mathbf{t}_n\}$ into an aggregated public key. We use a hash function H_{agg} to compute a small polynomial $a_i := \text{H}_{\text{agg}}(L,\mathbf{t}_i) \in C$ for each $\mathbf{t}_i \in L$. Then L is aggregated into $\tilde{\mathbf{t}} := \sum_{i=1}^n a_i \mathbf{t}_i$. Here L is an unordered set, and duplicate keys $\mathbf{t}_i = \mathbf{t}_j$ will make $a_i = a_j$.

Signature Generation. Now we describe the signing protocol of DualMS. In the protocol, each signer runs the same procedure, so we describe the protocol by showing the behavior of one signer. We assign the signer index 1. It has secret key $\mathbf{s}_1$ and public key $\mathbf{t}_1$. First, the signer computes the aggregated key $\tilde{\mathbf{t}} := \text{KAgg}(L)$. Then it uses a hash function H_{com} to derive a matrix $\mathbf{B} := \text{H}_{\text{com}}(\tilde{\mathbf{t}},\mu) \in R_q^{k \times l'}$ and lets $\bar{\mathbf{B}} := [\mathbf{B}|\mathbf{I}] \in R_q^{l'+k}$. It computes its commitment $\mathbf{w}_1 := \bar{\mathbf{A}}\mathbf{y}_1 + \bar{\mathbf{B}}\mathbf{r}_1$ with $\mathbf{y}_1 \leftarrow D_s^{l+k}$ and $\mathbf{r}_1 \leftarrow D_{s'}^{l'+k}$. It broadcasts $\mathbf{w}_1$ to other signers as its first-round protocol message.

Setup()

$\mathbf{A} \leftarrow\!\!\$\ R_q^{k \times l}$

$\bar{\mathbf{A}} := [\mathbf{A}|\mathbf{I}]$

return $\bar{\mathbf{A}}$

KGen()

$\mathbf{s} \leftarrow\!\!\$\ S_\eta^{l+k}$

$\mathbf{t} := \bar{\mathbf{A}}\mathbf{s}$

return $(\mathbf{s}, \mathbf{t})$

KAgg(L)

$\{\mathbf{t}_1, \ldots, \mathbf{t}_n\} := L$

for $i \in [n]$ do

$\quad a_i := \mathsf{H}_{\mathrm{agg}}(L, \mathbf{t}_i) \in C$

$\tilde{\mathbf{t}} := \sum_{i=1}^n a_i \mathbf{t}_i$

return $\tilde{\mathbf{t}}$

Vf($\mathsf{apk}, \mu, \tilde{\sigma}$)

$\tilde{\mathbf{t}} := \mathsf{apk}$

$(c, \tilde{\mathbf{z}}, \tilde{\mathbf{r}}, \tilde{\mathbf{e}}) := \tilde{\sigma}$

$\mathbf{B} := \mathsf{H}_{\mathrm{com}}(\tilde{\mathbf{t}}, \mu)$

$\tilde{\mathbf{w}} := \mathbf{A}\tilde{\mathbf{z}} + \mathbf{B}\tilde{\mathbf{r}} + \tilde{\mathbf{e}} - c\tilde{\mathbf{t}}$

return $[\![\|\tilde{\mathbf{z}}\|_2 \le B_n \wedge \|\tilde{\mathbf{r}}\|_2 \le B_n'$

$\quad \wedge \|\tilde{\mathbf{e}}\|_2 \le B_n'' \wedge \mathsf{H}_{\mathrm{sig}}(\tilde{\mathbf{t}}, \mu, \tilde{\mathbf{w}}) = c]\!]$

Sign$_1$(sk_1, L, μ)

$\mathbf{s}_1 := \mathsf{sk}_1$

$\{\mathbf{t}_1, \ldots, \mathbf{t}_n\} := L$

$a_1 := \mathsf{H}_{\mathrm{agg}}(L, \mathbf{t}_1)$

$\tilde{\mathbf{t}} := \mathsf{KAgg}(L)$

$\mathbf{B} := \mathsf{H}_{\mathrm{com}}(\tilde{\mathbf{t}}, \mu) \in R_q^{k \times l'}$

$\bar{\mathbf{B}} := [\mathbf{B}|\mathbf{I}] \in R_q^{k \times (l'+k)}$

$\mathbf{y}_1 \leftarrow D_s^{l+k}$

$\mathbf{r}_1 \leftarrow D_{s'}^{l'+k}$

$\mathbf{w}_1 := \bar{\mathbf{A}}\mathbf{y}_1 + \bar{\mathbf{B}}\mathbf{r}_1 \in R_q^k$

return $((\mathbf{s}_1, \tilde{\mathbf{t}}, \mu, a_1, \mathbf{y}_1, \mathbf{r}_1, \mathbf{w}_1), \mathbf{w}_1)$

Sign$_2$($\mathsf{st}_1, \{\mathsf{msg}_2, \ldots, \mathsf{msg}_n\}$)

$(\mathbf{s}_1, \tilde{\mathbf{t}}, \mu, a_1, \mathbf{y}_1, \mathbf{r}_1, \mathbf{w}_1) := \mathsf{st}_1$

for $i = 2, \ldots, n$ do $\mathbf{w}_i := \mathsf{msg}_i$

$\tilde{\mathbf{w}} := \sum_{i=1}^n \mathbf{w}_i$

$c := \mathsf{H}_{\mathrm{sig}}(\tilde{\mathbf{t}}, \mu, \tilde{\mathbf{w}}) \in C$

$\mathbf{z}_1 := \mathbf{y}_1 + a_1 c \mathbf{s}_1$

With prob. $\min(1, \frac{D_s^{l+k}(\mathbf{z}_1)}{M \cdot D_{a_1 c \mathbf{s}_1, s}^{l+k}(\mathbf{z}_1)})$:

$\quad$ return $(c, \mathbf{z}_1, \mathbf{r}_1)$

Otherwise:

$\quad$ return $\perp$

SAgg($\{\sigma_1, \ldots, \sigma_n\}$)

for $i = 1, \ldots, n$ do $(c_i, \mathbf{z}_i, \mathbf{r}_i) := \sigma_i$

if $\exists i \in [n], c_i \ne c_1$ then return $\perp$

for $i = 1, \ldots, n$ do

$\quad [\mathbf{z}_i'^\mathsf{T}, \mathbf{z}_i''^\mathsf{T}] := \mathbf{z}_i^\mathsf{T}$

$\quad [\mathbf{r}_i'^\mathsf{T}, \mathbf{r}_i''^\mathsf{T}] := \mathbf{r}_i^\mathsf{T}$

$\tilde{\mathbf{z}} := \sum_{i=1}^n \mathbf{z}_i' \in R^l$

$\tilde{\mathbf{r}} := \sum_{i=1}^n \mathbf{r}_i' \in R^{l'}$

$\tilde{\mathbf{e}} := \sum_{i=1}^n (\mathbf{z}_i'' + \mathbf{r}_i'') \in R^k$

return $(c_1, \tilde{\mathbf{z}}, \tilde{\mathbf{r}}, \tilde{\mathbf{e}})$

Fig. 3. Our DualMS scheme.

Table 1. Parameters of DualMS.

Parameter	Description
n	Number of parties
N	A power of two defining the degree of $f(X)$
$f(X) = X^N + 1$	The $2N$-th cyclotomic polynomial
$q = 5 \mod 8$	Prime modulus
$R = \mathbb{Z}[X]/f(X)$	Cyclotomic ring
$R_q = \mathbb{Z}_q[X]/f(X)$	Ring
k	The height of random matrix $\mathbf{A}$
l	The width of random matrix $\mathbf{A}$
$m = l + k \leq \mathrm{poly}(N)$	The width of matrix $\bar{\mathbf{A}}$
l'	The width of matrix $\mathbf{B}$ given by $\mathsf{H}_{\mathrm{com}}$
$m' = l' + k \leq \mathrm{poly}(N)$	The width of matrix $\bar{\mathbf{B}}$
γ	Parameters defining the tail bound of Lemma 4
$B = \gamma(s/\sqrt{2\pi})\sqrt{Nl}$	The maximum L^2-norm of response $\mathbf{z}'_1$
$B_n = \sqrt{n}B$	The maximum L^2-norm of aggregated response $\tilde{\mathbf{z}}$
$B' = \gamma(s'/\sqrt{2\pi})\sqrt{Nl'}$	The maximum L^2-norm of response $\mathbf{r}'_1$
$B'_n = \sqrt{n}B'$	The maximum L^2-norm of aggregated response $\tilde{\mathbf{r}}$
$B'' = \gamma(\sqrt{s^2 + s'^2}/\sqrt{2\pi})\sqrt{Nk}$	The maximum L^2-norm of error $\mathbf{z}''_1 + \mathbf{r}''_1$
$B''_n = \sqrt{n}B''$	The maximum L^2-norm of aggregated error $\tilde{\mathbf{r}}$
κ	The maximum L^1-norm of challenge vector c
$C = \{c \in R : \|c\|_\infty = 1 \wedge \|c\|_1 = \kappa\}$	Challenge set where $|C| = \binom{N}{\kappa}2^\kappa$
η	The maximum L^∞-norm of the secret $\mathbf{s}$
S_η	Key set
$T = \kappa^2\eta\sqrt{Nm}$	The maximum L^2-norm of $a_1c\mathbf{s}_1$
η'	The maximum L^∞-norm of the secret $\mathbf{u}$
$S_{\eta'}$	Dual key set
$T' = \kappa^2\eta'\sqrt{Nm'}$	The maximum L^2-norm of $a_1c\bar{\mathbf{u}}$
α	Parameter defining s and M based on Lemma 5
$t = \omega(\sqrt{\log(N)}) \wedge t = o(\log(N))$	Parameter defining M based on Lemma 5
$s > \max(\sqrt{2\pi}\alpha T, 2N \cdot q^{k/m+2/(Nm)})$	Deviation parameter of the Gaussian distribution of $\mathbf{y}_1$
$s' > \max(\sqrt{2\pi}\alpha T', 2N \cdot q^{k/m'+2/(Nm')})$	Deviation parameter of the Gaussian distribution of $\mathbf{r}_1$
$M = e^{t/\alpha + 1/(2\alpha^2)}$	The expected number of restarts of a single party
$M_n = M^n$	The expected number of restarts of all n parties

Once the signer receives all commitments $\mathbf{w}_2, \ldots, \mathbf{w}_n$ from the other signers, it aggregates them with its own commitment into an aggregated commitment $\tilde{\mathbf{w}} := \sum_{i=1}^n \mathbf{w}_i$. Then it uses a hash function $\mathsf{H}_{\mathrm{sig}}$ to derive a short challenge $c := \mathsf{H}_{\mathrm{sig}}(\tilde{\mathbf{t}}, \mu, \tilde{\mathbf{w}}) \in C$. It computes its response $\mathbf{z}_1 := \mathbf{y}_1 + a_1c\mathbf{s}_1$ where $a_1 = \mathsf{H}_{\mathrm{agg}}(L, \mathbf{t}_1)$. Here the distribution of $\mathbf{z}_1$ is discrete Gaussian centered at $a_1c\mathbf{s}_1$ depending on secret key $\mathbf{s}_1$. Following the FSwA paradigm [25,26], the signer runs a rejection sampling. Namely, it aborts except with probability $\min(1, D_s^{l+k}(\mathbf{z}_1)/(M \cdot D_{a_1c\mathbf{s}_1,s}^{l+k}(\mathbf{z}_1)))$. As a result, when it passes the rejection sampling, the distribution of $\mathbf{z}_1$ will center at $\mathbf{0}$, and thus $\mathbf{s}_1$ keeps secret. See a formal analysis in Sect. 4.1. The signer broadcasts $(c, \mathbf{z}_1, \mathbf{r}_1)$ as its individual signature if it does not abort. Otherwise, the signers may restart the protocol until no signer aborts here.

Finally, if all individual signatures have the same challenge c, then they can be aggregated into a multi-signature. This aggregating procedure does not involve any secret states of the signers and thus can be executed by a designated aggregator rather than the signers. The aggregator splits each $\mathbf{z}_i$ into $\mathbf{z}'_i \in R^l$ and $\mathbf{z}''_i \in R^k$ and similarly, $\mathbf{r}_i$ into $\mathbf{r}'_i \in R^{l'}$ and $\mathbf{r}''_i \in R^k$. Then it aggregates $\mathbf{z}'_1$, ..., $\mathbf{z}'_n$ into $\tilde{\mathbf{z}}$, $\mathbf{r}'_1$, ..., $\mathbf{r}'_n$ into $\tilde{\mathbf{r}}$, and the remaining k-dimensional vectors into $\tilde{\mathbf{e}}$.

In the aggregation procedure, we observe that $\mathbf{z}_i$ and $\mathbf{r}_i$ both contain a k-dimensional MLWE error term that will be multiplied by $\mathbf{I}$ for verification. We therefore optimize the scheme by aggregating all the k-dimensional error terms. Compared to directly aggregating $\mathbf{z}_i$'s and $\mathbf{r}_i$'s separately, the optimization cuts k dimensions from the final signature. Note that we only apply the optimization in the very last step. Alternatively, we can also let each signer just produce one error vector at the beginning. That will further improve efficiency a bit while complicate the presentation hereinafter. See the full version of this paper [10] for a more detailed discussion.

Verification. Given an aggregated key $\tilde{\mathbf{t}}$, a message μ and a multi-signature $(c, \tilde{\mathbf{z}}, \tilde{\mathbf{r}}, \tilde{\mathbf{e}})$, the verifier recovers the aggregated commitment $\tilde{\mathbf{w}} := \mathbf{A}\tilde{\mathbf{z}} + \mathbf{B}\tilde{\mathbf{r}} + \tilde{\mathbf{e}} - c\tilde{\mathbf{t}}$. It then verifies that $c = \mathsf{H}_{\mathrm{sig}}(\tilde{\mathbf{t}}, \mu, \tilde{\mathbf{w}})$ and that $\tilde{\mathbf{z}}$, $\tilde{\mathbf{r}}$, and $\tilde{\mathbf{e}}$ are short enough. We will show the completeness of DualMS in the next subsection.

Simulation. We will give a formal security proof for DualMS in the next section. Here let us briefly sketch how the reduction performs straight-line simulation. When the adversary queries $\mathsf{H}_{\mathrm{com}}$, the reduction answers with $\mathbf{B} := [\mathbf{b}|\hat{\mathbf{B}}]$, where $\hat{\mathbf{B}}$ is uniformly chosen from $R_q^{k \times (l'-1)}$ and $\mathbf{b} := \mathbf{t}_1 - [\hat{\mathbf{B}}|\mathbf{I}]\mathbf{u}$ with $\mathbf{u} \leftarrow_\$ S_{\eta'}^{l'-1+k}$. Consequently, the reduction knows a dual secret key $\bar{\mathbf{u}} := [1, \mathbf{u}^\mathsf{T}]^\mathsf{T}$ satisfying $\bar{\mathbf{B}}\bar{\mathbf{u}} = \mathbf{t}_1$.

In the signing protocol, the reduction computes its commitment as $\mathbf{w}_1 := \bar{\mathbf{A}}\mathbf{z}_1 + \bar{\mathbf{B}}\mathbf{p}$ with $\mathbf{z}_1 \leftarrow D_s^{l+k}$ and $\mathbf{p} \leftarrow D_{s'}^{l'+k}$. In the second stage, the reduction generates its individual signature with $\mathbf{r}_1 := \mathbf{p} + a_1 c \bar{\mathbf{u}}$. The reduction also performs rejection sampling here to keep $\bar{\mathbf{u}}$ secret.

3.2 Correctness and Number of Repetitions

We show that DualMS is correct and the expected number of restarts is approximately M_n, i.e., DualMS is ε-complete with $\varepsilon \approx 1/M_n$.

We need the following results implied by Lemma 14 in Sect. 4.1: conditioned on any commitment $\mathbf{w}_1$ sent out in the first round and any a_1, c: 1) the signer passes rejection sampling with probability approximately $1/M$; 2) the distribution of $\mathbf{z}_1$ is statistically close to D_s^{l+k}. The fact that these results hold for any $\mathbf{w}_1$, a_1, and c_1 means that no malicious signer can affect them. We know immediately from the first result that all signers pass rejection sampling together with probability about $1/M_n$.

Then we show that if no signer aborts, then the signing protocol outputs a valid multi-signature except with small probability bounded by Lemma 4. Consider each individual signature produced by the signing protocol, for all $i \in [n]$ we have

$$\mathbf{w}_i = \bar{\mathbf{A}}\mathbf{y}_i + \bar{\mathbf{B}}\mathbf{r}_i = \bar{\mathbf{A}}(\mathbf{z}_i - a_i c \mathbf{s}_i) + \bar{\mathbf{B}}\mathbf{r}_i$$
$$= \bar{\mathbf{A}}\mathbf{z}_i + \bar{\mathbf{B}}\mathbf{r}_i - a_i c \mathbf{t}_i = \mathbf{A}\mathbf{z}_i' + \mathbf{B}\mathbf{r}_i' + \mathbf{z}_i'' + \mathbf{r}_i'' - a_i c \mathbf{t}_i.$$

For the multi-signature given by the protocol, we have

$$\tilde{\mathbf{w}} = \sum_{i=1}^{n} \mathbf{w}_i = \mathbf{A}\sum_{i=1}^{n} \mathbf{z}_i' + \mathbf{B}\sum_{i=1}^{n} \mathbf{r}_i' + \sum_{i=1}^{n}(\mathbf{z}_i'' + \mathbf{r}_i'') - c\sum_{i=1}^{n} a_i \mathbf{t}_i = \mathbf{A}\tilde{\mathbf{z}} + \mathbf{B}\tilde{\mathbf{r}} + \tilde{\mathbf{e}} - c\tilde{\mathbf{t}}.$$

Thus, the verifier correctly recovers the aggregated commitment given such a multi-signature, so the condition $c = \mathsf{H}_{\mathrm{sig}}(\tilde{\mathbf{t}}, \mu, \tilde{\mathbf{w}})$ always holds.

It remains to consider conditions $\|\tilde{\mathbf{z}}\|_2 \leq B_n$, $\|\tilde{\mathbf{r}}\|_2 \leq B_n'$, and $\|\tilde{\mathbf{e}}\|_2 \leq B_n''$. For all $i \in [n]$, we know that $\mathbf{r}_i$ is sampled from $D_{s'}^{l'+k}$, and by Lemma 14, the distribution of $\mathbf{z}_i$ is statistically close to D_s^{l+k}. By Lemma 3, the distributions of $\tilde{\mathbf{z}}$, $\tilde{\mathbf{r}}$, and $\tilde{\mathbf{e}}$ are statistically close to $D_{s\sqrt{n}}^l$, $D_{s'\sqrt{n}}^{l'}$, and $D_{\sqrt{n(s^2+s'^2)}}^k$ respectively. Then Lemma 4 bounds the probability that $\|\tilde{\mathbf{z}}\|_2$, $\|\tilde{\mathbf{r}}\|_2$, and $\|\tilde{\mathbf{e}}\|_2$ exceed B_n, B_n', B_n'', respectively. Setting the parameter γ in Lemma 4 as 1.1 gives a reasonably small probability, and $\gamma = \sqrt{3}$ is enough to yield an unnecessarily small bound $(\sqrt{3}/e)^{Nm}$.

3.3   Security

We have the following security result for DualMS.

Theorem 12 (UF-CMA of DualMS). *For any τ-time adversary $\mathcal{A}$ against the UF-CMA of DualMS that makes at most Q_h queries to each random oracle and launches at most Q_s sessions with the signing oracles, there exist algorithms $\mathcal{B}$, $\mathcal{D}$, and $\mathcal{D}'$ such that*

$$\mathbf{Adv}_{\mathsf{DualMS}}^{\mathsf{UF\text{-}CMA}}(\mathcal{A}) \leq Q_h \cdot \left(\sqrt{\frac{Q_h^2}{|C|} + Q_h \sqrt{Q_h \mathbf{Adv}_{\mathsf{MSIS}_{q,k,1+l+l',\beta}}(\mathcal{B})}} \right.$$
$$+ \mathbf{Adv}_{\mathsf{MLWE}_{q,k,l,\eta}}(\mathcal{D}) + (Q_h - 1)\mathbf{Adv}_{\mathsf{MLWE}_{q,k,l'-1,\eta'}}(\mathcal{D}')$$
$$\left. + Q_s\left(\frac{3\epsilon}{2M} + 2^{-\Omega(N)}\right) + \frac{2Q_h^2}{|C|} + 3\left(\frac{2}{q^{N/2}}\right)^k \right),$$

where $\beta = 8\kappa\sqrt{\hat{n}^2\kappa^3 + B_n^2 + B_n'^2 + B_n''^2}$, $\hat{n}$ is the maximum number of duplicate keys in a public key list, $\epsilon = 2e^{-t^2/2}$, t is a parameter as specified in Table 1, and the running time of $\mathcal{B}$, $\mathcal{D}$, and $\mathcal{D}'$ are essentially 4τ, τ, and τ, respectively.

Let us explain the security guarantees given by this theorem. We can choose t to make ϵ and hence the term $Q_s(2\epsilon/M + 2^{-\Omega(N)})$ small enough. The term $3(2/q^{N/2})^k$ is clearly small. We also set κ to make $|C|$ large enough. A common setting when $N = 256$ is $\kappa = 60$, which gives $|C| > 2^{256}$. Among the two $Q_h^2/|C|$ terms in the formula, the square-rooted one is dominant. Due to the quadratic loss and the outer factor Q_h, $|C| > 2^{256}$ only permits at most

64 bits of security (i.e., the adversary need $Q_h \geq 2^{64}$ to achieve constant success probability). It remains to set the parameters to make $\mathsf{MSIS}_{q,k,1+l+l',\beta}$, $\mathsf{MLWE}_{q,k,l,\eta}$, and $\mathsf{MLWE}_{q,k,l'-1,\eta'}$ hard enough. Note that $\mathbf{Adv}_{\mathsf{MSIS}_{q,k,1+l+l',\beta}}(\mathcal{B})$ is also affected by quadratic and multiplicative loss. For about 64-bit security, we need $\mathbf{Adv}_{\mathsf{MSIS}_{q,k,1+l+l',\beta}}(\mathcal{B}) \approx 2^{-448}$. $\mathbf{Adv}_{\mathsf{MLWE}_{q,k,l'-1,\eta'}}(\mathcal{D}')$ is affected by an extra factor $(Q_h - 1)$ compared to $\mathbf{Adv}_{\mathsf{MLWE}_{q,k,l,\eta}}(\mathcal{D})$. They are required to be about 2^{-128} and 2^{-64} respectively.

Our scheme allows duplicate public keys unlike [9]. We consider the number of duplicates as an extra parameter $\hat{n}$. By doing this we can more accurately show how security is affected by allowing duplicates.

An important type of attacks against multi-signature schemes is to concurrently launch many signing sessions and linearly combine those signatures from the honest signer into a forged one [6,13]. Our scheme resists such attacks for a similar reason to [4,12,13]. Linear combination works only when matrix $\bar{\mathbf{A}}$ and $\bar{\mathbf{B}}$ are both fixed. However, different messages lead to different matrix $\bar{\mathbf{B}}$ with high probability, which prevents the attacker from forging signatures on new messages.

4 Proof of Security

In this section, we prove Theorem 12.

Assumptions About Random Oracle Queries. Before we begin our proofs, let us make the following assumptions about the adversary's random oracle queries.

- The adversary queries $\mathsf{H}_{\mathrm{com}}(\tilde{\mathbf{t}}, \mu)$ before it queries $\mathsf{H}_{\mathrm{sig}}(\tilde{\mathbf{t}}, \mu, \tilde{\mathbf{w}})$ for any $\tilde{\mathbf{w}}$.
- The adversary queries $\mathsf{H}_{\mathrm{agg}}(L, \mathbf{t}_i)$ for every $\mathbf{t}_i \in L$ before it makes signing query $\mathrm{SIGN}_1(\{\mathbf{t}_2, \ldots, \mathbf{t}_n\}, \mu)$, where $L = \{\mathbf{t}_1^*, \mathbf{t}_2, \ldots, \mathbf{t}_n\}$.
- The adversary queries $\mathsf{H}_{\mathrm{sig}}(\tilde{\mathbf{t}}, \mu, \tilde{\mathbf{w}})$ before it queries $\mathrm{SIGN}_2(sid, \{\mathbf{w}_2, \ldots, \mathbf{w}_n\})$, where $\tilde{\mathbf{t}}$ is the aggregated public key corresponding to that signing session, $\tilde{\mathbf{w}} = \sum_{i=1}^{n} \mathbf{w}_i$, and $\mathbf{w}_1$ is the nonce returned by SIGN_1 in that session.
- The adversary queries all hash queries that related to its forgery (i.e., all queries that will be made in verification) before it outputs the forgery.

These assumptions are without loss of generality in the sense that given an arbitrary adversary $\mathcal{A}$ making at most Q_h queries to each random oracles and launching Q_s sessions with the signing oracles, we can easily construct an adversary $\mathcal{A}'$ as a "random oracle middle man" that satisfies the assumptions, wins with the same probability as $\mathcal{A}$, and makes at most $2Q_h + n(Q_s + 1)$ queries to each random oracles. It is reasonable to consider Q_h as the dominant term, as Q_h is related to the local computation time of a real-world attacker. Hence, the security loss introduced here is not essential.

Selective Security. We prove Theorem 12 in a modular way. We first reduce UF-CMA to *selective UF-CMA (sel-UF-CMA)* (Lemma 13), then sel-UF-CMA to *selective UF-KOA (sel-UF-KOA)* and MLWE (Lemma 15), and finally sel-UF-KOA to MSIS and MLWE (Lemma 16). Let us define the sel-UF-CMA and the sel-UF-KOA of our DualMS. In the selective security game, the adversary selects at the beginning the index of a H_{com} query, and its goal is to forge a multi-signature corresponding to that H_{com} query. Precisely, the sUF-CMA$_{DualMS}$ security game has the following differences from UF-CMA$_{DualMS}$. The adversary $\mathcal{A} = (\mathcal{A}_1, \mathcal{A}_2)$ is split into two stages. The first stage $\mathcal{A}_1$ outputs an index i^* without making any oracle queries. The second stage $\mathcal{A}_2$ has the access to the random oracles and the signing oracles and outputs its forgery but without a message (namely, it outputs a public-key list L^* and a multi-signature $\tilde{\sigma}^*$). Suppose the i^*-th H_{com} query is $H_{com}(\tilde{\mathbf{t}}^*, \mu^*)$. For $\mathcal{A}$ to win, we require that L^* includes target public key $\mathbf{t}_1^*$, $\mathcal{A}$ has not queried (L^*, μ^*) to the signing oracle, L^* is aggregated into $\tilde{\mathbf{t}}^*$, and $\mathsf{Vf}(\tilde{\mathbf{t}}^*, \mu^*, \tilde{\sigma}^*) = 1$. Also see the definition in Fig. 5 where G_0 is exactly sUF-CMA$_{DualMS}$. The sUF-KOA$_{DualMS}$ security game is sUF-CMA$_{DualMS}$ without the signing oracles.

Apparently, UF-CMA reduces to sel-UF-CMA with factor Q_h loss of success probability. A reduction that guesses $i^* \in [Q_h]$ at the beginning is sufficient to prove that.

Lemma 13 (UF-CMA to sel-UF-CMA). *For any τ-time adversary $\mathcal{A}$ against the UF-CMA of DualMS that makes at most Q_h queries to each random oracle, there exists an adversary $\mathcal{B}$ such that* $\mathbf{Adv}_{DualMS}^{UF\text{-}CMA}(\mathcal{A}) \leq Q_h \cdot \mathbf{Adv}_{DualMS}^{sUF\text{-}CMA}(\mathcal{B})$ *and the running time of $\mathcal{B}$ is essentially τ.*

4.1   Straight-Line Simulation

This subsection is a preparation for reducing sel-UF-CMA to sel-UF-KOA. We bound the statistical distance between the output distributions of the normal signing oracle and the simulated one. Note that an adversary can query SIGN$_1$ to obtain a commitment $\mathbf{w}$ and then choose what challenge c it wants SIGN$_2$ to respond according to $\mathbf{w}$. We have to prevent the adversary from distinguishing the output distributions of SIGN$_2$ with strategically chosen c. Therefore, we need to analyze: 1) the distributions of $\mathbf{w}$ output by SIGN$_1$ and 2) the distributions of $\mathbf{z}$ and $\mathbf{r}$ output by SIGN$_2$ for any c, conditioned on any $\mathbf{w}$ output by SIGN$_1$ in the same session.

We define two procedures Trans and Sim in the following lemma, corresponding to the normal signing procedure and the dual signing simulation of DualMS, respectively. In both procedures, out$_1$, out$_2$ correspond to the output of SIGN$_1$, SIGN$_2$, respectively. Besides bounding the statistical distance between normal and simulated signing, the lemma also bounds the success probability of rejection sampling.

Lemma 14. *Let integers k, l, l', m, and m' satisfy $l + k = m \leq \mathsf{poly}(N)$ and $l' + k = m' \leq \mathsf{poly}(N)$. Fix some t such that $t = \omega(\sqrt{\log(N)})$ and $t = \omega(\sqrt{\log(N)})$ and $t = o(\log(N))$.[2] Let $T = \kappa^2 \eta \sqrt{N(l+k)} \geq \max \|c\mathbf{s}\|_2$*

---

[2] Since $m \leq \mathsf{poly}(N)$ and $m' \leq \mathsf{poly}(N)$, we have $\log(Nm) = \Theta(\log N)$ and $\log(Nm') = \Theta(\log N)$, so $t = o(\log(N))$ is enough for invoking Lemma 5.

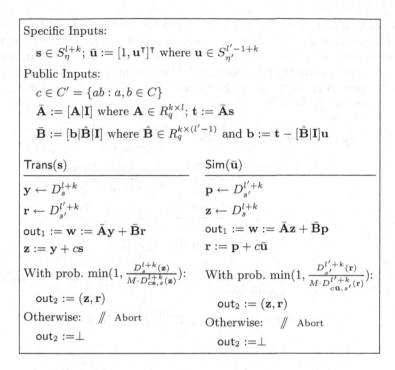

Fig. 4. Procedures Trans and Sim of Lemma 14.

and $T' = \kappa^2 \eta' \sqrt{N(l'+k)} \geq \max \|c\bar{\mathbf{u}}\|_2$. For any α, let $s > \max(\sqrt{2\pi}\alpha T, 2N \cdot q^{k/m+2/(Nm)})$, $s' > \max(\sqrt{2\pi}\alpha T', 2N \cdot q^{k/m'+2/(Nm')})$, $M = e^{t/\alpha + 1/(2\alpha^2)}$, and $\epsilon = 2e^{-t^2/2}$. Let Trans and Sim be procedures with specific and public inputs as described in Fig. 4. Then with probability $1 - 2^{-\Omega(N)}$ over the choices of $\mathbf{A}$ and $\hat{\mathbf{B}}$ uniformly over $R_q^{k \times l} \times R_q^{k \times (l'-1)}$, for any $\mathbf{s} \in S_\eta^{l+k}$, $\mathbf{u} \in S_{\eta'}^{l'-1+k}$, the following claims hold:

1. The distributions of out_1 (i.e., $\mathbf{w}$) in Trans and Sim are identical.
2. In both Trans and Sim, for any $c \in C'$ and conditioned on any out_1 (i.e., $\mathbf{w}$), it holds that

$$\frac{1-\epsilon}{M} - 2^{-\Omega(N)} \leq \Pr[\mathsf{out}_2 \neq\perp | \mathbf{w}] \leq \frac{1}{M} + 2^{-\Omega(N)}.$$

3. For any $c \in C'$ and conditioned on any out_1 (i.e., $\mathbf{w}$), the statistical distance between the distributions of out_2 in Trans and Sim is at most $3\epsilon/(2M) + 2^{-\Omega(N)}$.

Proof. Claim 1 is obvious, as $\mathbf{y}, \mathbf{r}$ in Trans are identical to $\mathbf{z}, \mathbf{p}$ in Sim. However, we still need to examine the distribution of $\mathsf{out}_1 = \mathbf{w}$ for proving other claims. We first look at $\mathbf{w}$ in Trans. Split $\mathbf{r}$ into $\mathbf{r} = [r_1, \mathbf{r}_2^\mathsf{T}]^\mathsf{T}$. Then we have

$$\bar{\mathbf{B}}\mathbf{r} = r_1(\mathbf{t} - [\hat{\mathbf{B}}|\mathbf{I}]\mathbf{u}) + [\hat{\mathbf{B}}|\mathbf{I}]\mathbf{r}_2.$$

By Lemma 6, with probability $1 - 2^{-\Omega(N)}$ over the choice of $\hat{\mathbf{B}}$, $[\hat{\mathbf{B}}|\mathbf{I}]\mathbf{r}_2$ is within statistical distance $2^{-\Omega(N)}$ of the uniform distribution. Hence, $\bar{\mathbf{B}}\mathbf{r}$ and $\mathbf{w}$ are also within distance $2^{-\Omega(N)}$ of the uniform distribution. Similarly, in Sim, $\bar{\mathbf{A}}\mathbf{z}$ and $\mathbf{w}$ are within statistical distance $2^{-\Omega(N)}$ of the uniform distribution.

Let us turn to claim 2 and look at Trans first. The conditional distribution of $\mathbf{y}$ on any $\mathbf{w}$ is within statistical distance $2^{-\Omega(N)}$ of D_s^m, since[3]

$$
\begin{aligned}
\Pr[\mathbf{y} = \mathbf{y}^* \mid \mathbf{w} = \mathbf{w}^*] &= \frac{\Pr[\mathbf{w} = \mathbf{w}^* \mid \mathbf{y} = \mathbf{y}^*] \cdot \Pr[\mathbf{y} = \mathbf{y}^*]}{\Pr[\mathbf{w} = \mathbf{w}^*]} \\
&= \frac{\Pr[\bar{\mathbf{B}}\mathbf{r} = \mathbf{w}^* - \bar{\mathbf{A}}\mathbf{y}^*] \cdot \Pr[\mathbf{y} = \mathbf{y}^*]}{\Pr[\mathbf{w} = \mathbf{w}^*]} \\
&= \frac{(1 \pm 2^{-\Omega(N)})q^{-Nk} \cdot D_s^m(\mathbf{y}^*)}{(1 \pm 2^{-\Omega(N)})q^{-Nk}} \\
&= (1 \pm 2^{-\Omega(N)})D_s^m(\mathbf{y}^*).
\end{aligned}
$$

Consider an arbitrary $c \in C'$. Let $\mathbf{v} = c\mathbf{s}$, and $S_{\mathbf{v}} = \{\mathbf{z} \in R^m : M \cdot D_{\mathbf{v},s}^m(\mathbf{z}) \geq D_s^m(\mathbf{z})\}$. Since $\mathbf{z} = \mathbf{y} + c\mathbf{s}$, we have

$$
\Pr[\mathbf{z} = \mathbf{z}^* \mid \mathbf{w}] = (1 \pm 2^{-\Omega(N)})D_{\mathbf{v},s}^m(\mathbf{z}^*). \tag{1}
$$

Thus,

$$
\begin{aligned}
\Pr[\mathrm{out}_2 \neq \perp \mid \mathbf{w}] &\geq \sum_{\mathbf{z} \in R^m} (1 - 2^{-\Omega(N)})D_{\mathbf{v},s}^m(\mathbf{z}) \cdot \min(1, \frac{D_s^m(\mathbf{z})}{M \cdot D_{\mathbf{v},s}^m(\mathbf{z})}) \\
&\geq \sum_{\mathbf{z} \in S_{\mathbf{v}}} \frac{D_s^m(\mathbf{z})}{M} + \sum_{\mathbf{z} \notin S_{\mathbf{v}}} D_{\mathbf{v},s}^m(\mathbf{z}) - 2^{-\Omega(N)} \\
&\geq \sum_{\mathbf{z} \in S_{\mathbf{v}}} \frac{D_s^m(\mathbf{z})}{M} - 2^{-\Omega(N)} \geq \frac{1 - \epsilon}{M} - 2^{-\Omega(N)}.
\end{aligned}
$$

In the last inequality, we have used Lemma 5. It also holds that

$$
\begin{aligned}
\Pr[\mathrm{out}_2 \neq \perp \mid \mathbf{w}] &\leq \sum_{\mathbf{z} \in R^m} (1 + 2^{-\Omega(N)})D_{\mathbf{v},s}^m(\mathbf{z}) \cdot \min(1, \frac{D_s^m(\mathbf{z})}{M \cdot D_{\mathbf{v},s}^m(\mathbf{z})}) \\
&\leq \sum_{\mathbf{z} \in R^m} D_{\mathbf{v},s}^m(\mathbf{z}) \cdot \frac{D_s^m(\mathbf{z})}{M \cdot D_{\mathbf{v},s}^m(\mathbf{z})} + 2^{-\Omega(N)} = \frac{1}{M} + 2^{-\Omega(N)}.
\end{aligned}
$$

Similar arguments can show that in Sim, the conditional distribution of $\mathbf{p}$ on any $\mathbf{w}$ is within statistical distance $2^{-\Omega(N)}$ of $D_{s'}^{m'}$ and give the same bound for $\Pr[\mathrm{out}_2 \neq \perp \mid \mathbf{w}]$.

It remains to prove claim 3. We already have $\Pr[\mathrm{out}_2 = \perp \mid \mathbf{w}]$ in Trans and Sim. It suffices to only consider $\Pr[\mathrm{out}_2 = (\mathbf{z}, \mathbf{r}) \mid \mathbf{w}]$ with $\mathbf{z} \in R^m$ and $\mathbf{r} \in R^{m'}$.

---

[3] In this proof, notation $\mathbf{y}^*$ (and $\mathbf{z}^*$, $\mathbf{r}^*$, $\mathbf{w}^*$, etc.) appear in an equation to denote some specific value if we view $\mathbf{y}$ as a random variable distributed according to the Trans or Sim.

In both procedures, $\Pr[\text{out}_2 = (\mathbf{z}, \mathbf{r}) \mid \mathbf{w}] = 0$ when $\bar{\mathbf{A}}\mathbf{z} + \bar{\mathbf{B}}\mathbf{r} \neq \mathbf{w} + c\mathbf{t}$. Define function P over $R^m \times R^{m'}$ as

$$P(\mathbf{z}, \mathbf{r}) = \frac{D_s^m(\mathbf{z}) D_{s'}^{m'}(\mathbf{r})}{M q^{-Nk}}.$$

We are going to show that both in Trans and Sim,

$$\sum_{\substack{\mathbf{z} \in R^m, \mathbf{r} \in R^{m'} \\ \bar{\mathbf{A}}\mathbf{z} + \bar{\mathbf{B}}\mathbf{r} = \mathbf{w} + c\mathbf{t}}} |\Pr[\text{out}_2 = (\mathbf{z}, \mathbf{r}) \mid \mathbf{w}] - P(\mathbf{z}, \mathbf{r})| \leq \frac{\epsilon}{M} + 2^{-\Omega(N)}. \tag{2}$$

This will prove claim 3 when combined with claim 2. Again, we prove the bound for Trans, and a similar argument applies to Sim.

Define $P_{\mathbf{w}}$ as

$$P_{\mathbf{w}}(\mathbf{z}^*, \mathbf{r}^*) = \frac{D_s^m(\mathbf{z}^*) \cdot D_{s'}^{m'}(\mathbf{r}^*)}{M \cdot \Pr[\bar{\mathbf{B}}\mathbf{r} = \mathbf{w} + c\mathbf{t} - \bar{\mathbf{A}}\mathbf{z}^*]},$$

and $P_{\mathbf{w}}'$ as

$$P_{\mathbf{w}}'(\mathbf{z}^*, \mathbf{r}^*) = D_{v,s}^m(\mathbf{z}^*) \cdot \min(1, \frac{D_s^m(\mathbf{z}^*)}{M \cdot D_{cs,s}^m(\mathbf{z}^*)}) \cdot \frac{D_{s'}^{m'}(\mathbf{r}^*)}{\Pr[\bar{\mathbf{B}}\mathbf{r} = \mathbf{w} + c\mathbf{t} - \bar{\mathbf{A}}\mathbf{z}^*]}.$$

By Lemma 6, we have

$$\sum_{\substack{\mathbf{z} \in R^m, \mathbf{r} \in R^{m'} \\ \bar{\mathbf{A}}\mathbf{z} + \bar{\mathbf{B}}\mathbf{r} = \mathbf{w} + c\mathbf{t}}} |P_{\mathbf{w}}(\mathbf{z}, \mathbf{r}) - P(\mathbf{z}, \mathbf{r})| \leq 2^{-\Omega(N)}. \tag{3}$$

For $\mathbf{z}^*$ and $\mathbf{r}^*$ satisfying $\bar{\mathbf{A}}\mathbf{z}^* + \bar{\mathbf{B}}\mathbf{r}^* = \mathbf{w} + c\mathbf{t}$, we have

$$\Pr[\text{out}_2 = (\mathbf{z}^*, \mathbf{r}^*) \mid \mathbf{w}]$$
$$= \Pr[\mathbf{z} = \mathbf{z}^* \wedge \text{out}_2 \neq \perp \mid \mathbf{w}] \cdot \Pr[\mathbf{r} = \mathbf{r}^* \mid \mathbf{w} \wedge \mathbf{z} = \mathbf{z}^*]$$
$$= \Pr[\mathbf{z} = \mathbf{z}^* \wedge \text{out}_2 \neq \perp \mid \mathbf{w}] \cdot \Pr[\mathbf{r} = \mathbf{r}^* \mid \bar{\mathbf{B}}\mathbf{r} = \mathbf{w} + c\mathbf{t} - \bar{\mathbf{A}}\mathbf{z}^*]$$
$$= \Pr[\mathbf{z} = \mathbf{z}^* \mid \mathbf{w}] \cdot \min(1, \frac{D_s^m(\mathbf{z}^*)}{M \cdot D_{v,s}^m(\mathbf{z}^*)}) \cdot \frac{D_{s'}^{m'}(\mathbf{r}^*)}{\Pr[\bar{\mathbf{B}}\mathbf{r} = \mathbf{w} + c\mathbf{t} - \bar{\mathbf{A}}\mathbf{z}^*]}.$$

By Eq. (1),

$$\sum_{\substack{\mathbf{z} \in R^m, \mathbf{r} \in R^{m'} \\ \bar{\mathbf{A}}\mathbf{z} + \bar{\mathbf{B}}\mathbf{r} = \mathbf{w} + c\mathbf{t}}} |\Pr[\text{out}_2 = (\mathbf{z}, \mathbf{r}) \mid \mathbf{w}] - P_{\mathbf{w}}'(\mathbf{z}, \mathbf{r})| \leq 2^{-\Omega(N)}. \tag{4}$$

Finally,

$$\sum_{\substack{\mathbf{z}^*\in R^m, \mathbf{r}^*\in R^{m'} \\ \bar{\mathbf{A}}\mathbf{z}^*+\bar{\mathbf{B}}\mathbf{r}^*=\mathbf{w}+ct}} |P'_{\mathbf{w}}(\mathbf{z}^*, \mathbf{r}^*) - P_{\mathbf{w}}(\mathbf{z}^*, \mathbf{r}^*)|$$

$$= \sum_{\substack{\mathbf{z}^*\in R^m, \mathbf{r}^*\in R^{m'} \\ \bar{\mathbf{A}}\mathbf{z}^*+\bar{\mathbf{B}}\mathbf{r}^*=\mathbf{w}+ct}} \frac{D_{s'}^{m'}(\mathbf{r}^*)}{\Pr[\bar{\mathbf{B}}\mathbf{r} = \mathbf{w} + ct - \bar{\mathbf{A}}\mathbf{z}^*]}$$

$$\cdot \left| D_{\mathsf{v},s}^m(\mathbf{z}^*) \cdot \min(1, \frac{D_s^m(\mathbf{z}^*)}{M \cdot D_{\mathsf{v},s}^m(\mathbf{z}^*)}) - \frac{D_s^m(\mathbf{z}^*)}{M} \right|$$

$$= \sum_{\substack{\mathbf{z}^*\in S_{\mathsf{v}}, \mathbf{r}^*\in R^{m'} \\ \bar{\mathbf{A}}\mathbf{z}^*+\bar{\mathbf{B}}\mathbf{r}^*=\mathbf{w}+ct}} \frac{D_{s'}^{m'}(\mathbf{r}^*)}{\Pr[\bar{\mathbf{B}}\mathbf{r} = \mathbf{w} + ct - \bar{\mathbf{A}}\mathbf{z}^*]} \left| \frac{D_s^m(\mathbf{z}^*)}{M} - \frac{D_s^m(\mathbf{z}^*)}{M} \right|$$

$$+ \sum_{\substack{\mathbf{z}^*\notin S_{\mathsf{v}}, \mathbf{r}^*\in R^{m'} \\ \bar{\mathbf{A}}\mathbf{z}^*+\bar{\mathbf{B}}\mathbf{r}^*=\mathbf{w}+ct}} \frac{D_{s'}^{m'}(\mathbf{r}^*)}{\Pr[\bar{\mathbf{B}}\mathbf{r} = \mathbf{w} + ct - \bar{\mathbf{A}}\mathbf{z}^*]} \left| D_{\mathsf{v},s}^m(\mathbf{z}^*) - \frac{D_s^m(\mathbf{z}^*)}{M} \right|$$

$$\leq \sum_{\substack{\mathbf{z}^*\notin S_{\mathsf{v}}, \mathbf{r}^*\in R^{m'} \\ \bar{\mathbf{A}}\mathbf{z}^*+\bar{\mathbf{B}}\mathbf{r}^*=\mathbf{w}+ct}} \frac{D_s^m(\mathbf{z}^*)D_{s'}^{m'}(\mathbf{r}^*)}{M \cdot \Pr[\bar{\mathbf{B}}\mathbf{r} = \mathbf{w} + ct - \bar{\mathbf{A}}\mathbf{z}^*]}$$

$$= \frac{1}{M} \sum_{\mathbf{z}^*\notin S_{\mathsf{v}}} \frac{D_s^m(\mathbf{z}^*)}{\Pr[\bar{\mathbf{B}}\mathbf{r} = \mathbf{w} + ct - \bar{\mathbf{A}}\mathbf{z}^*]} \sum_{\substack{\mathbf{r}^*\in R^{m'} \\ \bar{\mathbf{B}}\mathbf{r}^*=\mathbf{w}+ct-\bar{\mathbf{A}}\mathbf{z}^*}} D_{s'}^{m'}(\mathbf{r}^*)$$

$$= \frac{1}{M} \sum_{\mathbf{z}^*\notin S_{\mathsf{v}}} D_s^m(\mathbf{z}^*) \leq \frac{\epsilon}{M}.$$

Combined with Eqs. (3) and (4), this proves Eq. (2). A similar argument can show Eq. (2) for Sim.

4.2   Reduction from Sel-UF-CMA to Sel-UF-KOA and MLWE

Lemma 15 (sel-UF-CMA to sel-UF-KOA and MLWE). *For any τ-time adversary $\mathcal{A}$ against the sel-UF-CMA of DualMS that makes at most Q_h queries to each random oracle and launches at most Q_s sessions with the signing oracles, there exist algorithms $\mathcal{B}$ and $\mathcal{D}$ such that*

$$\mathbf{Adv}_{\mathsf{DualMS}}^{\mathsf{sUF\text{-}CMA}}(\mathcal{A}) \leq \mathbf{Adv}_{\mathsf{DualMS}}^{\mathsf{sUF\text{-}KOA}}(\mathcal{B}) + (Q_h - 1)\mathbf{Adv}_{\mathsf{MLWE}_{q,k,l'-1,\eta'}}(\mathcal{D})$$

$$+ Q_s(\frac{3\epsilon}{2M} + 2^{-\Omega(N)}) + \frac{Q_h(Q_h - 1)}{|C|} + (\frac{2}{q^{N/2}})^k,$$

where $\epsilon = 2e^{-t^2/2}$, t is a parameter as specified in Table 1, and the running time of $\mathcal{B}$ and $\mathcal{D}$ are essentially τ.

Proof. Let G_0 be the original sUF-CMA$_{\mathsf{DualMS}}$ game. We define a series of hybrid games G_1, $G_{2,0}$, ..., G_{2,Q_h}, and G_3. They are all described in Fig. 5, where we omit normal random oracles H_{agg} and H_{sig}.

G_1 differs from G_0 only in H_{com}. In G_0, on any fresh query, H_{com} returns $\mathbf{B}$ uniformly chosen from $R_q^{k \times l'}$. In G_1, except on the i^*-th fresh query, the first column $\mathbf{b}$ of $\mathbf{B}$ is instead decided by $\mathbf{b} := \mathbf{t}_1^* - \mathbf{v}$ with $\mathbf{v} \leftarrow_\$ R_q^k$. Apparently the view of $\mathcal{A}$ in G_0 and G_1 are identical, so we have

$$\Pr[G_0(\mathcal{A}) = 1] = \Pr[G_1(\mathcal{A}) = 1].$$

$G_{2,0}$ only differs from G_1 in the game initialization. To set up, $G_{2,0}$ initializes an empty table $\mathcal{T}_\mathbf{u}$. For $1 \le j \le Q_h$, $G_{2,j}$ differs from $G_{2,j-1}$ in the j-th fresh H_{com} query. To answer the j-th fresh H_{com} query in $G_{2,j-1}$, if $j \ne i^*$, then the first column of $\mathbf{B} = [\mathbf{b}|\hat{\mathbf{B}}]$ is decided by $\mathbf{b} := \mathbf{t}_1^* - \mathbf{v}$ with uniform $\mathbf{v}$. In $G_{2,j}$, $\mathbf{v}$ is instead decided by $\mathbf{v} := [\hat{\mathbf{B}}|\mathbf{I}]\mathbf{u}$ with a short $\mathbf{u}$ uniformly chosen from $S_{\eta'}^{l'-1+k}$. Then $\mathbf{u}$ is stored in $\mathcal{T}_\mathbf{u}[\tilde{\mathbf{t}}, \mu]$.

Note that $\hat{\mathbf{B}}$ and $\mathbf{v}$ constitute a MLWE$_{q,k,l'-1,\eta'}$ instance. A distinguisher $\mathcal{D}$ against MLWE$_{q,k,l'-1,\eta'}$ can simulate $G_{2,j-1}$ / $G_{2,j}$ for $1 \le j \le Q_h$ and $j \ne i^*$ for $\mathcal{A}$, since in $G_{2,j}$ the short secret $\mathbf{u}$ is never used elsewhere. Thus, we have

$$\Pr[G_{2,0}(\mathcal{A}) = 1] = \Pr[G_1(\mathcal{A}) = 1], \quad \Pr[G_{2,i^*}(\mathcal{A}) = 1] = \Pr[G_{2,i^*-1}(\mathcal{A}) = 1],$$

and for $1 \le j \le Q_h$ and $j \ne i^*$

$$\Pr[G_{2,j-1}(\mathcal{A}) = 1] - \Pr[G_{2,j}(\mathcal{A}) = 1] \le \mathbf{Adv}_{\mathsf{MLWE}_{q,k,l'-1,\eta'}}(\mathcal{D}).$$

G_3 differs from G_{2,Q_h} only in the signing oracles. In G_{2,Q_h}, the signing oracles use the secret key $\mathbf{s}_1$ to execute the signing protocol like an honest party. In G_3, the signing oracles retrieve $\mathbf{u} = \mathcal{T}_\mathbf{u}[\tilde{\mathbf{t}}, \mu]$ to obtain a vector $\bar{\mathbf{u}} = [1, \mathbf{u}^\intercal]^\intercal$. Unless $H_{\mathrm{com}}(\tilde{\mathbf{t}}, \mu)$ is the i^*-th fresh H_{com} query, $\bar{\mathbf{B}}$ and $\bar{\mathbf{u}}$ will have relation as specified in Fig. 4. The oracles use $\bar{\mathbf{u}}$ to perform straight-line simulation following algorithm Sim in Fig. 4. There will be no item $\mathcal{T}_\mathbf{u}[\tilde{\mathbf{t}}^*, \mu^*]$ in $\mathcal{T}_\mathbf{u}$, so the signing oracles in G_3 fail when dealing with $(\tilde{\mathbf{t}}, \mu) = (\tilde{\mathbf{t}}^*, \mu^*)$.

In each signing session, if $(\tilde{\mathbf{t}}, \mu) \ne (\tilde{\mathbf{t}}^*, \mu^*)$, it can be verified that the outputs of the signing oracles in G_{2,Q_h} and G_3 are distributed respectively according to Trans and Sim in Fig. 4. We already bounded their statistical distance by $3\epsilon/(2M) + 2^{-\Omega(N)}$. On the other hand, G_3 will be distinguishable from G_{2,Q_h} if $(\tilde{\mathbf{t}}, \mu) = (\tilde{\mathbf{t}}^*, \mu^*)$. Nevertheless, in this case G_{2,Q_h} outputs 1 only if $\mathcal{A}$ at the end outputs a different L^* from the queried public-key list L satisfying $\mathsf{KAgg}(L^*) = \mathsf{KAgg}(L) = \tilde{\mathbf{t}}^*$. Let AggCol denote the event that $\mathcal{A}$ ever queried two different public-key lists $L^* \ne L$ satisfying $\mathsf{KAgg}(L^*) = \mathsf{KAgg}(L)$. It is shown in [9] and the full version of this paper [10] that the probability of AggCol can be bounded by $Q_h(Q_h - 1)/|C| + (2/q^{N/2})^k$. Therefore, we have

$$\Pr[G_{2,Q_h}(\mathcal{A}) = 1] - \Pr[G_3(\mathcal{A}) = 1] \le Q_s(\frac{3\epsilon}{2M} + 2^{-\Omega(N)}) + \frac{Q_h(Q_h - 1)}{|C|} + (\frac{2}{q^{N/2}})^k.$$

$G_0(\mathcal{A}) - G_3(\mathcal{A})$

$\mathbf{A} \leftarrow\!\!\$\ R_q^{k \times l}$
$\bar{\mathbf{A}} := [\mathbf{A}|\mathbf{I}]$
$\mathbf{s}_1 \leftarrow\!\!\$\ S_\eta^{l+k}$
$\mathbf{t}_1^* \leftarrow\!\!\$\ \bar{\mathbf{A}}\mathbf{s}_1$
$\mathcal{T}_u := \emptyset$ // $G_{2,0} - G_3$
$\mathrm{ctr} := 0;\ \mathcal{S} := \emptyset;\ \mathcal{Q} := \emptyset$
$\mathrm{ORC} := \{\mathrm{SIGN}_1, \mathrm{SIGN}_2,$
   $\mathsf{H}_{\mathrm{agg}}, \mathsf{H}_{\mathrm{com}}, \mathsf{H}_{\mathrm{sig}}\}$
$(\mathrm{st}, i^*) \leftarrow \mathcal{A}_1(\bar{\mathbf{A}}, \mathbf{t}_1)$ // selective
$(L^*, \tilde{\sigma}^*) \leftarrow \mathcal{A}_2^{\mathrm{ORC}}(\mathrm{st})$
if $\mathbf{t}_1^* \notin L^* \vee (L^*, \mu^*) \in \mathcal{Q}$
   $\vee \mathsf{KAgg}(L^*) \neq \tilde{\mathbf{t}}^*$ then
   return 0
return $\mathsf{Vf}(\tilde{\mathbf{t}}^*, \mu^*, \tilde{\sigma}^*)$

$\mathsf{H}_{\mathrm{com}}(\tilde{\mathbf{t}}, \mu)$

if $\mathcal{T}_{\mathrm{com}}[\tilde{\mathbf{t}}, \mu] \neq\ \bot$ then
   return $\mathcal{T}_{\mathrm{com}}[\tilde{\mathbf{t}}, \mu]$
$\mathbf{B} \leftarrow\!\!\$\ R_q^{k \times l'}$ // G_0
if $|\mathcal{T}_{\mathrm{com}}| = i^* - 1$ then   // $G_1 - G_3$
   $\mathbf{B} \leftarrow\!\!\$\ R_q^{k \times l'}$ // $G_1 - G_3$
else   // $G_1 - G_3$
   $\hat{\mathbf{B}} \leftarrow\!\!\$\ R_q^{k \times (l'-1)}$ // $G_1 - G_3$
   $\mathbf{v} \leftarrow\!\!\$\ R_q^k$ // G_1
   if $|\mathcal{T}_{\mathrm{com}}| < j$ then   // $G_{2,j} - G_3$
      $\mathbf{u} \leftarrow\!\!\$\ S_{\eta'}^{l'-1+k}$ // $G_{2,j} - G_3$
      $\mathcal{T}_u[\tilde{\mathbf{t}}, \mu] := \mathbf{u}$ // $G_{2,j} - G_3$
      $\mathbf{v} := [\hat{\mathbf{B}}|\mathbf{I}]\mathbf{u}$ // $G_{2,j} - G_3$
   else   // $G_{2,j} - G_3$
      $\mathbf{v} \leftarrow\!\!\$\ R_q^k$ // $G_{2,j} - G_3$
   $\mathbf{b} := \mathbf{t}_1^* - \mathbf{v}$ // $G_1 - G_3$
   $\mathbf{B} := [\mathbf{b}|\hat{\mathbf{B}}]$ // $G_1 - G_3$
$\mathcal{T}_{\mathrm{com}}[\tilde{\mathbf{t}}, \mu] := \mathbf{B}$
if $|\mathcal{T}_{\mathrm{com}}| = i^*$ then
   $(\tilde{\mathbf{t}}^*, \mu^*) := (\tilde{\mathbf{t}}, \mu)$ // selective
return $\mathcal{T}_{\mathrm{com}}[\tilde{\mathbf{t}}, \mu]$

$\mathrm{SIGN}_1(\{\mathbf{t}_2, \ldots, \mathbf{t}_n\}, \mu)$ // G_0

$\mathrm{ctr} := \mathrm{ctr} + 1$
$\mathrm{sid} := \mathrm{ctr};\ \mathcal{S} := \mathcal{S} \cup \{\mathrm{sid}\}$
$L := \{\mathbf{t}_1^*, \ldots, \mathbf{t}_n\}$
$\mathcal{Q} := \mathcal{Q} \cup \{(L, \mu)\}$
$\tilde{\mathbf{t}} := \mathsf{KAgg}(L)$
if $(\tilde{\mathbf{t}}, \mu) = (\tilde{\mathbf{t}}^*, \mu^*)$ then   // G_3
   return $\bot$ // G_3
$a_1 := \mathsf{H}_{\mathrm{agg}}(L, \mathbf{t}_1^*)$
$\mathbf{B} := \mathsf{H}_{\mathrm{com}}(\tilde{\mathbf{t}}, \mu)$
$\bar{\mathbf{B}} := [\mathbf{B}|\mathbf{I}]$
$\mathbf{y}_1 \leftarrow D_s^{l+k}$ // $G_0 - G_{2,Q_h}$
$\mathbf{r}_1 \leftarrow D_{s'}^{l'+k}$ // $G_0 - G_{2,Q_h}$
$\mathbf{w}_1 := \bar{\mathbf{A}}\mathbf{y}_1 + \bar{\mathbf{B}}\mathbf{r}_1$ // $G_0 - G_{2,Q_h}$
$\mathrm{st}_{\mathrm{sid}} := (\tilde{\mathbf{t}}, \mu, a_1, \mathbf{y}_1, \mathbf{r}_1, \mathbf{w}_1)$ // $G_0 - G_{2,Q_h}$
$\mathbf{p} \leftarrow D_{s'}^{l'+k}$ // G_3
$\mathbf{z}_1 \leftarrow D_s^{l+k}$ // G_3
$\mathbf{w}_1 := \bar{\mathbf{A}}\mathbf{z}_1 + \bar{\mathbf{B}}\mathbf{p}$ // G_3
$\mathrm{st}_{\mathrm{sid}} := (\tilde{\mathbf{t}}, \mu, a_1, \mathbf{p}, \mathbf{z}_1, \mathbf{w}_1)$ // G_3
return $\mathbf{w}_1$

$\mathrm{SIGN}_2(\mathrm{sid}, \{\mathbf{w}_2, \ldots, \mathbf{w}_n\})$

if $\mathrm{sid} \notin \mathcal{S}$ then return $\bot$
$\mathcal{S} := \mathcal{S} \setminus \{\mathrm{sid}\}$
$(\tilde{\mathbf{t}}, \mu, a_1, \mathbf{y}_1, \mathbf{r}_1, \mathbf{w}_1) := \mathrm{st}_{\mathrm{sid}}$ // $G_0 - G_{2,Q_h}$
$(\tilde{\mathbf{t}}, \mu, a_1, \mathbf{p}, \mathbf{z}_1, \mathbf{w}_1) := \mathrm{st}_{\mathrm{sid}}$ // G_3
$\tilde{\mathbf{w}} := \sum_{i=1}^n \mathbf{w}_i$
$c := \mathsf{H}_{\mathrm{sig}}(\tilde{\mathbf{t}}, \mu, \tilde{\mathbf{w}})$
$\mathbf{z}_1 := \mathbf{y}_1 + a_1 c \mathbf{s}_1$ // $G_0 - G_{2,Q_h}$
$\mathbf{u} := \mathcal{T}_u[\tilde{\mathbf{t}}, \mu]$ // G_3
$\bar{\mathbf{u}} := [1, \mathbf{u}^\mathsf{T}]^\mathsf{T}$ // G_3
$\mathbf{r}_1 := \mathbf{p} + a_1 c \bar{\mathbf{u}}$ // G_3
With prob. $\min(1, \frac{D_s^{l+k}(\mathbf{z}_1)}{M \cdot D_{a_1 c \mathbf{s}_1, s}^{l+k}(\mathbf{z}_1)})$:   // $G_0 - G_{2,Q_h}$

With prob. $\min(1, \frac{D_{s'}^{l'+k}(\mathbf{r}_1)}{M \cdot D_{a_1 c \bar{\mathbf{u}}, s'}^{l'+k}(\mathbf{r}_1)})$:   // G_3

   return $(c, \mathbf{z}_1, \mathbf{r}_1)$
Otherwise:
   return $\bot$

Fig. 5. The hybrid games $G_0 - G_3$.

Finally, note that $\mathbf{s}_1$ is only used to compute $\mathbf{t}_1^*$ in G_3. Hence, an adversary $\mathcal{B}$ against the sel-UF-KOA of DualMS can perfectly simulate G_3 for $\mathcal{A}$. It uses the corresponding random oracle responses in its own sel-UF-KOA game to answer

$\mathsf{H}_{\mathrm{agg}}$ and $\mathsf{H}_{\mathrm{sig}}$ queries from $\mathcal{A}$ and to answer the i^*-th fresh query to $\mathsf{H}_{\mathrm{com}}$. It outputs the same i^*, L^*, and $\tilde{\sigma}^*$ as $\mathcal{A}$. Consequently, we have

$$\mathbf{Adv}_{\mathsf{DualMS}}^{\mathsf{sUF\text{-}CMA}}(\mathcal{A}) \leq \mathbf{Adv}_{\mathsf{DualMS}}^{\mathsf{sUF\text{-}KOA}}(\mathcal{B}) + (Q_{\mathrm{h}} - 1)\mathbf{Adv}_{\mathsf{MLWE}_{q,k,l'-1,\eta'}}(\mathcal{D})$$
$$+ Q_{\mathrm{s}}(\frac{3\epsilon}{2M} + 2^{-\Omega(N)}) + \frac{Q_{\mathrm{h}}(Q_{\mathrm{h}} - 1)}{|C|} + (\frac{2}{q^{N/2}})^k.$$

4.3   Reduction from sel-UF-KOA to MSIS and MLWE

Lemma 16 (sel-UF-KOA to MSIS and MLWE). *For any τ-time adversary $\mathcal{A}$ against the sel-UF-KOA of* DualMS *that makes at most Q_h queries to each random oracle, there exist algorithms $\mathcal{B}$ and $\mathcal{D}$ such that*

$$\mathbf{Adv}_{\mathsf{DualMS}}^{\mathsf{sUF\text{-}KOA}}(\mathcal{A}) \leq \sqrt{\frac{Q_h^2}{|C|} + Q_h\sqrt{Q_h\mathbf{Adv}_{\mathsf{MSIS}_{q,k,1+l+l',\beta}}(\mathcal{B})}}$$
$$+ \mathbf{Adv}_{\mathsf{MLWE}_{q,k,l,\eta}}(\mathcal{D}) + \frac{Q_h(Q_h + 1)}{|C|} + 2(\frac{2}{q^{N/2}})^k,$$

where $\beta = 8\kappa\sqrt{\hat{n}^2\kappa^3 + B_n^2 + B_n'^2 + B_n''^2}$, $\hat{n}$ is the maximum number of duplicate keys in a public key list, and the running time of $\mathcal{B}$ and $\mathcal{D}$ are essentially 4τ and τ, respectively.

The proof follows the "double forking" framework of [9,31,35]. In particular, a double-forking proof for lattice-based scheme was given in [9], and our proof is analogous to theirs. Therefore, we only sketch the proof here and defer the complete proof to the full version of this paper [10]. We first consider the inner forking algorithm $\mathcal{B}'$ that runs $\mathcal{A}$ twice. If adversary $\mathcal{A}$ wins in the first time, $\mathcal{B}'$ can obtain L^*, $\tilde{\mathbf{t}}^*$ μ, $\tilde{\mathbf{w}}$, $\tilde{\mathbf{z}}$, $\tilde{\mathbf{r}}$, and $\tilde{\mathbf{e}}$ satisfying $\tilde{\mathbf{t}}^* = \mathsf{KAgg}(L^*)$ and

$$\mathbf{A}\tilde{\mathbf{z}} + \mathbf{B}\tilde{\mathbf{r}} + \tilde{\mathbf{e}} = \tilde{\mathbf{w}} + c\tilde{\mathbf{t}}^*,$$

where $c = \mathsf{H}_{\mathrm{sig}}(\tilde{\mathbf{t}}, \mu, \tilde{\mathbf{w}})$ is what we call the "crucial" query corresponding to the forgery. Algorithm $\mathcal{B}'$ then forks the adversary at the crucial query, assigning another hash value c' to $\mathsf{H}_{\mathrm{sig}}(\tilde{\mathbf{t}}, \mu, \tilde{\mathbf{w}})$ in the second execution. In this execution, with probability lower-bounded by the forking lemma [5,39], we have $c \neq c'$, $\mathcal{A}$ wins, and $\mathsf{H}_{\mathrm{sig}}(\tilde{\mathbf{t}}, \mu, \tilde{\mathbf{w}})$ is again the crucial query. In this case, $\mathcal{B}'$ obtains another tuple of responses $\tilde{\mathbf{z}}'$, $\tilde{\mathbf{r}}'$, and $\tilde{\mathbf{e}}'$ satisfying

$$\mathbf{A}\tilde{\mathbf{z}}' + \mathbf{B}\tilde{\mathbf{r}}' + \tilde{\mathbf{e}}' = \tilde{\mathbf{w}} + c'\tilde{\mathbf{t}}^*.$$

Combine the two equations, and then we have

$$\mathbf{A}\hat{\mathbf{z}} + \mathbf{B}\hat{\mathbf{r}} + \hat{\mathbf{e}} = \hat{c}\tilde{\mathbf{t}}^*,$$

where $\hat{\mathbf{z}} = \tilde{\mathbf{z}} - \tilde{\mathbf{z}}'$, $\hat{\mathbf{r}} = \tilde{\mathbf{r}} - \tilde{\mathbf{r}}'$, $\hat{\mathbf{e}} = \tilde{\mathbf{e}} - \tilde{\mathbf{e}}'$ and $\hat{c} = c - c' \neq 0$.

Now we consider the outer forking algorithm $\mathcal{B}$ that runs $\mathcal{B}'$ twice. Note that $\tilde{\mathbf{t}}^* = \mathsf{KAgg}(L^*) = n^* a_1 \mathbf{t}_1^* + \sum_{\mathbf{t}_i \in L^* \wedge \mathbf{t}_i \neq \mathbf{t}_1^*} a_i \mathbf{t}_i$, where n^* is the number of times that $\mathbf{t}_1^*$ occurs in L^*. Thus, the earlier equation becomes

$$\mathbf{A}\hat{\mathbf{z}} + \mathbf{B}\hat{\mathbf{r}} + \hat{\mathbf{e}} = \hat{c}(n^* a_1 \mathbf{t}_1^* + \sum_{\mathbf{t}_i \in L^* \wedge \mathbf{t}_i \neq \mathbf{t}_1^*} a_i \mathbf{t}_i).$$

This time we regard $a_1 = \mathsf{H}_{\mathrm{agg}}(L^*, \mathbf{t}_1^*)$ as the crucial query. Algorithm $\mathcal{B}$ runs $\mathcal{B}'$ another time and assigns another value a_1' to $\mathsf{H}_{\mathrm{agg}}(L^*, \mathbf{t}_1^*)$. With the probability given by the forking lemma, we have $a_1 \neq a_1'$, again $\mathcal{B}'$ succeeds, and $\mathsf{H}_{\mathrm{agg}}(L^*, \mathbf{t}_1^*)$ is the crucial query. Then $\mathcal{B}$ obtains $\hat{c}'$, $\hat{\mathbf{z}}'$, $\hat{\mathbf{r}}'$, and $\hat{\mathbf{e}}'$ satisfying

$$\mathbf{A}\hat{\mathbf{z}}' + \mathbf{B}\hat{\mathbf{r}}' + \hat{\mathbf{e}}' = \hat{c}'(n^* a_1' \mathbf{t}_1^* + \sum_{\mathbf{t}_i \in L^* \wedge \mathbf{t}_i \neq \mathbf{t}_1^*} a_i \mathbf{t}_i).$$

Multiply the first equation by $\hat{c}'$ and the second by $\hat{c}$ and subtract the second from the first, and then we have

$$\mathbf{A}(\hat{c}'\hat{\mathbf{z}} - \hat{c}\hat{\mathbf{z}}') + \mathbf{B}(\hat{c}'\hat{\mathbf{r}} - \hat{c}\hat{\mathbf{r}}') + \hat{c}'\hat{\mathbf{e}} - \hat{c}\hat{\mathbf{e}}' = n^* \hat{c}\hat{c}'(a_1 - a_1')\mathbf{t}_1^*.$$

Rearrange the equation, and we have

$$[\mathbf{t}_1^* | \mathbf{A} | \mathbf{B} | \mathbf{I}] \begin{bmatrix} n^* \hat{c}\hat{c}'(a_1 - a_1') \\ \hat{c}'\hat{\mathbf{z}} - \hat{c}\hat{\mathbf{z}}' \\ \hat{c}'\hat{\mathbf{r}} - \hat{c}\hat{\mathbf{r}}' \\ \hat{c}'\hat{\mathbf{e}} - \hat{c}\hat{\mathbf{e}}' \end{bmatrix} = 0.$$

By Lemma 1, none of $\hat{c}$, $\hat{c}'$, and $a_1 - a_1'$ are zero-divisors. Hence, $n^* \hat{c}\hat{c}'(a_1 - a_1') \neq 0$, and $\mathcal{B}$ obtains a MSIS solution with respect to the matrix $[\mathbf{t}_1^* | \mathbf{A} | \mathbf{B}]$. Here we replace $\mathbf{t}_1^* = \bar{\mathbf{A}}\mathbf{s}_1$ with a random $\mathbf{t}_1^*$ independent of $\mathbf{A}$ by MLWE.

We need to be careful with the possibility that $\mathcal{B}'$ obtains different public-key sets from the two executions of $\mathcal{A}$. The consequence is that there will not be a unique crucial query $\mathsf{H}_{\mathrm{agg}}(L^*, \mathbf{t}_1^*)$ for $\mathcal{B}$ to fork. Fortunately, such an event is unlikely, because KAgg is somehow "collision resistant". We will formally define the relative bad events and bound their probabilities in the full version of this paper [10].

5   Concrete Parameters and Comparison

In this section, we provide two sample concrete parameter settings for DualMS, aiming at about 128 classical bits of security. We consider the number of signers $n = 32$ and $n = 1024$. We also provide parameters for MuSig-L for comparison.

Choosing parameters. For both schemes, we fix $N = 256$. Then we let $\kappa = 60$ for 256 bits of entropy. We set $t = 13.5$ aiming at 128-bit security and $\gamma = 1.1$ to let the bound given by Lemma 4 small enough.

For DualMS, we fix $l' = l + 1$, $\eta' = \eta$ and set $\alpha = 8.5n$ for an expected repetition number ≈ 5. It remains for us to choose main parameters q, k, l, and η. We consider the following security criteria:

- The hardness of forging a multi-signature on a new message. Based on the security of hash functions, this is conjectured to be as hard as choosing the inputs to hash functions to fix a target $\mathbf{t}' = \tilde{\mathbf{w}} + c\tilde{\mathbf{t}}$ and finding $\mathbf{z}$, $\mathbf{r}$, and $\mathbf{e}$ satisfying $\mathbf{A}\mathbf{z} + \mathbf{B}\mathbf{r} + \mathbf{e} = \mathbf{t}'$ [14]. This implies solving $\mathsf{MSIS}_{q,k,l+l'+1,\beta} = \mathsf{MSIS}_{q,k,2l+2,\beta}$, where $\beta \approx \sqrt{B_n^2 + B_2'^2 + B_2''^2}$.
- The pseudorandomness of the public key, which is related to the hardness of $\mathsf{MLWE}_{q,k,l,\eta}$.
- The "zero-knowledge" of signatures, i.e., how well the signatures hide useful information from the adversary, which is related to $\mathsf{MLWE}_{q,k,l'-1,\eta'} = \mathsf{MLWE}_{q,k,l,\eta}$ required by the signature simulation.

For MuSig-L, we consider an optimized scheme with computational instead of statistical trapdoor indistinguishability. Similarly, we estimate the hardness of forging a multi-signature related to MSIS, the pseudorandomness of the public key related to MLWE, and the trapdoor indistinguishability required by signature simulation. Remarkably, the simulation of MuSig-L requires the Gaussian width s to be so large that the protocol almost always succeeds. See more details about the parameters of MuSig-L in the full version of this paper [10].

We estimate the hardness of MSIS and MLWE using the security estimator of CRYSTALS.[4] Size of the challenge in the signature is estimated as 32 bytes as in [14]. Sizes of Gaussian responses in the signature are simply estimated based on B_n, B_n', and B_n'' and their dimensions based on Lemma 2 of [3]. The main parameters are chosen to minimize public-key size + signature size while satisfying the required security level.

Comparison. Table 2 summarizes our sample parameters. It shows that, aiming at approximately 128-bit security, public-key size + signature size of DualMS is about 4.7x times smaller than MuSig-L when $n = 32$ and about 3.4x smaller when $n = 1024$.

The comparison in Gaussian width s explains such differences. Relatively large Gaussian width of MuSig-L is somehow inherent in its construction and simulation technique. The large Gaussian width is directly related to the signature size. Moreover, it makes the underlying MSIS problem easier and thus requires to raise the main parameters.

Let us give a more detailed discussion. In DualMS, like typical FSwA signature schemes, the Gaussian width s of responses is decided by the requirement of hiding secret keys using rejection sampling. However, the construction of MuSig-L introduces another dominant requirement on the width that grows with $q^{k/(l+k)}$. The consequences include unusually large s and almost no rejection, large l and unnecessarily hard MLWE. Our understanding is that, while MuSig-L enables a clever straight-line simulation, it goes toward the opposite direction of Lyubashevsky's FSwA signatures [25,26], which introduce rejection sampling and LWE for a smaller Gaussian width and narrower matrix. On the other hand, the extra lower-bound of s in MuSig-L is independent of $\alpha \propto n$, so the growth of n affects MuSig-L less than DualMS when n is not too large.

---

[4] https://github.com/pq-crystals/security-estimates.

Table 2. Summary of the concrete parameters. "PK" refers to public-key size, and "Sig" refers to signature size, both measured in kB. "MSIS" refers to the hardness of MSIS related to signature forgery. Variable s refers to Gaussian width of the response in the signature. For DualMS, it actually refers to s' which is slightly larger than s. "MLWE" refers to the hardness of MLWE related to the pseudorandomness of public keys (and the indistinguishability of simulation for DualMS). We do not show the hardness of MLWE related to the indistinguishability of simulation of MuSig-L, since it can be set to sufficiently hard with a very small effect on the efficiency (see the full version of this paper [10]).

Params	MuSig-L	DualMS	MuSig-L	DualMS
n	32	32	1024	1024
N	256	256	256	256
$\lceil \log(q) \rceil$	104	37	104	48
k	8	6	10	7
l	42	7	38	9
η	1	1	1	1
PK	26	6.94	32.5	10.5
Sig	98.47	19.72	106.53	30.91
PK+Sig	124.47	26.66	139.03	41.41
$\log(s)$	60.04	27.13	65.54	32.27
MSIS	125	130	126	132
MLWE	>700	130	>500	131

We point out that we do not apply practical optimizations to DualMS and MuSig-L. We believe there is a lot of room for improvement of the concrete efficiency of both schemes. Our sample parameters provide more a proof of concept than practical meanings. Especially, parameter setting for MuSig-L is more involved. The authors of [9] did not provide concrete parameters, and our parameters could be non-optimal. We leave further optimizations and more comparison with different settings, such as security levels and number of signers, as future work.

Despite the advantages in efficiency of DualMS, we stress again that MuSig-L is irreplaceable so far if one wants the first round to be offline. Our estimation shows that the online-offline property could be expensive in lattice setting.

Communication and Round Complexity. Note that despite being two-round, the signing protocol succeeds in returning a valid signature only with some probability. Hence, the actual round complexity to produce a signature is larger. The naive way to produce a valid signature is to sequentially repeat the signing protocol until getting one. In this case, the protocol round complexity (2 for our scheme) should be multiplied by the expected times of repetitions. In fact, we can also repeat the protocol in parallel, which increases the communication while reduce the actual round number. That is, outside the signing protocol, there is always a trade-off between communication and round complexity.

We provide some examples for our parameter setting. We set the success probability to be around $1/5$, so sequential repetitions make the expected round number to be about $5 \times 2 = 10$. If we repeat the protocol for 5 times in parallel, then the success probability will be amplified to more than $2/3$, which yields an expected round number of about $1.5 \times 2 = 3$. If we want the success probability to be about 0.99 so that the actual round number is virtually 2, then it will suffice to run 20 parallel repetitions.

Let us roughly compare the communication cost of DualMS and MuSig-L. In MuSig-L, each signer broadcasts in the first round more than $\log q$ many commitments, each of equal size to a public key, and in the second round roughly a signature. In DualMS, each signer broadcasts only one commitment in the first round. The second-round message is k dimensions longer than a signature but is only output with probability about $1/5$. Suppose DualMS is executed in parallel 20 times, and MuSig-L is run only once since it almost never rejects. Then in our parameter settings with $n = 32$ for DualMS and MuSig-L, respectively, each signer broadcasts about <300 kB vs. >2800 kB to produce one valid signature. When $n = 1024$, the number is <400 kB vs. >3500 kB.

Here we also mention a possible trick to reduce the second round communication of DualMS: generate a pseudorandom $\mathbf{r}_1$ and only broadcast the seed in the second round.

Comparison with DOTT. DualMS has a closer structure to DOTT than MuSig-L. They are likely to have similar public size and communication, while the main difference is the signature size. Compared to DOTT, DualMS basically replaces the opening of a commitment scheme with a partial response of Dilithium (the vector $\mathbf{r}$) in the signature.

We do not make concrete comparison with DOTT. As it is a generic construction using homomorphic equivocable trapdoor commitments as a building block, the concrete efficiency will vary according to different instantiations of the commitment scheme. On the other hand, we argued in Sect. 1 that the instantiations from MSIS and MLWE of such commitment schemes so far give a significantly larger opening size compared to a Dilithium-G signature.

Here, we provide some evidence of the advantage of DualMS over DOTT from their constructions: DualMS can be seen as an instantiation of DOTT, with a much weaker "commitment". In other words, DOTT overstrikes the target of a multi-signature scheme using an unnecessarily powerful building block.

Specifically, if we view $\mathbf{w} = \bar{\mathbf{A}}\mathbf{y} + \bar{\mathbf{B}}\mathbf{r}$ as a commitment to $\bar{\mathbf{A}}\mathbf{y}$ with commitment key $\bar{\mathbf{B}}$ and randomness $\mathbf{r}$, then DualMS is an instantiation of the generic construction of DOTT. However, the properties of such a "commitment" scheme have two main differences compared to the requirements of the security analysis of DOTT.

- The commitment is not binding, while the security of DOTT is reduced to the binding of the commitment scheme. Clearly, one can open $\mathbf{w}$ to some random vector by sampling random $\mathbf{r}$.

– The equivocability is much weaker. An equivocable commitment scheme generally allows the trapdoor-holder to open a commitment to any vector. In our commitment scheme, the trapdoor is a short vector $\bar{u}$ satisfying $\bar{B}\bar{u} = t$. It only allows the trapdoor-holder to commit to a vector $\bar{A}y$ and then equivocate it to some related vector, namely $\bar{A}y - ct$, where c is from a much smaller set than the whole vector space. Moreover, rejection sampling is necessary to keep the trapdoor secret, so the equivocation can fail. It was also shown in Schnorr-based constructions that weaker equivocability is enough for multi-signatures [2,38].

The security proof of DOTT cannot work with our weaker equivocable commitment. Thus, it is necessary for us to provide a new proof for DualMS.

Acknowledgement. We thank Andrej Bogdanov for his helpful advice throughout this work. We thank Yunlei Zhao for letting us know this topic and the trick that reduces communication and Zhichuang Liang for his help in parameter setting. We thank the anonymous reviewers of PKC 2023 and Crypto 2023 for their constructive comments and suggestions.

References

1. Kılınç Alper, H., Burdges, J.: Two-round trip schnorr multi-signatures via delinearized witnesses. In: Malkin, T., Peikert, C. (eds.) CRYPTO 2021. LNCS, vol. 12825, pp. 157–188. Springer, Cham (2021). https://doi.org/10.1007/978-3-030-84242-0_7

2. Bagherzandi, A., Cheon, J.H., Jarecki, S.: Multisignatures secure under the discrete logarithm assumption and a generalized forking lemma. In: Ning, P., Syverson, P.F., Jha, S. (eds.) ACM CCS 2008, pp. 449–458. ACM Press (Oct 2008). https://doi.org/10.1145/1455770.1455827

3. El Bansarkhani, R., Buchmann, J.: Improvement and efficient implementation of a lattice-based signature scheme. In: Lange, T., Lauter, K., Lisoněk, P. (eds.) SAC 2013. LNCS, vol. 8282, pp. 48–67. Springer, Heidelberg (2014). https://doi.org/10.1007/978-3-662-43414-7_3

4. Bellare, M., Dai, W.: Chain reductions for multi-signatures and the HBMS scheme. In: Tibouchi, M., Wang, H. (eds.) ASIACRYPT 2021. LNCS, vol. 13093, pp. 650–678. Springer, Cham (2021). https://doi.org/10.1007/978-3-030-92068-5_22

5. Bellare, M., Neven, G.: Multi-signatures in the plain public-key model and a general forking lemma. In: Juels, A., Wright, R.N., De Capitani di Vimercati, S. (eds.) ACM CCS 2006, pp. 390–399. ACM Press (Oct / Nov 2006). https://doi.org/10.1145/1180405.1180453

6. Benhamouda, F., Lepoint, T., Loss, J., Orrù, M., Raykova, M.: On the (in)security of ROS. In: Canteaut, A., Standaert, F.-X. (eds.) EUROCRYPT 2021. LNCS, vol. 12696, pp. 33–53. Springer, Cham (2021). https://doi.org/10.1007/978-3-030-77870-5_2

7. Boneh, D., Kim, S.: One-time and interactive aggregate signatures from lattices. https://crypto.stanford.edu/Simskim13/agg_ots.pdf (2020)

8. Boschini, C., Takahashi, A., Tibouchi, M.: MuSig-L: Lattice-based multi-signature with single-round online phase. In: Dodis, Y., Shrimpton, T. (eds.) CRYPTO 2022,

Part II. LNCS, vol. 13508, pp. 276–305. Springer, Heidelberg (2022). https://doi.org/10.1007/978-3-031-15979-4_10

9. Boschini, C., Takahashi, A., Tibouchi, M.: MuSig-L: Lattice-based multi-signature with single-round online phase. Cryptology ePrint Archive, Report 2022/1036 (2022), https://eprint.iacr.org/2022/1036

10. Chen, Y.: DualMS: Efficient lattice-based two-round multi-signature with trapdoor-free simulation. Cryptology ePrint Archive, Report 2023/263 (2023). https://eprint.iacr.org/2023/263

11. Damgård, I., Orlandi, C., Takahashi, A., Tibouchi, M.: Two-Round n-out-of-n and multi-signatures and trapdoor commitment from lattices. In: Garay, J.A. (ed.) PKC 2021. LNCS, vol. 12710, pp. 99–130. Springer, Cham (2021). https://doi.org/10.1007/978-3-030-75245-3_5

12. Damgård, I., Orlandi, C., Takahashi, A., Tibouchi, M.: Two-round n-out-of-n and multi-signatures and trapdoor commitment from lattices. J. Cryptol. **35**(2), 14 (2022)

13. Drijvers, M., et al.: On the security of two-round multi-signatures. In: 2019 IEEE Symposium on Security and Privacy, pp. 1084–1101. IEEE Computer Society Press (May 2019). https://doi.org/10.1109/SP.2019.00050

14. Ducas, L., et al.: Crystals-dilithium "c algorithm specifications and supporting documentation (version 3.1) (2021). https://pq-crystals.org/dilithium/data/dilithium-specification-round3-20210208.pdf

15. Ducas, L., Lepoint, T., Lyubashevsky, V., Schwabe, P., Seiler, G., Stehle, D.: CRYSTALS - Dilithium: Digital signatures from module lattices. Cryptology ePrint Archive, Report 2017/633 (2017). https://eprint.iacr.org/2017/633

16. El Bansarkhani, R., Sturm, J.: An efficient lattice-based multisignature scheme with applications to bitcoins. In: Foresti, S., Persiano, G. (eds.) CANS 2016. LNCS, vol. 10052, pp. 140–155. Springer, Cham (2016). https://doi.org/10.1007/978-3-319-48965-0_9

17. Fiat, A., Shamir, A.: How to prove yourself: practical solutions to identification and signature problems. In: Odlyzko, A.M. (ed.) CRYPTO 1986. LNCS, vol. 263, pp. 186–194. Springer, Heidelberg (1987). https://doi.org/10.1007/3-540-47721-7_12

18. Fleischhacker, N., Simkin, M., Zhang, Z.: Squirrel: Efficient synchronized multi-signatures from lattices. In: Yin, H., Stavrou, A., Cremers, C., Shi, E. (eds.) ACM CCS 2022, pp. 1109–1123. ACM Press (Nov 2022). https://doi.org/10.1145/3548606.3560655

19. Fukumitsu, M., Hasegawa, S.: A tightly-secure lattice-based multisignature. In: Emura, K., Mizuki, T. (eds.) Proceedings of the 6th on ASIA Public-Key Cryptography Workshop, APKC@AsiaCCS 2019, Auckland, New Zealand, 8 July 2019, pp. 3–11. ACM (2019). https://doi.org/10.1145/3327958.3329542

20. Fukumitsu, M., Hasegawa, S.: A lattice-based provably secure multisignature scheme in quantum random oracle model. In: Nguyen, K., Wu, W., Lam, K.Y., Wang, H. (eds.) ProvSec 2020. LNCS, vol. 12505, pp. 45–64. Springer, Cham (2020). https://doi.org/10.1007/978-3-030-62576-4_3

21. Gentry, C., Peikert, C., Vaikuntanathan, V.: Trapdoors for hard lattices and new cryptographic constructions. In: Ladner, R.E., Dwork, C. (eds.) 40th ACM STOC, pp. 197–206. ACM Press (May 2008). https://doi.org/10.1145/1374376.1374407

22. Gorbunov, S., Vaikuntanathan, V., Wichs, D.: Leveled fully homomorphic signatures from standard lattices. In: Servedio, R.A., Rubinfeld, R. (eds.) 47th ACM STOC, pp. 469–477. ACM Press (Jun 2015). https://doi.org/10.1145/2746539.2746576

23. Itakura, K., Nakamura, K.: A public-key cryptosystem suitable for digital multisignatures. NEC Res. Developm. **71**, 1–8 (1983)
24. Libert, B., Nguyen, K., Tan, B.H.M., Wang, H.: Zero-knowledge elementary databases with more expressive queries. In: Lin, D., Sako, K. (eds.) PKC 2019. LNCS, vol. 11442, pp. 255–285. Springer, Cham (2019). https://doi.org/10.1007/978-3-030-17253-4_9
25. Lyubashevsky, V.: Fiat-Shamir with aborts: applications to lattice and factoring-based signatures. In: Matsui, M. (ed.) ASIACRYPT 2009. LNCS, vol. 5912, pp. 598–616. Springer, Heidelberg (2009). https://doi.org/10.1007/978-3-642-10366-7_35
26. Lyubashevsky, V.: Lattice signatures without trapdoors. In: Pointcheval, D., Johansson, T. (eds.) EUROCRYPT 2012. LNCS, vol. 7237, pp. 738–755. Springer, Heidelberg (2012). https://doi.org/10.1007/978-3-642-29011-4_43
27. Lyubashevsky, V., Neven, G.: One-shot verifiable encryption from lattices. In: Coron, J.-S., Nielsen, J.B. (eds.) EUROCRYPT 2017. LNCS, vol. 10210, pp. 293–323. Springer, Cham (2017). https://doi.org/10.1007/978-3-319-56620-7_11
28. Lyubashevsky, V., Peikert, C., Regev, O.: A toolkit for ring-LWE cryptography. In: Johansson, T., Nguyen, P.Q. (eds.) EUROCRYPT 2013. LNCS, vol. 7881, pp. 35–54. Springer, Heidelberg (2013). https://doi.org/10.1007/978-3-642-38348-9_3
29. Ma, C., Jiang, M.: Practical lattice-based multisignature schemes for blockchains. IEEE Access **7**, 179765–179778 (2019)
30. Ma, C., Weng, J., Li, Y., Deng, R.H.: Efficient discrete logarithm based multisignature scheme in the plain public key model. Des. Codes Cryptogr. **54**(2), 121–133 (2010)
31. Maxwell, G., Poelstra, A., Seurin, Y., Wuille, P.: Simple schnorr multi-signatures with applications to bitcoin. Des. Codes Cryptogr. **87**(9), 2139–2164 (2019)
32. Micciancio, D., Peikert, C.: Trapdoors for lattices: simpler, tighter, faster, smaller. In: Pointcheval, D., Johansson, T. (eds.) EUROCRYPT 2012. LNCS, vol. 7237, pp. 700–718. Springer, Heidelberg (2012). https://doi.org/10.1007/978-3-642-29011-4_41
33. Micciancio, D., Peikert, C.: Hardness of SIS and LWE with small parameters. In: Canetti, R., Garay, J.A. (eds.) CRYPTO 2013. LNCS, vol. 8042, pp. 21–39. Springer, Heidelberg (2013). https://doi.org/10.1007/978-3-642-40041-4_2
34. Micciancio, D., Regev, O.: Worst-case to average-case reductions based on Gaussian measures. In: 45th FOCS, pp. 372–381. IEEE Computer Society Press (Oct 2004). https://doi.org/10.1109/FOCS.2004.72
35. Nick, J., Ruffing, T., Seurin, Y.: MuSig2: simple two-round schnorr multisignatures. In: Malkin, T., Peikert, C. (eds.) CRYPTO 2021. LNCS, vol. 12825, pp. 189–221. Springer, Cham (2021). https://doi.org/10.1007/978-3-030-84242-0_8
36. Nick, J., Ruffing, T., Seurin, Y., Wuille, P.: MuSig-DN: Schnorr multi-signatures with verifiably deterministic nonces. In: Ligatti, J., Ou, X., Katz, J., Vigna, G. (eds.) ACM CCS 2020, pp. 1717–1731. ACM Press (Nov 2020). https://doi.org/10.1145/3372297.3417236
37. Okamoto, T.: Provably secure and practical identification schemes and corresponding signature schemes. In: Brickell, E.F. (ed.) CRYPTO 1992. LNCS, vol. 740, pp. 31–53. Springer, Heidelberg (1993). https://doi.org/10.1007/3-540-48071-4_3
38. Pan, J., Wagner, B.: Chopsticks: Fork-free two-round multi-signatures from non-interactive assumptions. In: Hazay, C., Stam, M. (eds.) EUROCRYPT 2023, Part V. LNCS, vol. 14008, pp. 597–627. Springer, Heidelberg (2023). https://doi.org/10.1007/978-3-031-30589-4_21

39. Pointcheval, D., Stern, J.: Security proofs for signature schemes. In: Maurer, U. (ed.) EUROCRYPT 1996. LNCS, vol. 1070, pp. 387–398. Springer, Heidelberg (1996). https://doi.org/10.1007/3-540-68339-9_33

40. Ristenpart, T., Yilek, S.: The power of proofs-of-possession: securing multiparty signatures against rogue-key attacks. In: Naor, M. (ed.) EUROCRYPT 2007. LNCS, vol. 4515, pp. 228–245. Springer, Heidelberg (2007). https://doi.org/10.1007/978-3-540-72540-4_13

41. Syta, E., et al.: Keeping authorities "honest or bust" with decentralized witness cosigning. In: 2016 IEEE Symposium on Security and Privacy, pp. 526–545. IEEE Computer Society Press (May 2016). https://doi.org/10.1109/SP.2016.38

42. Tessaro, S., Zhu, C.: Threshold and multi-signature schemes from linear hash functions. In: Hazay, C., Stam, M. (eds.) EUROCRYPT 2023, Part V. LNCS, vol. 14008, pp. 628–658. Springer, Heidelberg (2023). https://doi.org/10.1007/978-3-031-30589-4_22

Revisiting Security Estimation for LWE with Hints from a Geometric Perspective

Dana Dachman-Soled[1]([envelope])[ID], Huijing Gong[2][ID], Tom Hanson[1][ID], and Hunter Kippen[1][ID]

[1] University of Maryland, College Park, USA
{danadach,thanson,hkippen}@umd.edu
[2] Intel Labs, Hillsboro, USA
huijing.gong@intel.com

Abstract. The Distorted Bounded Distance Decoding Problem (DBDD) was introduced by Dachman-Soled et al. [Crypto '20] as an intermediate problem between LWE and unique-SVP (uSVP). They presented an approach that reduces an LWE instance to a DBDD instance, integrates side information (or "hints") into the DBDD instance, and finally reduces it to a uSVP instance, which can be solved via lattice reduction. They showed that this principled approach can lead to algorithms for side-channel attacks that perform better than ad-hoc algorithms that do not rely on lattice reduction.

The current work focuses on new methods for integrating hints into a DBDD instance. We view hints from a geometric perspective, as opposed to the distributional perspective from the prior work. Our approach provides the rigorous promise that, as hints are integrated into the DBDD instance, the correct solution remains a lattice point contained in the specified ellipsoid.

We instantiate our approach with two new types of hints: (1) Inequality hints, corresponding to the region of intersection of an ellipsoid and a halfspace; (2) Combined hints, corresponding to the region of intersection of two ellipsoids. Since the regions in (1) and (2) are not necessarily ellipsoids, we replace them with ellipsoidal approximations that circumscribe the region of intersection. Perfect hints are reconsidered as the region of intersection of an ellipsoid and a hyperplane, which is itself an ellipsoid. The compatibility of "approximate," "modular," and "short vector" hints from the prior work is examined.

We apply our techniques to the decryption failure and side-channel attack settings. We show that "inequality hints" can be used to model decryption failures, and that our new approach yields a geometric analogue of the "failure boosting" technique of D'anvers et al. [ePrint,'18].

The full version of this paper can be found in [18].

D. Dachman-Soled—This project is supported in part by NSF grant #CNS-1453045 (CAREER), by financial assistance awards 70NANB15H328 and 70NANB19H126 from the U.S. Department of Commerce, National Institute of Standards and Technology, and by Intel through the Intel Labs Crypto Frontiers Research Center.

H. Kippen—Supported in part by the Clark Doctoral Fellowship from the Clark School of Engineering, University of Maryland, College Park.

H. Handschuh and A. Lysyanskaya (Eds.): CRYPTO 2023, LNCS 14085, pp. 748–781, 2023.
https://doi.org/10.1007/978-3-031-38554-4_24

We also show that "combined hints" can be used to fuse information from a decryption failure and a side-channel attack, and provide rigorous guarantees despite the data being non-Gaussian. We provide experimental data for both applications. The code that we have developed to implement the integration of hints and hardness estimates extends the Toolkit from prior work and has been released publicly.

1 Introduction

LWE-based cryptosystems are among the foremost candidates for post-quantum standardization and, as such, are expected to be deployed in the next few years. It is therefore critical to understand the *concrete security* of LWE, i.e., exactly how much computational cost is needed to solve an LWE instance for a particular choice of parameters. Parameters for standardized cryptosystems are typically set so that the *best known (quantum) attack* in a given computational model requires some minimum amount of time (e.g. a common target is "128-bit security"). If the state-of-the-art algorithm for solving LWE is significantly improved, parameter settings of all cryptosystems relying on LWE must be modified in order to retain their security guarantees.

One of the commonly used algorithms for solving LWE follows this template: (1) Embed the LWE instance into a uSVP instance, which asks to find the shortest non-zero vector in a *lattice*, and then (2) solve the uSVP instance using a type of algorithm known as *lattice reduction*. In this work, we consider algorithms that follow the above template, and our goal is to develop improved methods for the first step—in the case that side information about the LWE secret or error is available. While side-channel information is not considered as part of the standard security model, it remains an important practical consideration, especially for standardized cryptosystems which will be widely deployed in a range of settings. Indeed, Round 3 of the NIST post-quantum cryptography (PQC) standardization effort focused attention on resistance to side-channel attacks [1].

Dachman-Soled et al. [17] created a toolkit for integrating so-called "hints" into uSVP instances that can then be solved via lattice-reduction algorithms. To achieve this, they introduced an intermediate lattice problem known as DBDD (Distorted Bounded Distance Decoding). A DBDD instance consists of three parts: A lattice Λ, a mean vector μ, and a covariance matrix Σ. The original lattice Λ represents the lattice obtained through Kannan's embedding—which is a way to construct a lattice in which the LWE secret/error is the shortest non-zero vector. Subsequently, side information can sometimes be used to sparsify or reduce the dimension of the original lattice. The remaining parts of the instance (μ, Σ), correspond to a mean vector and covariance matrix, and these represent distributional information known about the LWE secret/error. (μ, Σ) originally represents the fact that the secret/error is drawn from a distribution with known mean/covariance determined by the specifications of the cryptosystem. Subsequently, it captures the conditional distribution on the secret/error, given the side information, in cases where this conditional distribution remains well approximated by a Gaussian. Thus, certain types of information on the structure or on the distribution of the secret can be integrated into a DBDD instance, starting with the original instance, and then modifying Λ, and/or (μ, Σ) appropriately. A DBDD instance can then be converted into a uSVP instance using *homogenization*—centering the ellipsoid at the origin—and *isotropization*—applying a linear transformation that simultaneously transforms the ellipsoid into a ball and transforms the lattice into a different lattice with higher volume. Finally, the resulting uSVP instance is fed into the BKZ [50] lattice reduction algorithm to obtain the shortest non-zero vector in the transformed lattice. This short non-zero vector allows direct recovery of the LWE secret/error. [17] demonstrated their methodology with numerous examples, and provided an open-source implementation to predict the security decay (i.e. reduction in the BKZ blocksize, β, required for key recovery) of an LWE instance given a set of hints.

The approach of the current work is to provide an alternate geometric interpretation to the distributional approach considered in [17]. We alter the reduction from LWE to DBDD, by viewing the solution of an LWE instance (with secret of dimension n and error of dimension m, for a total dimension $d = n + m$) as the (unique) integer point contained in an ellipsoid that is constructed from the given LWE instance. Thus, the problem of finding the unique integer point is captured by the DBDD instance $(\mathbb{Z}^d, \mu, \Sigma)$. Here, μ and Σ are the center and the positive semidefinite "shape" matrix defining the ellipsoid. Interestingly, this geometric interpretation appears to have a connection with quadratic forms in lattices (e.g., [24]), warranting further investigation.

We now view "hints" as geometric operations on the DBDD ellipsoid, as opposed to inducing a conditional probability distribution (represented by a mean and covariance) on the secret/error. In our framework, the information obtained from a hint corresponds to the intersection of the DBDD ellipsoid with another convex body such as a hyperplane (*perfect hints*), halfspace (*inequality hints*), or another ellipsoid (*combined hints*). This region of intersection is itself a convex body, but may not be an ellipsoid. Thus, to obtain the updated DBDD instance, we compute (an approximation of) the minimal volume ellipsoid that circumscribes the region of intersection. Such ellipsoids are well-studied in the literature on convex geometry and are known as Löwner-John ellipsoids. Since the ellipsoid circumscribes the region of intersection, replacing the original DBDD ellipsoid with the new ellipsoid provably maintains the DBDD invariant that the LWE secret corresponds to a lattice point contained in the ellipsoid.

1.1   Benefits and Drawbacks of Our Geometric Approach

Our approach establishes a connection between ellipsoidal approximations in convex geometry and analysis of the impact of side information on the concrete hardness of an LWE instance. This opens up a body of literature which we only begin to tap into in this work.

One benefit of our geometric approach is that in some cases it can more naturally handle the type of information obtained from side channels. For example, in decryption failure attacks, the type of information obtained is exactly an inequality hint on the LWE secret and error. The prior work of [17] proposed an ingenious way of capturing the information obtained from a decryption failure, without the direct use of inequality hints. As we describe in more detail in Sect. 1.2, our framework allows for direct incorporation of inequality hints as they correspond to the region of intersection of an ellipsoid and a halfspace. Our approach is also inherently compatible with continuous variants of LWE (see Remark 4 for further details).

Another benefit is that our approach removes the need for the Gaussian assumption. Not all natural distributions on the LWE secret and error are Gaussian. For example, the data obtained from the side-channel attack (SCA) of Bos et al. [13] (which we use for experimentation in Sect. 5.3) gives rise to a probability distribution on each secret key coordinate that is far from a Gaussian distribution. What does one do now if one would like to initialize a DBDD instance with this SCA distribution and then integrate additional hints? One approach is to simply treat the SCA distribution as a Gaussian and apply the hint formulas based on conditional Gaussians from the prior work. In this case, however, there are no guarantees that the DBDD invariant—that the LWE secret corresponds to a lattice point contained in the ellipsoid—holds after hint integration, and so the obtained BKZ-β estimates may be inaccurate (see Fig. 2 for a case where underestimation of the ellipsoid norm impacts the accuracy of BKZ-β estimates). Our method provides rigorous guarantees even when the data distribution is non-Gaussian. Specifically, our approach can be viewed as a "worst case" approach that guarantees that the secret is contained in the evolving DBDD ellipsoid, even for the "worst case" distribution over the secret.

We show that in the perfect hint setting, even though the data *is* (approximately) Gaussian, our modeling leads to slightly more accurate estimates of β in certain regimes.[1] Further, despite being a worst-case approach, we are able to show a setting in which our approach yields a decreased predicted BKZ-β, as compared to the prior work of [17]. This is possible since our modeling in that setting is fundamentally different from the prior work (we model decryption failures as inequality hints versus full dimensional approximate hints) so that the two approaches no longer correspond to worst-case/average-case estimates for the same process. Finally, we analyze a setting in which the distribution on the LWE secret, due to incorporation of side-channel data, is far from a Gaussian distribution. We show that our approach allows combining this SCA data with side information from an independent source, without resorting to Gaussian models. We elaborate on these examples in Sect. 1.2 as well as in Sects. 5.1, 5.2, and 5.3, respectively. Direct comparisons with the prior work of [17] can be found in Figs. 1 (in the perfect hints plot), 2, 3, and 5, respectively.

---

[1] We believe our improved accuracy is due to the fact that our modeling incorporates the true distances (w.r.t. the ellipsoid norm) of the intersecting hyperplanes from the center of the ellipsoid with each successive hint, whereas the average-case approach can be viewed as incorporating the expected distance each time.

A drawback of our approach is that due to our worst-case modeling, we can get "stuck" and not make progress when integrating new hints. This occurs when the minimal circumscribing ellipsoid works out to be *equivalent* to the original ellipsoid. In Sect. 5.2 such a situation occurred in our experiments and we provide some techniques based on the unique geometry of the problem to allow for continued progress. We discuss constraints on hints for which this situation can occur at the end of Sects. 2.3.1 and in Sect. 4.2 (see Theorem 4.1). In Sect. 1.3 we discuss additional approaches for circumventing this issue.

Further, since our ellipsoids no longer represent Gaussian distributions, we cannot necessarily predict the expected length of the secret (with respect to the "ellipsoid norm") in the evolving DBDD instances. In some cases, we therefore need to scale the DBDD instance (in a way that depends on the actual LWE secret) in order to make accurate predictions on the hardness. We note that this additional scaling is needed only for hardness *estimates* (in which case the LWE secret is, in fact, known) but is not needed to launch a full attack, since the BKZ-β is agnostic to scaling of the instance. See Sect. 5.1 for a more detailed discussion of this phenomenon for the case of inequality hints.

1.2   Instantiations of Our Approach

Inequality Hints. Here we consider the leakage of the information that $\langle v, s \rangle \geq \gamma$, where v is known and s is the LWE secret/error vector. Given our geometric perspective, this hint now exactly corresponds to the information that the LWE secret is contained in the intersection of the initial ellipsoid and the half-space $\{x \in \mathbb{R}^d \mid \langle x, v \rangle \geq \gamma\}$. Unfortunately, the geometric perspective does not seem helpful, as this region of intersection is no longer an ellipsoid! Instead, we *approximate* the region of intersection with an ellipsoid. We use the fact that one can efficiently compute the minimal volume ellipsoid (called the Löwner-John ellipsoid) that circumscribes the intersection of an ellipsoid and a halfspace [12]. Using this circumscribed ellipsoid in our DBDD instance maintains our required invariant, yet the new ellipsoid has *smaller volume* (under the constraints given in Sect. 2.3.1), making the resulting uSVP problem easier. See Sect. 4.1 for details on integration of inequality hints and Sect. 5.1 for validation of our β estimates for these hints.

Inequality hints are useful in the decryption failure setting since the information that is learned from a decryption failure is exactly of the form of an inequality hint. We show that this yields improved estimation accuracy (see Fig. 2) compared to modeling decryption failures as full dimensional approximate hints as in [17]. We then show our approach reduces the predicted β value required for key recovery, given a fixed number of decryption failures. We further describe a new, geometric-based failure boosting technique[2] obtained from our approach. See Sect. 5.2 for details and experimental results.

---

[2] The term "failure boosting" (see [21]) refers to techniques that use information from previous decryption failures to increase the failure rate for subsequent queries.

Combined Hints. Combined hints provide a way to "fuse" information from two DBDD instances into a single instance. To motivate this type of hint, consider a situation where we have two sources of side information for a single LWE secret/error, such as data from decryption failures, and data from a side-channel attack. The information from these sources is captured by the two DBDD instances $(\Lambda, \mu_1, \Sigma_1)$ and $(\Lambda, \mu_2, \Sigma_2)$ (for purposes of this example we assume the two lattices are equal in the two instances, but our techniques extend to the case in which the lattice differ).

One might consider using the conditional approximate hints of [17] to integrate the information from the second instance (μ_2, Σ_2) into the first instance (μ_1, Σ_1). However, the formulas for conditional approximate hints given by [17] require both distributions to be Gaussian. If those formulas are applied when one or both sources are not well-approximated by a Gaussian, then the DBDD invariant may no longer hold for the evolved instance. In cases where the distribution over individual secret/error coordinates are independent, it is possible to use the *a posteriori* approximate hints of [17], even when the distributions are non-Gaussian. This approach essentially erases certain information from (μ_1, Σ_1), and replaces it with corresponding information from (μ_2, Σ_2). Our approach, which we discuss next, combines information from the two instances more effectively, rather than simply replacing one with the other.

We first observe that even when no distributional information is available, given the promise of the two DBDD instances, we can conclude that the LWE secret/error vector s lies in the intersection of the two ellipsoids corresponding to (μ_1, Σ_1) and (μ_2, Σ_2). This region is not necessarily an ellipsoid, so we cannot simply obtain a new DBDD instance by intersecting the ellipsoids. Instead, we adopt the "fusion" approach [49,54] which is to find the convex combination of the two ellipsoids that optimizes the volume of the resulting ellipsoid. The optimal convex combination has the following properties: (1) It is an ellipsoid, (2) It is guaranteed to contain the intersection of the two ellipsoids, (3) It does not contain points that are outside both ellipsoids, and (4) Points on the surface of both ellipsoids are on the surface of the resulting ellipsoid. This approach is attractive since the fused ellipsoid can be obtained by solving a one-dimensional convex optimization problem, which is computationally feasible. Further, the approach was shown to be equivalent to several other proposed relaxation methods for finding the optimal circumscribing ellipsoid [54]. See Sect. 4.2 for details on integration of combined hints and discussion of when the resulting ellipsoid achieves smaller volume than both input ellipsoids. Validation of our β estimates for these hints can be found in Sect. 5.1.

We illustrate our approach by using it to fuse information from decryption failures and side-channel leakage, reducing the predicted β value required to recover the secret as compared to the naive approach of combining the information. See Sect. 5.3 for details and experimental results.

Revisiting Perfect Hints. Once a DBDD instance has evolved via the integration of inequality or combined hints, we can no longer make the Gaussian assumption from the prior work. This means that if there are additional perfect hints, they can no longer be integrated using the prior method. We present a new algorithm for integrating "perfect hints" into an LWE instance that does not require any distributional assumptions. A perfect hint is the leakage of the information that $\langle v, s \rangle = \gamma$, where v is known and s is the LWE secret/error vector. We now view this hint as consisting of the information that the LWE secret lies in the the intersection of the current DBDD ellipsoid and the hyperplane $H := \{s : \langle v, s \rangle = \gamma\}$. We note that the resulting intersection is itself an ellipsoid, thus maintaining our DBDD invariant. We also propose a different way to deal with non-homogenized perfect hints. All perfect hints from [17] were homogenized so that the incorporated hint was $\langle v', s' \rangle = 0$ with $\gamma = 0$. This was needed in order to maintain the invariant that the lattice part of the DBDD instance remains a lattice, and not a lattice coset. However, it also had the by-product that the hint vector v' is not in the span of Σ, the shape matrix of the ellipsoid corresponding to the DBDD instance. For consistency with our geometric approach we require that our hint vectors $v \in \mathsf{Span}(\Sigma)$, and so we suggest an alternative technique for dealing with non-homogenized perfect hints. See the full version of this work for more details [18].

Experimental results show that our β estimates improve accuracy when more hints are integrated, compared to the estimates of [17]. Specifically, when the γ from the perfect hint $\langle v, s \rangle = \gamma$ is large, the hyperplane is far from the center of the ellipsoid, resulting in a smaller ellipsoid compared to the one obtained using the conditional Gaussian formulas described in [17]. The actual β needed to recover the secret are the same across the two techniques, since the generated instances differ only by a scaling factor. See Sect. 5.1 for validation of our β estimates for these hints and comparison with the β estimates from [17].

Compatibility with Approximate, Modular, and Short Vector Hints. We outline compatibility of our framework with approximate, modular and short hints in the full version of this work [18].

1.3   Future Work

In this initial work, our main goal is to establish a connection between techniques in convex geometry and analysis of the security loss of LWE with side information. We believe that this connection can be further explored in several ways.

The Maximal Inscribed Ellipsoid. The Löwner-John ellipsoids we have dealt thus far correspond to the minimal volume ellipsoid circumscribing a convex body. The literature also explores the *maximal* volume ellipsoid that can be *inscribed* in a convex body. For such ellipsoids, closed-form formulas for the case of inequality hints can be obtained from the more general formulas for ellipsoidal slabs [28]. As suggested to us by an anonymous reviewer, security estimations based on the maximal volume inscribed ellipsoid can be viewed as upper bounds on the strength of the optimal algorithm for recovering the LWE secret via lattice-reduction. Combining such estimates with our prior techniques, we would obtain both upper and lower bounds on the optimal algorithm that follows the attack template under consideration.

We note that both in the case of inequality hints and combined hints, it is possible that, while the volume of the intersected region is smaller, the minimal circumscribing ellipsoid is nevertheless equal to the original ellipsoid. This means that the hint yields no progress in our current framework. This, however, cannot occur with the maximal volume inscribed ellipsoid. Thus, we plan to explore using the maximal inscribed ellipsoid in cases where no progress can be made with the minimal circumscribing ellipsoid. One such example is inequality hints that carry little information about the secret.

Incorporating Techniques from Control Theory. There is a rich body of literature in control theory dealing with the "state estimation" problem in which the goal is to integrate new information (obtained from noisy measurements) into a current model of a system. Indeed, the conditional approximate hints from the prior work [17] can be viewed as a special case of the celebrated Kalman filter [35] from control theory (which assumes that all measurements are linear and all noise is Gaussian). A more recent line of work [41,49,54] studies the case in which the noise is not guaranteed to be Gaussian (and may even be deterministic) and uses a set of fundamental ellipsoidal operations (known as an "Ellipsoidal Calculus") to combine the information. Hybrid models (where some of the noise is assumed to be Gaussian, whereas worst-case assumptions are made for the rest) have also been studied [31]. We plan to explore further connections with the control theory literature, to understand better the tradeoffs of using worst-case/average-case assumptions to analyze a system.

Toolkit Extension. Alongside this paper, we release an extension to the original python/sage 9.0 toolkit from [17][3]. We provide an updated API (which simplifies further extensions to the toolkit), and several new class files. The new EBDD.sage class is *fully-featured* implementation of our geometric approach. It maintains all information about the instance: the lattice Λ, and the (rank-scaled) ellipsoid $E^{(\mathrm{Rank})}(\boldsymbol{\mu}, \boldsymbol{\Sigma})$ as hints are integrated. We leave the lightweight implementations of this extension to future work, as the full implementation is presently required to perform accurate estimation of the hardness loss resulting from our (more-general) geometry-based hints.

1.4 Related Work

Concrete Security of Lattice Based Cryptosystems. Two LWE attack templates considered in the literature are known as the *primal*, and *dual* attacks. Both of these attack templates reduce the task of breaking LWE to solving an SVP instance. The SVP problem is a long-standing problem that has attracted much attention from the cryptographic as well as quantum communities. The current asymptotically best SVP algorithms (for classical and quantum computers) include [3,10,32,42]. In practice, the BKZ algorithm [50] was found to perform well on parameter regimes of interest, though it is not amenable

---

[3] The updated toolkit can be found at https://github.com/hunterkipt/Geometric-LWE-Estimator.

to provable guarantees on its asymptotic performance. The BKZ algorithm on dimension d includes as a core subroutine an SVP solving step on a smaller block-size $\beta \ll d$. It is compatible with both classical and quantum algorithms for solving the smaller blocksize SVP-β instances. NIST post quantum (PQC) candidates have used the runtime estimates for the BKZ algorithm to inform the setting of their concrete parameters [1]. Several works have sought to create models to accurately predict the behavior of the BKZ algorithm in parameter regimes of interest [5,8,16]. Finally, there has been some work on comparing the lattice reduction-based algorithms described up to now with combinatorial algorithms [2,4].

Sice-Channel Attacks (SCA). There are various ways in which an attacker can obtain "side-channel" information about the secret key of a cryptographic scheme, greatly reducing the security of the scheme, or even allowing for a full key recovery. These methods include timing attacks [39], power analysis attacks [40], cache side-channel attacks [52], and microarchitectural attacks [38,43]. Side-channel attacks on NIST PQC candidates include attacks on (earlier versions of) Dilithium, which was recently announced as a selected digital signature algorithm [47,48], qTESLA [48], NTRUEncrypt [51], as well as Rainbow, NTRU, and McEliece [53]. Template attacks were introduced by [15], who used a device identical to the target to generate a precise "template" of the noise. When noisy side-channel data is obtained, the template can be used to learn information about the secret. Bos et al. [13] applied this approach to FrodoKEM, a Round 3 PQC alternate candidate, simulating a single trace power attack using ELMO [44]. We use their side channel attack as the starting point of our experiments in Sect. 5.3. Other research has focused on active side-channel attacks, where faults are injected during computation involving the secret key, such as RowHammer. Such attacks were performed on the LUOV signature scheme, a Round 2 PQC candidate [45], as well as Dilithium [33].

Decryption Failures. A decryption failure is when the decryption process returns an incorrect message on a validly encrypted ciphertext. Since most lattice-based cryptographic KEM schemes have a non-zero decryption failure rate, several prior works have investigated the possibility of decryption failure attacks. Specifically, decryption failures leak information about the secret key, and in some cases can be used to fully recover the secret. These attacks were first applied on CPA-secure schemes [9,22,23,26,37,46]. However, CCA-secure schemes use a Fujisaki-Okamoto transform which protects against such attacks and ensures that even a malicious attacker can only cause decryption failures with extremely low probability. Several methods have been suggested to boost the rate at which decryption failures occur, thereby lowering the complexity of the attack [11,19–21,29]. Recently, Fahr et al. [25] combined SCA and Decryption Failure attacks by using a Rowhammer attack—which induces bit flips in memory—to artificially boost the failure rate of NIST PQC candidate FrodoKEM. This allowed an end-to-end key recovery attack on Frodo-640.

1.5 Organization

In Sect. 2, we present notation and provide necessary background in linear algebra (Sect. 2.2), and geometry (Sect. 2.3). Lattice preliminaries and background on the ellipsoid method can be found in [18]. Section 3 defines the DBDD problem, as well as a new variant of the DBDD problem. The reduction from DBDD to uSVP is given in Sect. 3.1, and Sect. 3.2 presents security estimates for the uSVP problem. Section 3.3 presents the initial embedding we use in this work from LWE to DBDD.

Section 4 introduces inequality hints (Sect. 4.1), and combined hints (Sect. 4.2). The revisit of perfect and short vector hints are presented in the full version [18]. Section 5 presents experimental validation of our β estimates (Sect. 5.1), applications of our new types of hints to the decryption failure setting (Sect. 5.2), and to combining decryption failure and side-channel information (Sect. 5.3).

2 Preliminaries

2.1 Notation

We use bold lower case letters to denote vectors, and bold upper case letters to denote matrices. We use row notation for vectors, and start indexing from 1. We denote by I_d the d-dimensional identity matrix and denote by $\langle x, y \rangle$ the inner product of vectors x, y of the same dimension. We denote by $(x\|y)$ the concatenation of two row vectors x, y. For $v \in \mathbb{R}^d$, $\|v\|$ denotes the ℓ_2 norm of the vector. For a vector v, we use both v_i and $v[i]$ to denote the i-th coordinate of the vector. For a matrix M we use $M[i][j]$ to denote the (i, j)-th position of the matrix. Random variables—i.e. variables whose values depend on outcomes of a random experiment—are denoted with lowercase calligraphic letters e.g. a, b, e, while random vectors are denoted with uppercase calligraphic letters e.g. $\mathcal{C}, \mathcal{X}, \mathcal{Z}$.

2.2 Linear Algebra

Definition 2.1 (Positive Semidefinite). *A $n \times n$ symmetric real matrix M is positive semidefinite if the scalar quantity $x M x^T \geq 0 \forall x \in \mathbb{R}^n$; if so, we write $M \geq 0$. Given two $n \times n$ real matrices A and B, we note that $A \geq B$ if $A - B$ is positive semidefinite.*

Definition 2.2. *M is a square root of Σ, denoted $\sqrt{\Sigma}$, if $M^T \cdot M = \Sigma$.*

As in the prior work [17], we make use of a generalized notion of the inverse and determinant, where these operations are restricted to operate on the row span of the input matrix. For $X \in \mathbb{R}^{d \times k}$ (with any $d, k \in \mathbb{N}$), we denote by Π_X the orthogonal projection matrix onto $\mathsf{Span}(X)$. More formally, let Y be a maximal set of independent row-vectors of X; the orthogonal projection matrix is given by $\Pi_X = Y^T \cdot (Y \cdot Y^T)^{-1} \cdot Y$. Its complement (the projection orthogonally to $\mathsf{Span}(X)$) is denoted by $\boldsymbol{\Pi}_X^\perp := \boldsymbol{I}_d - \boldsymbol{\Pi}_X$. We naturally extend the notation $\boldsymbol{\Pi}_F$ and $\boldsymbol{\Pi}_F^\perp$ to subspaces $F \subset \mathbb{R}^d$. By definition, the projection matrices satisfy $\boldsymbol{\Pi}_F^2 = \boldsymbol{\Pi}_F$, $\boldsymbol{\Pi}_F^T = \boldsymbol{\Pi}_F$ and $\boldsymbol{\Pi}_F \cdot \boldsymbol{\Pi}_F^\perp = \boldsymbol{\Pi}_F^\perp \cdot \boldsymbol{\Pi}_F = \mathbf{0}$.

Definition 2.3 (Restricted Inverse and Determinant [17]). *Let $\boldsymbol{\Sigma}$ be a symmetric matrix. We denote a restricted inverse denoted $\boldsymbol{\Sigma}^\sim$ as*

$$\boldsymbol{\Sigma}^\sim := (\boldsymbol{\Sigma} + \boldsymbol{\Pi}_{\boldsymbol{\Sigma}}^\perp)^{-1} - \boldsymbol{\Pi}_{\boldsymbol{\Sigma}}^\perp.$$

It satisfies $\mathsf{Span}(\boldsymbol{\Sigma}^\sim) = \mathsf{Span}(\boldsymbol{\Sigma})$ *and* $\boldsymbol{\Sigma} \cdot \boldsymbol{\Sigma}^\sim = \boldsymbol{\Pi}_{\boldsymbol{\Sigma}}$.
We denote by $\mathsf{rdet}(\boldsymbol{\Sigma})$ *the restricted determinant:* $\mathsf{rdet}(\boldsymbol{\Sigma}) := \det(\boldsymbol{\Sigma} + \boldsymbol{\Pi}_{\boldsymbol{\Sigma}}^\perp)$.

2.3 Geometry

Definition 2.4 (Ellipsoid [27]). *A set $E \subseteq \mathbb{R}^d$ is a (possibly degenerate) **ellipsoid** if there exist a vector $\boldsymbol{\mu} \in \mathbb{R}^d$ and a positive (semi-)definite $d \times d$-matrix $\boldsymbol{\Sigma}$ such that*

$$E = E(\boldsymbol{\mu}, \boldsymbol{\Sigma}) := \{\boldsymbol{x} \in \boldsymbol{\mu} + \mathsf{Span}(\boldsymbol{\Sigma}) \mid (\boldsymbol{x} - \boldsymbol{\mu})\boldsymbol{\Sigma}^\sim(\boldsymbol{x} - \boldsymbol{\mu})^T \le 1\}. \quad (1)$$

Definition 2.4 generalizes the traditional non-degenerate ellipsoid. Note that if $\boldsymbol{\Sigma}$ is full rank, then $\boldsymbol{\mu} + \mathsf{Span}(\boldsymbol{\Sigma}) = \mathbb{R}^d$, and the restricted inverse becomes the regular matrix inverse. Equivalently, a (non-degenerate) ellipsoid can be described by the norm $\| \cdot \|_{\boldsymbol{\Sigma}}$ on $\mathbb{R}^d$

$$E(\boldsymbol{\mu}, \boldsymbol{\Sigma}) = \{\boldsymbol{x} \in \mathbb{R}^d \mid \|\boldsymbol{x} - \boldsymbol{\mu}\|_{\boldsymbol{\Sigma}} \le 1\}$$

thus, the ellipsoid $E(\boldsymbol{\mu}, \boldsymbol{\Sigma})$ is the unit ball around $\boldsymbol{\mu}$ in the vector space $\mathbb{R}^d$ endowed with the norm $\| \cdot \|_{\boldsymbol{\Sigma}}$. In particular, the unit ball around $\mathbf{0}$ in the traditional Euclidean norm is $E(\mathbf{0}, \boldsymbol{I}_d)$. As $\boldsymbol{\Sigma}$ is positive definite, the matrix square root exists. As such, we can express an ellipsoid via the following relation

$$E(\boldsymbol{\mu}, \boldsymbol{\Sigma}) = \boldsymbol{\Sigma}^{1/2} E(\mathbf{0}, \boldsymbol{I}_d) + \boldsymbol{\mu}$$

making every ellipsoid the image of the unit ball under a bijective affine transformation. These alternative views of an ellipsoid can also be generalized to work with the degenerate case in a similar fashion to the generalized definition.

Definition 2.5 (Volume of a full-rank ellipsoid). *A full-rank ellipsoid $E(\boldsymbol{\mu}, \boldsymbol{\Sigma})$ of dimension d has volume $\mathsf{Vol}(E(\boldsymbol{\mu}, \boldsymbol{\Sigma})) = \sqrt{\det(\boldsymbol{\Sigma})} \cdot V_d$, where V_d is the volume of the d-dimensional unit ball.*

Definition 2.6 (Ellipsoid norm). *Let $\boldsymbol{x} \in \boldsymbol{\mu} + \mathsf{Span}\,\boldsymbol{\Sigma}$. We define the **ellipsoid norm** of $\boldsymbol{x}$ with respect to ellipsoid $E(\boldsymbol{\mu}, \boldsymbol{\Sigma})$ to be the quantity $(\boldsymbol{x} - \boldsymbol{\mu})\boldsymbol{\Sigma}^\sim(\boldsymbol{x} - \boldsymbol{\mu})^T$. Note that $\boldsymbol{x}$ is contained in $E(\boldsymbol{\mu}, \boldsymbol{\Sigma})$ if and only if its ellipsoid norm with respect to $E(\boldsymbol{\mu}, \boldsymbol{\Sigma})$ is at most 1.*

Remark 1 (Ellipsoid Scaling). Throughout the paper, we make use of two different ellipsoid scalings. For ellipsoid operations defined by the ellipsoid method (Sect. 2.3.1) or ellipsoid fusion (Sect. 4.2), we make use of the traditional scaling factor of 1 in (1). However, the invariant of the DBDD problem (Sect. 3) requires that the ellipsoid be scaled such that the right hand side of (1) is $\mathsf{Rank}(\boldsymbol{\Sigma})$. To remain consistent with prior work [17], we will treat these ellipsoids as a separate object, the *rank-scaled ellipsoid.*

Definition 2.7 (Rank-scaled Ellipsoid). *A set $E^{(\mathsf{Rank})} \subseteq \mathbb{R}^d$ is a (possibly degenerate) **rank-scaled ellipsoid** if there exist a vector $\boldsymbol{\mu} \in \mathbb{R}^d$ and a positive semidefinite $d \times d$-matrix $\boldsymbol{\Sigma}$ such that*

$$E^{(\mathsf{Rank})} = E^{(\mathsf{Rank})}(\boldsymbol{\mu}, \boldsymbol{\Sigma}) := \{\boldsymbol{x} \in \boldsymbol{\mu} + \mathsf{Span}(\boldsymbol{\Sigma}) \mid (\boldsymbol{x} - \boldsymbol{\mu})\boldsymbol{\Sigma}^{\sim}(\boldsymbol{x} - \boldsymbol{\mu})^T \leq \mathsf{Rank}(\boldsymbol{\Sigma})\}. \tag{2}$$

Converting a traditional ellipsoid into a rank-scaled ellipsoid follows from the definition. Given a rank-scaled ellipsoid, $E^{(\mathsf{Rank})}(\boldsymbol{\mu}, \boldsymbol{\Sigma})$, it is equivalent to the traditional ellipsoid $E(\boldsymbol{\mu}, \boldsymbol{\Sigma} \cdot \mathsf{Rank}(\boldsymbol{\Sigma}))$. As the mean of the ellipsoid remains the same, let

$$\mathcal{F} : \mathbb{R}^{d \times d} \mapsto \mathbb{R}^{d \times d}, \ \mathcal{F}(\boldsymbol{\Sigma}) = \boldsymbol{\Sigma} \cdot \mathsf{Rank}(\boldsymbol{\Sigma}) \tag{3}$$

denote the transformation between the covariance matrices.

Definition 2.8 (Hyperplane). *A set $H \subseteq \mathbb{R}^d$ is a **hyperplane** if there exist a vector $\boldsymbol{v} \in \mathbb{R}^d$ and a scalar threshold $\gamma \in \mathbb{R}$ such that*

$$H = H(\boldsymbol{v}, \gamma) := \{\boldsymbol{x} \in \mathbb{R}^d \mid \langle \boldsymbol{x}, \boldsymbol{v} \rangle = \gamma\}.$$

Definition 2.9 (Halfspace). *Without loss of generality, A set $H^{\leq} \subseteq \mathbb{R}^d$ is a **halfspace** if there exist a vector $\boldsymbol{v} \in \mathbb{R}^d$ and a scalar threshold $\gamma \in \mathbb{R}$ such that*

$$H^{\leq} := \{\boldsymbol{x} \in \mathbb{R}^d \mid \langle \boldsymbol{x}, \boldsymbol{v} \rangle \leq \gamma\}.$$

2.3.1 Ellipsoid Halfspace and Hyperplane Intersection

The algorithms in some of our applications are reminiscent of the *ellipsoid method*, the first provably polynomial time algorithm for solving linear programs [36]. While our goal is to solve an *integer program*—a harder problem than linear programming—it is well-known (s.f. [34]) that the ellipsoid method can be combined with lattice reduction to solve integer programs. In practice, however, this method is both inefficient and prone to numerical errors. So we must make crucial changes for the approach to be viable in our setting (see Sect. 5.2). For an overview of the ellipsoid method, see Appendix A of the full version [18].

The main update procedure of the ellipsoid method calculates the Löwner-John ellipsoid corresponding to the intersection of an ellipsoid and halfspace. Given an ellipsoid $E(\boldsymbol{\mu}, \boldsymbol{\Sigma})$ and a halfspace $\{\boldsymbol{x} \in \mathbb{R}^d \mid \langle \boldsymbol{x}, \boldsymbol{v} \rangle \leq \gamma\}$ (where $\boldsymbol{v} \in$

Span(Σ)), the Löwner-John ellipsoid of the intersection $E(\mu', \Sigma')$ is:

$$\mu' = \mu - \tau \frac{v\Sigma}{\sqrt{v\Sigma v^T}}$$

$$\Sigma' = \delta \left(\Sigma - \sigma \frac{\Sigma v^T v \Sigma}{v \Sigma v^T} \right) \tag{4}$$

This expression generalizes the computation of multiple Löwner-John ellipsoids based on ellipsoid-X intersections. The exact intersection performed depends on the values of the three variables δ, σ, and τ. For a geometric interpretation of the effects of varying these parameters, see the survey on the ellipsoid method by Bland, Goldfarb, and Todd [12].

For an ellipsoid-halfspace intersection,

$$\tau = \frac{1+r\alpha}{r+1} \qquad \sigma = \frac{2(1+r\alpha)}{(r+1)(1+\alpha)} \qquad \delta = \frac{r^2}{r^2-1}(1-\alpha^2) \tag{5}$$

where r is the rank of Σ, and α is a distorted measure of the distance between the center of the ellipsoid and the separating hyperplane. In (5), α is defined as

$$\alpha = \frac{v\mu^T - \gamma}{\sqrt{v\Sigma v^T}}. \tag{6}$$

When $-1 < \alpha \leq 1$, the separating hyperplane intersects the ellipsoid. If $\alpha = 0$, the separating hyperplane bisects the ellipsoid through its center. The optimal circumscription when $-1 < \alpha < -1/r$ is simply the starting ellipsoid.

Ellipsoid-Hyperplane Intersection. The intersection between an ellipsoid $E(\mu, \Sigma)$ and a hyperplane $H(v, \gamma)$, where $v \in$ Span(Σ) can be obtained by plugging appropriate parameters into the formula for parallel cuts given in [12]. Doing so yields τ, δ, and σ:

$$\tau = \alpha \qquad \sigma = 1 \qquad \delta = \frac{r}{r-1}(1-\alpha^2) \tag{7}$$

where α remains the same as in (6). An ellipsoid-hyperplane intersection is itself an ellipsoid of one fewer dimension. As $\sigma = 1$, the rank one update of Σ in (4) reduces the rank of the intersection $E(\mu', \Sigma')$ by 1, and ensures it is flat in the direction of v. Here $-1 < \alpha \leq 1$, with no additional restrictions, as the hyperplane need simply intersect the starting ellipsoid.

It is possible to prove a tighter bound so that $\delta = (1 - \alpha^2)$, which is the setting of δ we will use in our implementation.

2.3.2   Ellipsoid Fusion

The intersection of two ellipsoids is not generally an ellipsoid, so as in the ellipsoid method, some optimal approximation must be used to compute a representation of the intersection efficiently. There are multiple measures of an ellipsoid's size that could be optimized to produce a good approximation. For our framework, we adopt the Ellipsoid Fusion procedure proposed by Ros et al. [49]. Ros et al. propose a measure based on the volume of a *convex combination* of the two input ellipsoids. This is done through the minimization of the determinant of the combined ellipsoid's covariance matrix.

Theorem 2.10 (Theorem 2 in [49]). *Given two (possibly degenerate) ellipsoids, $E(\boldsymbol{\mu}_1, \boldsymbol{\Sigma}_1)$ and $E(\boldsymbol{\mu}_2, \boldsymbol{\Sigma}_2)$, whose intersection is a nonempty bounded region, the region defined by*

$$\{\boldsymbol{x} \mid \lambda(\boldsymbol{x} - \boldsymbol{\mu}_1)\boldsymbol{\Sigma}_1^\sim(\boldsymbol{x} - \boldsymbol{\mu}_1)^T + (1 - \lambda)(\boldsymbol{x} - \boldsymbol{\mu}_2)\boldsymbol{\Sigma}_2^\sim(\boldsymbol{x} - \boldsymbol{\mu}_2)^T \leq 1\},$$

is a real ellipsoid, $E^\lambda(\boldsymbol{\mu}_0, \boldsymbol{\Sigma})$, which coincides with $E(\boldsymbol{\mu}_2, \boldsymbol{\Sigma}_2)$ or $E(\boldsymbol{\mu}_1, \boldsymbol{\Sigma}_1)$ for $\lambda = 1$ or $\lambda = 0$ respectively; and it is given by

$$\left.\begin{array}{l} \boldsymbol{\Sigma} = k\boldsymbol{X}^\sim \\ \boldsymbol{X} = \lambda\boldsymbol{\Sigma}_1^\sim + (1 - \lambda)\boldsymbol{\Sigma}_2^\sim \\ \boldsymbol{\mu}_0\boldsymbol{\Pi}_X = (\boldsymbol{\mu}_1\lambda\boldsymbol{\Sigma}_1^\sim + \boldsymbol{\mu}_2(1 - \lambda)\boldsymbol{\Sigma}_2^\sim)\,\boldsymbol{X}^\sim \\ k = 1 - \lambda(1 - \lambda)(\boldsymbol{\mu}_2 - \boldsymbol{\mu}_1)\boldsymbol{\Sigma}_2^\sim\boldsymbol{X}^\sim\boldsymbol{\Sigma}_1^\sim(\boldsymbol{\mu}_2 - \boldsymbol{\mu}_1)^T \end{array}\right\}$$

for $\lambda \in [0,1]$.

Note that $\boldsymbol{\mu}_0$ can be set arbitrarily so long as $\boldsymbol{\mu}_0\boldsymbol{\Pi}_X$ satisfies the above. While this combination is not necessarily the optimal circumscription, it does not contain points that are in neither $E(\boldsymbol{\mu}_1, \boldsymbol{\Sigma}_1)$ nor $E(\boldsymbol{\mu}_2, \boldsymbol{\Sigma}_2)$.

Definition 2.11 (Ellipsoid Fusion (Definition 5 in [49])). *The fusion of $E(\boldsymbol{\mu}_1, \boldsymbol{\Sigma}_1)$ and $E(\boldsymbol{\mu}_2, \boldsymbol{\Sigma}_2)$, whose intersection is a nonempty bounded region is $E^{\tilde{\lambda}}(\boldsymbol{\Sigma}, \boldsymbol{\mu}_0)$ for the value of $\tilde{\lambda} \in [0,1]$ that minimizes its volume.*

Theorem 2.12 (Fusion (Theorem 3 in [49])). *The fusion of $E(\boldsymbol{\mu}_1, \boldsymbol{\Sigma}_1)$ and $E(\boldsymbol{\mu}_2, \boldsymbol{\Sigma}_2)$ is: $E(\boldsymbol{\mu}_1, \boldsymbol{\Sigma}_1)$; or $E(\boldsymbol{\mu}_2, \boldsymbol{\Sigma}_2)$; or it is $E^{\tilde{\lambda}}(\boldsymbol{\Sigma}, \boldsymbol{\mu}_0)$ where $\tilde{\lambda}$ is the only root in $[0,1]$ of the following polynomial of degree $2n - 1$:*

$$k(\mathrm{rdet}(\boldsymbol{X}))\mathrm{Trace}(\boldsymbol{X}(\boldsymbol{\Sigma}_1^\sim - \boldsymbol{\Sigma}_2^\sim)) - n(\mathrm{rdet}(\boldsymbol{X}))^2(2\boldsymbol{\mu}_0\boldsymbol{\Sigma}_1^\sim\boldsymbol{\mu}_1^T$$
$$-2\boldsymbol{\mu}_0\boldsymbol{\Sigma}_2^\sim\boldsymbol{\mu}_2 + \boldsymbol{\mu}_0(\boldsymbol{\Sigma}_2^\sim - \boldsymbol{\Sigma}_1^\sim)\boldsymbol{\mu}_0^T - \boldsymbol{\mu}_1\boldsymbol{\Sigma}_1^\sim\boldsymbol{\mu}_1^T + \boldsymbol{\mu}_2\boldsymbol{\Sigma}_2^\sim\boldsymbol{\mu}_2^T) \quad (8)$$

3   The **DBDD** Problem

Definition 3.1 (Distorted Bounded Distance Decoding problem). *Let $\Lambda \subset \mathbb{R}^{d+1}$ be a lattice, $\boldsymbol{\Sigma} \in \mathbb{R}^{(d+1)\times(d+1)}$ be a symmetric matrix and $\boldsymbol{\mu} \in \mathsf{Span}(\Lambda) \subset \mathbb{R}^{(d+1)}$ such that*

$$\mathsf{Span}(\boldsymbol{\Sigma}) \subsetneq \mathsf{Span}(\boldsymbol{\Sigma} + \boldsymbol{\mu}^T \cdot \boldsymbol{\mu}) = \mathsf{Span}(\Lambda). \quad (9)$$

The Distorted Bounded Distance Decoding problem $\mathsf{DBDD}_{\Lambda,\boldsymbol{\mu},\boldsymbol{\Sigma}}$ *is:*

> *Given $\boldsymbol{\mu}, \boldsymbol{\Sigma}$ and a basis of Λ.*
> *Find the unique vector $\boldsymbol{x} \in \Lambda \cap E^{(\mathsf{Rank})}(\boldsymbol{\mu}, \boldsymbol{\Sigma})$*

where $E^{(\mathsf{Rank})}(\boldsymbol{\mu}, \boldsymbol{\Sigma})$ denotes the (possibly degenerate) rank-scaled ellipsoid

$$E^{(\mathsf{Rank})}(\boldsymbol{\mu}, \boldsymbol{\Sigma}) := \{\boldsymbol{x} \in \boldsymbol{\mu} + \mathsf{Span}(\boldsymbol{\Sigma}) \mid (\boldsymbol{x} - \boldsymbol{\mu})\boldsymbol{\Sigma}^{\sim}(\boldsymbol{x} - \boldsymbol{\mu})^T \leq \mathsf{Rank}(\boldsymbol{\Sigma})\}.$$

In [17], $E^{(\mathsf{Rank})}(\boldsymbol{\mu}, \boldsymbol{\Sigma})$ corresponds to knowing that the secret vector $\boldsymbol{x}$ to be recovered follows a Gaussian distribution of variance $\boldsymbol{\Sigma}$ and mean $\boldsymbol{\mu}$, and the expected value of $(\boldsymbol{x} - \boldsymbol{\mu})\boldsymbol{\Sigma}^{\sim}(\boldsymbol{x} - \boldsymbol{\mu})^T$ for a Gaussian $\boldsymbol{x}$ of variance $\boldsymbol{\Sigma}$ and mean $\boldsymbol{\mu}$ is $\mathsf{Rank}(\boldsymbol{\Sigma})$. In the current work, we do not view the ellipsoid in the DBDD instance as stemming from the covariance matrix of a multivariate Gaussian distribution. Rather, we view the ellipsoid as defining a region containing a feasible solution to a certain constraint satisfaction problem over the reals. Then we restrict the solutions to those that are also contained in some lattice.

In order to be consistent with the approaches in the literature on Löwner-John ellipsoids, it will be useful for us to consider instances DBDD instances of dimension one lower than those in the prior work. Further, we allow $\mathsf{Span}(\boldsymbol{\Sigma}) = \mathsf{Span}(\boldsymbol{\Sigma} + \boldsymbol{\mu}^T \cdot \boldsymbol{\mu}) = \mathsf{Span}(\Lambda)$, unlike in the prior work. For clarity we formally define below the DBDD variant that we consider in this work.

Definition 3.2 (A Variant of the Distorted Bounded Distance Decoding problem). *Let* $\Lambda \subset \mathbb{R}^d$ *be a lattice,* $\boldsymbol{\Sigma} \in \mathbb{R}^{d \times d}$ *be a symmetric matrix and* $\boldsymbol{\mu} \in \mathsf{Span}(\Lambda) \subset \mathbb{R}^d$. *such that*

$$\mathsf{Span}(\boldsymbol{\Sigma}) = \mathsf{Span}(\boldsymbol{\Sigma} + \boldsymbol{\mu}^T \cdot \boldsymbol{\mu}) = \mathsf{Span}(\Lambda). \tag{10}$$

The Distorted Bounded Distance Decoding problem $\mathsf{DBDD}_{\Lambda, \boldsymbol{\mu}, \boldsymbol{\Sigma}}$ *with respect to* $(\Lambda, \boldsymbol{\mu}, \boldsymbol{\Sigma})$ *defined as above is:*

> *Given $\boldsymbol{\mu}, \boldsymbol{\Sigma}$ and a basis of Λ.*
> *Find the unique vector $\boldsymbol{x} \in \Lambda \cap E^{(\mathsf{Rank})}(\boldsymbol{\mu}, \boldsymbol{\Sigma})$*

where $E^{(\mathsf{Rank})}(\boldsymbol{\mu}, \boldsymbol{\Sigma})$ *denotes the (possibly degenerate) rank-scaled ellipsoid*

$$E^{(\mathsf{Rank})}(\boldsymbol{\mu}, \boldsymbol{\Sigma}) := \{\boldsymbol{x} \in \mathsf{Span}(\boldsymbol{\Sigma}) \mid (\boldsymbol{x} - \boldsymbol{\mu})\boldsymbol{\Sigma}^{\sim}(\boldsymbol{x} - \boldsymbol{\mu})^T \leq \mathsf{Rank}(\boldsymbol{\Sigma})\}.$$

We can convert a DBDD instance $(\Lambda, \boldsymbol{\mu}, \boldsymbol{\Sigma})$ of the type considered above into a DBDD instance $(\Lambda', \boldsymbol{\mu}', \boldsymbol{\Sigma}')$ considered in the prior work as follows:

$$\Lambda' = \{(\boldsymbol{x}||z) \in \mathbb{R}^{d+1} : \boldsymbol{x} \in \Lambda, z \in \mathbb{Z}\}$$

$$\boldsymbol{\mu}' = (\boldsymbol{\mu}||1) \in \mathbb{R}^{d+1}$$

$$\boldsymbol{\Sigma}'[i][j] := \begin{cases} \boldsymbol{\Sigma}[i][j] & \text{if } i, j \leq d \\ 0 & \text{if } i = d+1 \text{ or } j = d+1. \end{cases}$$

3.1 Reduction from DBDD to uSVP

Following [17], the conversion of a DBDD instance $(\Lambda, \boldsymbol{\mu}, \boldsymbol{\Sigma})$ into a uSVP instance proceeds in two steps known as *homogenization* and *isotropization*.

Homogenization: The homogenization procedure takes an ellipsoid that is centered at $\boldsymbol{\mu}$ and converts it into an ellipsoid centered at $\mathbf{0}$. The zero-centered ellipsoid *contains* the ellipsoid centered at $\boldsymbol{\mu}$ (see [17] for the proof of this claim). The volume of the ellipsoid remains the same[4], and the rank of its covariance matrix goes up by 1. Specifically, the conversion is as follows:

$$(\Lambda, \boldsymbol{\mu}, \boldsymbol{\Sigma}) \mapsto (\Lambda, \mathbf{0}, \boldsymbol{\Sigma}' := \boldsymbol{\Sigma} + \boldsymbol{\mu}^T \cdot \boldsymbol{\mu}).$$

Isotropization: The isotropization procedure converts the covariance matrix $\boldsymbol{\Sigma}'$ into an isotropic matrix (i.e. with all its eigenvalues equal to 1), by applying an appropriate linear transformation to the input space. We then perform the same linear transformation on the lattice. Specifically, the conversion is as follows:

$$(\Lambda, \mathbf{0}, \boldsymbol{\Sigma}') \mapsto (\Lambda \cdot M, \mathbf{0}, M \cdot \boldsymbol{\Sigma}' \cdot M^T),$$

where $M = \sqrt{\boldsymbol{\Sigma}'}^{\sim}$. The above can be simplified to

$$(\Lambda \cdot M, \mathbf{0}, M \cdot \boldsymbol{\Sigma}' \cdot M^T) = (\Lambda \cdot M, \mathbf{0}, \boldsymbol{\Pi}_{\boldsymbol{\Sigma}'}) = (\Lambda \cdot M, \mathbf{0}, \boldsymbol{\Pi}_{\Lambda}),$$

see [17] for details on the above simplification. After homogenization and isotropization, we obtain the uSVP instance $\Lambda \cdot M$ (consisting of a lattice only). To complete the reduction, note that from a given solution, $\boldsymbol{x}$, to the uSVP$_{\Lambda \cdot M}$ problem, one can derive the solution, $\boldsymbol{x}' = \boldsymbol{x} \cdot M^{\sim}$, to the DBDD$_{\Lambda,\boldsymbol{\mu},\boldsymbol{\Sigma}}$ problem.

3.2 Security Estimates of uSVP

We briefly recap the way concrete hardness estimates are computed for a given uSVP instance. Specifically, we consider an attack that consists of applying BKZ-β to the uSVP lattice Λ for an appropriate block size parameter β. The cost of the attack grows with β, and, as in [17], we will treat β itself as a measurement of the security level in a unit called the *bikz*. Bikz-to-bit conversion can be performed using a conversion factor based on the current best algorithms for SVP in lattices of rank β. Typically, it is assumed that 1 bikz ≈ 0.265 bits. As in [17], the concrete security estimates given in this paper only concern the pure lattice attacks via the uSVP embedding discussed above.

Predicting β for a uSVP Instance. The state-of-the-art predictions for solving uSVP using BKZ were given in [5,7]: For a lattice Λ of dimension $\dim(\Lambda)$, it is predicted that BKZ-β can solve a uSVP$_{\Lambda}$ instance with secret $(e||s)$ when

$$\sqrt{\beta/\dim(\Lambda)} \cdot \|(e||s)\| \leq \delta_{\beta}^{2\beta - \dim(\Lambda) - 1} \cdot \mathsf{Vol}(\Lambda)^{1/\dim(\Lambda)} \qquad (11)$$

where δ_{β} is the so called root-Hermite-Factor of BKZ-β. For $\beta \geq 50$, the Root-Hermite-Factor is predictable using the Gaussian Heuristic [16]:

$$\delta_{\beta} = \left((\pi\beta)^{\frac{1}{\beta}} \cdot \frac{\beta}{2\pi e} \right)^{1/(2\beta - 2)} . \qquad (12)$$

---

[4] This assumes that $\boldsymbol{\mu}'$–corresponding to the first d coorindates of $\boldsymbol{\mu} \in \mathsf{Span}(\boldsymbol{\Sigma})$ and the final coordinate of $\boldsymbol{\mu}$ is equal to 1, which is the case for DBDD instances obtained from DBDD variant instances.

In [17], the uSVP instances obtained were always isotropic and centered so that the secret has covariance $\Sigma = I$ (or $\Sigma = \Pi_\Lambda$ if Λ is not of full rank) and $\mu = 0$. In this case, $\|(e\|s)\|^2 = \mathsf{Rank}(\Sigma) = \dim(\Lambda)$, in expectation, and β can be estimated as the minimum integer that satisfies

$$\sqrt{\beta} \leq \delta_\beta^{2\beta - \dim(\Lambda) - 1} \cdot \mathsf{Vol}(\Lambda)^{1/\dim(\Lambda)}. \tag{13}$$

Importantly, in our case where we do not enforce distributional assumptions, we can no longer assume that after isotropization the secret has covariance $\Sigma = I$ and $\mu = 0$, rather, we just know that the secret is contained in the ellipsoid $E^{(\mathsf{Rank})}(0, I)$, but its norm could be far smaller. Therefore, when performing our final hardness estimates, we sometimes need to take the length of the shortest vector into account (i.e. we will use Eq. (11)) in order to accurately predict β. Throughout the paper, whenever this is the case, we will make note of it. The default is to use the prediction from Eq. (13), which returns β that is at least as large as β from (11). As in [17], while β must be an integer as a BKZ parameter, we provide a continuous value.

Remark 2. To predict security, one does not need the basis of Λ, but only its dimension and its volume. Similarly, it is not necessary to explicitly compute the isotropization matrix M of Sect. 3.1: $\mathsf{Vol}(\Lambda \cdot M) = \det(M)\mathsf{Vol}(\Lambda) = \det(\Sigma')^{-1/2}\mathsf{Vol}(\Lambda)$.

Remark 3. Given a DBDD instance (Λ, μ, Σ), it is important to note that as the volume of the rank-scaled ellipsoid $E^{(\mathsf{Rank})}(\mu, \Sigma)$ *decreases*, the volume of the lattice $\Lambda \cdot M$ after homogenization and isotropization *increases*. Applying the hardness estimate from (13), this makes the resulting uSVP instance *easier* to solve. Our goal, therefore, when integrating "hints" is to ensure that the volume of the rank-scaled ellipsoid $E^{(\mathsf{Rank})}(\mu, \Sigma)$ *decreases* as much as possible.

3.3 Obtaining Our Initial DBDD Embedding

Recall that, in the prior work, Kannan's embedding was used to reduce LWE to DBDD. We next present a somewhat different embedding of LWE in DBDD.

The Geometric DBDD Embedding. Consider an LWE instance $sA^T + e = b$ mod q. We can remove the mod q and transform the above to a system of equations over the integers by adding the vector of variables c:

$$sA^T + e - qc = b.$$

Note that given an LWE instance A, b and a solution $(c\|s)$, there is an *affine* transformation to obtain a solution modulo q of the form $(e\|s)$. Specifically, $e = qc - sA^T + b$. Further, we assume that we can (w.h.p.) upper bound the squared norm of $(e\|s)$ by $\sigma^2(n + m) = \sigma^2 \cdot d$ (e.g. in standard LWE σ^2 is the variance of s, e). In matrix notation, we define B as:

$$B := \begin{bmatrix} qI_m & 0 \\ -A^T & I_n \end{bmatrix}. \tag{14}$$

We obtain the following constraint on the solution $(c||s)$ of the transformed system: $\left\| \left((c||s) \, B + (b||0) \right) \right\|^2 \leq \sigma^2 \cdot d$. The above defines a rank-scaled ellipsoid E with center $(-b||0) \, B^{-1}$:

$$E^{(\mathsf{Rank})}((-b||0, \sigma^2(BB^T)^{-1}) :=$$

$$\left\{ (c||s) \in \mathbb{R}^{n+m} : \left((c||s) - (-b)||0 \right) B^{-1} \frac{1}{\sigma^2} BB^T \left((c||s) - (b||0) \, B^{-1} \right)^T \leq d \right\}.$$

Our DBDD instance is therefore: $\left(\mathbb{Z}^d, (-b||0) \, B^{-1}, \sigma^2(BB^T)^{-1} \right)$.

Incorporating a Center and Shape Matrix for $(e||s)$. We consider here the case that we are given a center vector $(\mu_e||\mu_s) \in \mathsf{Span}(\Sigma)$, and a shape matrix Σ, along with the guarantee that w.h.p. $((e||s) - (\mu_e||\mu_s)) \, \Sigma^{\sim}$ $((e||s) - (\mu_e||\mu_s))^T \leq \mathsf{Rank}(\Sigma)$. As a special case, the above guarantee holds when $(e||s) \sim \mathcal{N}((\mu_e||\mu_s), \Sigma)$ follow a multivariate Gaussian distribution. Using the same B as in (14), we obtain the constraint:

$$\left\| \left(((c||s) \, B + (b||0)) \right) - (\mu_e||\mu_s) \right) \sqrt{\Sigma^{\sim}} \right\|^2 \leq \mathsf{Rank}(\Sigma).$$

This gives the rank-scaled ellipsoid:

$$E^{(\mathsf{Rank})}(((\mu_e - b)||\mu_s)B^{-1}, (B^T)^{-1}\Sigma(B)^{-1}) := \Big\{ (c||s) \in \mathsf{Span}((B^T)^{-1}\Sigma(B)^{-1}) :$$

$$\left((c||s) - ((\mu_e - b)||\mu_s) \, B^{-1} \right) B\Sigma^{\sim}B^T \left((c||s) - ((\mu_e - b)||\mu_s) \, B^{-1} \right)^T \leq \mathsf{Rank}(\Sigma) \Big\}.$$

Our DBDD instance is now: $\left(\mathbb{Z}^d, ((\mu_e - b)||\mu_s) \, B^{-1}, (B^T)^{-1}\Sigma(B)^{-1} \right)$. We can now apply hints to our initial DBDD instance.

Remark 4. Our DBDD embedding extends to s sampled from any distribution S whose support is contained in a lattice, and to $A^T \in \mathbb{R}^{n \times m}, e \in \mathbb{R}^m$ which are real-valued. Thus, our embedding captures the *Continuous LWE Problem* for secret distributions S as above [14, 30].

4   Hints

4.1   Inequality Hints

An inequality hint on the secret $(c||s)$ is the knowledge of $v \in \mathbb{R}^d$ and $l \in \mathbb{R}$, such that $\langle (c||s), v \rangle \leq \gamma$. In other words, inequality hints correspond to the knowledge that the secret lies on one side of a halfspace.

The process for integrating inequality hints relies on the ellipsoid-halfspace intersection procedure of the ellipsoid method (4, 5). Given a DBDD instance

$\text{DBDD}_{\Lambda,\mu,\Sigma}$, an inequality hint with $v \in \text{Span}(\Sigma)$ produces a new instance $\text{DBDD}_{\Lambda',\mu',\Sigma'}$,

$$\Lambda' = \Lambda \tag{15}$$

$$\mu' = \mu - \left(\frac{1+r\alpha}{r+1}\right)\frac{v\mathcal{F}(\Sigma)}{\sqrt{v\mathcal{F}(\Sigma)v^T}} \tag{16}$$

$$\Sigma' = \mathcal{F}^{-1}\left(\left(\frac{r^2}{r^2-1}(1-\alpha^2)\right)\left(\mathcal{F}(\Sigma) - \left(\frac{2(1+r\alpha)}{(r+1)(1+\alpha)}\right)\frac{\mathcal{F}(\Sigma)v^T v\mathcal{F}(\Sigma)}{v\mathcal{F}(\Sigma)v^T}\right)\right) \tag{17}$$

for $-1/r < \alpha \le 1$, where α is defined as in (6). and r is the rank of Σ. If $-1 < \alpha \le -1/r$, then $\Lambda' = \Lambda$, $\mu' = \mu$, and $\Sigma' = \Sigma$, meaning that for inequality hints with α in this range, we do not make progress under the approximation stemming from the ellipsoid method.

Quantitative Volume Reduction. Using the matrix determinant lemma and properties of rdet and $\Sigma^\sim$, we have that

$$\text{rdet}(\Sigma') = \left(\frac{r^2}{r^2-1}(1-\alpha^2)\right)^r \cdot \left(1 - \left(\frac{2(1+r\alpha)}{(r+1)(1+\alpha)}\right)\right) \cdot \text{rdet}(\Sigma).$$

Here we can clearly see the power of α on the volume. The closer α is to 1, the smaller the resulting volume of Σ' (yielding a larger decrease in security).

4.2   Combined Hints

We are given two DBDD instances, $(\Lambda_1, \mu_1, \Sigma_1), (\Lambda_2, \mu_2, \Sigma_2)$, with respect to the *same* secret $(c||s)$ (resp. $(e||s)$). Recall that DBDD instances (Λ, μ, Σ) provide the promise that the secret $(c||s) \in \Lambda$ and $(c||s) \in E^{(\text{Rank})}(\mu, \Sigma,)$ (resp. $(e||s) \in \Lambda$ and $(e||s) \in E^{(\text{Rank})}(\mu, \Sigma,)$).

Combined hints take the two DBDD instances and combine them into a single instance $(\Lambda', \mu', \Sigma')$ that captures the information from both. Specifically, Λ' will be equal to the intersection of the two lattices Λ_1, Λ_2. Since the intersection of two ellipsoids $E(\mu_1, \mathcal{F}(\Sigma_1)), E(\mu_2, \mathcal{F}(\Sigma_2))$ is not necessarily an ellipsoid, we define $E(\mu', \mathcal{F}(\Sigma'))$ to be an ellipsoid circumscribing their intersection. Exactly computing the minimal volume ellipsoid that circumscribes the intersection of two ellipsoids is computationally difficult. We instead use Theorem 2.10 to find $E(\mu', \mathcal{F}(\Sigma'))$.

$$\Lambda' = \Lambda_1 \cap \Lambda_2 \tag{18}$$

$$\mu' \Pi_X = \left(\mu_1 \tilde{\lambda}\mathcal{F}(\Sigma_1)^\sim + \mu_2(1-\tilde{\lambda})\mathcal{F}(\Sigma_2)^\sim\right)X^\sim \tag{19}$$

$$\Sigma' = \mathcal{F}^{-1}(kX^\sim), \tag{20}$$

where

$$X = \tilde{\lambda}\mathcal{F}(\Sigma_1)^\sim + (1-\tilde{\lambda})\mathcal{F}(\Sigma_2)^\sim,$$

$$k = 1 - \tilde{\lambda}(1 - \tilde{\lambda})(\boldsymbol{\mu}_2 - \boldsymbol{\mu}_1)\mathcal{F}(\boldsymbol{\Sigma}_2)^{\sim} \boldsymbol{X}^{\sim} \mathcal{F}(\boldsymbol{\Sigma}_1)^{\sim}(\boldsymbol{\mu}_2 - \boldsymbol{\mu}_1)^T$$

and $\tilde{\lambda}$ is the unique value between $[0,1]$ that minimizes the volume of $E(\boldsymbol{\mu}', \boldsymbol{\Sigma}')$. Theorem 2.12 provides a computationally efficient way to find $\tilde{\lambda}$. Given $\boldsymbol{\mu}' \Pi_X$, the mean $\boldsymbol{\mu}'$ can be recovered from the known linear constraints on the system.

When Does Fusion Yield a Volume Reduction? If $\tilde{\lambda} = 0$, then $\boldsymbol{\Sigma}' = \boldsymbol{\Sigma}_2$ and if $\tilde{\lambda} = 1$, then $\boldsymbol{\Sigma}' = \boldsymbol{\Sigma}_1$. Therefore, ellipsoid fusion does not always yield a reduction in volume. It is not hard to see that if $\boldsymbol{\Sigma}_1 = \boldsymbol{\Sigma}_2$, and if $\boldsymbol{\mu}_1 \neq \boldsymbol{\mu}_2$ are in the span of both $\boldsymbol{\Sigma}_1$ and $\boldsymbol{\Sigma}_2$, then the volume of $E^{(\mathsf{Rank})}(\boldsymbol{\mu}', \boldsymbol{\Sigma}')$ is strictly smaller than both the volume of $E^{(\mathsf{Rank})}(\boldsymbol{\mu}_1, \boldsymbol{\Sigma}_1)$ and of $E^{(\mathsf{Rank})}(\boldsymbol{\mu}_2, \boldsymbol{\Sigma}_2)$. We next show that fusion can lead to a volume reduction, even in case that the volume of $E^{(\mathsf{Rank})}(\boldsymbol{\mu}_2, \boldsymbol{\Sigma}_2)$ is strictly smaller than the volume of $E^{(\mathsf{Rank})}(\boldsymbol{\mu}_1, \boldsymbol{\Sigma}_1)$. In the following, we assume WLOG that $\boldsymbol{\mu}_1 = \boldsymbol{0}$ by applying a shift.

Theorem 4.1. *Let $\boldsymbol{c} \in \mathbb{R}^d$ denote the d-dimensional vector that has $c \in \mathbb{R}$ in each position. Let $\sigma_1^2, \sigma_2^2 \in \mathbb{R}$ be such that $\sigma_2^2 < \sigma_1^2$. Consider the rank-scaled ellipsoids $E^{(\mathsf{Rank})}(\boldsymbol{\mu}_1, \boldsymbol{\Sigma}_1) = E^{(\mathsf{Rank})}(\boldsymbol{0}, \sigma_1^2 \boldsymbol{I}_d)$ and $E^{(\mathsf{Rank})}(\boldsymbol{\mu}_2, \boldsymbol{\Sigma}_2) = E^{(\mathsf{Rank})}(\boldsymbol{c}, \sigma_2^2 \boldsymbol{I}_d)$. Then the volume of $E^{(\mathsf{Rank})}(\boldsymbol{\mu}', \boldsymbol{\Sigma}')$, where $\boldsymbol{\mu}'$ and $\boldsymbol{\Sigma}'$ are defined in Eqs. (19) and (20) respectively, is lower than both the volume of $E^{(\mathsf{Rank})}(\boldsymbol{\mu}_1, \boldsymbol{\Sigma}_1)$ and $E^{(\mathsf{Rank})}(\boldsymbol{\mu}_2, \boldsymbol{\Sigma}_2)$ if and only if $c^2 > \sigma_1^2 - \sigma_2^2$.*

The proof of Theorem 4.1 is available in Appendix B of the full version [18].

Remark 5. Consider the setting of Theorem 4.1 and let c be such that $(\sigma_1 - \sigma_2)^2 < c^2 < \sigma_1^2 - \sigma_2^2$. Note that $E^{(\mathsf{Rank})}(\boldsymbol{\mu}_2, \boldsymbol{\Sigma}_2) \not\subseteq E^{(\mathsf{Rank})}(\boldsymbol{\mu}_1, \boldsymbol{\Sigma}_1)$. This can be seen using the alternate definition of a rank-scaled ellipsoid as a linear transformation and shift of the ball of radius $\sqrt{r}$, where r is the rank. Specifically, since $\|\boldsymbol{1}\| = \sqrt{d}$ and since $\|\boldsymbol{1} \cdot \sqrt{\boldsymbol{\Sigma}_2} + \boldsymbol{\mu}_2\|^2 = d \cdot (\sigma_2 + c)^2 > d\sigma_1^2$, we have that the point $\boldsymbol{1} \cdot \sqrt{\boldsymbol{\Sigma}_2} + \boldsymbol{\mu}_2$ is contained in $E^{(\mathsf{Rank})}(\boldsymbol{\mu}_2, \boldsymbol{\Sigma}_2)$ but not in $E^{(\mathsf{Rank})}(\boldsymbol{\mu}_1, \boldsymbol{\Sigma}_1)$. On the other hand, the intersection of the two ellipsoids is not empty, since $\boldsymbol{\mu}_2$ is contained in both ellipsoids. Clearly $\boldsymbol{\mu}_2$ is contained in $E^{(\mathsf{Rank})}(\boldsymbol{\mu}_2, \boldsymbol{\Sigma}_2)$. We can see that it is contained in $E^{(\mathsf{Rank})}(\boldsymbol{\mu}_1, \boldsymbol{\Sigma}_1)$ since

$$\boldsymbol{\mu}_2 \boldsymbol{\Sigma}_1^{-1} \boldsymbol{\mu}_2^T = d \cdot c^2 \cdot \frac{1}{\sigma_1^2} < d \cdot \frac{\sigma_1^2 - \sigma_2^2}{\sigma_1^2} < d.$$

However, since $c^2 < \sigma_1^2 - \sigma_2^2$, we have by Theorem 4.1 that the volume of $E^{(\mathsf{Rank})}(\boldsymbol{\mu}', \boldsymbol{\Sigma}')$ does not decrease.

Importantly, this means that the ellipsoid fusion technique does not guarantee that we obtain a lower volume ellipsoid, even in the case that $E(\boldsymbol{\mu}_1, \boldsymbol{\Sigma}_1), E(\boldsymbol{\mu}_2, \boldsymbol{\Sigma}_2)$ are such that $E(\boldsymbol{\mu}_1, \boldsymbol{\Sigma}_1) \cap E(\boldsymbol{\mu}_2, \boldsymbol{\Sigma}_2) \neq \emptyset$, $E(\boldsymbol{\mu}_1, \boldsymbol{\Sigma}_1) \not\subseteq E(\boldsymbol{\mu}_2, \boldsymbol{\Sigma}_2)$, and $E(\boldsymbol{\mu}_2, \boldsymbol{\Sigma}_2) \not\subseteq E(\boldsymbol{\mu}_1, \boldsymbol{\Sigma}_1)$. This contradicts Theorem 3 of [49].

Remark 6. If $\boldsymbol{x}$ has ellipsoid norm $0 \leq a \leq 1$ with respect to $E(\boldsymbol{\mu}_1, \boldsymbol{\Sigma}_1)$ and ellipsoid norm $0 \leq b \leq 1$ with respect to $E(\boldsymbol{\mu}_2, \boldsymbol{\Sigma}_2)$, then its ellipsoid norm with respect to the fused ellipsoid is

$$0 \leq \frac{\tilde{\lambda}a + (1 - \tilde{\lambda})b + k - 1}{k} \leq 1.$$

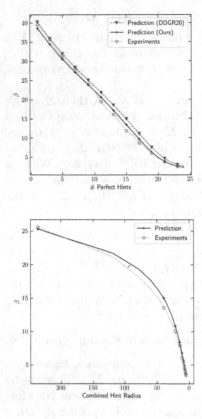

Fig. 1. Experimental verification of the bikz predictions for each type of hint. Each data point was averaged over 256 samples. Inequality and perfect hint validation were conducted by integrating successively larger numbers of hints. Combined hint validation was conducted by integrating instances with decreasing ellipsoid volume (see (21)).

For diagonal ellipsoids for which $0 \leq k \leq 1$, the above implies that the ellipsoid norm of x with respect to the fused ellipsoid is at most $\tilde{\lambda}a + (1-\tilde{\lambda})b \leq \max(a,b)$.

5   Experimental Validation and Applications

5.1   Experimental Validation

For (1) perfect hints, (2) inequality hints, (3) combined hints, we compare the bikz predicted by our tool with the bikz actually needed to launch the attack and recover the LWE secret/error. For (1) and (2), we choose the same set of LWE parameters for the initial instances as in [17], and integrate an increasing number of hints of each type.

For (1), the curve labeled "Prediction (DDGR20)" uses DBDD instances obtained by integrating perfect hints via the approach of [17], while "Prediction (Ours)" uses our new approach. We display a single "Experiments" curve since the EBDD and DBDD instances differ only by a scaling factor, which does not impact the bikz (as verified experimentally). To see why our predictions differ, compare the equations for Σ of the resulting distribution/ellipsoid, i.e., Eq. (10) in [17] and Eq. (7) in the current work. The main difference lies in the term $(1 - \alpha^2)$, where α represents the signed distance of the hyperplane from the center of the ellipsoid as defined in 6. Both the magnitude of γ and the length of v impact the value of α.

For (2), we create inequality hints by simulating a known (small) absolute error. Given a hint vector v, we create the hint $\langle v, (e||s) \rangle \geq \gamma - 2$, where γ is the inner product of v with the correct secret. Our predicted bikz–the "scaled" estimate–take into account the length of the shortest vector in our final lattice as in (11) as it deviates from the expected value assumed in (13). When integrating large numbers of inequality hints the ellipsoid norm of the secret w.r.t. the DBDD instance is significantly lower than the rank, while (13) holds under the assumption that the ellipsoid norm is approximately equal to the rank. This leads to overestimation of the hardness when applying (13)–the "unscaled" estimate. As such, we also use this calibration when examining the hardness loss resulting from decryption failures in Sect. 5.2.

For (3) we use the same set of LWE parameters to construct an initial DBDD (see Sect. 3.3) instance. We then perform combined hints with the initial DBDD instance and each of the DBDD instances corresponding to the ellipsoids

$$E^{(\text{Rank})}((c||s) + \mathcal{E}, (20/i) \cdot I_{m+n}), \tag{21}$$

where $\mathcal{E} \sim \mathcal{N}(0, (20/i) \cdot I_{m+n})$ for $i \in [1, 49]$. See Fig. 1 for details.

5.2 Decryption Failures, Revisited

Decryption failures exactly correspond to inequality hints from Sect. 4.1. Thus, the naive approach to running a decryption failure attack is to iteratively integrate each decryption failure as an inequality hint, obtaining a series of ellipsoids with volumes that are strictly decreasing. To test the efficacy of this approach, we mounted a decryption failure attack on a toy FrodoKEM [6] parameter set. We set $n = m = 80$ and $q = 2^{11}$, while we kept the secret/error distribution identical to that of the frodo-640 parameter set. This had the benefit of reducing the initial hardness of each instance to $\beta \approx 45$, while raising the empirical decryption failure rate to 0.44. We then generated a small database of 20 decryption failures for each of 50 different key pairs. For each key pair we integrated the decryption failures as both inequality hints and full dimensional approximate hints using the approach from [17]. After integrating each hint, we recorded both the predicted and experimental β as well as the ellipsoid norm for both approaches. A plot of the averages from all 50 key pairs can be seen in Fig. 2.

In the left figure, the ellipsoid norm of the LWE secret increases with the integration of approximate hints. An ellipsoid norm greater than 1 indicates that

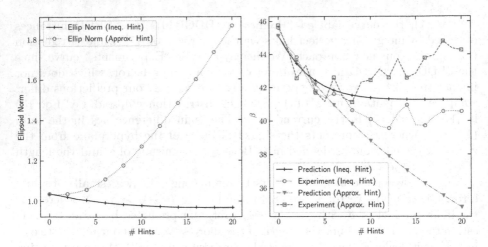

Fig. 2. 50 key pair average ellipsoid norm (left), predicted β and experimental β (right) for integrating up to 20 decryption failures from a toy frodo-80 parameter set with $n = m = 80$, $q = 2^{11}$. Inequality hints were integrated in order of decreasing α (as defined in (6)).

the secret is not contained in the DBDD ellipsoid. The formulation of decryption failures as approximate hints in [17] approximates the search space as spherical when in fact failures are biased in the direction of the secret. Thus, after a large number of integrated hints, the approximated search space no longer contains the secret. Since the hardness estimates depicted in the right figure assume that the secret *is* contained in the DBDD ellipsoid, they are far lower than the experimental BKZ-β.

With decryption failures modeled as inequality hints, the predicted loss in β is more modest, but the experimental β effectively matches the predictions. Note here, that compared to Fig. 1, inequality hints are more effective. When the hints are correlated with the secret, we find that α (6) is larger and therefore the volume reduction is larger (see (5)). The decrease in β levels off after around 10 inequality hints are integrated. For full-sized decryption failures (discussed next) we introduce a "regeneration" technique to allow for continued progress.

Full-Sized Decryption Failures. We experimented with applying our inequality hint approach to the recent decryption failure attack of Fahr et al. [25]. In their work, the public key of FrodoKEM [6] (NIST level 1 frodo-640) was altered by injecting faults via the Rowhammer exploit to significantly increase the decryption failure rate (by effectively lowering the decryption failure threshold). This enables an attacker to search for failing (honestly generated) ciphertexts in a reasonable amount of time and thus this scenario is more amenable for the experiments in this section.

When instantiating our naive approach in the Fahr et al. [25] setting, we find that while the first batch of hints reduce the volume as expected (e.g. for the first hint if a vector w causes decryption to fail with probability p over choice of secret key, then we see a reduction of volume by nearly a factor of p), hints quickly lose their efficacy, until almost no progress is made in terms of volume reduction as new hints are integrated. In fact, we found that the center of the successive ellipsoids obtained by integrating a sequence of inequality hints converges very quickly to a feasible solution (i.e. a solution that satisfies all the linear constraints). This is due to the one-sided nature of the linear inequalities corresponding to decryption failures. The intersection of a finite number of halfspaces pertaining to these inequalities is an unbounded region of space. Thus, a feasible solution sufficiently inside this region will not be affected by any new constraints of the same form.

After ≈ 200 hints for simulated failures on Frodo-640 [6] the center, μ itself satisfied *all prior and future* inequality hints, which corresponds to a terminating condition in the ellipsoid method. The full key recovery attack of Fahr et al. [25] required $\approx 100,000$ hints, so reaching a feasible solution after 200 hints is quite surprising. Unfortunately, the Euclidean distance between μ and the true LWE secret/error remained quite large, so μ itself was not a good candidate solution. Nevertheless, we found that μ contains a lot of information about s: We argue next that if μ satisfies all hints, then $\langle \mu, s \rangle \geq \langle s, s \rangle \approx \sigma_s^2 \cdot n$.

As observed in [17], the distribution of hint vectors w decomposes as $w = \alpha \cdot s/\|s\| + w'$, where α is a random variable with expectation $\approx t/\|s\|$ (where t is the decryption failure threshold) and w' is a zero-centered random variable orthogonal to s. So for a fixed center μ,

$$\mathbb{E}[\langle \mu, w \rangle] = \mathbb{E}[\alpha] \cdot \langle \mu, s \rangle / \|s\| \approx t \cdot \langle \mu, s \rangle / \|s\|^2 = t \cdot \langle \mu, s \rangle / \langle s, s \rangle.$$

If we find empirically, for a sufficiently large hint database, that $\mathbb{E}[\langle \mu, w \rangle] \geq t$– which occurs if μ satisfies all previous and future hint inequalities–it implies that $\langle \mu, s \rangle \geq \langle s, s \rangle$.

Inequality Hints with Regeneration. To solve the issue of stalled progress as well as issues of numerical precision, we developed the regeneration approach in Algorithm 1.

When the center μ of the successive ellipsoids becomes such that $\langle \mu, s \rangle \geq \sigma_s^2 \cdot d$, we simply use μ itself to perform an inequality hint on a fresh DBDD instance. Specifically, we regenerate the initial ellipsoid according to our embedding and integrate the hint $\langle \mu, s \rangle \geq \sigma_s^2 \cdot d$. Once this is done, we find that we can again make progress for some time by integrating more decryption failures. When progress stalls again, we simply regenerate again.

An attacker cannot directly check the condition for regeneration ($\langle \mu, s \rangle \geq \sigma_s^2 \cdot d$). Instead, the attacker can use the empirical value of $\mathbb{E}[\langle w, \mu \rangle]$, calculated using all w corresponding to failing ciphertexts in the attacker's database. In the case that $\langle \mu, s \rangle \geq \sigma_s^2 \cdot d$, we expect $\mathbb{E}[\langle w, \mu \rangle] \geq (1 + \epsilon) \cdot t$ where ϵ is a safety margin due to the uncertainty in the empirical expected value.

Algorithm 1 Integrating Decryption Failures Using Regeneration

Input: System of decryption failure hints: $(\boldsymbol{W}, \boldsymbol{\gamma})$, LWE instance,
      Maximum allowed regenerations: MaxRegen
Output: DBDD instance with integrated decryption failures
1:   $\boldsymbol{W}_{\mathsf{regen}} := [\,]$
2: **for** $i = 0$ to MaxRegen $- 1$ **do**
3:      DBDD $\leftarrow$ LWE.embed()
4:      **for** $j = 0$ to i **do**
5:          DBDD.IntegrateIneqHint($-\boldsymbol{W}_{\mathsf{regen}}[j]$, $-$LWE.$\sigma_s^2 \cdot$ LWE.d)
                                         ▷ *Inequality hints formulated for* $\leq$
6:      **while** Mean(DBDD.$\boldsymbol{\mu} \cdot \boldsymbol{W}^T$) $<$ LWE.t **do**   ▷ *Failure threshold*
7:          IntegrateNextHint(DBDD, $\boldsymbol{W}, \boldsymbol{\gamma}$)   ▷ *Use some hint integration strategy*
8:      append DBDD.$\boldsymbol{\mu}$ to $\boldsymbol{W}_{\mathsf{regen}}$
9: **return** DBDD

To evaluate the effectiveness of regeneration compared to the full dimensional approximate hint-based hardness estimates in [17], we continued to use the scenario of Fahr et al. [25]. For our experiment, we generated several simulated public keys (i.e. we directly modified honestly generated public keys to reproduce the result of the fault injection). Then, we searched for 4000 failing ciphertexts for each key. We integrated these 4000 hints as full-dimensional approximate hints and inequality hints with regeneration on two separate DBDD instances. We set the decryption failure threshold $t = 1024$ corresponding to the effect of the fault injection attack. The results can be seen in Fig. 3.

	Full-Dimen. Approx. Hints	Inequality Hints				
		Key 1	Key 2	Key 3	Key 4	Key 5
Initial BKZ–β	**487.08**	487.08	487.08	487.08	487.08	487.08
Ciphertexts	**4000**	1224	1106	959	986	965
Ellipsoid Norm	–	322.61	213.55	590.57	546.58	485.14
Final BKZ–β	**307.85**	295.68	279.78	284.47	283.67	284.70

Fig. 3. Comparison of BKZ blocksize β estimates for a fault injection assisted decryption failure attack using 4000 failing ciphertexts for 5 different (simulated) poisoned Frodo-640 public keys. The final scaled estimates result from shrinking the final ellipsoid by a factor of $\mathsf{Rank}(\boldsymbol{\Sigma})/\|\boldsymbol{s}\|_{\Sigma}$.

Since the obtained $E^{(\mathsf{Rank})}(\boldsymbol{\mu}, \boldsymbol{\Sigma})$ no longer represents a multivariate Gaussian distribution (unlike in [17]), the expected value of the rank-scaled ellipsoid norm of the LWE secret may be far less than the rank. Observe that in Fig. 3, the ellipsoid norm of the secret is less than half of the rank, which is 1279. To account for this, we compute the estimated BKZ–β using Eq. (11). This is equivalent to scaling the $E^{(\mathsf{Rank})}(\boldsymbol{\mu}, \boldsymbol{\Sigma})$ until the ellipsoid norm of the secret is equal to the rank, and then applying Eq. (13).

As highlighted in Sect. 4.1, the volume reduction incurred when integrating an inequality hint is almost entirely determined by the geometric parameter α defined in (6), since the determinant of Σ scales by $(1 - \alpha^2)^d$. Using our regeneration approach, we were able to achieve improved β levels compared to the full dimensional approximate hints approach of [17] by integrating only 959-1224 hints in total, as opposed to 4000 hints. To achieve this, we used a greedy algorithm that at each stage chose the hint with the largest α value to integrate.

We further note that while it is possible to obtain a β estimate using the full-dimensional approximate hint approach from the prior work by utilizing the ultra-lightweight version of the framework [17], it is not possible to compute the uSVP lattice basis itself required to run BKZ due to high computational overhead. In contrast, our new inequality hint-based method is more efficient and so allows us to compute the final ellipsoid covariance matrix necessary for the reduction from DBDD to uSVP, and consequently would allow one to run a full key recovery attack given a sufficient number of hints.

A Geometric Approach to Failure Boosting. The α value for a candidate hint, given the current information encapsulated by the ellipsoid, can be used as a proxy for the probability that the query will lead to decryption failure: The smaller α is, the higher the probability of decryption failure. Thus, computing this α value *before* submitting a decryption query provides a geometric analogue to the failure boosting approach of D'anvers et al. [21].

We tested this on a small scale by again using the scenario presented by Fahr et al. [25]. Here, instead of generating a database of 4000 failing ciphertexts, we generated a database of $100k$ candidate ciphertexts (note that in the Fahr et al. [25] there is a way to filter candidate ciphertexts that have a relatively high chance of causing a decryption failure). Of these, only 34 actually caused decryption failures (this is consistent with the decryption failure rate (DFR) for filtered ciphertexts reported by Fahr et al. [25]). We integrated these 34 failing ciphertexts as inequality hints in order of decreasing α, each time calculating the histogram of α values for the remaining ciphertext database. Figure 4 shows the evolution of the histogram as more hints are integrated.

Next, we looked to quantify the number of decryption queries required to find all 34 failures, compared to naively querying the database by a linear scan. All 34 failures had α values in the $[0.07, 0.12]$ range, so we only submitted decryption queries for ciphertexts with corresponding α values at each step sorted in ascending order. To obtain all 34 decryption failures in the database, we found that it took 39785 queries versus 94894 for a linear scan.

Essentially, we can profile the range of α values for the i-th hint and obtain a range $[\alpha_{\text{low}}^i, \alpha_{\text{high}}^i]$, for which a decryption failure is most likely. We can then run the following online algorithm when making decryption queries to find the i-th hint to integrate into the ellipsoid: Let S be the set of all failing decryption queries made up to this moment. First, search S to try to find a query with α value in the range $[\alpha_{\text{low}}^i, \alpha_{\text{high}}^i]$ with respect to the current ellipsoid. If such a query is found, integrate it into the ellipsoid. Otherwise, generate a set S' of candidate hints of some calibrated size s'. For each $w \in S'$, compute its α value.

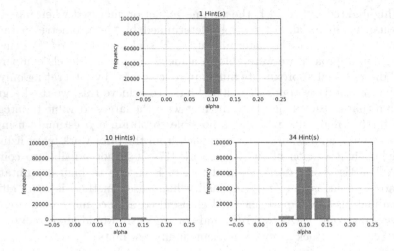

Fig. 4. Histograms of α values for a database of $100k$ ciphertexts after integrating 1 (top), 10 (bottom-left), and 34 (bottom-right) inequality hints based on the failing ciphertexts in the database.

If $\alpha \notin [\alpha_{\text{low}}^i, \alpha_{\text{high}}^i]$ then remove w from S'. Sort the entire set S' from smallest to largest α value. Make decryption queries in this order until a failing ciphertext is found. Once found, add w to S and integrate w into the current ellipsoid.

5.3   Combining Decryption Failure and SCA

We illustrate our "Combined Hints" approach from Sect. 4.2 by combining information on a single $(e\|s)$ pair from a decryption failure and a side-channel attack. In a recent work, Fahr et al. [25] showed that, for FrodoKEM, obtaining m' number of vectors corresponding to random decryption failures, scaling them by a constant that depends on the parameters of the cryptosystem, and taking their coordinate-wise mean, approximates a draw from the distribution $\mathcal{D}' := (e\|s) + \mathcal{W}''_{(m)}$, where the error $\mathcal{W}''_{(m)}$ is a d-dimensional Gaussian with mean $\mathbf{0}$ and covariance matrix $\sigma_{df}^2 \cdot \boldsymbol{I}_d$, where $\sigma_{df}^2 \leq d^2 \sigma_1^6/(t^2 m')$, σ_1^2 is the error of the original distribution, d is the dimension of the LWE secret/error, and t is the decryption failure threshold. Rearranging terms, given a draw $\boldsymbol{\mu}_{df} \sim \mathcal{D}'$, the secret is equal to $\boldsymbol{s} = \boldsymbol{\mu}_{df} + \mathcal{W}''_{(m)}$. This means that the secret is contained in the rank-scaled ellipsoid $E^{(\text{Rank})}(\boldsymbol{\mu}_{df}, \boldsymbol{\Sigma}_{df})$, where $\boldsymbol{\Sigma}_{df} = \sigma_{df}^2 \cdot \boldsymbol{I}_d$. Note that we could have used the results of Sect. 5.2 to obtain a DBDD instance with better parameters than the one corresponding to $E^{(\text{Rank})}(\boldsymbol{\mu}_{df}, \boldsymbol{\Sigma}_{df})$. Further, this instance would no longer correspond to a non-centered Gaussian distribution over the secret, and in fact the PDF of the secret would be unknown. Obtaining such a DBDD instance with the target σ_{df}^2 value needed for our experiment would be very computationally intensive. Therefore, for our illustration of the combined hints technique, we use the rank-scaled ellipsoid $E^{(\text{Rank})}(\boldsymbol{\mu}_{df}, \boldsymbol{\Sigma}_{df})$ described above to capture the DBDD instance obtained from the decryption failure information.

Bos et al. [13] studied the feasibility of single-trace power analysis of the Frodo Key Encapsulation Mechanism (FrodoKEM). Subsequently, Dachman-Soled et al. [17] used this information to conduct a side-channel attack on FrodoKEM on various parameter sets (CCS1, CCS2, CCS3, CCS4, NIST1, NIST2). Dachman-Soled et al. [17] used the score tables constructed from Bos et al. [13] to form an a posteriori distribution incorporating the side-channel information and used the information from the distribution tables to "guess" a large subset of coordinates when the confidence in the guess (where the confidence was calculated using the aforementioned score tables) was sufficiently high.

5.3.1   The Baseline Approach

The prior work [17] incorporated the side-channel information, represented by DBDD instance with $E^{(\mathrm{Rank})}(\boldsymbol{\mu}_{sc}, \boldsymbol{\Sigma}_{sc})$, using approximate *a posteriori hints*. In this method, the mean and covariance matrix of the a posteriori distribution (say on the $\boldsymbol{s}$ variables only) is calculated and then fully replaces the part of the covariance matrix in the DBDD instance that corresponds to the $\boldsymbol{s}$ variables. This method was suggested by [17] as an alternative to "conditioning" approximate hints. In our case, both $\boldsymbol{\Sigma}_{df}$ and $\boldsymbol{\Sigma}_{sc}$ are diagonal matrices. Therefore, the *a posteriori hints* approach, which we refer to as the *Baseline approach*, yields the following rank-scaled ellipsoid, $E^{(\mathrm{Rank})}(\boldsymbol{\mu}_{ba}, \boldsymbol{\Sigma}_{ba})$: For each $i \in [d]$, if $\boldsymbol{\Sigma}_{sc}[i][i] \leq \boldsymbol{\Sigma}_{df}[i][i]$, set $\boldsymbol{\Sigma}_{ba}[i][i] = \boldsymbol{\Sigma}_{sc}[i][i]$ and $\boldsymbol{\mu}_{ba}[i] = \boldsymbol{\mu}_{sc}[i]$. Otherwise, set $\boldsymbol{\Sigma}_{ba}[i][i] = \boldsymbol{\Sigma}_{df}[i][i]$ and $\boldsymbol{\mu}_{ba}[i] = \boldsymbol{\mu}_{df}[i]$.

5.3.2   Ellipsoid/Ellipsoid Intersection.

For an ellipsoid $E = (\mu, \Sigma)$ (resp. rank-scaled ellipsoid $E^{\mathrm{rank}} = (\mu, \Sigma)$), we denote by $E_S = (\mu_S, \Sigma_S)$ (resp. $E_S^{\mathrm{rank}} = (\mu_S, \Sigma_S)$) the ellipsoid (resp. rank-scaled ellipsoid) resulting from the restriction of the center and shape matrix of E (resp. E^{rank}) to a set of coordinates S. For an ellipsoid E, we denote by n_E the ellipsoid norm of the correct solution with respect to E. Let $E_{DF}^{\mathrm{rank}} = E^{(\mathrm{Rank})}(\boldsymbol{\mu}_{df}, \boldsymbol{\Sigma}_{df})$ and $E_B^{\mathrm{rank}} = E^{(\mathrm{Rank})}(\boldsymbol{\mu}_{ba}, \boldsymbol{\Sigma}_{ba})$. Restricting to the set S of secret (no error coordinates), let $E_{int,S}^{\mathrm{rank}} = E^{(\mathrm{Rank})}(\boldsymbol{\mu}_{int,S}, \boldsymbol{\Sigma}_{int,S})$ be the ellipsoid circumscribing the intersection of $E_{DF,S}^{\mathrm{rank}} = E^{(\mathrm{Rank})}(\boldsymbol{\mu}_{df,S}, \boldsymbol{\Sigma}_{df,S})$ and $E_{B,S}^{\mathrm{rank}} = E^{(\mathrm{Rank})}(\boldsymbol{\mu}_{ba,S}, \boldsymbol{\Sigma}_{ba,S})$. Let the diagonal of $\boldsymbol{\Sigma}_{ba,S}$ be denoted by $(\sigma_{2,1}^2, \ldots, \sigma_{2,n}^2)$. Let $\boldsymbol{c} = \boldsymbol{\mu}_{ba,S} - \boldsymbol{\mu}_{df,S}$. We simplify (19) and (20) as follows:

$$\mathcal{F}(\boldsymbol{\Sigma}_{int,S}) = k\boldsymbol{X}^{-1}; \qquad \boldsymbol{X} = \tilde{\lambda}\mathcal{F}(\boldsymbol{\Sigma}_{df,S})^{-1} + (1-\tilde{\lambda})\mathcal{F}(\boldsymbol{\Sigma}_{ba,S})^{-1}$$

$$\boldsymbol{\mu}_{int} = (\boldsymbol{\mu}_{df,S}\tilde{\lambda}\mathcal{F}(\boldsymbol{\Sigma}_{df,S})^{-1} + \boldsymbol{\mu}_{ba,S}(1-\tilde{\lambda})\mathcal{F}(\boldsymbol{\Sigma}_{df,S})^{-1})\boldsymbol{X}^{-1}$$

$$k = 1 - \tilde{\lambda}(1-\tilde{\lambda}) \cdot \frac{1}{n} \sum_{i \in [n]} \frac{c_i^2}{\tilde{\lambda}\sigma_{2,i}^2 + (1-\tilde{\lambda})\sigma_{df}^2}$$

and $\tilde{\lambda} \in [0,1]$ is the value that minimizes the determinant of $\boldsymbol{\Sigma}_{int,S}$. Specifically,

$$\det(\boldsymbol{\Sigma}_{int,S}) = k^n \cdot \prod_{i \in [n]} \left(\frac{\tilde{\lambda}}{\sigma_{df}^2} + \frac{1-\tilde{\lambda}}{\sigma_{s2,i}^2} \right)^{-1}. \tag{22}$$

	Baseline Approach	Combined Hints	
		Condition 1 unknown/known	Condition 2 unkown/known
Original BKZ–β	**268.83**	–	–
DF BKZ–β	**203.02**	–	–
SC BKZ–β before guess	**114.22**	–	–
SC BKZ–β after guess	**68.65**	–	–
$\ln(V_{int}/V_{base})$	–	-26.49/-30.47	-23.46/-32.24
BKZ–β before guesses	**97.86**	95.91/94.83	96.22/94.66
Number of guesses	**190**	190/190	190/190
Guess Success %	**0.76**	0.76/0.76	0.76/0.76
Final BKZ–β	52.20	50.19/ 49.18	50.50/ 49.00

Fig. 5. Comparison of bikz estimates for FrodoKEM with CCS1 parameters. Results are the average of 150 randomly generated instances. Starting from the top row, we report the original bikz, the bikz for only the decryption failure attack, and the bikz for only the side channel attack, before and after guesses (throughout we condition on all guesses being correct). We compare the baseline approach (Sect. 5.3.1) with two combined hints approaches using Condition 1 or 2 (Sect. 5.3.3) to select the set of coordinates for intersection. For each, we consider the known and unknown cases (Sect. 5.3.4). We next report the ln of the ratio of the volumes of the intersected and baseline ellipsoids (for the unknown case, these are reported after calibration (Sect. 5.3.4)). For each, we report the bikz without guesses, the number of guesses, the probability that all guesses are correct and the final bikz after guesses.

The terms in the product on the right side of Eq. (22) correspond to weighted harmonic means of σ_{df}^2 and $\sigma_{2,i}^2$, for each i. While the harmonic mean tends towards the smaller element, it is at least as large as the minimum of the two values. This is then compensated by multiplication by k, which is always at most 1. However, due to the negative influence of the harmonic mean on the final determinant, we experiment with intersecting only on coordinates i for which the gap between σ_{df}^2 and $\sigma_{2,i}^2$ is not too large.

5.3.3 Conditions 1 and 2.

We consider two candidate methods of performing intersection: In the first method, referred to as **Condition 1**, we restrict the intersection to the dimension $n - g$ ellipsoids (where g is the number of guesses) corresponding to the coordinates of the LWE secret (but not the error) that are not guessed. This is essentially equivalent to performing the intersection after guesses are made on the remaining coordinates of the LWE secret. For the remaining coordinates, we follow the baseline approach. In the second method, referred to as **Condition 2**, we restrict the intersection to the dimension n' ellipsoids corresponding to the coordinates i of the LWE secret (but not the error), for which $\sigma_{2,i}^2$ is in the range $[\frac{\sigma_{df}^2}{5}, \sigma_{df}^2]$. For the remaining coordinates, we again follow the baseline approach.

5.3.4   The Known and Unknown Cases.

Let $E_{DF,S} = E(\boldsymbol{\mu}_{df,S}, \mathcal{F}(\boldsymbol{\Sigma}_{df,S}))$ and $E_{B,S} = E(\boldsymbol{\mu}_{ba,S}, \mathcal{F}(\boldsymbol{\Sigma}_{ba,S}))$. We restrict ellipsoids $E_{DF,S}$ and $E_{B,S}$ to a set of coordinates $P \subseteq S$ corresponding to Condition 1 or 2, yielding $E_{DF,P}$ and $E_{B,P}$. These are then intersected to yield $E_{int,P}$, and $E_{int,P}$ is substituted for the set of P coordinates in $E_{B,S}$ yielding $E_{int,S}$. To maintain consistency of hardness estimates, we would like to keep $n_{E_{int,P}} = n_{E_{B,P}}$. Further, ellipsoid/ellipsoid intersection performs best when intersecting two ellipsoids $E_{DF,P}$ and $E_{B,P}$ such that $n_{E_{DF,P}} = n_{E_{B,P}} = 1$, since points on the surface of both $E_{DF,P}$ and $E_{B,P}$ also lie on the surface of $E_{int,P}$.

Assuming that $n_{E_{DF,P}}$ and $n_{E_{B,P}}$ are known, we scale $E_{DF,P}$ by $n_{E_{DF,P}}$ and $E_{B,P}$ by $n_{E_{B,P}}$, so that the correct solution lies on the surface of both scaled ellipsoids, and hence on the surface of $E_{int,P}$. We then scale $E_{int,P}$ by $1/n_{E_{B,P}}$, to ensure that $n_{E_{int,P}} = n_{E_{B,P}}$. This yields the optimal volume reduction while maintaining the norm constraint but requires knowledge of $n_{E_{DF,P}}$ and $n_{E_{B,P}}$. We refer to this case as the **known** case.

While $n_{E_{DF,P}}$ is fairly stable (since the decryption failure ellipsoid is a multivariate Gaussian in our experiments), $n_{E_{B,P}}$ can fluctuate. We therefore also explore the case in which the adversary is not presumed to know $n_{E_{DF,P}}$ and $n_{E_{B,P}}$. We refer to this case as the **unknown** case, and we next describe the algorithm for this case. We find experimentally that with probability at least $1/2$, $n_{E_{DF,P}} \leq 0.9 \cdot n_{E_{B,P}}$. We scale $E_{DF,P}$ by 0.9 before intersection. In the case that indeed $n_{E_{DF,P}} \leq 0.9 n_{E_{B,P}}$, we have by Remark 6, that $n_{E_{int,P}} \leq n_{E_{B,P}}$. In the case that $n_{E_{DF,P}} > 0.9 n_{E_{B,P}}$, it may be the case that $n_{E_{int,P}} > n_{E_{B,P}}$[5] To take into account the fact that $n_{E_{int,P}}$ can now be smaller or larger than $n_{E_{B,P}}$, we use Eq. (11) to calibrate the predicted β value with respect to the entire instance (including error coordinates).

We present our experimental results with decryption failure information modeled as described above, with $\sigma_{df}^2 = 0.25$, and with side-channel data obtained from the single trace attack of Bos et al. [13] on FrodoKEM. As in [17], we incorporate guesses when the side-channel distribution for a secret coordinate allows for a high confidence guess. Figure 5 displays the predicted hardness (in bikz) of the original and baseline DBDD instances, the intersected instances obtained using Condition 1 and 2, in both the known and unknown cases, both with and without guesses, for the CCS1 parameter set.[6] Our approach lowers the required number of bikz as compared to the baseline approach by 2–3 bikz.

Acknowledgements. We thank the anonymous reviewers for their insightful technical comments as well as their comments to improve the presentation. We would also like to thank Léo Ducas and Mélissa Rossi for helpful technical discussions.

---

[5] Note that in our experiments it was always the case that $1/0.9 n_{E_{DF,P}} \leq 1$ so the intersection is always non-empty.

[6] The number of bikz reported in our table for the SCA-only attack differs slightly from the bikz reported in [17], as we use the updated code found here: https://github.com/lducas/leaky-LWE-Estimator/tree/fix_extreme_hints2.

References

1. Alagic, G., et al.: Status report on the third round of the NIST post-quantum cryptography standardization process. Technical Report: NIST Internal Report (NISTIR) 8413, U.S. Department of Commerce, Washington, D.C. (2022)
2. Albrecht, M., Cid, C., Faugère, J.C., Fitzpatrick, R., Perret, L.: On the complexity of the Arora-Ge algorithm against LWE. In: 3rd International Conference on Symbolic Computation and Cryptography, SCC 2012, Castro Urdiales, Spain, July 2012, pp. 93–99 (2012)
3. Albrecht, M.R., Bai, S., Li, J., Rowell, J.: Lattice reduction with approximate enumeration oracles. In: Malkin, T., Peikert, C. (eds.) CRYPTO 2021. LNCS, vol. 12826, pp. 732–759. Springer, Cham (2021). https://doi.org/10.1007/978-3-030-84245-1_25
4. Albrecht, M.R., Cid, C., Faugère, J.C., Fitzpatrick, R., Perret, L.: On the complexity of the BKW algorithm on LWE. Cryptology ePrint Archive, Report 2012/636 (2012). https://eprint.iacr.org/2012/636
5. Albrecht, M.R., Göpfert, F., Virdia, F., Wunderer, T.: Revisiting the expected cost of solving uSVP and applications to LWE. In: Takagi, T., Peyrin, T. (eds.) ASIACRYPT 2017. LNCS, vol. 10624, pp. 297–322. Springer, Cham (2017). https://doi.org/10.1007/978-3-319-70694-8_11
6. Alkim, E., et al.: FrodoKEM: practical quantum-secure key encapsulation from generic lattices, April 2022
7. Alkim, E., Ducas, L., Pöppelmann, T., Schwabe, P.: Post-quantum key exchange - a new hope. In: Holz, T., Savage, S. (eds.) USENIX Security 2016: 25th USENIX Security Symposium, 10–12 August, pp. 327–343. USENIX Association, Austin (2016)
8. Bai, S., Stehlé, D., Wen, W.: Measuring, simulating and exploiting the head concavity phenomenon in BKZ. In: Peyrin, T., Galbraith, S. (eds.) ASIACRYPT 2018. LNCS, vol. 11272, pp. 369–404. Springer, Cham (2018). https://doi.org/10.1007/978-3-030-03326-2_13
9. Bauer, A., Gilbert, H., Renault, G., Rossi, M.: Assessment of the key-reuse resilience of NewHope. In: Matsui, M. (ed.) CT-RSA 2019. LNCS, vol. 11405, pp. 272–292. Springer, Cham (2019). https://doi.org/10.1007/978-3-030-12612-4_14
10. Becker, A., Ducas, L., Gama, N., Laarhoven, T.: New directions in nearest neighbor searching with applications to lattice sieving. In: Krauthgamer, R. (ed.) 27th Annual ACM-SIAM Symposium on Discrete Algorithms, pp. 10–24. Arlington, VA, USA, 10–12 January. ACM-SIAM (2016)
11. Bindel, N., Schanck, J.M.: Decryption failure is more likely after success. In: Ding, J., Tillich, J.-P. (eds.) PQCrypto 2020. LNCS, vol. 12100, pp. 206–225. Springer, Cham (2020). https://doi.org/10.1007/978-3-030-44223-1_12
12. Bland, R.G., Goldfarb, D., Todd, M.J.: The ellipsoid method: a survey. Oper. Res. **29**(6), 1039–1091 (1981)
13. Bos, J.W., Friedberger, S., Martinoli, M., Oswald, E., Stam, M.: Assessing the feasibility of single trace power analysis of Frodo. In: Cid, C., Jacobson Jr., M. (eds.) Selected Areas in Cryptography, SAC 2018. LNCS, vol. 11349, pp. 216–234. Springer, Cham (2019). https://doi.org/10.1007/978-3-030-10970-7_10
14. Bruna, J., Regev, O., Song, M.J., Tang, Y.: Continuous LWE. In: 53rd Annual ACM SIGACT Symposium on Theory of Computing, Virtual Event, STOC 2021, Italy, 21–25 June 2021, pp. 694–707 (2021)

15. Chari, S., Rao, J.R., Rohatgi, P.: Template attacks. In: Kaliski, B.S., Koç, K., Paar, C. (eds.) CHES 2002. LNCS, vol. 2523, pp. 13–28. Springer, Heidelberg (2003). https://doi.org/10.1007/3-540-36400-5_3

16. Chen, Y., Nguyen, P.Q.: BKZ 2.0: better lattice security estimates. In: Lee, D.H., Wang, X. (eds.) ASIACRYPT 2011. LNCS, vol. 7073, pp. 1–20. Springer, Heidelberg (2011). https://doi.org/10.1007/978-3-642-25385-0_1

17. Dachman-Soled, D., Ducas, L., Gong, H., Rossi, M.: LWE with side information: attacks and concrete security estimation. In: Micciancio, D., Ristenpart, T. (eds.) CRYPTO 2020. LNCS, vol. 12171, pp. 329–358. Springer, Cham (2020). https://doi.org/10.1007/978-3-030-56880-1_12

18. Dachman-Soled, D., Gong, H., Hanson, T., Kippen, H.: Revisiting security estimation for LWE with hints from a geometric perspective. Full version of this paper. Cryptology ePrint Archive, Paper 2022/1345 (2022). https://eprint.iacr.org/2022/1345

19. D'Anvers, J.-P., Guo, Q., Johansson, T., Nilsson, A., Vercauteren, F., Verbauwhede, I.: Decryption failure attacks on IND-CCA secure lattice-based schemes. In: Lin, D., Sako, K. (eds.) PKC 2019. LNCS, vol. 11443, pp. 565–598. Springer, Cham (2019). https://doi.org/10.1007/978-3-030-17259-6_19

20. D'Anvers, J.-P., Rossi, M., Virdia, F.: *(One) failure is not an option*: bootstrapping the search for failures in lattice-based encryption schemes. In: Canteaut, A., Ishai, Y. (eds.) EUROCRYPT 2020. LNCS, vol. 12107, pp. 3–33. Springer, Cham (2020). https://doi.org/10.1007/978-3-030-45727-3_1

21. D'Anvers, J.P., Vercauteren, F., Verbauwhede, I.: On the impact of decryption failures on the security of LWE/LWR based schemes. Cryptology ePrint Archive, Report 2018/1089 (2018). https://eprint.iacr.org/2018/1089

22. Ding, J., Alsayigh, S., RV, S., Fluhrer, S., Lin, X.: Leakage of signal function with reused keys in RLWE key exchange. Cryptology ePrint Archive, Report 2016/1176 (2016). https://eprint.iacr.org/2016/1176

23. Ding, J., Fluhrer, S., Rv, S.: Complete attack on RLWE key exchange with reused keys, without signal leakage. In: Susilo, W., Yang, G. (eds.) ACISP 2018. LNCS, vol. 10946, pp. 467–486. Springer, Cham (2018). https://doi.org/10.1007/978-3-319-93638-3_27

24. Ducas, L., Gibbons, S.: Hull attacks on the lattice isomorphism problem. In: Boldyreva, A., Kolesnikov, V. (eds.) Public-Key Cryptography, PKC 2023. LNCS, vol. 13940, pp. 177–204. Springer, Cham (2023). https://doi.org/10.1007/978-3-031-31368-4_7

25. Fahr Jr., M., et al.: When Frodo flips: end-to-end key recovery on FrodoKEM via Rowhammer. Cryptology ePrint Archive (2022)

26. Fluhrer, S.: Cryptanalysis of ring-LWE based key exchange with key share reuse. Cryptology ePrint Archive, Report 2016/085 (2016). https://eprint.iacr.org/2016/085

27. Grötschel, M., Lovász, L., Schrijver, A.: The ellipsoid method. In: Geometric Algorithms and Combinatorial Optimization. Algorithms and Combinatorics, vol. 2, pp. 64–101. Springer, Heidelberg (1988). https://doi.org/10.1007/978-3-642-97881-4_4

28. Güler, O., Gürtuna, F.: Symmetry of convex sets and its applications to the extremal ellipsoids of convex bodies. Optim. Meth. Softw. **27**(4–5), 735–759 (2012)

29. Guo, Q., Johansson, T., Nilsson, A.: A generic attack on lattice-based schemes using decryption errors with application to ss-ntru-pke. Cryptology ePrint Archive, Report 2019/043 (2019). https://eprint.iacr.org/2019/043

30. Gupte, A., Vafa, N., Vaikuntanathan, V.: Continuous LWE is as hard as LWE & applications to learning gaussian mixtures. Cryptology ePrint Archive, Report 2022/437 (2022). https://eprint.iacr.org/2022/437

31. Hanebeck, U.D., Horn, J.: Fusing information simultaneously corrupted by uncertainties with known bounds and random noise with known distribution. Inf. Fus. **1**(1), 55–63 (2000)

32. Herold, G., Kirshanova, E., Laarhoven, T.: Speed-ups and time–memory trade-offs for tuple lattice sieving. In: Abdalla, M., Dahab, R. (eds.) PKC 2018. LNCS, vol. 10769, pp. 407–436. Springer, Cham (2018). https://doi.org/10.1007/978-3-319-76578-5_14

33. Islam, S., Mus, K., Singh, R., Schaumont, P., Sunar, B.: Signature correction attack on Dilithium signature scheme (2022)

34. Lenstra, Jr., H.W.: Integer programming with a fixed number of variables. Math. Oper. Res. **8**(4), 538–548 (1983)

35. Kalman, R.E.: A new approach to linear filtering and prediction problems (1960)

36. Khachiyan, L.G.: A polynomial algorithm in linear programming. In: Doklady Akademii Nauk. Vol. 244, pp. 1093–1096. Russian Academy of Sciences (1979)

37. Kirkwood, D., Lackey, B.C., McVey, J., Motley, M., Solinas, J.A., Tuller, D.: Failure is not an option: standardization issues for post-quantum key agreement (2015). https://csrc.nist.gov/csrc/media/events/workshop-on-cybersecurity-in-a-post-quantum-world/documents/presentations/session7-motley-mark.pdf

38. Kocher, P., et al.: Spectre attacks: exploiting speculative execution. Commun. ACM **63**(7), 93–101 (2020)

39. Kocher, P.C.: Timing attacks on implementations of Diffie-Hellman, RSA, DSS, and other systems. In: Koblitz, N. (ed.) CRYPTO 1996. LNCS, vol. 1109, pp. 104–113. Springer, Heidelberg (1996). https://doi.org/10.1007/3-540-68697-5_9

40. Kocher, P., Jaffe, J., Jun, B.: Differential power analysis. In: Wiener, M. (ed.) CRYPTO 1999. LNCS, vol. 1666, pp. 388–397. Springer, Heidelberg (1999). https://doi.org/10.1007/3-540-48405-1_25

41. Kurzhanski, A.B.: Ellipsoidal calculus for estimation and feedback control. In: Byrnes, C.I., Datta, B.N., Martin, C.F., Gilliam, D.S. (eds.) Systems and Control in the Twenty-First Century. Systems & Control: Foundations & Applications, vol. 22, pp. 229–243. Birkhäuser, Boston, MA (1997). https://doi.org/10.1007/978-1-4612-4120-1_12

42. Laarhoven, T.: Search problems in cryptography: from fingerprinting to lattice sieving. PhD thesis (2015)

43. Lipp, M., et al.: Meltdown: reading kernel memory from user space. Commun. ACM **63**(6), 46–56 (2020)

44. McCann, D., Oswald, E., Whitnall, C.: Towards practical tools for side channel aware software engineering: 'grey box' modelling for instruction leakages. In: Kirda, E., Ristenpart, T. (eds.) 26th USENIX Security Symposium on USENIX Security 2017, Vancouver, BC, Canada, 16–18 August 2017, pp. 199–216. USENIX Association (2017)

45. Mus, K., Islam, S., Sunar, B.: QuantumHammer: a practical hybrid attack on the LUOV signature scheme. In: Ligatti, J., Ou, X., Katz, J., Vigna, G. (eds.) 27th Conference on Computer and Communications Security, ACM CCS 2020, Virtual Event, 9–13 November 2020, pp. 1071–1084, USA, ACM Press (2020)

46. Qin, Y., Cheng, C., Zhang, X., Pan, Y., Hu, L., Ding, J.: A systematic approach and analysis of key mismatch attacks on lattice-based NIST candidate KEMs. Cryptology ePrint Archive, Report 2021/123 (2021). https://eprint.iacr.org/2021/123

47. Ravi, P., Jhanwar, M.P., Howe, J., Chattopadhyay, A., Bhasin, S.: Side-channel assisted existential forgery attack on Dilithium - a NIST PQC candidate. Cryptology ePrint Archive, Report 2018/821 (2018). https://eprint.iacr.org/2018/821

48. Ravi, P., Jhanwar, M.P., Howe, J., Chattopadhyay, A., Bhasin, S.: Exploiting determinism in lattice-based signatures: practical fault attacks on pqm4 implementations of NIST candidates. In: Galbraith, S.D., Russello, G., Susilo, W., Gollmann, D., Kirda, E., Liang, Z. (eds.) 14th ACM Symposium on Information, ASIACCS 2019. Computer and Communications Security, Auckland, New Zealand, 9–12 July 2019, pp. 427–440. ACM Press (2019)

49. Ros, L., Sabater i Pruna, A., Thomas, F.: An ellipsoid calculus based on propagation and fusion. IEEE Trans. Syst. Man Cybern. Part B (Cybern.) **32**, 430–443 (2002)

50. Schnorr, C., Euchner, M.: Lattice basis reduction: improved practical algorithms and solving subset sum problems. Math. Program. **66**, 181–199 (1994)

51. Sepulveda, J., Zankl, A., Mischke, O.: Cache attacks and countermeasures for NTRUEncrypt on MPSoCs: post-quantum resistance for the IoT. In: 2017 30th IEEE International System-on-Chip Conference (SOCC), pp. 120–125 (2017)

52. Tsunoo, Y.: Crypt-analysis of block ciphers implemented on computers with cache. In: Proceedings of the ISITA2002, October 2002

53. Villanueva-Polanco, R.: Cold boot attacks on bliss. In: Schwabe, P., Thériault, N. (eds.) LATINCRYPT 2019. LNCS, vol. 11774, pp. 40–61. Springer, Cham (2019). https://doi.org/10.1007/978-3-030-30530-7_3

54. Wang, Z., Shen, X., Zhu, Y.: On equivalence of major relaxation methods for minimum ellipsoid covering intersection of ellipsoids. Automatica **103**, 337–345 (2019)

Lattice-Based Timed Cryptography

Russell W. F. Lai[1(✉)] and Giulio Malavolta[2]

[1] Aalto University, Espoo, Finland
russell.lai@aalto.fi
[2] Max Planck Institute for Security and Privacy, Bochum, Germany

Abstract. Timed cryptography studies primitives that retain their security only for a predetermined amount of time, such as proofs of sequential work and time-lock puzzles. This feature has proven to be useful in a large number of practical applications, e.g. randomness generation, sealed-bid auctions, and fair multi-party computation. However, the current state of affairs in timed cryptography is unsatisfactory: Virtually all efficient constructions rely on a single sequentiality assumption, namely that repeated squaring in unknown order groups cannot be parallelised. This is a single point of failure in the classical setting and is even false against quantum adversaries.

In this work we put forward a new sequentiality assumption, which essentially says that a repeated application of the standard lattice-based hash function cannot be parallelised. We provide concrete evidence of the validity of this assumption and, to substantiate its usefulness, we show how it enables a new proof of sequential work, with a stronger sequentiality guarantee than prior hash-based schemes.

1 Introduction

Timed cryptography studies a family of cryptographic primitives with diverse functionalities designed to meet their security goals only for a short (polynomial) amount of time. This includes, for example, time-lock puzzles [34], timed-commitments [11], proofs of sequential work [30], verifiable delay functions [10], and delay encryption [14]. This branch of cryptography has important theoretical implications in the context of non-malleable commitments [28] and in the average-case hardness of the class PPAD [8], which characterises the complexity of computing a Nash equilibrium. Furthermore, timed cryptography has attracted significant interest in the industry (e.g. [1]), in part due to their large number of practical applications (see [10,31] for a survey of applications).

The Repeated Squaring Assumption. The current state of affairs in timed cryptography is largely unsatisfactory: Virtually all efficient schemes are based on the hardness of a *single* problem (or variants thereof), namely the sequential squaring assumption. Loosely speaking, such an assumption postulates that the repeated application of the function

$$f_N(x) = x^2 \bmod N$$

© International Association for Cryptologic Research 2023
H. Handschuh and A. Lysyanskaya (Eds.): CRYPTO 2023, LNCS 14085, pp. 782–804, 2023.
https://doi.org/10.1007/978-3-031-38554-4_25

where $N = pq$ is an RSA modulus, is the fastest algorithm to compute $x^{2^T} \bmod N$ given x. In other words, there is no better algorithm than T-sequential iterations of f_N, provided that the order of the group is unknown by the evaluator. Unfortunately, this assumption is clearly false if we allow the attacker to run in *quantum* polynomial time. At present, there is no valid alternative sequential function with conjectured post-quantum security. Besides post-quantum security, the lack of other candidates places the entirety of efficient timed cryptography on thin foundations, and only one cryptanalytic breakthrough away from being wiped out. The goal of our work is to make progress on this front, and to establish broader foundations for timed cryptographic primitives.

1.1 Our Contributions

The contributions of this work can be summarised as follows. A more detailed technical overview is in Sect. 1.3.

A New Lattice-Based Sequential Function. We put forward a new candidate family of sequential functions, whose design is closely connected with lattice-based cryptography. Concretely, we define our new sequential function to be the T-fold repeated application of the binary decomposition operation followed by the SIS-based collision-resistant hash function [2,25], with parameters set in such a way to make the domain and the range of the function coincide. In other words, our base function $f_\mathbf{A} : \mathbb{Z}_q^n \to \mathbb{Z}_q^n$ is defined as

$$f_\mathbf{A}(\mathbf{x}) := \mathbf{A} \cdot \left(-\mathbf{G}^{-1}(\mathbf{x})\right) \bmod q$$

where $\mathbf{A} \leftarrow \mathbb{Z}_q^{n \times m}$, for $m \approx n \cdot \log q$, and $\mathbf{G}^{-1} : \mathbb{Z}_q^n \to \{0,1\}^m$ is the binary decomposition operator. Then we define $f_\mathbf{A}^T$ to be the T-fold repeated application of $f_\mathbf{A}$. Based on the observation that computing $\mathbf{y} = f_\mathbf{A}^T(\mathbf{x})$ is equivalent to establishing the satisfiability of a linear relation defined by $(\mathbf{A}, \mathbf{x}, \mathbf{y})$ by a binary vector $\mathbf{u}$, we conjecture that finding such $(\mathbf{u}, \mathbf{y})$ for random $(\mathbf{A}, \mathbf{x})$ is hard for (potentially quantum) circuits of depth less than T by some super-constant function in T.

Evidence of Sequentiality. The design of our new sequential function is motivated by concrete properties that one can prove about the base function, balanced with enough algebraic structure to enable advanced cryptographic applications. More specifically, the choice of our sequential function is based on the following guiding principles:

– Recursive composition: In order to have a succinct description, the sequential function is defined as the recursive application of a *base function* with cryptographic properties. There is evidence that this is a robust design principle: If the base function is modelled as a random oracle, then one can show that sequentiality holds unconditionally [19].

- Collision resistance: The base function must be collision-resistant (and one way). This is a property that is trivially satisfied by a random oracle and something that we can prove using standard computational assumptions.
- Uniformity preserving: Similar to a random oracle, the base function must map uniform distributions to uniform distributions over the specified domains and co-domains. Once again, we are able to prove that this property holds assuming the intractability of standard problems over lattices.
- Post-quantum security: Contrary to the sequential squaring problem, we want to conjecture that the sequentiality of our function holds also against *quantum* algorithms.
- Algebraic structure: Unlike a random oracle, we want our base function to have enough algebraic structure to produce relations that are amenable to efficient proofs.

In particular, we justify our assumption by showing that $f_{\mathbf{A}}$ is collision-resistant and uniformity preserving (for some choice of parameters) based on the standard lattice assumptions, suggesting other heuristic evidence, and discussing (failed) attack strategies.

Application: Proof of Sequential Work. To substantiate the usefulness of our new family of sequential functions, we construct a simple and efficient proof of sequential work (PoSW), where a prover can convince a verifier that it has performed a T-steps sequential computation. The runtime of the verifier is logarithmic in T, and the protocol is statistically sound. Compared to prior hash-based constructions, our PoSW has a potentially stronger sequentiality guarantee against a dishonest prover, depending on the strength of the sequentiality assumption. More concretely, in our approach, soundness holds against any adversary running in parallel time $(1 - \omega(1)) \cdot T$, whereas prior hash-based proofs of sequential work [19, 22, 30] are only sound against cheating provers who run in parallel time $(1 - \alpha) \cdot T$, for any constant $0 \le \alpha < 1$, where the verifier runtime is $\frac{1}{\log(1-\alpha)} \cdot O(\lambda)$.

On the Necessity of New Assumptions. We stress that we can only offer heuristic evidence for the sequentiality of our function family, and we are not able to reduce it to any "standard" computational problem. In fact, arguably the *only* "standard" computational assumption in timed cryptography is the repeated squaring assumption! Clearly, if we want to obtain a plausibly post-quantum candidate, new assumptions are necessary.

On the other hand, traditional computational assumptions in cryptography (such as LWE or DDH) do not make fine-grained distinctions on the parallelism of the attacker: The problem is assumed to be hard for all polynomial-size circuits, regardless of their depth/parallel runtime. In other words, such assumptions imply that $\mathsf{NP} \ne \mathsf{P}$ but do *not* imply that $\mathsf{NC} \ne \mathsf{P}$, which is a necessary condition for sequential functions to exist. Overall, this suggests that new assumptions may be necessary for timed cryptography, and we view our work as a promising first step towards a better understanding of this area.

1.2   Related Work

Besides works based on the repeated squaring assumption, there are various other approaches for constructing timed cryptographic primitives from different computational assumptions. In the following, we discuss the trade-offs when compared with our work.

Hash-Based Schemes. As alluded at earlier, random oracles are good candidates for constructing sequential functions, since the sequentiality of their repeated applications can be proven unconditionally. This approach has appealing properties: It offers a clean model to prove concrete statements, schemes are typically very efficient as they only involve symmetric-key operations, and one can conjecture (or even prove) post-quantum security. In fact, random oracles have been used to construct PoSW [19,22,30] with high concrete efficiency. However, when compared with our approach, the sequentiality guarantee that they offer is weaker: For any constant $0 \leq \alpha < 1$, the soundness of the scheme (parametrised by α) is only guaranteed against cheating provers who run in parallel time $(1 - \alpha) \cdot T$, where the verifier runtime is $\frac{1}{\log(1-\alpha)} \cdot O(\lambda)$. On the other hand, our approach allows us to catch any adversary running in parallel time $(1 - \omega(1)) \cdot T$, i.e. no adversary can speed up the computation by any additive factor super-constant in T, while the verifier runs in a fixed polynomial time.

Isogeny-Based Schemes. Recent works have explored constructions of timed cryptography from isogenies over elliptic curves [14,20]. This approach allows one to construct verifiable delay functions (VDF) [10] and even delay encryption [14]. However, such constructions are not post-quantum secure [20], or they rely on generic composition with succinct non-interactive arguments [15], making them impractical. Furthermore, the underlying assumptions have received substantially less scrutiny than sequential squaring.

Generic Approaches. Finally, we mention that one can use general-purpose cryptographic primitives to build timed cryptographic schemes. Assuming only the existence (but not knowledge) of an (iterative) sequential function, it is possible to provably construct an (iterative) sequential function from fully homomorphic encryption [26]. Incremental verifiable computation [36] can be immediately used to construct PoSWs and VDFs given a sequential function [10,21], and indistinguishability obfuscation can be used to construct time-lock puzzles [9]. While theoretically elegant, such generic constructions use heavy cryptographic machinery and result in schemes that are (concretely) prohibitively inefficient.

1.3   Technical Overview

In the following, we elaborate more on the results summarised in Sect. 1.1. For simplicity, the exposition in this technical overview is done over the set of rational integers, i.e. $\mathbb{Z}$. In the technical sections, we will be working over a ring of integers $\mathcal{R}$ of some cyclotomic field, which captures $\mathbb{Z}$ as a special case.

Lattice-based Sequential Function/Relation. We propose a new candidate sequential function defined as the T-fold repeated application of the binary decomposition operation followed by the SIS-based collision-resistant hash function [2,25], with parameters set in such a way to make the domain and the codomain of the function coincide. Concretely, (a special case of) our base function $f_{\mathbf{A}} : \mathbb{Z}_q^n \to \mathbb{Z}_q^n$ is defined as

$$f_{\mathbf{A}}(\mathbf{x}) := \mathbf{A} \cdot (-\mathbf{G}^{-1}(\mathbf{x})) \bmod q$$

where $\mathbf{A} \leftarrow \mathbb{Z}_q^{n \times m}$, for $m \approx n \cdot \log q$, and $\mathbf{G}^{-1} : \mathbb{Z}_q^n \to \{0,1\}^m$ is the binary decomposition operator. Below, we assume for simplicity that $m = n \cdot \log q$.

At first glance, it may seem that the function $f_{\mathbf{A}}$ is not proof-friendly, since $\mathbf{G}^{-1}$ is a highly non-linear operation. However, a few simple but crucial observations allow us to express the relations induced by $f_{\mathbf{A}}$ in a proof-friendly form. Specifically, we observe that a pair $(\mathbf{x}, \mathbf{y})$ satisfies $\mathbf{y} = f_{\mathbf{A}}(\mathbf{x})$ if and only if there exists a binary vector $\mathbf{u} \in \{0,1\}^m$ such that

$$\begin{pmatrix} \mathbf{G} \\ \mathbf{A} \end{pmatrix} \cdot \mathbf{u} = \begin{pmatrix} -\mathbf{x} \\ \mathbf{y} \end{pmatrix} \bmod q$$

where $\mathbf{G}$ is the binary reconstruction gadget matrix, which in particular is a linear operator.

Generalising, suppose $\mathbf{x}_T = f_{\mathbf{A}}^T(\mathbf{x}_0)$ is the T-fold repeated application of $f_{\mathbf{A}}$ on $\mathbf{x}_0$. Writing $\mathbf{x}_i = f_{\mathbf{A}}(\mathbf{x}_{i-1})$ and $\mathbf{u}_i = -\mathbf{G}^{-1}(\mathbf{x}_i)$, we observe the following equivalent relation:

$$\underbrace{\begin{pmatrix} \mathbf{G} & & & \\ \mathbf{A} & \mathbf{G} & & \\ & \mathbf{A} & \ddots & \\ & & \ddots & \mathbf{G} \\ & & & \mathbf{A} \end{pmatrix}}_{\mathbf{A}_T=:} \cdot \underbrace{\begin{pmatrix} \mathbf{u}_0 \\ \mathbf{u}_1 \\ \vdots \\ \\ \mathbf{u}_{T-1} \end{pmatrix}}_{\mathbf{u}=:} = \begin{pmatrix} -\mathbf{x}_0 \\ 0 \\ \vdots \\ 0 \\ \mathbf{x}_T \end{pmatrix} \bmod q \quad \text{and} \quad \underbrace{\begin{pmatrix} \mathbf{u}_0 \\ \mathbf{u}_1 \\ \vdots \\ \\ \mathbf{u}_{T-1} \end{pmatrix}} \in \{0,1\}^{mT}.$$

$$(1)$$

Looking ahead, to make the relation more proof-friendly, we relax the binary constraint, i.e. $\mathbf{u} \in \{0,1\}^{mT}$, to a bounded-norm constraint, i.e. $\|\mathbf{u}\| \le \beta$ for some $\beta \ll q$ where $\|\cdot\|$ denotes the infinity-norm.

We conjecture and give evidence that if the short integer solution problem $\mathsf{SIS}_{n,m,q,\beta}$ is hard, then for any $T \in \mathbb{N}$ and uniformly random $(\mathbf{A}, \mathbf{x}_0)$, it is infeasible for an adversary to find $(\mathbf{u}_0, \ldots, \mathbf{u}_{T-1}, \mathbf{x}_T)$ satisfying the above (relaxed) relation in parallel time $(1 - \omega(1)) \cdot T$. Reducing checking $\mathbf{y} = f_{\mathbf{A}}(\mathbf{x})$ to checking the satisfiability of a linear relation with a bounded-norm witness is the main leverage that will enable all applications in this work.

Proof of Sequential Work. In the sequential relation (Eq. (1)) proposed above, enforcing $\mathbf{u} \in \{0,1\}^{mT}$ ensures that for each instance $\mathbf{x}_0$ there exists a unique witness $(\mathbf{u}_0, \ldots, \mathbf{u}_{T-1}, \mathbf{x}_T)$. To construct a verifiable delay function (VDF), it suffices to prove the satisfiability of Eq. (1) with binary $(\mathbf{u}_0, \ldots, \mathbf{u}_{T-1})$ using a (preprocessing) succinct non-interactive argument (SNARG) with a (quasi-)

linear-time prover and a sublinear-time verifier (after preprocessing). Instantiating with a post-quantum-secure SNARG, which exists unconditionally in the quantum random oracle mode [17], we can obtain a candidate post-quantum VDF.

Although we believe that the above generic approach yields a somewhat efficient VDF, especially when instantiated with a SNARG optimised for proving the sequential relation, in this work we focus on constructing a tailor-made proof of sequential work (PoSW) which explicitly takes advantage of the block-bidiagonal structure of $\mathbf{A}_T$ in Eq. (1).

The main observation which underlies our PoSW construction is the following. When $T = 2t + 1$, the matrix $\mathbf{A}_T$ can be partitioned into

$$
\mathbf{A}_T = \left(
\begin{array}{c|c}
\mathbf{A}_t & \\
\hline
 & \begin{array}{c} \mathbf{G} \\ \hline \mathbf{A} \end{array} \\
\hline
 & \mathbf{A}_t
\end{array}
\right) .
$$

This structure allows us to construct a PoSW with a $O(\log T)$-time verifier in the random oracle model following the strategy in the (VDF) construction in [32].

In more detail, we sketch an interactive variant of the PoSW construction. Since the verifier is public-coin, the non-interactive variant follows from the Fiat-Shamir transform [6, 23] in the random oracle model. An instance of our PoSW is set up by sampling a random matrix $\mathbf{A} \leftarrow\!\!\$ \, \mathbb{Z}_q^{n \times m}$, which defines $\mathbf{A}_T$ for any T, and a random vector $\mathbf{x}_0 \leftarrow\!\!\$ \, \mathbb{Z}_q^n$. To convince the verifier that Eq. (1) holds for some $T \in \mathbb{N}$, the prover and the verifier engage in the following interactive protocol: We focus on the more interesting where $T = 2t + 1$ is odd[1]. The prover sends $\mathbf{u}_t$ to the verifier, reducing the linear relation in Eq. (1) to

$$
\mathbf{A}_t \cdot
\begin{pmatrix}
\mathbf{u}_0 & \mathbf{u}_{t+1} \\
\vdots & \vdots \\
\mathbf{u}_{t-1} & \mathbf{u}_{T-1}
\end{pmatrix}
=
\begin{pmatrix}
-\mathbf{x}_0 & -\mathbf{A} \cdot \mathbf{u}_t \\
0 & 0 \\
\vdots & \vdots \\
0 & 0 \\
-\mathbf{G} \cdot \mathbf{u}_t & \mathbf{x}_T
\end{pmatrix}
\mod q .
$$

The verifier checks that $\|\mathbf{u}_t\| \leq \beta$. If the check passes, the verifier sends a random challenge $r \in S \subseteq \mathbb{Z}$ chosen from challenge set S to the prover. The prover and verifier then engage in the same protocol but with parameter t for proving

---

[1] If T is even, the prover can reveal the last step of the computation. It then suffices for the prover to prove Eq. (1) for $T - 1$, which is odd.

$$\mathbf{A}_t \begin{pmatrix} \mathbf{u}_0 + \mathbf{u}_{t+1}r \\ \vdots \\ \mathbf{u}_{t-1} + \mathbf{u}_{T-1}r \end{pmatrix} = \begin{pmatrix} -(\mathbf{x}_0 + \mathbf{A}\mathbf{u}_t r) \\ 0 \\ \vdots \\ 0 \\ \mathbf{x}_T r - \mathbf{G}\mathbf{u}_t \end{pmatrix} \bmod q, \quad \left\| \begin{pmatrix} \mathbf{u}_0 + \mathbf{u}_{t+1}r \\ \vdots \\ \mathbf{u}_{t-1} + \mathbf{u}_{T-1}r \end{pmatrix} \right\| \leq \beta'$$

for an appropriately chosen $\beta' > \beta$. After recursing for $O(\log T)$ times, the prover and the verifier arrives at a statement of size independent of T for which the prover can simply send the witness to the verifier. Using standard techniques for arguing about security of (lattice-based) Σ-protocols (e.g. [3,4,12]), one could argue that (a parallel repetition [5] of) the above protocol allows to convince the verifier that the prover has knowledge of a witness satisfying Eq. (1) with certain norm bound $\beta^* > \beta$.

Note that even if we start with $\beta = 1$, the above protocol can only convince the verifier about the satisfiability of Eq. (1) with some $\beta^* > \beta$, with respect to which witnesses are not unique. This is the why our construction of PoSW does not yield a VDF, even though our construction is analogous to the VDF construction of [32].

2   Preliminaries

We denote by $\lambda \in \mathbb{N}$ the security parameter. A function $\mathsf{negl}(\cdot)$ is negligible if it vanishes faster than any polynomial. The cryptographic definitions in the paper follow the convention of modeling security against non-uniform adversaries. An efficient adversary $\mathcal{A}$ is modeled as a sequence of circuits $\mathcal{A} = \{\mathcal{A}_\lambda\}_{\lambda \in \mathbb{N}}$, such that the circuit $\mathcal{A}_\lambda$ is of polynomial size in λ. We define the *parallel* runtime of a given algorithm as the depth of the corresponding circuit, whereas the *total* runtime is determined by the size of the circuit. For a finite set S, we write $U(S)$ for the uniform distribution over S.

Lattice Background. Let $\mathcal{R} = \mathbb{Z}[\zeta]$ be the ring of integers of a cyclotomic field $\mathbb{Q}(\zeta)$, where $\zeta \in \mathbb{C}$ is a fixed ℓ-th primitive root of unity for some $\ell = \mathsf{poly}(\lambda)$.

An element $x \in \mathcal{R}$ is represented by its coefficients encoding $x = \sum_{i=0}^{\varphi(\ell)-1} x_i \cdot \zeta^i$, and its (infinity) norm is $\|x\| := \max_{i=0}^{\varphi(\ell)-1} |x_i|$. The norm extends naturally to vectors $\mathbf{u} = (u_1, \ldots, u_m) \in \mathcal{R}^m$, where $\|\mathbf{u}\| = \max_{i \in [m]} \|u_i\|$. The expansion factor of $\mathcal{R}$ is defined as $\gamma_{\mathcal{R}} := \max_{a,b \in \mathcal{R}} \frac{\|a \cdot b\|}{\|a\| \cdot \|b\|}$. We will always assume that ℓ is a prime-power, and in that case it is known that $\gamma_{\mathcal{R}} \leq 2\,\varphi(\ell)$ [3]. For $q \in \mathbb{N}$, define $\mathcal{R}_q := \mathcal{R}/q\mathcal{R}$. By a slight abuse of notation, we identify $\mathcal{R}_q$ by $\left\{ \sum_{i=0}^{\varphi(\ell)-1} x_i \cdot \zeta^i : x_i \in \{-\lceil q/2 \rceil + 1, \ldots, \lfloor q/2 \rfloor\} \right\}$, and thus $\|x\| \leq q/2$ for any $x \in \mathcal{R}_q$. The set of units in $\mathcal{R}$ is denoted by $\mathcal{R}^\times$. A set $S \subseteq \mathcal{R}$ is said to be subtractive if $(a - b) \in \mathcal{R}^\times$ for any distinct $a, b \in S$.

We recall the following useful fact.

Lemma 1 (Adapted from [13, Lemma 7]). *Let $n = \mathsf{poly}(\lambda)$, $p, q \in \mathbb{N}$, q prime, and $m \geq n \log_p q + \omega(\log \lambda)$. The following distributions are statistically close in λ:*

$$\left\{ (\mathbf{A}, \mathbf{v}) : \begin{array}{l} \mathbf{A} \leftarrow_{\$} \mathcal{R}_q^{n \times m} \\ \mathbf{u} \leftarrow_{\$} \mathcal{R}_p^m \\ \mathbf{v} := \mathbf{A} \cdot \mathbf{u} \bmod q \end{array} \right\} \quad and \quad \left\{ (\mathbf{A}, \mathbf{v}) : \begin{array}{l} \mathbf{A} \leftarrow_{\$} \mathcal{R}_q^{n \times m} \\ \mathbf{v} \leftarrow_{\$} \mathcal{R}_q^n \end{array} \right\}.$$

Gadget Matrices. For any $n, p, q \in \mathbb{N}$, let $\ell = \lceil \log_p q \rceil$ and $m = n \cdot \ell$. If $q < p^\ell$, write $q = \sum_{i=0}^{\ell-1} q_i \cdot p^i$ in p-ary expansion. If $q = p^\ell$, let $q_0 = \ldots = q_{\ell-2} = 0$ and $q_{\ell-1} = p$. Define the generalised "gadget vector" $\mathbf{g}_{p,q}$, generalised "gadget matrix" $\mathbf{G}_{p,q}$, and "parity-check matrix" $\mathbf{H}_{p,q}$ by

$$\mathbf{g}_{p,q}^{\mathsf{T}} := \begin{pmatrix} 1 \ p \ \ldots \ p^{\ell-1} \end{pmatrix}, \quad \mathbf{G}_{p,q} := \mathbf{I}_n \otimes \mathbf{g}_{p,q}^{\mathsf{T}}, \quad \mathbf{H}_{p,q} := \mathbf{I}_n \otimes \begin{pmatrix} p & & & q_0 \\ -1 & p & & q_1 \\ & -1 & \ddots & \vdots \\ & & \ddots & p & \vdots \\ & & & -1 & q_{\ell-1} \end{pmatrix}$$

respectively. Define the operator $\mathbf{G}_{p,q}^{-1} : \mathcal{R}_q^n \to \mathcal{R}_p^m$ which maps $\mathbf{v} = (v_i)_{i=0}^{n-1} \in \mathcal{R}_q^n$ to the concatenation of its p-ary representation $\left((v_{0,j})_{j=0}^{\ell-1}, \ldots, (v_{n-1,j})_{j=0}^{\ell-1} \right) \in \mathcal{R}_p^m$, i.e. $v_i = \sum_{j=0}^{\ell-1} v_{i,j} \cdot p^j$. The operator $\mathbf{G}_{p,q}^{-1}$ is naturally extended to act on any matrix $\mathbf{V}$ over $\mathcal{R}_q$ with n rows, with $\mathbf{G}_{p,q} \cdot \mathbf{G}_{p,q}^{-1}(\mathbf{V}) = \mathbf{V}$. Note that $\mathbf{G}_{p,q} \cdot \mathbf{H}_{p,q} = 0 \bmod q$. Indeed, $\mathbf{H}_{p,q}$ is a basis of the right-kernel of $\mathbf{G}_{p,q}$ over $\mathcal{K}$. When the choices of n, p, q are clear from the context, we omit the subscripts and write $\mathbf{G} := \mathbf{G}_{p,q}$.

Computational Assumptions. In the following we define the ring variant of the well-known short integer solution (SIS) problem [2].

Assumption 1 (Short Integer Solution). *The $\mathsf{SIS}_{\mathcal{R},n,m,q,\beta}$ assumption states that for any $\mathbf{v} \in \mathcal{R}_q^n$ and any PPT adversary $\mathcal{A}$ it holds that*

$$\Pr\left[\mathbf{A} \cdot \mathbf{u} = \mathbf{v} \bmod q \ \wedge \ \|\mathbf{u}\| \leq \beta \ \middle| \ \begin{array}{l} \mathbf{A} \leftarrow_{\$} \mathcal{R}_q^{n \times m} \\ \mathbf{u} \leftarrow \mathcal{A}(\mathbf{A}, \mathbf{v}) \end{array} \right] \leq \mathsf{negl}(\lambda).$$

We also recall the learning with errors (LWE) problem [33], and in particular the version over rings [29].

Assumption 2 (Learning with Errors). *The (normal form of the) $\mathsf{LWE}_{\mathcal{R},n,m,q,\chi}$ assumption states that for any PPT adversary $\mathcal{A}$ it holds that*

$$\left| \Pr\left[\mathcal{A}(\mathbf{A}, \mathbf{b}) = 1 \ \middle| \ \begin{array}{l} \mathbf{A} \leftarrow_{\$} \mathcal{R}_q^{n \times m} \\ \mathbf{s} \leftarrow_{\$} \chi^n \\ \mathbf{e} \leftarrow_{\$} \chi^m \\ \mathbf{b}^{\mathsf{T}} := \mathbf{s}^{\mathsf{T}} \cdot \mathbf{A} + \mathbf{e}^{\mathsf{T}} \bmod q \end{array} \right] - \Pr\left[\mathcal{A}(\mathbf{A}, \mathbf{b}) = 1 \ \middle| \ \begin{array}{l} \mathbf{A} \leftarrow_{\$} \mathcal{R}_q^{n \times m} \\ \mathbf{b} \leftarrow_{\$} \mathcal{R}_q^m \end{array} \right] \right|$$

$$\leq \mathsf{negl}(\lambda).$$

For convenience, we state here a decisional variant of the SIS problem, which is known to be as hard as LWE. For completeness, we recall also a proof of this fact.

Assumption 3 (Decisional Short Integer Solution). *The* $\mathsf{dSIS}_{\mathcal{R},n,m,q,\chi}$ *assumption states that for any PPT adversary* $\mathcal{A}$ *it holds that*

$$\left| \Pr\left[\mathcal{A}(\mathbf{A},\mathbf{v}) = 1 \middle| \begin{array}{l} \mathbf{A} \leftarrow_\$ \mathcal{R}_q^{n\times m} \\ \mathbf{u} \leftarrow_\$ \chi^m \\ \mathbf{v} := \mathbf{A}\cdot\mathbf{u} \bmod q \end{array} \right] - \Pr\left[\mathcal{A}(\mathbf{A},\mathbf{v}) = 1 \middle| \begin{array}{l} \mathbf{A} \leftarrow_\$ \mathcal{R}_q^{n\times m} \\ \mathbf{v} \leftarrow_\$ \mathcal{R}_q^n \end{array} \right] \right|$$
$$\le \mathsf{negl}(\lambda).$$

Lemma 2. *If* $m = n + \Omega(\lambda)$ *and the* $\mathsf{LWE}_{\mathcal{R},n,m,q,\chi}$ *assumption holds, then the* $\mathsf{dSIS}_{\mathcal{R},n,m,q,\chi}$ *assumption holds.*

Proof. Suppose there exists a PPT algorithm $\mathcal{A}$ which solves the $\mathsf{dSIS}_{\mathcal{R},n,m,q,\chi}$ problem. We construct a PPT algorithm $\mathcal{B}$ which solves the $\mathsf{LWE}_{\mathcal{R},n,m,q,\chi}$ problem. On input $(\bar{\mathbf{A}},\bar{\mathbf{b}}) \in \mathcal{R}_q^{n\times m} \times \mathcal{R}_q^m$, $\mathcal{B}$ samples $\mathbf{A} \leftarrow_\$ \mathcal{R}_q^{n\times m}$ uniformly conditioned on $\bar{\mathbf{A}}\cdot\mathbf{A}^\mathsf{T} = \mathbf{0} \bmod q$. It then computes $\mathbf{v} := \mathbf{A}\cdot\bar{\mathbf{b}} \bmod q$ and outputs $b \leftarrow \mathcal{A}(\mathbf{A},\mathbf{v})$.

We next analyse the distribution of $(\mathbf{A},\mathbf{v})$. First, since $\bar{\mathbf{A}}$ is uniformly random over $\mathcal{R}_q^{n\times m}$, so does $\mathbf{A}$. Furthermore, since $m = n + \Omega(\lambda)$, with overwhelming probability in λ we have that the columns of $\mathbf{A}$ spans $\mathcal{R}_q^n$. Conditioning on this, we show that $\mathcal{B}$ is given an LWE sample if and only if $\mathcal{B}$ gives a SIS sample to $\mathcal{A}$. Observe that if $(\bar{\mathbf{A}},\bar{\mathbf{b}})$ is an LWE sample, then $\bar{\mathbf{b}}$ is of the form $\bar{\mathbf{b}}^\mathsf{T} = \mathbf{s}^\mathsf{T}\cdot\bar{\mathbf{A}} + \mathbf{e}^\mathsf{T}$ for some $\mathbf{e} \leftarrow_\$ \chi^m$. It follows that $\mathbf{v}$ is of the form $\mathbf{v} = \mathbf{A}\cdot\mathbf{e} \bmod q$. If $(\bar{\mathbf{A}},\bar{\mathbf{b}})$ is a random sample, then $\mathbf{v} = \mathbf{A}\cdot\bar{\mathbf{b}} \bmod q$ is uniformly random. $\qquad\square$

3   A Lattice-Based Sequential Function/Relation

In what follows we formally define our family of sequential functions and state our conjecture regarding the sequentiality of the T-fold repetition of such functions.

Our Sequential Function/Relation. For any $\mathbf{A} \in \mathcal{R}_q^{n\times m}$, define the function $f_{\mathbf{A}} : \mathcal{R}_q^m \to \mathcal{R}_q^m$ as

$$f_{\mathbf{A}}(\mathbf{x}) := \mathbf{A}\cdot(-\mathbf{G}^{-1}(\mathbf{x})) \bmod q.$$

For $T \in \mathbb{N}$, denote by $f_{\mathbf{A}}^T$ the T-fold recursive evaluation of $f_{\mathbf{A}}$, i.e.

$$f_{\mathbf{A}}^T(\mathbf{x}) := \underbrace{f_{\mathbf{A}}(f_{\mathbf{A}}(\ldots(f_{\mathbf{A}}(\mathbf{x})))\ldots)}_{T \text{ times}}.$$

The results in this work are based on the conjecture that, for a uniformly random $\mathbf{A} \leftarrow_\$ \mathcal{R}_q^{n\times m}$, the evaluations of the functions $f_{\mathbf{A}}^T$ take sequential time at least

$\Omega(T)$. To formally state our conjecture, it is convenient to define the matrix

$$
A_T := \begin{pmatrix} G & & & \\ A & G & & \\ & A & \ddots & \\ & & \ddots & G \\ & & & A \end{pmatrix}
$$

$$\underbrace{\hphantom{\begin{pmatrix} G & & & \\ A & G & & \\ & A & \ddots & \\ & & \ddots & G \\ & & & A \end{pmatrix}}}_{T \text{ columns}}$$

and observe that if the evaluation of f_A is split into two steps as $\mathbf{u}_{i-1} = -\mathbf{G}^{-1}(\mathbf{x}_{i-1}) \in \mathcal{R}_p^m$ and $\mathbf{x}_i = \mathbf{A} \cdot \mathbf{u}_{i-1} \bmod q$ for all $i \in [T]$ then

$$
A_T \begin{pmatrix} \mathbf{u}_0 \\ \mathbf{u}_1 \\ \vdots \\ \mathbf{u}_{T-1} \end{pmatrix} = \begin{pmatrix} \mathbf{G} & & & \\ \mathbf{A} & \mathbf{G} & & \\ & \mathbf{A} & \ddots & \\ & & \ddots & \mathbf{G} \\ & & & \mathbf{A} \end{pmatrix} \begin{pmatrix} \mathbf{u}_0 \\ \mathbf{u}_1 \\ \vdots \\ \mathbf{u}_{T-1} \end{pmatrix} = \begin{pmatrix} -\mathbf{x}_0 \\ 0 \\ \vdots \\ 0 \\ \mathbf{x}_T \end{pmatrix} \bmod q, \ \left\| \begin{pmatrix} \mathbf{u}_0 \\ \mathbf{u}_1 \\ \vdots \\ \mathbf{u}_{T-1} \end{pmatrix} \right\| \le \beta
$$

for any $\beta \ge p/2$. Furthermore, if p is odd, $q = p^\ell$, and $\beta = p/2$, we observe that the preimage $(\mathbf{u}_0^\mathsf{T} \, \mathbf{u}_1^\mathsf{T} \, \dots \, \mathbf{u}_{T-1}^\mathsf{T})^\mathsf{T}$, and hence the evaluation result $\mathbf{x}_T$, are unique.[2]

Formally, we state a family of conjectures parametrised by n, p, q, β as follows.

Assumption 4 ($\sigma(\lambda, T)$-SIS-Sequentiality). *If the $\mathsf{SIS}_{\mathcal{R}, n, m, q, \beta}$ assumption holds for $m = n\lceil \log_p q \rceil$, then for all polynomial-size adversary $\mathcal{A}$ it holds that*

$$
\Pr \left[\begin{array}{l} A_{T(\lambda)} \cdot \mathbf{u} = \left(-\mathbf{x}^\mathsf{T} \, 0^\mathsf{T} \, \dots \, 0^\mathsf{T} \, \mathbf{y}^\mathsf{T}\right)^\mathsf{T} \bmod q \\ \wedge \ \|\mathbf{u}\| \le \beta \\ \wedge \ \mathsf{Depth}(\mathcal{A}) < \sigma(\lambda, T) \end{array} \middle| \begin{array}{l} \mathbf{A} \leftarrow_\$ \mathcal{R}_q^{n \times m} \\ \mathbf{x} \leftarrow_\$ \mathcal{R}_q^n \\ (\mathbf{y}, \mathbf{u}) = \mathcal{A}(\mathbf{A}, \mathbf{x}) \end{array} \right] \le \mathsf{negl}(\lambda).
$$

By the above discussion, $\{f_A^T\}_A$ induces a family of sequential relations. Although such a relation has potentially many solutions $(\mathbf{u}, \mathbf{y}) \in \mathcal{R}_p^{mT} \times \mathcal{R}_q^n$ to an input $\mathbf{x}$, each takes $\Omega(T)$ sequential steps to find under the SIS-sequentiality assumption.

3.1 Evidence of Sequentiality

To substantiate the plausibility of the SIS-sequentiality assumption, we shall offer some concrete evidence on the cryptographic properties satisfied by the function f_A. First we show that the function f_A is collision resistant.

Theorem 5 (Collision Resistance). *If the $\mathsf{SIS}_{\mathcal{R}, n, m, q, p}$ problem is hard for $m = n \cdot \lceil \log_p q \rceil$, then f_A is collision resistant.*

---

[2] For even p and $q = p^\ell$, we can replace the $\|(\mathbf{u}_0^\mathsf{T} \, \mathbf{u}_1^\mathsf{T} \, \dots \, \mathbf{u}_{T-1}^\mathsf{T})\| \le p/2$ check with the $(\mathbf{u}_0^\mathsf{T} \, \mathbf{u}_1^\mathsf{T} \, \dots \, \mathbf{u}_{T-1}^\mathsf{T}) \in \mathcal{R}_p^{mT}$ check to guarantee uniqueness.

Proof. The proof is a trivial reduction from the $\mathsf{SIS}_{\mathcal{R},n,m,q,p}$ problem. Let $\mathbf{A}$ be an instance of $\mathsf{SIS}_{\mathcal{R},n,m,q,p}$. If $\mathbf{x}, \mathbf{x}' \in \mathcal{R}_q^n$ are distinct vectors such that $f_\mathbf{A}(\mathbf{x}) = f_\mathbf{A}(\mathbf{x}')$, write $\mathbf{u} = -\mathbf{G}^{-1}(\mathbf{x})$ and $\mathbf{u}' = -\mathbf{G}^{-1}(\mathbf{x}')$, we have $\mathbf{A} \cdot \mathbf{u} = \mathbf{A} \cdot \mathbf{u}' \bmod q$. In other words, we have $\mathbf{A} \cdot (\mathbf{u} - \mathbf{u}') = \mathbf{0} \bmod q$ and $\|\mathbf{u} - \mathbf{u}'\| \le p$. □

Note that the same proof shows that $f_\mathbf{A}$ is one-way. Next, we show that the function $f_\mathbf{A}$ provably maps uniform distributions to distributions statistically or computationally close to uniform for certain parameter settings. It then follows from a standard hybrid argument that $f_\mathbf{A}^T$ also maps uniform distributions to near-uniform distributions for any polynomial T. First, we show that if q is super-polynomial and is smaller than a sufficiently large power of p by an additive polynomial factor, then the above claim holds statistically.

Theorem 6 (Uniformity Preserving for Large $q \lesssim p^k$). *Let q be a prime of the form $q = p^k - r$ where $k > \log_p q + 2\lambda/n$, $r = \mathsf{poly}(\lambda)$, $0 < r < p^k - p^{k-1}$, and $1/q = \mathsf{negl}(\lambda)$. The following distributions are statistically close in λ:*

$$\{\mathbf{y} : \mathbf{y} \leftarrow_\$ \mathcal{R}_q^n\} \approx \{f_\mathbf{A}(\mathbf{x}) : \mathbf{A} \leftarrow_\$ \mathcal{R}_q^{n \times m}, \mathbf{x} \leftarrow_\$ \mathcal{R}_q^n\}.$$

Proof. We first show that the distributions

$$\{\mathbf{u} \leftarrow_\$ \mathcal{R}_p^m\} \approx \{\mathbf{G}^{-1}(\mathbf{x}) : \mathbf{x} \leftarrow_\$ \mathcal{R}_q^n\}$$

are statistically close in λ. Let $d = \mathsf{poly}(\lambda)$ be the degree of the ring $\mathcal{R}$. The statistical distance of the two distributions is given by

$$
\begin{aligned}
\Delta &:= \frac{1}{2} \cdot \left(q^{dn} \cdot \left| \frac{1}{p^{dm}} - \frac{1}{q^{dn}} \right| + (p^{dm} - q^{dn}) \cdot \frac{1}{p^{dm}} \right) \\
&= \frac{1}{2} \cdot \left(1 - \frac{q^{dn}}{p^{dm}} + 1 - \frac{q^{dn}}{p^{dm}} \right) \\
&= 1 - \left(\frac{q^n}{p^m} \right)^d.
\end{aligned}
$$

Note that $m = n \cdot \lceil \log_p q \rceil = nk$. Since $p^k > q$ and $(1 + x)^n \ge 1 + nx$ for all $n \in \mathbb{N}$ and $x \ge -1$, we have

$$
\left(\frac{q^n}{p^m} \right)^d = \left(\frac{q^n}{q^{nk}} \right)^d = \left(\frac{q}{p^k} \right)^{dn} = \left(\frac{p^k - r}{p^k} \right)^{dn} = \left(1 - \frac{r}{p^k} \right)^{dn} > \left(1 - \frac{r}{q} \right)^{dn}
$$

$$
\ge 1 - \frac{rdn}{q} \ge 1 - \mathsf{negl}(\lambda).
$$

In other words, we have $\Delta \le \mathsf{negl}(\lambda)$. Since $k > \log_p q + 2\lambda/n$, we have $m = nk > n \log_p q + 2\lambda$. The result then follows from the leftover hash lemma (Lemma 1). □

Next, we show that if q is a power of p and an LWE assumption with uniform noise holds, then the claim holds computationally.

Theorem 7 (Uniformity Preserving for $q = p^k$). *Let $q = p^k$ for some $k \in \mathbb{N}$. If the $\mathsf{LWE}_{\mathcal{R},n,m,q,U(\mathcal{R}_p)}$ assumption holds for $m = nk$, then the following distributions are computationally indistinguishable:*

$$\left\{ \mathbf{y} : \mathbf{y} \leftarrow_\$ \mathcal{R}_q^n \right\} \approx \left\{ f_{\mathbf{A}}(\mathbf{x}) : \mathbf{A} \leftarrow_\$ \mathcal{R}_q^{n \times m}, \mathbf{x} \leftarrow_\$ \mathcal{R}_q^n \right\}.$$

Proof. Since $q = p^k$ is a power of p, $\mathbf{G}^{-1}$ is a bijection and thus the following distributions are identical:

$$\left\{ \mathbf{u} \leftarrow_\$ \mathcal{R}_p^m \right\} \equiv \left\{ \mathbf{G}^{-1}(\mathbf{x}) : \mathbf{x} \leftarrow_\$ \mathcal{R}_q^n \right\}.$$

The result then follows from the $\mathsf{LWE}_{\mathcal{R},n,m,q,U(\mathcal{R}_p)}$ assumption. □

We remark that the above proof would still go through for other choices of q, by making an LWE assumption with skewed uniform noise, i.e. $U((\mathbf{g}^\mathsf{T})^{-1}(\mathcal{R}_q))$.

More Heuristic Evidence. We offer more heuristic evidence that the function is indeed sequential. First, it was shown in [26] that a fully homomorphic encryption scheme (FHE) can be used to show the existence of a *universal* sequential function, i.e. a function that is sequential if and only if sequential functions exist at all. The evaluation algorithm of this construction consists of running an empty circuit homomorphically. Looking at a specific instantiation of an FHE scheme [24], the homomorphic evaluation algorithm consists exclusively of linear operations (over some ring), interleaved with binary decomposition. This bears strong resemblance with our candidate function, which also interleaves linear operations with p-ary decomposition, albeit with a fixed matrix $\mathbf{A}$. In this sense, our candidate can be seen as the *minimal* non-trivial operation that is performed in the FHE evaluation, which we conjecture to be already secure.

Another evidence for the cryptographic usefulness of binary decomposition is the recent work of Chen et al. [16] which shows that the binary decomposition operator can in some cases be used as a sound alternative to the Fiat-Shamir transformation, which is normally instantiated using a random oracle.[3] Here the heuristic argument that we propose is that binary decomposition bears similarities with random oracles (in the sense that they can be both used for Fiat-Shamir) and random oracles are known to be sequential. Thus, we can conjecture that binary decomposition also bears sequentiality properties.

3.2 Cryptanalysis

We discuss a few attack strategies and why they do not apply to our scheme.

Finding Associative Structure. One simple approach to attack the sequentiality of our scheme would be to find some associative structure in the computation. For example, say we omitted the decomposition operator $\mathbf{G}^{-1}$ from

---

[3] Although the signature scheme presented in [16] actually relies on random oracles, it is only used to upgrade random-message unforgeability to existential unforgeability, while the use of random oracles for the Fiat-Shamir transformation is eliminated.

the definition of $f_{\mathbf{A}}$ (adjusting the parameters suitably), then one could use the associativity of matrix multiplication to parallelise the computation, since the function

$$g_{\mathbf{A}}^T(\mathbf{x}) = \underbrace{\mathbf{A} \cdot \mathbf{A} \cdots \mathbf{A}}_{T\text{-times}} \cdot \mathbf{x} \bmod q$$

can be computed in parallel time $O(\log(T))$ by computing the matrix products in a tree fashion. However, the same attack does not appear to be viable once we interleave each multiplication with the operator $\mathbf{G}^{-1}$, since the composition of these two operations is not associative.

Gluing Parallel Threads. Another (related) attack strategy is to *glue together* two parallel computation transcripts. For example, suppose $T = 2t + 1$, the adversary may sample a random $\mathbf{x}^* \leftarrow_\$ \mathcal{R}_q^n$ declare it to be output of the function at time $t + 1$. Then it would spawn two parallel threads computing $\mathbf{x}_t \leftarrow f_{\mathbf{A}}^t(\mathbf{x})$ and $\mathbf{y} \leftarrow f_{\mathbf{A}}^t(\mathbf{x}^*)$. To obtain a consistent transcript, the adversary must now find a vector $\mathbf{u}_t \in \mathcal{R}^m$ such that:

$$\begin{pmatrix} \mathbf{G} \\ \mathbf{A} \end{pmatrix} \cdot \mathbf{u}_t = \begin{pmatrix} -\mathbf{x}_t \\ \mathbf{x}^* \end{pmatrix} \bmod q \qquad \text{and} \qquad \|\mathbf{u}_t\| \leq \beta,$$

which is not easier than solving $\mathsf{SIS}_{\mathcal{R},n,m,q,\beta}$. Note that this attack is only plausible when the solution to the sequential relation is not unique, e.g. when $\beta > p/2$.

Preprocessing Attack. If we were to *fix* a matrix $\mathbf{A}$, instead of sampling it as part of the instance, then it turns out that our sequentiality assumption does *not hold* unless SIS is easy for $\beta > (\gamma_{\mathcal{R}} \cdot p \cdot n \cdot \lceil \log q \rceil)/2$. The idea of the attack is to precompute a witness for $(\mathbf{A}, 2^i \cdot \mathbf{e}_j)$, for $i = 0, \ldots, \lceil \log q \rceil - 1$ and $j = 1, \ldots, n$ and where $\mathbf{e}_j \in \{0,1\}^n$ denotes the j-th unit vector. Let us denote the (i,j)-th precomputed witness by $(\mathbf{u}_0^{(i,j)}, \ldots, \mathbf{u}_{T-1}^{(i,j)}, \mathbf{y}^{(i,j)})$. Note that $\|\mathbf{u}_k^{(i,j)}\| \leq p/2$. Upon receiving $\mathbf{x} \in \mathcal{R}_q^n$, decompose $\mathbf{x}$ into

$$\mathbf{x} = \sum_{i=0}^{\lceil \log q \rceil - 1} \sum_{j=1}^{n} x^{(i,j)} \cdot 2^i \cdot \mathbf{e}_j$$

where $x^{(i,j)} \in \mathcal{R}_2$. Set the witness to

$$(\mathbf{u}_0, \ldots, \mathbf{u}_{T-1}, \mathbf{y}) := \sum_{i=0}^{\lceil \log q \rceil - 1} \sum_{j=1}^{n} x^{(i,j)} \cdot (\mathbf{u}_0^{(i,j)}, \ldots, \mathbf{u}_{T-1}^{(i,j)}, \mathbf{y}^{(i,j)}).$$

Note that $\|\mathbf{u}_k\| \leq (\gamma_{\mathcal{R}} \cdot p \cdot n \cdot \lceil \log q \rceil)/2$, and furthermore the parallel runtime of the attack (after the preprocessing phase) is $O(\log T)$. This would break a hypothetical version of our sequentiality assumption, where we fix $\mathbf{A}$ for all instances. Although we shall mention explicitly that, in the restrictive settings where we require the witness to be binary (i.e. we do not allow any slack), then the above attack does not seem to apply, even with a fixed $\mathbf{A}$.

In contrast, if we sample $\mathbf{A}$ as part of the instance (which is what we do in our actual assumption), then simple linearity attacks as above do not appear to be working. In particular, while we can decompose

$$\mathbf{A} = \sum_{i,j,k} a_{i,j,k} \cdot 2^k \cdot \mathbf{E}_{i,j}$$

where $\mathbf{E}_{i,j}$ is the matrix with the (i,j)-th entry being 1 and everywhere else being 0, we don't know how to decompose $\mathbf{G}$ consistently (while being able to evaluate the decomposition of $\mathbf{G}^{-1}$). Moreover, even if we can decompose the $\mathbf{G}$ matrix, the attack would need to perform a *bi-linear* combination on both the matrix and the preimage vector, which breaks the linear structure of the relation.

3.3 Verifiable Delay Functions

We shall remark that our sequential function can be combined with a succinct non-interactive argument with a (quasi-)linear-time prover to obtain a verifiable delay function. While this is a known implication [21], we explicitly mention this here since the statement to be proven has a particularly simple form. Specifically, for an input instance $\mathbf{x}$ and an output $\mathbf{y}$ the prover only needs to show the existence of a vector $\mathbf{u}$ such that:

$$\begin{pmatrix} \mathbf{G} & & & \\ \mathbf{A} & \mathbf{G} & & \\ & \mathbf{A} & \ddots & \\ & & \ddots & \mathbf{G} \\ & & & \mathbf{A} \end{pmatrix} \cdot \mathbf{u} = \begin{pmatrix} -\mathbf{x} \\ 0 \\ \vdots \\ \vdots \\ 0 \\ \mathbf{y} \end{pmatrix} \mod q \qquad \text{and} \qquad \mathbf{u} \in \mathcal{R}_p^{mT}.$$

In other words, the statement to be proven consists of a highly structured linear relation and a bounded-norm or set-membership constraint. For small p, e.g. $p = 2$, and ring $\mathcal{R}$ of low degree, e.g. $\mathcal{R} = \mathbb{Z}$, the latter can be viewed as a simple low-degree relation $(\prod_{a \in \mathcal{R}_p} (u_i - a) = 0)_{i=1}^{mT}$ which reduces to $(u_i \cdot (u_i - 1) = 0)_{i=1}^{mT}$ for $(p, \mathcal{R}) = (2, \mathbb{Z})$. We expect that recent constructions of efficient succinct arguments for structured relations, e.g. [7,18], can efficiently prove statements of this form without too much overhead needed to manipulate the statement. We leave exploring the concrete efficiency of this approach as future work.

4   Proof of Sequential Work

We recall the definition of proofs of sequential work (PoSW) and present a construction based on the new SIS-sequentiality assumption.

4.1   Definitions

We recall the definition of a proof of sequential work (PoSW).

Definition 1 ((Interactive) Proof of Sequential Work (PoSW)).
An (interactive) proof of sequential work (PoSW) is a tuple of PPT algorithms/protocols $(\mathsf{Gen}, \langle \mathsf{Eval}, \mathsf{Vf} \rangle)$ *with the following syntax:*

- $\mathsf{x} \leftarrow \mathsf{Gen}(1^\lambda)$: *The instance generation algorithm inputs the security parameter* $\lambda \in \mathbb{N}$ *and generates a problem instance* x.
- $b \leftarrow \langle \mathsf{Eval}(\mathsf{x}, 1^T), \mathsf{Vf}(\mathsf{x}, T) \rangle$: *The evaluation-verification protocol is run between the interactive evaluation and verification algorithms. Both algorithms input an instance* x. *The evaluation algorithm further inputs a time parameter* 1^T *in unary while the verification algorithm inputs* T *in binary. The protocol terminates when the verification algorithm returns a bit* $b \in \{0, 1\}$.

A PoSW is required to satisfy the following properties:

Efficiency. *For any* $\mathsf{x} \in \mathsf{Gen}(1^\lambda)$, *the circuit-depth of* Eval *(as a function of* (λ, T)*) satisfies*
$$\mathsf{Depth}(\mathsf{Eval}(\cdot, 1^T)) = T \cdot \mathsf{poly}(\lambda).$$

Completeness. *For any* $\lambda \in \mathbb{N}$, $\mathsf{x} \in \mathsf{Gen}(1^\lambda)$, *and* $T \in \mathbb{N}$, *it holds that*
$$\langle \mathsf{Eval}(\mathsf{x}, 1^T), \mathsf{Vf}(\mathsf{x}, T) \rangle = 1.$$

$\sigma(\lambda, T)$**-Sequential Soundness.** *For any pair of PPT adversaries* $(\mathcal{A}_0, \mathcal{A}_1)$ *it holds that*
$$\Pr\left[\begin{array}{c} \langle \mathcal{A}_1(\mathsf{x}), \mathsf{Vf}(\mathsf{x}, T) \rangle = 1 \\ \wedge \ \mathsf{Depth}(\mathcal{A}_1) < \sigma(\lambda, T)) \end{array} \middle| \begin{array}{c} \mathsf{x} \leftarrow \mathsf{Gen}(1^\lambda) \\ (\mathsf{st}, T) \leftarrow \mathcal{A}_0(1^\lambda) \end{array} \right] \leq \mathsf{negl}(\lambda).$$

The function σ *is called the sequentiality of the PoSW.*

4.2   Construction

Let $S \subseteq \mathcal{R}$ be a subtractive set where $\|r\| = 1$ for all $r \in S$. We first construct a core protocol $\langle \mathsf{P}(\mathbf{A}, (\mathbf{u}_i)_{i=0}^{T-1}, (\mathbf{x}_i)_{i=0}^T, \beta), \mathsf{V}(\mathbf{A}, \mathbf{x}_0, \mathbf{x}_T, \beta, T) \rangle$ recursively as follows:

- If $T = 1$, P sends $\mathbf{u}_0$ and V returns 1 if $\mathbf{A}_1 \cdot \mathbf{u}_0 = (-\mathbf{x}_0, \mathbf{x}_1) \bmod q$ and $\|\mathbf{u}_0\| \leq \beta$.[4]
- If $T > 1$ and T is even:
  - P sends $\mathbf{u}_{T-1}$.
  - V checks that $(\mathbf{x}_T \overset{?}{=} \mathbf{A} \cdot \mathbf{u}_{T-1})$, returns 0 if not.

---

[4] This step serves to make the security proof a bit simpler. Alternatively, P does not need to send anything and V could simply return $(\mathbf{x}_1 \overset{?}{=} -\mathbf{A} \cdot \mathbf{G}^{-1}(\mathbf{x}_0))$.

Gen(pp)	$\langle \mathsf{Eval}(\mathsf{x}, 1^T), \mathsf{Vf}(\mathsf{x}, T) \rangle$
$\mathbf{A} \leftarrow\!\!\$\ \mathcal{R}_q^{n \times m}$	Eval :
$\mathbf{x}_0 \leftarrow\!\!\$\ \mathcal{R}_q^n$	for $i \in \{0, \dots, T-1\}$ do
$\mathsf{x} := (\mathbf{A}, \mathbf{x}_0)$	$\mathbf{u}_i := -\mathbf{G}^{-1}(\mathbf{x}_i)$
return x	$\mathbf{x}_{i+1} := \mathbf{A} \cdot \mathbf{u}_i \bmod q$
	send $\mathbf{x}_T$
	$\langle \mathsf{Eval}, \mathsf{Vf} \rangle$:
	for $j \in [\lambda/\log \lambda]$ do
	$b_j \leftarrow \langle \mathsf{P}(\mathbf{A}, (\mathbf{u}_i)_{i=0}^{T-1}, (\mathbf{x}_i)_{i=0}^{T}, p/2), \mathsf{V}(\mathbf{A}, \mathbf{x}_0, \mathbf{x}_T, p/2, T) \rangle$
	$\mathsf{Vf} : \mathbf{return}\ (b_1 \wedge \dots \wedge b_{\lambda/\log\lambda})$

Fig. 1. Construction of proof of sequential work.

- P and V compute the following:
  * $\mathbf{x}_{T-1} = -\mathbf{G} \cdot \mathbf{u}_{T-1}$
- Run $\langle \mathsf{P}(\mathbf{A}, (\mathbf{u}_i)_{i=0}^{T-2}, (\mathbf{x}_i)_{i=0}^{T-1}, \beta), \mathsf{V}(\mathbf{A}, \mathbf{x}_0, \mathbf{x}_{T-1}, \beta, T-1) \rangle$.
- If $T > 1$ and T is odd:
  - Write $T = 2t + 1$.
  - P sends $\mathbf{u}_t$.
  - V checks that $\|\mathbf{u}_t\| \leq \beta$, returns 0 if not.
  - V samples $r \leftarrow\!\!\$\ S$ and sends r to P.
  - P and V compute the following:
    * $\mathbf{x}_0' := -\mathbf{x}_0 - \mathbf{A} \cdot \mathbf{u}_t \cdot r \bmod q$
    * $\mathbf{x}_t' := \mathbf{x}_T \cdot r - \mathbf{G} \cdot \mathbf{u}_t \bmod q$
    * $\beta' := 2 \gamma_{\mathcal{R}} \beta$
  - P computes $\mathbf{u}_i' := \mathbf{u}_i + \mathbf{u}_{t+i+1} \cdot r$ for all $i \in \{0, \dots, t-1\}$.
  - Run $\langle \mathsf{P}(\mathbf{A}, (\mathbf{u}_i')_{i=0}^{t-1}, (\mathbf{x}_i')_{i=0}^{t}, \beta'), \mathsf{V}(\mathbf{A}, \mathbf{x}_0', \mathbf{x}_t', \beta', t) \rangle$.

The PoSW protocol is then specified in Fig. 1.

Analysis. In the following we show that the above protocol is $(2, 2, \dots, 2)$-special sound. First, we recall the definition of special soundness and a useful fact from [3].

Definition 2 ($((k_1, \dots, k_\mu)$-out-of-$(N_1, \dots, N_\mu)$-Special Soundness [5]). *Let* $k_1, \dots, k_\mu, N_1, \dots, N_\mu \in \mathbb{N}$. *A $(2\mu+1)$-round public-coin protocol (P, V) for relation Φ, where V samples the i-th challenge from a set of cardinality $N_i \geq k_i$ for $i \in [\mu]$, is $(k_1, \dots, k_\mu)$-out-of-$(N_1, \dots, N_\mu)$-special-sound if there exists a polynomial-time algorithm that, on input a statement stmt and a $(k_1, \dots, k_\mu)$-tree of accepting transcripts, outputs a witness wit such that $(\mathsf{stmt}; \mathsf{wit}) \in \Phi$. We also say (P, V) is $(k_1, \dots, k_\mu)$-special-sound.*

For the (standard) definitions of public-coin protocol and trees of accepting transcripts we refer to [5].

Lemma 3 ([3]). *Let $\mathcal{R} = \mathbb{Z}[\zeta_{d+1}]$ be the $(d+1)$-th cyclotomic ring where $(d+1)$ is prime. The set $S = \{\mu_1, \ldots, \mu_d\} \subseteq \mathcal{R}^\times$ where $\mu_i = (\zeta^i - 1)/(\zeta - 1)$ is subtractive, i.e. for any $r_0, r_1 \in S$ it holds that $(r_1 - r_0)^{-1} \in \mathcal{R}$. Furthermore, for any $r_0, r_1 \in S$, we have $\|\frac{r_0}{r_1 - r_0}\| \le 1$, $\|\frac{r_1}{r_1 - r_0}\| \le 1$, and $\|\frac{1}{r_1 - r_0}\| \le 1$.*

Lemma 4 (Special Soundness). *The above folding argument is $(2, 2, \ldots, 2)$-special sound for the relation*

$$\left\{((\mathbf{A}, \mathbf{x}_0, \mathbf{x}_T); \mathbf{u}) : \; \mathbf{A}_T \mathbf{u} = (-\mathbf{x}_0, \mathbf{0}, \ldots, \mathbf{0}, \mathbf{x}_T) \bmod q \; \wedge \; \|\mathbf{u}\| \le (2\gamma_\mathcal{R})^{2\log T} \beta\right\}.$$

Proof. In this proof, we focus on the (more interesting) special case where $T = 2^{\mu+1} - 1$ for some $\mu \in \mathbb{N}$, so that $\frac{T-1}{2} = 2^\mu - 1$ is also an odd integer. It is clear that for such T the above folding argument is $(2\mu + 1)$-round. The general case can be dealt with analogously.

In the following, we construct an extractor $\mathcal{E}$ which extracts a witness $\mathbf{u}$ given a $(2, \ldots, 2)$-tree of accepting transcripts recursively from depth $i = \mu$ to depth $i = 1$. Let $T_i := 2^{\mu-i+1} - 1$ for $i \in \{0, \ldots, \mu\}$ so that $T_0 = T$ and $T_\mu = 1$. Note that $T_{i-1} = 2T_i + 1$ for all $i \in [\mu]$. Let node_0 and node_1 be siblings at depth-i associated with the challenges r_0 and r_1 respectively, and let node_ϵ be the parent node of node_0 and node_1. From the tree of accepting transcripts, $\mathcal{E}$ fetches the vectors $\mathbf{x}_0^{(\mathsf{node})}, \mathbf{x}_{T_{\mathsf{depth(node)}}}^{(\mathsf{node})}, \mathbf{u}_t^{(\mathsf{node})}$ associated to each node $\mathsf{node} \in \{\mathsf{node}_\epsilon, \mathsf{node}_0, \mathsf{node}_1\}$ recursively defined such that $\mathbf{x}_0^{\mathsf{root}} = \mathbf{x}_0$, $\mathbf{x}_{T_0}^{\mathsf{root}} = \mathbf{x}_T$, and

$$\begin{pmatrix} \mathbf{x}_0^{(\mathsf{node}_b)} \\ \mathbf{x}_{T_i}^{(\mathsf{node}_b)} \end{pmatrix} = \begin{pmatrix} \mathbf{x}_0^{(\mathsf{node}_\epsilon)} \\ -\mathbf{G} \cdot \mathbf{u}_{T_i}^{(\mathsf{node}_\epsilon)} \end{pmatrix} + \begin{pmatrix} \mathbf{A} \cdot \mathbf{u}_{T_i}^{(\mathsf{node}_\epsilon)} \\ \mathbf{x}_{T_{i-1}}^{(\mathsf{node}_\epsilon)} \end{pmatrix} \cdot r_b \bmod q.$$

Suppose the vector $(\mathbf{u}_0^{\mathsf{node}_b}, \ldots, \mathbf{u}_{T_i-1}^{\mathsf{node}_b})$ extracted at node_b for $b \in \{0, 1\}$ satisfies

$$\mathbf{A}_{T_i} \cdot \begin{pmatrix} \mathbf{u}_0^{\mathsf{node}_b} \\ \vdots \\ \mathbf{u}_{T_i-1}^{\mathsf{node}_b} \end{pmatrix} = \begin{pmatrix} -\mathbf{x}_0^{(\mathsf{node}_b)} \\ \mathbf{0} \\ \vdots \\ \mathbf{0} \\ \mathbf{x}_{T_i}^{(\mathsf{node}_b)} \end{pmatrix} \bmod q \quad \text{and} \quad \left\| \begin{pmatrix} \mathbf{u}_0^{\mathsf{node}_b} \\ \vdots \\ \mathbf{u}_{T_i-1}^{\mathsf{node}_b} \end{pmatrix} \right\| \le (2\gamma_\mathcal{R})^{2\mu-i} \cdot \beta.$$

Expanding the expressions, the L.H.S. becomes

$$\mathbf{A}_{T_i} \cdot \begin{pmatrix} \mathbf{u}_0^{\mathsf{node}_b} \\ \vdots \\ \mathbf{u}_{T_i-1}^{\mathsf{node}_b} \end{pmatrix} = \begin{pmatrix} -\mathbf{x}_0^{(\mathsf{node}_\epsilon)} \\ \mathbf{0} \\ \vdots \\ \mathbf{0} \\ -\mathbf{G} \cdot \mathbf{u}_{T_i}^{(\mathsf{node}_\epsilon)} \end{pmatrix} + \begin{pmatrix} -\mathbf{A} \cdot \mathbf{u}_{T_i}^{(\mathsf{node}_\epsilon)} \\ \mathbf{0} \\ \vdots \\ \mathbf{0} \\ \mathbf{x}_T^{(\mathsf{node}_\epsilon)} \end{pmatrix} \cdot r_b \bmod q.$$

Let

$$
\begin{pmatrix} \mathbf{u}_0 & \mathbf{u}_{t+1} \\ \vdots & \vdots \\ \mathbf{u}_{T_i-1} & \mathbf{u}_{T_i-1-1} \end{pmatrix} = \begin{pmatrix} \mathbf{u}_0^{\mathrm{node}_0} & \mathbf{u}_0^{\mathrm{node}_1} \\ \vdots & \vdots \\ \mathbf{u}_{T_i-1}^{\mathrm{node}_0} & \mathbf{u}_{T_i-1}^{\mathrm{node}_1} \end{pmatrix} \cdot \begin{pmatrix} \frac{r_1}{r_1-r_0} & \frac{-1}{r_1-r_0} \\ \frac{-r_0}{r_1-r_0} & \frac{1}{r_1-r_0} \end{pmatrix}.
$$

It follows that

$$
\mathbf{A}_{T_i} \cdot \begin{pmatrix} \mathbf{u}_0 & \mathbf{u}_{t+1} \\ \vdots & \vdots \\ \mathbf{u}_{T_i-1} & \mathbf{u}_{T_i-1-1} \end{pmatrix} = \begin{pmatrix} -\mathbf{x}_0^{(\mathrm{node}_\epsilon)} & -\mathbf{A} \cdot \mathbf{u}_t^{(\mathrm{node}_\epsilon)} \\ 0 & 0 \\ \vdots & \vdots \\ 0 & 0 \\ -\mathbf{G} \cdot \mathbf{u}_{T_i}^{(\mathrm{node}_\epsilon)} & \mathbf{x}_{T_i-1}^{(\mathrm{node}_\epsilon)} \end{pmatrix} \bmod q,
$$

or equivalently

$$
\mathbf{A}_{T_i-1} \cdot \begin{pmatrix} \mathbf{u}_0 \\ \vdots \\ \mathbf{u}_{T_i-1-1} \end{pmatrix} = \begin{pmatrix} -\mathbf{x}_0^{(\mathrm{node}_\epsilon)} \\ 0 \\ \vdots \\ 0 \\ \mathbf{x}_{T_i-1}^{(\mathrm{node}_\epsilon)} \end{pmatrix} \bmod q,
$$

and $\|(\mathbf{u}_0, \ldots, \mathbf{u}_{T-1})\| \leq (2\,\gamma_{\mathcal{R}})^{2\mu-i+1} \cdot \beta$, where the inequality is due to Lemma 3. By recursion, $\mathcal{E}$ extracts at the root node a vector $(\mathbf{u}_0, \ldots, \mathbf{u}_{T-1})$ satisfying

$$
\mathbf{A}_T \begin{pmatrix} \mathbf{u}_0 \\ \vdots \\ \mathbf{u}_{T-1} \end{pmatrix} = \begin{pmatrix} -\mathbf{x}_0 \\ 0 \\ \vdots \\ 0 \\ \mathbf{x}_T \end{pmatrix} \bmod q, \quad \left\| \begin{pmatrix} \mathbf{u}_0 \\ \vdots \\ \mathbf{u}_{T-1} \end{pmatrix} \right\| \leq (2\,\gamma_{\mathcal{R}})^{2\mu} \beta < (2\,\gamma_{\mathcal{R}})^{2\log T} \beta
$$

as desired.   □

Finally, we are ready to show that the construction is sound, which follows by invoking the extractor of the above protocol, which returns a valid computation transcript. Since the extractor runs in time sublinear in T, this contradicts the sequentiality of our function.

Theorem 8 (Soundness). *There exists* $p(\lambda) \in \mathrm{poly}(\lambda)$ *such that if* $\mathsf{SIS}_{\mathcal{R},n,m,q,\beta}$ *and the* $\sigma'(\lambda, T)$-*SIS-sequentiality assumption hold, then the PoSW constructed in Fig. 1 is* $\sigma(\lambda, T)$-*sequentially sound, where* $\sigma'(\lambda, T) = \sigma(\lambda, T) \cdot p(\lambda)$.

Proof (Sketch). The theorem follows from Lemma 4 and standard techniques. We provide a proof sketch. Since the above folding argument is $(2, 2, \ldots, 2)$-special-sound with a challenge set size of $\Omega(\lambda)$, it follows from [5] that the $(\lambda / \log \lambda)$-fold parallel repetition of it is knowledge-sound with negligible knowledge error. Furthermore, we observe that the extractor constructed in [5] is depth-preserving, i.e. there exists a polynomial $p(\lambda) \in \mathsf{poly}(\lambda)$ such that the knowledge extractor $\mathcal{E}_\mathcal{A}$ has depth $\mathsf{Depth}(\mathcal{E}_\mathcal{A}) \leq p(\lambda) \cdot \mathsf{Depth}(\mathcal{A})$. Suppose there exists a polynomial-size adversary $\mathcal{A}$ which breaks the $\sigma(\lambda, T)$-sequentially-soundness of the PoSW, then the above shows that $\mathcal{E}_\mathcal{A}$ is a polynomial-size adversary which breaks the $\sigma'(\lambda, T)$-SIS-sequentiality assumption. $\qquad\square$

In Appendix A, we discuss challenges of formally proving the security of our PoSW against quantum adversaries.

Acknowledgments. The authors wish to thank Andrej Bogdanov and Alon Rosen for insightful discussions and for comments on an earlier draft of this work. The authors are also grateful to the anonymous reviewers for suggesting the preprocessing attack described in Sect. 3.2.

G.M. is partially funded by the German Federal Ministry of Education and Research (BMBF) in the course of the 6GEM research hub under grant number 16KISK038 and by the Deutsche Forschungsgemeinschaft (DFG, German Research Foundation) under Germany's Excellence Strategy - EXC 2092 CASA - 390781972.

A   On Post-Quantum Security of Our PoSW

Formally showing that our PoSW is secure against quantum adversaries requires more work than what is presented in Sect. 4.2. A recent work [27] shows that protocols that satisfy special soundness and a particular notion of binding for the hash function (called *collapsing*) can be proven secure against quantum adversary (when sequentially repeated). Unfortunately, their result is not sufficient for our purposes, since the depth of the extractor scales with the size of the extraction tree, which in particular means that it is polynomial in T. Thus, we cannot hope to use this extractor to derive a contradiction against the sequentiality of our function. We leave proving a precise statement in the quantum settings as a fascinating open question. As a first step towards this, in the following we show that the hash function used at each round of our protocol is collapsing. Here we assume familiarity with the basics of quantum information and we refer the reader to [27] for precise definitions of the notions used here. First we recall below the notion of collapsing for hash functions [35].

Definition 3 (Collapsing). *Let* H *be a (keyed) hash function. We say that* H *is collapsing if for any efficient (quantum) adversary* $\mathcal{A}$

$$\left| \Pr\!\left[\mathsf{Collapsing}_\mathcal{A}^0(1^\lambda) = 1\right] - \Pr\!\left[\mathsf{Collapsing}_\mathcal{A}^1(1^\lambda) = 1\right] \right| \leq \mathsf{negl}(\lambda),$$

where the experiment $\mathsf{Collapsing}_\mathcal{A}^b$ *is defined as follows:*

$\underline{\mathsf{Collapsing}^b_{\mathcal{A}}(1^\lambda)}$:

- Sample a key k and send it over to $\mathcal{A}$.
- $\mathcal{A}$ replies with a classical bitstring y and a quantum state on a register $\mathcal{X}$.
- Let $U_{k,y}$ be the unitary that acts on $\mathcal{X}$ and a fresh ancilla, and CNOTs into the fresh ancilla the bit that determines whether the output of $\mathsf{H}_k(\cdot)$ equals y and the input belongs to the appropriate domain. Apply $U_{k,y}$, measure the ancilla, and apply $U^\dagger_{k,y}$.
- If the output of the measurement is 0, then abort the experiment. Else proceed.
- If $b = 0$ do nothing.
- If $b = 1$ measure the register $\mathcal{X}$ in the computational basis, discard the result.
- Return to $\mathcal{A}$ all registers and output whichever bit $\mathcal{A}$ outputs.

In [27] it is shown that the SIS-based hash function is collapsing, assuming the hardness of the LWE problem.

Lemma 5 ([27]). *If the LWE problem is hard, then the function $\mathsf{H}_{\mathbf{A}}$ defined as*

$$\mathsf{H}_{\mathbf{A}}(\mathbf{u}) = \mathbf{A} \cdot \mathbf{u} \bmod q$$

where $\mathbf{A} \leftarrow_{\$} \mathcal{R}_q^{n \times m}$, is collapsing.

We are now ready to prove that the hash function used in our folding argument is collapsing.

Lemma 6 (Collapsing). *Let t be a polynomial in the security parameter. If the LWE problem is hard, then the function $\mathsf{H}_{\mathbf{A}}$ defined as*

$$\mathsf{H}_{\mathbf{A}}(\mathbf{u}) = \underbrace{\begin{pmatrix} \mathbf{G} & & & & \\ \mathbf{A} & \mathbf{G} & & & \\ & \mathbf{A} & \ddots & & \\ & & \ddots & \mathbf{G} & \\ & & & \mathbf{A} & \end{pmatrix}}_{t \ columns} \cdot \mathbf{u} \bmod q$$

where $\mathbf{A} \leftarrow_{\$} \mathcal{R}_q^{n \times m}$, is collapsing.

Proof. The proof follows by a standard hybrid argument. Let us split the input $\mathbf{u} \in \mathcal{R}_p^{tm}$ in t blocks $(\mathbf{u}_1, \ldots, \mathbf{u}_t)$ where $\mathbf{u}_i \in \mathcal{R}_p^m$ and let $\mathcal{X}_1 \otimes \cdots \otimes \mathcal{X}_t$ be the corresponding registers. In the last hybrid, the challenger does not measure any of the registers (this corresponds to $\mathsf{Collapsing}^1_{\mathcal{A}}$). The i-th hybrid is defined as the previous one, except that the challenger only measures registers $\mathcal{X}_1 \otimes \cdots \otimes \mathcal{X}_i$ in the computational basis. Note that the 0-th hybrid corresponds to the experiment $\mathsf{Collapsing}^0_{\mathcal{A}}$. What is left to be shown is that consequent hybrids are computationally indistinguishable.

For hybrids t and $t-1$, indistinguishability follows directly from the collapsing property of $\mathbf{A}$ (Lemma 5). For other hybrids, it suffices to observe that the i-th block of the output $\mathbf{y} = (\mathbf{y}_1, \ldots, \mathbf{y}_t)$ is computed as:

$$\mathbf{y}_i = \mathbf{A} \cdot \mathbf{u}_i + \mathbf{G} \cdot \mathbf{u}_{i+1} \bmod q$$

$$\mathbf{y}_i - \mathbf{G} \cdot \mathbf{u}_{i+1} = \mathbf{A} \cdot \mathbf{u}_i \bmod q$$

and therefore indistinguishability follows one again by Lemma 5, since $\mathbf{u}_{i+1}$ can be computed as the result of the measurement on register $\mathcal{X}_{i+1}$ (which we assume it is measured).   □

References

1. VDF Alliance (2019). https://www.vdfalliance.org. Accessed June 2023
2. Ajtai, M.: Generating hard instances of lattice problems (extended abstract). In: 28th ACM STOC, pp. 99–108. ACM Press, May 1996. https://doi.org/10.1145/237814.237838
3. Albrecht, M.R., Lai, R.W.F.: Subtractive sets over cyclotomic rings. In: Malkin, T., Peikert, C. (eds.) CRYPTO 2021. LNCS, vol. 12826, pp. 519–548. Springer, Cham (2021). https://doi.org/10.1007/978-3-030-84245-1_18
4. Attema, T., Cramer, R., Kohl, L.: A compressed $\sum$-protocol theory for lattices. In: Malkin, T., Peikert, C. (eds.) CRYPTO 2021. LNCS, vol. 12826, pp. 549–579. Springer, Cham (2021). https://doi.org/10.1007/978-3-030-84245-1_19
5. Attema, T., Fehr, S.: Parallel repetition of $(k\_1, \ldots, k\_\mu)$-special-sound multi-round interactive proofs. In: Dodis, Y., Shrimpton, T. (eds.) CRYPTO 2022, Part I. LNCS, vol. 13507, pp. 415–443. Springer, Heidelberg (2022). https://doi.org/10.1007/978-3-031-15802-5_15
6. Attema, T., Fehr, S., Klooß, M.: Fiat-shamir transformation of multi-round interactive proofs. In: Kiltz, E., Vaikuntanathan, V. (eds.) TCC 2022, Part I. LNCS, vol. 13747, pp. 113–142. Springer, Heidelberg (2022). https://doi.org/10.1007/978-3-031-22318-1_5
7. Ben-Sasson, E., Chiesa, A., Goldberg, L., Gur, T., Riabzev, M., Spooner, N.: Linear-size constant-query IOPs for delegating computation. In: Hofheinz, D., Rosen, A. (eds.) TCC 2019. LNCS, vol. 11892, pp. 494–521. Springer, Cham (2019). https://doi.org/10.1007/978-3-030-36033-7_19
8. Bitansky, N., et al.: PPAD is as hard as LWE and iterated squaring. In: Kiltz, E., Vaikuntanathan, V. (eds.) TCC 2022, Part II. LNCS, vol. 13748, pp. 593–622. Springer, Heidelberg (2022). https://doi.org/10.1007/978-3-031-22365-5_21
9. Bitansky, N., Goldwasser, S., Jain, A., Paneth, O., Vaikuntanathan, V., Waters, B.: Time-lock puzzles from randomized encodings. In: Sudan, M. (ed.) ITCS 2016, pp. 345–356. ACM (2016). https://doi.org/10.1145/2840728.2840745
10. Boneh, D., Bonneau, J., Bünz, B., Fisch, B.: Verifiable delay functions. In: Shacham, H., Boldyreva, A. (eds.) CRYPTO 2018, Part I. LNCS, vol. 10991, pp. 757–788. Springer, Heidelberg (2018). https://doi.org/10.1007/978-3-319-96884-1_25
11. Boneh, D., Naor, M.: Timed commitments. In: Bellare, M. (ed.) CRYPTO 2000. LNCS, vol. 1880, pp. 236–254. Springer, Heidelberg (2000). https://doi.org/10.1007/3-540-44598-6_15
12. Bootle, J., Lyubashevsky, V., Nguyen, N.K., Seiler, G.: A non-PCP approach to succinct quantum-safe zero-knowledge. In: Micciancio, D., Ristenpart, T. (eds.) CRYPTO 2020, Part II. LNCS, vol. 12171, pp. 441–469. Springer, Heidelberg (2020). https://doi.org/10.1007/978-3-030-56880-1_16
13. Boudgoust, K., Jeudy, C., Roux-Langlois, A., Wen, W.: Towards classical hardness of module-LWE: the linear rank case. In: Moriai, S., Wang, H. (eds.) ASIACRYPT 2020, Part II. LNCS, vol. 12492, pp. 289–317. Springer, Heidelberg (2020). https://doi.org/10.1007/978-3-030-64834-3_10

14. Burdges, J., De Feo, L.: Delay encryption. In: Canteaut, A., Standaert, F.X. (eds.) EUROCRYPT 2021, Part I. LNCS, vol. 12696, pp. 302–326. Springer, Heidelberg (2021). https://doi.org/10.1007/978-3-030-77870-5_11

15. Chávez-Saab, J., Rodríguez-Henríquez, F., Tibouchi, M.: Verifiable isogeny walks: towards an isogeny-based postquantum VDF. In: AlTawy, R., Hülsing, A. (eds.) SAC 2021. LNCS, vol. 13203, pp. 441–460. Springer, Heidelberg (2022). https://doi.org/10.1007/978-3-030-99277-4_21

16. Chen, Y., Lombardi, A., Ma, F., Quach, W.: Does Fiat-Shamir require a cryptographic hash function? In: Malkin, T., Peikert, C. (eds.) CRYPTO 2021, Virtual Event, Part IV. LNCS, vol. 12828, pp. 334–363. Springer, Heidelberg (2021). https://doi.org/10.1007/978-3-030-84259-8_12

17. Chiesa, A., Manohar, P., Spooner, N.: Succinct arguments in the quantum random oracle model. In: Hofheinz, D., Rosen, A. (eds.) TCC 2019, Part II. LNCS, vol. 11892, pp. 1–29. Springer, Heidelberg (2019). https://doi.org/10.1007/978-3-030-36033-7_1

18. Cini, V., Lai, R.W.F., Malavolta, G.: Lattice-based succinct arguments from vanishing polynomials. In: CRYPTO 2023, vol. 14082, pp. 72–105. Springer, Hidelberg (2023)

19. Cohen, B., Pietrzak, K.: Simple proofs of sequential work. In: Nielsen, J.B., Rijmen, V. (eds.) EUROCRYPT 2018, Part II. LNCS, vol. 10821, pp. 451–467. Springer, Heidelberg (2018). https://doi.org/10.1007/978-3-319-78375-8_15

20. De Feo, L., Masson, S., Petit, C., Sanso, A.: Verifiable delay functions from supersingular isogenies and pairings. In: Galbraith, S.D., Moriai, S. (eds.) ASIACRYPT 2019, Part I. LNCS, vol. 11921, pp. 248–277. Springer, Heidelberg (2019). https://doi.org/10.1007/978-3-030-34578-5_10

21. Döttling, N., Garg, S., Malavolta, G., Vasudevan, P.N.: Tight verifiable delay functions. In: Galdi, C., Kolesnikov, V. (eds.) SCN 20. LNCS, vol. 12238, pp. 65–84. Springer, Heidelberg (2020). https://doi.org/10.1007/978-3-030-57990-6_4

22. Döttling, N., Lai, R.W.F., Malavolta, G.: Incremental proofs of sequential work. In: Ishai, Y., Rijmen, V. (eds.) EUROCRYPT 2019, Part II. LNCS, vol. 11477, pp. 292–323. Springer, Heidelberg (2019). https://doi.org/10.1007/978-3-030-17656-3_11

23. Fiat, A., Shamir, A.: How to prove yourself: practical solutions to identification and signature problems. In: Odlyzko, A.M. (ed.) CRYPTO'86. LNCS, vol. 263, pp. 186–194. Springer, Heidelberg (1987). https://doi.org/10.1007/3-540-47721-7_12

24. Gentry, C., Sahai, A., Waters, B.: Homomorphic encryption from learning with errors: conceptually-simpler, asymptotically-faster, attribute-based. In: Canetti, R., Garay, J.A. (eds.) CRYPTO 2013, Part I. LNCS, vol. 8042, pp. 75–92. Springer, Heidelberg (2013). https://doi.org/10.1007/978-3-642-40041-4_5

25. Goldreich, O., Goldwasser, S., Halevi, S.: Collision-free hashing from lattice problems. Cryptology ePrint Archive, Report 1996/009 (1996). https://eprint.iacr.org/1996/009

26. Jaques, S., Montgomery, H., Rosie, R., Roy, A.: Time-release cryptography from minimal circuit assumptions. In: Adhikari, A., Küsters, R., Preneel, B. (eds.) INDOCRYPT 2021. LNCS, vol. 13143, pp. 584–606. Springer, Cham (2021). https://doi.org/10.1007/978-3-030-92518-5_26

27. Lai, R.W.F., Malavolta, G., Spooner, N.: Quantum rewinding for many-round protocols. In: Kiltz, E., Vaikuntanathan, V. (eds.) TCC 2022, Part I. LNCS, vol. 13747, pp. 80–109. Springer, Heidelberg (2022). https://doi.org/10.1007/978-3-031-22318-1_4

28. Lin, H., Pass, R., Soni, P.: Two-round and non-interactive concurrent non-malleable commitments from time-lock puzzles. In: Umans, C. (ed.) 58th FOCS, pp. 576–587. IEEE Computer Society Press, October 2017. https://doi.org/10.1109/FOCS.2017. 59

29. Lyubashevsky, V., Peikert, C., Regev, O.: On ideal lattices and learning with errors over rings. In: Gilbert, H. (ed.) EUROCRYPT 2010. LNCS, vol. 6110, pp. 1–23. Springer, Heidelberg (2010). https://doi.org/10.1007/978-3-642-13190-5_1

30. Mahmoody, M., Moran, T., Vadhan, S.P.: Publicly verifiable proofs of sequential work. In: Kleinberg, R.D. (ed.) ITCS 2013. pp. 373–388. ACM (2013). https://doi. org/10.1145/2422436.2422479

31. Malavolta, G., Thyagarajan, S.A.K.: Homomorphic time-lock puzzles and applications. In: Boldyreva, A., Micciancio, D. (eds.) CRYPTO 2019, Part I. LNCS, vol. 11692, pp. 620–649. Springer, Heidelberg (2019). https://doi.org/10.1007/978-3-030-26948-7_22

32. Pietrzak, K.: Simple verifiable delay functions. In: Blum, A. (ed.) ITCS 2019. LIPIcs, vol. 124, pp. 60:1–60:15, January 2019. https://doi.org/10.4230/LIPIcs. ITCS.2019.60

33. Regev, O.: On lattices, learning with errors, random linear codes, and cryptography. In: Gabow, H.N., Fagin, R. (eds.) 37th ACM STOC, pp. 84–93. ACM Press, May 2005. https://doi.org/10.1145/1060590.1060603

34. Rivest, R.L., Shamir, A., Wagner, D.A.: Time-lock puzzles and timed-release crypto. Technical report (1996)

35. Unruh, D.: Computationally binding quantum commitments. In: Fischlin, M., Coron, J.S. (eds.) EUROCRYPT 2016, Part II. LNCS, vol. 9666, pp. 497–527. Springer, Heidelberg (2016). https://doi.org/10.1007/978-3-662-49896-5_18

36. Valiant, P.: Incrementally verifiable computation or proofs of knowledge imply time/space efficiency. In: Canetti, R. (ed.) TCC 2008. LNCS, vol. 4948, pp. 1–18. Springer, Heidelberg (2008). https://doi.org/10.1007/978-3-540-78524-8_1

A Lower Bound for Proving Hardness
of Learning with Rounding
with Polynomial Modulus

Parker Newton[✉] and Silas Richelson

University of California, Riverside, Riverside, CA 92521, USA
pnewt001@ucr.edu, silas@cs.ucr.edu

Abstract. Regev's Learning with Errors (LWE) problem (STOC 2005) is
a fundamental hardness assumption for modern cryptography. The Learning with Rounding (LWR) Problem was put forth by Banerjee, Peikert and
Rosen (Eurocrypt 2012) as an alternative to LWE, for use in cryptographic
situations which require determinism. The only method we currently have
for proving hardness of LWR is the so-called "rounding reduction" which
is a specific reduction from an analogous LWE problem. This reduction
works whenever the LWE error is small relative to the noise introduced by
rounding, but it fails otherwise. For this reason, all prior work on establishing hardness of LWR forces the LWE error to be small, either by setting
other parameters extremely large (which hurts performance), or by limit-
ing the number of LWR samples seen by the adversary (which rules out certain applications). Hardness of LWR is poorly understood when the LWE
modulus (q) is polynomial and when the number of LWE samples (m) seen
by the adversary is an unbounded polynomial. This range of parameters is
the most relevant for practical implementations, so the lack of a hardness
proof in this situation is not ideal.

In this work, we identify an obstacle for proving the hardness of LWR
from LWE in the above framework when q is polynomial and m is an
unbounded polynomial. Specifically, we show that any "pointwise" reduction from LWE to LWR (*i.e.*, any reduction which maps LWE samples independently to LWR samples) admits an efficient algorithm which
directly solves LWE (without the use of an LWR solver). Consequently,
LWE cannot be reduced to LWR in our pointwise reduction model with
our setting of q and m, unless LWE is easy. Our model of a pointwise
reduction from LWE to LWR captures all prior reductions from LWE to
LWR except the rejection sampling reduction of Bogdanov *et al.* (TCC
2016); while their reduction still operates in a pointwise manner, it can
reject an LWE sample instead of mapping it to an LWR sample. However
we conjecture that our result still holds in this setting.

Our argument proceeds roughly as follows. First, we show that any
pointwise reduction from LWE to LWR must have good agreement with
some affine map. Then, we use the affine agreement of a pointwise
reduction together with a type of Goldreich-Levin "prediction-implies-
inversion" argument to extract the LWE secret from LWE input samples.
Both components may be of independent interest.

Work completed prior to one of the co-authors joining Amazon.

H. Handschuh and A. Lysyanskaya (Eds.): CRYPTO 2023, LNCS 14085, pp. 805–835, 2023.
https://doi.org/10.1007/978-3-031-38554-4_26

Keywords: Learning with errors · Learning with rounding · Lattice problems · Lower bounds

1   Introduction

Regev's learning with errors (LWE) problem [19] is fundamental for modern cryptography due to its versatility and strong security guarantees. LWE asks an algorithm to solve a random noisy linear system of equations mod q: given integers n, q, m, an "error" distribution χ on $\mathbb{Z}_q$ and a uniform $\mathbf{s} \sim \mathbb{Z}_q^n$, recover $\mathbf{s}$ given samples

$$\{(\mathbf{a}_i, b_i = \langle \mathbf{a}_i, \mathbf{s} \rangle + e_i)\} \subset (\mathbb{Z}_q^n \times \mathbb{Z}_q)^m, \tag{1}$$

where the $\mathbf{a}_i$ are drawn uniformly from $\mathbb{Z}_q^n$ and the e_i are drawn according to χ. It is known that when q is sufficiently large compared to n, there are error distributions which make solving LWE efficiently given any number of samples as hard as solving computational problems on lattices in the worst case [9,17, 19]; such problems are conjectured to be hard even for quantum computers. In addition to the strong hardness guarantees, LWE has proven to be extremely useful for cryptography. Since its introduction, an immense research effort has established LWE-based constructions for most known cryptographic primitives (*e.g.*, [3,8,12,13,16,18] and many, many more).

The randomness inherent to the LWE problem (*i.e.*, the randomness used to draw the $e_i \sim \chi$) precludes straightforward constructions of certain cryptographic primitives which require determinism, such as PRFs. Banarjee, Peikert and Rosen [6] introduced the learning with rounding (LWR) problem in order to overcome this obstacle. LWR asks an algorithm to solve a random linear system with "deterministic noise": given n, p, q, m with $p < q$ and a uniform $\mathbf{s} \sim \mathbb{Z}_q^n$, recover $\mathbf{s}$ from

$$\{(\mathbf{a}_i, b_i = \lfloor \langle \mathbf{a}_i, \mathbf{s} \rangle \rceil_p)\} \subset (\mathbb{Z}_q^n \times \mathbb{Z}_p)^m, \tag{2}$$

where each $\mathbf{a}_i \sim \mathbb{Z}_q^n$ and where $\lfloor \cdot \rceil_p : \mathbb{Z}_q \to \mathbb{Z}_p$ is the function which, given $x \in \mathbb{Z}_q$, outputs the nearest integer to px/q. Since its introduction, LWR has been used in numerous works to give cryptographic constructions where determinism is mandatory (*e.g.*, [5,6,10], and more).

Hardness of LWR is established via the following reduction from LWE: given an LWE sample $(\mathbf{a}, b) \in \mathbb{Z}_q^n \times \mathbb{Z}_q$, round the second value and output $(\mathbf{a}, \lfloor b \rceil_p) \in \mathbb{Z}_q^n \times \mathbb{Z}_p$. In [6], it is shown that this reduction is valid whenever $q/p = n^{\omega(1)}$ (n the security parameter), and so establishes hardness of LWR for this parameter regime. In practice we would like to be able to use small q as this lends itself better to efficient implementations. So establishing hardness for LWR in the "polynomial modulus" setting, where $q = \mathsf{poly}(n)$, was an important open problem left by [6]. This direction was pursued in the follow-up works [1,2,7] where it is shown that if the number of LWR samples given to the solver (*i.e.*, m) is bounded, then the correctness proof of the above reduction goes through and one can establish hardness of LWR with polynomial modulus in the "bounded sample" setting. This is good enough for some cryptographic applications [2], but not for all, *e.g.*, PRFs.

The problem with the above reduction when q/p is small is that the error in the LWE sample might cause the rounding function to make a mistake. The reason for this is that the "threshold points" of the rounding function[1] $\lfloor \cdot \rceil_p$: $\mathbb{Z}_q \to \mathbb{Z}_p$ have density p/q in $\mathbb{Z}_q$, and so when $q/p \ll m$, some of the $\mathbf{a}_i$'s chosen will be such that their secret inner product $\langle \mathbf{a}_i, \mathbf{s} \rangle$ is close to a threshold point. Whenever this occurs, the reduction will make an error if $\langle \mathbf{a}_i, \mathbf{s} \rangle + e_i$ is on the opposite side of the threshold from $\langle \mathbf{a}_i, \mathbf{s} \rangle$. Prior work handles this issue by forcing q/p to be large relative to m (either by setting q/p to be superpolynomial, or by bounding m).

Getting a version of the above reduction to yield a hardness proof for LWR in the case when m is large compared to q/p is challenging because it requires dealing with situations where the LWE error creates a rounding problem. By definition, a reduction from LWE to LWR is an oracle algorithm which solves LWE when instantiated with access to any LWR solver, *including the pathological LWR solver who aborts whenever it sees a rounding error*. Specifically, suppose S is an algorithm which takes m LWR samples $\{(\mathbf{a}_i, b_i')\} \subset \mathbb{Z}_q \times \mathbb{Z}_p$, (somehow) recovers the hidden secret $\mathbf{s}$, then scans the m samples to make sure that $b_i' = \lfloor \langle \mathbf{a}_i, \mathbf{s} \rangle \rceil_p$ for all i, aborting if it finds an error, outputting $\mathbf{s}$ otherwise. It is clear that S will solve LWR when it is given true LWR samples, however in order for the reduction to make use of S's solving power to solve LWE, it must produce m LWR samples without making an error. This is the core challenge in proving hardness of LWR with polynomial modulus and unbounded samples.

1.1 Our Contribution

In this work we convert the above difficulty into a lower bound for proving hardness of LWR with polynomial modulus and an unbounded number of samples via reductions from LWE. Our barrier applies to any "pointwise" reduction from LWE to LWR, *i.e.*, any function $f : \mathbb{Z}_q^n \times \mathbb{Z}_q \to \mathbb{Z}_q^n \times \mathbb{Z}_p$. This includes and broadly extends the reduction $(\mathbf{a}, b) \mapsto (\mathbf{a}, \lfloor b \rceil_p)$ mentioned above. The starting observation for our work is that any pointwise reduction f which works in this parameter regime must implicitly be able to handle the "problematic" LWE pairs which are close to a rounding threshold. What we prove is essentially that f's understanding of how to handle these threshold samples can be *extracted* in the form of knowledge about the LWE secret. Our main theorem is the following.

Theorem 1 (Informal). *Let $n, q, p \in \mathbb{N}$ be integers such that $q = \mathsf{poly}(n)$ is prime and such that $q^{2/3+c} < p < q$ for a small constant $c > 0$. Let χ be an error distribution on $\mathbb{Z}_q$. Suppose an efficient function $f : \mathbb{Z}_q^n \times \mathbb{Z}_q \to \mathbb{Z}_q^n \times \mathbb{Z}_p$ is a pointwise reduction from $\mathsf{LWE}_{n,q,\chi}$ to $\mathsf{LWR}_{n,q,p}$. Then f can be used to design an efficient algorithm which solves $\mathsf{LWE}_{n,q,\chi}$.*

---

[1] By threshold points we mean the half integer multiples of q/p where the rounding function switches from rounding to adjacent values in $\mathbb{Z}_p$.

The Hypotheses of our Theorem. We view the requirements that q be prime and especially that $q^{2/3+c} < p$ as shortcomings of our work, and we believe it should be possible to improve our result to remove these extra hypotheses. Our proof requires q to be prime so that linear algebra works on the set $\mathbb{Z}_q^n$. The lower bound on p comes from one place in the proof where we use two LWE samples $(\mathbf{a}_0, b_0), (\mathbf{a}_1, b_1) \in \mathbb{Z}_q^n \times \mathbb{Z}_q$ to generate three LWR samples:

$$(\mathbf{a}_0', b_0') = f(\mathbf{a}_0, b_0); \; (\mathbf{a}_1', b_1') = f(\mathbf{a}_1, b_1); \; (\mathbf{a}_2', b_2') = f(\mathbf{a}_0 + \mathbf{a}_1, b_0 + b_1) \in \mathbb{Z}_q^n \times \mathbb{Z}_p,$$

and we require essentially that the three output values $b_0', b_1', b_2' \in \mathbb{Z}_p$ contain more information than the input values $b_0, b_1 \in \mathbb{Z}_q$. We suspect that a different proof technique could be used to improve the lower bound required of p or remove it altogether. We note however that our result does not require the amount of LWR "noise" (*i.e.*, q/p) to be small relative to the amount of LWE noise. In particular, our theorem applies in situations where q/p is much larger than the standard deviation of the discrete Gaussian used for the LWE noise.

Aborting Pointwise Reductions. Another way to relax the hypotheses of our main theorem would be to allow f to abort. In this case, the reduction works by applying the aborting pointwise function $f : \mathbb{Z}_q^n \times \mathbb{Z}_q \to (\mathbb{Z}_q^n \times \mathbb{Z}_p) \cup \{\bot\}$ to all LWE samples, and then invoking the LWR solver on all "non-bot" outputs. Such "aborting pointwise reductions" were considered in prior work [7] as a way to prove hardness of LWR in the polynomial modulus setting assuming hardness of LWE with uniform errors (uLWE). The key intuition behind the proof of our main theorem is that it is impossible for the reduction to correctly produce the LWR distribution given LWE samples because doing this would require converting the LWE error into the "rectangular" LWR error. In uLWE, the errors are already rectangular and the only difference between uLWE and LWR is that in uLWE the rectangles are centered around $\langle \mathbf{a}, \mathbf{s} \rangle$ while in LWR they are centered around the rounding points. Bogdanov *et al.* [7] showed that it is possible to fix this "rectangle center discrepancy" using rejection sampling and obtained an aborting pointwise reduction from uLWE to LWR. An interesting question is: *how much power do we get by allowing the reduction to abort?* Does aborting allow transforming Gaussian LWE errors to the rectangular LWR errors? Or does aborting *only* allow us to reposition the centers of the error distribution, *and not* convert non-rectangular errors to rectangular errors? We tend to believe that aborting reductions can only translate the errors, and cannot convert non-rectangular errors into rectangular errors. However, several parts of our proof break down if we allow the function to abort. We state the following conjecture.

Conjecture 1. *Let $n, p, q \in \mathbb{N}$ be integers such that such that $q = \mathsf{poly}(n)$ is prime and $2 \leq p < q$. Let χ be a discrete Gaussian distribution on $\mathbb{Z}_q$. Suppose an efficient function $f : \mathbb{Z}_q^n \times \mathbb{Z}_q \to (\mathbb{Z}_q^n \times \mathbb{Z}_p) \cup \{\bot\}$ is part of an aborting pointwise reduction from $\mathsf{LWE}_{n,q,\chi}$ to $\mathsf{LWR}_{n,q,p}$. Then f can be used to build an efficient algorithm $\mathcal{B}$ which solves $\mathsf{LWE}_{n,q,\chi}$.*

Compared to Theorem 1, Conjecture 1 removes the hypothesis that $q^{2/3+c} < p$ and allows f to abort, though focuses in on the case when χ is a discrete Gaussian. We tend to believe Conjecture 1 is true for any non-rectangular error distribution χ, in which case it combines with (a slight extension of) Theorem 5 of [7] to give a dichotomy: if $q = \mathsf{poly}(n)$ is prime and if there is an aborting pointwise reduction from $\mathsf{LWE}_{n,q,\chi}$ to $\mathsf{LWR}_{n,q,p}$ for $2 \le p < q$ then either 1) χ is rectangular; or 2) there is an efficient algorithm which solves $\mathsf{LWE}_{n,q,\chi}$.

Extensions of Our Reduction Model. One can ask whether our reduction holds for other extensions of our reduction model. For example, does our theorem hold for pointwise reductions between problems with different dimensions and moduli (*i.e.*, reductions from $\mathsf{LWE}_{n,q,\chi}$ to $\mathsf{LWR}_{n',q',p'}$)? Furthermore, our notion of pointwise reductions does not allow the reduction to use two or more LWE samples to produce an LWR sample. One might hope that a similar theorem to ours would hold for any "$k-\text{to}-\text{one}$" function $f : \left(\mathbb{Z}_q^n \times \mathbb{Z}_q\right)^k \to \mathbb{Z}_q^n \times \mathbb{Z}_p$ as long as k is small enough to ensure that $\mathbf{s}$ has sufficient entropy given k LWE samples. Note that if k is large enough so that k LWE samples determine $\mathbf{s}$ information theoretically, then one could imagine a function f which takes k LWE samples, (somehow) recovers $\mathbf{s}$, and outputs a single LWR sample with secret $\mathbf{s}$. While it feels like such a function is breaking LWE, it would be hard to prove a theorem like the above since it seems that in order to extract any knowledge about the LWE secret, one would have to solve LWR.

Interpreting Our Result. Our main theorem identifies a barrier to proving the hardness of LWR in certain practical parameter regimes via reductions from LWE. This explains, to some extent, why this problem has remained open for so long. Our result **does not** suggest that LWR is easy. Rather, it speaks to the fact that the current techniques we have available for deriving hardness from worst-case lattice problems are inherently probabilistic. Our work indicates that a reduction from a hard lattice problem to LWR with these parameter settings would be extremely interesting as it would likely contain significant new ideas.

1.2 Technical Overview

We now give a summary of our proof of Theorem 1 which says that a pointwise reduction from LWE to LWR can be used to design an algorithm which solves LWE. The proof consists of three main parts. First, we derive some basic combinatorial structure about the pointwise function which it must satisfy if it is to be part of a reduction. Next, building on this basic structure we show that in fact the pointwise function must very close to an affine function. Finally, we show how to use a pointwise function which has good affine agreement and which is part of a reduction to directly solve LWE.

Notation. Let $n, q, p \in \mathbb{N}$ such that $q = \mathsf{poly}(n)$ is prime, and $q^{2/3+c} < p < q$, for a small constant $c > 0$. Let χ be an error distribution on $\mathbb{Z}_q$. Let $f : \mathbb{Z}_q^n \times \mathbb{Z}_q \to \mathbb{Z}_q^n \times \mathbb{Z}_p$ be part of a pointwise reduction from $\mathsf{LWE}_{n,q,\chi}$ to $\mathsf{LWR}_{n,q,p}$ (formal definition is in Sect. 3). If $\mathbf{s} \in \mathbb{Z}_q^n$, then let $\mathsf{LWE}_\mathbf{s}$ denote the distribution which chooses $\mathbf{a} \sim \mathbb{Z}_q^n, e \sim \chi$, and outputs $(\mathbf{a}, b = \langle \mathbf{a}, \mathbf{s} \rangle + e) \in \mathbb{Z}_q^n \times \mathbb{Z}_q$. Likewise, if $\mathbf{s}' \in \mathbb{Z}_q^n$, then $\mathsf{LWR}_{\mathbf{s}'}$ draws $\mathbf{a}' \sim \mathbb{Z}_q^n$ and outputs $(\mathbf{a}', b' = \lfloor \langle \mathbf{a}', \mathbf{s}' \rangle \rceil_p) \in \mathbb{Z}_q^n \times \mathbb{Z}_p$. We write $(\mathbf{a}', b') \in \mathsf{LWR}_{\mathbf{s}'}$ if $b' = \lfloor \langle \mathbf{a}', \mathbf{s}' \rangle \rceil_p$. Finally, for $m \in \mathbb{N}$, let LWE_m (resp. LWR_m) be the distribution which draws $\mathbf{s} \sim \mathbb{Z}_q^n$ (resp. $\mathbf{s}' \sim \mathbb{Z}_q^n$) and outputs m samples from $\mathsf{LWE}_\mathbf{s}$ (resp. $\mathsf{LWR}_{\mathbf{s}'}$).

Establishing Basic Combinatorial Structure of f. The key observation which allows us to get started imposing structure on f is the following: *all statistics of the LWR distribution and the output distribution of f (given LWE samples as input) must be the same.* Indeed, if there is a statistic which differs between LWR_m and $f(\mathsf{LWE}_m)$, we can conceive of a "pathological LWR solver" which draws enough samples to approximate the statistic, aborting if it decides it is being fed with mapped LWE samples, solving if it decides it is being fed with true LWR samples.

For example, for all $\mathbf{s}' \in \mathbb{Z}_q^n$, clearly, $\Pr_{(\mathbf{a}', b') \sim \mathsf{LWR}_{\mathbf{s}'}} \left[(\mathbf{a}', b') \in \mathsf{LWR}_{\mathbf{s}'} \right] = 1$. Thus, if f is a reduction then the following *correctness condition* must hold: with non-negligible probability over $\mathbf{s} \sim \mathbb{Z}_q^n$ there must exist some $\mathbf{s}' \in \mathbb{Z}_q^n$ such that

$$\Pr_{(\mathbf{a}, b) \sim \mathsf{LWE}_\mathbf{s}} \left[f(\mathbf{a}, b) \in \mathsf{LWR}_{\mathbf{s}'} \right] = 1 - \mathsf{negl}(n).$$

If not, then consider the "pathological LWR solver" S which, given $(\mathbf{a}_1', b_1'), \ldots,$ $(\mathbf{a}_m', b_m') \in \mathbb{Z}_q^n \times \mathbb{Z}_p$ statistically recovers $\mathbf{s}' \in \mathbb{Z}_q^n$ such that $(\mathbf{a}_i', b_i') \in \mathsf{LWR}_{\mathbf{s}'}$ for all $i = 1, \ldots, m$ and outputs $\mathbf{s}'$ (outputting $\perp$ if no such $\mathbf{s}' \in \mathbb{Z}_q^n$ exists). Note, S does indeed solve LWR when fed with samples from LWR_m, however S outputs $\perp$ with high probability when fed with samples from $f(\mathsf{LWE}_m)$. This means that f is not a reduction since it is unable to make use of S's LWR solving power. The fact that f induces a mapping on secrets $\mathbf{s} \mapsto \mathbf{s}'$ (meaning that $f(\mathbf{a}, b) \in \mathsf{LWR}_{\mathbf{s}'}$ holds with high probability over $(\mathbf{a}, b) \sim \mathsf{LWE}_\mathbf{s}$) turns out to be immensely useful, as we will already see throughout the remainder of this overview. In Sect. 4, we use analogous "pathological solver" arguments to establish this and several other combinatorial properties of f which will be useful throughout the remainder of the paper.

Establishing High Affine Agreement of f. After establishing some basic statistics of f, the technical core of our paper involves proving that f has high agreement with an affine function. More specifically, we algorithmically recover a matrix $\mathbf{H} \in \mathbb{Z}_q^{n \times n}$ of rank $n - \mathcal{O}(1)$ and a constant dimensional vector space $\mathbf{V} \subset \mathbb{Z}_q^n$ such that

$$\Pr_{(\mathbf{a}, b) \sim \mathbb{Z}_q^n \times \mathbb{Z}_q} \left[\mathbf{a}' \in \mathrm{Span}(\mathbf{Ha}) + \mathbf{V} \right] \geq 1 - \eta,$$

for a small parameter $\eta > 0$, where $(\mathbf{a}', b') = f(\mathbf{a}, b)$. We prove this in two stages. First, we recover $\mathbf{V} \subset \mathbb{Z}_q^n$ of constant dimension such that f passes the following test with high probability.

– Draw $(\mathbf{a}_0, b_0), (\mathbf{a}_1, b_1) \sim \mathbb{Z}_q^n \times \mathbb{Z}_q$.
– Set $(\mathbf{a}_2, b_2) = (\mathbf{a}_0 + \mathbf{a}_1, b_0 + b_1)$ and $(\mathbf{a}'_i, b'_i) = f(\mathbf{a}_i, b_i) \in \mathbb{Z}_q^n \times \mathbb{Z}_p$ for $i = 0, 1, 2$.
– Pass if $\mathbf{a}'_2 \in \mathrm{Span}(\{\mathbf{a}'_0, \mathbf{a}'_1\}) + \mathbf{V}$, fail if not.

The idea here is that when f does not pass this test, it is using three linearly dependent relations about the LWE secret to generate three linearly independent relations about the LWR secret. Either this behavior must be extremely unlikely, or it must be that the map $\mathbf{s} \mapsto \mathbf{s}'$ mapping $\mathbf{s} \in \mathbb{Z}_q^n$ to $\mathbf{s}' \in \mathbb{Z}_q^n$ such that $\Pr_{(\mathbf{a}, b) \sim \mathsf{LWE}_\mathbf{s}}[f(\mathbf{a}, b) \in \mathsf{LWR}_{\mathbf{s}'}] = 1 - \mathsf{negl}(n)$ is many-to-one, which we show is impossible in Sect. 4.

We then prove a property testing-type result showing that any function f which passes this test with high probability must be close to some linear map in the above sense. For this we use techniques from the proof of the following "fundamental theorem of projective geometry" which says that any function $h : \mathbb{Z}_q^n \to \mathbb{Z}_q^n$ which maps lines to lines must be affine.

Proposition 1 (FTPG – [4], Sect. 2.10). *Let q be a prime and $h : \mathbb{Z}_q^n \to \mathbb{Z}_q^n$ be a function such that for any one-dimensional line $\ell \subset \mathbb{Z}_q^n$, the set $h(\ell) := \{f(\mathbf{x}) : \mathbf{x} \in \ell\} \subset \mathbb{Z}_q^n$ is also a line. Then h is affine.*

To see the connection between Proposition 1 and our setting, note that high probability of passing the above test in the simplified setting where $\mathbf{V} = \{0\}$ means that f is mapping 2−planes to 2−planes with high probability. The techniques used in this part of our analysis may be of independent interest.

Solving LWE Using an Affine Reduction. Finally, once we know that f has good affine agreement, we can use f to recover the LWR secret of the output samples using a Goldreich-Levin-type argument. Assume for simplicity that $\mathbf{a}' = \mathbf{H}\mathbf{a}$, rather than $\mathbf{a}' \in \mathrm{Span}(\mathbf{H}\mathbf{a}) + \mathbf{V}$ holds with high probability over $(\mathbf{a}, b) \sim \mathbb{Z}_q^n \times \mathbb{Z}_q$ where $(\mathbf{a}', b') = f(\mathbf{a}, b)$. The key point is that if $(\mathbf{a}', b') \in \mathsf{LWR}_{\mathbf{s}'}$ also holds with high probability over $(\mathbf{a}, b) \sim \mathsf{LWE}_\mathbf{s}$, then

$$b' = \lfloor \langle \mathbf{a}', \mathbf{s}' \rangle \rceil_p = \lfloor \langle \mathbf{a}, \mathbf{H}^\mathbf{t} \mathbf{s}' \rangle \rceil_p,$$

and so b' allows us to predict the inner product $\langle \mathbf{a}, \mathbf{H}^\mathbf{t} \mathbf{s}' \rangle$ with non-negligible advantage over guessing randomly (simply by drawing $x \sim \mathbb{Z}_q$ such that $\lfloor x \rceil_p = b'$). The Goldreich-Levin machinery can then be used to recover $\mathbf{H}^\mathbf{t} \mathbf{s}'$, which will allow recovering $\mathbf{s}'$ with non-negligible probability since $\mathbf{H}$ has nearly full rank.

Putting Everything Together. Suppose when playing the distinguishing game for LWE we are given samples $(\mathbf{a}_1, b_1), \ldots, (\mathbf{a}_m, b_m) \in \mathbb{Z}_q^n \times \mathbb{Z}_q$ which are either drawn from $\mathsf{LWE}_\mathbf{s}$ for a uniform $\mathbf{s} \sim \mathbb{Z}_q^n$, or from $\mathbb{Z}_q^n \times \mathbb{Z}_q$. We can use f to distinguish as follows.

– Let $(\mathbf{a}'_i, b'_i) = f(\mathbf{a}_i, b_i) \in \mathbb{Z}_q^n \times \mathbb{Z}_p$ for $i = 1, \ldots, m$.
– If the LWR secret reconstruction procedure succeeds in obtaining $\mathbf{s}' \in \mathbb{Z}_q^n$ proceed, if not output a random bit.

– Now check whether $(\mathbf{a}'_i, b'_i) \in \mathsf{LWR}_{\mathbf{s}'}$ holds for all $i = 1, \ldots, m$; if so output 0 (corresponding to LWE samples), otherwise output a random bit.

As discussed above, if we have been fed with LWE samples, then the LWR recovery procedure will work with non-negligible probability. On the other hand, a simple statistical argument (proven in Sect. 4) shows that there cannot exist $\mathbf{s}' \in \mathbb{Z}_q^n$ such that f maps uniform samples into $\mathsf{LWE}_{\mathbf{s}'}$ with high probability.

2 Preliminaries

Throughout this work, the integer n will denote the security parameter. We use boldface lower case for vectors, and boldface capitals for matrices (*e.g.*, $\mathbf{v}$ or $\mathbf{M}$). Given a distribution χ on a set X, we write $x \sim \chi$ to indicate that $x \in X$ is drawn according to χ; we write $x \sim X$ as shorthand for $x \sim \mathsf{Unif}(X)$, the uniform distribution on X.

2.1 Learning with Errors/Rounding

Definition 1 (The LWE/LWR Distributions). *Let* $n, q \in \mathbb{N}$, $\mathbf{s} \in \mathbb{Z}_q^n$, *and* χ *be a distribution on* $\mathbb{Z}_q$.

- **The LWE Distribution:** *The* learning with errors distribution $\mathsf{LWE}_{n,q,\mathbf{s},\chi}$ *works as follows:*
  - *draw* $\mathbf{a} \sim \mathbb{Z}_q^n$, $e \sim \chi$, *set* $b = \langle \mathbf{a}, \mathbf{s} \rangle + e$ *and output* $(\mathbf{a}, b) \in \mathbb{Z}_q^n \times \mathbb{Z}_q$.
- **The LWR Distribution:** *If* $p \in \mathbb{N}$ *such that* $2 \le p < q$, *then the* learning with rounding distribution $\mathsf{LWR}_{n,q,\mathbf{s},p}$ *is:*
  - *draw* $\mathbf{a} \sim \mathbb{Z}_q^n$, *set* $b = \lfloor \langle \mathbf{a}, \mathbf{s} \rangle \rceil_p$, *and output* $(\mathbf{a}, b) \in \mathbb{Z}_q^n \times \mathbb{Z}_p$, *where* $\lfloor \cdot \rceil_p$ *maps* $x \in \mathbb{Z}_q$ *to* $x \cdot (p/q)$ *rounded to the nearest integer* (mod p).

Given $m \in \mathbb{N}$, *the distributions* $\mathsf{LWE}_{n,q,m,\chi}$ *(resp.* $\mathsf{LWR}_{n,q,m,p}$) *work by drawing* $\mathbf{s} \sim \mathbb{Z}_q^n$ *and outputting* m *independent samples from* $\mathsf{LWE}_{n,q,\mathbf{s},\chi}$ *(resp.* $\mathsf{LWR}_{n,q,\mathbf{s},p}$).

Definition 2 (The LWE/LWR Problems). *Let* $n, q, m \in \mathbb{N}$ *and* χ *be a distribution on* $\mathbb{Z}_q$. *The* search/decisional *version of the* learning with errors/rounding problems *refer to the following computational tasks.*[2]

- **Search LWE:** *Given* $\{(\mathbf{a}_1, b_1), \ldots, (\mathbf{a}_m, b_m)\} \sim \mathsf{LWE}_{n,q,m,\chi}$, *output* $\mathbf{s}$.
- **Decisional LWE:** *Distinguish* $\mathsf{LWE}_{n,q,m,\chi}$ *from* $\mathsf{Unif}(\mathbb{Z}_q^n \times \mathbb{Z}_q)^m$.
- **Search LWR:** *If* $p \in \mathbb{N}$ *such that* $2 \le p < q$, *then given* $\{(\mathbf{a}_1, b_1), \ldots, (\mathbf{a}_m, b_m)\} \sim \mathsf{LWR}_{n,q,m,p}$, *output* $\mathbf{s}$.

---

[2] We will not need the decisional version of LWR in this work, so we do not give the definition.

Error Distributions and Rounding Subsets. The most common choice for the error distribution χ is a discrete Gaussian on $\mathbb{Z}_q$, centered at 0 with standard deviation αq for some $\alpha = 1/\mathsf{poly}(n)$. Hardness of decisional LWE with this error distribution is known assuming worst-case hardness of computational problems on lattices which are believed to be hard even for quantum computers [9,17,19]. The arguments in this work will apply equally well to any bounded error distribution which gives output in $\{-B, \ldots, B\} \subset \mathbb{Z}_q$ for $B \ll q$ with overwhelming probability $1 - 2^{-n}$.

Solvers and Distinguishers. Given $\varepsilon > 0$ and $m \in \mathbb{N}$, we say an algorithm S is an $(\varepsilon, m)-$*solver* for $\mathsf{LWE}_{n,q,\chi}$ (resp. $\mathsf{LWR}_{n,q,p}$) if it solves search LWE (resp. search LWR) with probability at least ε, given m samples:

$$\Pr_{\{(\mathbf{a}_i, b_i)\}_{i=1}^m \sim \mathsf{LWE}_{n,q,m,\chi}} \left[\mathsf{S}(\{(\mathbf{a}_i, b_i)\}_{i=1}^m) = \mathbf{s} \right] \geq \varepsilon,$$

and similarly for $\mathsf{LWR}_{n,q,m,p}$ except the probability is over $\{(\mathbf{a}_i, b_i)\}_{i=1}^m \sim \mathsf{LWR}_{n,q,m,p}$. Likewise, we say that an algorithm D is an $(\varepsilon, m)-$*distinguisher* for $\mathsf{LWE}_{n,q,\chi}$ if

$$\left| \Pr_{\{(\mathbf{a}_i, b_i)\}_{i=1}^m \sim \mathcal{D}_0} \left[\mathsf{D}(\{(\mathbf{a}_i, b_i)\}_i) = 1 \right] - \Pr_{\{(\mathbf{a}_i, b_i)\}_{i=1}^m \sim \mathcal{D}_1} \left[\mathsf{D}(\{(\mathbf{a}_i, b_i)\}) = 1 \right] \right| \geq \varepsilon,$$

where $\mathcal{D}_0 = \mathsf{LWE}_{n,q,m,\chi}$ and $\mathcal{D}_1 = (\mathbb{Z}_q^n \times \mathbb{Z}_q)^m$. We write the inputs to solvers and distinguishers as sets even though technically speaking they are lists: they have an ordering and they can contain duplicated elements (this distinction will not matter for us).

Definition 3 (Reduction from LWE to LWR). *Let $n, q, p \in \mathbb{N}$ be integers with $p < q$, and let χ be a distribution on $\mathbb{Z}_q$, and let $\ell_{\mathsf{err}} : \mathbb{R}_{>0} \times \mathbb{N} \to \mathbb{R}_{>0}$ and $\ell_{\mathsf{samp}} : \mathbb{R}_{>0} \times \mathbb{N} \to \mathbb{N}$ be functions. We say that a PPT oracle algorithm $\mathcal{A}$ is an $(\ell_{\mathsf{err}}, \ell_{\mathsf{samp}})-$reduction from $\mathsf{LWE}_{n,q,\chi}$ to $\mathsf{LWR}_{n,q,p}$ if the following holds: if S is an $(\varepsilon', m')-$ solver for $\mathsf{LWR}_{n,q,p}$, then $\mathcal{A}^{\mathsf{S}}$ (i.e., $\mathcal{A}$ instantiated with oracle access to S) is an $(\varepsilon, m)-$solver for $\mathsf{LWE}_{n,q,\chi}$, where $(\varepsilon, m) = (\ell_{\mathsf{err}}(\varepsilon', m'), \ell_{\mathsf{samp}}(\varepsilon', m'))$.*

Remark. We are interested in noticeable solvers which run in polynomial time; i.e., $(\varepsilon', m')-$solvers for $\varepsilon' = \mathsf{poly}(1/n)$ and $m' = \mathsf{poly}(n)$. In order to preserve this, our reductions will always have $\ell_{\mathsf{err}}(\varepsilon', m') = \mathsf{poly}(1/n, \varepsilon', 1/m')$ and $\ell_{\mathsf{samp}}(\varepsilon', m') = \mathsf{poly}(n, 1/\varepsilon', m')$. Thus, our reduction model requires $\mathcal{A}^{\mathsf{S}}$ to be a polynomial time noticeable solver for LWE whenever S is a polynomial time noticeable solver for LWR. As mentioned in the introduction, several prior works [2,5,7] prove hardness results for LWR with $q = \mathsf{poly}(n)$ via LWE hardness as long as there is a bound B on the overall number of samples given to the LWR solver. In the above language, these works give a reduction $\mathcal{A}$ such that $\mathcal{A}^{\mathsf{S}}$ is a polytime noticeable solver for LWE whenever S is a polytime noticeable solver for LWR which uses $m' \leq B$ samples.

2.2   Pseudorandomness

Definition 4 (Statistical Distance). *Let X and Y be random variables, both supported on the same set Ω. The statistical distance between X and Y, denoted $\Delta(X, Y)$, is equal to both of the following expressions:*

$$\max_{T \subset \Omega} \left| \Pr_{x \sim X} \left[x \in T \right] - \Pr_{y \sim Y} \left[y \in T \right] \right| = \frac{1}{2} \cdot \sum_{z \in \Omega} \left| \Pr_{x \sim X} \left[x = z \right] - \Pr_{y \sim Y} \left[y = z \right] \right|.$$

We will use a version of the fact that the inner product mod q is a good two-source extractor. The original proof of this fact when $q = 2$ is in [11]; see [15] for the following generalization to larger prime q.

Fact 1. *Let $n, q \in \mathbb{N}$ be such that q is prime, let $X \subset \mathbb{Z}_q^n$ be a subset, and let $\mathcal{D}$ be the distribution on $\mathbb{Z}_q^{n+1}$ which draws $\mathbf{a} \sim \mathbb{Z}_q^n$, $\mathbf{x} \sim X$ and outputs $(\mathbf{a}, \langle \mathbf{a}, \mathbf{x} \rangle)$. Then*

$$\Delta(\mathcal{D}, \mathsf{Unif}(\mathbb{Z}_q^{n+1}))^2 \leq \frac{q}{4|X|}.$$

The following corollary will be used several times throughout the paper. Intuitively, it says that any property which holds with good probability over $(\mathbf{a}, b) \sim \mathbb{Z}_q^n \times \mathbb{Z}_q$ holds with similar probability over $(\mathbf{a}, b) \sim \mathsf{LWE}_{n,q,\mathbf{s},\chi}$ for almost all $\mathbf{s} \in \mathbb{Z}_q^n$.

Corollary 1 (Sampling of LWE). *For any test set $T \subset \mathbb{Z}_q^n \times \mathbb{Z}_q$ of size $|T| = \tau \cdot q^{n+1}$, and any $e \in \mathbb{Z}_q$,*

$$\Pr_{\mathbf{s} \sim \mathbb{Z}_q^n} \left[\left| \Pr_{\mathbf{a} \sim \mathbb{Z}_q^n} \left[(\mathbf{a}, \langle \mathbf{a}, \mathbf{s} \rangle + e) \in T \right] - \tau \right| > q^{-n/4} \right] = q^{-\Omega(n)}.$$

In particular,

$$\Pr_{\mathbf{s} \sim \mathbb{Z}_q^n} \left[\left| \Pr_{(\mathbf{a},b) \sim \mathsf{LWE}_{\mathbf{s}}} \left[(\mathbf{a}, b) \in T \right] - \tau \right| > q^{-n/4} \right] = q^{-\Omega(n)}.$$

Proof. Fix $T \subset \mathbb{Z}_q^n \times \mathbb{Z}_q$ of size $|T| = \tau \cdot q^{n+1}$, and let $S \subset \mathbb{Z}_q^n$ be the set of $\mathbf{s} \in \mathbb{Z}_q^n$ such that $\Pr_{\mathbf{a} \sim \mathbb{Z}_q^n} \left[(\mathbf{a}, \langle \mathbf{a}, \mathbf{s} \rangle + e) \in T \right] > \tau + q^{-n/4}$ for some $e \in \mathbb{Z}_q$. We will prove $|S| < q^{n/2+3} = q^{-(n/2-3)} \cdot q^n$; the result follows since we can argue similarly for the set of $\mathbf{s} \in \mathbb{Z}_q^n$ such that for some $e \in \mathbb{Z}_q$, $\Pr_{\mathbf{a} \sim \mathbb{Z}_q^n} \left[(\mathbf{a}, \langle \mathbf{a}, \mathbf{s} \rangle + e) \in T \right] < \tau - q^{-n/4}$. For the part of the claim about LWE samples, note that if $\mathbf{s} \notin S$ then

$$\Pr_{(\mathbf{a},b) \sim \mathsf{LWE}_{\mathbf{s}}} \left[(\mathbf{a}, b) \in T \right] = \sum_{e \in \mathbb{Z}_q} \Pr \left[\chi = e \right] \cdot \Pr_{\mathbf{a} \sim \mathbb{Z}_q^n} \left[(\mathbf{a}, \langle \mathbf{a}, \mathbf{s} \rangle + e) \in T \right] \leq \tau + q^{-n/4}.$$

So it suffices to bound $|S|$. Let $S_e \subset S$ be the $\mathbf{s} \in S$ such that $\Pr_{\mathbf{a} \sim \mathbb{Z}_q^n} \left[(\mathbf{a}, \langle \mathbf{a}, \mathbf{s} \rangle + e) \in T \right] > \tau + q^{-n/4}$. For all $e \in \mathbb{Z}_q$, we have

$$\tau + q^{-n/4} < \Pr_{\mathbf{s} \sim S_e, \mathbf{a} \sim \mathbb{Z}_q^n} \left[(\mathbf{a}, \langle \mathbf{a}, \mathbf{s} \rangle) + (0, e) \in T \right] \leq \tau + \sqrt{\frac{q}{4|S_e|}},$$

where the inequality on the second line is Fact 1. Thus, $|S_e| \leq q^{n/2+1}/4$ holds for all $e \in \mathbb{Z}_q$, and so $|S| = \left| \bigcup_e S_e \right| \leq q^{n/2+2}$. The result follows.

3 Our Reduction Model and Main Theorem

3.1 Pointwise Reductions and Main Theorem Statement

In this section we define *pointwise reductions from LWE to LWR*, which are the reductions ruled out by our main theorem. To say that $\mathcal{A}$ is a pointwise reduction is to require that the LWE solver $\mathcal{A}^{\mathsf{S}}$ uses its oracle access to S in a precise way. First, $\mathcal{A}^{\mathsf{S}}$ must map its input LWE samples to LWR samples in a pointwise fashion (*i.e.*, using $f : \mathbb{Z}_q^n \times \mathbb{Z}_q \to \mathbb{Z}_q^n \times \mathbb{Z}_p$, applied pointwise on each of the input samples). Then $\mathcal{A}^{\mathsf{S}}$ invokes S on the outputs obtaining an LWR secret. Finally, $\mathcal{A}^{\mathsf{S}}$ outputs an LWE secret computed using the original LWE samples and the LWR secret.

Definition 5 (Point-Wise Reduction from LWE to LWR). *Let $n, p, q \in \mathbb{N}$ be integers such that $p < q$, let χ be a distribution on $\mathbb{Z}_q$, and let $\ell_{\mathsf{err}} : \mathbb{R}_{>0} \times \mathbb{N} \to \mathbb{R}_{>0}$ and $\ell_{\mathsf{samp}} : \mathbb{R}_{>0} \times \mathbb{N} \to \mathbb{N}$ be functions. We say the PPT oracle algorithm $\mathcal{A}$ is an $(\ell_{\mathsf{err}}, \ell_{\mathsf{samp}})$−pointwise reduction from $\mathsf{LWE}_{n,q,\chi}$ to $\mathsf{LWR}_{n,q,p}$ if it is a reduction per Definition 3 and, moreover, if there exists an efficiently computable function $f : \mathbb{Z}_q^n \times \mathbb{Z}_q \to \mathbb{Z}_q^n \times \mathbb{Z}_p$ and a PPT algorithm $\mathcal{B}$ such that for any (ε', m')−solver S for $\mathsf{LWR}_{n,q,p}$, the (ε, m)−solver $\mathcal{A}^{\mathsf{S}}$ for $\mathsf{LWE}_{n,q,\chi}$ works as follows where $(\varepsilon, m) = \big(\ell_{\mathsf{err}}(\varepsilon', m'), \ell_{\mathsf{samp}}(\varepsilon', m') \big)$.*

1. *Given $\{(\mathbf{a}_i, b_i)\}_{i=1}^m \subset \mathbb{Z}_q^n \times \mathbb{Z}_q$, compute $(\mathbf{a}_i', b_i') = f(\mathbf{a}_i, b_i) \in \mathbb{Z}_q^n \times \mathbb{Z}_p$ for $i = 1, \ldots, m$.*
2. *Call $\mathsf{S}(\{(\mathbf{a}_i', b_i')\})$ obtaining $\mathbf{s}' \in \mathbb{Z}_q^n \cup \{\bot\}$ (S reads only the first m' pairs; if fewer than m' pairs are given, S outputs $\bot$).*
3. *Compute $\mathcal{B}(\{(\mathbf{a}_i, b_i)\}, \mathbf{s}')$ obtaining $\mathbf{s} \in \mathbb{Z}_q^n \cup \{\bot\}$; output $\mathbf{s}$.*

Note that in a pointwise reduction, $m = \ell_{\mathsf{samp}}(\varepsilon', m') = m'$, since each LWE sample is mapped to an LWR sample which is then used by the LWR solver. For this reason, we usually ignore ℓ_{samp} when dealing with pointwise reductions.

Theorem 2 (Main). *Let $n, p, q \in \mathbb{N}$ be integers with $q = \mathsf{poly}(n)$ prime and $q^{2/3+c} < p < q = \mathsf{poly}(n)$ for a universal constant $c > 0$, and let χ be a distribution on $\mathbb{Z}_q$. Let $\ell_{\mathsf{err}} : \mathbb{R}_{>0} \times \mathbb{N} \to \mathbb{R}_{>0}$ be a function so $\ell_{\mathsf{err}}(\varepsilon', m') = \mathsf{poly}(1/n, 1/m', \varepsilon')$. Then any ℓ_{err}−pointwise reduction $\mathcal{A} = (f, \mathcal{B})$ from $\mathsf{LWE}_{n,q,\chi}$ to $\mathsf{LWR}_{n,q,p}$ can be used to build an efficient (ε, m)−distinguisher for $\mathsf{LWE}_{n,q,\chi}$ for some non-negligible $\varepsilon > 0$ and some $m = \mathsf{poly}(n)$.*

If the error distribution χ on $\mathbb{Z}_q$ is such that $\mathsf{LWE}_{n,q,m,\chi}$ is hard for all $m = \mathsf{poly}(n)$ (*e.g.*, if χ is a discrete Gaussian), then Theorem 2 says that it is impossible to reduce $\mathsf{LWE}_{n,q,\chi}$ to $\mathsf{LWR}_{n,q,p}$ in a pointwise fashion.

3.2 The LWR Secret Recovery Algorithm and Proof of Theorem 2

Notation. Let $n, p, q \in \mathbb{N}$ be integers such that q is prime such that $q^{2/3+c} < p < q$ for a small constant $c > 0$. Let $f : \mathbb{Z}_q^n \times \mathbb{Z}_q \to \mathbb{Z}_q^n \times \mathbb{Z}_p$ be part of a pointwise reduction from $\mathsf{LWE}_{n,q,\chi}$ to $\mathsf{LWR}_{n,q,p}$. Since n, p, q, χ are fixed throughout the remainder of the paper, we write $\mathsf{LWE_s}$ and $\mathsf{LWR_{s'}}$ instead of $\mathsf{LWE}_{n,q,\mathbf{s},\chi}$ and $\mathsf{LWR}_{n,q,\mathbf{s}',p}$, respectively. The lemmas in this section make reference to non-negligible quantities $\eta, \delta > 0$ which will be specified in the next section.

Lemma 1 (Main Technical Lemma). *Let notations be as above. There exists an efficient algorithm $\mathcal{A}$ with the following syntax and correctness guarantees.*

- **Syntax:** $\mathcal{A}$ *takes no input, gets oracle access to a* $\left(\mathbb{Z}_q^n \times \mathbb{Z}_q\right)-$*oracle and to* f, *and outputs a vector* $\mathbf{s}' \in \mathbb{Z}_q^n$.
- **Correctness:** *If $\mathcal{A}$ is run when given oracle access to $\mathsf{LWE_s}$ for a random* $\mathbf{s} \sim \mathbb{Z}_q^n$, *then with non-negligible probability (over $\mathbf{s} \sim \mathbb{Z}_q^n$ and the random coins of $\mathcal{A}$), $\mathcal{A}$ outputs $\mathbf{s}' \in \mathbb{Z}_q^n$ such that:*

$$\Pr_{(\mathbf{a},b)\sim\mathsf{LWE_s}} \left[b' = \left\lfloor \langle \mathbf{a}', \mathbf{s}' \rangle \right\rceil_p \right] \geq 1 - \eta, \tag{3}$$

where $(\mathbf{a}', b') = f(\mathbf{a}, b)$.

Lemma 2. *Assume $(f, \mathcal{B})$ is a pointwise reduction from $\mathsf{LWE}_{n,q,\chi}$ to $\mathsf{LWR}_{n,q,p}$. If there exists $\mathbf{s}' \in \mathbb{Z}_q^n$ such that*

$$\Pr_{(\mathbf{a},b)\sim\mathbb{Z}_q^n \times \mathbb{Z}_q} \left[b' = \left\lfloor \langle \mathbf{a}', \mathbf{s}' \rangle \right\rceil_p \right] \geq 1 - 2\eta,$$

where $(\mathbf{a}', b') = f(\mathbf{a}, b)$, then $\mathcal{B}$ is a $(\delta, m)-$solver for $\mathsf{LWE}_{n,q,\chi}$ for $m = n(1 + \log q)/\eta$.

Proof (Proof of Theorem 2 Assuming Lemmas 1 and 2). Let $\mathcal{A}$ denote the algorithm promised by Lemma 1. Consider the following distinguishing algorithm $\mathcal{D}$, which gets oracle access to a $\left(\mathbb{Z}_q^n \times \mathbb{Z}_q\right)-$oracle $\mathcal{O}$ and works as follows.

1. D instantiates $\mathcal{A}$ with oracle access to $\mathcal{O}$, obtaining output $\mathbf{s}' \in \mathbb{Z}_q^n$. If $\mathcal{A}$ fails to give output of the proper type, D outputs 0.
2. Now D draws samples $(\mathbf{a}_1, b_1), \ldots, (\mathbf{a}_N, b_N) \sim \mathcal{O}$ for $N = n/\eta$, and computes an approximation $\hat{\mathsf{P}}$ of the probability

$$\mathsf{P} := \Pr_{(\mathbf{a},b)\sim\mathcal{O}} \left[b' = \left\lfloor \langle \mathbf{a}', \mathbf{s}' \rangle \right\rceil_p \right],$$

where $(\mathbf{a}', b') = f(\mathbf{a}, b)$. If $\hat{\mathsf{P}} \geq 1 - 3\eta/4$, D outputs 1, otherwise D outputs 0.

We show that D outputs 0 with probability $1 - 2^{-\Omega(n)}$ when $\mathcal{O}$ is a random oracle, and outputs 1 with non-negligible probability when $\mathcal{O}$ is an LWE oracle. The theorem follows.

Uniform Samples. Consider the execution of D when $\mathcal{O}$ is a random oracle, and let $\mathbf{s}' \in \mathbb{Z}_q^n$ be the vector obtained by $\mathcal{A}$ in Step 1 (if $\mathcal{A}$ outputs $\perp$ during this step then D outputs a random bit). In this case, the Chernoff-Hoeffding inequality ensures that $|\hat{\mathsf{P}} - \mathsf{P}| < \eta/2$ holds with probability $1 - 2^{-\Omega(n)}$. Thus by Lemma 2, $\hat{\mathsf{P}} < 1 - 3\eta/2$ occurs with probability $1 - 2^{-\Omega(n)}$, and so D outputs a random bit with high probability.

LWE Samples. Now consider the execution of D when instantiated with a $\mathsf{LWE_s}$−oracle for a random $\mathbf{s} \sim \mathbb{Z}_q^n$. In this case, Lemma 1 ensures that with non-negligible probability, $\mathcal{A}$ outputs $\mathbf{s}' \in \mathbb{Z}_q^n$ such that $\mathsf{P} \geq 1 - \eta$. In this case, $\hat{\mathsf{P}}$ is again accurate to within $\pm \eta/2$ by the Chernoff bound, and so $\hat{\mathsf{P}} \geq 1 - 3\eta/2$ and D outputs 1 with non-negligible probability.

4   The Statistics of a Pointwise Reduction

In this section we begin to impose structure on $f : \mathbb{Z}_q^n \times \mathbb{Z}_q \to \mathbb{Z}_q^n \times \mathbb{Z}_p$ which is part of a pointwise reduction from $\mathsf{LWE}_{n,q,\chi}$ to $\mathsf{LWR}_{n,q,p}$. The fundamental intuition of this section is the following "meta" statement: *all statistics of the LWR distribution and the output distribution of f (given LWE samples as input) must be the same.* The reason for this is that any statistic which differs can be used to build a "pathological solver" which solves LWR but which will be useless for solving LWE via f. The solver simply draws enough samples to approximate the statistic, aborting if it decides it is being fed with mapped LWE samples, solving if it decides it is being fed with true LWR samples.

4.1   Non-Degeneracy

We prove that the distribution which draws $(\mathbf{a}, b) \sim \mathbb{Z}_q^n \times \mathbb{Z}_q$, computes $(\mathbf{a}', b') = f(\mathbf{a}, b)$ and outputs $\mathbf{a}' \in \mathbb{Z}_q^n$ cannot give non-negligible weight to any set $T \subset \mathbb{Z}_q^n$ with negligible density.

Definition 6. *Let $\zeta, \rho > 0$ be such that $\zeta > \rho$, and let $f : \mathbb{Z}_q^n \times \mathbb{Z}_q \to \mathbb{Z}_q^n \times \mathbb{Z}_p$ be a function. We say f is (ζ, ρ)−degenerate if there exists $T \subset \mathbb{Z}_q^n$ of density $|T|/q^n = \rho$ such that $\Pr_{(\mathbf{a},b) \sim \mathbb{Z}_q^n \times \mathbb{Z}_q} [\mathbf{a}' \in T] \geq \zeta$, where $(\mathbf{a}', b') = f(\mathbf{a}, b)$. We say that f is (ζ, ρ)−non-degenerate if it is not (ζ, ρ)−degenerate.*

Claim 1. Non-Degeneracy. *Let $n, q, p \in \mathbb{N}$ such that $p < q$ and χ be a distribution on $\mathbb{Z}_q$. Suppose $f : \mathbb{Z}_q^n \times \mathbb{Z}_q \to \mathbb{Z}_q^n \times \mathbb{Z}_p$ is part of a pointwise reduction $(f, \mathcal{B})$ from $\mathsf{LWE}_{n,q,\chi}$ to $\mathsf{LWR}_{n,q,p}$. Suppose f is $(\rho + \varepsilon, \rho)$−degenerate for $\rho, \varepsilon > 0$ with ε non-negligible. Then $\mathcal{B}$ is an (ε, m)−solver of $\mathsf{LWE}_{n,q,\chi}$, for $m = \max \{ qn(1 + \log q), n/(\rho \varepsilon^2) \}$.*

Proof. Let $\varepsilon > 0$ be non-negligible and suppose $(f, \mathcal{B})$ is a pointwise reduction from $\mathsf{LWE}_{n,q,\chi}$ to $\mathsf{LWR}_{n,q,p}$ which is $(\rho + \varepsilon, \rho)$−degenerate. Let $\mathcal{D}$ be the distribution on $\mathbb{Z}_q^n$ which draws $(\mathbf{a}, b) \sim \mathbb{Z}_q^n \times \mathbb{Z}_q$, computes $(\mathbf{a}', b') = f(\mathbf{a}, b)$, and outputs $\mathbf{a}'$. By definition, there exists $T \subset \mathbb{Z}_q^n$ of density ρ such that $\Pr_{\mathcal{D}} [\mathbf{a}' \in T] \geq \rho + \varepsilon$. Let S be the pathological $(1 - 2^{-\Omega(n)}, m)$−solver for $\mathsf{LWR}_{n,q,p}$ which, on input $\{(\mathbf{a}_i', b_i')\}_{i=1}^m \subset \mathbb{Z}_q^n \times \mathbb{Z}_p$, computes $t := {}^{\#}\{i : \mathbf{a}_i' \in T\}$ and outputs $\perp$ if $t \geq (\rho + \varepsilon/2)m$; otherwise if $t < (\rho + \varepsilon/2)m$, S outputs the unique $\mathbf{s}' \in \mathbb{Z}_q^n$ such that $b_i' = \lfloor \langle \mathbf{a}_i', \mathbf{s}' \rangle \rceil_p$ for all $i = 1, \ldots, m$ (if no such $\mathbf{s}'$ exists or if more than one such $\mathbf{s}'$ exists, S outputs $\perp$). Note that when S is fed with LWR samples $t = \rho m$ in expectation as the $\mathbf{a}_i' \sim \mathbb{Z}_q^n$ are uniform. By the

Chernoff-Hoeffding inequality, $t < (\rho + \varepsilon/2)m$ holds with probability $1 - 2^{-\Omega(n)}$ (since $m \geq n/(\rho\varepsilon^2)$). As $m \geq nq(1 + \log q)$, with probability at least $1 - 2^{-\Omega(n)}$, there exists exactly one $\mathbf{s}' \in \mathbb{Z}_q^n$ such that $b_i' = \lfloor \langle \mathbf{a}_i', \mathbf{s}' \rangle \rceil_p$ for all $i = 1, \ldots, m$. Therefore, when S is fed with LWR samples it outputs the LWR secret $\mathbf{s}'$ with high probability.

On the other hand, when m LWE samples are chosen and S is fed with $\{f(\mathbf{a}_i, b_i)\}$, $t \geq (\rho + \varepsilon)m$ in expectation, and so by the Chernoff-Hoeffding inequality, $t \geq (\rho + \varepsilon/2)m$ holds with probability $1 - 2^{-\Omega(n)}$ (since $m \geq n/(\rho\varepsilon^2) \geq n/(\rho + \varepsilon)$). Therefore, S outputs $\bot$ with high probability when fed with mapped LWE samples. As $(f, \mathcal{B})$ is a pointwise reduction from $\mathsf{LWE}_{n,q,\chi}$ to $\mathsf{LWR}_{n,q,p}$, $\mathcal{B}$ outputs the LWE secret with non-negligible probability when fed with $(\{(\mathbf{a}_i, b_i)\}, \bot)$, where the $(\mathbf{a}_i, b_i)$ are LWE samples and the $\bot$ is the output of S on their images under f. Thus $\mathcal{B}$ solves $\mathsf{LWE}_{n,q,m,\chi}$ with non-negligible probability.

4.2   Good LWE Secrets

We now identify a non-negligible subset $\mathsf{G} \subset \mathbb{Z}_q^n$ of *good* LWE secrets, where $\mathbf{s} \in \mathsf{G}$ guarantees some good behavior from f when fed with samples from $\mathsf{LWE}_{n,q,\mathbf{s},\chi}$.

The Secret Graph. The secret graph is a weighted complete bipartite graph whose left and right vertex sets (X and Y, respectively) are both $\mathbb{Z}_q^n$, and where the weight of the edge $(\mathbf{s}, \mathbf{s}') \in X \times Y$ is $\mathsf{p}_{(\mathbf{s},\mathbf{s}')} := \Pr_{(\mathbf{a},b) \sim \mathsf{LWE}_\mathbf{s}}[b' = \lfloor \langle \mathbf{a}', \mathbf{s}' \rangle \rceil_p]$, where $(\mathbf{a}', b') = f(\mathbf{a}, b)$. For $\mathbf{s} \in X$ and $\varepsilon > 0$, we write $Y_\varepsilon(\mathbf{s}) = \{\mathbf{s}' \in Y : \mathsf{p}_{(\mathbf{s},\mathbf{s}')} \geq 1 - \varepsilon\}$. Likewise, given $\mathbf{s}' \in Y$ and $\varepsilon > 0$, $X_\varepsilon(\mathbf{s}') = \{\mathbf{s} \in X : \mathsf{p}_{(\mathbf{s},\mathbf{s}')} \geq 1 - \varepsilon\}$. So intuitively, $Y_\varepsilon(\mathbf{s})$ is the subset of $\mathbf{s}$'s neighborhood which is connected to $\mathbf{s}$ by an edge with weight at least $1 - \varepsilon$; and similarly for $X_\varepsilon(\mathbf{s}')$.

Parameters. In addition to the parameters mentioned above, the good secrets are defined in terms of three non-negligible values $\delta, \eta, \sigma > 0$. The quantity δ is defined using the error loss function ℓ_{err} of the pointwise reduction $(f, \mathcal{B})$. Specifically, $2\delta = \ell_{\mathsf{err}}(1/3, m)$ where $m = 2n(1 + \log q)/\eta$, so that if S is a $(\frac{1}{3}, m)$-solver for $\mathsf{LWR}_{n,q,p}$, $\mathcal{B}^\mathsf{S}$ is a 2δ-solver for $\mathsf{LWE}_{n,q,\chi}$. Given δ, we set $\sigma = \delta/2nq(1 + \log q)$ and $\eta = \min\{\sigma, (1/3nq)^3\}$. The reader is encouraged on a first pass to just think of δ, η, σ all as arbitrarily small, but non-negligible, quantities.

Definition 7 (Good LWE Secrets). *With the above notation and conventions, we say that $\mathbf{s} \in \mathbb{Z}_q^n$ is good, and write $\mathbf{s} \in \mathsf{G}$, if the following three conditions hold:*

$$(1)\ |Y_\eta(\mathbf{s})| = 1; \quad (2)\ |Y_\sigma(\mathbf{s})| \leq 1; \quad (3)\ |X_\eta(\mathbf{s}')| = 1.$$

In point (3), $\mathbf{s}' \in \mathbb{Z}_q^n$ is the LWR secret for which $Y_\eta(\mathbf{s}) = \{\mathbf{s}'\}$.

Note that Points (1) and (3) together establish that the edges in the secret graph with weight above $1 - \eta$ induce a matching between good LWE secrets and (a subset of) LWR secrets.

Claim 2. *Suppose $(f, \mathcal{B})$ is a pointwise reduction from $\mathsf{LWE}_{n,q,\chi}$ to $\mathsf{LWR}_{n,q,p}$. Then either $|G| \geq \delta \cdot q^n$, or $\mathcal{B}$ is a (δ, m)-solver for $\mathsf{LWE}_{n,q,\chi}$ for $m = 2n(1 + \log q)/\eta$.*

Proof. Let $m = n(1 + \log q)/\eta$, and let S be the pathological solver for $\mathsf{LWR}_{n,q,p}$ which, on input $\{(\mathbf{a}'_i, b'_i)\}_{i=1}^m$, does the following:

(i) it looks at the first $nq(1 + \log q)$ samples (this is less than m since $\eta \leq 1/q$) and checks whether there exist distinct $\mathbf{s}', \mathbf{s}'' \in \mathbb{Z}_q^n$ such that $\lfloor \langle \mathbf{a}'_i, \mathbf{s}' \rangle \rceil_p = b'_i = \lfloor \langle \mathbf{a}'_i, \mathbf{s}'' \rangle \rceil_p$ holds for all $i = 1, \ldots, nq(1 + \log q)$; if so, S outputs $\perp$;

(ii) S computes the unique $\mathbf{s}' \in \mathbb{Z}_q^n$ such that $b'_i = \lfloor \langle \mathbf{a}'_i, \mathbf{s}' \rangle \rceil_p$ holds for all $i = 1, \ldots, m$, if no such $\mathbf{s}'$ exists, S outputs $\perp$;

(iii) using the $\mathbf{s}' \in \mathbb{Z}_q^n$ just computed, S checks if $\#\{\mathbf{s} \in \mathbb{Z}_q^n : |Y_\eta(\mathbf{s})| = 1 \ \& \ \mathsf{p}_{(\mathbf{s}, \mathbf{s}')} \geq 1 - \eta\} \geq 2$; if so S outputs $\perp$;

(iv) if it has not already aborted, S outputs $\mathbf{s}' \in \mathbb{Z}_q^n$ recovered in Step (ii).

Assume $|G| < \delta \cdot q^n$. We will prove the following two points.

1. if S is called on $\{(\mathbf{a}'_i, b'_i)\} \sim \mathsf{LWR}_{n,q,m,p}$, then S outputs the secret $\mathbf{s}'$ with probability at least $1/3$;
2. if S is called on $\{(\mathbf{a}'_i, b'_i)\}$ for $\{(\mathbf{a}_i, b_i)\} \sim \mathsf{LWE}_{n,q,m,\chi}$ and $(\mathbf{a}'_i, b'_i) = f(\mathbf{a}_i, b_i)$, then S outputs $\perp$ with probability at least $1 - \delta$.

Just as in Claim 1, these two points suffice. Point 1 says that S is a $(\frac{1}{3}, m)$-solver for $\mathsf{LWR}_{n,q,m,p}$. As $(f, \mathcal{B})$ is a pointwise reduction, with probability at least $2\delta = \ell_{\mathrm{err}}(1/3)$ over $\{(\mathbf{a}_i, b_i)\} \sim \mathsf{LWE}_{n,q,m,\chi}$, $\mathcal{B}$ outputs the LWE secret given $\{(\mathbf{a}_i, b_i)\}$ and $\mathsf{S}(\{(\mathbf{a}'_i, b'_i)\})$. By point 2, the probability that $\mathcal{B}$ recovers the LWE secret without the second argument is at least δ. It remains to establish the two points.

Point 1 — S on LWR Samples: If S is fed with LWR instances, then certainly there exists $\mathbf{s}' \in \mathbb{Z}_q^n$ such that $b'_i = \lfloor \langle \mathbf{a}'_i, \mathbf{s}' \rangle \rceil_p$ for all i (namely, the LWR secret). So S will solve LWR in step (ii) and give correct output as long as it does not abort in steps (i) or (iii). Just as in the proof of Claim 1, the probability that S outputs $\perp$ in Step (i) because it finds distinct $\mathbf{s}' \neq \mathbf{s}''$ such that $\lfloor \langle \mathbf{a}'_i, \mathbf{s}' \rangle \rceil_p = b'_i = \lfloor \langle \mathbf{a}'_i, \mathbf{s}'' \rangle \rceil_p$ for $i = 1, \ldots, m$ is $2^{-\Omega(n)}$. Moreover, note that

$$\#\{\mathbf{s} \in \mathbb{Z}_q^n : |Y_\eta(\mathbf{s})| = 1 \ \& \ \mathsf{p}_{(\mathbf{s}, \mathbf{s}')} \geq 1 - \eta\} \geq 2$$

holds for at most half of the $\mathbf{s}' \in \mathbb{Z}_q^n$. Therefore S aborts given LWR samples with probability at most $1/2 + 2^{-\Omega(n)} \leq 2/3$, and otherwise solves LWR.

Point 2 — S on Mapped LWE Samples: If S is fed with mapped LWE instances, then some $\mathbf{s} \sim \mathbb{Z}_q^n$ is chosen, $\{(\mathbf{a}_i, b_i)\}_{i=1}^m \sim \mathsf{LWE}_{n,q,\mathbf{s},\chi}$ are drawn, and $(\mathbf{a}'_i, b'_i) = f(\mathbf{a}_i, b_i)$ are computed and fed to S. With probability at least $1 - \delta$, $\mathbf{s} \notin G$ in which case one of the properties (1), (2) and (3) does not hold. If (1) does not hold, then $\mathsf{p}_{(\mathbf{s}, \mathbf{s}')} < 1 - \eta$ for all $\mathbf{s}' \in \mathbb{Z}_q^n$ and so

$$\Pr_{\{(\mathbf{a}_i, b_i)\}_{i=1}^m \sim \mathsf{LWE}_{n,q,\mathbf{s},\chi}} \left[\exists \, \mathbf{s}' \in \mathbb{Z}_q^n \text{ st } b'_i = \lfloor \langle \mathbf{a}'_i, \mathbf{s}' \rangle \rceil_p \ \forall \, i = 1, \ldots, m \right] < q^n \cdot (1 - \eta)^m$$

which is at most 2^{-n} since $m = n(1 + \log q)/\eta$, and so S outputs $\perp$ in Step (ii) with high probability $1 - 2^{-n}$. On the other hand, if (2) does not hold then there exist distinct $\mathbf{s}', \mathbf{s}'' \in \mathbb{Z}_q^n$ such that $\mathsf{p}_{(\mathbf{s},\mathbf{s}')}, \mathsf{p}_{(\mathbf{s},\mathbf{s}'')} \geq 1 - \sigma$ both hold. In this case,

$$\Pr\nolimits_{\{(\mathbf{a}_i,b_i)\}_{i=1}^m \sim \mathsf{LWE}_{n,q,\mathbf{s},\chi}} \left[\left\lfloor \langle \mathbf{a}_i', \mathbf{s}' \rangle \right\rfloor_p = b_i' = \left\lfloor \langle \mathbf{a}_i', \mathbf{s}'' \rangle \right\rfloor_p \ \forall \ i \right] \geq 1 - 2nq(1 + \log q)\sigma$$

which is at least $1 - \delta$ (using $\sigma \leq \delta/2nq(1 + \log q)$), and so S outputs $\perp$ in Step (i) with probability $1 - \delta$. Finally, suppose that (1) and (2) both hold and that S does not abort in Steps (i) or (ii) but that (3) does not hold. Note that $|X_\eta(\mathbf{s}')| \geq 1$ since $\mathbf{s} \in X_\eta(\mathbf{s}')$, thus if (3) does not hold then it must be that $|X_\eta(\mathbf{s}')| \geq 2$. In this case S simply outputs $\perp$ in Step (iii). So we have shown that when $\mathbf{s} \notin \mathsf{G}$, S outputs $\perp$ with probability at least $1 - \delta$, as desired.

4.3   Proof of Lemma 2

Claim 2 imposes quite a lot of structure on a pointwise reduction. We will refer to Claim 2 repeatedly throughout the remainder of the paper. Additionally, we can already derive Lemma 2 as a corollary (we defer the proof of Lemma 2 to the full version of our paper).

4.4   Outline of the Proof of Lemma 1

At this point we have reduced our main result (Theorem 2) to proving Lemma 1; namely we must design an algorithm which, given oracle access to $\mathsf{LWE}_\mathbf{s}$ for some uniform secret $\mathbf{s} \sim \mathbb{Z}_q^n$, reconstructs the LWR secret $\mathbf{s}' \in \mathbb{Z}_q^n$ of the mapped LWE pairs. We have also already proved a key claim, Claim 2, which specifies a notion of "good" behavior from an LWE secret $\mathbf{s}$ and proves that the set of good secrets $\mathsf{G} \subset \mathbb{Z}_q^n$ comprises a non-negligible fraction of the entire space. Intuitively, $\mathbf{s} \in \mathsf{G}$ if there exists a unique $\mathbf{s}' \in \mathbb{Z}_q^n$ such that

$$\mathsf{p}_{(\mathbf{s},\mathbf{s}')} := \Pr\nolimits_{(\mathbf{a},b) \sim \mathsf{LWE}_\mathbf{s}} \left[b' = \left\lfloor \langle \mathbf{a}', \mathbf{s}' \rangle \right\rfloor_p \right] \geq 1 - \eta,$$

and, moreover, if this $\mathbf{s}'$ is unique to $\mathbf{s}$ (i.e., so $\mathsf{p}_{(\mathbf{s}^*,\mathbf{s}')} < 1 - \eta$ for all $\mathbf{s}^* \neq \mathbf{s}$). The algorithm of Lemma 1 will aim to recover $\mathbf{s}'$ whenever $\mathbf{s} \in \mathsf{G}$.

The bulk of the technical work of the remainder of the paper will go into proving the following lemma. Recall the notation of Lemma 1: $n, p, q \in \mathbb{N}$ are integers such that q is prime and $q^{2/3+c} < p < q$; $\nu = \nu(n) > 0$ is non-negligible and $f : \mathbb{Z}_q^n \times \mathbb{Z}_q \to \mathbb{Z}_q^n \times \mathbb{Z}_p$ is part of a pointwise reduction from $\mathsf{LWE}_{n,q,\chi}$ to $\mathsf{LWR}_{n,q,p}$. Recall also that we inherited the non-negligible parameters $\delta, \eta, \sigma > 0$ from Claim 2.

Lemma 3. *Assume the above setup. There exists an efficient algorithm $\mathcal{A}_{\mathsf{AffRec}}$ which takes no input, gets oracle access to f, and outputs a pair $(\mathbf{H}, \mathbf{V})$ where $\mathbf{H} \in \mathbb{Z}_q^{n \times n}$ and $\mathbf{V} \subset \mathbb{Z}_q^n$ is a constant dimensional vector space such that with non-negligible probability (over the random coins of $\mathcal{A}_{\mathsf{AffRec}}$) the following holds:*

$$\Pr\nolimits_{(\mathbf{a},b) \sim \mathbb{Z}_q^n \times \mathbb{Z}_q} \left[\mathbf{a}' \in \mathrm{Span}(\mathbf{H}\mathbf{a}) + \mathbf{V} \right] \geq 1 - \tau,$$

where $(\mathbf{a}', b') = f(\mathbf{a}, b)$ *and* $\tau = nq^2\eta^{1/12t}\sqrt{178n}$, *and* $t \in \mathbb{N}$ *minimal such that* $t \geq \frac{\log_q(1/\delta)+2}{3c}$ *holds.*

As mentioned in Sect. 1.2, once we know that $\mathbf{a}' \in \mathrm{Span}(\mathbf{Ha}) + \mathbf{V}$ holds with high probability, we can recover $\mathbf{s}'$ using a Goldreich-Levin-type argument. This part of our proof is in Sect. 5. Also as mentioned in Sect. 1.2, the proof of Lemma 3 consists of two separate pieces. First, we show that f passes a certain "property test" with high probability, then we show that any function which passes the test must have good agreement with an affine function. See Sect. 6 for a detailed overview and the formal proofs.

5   Recovering the LWR Secret via Goldreich-Levin Inversion

In this section we show how to use the Goldreich-Levin (GL) inversion technique [14] to recover the LWR secret. We begin by recalling the parameters and notations which we will use in this section.

Notations. We have integers $n, p, q \in \mathbb{N}$ such that q is prime and $q^{2/3+c} < p < q$ for some small constant $c > 0$. Additionally, $f : \mathbb{Z}_q^n \times \mathbb{Z}_q \to \mathbb{Z}_q^n \times \mathbb{Z}_p$ is part of a pointwise reduction from $\mathsf{LWE}_{n,q,\chi}$ to $\mathsf{LWR}_{n,q,p}$. We have non-negligible parameters $\delta, \eta, \sigma > 0$ from Claim 2, and a set of "good" LWE secrets $\mathsf{G} \subset \mathbb{Z}_q^n$ from Sect. 4.2. Additionally, we have an additional non-negligible $\tau > 0$ and $(\mathbf{H}, \mathbf{V})$ where $\mathbf{H} \in \mathbb{Z}_q^{n \times n}$ and $\mathbf{V} \subset \mathbb{Z}_q^n$ is a constant dimensional subspace such that

$$\mathsf{P}(\mathbf{H}, \mathbf{V}) := \Pr_{(\mathbf{a},b) \sim \mathbb{Z}_q^n \times \mathbb{Z}_q}\left[\mathbf{a}' \in \mathrm{Span}(\mathbf{Ha}) + \mathbf{V}\right] \geq 1 - \tau,$$

where $(\mathbf{a}', b') = f(\mathbf{a}, b)$. For $\mathbf{s} \in \mathbb{Z}_q^n$ and $e \in \mathbb{Z}_q$, let $\mathsf{P}_{\mathbf{s},e}(\mathbf{H}, \mathbf{V}) := \Pr_{\mathbf{a} \sim \mathbb{Z}_q^n}[\mathbf{a}' \in \mathrm{Span}(\mathbf{Ha}) + \mathbf{V}]$, where $(\mathbf{a}', b') = f(\mathbf{a}, \langle \mathbf{a}, \mathbf{s} \rangle + e)$. It follows immediately from Corollary 1 that for at most a $q^{-\Omega(n)}$–fraction of $\mathbf{s} \in \mathbb{Z}_q^n$, there exists an $e \in \mathbb{Z}_q$ such that $\mathsf{P}_{\mathbf{s},e}(\mathbf{H}, \mathbf{V}) < 1 - 2\tau$. So let us remove all such $\mathbf{s}$ from G; G will still comprise a non-negligible fraction of $\mathbb{Z}_q^n$. At this point what we will need from $\mathbf{s} \in \mathsf{G}$ is that the following points both hold:

$$(1)\ \exists \text{ unique } \mathbf{s}' \in \mathbb{Z}_q^n \text{ st } \mathsf{p}_{(\mathbf{s},\mathbf{s}')} \geq 1 - \eta;\ (2)\ \mathsf{P}_{\mathbf{s},e}(\mathbf{H}, \mathbf{V}) \geq 1 - 2\tau\ \forall\, e$$

5.1   A Goldreich-Levin Theorem for LWE Samples

In this section, we state and prove a Goldreich-Levin-type theorem which will allow us to recover $\mathbf{H}^t\mathbf{s}'$ given oracle access to $\mathsf{LWE}_\mathbf{s}$ for unknown $\mathbf{s}$.

Lemma 4 (A Goldreich-Levin Theorem for LWE Samples). *Let* $n, q \in \mathbb{N}$ *be such that* $q = \mathsf{poly}(n)$ *is prime,* $\zeta \in (0, 1)$. *For a function* $\mathsf{Pred} : \mathbb{Z}_q^n \times \mathbb{Z}_q \to \mathbb{Z}_q$, *and quantities* $(\mathbf{s}, e, \bar{\mathbf{s}}, \gamma) \in \mathbb{Z}_q^n \times \mathbb{Z}_q \times \mathbb{Z}_q^n \times \mathbb{Z}_q$, *define:*

- $\mathsf{P}_{\mathbf{s},e}(\bar{\mathbf{s}}, \gamma) := \Pr_{\mathbf{a} \sim \mathbb{Z}_q^n}\left[\mathsf{Pred}(\mathbf{a}, \langle \mathbf{a}, \mathbf{s} \rangle + e) = \langle \mathbf{a}, \bar{\mathbf{s}} \rangle + \gamma\right].$

$$- \mathsf{P_s}(\bar{\mathbf{s}}, \gamma) := \Pr_{(\mathbf{a},b) \sim \mathsf{LWE_s}} \left[\mathsf{Pred}(\mathbf{a}, b) = \langle \mathbf{a}, \bar{\mathbf{s}} \rangle + \gamma \right].$$

Then there exists a randomized algorithm Inv *which takes* $\{(\mathbf{a}_i, b_i)\}_{i=1}^m \in (\mathbb{Z}_q^n \times \mathbb{Z}_q)^m$ *as input, outputs* $\bar{\mathbf{s}}^* \in \mathbb{Z}_q^n$, *runs in time* $\mathsf{poly}(n, q, 1/\zeta, \mathsf{T_{Pred}})$ *where* $\mathsf{T_{Pred}}$ *is the running time of* Pred, *and has the following correctness guarantee.*

- **Correctness:** *Suppose that* $\mathbf{s}, \bar{\mathbf{s}} \in \mathbb{Z}_q^n$ *are such that both of the following hold:*
  - *for all* $e \in \mathbb{Z}_q$ *such that* $\Pr[\chi = e] \geq \frac{4\zeta}{5qn^2}$, *and non-zero* $\gamma \in \mathbb{Z}_q^*$, $\mathsf{P_{s,e}}(\bar{\mathbf{s}}, 0) \geq \mathsf{P_{s,e}}(\bar{\mathbf{s}}, \gamma) - \zeta$;
  - *for all non-zero* $\gamma \in \mathbb{Z}_q^*$, $\mathsf{P_s}(\bar{\mathbf{s}}, 0) \geq \mathsf{P_s}(\bar{\mathbf{s}}, \gamma) + 10\zeta$.
  Then

$$\Pr_{\{(\mathbf{a}_i, b_i)\}_{i=1}^m \sim \mathsf{LWE_{s,\chi}}} \left[\mathsf{Inv}(\{(\mathbf{a}_i, b_i)\}) = \bar{\mathbf{s}} \right] \geq \frac{8\zeta^6}{9n^4 q^6}.$$

Remark 1. Intuitively, the requirement $\mathsf{P_s}(\bar{\mathbf{s}}, 0) \geq \mathsf{P_s}(\bar{\mathbf{s}}, \gamma) + 10\zeta$ means that the most likely output of the predictor on samples from $\mathsf{LWE_s}$ is $\bar{\mathbf{s}}$. The additional requirement that $\mathsf{P_{s,e}}(\bar{\mathbf{s}}, 0) \geq \mathsf{P_{s,e}}(\bar{\mathbf{s}}, \gamma) - \zeta$ means that the predictor performs pretty well regardless of the LWE error. Note that the most likely output of the "trivial" predictor $\mathsf{Pred}(\mathbf{a}, b) = b$ is $\langle \mathbf{a}, \mathbf{s} \rangle$ (assuming $e = 0$ is the most likely LWE error, which is standard). However, as soon as $e \neq 0$, the trivial predictor starts performing extremely badly, always outputting the wrong value. Clearly if $\mathbf{s}$ could be recovered from the trivial predictor then LWE would be efficiently solvable. Thus the requirement that the predictor perform well for all errors is a critical hypothesis for the above lemma.

Proof. Let $m = n^2/4\zeta$ and $k = 1 + \lceil \log_q(3mq/\zeta^2) \rceil$; Inv works as follows.

Input: Inv gets input $\{(\mathbf{a}_i, b_i)\}_{i=1}^m \in (\mathbb{Z}_q^n \times \mathbb{Z}_q)^m$ and uses an algorithm for Pred as a subroutine.
Output: Inv outputs $\bar{\mathbf{s}}^* \in \mathbb{Z}_q^n$.

1. Choose $\mathbf{x}_1, \ldots, \mathbf{x}_k \sim \mathbb{Z}_q^n$, $g_1, h_1, \ldots, g_k, h_k \sim \mathbb{Z}_q$. For all $\mathbf{u} = (u_1, \ldots, u_k) \in \mathbb{Z}_q^k$, let

$$\mathbf{x_u} := \sum_{j=1}^k u_j \mathbf{x}_j \in \mathbb{Z}_q^n; \quad g_\mathbf{u} := \sum_{j=1}^k u_j g_j \in \mathbb{Z}_q; \quad \text{and} \quad h_\mathbf{u} := \sum_{j=1}^k u_j h_j \in \mathbb{Z}_q.$$

2. For all $i = 1, \ldots, m$, do the following:
   - for each $\beta \in \mathbb{Z}_q$, compute $\hat{\mathsf{p}}_i(\beta) := \Pr_{\mathbf{u} \sim \mathbb{Z}_q^k \setminus \{0\}} \left[\mathsf{Pred}(\mathbf{a}_i + \mathbf{x_u}, b_i + g_\mathbf{u}) - h_\mathbf{u} = \beta \right]$;
   - if there exists $\beta \in \mathbb{Z}_q$ such that $\hat{\mathsf{p}}_i(\beta) \geq \hat{\mathsf{p}}_i(\beta') + 3\zeta$ for all $\beta' \neq \beta$, set $w_i = \beta$; otherwise set $w_i = \bot$.
3. Finally, let $W = \{i \in \{1, \ldots, m\} : w_i \neq \bot\}$, and let $\{i_1, \ldots, i_n\} \subset W$ be such that $\{\mathbf{a}_{i_1}, \ldots, \mathbf{a}_{i_n}\}$ is linearly independent (if no such subset exists, output the failure symbol $\bot$). Let $(\mathbf{A}, \mathbf{w}) \in \mathbb{Z}_q^{n \times n} \times \mathbb{Z}_q^n$ be such that the t-th row (resp., coordinate) of $\mathbf{A}$ (resp., $\mathbf{w}$) is $\mathbf{a}_{i_t}$ (resp., w_{i_t}). Output $\bar{\mathbf{s}}^* = \mathbf{A}^{-1}\mathbf{w} \in \mathbb{Z}_q^n$.

It is clear that Inv runs in time $\mathsf{poly}(n, q, 1/\zeta, \mathsf{T_{Pred}})$. Assume that $\mathbf{s}, \bar{\mathbf{s}} \in \mathbb{Z}_q^n$ are such that both correctness hypotheses hold. We will show that Inv outputs $\bar{\mathbf{s}}^* = \bar{\mathbf{s}}$ with probability at least $1/2q^{2k}$. Consider first the random choices $(\mathbf{x}_j, g_j, h_j) \sim \mathbb{Z}_q^n \times \mathbb{Z}_q \times \mathbb{Z}_q$ drawn during Step 1. Let us say that these random choices are *correct* if:

$$g_j = \langle \mathbf{x}_j, \mathbf{s} \rangle \text{ and } h_j = \langle \mathbf{x}_j, \bar{\mathbf{s}} \rangle \ \forall \ j = 1, \dots, k.$$

Note these random choices are correct with probability q^{-2k}. When the random choices are correct, we have $g_\mathbf{u} = \langle \mathbf{x}_\mathbf{u}, \mathbf{s} \rangle$ and $h_\mathbf{u} = \langle \mathbf{x}_\mathbf{u}, \bar{\mathbf{s}} \rangle$ for all $\mathbf{u} \in \mathbb{Z}_q^k$. Consider now the values $\hat{\mathsf{p}}_i(\beta)$ for $\beta \in \mathbb{Z}_q$ and $i \in \{1, \dots, m\}$ computed in Step 2, and let us interpret the $\hat{\mathsf{p}}_i(\beta)$ as random variables over $\mathbf{x}_j \sim \mathbb{Z}_q^n$. Note that if the choices are correct, then $(\mathbf{a}_i + \mathbf{x}_\mathbf{u}, b_i + g_\mathbf{u})$ is a random $\mathsf{LWE_s}$ pair with the same error as $(\mathbf{a}_i, b_i)$; thus the expectation of $\hat{\mathsf{p}}_i(\langle \mathbf{a}_i, \bar{\mathbf{s}} \rangle + \gamma)$ is $\mathsf{P}_{\mathbf{s}, e_i}(\bar{\mathbf{s}}, \gamma)$ for all $\gamma \in \mathbb{Z}_q$ and $i \in \{1, \dots, m\}$, where $e_i = b_i - \langle \mathbf{a}_i, \mathbf{s} \rangle$. We will prove a concentration bound using the pairwise independence of $(\mathbf{x}_\mathbf{u}, \mathbf{x}_{\mathbf{u}'})$ for $\mathbf{u} \neq \mathbf{u}' \in \mathbb{Z}_q^k$ which will guarantee that with probability at least $2/3$ (conditioned on correctness), $\left| \hat{\mathsf{p}}_i(\langle \mathbf{a}_i, \bar{\mathbf{s}} \rangle + \gamma) - \mathsf{P}_{\mathbf{s}, e_i}(\bar{\mathbf{s}}, \gamma) \right| < \zeta$ holds for all $i = 1, \dots, m$ and $\gamma \in \mathbb{Z}_q$. Let us first show how this completes the analysis of Inv.

Assume that the error term e_i is such that $\Pr[\chi = e_i] \geq \frac{1}{5qm}$; by the union bound the probability that this holds for all $i = 1, \dots, m$ is at least $4/5$. The first observation is that for all $i \in \{1, \dots, m\}$ and non-zero $\gamma \in \mathbb{Z}_q^*$, we have

$$\hat{\mathsf{p}}_i(\langle \mathbf{a}_i, \bar{\mathbf{s}} \rangle) > \mathsf{P}_{\mathbf{s}, e_i}(\bar{\mathbf{s}}, 0) - \zeta \geq \mathsf{P}_{\mathbf{s}, e_i}(\bar{\mathbf{s}}, \gamma) - 2\zeta > \hat{\mathsf{p}}_i(\langle \mathbf{a}_i, \bar{\mathbf{s}} \rangle + \gamma) - 3\zeta.$$

This means that Step 2 never sets w_i to be any value other than $\langle \mathbf{a}_i, \bar{\mathbf{s}} \rangle$. Likewise, we have the bound $\mathsf{P}_\mathbf{s}(\bar{\mathbf{s}}, 0) - \mathsf{P}_\mathbf{s}(\bar{\mathbf{s}}, \gamma) \geq 10\zeta$ for non-zero $\gamma \in \mathbb{Z}_q^*$ means that $\mathsf{P}_{\mathbf{s}, e_i}(\bar{\mathbf{s}}, 0) - \mathsf{P}_{\mathbf{s}, e_i}(\bar{\mathbf{s}}, \gamma) \geq 5\zeta$ holds with probability at least 5ζ over $e \sim \chi$. By Chernoff, the probability that $\mathsf{P}_{\mathbf{s}, e_i}(\bar{\mathbf{s}}, 0) - \mathsf{P}_{\mathbf{s}, e_i}(\bar{\mathbf{s}}, \gamma) \geq 5\zeta$ holds for at least $4\zeta m = n^2$ of the input LWE pairs $(\mathbf{a}_i, b_i)$ is $1 - 2^{-\Omega(n)}$. The probability that n^2 random vectors in $\mathbb{Z}_q^n$ span a proper subspace is at most $q^{-\Omega(n)}$; thus with probability at least $1 - 2^{-\Omega(n)}$, there exist n input samples $(\mathbf{a}_{i_1}, b_{i_1}), \dots, (\mathbf{a}_{i_n}, b_{i_n})$ such that $\mathsf{Span}(\{\mathbf{a}_{i_1}, \dots, \mathbf{a}_{i_n}\}) = \mathbb{Z}_q^n$ and such that each error term e satisfies $\mathsf{P}_{\mathbf{s}, e}(\bar{\mathbf{s}}, 0) - \mathsf{P}_{\mathbf{s}, e}(\bar{\mathbf{s}}, \gamma) \geq 5\zeta$ for all non-zero $\gamma \in \mathbb{Z}_q^*$. For each $i \in \{i_1, \dots, i_n\}$,

$$\hat{\mathsf{p}}_i(\langle \mathbf{a}_i, \bar{\mathbf{s}} \rangle) > \mathsf{P}_{\mathbf{s}, e_i}(\bar{\mathbf{s}}, 0) - \zeta \geq \mathsf{P}_{\mathbf{s}, e_i}(\bar{\mathbf{s}}, \gamma) + 4\zeta > \hat{\mathsf{p}}_i(\langle \mathbf{a}_i, \mathbf{s} \rangle + \gamma) + 3\zeta,$$

and so Inv sets $w_i = \langle \mathbf{a}_i, \bar{\mathbf{s}} \rangle$ during Step 2. So we have shown that, conditioned on the random choices in Step 1 being correct, Inv never sets w_i equal to anything but $\langle \mathbf{a}_i, \bar{\mathbf{s}} \rangle$ in Step 2, and furthermore, with probability at least $4/5 - 2^{-\Omega(n)} \geq 3/4$, Inv sets $w_i = \langle \mathbf{a}_i, \bar{\mathbf{s}} \rangle$ for at least n values of $i \in \{1, \dots, m\}$ such that the corresponding $\mathbf{a}_i$'s span $\mathbb{Z}_q^n$. Thus, once we show that $\left| \hat{\mathsf{p}}_i(\langle \mathbf{a}_i, \bar{\mathbf{s}} \rangle + \gamma) - \mathsf{P}_{\mathbf{s}, e_i}(\bar{\mathbf{s}}, \gamma) \right| < \zeta$ holds simultaneously for all $i = 1, \dots, m$ and $\gamma \in \mathbb{Z}_q$ with probability at least $2/3$, we will have shown that Inv recovers $\bar{\mathbf{s}}$ with probability at least $q^{-2k}/2$, as desired.

So fix an LWE sample $(\mathbf{a}, b)$ and $\gamma \in \mathbb{Z}_q$, and let $\mathbb{1}(\mathbf{u})$ be the $0/1$ random variable which outputs 1 if $\mathsf{Pred}(\mathbf{a} + \mathbf{x}_\mathbf{u}, b + g_\mathbf{u}) - h_\mathbf{u} = \langle \mathbf{a}, \bar{\mathbf{s}} \rangle + \gamma$ and 0 otherwise.

Let $Q := \Pr\left[|\hat{p}(\langle \mathbf{a}, \bar{\mathbf{s}} \rangle + \gamma) - P_{\mathbf{s},e}(\bar{\mathbf{s}}, \gamma)| > \zeta\right]$ be shorthand. We have

$$\zeta^2 Q \leq \mathbb{E}\left[\hat{p}(\langle \mathbf{a}, \bar{\mathbf{s}} \rangle + \gamma)^2\right] - P_{\mathbf{s},e}(\bar{\mathbf{s}}, \gamma)^2$$

$$= \frac{1}{(q^k-1)^2} \cdot \sum_{\mathbf{u} \neq \mathbf{u}' \in \mathbb{Z}_q^k \setminus \{0\}} \mathbb{E}\left[\mathbb{1}(\mathbf{u}) \cdot \mathbb{1}(\mathbf{u}')\right] - P_{\mathbf{s},e}(\bar{\mathbf{s}}, \gamma)^2 + \frac{1}{(q^k-1)}$$

$$\leq \frac{1}{(q^k-1)},$$

and so $Q \leq \frac{1}{\zeta^2(q^k-1)} \leq \frac{1}{3mq}$. So the concentration bound holds simultaneously for all $i \in \{1, \ldots, m\}$ and $\gamma \in \mathbb{Z}_q$ with probability at least $2/3$ by the union bound. The result follows.

5.2   The Natural Predictor

Let notations be as specified at the beginning of this section. So, $f : \mathbb{Z}_q^n \times \mathbb{Z}_q \to \mathbb{Z}_q^n \times \mathbb{Z}_p$ is part of a pointwise reduction, and $(\mathbf{H}, \mathbf{V})$ are such that $\mathbf{H} \in \mathbb{Z}_q^{n \times n}$ and $\mathbf{V} \subset \mathbb{Z}_q^n$ is a constant dimensional vector space such that $P(\mathbf{H}, \mathbf{V}) \geq 1 - \tau$. Let $\{\mathbf{v}_1, \ldots, \mathbf{v}_d\}$ be a basis for $\mathbf{V}$. Given such setup, we now describe the "natural predictor", which given samples $(\mathbf{a}, b) \sim \mathsf{LWE}_{\mathbf{s}}$ for sufficiently good $\mathbf{s} \in \mathbf{G}$, predicts the inner product $\langle \mathbf{a}, \mathbf{H}^t\mathbf{s}' \rangle$ well enough so that it is possible to use Lemma 4 to recover $\mathbf{H}^t\mathbf{s}'$.

The Natural Predictor. The predictor function $\mathsf{Pred} : \mathbb{Z}_q^n \times \mathbb{Z}_q \to \mathbb{Z}_q$ works as follows.

- The natural predictor is parametrized by $\alpha_1, \ldots, \alpha_d \in \mathbb{Z}_q$.
- Given $(\mathbf{a}, b) \in \mathbb{Z}_q^n \times \mathbb{Z}_q$, Pred computes $(\mathbf{a}', b') = f(\mathbf{a}, b)$; if $\mathbf{a}' = \alpha \mathbf{H}\mathbf{a} + \mathbf{v}$ for $\alpha \in \mathbb{Z}_q^*$ and $\mathbf{v} = \sum_{i=1}^d c_i \mathbf{v}_i \in \mathbf{V}$, then output $\alpha^{-1}\left(x - \sum_{i=1}^d c_i \alpha_i\right)$ where $x \sim \mathbb{Z}_q$ is random such that $\lfloor x \rfloor_p = b'$.
- If $\mathbf{a}' \notin \mathrm{Span}(\mathbf{H}\mathbf{a}) + \mathbf{V}$, output a random $x \sim \mathbb{Z}_q$.

Note that whenever $b' = \lfloor \langle \mathbf{a}', \mathbf{s}' \rangle \rfloor_p$ and $\mathbf{a}' = \alpha \mathbf{H}^t\mathbf{a} + \mathbf{v}$ both hold, $b' = \lfloor \alpha \langle \mathbf{a}, \mathbf{H}^t\mathbf{s}' \rangle + \langle \mathbf{v}, \mathbf{s}' \rangle \rfloor_p$ also holds; so when the natural predictor draws x, a random rounding preimage of b' and outputs $\alpha^{-1}\left(x - \sum_i c_i \alpha_i\right)$, it has probability roughly $p/q \gg 1/q$ of outputting $\langle \mathbf{a}, \mathbf{H}^t\mathbf{s}' \rangle$ as long as $\alpha_i = \langle \mathbf{v}_i, \mathbf{s}' \rangle$ for all $i = 1, \ldots, d$. The following claim proves that this predictor satisfies the hypotheses of Lemma 4, and so can be used to recover $\mathbf{H}^t\mathbf{s}'$.

Claim 3. *Let notations be as above. Suppose that the natural predictor is fed with inputs from an $\mathsf{LWE}_{\mathbf{s}}$–oracle for some unknown $\mathbf{s} \in \mathbf{G}$ such that for all $\beta \in \mathbb{Z}_q$, $\Pr\left[\mathcal{D}_{\mathbf{s}} = \beta\right] \geq \frac{1}{q^2}$, where $\mathcal{D}_{\mathbf{s}}$ is the distribution which draws $(\mathbf{a}, b) \sim \mathsf{LWE}_{\mathbf{s}}$ such that $\mathbf{a}' \in \mathrm{Span}(\mathbf{H}\mathbf{a}) + \mathbf{V}$, and outputs $\langle \mathbf{a}, \mathbf{H}^t\mathbf{s}' \rangle$. Assume furthermore that the parameters of the predictor are $\alpha_i = \langle \mathbf{v}_i, \mathbf{s}' \rangle$ for all $i = 1, \ldots, d$. Then both of the correctness hypotheses of Lemma 4 are satisfied for $\bar{\mathbf{s}} = \mathbf{H}^t\mathbf{s}'$.*

Proof. Fix $\zeta = \frac{1-2\tau-q^2\eta}{11q^3}$. We must show two points:

· for all $e \in \mathbb{Z}_q$ with $\Pr[\chi = e] \geq \frac{4\zeta}{5qn^2}$ and all non-zero $\gamma \in \mathbb{Z}_q^*$, $P_{\mathbf{s},e}(\mathbf{H^t s'}, 0) \geq P_{\mathbf{s},e}(\mathbf{H^t s'}, \gamma) - \zeta$;

· for all non-zero $\gamma \in \mathbb{Z}_q^*$, $P_{\mathbf{s}}(\mathbf{H^t s'}, 0) - P_{\mathbf{s}}(\mathbf{H^t s'}, \gamma) \geq 10\zeta$;

where $P_{\mathbf{s},e}(\mathbf{H^t s'}, \gamma)$ and $P_{\mathbf{s}}(\mathbf{H^t s'}, \gamma)$ are the notations from Lemma 4:

$$P_{\mathbf{s},e}(\mathbf{H^t s'}, \gamma) := \Pr_{\mathbf{a} \sim \mathbb{Z}_q^n}\left[\mathsf{Pred}(\mathbf{a}, \langle \mathbf{a}, \mathbf{s}\rangle + e) = \langle \mathbf{a}, \mathbf{H^t s'}\rangle + \gamma\right],$$

and $P_{\mathbf{s}}(\mathbf{H^t s'}, \gamma)$ is the same except the probability is over $(\mathbf{a}, b) \sim \mathsf{LWE_s}$. Let us simplify the shorthand by writing $P_e^{(1)}(\gamma)$ and $P^{(1)}(\gamma)$ instead of $P_{\mathbf{s},e}(\mathbf{H^t s'}, \gamma)$ and $P_{\mathbf{s}}(\mathbf{H^t s'}, \gamma)$. Note

$$P_e^{(1)}(\gamma) = \left(1 - P_{\mathbf{s},e}(\mathbf{H}, \mathbf{V})\right) \cdot \frac{1}{q}$$
$$+ \Pr_{\mathbf{a} \sim \mathbb{Z}_q^n}\left[\mathsf{Pred}(\mathbf{a}, \langle \mathbf{a}, \mathbf{s}\rangle + e) = \langle \mathbf{a}, \mathbf{H^t s'}\rangle + \gamma \ \& \ \mathbf{a'} \in \mathsf{Span}(\mathbf{Ha}) + \mathbf{V}\right],$$

where $(\mathbf{a'}, b') = f(\mathbf{a}, \langle \mathbf{a}, \mathbf{s}\rangle + e)$. So if we shorthand the second term by $P_e^{(2)}(\gamma)$, then we get that $P_e^{(1)}(0) - P_e^{(1)}(\gamma) = P_e^{(2)}(0) - P_e^{(2)}(\gamma)$. Now let

$$P_e^{(3)}(\gamma) := \Pr_{\mathbf{a} \sim \mathbb{Z}_q^n}\left[\mathsf{Pred}(\mathbf{a}, \langle \mathbf{a}, \mathbf{s}\rangle + e) = \langle \mathbf{a}, \mathbf{H^t s'}\rangle + \gamma \right.$$
$$\left. \& \ b' = \lfloor\langle \mathbf{a'}, \mathbf{s'}\rangle\rceil_p \ \& \ \mathbf{a'} \in \mathsf{Span}(\mathbf{Ha}) + \mathbf{V}\right],$$

where $(\mathbf{a'}, b') = f(\mathbf{a}, \langle \mathbf{a}, \mathbf{s}\rangle + e)$. If $\Pr[\chi = e] \geq \frac{4\zeta}{5qn^2}$, $P_3^{(2)} - \frac{5qn^2\eta}{4\zeta} \leq P_e^{(3)}(\gamma) \leq P_e^{(2)}(\gamma)$, since $\mathbf{s} \in \mathbf{G}$ and so $p_{(\mathbf{s}, \mathbf{s'})} \geq 1 - \eta$. Therefore, $P_e^{(2)}(0) - P_e^{(2)}(\gamma) \geq P_e^{(3)}(0) - P_e^{(3)}(\gamma) - \zeta$, using $\eta \leq \frac{4\zeta^2}{5qn^2}$. To bound the $P^{(3)}$ terms, recall that when $\mathbf{a'} = \alpha\mathbf{Ha} + \mathbf{v}$ for $\mathbf{v} = \sum_i c_i \mathbf{v}_i \in \mathbf{V}$, Pred outputs $\alpha^{-1}(x - \sum_i c_i \alpha_i)$ for a random $x \sim \mathbb{Z}_q$ such that $\lfloor x\rceil_p = b'$. Therefore, when $b' = \lfloor\langle \mathbf{a'}, \mathbf{s'}\rangle\rceil_p = \lfloor\alpha\langle \mathbf{a}, \mathbf{H^t s'}\rangle + \langle \mathbf{v}, \mathbf{s'}\rangle\rceil_p$, Pred outputs $\langle \mathbf{a}, \mathbf{H^t s'}\rangle$ with probability roughly p/q when $\lfloor\alpha(\langle \mathbf{a}, \mathbf{H^t s'}\rangle + \gamma) + \langle \mathbf{v}, \mathbf{s'}\rangle\rceil_p = \lfloor\alpha\langle \mathbf{a}, \mathbf{H^t s'}\rangle + \langle \mathbf{v}, \mathbf{s'}\rangle\rceil_p$, and with probability 0 otherwise. It follows that $P_e^{(3)}(0) - P_e^{(3)}(\gamma)$ is roughly

$$\frac{p}{q} \cdot \Pr_{\mathbf{a} \sim \mathbb{Z}_q^n}\left[\lfloor\alpha(\langle \mathbf{a}, \mathbf{H^t s'}\rangle + \gamma) + \langle \mathbf{v}, \mathbf{s'}\rangle\rceil_p \neq \lfloor\alpha\langle \mathbf{a}, \mathbf{H^t s'}\rangle + \langle \mathbf{v}, \mathbf{s'}\rangle\rceil_p\right.$$
$$\left. \& \ \mathbf{a'} \in \mathsf{Span}(\mathbf{Ha}) + \mathbf{V}\right] \geq 0.$$

Thus, $P_e(0) \geq P_e(\gamma) - \zeta$ for all non-zero $\gamma \in \mathbb{Z}_q^*$, which establishes the first point.

For the second point, we can define $P^{(2)}(\gamma), P^{(3)}(\gamma)$ analogously to how we defined $P_e^{(2)}(\gamma), P_e^{(3)}(\gamma)$, respectively (except probability is over $(\mathbf{a}, b) \sim \mathsf{LWE_s}$), and we get $P^{(1)}(0) - P^{(1)}(\gamma) = P^{(2)}(0) - P^{(2)}(\gamma) \geq P^{(3)}(0) - P^{(3)}(\gamma) - \eta \geq P^{(3)}(0) - P^{(3)}(\gamma) - \zeta$. Now, let us write $P^{(3)}(\gamma) = \sum_{\beta \in \mathbb{Z}_q} S_\beta(\gamma)$ where each $S_\beta(\gamma)$ is the product of the following four terms:

- $\Pr_{(a,b)\sim\mathsf{LWE_s}}\left[a' \in \mathrm{Span}(\mathbf{Ha}) + \mathbf{V}\right] =: \mathsf{P_s}(\mathbf{H}, \mathbf{V});$
- $\Pr_{(a,b)\sim\mathsf{LWE_s}}\left[\langle a, \mathbf{H^ts'}\rangle = \beta | a' \in \mathrm{Span}(\mathbf{Ha}) + \mathbf{V}\right];$
- $\Pr_{(a,b)\sim\mathsf{LWE_s}}\left[b' = \lfloor\langle a', s'\rangle\rceil_p | \langle a, \mathbf{H^ts'}\rangle = \beta \ \& \ a' \in \mathrm{Span}(\mathbf{Ha}) + \mathbf{V}\right];$
- $\Pr_{(a,b)\sim\mathsf{LWE_s}}\left[\mathsf{Pred}(a, b) = \langle a, \mathbf{H^ts'}\rangle + \gamma | b' = \lfloor\langle a', s'\rangle\rceil_p \ \& \ \langle a, \mathbf{H^ts'}\rangle = \beta \ \& \ a' \in \mathrm{Span}(\mathbf{Ha}) + \mathbf{V}\right].$

Let $\mathsf{Q}_\beta(\gamma)$ be shorthand for the fourth term; as noted above, $\mathsf{Q}_\beta(\gamma)$ is roughly equal to $\frac{p}{q} \cdot \mathbb{1}(\beta, \gamma)$ where $\mathbb{1}(\beta, \gamma) = 1$ if $\lfloor\alpha(\beta+\gamma)+\sum_i c_i\alpha_i\rceil_p = \lfloor\alpha\beta+\sum_i c_i\alpha_i\rceil_p$, and is zero otherwise. The second term is $\Pr[\mathcal{D}_s = \beta]$, where $\mathcal{D}_s$ is the distribution defined in the claim statement. Finally, note that the third term is at least $1 - \frac{q^2\eta}{\mathsf{P_s}(\mathbf{H}, \mathbf{V})}$. Thus, for non-zero $\gamma \in \mathbb{Z}_q^*$,

$$\mathsf{P}^{(3)}(0) - \mathsf{P}^{(3)}(\gamma) \geq \left(\mathsf{P_s}(\mathbf{H}, \mathbf{V}) - q^2\eta\right) \cdot \sum_{\beta \in \mathbb{Z}_q} \Pr[\mathcal{D}_s = \beta] \cdot (\mathsf{Q}_\beta(0) - \mathsf{Q}_\beta(\gamma))$$

$$\geq \left(\frac{\mathsf{P_s}(\mathbf{H}, \mathbf{V})}{q^2} - \eta\right) \cdot \sum_{\beta:\mathbb{1}(\beta,\gamma)=0} \frac{1}{q} \geq \left(\frac{1 - 2\tau - q^2\eta}{q^3}\right) = 11\zeta,$$

where the second inequality on the second line holds since when $\gamma \neq 0$ there exists at least one β such that $\mathbb{1}(\beta, \gamma) = 0$. Hence we have that $\mathsf{P}^{(1)}(0) - \mathsf{P}^{(1)}(\gamma) \geq (1 - (2\tau + q^2\eta))/q^3 - \zeta \geq 10\zeta$, which completes the proof of the second point.

5.3   Proving Lemma 1 Assuming Lemma 3

Lemma 1 (Restated). Assume the notations described in the beginning of the section. So specifically, $f : \mathbb{Z}_q^n \times \mathbb{Z}_q \to \mathbb{Z}_q^n \times \mathbb{Z}_p$ is part of a pointwise reduction and $(\mathbf{H}, \mathbf{V})$ are such that $\mathsf{P}(\mathbf{H}, \mathbf{V}) \geq 1 - \tau$. Then there exists an algorithm which, given oracle access to an $\mathsf{LWE_s}-oracle$ for a random $s \sim G$, outputs $\mathbf{H^ts'}$ with non-negligible probability over $s \sim G$ and the random coins.

Proof. By Claim 3 and Lemma 4, it suffices simply to show that for an overwhelming fraction of the $s \in G$ have $\Pr[\mathcal{D}_s = \beta] \geq \frac{1}{q^2}$ for all $\beta \in \mathbb{Z}_q$ where $\mathcal{D}_s$ is the distribution which draws $(a, b) \sim \mathsf{LWE_s}$ such that $a' \in \mathrm{Span}(\mathbf{Ha}) + \mathbf{V}$ and outputs $\langle a, \mathbf{H^ts'}\rangle$. Since $\mathsf{P_s}(\mathbf{H}, \mathbf{V}) \geq 1 - 2\tau$, $\mathcal{D}_s$ is within statistical distance 2τ of the distribution $\hat{\mathcal{D}}_s$ which simply draws $a \sim \mathbb{Z}_q^n$ and outputs $\langle a, \mathbf{H^ts'}\rangle$. For $\beta \in \mathbb{Z}_q$, define the sets:

$$X_\beta := \left\{s \in G : \Pr_{a\sim\mathbb{Z}_q^n}[\langle a, \mathbf{H^ts'}\rangle = \beta] < q^{-2}\right\}; \text{ and } Y_\beta := \{\mathbf{H^ts'} : s \in X_\beta\},$$

and consider the distribution $\mathcal{D}_\beta$, which draws $a \sim \mathbb{Z}_q^n$, $s \sim X_\beta$ and outputs $\langle a, \mathbf{H^ts'}\rangle$. We have

$$\frac{1}{q} - \frac{1}{q^2} - 2\tau < \Delta(\mathcal{D}_\beta, \mathsf{Unif}(\mathbb{Z}_q)) \leq q^c\Delta(\langle\mathsf{Unif}(\mathbb{Z}_q^n), \mathsf{Unif}(Y_\beta)\rangle, \mathsf{Unif}(\mathbb{Z}_q)) \leq \sqrt{\frac{q}{4|Y_\beta|}}.$$

The first inequality used the definition of X_β; the second used that $\mathbf{H}$ has rank $n - c$ for some constant c (since otherwise f would be degenerate), and that

G induces a perfect matching between LWE secrets and LWR secrets; and the last inequality is Fact 1. It follows that $|Y_\beta| = q^{\mathcal{O}(1)}$, and thus so are $|X_\beta|$, and $\bigcup_\beta X_\beta$. Therefore, $\Pr[\mathcal{D}_\mathbf{s} = \beta] \geq \frac{1}{q^2}$ holds for all $\beta \in \mathbb{Z}_q$ for an overwhelming fraction of the $\mathbf{s} \in G$. Lemma 1 follows.

6   Proof of Lemma 3

Notation. Recall we have integers $n, p, q \in \mathbb{N}$ such that q is prime and $q^{2/3+c} < p < q$ for some small constant $c > 0$. Additionally, $f : \mathbb{Z}_q^n \times \mathbb{Z}_q \to \mathbb{Z}_q^n \times \mathbb{Z}_p$ is part of a pointwise reduction from $\mathsf{LWE}_{n,q,\chi}$ to $\mathsf{LWR}_{n,q,p}$. Recall from Sect. 4.2, we have a set $G \subset \mathbb{Z}_q^n$ of "good secrets"; this set has size at least $|G| \geq \delta q^n$ for non-negligible $\delta > 0$ and for each $\mathbf{s} \in G$ there exists a unique $\mathbf{s}' \in \mathbb{Z}_q^n$ such that $\mathsf{p}_{(\mathbf{s},\mathbf{s}')} \geq 1 - \eta$ for non-negligible $\eta > 0$. It was also shown in Claim 1 that for all subset $S \subset \mathbb{Z}_q^n$ of size $|S| = \rho q^n$, and non-negligible $\nu > 0$, $\Pr_{(\mathbf{a},b)\sim\mathbb{Z}_q^n\times\mathbb{Z}_q}[\mathbf{a}' \in S] \leq \rho + \nu$. We have been calling this the "non-degenerate" property of f; this will play a major role in this section. Our goal in this section is to algorithmically recover $(\mathbf{H}, \mathbf{V})$ such that $\mathbf{H} \in \mathbb{Z}_q^{n \times n}$ and $\mathbf{V} \subset \mathbb{Z}_q^n$ is a constant dimensional vector subspace such that

$$\mathsf{P}(\mathbf{H}, \mathbf{V}) := \Pr_{(\mathbf{a},b)\sim\mathbb{Z}_q^n\times\mathbb{Z}_q}[\mathbf{a}' \in \mathrm{Span}(\mathbf{Ha}) + \mathbf{V}] \geq 1 - \tau,$$

where $(\mathbf{a}', b') = f(\mathbf{a}, b)$, and $\tau = nq^2 \eta^{1/12t}\sqrt{178n}$, where $t \in \mathbb{N}$ is a new parameter; it is the minimal integer such that $t \geq \frac{\log_q(1/\delta)+2}{3c}$ holds. Note $t = \mathcal{O}(1)$.

The Function h. We introduce the function $h : \mathbb{Z}_q^n \to \mathbb{Z}_q^n$ which is defined from f as follows. First, if $b \in \mathbb{Z}_q$, then define the function $h_b : \mathbb{Z}_q^n \to \mathbb{Z}_q^n$ by $h_b(\mathbf{a}) = \mathbf{a}'$ such that $(\mathbf{a}', b') = f(\mathbf{a}, b)$. If $\mathbf{a} \sim \mathbb{Z}_q^n$, then $h(\mathbf{a})$ chooses $b \sim \mathbb{Z}_q$ and outputs $h_b(\mathbf{a}) \in \mathbb{Z}_q^n$. However, if $\mathbf{a}_1, \ldots, \mathbf{a}_n \sim \mathbb{Z}_q^n$, and $\alpha_1, \ldots, \alpha_n \in \mathbb{Z}_q$, then we define

$$h\left(\sum_i \alpha_i \mathbf{a}_i\right) = h_{\sum_i \alpha_i b_i}\left(\sum_i \alpha_i \mathbf{a}_i\right),$$ where each $b_i \in \mathbb{Z}_q$ is the randomness chosen

in the computation of $h(\mathbf{a}_i)$. In this section, it will be considerably simpler to work with h rather than f. The non-degeneracy property framed in terms of h asserts that for all $S \subset \mathbb{Z}_q^n$ of size $|S| = \rho q^n$, and non-negligible $\nu > 0$, $\Pr_{\mathbf{a}\sim\mathbb{Z}_q}[h(\mathbf{a}) \in S] \leq \rho + \nu$.

6.1   Proof Overview

We first provide a brief high-level overview of the proof of Lemma 3. We prove Lemma 3 in two parts. First, we show there exists an efficiently computable subspace $\mathbf{V} \subset \mathbb{Z}_q^n$ of constant dimension such that

$$\Pr_{\substack{\mathbf{a}_1, \mathbf{a}_2 \sim \mathbb{Z}_q^n \\ (\alpha_1, \alpha_2) \sim \mathbb{Z}_q^2 \\ \text{s.t. } (\alpha_1, \alpha_2) \neq (0,0)}} \left[h(\alpha_1\mathbf{a}_1 + \alpha_2\mathbf{a}_2) \in \mathrm{Span}(\{h(\mathbf{a}_1), h(\mathbf{a}_2)\}) + \mathbf{V}\right] \geq 1 - 2\sqrt{\nu},$$

for a non-negligible quantity $\nu = \nu(n)$. Next, we prove an affine linearity testing theorem to show there exists an efficiently computable matrix $\mathbf{H} \in \mathbb{Z}_q^{n \times n}$ such that $\mathsf{P}(\mathbf{H}, \mathbf{V}) \geq 1 - \tau$, as desired.

Part I: h Passes an Affine Linearity Test with High Probability. Towards proving the first point, we consider the experiment which, for all $i \in [t]$:

1. Chooses $\mathbf{a}_{i,0}, \mathbf{a}_{i,1} \sim \mathbb{Z}_q^n$, $\alpha_{i,0}, \alpha_{i,1} \sim \mathbb{Z}_q$;
2. Sets $\mathbf{a}_{i,2} = \alpha_0 \mathbf{a}_0 + \alpha_1 \mathbf{a}_1 \in \mathbb{Z}_q^n$;
3. Computes $\mathbf{a}'_{i,j} = h(\mathbf{a}_{i,j})$, $\forall j \in \{0, 1, 2\}$;

and then outputs $\{\mathbf{a}'_{i,j}\}_{\substack{i \in [t], \\ j \in \{0,1,2\}}} \subset \mathbb{Z}_q^n$. Suppose that

$$d := \dim \left(\mathrm{Span}(\{\mathbf{a}'_{i,j}\}_{\substack{i \in [t], \\ j \in \{0,1,2\}}}) \right) = 3t.$$

For ease of presentation, suppose furthermore that $\dim \left(\mathrm{Span}(\{\mathbf{a}_{i,j}\}_{\substack{i \in [t], \\ j \in \{0,1\}}}) \right) = 2t$. Since $\{(\mathbf{a}_{i,j}, b_{i,j})\}_{\substack{i \in [t] \\ j \in \{0,1\}}}$ is statistically close to $2t$ LWE$_\mathbf{s}$ samples, for some $\mathbf{s} \in \mathbb{Z}_q^n$, by the correctness of f it follows that f generates $3t$ LWR$_{\mathbf{s}'}$ samples from the $2t$ LWE$_\mathbf{s}$ samples, where $\mathbf{s}' \in \mathbb{Z}_q^n$ is the unique right neighbor of $\mathbf{s}$ in G. But, letting $e_{i,j} \in \mathbb{Z}_q$ be the LWE error term of each sample $(\mathbf{a}_{i,j}, b_{i,j})$ $(i \in [t], j \in \{0,1\})$, observe that

$$\frac{\#\{\mathbf{s} \in \mathbb{Z}_q^n : b_{i,j} - e_{i,j} = \langle \mathbf{a}_{i,j}, \mathbf{s} \rangle \in \mathbb{Z}_q \ \forall i \in [t], j \in \{0,1\}\}}{\#\{\mathbf{s}' \in \mathbb{Z}_q^n : b'_{i,j} = \lfloor \langle \mathbf{a}_{i,j}, \mathbf{s}' \rangle \rceil_p \in \mathbb{Z}_p \ \forall i \in [t], j \in \{0,1,2\}\}} \geq \frac{q^{n-2t}}{(q/p)^{3t} q^{n-3t}}$$

$$= \frac{p^{3t}}{q^{2t}} \geq q^{3ct} > 1,$$

hence at least two distinct good LWE secrets in G must map to the same right-vertex $\mathbf{s}'$, contradicting the definition of G. Hence $d < 3t$.

In reality, our full proof actually shows that $d < 3t$ with probability at least $1 - \nu^t$ over our experiment. A routine counting argument then shows $\exists r \in \{0, 1, \dots, t-1\}$ such that

$$1 - \nu \leq \Pr\left[\dim \left(\mathrm{Span}(\{\mathbf{a}'_{i,0}, \mathbf{a}'_{i,1}, \mathbf{a}'_{i,2}\}_{i \leq r+1}) \right) < 3(r+1) \ \middle|\right.$$

$$\left. \dim \left(\mathrm{Span}(\{\mathbf{a}'_{i,0}, \mathbf{a}'_{i,1}, \mathbf{a}'_{i,2}\}_{i \leq r}) \right) = 3r \right]$$

$$\leq \Pr\left[\mathbf{a}'_{r+1,0} \in \mathbf{V} \right] + \Pr\left[\mathbf{a}'_{r+1,1} \in \mathrm{Span}(\{\mathbf{a}'_{r+1,0}\}) + \mathbf{V} \right]$$

$$+ \Pr\left[\mathbf{a}'_{r+1,2} \in \mathrm{Span}(\{\mathbf{a}'_{r+1,0}, \mathbf{a}'_{r+1,1}\}) + \mathbf{V} \right]$$

$$\leq 2\nu + q^{-\Omega(n)} + \Pr\left[\mathbf{a}'_{r+1,2} \in \mathrm{Span}(\{\mathbf{a}'_{r+1,0}, \mathbf{a}'_{r+1,1}\}) + \mathbf{V} \right],$$

where the probabilities are all over the randomness of our experiment, $\mathbf{V} = \mathrm{Span}(\{\mathbf{a}'_{i,0}, \mathbf{a}'_{i,1}, \mathbf{a}'_{i,2}\}_{i \leq r})$, and the last inequality follows from the non-degeneracy of h. Hence

$$\Pr\left[\mathbf{a}'_{r+1,2} \in \mathrm{Span}(\{\mathbf{a}'_{r+1,0}, \mathbf{a}'_{r+1,1}\}) + \mathbf{V} \right] \geq 1 - 4\nu,$$

which implies that with probability at least $1 - 2\sqrt{\nu}$ over $\mathbf{V}$ it holds that

$$\Pr_{\substack{\mathbf{a}_1, \mathbf{a}_2 \sim \mathbb{Z}_q^n \\ (\alpha_1, \alpha_2) \in \mathbb{Z}_q^2 \\ \text{s.t.} (\alpha_1, \alpha_2) \neq (0,0)}} \left[h(\alpha_1 \mathbf{a}_1 + \alpha_2 \mathbf{a}_2) \in \text{Span}(h(\mathbf{a}_1), h(\mathbf{a}_2)) + \mathbf{V} \right] \geq 1 - 2\sqrt{\nu}.$$

Our algorithm then simply chooses $r^* \sim \{0, 1, \ldots, t - 1\}$ as a guess for r, repeats our experiment substituting r^* for t, and outputs $\mathbf{V} :=$ $\text{Span}(\{\mathbf{a}'_{i,0}, \mathbf{a}'_{i,1}, \mathbf{a}'_{i,2}\}_{i \leq r^*})$. See Sect. 6.2 for the full proof.

Part II: Recovering H via an Affine Linearity Testing Theorem. In Part I of this proof overview, we showed that the function h satisfies a type of affine linearity test. Specifically, we showed there exists an efficiently computable subspace $\mathbf{V} \subset \mathbb{Z}_q^n$ of constant dimension such that

$$\Pr_{\substack{\mathbf{a}_1, \mathbf{a}_2 \sim \mathbb{Z}_q^n \\ (\alpha_1, \alpha_2) \sim \mathbb{Z}_q^2 \\ \text{s.t.} (\alpha_1, \alpha_2) \neq (0,0)}} \left[h(\alpha_1 \mathbf{a}_1 + \alpha_2 \mathbf{a}_2) \in \text{Span}(\{h(\mathbf{a}_1), h(\mathbf{a}_2)\} + \mathbf{V}) \right] \geq 1 - 2\sqrt{\nu}. \quad (4)$$

Now, we outline an affine linearity testing theorem which concludes there exists an efficiently computable matrix $\mathbf{H} \in \mathbb{Z}_q^{n \times n}$ such that

$$\Pr_{\mathbf{a} \sim \mathbb{Z}_q^n} \left[h(\mathbf{a}) \in \text{Span}(\{\mathbf{Ha}\}) + \mathbf{V} \right] \geq 1 - \tau.$$

The high-level idea is that we compute a random basis $\{\mathbf{a}_1, \ldots, \mathbf{a}_n\} \subset \mathbb{Z}_q^n$ of $\mathbb{Z}_q^n$, and then compute $\{\mathbf{a}'_1, \ldots, \mathbf{a}'_n\} \subset \mathbb{Z}_q^n$ that

$$\Pr_{\alpha \sim \mathbb{Z}_q^n} \left[h\left(\sum_{i=1}^{n} \alpha_i \mathbf{a}_i \right) \in \text{Span}\left(\left\{ \sum_{i=1}^{n} \alpha_i \mathbf{a}'_i \right\} \right) + \mathbf{V} \right] \geq 1 - \tau.$$

Then, we construct an algorithm which simply computes the matrices $\mathbf{A}, \mathbf{A}' \in \mathbb{Z}_q^{n \times n}$ where the ith column of $\mathbf{A}$ (resp., $\mathbf{A}'$) is $\mathbf{a}_i$ (resp., $\mathbf{a}'_i$), and outputs the matrix $\mathbf{H} = \mathbf{A}'\mathbf{A}^{-1} \in \mathbb{Z}_q^{n \times n}$.

For the purpose of this proof overview, we assume that the hypothesis (4) of the affine linearity holds with probability 1, and that $\mathbf{V} = \{\mathbf{0}\}$. Let $\{\mathbf{a}_1, \ldots, \mathbf{a}_n\} \subset \mathbb{Z}_q^n$ is a basis for $\mathbb{Z}_q^n$. We additionally assume that $\{h(\mathbf{a}_1), \ldots, h(\mathbf{a}_n)\} \subset \mathbb{Z}_q^n$ is linearly independent. Finally, for simplicity, here we'll actually show there exists $\{\mathbf{a}'_1, \mathbf{a}'_2, \mathbf{a}'_3\} \subset \mathbb{Z}_q^n$ such that $\forall (\alpha_1, \alpha_2, \alpha_3) \in (\mathbb{Z}_2 \times \mathbb{Z}_q \times \mathbb{Z}_q) \setminus \{(0, 0, 0)\}$,

$$h(\alpha_1 \mathbf{a}_1 + \alpha_2 \mathbf{a}_2 + \alpha_3 \mathbf{a}_3) \in \text{Span}(\{\alpha_1 \mathbf{a}'_1 + \alpha_2 \mathbf{a}'_2 + \alpha_3 \mathbf{a}'_3\}).$$

Our techniques follow those in the proof of a major result in algebraic geometry called the Fundamental Theorem of Projective Geometry [4]. As we will see, our argument assumes a polynomially bounded number of events, each of which in reality occurs with high probability. So, in our full proof, we can assume all of these events hold simultaneously, allowing us to adapt these techniques while applying the union bound to obtain the conclusion with probability $1 - \tau$. For the full proof, see Sect. 6.3.

We begin by setting $\mathbf{a}_1' = h(\mathbf{a}_1) \in \mathbb{Z}_q^n$. Observe that since $h(\mathbf{a}_1 + \mathbf{a}_2) \in$ Span$(\{\mathbf{a}_1', h(\mathbf{a}_2)\})$, then we can define $\mathbf{a}_2' \in \mathbb{Z}_q^n$ such that $h(\mathbf{a}_1+\mathbf{a}_2) \in$ Span$(\{\mathbf{a}_1' + \mathbf{a}_2'\})$ ($\mathbf{a}_2'$ is well-defined since $\{h(\mathbf{a}_1), h(\mathbf{a}_2)\}$ are linearly independent). We similarly define $\mathbf{a}_3' \in \mathbb{Z}_q^n$ such that $h(\mathbf{a}_1 + \mathbf{a}_3) \in$ Span$(\{\mathbf{a}_1' + \mathbf{a}_3'\})$. Note that $\{\mathbf{a}_1', \mathbf{a}_2', \mathbf{a}_3'\} \subset \mathbb{Z}_q^n$ are linearly independent. Now, for each $i \in \{2, 3\}$, we can similarly define a map $\pi_i : \mathbb{Z}_q \to \mathbb{Z}_q$ by $\pi_i(\alpha) = \beta \in \mathbb{Z}_q$ such that $h(\mathbf{a}_1 + \alpha \mathbf{a}_i) \in$ Span$(\{\mathbf{a}_1' + \beta \mathbf{a}_i'\})$. Observe that $\pi_i(0) = 0$ and $\pi_i(1) = 1$. Moreover, if $\alpha_2, \alpha_3 \in \mathbb{Z}_q$, then by rewriting $\mathbf{a}_1 + \alpha_2 \mathbf{a}_2 + \alpha_3 \mathbf{a}_3 = (\mathbf{a}_1 + \alpha_2 \mathbf{a}_2) + \alpha_3 \mathbf{a}_3 = (\mathbf{a}_1 + \alpha_3 \mathbf{a}_3) + \alpha_2 \mathbf{a}_2 \in \mathbb{Z}_q^n$, we see that

$$h(\mathbf{a}_1 + \alpha_2 \mathbf{a}_2 + \alpha_3 \mathbf{a}_3) \in \text{Span}(\{\mathbf{a}_1' + \pi_2(\alpha_2)\mathbf{a}_2', \mathbf{a}_3'\}) \cap \text{Span}(\{\mathbf{a}_1' + \pi_3(\alpha_3)\mathbf{a}_3', \mathbf{a}_2'\})$$
$$= \text{Span}(\{\mathbf{a}_1' + \pi_2(\alpha_2)\mathbf{a}_2' + \pi_3(\alpha_3)\mathbf{a}_3'\}).$$

Next, let $(\alpha_2, \alpha_3) \in \mathbb{Z}_q^2 \backslash \{(0,0)\}$, and let $\mathbf{x} = \alpha_2 \mathbf{a}_2 + \alpha_3 \mathbf{a}_3 \in \mathbb{Z}_q^n$. We'll show that $h(\mathbf{x}) \in$ Span$(\{\pi_2(\alpha_2)\mathbf{a}_2' + \pi_3(\alpha_3)\mathbf{a}_3'\})$. Note that we have $h(\mathbf{x}) \in$ Span$(\{\mathbf{a}_2', \mathbf{a}_3'\})$. On the other hand, we can write $\mathbf{x} = (\mathbf{a}_1 + \alpha_2 \mathbf{a}_2 + \alpha_3 \mathbf{a}_3) - \mathbf{a}_1$, hence $h(\mathbf{x}) \in$ Span$(\{h(\mathbf{a}_1 + \alpha_2 \mathbf{a}_2 + \alpha_3 \mathbf{a}_3), \mathbf{a}_1'\}) \subset$ Span$(\{\mathbf{a}_1' + \pi_2(\alpha_2)\mathbf{a}_2' + \pi_3(\alpha_3)\mathbf{a}_3', \mathbf{a}_1'\})$. So, we have

$$h(\mathbf{x}) \in \text{Span}(\{\mathbf{a}_2', \mathbf{a}_3'\}) \cap \text{Span}(\{\mathbf{a}_1' + \pi_2(\alpha_2)\mathbf{a}_2' + \pi_3(\alpha_3)\mathbf{a}_3', \mathbf{a}_1'\})$$
$$= \text{Span}(\{\pi_2(\alpha_2)\mathbf{a}_2' + \pi_3(\alpha_3)\mathbf{a}_3'\}).$$

Finally, we show that each map π_i is actually the identity map on $\mathbb{Z}_q$, which completes the proof. Consider the map π_2 (a similar symmetric argument holds for π_3). We proceed by induction on $\alpha \in \mathbb{Z}_q$. The base cases in which $\alpha \in \{0, 1\}$ follow from the above discussion. Suppose that $\pi_2(\alpha - 1) = \alpha - 1$. Let $\mathbf{x} = \mathbf{a}_1 + \alpha \mathbf{a}_2 + \mathbf{a}_3 \in \mathbb{Z}_q^n$. We can first write $\mathbf{x} = (\mathbf{a}_1 + \pi_2(\alpha)\mathbf{a}_2) + \mathbf{a}_3 \in \mathbb{Z}_q^n$, hence $h(\mathbf{x}) \in$ Span$(\{\mathbf{a}_1' + \pi_2(\alpha)\mathbf{a}_2', \mathbf{a}_3'\})$, so $\exists(\beta_1, \beta_2) \in \mathbb{Z}_q^2$ such that $h(\mathbf{x}) = \beta_1(\mathbf{a}_1' + \pi_2(\alpha)\mathbf{a}_2') + \beta_2 \mathbf{a}_3' \in \mathbb{Z}_q^n$. On the other hand, we can write also write $\mathbf{x} = (\mathbf{a}_1 + (\alpha - 1)\mathbf{a}_2) + (\mathbf{a}_2 + \mathbf{a}_3)$, hence $h(\mathbf{x}) \in$ Span$(\{\mathbf{a}_1' + (\alpha - 1)\mathbf{a}_2', \mathbf{a}_2' + \mathbf{a}_3'\})$, where we have used the induction hypothesis, the conclusion of the previous paragraph, and the base case. So, $\exists(\gamma_1, \gamma_2) \in \mathbb{Z}_q^2$ such that $h(\mathbf{x}) = \gamma_1(\mathbf{a}_1' + (\alpha - 1)\mathbf{a}_2') + \gamma_2(\mathbf{a}_2' + \mathbf{a}_3') \in \mathbb{Z}_q^n$. Finally, we can write $\mathbf{x} = (\mathbf{a}_1 + \mathbf{a}_3) + \alpha_2 \mathbf{a}_2 \in \mathbb{Z}_q^n$, and so $h(\mathbf{x}) \in$ Span$(\{\mathbf{a}_1' + \mathbf{a}_3', \mathbf{a}_2'\})$. Then $\exists(\delta_1, \delta_2) \in \mathbb{Z}_q^2$ such that $h(\mathbf{x}) = \delta_1(\mathbf{a}_1' + \mathbf{a}_3') + \delta_2 \mathbf{a}_2 \in \mathbb{Z}_q^n$. By equating these three representations of $h(\mathbf{x})$, and by the linear independence of $\{\mathbf{a}_1', \mathbf{a}_2', \mathbf{a}_3'\}$, it follows that $\gamma_1(\alpha - 1) + \gamma_2 = \beta_1 \pi_2(\alpha)$, $\gamma_1 = \beta_1$, and $\gamma_2 = \delta_1 = \gamma_1$. Hence $\gamma_1 \alpha = \gamma_1 \pi_2(\alpha)$, and so $\alpha = \pi_2(\alpha)$ when $\gamma_1 \neq 0$. Indeed, it can be shown that $\gamma_1 \neq 0$ (with overwhelming probability) since h is non-degenerate.

6.2   Recovering V

The Algorithm to Recover **V**. Let notations be as above. We recover **V** as follows.

1. Initialize $\mathbf{V} = \{\mathbf{0}\}$; choose $r \sim \{1, \ldots, t\}$; for $i = 1, \ldots, r$, do the following:

- choose $\mathbf{a}_{i,0}, \mathbf{a}_{i,1} \sim \mathbb{Z}_q^n$ and $(\alpha_{i,0}, \alpha_{i,1}) \sim \mathbb{Z}_q^2 \setminus \{(0,0)\}$;
- compute $\mathbf{a}_{i,j}' = h(\mathbf{a}_{i,j})$ for $j = 0, 1, 2$, where $\mathbf{a}_{i,2} = \alpha_{i,0} \mathbf{a}_{i,0} + \alpha_{i,1} \mathbf{a}_{i,1}$;
- update $\mathbf{V} := \mathbf{V} + \mathrm{Span}(\{\mathbf{a}_{i,0}', \mathbf{a}_{i,1}', \mathbf{a}_{i,2}'\})$.

2. Output $\mathbf{V}$.

Claim 4. *Let $\mathcal{D}_r$ denote the random procedure used to generate the vectors $\{\mathbf{a}_{i,0}', \mathbf{a}_{i,1}', \mathbf{a}_{i,2}'\}_{i=1,\ldots,r}$. Suppose the function $h : \mathbb{Z}_q^n \to \mathbb{Z}_q^n$ is such that $\mathrm{Pr}_{\mathcal{D}_t}[\dim \mathrm{Span}(\{\mathbf{a}_{i,j}'\}_{i,j}) = 3t] < \eta^{1/3}$. Then with non-negligible probability, the vector space $\mathbf{V}$ output above satisfies $\mathsf{P}(\mathbf{V}) \geq 1 - 4\eta^{1/6t}$, where*

$$\mathsf{P}(\mathbf{V}) := \Pr_{\substack{\mathbf{a}_1, \mathbf{a}_2 \sim \mathbb{Z}_q^n \\ (\alpha_1 \alpha_2) \sim \mathbb{Z}_q^2 \setminus \{(0,0)\}}} \left[h(\alpha_1 \mathbf{a}_1 + \alpha_2 \mathbf{a}_2) \in \mathrm{Span}(\{h(\mathbf{a}_1), h(\mathbf{a}_2)\}) + \mathbf{V} \right].$$

Proof. Let $\nu > 0$ be such that $\nu^{3t} = \eta$. Consider an execution of $\mathcal{D}_t$; for $i = 0, \ldots, t$, let $\mathbf{V}_i$ denote the vector space $\mathbf{V}$ after the i-th iteration, and let $d_i = \dim(\mathbf{V}_i)$. We are given that $\Pr[d_t = 3t] < \nu^t$; let $r \in \{0, 1, \ldots, t-1\}$ be maximal such that $\Pr[d_r = 3r] \geq \nu^r$. We have

$$\nu^{r+1} > \Pr[d_{r+1} = 3(r+1)] = \Pr[d_{r+1} = 3(r+1) | d_r = 3r] \cdot \Pr[d_r = 3r]$$
$$\geq \Pr[d_{r+1} = 3(r+1) | d_r = 3r] \cdot \nu^r,$$

and so $\Pr[d_{r+1} < 3(r+1) | d_r = 3r] \geq 1 - \nu$. Let $\mathbf{a}_0, \mathbf{a}_1 \in \mathbb{Z}_q^n$ and $(\alpha_0, \alpha_1) \in \mathbb{Z}_q^2 \setminus \{(0,0)\}$ be the vectors and scalars drawn during the $(r+1)$-th round of $\mathcal{D}_t$. Note if $d_{r+1} < 3(r+1)$ then it must be that at least one of the following occurs:

(1) $\mathbf{a}_0' \in \mathbf{V}_r$; (2) $\mathbf{a}_1' \in \mathbf{V}_r + \mathrm{Span}(\mathbf{a}_0')$; (3) $\mathbf{a}_2' \in \mathbf{V}_r + \mathrm{Span}(\{\mathbf{a}_0', \mathbf{a}_1'\})$.

By non-degeneracy, the first two points happen with probability at most $\nu + q^{-\Omega(n)}$. Thus, the third point holds with probability at least $1 - 3\nu - q^{-\Omega(n)} \geq 1 - 4\nu$, and so it holds with probability $1 - 2\sqrt{\nu}$ over $\mathbf{V}_r$ that

$$\mathsf{P}(\mathbf{V}_r) = \Pr_{\substack{\mathbf{a}_0, \mathbf{a}_1 \sim \mathbb{Z}_q^n \\ (\alpha_0, \alpha_1) \sim \mathbb{Z}_q^2 \setminus \{(0,0)\}}} \left[h(\alpha_0 \mathbf{a}_0 + \alpha_1 \mathbf{a}_1) \in \mathrm{Span}(\{h(\mathbf{a}_0), h(\mathbf{a}_1)\}) + \mathbf{V}_r \right]$$
$$\geq 1 - 2\sqrt{\nu}.$$

The probability that the above algorithm chooses this r is $1/t$. The claim follows.

Claim 5. *Let notations be as above. Then $\mathrm{Pr}_{\mathcal{D}_t}[\dim(\mathbf{V}) = 3t] < \eta^{1/3}$.*

Remark 2. This is the only place in the paper where we need to use the assumption that $q^{2/3+c} < p < q$.

Proof. Let $\mathcal{D}$ be the distribution which runs the same random procedure as in $\mathcal{D}_t$ except which also outputs the $\{\mathbf{a}_{i,j}\}$, and additionally which outputs the $\{b_{i,j}\}$ and $\{b_{i,j}'\}$ used to compute h. So specifically, $\mathcal{D}$ outputs

$$\left\{ (\mathbf{a}_{i,j}, b_{i,j}), (\mathbf{a}_{i,j}', b_{i,j}') \right\}_{\substack{i=1,\ldots,t \\ j=0,1,2}} \subset \left(\mathbb{Z}_q^n \times \mathbb{Z}_q \right)^3 \times \left(\mathbb{Z}_q^n \times \mathbb{Z}_p \right)^3$$

where for all $i = 1, \ldots, t$:

- $(\mathbf{a}_{i,0}, b_{i,0}), (\mathbf{a}_{i,1}, b_{i,1}) \sim \mathbb{Z}_q^n \times \mathbb{Z}_q$;
- $(\alpha_{i,0}, \alpha_{i,1}) \sim \mathbb{Z}_q^2 \setminus \{(0,0)\}$ and $(\mathbf{a}_{i,2}, b_{i,2}) = (\alpha_{i,0}\mathbf{a}_{i,0} + \alpha_{i,1}\mathbf{a}_{i,1}, \alpha_{i,0}b_{i,0} + \alpha_{i,1}b_{i,1})$;
- $(\mathbf{a}'_{i,j}, b'_{i,j}) = f(\mathbf{a}_{i,j}, b_{i,j})$.

Consider a draw $(\{(\mathbf{a}_{i,j}, b_{i,j})\}, \{(\mathbf{a}'_{i,j}, b'_{i,j})\}) \sim \mathcal{D}$, let $d := \dim(\text{Span}(\{\mathbf{a}'_{i,j}\}))$, and let $S, S' \subset \mathbb{Z}_q^n$ be the following subsets of LWE and LWR secrets:

$$S := \{\mathbf{s} \in \mathsf{G} : b_{i,j} = \langle \mathbf{a}_{i,j}, \mathbf{s} \rangle \ \forall \ i, j\},$$

$$S' := \{\mathbf{s}' \in \mathbb{Z}_q^n : b'_{i,j} = \lfloor \langle \mathbf{a}'_{i,j}, \mathbf{s}' \rangle \rceil_p \ \forall \ i, j\}.$$

Consider the following three events:

- $\mathbf{E}_1$: $d = 3t$;
- $\mathbf{E}_2$: $|S| \geq q^{-2t-1} \cdot |\mathsf{G}|$;
- $\mathbf{E}_3$: $\text{Pr}_{\mathbf{s} \sim S}[\mathbf{s}' \in S'] \geq 1 - \sqrt{3tq\eta}$, where $\mathbf{s}' \in \mathbb{Z}_q^n$ is the unique LWR secret st $\mathsf{p}_{(\mathbf{s}, \mathbf{s}')} \geq 1 - \eta$.

Note that all three events cannot occur simultaneously. Indeed, the events $\mathbf{E}_2$ and $\mathbf{E}_3$ together imply that $\#\{\mathbf{s} \in S : \mathbf{s}' \in S'\} \geq (1 - \sqrt{3tq\eta}) \cdot q^{-2t-1} \cdot |\mathsf{G}| \geq \frac{1}{2} \cdot q^{-2t-1} \cdot |\mathsf{G}|$, while $\mathbf{E}_1$ implies that $|S'| = (q/p)^{3t} \cdot q^{-3t} \cdot q^n = p^{-3t} \cdot q^n$. If all three hold then

$$\frac{\#\{\mathbf{s} \in S : \mathbf{s}' \in S'\}}{|S'|} \geq \frac{q^{-2t-1} \cdot \delta}{2 \cdot p^{-3t}} > \frac{q^{3tc-1} \cdot \delta}{2} > 1,$$

which violates property 3 of G since it means some $\mathbf{s}' \in S'$ has $\#\{\mathbf{s} \in S : \mathsf{p}_{(\mathbf{s}, \mathbf{s}')} \geq 1 - \eta\} \geq 2$. We finish by claiming that $\mathbf{E}_2$ and $\mathbf{E}_3$ occur with probability at least $1 - q^{-n/3}$ and $1 - \sqrt{3tq\eta}$, respectively (we defer the proofs of these claims to the full version of our paper). Then, it follows that $\text{Pr}_{\mathcal{D}}[\mathbf{E}_2 \& \mathbf{E}_3] > 1 - \eta^{1/3}$. Since all three events cannot occur simultaneously, $\text{Pr}_{\mathcal{D}}[\mathbf{E}_1] < \eta^{1/3}$ must hold.

6.3   Recovering H

In the previous section we showed how to recover a constant dimensional subspace $\mathbf{V} \subset \mathbb{Z}_q^n$ such that $\mathsf{P}(\mathbf{V}) \geq 1 - 4\gamma$, where $\gamma = \eta^{1/6t}$. Here, we show how to use h such that $\mathsf{P}(\mathbf{V}) \geq 1 - 4\gamma$ holds to recover $\mathbf{H} \in \mathbb{Z}_q^{n \times n}$ such that $\mathsf{P}(\mathbf{H}, \mathbf{V}) \geq 1 - \tau$ holds where $\tau = nq^2\sqrt{178n\gamma}$. This completes the proof of Lemma 3, and thus also the proof of Theorem 2. Rather than directly recovering $\mathbf{H} \in \mathbb{Z}_q^{n \times n}$, our algorithm will recover vectors $\{\mathbf{a}_i, \mathbf{a}'_i\}_{i=1}^n \subset \mathbb{Z}_q^n$ such that $\{\mathbf{a}_i\}_i$ is linearly independent and such that

$$\text{Pr}_{\alpha_1, \dots, \alpha_n \sim \mathbb{Z}_q}\left[h(\alpha_1 \mathbf{a}_1 + \cdots + \alpha_n \mathbf{a}_n) \in \text{Span}(\alpha_1 \mathbf{a}'_1 + \cdots + \alpha_n \mathbf{a}'_n) + \mathbf{V}\right] \geq 1 - \tau. \quad (5)$$

Given such $\{\mathbf{a}_i, \mathbf{a}'_i\}_i$, we let $\mathbf{H} \in \mathbb{Z}_q^{n \times n}$ be the linear map which sends $\mathbf{a}_i$ to $\mathbf{a}'_i$ for all $i = 1, \dots, n$; $\mathsf{P}(\mathbf{H}, \mathbf{V}) \geq 1 - \tau$ follows from (5).

The Algorithm to Recover $\{\mathbf{a}_i, \mathbf{a}_i'\}_i$. Let notations be as above. We recover $\{\mathbf{a}_i, \mathbf{a}_i'\}_i$ as follows.

1. Choose $\mathbf{a}_1, \ldots, \mathbf{a}_n \sim \mathbb{Z}_q^n$ such that $\{\mathbf{a}_1, \ldots, \mathbf{a}_n\}$ is linearly independent.
2. For $i = 1, \ldots, n$, set $\mathbf{a}_i' = \lambda_i h(\mathbf{a}_i) \in \mathbb{Z}_q^n$ for scalars $\{\lambda_i\}_{i=1}^n$ computed as follows:
   · set $\lambda_1 = 1$;
   · for $i \geq 2$, let $\lambda_i \in \mathbb{Z}_q$ be the unique scalar such that $h(\mathbf{a}_1 + \mathbf{a}_i) \in \mathrm{Span}(\mathbf{a}_1' + \lambda_i h(\mathbf{a}_i)) + \mathbf{V}$; if no such λ_i exists, or if more than one such λ_i exists, halt and give no output.
3. Output $\{\mathbf{a}_i, \mathbf{a}_i'\}_{i=1}^n$.

Note that $h(\mathbf{a}_1 + \mathbf{a}_i) \in \mathrm{Span}(\{\mathbf{a}_1', h(\mathbf{a}_i)\}) + \mathbf{V}$ holds for all $i \in \{2, \ldots, n\}$ with probability at least $1 - 4(n-1)q^2\gamma$, since $\mathrm{P}(\mathbf{V}) \geq 1 - 4\gamma$. In this case, for all i, there exist scalars (β_1, β_i) such that $h(\mathbf{a}_1 + \mathbf{a}_i) \in \beta_1 \mathbf{a}_1' + \beta_i h(\mathbf{a}_i) + \mathbf{V}$. If $\beta_1 = 0$ then $h(\mathbf{a}_1 + \mathbf{a}_i) \in \mathrm{Span}(h(\mathbf{a}_i)) + \mathbf{V}$; this happens only with negligible probability since h is non-degenerate. If $\beta_1 \neq 0$ then there exists some scalar $\lambda_i \in \mathbb{Z}_q$ such that $h(\mathbf{a}_1 + \mathbf{a}_i) \in \mathrm{Span}(\mathbf{a}_1' + \lambda_i h(\mathbf{a}_i)) + \mathbf{V}$. Note, it is only possible for there to exist two such scalars, $\lambda_i \neq \lambda_i'$ such that

$$h(\mathbf{a}_1 + \mathbf{a}_i) \in \Big(\mathrm{Span}(\mathbf{a}_1' + \lambda_i h(\mathbf{a}_i)) + \mathbf{V}\Big) \cap \Big(\mathrm{Span}(\mathbf{a}_1' + \lambda_i' h(\mathbf{a}_i)) + \mathbf{V}\Big),$$

if $h(\mathbf{a}_i) \in \mathrm{Span}(\mathbf{a}_1') + \mathbf{V}$. This also occurs with negligible probability since h is non-degenerate. Thus, the above algorithm completes and gives output without aborting with probability at least $1 - (n/q + 4nq^2\gamma)$.

Henceforth, if $\mathbf{a}_1, \ldots, \mathbf{a}_n \sim \mathbb{Z}_q^n$, then we will implicitly condition on $\{\mathbf{a}_1, \ldots, \mathbf{a}_n\}$ being linearly independent and computing $\{\mathbf{a}_1', \ldots, \mathbf{a}_n'\}$ as above. Specifically, we'll show that

$$\Pr_{\substack{\mathbf{a}_1, \ldots, \mathbf{a}_n \sim \mathbb{Z}_q^n \\ (\alpha_1, \ldots, \alpha_n) \sim \mathbb{Z}_q^n \setminus \{0\}}} \left[h\Big(\sum_i \alpha_i \mathbf{a}_i\Big) \in \mathrm{Span}\Big(\Big\{\sum_i \alpha_i \mathbf{a}_i'\Big\}\Big) + \mathbf{V} \right] \geq 1 - 178n^3q^4\gamma,$$

hence with non-negligible probability over $\mathbf{a}_1, \ldots, \mathbf{a}_n \sim \mathbb{Z}_q^n$, it follows that $\{\mathbf{a}_1, \ldots, \mathbf{a}_n\}$ is linearly independent, our above algorithm outputs $\{\mathbf{a}_1', \ldots, \mathbf{a}_n'\}$ as desired, and (5) holds.

We'll use induction on $r \in \{3, \ldots, n\}$ to show that

$$\mathsf{P}_r := \Pr_{\substack{\mathbf{a}_1, \ldots, \mathbf{a}_n \sim \mathbb{Z}_q^n \\ (\alpha_1, \ldots, \alpha_n) \sim \mathbb{Z}_q^n \setminus \{0\}}} \left[h\Big(\sum_{i=1}^r \alpha_i \mathbf{a}_i\Big) \in \mathrm{Span}\Big(\Big\{\sum_{i=1}^r \alpha_i \mathbf{a}_i'\Big\}\Big) + \mathbf{V} \right]$$
$$\geq 1 - (80n^2q^4\gamma + 89(r-3)n^2q^4\gamma),$$

hence $\mathsf{P}_n \geq 1 - 178n^3q^4\gamma$ as desired. We begin with the following key technical claim, whose proof we defer to the full version of our paper.

Claim 6. *For all distinct* $i, j \in \{2, \ldots, n\}$, *and* $(\alpha_1, \alpha_i, \alpha_j) \in \mathbb{Z}_q^3 \setminus \{0\}$,

$$h(\alpha_1 \mathbf{a}_1 + \alpha_i \mathbf{a}_i + \alpha_j \mathbf{a}_j) \in \mathrm{Span}(\{\alpha_1 \mathbf{a}_1' + \alpha_i \mathbf{a}_i' + \alpha_j \mathbf{a}_j'\}) + \mathbf{V},$$

holds with probability at least $1 - 80n^2q^4\gamma$ *over* $\{\mathbf{a}_i\}_{i=1}^n$.

The base case of $r = 3$ follows immediately from Claim 6. For the induction step, assume that $\mathsf{P}_{r-1} \geq 80n^2q^4\gamma + 89(r-4)n^2q^4\gamma$. Since the probability P_r over $\mathbf{a}_1, \ldots, \mathbf{a}_n \sim \mathbb{Z}_q^n, (\alpha_1, \ldots, \alpha_n) \sim \mathbb{Z}_q^n \backslash \{\mathbf{0}\}$, we will assume WLOG that $\alpha_1 \neq 0$. Observe that we can write $\mathbf{z} := h(\alpha_1\mathbf{a}_1 + \cdots + \alpha_r\mathbf{a}_r) = h\big((\alpha_1\mathbf{a}_1 + \cdots + \alpha_{r-1}\mathbf{a}_{r-1}) + \alpha_r\mathbf{a}_r\big) \in \mathrm{Span}\big(\{h(\alpha_1\mathbf{a}_1 + \cdots + \alpha_{r-1}\mathbf{a}_{r-1}), h(\mathbf{a}_r)\}\big) + \mathbf{V} \subset \mathrm{Span}\big(\{\alpha_1\mathbf{a}_1' + \cdots + \alpha_{r-1}\mathbf{a}_{r-1}', \mathbf{a}_r'\}\big) + \mathbf{V}$, except with probability $4\gamma + (80n^2q^4\gamma + 89(r-4)n^2q^4\gamma)$ (here we have invoked the induction hypothesis). On the other hand, we can write $\mathbf{z} = h\big((\alpha_1\mathbf{a}_1 + \alpha_r\mathbf{a}_r) + (\alpha_2\mathbf{a}_2 + \cdots + \alpha_{r-1}\mathbf{a}_{r-1})\big) \in \mathrm{Span}\big(\{h(\alpha_1\mathbf{a}_1 + \alpha_r\mathbf{a}_r), \mathbf{y}\}\big) + \mathbf{V} \subset \mathrm{Span}\big(\{\alpha_1\mathbf{a}_1' + \alpha_r\mathbf{a}_r', \mathbf{y}\}\big) + \mathbf{V}$, except with probability $4\gamma + 80n^2q^4\gamma$, by Claim 6. Hence $\exists \beta_1, \beta_2, \beta_3, \beta_4 \in \mathbb{Z}_q, \mathbf{v}_1, \mathbf{v}_2 \in \mathbf{V}$ such that

$$\beta_1(\alpha_1\mathbf{a}_1' + \cdots + \alpha_{r-1}\mathbf{a}_{r-1}') + \beta_2\mathbf{a}_r' + \mathbf{v}_1 = \mathbf{z} = \beta_3(\alpha_1\mathbf{a}_1' + \alpha_r\mathbf{a}_r') + \beta_4\mathbf{y} + \mathbf{v}_2,$$

and since the distribution of $\mathbf{y}$ is independent of $\{\mathbf{a}_1, \mathbf{a}_r\}$, it follows from the non-degeneracy of h that with overwhelming probability $\beta_1\alpha_1 = \beta_3\alpha_1$ and $\beta_2 = \beta_3\alpha_r$. Since $\alpha_1 \neq 0$ we thus have that $\beta_1 = \beta_3$ and so $\beta_2 = \beta_1\alpha_r$, hence $\mathbf{z} \in \mathrm{Span}\big(\{\alpha_1\mathbf{a}_1' + \cdots + \alpha_r\mathbf{a}_r'\}\big) + \mathbf{V}$ with probability $1 - (4\gamma + (80n^2q^4\gamma + 89(r-4)n^2q^4\gamma) + 4\gamma + 80n^2q^4\gamma + \mathsf{negl}(n)) \geq 1 - (80n^2q^4\gamma + 89(r-3)n^2q^4\gamma)$, which completes the induction step.

References

1. Alperin-Sheriff, J., Apon, D.: Dimension-preserving reductions from LWE to LWR. IACR Cryptol. ePrint Arch., p. 589 (2016). http://eprint.iacr.org/2016/589
2. Alwen, J., Krenn, S., Pietrzak, K., Wichs, D.: Learning with rounding, revisited. In: Canetti, R., Garay, J.A. (eds.) CRYPTO 2013, Part I. LNCS, vol. 8042, pp. 57–74. Springer, Heidelberg (2013). https://doi.org/10.1007/978-3-642-40041-4_4
3. Applebaum, B., Cash, D., Peikert, C., Sahai, A.: Fast cryptographic primitives and circular-secure encryption based on hard learning problems. In: Halevi, S. (ed.) CRYPTO 2009. LNCS, vol. 5677, pp. 595–618. Springer, Heidelberg (2009). https://doi.org/10.1007/978-3-642-03356-8_35
4. Artin, E.: Geometric Algebra (1957)
5. Bai, S., Langlois, A., Lepoint, T., Stehlé, D., Steinfeld, R.: Improved security proofs in lattice-based cryptography: using the rényi divergence rather than the statistical distance. IACR Cryptol. ePrint Arch. 2015, 483 (2015). http://eprint.iacr.org/2015/483
6. Banerjee, A., Peikert, C., Rosen, A.: Pseudorandom functions and lattices. In: Pointcheval, D., Johansson, T. (eds.) EUROCRYPT 2012. LNCS, vol. 7237, pp. 719–737. Springer, Heidelberg (2012). https://doi.org/10.1007/978-3-642-29011-4_42
7. Bogdanov, A., Guo, S., Masny, D., Richelson, S., Rosen, A.: On the hardness of learning with rounding over small modulus. In: Kushilevitz, E., Malkin, T. (eds.) TCC 2016. LNCS, vol. 9562, pp. 209–224. Springer, Heidelberg (2016). https://doi.org/10.1007/978-3-662-49096-9_9
8. Brakerski, Z., Gentry, C., Vaikuntanathan, V.: Fully homomorphic encryption without bootstrapping. IACR Cryptol. ePrint Arch. 2011, 277 (2011). http://eprint.iacr.org/2011/277

9. Brakerski, Z., Langlois, A., Peikert, C., Regev, O., Stehlé, D.: Classical hardness of learning with errors. CoRR abs/1306.0281 (2013). http://arxiv.org/abs/1306.0281

10. Brakerski, Z., Vaikuntanathan, V.: Constrained key-homomorphic PRFs from standard lattice assumptions. In: Dodis, Y., Nielsen, J.B. (eds.) TCC 2015, Part II. LNCS, vol. 9015, pp. 1–30. Springer, Heidelberg (2015). https://doi.org/10.1007/978-3-662-46497-7_1

11. Chor, B., Goldreich, O.: Unbiased bits from sources of weak randomness and probabilistic communication complexity. SIAM J. Comput. **17**(2), 230–261 (1988). https://doi.org/10.1137/0217015

12. Gentry, C., Peikert, C., Vaikuntanathan, V.: Trapdoors for hard lattices and new cryptographic constructions. In: Dwork, C. (ed.) Proceedings of the 40th Annual ACM Symposium on Theory of Computing, Victoria, British Columbia, Canada, 17–20 May 2008, pp. 197–206. ACM (2008). https://doi.org/10.1145/1374376.1374407

13. Gentry, C., Sahai, A., Waters, B.: Homomorphic encryption from learning with errors: conceptually-simpler, asymptotically-faster, attribute-based. In: Canetti, R., Garay, J.A. (eds.) CRYPTO 2013, Part I. LNCS, vol. 8042, pp. 75–92. Springer, Heidelberg (2013). https://doi.org/10.1007/978-3-642-40041-4_5

14. Goldreich, O., Levin, L.A.: A hard-core predicate for all one-way functions. In: Johnson, D.S. (ed.) Proceedings of the 21st Annual ACM Symposium on Theory of Computing, 14–17 May 1989, Seattle, Washigton, USA, pp. 25–32. ACM (1989). https://doi.org/10.1145/73007.73010

15. Lee, C., Lu, C., Tsai, S., Tzeng, W.: Extracting randomness from multiple independent sources. IEEE Trans. Inf. Theor. **51**(6), 2224–2227 (2005). https://doi.org/10.1109/TIT.2005.847746

16. Micciancio, D., Peikert, C.: Trapdoors for lattices: simpler, tighter, faster, smaller. In: Pointcheval, D., Johansson, T. (eds.) EUROCRYPT 2012. LNCS, vol. 7237, pp. 700–718. Springer, Heidelberg (2012). https://doi.org/10.1007/978-3-642-29011-4_41

17. Peikert, C.: Public-key cryptosystems from the worst-case shortest vector problem: extended abstract. In: Mitzenmacher, M. (ed.) Proceedings of the 41st Annual ACM Symposium on Theory of Computing, STOC 2009, Bethesda, MD, USA, 31 May–2 June 2009, pp. 333–342. ACM (2009). https://doi.org/10.1145/1536414.1536461

18. Peikert, C., Shiehian, S.: Noninteractive zero knowledge for NP from (plain) learning with errors. In: Boldyreva, A., Micciancio, D. (eds.) CRYPTO 2019. LNCS, vol. 11692, pp. 89–114. Springer, Cham (2019). https://doi.org/10.1007/978-3-030-26948-7_4

19. Regev, O.: On lattices, learning with errors, random linear codes, and cryptography. In: Gabow, H.N., Fagin, R. (eds.) Proceedings of the 37th Annual ACM Symposium on Theory of Computing, Baltimore, MD, USA, 22–24 May 2005, pp. 84–93. ACM (2005). https://doi.org/10.1145/1060590.1060603

Reductions from Module Lattices to Free Module Lattices, and Application to Dequantizing Module-LLL

Gabrielle De Micheli[1], Daniele Micciancio[1], Alice Pellet-Mary[2], and Nam Tran[3,4(✉)]

[1] University of California, San Diego, USA
gdemicheli@ucsd.edu, daniele@cs.ucsd.edu
[2] Univ. Bordeaux, CNRS, INRIA, Bordeaux INP, IMB, Talence, France
alice.pellet-mary@math.u-bordeaux.fr
[3] Institute of Cybersecurity and Cryptology, School of Computing and Information Technology, University of Wollongong, Wollongong, Australia
ndt141@uowmail.edu.au
[4] CSIRO Data61, Eveleigh, Australia

Abstract. In this article, we give evidence that free modules (i.e., modules which admit a basis) are no weaker than arbitrary modules, when it comes to solving cryptographic algorithmic problems (and when the rank of the module is at least 2). More precisely, we show that for three algorithmic problems used in cryptography, namely the shortest vector problem, the Hermite shortest vector problem and a variant of the closest vector problem, there is a reduction from solving the problem in any module of rank $n \geq 2$ to solving the problem in any *free* module of the same rank n. As an application, we show that this can be used to dequantize the LLL algorithm for module lattices presented by Lee et al. (Asiacrypt 2019).

Keywords: lattices · module lattices · shortest vector problem

1 Introduction

Lattice-based algorithmic problems using algebraic lattices, such as the NTRU problem [HPS06], the Ring LWE [SSTX09,LPR13] and Ring SIS [LM06,PR06] problems, or the Module LWE and Module SIS problems [BGV14,LS15], have been used as security foundation for many cryptographic primitives. As an example of the importance of such problems, 3 out of 4 algorithms standardized by NIST in July 2022 are based on one of these algebraic lattice problems.[1] One of the main advantages of using algebraic lattices compared to standard lattices is that the extra structure added to the lattices allows for less resource

---

[1] https://csrc.nist.gov/projects/post-quantum-cryptography.

© International Association for Cryptologic Research 2023
H. Handschuh and A. Lysyanskaya (Eds.): CRYPTO 2023, LNCS 14085, pp. 836–865, 2023.
https://doi.org/10.1007/978-3-031-38554-4_27

for storage and enables faster algorithms for computation, thus improving efficiency. Another advantage of the algebraic structure is that it allows to multiply elements, which can be useful for applications like homomorphic encryption [Gen09a, Gen09b] or obfuscation [GGH+16].

All the five algorithmic problems mentioned above enjoy reductions from (various) worst-case problems over algebraically structured lattices, called module and ideal lattices (see [PS21, FPS22] for the reductions to the NTRU problem, [LM06, PR06] for Ring SIS, [SSTX09, LPR13] for Ring LWE, and [LS15] for module SIS and module LWE). These worst-case algorithmic problems over modules and ideals provide lower bounds on the hardness of the NTRU, Ring/Module SIS and Ring/Module LWE problems, and hence on the security of the schemes based upon them. At a high level, a module can be seen as a lattice, but defined over a ring which is not the ring $\mathbb{Z}$. More formally, let K be a number field of degree d. For simplicity in this introduction, we will focus on $K = \mathbb{Q}[X]/(X^d+1)$ with d a power-of-two, which is a cyclotomic field. This field has a ring of integers $\mathcal{O}_K$, which in our example is equal to $\mathbb{Z}[X]/(X^d+1)$. An $\mathcal{O}_K$-module M in K^m (which we will simply call "a module" in the rest of this article) is a subset of K^m generated by a finite set of vectors $\mathbf{v}_1, \ldots, \mathbf{v}_k \in K^m$, i.e.,

$$M := \{\alpha_1 \mathbf{v}_1 + \ldots + \alpha_k \mathbf{v}_k : \alpha_1, \ldots, \alpha_k \in \mathcal{O}_K\}.$$

An ideal is a special case of the above definition, corresponding to the case where the generating set is a finite subset of K (i.e., $m = 1$ in the definition above). An important remark in this definition is that the vectors $\mathbf{v}_1, \ldots, \mathbf{v}_k$ are not required to be linearly independent: they generate the module, but they might not be a basis of the module.

This remark actually highlights a key difference between modules over the ring of integers $\mathcal{O}_K$ and lattices over the ring $\mathbb{Z}$. Indeed, the ring $\mathcal{O}_K$ is usually not a principal ideal domain (at least for our illustrating example where K is cyclotomic). This means that module lattices do not always have bases over $\mathcal{O}_K$ (contrary to lattices which always have bases over $\mathbb{Z}$). Instead, a module M over $\mathcal{O}_K$ admits pseudo-bases, which consist in n linearly independent vectors $\mathbf{b}_1, \ldots, \mathbf{b}_n$ of K^m and n ideals $I_1, \ldots, I_n$ such that $M = \{\sum_i x_i \mathbf{b}_i \mid x_i \in I_i\}$. The integer n is called the rank of the module M.

In some cases, a module M admits a basis, that is, a pseudo-basis where all the coefficient ideals I_i are equal to $\mathcal{O}_K$. In this case, M is said to be a *free module*. In the case of ideals (i.e., modules included in K), an ideal admitting a basis is called a *principal ideal*. We note that, in our example rings, free modules represent a very small portion of the set of all modules.[2] Moreover, even when a module M is free, computing a basis from a given generating set (or a pseudo-basis) of M might be challenging. It can be performed in *quantum* polynomial time, but only in subexponential classical time so far (more details can be found

---

[2] In the case of ideals for instance, we know that the proportion of principal ideals among all ideals is equal to $1/h_K$, where h_K is a quantity called the class number of the field K. When K is a cyclotomic field, it is known that h_K grows more than exponentially in the degree d of the number field (see, e.g., [Was97, Proposition 11.15]).

in preliminaries). In this article, the main question we try to answer is the following: if we restrict ourselves to free modules represented by a basis (and not any pseudo-basis), are algorithmic problems like the shortest vector problem or the closest vector problem easier to solve? (When compared to the problems over arbitrary modules, represented by a pseudo-basis.)

So far, the answer to this question is not so clear. There have been some algorithms exploiting the specific structure of free modules or principal ideals, but most of these algorithms were later extended to all modules or all ideals. For example, [CDPR16] introduced in 2016 an algorithm to compute relatively short elements in *principal ideals* of a cyclotomic field, which was generalized to all ideals one year later in [CDW17]. To the best of our knowledge, the only algorithm which (still) behaves significantly better for free modules than for arbitrary modules is the LLL algorithm for module lattices from [LPSW19] (referred to as module-LLL below). This oracle-based algorithm runs in classical polynomial time when given as input any free module (represented by a basis) but only in quantum polynomial time when given as input an arbitrary module.

Contributions. In this article, we give evidence that free modules already capture all the hardness contained in arbitrary modules, for modules of rank ≥ 2. More formally, we prove that it is possible to reduce three algorithmic problems from their variant over module lattices to their variant over free-module lattices (represented by a basis). The three problems we consider in this work are: the shortest vector problem (SVP), the Hermite shortest vector problem (HSVP) and a variant of the closest vector problem ($\mathrm{CVP_{cov}}$). In the variant of CVP we consider, we want to find a lattice point $\mathbf{s}$ close to a target $\mathbf{t}$, such that $\|\mathbf{t} - \mathbf{s}\| \leq \gamma \cdot \mathrm{cov}(\mathcal{L})$, where $\gamma \geq 1$ is some approximation factor and $\mathrm{cov}(\mathcal{L})$ is the covering radius of the lattice $\mathcal{L}$ (in the standard CVP problem, we usually asks that $\|\mathbf{t} - \mathbf{s}\| \leq \gamma \cdot \mathrm{dist}(\mathbf{t}, \mathcal{L})$, where $\mathrm{dist}(\mathbf{t}, \mathcal{L})$ is the minimal distance between $\mathbf{t}$ and a point of $\mathcal{L}$).

For an algorithmic problem $\mathcal{P}$, let us write n-module-$\mathcal{P}$ the worst-case problem $\mathcal{P}$ restricted to module lattices of rank n included in K^n, and n-free-module-$\mathcal{P}$ the worst-case problem $\mathcal{P}$ restricted to free-module lattices of rank n included in K^n and represented by a basis. We prove the following theorem.

Theorem 1.1 (Informal, see Theorems 6.1, 6.2 **and** 6.3**).** *Let $n \geq 2$ be an integer. Then, there exist probabilistic polynomial time reductions*

- *from n-module-SVP to n-free-module-SVP;*
- *from n-module-HSVP to n-free-module-HSVP;*
- *from n-module-CVP_{cov} to n-free-module-CVP_{cov}.*

The approximation factors achieved by these reductions are polynomial in some quantities depending on the number fields, in n, and in the approximation factor of the oracle solving the problem in free modules (see Theorems 6.1, 6.2, 6.3 for more details). Moreover, one can check that the reductions from the theorem require only two calls to an oracle solving the free-module-$\mathcal{P}$ problem in order to solve one instance of the module-$\mathcal{P}$ problem (where $\mathcal{P} \in \{\mathrm{SVP}, \mathrm{HSVP}, \mathrm{CVP_{cov}}\}$).

As an application, we show how the reduction from n-module-SVP to n-free-module-SVP can be used to dequantize the module-LLL algorithm from [LPSW19] for *all modules*.[3] This closes the gap between free and arbitrary module for this algorithm.

Techniques. The three reductions, for SVP, HSVP and CVP_{cov} follow the same framework. Let $\mathcal{P}$ be one of the three problems. We first reduce $\mathcal{P}$ in modules to $\mathcal{P}$ is free modules *and* HSVP in ideals (Sect. 3). Then, we reduce HSVP in ideals to $\mathcal{P}$ in free modules of rank 2 (Sect. 4). Finally, we reduce $\mathcal{P}$ in free modules of rank 2 to $\mathcal{P}$ in free modules of rank $n \geq 2$ (Sect. 5). Combining these three reductions, we obtain a reduction from $\mathcal{P}$ in modules of rank n to $\mathcal{P}$ in free modules of rank n for any $n \geq 2$.

Let us focus a bit more on each of the three subreductions. For the reduction from module-$\mathcal{P}$ to free-module-$\mathcal{P}$ and HSVP in ideal lattices, the main idea is to use an *almost-free representation* of the input module M, that is, a pseudo-basis of M of the form $((\mathbf{b}_i, I_i))_{1 \leq i \leq n}$ with $I_i = \mathcal{O}_K$ for all $i \leq n-1$. Such a pseudo-basis can be computed in probabilistic polynomial time from any pseudo-basis of M. Then, we use the oracle solving HSVP in ideals to compute a short element $x \in I_n$, and we consider the free module N given by the basis $(\mathbf{c}_i)_{1 \leq i \leq n}$, where $\mathbf{c}_i = \mathbf{b}_i$ for $i \leq n-1$ and $\mathbf{c}_n = x \cdot \mathbf{b}_n$. One can check that N is a free module included in M. It can also be checked that N is not much sparser than M. Both properties imply that solving $\mathcal{P}$ in N also provides a solution to $\mathcal{P}$ in M, with some controlled loss in the approximation factor.

In the second step of the reduction, we want to find a short element of an ideal, given access to an oracle solving $\mathcal{P}$ in free modules of rank 2. Here, the main idea is to consider a *two-element representation* of the input ideal, that is, two elements of K that, together, generate the ideal. This two-element representation can be computed in probabilistic polynomial time from any basis of the ideal (see Theorem 2.2). We then show that, by solving a free-module-$\mathcal{P}$ instance in a free module of rank 2 constructed from the two elements found before, it is possible to find a short element of the input ideal. Similar techniques were used in [DM22] in order to transform modules of rank 2 into free modules of rank 4.

Finally, the last part of the reduction is to reduce $\mathcal{P}$ from free modules of rank 2 to free modules of rank $n \geq 2$. The strategy here is quite natural: we embed the input module of rank 2 into a larger module of rank n. The naive strategy is, for instance, to consider the direct orthogonal sum of the input module M with the free module $\mathcal{O}_K^{n-1}$ of rank $n-2$ (possibly scaled). This works well for SVP and CVP_{cov}, but surprisingly, this does not seem to work for HSVP. Instead, for HSVP, we construct a module of rank n from M by gluing $\lfloor n/2 \rfloor$ orthogonal copies of M together, and adding an extra orthogonal copy of $\mathcal{O}_K$ if n is odd. This provides a reduction for HSVP which has some significant loss in the approximation factor when n is odd (whereas we had almost no loss for SVP and CVP_{cov}). We believe that it would be an interesting open problem to reduce this loss in the HSVP case (or, on the contrary, show that this loss is mandatory).

---

[3] Recall that in this article, modules are always included in K^m for some $m > 0$.

The dequantization of the module-LLL algorithm from [LPSW19] is obtained almost immediately as a corollary of the reduction from module-SVP to free-module-SVP. Indeed, recall that the module-LLL algorithm from [LPSW19] (solving SVP in module lattices) is by default a quantum algorithm (when given as input a pseudo-basis of a module), but can be run by a classical computer in the specific case where the input module is free and represented by a basis. Combining this classical algorithm for free-module-SVP with the reduction from module-SVP to free-module-SVP provides an algorithm for arbitrary modules.

Discussion. In this introduction, we focused on the special case of cyclotomic number fields. However, our results are not restricted to cyclotomic number fields, but can be used in any number field K. For example, our results might be interesting even in number fields with class number one (i.e., whose ring of integers $\mathcal{O}_K$ is principal). In these special cases, all modules are free, but we have seen that it is in general hard to compute a basis of a free module without a quantum computer. Our reduction provides a way to transform *classically* a problem over a free module represented by a pseudo-basis into two instances of the same problem over free modules represented by a basis.

In this article, we restricted ourselves to prove reductions for three lattice problems, namely SVP, HSVP and CVP_{cov}, which we thought were somewhat standard and representative of the variety of lattice problems. We did not try to see if our reduction framework could be adapted to the large set of other lattice problems (see, e.g., [Ste15, page 1] for a non-exhaustive list of problems). However, we did try to use our framework to prove a reduction for the standard CVP problem,[4] instead of the variant CVP_{cov} that we used, but did not succeed. The issue with the standard formulation of CVP stems from the fact that if a target is unexpectedly close to a lattice point, then we may have to find a lattice point whose distance to the target is significantly smaller than the covering radius of the lattice. Interestingly, it seems that our framework can be used in the cases where the target is very close to the lattice (closer than the minimal distance of the lattice) or relatively far away (at a distance of the order of the covering radius of the lattice), but we do not know how to handle the cases in between. We leave it as an open problem to obtain a reduction similar to ours, for the standard CVP problem.

Finally, we remark that another way to obtain reductions from (non free) module problems to free module problems could be to use the reductions from worst-case ideal/module problems to NTRU, Ring/Module LWE or Ring/Module SIS. Indeed, the NTRU, Ring/Module LWE and Ring/Module SIS problems can be reduced to problems over modules (either the shortest vector problem or the bounded distance decoding problem), and the modules that are produced by these reductions are often free and with an easily computable basis. As an example, a Ring LWE instance with good parameters can be reduced to

---

[4] Recall that the standard CVP problem asks, given as input a target $\mathbf{t}$, to find a point $\mathbf{s}$ of the lattice $\mathcal{L}$ such that $\|\mathbf{t} - \mathbf{s}\| \leq \gamma \cdot \mathrm{dist}(\mathbf{t}, \mathcal{L})$, for some approximation factor γ.

a bounded distance decoding problem in a module M of rank 2 in $\mathcal{O}_K^2$ spanned by three vectors $(a_1, a_2)^T$, $(q, 0)^T$ and $(0, q)^T$. If a_1 is coprime with q (which should happen with relatively high probability), then there exists $u, v \in \mathcal{O}_K$ such that $u a_1 + v q = 1$ and in this case the two vectors $(1, u a_2)^T$ and $(0, q)^T$ form a basis of the module M (which is then free). Even if this approach seems a possible alternative way to obtain reductions from arbitrary modules to free modules, we would like to highlight some advantages of the approach we chose in this article. First of all, the reductions from worst-case ideal/module problems to Ring/Module LWE and Ring/Module SIS do not preserve the rank of the modules, whereas our reductions transform modules into free modules of the same rank (this is also a limitation for the reduction to NTRU from [PS21], but not for the reduction from [FPS22], which preserves the rank). Another limitation of the approach using Ring/Module LWE is that the reductions from worst-case problem to Ring/Module LWE are quantum, whereas our reductions are classical (this is a limitation only for Ring/Module LWE, not for NTRU or Ring/Module SIS which enjoy classical reductions). Finally, one last advantage of our reductions is that the framework is quite simple, and does not require the heavy machinery of the worst-case to average-case reductions of NTRU, Ring/Module LWE and Ring/Module SIS. In particular, our reduction could be easily implemented, and should be quite efficient. Also, we believe that the general framework we describe might be used to derive reductions for other algorithmic problems, in case they are needed.

Previous Versions. This article is the result of a merge between [DM22] and [PT23]. The first article showed how to dequantize the module-LLL algorithm, by using the two-element representation of ideals in order to transform arbitrary rank-2 modules into free rank-4 modules. The second article extended the techniques to obtain reductions from problems over arbitrary modules to problems over free modules of the same rank. The merged article mostly contains material from [PT23], since it mostly subsumes [DM22].

2 Preliminaries

We let $\mathbb{Z}, \mathbb{Q}, \mathbb{R}, \mathbb{C}$ denote the set of integers, rationals, real and complex numbers respectively. For a positive real number x, we let $\log(x)$ denote the logarithm of x in base 2. Throughout this article, we let bold lowercase letters denote vectors. All vectors are column vectors with the coordinates denoted by normal lowercase letter with subsripted index, for example

$$\mathbf{v} = \begin{pmatrix} v_1 \\ \vdots \\ v_d \end{pmatrix} \in \mathbb{R}^d$$

is a column vectors with coordinates $v_1, \dots, v_d \in \mathbb{R}$. We let $\mathbf{v}^T$ denote the transpose of $\mathbf{v}$. We write $\|\mathbf{v}\|_2 = \sqrt{\sum_i v_i^2}$ and $\|\mathbf{v}\|_\infty = \max_i |v_i|$ to denote the ℓ_2-norm and the ℓ_∞-norm respectively. We mostly work with the ℓ_2-norm and ignore the subscript index when there is no confusion.

2.1   Lattices

A lattice $\mathcal{L}$ is a set of linear combinations with integer coefficients of $\mathbb{R}$-linearly independent vectors $\mathbf{b}_1, \ldots, \mathbf{b}_n \in \mathbb{R}^m$.

$$\mathcal{L} = \{a_1 \mathbf{b}_1 + \ldots + a_n \mathbf{b}_n \; : \; a_1, \ldots, a_n \in \mathbb{Z}\}.$$

The (ordered) set of vectors $\{\mathbf{b}_1, \ldots, \mathbf{b}_n\}$ forms a *basis* of $\mathcal{L}$, and can be represented by a matrix $\mathbf{B} \in \mathbb{R}^{m \times n}$ whose columns are the vectors $\mathbf{b}_1, \ldots, \mathbf{b}_n$. The integer n is the rank of the lattice $\mathcal{L}$. When $n = m$, $\mathcal{L}$ is said to be *full-rank*. Given a basis $\mathbf{B} \in \mathbb{R}^{m \times n}$ of $\mathcal{L}$, the determinant (or volume) $\det(\mathcal{L})$ is defined as $\det(\mathbf{B}^T \mathbf{B})^{1/2}$. The determinant of a lattice is invariant with respect to any choice of its basis.

For a lattice $\mathcal{L}$ and $i \in \{2, \infty\}$, we let $\lambda_1^{(i)}(\mathcal{L}) = \min\{\|\mathbf{v}\|_i : \mathbf{v} \in \mathcal{L} \backslash \{\mathbf{0}\}\}$ be the length of a shortest non-zero vector of $\mathcal{L}$ with respect to the ℓ_i-norm. We will also use $\lambda_n^{(i)}(\mathcal{L})$, where n is the rank of $\mathcal{L}$, which is the smallest radius $r > 0$ such that there exists n linearly independent vectors in $\mathcal{L}$ of ℓ_i-norm $\leq r$. Again, we mostly work with the ℓ_2-norm and we drop the superscript index when there is no confusion.

Theorem 2.1 (Minkowski's bound). *For a rank-n lattice $\mathcal{L}$, we have*

$$\lambda_1^{(\infty)}(\mathcal{L}) \leq \det(\mathcal{L})^{1/n};$$
$$\lambda_1^{(2)}(\mathcal{L}) \leq \sqrt{n} \cdot \det(\mathcal{L})^{1/n}.$$

We write $\mathrm{Span}_{\mathbb{R}}(\mathcal{L})$ the real span of a lattice $\mathcal{L}$ (not necessarily full rank). The covering radius $\mathrm{cov}(\mathcal{L})$ of a (not necessarily full rank) lattice $\mathcal{L}$ is defined as $\mathrm{cov}(\mathcal{L}) = \max_{\mathbf{t} \in \mathrm{Span}_{\mathbb{R}}(\mathcal{L})} \min_{\mathbf{s} \in \mathcal{L}} \|\mathbf{t} - \mathbf{s}\|$. Equivalently, $\mathrm{cov}(\mathcal{L})$ is the minimal real number $r > 0$ such that for all $\mathbf{t} \in \mathrm{Span}_{\mathbb{R}}(\mathcal{L})$, there exists $\mathbf{s} \in \mathcal{L}$ with $\|\mathbf{t} - \mathbf{s}\| \leq r$. The covering radius of a lattice is a priori hard to compute, but we can show that for any rank-n lattice $\mathcal{L}$, it holds that

$$\mathrm{cov}(\mathcal{L}) \leq n \cdot \lambda_n^{(2)}(\mathcal{L}). \tag{1}$$

Indeed, let $\mathbf{b}_1, \cdots, \mathbf{b}_n$ be linearly independent vectors of $\mathcal{L}$ satisfying $\|\mathbf{b}_i\| \leq \lambda_n^{(2)}(\mathcal{L})$ and let $\mathbf{t} = \sum_i t_i \mathbf{b}_i \in \mathrm{Span}_{\mathbb{R}}(\mathcal{L})$. Then $\mathbf{s} = \sum_i \lfloor t_i \rfloor \mathbf{b}_i \in \mathcal{L}$ and satisfies $\|\mathbf{t} - \mathbf{s}\| \leq \sum_i \|\mathbf{b}_i\| \leq n \cdot \lambda_n^{(2)}(\mathcal{L})$.

On the other hand, we also know that $\mathrm{cov}(\mathcal{L}) \geq 1/2 \cdot \lambda_1^{(2)}(\mathcal{L})$. Indeed, if $\mathbf{s}$ is a shortest nonzero vector of $\mathcal{L}$, then $1/2 \cdot \mathbf{s}$ has to be at distance $\geq \lambda_1^{(2)}(\mathcal{L})/2$ from any lattice point, since otherwise we would have a nonzero vector in $\mathcal{L}$ of euclidean norm $< \lambda_1^{(2)}(\mathcal{L})$.

2.2   Number Fields

Let K be a number field of degree d and $\mathcal{O}_K$ be its ring of integers. The ring $\mathcal{O}_K$ is a free $\mathbb{Z}$-module of rank d. There exists d embeddings from K to $\mathbb{C}$, denoted by $\sigma_1, \ldots, \sigma_d$. The canonical embedding σ is defined as

$$\forall x \in K, \sigma(x) = (\sigma_1(x), \ldots, \sigma_d(x)) \in \mathbb{C}^d.$$

The number field K, embedded into $\mathbb{C}^d$ via the canonical embedding, has a geometry induced by the geometry of $\mathbb{C}^d$. For $x \in K$, the ℓ_2-norm of x, denoted by $\|x\|$, is defined as the (Hermitian) ℓ_2-norm of the vector $\sigma(x)$ in the space $\mathbb{C}^d$, i.e., $\|x\| := \|\sigma(x)\|$. A similar definition also applies for the ℓ_∞-norm, i.e., $\|x\|_\infty := \|\sigma(x)\|_\infty$ for $x \in K$. For $x, y \in K$, we have the following bound

$$\|xy\| \leq \|x\|_\infty \cdot \|y\| \leq \|x\| \cdot \|y\| \, .$$

The image $\sigma(\mathcal{O}_K)$ is a rank-d lattice, living in $\mathbb{C}^d \simeq \mathbb{R}^{2d}$ (it is not a full rank lattice in $\mathbb{C}^d$). The volume of $\sigma(\mathcal{O}_K)$ is equal to $\Delta_K^{1/2}$, where Δ_K is the *absolute discriminant* of the number field K and is given by

$$\Delta_K = \left| \det \left(\sigma_i(r_j) \right)_{1 \leq i,j \leq d} \right|^2 \, ,$$

where $r_1, \ldots, r_d$ is a $\mathbb{Z}$-basis of $\mathcal{O}_K$. The value of Δ_K is invariant from the choice of the basis $r_1, \ldots, r_d$ of $\mathcal{O}_K$. We will also consider the quantity $\lambda_d^\infty(\sigma(\mathcal{O}_K))$, which we will write $\lambda_d^{(\infty)}(\mathcal{O}_K)$ to simplify notations. In the case of cyclotomic fields, we know that $\lambda_d^{(\infty)}(\mathcal{O}_K) = 1$ (since there is a basis of $\mathcal{O}_K$ made of roots of unity). For general number fields, the quantity $\lambda_d^{(\infty)}(\mathcal{O}_K)$ can be larger, but it cannot be too large, as stated in the following lemma from [BST+20] (the original result from [BST+20] only states that $\lambda_d^\infty(\mathcal{O}_K) = O(\Delta_K^{1/d})$, but the constant in the big O can be worked out [Boe22, Theorem A.4]).

Lemma 2.1 ([Boe22, Theorem A.4], adapted from [BST+20, Theorem 3.1]). *For any number field K, it holds that $\lambda_d^\infty(\mathcal{O}_K) \leq \Delta_K^{1/d}$.*

Algorithms. In this article, when we say that an algorithm is *probabilistic polynomial time*, we mean that the algorithm is a Las Vegas type algorithm,[5] whose expected running time is polynomial in the input size of the algorithm and in $\log \Delta_K$. We emphasize that even when Δ_K is not part of the input of the algorithm, we consider that $\log \Delta_K$ is a polynomial quantity.

2.3 Ideals

A fractional ideal I of K is an $\mathcal{O}_K$-submodule of K for which there exists $a \in \mathcal{O}_K \backslash \{0\}$ such that $aI \subset \mathcal{O}_K$. When $I \subset \mathcal{O}_K$, we say that I is an *integral* ideal. The sum and product of two fractional ideals I and I', defined as,

$$I + I' := \{x + y : x \in I, y \in I'\}$$

$$II' := \left\{ \sum_{i=1}^n x_i y_i : n \in \mathbb{Z}_{>0}, x_i \in I, y_i \in I' \right\}$$

---

[5] That is, an algorithm whose output is always correct, but whose running time is a random variable.

are also fractional ideals. Any non-zero fractional ideal I of K is invertible, meaning that there exists some fractional ideal I^{-1} such that $I \cdot I^{-1} = \mathcal{O}_K$. An ideal $\mathfrak{p}$ is said to be prime if the quotient ring $\mathcal{O}_K/\mathfrak{p}$ is an integral domain. For $x \in K$, we write $\langle x \rangle = x\mathcal{O}_K$ to denote the principal ideal generated by x. We remark that $\mathcal{O}_K$ is a Dedekind domain, in which nonzero proper ideals are uniquely factorized into product of power of prime ideals (the uniqueness is up to the order of the prime factors).

Ideal Lattices and Algebraic Norm. The image $\sigma(I)$ of a fractional ideal I is a rank-d lattice of $\mathbb{C}^d$. We also refer to such lattices as *ideal lattices*. The algebraic norm of a fractional ideal I, denoted by $\mathcal{N}(I)$, is defined to be the determinant of the lattice $\sigma(I)$ divided by $\Delta_K^{1/2}$. Note that if I is integral, then $\mathcal{N}(I)$ is the index $[\mathcal{O}_K : I]$. The ideal norm is multiplicative, i.e. $\mathcal{N}(IJ) = \mathcal{N}(I) \cdot \mathcal{N}(J)$ for fractional ideals I, J. For a principal ideal $\langle x \rangle$, we write $\mathcal{N}(x)$ to denote the algebraic norm of $\langle x \rangle$. This corresponds to the absolute value of the usual definition of the algebraic norm of an element, i.e., $\mathcal{N}(x) = \left| \prod_{i=1}^{d} \sigma_i(x) \right|$.

For any non-zero element $x \in K$, we have the following relation between the algebraic norm and euclidean norm of x, which is obtained from the inequality of arithmetic and geometric means applied to $(|\sigma_i(x)|^2)_i$.

$$\sqrt{d} \cdot \mathcal{N}(x)^{1/d} \leq \|x\|. \tag{2}$$

This implies in particular that for any element $x \in \mathcal{O}_K$, we have $\|x\| \geq \sqrt{d}$.

For any fractional ideal I, it holds that $\lambda_d(I) \leq \lambda_1(I) \cdot \lambda_d^{(\infty)}(\mathcal{O}_K)$. Indeed, if $s \in I$ is a shortest nonzero element of I for the euclidean norm, and $r_1, \ldots, r_d$ are d linearly independent elements of $\mathcal{O}_K$ satisfying $\|r_i\|_\infty \leq \lambda_d^{(\infty)}(\mathcal{O}_K)$ for all i's, then the elements $r_i \cdot s$ are d linearly independent elements of I and satisfy $\|r_i \cdot s\| \leq \|r_i\|_\infty \cdot \|s\| \leq \lambda_1(I) \cdot \lambda_d^{(\infty)}(\mathcal{O}_K)$. Combining this with Minkowski's inequality and Eq. (1) yields

$$\mathrm{cov}(I) \leq d^{3/2} \cdot \lambda_d^{(\infty)}(\mathcal{O}_K) \det(I)^{1/d}. \tag{3}$$

If $I = x\mathcal{O}_K$ is principal, using (2) this can be rewritten

$$\mathrm{cov}(x\mathcal{O}_K) \leq d \cdot \lambda_d^{(\infty)}(\mathcal{O}_K) \cdot \Delta_K^{1/2d} \cdot \|x\|. \tag{4}$$

Two Elements Representation. Every fractional ideal I in K admits a *two-element representation*, which is a way to write I as a sum of two principal ideals $\langle x \rangle$ and $\langle y \rangle$. The following result states that the two-element representation of an ideal can be computed in expected polynomial time.

Theorem 2.2 (Adapted from Lemma 2.6 of [PS21]). *There exists a probabilistic polynomial time algorithm taking a fractional ideal $I \subset K$ and a nonzero $x \in I$ as inputs, and computing $y \in I$ such that $I = \langle x \rangle + \langle y \rangle$.*

Proof. The proof is nearly identical to that in [PS21], except that we repeat the algorithm until it outputs a valid pair (x, y), instead of allowing the algorithm to fail with small probability. Unwrapping the proof, one can see that the algorithm in [PS21] is obtained by taking the algorithm from [FS10, Fig. 1], and setting the element x_1 to be the input x in Step 1. In [FS10], it is proven that the probability p that the algorithm does not fail is at least $1/e$. Hence, the expected number of iterations of our algorithm is $1/p \leq e$.   □

2.4 Modules

Below, we recall the main results about modules that we will need in this article. For more detailed references about the theoretical and computational aspects of modules over Dedekind domain, we refer the reader to [Hop98, Chapter 4] and [Coh12, Chapter 1].

Let $M \subset K^m$ be a finitely generated $\mathcal{O}_K$-module,[6] then there exist K-linearly independent vectors $\mathbf{b}_1, \ldots, \mathbf{b}_n$ of K^m and fractional ideals $I_1, \ldots, I_n$ such that

$$M = I_1\mathbf{b}_1 + \ldots + I_n\mathbf{b}_n.$$

The set of tuples $((I_i, \mathbf{b}_i))_{i \leq n}$ is called a *pseudo-basis* of M, the positive integer n is called the *rank* of M. In particular, fractional ideals of K are rank-1 $\mathcal{O}_K$-modules. For any rank-n module M in K^m, there exists a canonical pseudo-basis, called the HNF basis of M, which can be computed in polynomial time from any pseudo-basis of M (see, e.g., [Coh12]).

Free Modules. A free module is a module M which has a pseudo basis $((I_i, \mathbf{b}_i))_{i \leq n}$ with all the ideals I_i equal to $\mathcal{O}_K$. When this is the case, we say that $(\mathbf{b}_1, \ldots, \mathbf{b}_n)$ is a *free basis* of M.[7] We emphasize here that even if the module M is free, not all pseudo-bases of M are free bases. In particular, the HNF basis of a free module has no reason to be a free basis. Moreover, computing a free basis of a free module given as input an arbitrary pseudo-basis is not known to be doable in classical polynomial time. Indeed, computing a free basis of a free module amounts to computing generators of principal ideals, given as input an arbitrary $\mathbb{Z}$-basis of the ideals (since one can efficiently transform any pseudo-basis of a free module into a new pseudo-basis where all the coefficient ideals are principal, using, e.g., the almost free representation discussed in the next section). This can be done in quantum polynomial time [BS16] but only in sub-exponential classical time [BF14] so far.

Almost Free Representations. For any rank-n module M, there exist pseudo-bases of the form $((\mathbf{b}_i, I_i))_i$, with $I_i = \mathcal{O}_K$ for all $i = 1$ to $n - 1$ (i.e., only the last ideal is non-trivial). Such pseudo-bases are called *almost-free representations*

---

[6] In this article, when we say that M is a module, we always mean an $\mathcal{O}_K$-module included in K^m for some $m > 0$.

[7] Those are usually simply called "bases", by opposition to the pseudo-bases. But we prefer to add the adjective "free" in this work, to make the distinction even clearer.

of M (or *Steinitz form*). We denote this representation by $(\mathbf{b}_1, \ldots, \mathbf{b}_n, I)$, where I is the coefficient ideal corresponding to $\mathbf{b}_n$. Note that, contrary to the HNF basis, the almost-free representation is not unique: for a given module M, there are many pseudo-bases satisfying $I_i = \mathcal{O}_K$ for all $i = 1$ to $n - 1$. Still, it is efficiently computable, as stated in the following lemma.

Lemma 2.2 ([BHJ22, Corollary A.3]).   *There is a probabilistic polynomial time algorithm that takes as input any pseudo-basis of a rank-n module M in K^n for some $n \geq 1$, and returns an almost-free representation of M.*

Module Lattices. The canonical embedding can be extended to K^m, by defining $\sigma(\mathbf{v})$ for $\mathbf{v} = (v_1, \ldots, v_m)^T \in K^m$ to be the concatenation of $\sigma(v_i)$. Then $\sigma(\mathbf{v})$ is a vector of $\mathbb{C}^{md}$ and $\sigma(M)$ is a lattice of rank nd (i.e., non full rank). We refer to such lattices as *module lattices*. We will again abuse notations and write $\|\mathbf{v}\|_2 := \|\sigma(\mathbf{v})\|_2$ and $\|\mathbf{v}\|_\infty := \|\sigma(\mathbf{v})\|_\infty$ for vectors $\mathbf{v} \in K^m$. Similarly, we use M instead of $\sigma(M)$ when we view M as a lattice (e.g., $\lambda_1(M)$, $\det(M)$, $\ldots$). In the rest of the article, we will use the observation that $\mathrm{Span}_{\mathbb{Q}}(\sigma(M)) = \sigma(\mathrm{Span}_K(M))$, and we will again abuse notation and write $\mathrm{Span}_K(M)$ for both.

For a rank-n module M in K^n (i.e., a full rank module), we define the norm of M to be

$$\mathcal{N}(M) = \mathcal{N}(\det \mathbf{B}) \cdot \prod_i \mathcal{N}(I_i),$$

where $((\mathbf{b}_i, I_i))_i$ is a pseudo-basis of M and $\mathbf{B}$ is the $n \times n$ matrix with columns $\mathbf{b}_i$'s (so $\det(\mathbf{B})$ is an element of K). This quantity does not depend on the choice of the pseudo-basis. It is related to the volume of the lattice $\sigma(M)$ by the formula $\det(\sigma(M)) = \Delta_K^{n/2} \cdot \mathcal{N}(M)$.

2.5   Algorithmic Problems over Module and Ideal Lattices

We will consider the following algorithmic problems over module and ideal lattices. These problems are worst-case, which means that we want an algorithm that succeeds on any possible input.

Definition 2.1 (module-SVP). *For $\gamma \geq 1$ and a positive integer n, the module shortest vector problem (γ, n)-module-SVP asks, given as input any pseudo-basis of any rank-n module M in K^n, to find a nonzero vector $\mathbf{s}$ of M such that $\|\mathbf{s}\| \leq \gamma \cdot \lambda_1(M)$.*

Definition 2.2 (free-module-SVP). *For $\gamma \geq 1$ and a positive integer n, the free module shortest vector problem (γ, n)-free-module-SVP asks, given as input any free basis of any rank-n free module M in K^n, to find a nonzero vector $\mathbf{s}$ of M such that $\|\mathbf{s}\| \leq \gamma \cdot \lambda_1(M)$.*

Note that, for simplicity, we restricted our problems to full-rank modules, i.e., to modules of rank n living in K^n. Regarding the choice of the input pseudo-basis, we note that for the module-SVP problem, we can always assume that the module is represented by its HNF pseudo-basis, since it can be computed efficiently from any pseudo-basis. Doing so, we could define the problem as being worst-case only on the choice of the module. In the case of free-module-SVP however, we cannot do the same, since the module has to be represented by a *free basis* (recall that HNF bases are in general not free, even for free modules). In this definition, it is important that the algorithm succeeds for any free basis of a module.

We also define Hermite analogues of these two problems, by replacing $\lambda_1(M)$ by $\sqrt{nd} \cdot \det(M)^{1/(nd)}$ in the definitions above.

Definition 2.3 ((free)-module-HSVP). *For $\gamma \geq 1$ and a positive integer n, the module Hermite shortest vector problem (γ, n)-module-HSVP asks, given as input any pseudo-basis of any rank-n module M in K^n, to find a nonzero vector s of M such that $\|s\| \leq \gamma \cdot \sqrt{nd} \cdot \det(M)^{1/(nd)}$.*
The free-module Hermite shortest vector problem (γ, n)-free-module-HSVP is defined analogously, by restricting the input module to being free and represented by (any) free basis.

Note that by Minkowski's bound, we have immediate reductions from module-HSVP to module-SVP, and from free-module-HSVP to free-module-SVP, which preserve the rank of the module and the approximation factor. When $n = 1$, the modules are ideals and we use the terminology γ-ideal-HSVP instead of $(\gamma, 1)$-module-HSVP.[8]

Finally, we define a variant of the CVP problem over modules, which we call CVP_{cov}. In the CVP_{cov} problem, the approximation factor is usually defined by comparing the distance between the target and the solution with the minimal distance from the target to the lattice. In the variant of CVP_{cov} we consider, we instead compare this with the covering radius of the lattice. We believe that this variant is quite natural: this covers the "standard situation", where the target vector t has no reason to be particularly close to a lattice vector. This is in a sense similar to the Hermite variant of the shortest vector problem: we consider the expected distance from the target to the lattice (or the expected length of a shortest nonzero vector) instead of the actual distance to the lattice (or the actual length of a shortest vector).

Definition 2.4 ((free-)module-CVP$_{\text{cov}}$). *For $\gamma \geq 1$ and a positive integer n, the module closest vector problem with respect to the covering radius (γ, n)-module-CVP$_{cov}$ asks, given as input any pseudo-basis of any rank-n module M in K^n and any target vector $t \in \text{Span}_K(M)$, to find a vector s of M such that $\|t - s\| \leq \gamma \cdot \text{cov}(M)$.*
The free-module closest vector problem with respect to the covering radius (γ, n)-free-module-CVP$_{cov}$ is defined analogously, by restricting the input module to being free and represented by (any) free basis.

---

[8] The other problems will not be used for ideal lattices, so we do not give them a special name.

3   From Module Problems to Free-Module Problems and Ideal-HSVP

In this section, we show that solving SVP (respectively HSVP, CVP_{cov}) in modules can be reduced to solving SVP (respectively HSVP, CVP_{cov}) in free modules *and* solving HSVP in ideals. The three reductions have exactly the same structure, hence we present the reductions in a unique algorithm, namely Algorithm 3.1 below, making queries to an oracle that solves either SVP, HSVP or CVP_{cov} in free modules. We then present the analysis of the three different cases in separate subsections, since these analyses differ.

The high level idea of the reductions is as follows. First, we compute an almost free basis of our input module, namely $(\mathbf{b}_1, \ldots, \mathbf{b}_n, I)$. Then, we solve HSVP in the ideal I to obtain a short element $\alpha \in I$. The reduction finally calls the oracle solving SVP (respectively HSVP, CVP_{cov}) in free modules on the free module N with basis $(\mathbf{b}_1, \ldots, \alpha \mathbf{b}_n)$. This free module is a submodule of M, and so a solution to SVP (respectively HSVP, CVP_{cov}) in N is in particular also a solution in M. Analysing how much one loses during this reduction depends on the choice of the problem (SVP, HSVP, CVP_{cov}), and will be done in separate propositions.

Let us first describe the reduction algorithm formally.

Algorithm 3.1: Reduction from module-SVP/HSVP/CVP_{cov} to free-module-SVP/HSVP/CVP_{cov}

Oracles: $\mathcal{O}_{id}$ an oracle solving γ_{id}-ideal-HSVP and $\mathcal{O}$ an oracle solving (γ, n)-free-module-SVP (or HSVP, or CVP_{cov})
Input: A pseudo-basis $(\mathbf{c}_i, I_i)_{1 \le i \le n}$ of a rank-n module $M \subset K^n$;
optionally a target vector $\mathbf{t} \in \text{Span}_K(M)$ if $\mathcal{O}$ solves
free-module-CVP_{cov}
Output: A vector $\mathbf{s} \in M$

1 Compute an almost-free representation $(\mathbf{b}_1, \cdots, \mathbf{b}_n, I)$ of M;
2 Run $\mathcal{O}_{id}$ on I to obtain $\alpha \in I \setminus \{0\}$;
3 Let N be the free module spanned by $\mathbf{b}_1, \ldots, \mathbf{b}_{n-1}, \alpha \mathbf{b}_n$;
4 Run $\mathcal{O}$ on N (and optionally $\mathbf{t}$ in the case of CVP_{cov}) to obtain $\mathbf{s} \in N$;
5 **return** $\mathbf{s}$.

Proposition 3.1. *Let $n \ge 1$ be an integer and $\gamma_{id}, \gamma \ge 1$ be real numbers. Let $\mathcal{O}_{id}$ be an oracle solving γ_{id}-ideal-HSVP and $\mathcal{O}$ be an oracle solving (γ, n)-free-module-SVP (respectively (γ, n)-free-module-HSVP, (γ, n)-free-module-CVP_{cov}). Then given access to $\mathcal{O}_{id}$ and $\mathcal{O}$, Algorithm 3.1 runs in probabilistic polynomial time, and makes one call to $\mathcal{O}_{id}$ and one call to $\mathcal{O}$.*

Proof. The only step of the algorithm which does not consist in calling an oracle is the computation of the almost-free pseudo-basis in the first step. This can be done in expected polynomial time thanks to Lemma 2.2.   □

We will now analyze the correctness and the loss of the reductions.

3.1   The Case of SVP

We start by an auxiliary lemma.

Lemma 3.1. *Using the same notations as in Algorithm 3.1, we have* $\lambda_1(N) \leq \gamma_{id} \cdot \Delta_K^{1/d} \cdot \lambda_1(M)$.

Proof. Take $\mathbf{v} \in M \backslash \{\mathbf{0}\}$ such that $\|\mathbf{v}\| = \lambda_1(M)$. We have $\mathbf{v} = \alpha_1 \mathbf{b}_1 + \ldots + \alpha_n \mathbf{b}_n$, where $\alpha_1, \ldots, \alpha_{n-1} \in \mathcal{O}_K$ and $\alpha_n \in I$. Note that since $\alpha \in I$, there exists some integral ideal J such that $\langle \alpha \rangle = IJ$. Since α is a solution to γ_{id}-HSVP in I, we have $\|\alpha\| \leq \gamma_{id} \cdot \sqrt{d} \cdot \Delta_K^{1/(2d)} \cdot \mathcal{N}(I)^{1/d}$, which implies

$$\mathcal{N}(J) = \frac{\mathcal{N}(\alpha)}{\mathcal{N}(I)} \leq \frac{\|\alpha\|^d}{\sqrt{d}^d \cdot \mathcal{N}(I)^d} \leq \gamma_{id}^d \cdot \Delta_K^{1/2},$$

where the first inequality is obtained from Eq. (2).

Let $u \in J \backslash \{0\}$ such that $\|u\| = \lambda_1(J)$, then $u \in \mathcal{O}_K$ (recall that J is integral) and $\alpha_n u \in \langle \alpha \rangle$. This implies that

$$u\mathbf{v} = \alpha_1 u \mathbf{b}_1 + \ldots + \alpha_n u \mathbf{b}_n \in N.$$

From this and Minkowski's bound for ℓ_∞-norm (Theorem 2.1) we finally obtain that

$$\begin{aligned}
\lambda_1(N) \leq \|u\mathbf{v}\| \leq \|u\|_\infty \cdot \|\mathbf{v}\| &\leq \lambda_1^{(\infty)}(J) \cdot \lambda_1(M) \\
&\leq \Delta_K^{1/2d} \cdot \mathcal{N}(J)^{1/d} \cdot \lambda_1(M) \\
&\leq \gamma_{id} \cdot \Delta_K^{1/d} \cdot \lambda_1(M).
\end{aligned}$$

$\square$

Proposition 3.2. *If $\mathcal{O}$ solves (γ, n)-free-module-SVP, then given as input a pseudo-basis of a rank-n module M in K^n, Algorithm 3.1 outputs $\mathbf{s} \in M \backslash \{0\}$ such that $\|\mathbf{s}\| \leq \gamma \cdot \gamma_{id} \cdot \Delta_K^{1/d} \cdot \lambda_1(M)$.*

Proof. Observe first that N is a submodule of M, hence a non-zero vector of N is also a non-zero vector of M, and $\mathbf{s} \in M \backslash \{0\}$ as desired. The upper bound on $\|\mathbf{s}\|$ comes from the fact that $\mathbf{s}$ is a solution to (γ, n)-free-module-SVP in N, i.e., $\|\mathbf{s}\| \leq \gamma \cdot \lambda_1(N)$, and the upper bound on $\lambda_1(N)$ from Lemma 3.1. $\square$

Combining Proposition 3.2 with Proposition 3.1, we obtain the following corollary.

Corollary 3.1. *Let $\gamma, \gamma_{id} \geq 1$ and $n \geq 1$ be an integer. For any $\gamma' \geq \gamma \cdot \gamma_{id} \cdot \Delta_K^{1/d}$, there is a probabilistic, polynomial-time reduction from solving (γ', n)-module-SVP in K^n to solving (γ, n)-free-module-SVP in K^n and γ_{id}-ideal-HSVP.*

3.2   The Case of HSVP

As in the SVP case, we start by an auxiliary lemma.

Lemma 3.2. *Using the same notations as in Algorithm 3.1, we have* $\det(N) \leq \gamma_{id}^d \cdot \Delta_K^{1/2} \cdot \det(M)$.

Proof. We know from preliminaries that

$$\frac{\det N}{\det M} = \frac{\mathcal{N}(N)}{\mathcal{N}(M)} = \frac{\mathcal{N}(\alpha)}{\mathcal{N}(I)} \leq \gamma_{id}^d \cdot \Delta_K^{1/2},$$

where the last inequality was proven in the proof of Lemma 3.1.   □

Proposition 3.3. *If $\mathcal{O}$ solves (γ, n)-free-module-HSVP, then on input a pseudo-basis of a rank-n module M, Algorithm 3.1 outputs $\mathbf{s} \in M \setminus \{0\}$ such that $\|\mathbf{s}\| \leq \gamma_{id}^{1/n} \cdot \gamma \cdot \Delta_K^{1/2nd} \cdot \sqrt{nd} \cdot (\det M)^{1/nd}$.*

Proof. Let N be as in Algorithm 3.1. Observe that N is a submodule of M, hence a non-zero vector of N is also a non-zero vector of M, and $\mathbf{s} \in M \setminus \{0\}$ as desired. From Lemma 3.2, we know that $\det(N) \leq \gamma_{id}^d \cdot \Delta_K^{1/2} \cdot \det(M)$, hence it follows that

$$\|\mathbf{s}\| \leq \gamma \cdot \sqrt{nd} \cdot (\det N)^{1/nd}$$
$$\leq \gamma_{id}^{1/n} \cdot \gamma \cdot \Delta_K^{1/2nd} \cdot \sqrt{nd} \cdot (\det M)^{1/nd}$$

as desired.   □

Combining Propositions 3.3 and 3.1, we obtain the following corollary.

Corollary 3.2. *Let $\gamma, \gamma_{id} \geq 1$ and $n \geq 1$ be an integer. For any $\gamma' \geq \gamma_{id}^{1/n} \cdot \gamma \cdot \Delta_K^{1/2nd}$, there is a probabilistic, polynomial-time reduction from solving (γ', n)-module-HSVP in K^n to solving (γ, n)-free-module-HSVP in K^n and γ_{id}-ideal-HSVP.*

3.3   The Case of CVP$_{cov}$

Similarly to the two previous cases, we start by an auxiliary lemma.

Lemma 3.3. *Using the same notations as in Algorithm 3.1, we have $\text{cov}(N) \leq \gamma_{id} \cdot \Delta_K^{1/d} \cdot \text{cov}(M)$.*

Proof. Let $\mathbf{t} \in \text{Span}_K(N)$. We want to prove the existence of a vector $\mathbf{s} \in N$ with $\|\mathbf{t} - \mathbf{s}\| \leq \gamma_{id} \cdot \Delta_K^{1/d} \cdot \text{cov}(M)$.

Let $u \in \alpha \cdot I^{-1}$ be a shortest nonzero vector of $\alpha \cdot I^{-1}$ for the infinity norm. By Minkowski's theorem, we know that

$$\|u\|_\infty \leq \det(\alpha \cdot I^{-1})^{1/d} = \Delta_K^{1/2d} \cdot \mathcal{N}(\alpha \cdot I^{-1})^{1/d} \leq \gamma_{id} \cdot \Delta_K^{1/d},$$

where the last inequality was proven in the proof of Lemma 3.1. Note that since $\alpha \in I$, then the ideal $\alpha \cdot I^{-1}$ is integral and so in particular $u \in \mathcal{O}_K$. This in turn, implies that for any $\mathbf{x} \in M$, we have $u \cdot \mathbf{x} \in N$.

Now, let us define $\mathbf{t}' = u^{-1} \cdot \mathbf{t}$. It holds that $\mathbf{t}' \in \mathrm{Span}_K(N) = \mathrm{Span}_K(M)$, so by definition of the covering radius, there exists $\mathbf{s}' \in M$ such that $\|\mathbf{t}' - \mathbf{s}'\| \leq \mathrm{cov}(M)$. From what we have seen above, $\mathbf{s} = u \cdot \mathbf{s}'$ is then a vector of N, and from the bound on $\|u\|_\infty$ we finally obtain

$$\|\mathbf{t} - \mathbf{s}\| \leq \|u\|_\infty \cdot \|\mathbf{t}' - \mathbf{s}'\| \leq \gamma_{id} \cdot \Delta_K^{1/d} \cdot \mathrm{cov}(M),$$

as desired.   □

Proposition 3.4. *If $\mathcal{O}$ solves (γ, n)-free-module-CVP_{cov}, then on input a pseudo-basis of a rank-n module M and a target vector $\mathbf{t} \in \mathrm{Span}_K(M)$, Algorithm 3.1 outputs $\mathbf{s} \in M$ such that $\|\mathbf{t} - \mathbf{s}\| \leq \gamma \cdot \gamma_{id} \cdot \Delta_K^{1/d} \cdot \mathrm{cov}(M)$.*

Proof. Let N be as in Algorithm 3.1. Since N is a submodule of M, and $\mathbf{s} \in N$, then in particular we have $\mathbf{s} \in M$. Moreover, from Lemma 3.3, we know that $\mathrm{cov}(N) \leq \gamma_{id} \cdot \Delta_K^{1/d} \cdot \mathrm{cov}(M)$, hence it follows that

$$\|\mathbf{t} - \mathbf{s}\| \leq \gamma \cdot \mathrm{cov}(N)$$
$$\leq \gamma \cdot \gamma_{id} \cdot \Delta_K^{1/d} \cdot \mathrm{cov}(N),$$

as desired.   □

Combining Propositions 3.4 and 3.1, we obtain the following corollary.

Corollary 3.3. *Let $\gamma, \gamma_{id} \geq 1$ and $n \geq 1$ be an integer. For any $\gamma' \geq \gamma \cdot \gamma_{id} \cdot \Delta_K^{1/d}$, there is a probabilistic, polynomial-time reduction from solving (γ', n)-module-CVP_{cov} in K^n to solving (γ, n)-free-module-CVP_{cov} in K^n and γ_{id}-ideal-HSVP.*

4   From Ideal-HSVP to Rank-2 Free-Module Problems

In this section, we show that solving ideal-HSVP can be reduced to solving free-module-SVP (respectively free-module-HSVP, free-module-CVP_{cov}) in modules of rank 2. Since HSVP reduces to SVP in the same lattice by Minkowski's theorem, we actually only need to prove two reductions, one to free-module-HSVP and one to free-module-CVP_{cov}. We do so in the two subsections below.

4.1   The Case of HSVP (and SVP)

In this subsection, we reduce ideal-HSVP to free-module-HSVP in modules of rank 2. The high level idea is to use a two-element representation of the input ideal to transform it into a free rank-2 module, such that any short vector of this free rank-2 module can be transformed back into a short vector of the input ideal. Similar ideas were used in [DM22] in order to transform a rank-2 module into a free rank-4 module.

More precisely, given an ideal I, we compute a two-element representation $I = \langle a \rangle + \langle b \rangle$ and construct the free module M with a basis consisting of the columns of the following matrix

$$\begin{pmatrix} a & b \\ 0 & \varepsilon \end{pmatrix},$$

where $\varepsilon > 0$ is a rational number to be specified later. Observe that every $\mathbf{s} \in M$ is of the form $(x \; y)^T$ for $x \in I$ and $y \in \langle \epsilon \rangle$. Hence, if $\mathbf{s}$ is small, then its first coordinate x is a small element of I. Here, since the size of $\mathbf{s}$ is related to the determinant of M, which depends on the choice of ε, we want to take ε as small as possible. However, M also contains vectors of the form $(0 \; v\varepsilon)^T$ for $v \in \mathcal{O}_K$, so if ε is too small then the short vectors of M are of this form and result in $x = 0$. To avoid this case, we observe that when $(0 \; v\varepsilon)^T$ is a short vector of M then ε can be upper bounded by a quantity depending only on K, I and a. Thus by choosing ε greater than this quantity, we avoid the case where short vectors of M have their first coordinate equal to 0.

Proposition 4.1. *For any $\gamma \geq 1$ and $\gamma' > 2\gamma^2 \cdot \Delta_K^{1/2d}$, there exists a probabilistic polynomial-time reduction from solving γ'-ideal-HSVP to solving $(\gamma, 2)$-free-module-HSVP in K^2.*

Proof. Let I be a non-zero ideal of K, without loss of generality we can assume that I is integral (otherwise we scale it to an integral ideal, which does not change its geometry). Compute a two-element representation $I = \langle a \rangle + \langle b \rangle$ with $a \neq 0$ using the algorithm of Theorem 2.2 and consider the free module $M \subset K^2$ generated by the free basis (in columns)

$$\begin{pmatrix} a & b \\ 0 & \varepsilon \end{pmatrix},$$

for some $\varepsilon > 0$, rational, to be determined. We want to prove that any solution to γ-HSVP in M is of the form $(x \; y)^T$, with x a solution to γ'-ideal-HSVP in I. Since a free basis of M is efficiently computable from I (in probabilistic polynomial time), this will give us a probabilistic polynomial time reduction from γ'-ideal-HSVP to $(\gamma, 2)$-free-module-HSVP as desired.

Let us first prove that if ε is large enough, then all solutions to γ-HSVP in M are of the form $(x \; y)^T$ with x non-zero. To do so, assume for a contradiction that $(0 \; v\varepsilon)^T$ is a solution to γ-HSVP in M, then $v \in \mathcal{O}_K \setminus \{0\}$ and there exists $u \in \mathcal{O}_K$ such that $ua + vb = 0$. By definition of γ-HSVP, we have

$$\varepsilon \cdot \|v\| \leq \gamma \cdot \sqrt{2d} \cdot \Delta_K^{1/2d} \cdot \mathcal{N}(M)^{1/2d} = \gamma \cdot \sqrt{2d} \cdot \Delta_K^{1/2d} \cdot \varepsilon^{1/2} \cdot \mathcal{N}(a)^{1/2d}.$$

Next, we want to show that because of the equality $ua + vb = 0$, then v has to be quite large, and the inequality above cannot be satisfied. The equality $ua + vb = 0$

implies that $\langle u \rangle \langle a \rangle = \langle v \rangle \langle b \rangle$. Assume for the moment that $b \neq 0$. Then, all ideals in the equation above are nonzero (since both a and b are nonzero, and v should also be nonzero). Since $I = \langle a \rangle + \langle b \rangle$, there exist nonzero integral ideals J_1, J_2 such that $\langle a \rangle = IJ_1$, $\langle b \rangle = IJ_2$ and J_1, J_2 do not have any common factor in their factorization into prime ideals. Since I is invertible (because it is non-zero), the equality $\langle u \rangle \langle a \rangle = \langle v \rangle \langle b \rangle$ can be rewritten as $\langle u \rangle J_1 = \langle v \rangle J_2$. Note that all ideals involved in this equality are integral (because u and v are in $\mathcal{O}_K$). Since J_1 and J_2 are coprime, it must be that J_1 divides $\langle v \rangle$, which implies in particular that $\mathcal{N}(v) \geq \mathcal{N}(J_1) = \mathcal{N}(a)/\mathcal{N}(I)$, where the last equality comes from the definition of J_1. Finally, recall from Eq. (2) that $\|v\| \geq \sqrt{d} \cdot \mathcal{N}(v)^{1/d}$, which gives us

$$\|v\| \geq \sqrt{d} \cdot \left(\frac{\mathcal{N}(a)}{\mathcal{N}(I)} \right)^{1/d}.$$

In the case $b = 0$, then $\mathcal{N}(a) = \mathcal{N}(I)$ and thus the inequality still holds, since $v \in \mathcal{O}_K$. Combining this inequality with the one above we obtain

$$\sqrt{d} \cdot \left(\frac{\mathcal{N}(a)}{\mathcal{N}(I)} \right)^{1/d} \leq \|v\| \leq \frac{\gamma \cdot \sqrt{2d} \cdot \Delta_K^{1/2d} \cdot \mathcal{N}(a)^{1/2d}}{\varepsilon^{1/2}},$$

which results in

$$\varepsilon \leq 2\gamma^2 \Delta_K^{1/d} \cdot \frac{\mathcal{N}(I)^{2/d}}{\mathcal{N}(a)^{1/d}}.$$

Therefore choosing $\varepsilon > 2\gamma^2 \Delta_K^{1/d} \mathcal{N}(I)^{2/d}/\mathcal{N}(a)^{1/d}$ guarantees that the solution $\mathbf{s} = (x \ y)^T$ to γ-SVP over M satisfies $x \neq 0$.

Now, we also choose ε such that

$$\varepsilon \leq \frac{\gamma'^2}{2\gamma^2} \cdot \frac{\mathcal{N}(I)^{2/d}}{\mathcal{N}(a)^{1/d}}.$$

Note that $\gamma' > 2\gamma^2 \cdot \Delta_K^{1/2d}$ implies the existence of such ε. Calling the free-module-HSVP oracle on input M, let $\mathbf{s}$ be the output and x be the first coordinate of $\mathbf{s}$. The choice of ε guarantees that $x \in I \backslash \{0\}$ and

$$\|x\| \leq \|\mathbf{s}\| \leq \gamma \cdot \sqrt{2d} \cdot \Delta_K^{1/2d} \cdot \varepsilon^{1/2} \cdot \mathcal{N}(a)^{1/2d}$$
$$\leq \gamma' \cdot \sqrt{d} \cdot \Delta_K^{1/2d} \cdot \mathcal{N}(I)^{1/d} = \gamma' \cdot \sqrt{d} \cdot \det(I)^{1/d}.$$

Hence x is a solution to γ'-ideal-HSVP over I. □

Since $(\gamma, 2)$-free-module-HSVP reduces to $(\gamma, 2)$-free-module-SVP (by definition and by Minkowski's bound), Proposition 4.1 implies the following proposition.

Proposition 4.2. *For any $\gamma \geq 1$ and $\gamma' > 2\gamma^2 \cdot \Delta_K^{1/2d}$, there exists a probabilistic polynomial-time reduction from solving γ'-ideal-HSVP to solving $(\gamma, 2)$-free-module-SVP in K^2.*

4.2   The Case of CVP$_{cov}$

Let us now consider the reduction to CVP$_{cov}$ in free-modules of rank 2. The main ideas of the reduction are similar to the SVP/HSVP case, but the analysis is a bit different.

The idea is again to consider the free rank-2 module M spanned by the columns of the matrix $\begin{pmatrix} a & b \\ 0 & \varepsilon \end{pmatrix}$, where $I = \langle a \rangle + \langle b \rangle$ and ε is small. We show that if ε is sufficiently small, then the covering radius of this lattice is roughly equal to $\det(I)^{1/d}$ (up to polynomial factors). Note that, contrary to the SVP/HSVP case, we have no lower bound on ε here. The ideal case would be $\varepsilon = 0$, but this would lead to a (non free) module of rank 1. Ensuring that the module has rank 2 is the only reason we take $\varepsilon \neq 0$.

Then, in order to find a short vector in I, we simply solve CVP$_{cov}$ in M with a target vector of the form $\mathbf{t} = (t_0, 0)^T$, where we choose t_0 just slightly above the covering radius of M, so that any solution $\mathbf{s} = (s_0, s_1)^T$ has $s_0 \neq 0$, and $s_0 \in I$ is somewhat short.

Proposition 4.3. *For any $\gamma \geq 1$ and $\gamma' \geq 5 \cdot \gamma \cdot d \cdot \lambda_d^{(\infty)}(\mathcal{O}_K)$, there exists a probabilistic polynomial-time reduction from solving γ'-ideal-HSVP to solving $(\gamma, 2)$-free-module-CVP$_{cov}$ in K^2.*

Proof. Let I be an integral ideal in $\mathcal{O}_K$ (we can assume that I is integral without loss of generality, if it is not we scale it). Let $a, b \in \mathcal{O}_K$ be such that $I = \langle a \rangle + \langle b \rangle$ (with $a \neq 0$), and $\varepsilon > 0$ be some rational number. Let M be the rank-2 free module spanned by the basis $\begin{pmatrix} a & b \\ 0 & \varepsilon \end{pmatrix}$. First, let us prove that

$$\text{cov}(M) \leq \varepsilon \cdot \left(d \cdot \lambda_d^{(\infty)}(\mathcal{O}_K) \cdot \Delta_K^{1/2d} \cdot (\sqrt{d} + \|a\|) \right) + d^{3/2} \cdot \lambda_d^{(\infty)}(\mathcal{O}_K) \cdot \det(I)^{1/d}.$$

Let $\mathbf{t} = (t_0, t_1)^T \in \text{Span}_K(M) = K^2$. Let $w \in \mathcal{O}_K$ be such that $\|w\varepsilon - t_1\| \leq \text{cov}(\varepsilon\mathcal{O}_K)$ (i.e., $w\varepsilon$ is a closest point to t_1 in the ideal $\varepsilon\mathcal{O}_K$). If we subtract $w \cdot (b, \varepsilon)^T$ to $\mathbf{t}$, we obtain a new vector $\mathbf{t}' = (t_0', t_1')^T$, which is at the same distance to M as $\mathbf{t}$ (since $w \cdot (b, \varepsilon)^T \in M$), but whose second coordinate is small, namely $\|t_1'\| \leq \text{cov}(\varepsilon\mathcal{O}_K)$.

Let us now reduce the first coordinate. Let $\alpha \in I$ be a closest vector to t_0', that is, $\|\alpha - t_0'\| \leq \text{cov}(I)$. Since I is generated by a and b, there exists u_0 and v_0 in $\mathcal{O}_K$ such that $\alpha = u_0 a + v_0 b$. We would like to take v_0 as small as possible (since adding v_0 times the second basis vector will make the second coordinate of our vector increase again). We know that any $(u, v) = (u_0 + kb, v_0 - ka)$ with $k \in \mathcal{O}_K$ also satisfies $\alpha = ua + vb$. Hence, we can always reduce v modulo a and ensure that $\|v\| = \|v_0 - ka\| \leq \text{cov}(a\mathcal{O}_K)$.

Overall, we obtain $(u, v) \in \mathcal{O}_K^2$ with $\|v\| \leq \text{cov}(a\mathcal{O}_K)$ such that $\|ua + vb - t_0'\| \leq \text{cov}(I)$. Taking $\mathbf{s} = u(a, 0)^T + (v + w)(b, \varepsilon)^T \in M$ finally gives us

$$\|\mathbf{t} - \mathbf{s}\| = \|\mathbf{t}' - u(a, 0)^T - v(b, \varepsilon)^T\|$$
$$= \|(t_0' - \alpha, t_1' - \varepsilon v)^T\|$$
$$\leq \|t_0' - \alpha\| + \|t_1'\| + \varepsilon\|v\|$$
$$\leq \text{cov}(I) + \text{cov}(\varepsilon\mathcal{O}_K) + \varepsilon \cdot \text{cov}(a\mathcal{O}_K).$$

To conclude, recall from preliminaries (Eqs. (3) and (4)) that

$$\text{cov}(I) \leq d^{3/2} \cdot \lambda_d^{(\infty)}(\mathcal{O}_K) \cdot \det(I)^{1/d},$$
$$\text{cov}(a\mathcal{O}_K) \leq d \cdot \lambda_d^{(\infty)}(\mathcal{O}_K) \cdot \Delta_K^{1/2d} \cdot \|a\|,$$
$$\text{cov}(\varepsilon\mathcal{O}_K) \leq \varepsilon \cdot d^{3/2} \cdot \lambda_d^{(\infty)}(\mathcal{O}_K) \cdot \Delta_K^{1/2d},$$

where in the last inequality we used the fact that ε is rational and so $\|\varepsilon\| = \varepsilon\sqrt{d}$. Combining everything, we obtain the desired upper bound on $\text{cov}(M)$.

We can now describe our reduction from ideal-HSVP to free-module-CVP$_{\text{cov}}$ in modules of rank 2. Our algorithm takes as input some integral ideal I. It computes in probabilistic polynomial time a and b in $\mathcal{O}_K$ such that $I = \langle a \rangle + \langle b \rangle$, with $a \neq 0$ (see Lemma 2.2). Then, it sets $\varepsilon > 0$ rational such that $\varepsilon \leq \left(\Delta_K^{1/(2d)} \cdot (\sqrt{d} + \|a\|)\right)^{-1} \cdot \det(I)^{1/d}$, and compute the free basis $\begin{pmatrix} a & b \\ 0 & \varepsilon \end{pmatrix}$, spanning some rank-2 module M.

The reduction also creates the target vector $\mathbf{t} = (\delta, 0)^T$, with $\delta \in \mathbb{Q}$ such that $\delta \in (2, 3] \cdot \gamma \cdot d\lambda_d^{(\infty)}(\mathcal{O}_K) \cdot \det(I)^{1/d}$. The reduction then runs the $(\gamma, 2)$-free-module-CVP$_{\text{cov}}$ oracle on input M and $\mathbf{t}$, to obtain a vector $\mathbf{s} = (s_0, s_1)^T$, and it outputs s_0.

One can check that the reduction in probabilistic polynomial time. Let us now prove that s_0 is a solution to γ'-HSVP in I with γ' as in the theorem statement.

First, $s_0 \in I$ since a and b are both in I. Also, by choice of ε and using what we have proven above, we know that $\text{cov}(M) \leq 2d^{3/2} \cdot \lambda_d^{(\infty)}(\mathcal{O}_K) \cdot \det(I)^{1/d}$. This implies that

$$\|s_0 - \delta\| \leq \|\mathbf{s} - \mathbf{t}\| \leq \gamma \cdot \text{cov}(M) < \|\delta\|,$$

using the fact that $\|\delta\| = \sqrt{d}\delta$ since $\delta \in \mathbb{Q} \subseteq K$. This means that s_0 is nonzero, and $\|s_0\| \leq \|\delta\| + \gamma \cdot \text{cov}(M) \leq 5\gamma \cdot d \cdot \lambda_d^{(\infty)}(\mathcal{O}_K) \cdot \sqrt{d} \cdot \det(I)^{1/d}$, as desired. $\square$

5   From Rank-2 Free-Module Problems to Rank-n Free-Module Problems

We conclude the reductions by proving a reduction from free-module-SVP (respectively HSVP, CVP$_{\text{cov}}$) in modules of rank 2 to free-module-SVP (respectively HSVP, CVP$_{\text{cov}}$) in modules of rank $n \geq 2$. These reductions are not surprising, since they follow the intuition that the hardness of module problems increase when the rank of the module increases (for a fixed underlying field). Following this intuition, the reductions for SVP and CVP_{cov} are easily obtained by embedding the rank 2 input module into a larger rank module, and padding the extra dimensions with dummy vectors. Surprisingly however, the reduction for HSVP is not as easy as the other two, and we even have some significant loss in the approximation factor when reducing to modules of rank n with n odd. The proof of Proposition 5.2 (the HSVP reduction) is the most interesting one of this section. We believe that improving the reduction for HSVP to obtain a smaller loss is an interesting open problem.

5.1   The Case of SVP

In this subsection, we reduce SVP in rank-2 free modules in K^2 to SVP in rank-n free module, where $n \geq 2$. This is naturally done by embedding the rank 2 free module into a larger rank free module.

Let $M_1 \subset K^2$ be a rank-2 free modules with a free basis $\mathbf{B}' \in K^{2 \times 2}$. We construct a rank-$n$ free module $M \subset K^n$ generated by the columns of the following block matrix

$$\mathbf{B} = \left(\begin{array}{c|c} \mathbf{B}' & 0 \\ \hline 0 & \delta I_{n-2} \end{array} \right) \in K^{n \times n}$$

where δ is a positive, rational number, to be determined later. Note that M_1 is the rank-2 free module generated by the first two columns of $\mathbf{B}$. If we let M_2 be the rank-$(n-2)$ free module generated by the remaining $n-2$ columns of B, then we see that $M = M_1 \oplus M_2$, and the sum is orthogonal.

Lemma 5.1. *With the above notations, $\lambda_1(M) = \min\{\lambda_1(M_1), \lambda_1(M_2)\}$.*

Proof. Let $\mathbf{s} \in M \backslash \{\mathbf{0}\}$ be a shortest vector, we have $\mathbf{s} = \mathbf{s}_1 + \mathbf{s}_2$, where $\mathbf{s}_1 \in M_1$, $\mathbf{s}_2$ in M_2 and $\mathbf{s}_1, \mathbf{s}_2$ are orthogonal (when viewed as vectors in $\mathbb{C}^{nd}$). If both $\mathbf{s}_1$ and $\mathbf{s}_2$ are nonzero vectors, then $\lambda_1(M) = \|\mathbf{s}\| > \min\{\|\mathbf{s}_1\|, \|\mathbf{s}_2\|\}$, which is absurd. Thus one of $\mathbf{s}_1$ and $\mathbf{s}_2$ is zero vector, and the conclusion follows.   □

Suppose that we have access to an oracle solving (γ, n)-free-module-SVP on input any free basis of any rank-n module in K^n. Calling this oracle on input $\mathbf{B}$ will give a short vector $\mathbf{s}$ of M. The idea is to choose δ large enough such that M_2 does not contain any relatively short vector of M and thus the short vectors of M should be the short vectors of M_1. In particular, if we choose δ such that $\lambda_1(M_2) \geq \gamma \lambda_1(M_1)$, then a solution $\mathbf{s}$ to γ-SVP in M is also a solution to γ-SVP in M_1 (when projecting on the first two coordinates).

Lemma 5.2. *If $\delta > \gamma \cdot \sqrt{2} \cdot \det(M_1)^{1/(2d)}$, then $\lambda_1(M_2) > \gamma \cdot \lambda_1(M_1)$.*

Proof. Let $\mathbf{s} = (0, 0, s_1 \delta, \ldots, s_{n-2} \delta)^T \in M_2$ be a shortest nonzero vector of M_2, where $s_i \in \mathcal{O}_K$. Observe that there exists some $i \in \{1, \ldots, n-2\}$ such that $s_i \neq 0$, then

$$\lambda_1(M_2) = \|\mathbf{s}\| \geq \delta \cdot \|s_i\| \geq \delta \cdot \sqrt{d} > \gamma \cdot \sqrt{2d} \cdot \det(M_1)^{1/(2d)}.$$

By Minkowski's bound, it follows that $\lambda_1(M_2) > \gamma\lambda_1(M_1)$.   □

We can now prove our reduction from rank 2 to rank n free modules.

Proposition 5.1. *Let $\gamma \geq 1$ be a reaul number and $n \geq 2$ be an integer. There is a polynomial-time (deterministic) reduction from solving $(\gamma, 2)$-free-module-SVP in K^2 to (γ, n)-free-module-SVP in K^n.*

Proof. Consider a rank-2 free module M_1 given by a basis $\mathbf{B}' \in K^{2\times 2}$. We set $\delta = \lceil \gamma \cdot 2 \cdot \det(M_1)^{1/(2d)} \rceil$ and construct the block matrix

$$\mathbf{B} = \left(\begin{array}{c|c} \mathbf{B}' & 0 \\ \hline 0 & \delta I_{n-2} \end{array} \right) \in K^{n\times n}$$

as above. Note that computing δ and constructing $\mathbf{B}$ can be performed in time polynomial in the size of $\mathbf{B}'$ and in $\log \Delta_K$ (and the size of $\mathbf{B}$ is polynomial in these two quantities). We observe also that $\mathbf{B}$ is a free basis of a rank n module in K^n. Calling the (γ, n)-free-module-SVP oracle on this module produces $\mathbf{s} = (s_1, s_2, \ldots, s_n) \in K^n$. Our reduction algorithm then outputs the vector formed by the first two coordinates of $\mathbf{s}$.

We have seen that this procedure is polynomial time. Let us now show that the output vector is a solution to γ-SVP in M_1. Since δ satisfies the condition of Lemma 5.2, we have $\lambda_1(M_2) > \gamma\lambda_1(M_1) \geq \lambda_1(M_1)$. By Lemma 5.1, it follows that $\lambda_1(M) = \lambda(M_1)$. The output $\mathbf{s}$ of the oracle then satisfies $\|\mathbf{s}\| \leq \gamma \cdot \lambda_1(M_1) < \lambda_1(M_2)$. This implies that $\mathbf{s}' = (s_1, s_2)^T$ is nonzero, in M_1 and of euclidean norm $\leq \gamma \cdot \lambda_1(M_1)$ as desired.   □

5.2 The Case of HSVP

In this section, we reduce HSVP in free modules of rank 2 to HSVP in free modules of rank $n \geq 2$. The strategy is somewhat similar to the SVP case: we embed our rank-2 module into a rank-n module and use the oracle in this rank-n module. However, in the HSVP case, padding the extra dimensions of the modules with (scaled) identity vectors does not seem to work. Hence, we instead copy our rank-2 modules into $n/2$ orthogonal copies of itself. For this reason, the case with n odd behaves differently from the case with n even, and we obtain a worse approximation factor in this case of n odd (this is the only reduction in this section, where the new approximation factor is more than linear in the original approximation factor).

Proposition 5.2. *Let $n \geq 2$ be an integer and define $\varepsilon_n = 0$ if n is even and $\varepsilon_n = 1/(n-1)$ if n is odd. For any real numbers $\gamma \geq 1$ and $\gamma' \geq \gamma^{1+\varepsilon_n} \cdot \sqrt{n}^{1+\varepsilon_n} \cdot \Delta_K^{\varepsilon_n/2d}$, there exists a (deterministic) polynomial time reduction from solving $(\gamma', 2)$-free-module-HSVP to solving (γ, n)-free-module-HSVP.*

Note that the quantity ε_n in the theorem is always $\leq 1/2$, so by taking $\gamma' \geq \gamma^{3/2} \cdot n^{3/4} \cdot \Delta_K^{1/4d}$, the theorem's requirement is fulfilled.

Proof. Consider a rank-2 free module M_1 given by a basis $\mathbf{B}' \in K^{2\times 2}$. Consider the case when n is even, we construct the block matrix

$$\mathbf{B} = \begin{pmatrix} \mathbf{B}' & 0 & \cdots & 0 \\ 0 & \mathbf{B}' & \cdots & 0 \\ \vdots & \vdots & \ddots & \vdots \\ 0 & 0 & \cdots & \mathbf{B}' \end{pmatrix} \in K^{n\times n},$$

which is a block diagonal matrix with diagonal elements consisting of $n/2$ blocks of $\mathbf{B}'$. Observe the cost of constructing $\mathbf{B}$ and the size of $\mathbf{B}$ is polynomial in the size of $\mathbf{B}'$. We observe also that $\mathbf{B}$ is a free basis of a rank n module in K^n. Calling the (γ, n)-free-module-HSVP oracle on this module produces $\mathbf{s} = (s_1, s_2, \ldots, s_n) \in K^n$ satisfying $\|\mathbf{s}\| \leq \gamma \cdot \sqrt{nd} \cdot \det(M)^{1/nd}$. Our reduction algorithm then selects an odd index i such that (s_i, s_{i+1}) is nonzero and outputs $\mathbf{s}' = (s_i, s_{i+1})$. Such i always exists since $\mathbf{s}$ is nonzero, and $\mathbf{s}' \in M_1$ and satisfies

$$\|\mathbf{s}'\| \leq \|\mathbf{s}\| \leq \gamma \cdot \sqrt{nd} \cdot \det(M)^{1/nd}$$
$$= \gamma \cdot \sqrt{nd} \cdot \left(\Delta_K^{n/2} \cdot \mathcal{N}(\det \mathbf{B}) \right)^{1/nd}$$
$$= \gamma \cdot \sqrt{nd} \cdot \Delta_K^{1/2d} \cdot \left(\mathcal{N}(\det \mathbf{B}')^{n/2} \right)^{1/nd}$$
$$= \gamma \cdot \sqrt{nd} \cdot \det(M_1)^{1/2d} \leq \gamma' \cdot \sqrt{2d} \cdot \det(M_1)^{1/2d},$$

the last inequality is obtained by the fact that $\gamma' = \gamma\sqrt{n} \geq \gamma \cdot \sqrt{n/2}$ when n is even. Hence, $\mathbf{s}'$ is a solution to γ'-HSVP in M_1 as desired. Now consider the case when n is odd, we construct the block matrix

$$\mathbf{B} = \begin{pmatrix} \mathbf{B}' & 0 & 0 & \cdots & 0 & 0 \\ 0 & \mathbf{B}' & 0 & \cdots & 0 & 0 \\ 0 & 0 & \mathbf{B}' & \cdots & 0 & 0 \\ \vdots & \vdots & \vdots & \ddots & \vdots & \vdots \\ 0 & 0 & 0 & \cdots & \mathbf{B}' & 0 \\ 0 & 0 & 0 & \cdots & 0 & \delta \end{pmatrix} \in K^{n\times n},$$

where δ is a rational number satisfying $\delta_0 < \delta \leq 2\delta_0$, for

$$\delta_0 = \gamma^{n/(n-1)} \cdot \Delta_K^{n/2d(n-1)} \cdot (\sqrt{n})^{n/(n-1)} \cdot \mathcal{N}(\det \mathbf{B}')^{1/2d}.$$

Note that $\mathbf{B}$ is a block diagonal matrix with diagonal elements consisting of $(n-1)/2$ blocks of $\mathbf{B}'$ and δ. Similarly to the case where n is even, $\mathbf{B}$ is a free basis of a rank n module in K^n; the cost of constructing $\mathbf{B}$ and the size of $\mathbf{B}$ is polynomial in the size of $\mathbf{B}'$ and $\log \Delta_K$. Calling the (γ, n)-free-module-HSVP oracle on this module produces $\mathbf{s} = (s_1, s_2, \ldots, s_n) \in K^n$ satisfying $\|\mathbf{s}\| \leq \gamma \cdot \sqrt{nd} \cdot \det(M)^{1/nd}$. Our reduction algorithm now select an odd index $i < n$ such that (s_i, s_{i+1}) is nonzero and outputs $\mathbf{s}' = (s_i, s_{i+1})$.

Now we show that such choice of i can always be made. Suppose by contradiction that the (γ, n)-free-module-SVP outputs $\mathbf{s} = (0, \ldots, 0, \delta u) \in K^n$, where $u \in \mathcal{O}_K \backslash \{0\}$. Note that we have

$$\delta \cdot \|u\| \leq \gamma \cdot \sqrt{nd} \cdot (\det M)^{1/nd} = \gamma \cdot \sqrt{nd} \cdot \Delta_K^{1/2d} \cdot \mathcal{N}(\det \mathbf{B}')^{(n-1)/2nd} \cdot \delta^{1/n}.$$

Since $u \in \mathcal{O}_K \backslash \{0\}$, we have $\|u\| \geq \sqrt{d}$, which implies

$$\delta \leq \gamma^{n/(n-1)} \cdot \Delta_K^{n/2d(n-1)} \cdot (\sqrt{n})^{n/(n-1)} \cdot \mathcal{N}(\det \mathbf{B}')^{1/2d} = \delta_0.$$

This contradicts the choice of δ. Thus the reduction algorithm in case n is odd can always outputs $\mathbf{s}'$ which is a nonzero vector of M_1 and satisfies

$$\begin{aligned}
\|\mathbf{s}'\| \leq \|\mathbf{s}\| &\leq \gamma \cdot \sqrt{nd} \cdot \det(M)^{1/nd} \\
&= \gamma \cdot \sqrt{nd} \cdot \Delta_K^{1/2d} \cdot \mathcal{N}(\det \mathbf{B}')^{(n-1)/2nd} \cdot \delta^{1/n} \\
&\leq \gamma \cdot \sqrt{nd} \cdot \Delta_K^{1/2d} \cdot \mathcal{N}(\det \mathbf{B}')^{(n-1)/2nd} \cdot 2^{1/n} \cdot \gamma^{\varepsilon n} \cdot \Delta_K^{\varepsilon n/2d} \cdot \sqrt{n}^{\varepsilon n} \cdot \mathcal{N}(\det \mathbf{B}')^{1/2nd} \\
&\leq \gamma^{1+\varepsilon n} \cdot \sqrt{n}^{1+\varepsilon n} \Delta_K^{\varepsilon n/2d} \cdot \sqrt{2d} \cdot \Delta_K^{1/2d} \cdot \mathcal{N}(\det \mathbf{B}')^{1/2d} \\
&\leq \gamma' \cdot \sqrt{2d} \cdot \det(M_1)^{1/2d},
\end{aligned}$$

as desired. $\square$

5.3   The Case of CVP$_{\text{cov}}$

In this subsection, we reduce CVP$_{\text{cov}}$ in free modules of rank 2 to CVP$_{\text{cov}}$ in free modules of rank $n \geq 2$. This is probably the simplest of the three reductions from this section. Like in the SVP case, we simply embed our rank—2 module M_1 into a rank-n module by padding the extra dimensions with (scaled) identity vectors. We only need to ensure that these vectors are smaller than the covering radius of M_1, to be sure that these extra dimensions do not increase the covering radius of our module too much. Then, we create a target vector by padding zeros to the original target vector. Overall, we prove the following reduction.

Proposition 5.3. *Let $\gamma \geq 1$ a real number and $n \geq 2$ an integer. There is a (deterministic) polynomial-time reduction from solving $(\gamma', 2)$-free-module-CVP$_{\text{cov}}$ in K^2 to (γ, n)-free-module-CVP$_{\text{cov}}$ in K^n, for any $\gamma' \geq \sqrt{2} \cdot \gamma$.*

Proof. Consider a rank-2 free module M_1 given by a basis $\mathbf{B}' \in K^{2\times 2}$ and a target vector $\mathbf{t}_1 \in \text{Span}_K(M_1) = K^2$. Let us assume without loss of generality that $M_1 \subseteq \mathcal{O}_K^2$.

The reduction algorithm computes $\delta \leq (dn \cdot \lambda_d(\mathcal{O}_K))^{-1}$ rational and constructs the block matrix (spanning a module called M)

$$\mathbf{B} = \left(\begin{array}{c|c} \mathbf{B}' & 0 \\ \hline 0 & \delta \cdot I_{n-2} \end{array} \right) \in K^{n\times n}.$$

and the target vector $\mathbf{t} = (\mathbf{t_1}^T, 0, \ldots, 0)^T$ (with $n-2$ zeros). The reduction then calls the oracle solving (γ, n)-free-module-CVP$_{\mathrm{cov}}$ on input $\mathbf{B}$ and $\mathbf{t}$, which outputs a vector $\mathbf{s}$. Let us call $\mathbf{s_1}$ the vector formed by the first two coordinates of $\mathbf{s}$. The reduction algorithm finally outputs $\mathbf{s_1}$.

One can check that computing an appropriate value of δ can be done in polynomial time since we know from Lemma 2.1 that $\lambda_d^{(\infty)}(\mathcal{O}_K) \le \Delta_K^{1/d}$. Constructing $\mathbf{B}$ and $\mathbf{t}$ can also be performed in polynomial time, hence our reduction runs in polynomial time.

Let us now focus on correctness. From the definition of $\mathbf{B}$, we know that $\mathbf{s_1} \in M_1$. We also know that

$$\|\mathbf{t_1} - \mathbf{s_1}\| \le \|\mathbf{t} - \mathbf{s}\| \le \gamma \cdot \mathrm{cov}(M).$$

Let us analyse $\mathrm{cov}(M)$. Because of the special shape of $\mathbf{B}$, we know that

$$\mathrm{cov}(M) = \sqrt{\mathrm{cov}(M_1)^2 + \delta^2 \cdot \mathrm{cov}(\mathcal{O}_K^{n-2})^2}$$
$$\le \sqrt{\mathrm{cov}(M_1)^2 + (\delta \cdot dn \cdot \lambda_d(\mathcal{O}_K))^2} \le \sqrt{\mathrm{cov}(M_1)^2 + 1}$$

Moreover, we know from preliminaries that $\mathrm{cov}(M_1) \ge 1/2 \cdot \lambda_1(M_1) \ge \sqrt{d}/2$, where the last inequality follows from the fact that $M_1 \subseteq \mathcal{O}_K^2$. Combining this with the previous inequality yields

$$\mathrm{cov}(M) \le \sqrt{2} \cdot \mathrm{cov}(M_1).$$

Hence, our reduction solves $(\sqrt{2}\gamma, 2)$-CVP$_{\mathrm{cov}}$ in M_1 as desired. $\square$

6   Combining the Reductions

In this last section, we combine the three reductions from Sects. 3, 4 and 5 to prove our main theorems.

Theorem 6.1. *Let $\gamma \ge 1$ and $n \ge 2$ be an integer. For any $\gamma' > 2 \cdot \gamma^3 \cdot \Delta_K^{3/2d}$, there is a probabilistic, polynomial-time reduction from solving (γ', n)-module-SVP in K^n to solving (γ, n)-free-module-SVP in K^n.*

Theorem 6.2. *Let $\gamma \ge 1$ and $n \ge 2$ be an integer. For any $\gamma' > \gamma^2 \cdot \sqrt{2n} \cdot \Delta_K^{1/2d}$, there is a probabilistic, polynomial-time reduction from solving (γ', n)-module-HSVP in K^n to solving (γ, n)-free-module-HSVP in K^n.*

Theorem 6.3. *Let $\gamma \ge 1$ and $n \ge 2$ be an integer. For any $\gamma' \ge \gamma^2 \cdot 5\sqrt{2} \cdot d \cdot \Delta_K^{2/d}$, there is a probabilistic, polynomial-time reduction from solving (γ', n)-module-CVP$_{cov}$ in K^n to solving (γ, n)-free-module-CVP$_{cov}$ in K^n.*

We note that, in the statements above, we chose to make the lower bound on γ' as simple as possible, but not necessarily as tight as possible. If the reader is interested in tighter bounds, it might be worth combining the reductions from the previous sections in a more careful way.

Interestingly, the reduction for SVP is the less tight of the three reductions, if we ignore the factors depending on the field and the module rank. Indeed, in the SVP case, the new approximation factor γ' is cubic in the original approximation factor γ, when for the other two reductions, the new approximation factor γ' is only quadratic in γ. We do not know whether it is possible to decrease the loss to quadratic in γ in the SVP case too, and leave it as an open problem.

Proof (Proof of Theorem 6.1). Let $\gamma_1 = \gamma'$, $\gamma_2 = \frac{\gamma'}{\gamma \Delta_K^{1/d}}$ and $\gamma_3 = \gamma_4 = \gamma$. It holds by definition that $\gamma_1 \geq \gamma_4 \cdot \gamma_2 \cdot \Delta_K^{1/d}$ hence, by Corollary 3.1, we have a reduction from (γ_1, n)-module-SVP to (γ_4, n)-free-module-SVP and γ_2-ideal-HSVP. Then, observe that because of the lower bound on γ' in the theorem statement, we have $\gamma_2 > 2\gamma_3^2 \cdot \Delta_K^{1/2d}$, so by Proposition 4.2 there is a reduction from γ_2-ideal-HSVP to $(\gamma_3, 2)$-free-module-SVP. Finally, by Proposition 5.1, there is a reduction from $(\gamma_3, 2)$-free-module-SVP to (γ_4, n)-free-module-SVP. Combining the three reductions provides a reduction from (γ_1, n)-module-SVP to (γ_4, n)-free-module-SVP as required. □

Proof (Proof of Theorem 6.2). Let $\gamma_1 = \gamma'$, $\gamma_2 = \left(\frac{\gamma'}{\gamma}\right)^n \cdot \Delta_K^{-1/2d}$ and $\gamma_4 = \gamma$. For γ_3, we treat the case $n = 2$ separately: if $n = 2$, we let $\gamma_3 = \gamma \cdot \sqrt{n}$ and if $n \geq 3$ we take $\gamma_3 = \gamma^{3/2} \cdot n^{3/4} \cdot \Delta_K^{1/4d}$.

First, let us observe that by definition of γ_1, γ_2 and γ_4, it holds that $\gamma_1 \geq \gamma_2^{1/n} \cdot \gamma_4 \cdot \Delta_K^{1/2nd}$. Hence, by Corollary 3.2, there is a reduction from (γ_1, n)-module-HSVP to (γ_4, n)-free-module-HSVP and γ_2-ideal-HSVP.

Then, observe that thanks to the lower bound on γ' in the theorem's statement, we have that $\gamma_2 > 2 \cdot (\gamma^{3/2} \cdot n^{3/4} \cdot \Delta_K^{1/4d})^2 \cdot \Delta_K^{1/2d}$ when $n \geq 3$ and $\gamma_2 > 2 \cdot (\gamma \cdot \sqrt{n})^2 \cdot \Delta_K^{1/2d}$ when $n = 2$. In both cases, by choice of γ_3, it holds that $\gamma_2 > 2\gamma_3^2 \cdot \Delta_K^{1/2d}$ and so from Proposition 4.1, we have a reduction from γ_2-ideal-HSVP to $(\gamma_3, 2)$-free-module-HSVP.

Finally, let ε_n be as in Proposition 5.2, that is $\varepsilon_n = 0$ if n is even and $\varepsilon_n = 1/(n - 1)$ if n is odd. Note that $\varepsilon_n = 0$ when $n = 2$ and $\varepsilon_n \leq 1/2$ when $n \geq 3$. With this in mind, one can check that $\gamma_3 \geq \gamma_4^{1+\varepsilon_n} \cdot \sqrt{n}^{1+\varepsilon_n} \cdot \Delta_K^{\varepsilon_n/2d}$ in both cases $n = 2$ and $n \geq 3$. From Proposition 5.2, this implies the existence of a reduction from $(\gamma_3, 2)$-free-module-HSVP to (γ_4, n)-free-module-HSVP. Combining the three reductions provides a reduction from (γ_1, n)-module-HSVP to (γ_4, n)-free-module-HSVP as required. □

Proof (Proof of Theorem 6.3). Let $\gamma_1 = \gamma'$, $\gamma_2 = \gamma \cdot 5\sqrt{2} \cdot d \cdot \Delta_K^{1/d}$, $\gamma_3 = \sqrt{2}\gamma$ and $\gamma_4 = \gamma$. By definition and from the lower bound on γ' in the theorem statement, it holds that $\gamma_1 \geq \gamma_4 \cdot \gamma_2 \cdot \Delta_K^{1/d}$ hence, by Corollary 3.3, we have a reduction from (γ_1, n)-module-CVP$_{\text{cov}}$ to (γ_4, n)-free-module-CVP$_{\text{cov}}$ and γ_2-ideal-HSVP. Then, by definition of γ_2 and using the fact that $\lambda_d^{(\infty)}(\mathcal{O}_K) \leq \Delta_K^{1/d}$ (see Lemma 2.1), we have $\gamma_2 \geq 5\gamma_3 \cdot d \cdot \lambda_d^{(\infty)}(\mathcal{O}_K)$, so by Proposition 4.3 there is a reduction from γ_2-ideal-HSVP to $(\gamma_3, 2)$-free-module-CVP$_{\mathrm{cov}}$. Finally, we have $\gamma_3 \geq \sqrt{2} \cdot \gamma_4$ and so by Proposition 5.3, there is a reduction from $(\gamma_3, 2)$-free-module-CVP$_{\mathrm{cov}}$ to (γ_4, n)-free-module-CVP$_{\mathrm{cov}}$. Combining the three reductions provides a reduction from (γ_1, n)-module-CVP$_{\mathrm{cov}}$ to (γ_4, n)-free-module-CVP$_{\mathrm{cov}}$ as required. $\square$

7   Application: Dequantizing Module-LLL

One of the main application of our reductions (and more precisely of the reduction for SVP from Theorem 6.1) is a de-quantized, *i.e.*, classical version of the LLL algorithm for modules lattices from [LPSW19] (which we refer to as module-LLL). Module-LLL is an oracle-based algorithm which, on input a pseudo-basis of a rank-n module $M \subset K^m$, outputs a somewhat short vector of the module. The algorithm is heuristic and runs in quantum polynomial time, provided it is given access to an oracle solving the closest vector problem in a fixed (field dependent) lattice L_K. The authors of [LPSW19] also showed that module-LLL can be made classical if the input module is free and represented by a basis, but they were unable to de-quantize the algorithm in the generic case. The following theorem was proved in [LPSW19].

Theorem 7.1 (Heuristic [LPSW19, Theorem 5.1]). *For any sequence of number fields K and any $\eta > 0$, there exist a sequence of lattices L_K of dimension $O((\log \Delta_K)^{2+\eta})$, an approximation factor $\gamma = 2^{\tilde{O}(\log \Delta_K)/d}$ and an algorithm $\mathcal{A}$ such that (under some heuristics):*

- *Algorithm $\mathcal{A}$ solves (γ^n, n)-free-module-SVP in K^n;*
- *Algorithm $\mathcal{A}$ makes a number of queries to an oracle solving the closest vector problem in L_K and requires a total number of classical operations that are both polynomial in $\log \Delta_K$ and the input bit-length.*

Note that our formulation of Theorem 7.1 is slightly different from the one of Theorem 5.1 from [LPSW19]. In particular, we state the theorem only for full rank modules and we use the recent result from [BST+20] to simplify some of the bounds. More precisely, in [LPSW19, Theorem 5.1], both the dimension of the lattice L_K and the approximation factor γ involved the quantity $d \log(\mathrm{cov}(\mathcal{O}_K))$. By combining Lemma 2.1 and Eq. (3), we can see that $\mathrm{cov}(\mathcal{O}_K) \leq d^{3/2} \cdot \Delta_K^{3/(2d)}$, which implies that $d \log(\mathrm{cov}(\mathcal{O}_K)) = \tilde{O}(\log \Delta_K)$, and leads to our simplification.

We now show in the following theorem that there exists a classical module-LLL algorithm that solves an approximate version of the module-SVP problem, regardless of the fact that the input module is free or not. The only difference between Theorem 7.2 below and Theorem 7.1 above is that $\mathcal{A}$ now solves module-SVP, instead of free-module-SVP.

Theorem 7.2. *For any sequence of number fields K and any $\eta > 0$, there exist a sequence of lattices L_K of dimension $O((\log \Delta_K)^{2+\eta})$, an approximation factor $\gamma' = 2^{\tilde{O}(\log \Delta_K)/d}$ and an algorithm $\mathcal{A}$ such that (under some heuristics):*

- *Algorithm $\mathcal{A}$ solves $((\gamma')^n, n)$-module-SVP in K^n;*
- *Algorithm $\mathcal{A}$ makes a number of queries to an oracle solving the closest vector problem in L_K and requires a total number of classical operations that are both polynomial in $\log \Delta_K$ and the input bit-length.*

Proof. Combine Theorem 7.1 with Theorem 6.1.

Note that, due to the reduction, the approximation factor γ' from Theorem 7.2 is a priori slightly worse than the approximation factor γ in Theorem 7.1 (we have, e.g., $\gamma' = 3 \cdot \gamma^3 \cdot \Delta_K^{3/2d}$), but the difference is hidden in the soft O notation that is used in both statements.

Acknowledgements. Gabrielle De Micheli is supported in part by the Swiss National Science Foundation Early Postdoc.Mobility fellowship. Daniele Micciancio is supported by the NSF Award 1936703, Samsung and Intel. Alice Pellet-Mary is supported by the CHARM ANR-NSF grant (ANR-21-CE94-0003) and by the PEPR quantique France 2030 programme managed by the ANR (ANR-22-PETQ-0008 PQ-TLS). Nam Tran is supported by CSIRO Data61 PhD Scholarship and CSIRO Data61 Top-up Scholarship. This work was done when Nam Tran was a Master student in the University of Limoges (France) and doing his internship at Institute of Mathematics of Bordeaux (IMB, France), founded by IMB.

References

[BF14]   Biasse, J.F., Fieker, C.: Subexponential class group and unit group computation in large degree number fields. LMS J. Comput. Math. **17**(A), 385–403 (2014)

[BGV14] Brakerski, Z., Gentry, C., Vaikuntanathan, V.: (Leveled) fully homomorphic encryption without bootstrapping. ACM Trans. Comput. Theory (TOCT) **6**(3), 1–36 (2014)

[BHJ22] Bley, W., Hofmann, T., Johnston, H.: Computation of lattice isomorphisms and the integral matrix similarity problem. In: Forum of Mathematics, Sigma, vol. 10, p. e87. Cambridge University Press, Cambridge (2022)

[Boe22] de Boer, K.: Random walks on Arakelov class groups. PhD thesis, Leiden University (2022)

[BS16]   Biasse, J.F., Song, F.: Efficient quantum algorithms for computing class groups and solving the principal ideal problem in arbitrary degree number fields. In: Proceedings of the Twenty-Seventh Annual ACM-SIAM Symposium on Discrete Algorithms, pp. 893–902. SIAM (2016)

[BST+20] Bhargava, M., Shankar, A., Taniguchi, T., Thorne, F., Tsimerman, J., Zhao, Y.: Bounds on 2-torsion in class groups of number fields and integral points on elliptic curves. J. Am. Math. Soc. **33**(4), 1087–1099 (2020)

[CDPR16] Cramer, R., Ducas, L., Peikert, C., Regev, O.: Recovering short generators of principal ideals in cyclotomic rings. In: Fischlin, M., Coron, J.-S. (eds.) EUROCRYPT 2016. LNCS, vol. 9666, pp. 559–585. Springer, Heidelberg (2016). https://doi.org/10.1007/978-3-662-49896-5_20

[CDW17] Cramer, R., Ducas, L., Wesolowski, B.: Short Stickelberger class relations and application to ideal-SVP. In: Coron, J.-S., Nielsen, J.B. (eds.) EUROCRYPT 2017. LNCS, vol. 10210, pp. 324–348. Springer, Cham (2017). https://doi.org/10.1007/978-3-319-56620-7_12

864   G. De Micheli et al.

[Coh12] Cohen, H.: Advanced Topics in Computational Number Theory, vol. 193. Springer, Heidelberg (2012). https://doi.org/10.1007/978-1-4419-8489-0

[DM22] De Micheli, G., Micciancio, D.: A fully classical LLL algorithm for modules. Cryptology ePrint Archive (2022)

[FPS22] Felderhoff, J., Pellet-Mary, A., Stehlé, D.: On module unique-SVP and NTRU. In: Advances in Cryptology-ASIACRYPT 2022: 28th International Conference on the Theory and Application of Cryptology and Information Security, Taipei, Taiwan, 5–9 December 2022, Proceedings, Part III, pp. 709–740. Springer, Heidelberg (2022)

[FS10] Fieker, C., Stehlé, D.: Short bases of lattices over number fields. In: Hanrot, G., Morain, F., Thomé, E. (eds.) ANTS 2010. LNCS, vol. 6197, pp. 157–173. Springer, Heidelberg (2010). https://doi.org/10.1007/978-3-642-14518-6_15

[Gen09a] Gentry, C.: A fully homomorphic encryption scheme. PhD thesis, Stanford University (2009)

[Gen09b] Gentry, C.: Fully homomorphic encryption using ideal lattices. In: Proceedings of the Forty-First Annual ACM Symposium on Theory of Computing, pp. 169–178 (2009)

[GGH+16] Garg, S., Gentry, C., Halevi, S., Raykova, M., Sahai, A., Waters, B.: Candidate indistinguishability obfuscation and functional encryption for all circuits. SIAM J. Comput. 45(3), 882–929 (2016)

[Hop98] Hoppe, A.: Normal forms over Dedekind domain, efficient implementation in the computer algebra system KANT. PhD thesis, TU Berlin (1998)

[HPS06] Hoffstein, J., Pipher, J., Silverman, J.H.: NTRU: a ring-based public key cryptosystem. In: Buhler, J.P. (ed.) ANTS 1998. LNCS, vol. 1423, pp. 267–288. Springer, Heidelberg (1998). https://doi.org/10.1007/BFb0054868

[LM06] Lyubashevsky, V., Micciancio, D.: Generalized compact knapsacks are collision resistant. In: Bugliesi, M., Preneel, B., Sassone, V., Wegener, I. (eds.) ICALP 2006. LNCS, vol. 4052, pp. 144–155. Springer, Heidelberg (2006). https://doi.org/10.1007/11787006_13

[LPR13] Lyubashevsky, V., Peikert, C., Regev, O.: On ideal lattices and learning with errors over rings. J. ACM (JACM) 60(6), 1–35 (2013)

[LPSW19] Lee, C., Pellet-Mary, A., Stehlé, D., Wallet, A.: An LLL algorithm for module lattices. In: Galbraith, S.D., Moriai, S. (eds.) ASIACRYPT 2019. LNCS, vol. 11922, pp. 59–90. Springer, Cham (2019). https://doi.org/10.1007/978-3-030-34621-8_3

[LS15] Langlois, A., Stehlé, D.: Worst-case to average-case reductions for module lattices. Des. Codes Cryptogr. 75(3), 565–599 (2015)

[PR06] Peikert, C., Rosen, A.: Efficient collision-resistant hashing from worst-case assumptions on cyclic lattices. In: Halevi, S., Rabin, T. (eds.) TCC 2006. LNCS, vol. 3876, pp. 145–166. Springer, Heidelberg (2006). https://doi.org/10.1007/11681878_8

[PS21] Pellet-Mary, A., Stehlé, D.: On the hardness of the NTRU problem. In: Tibouchi, M., Wang, H. (eds.) ASIACRYPT 2021. LNCS, vol. 13090, pp. 3–35. Springer, Cham (2021). https://doi.org/10.1007/978-3-030-92062-3_1

[PT23] Pellet-Mary, A., Tran, N.: Reductions from module lattices to free module lattices (2023). https://hal.science/hal-04119912/document

[SSTX09] Stehlé, D., Steinfeld, R., Tanaka, K., Xagawa, K.: Efficient public key encryption based on ideal lattices. In: Matsui, M. (ed.) ASIACRYPT 2009. LNCS, vol. 5912, pp. 617–635. Springer, Heidelberg (2009). https://doi.org/10.1007/978-3-642-10366-7_36

[Ste15] Stephens-Davidowitz, N.: Dimension-preserving reductions between lattice problems (2015). http://noahsd.com/latticeproblems.pdf

[Was97] Washington, L.C.: Introduction to Cyclotomic Fields, vol. 83, p. 104. Springer, Heidelberg (1997). https://doi.org/10.1007/978-1-4612-1934-7

Author Index

© International Association for Cryptologic Research 2023
H. Handschuh and A. Lysyanskaya (Eds.): CRYPTO 2023, LNCS 14085, pp. 867–868, 2023.
https://doi.org/10.1007/978-3-031-38554-4

Printed in the United States
by Baker & Taylor Publisher Services